HUDSONS

Historic Houses & Gardens

Castles and Heritage Sites

HERITAGE HOUSE GROUP

2008

Gosford House, Edinburgh

Foreword by Dr Simon Thurley

Visiting houses, castles, abbeys and gardens is one of the world's oldest pleasures. For hundreds of years people have gone out of their way to see great historic buildings, to peer through their windows and, if possible, get inside. While the gentry tipped the housekeepers of the great country houses for a glimpse of their treasures, ordinary people queued up at ancient sites to gasp in amazement at ghost stories.

I have been visiting historic places since I was a small boy, and for the last 20 years a copy of *Hudson's* has been my companion. Over the last few years *Hudson's* (like many of us) has got fatter; it has included more and more sites, most of which are privately owned. The entries in this book are now a representative snapshot of this country's extraordinary heritage. They are our country's history in brick, stone and earth. They have been the setting for some of the most important, most poignant and most terrible events in our history. That is why they matter.

We have a shared responsibility to make sure that future generations can enjoy them as we do. The owners who are listed in these pages shoulder most of the burden – by visiting these places, by buying a postcard and licking an ice cream, we can help.

So we should remember that visiting one of these wonderful sites is not only one of the nicest ways of spending a day out, it is also a small contribution to saving them for people who come after us.

Simon Thurley.

Dr Simon Thurley
Chief Executive
English Heritage

HUDSON's

From the editor

My original and largely unchanged objective in publishing *Hudson's* was to inform people, and those in the travel trade in particular, about the enormous number of historic properties in Britain available to be visited. Many were, and still are, comparatively unknown.

Many of the properties in *Hudson's* are in public or charitable ownership. While great organisations such as the National Trust or English Heritage come readily to mind in this context, some people are surprised to discover that the majority of historic houses open to the public, or made available for various uses, are still privately owned. Since the 18th century owners have welcomed visitors. During the past 60 years this has greatly expanded and is now on a much more commercial basis than hitherto. The income from admission fees and secondary spend has made an important contribution to the enormous cost of upkeep.

Initially properties were mainly opened primarily for viewing. But over the last 20 years they have also been made increasingly available for weddings, functions, as film locations and as venues for a variety of events. In tune with this, *Hudson's* has also adapted so as to provide additional information about these wider categories of use.

While my first objective has in large measure been achieved, there are always new horizons. As has always been the case, the use of properties has evolved in response to the interests of conservation, the needs of the owners and the visiting public, and the requirement to generate income to ensure sustainability.

New opportunities arise, and new markets can be found to make greater use of heritage properties for education, cultural enrichment and pure enjoyment of their style and beauty. It has been my hope that *Hudson's* will continue, beyond my involvement, to contribute to this scene. To that end, I have transferred *Hudson's* to a larger organisation, confident that they will further expand the way in which it can serve the interests of owners of heritage property, and those who visit and also enjoy and make use of them. *Hudson's* is now part of the Heritage House Group with Kate Kaegler as Publisher. However, I am delighted I will continue to be involved in an advisory capacity.

Norman Hudson OBE

Hudson's Historic Houses & Gardens

2008 edition produced by Norman Hudson & Co for Heritage House Group

Publisher	Kate Kaegler
Administration	Sarah Phillips
Design	Cameron Buxton
Maps	Maps in Minutes™
HHG Director	Kelvin D Ladbrook
Printed by	Wyndeham Heron
UK & European Distribution	Portfolio (tel 020 8997 9000)
US Distribution	The History Press, Inc (843 577 5971)

Published by:
Heritage House Group
Heritage House
Lodge Lane
Derby DE1 3HE

Tel: 01332 347087
Fax: 01332 290688
E-mail: hudsons@hhgroup.co.uk
Web: www.hudsonsguide.co.uk

Contents

2008

'Full Moon Circle' by Richard Long

Houghton Hall

where history meets contemporary art

Houghton Hall – an 18th century palace where the addition of a number of contemporary works of art, both to the grounds and to the wider parkland area, is an exciting example of modern stewardship and patronage.

Built by Sir Robert Walpole the first *de facto* British Prime Minister, as a statement of power and wealth, Houghton Hall stands in a quiet part of rural north-west Norfolk. The Hall and its surroundings have changed little since the early 18th century despite long periods of neglect. Most of the original furniture is still in its intended place. Houghton was inherited by the 1st Marquess of Cholmondeley in 1797. He saved the contents and much of the estate from sale but at that time the family were concentrating their efforts on the rebuilding of Cholmondeley Castle in Cheshire. Houghton only came to life again in 1919 when the 5th Marquess of Cholmondeley and his wife, Sybil Sassoon, took over.

Over the last 15 years or so much work has been undertaken by their grandson, the 7th Marquess, continuing the restoration of the Hall and conserving its contents. With the major work now largely completed, the focus moved to restoring the important 18th century landscape that was designed by Charles Bridgeman in the 1720s. The park on the west side of the house had been ploughed up in the 19th century. This has been reinstated with a number of 18th century features such as avenues of pleached limes flanking the west view, and the Wildernesses relaid behind them. This has nearly doubled the size of the park, with the Hall standing at its centre, a deer park on the east side, and the park on the west grazed by Longhorn cattle, Norfolk Horn and Southdown flocks of sheep. The great ha-ha on the west side of the Hall was also rebuilt, separating the gardens from the park. The five acre formal walled garden has been redesigned and laid out as a series of gardens by Lord Cholmondeley as a memorial to his grandmother. At the south end is a new Rustic Temple with oak Tuscan pillars and

'Sky Space' by James Turrell

'Interior Space' by Stephen Cox

5

pediment filled with deer antlers, which has been designed by Julian and Isobel Bannerman.

With the Hall and its gardens and landscape restored, it was clear from 18th century plans of Houghton that the gardens and park contained several architectural elements within the framework of formal and ornate planting. Whether these consisted of Temples, Follies or water features is unclear; but it seemed to Lord Cholmondeley appropriate to reinterpret the idea for our own time and in this spirit he has recently added a number of contemporary works of art, both to the grounds and the park.

Artists such as Richard Long and James Turrell were invited to create pieces for specific areas, while sculptures by Stephen Cox have been placed with the artist's involvement.

The first work to be commissioned was James Turrell's "Skyspace" which has been built in the North Wilderness on the west front. The building itself is clad in oak, rising through a canopy of trees. Within the structure is a chamber containing only seating, lighting and an aperture in the ceiling. Visitors can sit and gaze at the sky, whilst experiencing the balance between interior and exterior light and given space for contemplation.

A second piece by James Turrell was also commissioned and has been constructed within the 18th century Water Tower. "St Elmo's Breath" is planned to be open for viewing on a limited basis.

On the east view is Richard Long's "Full Moon Circle", a dramatic yet subtle addition to this vista. Stephen Cox's interior space stands within the Pleasure Grounds on the west side of the Hall within a piece of woodland that has the nave-like qualities of a cathedral. Other works are planned, including "Four Side Pyramid" by the late Sol LeWitt, "Water Flame" by Jeppe Hein and a piece by Anya Gallaccio.

These important contemporary works embellish the 18th century designed landscape without imposing themselves upon it, and create a new and exciting layer on this historic park.

The Saloon

The Green Velvet Bedchamber

6

Pleached Limes

James Turrell (b 1943, USA)

James Turrell works with light and space. He has held a pilot's licence since the age of 16 and his visual experiences whilst flying have greatly influenced his work. He creates spaces which enable the view to study particular qualities and variations in the light that is all around us, that we often take for granted. He has worked in galleries, building spaces and lighting them in a way that breaks down the viewer's preconceptions about the relationship between light and space and creates a sense of wonder at the way in which we perceive light and colour. At Houghton he has created a "Skyspace", a context for viewing the sky. Light and colour is perceived by each person uniquely.

Stephen Cox (b 1946, UK)

Stephen Cox comes out of the minimalist tradition. Since the 1970s he has made sculptures out of stone and has been inspired by the stone carvings of earlier times. He is well known for working with unusual stones and those that are extremely difficult to carve. His recent works are monumental in character and include a series that have been inspired by tombs and tomb culture – his "Interior Space" may be seen at Houghton.

Richard Long (b 1945, UK)

Richard Long's work is inspired by his personal, direct experience of the landscape through the activity of walking. His sculptures are made by arranging natural materials, usually stone or wood, into a shape onto the floor or ground: a circle, line, spiral or cross. At Houghton is his "Full Moon Circle", constructed from Cornish slate.

The Rustic Temple   © Jerry Harpur

Houghton Hall West Front

The Rose Garden

The headline-grabbing castles of Wales rightly deserve their impressive reputations, but there are also a number of somewhat smaller, yet no less important, historic houses in the care of Cadw, the Welsh Assembly Government's historic environment service. These provide the visitor with a unique insight into the development of the domestic house in Wales.

The front cover of the Cadw publication *Living Rooms — Interior Decoration in Wales 400-1960*

Domestic living, Cadw style

Through rare examples of surviving high status domestic houses such as Penarth Fawr, near Criccieth, Hafoty in Anglesey and Plas Mawr in Conwy, we can trace the progression from open hall to storeyed mansion, displaying how the aristocracy and gentry of Wales lived in the 14th century (Hafoty), 15th century (Penarth Fawr) and later 16th century (Plas Mawr).

It is fair to say that any house, whatever its scale, is a mirror to the lives and ambitions of its occupiers. This can be reflected in the way space is arranged as well as in the quality of construction and decoration. The contrast between Penarth Fawr or Hafoty and Plas Mawr marks a major landmark in the evolution of the house from the relative simplicity of the hall house with its limited number of rooms, to the later sophisticated complexity of Plas Mawr.

The ways in which these buildings changed, through the placing of fireplaces into the open halls or the insertion of floors, also indicated changing ideas about how to live, and changing needs for space. The increasing elaboration and sophistication of these buildings also has a lot to say about the increasing wealth and status of their gentry builders.

Whilst Plas Mawr is a particularly dramatic testimony to the new wealth available to the Tudor gentry in Wales after the Act of Union and is architecturally more elaborate than either Hafoty or Penarth Fawr, each in turn successfully displays a potent expression of status.

Above, Left and Right: Plas Mawr, Conwy, North Wales

11

This is most obvious at Plas Mawr with its lavish interior decoration, its ornate fireplaces and colourful intricate plasterwork, but it is also apparent in the quality of carpentry in Hafoty and Penarth Fawr - two houses which formed the centre–piece of rural estates. Plas Mawr however was a townhouse which would have functioned in rather a different way in its urban cultural context and is still today exceptional for its size and completeness.

Other property in the Cadw estate shows the emergence of domestic architecture from other origins, primarily defensive in nature. For example, at Tretower, near Crickhowell, the Court was built from the 15th century as a direct replacement of the castle, and in its layout and architectural detail it reveals the status of its owners and demonstrates particular patterns of use. The transformation of Raglan Castle in Monmouthshire into an Elizabethan mansion also shows the triumph of a particular domestic gentry culture.

Such themes and the visual evidence for this can be examined in greater detail in 'Living Rooms', a Cadw publication which focuses on interior decoration in Wales from 400-1960 and which strives to dispel any perception that the people of pre-industrial Wales lived either in stark fortresses or filthy hovels, both devoid of comfort, colour and decoration. At Plas Mawr in particular Cadw pioneered the historically accurate re-creation of rooms with their original vibrant colours. Magnolia it most definitely isn't!

For more information on Cadw, visit www.cadw.wales.gov.uk. All images © Cadw Crown Copyright

Penarth Fawr, Criccieth, North Wales

Plas Mawr, Conwy, North Wales

'exquisite craftsmanship'
All Saints,
Cambridge CB5 8BS

'medieval magnificence'
Holy Trinity,
Torbryan, Devon TQ12 5UR

'fascinating monuments'
All Saints,
Harewood Park, Leeds LS17 9LX

'Georgian gem'
St John the Evangelist,
Chichester PO19 1UR

**THE CHURCHES
CONSERVATION TRUST**

1 West Smithfield London EC1A 9EE

The Churches Conservation Trust is the national charity which cares for churches of outstanding historical, architectural or archaeological importance which are no longer needed for regular worship.

We receive limited statutory funds which we use to ensure that the structure of our buildings is safe and watertight. However, we rely on voluntary contributions to make significant repairs to these beautiful buildings in our care, including specialist conservation work to wall paintings, textiles, stained glass and monuments.

We need your support to save the centuries of irreplaceable art, architecture and heritage embodied in these historic churches.

A thousand years of English history awaits you …

The historic churches of England are quintessential features of our towns, villages and countryside. Wherever you go, you are rarely far from one of the 340 historic and beautiful churches in the care of The Churches Conservation Trust.

Each church has something very special to offer – breathtaking architecture, a glorious setting, exquisite craftsmanship, brilliant stained glass, fascinating monuments. A thousand years of English history awaits you within their walls.

Why not include a visit to one of these memorable buildings on your next outing or holiday. Everyone is welcome, and entry is free to all.

You will find full details, maps, and access information about all Trust churches on our website. These unique and wonderful buildings are waiting for you to discover and enjoy.

www.visitchurches.org.uk.

Yes, I would like to support The Churches Conservation Trust

Title _____ First Name _____

Surname _____

Address _____

Postcode _____

Daytime phone _____

Email address _____

Please send me information on:

☐ List of all CCT churches

☐ List of CCT churches in _____
(specify county)

☐ Becoming a volunteer

☐ CCT's Supporter Scheme

Please return the completed form to: Freepost RLXX-KXLT-XJYK,
The Churches Conservation Trust, 1 West Smithfield, London EC1A 9EE

The Churches Conservation Trust is a registered charity number 258612

Please accept my gift of £ _____

Please tick payment method

☐ Cheque   ☐ Credit card   ☐ Debit card

If you would like to pay by cheque, please make payable to The Churches Conservation Trust.

To pay by debit or credit card please fill in the following.

Card number:

☐☐☐☐ ☐☐☐☐ ☐☐☐☐ ☐☐☐☐

Issue number: | Valid from: | Expiry date: | Security number:

☐☐☐☐ | ☐☐☐☐ | ☐☐☐☐ | ☐☐☐☐

Card holder's name: _____

Card holder's signature: _____

HH08

13

With over 400 properties to explore across the country and with special events throughout the year, English Heritage has something for everyone – from days out with the family to inspirational trips for those with an interest in history. At some English Heritage properties there are now holiday cottages, for a memorable weekend away or for a longer stay.

ENGLISH HERITAGE

Days out worth talking about.

What's new for 2008 at English Heritage
properties

Historic Places to stay

Each of the 12 English Heritage cottages and apartments is located at the heart of a remarkable property where history, discovery and enjoyment are on the doorstep. They offer the unique opportunity to experience a very special place in peace and privacy. When the property closes for the day and the visitors go home, there is the joy of having the gardens and grounds almost to yourself (more information is available at **www.english-heritage.org.uk/holidaycottages**; booking office 0870 3331187).

Bringing History to Life

English Heritage has the largest events programme in Europe, from Battle Boot Camps to Medieval Jousts and Knight Schools. The **St George's Day Festival** celebrates England through the ages, with dramatic equestrian displays, falconry, children's theatre and an historic market. Visitors can try traditional games and make mischief with the jugglers, visit the raucous Romans or root for St George as he battles it out with the dastardly dragon. This all takes place at **Wrest Park**, Bedfordshire on Saturday 19 and Sunday 20 April.

The flagship event, with a cast of thousands, is the **Festival of History** which takes place at **Kelmarsh Hall**, Northamptonshire on Saturday 19 and Sunday 20 July. This takes visitors on an action-packed journey through 2,000 years of history. Nowhere else will you be able to enjoy spectacular battle re-enactments, colourful living history encampments, street markets, music, dance and jousting. This year's event will also include a Gladiator Show, World War I Trench Experience and Tank Display, and the Knights' Tournament (for more information visit **www.festivalofhistory.org.uk**).

The annual re-enactment of England's most famous battle, the **Battle of Hastings**, provides all the tension and atmosphere of medieval battle as 200 soldiers from the armies of King Harold and William the Conqueror clash on the very site where it took place 942 years ago. Visitors can soak up Saxon life as they walk through the living history encampments and authentic medieval market with its displays of unusual wares. This takes place on Saturday 11 and Sunday 12 October at the **1066 Battle of Hastings Abbey & Battlefield**, East Sussex.

Left: The St George's Day Festival at Wrest Park

Right: The Festival of History at Kelmarsh Hall

English Heritage's work to restore, refurbish and authentically improve historic properties to increase visitors' enjoyment is continuous. Across the country the results of recent work will be revealed in Spring 2008.

At **Framlingham Castle**, Suffolk visitors will be able to explore life at the Castle in a new introductory exhibition in the Poor House, which tells the story of the people who lived in this great castle through its 800 year history.

 Just a little further south in Essex, Spring 2008 will see the opening of the **Audley End House Service Wing**, revealing life behind the scenes for servants during Audley End's Victorian heyday. Rooms within the Service Wing including the Scullery, Dairy, Meat and Game Larders and Laundries, will be open to the public for the first time and vividly animated with lifelike sights and sounds, film projection, and even examples of original food from the era.

In the South East, after extensive improvements, from late May 2008 **Lullingstone Roman Villa** will reopen for visitors who will be able to discover much more about this important archaeological site. An atmospheric sound and light show, delivered from a platform overlooking the Villa, will provide a lively history and many impressive and intricate artefacts will be on display for the first time.

Further north at **Brodsworth Hall** in Yorkshire, Spring 2008 will see another Wing of the Hall being opened to visitors. Restored and furnished, the four new rooms include 'Emily's Kitchen' or 'The Still Room' (used for jam-making, preserving and custards in Victorian times) plus the Scullery as well as two comfortable chintzy bedrooms. A new exhibition and trail through the house and gardens was put in place last year. This featured recorded memories, original photographs, costumed actors in a series of talks and tours by curators, and looks into the private lives of the family, servants and estate workers who lived at Brodsworth in its Victorian heyday. Outside extensive restoration work has returned the gardens to the 1890s, with an Alpine Garden planted for Spring 2008.

Drawing Room, Brodsworth Hall, Yorkshire

Enjoy great days out throughout the year when you join English Heritage.

Enjoy great days out throughout the year when you join English Heritage. Membership gives you free or reduced-price entry to our events as well as free entry to all our properties. And the benefits of membership don't end there. Members receive our award-winning quarterly magazine, Heritage Today. What's more, members can take children under 19 with them for free.*

Every penny from your membership makes a difference to our work in conserving England's historic environment. In return, we hope you'll gain a great deal of enjoyment from your membership.

Call 0870 333 1181 quoting HUDS3 to join today, or visit www.english-heritage.org.uk/membership to find out more.

*Membership allows free admission for you and up to six accompanying children within your family group.

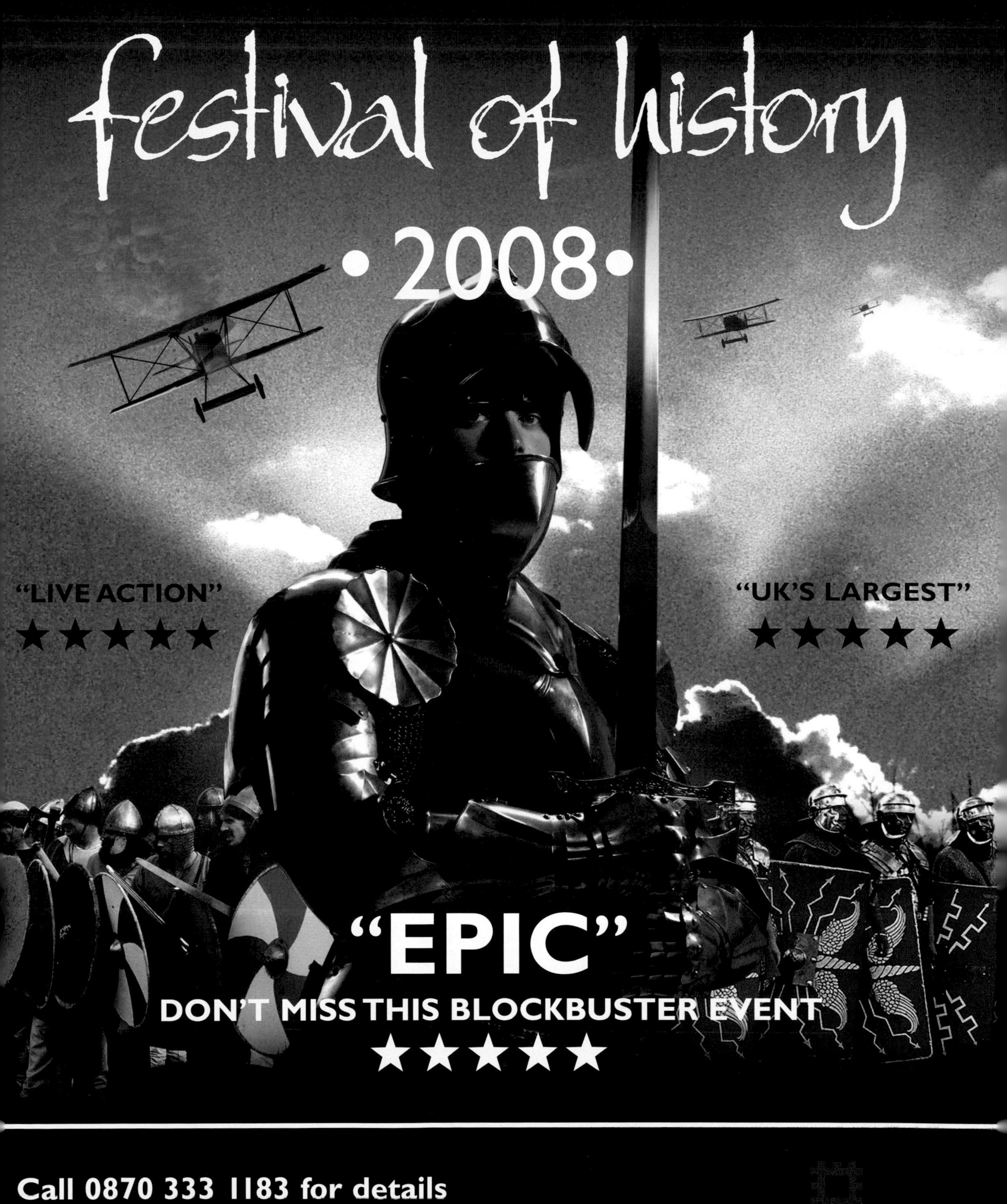
festival of history
• 2008 •
"LIVE ACTION"
★★★★★
"UK'S LARGEST"
★★★★★
"EPIC"
DON'T MISS THIS BLOCKBUSTER EVENT
★★★★★

A new visitor centre for the
Castle of Mey

A new Visitor Centre at the Castle of Mey, the most northerly castle on the British mainland, has been sensitively designed to merge with its surroundings and provide visitors with shelter, refreshment and dramatic views over the Pentland Firth to Orkney.

Left (main image): The Castle of Mey and Gardens, Highlands & Skye © Nick McCann

Above and left: The new Visitor Centre, The Castle of Mey, Highlands & Skye © Nick McCann

The only property that Queen Elizabeth, the Queen Mother ever actually owned was the Castle of Mey, on the north coast of Scotland overlooking the sea. She saw it on her first visit to Caithness in 1952 while mourning the death of her husband, King George VI and when staying with her friends, Commander and Lady Dorothy Vyner, who had a house nearby at Dunnet. At that time, although the windswept exterior of the castle was largely intact, the interior, following occupation by troops during World War II, was in a poor state. It had no bathrooms, no electricity, but it did have an exciting and wild location. She fell for its ruined isolated charm. It was also for sale.

The Queen Mother bought the castle and began the process of restoration and renovation, transforming a near-derelict building to a welcoming and comfortable holiday home. For almost half a century she spent many happy summers there, until her death in 2002 at the age of 101.

The gardens at the Castle of Mey, with their daunting and inhospitable climate, are testament to the Queen Mother's experience and enthusiasm. The garden wall, the 15' high 'Great Wall of Mey' provides protection from the fierce gales and sea spray that blow in from the Pentland Firth. The gardens, in which her grandson Prince Charles now takes a great interest, are as great a source of delight for visitors as they were to the Queen Mother.

In 2002 the Castle and Gardens at Mey were opened regularly to the public. It was soon clear that a Visitor Centre with a tearoom and shop was an important requirement of visitors. Plans designed by ANTA of Fearn, Ross-shire, were agreed in January 2006 and construction by D M Geddes, a Caithness firm, started in February 2006. Constructed of Caithness stone and using lime mortar (not cement), with a Caithness slate roof, the new building nestles into the seaward side of the Great Garden Wall. It merges so well into its surroundings that some visitors are surprised that it opened only in May 2007 and has not always been there. Inside, with the high standard of contemporary design, they would know otherwise. There are immense Douglas Fir beams, with the walls lined in Larch and insulated with 80 cubic metres of sheep's wool. The floor is of Caithness flagstone with under-floor heating provided by a geo-thermal system that has five boreholes, each sunk to a depth of 100 metres.

Nick McCann © The Queen Elizabeth Castle of Mey Trust

A garden
for all seasons

When you think of The National Trust your first thought is probably of the historic houses and castles with the gardens a pretty afterthought – but it is these very gardens that can often breathe life into a visit. More than 450 expert gardeners and over 1500 willing volunteers dedicate themselves to looking after one of the greatest collections of historic gardens and cultivated plants in the world, spanning over 36,000 acres and encompassing over 400 years of history.

A group of Galanthus nivalis var .' viridapicis' or common snowdrop growing in the garden at Kingston Lacy

©NTPL/Stephen Robson

The sheer variety of the gardens looked after by The National Trust across England, Wales and Northern Ireland means that whatever time of year you visit you will be struck by a seasonal extravaganza. During the early stirrings of spring, garden lovers will have their senses seduced by spectacular displays of rhododendrons bursting onto the scene. With an abundance of beautiful canopies and walks to enjoy, it's a great time of year to visit and explore a Victorian fascination which continues to delight today.

Such a vista can be enjoyed at the famous gardens at Mount Stewart in County Down, Northern Ireland. Planted in the 1920s by Lady Edith Londonderry, the gardens have since been nominated a World Heritage Site. A rhododendron spectacular is also offered to visitors to Lyme Park in Cheshire, a great estate famed for its fine gardens, surrounded by a medieval deer park.

Nymans, one of the great gardens of the Sussex Weald and internationally known for its beauty, atmosphere and collection of rare plants, is a haven in the summer months. The achievement of three generations of the Messel family over more than 100 years, Nymans was one of the first gardens to come to the National Trust in 1953. The vibrant seasonal colours are heightened by the stunning yew topiary.

Summer is also the season for many National Trust gardens to come alive with the sights and sounds of outdoor theatre. Picnic hampers are the order of the day as families and friends enjoy the favourites of Shakespeare, children's classics and even the odd murder mystery tale set against some of the most beautiful backdrops the country has to offer.

As the days begin to draw in with the golden glow of autumnal light and the leaves turn a rainbow of reds, russets and browns you may think it's the perfect excuse to stay indoors, but you'd be wrong! At Stourhead you could

Nymans Garden, a gravel path bordered by colourful summer flowers leading to an ornate archway.

A view over the vegetable beds and runner bean tripods in the kitchen garden at Calke Abbey   ©NTPL/Stephen Robson

wonder if there is a more entrancing autumnal view than the tulip tree on the ornamental lake turning to a shimmering gold. Gentle lakeside paths lead past classical temples and follies, set against a backdrop of beautiful and exotic trees including the Japanese maples.

As autumn makes way for the frosted landscape of winter, many properties offer guided walks with the Head Gardener, where you can pick up tips on winter garden highlights and ideas to take into spring. The gardens at Kingston Lacy in Dorset provide a wonderful wintry carpet of over six million snowdrops bursting into life, and every year the Trust introduces new snowdrop varieties.

However stunning and inspiring they are, the value of National Trust gardens goes way beyond the aesthetic. Over 50 working and ornamental kitchen gardens are looked after by the Trust not only providing local and seasonal produce to our restaurants, tea rooms and cafés, but also enabling visitors to learn about traditional food production techniques, and many run 'Plot to Plate' events for visitors. So, if you're keen to get back to basics and grow your own produce then a visit to one of these gardens is a must for inspirational ideas.

At Sizergh Castle in Cumbria the Kitchen Garden grows soft fruits including strawberries, raspberries, loganberries and redcurrants; another of the beds is used to sow annuals to produce cut flowers for the Castle.

At Clumber Park in Nottinghamshire the Walled Kitchen Garden, constructed in 1772, encloses four acres and has one of the longest glasshouses in National Trust ownership, where vines, figs and peaches are grown and used in the restaurant and sold to visitors.

Many National Trust gardens are also havens for wildlife and this has prompted the Trust to launch a scheme to discover and celebrate the wildlife that occurs in its heritage gardens that are open to visitors. Specialist surveys in 2003 found three species of insect new to Britain in National Trust gardens – a paper wasp at Ham House and a mistletoe bug at both Barrington Court and Tintinhull.

Rhododendrons at Lyme Park

©NTPL

The Liriodendron tulipifera (tulip tree) on the island in the lake at Stourhead has brilliant autumn foliage.

©NTPL/Stephen Robson

The Trust is encouraging naturalists visiting its gardens to record interesting wildlife they see and forward the information to the Trust via a special email address – gardenswildlifesurvey@nationaltrust.org.uk. Information will be collated and processed by volunteers, co-ordinated by the central National Trust Nature Conservation team. This information can then be sent to the properties and used in interpretation and education activities.

The major issue of climate change is also being tackled in many National Trust gardens, with gardeners and their teams adapting techniques and introducing new initiatives to help combat the changes occurring as a result. Many of the initiatives, such as collecting rain in water-butts for use during drought and using stakes to support plants and shrubs during stormy weather can be replicated in visitors' own gardens.

So if it's unearthing curious facts about the gardens' origins, exotic planting schemes and picking up tips from our garden staff or simply catching up on some quality time with friends and family, a National Trust garden is the perfect place to spend the day.

For all National Trust Property opening times, entry prices and travel directions visit www.nationaltrust.org.uk, call 0870 458 4000 or see entries in this guide.

Laura Brown
Visitor Marketing PR Officer

The Glasshouse at Clumber Park is one of the longest glasshouses in National Trust ownership.

Making
movies

'On second thought, let's not go to Camelot. It is a silly place.' Monty Python and the Holy Grail (1975)

In any plot line, with any script, the success of the production can depend on a good many things. Perhaps the most important influence is that of the canvas on which the story is portrayed. In the world of moving pictures, the scenery is already there, it simply has to be found.

Historic Scotland's extensive and diverse portfolio of heritage attractions offers a rich source of locations suitable for filming. Such projects not only enable more people and wider audiences to experience and appreciate wonderful heritage sites, but allow future generations to enjoy the reality of visiting the actual locations where filming history was made (eg Doune Castle in Stirlingshire, the location for *Monty Python and the Holy Grail*).

This inspirational backdrop certainly inspired the Monty Python producers, as rather than using numerous locations, they instead utilised many different areas of Doune Castle itself for their needs. Keeping the shots tight made sure that the attraction could easily transform into the various fictional castles within the film. Today, Doune remains an important place of pilgrimage for Python fans the world over. Approaching the Castle is an almost euphoric moment for many, as they instantly picture the opening scene of the film as King Arthur and Patsy 'ride' into the Castle, heralded only by the clip clop of coconuts. Doune, with its 100 foot high gatehouse high gatehouse, is breathtaking in itself but with the added interest brought by the film, its legendary status in the world was confirmed.

Scotland provides an often instantly recognisable film backdrop with a strong identity and character. Films such as *Greyfriars Bobby* (2005) for example, highlight Scottish culture and heritage. Shot at Holyrood Park and Edinburgh Castle, it was at Stirling Castle that filming of this heartwarming tale really made an impact. The Castle, with its magnificent Renaissance architecture, beautiful tapestries and paintings, is more akin to the beautiful sounds of harpsichord music drifting out of the Great Hall and the

Left & above: Crichton Castle.

All images © Crown Copyright

soft tones of visitors as they wander through the cobbled wynds; than the snorting and hooves of a bull and other animals, as it was transformed into a market place film set for two weeks.

Major films such as *Braveheart* and *Rob Roy* have been significant vehicles in highlighting the profile and appeal of Scotland and promoting the country as a holiday destination, the latter film using Historic Scotland's Crichton Castle as a location. Crichton's exceptional isolation, despite being just 15 miles from the capital city of Edinburgh, allowed the film makers to capture the remoteness of 17th century Scotland needed for the film. During filming of the BBC production of *Ivanhoe* (1997) starring Christopher Lee, extensive internal areas of Craigmillar Castle were used with many of the rooms being turned into small cottages, with thatch materials for the roof having to be added to complete the effect. An area was also dressed to portray a soldiers' barracks.

From cult comedy classics to children's tales to Shakespearean tragedies, heritage sites have the versatility to cater for all genres, and nothing is quite as diverse and distinct as one of the latest filming projects to take place at Blackness Castle. This striking, dominant fortress on the banks of the Firth of Forth is a formidable sight on approach. So when looking for a location for *Doomsday*, the action thriller which documents the spread of a lethal virus throughout a major country, the intimidating, magnificent Blackness Castle proved to be the perfect setting. Due to the scale of production, the Castle was closed to the public for the duration of filming, only the second time this had happened in its history, the first occurring as part of filming for Franco Zeffirelli's *Hamlet* starring Mel Gibson. As one of the strongest artillery fortifications of its age as well as a state prison, the Castle served the purpose well, its impenetrable defences proving the perfect atmosphere for such an ominous, yet thought-provoking film.

Over the last ten years, Historic Scotland has built up a positive relationship with all of the main bodies promoting filming in Scotland. This has enabled filmmakers to turn their location wish-list into a reality for over 200 projects a year. From castles to abbeys to cathedrals to prehistoric settlements to palaces to the mightiest artillery fortification in Europe, each attraction has individual character, whether it is on a grand scale such as Edinburgh, Stirling and Urquhart Castles or small, such as Corgarff Castle, Smailholm Tower and New Abbey Corn Mill. Whatever the location, Historic Scotland remains committed to maximising the possibilities for filmmakers…and that's a wrap.

Stirling Castle.

Great Hall, Stirling Castle.

For more information on filming at Historic Scotland attractions, please visit www.historic-scotland.gov.uk/filming or call 0131 668 8688.

Glasshouses
a glimpse of history

By May Woods

Of all garden buildings, decorative or functional, glasshouses
are unique. Their form keeps evolving as man's ability to
deliver the ideal environment for plants keeps improving

Davies Alpine House and Princess of Wales Conservatory, Kew Gardens, Surrey   © RBG Kew

Gardeners have always been ingenious, so glasshouse history is a tale of experiments in design, orientation, materials, heating and shading. The story starts with wooden sheds built round plants in winter and continues through to the latest ideas in the Alpine House at the Royal Botanic Gardens, Kew.

Citrus were, and still are, a vital feature of Italian gardens. At first, in Renaissance Italy, oranges and lemons, oleanders, pomegranates and myrtles were protected in winter with timber boards in gardens around Rome, but in Florence and further north they were taken into cellars to escape the colder winters. Lack of light in winter is no great disadvantage, provided humidity is low. The fashionable citruses were soon brought north to grace gardens in France, and then on to England. Sir William Cecil, Lord Burghley, sent to Paris in 1562 for a lemon tree and two myrtles, and probably kept them at Cecil House in the Strand; while by the late 16th century, Sir Francis Carew had a celebrated forest of orange trees at Beddington in Surrey. In winter, these trees were protected by large wooden sheds built up around them each autumn, and heated by two iron stoves.

Most tender plants, however, were kept in a frost proof shed or dark dry cellar, but one of the earliest illustrated houses for citrus plants was at Wimbledon Manor, put up for Queen Henrietta Maria in 1642. It was inspired by those in France, built in brick and it had a tiled roof and glass doors along the south facade to capture winter sunshine.

By the early 1700s there were many such brick buildings, known as greenhouses as they protected many tender evergreens as well as the ever popular citrus. Some were designed by architects and were exceedingly handsome, such as at Powis Castle, by William Winde, and Queen Anne's greenhouse at Kensington Palace by Vanbrugh and Hawksmoor, and there were plainer versions at the Chelsea Physic Garden and Lambeth Palace, and at Ham House in Surrey.

During the course of the 18th century the greenhouse became essential in every well appointed garden, from Bowood in Wiltshire to Kenwood in Hampstead; from Blenheim in Oxfordshire to Attingham Park in Shropshire; from Hanbury Hall in Worcestershire to Norton Conyers in Yorkshire; and in Scotland, at Arniston in Midlothian. All of these, and many more, are still in existence.

Left: Tropical section of the Glasshouse at Wisley, Surrey   © Mike Sleigh

The exterior of the Glasshouse at Wisley, Surrey   © Paul Upward

Meanwhile, inside the great walled gardens, tropical fruit and flowers were cherished with enthusiasm during the 18th century in timber framed glass roofed houses. Exotic fruit and deliciously scented flowers were collectors' items. The Bishop of London at Fulham Palace was growing pineapples, the Duchess of Beaufort had fruiting papaya and guavas and at the Chelsea Physic Garden Philip Miller was experimenting with heated floors and later heated rear walls, while avocado pears, coconuts, ginger and mahogany grew inside. These tropical plant houses were called stove houses, with cactus and aloes in the Dry Stove and humidity loving plants in the Hot Stove.

Around the beginning of the 19th century several important changes took place. Firstly, the value of overhead light for all plants was acknowledged, even in winter, so new greenhouses were built with glass roofs, such as Lord Brownlow's at Belton in Lincolnshire, and the Duke of Bedford's at Woburn Abbey in Bedfordshire. Secondly, improved techniques in the manufacture of cast iron allowed it to be easily moulded into any shape while retaining its strength, so it was ideal for slender, curving glazing bars. This development liberated design from the constraints of brick and wood, and led eventually, with larger panes of glass developed in the 1830s, to the soaring curves of the Palm House at Kew Gardens.

Thirdly, also in the 1830s, the system of heating with hot water pipes was perfected so that heat could be easily controlled and entirely reliable. Fourthly, the glorious profusion of exotic flowers in the walled garden was too distant from the house, so conservatories adjoining the drawing room were built to show them off to everyone. New country houses, like Ashridge Park in Hertfordshire, included attached conservatories, and older houses, like Broughton Hall in Yorkshire and Hurlingham House in Fulham, had conservatories added to them. Finally, terminology underwent a slightly confusing change. The greenhouse of the 18th century was renamed an orangery; and the term greenhouse was transferred to an all-glass house, be it in a walled or suburban garden.

By the middle of the 19th century, the well-appointed country house would have a conservatory attached to or near the house, an orangery across the lawns, greenhouses in the walled garden, plus a fernery and a peach house, hothouses, melon beds, pineries and vineries. After the Great War, all too many decayed into twisted skeletons, and were dismantled. Felbrigg Hall in Norfolk still has its handsome greenhouse in the flower garden, but the Great Stove at Chatsworth in Derbyshire and the Winter Garden at Somerleyton in Suffolk are both long gone.

The Orangery, Belton House, Lincolnshire

Norton Conyers, Yorkshire

Since the 1980s, both public and private glasshouses have enjoyed a great revival in popularity. Once again, a conservatory is a fashionable addition, for living space more than for plants, whether tucked on the back of a town house or gracing a country manor. But our gardening traditions have been rediscovered too as we look at the skills and techniques of our predecessors. A set of 19th century glasshouses was discovered in 1991 at Heligan in Cornwall. Brambles and ivy had smothered their timber frames, splintered glass and old heating pipes, but now they are gleaming again and wonderfully productive, including even the pineapple pit. The old greenhouses at Tatton Park in Cheshire are back in action again producing peaches and grapes, and pineapples are due to fruit in 2009.

Birmingham, Sheffield, Edinburgh, Glasgow and many other cities have maintained or restored their impressive 19th century heritage and at Kew, the superbly graceful Palm House of the 1840s has been rebuilt and planted afresh. Again at Kew, the Princess of Wales Conservatory was completed in 1987 with ten separate climate zones, using an energy conscious design.

The Eden Project has the largest hothouse in the world, not made of glass as it would be too heavy, but instead covered with three layers of a type of polythene. Under its interlocking hexagons grows a tropical jungle of the fruit and vegetables we eat, and the plants we use for raw materials. The newest shining example is the glasshouse at the Royal Horticultural Society's gardens at Wisley in Surrey. Although only opened in the summer of 2007, the vegetation is already abundantly lush and floriferous in the tropical and temperate zones, with climbers racing up columns and carpets of flowers tumbling over rocks.

Back at the Royal Botanic Gardens at Kew is a most interesting new Alpine House, opened in 2006. Alpines are often protected from extreme cold in winter by a blanket of snow which melts in the spring, so they need to be dry in winter and moist in spring and early summer. Planted in poor soil, they are used to wind and sun but not great heat, hard to avoid in a traditional glass house. Architects Wilkinson Eyre calculated that 10 metres was the height necessary for warm air to exit naturally and quickly through roof vents and for cooler air to be drawn in at ground level. The higher are the vents, the quicker is the process. In addition, a fan blows cool air over the alpines, drawn in from outside and cooled by 3 or 4 degrees C by passing through a labyrinth of chambers under the floor. Shading helps to keep the temperature down to 30 degrees in summer.

The colours, shapes, scents, and forms of the myriad plants in the world still inspire new designs for botanic glasshouses, while ingenuity and experimentation are still essential for the glasshouse gardener striving to mimic the climates of origin. As a result, plants from all around the globe are here in this country for us all to enjoy.

May Woods is the author of Visions of *Arcadia: European Gardens from Renaissance to Rococo* (Aurum Press, 1996) and co-author with Arete Warren of *Glass Houses: a History of Orangeries, Greenhouses and Conservatories* (Aurum Press, 1988).

Broughton Hall, Yorkshire

Princess of Wales Conservatory, Kew Gardens, Surrey   © RBG Kew

An aerial shot of the Eden Project, Cornwall   © Ben Foster

Shooting Granada TV's "Henry VIII" at Berkeley Castle, Gloucestershire

As seen on TV

Filming on location provides an authenticity that cannot be achieved with studio sets. Actors often find it easier. They can imbibe the atmosphere of a place, which not only helps them to be totally natural but is also conducive to their performance. They don't have to imagine that a building actually extends beyond the studio wall. That is why historic houses, their exteriors and interiors, their landscaped parks, gardens and ancillary buildings are regularly in demand by commercial film makers for use as locations.

But for the house owner, it can be alarming. Some have likened the arrival of a film crew to that of a circus coming to town! Space has to be found for mobile canteens, make-up and hairdressing caravans, props, generators, wardrobes and artists' trailers, and a production office. Those who are unfamiliar with the filming of a full-scale drama for the cinema or TV will have no idea of how demanding and destructive to normal life location work can be. Nevertheless there is a financial incentive and it can be fun. Moreover, if the film is a success and the house is open to the public, it adds further interest for the visitor.

Some properties, like Dorney Court (Windsor), Knebworth (Hertfordshire) and Eltham Palace, being close to London and film studios, have been particularly convenient and much used.

The Midlands and the West Country have also provided a rich crop of locations. Further north, Castle Howard (Yorkshire) has featured in many films and TV series, the most famous of which was Granada TV's filming of Evelyn Waugh's novel "Brideshead Revisited" in 1981. Now, even though it is unlikely that Waugh identified his "Brideshead" with a building like Castle Howard, it has just been used again in the summer of 2007 for a new making of "Brideshead Revisited". The original production, starring Anthony Andrews, Jeremy Irons and Diana Quick, achieved symbolic status as one of the great costume dramas and has been seen by millions across the world. The new film, to be released in late 2008, features Michael Gambon and Emma Thompson as Lord and Lady Marchmain, Matthew Goode as Charles Ryder, Ben Wishaw as Sebastian Flyte and Hayley Atwell as Julia Flyte.

Below: Filming of the new "Brideshead Revisted" at Castle Howard in Yorkshire

The Hartland Abbey estate, in a beautiful situation on the North Devon coast, has been used for a diverse selection of productions. Three years ago part of "The Shellseekers" by Rosamund Pilcher was filmed at Hartland with Vanessa Redgrave playing the main role. It was not so much the Abbey that was used, but a 15th cottage at Blackpool Mill by the rocky Atlantic cove familiar to those visitors to the Abbey who enjoy the walk to the beach.

Last year Hartland was used to film part of multi-award-winning writer Andrew Davies' ("Bleak House", "Pride and Prejudice") romantic, witty and stylish new three-part adaptation of Jane Austen's "Sense and Sensibility", a BBC drama production to be shown on BBC1 in Spring 2008. Andrew Davies says, "The novel is as much about sex and money as social conventions. This drama is more overtly sexual than most previous Austen adaptations seen on screen and gets to grip with the dark underbelly of the book".

The production has an all-star cast but the restrained, rational Elinor Dashwood and the wildly romantic, impulsive Marianne Dashwood are played by sensational newcomers, Hattie Morahan (Elinor) and Charity Wakefield (Marianne). Coincidentally, Hattie Morahan's father, the well-known film director Christopher Morahan, had been evacuated to Hartland Abbey during the War. Lady Stucley, whose home is at Hartland Abbey, said that "working with the BBC on this production was a joy. Even though the weather was unfavourable from day one which could have resulted in mayhem, the brilliant location manager, Rupert Bray, was so organised that everything ran smoothly. The crew and actors were fantastic, our car park on the lawn next to the house was the unit base including delicious catering in a double-decker bus. Our visitors adored bumping into actors in period costumes or seeing coachmen queuing for ice creams".

Broughton Castle in North Oxfordshire has long been a favourite location both for historical drama and contemporary films. Adaptability is important and its variety of rooms, broad moat, gatehouse, parkland and nearby church, offer many opportunities. Its Oak Room and Great Hall featured in the sumptuous 1998 production of "Shakespeare in Love" with Joseph Fiennes (related to the Fiennes family who live at Broughton) and Gwyneth Paltrow. The Dining Room was turned into the King's bedroom at one end and Queen Charlotte's bedroom at the other for "The Madness of King George" (1994) and recently it was the location for Stephen Poliakoff's "Friends and Crocodiles".

The Weald & Downland Open Air Museum near Chichester, Sussex has over 45 original historic buildings re-erected on site here being shown for the filming of Granada TV's "Henry VIII"

Keira Knightley, who received an Academy Award nomination for her role as Elizabeth Bennet in "Pride and Prejudice" has, in her comparatively short career, experienced a large number of historic house locations. In "Pride and Prejudice" Basildon Park (Berkshire) featured as 'Netherfield'; Chatsworth as 'Pemberley' home of Mr Darcy and Burghley House (Lincolnshire) as the home of Lady Catherine de Burgh (played by Dame Judi Dench).

"Pride and Prejudice" at Basildon Park

Filming in the Heaven Room at Burghley House.

Below: The Hartland Abbey Estate in Devon used as a location for "Sense and Sensibility".

In "Atonement", the film released in 2007, the major location was Stokesay Court in Shropshire which is featured for the first time in this edition of *Hudson's*.

Keira Knightley has recently been playing Georgiana, the 5th Duchess of Devonshire and great-great-great-great aunt of Diana, Princess of Wales. A number of scenes have appropriately been filmed at Chatsworth. The script for the movie "The Duchess" has been adapted from Amanda Forman's biography of the 18th century aristocrat who endured her husband, the Duke of Devonshire's affair with her best friend, Lady Elizabeth 'Bess' Foster. Their unhappy marriage inspired Richard Brinsley Sheridan's play "School for Scandal". Ralph Fiennes is playing Knightley's on-screen husband while Charlotte Rampling is playing Lady Spencer.

Another actress familiar with historic locations is Cate Blanchett. When starring in "Elizabeth" (1998), the film was shot around the UK at locations which included Alnwick Castle, the beach below Bamburgh Castle, Aydon Castle, Warkworth Castle (all in Northumberland), Haddon Hall (Derbyshire) and the Tower of London. She has recently finished filming "Elizabeth: the Golden Age", a gripping historical thriller documenting Queen Elizabeth I's reign, being filmed and set in a number of locations around the UK including Hatfield House (Hertfordshire), Winchester Cathedral (Hampshire), Leeds Castle (Kent), Burghley House (Lincolnshire), Petworth House (Sussex) and Dorney Court (Berkshire).

Stokesay Court in Shropshire was the main location for the film "Atonement".

The Historic Chapels Trust
Preserving places of worship in England

The Historic Chapels Trust was established to take into ownership redundant chapels and other places of worship in England which are of outstanding architectural and historic interest – securing for public benefit their preservation, repair and regeneration.

Below are 14 of the chapels in the care of HCT which you can visit on application to the keyholder. Farfield and Coanwood are, experimentally, left open.

Biddlestone RC Chapel, Northumberland 01665 574420, 01669 630270, 01669 620230

Coanwood Friends Meeting House, Northumberland 01434 321316

Cote Baptist Chapel, Oxfordshire 01993 850901

Farfield Friends Meeting House, West Yorkshire 01756 710587

The Dissenters' Chapel, Kensal Green Cemetery, London 020 7602 0173

Penrose Methodist Chapel, St Ervan, Cornwall 01841 540737

Salem Chapel, East Budleigh, Devon 01395 446189, 01395 445236

Shrine of Our Lady of Lourdes, Blackpool, Lancashire 01253 302373

St Benet's Chapel, Netherton, Merseyside 0151 520 2600

St George's German Lutheran Church, Tower Hamlets, London 020 7481 0533

Todmorden Unitarian Church, West Yorkshire 01706 815407

Wainsgate Baptist Church, West Yorkshire 01422 843315

Wallasey Unitarian Church, Merseyside 0151 639 9707

Walpole Old Chapel, Suffolk 01986 798308

For further information please visit our website: www.hct.org.uk or telephone: 020 7481 0533

Historic Chapels Trust, St George's German Lutheran Church, 55 Alie Street, London E1 8EB
Tel: 020 7481 0533   **Fax:** 020 7488 3756   **E-mail:** chapels@hct.org.uk   **Web:** www.hct.org.uk
Company No. 2778395 Registered Charity No. 1017321

Votive Shrine of Our Lady of Lourdes

Pulpit, Wallasey Memorial Unitarian Church

St George's German Lutheran Church.

Salem Chapel

Cote Chapel

Biddlestone Chapel

Liverpool's 800th Birthday Celebrations, 2007

A company that inspires passion
Fantastic Fireworks

Brocket Hall Private Party

There are many beautiful things in the world which inspire passion but few can match the impact of fireworks. Feelings of joy, pride and excitement are just some of the emotions stirred up by the sight of those huge starbursts exploding in the sky. When you add the chest-thumping booms which accompany them, the feeling of overwhelming pleasure is complete.

Leeds Castle Summer Concert

At Fantastic Fireworks we have more than 20 years' experience in creating such emotions. From Blenheim Palace in Oxfordshire to Chatsworth in Derbyshire we have entertained Russian billionaires celebrating a birthday, concert audiences enjoying a last night of the proms and wedding guests bidding a spectacular farewell to the bride and groom. Whatever the event our team of experts pay special attention not only to the needs of the client but of the venue as well.

We are very aware that venues are open all year round and that fireworks play only a small part in their busy schedule. This is why we take special care to clear up thoroughly after our displays - often at first light the following day - in order to ensure the grounds are left as we found them, for the pleasure of visitors. We are also sensitive to the issue of noise. For venues where this is a problem, we have created The Quiet Collection™, a series of firework sequences which are still beautiful to behold but which do not rattle the window panes!

Many of our displays are choreographed to both live and recorded music. For live music performances such as outdoor concerts we work with Musical Directors to ensure sympathetic treatment and perfect choreography. For recorded music we will work closely with the client, suggesting and creating soundtracks individually tailored to the occasion and the venue. If there is a lake we will use fireworks whose reflections make a breathtaking impact. For company occasions we can create logos in glittering fireworks. All this is achieved using the latest computerised firing systems.

However it is not the technology which makes Fantastic Fireworks the country's leading name in pyrotechnics, it is our people and our imagination. Please call us to see how we can create something beautiful for you.

Fantastic Fireworks
It's what we do

Fantastic Fireworks, Rocket Park, Pepperstock, Herts LU1 4LL Tel 01582 485555 Fax 01582 485545
email info@fantasticfireworks.co.uk
web: www.fantasticfireworks.co.uk

The Landmark Trust

Preserving our past
for the future

The Landmark Trust is a charity with two purposes.
The first is to rescue worthwhile buildings and their
surroundings from neglect. The second is to promote the
enjoyment of such places, mainly by letting them for holidays.

The West Blockhouse before and after restoration

A bedroom at Cawood Castle

Since its foundation in 1965 the Landmark Trust has saved over 200 buildings of historic interest or architectural importance from decay or unsympathetic alteration. More than 20 are Grade I Listed and over 180 have been made available to stay in. In this way, many different people find themselves for a short time the owners of a fine old building.

By sleeping under its roof visitors profit far more from each place than by looking at it only; they can study it at leisure, be there early and late, in all lights and weathers. They will see, too, what can be done by the modern architects and builders, and craftsmen and women, who have worked on its repair. Whether they are already enthusiasts or simply want a holiday in beautiful surroundings, the chances are that they will return with their interest roused.

Being let for holidays also has advantages for the building. It is constantly used and shared by a wide variety of people. An income is generated for its upkeep in the future. Each building has modern bathrooms and heating, sheets and towels, open fires wherever possible and a well-equipped kitchen. There will also be good furniture and interesting pictures, specially chosen books and a history album revealing the secrets of the building's past.

What sort of buildings does Landmark take on? The answer is almost anything that is good of its kind and which, for whatever reason, is now at risk. For over forty years it has championed the humble and the functional – simple cottages in unspoiled but fragile settings, survivors of past industries, fortifications of any period – and remain firmly committed to their cause. Alongside these are the many ornamental buildings whose excuse for existing was little more than to amuse, entertain or impress.

Landmark is seldom able to resist the curious and the highly individual, but are fond too of buildings once so ordinary as to be taken for granted but which, swept aside by changes in fashion, are now rare. These include vernacular buildings and those on the old canal and railway systems and one of its latest projects, Stoker's Cottage in Cambridgeshire, part of the Fenland's rich industrial history. Here lived the stoker, who kept the boilers topped up with coal at the Stretham Steam Engine (now disused) next door.

The Pineapple

Stoker's Cottage, Cambridgeshire

Some of Landmark's buildings have been larger undertakings such as the recent restoration of The Grange, the house designed and lived in by architect and designer Augustus Pugin and the current restoration of Silverton Park Stables in Devon, the unfinished stable block built in monumental style by the 4th Earl of Egremont. It is all that remains of Silverton Park which was never fully completed and the house itself was demolished within 50 years of being built.

Silverton Park Stables, Devon, under current construction

For further details about the work of the Landmark Trust visit **www.landmarktrust.org.uk** or telephone **01628 825925**. The 22nd edition of the Landmark Trust Handbook, which contains details of all 184 buildings, can be purchased for £11.50 (refundable on a booking).

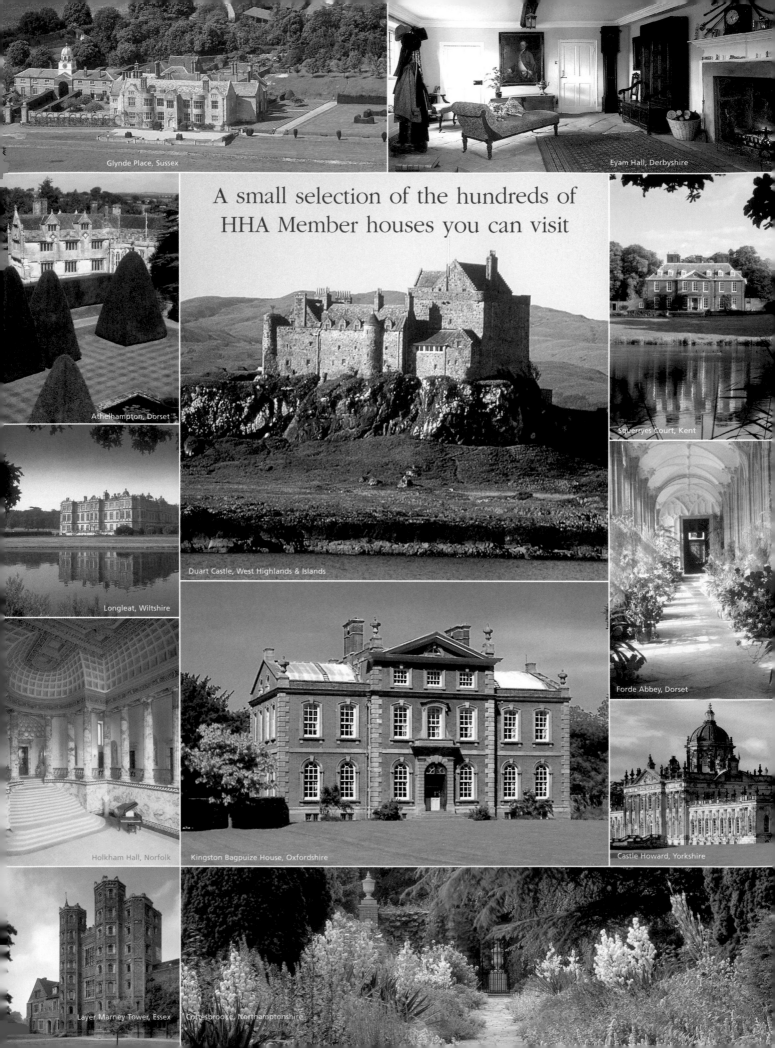

Glynde Place, Sussex

Eyam Hall, Derbyshire

A small selection of the hundreds of HHA Member houses you can visit

Athelhampton, Dorset

Squerryes Court, Kent

Duart Castle, West Highlands & Islands

Longleat, Wiltshire

Forde Abbey, Dorset

Holkham Hall, Norfolk

Kingston Bagpuize House, Oxfordshire

Castle Howard, Yorkshire

Layer Marney Tower, Essex

Cottesbrooke, Northamptonshire

HISTORIC HOUSES ASSOCIATION

Cottesbrooke, Northamptonshire

Become a Friend of the HHA and visit nearly 300 privately owned houses and gardens FREE

From just £36 for an annual membership, we offer free access to more houses than in the ownership of the National Trust and English Heritage combined.

Friends Membership benefits include:-
- Free entry to nearly 300 houses, parks and gardens
- 4 magazines a year
- Opportunities to join tours to see houses not usually open to the public

There is a fascinating diversity of properties to visit free with a Friends of the HHA card – from the great treasure houses such as Burghley and Woburn Abbey to intimate manor houses, such as Athelhampton and Owlpen. What makes these places so special is their individuality and the fact that they are generally still lived in – often by the same family that has owned them through centuries of British history. As well as the beautiful gardens which surround the houses, there are over 60 additional wonderful gardens to visit.

The subscription rate remains outstanding value for money. Individual Friend: £36. Double Friends living at the same address: £58 (each additional Friend living at same address, £17.50 – only available to holders of a Double Membership or for children (under 16) of holders of Individual Memberships). If you wish to become a Friend of the HHA, then you can join, using your credit/debit card by calling 01462 896688 or simply fill in the form below.

You can also join online at www.hha.org.uk

Members of NADFAS, CLA and The Art Fund are offered special rates of £33 Individual and £55 Double (at same address).

FRIENDS APPLICATION FORM   HHHG/08

PLEASE USE BLOCK CAPITALS   *DELETE AS APPROPRIATE

MR/MRS/MS or MR & MRS*   INITIALS _____

SURNAME _____

ADDRESS _____

_____

_____

POST CODE _____

ADDITIONAL FRIENDS AT SAME ADDRESS

_____

DATES OF BIRTH OF CHILDREN UNDER 16

_____

I/We* are members of NADFAS / CLA / The Art Fund (please circle name of organisation to which you belong) our membership number is: _____

☐ I/We* enclose remittance of £ _____ payable to the Historic Houses Association.

☐ I/We* have completed the direct debit adjacent.

Please return to:
HHA, Friends Membership Dept, Heritage House, PO Box 21, Baldock, Hertfordshire SG7 5SH.
Telephone: 01462 896688

INSTRUCTION TO YOUR BANK TO PAY DIRECT DEBITS

Please complete Parts 1 to 5 to instruct your Bank to make payments directly from your account. Then return the form to: **Historic Houses Association, Membership Dept, Heritage House, PO Box 21, Baldock, Hertfordshire, SG7 5SH.**

1. Name and full postal address of your Bank

_____

_____

Your Bank may decline to accept instructions to pay Direct Debits from some types of accounts.

2. Account holder name

_____

3. Account number

4. Bank sort code

Originator's identification No.   `9 3 0 5 8 7`

Originator's reference
(office use only)

5. Your instructions to the Bank and signature.

■ I instruct you to pay Direct Debits for my annual subscription from my account at the request of the Historic Houses Association.

■ The amounts are variable and may be debited on various dates.

■ I understand that the Historic Houses Association may change the amounts and dates only after giving me prior notice of not less than 21 days.

■ Please cancel all previous Standing Order and Direct Debiting instructions in favour of the Historic Houses Association.

■ I will inform the Bank in writing if I wish to cancel this instruction.

■ I understand that if any Direct Debit is paid which breaks the terms of the instruction, the Bank will make a refund.

Signature(s)

_____

Date: _____

DIRECT Debit Completion of the form above ensures that your subscription will be paid automatically on the date that it is due. You may cancel the order at any time. The Association guarantees that it will only use this authority to deduct annually from your account an amount equal to the annual subscription then current for your class of membership.

PHOTOCOPIES OF THIS FORM ARE ACCEPTABLE

IF COMPLETING THE DIRECT DEBIT FORM, YOU MUST ALSO COMPLETE THE APPLICATION FORM.

The Principal Rooms

The selection, size and arrangement of rooms in the country house reflect the personal demands and expectations of the owner, his family and his guests. No one house is the same as another. There were, however, certain fashionable room types although the date at which they appear can vary greatly, as with all parts of the house, depending on how close the property was to major cities and the owner to court and political life.

This chapter will look at the most common room types, the general dates at which they were popular and features to look out for within.

It is worth noting though that despite these periodic changes the rooms on show in many houses today will have been laid out in the 19th and early 20th century and often seem like a procession of similar, lavishly decorated voids. Although some bodies like the National Trust have endeavoured to return interiors to earlier periods in the history of a house, the original use of the room may only be discernible from its size, position within the layout or the detailing in its decoration.

THE HALL

Whether it was a medieval knight stepping through the timber doorway into his lord's manor house or a Georgian gentleman entering a fellow aristocrat's mansion from under a towering portico, their first impression of their host's power or refinement would be cast by the hall. Yet this room was originally much more than somewhere to take off your coat, more than just a vestibule full of sculptures and portraits, in fact it started its life as the very house itself.

The Saxon or Norman manor house would usually have consisted of one large building, very much like a barn, surrounded by lesser structures and an external face or wall. This principal building was the hall. The lord, his fellow nobles, personal army, and servants would eat, drink and sleep in this one cavernous space. In the middle was a hearth with the fumes from the fire drifting up through blackened timbers and a gap in the roof, while at one end was a raised platform, the dais, from which the lord dealt justice, gathered men in arms, managed his farmland and was entertained. The hall was a bedroom, dining room, a theatre and a courtroom. It was the centre of the community and all were welcome.

However, sleeping with a group of belching servants, snoring soldiers and scratching dogs, upon filthy and muck ridden straw, somehow lost is appeal for later medieval lords! They built wings and extensions onto their halls to create private rooms in what is called the solar. At the other end a buttery and

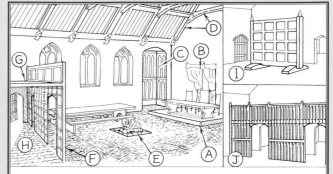

Fig 8.2: *A view of a late medieval hall with elaborate window openings and straw covering the floor. The dais (A) has upon it the lord's seat with its canopy (B) to keep out the chills and a large oriel window (C) illuminating this end of the room. Above are the trusses (D) supporting the roof timbers, while in the middle is the central hearth (E). At the entrance end of the hall is the screen (F) the inserting of which has formed a minstrels' gallery above (G) and a passage below (H). The earliest screens were free-standing and portable (I), while later fixed ones featured beautiful carving (J).*

pantry were added, often with a passage between to access the separate kitchen. The later Middle Ages were also a time of great social changes accelerated by the Black Death, which saw the breaking down of the old feudal system and the renting out of manor lands. Decisions on managing the fields were increasingly made by the new yeoman farmers and therefore the hall's role as the centre of the estate and community faded. By the 15th and 16th centuries the hearths were being removed to the sides, ceiling inserted and rooms created above. Note though that these changes to the running of the estate occurred at different times across the country, and the hall may have still been fulfilling its communal role in some areas at a later date.

Those genuine medieval halls which survive today usually have the whitewash and paintwork stripped from their walls, stone slabs on the floor where straw and earth sufficed and glass in windows where once oiled cloth or shutters kept out the cold. Despite this it would be difficult not to be impressed by the scale of the room and the impressive timber trusses which support the roof above. Another area where the carver could show off his skill with wood was on the screen. Keeping warm was a major problem in such a large room, so to reduce the draughts which would come howling through the main doorway a screen was built, at first a movable one but later fixed, which created a passage at one end of the hall (screens passage). By the 16th century these screens had become elaborately carved, often with a platform above from which minstrels could play. A popular piece of decoration in the medieval hall was the lord's coat of arms, which not only represented his high status but also, when formed into a family tree of arms (often in the stained glass of oriel windows) displayed his links to important or powerful families.

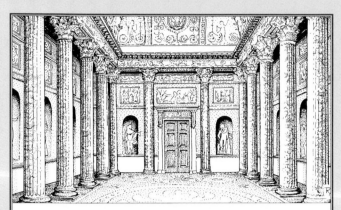

Fig 8.4: Kedleston Hall, Derbyshire
In the 18th century fantastic marble and stone halls were a feature of Palladian houses. This example by Robert Adam has columns made from local alabaster (a form of gypsum or limestone) with flutings which were cut on site, arched niches containing sculptures and a huge coffered ceiling above.

At the same time as many peasants were still enjoying the hospitality of their lord, Renaissance aristocrats and gentlemen were erecting new houses for display, with a series of refined, classically decorated rooms with which to impress their guests. The hall was often still the centre of the house and placed lengthways across it when viewed from the front. For the first time though at Hardwick Hall it was turned 90° and became the long, thin entrance room we associate it with today. As the hall was now one of the rooms through which guests passed, you would hardly want servants eating and sleeping within, so gradually separate accommodation and a servants' hall in which they could take meals were created.

The 17th century hall would usually be wood panelled with a new patterned plaster ceiling. It would have within it, or off to one end, a beautifully carved staircase by which guests could ascend to the state rooms. By the 18th century it had risen in importance again, forming part of the piano nobile on the first floor with usually external steps leading up to it. The vivid colours which were popular in Palladian houses, to best display gilt-framed pictures, gradually made way for pale, plastered walls with columns and a floor of light coloured stone and marble. These cool rooms could also be used for dining in the heat of summer as well as being spacious enough to welcome a party of guests or to serve as an antechamber. Later, the assortment of styles available to the Victorian gentleman resulted in halls of medieval grandeur in mock Tudor houses, as well as ones that were more of an extended stairwell with illumination from above.

▓ THE GREAT CHAMBER

One of the first rooms to appear when the owner sought more privacy from his medieval hall was an upper chamber in which he could dine and sleep called the solar (from the Latin word 'solarium', with the root 'sol', meaning sun). Food was brought up in a procession from the service rooms at the other end of the hall, past his household sitting along tables in the hall and then up a staircase at the side of the dais. By the later Middle Ages though, the lord was likely to be receiving guests in the solar and eating in state so with its increased status the room became more lavishly decorated and had a separate bedchamber leading off it. Around this time it became known as the great chamber.

The great chamber was popular during the 16th and early 17th century and it could usually be found upstairs in a crosswing or built directly above the hall when this was divided horizontally by inserting a ceiling. Displaying hanging tapestries or family portraits, it was used for important meals and sometimes for music, plays and dancing. Wood panelling was added to the walls and the chairs would have had horsehair covers (which did not retain the smell of food). Details like royal coats of arms above the chimneypiece and hunting themes in the decoration were popular. Later chambers started to increase in scale with coved ceilings while paintings were built in above the chimneypiece and carved features such as fruit, flowers and birds adorned the panelling.

Fig 8.6: Calke Abbey, Derbyshire
The dining room created in 1794 is decorated with plaster mouldings framing small inset pictures, while the alcove behind the columns features a sideboard which could be used when serving meals. Note the door just behind the right-hand column which could give servants a discreet access to the room.

THE BANQUETING HALL

In the later medieval hall, once the dignitaries had finished their main course they could retire to a separate room to eat a luxurious selection of wafers and spices. In the 16th century this was also referred to as a 'banquet' (and not just the huge meal which we associate with the word), and in some larger houses an impressive room was constructed specifically for it. The banqueting hall often had access to the roof, or in some cases was even built on top of it so the relaxing diners could admire the views. Whole banqueting houses were sometimes built as separate structures out in the garden.

THE PARLOUR

Such a large room was excessive for everyday meals, so a parlour would have been provided for the family. Parlour comes from the French verb 'parler', to speak, and it could have also been a room in which to hold private conversation. They can be found in country houses from the 15th century and were usually simply decorated with an oval gate leg able which could be removed when required. There was little other furniture as masses of plates and cutlery were not used at this time; the guest brought their own knife and spoon, and forks were not in general use until the 18th century. Larger houses may have had more than one, perhaps a great and little parlour, while in 18th and 19th century houses you will probably find a selection of rooms intended for the family to dine in, often labelled by the certain times of the day or season in which they were used (for example, 'breakfast room').

THE DINING ROOM

By the 18th century a new room within the state apartments on the piano nobile began to appear. The dining room replaced the great chamber as the place where important meals were held, becoming a major element in 19th century houses where it was as much for show as for eating. Walls were usually plastered or stuccoed with floral, fruit and animal designs around the cornice and friezes while shutters were recommended in place of curtains to avoid lingering food odours.

Victorians were better at ergonomics than their predecessors and would rather receive their meals hot, so the dining room would not be positioned too far from the kitchen. A serving area would be nearby where the different parts of the meal were collected before they were brought into the room. Some even had hidden doorways so that servants could emerge to remove dishes with minimal fuss. It was only in the 19th century that the table became a fixed piece of furniture in the middle of what was now a permanent dining room, rather than the previous gate leg type which could be removed and the chairs pushed up against the walls when the room was to be used for another purpose.

THE SALOON

The great chamber died out from the late 17th century, its rôle being taken over by the dining room and saloon in the state apartments of Baroque and Palladian houses. The saloon (a French word derived from the Italian 'sala', meaning a hall) was ideally placed centrally, behind the entrance hall, with the dining room and drawing room on each side and views over the garden to the rear. This room was regarded as essential in 18th century houses and would be as tall as the hall, even if this meant lifting the floor of the room above. Architects could make use of its grand scale and produced domed round rooms or large double cubed spaces with alcoves and apses, with huge coffered ceilings and shallow bowed windows.

It was here that the best pieces of artwork, sculpture and furniture could be displayed, and concerts, balls and other entertainment held. As the room was not used for dining, the walls could be covered in delicate fabrics and paintings hung upon them. By the 19th century many saloons had become no more than picture galleries, and were referred to as such, with glass panels in the ceiling, very much like a Victorian museum, whiles dances and great gatherings could take place in a separate ballroom.

WITHDRAWING ROOMS

As the medieval solar developed into the more luxurious great chamber, a separate bedroom was usually built off it for the owner. Between these rooms an antechamber was supplied where he could take a private meal in the days before a parlour, and his servant could sleep on a straw pallet and guard the door to his bedroom. This room was referred to as the withdrawing room.

By the late 16th and early 17th century the room had become more of a private sitting room where the owner could hang his

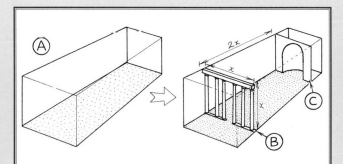

Fig 8.7: *State rooms like the hall, saloon and dining rooms of new 18th century country houses would preferably form a single or double cube. When refitting an existing house, however, moving walls to create these proportions was not usually practical. At Syon House, London, Robert Adam was faced with a long thin room (A), so he ingeniously inserted a screen of columns (B) and an apse (C), thus making the space between them a double cube.*

favourite or best pieces of art. In Baroque houses though it formed part of the state apartments and was nearly always positioned between the saloon and the bedchambers. In 18th century houses it was still expected to be an intimate room, often with a lower ceiling than the saloon and hall, delicate fabrics on the walls and curtains with pelmets around the windows (before it became fashionable to hang them in all rooms). It was regarded as a feminine room; while the men stayed on to smoke and drink in the dining room, the ladies would retire to what was now generally referred to as the drawing room. Its role was vague – you could find card tables, spinning wheels or a piano within, music often being the decorative theme. Through the Regency period the informality grew with chairs in groups around the room rather than up against the walls; the French fashion for hanging a mirror above the fireplace became popular and there was increased comfort and luxury with large draped pelmets gathered above the curtains. Today, the drawing room has become a place with no specific purpose and rooms where their original role has been forgotten are often labelled as such.

❧ BEDCHAMBERS

The most recognised symbol of a country house bedroom is the four poster bed. They became common by the 16th century, giving the occupants a form of draught exclusion and some much needed privacy in bedrooms, which even when separated from the old great chambers still had a medley of servants buzzing around through the day. Four posters became the single most expensive item of furniture in a house and were usually positioned on the opposite side of the room from the windows which had a dressing table and looking glass on the wall between them. By the late 17th century a separate room for dressing was provided so the table became more of a showpiece.

In the Baroque houses of this date the state bedchamber was at the end of the enfilade after the saloon and withdrawing rooms, although it was less ornate than those which preceded it. In late 17th and early 18th century bedchambers there was a fashion for positioning the four poster behind rails or within an alcove divided off from the rest of the room by columns. This helped keep the room clear for other uses through the day, and made a grand climax to the procession of retiring to the state bed, although there may have also been a door to the side of the alcove for the occupant to access another more private bed after the ceremony.

With the end of the piano nobile in the 19th century and the resiting of the principal rooms on the ground floor, the bedrooms went upstairs, although it was usual to retain a bedchamber on the ground floor for infirm or elderly members of the family. These new rooms tended to be smaller than the old state bedchambers but more numerous as the Victorian gentleman was likely to be entertaining large parties of guests rather than smaller family groups.

Going back to the late 17th century, additional rooms off the bedchamber were being provided for dressing, where possible at the far end of the enfilade. In the case of a lady there was a dressing room, while the gentleman's version was known as a cabinet. William III met his closest circle of ministers within his cabinet and the name still refers to the group of senior ministers in government today. Corner fireplaces and oriental artwork were popular and small pictures were often hung here as these rooms tended to have lower ceilings than the bedroom. This meant that a space above could be provided for the servants. By the later 18th century ladies were likely to have a boudoir (from the French word 'bouder', meaning sulk!), a private sitting room where they could sew or read in increasing luxury. As bedchambers moved upstairs and became the conventional bedroom the male cabinets next to them were known simply as dressing rooms.

Another bedroom off the bedchamber or dressing room was the closet, a room for keeping the close stool (basically a chamber pot covered by a closed top with a hole in it). In earlier medieval houses a chamber pot would have been used in the great chamber while separate garderobes may have been provided elsewhere. These were tiny rooms with a simple hole in a board to form a toilet seat and either earth below which could afterwards be used as fertiliser, or a drop down directly into the moat. In 16th century country house the closet may have been no more than a cupboard sized room with no light or ventilation. This was bad enough for the dignitary who had to use it, even worse for the poor servant who had to walk through the house with a pot full of effluent afterwards! By the later 17th century the closet had become more of a private sanctuary, a larger room were the owner could expect to be seated on something more

Fig 8.9: *A bedchamber with a rail closing off the alcove containing the four poster bed, with a doorway to the left of it giving access to a private sleeping room. These rails were only a short-lived fashion and rarely survive today although the bed may still be found in an alcove.*

Fig 8.10: Little Moreton Hall, Cheshire
The left-hand photograph shows the garderobes extension which protrudes from the front of the building. The right-hand picture shows the interior of one of the garderobes with the toilet seat hole leading directly down into the moat which runs below.

luxurious, like veneered wood or even a velvet seat, while his waste would be carried away with more privacy. The invention of flushing toilets and bathrooms in the 19th century made closets a thing of the past.

THE LONG GALLERY

Today's glass-roofed leisure parks are not the bright new idea they might appear. Elizabethans were well aware of the limitations of the English weather and built themselves huge long rooms for recreational use, illuminated by masses of glass windows. These long galleries were in high fashion for a relatively short period from the mid 16th to mid 17th century, yet their distinctive long, thin form are a notable feature of numerous country houses even after later alterations. They can be more than 170ft in length, have at least two walls full of glass, with wood panelling elsewhere, so the family and their guests could admire the view while promenading along the boarded floor. The rooms were used for sports like real tennis, games including billiards or shove halfpenny on long shuffleboards, and even workouts on early dumb bells or exercise chairs! Others were more educational with portraits of important dignitaries lining one of the walls and symbols with hidden meanings in the plasterwork. They were a gym, sports hall, art gallery and viewing tower all in one.
Their shape, however, did not fit easily into the later Baroque houses and although some were built in the 18th century for artwork, dances and after dinner chats, many of the existing ones became libraries or pictures galleries. By the Victorian period their rôle, as was usual, had been absorbed by numerous smaller rooms, with the children now playing in the nursery, male recreation taking place in the billiards room, the ladies using their boudoir or drawing room, topical discussions being held in the study and dancing in the ballroom.

LIBRARY

The 17th century gentleman who collected curiosities usually stored them in his cabinet (off the bedchamber) but the 18th century connoisseur who bought up much larger works of art, sculpture and literature would have to find more room. The spacious Palladian halls, saloons, drawing rooms and dining rooms would house his artworks, but a separate library would now be required for his books.

At this time collecting books was a new fashion inspired by an intellectual thirst for Art and Politics, but in medieval or Tudor households they were rarely found, not only because few ere made but also because prowess on the field of arms was more important than gaining knowledge. The Renaissance man educated in the Humanities may have started gathering some volumes but these precious items would not be kept in one particular place. In the 17th century, especially after the founding of scientific societies, more books were likely to be collected and were usually stored in the gentlemen's closet (keeping a book or newspaper in the toilet today is not such a new idea). In fact early libraries, which at the time were very much male preserves, can often be found built off the closet.

By the 18th century though, the importance of literature had elevated the library to a state room, increasingly used by all the family as a place for letter writing, playing cards or as a meeting place for guests. Open bookcases became popular from the mid 1700s, replacing earlier glass cabinets, while the awakening of interest in English history and literature later in the century inspired a fashion of Gothic styles libraries.

CHAPEL

The importance of religion in daily life in medieval England meant that it would be unthinkable not to have a chapel or church, and usually both, at hand for the lord and his household. The private chapel was used for daily prayers while the parish church next door would be attended by the owner, his family and household along with the parish every Sunday. In larger houses the chapel would usually have a comfortable gallery above for the lord and his family, which could be accessed from their private apartments, while the household could use the main body of the room below.

Chapels that survive today are often in the earliest part of a house, as very few were built after the Reformation of the 1530s, although many had a later flamboyant Baroque or cool Classical refit. These impressively decorated chapels were often partly a show of anti Catholic feeling, but when this religious fever of the 1600s died down in the following century there was a lack of interest in chapel and church building generally. However, the situation was very different for the suppressed Catholics. Ever since the Reformation there had been a constant battle between the Catholics who pledged allegiance to the

Pope and those who protested against him, the Protestants. England was not a powerful country in the 16th century, so when the Catholic Mary, Queen of Scots was executed in 1587 and Catholic Spain dispatched the Armada for revenge, there was great fear in the country. This fuelled a witch hunt with the express intention of destroying Popery. Legislation for the conviction of Catholics and to reward those who betrayed them was set in place.

It was from this date and into the 17th century that priest holes were built in the homes of practising Catholics. Their sons were sent abroad to become priests and then returned as secret missionaries, often basing themselves at remote homes of staunch supporters and from here visiting local Catholics. Ingenious hiding places were thus required in which they could secrete themselves when the dreaded Pursuivants (priest hunters) came knocking. Many timber framed and stone Tudor mansions have more than one hidden passage or secret chamber still to be found today.

As previously mentioned though, the religious fever calmed down in the 1700s and by the latter part of the century Catholics were permitted to have a chapel, perhaps just a converted room, although it was not allowed to be visible as such from the outside. It was not until the Catholic Emancipation Act of 1829 that they could once again build new chapels and churches.

Fig 8.12: Baddesley Clinton, Warwickshire
The sacristy, a room off the chapel where the vestments and sacred vessels were stored, has an innocent looking box with a cross upon it on the far wall. This, however, covers a secret passage leading to a priest hole which was used when the house was raided in 1591. The Catholic fugitives may have hesitated, though, if they had realised that the hole they were dropping down was previously the garderobe shaft!

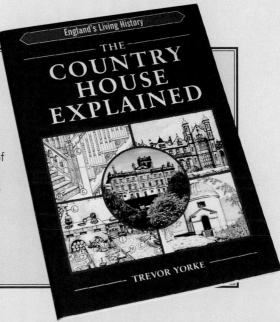

This article is taken from *The Country House Explained* by Trevor Yorke, published by Countryside Books, price £9.95.

READER OFFER
The publishers Countryside Books are offering copies of *The Country House Explained* to *Hudson's Historic Houses & Gardens* readers at a special price of £7.95 – £2 off the cover price of £9.95 – inclusive of postage and packing. If you would like a copy, please print your name, address and the title of the book clearly on a sheet of paper and send it with a cheque (payable to Countryside Books) to: **Hudson's Historic Houses & Gardens Offer**, Countryside Books, 2 Highfield Avenue, Newbury, Berkshire RG14 5DS. Please allow 10 days for receipt.

Overleaf, see how an imagined property might have changed over the centuries, and find a Glossary of Terms used in Trevor Yorke's Book

Exemplar Hall

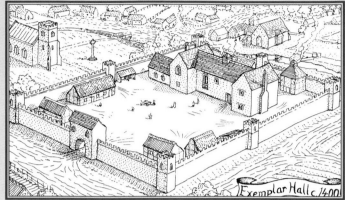

c1400

So, imagine yourself approaching Exemplar Hall, passing along a muddy, rutted road lined with a mix of low, timber framed cottages and a few taller, sturdy houses until you reach its imposing crenellated walls. You turn in, under the gatehouse, into a courtyard surrounded by an array of buildings with household staff busy crossing between them. The old hall is in front of you, recognisable by its large window and louvre in the roof, while behind it is the kitchen, which is separate from the main building due to its inflammable nature. To the left of the hall is a small private chapel for the use of the owner of the house. Your impression is of a scattered range of buildings with your eye drawn to the decorative incidental parts rather than the whole composition.

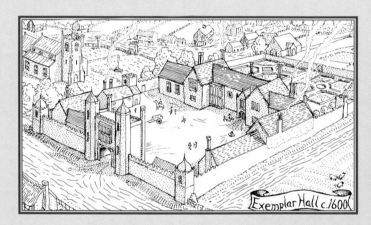

c1600

Two hundred years have passed and the recent lords of the manor have made modest progress and have embellished their family home rather than rebuilding it. The entrance is marked by an impressive brick gatehouse with the courtyard beyond now lined with new lodgings and service buildings. A small concession to symmetry appears on the front of the main hall which has a large bay window to the left and a tall porch balancing it to the right. A new kitchen has been built on the right side of the house and the area at the rear where it previously stood has now become a garden.

c1700

The rambling collection of medieval and Tudor buildings has been swept aside to make way for a new Dutch style house financed by the current lord of the manor's foreign investments. The old chapel which is just to the left of the main building is the only part retained, while the parish church on the other side of the wall is looking neglected. A new stable courtyard with an arched entrance has been erected.

The garden has been terraced and the main estate farm (Home Farm) has been masked off by trees and landscaping. Some of the old cottages have been removed to achieve a better view from the front of the house. The separation between manor house and village is growing, with only a few larger farms remaining.

c1800

Few changes have been made to the main house, other than to give it a Classical makeover and stick a portico on the front. However, the surroundings have changed dramatically. A new wing with extra accommodation has been added on the foundations of the entrance to the stable block. A courtyard in the foreground houses service rooms and stables while the emphasis of the house is now geared towards the garden at the rear.

The previous lord of the manor bought up the old village properties, cleared them out of the way and had a picturesque landscape garden laid out complete with temples and ruins. The old stream, which in the medieval and Tudor views fed the fishponds behind the house, has now been flooded to form a lake over which a Classical style bridge stands.

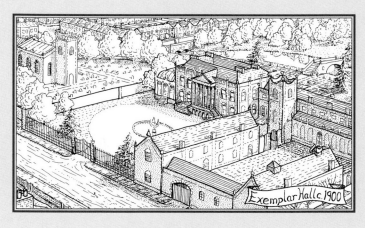

c1900

Some forty years before this view is dated, the owner embarked on another face-lift and expansion of the property. The wing to the right of the picture was extended to create additional rooms for leisure and guest accommodation, a tower was constructed to hold the water tank and the service courtyard in the foreground was enlarged, with a walled kitchen garden just in the bottom right corner of the picture.

This was a time of great prosperity on the estate due to high agricultural returns, but by 1900 a sharp downturn in fortunes has resulted in the sale of much of the farm and parkland. At the same time the small mill town where the evicted villagers had resettled has expanded rapidly and new villas for the successful businessmen have encroached in the top and bottom left of the picture.

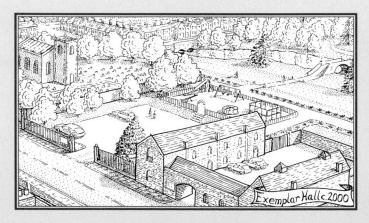

c2000

Tragedy struck one winter's day in 1917 when news reached the family that the young lord had been killed in action in a Flanders field. Here, as with many country estates, the loss of young men in World War I would have devastating effects. Exemplar's owner died shortly after the end of the conflict and as he left no heir and mounting debts it was sold off and became a private school. This was poorly run and by the time of the Second World War the property was in the hands of the armed forces as a training centre. After these hostilities the local town council purchased the site but the lack of maintenance had left the old hall unsafe and the majority of the building was demolished. Only the old kitchen courtyard was retained and has become offices while the remainder of the estate is now a public park. After all these years only the church and its surrounding boundary have survived from the original scene in 1400.

Glossary

Abutment A wall which supports the arch of a bridge or a vaulted ceiling.

Aisle A side space running along a hall and separated by a row of posts (hence aisled hall).

Anthemion A decorative honeysuckle flower.

Apse A semi-circular area at one end of a church or room.

Arcade A row of arches or columns.

Architrave The lowest part of the entablature and the surround of a doorway.

Ashlar A type of smooth stone masonry with fine joints.

Atrium A top lit court rising through a number of storeys.

Balustrade A row of decorated uprights (balusters) with a rail along the top.

Bolection moulding A curved shaped moulding used to cover the joint between tow different surface levels. Popular in the late 17th and early 18th century and often found surrounding three sides of the opening of a fireplace.

Bonding The way bricks are laid in a wall which can be recognised by the pattern made by the headers (short end of a brick) and stretchers (long side of a brick).

Capital The decorated top of a column.

Cartouche A usually oval-shaped tablet featuring a coat of arms.

Caryatids Female figures supporting an entablature.

Casement A window which is hinged at the side.

Castellated A battlemented feature.

Coffered ceiling A ceiling with sunken panels (coffers).

Console An ornamental bracket with an S-shaped centre.

Cornice The top section of an entablature which also features around the top of interior and exterior walls.

Cupola A small, domed, round or polygonal tower which stands on top of a roof or dome.

Daub A mixture of clay and mud (usually with straw or animal hair for increased strength) which was used to cover the wattle strips which filled in the gaps in a timber framed house.

Dormer window An upright window set in the angle of the roof casting light into attic rooms which were usually used for sleeping quarters (from French verb 'to sleep').

Double pile A house which is two rooms deep.

Drip moulding A moulding running along the top of a window to protect it from rain.

Eaves The roof overhang projecting over the wall.

Enfilade The French fashion for arranging doors in a line (usually near the windows) so that when they are opened a long view down the length of the house can be achieved. Popular in the 17th and early 18th century Baroque houses.

Fluting Vertical concave grooves running up a column or pilaster.

Frieze The middle of the entablature.

Gable The triangular-shaped top of an end wall between the slopes of a roof.

Garderobe The medieval word for a lavatory.

Hipped roof A roof with a slope on all four sides. A gabled roof has two vertical end walls (gables).

Jambs The sides of an opening for a door or window.

Keystone The top middle stone of an arch, which can be projected out as a feature.

Knot garden A formal arrangement of patterned areas in gravel or grass and surrounded by low clipped hedges. Popular in the 16th century.

Lantern A small tower on top of a dome which lets light in, illuminating the interior.

Lintel A flat beam which is fitted above a doorway or window to take the load of the wall above.

Loggia A gallery or corridor opened on one side with a row of columns.

Louvre An opening, usually with slats, through which smoke can escape from a hearth.

Mansard roof A roof with a steep-sided lower section and low-pitched top part which creates more room in the attic below (named after the French architect Francois Mansard).

Mullion A vertical bar in a window.

Oratory A small private chapel.

Oriel window A large projecting window.

Palisade A fence comprising pales, pointed pieces of wood, and often mounted on a ban surrounding a fortified site or deer park.

Parapet A low wall running along the edge of the roof above the main wall, or along the top of a hipped roof on 17th century Dutch style houses.

Parterre A level piece of land within a garden (from the French for 'on the ground'). A series of parterres, often in steps if the land sloped, with arrangements of flowerbeds, were popular in 17th century and early 18th century gardens.

Pediment A low-pitched triangular feature supported by columns on the top of a portico or a Classical doorway.

Piano nobile The floor on which the principal rooms are contained, usually above a raised basement or ground floor.

Portico A porch with a flat entablature or triangular pediment supported on columns.

Quoins Dressed stones at the corners of buildings.

Rotunda A circular building with a dome on top.

Rustication The cutting of masonry into blocks separated by deep lines and sometimes with a rough hewn finish. Often used to distinguish the basement of Palladian houses.

Sash A window which slides vertically (a Yorkshire sash slides horizontally).

Screens passage The space between opposing doorways at the other end of the hall from where the lord sat, which was partially closed off from the room by a wooden screen. This could be portable but was usually later fixed with two openings and a gallery above for musicians.

Sill The horizontal beam at the bottom of a window, door or timber framed wall.

Solar An upper withdrawing room behind the lord's end of a medieval hall.

State apartments The principal rooms within a major house, for impressing and accommodating visiting dignitaries and for ceremonial occasions.

String course A thin moulding which runs horizontally around a building.

Stucco A durable smooth plaster coating applied to the outside of houses often over brick in lieu of stone. It was particularly popular in the Regency period.

Swag A popular ornament in the form of a piece of fabric draped from two horizontal points, which is often found on friezes and panels especially in later 17th and 18th century decoration. A garland of fruit or flowers was sometimes used in place of the fabric, though this is usually termed a festoon.

Tracery The ribs at the top of a stone window which are formed into patterns (usually on churches, chapels and medieval halls).

Transom A horizontal bar in a window.

Tympanum The flat triangular space within a pediment.

Vault An arched ceiling formed from brick or stone, and sometimes imitated in plaster and wood.

Venetian window A window in three vertical sections, the centre one being taller and arched.

Voussoir A wedge-shaped stone used in the making of an arch.

Wilderness Originally an area of tall clipped trees, which could be formally arranged and was popular in late 17th and early 18th century garden schemes. Where they survive today, they tend to be more wild, wooded areas.

52

Royal Horticultural Society

BE INSPIRED
AT THE RHS FLOWER SHOWS 2008

18th – 20th April, RHS SPRING FLOWER SHOW, CARDIFF
Bute Park, by Cardiff Castle. To book call 0870 040 0286

8th – 11th May, MALVERN SPRING GARDENING SHOW
The Showground, Malvern, Worcs. To book call 01684 584 924

20th – 24th May, RHS CHELSEA FLOWER SHOW
The Royal Hospital, Chelsea, London. To book call 0870 842 2223

11th – 15th June, BBC GARDENERS' WORLD LIVE
The NEC, Birmingham. To book call 0870 040 0370

8th – 13th July, HAMPTON COURT PALACE FLOWER SHOW
Hampton Court Palace, East Molesey, Surrey. To book call 0870 842 2223

23rd – 27th July, RHS FLOWER SHOW AT TATTON PARK
Tatton Park, nr Knutsford, Cheshire. To book call 0870 842 2223

27th – 28th September, MALVERN AUTUMN SHOW
The Showground, Malvern, Worcs. To book call 01684 584 924

Registered Charity No: 222879/SCO38262

For further information visit **www.rhs.org.uk/flowershows**
or call the RHS recorded Show Information line **020 7649 1885** (24hr)

The Tower of London © Historic Royal Palaces

London

England's vibrant capital city contains not just the 'must-see' attractions such as Buckingham Palace and the Tower of London, but also many smaller and no less interesting properties. London's parks are the lungs of the city. From Regent's Park in the north to Battersea Park south of the river, via Hyde Park and St James's it is possible to walk for miles, hardly touching a pavement.

Syon Park

©English Heritage Photo Library/Nigel Corrie

■ **Owner**
English Heritage

■ **Contact**
House Manager
Apsley House
Hyde Park Corner
London W1J 7NT

Tel: 020 7499 5676
Fax: 020 7493 6576

■ **Location**
MAP 20:L8
OS Ref. TQ284 799

N. side of
Hyde Park Corner.

Underground:
Hyde Park Corner exit 1
Piccadilly Line.

Bus:
9,22, 148.

■ **Opening Times**
21 March–31 October
Wed–Sun & BHs
11am–5pm.
1 November–31 March
Wed–Sun, 11am–4pm.
Closed 24–26 Dec
& 1 Jan.

■ **Admission**
Adult	£5.50
Children	£2.80
Child (under 5yrs)	Free
Conc.	£4.40

Joint ticket with
Wellington Arch
(Wed–Sun):

Adult	£6.90
Children	£3.50
Child (under 5yrs)	Free
Conc.	£5.50
Family	£17.30

15% discount for groups
(11+). Free for English
Heritage members and
for Overseas Visitor Pass
holders.

APSLEY HOUSE ⊞

www.english-heritage.org.uk/apsley

Apsley House (also known as No. 1 London) is the former residence of the first Duke of Wellington.

The Duke made Apsley House his London home after a dazzling military career culminating in his victory over Napoleon at Waterloo in 1815. Wellington enlarged the house (originally designed and built by Robert Adam between 1771–78) adding the magnificent Waterloo Gallery by Benjamin Dean Wyatt which holds many of the masterpieces from the Duke's extensive painting collection. It has been the London home of the Dukes of Wellington ever since.

The seventh Duke gave the house and contents to the Nation in 1947, with apartments retained for the family. With its collections of outstanding paintings, porcelain, silver, sculpture, furniture, medals and memorabilia largely intact and the family still in residence, Apsley House is the last great aristocratic town house in London.

©English Heritage Photo Library/Nigel Corrie

ℹ No photography in house.

🛍 Partial.

♿ By arrangement.

🎧 Free. English, French,
Spanish & German.

🅿 In Park Lane.

🐕 Guide dogs only

❄

🎭

© English Heritage Photo Library

Owner
English Heritage

Contact
Visits:
House Manager
Chiswick House
Burlington Lane
London W4 2RP

Tel: 020 8995 0508

Venue Hire and Hospitality:
Hospitality Manager
Tel: 020 7973 3292

Location
MAP 19:C8
OS Ref: TQ210 775

Burlington Lane
London W4.

Rail: ½ mile NE of Chiswick Station.

Tube:
Turnham Green, ¾ mile

Bus: 190, E3.

Opening Times
Summer
21 March–31 October
Sun–Wed & BHs,
10am–5pm.

Winter
1 November–
21 December. Pre-booked appointments only.
22 December–31 March, closed.

Admission
Adult	£4.20
Child (5–15yrs)	£2.10
Conc	£3.40
Family	£10.50

Groups (11+)
15% discount.

EH Members free.

CHISWICK HOUSE ⊞

www.english-heritage.org.uk/chiswickhouse

Chiswick House is internationally renowned as one of the first and finest English Palladian villas. Lord Burlington, who built the villa from 1725–1729, was inspired by the architecture and gardens of ancient Rome and this house is his masterpiece. His aim was to create a fit setting to show his friends his fine collection of art and his library. The opulent interior features gilded decoration, velvet walls and painted ceilings. The important 18th century gardens surrounding Chiswick House have, at every turn, something to surprise and delight the visitor from the magnificent cedar trees to the beautiful Italianate gardens with their cascade, statues, temples, urns and obelisks.

The Chiswick House & Gardens Trust (reg. charity 1109239) has been set up to lead a major restoration project to restore the historic gardens and improve visitor facilities. Visit www.chtg.org.uk for details.

© English Heritage Photo Library

© English Heritage Photo Library

 WCs. Filming, plays, photographic shoots.

Private & corporate hospitality.

Please call in advance. WC.

Café in grounds not managed by English Heritage.

Personal guided tours must be booked in advance.

Free audio tours in English, French & German.

Free if booked in advance. Tel: 020 7973 3485.

Guide dogs in grounds.

58

English Heritage Photo Library/Jonathan Bailey

ELTHAM PALACE ⌗

www.english-heritage.org.uk/eltham

English Heritage Photo Library/Jonathan Bailey

The epitome of 1930s chic, Eltham Palace dramatically demonstrates the glamour and allure of the period.

Bathe in the light flooding from a spectacular glazed dome in the Entrance Hall as it highlights beautiful blackbeam veneer and figurative marquetry. It is a *tour de force* only rivalled by the adjacent Dining Room – where an Art Deco aluminium-leafed ceiling is a perfect complement to the bird's-eye maple walls. Step into Virginia Courtauld's magnificent gold-leaf and onyx bathroom and throughout the house discover lacquered, 'ocean liner' style veneered walls and built-in furniture.

A Chinese sliding screen is all that separates chic Thirties Art Deco from the medieval Great Hall. You will find concealed electric lighting, centralised vacuum cleaning and a loud-speaker system that allowed music to waft around the house. Authentic interiors have been recreated by the finest contemporary craftsmen. Their appearance was painstakingly researched from archive photographs, documents and interviews with friends and relatives of the Courtaulds.

Outside you will find a delightful mixture of formal and informal gardens including a rose garden, pergola and loggia, all nestled around the extensive remains of the medieval palace.

New to the Palace: The Courtaulds' Home Movie, rare footage showing Eltham in its heyday.

Owner
English Heritage

Contact
Eltham Palace
Court Yard
Eltham
London SE9 5QE

Visits:
Property Secretary
Tel: 020 8294 2548

Venue Hire and Hospitality:
Hospitality Manager
Tel: 020 8294 2577

Location
MAP 19:F8
OS Ref. TQ425 740

M25/J3, then A20 towards Eltham. The Palace is signposted from A20 and from Eltham High Street.
A2 from Central London.

Rail: 30 mins from Victoria or London Bridge Stations to Eltham or Mottingham, then 15 mins walk.

Opening Times
21 March–31 October
Sun–Wed
10am–5pm.

1 November–21 December
Sun–Wed
11am–4pm.

Closed 22 December–31 January.

1 February–31 March
Sun–Wed
11am–4pm.

Groups visits must be booked two weeks in advance.

Venue Hire and Hospitality
English Heritage offers exclusive use of the Palace on Thu, Fri or Sat for daytime conferences, meetings and weddings and in the evenings for dinners, concerts and receptions.

Admission
House and Garden
Adult	£8.20
Child	£4.10
Conc.	£6.60
Family (2+3)	£20.50

Garden only
Adult	£5.10
Child	£2.60
Conc.	£4.10

EH Members free.

Group discount available.

  WCs. Filming, plays and photographic shoots.

Exclusive private and corporate hospitality.

WC.

  Guided tours on request.

Free. English, German & French.

Coaches must book.

Conference/Function

ROOM	MAX CAPACITY
Great Hall	300 standing 200 dining
Entrance Hall	100 seated
Drawing Room	120 standing 80 theatre-style
Dining Room	80 standing 10 dining

■ Owner
English Heritage

■ Contact
Kenwood House
Hampstead Lane
London NW3 7JR

Visits:
The House Manager
Tel: 020 8348 1286

■ Location
MAP 20:K1
OS Ref. TQ271 874

M1/J2. Signed off A1, on leaving A1 turn right at junction with Bishop's Ave, turn left into Hampstead Lane. Visitor car park on left.

Bus: London Transport 210.

Rail: Hampstead Heath.

Underground:
Archway or Golders Green Northern Line then bus 210.

■ Opening Times
All year, daily.
11.30am–4pm.

Closed 24–26 December & 1 January.

The Park stays open later, please see site notices. House and grounds free; donations welcome. Pre-booked group tours available.

Venue Hire and Hospitality
Events are available for up to 100 guests in the Service Wing. Please ring Company of Cooks on 020 8341 5384.

■ Admission
House & Grounds
Free. Donations welcome.

KENWOOD HOUSE ⊞
www.english-heritage.org.uk/kenwoodhouse

Kenwood, one of the treasures of London, is an idyllic country retreat close to the popular villages of Hampstead and Highgate.

The house was remodelled in the 1760s by Robert Adam, the fashionable neo-classical architect. The breathtaking library or 'Great Room' is one of his finest achievements.

Kenwood is famous for the internationally important collection of paintings bequeathed to the nation by Edward Guinness, 1st Earl of Iveagh. Some of the world's finest artists are represented by works such as a Rembrandt *Self Portrait*, Vermeer's *The Guitar Player*; *Mary, Countess Howe* by Gainsborough and paintings by Turner, Reynolds and many others.

As if the house and its contents were not riches enough, Kenwood stands in 112 acres of landscaped grounds on the edge of Hampstead Heath, commanding a fine prospect towards central London. The meadow walks and ornamental lake of the park, designed by Humphry Repton, contrast with the wilder Heath below.

 WCs. Concerts, exhibitions, filming. No photography in house.

Exclusive private and corporate hospitality.

Ground floor access. WC. Visitors can be dropped off in front of the House. Mobility vehicle provided for those who have difficulty with the walk from the car park to the House.

Available in the Brew House.

Available on request (in English). Please call for details.

West Lodge car park (Pay & Display) on Hampstead Lane. Parking for the disabled.

Free when booked in advance on 020 7973 3485.

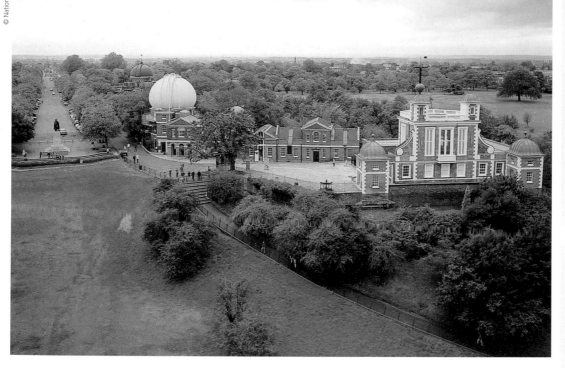

© National Maritime Museum

■ Owner
National Maritime
Museum

■ Contact
Groups: Robin Scates
Events: Jo Rough
Park Row
Greenwich
London SE10 9NF

Tel: 020 8858 4422
Fax: 020 8312 6632

Visit Bookings:
Tel: 020 8858 4422
Fax: 020 8312 6522
E-mail:
bookings@nmm.ac.uk

Functions:
Tel: 020 8312 8517
Fax: 020 8312 6572
E-mail:
events@nmm.ac.uk

■ Location
MAP 19·F7
OS Ref. TQ388 773

Within Greenwich Park
on the S bank of the
Thames at Greenwich.
Travel by river cruise or
Docklands Light Railway
(Cutty Sark station).
M25 (S) via A2. From
M25 (N) M11, A12 and
Blackwall Tunnel.

■ Opening Times
Daily, 10am–5pm (later
opening in summer). Last
admission 30 mins prior.
Varies at New Year and
Marathon Day (13 April).

Closed 24–26 December.

Gallery talks and drama
(see notices on arrival).

Special Exhibitions
Art for the Nation
(all year)

Atlantic Worlds
(all year)

Esther Shelev-Gerz
(to 2 March)

■ Admission
Free admission except
for Planetarium shows.

ROYAL OBSERVATORY, NATIONAL MARITIME MUSEUM & QUEEN'S HOUSE

www.nmm.ac.uk

The Royal Park at Greenwich provides a beautiful backdrop to the architectural landscape of Greenwich, now a World Heritage Site. The Tudor palace of Placentia, in which Henry VIII, Mary Tudor and Elizabeth I were born, is now covered by the 17th-century Old Royal Naval College with its Painted Hall and Chapel.

Illustrated above is Flamsteed House (Wren 1675), built to accommodate the first Astronomer Royal. It was restored for 2006 with new presentations of significant time-keepers, including those of John Harrison, and the story of Greenwich Mean Time. The Meridian Line, Longitude 0°, is marked in the courtyard as the base point for the calculation of the World's time zones and the 1833 timeball still drops punctually at 1 o'clock. The new Peter Harrison Planetarium and an Astronomy Centre with a café has now opened.

The modern National Maritime Museum charts Britain's history of seafaring and empire. Nelson's uniform coat is on display and portraits and artefacts from various military and civil expeditions tell the human stories behind many great events. Contemporary themes are tackled including the ocean environment, slavery and travel at sea. Stained glass from the destroyed Baltic Exchange is in a separate memorial gallery. There are frequent events and talks for adults and children.

The Queen's House (Inigo Jones 1635) is significant as the first classical house in England. Introducing the Palladian style to England, it was called a 'House of Delights' by Henrietta Maria and was used for court entertainments and balls. The Great Hall, Orangery and 'Tulip' stairs provide an elegant setting for fine and contemporary art displays, occasional exhibitions and private functions.

© NMM

The Restored Baltic Glass at the National Maritime Museum

 No photography.

 Partial. WC.

Licensed.

  Limited for coaches.

 Guide dogs only.

Conference/Function

ROOM	SIZE	MAX CAPACITY
Queen's House	40' x 40'	Dining 120 Standing 200 Conference 120
Observatory, Octagon Rm	25' x 25'	Dining 60 Standing 120
NMM Upper Deck	140' x 70'	Dining 500 Standing 800
NMM Lecture Theatre		Conference 120

The Choir Stalls looking east towards the High Altar

■ Owner
Dean & Chapter of
St Paul's Cathedral

■ Contact
The Chapter House
St Paul's Churchyard
London EC4M 8AD

Tel: 020 7246 8350
020 7236 4128
Fax: 020 7248 3104
E-mail: chapter@
stpaulscathedral.org.uk

■ Location
MAP 20:N7
OS Ref. TQ321 812

Central London.

Underground:
St Paul's, Mansion
House, Blackfriars, Bank.

Rail: Blackfriars,
City Thameslink.

Air: London Airports.

■ Opening Times
Mon–Sat, 8.30am–
4.30pm, last admission
4pm.

Guided tours: Mon–Sat,
11am, 11.30am,1.30pm
& 2pm.

Tours of the Triforium:
Mon & Tues, 11.30am &
2pm. Fri, 2pm.

All tours are subject to
an additional charge.

**Cathedral Shop
& Café:**
Mon–Sat, 9am–5pm,
Sun, 10am–5pm.

Restaurant:
Mon–Sat, 10am–5pm.
Sun,12noon–5pm.

■ Service Times
Mon–Sat, 7.30am
Mattins (Sat 8.30am)
8am Holy Communion
(said), 12.30pm Holy
Communion (said)
5pm Choral Evensong

Sun: 8am Holy
Communion (said)
10.15am Choral Mattins
& sermon, 11.30am
Choral Eucharist &
sermon, 3.15pm Choral
Evensong & sermon
6pm Evening service

The Cathedral may be
closed to tourists on
certain days of the year.
It is advisable to phone
or check our website for
up-to-date information.

■ Admission
Adult	£10.00
Child	£3.50
OAP	£9.00
Student	£8.50
Family	£23.50
Groups (10+)	
Adult	£9.00
Child	£3.00
OAP	£8.00
Student	£7.50

Conference/Function
ROOM	MAX CAPACITY
Conference Suite	100 (standing)

ST PAUL'S CATHEDRAL
www.stpauls.co.uk

St Paul's, with its world-famous Dome, is an iconic feature of the London skyline, but there is much more to Sir Christopher Wren's masterpiece than its impressive façade.

A spiritual focus for the nation since its first service in 1697, many important events have taken place within its walls, from State funerals of Lord Nelson, the Duke of Wellington and Sir Winston Churchill to the wedding of the Prince of Wales to Lady Diana Spencer and the Thanksgiving services for Her Majesty the Queen's Golden Jubilee and 80th Birthday.

The Cathedral is currently in the process of being restored and the results so far are breathtaking.

The West front, once blackened and damaged, now rises majestically at the top of Ludgate Hill and details previously hidden stand out crisp and proud. The interior has been transformed by state-of-the-art restoration techniques and the light that now floods the space, highlights the luminescent Portland stone and brings mosaics, carvings and sculpture to life. In the Dome, exquisite 18th century paintings by Sir James Thornhill, showing scenes from the life of St Paul, have been returned to their original beauty.

But of course, the pinnacle of any trip to St Paul's has to be the winding journey up the spiral staircase to the Whispering Gallery, to sample its unique audio effects before traveling up and out to the Stone and Golden Galleries, which afford a panoramic view of London that is second to none.

The High Altar

The West Front

 No photography, video or mobile phones.

 Partial.

Licensed.

 None for cars, limited for coaches.

 Guide dogs only.

©James Brittain

SOMERSET HOUSE

www.somersethouse.org.uk

Home to The Courtauld Gallery (www.courtauld.ac.uk) and the Gilbert Collection (www.gilbert-collection.co.uk).

The original Somerset House, built in 1573 and used first as a private home and then a royal residence, had by 1776 fallen into such disrepair that George III commissioned Sir William Chambers to replace it with the Palladian-style masterpiece we see today.

Over the next 200 years, its imposing architecture housed the Navy Board, the Royal Academy and Royal Society, as well as 'publick offices' such as the Registry of Births, Marriages, and Deaths. The end of the 20th century saw a major refurbishment to the complex of buildings with the new Edmond J. Safra Fountain Court at its heart, and a year-round programme of visual and live arts that brings the building to life with surprising and original events.

The world-renowned Courtauld Gallery houses iconic Impressionist and Post-Impressionist masterpieces, as well as numerous other important paintings and works on paper from the Renaissance through to the 20th century.

The Gilbert Collection was formed over four decades by the late Sir Arthur Gilbert, who first started to collect English silver before his passion for great craftsmanship led him to collect Italian mosaics, gold boxes, portrait miniatures and Roman enamel mosaics.

This is a spectacular venue for open air films and concerts in the summer, and the capital's premier winter ice rink. With education projects, family events, cafés and a restaurant, Somerset House is a thriving centre for inspiration and relaxation in the heart of London's West End.

Self Portrait – Van Gogh

© The Samuel Courtauld Trust, Courtauld Institute of Art Gallery

A Bar at The Folies-Bergère – Manet

 Licensed.
 Licensed.
 By arrangement.
 None.
Guide dogs only.

■ **Owner**
Somerset House Trust

■ **Contact**
Director
Somerset House Trust
Strand
London WC2R 1LA

Tel: 020 7845 4600
Fax: 020 7836 7613
E-mail:
info@somersethouse.
org.uk

■ **Location**
MAP 20:N7
OS Ref. TQ308 809

In the West End of London, overlooking the Thames, by Waterloo Bridge.

Entrances on Strand, Embankment and Waterloo Bridge.

Underground: Temple, Embankment, Charing Cross, Covent Garden.

■ **Opening Times**
Somerset House
Daily, 10am–6pm. Extended hours apply for the courtyard, river terrace and restaurants.

Galleries
Daily, 10am–6pm (last admission: Courtauld 5.30pm, Gilbert Collection 5.15pm).

Seasonal opening times apply 24–26 December and 1 January – check website for details

■ **Admission**
Entry to Somerset House is free

Galleries
One Collection:
Adult   £5.00
Conc.   £4.00

Two Collections:
Adult   £8.00
Conc.   £7.00

Three Collections:
Adult   £12.00
Conc.   £11.00

Galleries are free for under 18s, full-time UK students and registered unwaged.

© Spencer House / Mark Fiennes

■ Contact
Jane Rick
Director
Spencer House
27 St James's Place
London SW1A 1NR

Tel: 020 7514 1958
Fax: 020 7409 2952
Info Line:
020 7499 8620

■ Location
MAP 20:L8
OS Ref. TQ293 803

Central London:
off St James's Street,
overlooking
Green Park.

Underground:
Green Park.

■ Opening Times
All Year (except January
& August) Suns,
10.30am–5.45pm.

Last tour 4.45pm.

Regular tours
throughout the day.
Maximum number on
each tour is 20.

Mon mornings for
pre-booked groups only.

Open for corporate
hospitality except
during January & August.

■ Admission
Adult   £9.00
Conc.*   £7.00

*Students, Friends of the
V&A, Friends of the Tate,
Friends of the Royal
Academy and senior
citizens (only on
production of valid
identification), children
under 16. No children
under 10 admitted.
Group size: min 15–60.

Prices include guided
tour.

Specific Sundays
The authentically
restored garden of this
18th century London
palace will be open to
the public on specific
Sundays during Spring
and Summer.

For updated information
telephone 020 7499
8620 or view
www.spencerhouse.co.uk

All images are copyright
of Spencer House
Limited and may not be
used without the
permission of Spencer
House Limited.

SPENCER HOUSE

www.spencerhouse.co.uk

Spencer House, built 1756–66 for the first Earl Spencer, an ancestor of Diana, Princess of Wales (1961–97), is London's finest surviving 18th century town house. The magnificent private palace has regained the full splendour of its late 18th century appearance, after a painstaking ten-year restoration programme.

Designed by John Vardy and James 'Athenian' Stuart, the nine State rooms are amongst the first neo-classical interiors in Europe. Vardy's Palm Room, with its spectacular screen of gilded palm trees and arched fronds, is a unique Palladian set-piece, while the elegant mural decorations of Stuart's Painted Room reflect the 18th century passion

for classical Greece and Rome. Stuart's superb gilded furniture has been returned to its original location in the Painted Room by courtesy of the V&A and English Heritage. Visitors can also see a fine collection of 18th century paintings and furniture, specially assembled for the house, including five major Benjamin West paintings, graciously lent by Her Majesty The Queen.

The State rooms are open to the public for viewing on Sundays. They are also available on a limited number of occasions each year for private and corporate entertaining during the rest of the week.

© Spencer House / Mark Fiennes

© Spencer House / Mark Fiennes

ℹ No photography inside House or Garden.

🍽 House only, ramps and lifts. WC.

🚶 Obligatory. Comprehensive colour guidebook.

🅿 None.

Conference/Function

ROOM	MAX CAPACITY
Receptions	400
Lunches & Dinners	130
Board Meetings	40
Theatre-style Meetings	100

SYON PARK

www.syonpark.co.uk

Described by John Betjeman as the 'Grand Architectural Walk', Syon House and its 200-acre park is the London home of the Duke of Northumberland, whose family, the Percys, have lived here for 400 years.

Originally the site of a late medieval monastery, excavated by Channel 4's *Time Team*, Syon Park has a fascinating history. The present house has Tudor origins but contains some of Robert Adam's finest interiors, which were commissioned by the 1st Duke in the 1760s. The private apartments and State bedrooms are available to view. The house can be hired for filming and photo shoots subject to availability.

Within the 'Capability' Brown landscaped park are 40 acres of gardens which contain the spectacular Great Conservatory designed by Charles Fowler in the 1820s. The House and Great Conservatory are available for corporate and private hire.

The Northumberland Room in Syon House is an excellent venue for conferences, meetings, lunches and dinners (max 60). The State Apartments make a sumptuous setting for dinners, concerts, receptions, launches and wedding ceremonies (max 120). Marquees can be erected on the lawn adjacent to the house for balls and corporate events. The Great Conservatory is available for summer parties, launches, filming, photoshoots and wedding receptions (max 150).

■ Owner
The Duke of Northumberland

■ Contact
Estate Office
Syon House
Syon Park
Brentford
TW8 8JF

Tel: 020 8560 0882
Fax: 020 8568 0936
E-mail: info@
syonpark.co.uk

■ Location
MAP 19:B8
OS Ref. TQ173 767

Between Brentford and Twickenham, off the A4, A310 in SW London.

Rail: Kew Bridge or Gunnersbury Underground then Bus 237 or 267.

Air: Heathrow 8m.

■ Opening Times
Syon House
19 March–26 October
Wed, Thur, Sun & BHs
11am–5pm
(open Good Fri & Easter Sat).

Other times by appointment for groups.

Gardens only
April–October
Daily, 10.30am–5pm
November–March
Sats & Suns, &
New Year's day,
10.30am–4pm or dusk, whichever is earlier.

Last admissions House & Gardens ¾ hr before closing.

■ Admission
House and Gardens
Adult	£8.00
Child	£4.00
Conc.	£7.00
Family (2+2)	£18.00

Group bookings (15–50)	
Adult	£7.50
Conc.	£6.50
School Group	£2.00

Gardens & Great Conservatory
Adult	£4.00
Conc.	£2.50
Family (2+2)	£9.00

Group bookings (15–50)
Price on application
(please telephone).

Syon Park Holdings Ltd. & The Lovaine Trust reserve the right to alter opening times.

No photography in house. Indoor adventure playground.

Garden centre.

Partial.

By arrangement.

P

Guide dogs only.

Conference/Function

ROOM	SIZE	MAX CAPACITY
Great Hall	50' x 30'	120
Great Conservatory	60' x 40'	150
Northumberland Room	35' x 20'	60
Marquee		1000

2 WILLOW ROAD

HAMPSTEAD, LONDON NW3 1TH

Tel: 020 7435 6166 **E-mail:** 2willowroad@nationaltrust.org.uk

Owner: The National Trust **Contact:** The Custodian

The former home of Ernö Goldfinger, designed and built by him in 1939. A three-storey brick and concrete rectangle, it is one of Britain's most important examples of modernist architecture and is filled with furniture also designed by Goldfinger. The interesting art collection includes works by Henry Moore and Max Ernst.

Location: MAP 20:J2, OS Ref. TQ270 858. Hampstead, London.

Open: 1–15 Mar & 8–29 Nov: Sats, 11am–5pm. 20 Mar–1 Nov: Thurs & Fri, 12 noon–5pm, Sats, 11am–5pm. Open Good Friday. Entry by timed tour only at 12 noon, 1 & 2pm (plus 11am on Sats). Places on tours limited and available on a first come first served basis on the day. Non-guided viewing 3–5pm with timed entry when busy.

Admission: Adult £5.10, Child £2.60, Family £12.80. Joint ticket with Fenton House £7.30. Private groups are welcome to book visits between Mar–Nov outside public opening times. Groups must be 5+, booking essential. Free to NT Members.

Small ground floor area accessible. Filmed tour of whole house available.

7 HAMMERSMITH TERRACE – HOME OF EMERY WALKER

7 Hammersmith Terrace, London W6 9TS

Tel: 020 8741 4104 **E-mail:** admin@emerywalker.org.uk

www.emerywalker.org.uk

Owner: The Emery Walker Trust **Contact:** The Administrator

Emery Walker, friend and advisor to William Morris, lived in this riverside house for 30 years and it preserves the only authentic Arts and Crafts urban interior in Britain, with furniture, wallpapers, textiles and ceramics by Morris & Co, Philip Webb, William de Morgan, etc. Small, pretty garden.

Location: MAP 3:H1, OS Ref. TQ221 782. Between Chiswick Mall and South Black Lion Lane in Hammersmith, parallel with King Street (Buses 27, 190, 267, 391, H91). Underground: Stamford Brook or Ravenscourt Park (District Line, both 7 mins walk) or Hammersmith (Piccadilly Line, 15 mins walk). Very limited metered on-street parking.

Open: Apr Jul & September. Guided tour. Please visit website for times, dates and booking arrangements. Admission strictly by pre-booked timed ticket.

Admission: Adult £10, Student £5. No children under 12yrs. Groups (max 8).

No photography inside house. No WC. Refreshments available locally.

Limited access to ground floor, no access to garden. Obligatory.

18 FOLGATE STREET

Spitalfields, East London E1 6BX

Tel: 020 7247 4013 **Fax:** 020 7377 5548 **www.dennissevershouse.co.uk**

Owner: Spitalfields Historic Buildings Trust **Contact:** Mick Pedroli

A time capsule furnished and decorated to tell the story of the Jervis family, Huguenot silk weavers from 1724–1919.

Location: MAP 20:P6, OS Ref. TQ335 820. ½m NE of Liverpool St. Station. E of Bishopsgate (A10), just N of Spitalfields Market.

Open: "Silent Night" every Mon evening. Booking required. 1st & 3rd Sun each month: 2–4pm. Mons following these Suns 12 noon–2pm.

Admission: "Silent Night" Mons £12 (pm £5), Suns £8. Christmas prices may vary.

Partial. Obligatory by private bookings.

ALBERT MEMORIAL

Princes Gate, Kensington Gore SW7 2AN

Tel: Bookings – 020 7495 0916. Enquiries – 020 7495 5504

An elaborate memorial by George Gilbert Scott to commemorate the Prince Consort.

Location: MAP 20:J8, OS Ref. TQ266 798. Victoria Station 1½m, South Kensington Tube ½m.

Open: All visits by booked guided tours; first Sun of the month Mar–Dec, 2pm & 3pm. Tours last 45 mins.

Admission: Adult £4.50, Conc £4. Booking advisable for groups (10+). (2007 prices).

APSLEY HOUSE

See page 57 for full page entry.

THE BANQUETING HOUSE

WHITEHALL, LONDON SW1A 2ER

www.banqueting-house.org.uk

Owner: Historic Royal Palaces

Contact: General Enquiries: 0844 482 7777 **Functions:** 020 3166 6150 / 6151

This revolutionary building, the first in England to be designed in a Palladian style by Inigo Jones, was finished in 1622 for James I. Intended for the splendour and exuberance of court masques, the Banqueting House is probably most famous for the one real life drama: the execution of Charles I which took place here in 1649 to the *"dismal, universal groan"* of the crowd. One of Charles' last sights as he walked through the Banqueting House to his death was the magnificent ceiling, painted by Peter Paul Rubens in 1630–4.

Location: MAP 20:M8, OS Ref. TQ302 80, Underground: Westminster, Embankment and Charing Cross. Rail: Charing Cross.

Open: All year, Mon–Sat, 10am–5pm. Last admission 4.30pm. Closed 24 Dec–1 Jan, Good Friday and other public holidays. NB. Liable to close at short notice for Government functions.

Admission: Enquiry line for admission prices: 0844 482 7777.

Concerts. No photography inside. Undercroft suitable. Video and audio guide. None.

BLEWCOAT SCHOOL

23 Caxton Street, Westminster, London SW1H 0PY
Tel: 020 7222 2877
Owner: The National Trust   **Contact:** Janet Bowden
Built in 1709 at the expense of William Green, a local brewer, to provide an education for poor children. Used as a school until 1926, it is now the NT London Gift Shop and Information Centre.
Location: MAP 20:L9, OS Ref. TQ295 794. Near the junction with Buckingham Gate.
Open: All year: Mon–Fri, 10am–5.30pm. Easter–Christmas: Thurs, 10am–7pm.
17 Nov–22 Dec: Sats, 10am–4pm. Closed BHs.

BOSTON MANOR HOUSE

Boston Manor Road, Brentford TW8 9JX
Tel: 0845 456 2824   **E-mail:** info@cip.org.uk
Owner: Hounslow Cultural & Community Services
A fine Jacobean house built in 1623.
Location: MAP 19:B7, OS Ref. TQ168 784. 10 mins walk S of Boston Manor Station (Piccadilly Line) and 250yds N of Boston Manor Road junction with A4 Great West Road, Brentford.
Open: Apr–end Oct: Sat, Sun & BHs, 2.30–5pm. Park open daily.
Admission: Free.

BRUCE CASTLE MUSEUM

Haringey Libraries, Archives & Museum Service, Lordship Lane, London N17 8NU
Tel: 020 8808 8772   **Fax:** 020 8808 4118   **E-mail:** museum.services@haringey.gov.uk
Owner: London Borough of Haringey
A Tudor building. Sir Rowland Hill (inventor of the Penny Post) ran a progressive school at Bruce Castle from 1827.
Location: MAP 19:E6, OS Ref. TQ335 906. Corner of Bruce Grove (A10) and Lordship Lane, 600yds NW of Bruce Grove Station.
Open: All year: Wed–Sun & Summer BHs (except Good Fri), 1–5pm. Organised groups by appointment.
Admission: Free.

BUCKINGHAM PALACE

London SW1A 1AA
Tel: 020 7766 7300   **E-mail:** bookinginfo@royalcollection.org.uk
Owner: Official Residence of Her Majesty The Queen
Contact: Ticket Sales & Information Office
Buckingham Palace is the official London residence of Her Majesty The Queen and serves as both home and office. Its 19 State Rooms, which open for eight weeks a year, form the heart of the working palace. The garden walk offers superb views of the Garden Front of the Palace and the 19th-century lake.
Location: MAP 20:L8, OS Ref. TQ291 796. Underground: Green Park, Victoria, St James's Park.
Open: Contact information office.
Admission: Contact information office.

BURGH HOUSE

New End Square, Hampstead, London NW3 1LT
Tel: 020 7431 0144   **Buttery:** 020 7431 2516   **Fax:** 020 7435 8817
E-mail: burghhouse@talk21.com   **www.burghhouse.org.uk**
Owner: London Borough of Camden   **Contact:** General Manager
A Grade I listed building of 1703 in the heart of old Hampstead with original panelled rooms, "barley sugar" staircase banisters and a music room. Child-friendly, refurbished Hampstead Museum, permanent and changing exhibitions. Prize-winning terraced garden. Regular programme of concerts, art exhibitions, and meetings. Receptions, seminars and conferences. Rooms for hire. Special facilities for schools visits. Wedding receptions.
Location: MAP 20:J2, OS Ref. TQ266 859. New End Square, E of Hampstead Underground station.
Open: All year: Wed–Sun, 12 noon–5pm. Sats by appointment only. BH Mons, 2–5pm. Closed Christmas fortnight, Good Fri & Easter Mon. Groups by arrangement. Buttery: Wed–Sun, 11am–5.30pm. BHs, 11am–4pm.
Admission: Free.
⬚ ⬚ ⬚ Ground floor & grounds. WC. ⬚ Licensed buttery. ⬚ ⬚ By arrangement.
⬚ None. ⬚ By arrangement. ⬚ Guide dogs only. ⬚ ⬚

CAPEL MANOR GARDENS

BULLSMOOR LANE, ENFIELD EN1 4RQ

www.capelmanorgardens.co.uk

Tel: 08456 122122   **Fax:** 01992 717544
Owner: Capel Manor Charitable Organisation   **Contact:** Miss Julie Ryan
These extensive, richly planted gardens are delightful throughout the year offering inspiration, information and relaxation. The gardens include various themes - historical, modern, walled, rock, water, sensory and disabled and an Italianate Maze, Japanese Garden and 'Gardening Which?' demonstration and trial gardens. Capel Manor is a College of Horticulture and runs a training scheme for professional gardeners originally devised in conjunction with the Historic Houses Association.
Location: MAP 19:E4, OS Ref. TQ344 997. Minutes from M25/J25. Tourist Board signs posted.
Open: Daily in summer: 10am–6pm. Last ticket 4.30pm. Check for winter times.
Admission: Adult £6, Child £3, Conc. £5, Family £15. Charges alter for special show weekends and winter months.
⬚ ⬚ Grounds. WC. ⬚ ⬚ ⬚ ⬚ In grounds, on leads. ⬚ ⬚

CAREW MANOR DOVECOTE

Church Road, Beddington SM6 7NH
Tel: 020 8770 4781   **Fax:** 020 8770 4777   **E-mail:** valary.murphy@sutton.gov.uk
www.sutton.gov.uk
Owner: London Borough of Sutton   **Contact:** Ms V Murphy
An early 18th century octagonal brick dovecote with around 1200 nesting boxes and the original potence (circular ladder). Opened for tours with the adjacent late medieval Grade I listed Great Hall of Carew Manor.
Location: MAP 19:D9, OS Ref. TQ295 652. Just off A232 at entrance to Beddington Park.
Open: Tours: Suns only.
Admission: Adult £4, Child £2.

CARLYLE'S HOUSE

24 Cheyne Row, Chelsea, London SW3 5HL
Tel: 020 7352 7087   **Fax:** 020 7352 5108   **E-mail:** carlyleshouse@nationaltrust.org.uk
Owner: The National Trust   **Contact:** The Custodian
Atmospheric home of the writer Thomas Carlyle and his wife Jane from 1834–1881. There is a small walled garden and the surrounding streets are rich in literary and artistic associations.
Location: MAP 20:K10, OS Ref. TQ272 777. Off the King's Road and Oakley Street, or off Cheyne Walk between Albert Bridge and Battersea Bridge on Chelsea Embankment.
Open: 12 Mar–2 Nov: Wed–Fri (incl. Good Fri), 2–5pm; Sat, Sun & BH Mons, 11am–5pm. Last admission 4.30pm.
Admission: Adult £4.75, Child £2.40, Family £11.90. Tel for groups visits and guided tours. Free to NT Members.
⬚ By arrangement for groups. ⬚

CHAPTER HOUSE ⚏

East Cloisters, Westminster Abbey, London SW1P 3PA
Tel: 020 7654 4900   www.english-heritage.org.uk/chapter
Owner: English Heritage   **Managed by:** Dean & Chapter of Westminster

The Chapter House, built by the Royal masons c1250 and faithfully restored in the 19th century, contains some of the finest medieval sculpture to be seen and spectacular wall paintings. The building is octagonal, with a central column, and still has its original floor of glazed tiles, which have been newly conserved. Its uses have varied and in the 14th century it was used as a meeting place for the Benedictine monks of the Abbey as well as for Members of Parliament.

Location: MAP 20:M8, OS Ref. TQ301 795.
Open: All year: Daily, 10am–4pm. May close at short notice on State and religious occasions. Closed Good Fri, 24–26 Dec & 1 Jan.
Admission: Integral part of tour of Westminster Abbey www.westminster-abbey.org.

CHELSEA PHYSIC GARDEN

SWAN WALK (OFF ROYAL HOSPITAL ROAD), LONDON SW3 4HS

www.chelseaphysicgarden.co.uk

Tel: 020 7352 5646   **Fax:** 020 7376 3910
E-mail: enquiries@chelseaphysicgarden.co.uk
Owner: Chelsea Physic Garden Company

In the heart of London, hidden behind high walls beside the Thames and not far from the site of the world famous Chelsea Flower Show, there is a magical secret garden. Over 300 years old, it has been the scene of some of the most important developments in the history of horticulture, medicine and agriculture. Enjoy free guided tours with entertaining guides, delicious refreshments at the Garden's renowned tearoom, and browse the eclectic selection of garden-related gifts in the shop.

Location: MAP 20:L10, OS Ref. TQ277 778. Off Embankment between Chelsea & Albert Bridges. Underground Sloane Square/South Kensington. 239 Bus from Victoria and Clapham Junction to the Garden.
Open: 19 Mar–31 Oct: Wed–Fri, 12 noon–5pm. Sun, Good Friday & BHs: 12 noon–6pm. Special Winter openings: 2/3 Feb & 9/10 Feb 10am–4 pm. Chelsea Flower Show week. 19 22 May, 12 noon–5pm. Late opening Jul/Aug, Weds until 10pm.
Admission: Adult £7, Conc. £4, Carers for disabled: Free.

🖥 🚼 🍴 ♿ Partial. WCs. 🖤 🎦 By arrangement. 📷 📹 Guide dogs only. 🐚

CHISWICK HOUSE ⚏

See page 58 for full page entry.

COLLEGE OF ARMS

Queen Victoria Street, London EC4V 4BT
Tel: 020 7248 2762   **Fax:** 020 7248 6448   **E-mail:** enquiries@college-of-arms.gov.uk
Owner: Corp. of Kings, Heralds & Pursuivants of Arms   **Contact:** The Officer in Waiting
Mansion built in 1670s to house the English Officers of Arms and their records.
Location: MAP 20:O7, OS Ref. TQ320 810. On N side of Queen Victoria Street, S of St Paul's Cathedral.
Open: Earl Marshal's Court only; open all year (except BHs, State and special occasions) Mon–Fri, 10am–4pm. Group visits (up to 10) by arrangement only. Record Room: open for tours (groups of up to 20) by special arrangement in advance with the Officer in Waiting.
Admission: Free (groups by negotiation)

EASTBURY MANOR HOUSE 🦋

Eastbury Square, Barking, Essex IG11 9SN
Tel: 020 8724 1000   **Fax:** 020 8724 1003   **E-mail:** eastburyhouse@lbbd.gov.uk
www.barking-dagenham.gov.uk
Owner: The National Trust   **Contact:** Julie Packham

Eastbury Manor is a unique example of a medium sized Elizabethan Manor House with attractive grounds. Leased to the London Borough of Barking and Dagenham and used for a variety of events and arts and heritage activites. In addition Eastbury can be hired for business conferences, Civil wedding and Civil partnership ceremonies, and education days. Extensive building works planned for 2008.

Location: MAP 19:F7, OS TQ457 838. In Eastbury Square off Ripple Road off A13, 10 mins S from Upney Station. Buses 287, 368 or 62.
Open: All year: Mons & Tues and 1st & 2nd Sat of the month, 10am–4pm.
Admission: Adult £2.50, Child 65p, Conc. £1.25, Family £5. Groups (15+) by arrangement: £2pp. Free to NT Members.

🖥 ♿ 🖤 🎦 🅿 In Eastbury Square. 📷 📹 In grounds only. 🔺 ❋ 🐚

ELTHAM PALACE ⚏

See page 59 for full page entry.

Chelsea Physic Garden

FENTON HOUSE ❧
WINDMILL HILL, HAMPSTEAD, LONDON NW3 6RT

Tel/Fax: 020 7435 3471   **Infoline:** 01494 755563
E-mail: fentonhouse@nationaltrust.org.uk
Owner: The National Trust   **Contact:** The Custodian
A delightful late 17th century merchant's house, set among the winding streets of Old Hampstead. The charming interior contains an outstanding collection of Oriental and European porcelain, needlework and furniture. The Benton Fletcher Collection of beautiful early keyboard instruments is also housed at Fenton and the instruments are sometimes played by music scholars during opening hours. Since 2006 the house has been home to the Peter Barkworth collection of pictures, including works by Sickert and Constable. The walled garden has a formal lawn and walks, an orchard and

vegetable garden and fine wrought-iron gates. Telephone for details of demonstrations and other events.
Location: MAP 20:J2, OS Ref. TQ262 860. Visitors' entrance on W side of Hampstead Grove. Hampstead Underground station 300 yds.
Open: 1–16 Mar: Sat & Sun, 2–5pm; 19 Mar–2 Nov: Wed–Fri, 2–5pm; Sat, Sun & BHs, 11am–5pm. Groups at other times by appointment.
Admission: Adult £5.40, Child £2.70, Family £13, Groups (15+) £4.60. Joint ticket with 2 Willow Road, £7.30. Garden only: Adult £1. Free to NT Members.
ⓘ No picnics in grounds. Ⓖ Ground floor. Braille guide. Ⓣ Demonstration tours. Ⓟ None. ⊠ ✉ Send SAE for details.

FITZROY HOUSE
35–37 FITZROY STREET, FITZROVIA, LONDON W1T 6DX
www.fitzroyhouse.org

Tel/Fax: 0207 255 2422   **E-mail:** tours@fitzroyhouse.org
Owner: Heritage Properties International   **Contact:** Sarah Borburg
Set in the heart of Fitzrovia, famed for its writers and artists, Fitzroy House was built in 1791 shortly after development was undertaken of this area. The original interior and current exterior imitate the designs of Robert Adam, celebrated Georgian-period architect. Fitzroy House is also where writer and philosopher L Ron Hubbard, founder of Scientology, worked in the 1950s. The library displays the hundreds of Mr Hubbard's published works for which he was awarded "Most Published Author" by the Guinness

Book of World Records. The building is reminiscent of the 1950s, complete with Adler typewriters, Grundig tape recorders, and Western Union telefax.
Location: MAP 20:L6, OS Ref. TQ291 820. Warren St Underground.
Open: The house is open every day of the year by appointment between 11am–5pm. Groups are welcome.
Admission: Free.
▣ Morning coffee and afternoon tea is served. Ⓣ Obligatory. ⊠ ❄

FORTY HALL
FORTY HILL, ENFIELD, MIDDLESEX EN2 9HA
www.enfield.gov.uk/fortyhall

Tel: 020 8363 8196 **Fax:** 020 8367 9098 **E-mail:** forty.hall@enfield.gov.uk
Contact: London Borough of Enfield **Contact:** Gavin Williams
This beautiful Grade I listed Jacobean House was built in 1629 for Sir Nicholas Rainton, Lord Mayor of London. He made his fortune as a Haberdasher, importing silks and taffeta from Italy. It has passed through many different owners who have made substantial changes to the Hall, both internally and externally.
It is now a location for festivals, events and guided tours throughout the year. The 273-acre estate includes formal gardens, wildflower meadows and the site of Elsyng Palace, owned by Henry VIII and Elizabeth I.

The Courtyard Café offers a selection of hot food, light snacks, and refreshments.
Location: MAP 19:E5, OS Ref. TQ336 985. 1m from M25/J25, just off A10. Tourist Board sign posted.
Open: All year: Wed–Sun, 11am–4pm.
Admission: Free. Groups welcome.
🔲 ♿ Partial. WCs. 💷 🅵 By arrangement. 🅿 Ample for cars. Limited for coaches.
🔳 🐕 In grounds, on leads. ✳ 🅼

THE FOUNDLING MUSEUM

40 Brunswick Square, London WC1N 1AZ
Tel: 020 7841 3600 **Fax:** 020 7841 3601
Owner: The Foundling Museum
Site of London's first home for abandoned children. Established in 1739. The museum charts the history of the Foundling Hospital and its residents.
Location: MAP 20:M6, OS Ref. TQ303 822. Underground: Russell Square.
Open: Tues–Sat, 10am–6pm; Sun, 12 noon–6pm.
Admission: Adult £5, Child up to 16yrs Free, Conc. £4. Special rates for groups & schools.

BENJAMIN FRANKLIN HOUSE

36 Craven Street, London WC2N 5NF
Tel: 020 7930 2000 (Box Office) **www.BenjaminFranklinHouse.org**
Owner: The Friends of Benjamin Franklin House **Contact:** Dr Marcia Balisciano
Benjamin Franklin's only surviving residence. A dynamic museum and educational facility. The 'museum as theatre' Historical Experience takes visitors on a journey through three prime floors, blending live interpretation, leading-edge lighting, sound and visual projection to tell the rich story of Franklin in London in his own words.
Location: MAP 20:N7, OS Ref. TQ302 804. Nr Charing Cross Station.
Open: All year: Wed–Sun, 10.30am–5pm. Historical Experience Show, 12 noon, 1, 2, 3.15 and 4.15pm.
Admission: Summer: Adult £7,.Child up to 16yrs Free.
🍴 🔳 ✳ 🅼

FULHAM PALACE & MUSEUM

Bishop's Avenue, Fulham, London SW6 6EA
Tel: 020 7736 3233
Owner: London Borough of Hammersmith & Fulham & Fulham Palace Trust
Former home of the Bishops of London (Tudor with Georgian additions and Victorian Chapel). Set in gardens with a collection of rare trees. Museum, contemporary art gallery.
Location: MAP 20:I12, OS Ref. TQ240 761.
Open: Museum: Mons & Tues, 12 noon–4pm; Sats, 11am–2pm; Suns, 11.30am–3.30pm. Café: daily, 9am–5pm.
Admission: Palace & Gardens: Free.

GUNNERSBURY PARK & MUSEUM

Gunnersbury Park, London W3 8LQ
Tel: 020 8992 1612 **Fax:** 020 8752 0686 **E-mail:** gp-museum@cip.org.uk
Owner: Hounslow and Ealing Councils **Contact:** Lynn Acum
Built in 1802 and refurbished by Sydney Smirke for the Rothschild family.
Location: MAP 19:B7, OS Ref. TQ190 792. Acton Town Underground station. ¼m N of the junction of A4, M4 North Circular.
Open: Apr–Oct: daily: 11am–5pm. Nov–Mar: daily: 11am–4pm. Victorian kitchens summer weekends only. Closed Christmas Day & Boxing Day. Park: open dawn–dusk.
Admission: Free. Donations welcome.

G F Handel (after Thomas Hudson) - Handel House Museum
The Royal Collection © 2001, HM Queen Elizabeth II

HAM HOUSE & GARDEN 🌾

HAM, RICHMOND, SURREY TW10 7RS

www.nationaltrust.org.uk/hamhouse

Tel: 020 8940 1950 **Fax:** 020 8439 8241 **E-mail:** hamhouse@nationaltrust.org.uk
Owner: The National Trust **Contact:** The Property Manager

Ham House, set on the banks of the Thames near Richmond, is perhaps the most remarkable Stuart house in the country. Formerly the home of the influential Duke and Duchess of Lauderdale, Ham was a centre for Court intrigue throughout the 17th century. In its time, the house was at the forefront of fashion and retains much of its interior decoration from that period. Sumptuous textiles, furniture and paintings collected by the couple are shown in 26 rooms.

The garden is a remarkable survival of English formal gardening and is being gradually restored to its former glory. The unusual 18th century dairy is decorated with cast iron cows' legs supporting marble surfaces and hand-painted Wedgwood tiles. Rare 17th century still house, originally used for distilling alcohol and perfumes.

Programme of events throughout the year, including open air theatre, guided tours, Christmas specific events and children's activities.

Location: MAP 19:B8, OS Ref. TQ172 732. 1½ m from Richmond and 2m from Kingston. On the S bank of the River Thames, W of A307 at Petersham.
Open: House: 15 Mar–2 Nov: Sat–Wed, 12–4pm. Gardens: All year, Sat–Wed, 11am–6pm. Closed 25/26 Dec & 1 Jan. Special Christmas openings for house, café and gift shop and Christmas lunches in December.
Admission: House & Garden: Adult £9.90, Child £5.50, Family £25.30. Garden only: Adult £3.30, Child £2.20, Family £8.80. Family group tickets include 2 adults and children under 16. Free to NT Members. Pre-booked groups during opening hours (15+) Adult £8.50, Child £5, outside normal hours £14. *includes a voluntary 10% donation but visitors can choose to pay the standard prices displayed at the property and on the website.

🔲 ⚡ 🚻 ♿ Partial. WC. 🐕 ⓘ 🅿 🔲 🐾 Guide dogs. 🔲🔲

HANDEL HOUSE MUSEUM

25 BROOK STREET, LONDON W1K 4HB

www.handelhouse.org

Tel: 020 7495 1685 **Fax:** 020 7495 1759 **E-mail:** mail@handelhouse.org
Owner: The Handel House Trust Ltd **Contact:** Shuk Kwan Liu

Handel House Museum is a beautifully restored Georgian townhouse where the famous composer George Frideric Handel lived for 36 years and composed timeless masterpieces such as *Messiah* and *Zadok the Priest*. The elegantly refurbished interiors create the perfect setting for 18th century fine art and furniture, evoking the spirit of Georgian London. Portraits and paintings of Handel and his contemporaries illustrate Handel's London life and the House is as vibrant with music as it was in Handel's day. Weekly Thursday evening recitals and regular weekend events are held in Handel's intimate music room (booking recommended).

Location: MAP 20:K7, OS Ref. TQ286 809. Central London, between New Bond St and Grosvenor Square. Entrance in Lancashire Court. Bond Street Tube.
Open: All year, Tue–Sat, 10am–6pm (8pm Thur). Suns, 12 noon–6pm. Closed Mons. Groups by arrangement. Last entry 30 mins before closing.
Admission: Adult £5, Child £2 (Free on Sat), Conc. £4.50. The Art Fund cardholders Free.

ⓘ No inside photography. 🔲 ♿ ⓘ By arrangement. 🐾 Guide dogs only. 🔲🔲

HONEYWOOD

Honeywood Walk, Carshalton SM5 3NX
Tel: 020 8770 4297 **Fax:** 020 8770 4297 **E-mail:** lbshoneywood@btconnect.com
www.sutton.gov.uk www.friendsofhoneywood.co.uk
Owner: London Borough of Sutton **Contact:** The Curator

Local history museum in a 17th century listed building next to the picturesque Carshalton Ponds, containing displays on many aspects of the history of the London Borough of Sutton plus a changing programme of exhibitions and events on a wide range of subjects. Attractive garden at rear.

Location: MAP 19:D9, OS Ref. TQ279 646. On A232 approximately 4m W of Croydon.
Open: Wed–Fri, 11am–5pm. Sat, Suns & BH Mons, 10am–5pm. Free admission to shop.
Admission: Adult £1.60, Child 80p, under 5 Free. Groups by arrangement.

🔲 ♿ Ground floor. WC. ⓘ 🅿 Limited. 🔲 🐾 Guide dogs only. 🔲🔲

JEWEL TOWER ⚑

Abingdon Street, Westminster, London SW1P 3JX
Tel: 020 7222 2219 **www.english-heritage.org.uk/jeweltower**
Owner: English Heritage **Contact:** Visitor Operations Team

Built c1365 to house the personal treasure of Edward III. One of two surviving parts of the original Palace of Westminster. Now houses an exhibition on 'Parliament Past and Present'. The second floor now includes new illustrated panels, telling the story of this small but important building.

Location: MAP 20:M8, OS Ref. TQ302 794. Opposite S end of Houses of Parliament (Victoria Tower).
Open: 21 Mar–31 Oct: daily, 10am–5pm. 1 Nov–31 Mar: daily, 10am–4pm. Closed 24–26 Dec & 1 Jan.
Admission: Adult £3, Child £1.50, Conc. £2.40. EH Members free. Group discount available.

🔲 🐾 🔲🔲

See which properties offer **educational facilities** or **school visits** in our index at the end of the book.

DR JOHNSON'S HOUSE

17 Gough Square, London EC4A 3DE
Tel: 020 7353 3745 **E-mail:** curator@drjohnsonshouse.org
Owner: The Trustees
Fine 18th century house, once home to Dr Samuel Johnson, the celebrated literary figure, famous for his English dictionary.
Location: MAP 20:N7, OS Ref. TQ314 813. N of Fleet Street.
Open: Oct–Apr: Mon–Sat, 11am–5pm. May–Sept: Mon–Sat, 11am–5.30pm. Closed BHs.
Admission: Adult £4.50, Child £1.50 (under 10yrs Free), Conc. £3.50. Family £10. Groups: £3.50.

KENWOOD HOUSE ⌗

See page 60 for full page entry.

2 Willow Road

KEATS HOUSE
KEATS GROVE, HAMPSTEAD, LONDON NW3 2RR

www.cityoflondon.gov.uk/keats

Tel: 020 7435 2062 **Fax:** 020 7431 9293 **E-mail:** keatshouse@cityoflondon.gov.uk
Owner: City of London **Contact:** The Manager
This Grade I listed Regency house is where the poet John Keats lived from 1818 to 1820 with his friend Charles Brown. Here he wrote '*Ode to a Nightingale*' and met and fell in love with Fanny Brawne. Suffering from tuberculosis, Keats left for Italy, where he died aged twenty-five.
Location: MAP 20:K3, OS Ref. TQ272 856. Hampstead, NW3. Nearest Underground: Belsize Park & Hampstead.
Open: Keats House will be closed on 31 Oct 2007–Autumn 2008 for a Heritage Lottery Funded transformation. Please see website for details.
Admission: Please see website for details.
🔲 🔳 Ground floor & garden. 🅿 None. 🔳 🔳 Guide dogs only.

KENSINGTON PALACE
LONDON W8 4PX

www.kensington-palace.org.uk

Tel Information line: 0844 482 7777
Venue Hire and Corporate Hospitality: 020 3166 6104
Owner: Historic Royal Palaces
The feminine influence of generations of royal women have shaped this stylish palace and elegant gardens. The birthplace and childhood home of Queen Victoria, the palace first became a royal residence for William and Mary in 1689. Mary felt 'shut in' at Whitehall and much preferred her new Kensington home, which was enlarged by Sir Christopher Wren. The famous Orangery was built in 1704 in by Queen Anne, and George II's wife, Queen Caroline, another keen gardener, added further improvements. Today, the palace houses a stunning permanent display of fashionable and formal dresses, the Royal Ceremonial Dress Collection, which includes dresses worn by Diana, Princess of Wales.
Location: MAP 20:I8, OS Ref. TQ258 801 In Kensington Gardens. Underground: Queensway on Central Line, High Street Kensington on Circle & District Line.
Open; Mar–Oct: daily, 10am–6pm (last admission 5pm) Nov–Feb: daily, 10am–5pm (last admission 4pm) Closed 24–26 Dec.
Admission: Telephone Information Line for admission prices: 0844 482 7777. Advance Ticket Sales: 0844 482 7799. Group bookings 0844 482 7770. Quote Hudson's.
ℹ️ No photography indoors. 🔲 🔳 🔳 🍴 🔳 Partial. 🔲 🅿 Nearby. 🔳 Please book, 0844 482 7777. 🔳 In grounds, on leads. Guide dogs only in Palace. 🔆

LEIGHTON HOUSE MUSEUM
12 HOLLAND PARK ROAD, KENSINGTON, LONDON W14 8LZ

www.rbkc.gov.uk/leightonhousemusem

Tel: 020 7602 3316 **Fax:** 020 7371 2467
E-mail: museums@rbkc.gov.uk
Owner: Royal Borough of Kensington & Chelsea
Contact: Curator

Leighton House was the home of Frederic, Lord Leighton 1830–1896, painter and President of the Royal Academy, built between 1864–1879. It was a palace of art designed for entertaining and to provide a magnificent working space in the studio, with great north windows and a gilded apse. The Arab Hall is the centrepiece of the house, containing Leighton's collection of Islamic tiles, a gilt mosaic frieze and a fountain. Victorian paintings by Leighton, Millais and Burne-Jones are on display.

Location: MAP 20:I9, OS Ref. TQ247 793. Nearest underground: High Street Kensington (exit staircase turn left, take first right for Melbury Road after Commonwealth Institute. Leighton House is located in Holland Park Road, the first left. Bus: 9, 10, 27, 28, 33, 49, 328 (to Commonwealth Institute).

Open: Daily, except Tues, 11am–5.30pm. Also open Spring/Summer BHs. Guided tours on Wed & Thur, 2.30pm. Closed 25/26 Dec.

Admission: Adult £3, Conc £1. Family £6. Guided tours free on Weds & Thurs. Joint group guided tour with Linley Sambourne House £10pp.
ⓘ No photography. 🅾 🆃 ♿ Unsuitable. 👣 Wed & Thurs at 2.30pm. 🅿 None.

LINLEY SAMBOURNE HOUSE
18 STAFFORD TERRACE, LONDON W8 7BH

www.rbkc.gov.uk/linleysambournehouse

Info: 020 7602 3316 (ext 300 Mon–Fri) or 020 7938 1295 (Sats & Suns)
Fax: 020 7371 2467 **E-mail:** museums@rbkc.gov.uk
Owner: The Royal Borough of Kensington & Chelsea **Contact:** Curatorial staff

Linley Sambourne House is the former home of the Punch cartoonist Edward Linley Sambourne and his family. Almost unchanged over the course of the last century, the house provides a unique insight into the life of an artistic middle-class family. The majority of the original decoration and furnishings remain in situ exactly as left by the Sambournes. All visits are by guided tour with special dramatic tours available and an introductory video. Larger groups can visit jointly with Leighton House Museum just 10 minutes walk away.

Location: MAP 20:I8, OS Ref. TQ252 794. Parallel to Kensington High St, between Phillimore Gardens & Argyll Rd. Bus: 9, 10, 27, 28, 31, 49, 52, 70 & C1. Underground: Kensington High St. Parking on Sun in nearby streets.

Open: Mid Mar–mid Dec: Sats & Suns; tours leaving 11.15am, 1pm, 2.15pm and 3.30pm. Pre-booking is advised. At other times for booked groups (10+), by appointment. Larger groups (12+) will be divided for tours of the House. Access for Group tours: Mon–Fri.

Admission: Adult £6, Child (under 18yrs) £1, Conc £4. Groups (12+): Min £72. Joint group (10+) guided tour with Leighton House Museum £10pp.
ⓘ No photography. 🅾 👣 Obligatory. 🅿 None. 🔲 🅱 Guide dogs only. ✱

LITTLE HOLLAND HOUSE

40 Beeches Avenue, Carshalton SM5 3LW
Tel: 020 8770 4781 **Fax:** 020 8770 4777
E-mail: valary.murphy@sutton.gov.uk
www.sutton.gov.uk
Owner: London Borough of Sutton **Contact:** Ms V Murphy
The home of Frank Dickinson (1874–1961) artist, designer and craftsman, who dreamt of a house that would follow the philosophy and theories of William Morris and John Ruskin. Dickinson designed, built and furnished the house himself from 1902 onwards. The Grade II* listed interior features handmade furniture, metal work, carvings and paintings produced by Dickinson in the Arts and Crafts style.
Location: MAP 19:D9, OS Ref. TQ275 634. On B278 1m S of junction with A232.
Open: First Sun of each month & BH Suns & Mons (excluding Christmas & New Year), 1.30–5.30pm.
Admission: Free. Groups by arrangement, £4pp (includes talk and guided tour).
🛈 No photography in house. 🅖 Ground floor. 🅣 By arrangement.
🐕 Guide dogs only. ❋

English Heritage Photo Library

MARBLE HILL HOUSE ⌗

RICHMOND ROAD, TWICKENHAM TW1 2NL

www.english-heritage.org.uk/marblehillhouse

Tel: 020 8892 5115
Owner: English Heritage **Contact:** Visitor Operations Team
This beautiful villa beside the Thames was built in 1724–29 for Henrietta Howard, mistress of George II. Here she entertained many of the poets and wits of the Augustan age including Alexander Pope and later Horace Walpole. The perfect proportions of the villa were inspired by the work of the 16th century Italian architect, Palladio. Today this beautifully presented house contains an important collection of paintings and furniture, including some pieces commissioned for the villa when it was built. A recent installation recreates the Chinese wallpaper Henrietta Howard hung in the Dining Room in 1751. Summer concerts.
Location: MAP 19:B8, OS Ref. TQ174 736. A305, 600yds E of Orleans House.
Open: 21 Mar–31 Oct: Sat, 10am–2pm. Suns & BHs, 10am–5pm. 1 Nov–21 Dec & Mar: by appointment only. Closed 22 Dec–28 Feb 09.
Admission: Adult £4.20, Child £2.10, Conc. £3.40, Family £10.50. EH Members free. Group discount available.
🗗 🅣 🅖 Ground floor. WC. 🛒 Summer only. 🅟 🐕 🖼 🎧

MORDEN HALL PARK 🌿

Morden Hall Road, Morden SM4 5JD
Tel: 020 8545 6850 **Fax:** 020 8417 8091
E-mail: mordenhallpark@nationaltrust.org.uk
Owner: The National Trust **Contact:** The Property Manager
Former deer park centred around historic snuff mills and rose garden featuring an extensive network of waterways, ancient hay meadows and wetlands. Workshops now house local craftworkers.
Location: MAP 19:D8, OS Ref. TQ261 684. Off A24 and A297 S of Wimbledon, N of Sutton.
Open: All year: daily. NT gift shop & Riverside Café: 10am–5pm (closed: 25/26 Dec & 1 Jan). Car park closes 6pm.
Admission: Free.

WILLIAM MORRIS GALLERY

Lloyd Park, Forest Road, Walthamstow, London E17 4PP
Tel: 020 8527 3782 **Fax:** 020 8527 7070
Owner: London Borough of Waltham Forest **Contact:** The Keeper
Location: MAP 19:F6, OS Ref. SQ372 899. 15 mins walk from Walthamstow tube (Victoria line). 5–10 mins from M11/A406.
Open: Tue–Sat and first Sun each month, 10am–1pm and 2–5pm.
Admission: Free for all visitors but a charge is made for guided tours which must be booked in advance.

MYDDELTON HOUSE GARDENS

BULLS CROSS, ENFIELD, MIDDLESEX EN2 9HG

www.leevalleypark.org.uk

Tel: 01992 702200
Owner: Lee Valley Regional Park Authority
Created by the famous plantsman and Fellow of the Royal Horticultural Society, E A Bowles, the gardens contain year round interest. From the January snowdrops, through the springtime flowering daffodils to the summer roses and beyond to the autumn crocus, there's always something in the gardens to interest the visitor. The gardens are an ideal place to draw, paint, photograph or picnic. Woodland walks. Carp lake. National Collection of award-winning Bearded Iris. Guided walks available.
Location: MAP 19:D4, OS Ref. TQ342 992. ¼m W of A10 via Turkey St. ¾m S M25/J25.
Open: Apr–Sept: Mon–Fri, 10am–4.30pm, Suns & BH Mons & NGS days, 12 noon–4pm. Oct–Mar: Mon–Fri, 10am–3pm. Last admission 30 mins before closing. Closed Christmas.
Admission: Adult £2.60, Conc. £2.00. Prices subject to change April 2008. Separate charge for guided walks.
🗗 🅣 🅖 Some paths. 🛒 🅣 Please ring 01992 702200. 🅟 🐕 Guide dogs only. ❋

THE OCTAGON, ORLEANS HOUSE GALLERY

Riverside, Twickenham, Middlesex TW1 3DJ
Tel: 020 8831 6000 **Fax:** 020 8744 0501 **E-mail:** galleryinfo@richmond.gov.uk
Owner: London Borough of Richmond-upon-Thames **Contact:** The Curator
Outstanding example of baroque architecture by James Gibbs c1720. Art gallery.
Location: MAP 19:B8, OS Ref. TQ168 734. On N side of Riverside, 700yds E of Twickenham town centre, 400yds S of Richmond Road. Vehicle access via Orleans Rd only.
Open: Tue–Sat, 1–5.30pm, Sun & BHs, 2–5.30pm (Oct–Mar closes 4.30pm). Closed Mons. Garden: open daily, 9am–sunset.
Admission: Free.

© NTPL

© NTPL/Bill Batten

OSTERLEY PARK AND HOUSE ⚘
JERSEY ROAD, ISLEWORTH, MIDDLESEX TW7 4RB
www.nationaltrust.org.uk/osterley/

Tel: 020 8232 5050   **Fax:** 020 8232 5080   **Infoline:** 01494 755566
E-mail: osterley@nationaltrust.org.uk
Owner: The National Trust   **Contact:** Visitor Services Manager
Osterley's four turrets look out across one of the last great 'Landscape' parks in suburban London, its trees and lakes an unexpected haven of green. Originally built in 1575, the mansion was transformed in the 18th century into an elegant villa by architect Robert Adam. The classical interior, designed for entertaining on a grand scale, still impresses with its specially made tapestries, furniture and plasterwork. The magnificent 16th century stables survive largely intact.

Location: MAP 19:B7, OS Ref. TQ146 780. Access via Thornbury Road on N side of A4.
Open: House: 12 Mar–2 Nov: Wed–Sun & BHs, 1–4.30pm. 6–21 Dec: Sat & Sun, 12.30–3.30pm. Garden: 12 Mar–2 Nov: Wed–Sun & BHs, 11am–5pm.
Park: All year, daily, 8am–7.30pm (closes 6pm in winter).
*Admission: House and Garden: Adult £8, Child £4, Family £20, Groups (15+) £6.80. Garden: Adult £3.50, Child £1.75. Park: Free. Car Park: £3.50. Free to NT Members. *includes a voluntary 10% donation but visitors can choose to pay the standard prices displayed at the property and on the website.
▢ T &. Tel for details. ☻ P ▦ ▧ On leads in park. ▲ ✳ ♨

PALACE OF WESTMINSTER

London SW1A 0AA

Tel: 020 7219 3000 / 0870 906 3773   **Info:** 020 7219 4272
Fax: 020 7219 5839   **Contact:** Information Office
The first Palace of Westminster was erected on this site by Edward the Confessor in 1042 and the building was a royal residence until a devastating fire in 1512. After this, the palace became the two-chamber Parliament for government – the House of Lords and the elected House of Commons. Following a further fire in 1834, the palace was rebuilt by Sir Charles Barry and decorated by A W Pugin.

Location: MAP 20:M8, OS Ref. TQ303 795. Central London, W bank of River Thames. 1km S of Trafalgar Square. Underground: Westminster.
Open: Aug–Sept (please ring for details). At other times by appointment. Please telephone Info line.
Admission: Aug–Sept: Adult £12, Conc. £8, Child £5 (under 5yrs Free), At other times Free.

PITZHANGER MANOR-HOUSE

Walpole Park, Mattock Lane, Ealing W5 5EQ

Tel: 020 8567 1227   **Fax:** 020 8567 0595
E-mail: pmgallery&house@ealing.gov.uk **www.ealing.gov.uk/pmgalleryandhouse**
Owner: London Borough of Ealing   **Contact:** Anne Ninivin
Pitzhanger Manor House is a restored Georgian villa, once owned and designed by the architect Sir John Soane (1753–1837). Rooms in the house have been restored using Soane's highly individual ideas in design and decoration. Exhibitions of contemporary art are programmed year-round, sited in the adjacent Gallery and often also in the House.

Location: MAP 19:B7, OS Ref. TQ176 805. Ealing, London.
Open: All year: Tue–Fri, 1–5pm. Sat, 11am–5pm. Summer Sunday Openings, please ring for details. Closed Christmas, Easter, New Year and BHs.
Admission: Free.
T &. By arrangement. ▢ ▦ ▧ In grounds, on leads. ▲ ✳

RED HOUSE ⚘

Red House Lane, Bexleyheath DA6 8JF

Tel: 020 8304 9878 (Booking line: Tues–Sat, 9.30am–1.30pm)
Owner: The National Trust
Commissioned by William Morris in 1859 and designed by Philip Webb, Red House is of enormous international significance in the history of domestic architecture and garden design. The garden was designed to "clothe" the house with a series of sub-divided areas that still clearly exist today. Inside, the house retains many of the original features and fixed items of furniture designed by Morris and Webb, as well as wall paintings and stained glass by Burne-Jones.

Location: MAP 19:G8, OS Ref. TQ48 1750. Off A221 Bexleyheath. Visitors will be advised on how to reach the property when booking. Nearest rail station Bexleyheath, 20 mins' walk.
Open: Mar–Dec: Wed–Sun, 11am–4.45pm. Closed 22 Dec–4 Mar. Open Easter Sun, Good Fri, BH Mons. Admission by pre-booked guided tour.
Admission: Adult £6.60, Child £3.30, Family £16.50. NT Members Free.
ⓘ No WC. &. Ground floor only. ☻ Limited. P No parking on site. Disabled drivers can pre-book (limited parking). Parking at Danson Park (15 min walk). Parking charge at weekends and BHs. See Danson House (Kent section).

ROYAL OBSERVATORY
NATIONAL MARITIME MUSEUM
& QUEEN'S HOUSE

See page 61 for full page entry.

ST GEORGE'S CATHEDRAL, SOUTHWARK

Westminster Bridge Road, London SE1 7HY

Tel: 020 7928 5256   **Fax:** 020 7202 2189
E-mail: info@southwark-rc-cathedral.org.uk   **Contact:** Canon James Cronin
Neo-Gothic rebuilt Pugin Cathedral bombed during the last war and rebuilt by Romily Craze in 1958.

Location: MAP 20:N9, OS Ref. TQ315 794. Near Imperial War Museum. ½m SE of Waterloo Stn.
Open: 8am–6pm, every day, except BHs.
Admission: Free.

ST JOHN'S GATE
MUSEUM OF THE ORDER OF ST JOHN
ST JOHN'S GATE, LONDON EC1M 4DA

www.sja.org.uk/museum

Tel: 020 7324 4005 **Fax:** 020 7336 0587 **E-mail:** museum@nhq.sja.org.uk
Owner: The Order of St John **Contact:** Pamela Willis
Early 16th century Gatehouse (built 1504), Priory Church and Norman Crypt. The remarkable history of the Knights Hospitaller, dedicated to caring for the sick and dating back to the 11th century, is revealed in collections including furniture, paintings, armour, stained glass and other items. Notable associations with Shakespeare, Hogarth, Edward Cave, Dr Johnson, Dickens, David Garrick and many others. In Victorian times, St John Ambulance was founded here and a modern interactive gallery tells its story.
Location: MAP 20:N6, OS Ref. TQ317 821. St. John's Lane, Clerkenwell. Nearest Underground: Farringdon.
Open: Mon–Fri: 10am–5pm. Sat: 10am–4pm. Closed BHs & Sat of BH weekend. Tours: Tue, Fri & Sat at 11am & 2.30pm. Reference Library: Open by appointment.
Admission: Museum Free. Tours of the building: £5, OAP £4 (donation).
⬚ 🅖 Ground floor. WC. 🄵 ▣ 🄼 Guide dogs only. ✳   Reg. Charity No. 1077265

ST PAUL'S CATHEDRAL   *See page 62 for full page entry.*

SIR JOHN SOANE'S MUSEUM

13 Lincoln's Inn Fields, London WC2A 3BP
Tel: 020 7405 2107 **Fax:** 020 7831 3957 **www.soane.org**
Owner: Trustees of Sir John Soane's Museum **Contact:** Julie Brock
The celebrated architect Sir John Soane built this in 1812 as his own house. It now contains his collection of antiquities, sculpture and paintings.
Location: MAP 20:M6, OS Ref. TQ308 816. E of Kingsway, S of High Holborn.
Open: Tue–Sat, 10am–5pm. 6–9pm, first Tue of the month. Closed BHs & 24 Dec.
Admission: Free. Possible charge for first Tue. Groups must book.

SOMERSET HOUSE   *See page 63 for full page entry.*

Carlyle's House

SOUTHSIDE HOUSE 🏛
3 WOODHAYES ROAD, WIMBLEDON, LONDON SW19 4RJ

www.southsidehouse.com

Tel: 020 8946 7643 **E-mail:** info@southsidehouse.com
Owner: The Pennington-Mellor-Munthe Charity Trust **Contact:** The Administrator
Described by connoisseurs as an unforgettable experience, Southside House provides an enchantingly eccentric backdrop to the lives and loves of generations of the Pennington Mellor Munthe families. Maintained in traditional style, without major refurbishment, and crowded with the family possessions of centuries, Southside offers a wealth of fascinating family stories.
Behind the long façade are the old rooms, still with much of the original furniture and a superb collection of art and historical objects. John Pennington-Mellor's daughter, Hilda, married Axel Munthe, the charismatic Swedish doctor and philanthropist. The preservation of the house was left to their youngest son who led a life of extraordinary adventure during the Second World War. Malcolm Munthe's surviving children continue to care for the property.
The gardens are as fascinating as the house, with a series of sculptural "rooms" linked by water and intriguing pathways.

Location: MAP 20:D8, OS Ref. TQ234 706. On S side of Wimbledon Common (B281), opposite Crooked Billet Inn.
Open: Easter Sun–30 Sept: Weds, Sats, Suns & BH Mons. Closed during Wimbledon fortnight in July. Guided tours on the hour 2, 3 & 4pm. Other times throughout the year by arrangement with the Administrator.
Admission: Adult £5, Child £2.50 (must be accompanied by an adult), Conc. £4, Family £10.
ℹ No photography inside house. 🅖 Unsuitable. 🄵 Obligatory. 🅿 Limited. ▣
🄼 In grounds on leads. ♿

SOUTHWARK CATHEDRAL

London Bridge, London SE1 9DA
Tel: 020 7367 6700 **Fax:** 020 7367 6730 **Visitors' Officer:** 020 7367 6734
E-mail: cathedral@southwark.anglican.org **www.southwark.anglican.org/cathedral**
Owner: Church of England **Contact:** Visitors' Officer

London's oldest gothic building and a place of worship for over 1,400 years, Southwark Cathedral has connections with Chaucer, Shakespeare, Dickens and John Harvard. Included in the new riverside Millennium buildings are: the Cathedral Shop, Refectory, and Archaeological Chamber.

Location: MAP 20:O8, OS Ref. TQ327 803. South side of London Bridge, near Shakespeare's Globe and Tate Modern.

Open: Daily: 8.30am–6pm. Weekday services: 8am, 12.30pm and 5.30pm. Sat services, 9am and 4pm. Sun services: 9am, 1am, 3pm & 6.30pm. Cathedral Shop: daily, 10am–6pm, Sun, 12 noon–6pm.

Admission: Recommended donation of £4 per person. Booked groups (min 10): Adult £4, Child £2, Conc. £3.50. Trade discounts available.

ℹ️ Indoor photography & video recording with permit. ⬜ 🅃 🅰 Partial. WCs.
▣ 🍴 Licensed. 🅵 By arrangement. 🅾 🅿 None. 🔳 🔲 Guide dogs only. ✳ 🔳

SPENCER HOUSE

See page 64 for full page entry.

STRAWBERRY HILL

St Mary's, Strawberry Hill, Waldegrave Road, Twickenham TW1 4SX
Tel: 0870 626 0402
Owner: Strawberry Hill Trust **Contact:** The Administrator
Location: MAP 19:B8, OS Ref. TQ158 722. Off A310 between Twickenham & Teddington. From Oct 2008 Horace Walpole's Villa at Strawberry Hill will be closed for a major conservation programme. The re-opening is planned for 2010. For further information please contact Strawberrytours on 0208 892 2804. The Waldegrave Wing remains available for weddings and corporate functions. Telephone The Conference Office: 020 8240 4044.

© NTPL/Geoffrey Frosh

SUTTON HOUSE 🌼

2 & 4 HOMERTON HIGH STREET, HACKNEY, LONDON E9 6JQ
Tel: 020 8986 2264 **E-mail:** suttonhouse@nationaltrust.org.uk
Owner: The National Trust **Contact:** The Custodian

A rare example of a Tudor red-brick house, built in 1535 by Sir Ralph Sadleir, Principal Secretary of State for Henry VIII, with 18th century alterations and later additions. Restoration revealed many 16th century details, even in rooms of later periods. Notable features include original linenfold panelling and 17th century wall paintings.

Location: MAP 20:P3, OS Ref. TQ352 851. At the corner of Isabella Road and Homerton High St.

Open: Historic rooms: 1 Feb–21 Dec: Thur–Sun, 12.30–4.30pm. Café, Shop & Art Gallery: 1 Feb–23 Dec: Thur–Sun, 12 noon–4.30pm. Last admission 4pm. Open BH Mons, closed Good Fri.

Admission: Adult £2.80, Child 70p, Family £6.30. Group £2.40. Free to NT Members.

⬜ 🅰 Ground floor only. WC. ▣ 🅵 🅿 None. 🔳 🔺 ✳ 🔳

SYON PARK 🏛

See page 65 for full page entry.

THE TOWER BRIDGE EXHIBITION

Tower Bridge, London SE1 2UP
Tel: 0207 403 3761 **Fax:** 020 7357 7935
Owner: Corporation of London **Contact:** Emma Parlow

One of London's most unusual and exciting exhibitions is situated inside Tower Bridge. Enjoy spectacular views from the high level walkways.

Location: MAP 20:P8, OS Ref. TQ337 804. Adjacent to Tower of London, nearest Underground: Tower Hill.

Open: 1 Apr–30 Sep: 10am–5.30pm (last ticket). 1 Oct–31 Mar: 9.30am–5pm (last ticket). Closed 24–26 Dec.

Admission: Adult £6, Child £3, Conc. £4.50. (Prices may change April 2008.)

18 Folgate Street

TOWER OF LONDON
LONDON EC3N 4AB
www.tower-of-london.org.uk

Tel Information Line: 0844 482 7777
Venue Hire and Corporate Hospitality: 020 3166 6207
Owner: Historic Royal Palaces

The ancient stones reverberate with dark secrets, priceless jewels glint in fortified vaults and pampered ravens strut the grounds. The Tower of London, founded by William the Conqueror in 1066–7, is one of the world's most famous fortresses, and Britain's most visited historic site. Despite a grim reputation for a place of torture and death, there are so many more stories to be told about the Tower. This powerful and enduring symbol of the Norman Conquest has been enjoyed as a royal palace, served as an armoury and, for a few years in the 1830s, even housed a zoo! An intriguing cast of characters have played their part: including the dastardly jewel-thief Colonel Blood, tragic Lady Jane Grey and maverick zoo keeper Albert Cops.

Location: MAP 20:P7, OS Ref. TQ336 806, Underground: Tower Hill on Circle/District Line. Docklands Light Railway: Tower Gateway Station. Rail: Fenchurch Street Station and London Bridge Station. Bus: 15, 25, 42, 78, 100, D1, RV1. Riverboat: From Charing Cross, Westminster or Greenwich to Tower Pier. London Eye to Tower of London Express.

Open: Summer: 1 Mar–31 Oct, Daily, Tues–Sat: 9am–6pm (last admission 5pm), Mons & Suns: 10am–6pm (last admission 5pm). Winter: 1 Nov–28 Feb, Tues–Sat: 9am–5pm, Mons & Suns: 10am–5pm (last admission 4pm). Closed 24–26 Dec and 1 Jan. Buildings close 30 minutes after last admission.

Admission: Telephone Information Line for admission prices: 0844 482 7777. Advance Ticket Sales: 0844 482 7799. Group bookings: 0844 482 7770. Quote Hudson's.
ℹ️ No photography in Jewel House. 📷 📞 020 3166 6311. ♿ Partial. WC. ☕ 🍴
🎭 Yeoman Warder tours are free and leave front entrance every ½ hr. 🎧
🅿️ None for cars. Coach parking nearby. 🚌 To book 0844 482 7777.
🐕 Guide dogs only. ✳️ ♿

The Tulip Staircase, The Queen's House, Greenwich

WELLINGTON ARCH ⌗

HYDE PARK CORNER, LONDON W1J 7JZ

www.english-heritage.org.uk/wellingtonarch

Tel: 020 7930 2726   **Venue Hire and Hospitality:** 020 7973 3292
Owner: English Heritage   **Contact:** Visitor Operations Team
Set in the heart of Royal London at Hyde Park Corner, Wellington Arch is a landmark for Londoners and visitors alike. George IV originally commissioned this massive monument as a grand outer entrance to Buckingham Palace. It was completed in 1830 by architect Decimus Burton, and moved to its present site in 1882. Take a lift to the balconies just below the spectacular bronze sculpture, which tops the imposing monument, for glorious views over London's Royal Parks and the Houses of Parliament. The statue is the largest bronze sculpture in Europe, and depicts the angel of Peace descending on the chariot of war. Inside the Arch, three floors of exhibits tell its fascinating history.
Location: MAP 20:L8, OS Ref. TQ285 798. Hyde Park Corner Tube Station.
Open: 21 Mar–31 Oct: Wed–Sun & BHs, 10am–5pm. 1 Nov–31 Mar: Wed–Sun, 10am–4pm. Closed 24–26 Dec & 1 Jan. May close at short notice, please tel for details.
Admission: Adult £3.30, Child £1.70, Conc. £2.60. Groups (11+) 15% discount. Joint ticket available with Apsley House. EH Members free.
◻ T ♿ 🅸 Mondays for groups only. ✳ ♥

THE 'WERNHER COLLECTION' AT RANGER'S HOUSE ⌗

Chesterfield Walk, Blackheath, London SE10 8QX
Tel: 020 8853 0035   www.english-heritage.org.uk/rangershouse
Owner: English Heritage   **Contact:** House Manager
This attractive red-brick villa built c1700 on the edge of Greenwich Park houses the 'Wernher Collection': the life-time collection of self-made millionaire, Julius Wernher. A superb display of fine and decorative arts with objects dating from 3BC to the 19th-century, and including a stunning array of Renaissance jewellery as well as paintings, sculpture, furniture, tapestries, enamels and ivories.
Location: MAP 4:I2, OS Ref. TQ388 768. N of Shooters Hill Road.
Open: 21 Mar–30 Sept: Sun–Wed, 10am–5pm, Thurs pre-booked groups only. 1–31 Oct closed. 1 Nov—21 Dec: by appointment only. Closed 22 Dec–28 Feb.
Admission: Adult £5.50, Child £2.80, Conc. £4.40. EH Members free. Group discount available.
🅸 WC. ◻ T ♿ Limited, lift available. 🅿 ■ ♥ Guide dogs only.

WESTMINSTER CATHEDRAL

Victoria, London SW1P 1QW
Tel: 020 7798 9055   **Fax:** 020 7798 9090   www.westminstercathedral.org.uk
Owner: Diocese of Westminster   **Contact:** Revd Mgr Mark Langham
The Roman Catholic Cathedral of the Archbishop of Westminster. Spectacular building in the Byzantine style, designed by J F Bentley, opened in 1903, famous for its mosaics, marble and music.
Location: MAP 20:L9, OS Ref. TQ293 791. Off Victoria Street, between Victoria Station and Westminster Abbey.
Open: All year: 7am–7pm. Please telephone for times at Easter & Christmas.
Admission: Free. Tower lift/viewing gallery charge: Adult £5. Family (2+4) £11. Conc. £2.50
◻ ♿ Ground floor. ● 🅸 Booking required. 🅿 None. ■ Worksheets & tours.
♥ Guide dogs only. ✳

WHITEHALL

1 Malden Road, Cheam SM3 8QD
Tel/Fax: 020 8643 1236   **E-mail:** whitehallcheam@btconnect.com
www.sutton.gov.uk   www.friendsofwhitehallcheam.co.uk
Owner: London Borough of Sutton   **Contact:** The Curator
A Tudor timber-framed house, c1500 with later additions, in the heart of Cheam Village conservation area. Displays on the history of the house and the people who lived here, plus nearby Nonsuch Palace, Cheam School and William Gilpin (Dr Syntax). Changing exhibition programme and special event days throughout the year. Attractive rear garden features medieval well from c1400.
Location: MAP 19:C9, OS Ref. TQ242 638. Approx. 2m S of A3 on A2043 just N of junction with A232.
Open: Wed–Fri, 2–5pm; Sat, 10am–5pm; Sun & BH Mons, 2–5pm.
Admission: Adult £1.60, Child (6-16yrs) 80p, under 5yrs Free. Groups by appt.
◻ ♿ Ground floor. ● 🅸 ◻ ■ ♥ Guide dogs only. ✳ ♥

7 Hammersmith Terrace – Home of Emery Walker

Hole Park, Kent

South East

Eight counties make up the this region. In each you can find world-famous properties such as Windsor Castle, Blenheim Palace and Leeds Castle – and lesser known treasures such as Belmont, Broughton Castle and Great Dixter House & Gardens that give a deeper insight into Britain's heritage and history both architectural and horticultural.

Berkshire

Buckinghamshire

Hampshire

Kent

Oxfordshire

Surrey

Sussex

Isle of Wight

The Oaks

Owner
The Crown Estate

Contact
The Savill Garden
Wick Lane
Englefield Green
Surrey TW20 0UU

Tel: 01784 435544
Fax: 01784 439746
E-mail: enquiries@
theroyallandscape.co.uk

Location
MAP 3:G2
OS Ref. SU977 706

Sign posted off A30,
M25 Junction 13 or M4
Junction 6.

Rail: Windsor Central or
Egham.

Opening Times
Daily. March–October:
10am–6pm.
November–February:
10am–4:30pm.
Closed Christmas Day
and Boxing Day.

Admission
Winter

Adult	£5.00
Child under 6	Free
Child (6–16yrs)	£2.00
Seniors	£4.50
Groups (10+)	£4.00

Summer

Adult	£7.00
Child under 6	Free
Child (6–16yrs)	£3.50
Seniors	£6.50
Groups (10+)	£5.50

Groups should pre-book.
Guided tours available at
additional cost.
Family ticket concessions
available. For prices from
November 2008, please
telephone or email.
Annual Memberships
available from £40.

Special Events
The Savill Garden is
constantly being
developed but some of
the popular highlights are:
Feb–Mar:
Camellias and the carpet
of daffodils in The Glades.
Apr–May:
Azalea and
rhododendrons.
June–Jul:
Rose Garden, Hidden
Gardens and Golden
Jubilee Garden.
Aug–Sept:
Herbaceous borders, the
Dry Garden and
hydrangeas.
Oct–Nov:
The New Zealand Garden
and the spectacle of the
American and Asian
deciduous woodland.
Dec–Jan:
National Collection of
Mahonias and a packed
programme of Christmas
festivities in the Savill
Building.

See our website for our
exciting events
programme.

THE SAVILL GARDEN
(WINDSOR GREAT PARK, BERKSHIRE)
www.theroyallandscape.co.uk

World-renowned 35 acres of ornamental gardens and woodland, including National Collections and rare international species, The Savill Garden provides a wealth of beauty and interest in all seasons.

Spring in The Savill Garden is heralded by hosts of daffodils, marvellous magnolias and the wonderful perfume of the varieties of rhododendrons and azaleas. Summer brings a contrast of colour with the floral vibrancy of the borders and the tranquil, pastel shades of the Golden Jubilee Garden. The glorious displays of autumn in the Garden are a joy to behold as many of the plants perform one last splendid encore before winter.

The Savill Garden takes the visitor on a journey through 10 subtly different 'gardens within a garden,' including the recent addition of the unique New Zealand Garden in 2007, which houses nearly 3,000 native plants.

Visit the iconic Savill Building, with its award winning grid-shell roof structure, fabricated from sustainable sources from forests within Windsor Great Park. This impressive visitor centre is the gateway to The Royal Landscape, and also offers excellent shopping, boutique plant sales and a terraced restaurant.

The Spring Wood

The Herbaceous Borders

ℹ️	Film & photographic shoots.	🏃	For groups, by appointment.
🛍️		P	
🌱	Plant centre.	🐕	Guide dogs only.
🍷		❄️	
♿	Grounds. WC.		
☕		🗑️	
🍴	Licensed.		

BASILDON PARK

BASILDON PARK, LOWER BASILDON, READING, BERKSHIRE RG8 9NR

www.nationaltrust.org.uk/basildonpark

Tel: 0118 984 3040 **Fax:** 0118 976 7370 **E-mail:** basildonpark@nationaltrust.org.uk
Owner: The National Trust **Contact:** The Property Manager

This beautiful Palladian mansion stars as 'Netherfield' in the recent feature film adaptation of Jane Austen's classic novel *Pride and Prejudice*. It is an elegant, classical house designed in the 18th century by John Carr of York and set in rolling parkland in the Thames Valley. The house has rich interiors with fine plasterwork, pictures and furniture, and includes an unusual Octagon Room and decorative Shell Room. Basildon Park has connections with the East through its builder and was the home of a wealthy industrialist in the 19th century. Flower gardens, pleasure grounds, 400 acres of parkland with woodland walks.

Location: MAP 3:E2 OS Ref. SU611 782. 2½m NW of Pangbourne, W of A329, 7m from M4/J12.
Open: 19 Mar–26 Oct: daily except Mon & Tue (open BH Mons), 12 noon–5pm. Property closes at 4pm 15–17 Aug. Park; Garden, Woodland Walk & Restaurant: as house, 11am–5pm. Shop: as house plus 29 Oct–21 Dec, Wed–Sun 12 noon–4pm.
***Admission:** House, Park & Garden: Adult £6.60 Child £3.30 Family £16.50 Park & Garden only: Adult £3.30 Child £1.65 Family £8.25, Groups (15+) by appointment £5. Free to NT Members. All information correct at time of going to print. *includes a voluntary 10% donation but visitors can choose to pay the standard prices displayed at the property and on the website.

🖾 🕹 🍴 🅿 In grounds. 📷 By appointment. 🐾 On leads, in grounds only. 🔺

DONNINGTON CASTLE ⊞

Newbury, Berkshire
Tel: 01424 775705 **www.english-heritage.org.uk/donnington**
Owner: English Heritage **Contact:** 1066 Battle Abbey

Built in the late 14th century, the twin towered gatehouse of this heroic castle survives amidst some impressive earthworks.
Location: MAP 3:D2, OS Ref. SU461 692. 1m N of Newbury off B4494.
Open: All year: Any reasonable time (exterior viewing only).
Admission: Free.
🕹 Steep slopes within grounds. 🅿 🐾 On leads. ✳

DORNEY COURT 🏠

Nr WINDSOR, BERKSHIRE SL4 6QP

www.dorneycourt.co.uk

Tel: 01628 604638 **E-mail:** palmer@dorneycourt.co.uk
Owner/Contact: Mrs Peregrine Palmer

Just a few miles from the heart of bustling Windsor lies "one of the finest Tudor Manor Houses in England", *Country Life*. Grade I listed with the added accolade of being of outstanding architectural and historical importance, the visitor can get a rare insight into the lifestyle of the squirearchy through 550 years, with the Palmer family, who still live there today, owning the house for 450 of these years. The house boasts a magnificent Great Hall, family portraits, oak and lacquer furniture, needlework and panelled rooms. A private tour on a 'non-open day' takes around 1½ hours, but when open to the public this is reduced to around 40 mins. The adjacent 13th century Church of St James, with Norman font and Tudor tower can also be visited, as well as the adjoining Plant Centre in our walled garden where light lunches and full English cream teas are served in a tranquil setting throughout the day. Highly Commended by Country Life – The Nation's Finest Manor House – 2006.
Location: MAP 3:G2, OS Ref. SU926 791. 5 mins off M4/J7, 10mins from Windsor, 2m W of Eton.
Open: May: BH Suns & Mons; Aug: daily except Sats, 1.30–4pm (last admission).
Admission: Adult: £6.50, Child (10yrs +) £4.50. Groups (10+): £6 when house is open to public. Private group rates at other times.

ℹ Film & photographic shoots. No stiletto heels. 🌱 Garden centre.
🍽 Wedding receptions. 🕹 Garden centre. 🖾 📷 🅿 🐾 Guide dogs only. ✳

Eton College

ETON COLLEGE

Windsor, Berkshire SL4 6DW
Tel: 01753 671177 **Fax:** 01753 671029 **www.etoncollege.com**
E-mail: r.hunkin@etoncollege.org.uk
Owner: Provost & Fellows **Contact:** Rebecca Hunkin
Eton College, founded in 1440 by Henry VI, is one of the oldest and best known schools in the country. The original and subsequent historic buildings of the Foundation are a part of the heritage of the British Isles and visitors are invited to experience and share the beauty of the ancient precinct which includes the magnificent College Chapel, a masterpiece of the perpendicular style.
Location: MAP 3:G2, OS Ref. SU967 779. Off M4/J5. Access from Windsor by footbridge only. Vehicle access from Slough 2m N.
Open: Mar - early Oct: Times vary, please check with the Visits Office. Pre-booked groups welcome all year.
Admission: Ordinary admissions and daily guided tours during the season at 2.15pm and 3.15pm. Groups by appointment only. Rates vary according to type of tour.
Ground floor. WC. Limited. Guide dogs only.

SAVILL GARDEN

See page 82 for full page entry.

TAPLOW COURT

BERRY HILL, TAPLOW, Nr MAIDENHEAD, BERKS SL6 0ER

www.sgi-uk.org

Tel: 01628 591230/209 **Fax:** 01628 773055
Owner: SGI-UK **Contact:** Michael Yeadon
Set high above the Thames, affording spectacular views. Remodelled mid-19th century by William Burn. Earlier neo-Norman Hall. 18th century home of Earls of Orkney and more recently of Lord and Lady Desborough who entertained 'The Souls' here. Tranquil gardens and grounds. Anglo-Saxon burial mound. Permanent and temporary exhibitions.
Location: MAP 3:F1, OS Ref. SU907 822. M4/J7 off Bath Road towards Maidenhead. 6m off M40/J2.
Open: Grounds: 1 Mar–30 Sept: Suns & BH Mons, 2–5.30pm. House: tel for opening times. Groups at other times by appointment.
Admission: No charge. Free parking.
Guide dogs only.

WELFORD PARK

NEWBURY, BERKSHIRE RG20 8HU

www.welfordpark.co.uk

Tel: 01488 608203 / 608691
Owner/Contact: Mr & Mrs J H L Puxley
A Queen Anne house with attractive gardens and grounds. Riverside walks. Wonderful snowdrops during February.
Location: MAP 3:C2, OS Ref: SU409 731. On Lambourn Valley Road. 6m NW of Newbury.
Open: 2–27 Jun (except Suns) & 30 Jun–4 Jul, 11am to 5pm. Grounds open in Feb 11am–4pm. (closed Mon & Fri) for snowdrop woods and aconite riverbanks.
Admission: Booked House Tour: Adult £5, Children under 16yrs Free. Grounds free except when open in the aid of charities & in Feb. Grounds: Adults £4, Concs. £3. Tearoom serves home-made lunches and teas during Feb.
Grounds. Home-made lunches & teas, must book in advance (except Feb). On leads, in grounds. Obligatory.

WINDSOR CASTLE

Windsor, Berkshire SL4 1NJ
Tel: 020 7766 7304 **E-mail:** bookinginfo@royalcollection.org.uk
Owner: Official Residence of Her Majesty The Queen
Contact: Ticket Sales & Information Office
Windsor Castle, along with Buckingham Palace and the Palace of Holyroodhouse in Edinburgh, it is one of the official residences of Her Majesty The Queen. The magnificent State Rooms are furnished with some of the finest works of art from the Royal Collection.
Location: MAP 3:G2, OS Ref. SU969 770. M4/J6, M3/J3. 20m from central London.
Open: Contact information office.
Admission: Contact information office.

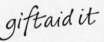 Some properties will be operating the Gift Aid on Entry scheme at their admission points. Where the scheme is operating, visitors are offered a choice between paying the standard admission price or paying the 'Gift Aid Admission' which includes a voluntary donation of at least 10%. Gift Aid Admissions enable the charity to reclaim tax on the whole amount paid* - an extra 28% - potentially a very significant boost to property funds. Money raised from paying visitors in this way will go towards restoration projects at the property and will be very welcome.
Where shown, the admission prices are inclusive of the 10% voluntary donation where properties are operating the Gift Aid on Entry scheme, but both the standard admission price and the Gift Aid Admission will be displayed at the property and on their website.

*Gift Aid donations must be supported by a valid Gift Aid declaration and a Gift Aid declaration can only cover donations made by an individual for him/herself or for him/herself and members of his/her family.

Dorney Court

The Golden Jubilee Fountain, Savill Garden.
©The Royal Landscape Media Library

■ Owner

Stowe House
Preservation Trust

■ Contact

Visitor Services Manager
Stowe School
Buckingham
MK18 5EH

Tel: 01280 818229
Fax: 01280 818186
House only
E-mail:
amcevoy@stowe.co.uk

■ Location

MAP 7:C10
OS Ref. SP666 366

From London, M1 to
Milton Keynes, 1½ hrs
or Banbury 1¼ hrs,
3m NW of Buckingham.

Bus: Buckingham 3m.

Rail: Milton Keynes 15m.

Air: Heathrow 50m.

■ Opening Times

House:
Easter & Summer
School Holidays.
Wed–Sun 12noon–5pm
(last admission 4pm),
Guided tour at 2pm &
also in term times, please
check website or
telephone for further
details 01280 818166.

■ Admission

**House (including
optional tour)**
Adult £4.00
Child (5–16yrs) £2.50
Adult NT members £3.00
Child NT members £2.00
Family (2+3) £12.00
 (NT members) £10.00
Children under 5yrs Free

Open to private groups
(15–60 persons), all year
round at discounted rates.
Please telephone 01280
818229 to pre-book.

Visit both the Landscape
Gardens and the House.
For Landscape Gardens
opening times telephone
01280 822850 or visit
www.nationaltrust.org.uk/
stowegardens
Joint tickets available.

Conference/Function

ROOM	MAX CAPACITY
Roxburgh Hall	350
Music Room	100
Marble Hall	200
State Dining Rm	200

STOWE HOUSE 🏛

www.shpt.org

Stowe owes its pre-eminence to the vision and wealth of two great owners. From 1715 to 1749 Viscount Cobham, one of Marlborough's Generals, continuously improved his estate, calling in the leading designers of the day to lay out the Gardens and commissioning several leading architects – Vanburgh, Gibbs, Kent and Leoni – to decorate them with garden temples. From 1750 to 1779 Earl Temple, his nephew and heir, continued to expand and embellish both the House and Gardens. As the estate was expanded, and political and military intrigues followed, the family eventually fell into debt, resulting in two great sales – 1848 when all the contents were sold and 1922 when the contents and the estate were sold off separately. The House is now part of a major public school, since 1923, and owned by Stowe House Preservation Trust, since 2000. Over the last four years, through the Trust, the House has under gone two phases of a six phase restoration – the North Front and Colonnades, the Central Pavilion and South Portico and the absolutely spectacular Marble Saloon, dating from the 1770s. Around the mansion is one of Britain's most magnificent and complete landscape gardens, taken over from the School by the National Trust in 1989. The Gardens have since undergone a huge, and continuing, restoration programme, and with the House restoration, Stowe is slowly being returned to its 18th century status as one of the most complete neo-classical estates in Europe.

Jerry Hardman-Jones / SHPT

ℹ️ Indoor swimming pool, sports hall, tennis court, squash courts, astroturf, parkland, cricket pitches and golf course.

🍴 International conferences, private functions, weddings, and prestige exhibitions. Catering on request.

♿ Visitors may alight at entrance, tel. 01280 818229 for details. Allocated parking. WC. 'Batricars' available (from NT – tel. 01280 818825).

☕ NT tearooms.

🍴 Morning coffee, lunch and afternoon tea available at the House by pre-arrangement only, for up to 80.

🚶 For parties of 15–60 at group rate. Tour time: house and garden 2½–4½ hrs, house only 1¼ hrs.

🅿️ Ample.

♿

🐕 In grounds on leads.

🔔 Civil Wedding Licence.

🏠 Available.

❄️ House open to groups all year, tel for details.

📅 Please check website for 2008 events: www.stoweevents.co.uk

© The National Trust, Waddesdon Manor/Barry Keen

WADDESDON MANOR

www.waddesdon.org.uk

Waddesdon Manor was built (1874–89) by Baron Ferdinand de Rothschild to display his outstanding collection of art treasures and to entertain the fashionable world. The 45 rooms on view combine the highest quality French furniture and decorative arts from the 18th century with magnificent portraits by Gainsborough and Reynolds, works by Dutch and Flemish Masters of the 17th century; Savonnerie carpets and Sèvres porcelain.

The Victorian gardens are considered some of the finest in Britain renowned for the colourful parterre, seasonal displays, statuary and fountains, walks and wonderful views across the Vale of Aylesbury. At the heart of the gardens lies the rococo-style aviary which houses a splendid collection of exotic birds and is well known for breeding endangered species. The Wine Cellars, modelled on the private cellars at Château Lafite Rothschild, contain thousands of bottles of Rothschild wines dating back to 1868.

Top quality food and wines are served throughout the day in the restaurants and the shops offer a superb range of gifts and wines, many of which are unique to Waddesdon. A full programme of events is organised throughout the year. Conveniently situated for London, Oxford and Milton Keynes, Waddesdon offers a memorable day out for all the family.

© The National Trust, Waddesdon Manor/Rob Judges

ℹ️ No photography in House. NT members free. HHA Members free entry to grounds. RHS members free to grounds in Mar, Sept & Oct. Children welcomed under parental supervision in the House. Babies must be carried in a front-sling.

🎁 Gift and Wine Shops.

✳️ Plant Sales

🍽️ Conferences, corporate hospitality.

♿ WCs. Parking.

🍴 Licensed.

🍽️ Licensed. Reservations can be made at the Manor Restaurant. Tel: 01296 653242

🚶 By arrangement.

🎧 Audio Tours

🅿️ Ample for coaches and cars.

🐕 Assistance dogs only.

🔔

🍷 Wine Tasting, Special Interest Days, Family Events. Please telephone 01296 653226 for details.

Contact

Waddesdon
Nr Aylesbury
Buckinghamshire
HP18 0JH
Tel: 01296 653211
Booking & Info:
(Mon–Fri 10am–4pm):
01296 653226
Fax: 01296 653212
E-mail: waddesdonmanor
@nationaltrust.org.uk

Location

MAP 7:C11
OS Ref. SP740 169

Between Aylesbury &
Bicester, off A41.

Rail: Aylesbury 6m.

Opening Times

**Gardens, Aviary,
Restaurants, Shops &
Woodland Playground**
5 Jan–16 Mar: Sats & Suns;
19 Mar–23 Dec, 22/23,
29/30 Dec, Wed–Sun & BH
Mons, 10am–5pm.

**House & Gardens,
Wine Cellars, Aviary,
Woodland Playground,
Shops & Restaurants**
19 Mar–26 Oct, Wed–Sun
& BH Mons, 12noon–4pm
(11am Sats & Suns). Last
rec adm. 2.30pm.

Bachelors' Wing
19 Mar–26 Oct: Wed–Fri
12noon–4pm. Limited
space, entry cannot be
guaranteed.

**Christmas Season
(East Wing decorated
for the festive season)**
12 Nov–21 Dec, Wed–Fri
12 noon–4pm. Sats &
Suns 11am–4pm. Timed
tickets to house avail.
Booking fee £3 per
transaction. Please call
Booking Office.

*Admission

**House & Gardens,
Wine Cellars, Aviary,
Woodland Playground,
Shops & Restaurants**
Adult Wed–Fri   £13.20
 Sats, Suns & BHs £15.00
Child† Wed–Fri   £9.35
 Sats, Suns & BHs £11.00

Christmas Season special
rates apply.

**Gardens, Aviary,
Woodland Playground,
Shops & Restaurants**
Adult Wed–Fri   £5.50
 Sats, Suns & BHs £7.00
Child† Wed–Fri   £2.75
 Sats, Suns & BHs £3.50

5 Jan–16 Mar, Sats/Suns
 Adult   £5.50
 Child†   £2.75

Bachelors' Wing £3.30

†Child (5–16 yrs).
Children under 5 Free.

Group rates available.

*includes a voluntary
donation but visitors can
choose to pay standard
prices displayed at
property and on website.

ASCOTT

Wing, Leighton Buzzard, Buckinghamshire LU7 0PS
Tel: 01296 688242   **Fax:** 01296 681904
E-mail: info@ascottestate.co.uk   **www.ascottestate.co.uk**
Owner: The National Trust   **Contact:** Resident Agent

Originally a half-timbered Jacobean farmhouse, Ascott was bought in 1876 by the de Rothschild family and considerably transformed and enlarged. It now houses a quite exceptional collection of fine paintings, Oriental porcelain and English and French furniture. The extensive gardens are a mixture of the formal and natural, containing specimen trees and shrubs, as well as an herbaceous walk, lily pond, Dutch garden and remarkable topiary sundial.

Location: MAP 7:D11, OS Ref. SP891 230. ½ m E of Wing, 2m SW of Leighton Buzzard, on A418.

Open: House & Garden: 25 Mar–27 Apr: daily except Mons, 2–6pm. 29 Apr–24 Jul: Tues–Thurs, 2–6pm. 29 Jul–12 Sept daily except Mons, 2–6pm. Last admission 5pm.

Admission: Adult £8, Child £4. Garden only: £4, Child £2. No reduction for groups which must book. NT members free (except NGS days) 5 May & 25 Aug.

  Ground floor & grounds with assistance. 3 wheelchairs available. WCs.
  220 metres. In car park only, on leads.

BOARSTALL DUCK DECOY

Boarstall, Aylesbury, Buckinghamshire HP18 9UX
Tel: 01844 237488 / 01280 822850 (Visitor Services Manager Mon–Fri)
E-mail: boarstalldecoy@nationaltrust.org.uk
Owner: The National Trust   **Contact:** Visitor Services Manager

A rare survival of a 17th century decoy in working order, set on a tree-fringed lake, with nature trail and exhibition hall.

Location: MAP 7:B11, OS Ref. SP624 151. Midway between Bicester and Thame, 2m W of Brill.

Open: 5 Apr–25 Aug: Sats & Suns, 10am–4pm; 9 Apr–20 Aug: Weds, 3.30–6pm; BH Mons 10am–4pm. Displays on Sats, Suns, & BH Mons: 11am & 3pm; Weds: 3.30pm. Bird walks and woodland talks occasionally, please telephone for details. Please telephone for winter opening details. Free to NT members.

Admission: Adult £2.50, Child £1.20. Family £6. Groups (6+) must book: £1.50.

  Partial. By arrangement. In car park only, on leads.

BOARSTALL TOWER

Boarstall, Aylesbury, Buckinghamshire HP18 9UX
Tel: 01280 822850 (Mon–Fri)   **E-mail:** boarstalltower@nationaltrust.org.uk
Owner: The National Trust   **Contact:** Visitor Services Manager

The stone gatehouse of a fortified house long since demolished. It dates from the 14th century, and was altered in the 16th and 17th centuries, but retains its crossloops for bows. The gardens are surrounded by a moat on three sides.

Location: MAP 7:B11, OS Ref. SP624 141. Midway between Bicester and Thame, 2m W of Brill.

Open: 2 Apr–29 Oct: Weds, 2–6pm. BH Sats: 11am–4pm & BH Mons: 2–6pm.

Admission: Adult £2.50, Child £1.20, Family £6. Free to NT members.

  No WC. Ground floor & garden (steps to entrance). In car park only.

BUCKINGHAM CHANTRY CHAPEL

Market Hill, Buckingham
Tel: 01280 822850 (Mon–Fri)   **Fax:** 01280 822437
Owner: The National Trust   **Contact:** The National Trust

Rebuilt in 1475 and retaining a fine Norman doorway. The chapel was restored by Gilbert Scott in 1875, at which time it was used as a Latin or Grammar School.

Location: MAP 7:B10, OS Ref. SP693 340. In narrow lane, NW of Market Hill.

Open: By appointment with the The National Trust.

Admission: Free. Donations welcome.

  No WCs.

For **accommodation** in the South East, see our special index at the end of the book.

CHENIES MANOR HOUSE

CHENIES, BUCKINGHAMSHIRE WD3 6ER

www.cheniesmanorhouse.co.uk

Tel: 01494 762888   **E-mail:** macleodmatthews@btinternet.com
Owners: Mrs E MacLeod Matthews & Mr C MacLeod Matthews
Contact: Susan Brock

Home of the MacLeod Matthews family, this 15th & 16th century Manor House with fortified tower is the original home of the Earls of Bedford. Visited by Henry VIII and Elizabeth I. She was a frequent visitor, first coming as an infant in 1534 and as Queen she visited on several occasions, once being for a six week period. The Bedford Mausoleum is in the adjacent church. The House contains tapestries and furniture mainly of the 16th and 17th centuries, hiding places, and a collection of antique dolls. Art Exhibitions are held throughout the season in the newly restored 16th century Pavilion with its unusual cellars. The Manor is surrounded by enchanting gardens, famed for the spring display of tulips, which have been featured in many publications and on television. From early June there is a succession of colour in the Tudor Sunken Garden, The White Garden, Herbaceous Borders and Fountain Court. The Physic Garden contains a wide selection of medicinal and culinary herbs. The Parterre has an ancient oak and complicated Yew Maze while the Kitchen Garden is in Victorian style with unusual vegetables and fruit. Attractive dried and fresh flower arrangements decorate the house.

Location: MAP 7:D12, OS Ref TQ016 984. N of A404 between Amersham & Rickmansworth. M25—Ext 18 3m

Open: 2 Apr–30 Oct: Wed & Thurs and BH Mons, 2–5pm. Last entry to House: 4.15pm.

Admission: House & Garden: Adult £5.50, Child £3, Garden only: Adult £4, Child £2, Groups (20+) by arrangement throughout the year (half price during Oct).

  24 Mar Easter Fun for Children 2–5pm. 5 May, Tulip Festival. 2–5pm 26th May, Special entertainment 2–5pm. 20th Jul, Plant and Garden Fair 10am–5pm (The Manor House opens at 2pm). Rare and exceptional plants, topiary and trees from specialist nurseries. Gardening advice, sculpture, garden furniture. Lunch and refreshments. Children's entertainer. 25th Aug, Special entertainment 2–5pm.

CHILTERN OPEN AIR MUSEUM

Newland Park, Gorelands Lane, Chalfont St Giles, Buckinghamshire HP8 4AB
Tel: 01494 871117 **Fax:** 01494 872774
Owner: Chiltern Open Air Museum Ltd **Contact:** Phil Holbrook
A museum of historic buildings showing their original uses including a blacksmith's forge, stables, barns etc.
Location: MAP 3:G1, OS Ref. TQ011 938. At Newland Park 1½ m E of Chalfont St Giles, 4½ m from Amersham. 3m from M25/J17.
Open: Apr–Oct: daily. Please telephone for details.
Admission: Adult £7.50, Child (5–16yrs) £4.50, Child under 5yrs Free, OAP £6.50, Family (2+2) £21.50. Groups discount available on request. 2007 prices.

The Temple of Venus, Stowe Landscape Gardens & Park

CLAYDON HOUSE

MIDDLE CLAYDON, Nr BUCKINGHAM MK18 2EY

Tel: 01296 730349 **Fax:** 01296 738511 **Infoline:** 01494 755561
E-mail: claydon@nationaltrust.org.uk
Owner: The National Trust **Contact:** The House and Premises Manager
Home of the Verney family for more than 400 years, the extraordinary interiors of Claydon House, built 1759–69, represent a veritable three-dimensional pattern book of 18th-century decorative styles. Outstanding features include the astonishingly lavish wood carving in the Chinese Room and the fine parquetry grand staircase. Claydon has strong associations with Florence Nightingale, who was sister-in-law to Sir Harry Verney. She was a regular visitor to the house, which contains many of her personal belongings. Claydon House is set within 21 hectares of unspoilt parkland with far-reaching views and lakeside walks. The courtyard comtains a second-hand bookshop and craft galleries, as well as a restaurant and tearoom (not NT). The private gardens and kitchen garden are open to visitors at an additional charge.

Location: MAP 7:C11, OS Ref. SP720 253. In Middle Claydon, 13m NW of Aylesbury, signposted from A413 and A41. 3½ m SW of Winslow.
Open: House: 15 Mar–2 Nov, daily except Thu & Fri (open Good Friday), 1–5pm, last admission 4.30pm. Grounds, Private Garden, Bookshop, Church & facilities: As house, 12 noon–5pm.
Admission: Adult £5.75, Child £2.80, Family £14. Groups: Adult £4.75 (£1 extra for guided tour). Private Gardens: Adult £3.50, including NT Members, under 5s free.
ⓘ No photography. No pushchairs. No backpacks. No large bags. 🛍 Second-hand books, pottery & art gallery. 🚻♿ Ground floor only. WC. Braille guide. Photograph album. Ramp. 🍴 👥 For groups only, by arrangement. 🅿 Limited for coaches. 🐕 In parkland only, on leads.
🖥 For details visit www.nationaltrust.org.uk.

© The National Trust

Waddesdon Manor

CLIVEDEN ❧
TAPLOW, MAIDENHEAD SL6 0JA

Tel: 01628 605069 **Infoline:** 01494 755562 **Fax:** 01628 669461
E-mail: cliveden@nationaltrust.org.uk
Owner: The National Trust **Contact:** Property Manager

152 hectares of gardens and woodland. A water garden, 'secret' garden, herbaceous borders, topiary, a great formal parterre, and informal vistas provide endless variety. The garden statuary is one of the most important collections in the care of The National Trust and includes many Roman antiquities collected by 1st Viscount Astor. The Octagon Temple (Chapel) with its rich mosaic interior is open on certain days, as is part of the house (see below).

Location: MAP 3:F1, OS Ref. SU915 851. 3m N of Maidenhead, M4/J7 onto A4 or M40/J4 onto A404 to Marlow and follow signs. From London by train take Thames Train service from Paddington to Burnham (taxi rank and office adjacent to station).
Open: Estate & Garden: 1 Mar–26 Oct, daily, 11am–6pm; 27 Oct–23 Dec, daily, 11am–4pm. House (part) & Octagon Temple (Chapel): 1 Apr–31 Oct: Thurs & Sun, 3–5.30pm. Admission to house by timed ticket, from Information Centre only. Woodlands: 1 Mar–26 Oct, daily, 11am–5.30pm; 27 Oct–23 Dec, daily, 11am–4pm. Restaurant: 1 Mar–26 Oct, daily, 11am–5pm; 27 Oct–2 Nov, daily, 11am–4pm; 8 Nov–21 Dec, Sat/Sun 11am–3pm. Shop: as Woodland. Some areas of formal garden may be roped off when ground conditions are bad.
Admission: Grounds: Adult £7.50 Child £3.70, Family £18.70, Groups (must book) £6.50 House: £1 extra, Child 50p extra.* Note: Mooring charge on Cliveden Reach. *Free to NT members.

◻ ⬇ Partial. WC. ⏍ Licensed. ⌨ Specified woodlands only. ✱ ☞

COWPER & NEWTON MUSEUM

Home of Olney's Heritage, Orchard Side, Market Place, Olney MK46 4AJ
Tel: 01234 711516 **E-mail:** cnm@mkheritage.co.uk
www.cowperandnewtonmuseum.org.uk
Owner: Board of Trustees **Contact:** Mrs S Whyte, House Manager

Once the home of 18th century poet and letter writer William Cowper and now containing furniture, paintings and belongings of both Cowper and his ex-slave trader friend, Rev John Newton (author of "Amazing Grace"). Attractions include re-creations of a Victorian country kitchen and wash-house, two peaceful gardens and Cowper's restored summerhouse. Costume gallery, important collections of dinosaur bones and bobbin lace, and local history displays.

Location: MAP 7:D9, OS Ref. SP890 512. On A509, 6m N of Newport Pagnell, M1/J14.
Open: 1 Mar–23 Dec: Tue–Sat & BH Mons, 10.30am–4.30pm. Closed on Good Fri.
Admission: Adult £3, Conc/Students (with card) £2, Children under 12 yrs Free, Garden only £1.

ⓘ No photography. ◻ ⬇ Gardens. ⌧ By arrangement. ⌨ Guide dogs only.

FORD END WATERMILL

Station Road, Ivinghoe, Buckinghamshire
Tel: 01296 661997 **Contact:** John Wallis

The Watermill, a listed building, was recorded in 1616 but is probably much older.
Location: MAP 7:D11, OS Ref. SP941 166. 600 metres from Ivinghoe Church along B488 (Station Road) to Leighton Buzzard.
Open: Easter Mon–end Sept: 2nd & 4th Suns of each month & BHs, 2.30–5.30pm. Milling between 3–5pm on BHs and the 2nd Sun in May (National Mills Day) and 4th Sun in July and Sept.
Admission: Adult £1.50, Child 50p (5–15yrs). Schools: Child 75p, Adults Free.

Chenies Manor House

visit hudsons guide online

©NTPL /Paul Watson

©NTPL /David Watson

HUGHENDEN MANOR

HIGH WYCOMBE HP14 4LA

Tel: 01494 755573/ 755565 - Infoline **Fax:** 01494 474284
E-mail: hughenden@nationaltrust.org.uk
Owner: The National Trust **Contact:** The Property Manager

Home of Prime Minister Benjamin Disraeli from 1848–1881. The interior is a comfortable Victorian home and still holds many of Disraeli's pictures, books and furniture. The surrounding park and woodland have lovely walks, and the formal garden has been recreated in the spirit of Mary Anne Disraeli's colourful designs.

Location: MAP 3:F1, OS 165 Ref. SU866 955. 1½ m N of High Wycombe on the W side of the A4128.

Open: House: 1 Mar–2 Nov, 1–5pm (11.30am by guided tour only). Wed–Sun & BH Mon. Open Good Fri. On BHs and busy days entry is by timed ticket. 6–21 Dec, Sat & Sun. Gardens open same days as house, 11am–5pm. Shop and Restaurant: open 11am–5pm also weekends 5 Nov–21 Dec, 11am–3.30pm. Park & Woodland: All year.

***Admission:** House & Garden: Adult £7, Child £3.50, Family £17.50. Garden only: Adult £2.90, Child £2.10. Park & Woodland Free. Groups: Adult £5.50. No groups at weekends or BHs. £1 off if arriving by public transport. Free to NT Members. *includes a voluntary 10% donation but visitors can choose to pay the standard prices displayed at the property and on the website.

Ground floor only. WC. For booked groups. In grounds, on leads. Guide dogs in house & formal gardens.

THE KING'S HEAD

King's Head Passage, Market Square, Aylesbury, Buckinghamshire HP20 2RW
Tel: 01296 381501 **Fax:** 01296 381502 **E-mail:** kingshead@nationaltrust.org.uk
Owner: The National Trust **Contact:** The Custodian

This enchanting restored coaching inn dates from 1455 and its noteworthy architectural features include medieval stained glass windows, extensive timber framing and a central cobbled courtyard. It has strong associations with the Civil War, as it is believed that Oliver Cromwell once used it as a base, and with the Rothschild Family. There is a second-hand bookshop, coffee shop and the Farmers' Bar is run by the Chiltern Brewery.

Location: MAP 7:C11, OS Ref. SP818 138. At NW corner of Aylesbury Market Square.

Open: All year: Mon–Sat (except BH Mons). Visitor Reception 9am–4pm. Bookshop & coffee shop 10.30am–4pm. Farmers' Bar licensing hours all year. Guided tours on Wed, Fri & Sat at 2pm.

Admission: Adult £3 (incl tour) booking necessary. NT members Free.

Partial. WC. Licensed. Obligatory. None. Guide dogs only.

LONG CRENDON COURTHOUSE

High St, Long Crendon, Buckinghamshire
Tel: 01280 822850 (Mon–Fri) **E-mail:** stowegarden@nationaltrust.org.uk
www.nationaltrust.org.uk
Owner: The National Trust **Contact:** Visitor Services Manager

A fantastic opportunity to see very clearly a 15th century building. The exposed timber beams and early oak floorboards are a rare sight.

Location: MAP 7:B11, OS Ref. SP698 091. 3miles N of Thame.

Open: 5 Apr–28 Sept: Weds: 2–6pm. Sats, Suns & BH Mons, 11am–6pm.

Admission: Adult £1, Child 50p. Free to NT Members.

For unique **Civil wedding** venues see our index at the end of the book.

JOHN MILTON'S COTTAGE

21 Deanway, Chalfont St. Giles, Buckinghamshire HP8 4JH
Tel: 01494 872313 **E-mail:** info@miltonscottage.org **www.miltonscottage.org**
Owner: Milton Cottage Trust **Contact:** Mr E A Dawson

Grade I listed 16th century cottage where John Milton lived and completed 'Paradise Lost' and started 'Paradise Regained'. Four ground floor museum rooms contain important first editions of John Milton's 17th century poetry and prose works. Amongst many unique items on display is the portrait of John Milton by Sir Godfrey Kneller. Well stocked, attractive cottage garden, listed by English Heritage. 2008 is the quatercentenary of Milton's birth and celebrations at the Cottage, in the city of London and at Cambridge are taking place.

Location: MAP 3:G1, OS Ref. SU987 933. ½ m W of A413. 3m N of M40/J2. S side of street.

Open: 1 Mar–31 Oct: Tue–Sun, 10am–1pm & 2–6pm. Closed Mons (open BH Mons). Coach parking by prior arrangement only.

Admission: Adult £4, under 15s £2, Groups (20+) £3.

Ground floor. Talk followed by free tour.

NETHER WINCHENDON HOUSE

Nether Winchendon, Nr Aylesbury, Buckinghamshire HP18 ODY
Tel: 01844 290101 **Fax:** 01844 290199
www.netherwinchendonhouse.com www.timelessweddingvenues.com
Owner/Contact: Mr Robert Spencer Bernard

Medieval and Tudor manor house. Great Hall. Dining Room with fine 16th century frieze, ceiling and linenfold panelling. Fine furniture and family portraits. Home of Sir Francis Bernard Bt (d1779), the last British Governor of Massachussetts Bay. Continuous family occupation since mid-16th century. House altered in late 18th century in the Strawberry Hill Gothick style. Interesting garden (5 acres) and specimen trees.

Location: MAP 7:C11, OS Ref. SP734 121. 2m N of A418 equidistant between Thame & Aylesbury.

Open: 3–31 May & 25 Aug '08: 2.30–5.30pm (conducted tours only at ¼ to each hour). Groups at any time by prior written agreement (minimum charge £100, no concessions).

Admission: Adult £5, OAP £4 (no concession at weekends or BHs), Child (under 12yrs) £2. HHA members free (not on special groups).

Please tel in advance. WC. By arrangement. Obligatory.

PITSTONE WINDMILL

Ivinghoe, Buckinghamshire
Tel: 01442 851227   **Group organisers:** 01296 668223   **Fax:** 01442 850000
E-mail: pitstonemill@nationaltrust.org.uk
Owner: The National Trust
One of the oldest post mills in Britain; in view from Ivinghoe Beacon.
Location: MAP 7:D11, OS Ref. SP946 158. 1/2 m S of Ivinghoe, 3m NE of Tring.
Just W of B488.
Open: 1 Jun–31 Aug, Sun & BHs, 2.30–6pm. Last admission, 5.30pm.
Admission: Adult £1.50, Child 70p. Free to NT members.
ⓘ No WC. ♿ Difficult access. ⓟ

John Milton's Cottage

STOWE LANDSCAPE GARDENS & PARK ✿

Nr BUCKINGHAM MK18 5EH

www.nationaltrust.org.uk/stowegardens

Tel: 01280 822850   **Infoline:** 01494 755568   **Fax:** 01280 822437
Group Visits: 01280 822850   **E-mail:** stowegarden@nationaltrust.org.uk
Owner: The National Trust   **Contact:** The Property Manager
Discover one of Europe's most influential landscape gardens. Hidden amongst spectacular views and vast open spaces there are magical secret corners, hidden meanings, and over 40 monuments and temples waiting to be discovered. Visitors can also take a tour of Stowe House or explore the 750 acres of surrounding historic parkland, including the newly restored 250 acre Deer Park. Stowe is the perfect setting for a family picnic or those seeking peace and tranquility, with walks and trails for all to enjoy. With the changing seasons, continuing restoration and a calendar of events for all the family, each visit provides something new to discover. Recent restoration: return of statues of Mercury and the Shepherd and Shepherdess.
Location: MAP 7:C10, OS Ref. SP665 366. Off A422 Buckingham – Banbury Rd. 3m NW of Buckingham.

Open: Gardens, Shop & Tearooms: 5 Jan–2 Mar & 8 Nov–1 Feb '09, Sat & Sun, Gardens & Shop 10.30am–4pm; Tearooms 10.30am–3.30 pm. 5 Mar–2 Nov, Wed–Sun; Gardens & Shop 10.30am–5.30pm, Tearooms 10.30am–5pm. Open BH Mons. Last admission 1½hrs before closing. Shop also open 5 Nov–19 Dec, 11am–3pm. May close in extreme weather conditions. House not NT.
*Admission: Gardens: Adult £6.90, Child £3.50, Family £17.10. Free to NT Members. 15% discount for booked groups. House admission payable at NT reception. *includes a voluntary donation but visitors can choose to pay the standard prices displayed at the property and on the website.
🅿 ♿ Pre-booked self-drive powered chairs available. WC. ▣ 🎫 Free in gardens, 11am and 2pm most days. By arrangement for groups. ▣ ▦ ▨ In grounds, on leads. ▲ ❋ ☻ For details visit www.nationaltrust.org.uk/stowegardens.

STOWE HOUSE 🏛   *See page 86 for full page entry.*

WADDESDON MANOR ✿   *See page 87 for full page entry.*

See which properties offer **educational facilities** or **school visits** in our index at the end of the book.

©NTPL/Matthew Antrobus
Hughenden Manor

WEST WYCOMBE PARK 🌿

WEST WYCOMBE, HIGH WYCOMBE, BUCKINGHAMSHIRE HP14 3AJ

Tel: 01494 513569

Owner: The National Trust   **Contact:** The Head Guide

A perfectly preserved rococo landscape garden, created in the mid-18th century by Sir Francis Dashwood, founder of the Dilettanti Society and the Hellfire Club. The house is among the most theatrical and Italianate in England, its façades formed as classical temples. The interior has Palmyrene ceilings and decoration, with pictures, furniture and sculpture dating from the time of Sir Francis.

Location: MAP 3:F1, OS Ref. SU828 947. At W end of West Wycombe S of the A40.

Open: House & Grounds: 1 Jun–31 Aug: daily except Fri & Sat, 2–6pm. Weekday entry by guided tour only every 20 mins (approx), last admission 5.15pm. Grounds only: 1 Apr–29 May: daily except Fri & Sat, 2–6pm.

Admission: House & Grounds: Adult £6.30, Child £3.15, Family £15.75. Groups £4.90. Grounds only: Adult £3.15, Child £1.60. Free to NT Members. Groups by arrangement. Note: The West Wycombe Caves and adjacent café are privately owned and NT members must pay admission fees.

🔹 Grounds partly suitable. 🔹 Obligatory on weekdays. 🔹 In car park only, on leads.

WOTTON HOUSE

Wotton Underwood, Aylesbury, Buckinghamshire HP18 0SB

Tel: 01844 238363   **Fax:** 01844 238380   **E-mail:** david.gladstone@which.net

Owner/Contact: David Gladstone

The Capability Brown Pleasure Grounds at Wotton, currently undergoing restoration, are related to the Stowe gardens, both belonging to the Grenville family when Brown laid out the Wotton grounds between 1750 and 1767. A series of man-made features on the 3 mile circuit include bridges, follies and statues.

Location: MAP 7:B11, OS Ref. 468576, 216168. Either A41 turn off Kingswood, or M40/J7 via Thame. Rail: Haddenham & Thame 6m.

Open: 9 Apr–10 Sept: Weds only, 2–5pm. Also 22 Mar, 5 May, 5 Jul, 2 Aug, 6 Sept: 2–5pm.

Admission: Adult £6, Child Free, Conc. £3. Groups (max 25).

🔹 Obligatory. 🅿 Limited. 🔹

WYCOMBE MUSEUM

Priory Avenue, High Wycombe, Buckinghamshire HP13 6PX

Tel: 01494 421895   **E-mail:** museum@wycombe.gov.uk

Owner: Wycombe District Council   **Contact:** Grace Wison

Set in historic Castle Hill House and surrounded by peaceful and attractive gardens.

Location: MAP 3:F1, OS Ref. SU867 933. Signposted off the A404 High Wycombe/Amersham road. The Museum is about 5mins walk from the town centre and railway station.

Open: Mon–Sat, 10am–5pm. Suns, 2–5pm. Closed BHs.

Admission: Free.

©NTPL /John Hammond

Lady Mary Wortley Montagu – West Wycombe Park

■ Owner
Lord Montagu

■ Contact
John Montagu Building
Beaulieu
Brockenhurst
Hampshire SO42 7ZN

Tel: 01590 614769/87
Fax: 01590 612624
E-mail: conference@
beaulieu.co.uk

■ Location
MAP 3:C6
OS Ref. SU387 025

M27 to J2, A326, B3054
follow brown signs.

Bus: Local service within
the New Forest.

Rail: Stations at
Brockenhurst 7m away.

■ Opening Times
Summer
May–September
Daily, 10am–6pm.

Winter
October–April
Daily, 10am–5pm.

Closed Christmas Day.

■ Admission
All year

Individual rates upon
application.

Groups (15+)
Rates upon application.

■ Special Events
April 27
Boatjumble & Boatworld

May 17/18
Spring Motormart &
Autojumble

June 28/29
Motorcycle World

September 13/14
International Autojumble

October 25
Fireworks Spectacular

All enquiries should be
made to our Special
Events Booking Office
where advance tickets can
be purchased. The
contact telephone is
01590 612888.

BEAULIEU 🏛
www.beaulieu.co.uk

The Beaulieu Estate has been owned by the same family since 1538 and is still the private home of the Montagus. Thomas Wriothesley, who later became the 1st Earl of Southampton, acquired the estate at the time of the Dissolution of the Monasteries when he was Lord Chancellor to Henry VIII.

Palace House, overlooking the Beaulieu River, was once the Great Gatehouse of Beaulieu Abbey with its monastic origins reflected in the fan vaulted ceilings of the 14th Century Dining Hall and Lower Drawing Room. The rooms are decorated with furnishings, portraits and treasures collected by past and present generations of the family. Visitors can enjoy the fine gardens or take a riverside walk around the Monks' Mill Pond.

Beaulieu Abbey was founded in 1204 when ing John gave the land to the Cistercians and although most of the buildings have now been destroyed, much of the beauty and interest remains. The former Monks' Refectory is now the local parish church and the Domus, which houses an exhibition and video presentation of monastic life, is home to beautiful wall hangings.

Beaulieu also houses the world famous National Motor Museum which traces the story of motoring from 1894 to the present day. 250 vehicles are on display including legendary world record breakers plus veteran, vintage and classic cars and motorcycles.

The modern Beaulieu is very much a family destination with many free and unlimited rides on a transportation theme to be enjoyed, including a mile long, high-level monorail and replica 1912 London open-topped bus.

Conference/Function

ROOM	SIZE	MAX CAPACITY
Brabazon (x3)	40' x 40'	85 (x3)
Domus	69' x 27'	150
Theatre		200
Palace House		60
Motor Museum		250

BEAULIEU ...

Catering and Functions

Beaulieu also offers a comprehensive range of facilities for conferences, company days out, product launches, management training, corporate hospitality, promotions, film locations, exhibitions and outdoor events.

The National Motor Museum is a unique venue for drinks receptions, evening product launches and dinners or the perfect complement to a conference as a relaxing visit.

The charming 13th century Domus hall with its beautiful wooden beams, stone walls and magnificent wall hangings, is the perfect setting for weddings, conferences, dinners, buffets or themed evenings.

Palace House, the ancestral home of Lord Montagu is an exclusive setting for smaller dinners, buffets and receptions. With a welcoming log fire in the winter and the coolness of the courtyard fountain in the summer, it offers a relaxing yet truly 'stately' atmosphere to ensure a memorable experience for your guests whatever the time of year.

A purpose-built theatre, with tiered seating, can accommodate 200 people whilst additional meeting rooms can accommodate from 20 to 200 delegates. Bespoke marquees can also be erected in a charming parkland setting, for any event or occasion. With the nearby Beaulieu River offering waterborne activities and the Beaulieu Estate, with its purpose-built off road course, giving you the opportunity of indulging in a variety of country pursuits and outdoor management training, Beaulieu provides a unique venue for your conference and corporate hospitality needs.

i Allow 3 hrs or more for visits. Last adm. 40 mins before closing. Helicopter landing point. When visiting Beaulieu arrangements can be made to view the Estate's vineyards. Visits, which can be arranged between Apr–Oct, must be pre-booked at least one week in advance with Beaulieu Estate Office.

Palace House Shop and Kitchen Shop plus Main Reception Shop.

Disabled visitors may be dropped off outside Visitor Reception before parking. WC. Wheelchairs can be provided free of charge in Visitor Reception by prior booking.

The Brabazon restaurant seats 250. Prices start at £18.95. Further details and menus from the Sales Office: 01590 614769.

Attendants on duty. Guided tours by prior arrangement for groups.

P 1,500 cars and 30 coaches. During the season the busy period is from 11.30am to 1.30pm. Coach drivers should sign in at Information Desk. Free admission for coach drivers plus voucher which can be exchanged for food, drink and souvenirs.

Professional staff available to assist in planning of visits. Services include introductory talks, films, guided tours, rôle play and extended projects. In general, educational services incur no additional charges and publications are sold at cost. Information available from Education at Beaulieu, John Montagu Building, Beaulieu, Hants SO42 7ZN.

In grounds, on leads only.

■ Owner
Earl of Carnarvon

■ Contact
The Castle Office
Highclere Castle
Newbury
Berkshire RG20 9RN

Tel: 01635 253210
Fax: 01635 255315
E-mail: theoffice@
highclerecastle.co.uk

■ Location
MAP 3:D3
OS Ref. SU445 587

M4/J13–A34 south,
M3/J8–A303–A34 north.

Air: Heathrow M4
45 mins.

Rail: Paddington –
Newbury 45 mins.

Taxi: 4½m
07778 156392.

■ Opening Times
Easter
23 Mar–10 April,
Sunday–Thursday.

May Bank Holidays
4/5 May,
Sunday & Monday,

26/27 May,
Monday/Tuesday

Summer
1 July–31 August,
Sunday–Thursday

11am–4.30pm
(Gates open 10.30am)
last admission 3.30pm.

This information is correct
at the time of publication.
However it may be
subject to change so
please check in advance
of your visit.

■ Admission
Adult	£8.00
Child (4–15)	£4.00
Concession	£7.00
Family (2+3/1+4)	£20.00

Free to members of HHA

**Grounds & Gardens
only**
Adult	£3.00
Child (4–15)	£1.00

Groups (20+)
Adult	£7.00
Child (4–15)	£3.50
Concession	£6.00

Private guided tours at
other times may be
arranged subject to
availability at a minimum
cost for up to 40 persons
of £600 plus VAT; each
additional person £15
plus VAT.

Conference/Function

ROOM	SIZE	MAX CAPACITY
Library	43' x 21'	140
Saloon	42' x 29'	120
Dining Rm	37' x 18'	70
Library, Saloon, Drawing Rm, Music Rm, Smoking Rm		500

HIGHCLERE CASTLE & GARDENS

www.highclerecastle.co.uk

Highclere Castle was designed by Charles Barry in the 1830s at the same time as he was building the Houses of Parliament. This soaring pinnacled mansion provided a perfect setting for the 4th Earl of Carnarvon, one of the great hosts of Queen Victoria's reign. The extravagant interiors range from church Gothic through Moorish flamboyance and Rococo Revival to the solid masculinity in the long Library. Old Master paintings mix with portraits by Van Dyck and 18th century painters. Napoleon's desk and chair, rescued from St Helena, sit with other 18th and 19th century furniture. The 5th Earl of Carnarvon, together with Howard Carter, discovered the tomb of Tutankhamun and the Castle houses a unique exhibition of some of his earlier discoveries. The 8th Earl and Countess take a very personal interest in the Castle and are often to be seen around their home, grounds and gardens.

Gardens
The magnificent parkland, with its massive cedars, was designed by 'Capability' Brown. The walled gardens also date from an earlier house at Highclere, but the dark yew walks are entirely Victorian in character. The Secret Garden has a romance of its own with a beautiful curving lawn surrounded by densely planted herbaceous gardens, a place for romantics and poets.

 Conferences, exhibitions, filming, fairs, and concerts (cap. 8000). No photography in the house.

Receptions, dinners, corporate hospitality.

Visitors may alight at the entrance. WC. A necessary companion of a paying disabled visitor will be admitted free of charge.

Tearooms, licensed. Lunches for 20+ can be booked.

P Ample.

Egyptian Exhibition: £4.50 + VAT per child. 1 adult free per every 10 children, extra adults at child rate, by prior arrangement – includes playgroups, Brownie packs, Guides etc. Nature walks, beautiful old follies, Secret Garden.

In grounds, on leads.

 Please visit website.

JANE AUSTEN'S HOUSE

CHAWTON, ALTON, HAMPSHIRE GU34 1SD

www.jane-austens-house-museum.org.uk

Tel: 01420 83262 **E-mail:** enquiries@jahmusm.org.uk

Owner: Jane Austen Memorial Trust **Contact:** Ann Channon

17th century house where Jane Austen wrote or revised her six great novels. Contains many items associated with her and her family, documents and letters, first editions of the novels, pictures, portraits and furniture. Pleasant garden, suitable for picnics, bakehouse with brick oven and wash tub, houses Jane's donkey carriage.

Location: MAP 3:E4, OS Ref. SU708 376. Just S of A31, 1m SW of Alton, signposted Chawton.

Open: Jan/Feb: Sats & Suns, 10.30am–4.30pm. Mar–end May: daily, 10.30am–4.30pm. June–Aug: daily, 10am–5pm. Sept–end Dec: daily, 10.30am–4.30pm. Closed 25/26 December.

Admission: Fee charged.

⬚ Bookshop. ⬚ Ground floor & grounds. WC. ⬚ Opposite house. ⬚ Opposite house. ⬚ ⬚ Guide dogs only. ⬚ ⬚

Beaulieu Palace House

AVINGTON PARK 🏛

WINCHESTER, HAMPSHIRE SO21 1DB

www.avingtonpark.co.uk

Tel: 01962 779260 **E-mail:** enquiries@avingtonpark.co.uk

Owner/Contact: Mrs S L Bullen

Avington Park, where Charles II and George IV both stayed at various times, dates back to the 11th century. The house was enlarged in 1670 by the addition of two wings and a classical Portico surmounted by three statues. The State rooms are magnificently painted and lead onto the unique pair of conservatories flanking the South Lawn. The Georgian church, St. Mary's, is in the grounds.

Avington Park is a privately owned stately home and is a most prestigious venue in peaceful surroundings. It is perfect for any event from seminars, conferences and exhibitions to wedding ceremonies and receptions, dinner dances and private parties. The Conservatories and the Orangery make a delightful location for summer functions, whilst log fires offer a welcome during the winter. Excellent caterers provide for all types of occasion, ranging from breakfasts and light lunches to sumptuous dinners. All bookings at Avington are individually tailor-made and only exclusive use is offered. Several rooms are licensed for Civil wedding ceremonies and a delightful fully-equipped apartment is available for short stays.

Location: MAP 3:D4, OS Ref. SU534 324. 4m NE of Winchester ½m S of B3047 in Itchen Abbas.

Open: May–Sept: Suns & BH Mons plus Mons in Aug, 2.30–5.30pm. Last tour 5pm. Other times by arrangement, coach parties welcome by appointment all year.

Admission: Adult £4.50, Child £2.

ⓘ Conferences. ⬚ ⬚ Partial. WC. ⬚ ⬚ Obligatory. ⬚ ⬚ In grounds, on leads. Guide dogs only in house. ⬚ ⬚

BASING HOUSE

Redbridge Lane, Basing, Basingstoke RG24 7HB
Tel: 01256 467294
Owner: Hampshire County Council **Contact:** Alan Turton
Ruins, covering 10 acres, of huge Tudor palace. Recent recreation of Tudor formal garden.
Location: MAP 3:E3, OS Ref. SU665 526. 2m E from Basingstoke town centre. Signposted car parks are about 5 or 10 mins walk from entrance.
Open: Apr–Sept: Wed–Sun & BHs, 2–6pm.
Admission: Adult £2, Conc. £1.

BEAULIEU 🏛

See pages 94/95 for double page entry.

BISHOP'S WALTHAM PALACE ⌗

Bishop's Waltham, Hampshire SO32 1DH
Tel: 01489 892460 **www.english-heritage.org.uk/bishop**
Owner: English Heritage **Contact:** Visitor Operations Team
This medieval seat of the Bishops of Winchester once stood in an enormous park. Wooded grounds, the remains of the Great Hall and the three storey tower can still be seen. Dower House furnished as a 19th-century farmhouse.
Location: MAP 3:D5, OS Ref. SU552 174. In Bishop's Waltham, 5 miles NE from M27/J8.
Open: Grounds: 1 May–30 Sept: Sun–Fri, 10am–5pm. Farmhouse: by request. Guided tours: Aug, Suns, 11am.
Admission: Free.
ℹ WCs. Exhibition. 🅿 🛆 Grounds. 🅿 🛋 Grounds only, on leads. 🐕

BREAMORE HOUSE & MUSEUM 🏛

BREAMORE, FORDINGBRIDGE, HAMPSHIRE SP6 2DF

www.breamorehouse.com

Tel: 01725 512468 **Fax:** 01725 512858 **E-mail:** breamore@btinternet.com
Owner/Contact: Sir Edward Hulse Bt
Elizabethan manor with fine collections of pictures and furniture. Countryside Museum takes visitors back to the time when a village was self-sufficient.
Location: MAP 3:B5, OS Ref. SU152 191. W Off the A338, between Salisbury and Ringwood.
Open: Easter weekend; Apr: Tue & Sun; May–Sept: Tue/Wed, Thur, Sat/Sun & BHs. House: 2–5pm. Countryside Museum: 1–5.30pm. Last admission 4pm.
Admission: Combined ticket for house and museum: Adult £7, Child £5, OAP £6, Family £17.
🅿 🛆 Ground floor & grounds. WC. 🐾 🛋

© Lord Romsey

BROADLANDS

ROMSEY, HAMPSHIRE SO51 9ZD

www.broadlands.net

Tel: 01794 505010 **Event Enquiry Line:** 01794 505020 **Fax:** 01794 529755
E-mail: admin@broadlands.net
Owner: Lord & Lady Brabourne **Contact:** Estate Manager
Broadlands, the home of Lord and Lady Brabourne by descent from Prime Minister Viscount Palmerston and The Earl Mountbatten of Burma, is open to the public by guided tour only. The Mountbatten Exhibition depicts the life and times of Lord and Lady Mountbatten. Limited tours, which include items normally available by appointment, are offered on certain days.
Location: MAP 3:C5, OS Ref. SU355 204. On A3090 at Romsey.
Open/Admission: Details of opening times and admission charges can be obtained from the website, or by telephone.
🛗 🛆 Ground floor. WC. 🚶 Obligatory. 🛋 Guide dogs only.

CALSHOT CASTLE ⌗

Calshot, Fawley, Hampshire SO45 1BR
Tel: 02380 892023 **www.english-heritage.org.uk/calshot**
Owner: English Heritage **Contact:** Hampshire County Council
Henry VIII built this coastal fort in an excellent position, commanding the sea passage to Southampton. The fort houses an exhibition and recreated pre-World War I barrack room.
Location: MAP 3:D6, OS Ref. SU489 025. On spit 2 miles SE of Fawley off B3053.
Open: 21 Mar–31 Oct: daily, 10am–4pm.
Admission: Adult £2.50, Child £1.50, Conc. £1.80, Family £6. EH Members Free. Group discount available.
ℹ WCs. 🅿 🅿 🛋

ELING TIDE MILL

The Toll Bridge, Eling, Totton, Southampton, Hampshire SO40 9HF
Tel: 023 8086 9575 **E-mail:** info@elingtidemill.org.uk
Owner: Eling Tide Mill Trust Ltd & New Forest District Council
Contact: Mr David Blackwell-Eaton
Location: MAP 3:C5, OS Ref. SU365 126. 4m W of Southampton. ½m S of the A35.
Open: All year: Wed–Sun and BH Mons, 10am–4pm. Closed 25/26 Dec.
Admission: Adult £2.30, Child £1.30, OAP £1.80, Family £6. Group rates on application. Prices may change Apr 2008. Please telephone for details.

Avington Park

Kevan Brewar

EXBURY GARDENS & STEAM RAILWAY
EXBURY, SOUTHAMPTON, HAMPSHIRE SO45 1AZ

www.exbury.co.uk

Tel: 023 8089 1203 **Fax:** 023 8089 9940

Owner: Edmund de Rothschild Esq **Contact:** Estate Office

HHA/Christie's *Garden of the Year* 2001. A spectacular 200-acre woodland garden showcasing the world famous Rothschild Collection of rhododendrons, azaleas magnolias, camellias, rare trees and plants. Enchanting river walks, ponds and cascades. Daffodil Meadow, Rock and Heather Gardens, exotic plantings and herbaceous borders ensure year-round interest. The Steam Railway enchants visitors of all ages, passing through a Summer Garden, and featuring a bridge, tunnel, viaduct and causeway. Licensed for Civil weddings in three venues on site. Excellent Restaurant and Tearooms.

Location: MAP 3:D6, OS Ref. SU425 005. 11m SE of Totton (A35) via A326 & B3054 & minor road. In New Forest.

Open: 8 Mar–9 Nov: daily, 10am–5.30pm (dusk in Nov). Please call for details of Santa Steam Specials in December.

Admission: Adult £7.50, Child (3–15yrs) £1.50, OAP/Group £7, Family (2+3) £17.50; Railway +£3, Rover Ticket £4.50. Child under 3yrs Free. Buggy tours +£3/£3.50. RHS Members Free Mar & Sept.

🖼 🚻 🍴 ⚐ ♿ 🍽 Licensed. 🅧 By arrangement. 🅿 🐕 In grounds, on leads. 🔺 ♿

FORT BROCKHURST ♯

Gunner's Way, Gosport, Hampshire PO12 4DS

Tel: 02392 581059 www.english-heritage.org.uk/fortbrockhurst

Owner: English Heritage **Contact:** Visitor Operations Team

This 19th-century fort was built to protect Portsmouth. Today it houses a display of extraordinary objects found at sites across the region, including stonework, jewellery, textiles and furniture from various periods. Tours of the fort introduce the visitor to these hidden stores and will explain the exciting history of the site and the legend behind the ghostly activity in cell no. 3.

Location: MAP 3:E6, OS196, Ref. SU596 020. Off A32, in Gunner's Way, Elson on N side of Gosport.

Open: Heritage Open Days (6–9 Sept) and Feb–Oct, 2nd Fri of each month for tours and handling sessions. 12 noon–3pm. Available for private hire, telephone for details.

Admission: Please telephone for details.

ℹ WCs. 🚻 ♿ Grounds and ground floor only. 🐕 Dogs on leads (restricted areas).

FURZEY GARDENS

Minstead, Lyndhurst, Hampshire SO43 7GL

Tel: 023 8081 2464 **Fax:** 023 8081 2297

Owner: Furzey Gardens Charitable Trust **Contact:** Maureen Cole

Location: MAP 3:C5, OS Ref. SU273 114. Minstead village ½m N of M27/A31 junction off A337 to Lyndhurst.

Open: Mar–Oct: daily, 10am–5pm.

Admission: Please contact property for prices.

See which properties offer **educational facilities** or **school visits** in our index at the end of the book.

GILBERT WHITE'S HOUSE & THE OATES MUSEUM
THE WAKES, HIGH STREET, SELBORNE, ALTON GU34 3JH

www.gilbertwhiteshouse.org.uk

Tel: 01420 511275 **E-mail:** info@gilbertwhiteshouse.org.uk

Owner: Oates Memorial Trust **Contact:** Duty Manager

Gilbert White's House & The Oates Museum is a charming 18th century house, home of the famous naturalist, the Rev Gilbert White, the author of *The Natural History and Antiquities of Selborne*. Over 20 acres of garden and parkland restored to how it would have looked in Gilbert White's day, including an orchard, vegetable plot, flower gardens and shrubberies, and a small scale landscape garden with ha-ha. The core of the house dates back to the 17th century and recreates how Gilbert would have lived. The building also houses a separate exhibition on the Victorian explorer Frank Oates and his nephew Captain Lawrence Oates, and his part in Scott's ill fated expedition to the South Pole in 1911. Facilities include a tea parlour serving 18th century fare such as Homity Pie and Toasted Wigs and an excellent Museum shop stocking unusual gifts such as Medlar Jelly from our orchard.

Open: 1 Jan–23 Dec: Tue–Sun, 11am–5pm. Also open Mons Jun, Jul and Aug.

Admission: Adults £6.50, Conc. £5.50, Child Free (2007 prices). Reductions are available for pre-booked groups of over 10 people, including a free introductory talk.

ℹ No photography in house. 🖼 🚻 ♿ Partial. ⚐ 🅧 By arrangement. 🅿 🐕 Guide dogs only. ✱ ♿

GREAT HALL & QUEEN ELEANOR'S GARDEN

WINCHESTER CASTLE, WINCHESTER SO23 8UJ

www.hants.gov.uk/greathall

Tel: 01962 846476   **Fax:** for bookings 01962 841326
Owner: Hampshire County Council   **Contact:** Custodian

The only surviving part of Henry III's medieval castle at Winchester, this 13th century hall was the centre of court and government life. The Round Table closely associated with the legend of King Arthur has hung here for over 700 years. Queen Eleanor's garden is a faithful representation of the medieval garden visited by Kings and Queens of England.

Location: MAP 3:D4, OS Ref. SU477 295. Central Winchester. SE of Westgate archway.
Open: Mar–Oct daily, 10am–5pm. Nov–Feb: daily 10am–4pm. Closed 25/26 Dec and for Civic events only – see website for details.
Admission: Free. Donations appreciated towards the upkeep of the Great Hall.
By arrangement.

HIGHCLERE CASTLE
& GARDENS

See page 96 for full page entry.

For rare and unusual plants visit the **plant sales** index at the end of the book.

©Kevan Brewar

Exbury Gardens

©NTPL/Stephen Robson

HINTON AMPNER ✂
BRAMDEAN, ALRESFORD, HAMPSHIRE SO24 0LA
www.nationaltrust.org.uk

Tel: 01962 771305 **Fax:** 01962 793101 **E-mail:** hintonampner@nationaltrust.org.uk

Owner: The National Trust **Contact:** The Property Manager

"I have learned during the past years what above all I want from a garden: this is tranquillity". So said Ralph Dutton, 8th and last Lord Sherborne, of his garden at Hinton Ampner. He created one of the great gardens of the 20th century, a masterpiece of design based upon the bones of a Victorian garden, in which he united a formal layout with varied and informal planting in pastel shades. It is a garden of all year round interest with scented plants and magnificent vistas over the park and surrounding countryside.

The garden forms the link between the woodland and parkland planting, which he began in 1930, and the house, which he remodelled into a small neo-Georgian manor house in 1936. He made further alterations when the house was reconstructed after a fire in 1960. Today it contains his very fine collection of English furniture, Italian paintings and hard-stones. Both his collection and every aspect of the decoration at Hinton Ampner reflects Ralph Dutton's sure eye and fine aesthetic judgement.

He placed the whole within the rolling Hampshire landscape that he loved and understood so well.

Location: MAP 3:E4, OS Ref. SU597 275. M3/J9 follow signs to Petersfield. On A272, 1m W of Bramdean village, 8m E of Winchester.

Open: House: 15 Mar–2 Nov: Tues, Wed, Sat & Sun, 12noon–5pm. Garden: 15 Mar–2 Nov, daily except Thur & Fri, 11am–5pm.

Admission: House & Garden: Adult £7.50, Child (5–16yrs) £3.75. Garden only: Adult £6.50, Child (5–16yrs) £3.25, Free to NT Members. *includes a voluntary 10% donation but visitors can choose to pay the standard prices displayed at the property and on the website.

◻ ⬚ ⬚ **P** Limited for coaches. 🐕 Guide dogs only.

HOUGHTON LODGE GARDENS 🏛
STOCKBRIDGE, HAMPSHIRE, SO20 6LQ
www.houghtonlodge.co.uk

Tel: 01264 810502 **Fax:** 01264 810063 **E-mail:** info@houghtonlodge.co.uk

Owner/Contact: Captain M W Busk

A haven of peace above the tranquil beauty of the River Test. 12 acres of Grade II* Gardens with fine trees surround an enchanting and unique example of an 18th Century *Cottage Ornée*. Chalk Cob walls enclose traditional Kitchen Garden with espaliers, herbs and heated greenhouses, hydroponicum and orchid collection. Gardens both formal and informal. 14 acres adjoining the garden provide an experience of the natural world with meadow walks through the peaceful and unspoiled surroundings of the River Test. Come and meet Tom and Dick, our new Alpacas. Popular TV/Film location.

Location: MAP 3:C4, OS Ref. SU344 332. 1½m S of Stockbridge (A30) on minor road to Houghton village.

Open: 1 Mar–31 Oct, daily, 10am–5pm. Weds & House by appointment.

Admission: Adult £5, Children under 14 Free. Pre-booked groups welcome at special rates.

⬚ ⬚ Self-service teas & coffees, home-made cakes. 🎨 By arrangement. **P** 🐕 In grounds, on leads. ⬚

HURST CASTLE ⌗

Keyhaven, Lymington, Hampshire SO41 0TP

Tel: 01590 642344 www.english-heritage.org.uk/hurstcastle

Owner: English Heritage **Contact:** (Managed by) Hurst Castle Services

This was one of the most sophisticated fortresses built by Henry VIII, and later strengthened in the 19th and 20th centuries, to command the narrow entrance to the Solent. There is an exhibition in the castle, and two huge 38-ton guns form the fort's armaments.

Location: MAP 3:C7, OS196 Ref. SZ318 897. On Pebble Spit S of Keyhaven. Best approach by ferry from Keyhaven. 4 miles SW of Lymington.

Open: 6 Apr–31 Oct: daily, 10.30am–5.30pm. Café: open Apr–May weekends & Jun–Sept: daily.

Admission: Adult £3.20, Child £1.80, Conc. £2.80. EH Members free. Group discount available.

ⓘ WCs. ⬚ Unsuitable. ⬚ 🐕 Dogs on leads (restricted areas).

©English Heritage Photo Library/Jonathan Bailey

Hurst Castle

KING JOHN'S HOUSE & HERITAGE CENTRE

CHURCH STREET, ROMSEY, HAMPSHIRE SO51 8BT

www.kingjohnshouse.org.uk

Tel: 01794 512200 **E-mail:** annerhc@aol.com
Owner: King John's House & Tudor Cottage Trust Ltd   **Contact:** Anne James
Three historic buildings on one site: Medieval King John's House, containing 14th-century graffiti and rare bone floor, Tudor Cottage complete with traditional tea room and Victorian Heritage Centre with recreated shop and parlour. Beautiful period gardens, special events/exhibitions and children's activities. Gift shop and Tourist Information Centre. Receptions and private/corporate functions.
Location: MAP 3:C5, OS Ref. SU353 212. M27/J3. Opposite Romsey Abbey, next to Post Office.
Open: Apr–Sept: Mon–Sat, 10am–4pm. Oct–Mar: Heritage Centre only. Limited opening on Sundays. Evenings also for pre-booked groups.
Admission: Adult £2.50, Child 50p, Conc. £2. Heritage Centre only: Adult £1.50, Child 50p, Conc. £1. Discounted group booking by appointment.
⬜ 🔲 🔲 Partial. ⬛ 🔲 By arrangement.
🅿 Off Latimer St with direct access through King John's Garden.
🔲 🔲 Guide dogs only. 🔲 🔲

MEDIEVAL MERCHANTS HOUSE ⌗

58 French Street, Southampton, Hampshire SO1 0AT
Tel: 02380 221503   www.english-heritage.org.uk/medievalmerchant
Owner: English Heritage   **Contact:** Visitor Operations Team
The life of a prosperous merchant in the Middle Ages is vividly evoked in this recreated, faithfully restored 13th-century townhouse.
Location: MAP 3:D5, OS Ref. SU419 112. 58 French Street. ¼m S of Bargate off Castle Way. 150yds SE of Tudor House.
Open: 21 Mar–30 Sept: Fri–Sun & BHs, 12noon–6pm.
Admission: Adult £3.70, Child £1.90, Conc. £3. EH Members free.
⬜ 🔲 🔲 🔲

Broadlands

©NTPL/David Watson

MOTTISFONT ABBEY & GARDEN 🌿

MOTTISFONT, Nr ROMSEY, HAMPSHIRE SO51 0LP

www.nationaltrust.org.uk/mottisfontabbey

Tel: 01794 340757 **Fax:** 01794 341492 **Recorded Message:** 01794 341220
E-mail: mottisfontabbey@nationaltrust.org.uk
Owner: The National Trust   **Contact:** The Property Manager
The Abbey and Garden form the central point of an 809 ha estate including most of the village of Mottisfont, farmland and woods. A tributary of the River Test flows through the garden forming a superb and tranquil setting for a 12th century Augustinian priory which, after the Dissolution, became a house. It contains the spring or "font" from which the place name is derived. The magnificent trees, walled gardens and the National Collection of Old-fashioned Roses combine to provide interest throughout the seasons. The Abbey contains a drawing room decorated by Rex Whistler and the cellarium of the old Priory. In 1996 the Trust acquired Derek Hill's 20th century picture collection.
Location: MAP 3:C5, OS185 Ref. SU327 270. Signposted off A3057 Romsey to Stockbridge road, 4½m N of Romsey. Also signposted off B3084 Romsey to Broughton. Station: Dunbridge (U) ¾m.
Open: Garden: 2–23 Feb, 1 Nov–21 Dec, Sat–Sun, 11am–4pm. 1 Mar–3 Apr, 21 Apr–25 May, 23 Jun–30 Oct, Sat–Thurs, 11am–5pm. 26 May–23 Jun, daily, 11am–5pm. (31 May–23 Jun, Mon–Sat, 11am–8pm). House: as garden (26 May–23 Jun, closes 5pm). Shop / Café: As garden. Car park gates close at 6pm except in June. Access to some showrooms in the house may be limited occasionally due to weddings.
***Admission:** Adult £7.50, Child (5-18yrs) £3.80, Family £18.80. During June Rose Season: Adult £8.50. Group discount, rate on application. Free to NT Members.
*includes a voluntary donation but visitors can choose to pay the standard prices displayed at the property and on the website.
⬜ 🔲 Partial. ⬛ 🔲 Licensed. 🅿 🔲 Guide dogs only. 🔲 🔲 🔲

NETLEY ABBEY ⌗

Netley, Southampton, Hampshire
Tel: 02392 378291   www.english-heritage.org.uk/netleyabbey
Owner: English Heritage   **Contact:** Portchester Castle
A peaceful and beautiful setting for the extensive ruins of this 13th-century Cistercian abbey converted in Tudor times for use as a house. Even in ruins, the abbey continues to be influential, inspiring romantic writers and poets.
Location: MAP 3:D6, OS Ref. SU453 089. In Netley, 4 miles SE of Southampton, facing Southampton Water.
Open: 6 Apr–30 Sept: daily, 10am–6pm. 1 Oct–31 Mar '09: Sats & Suns, 10am–3pm. Closed 24–26 Dec & 1 Jan. Guided tours Sats 11am during Aug.
Admission: Free.
🔲 🔲 🅿 🔲 Dogs on leads. 🔲

NORTHINGTON GRANGE ⌗

New Alresford, Hampshire
Tel: 01424 775705   www.english-heritage.org.uk/northingtongrange
Owner: English Heritage   **Contact:** 1066 Battle Abbey
Northington Grange and its landscaped park as you see it today, formed the core of the house as designed by William Wilkins in 1809. It is one of the earliest Greek Revival houses in Europe.
Location: MAP 3:E4, OS 185, SU562 362. 4 miles N of New Alresford off B3046 along farm track – 550 metres.
Open: Grounds only: 21 Mar–30 Sept: daily, 10am–6pm. (3pm Jun & July). 1 Nov–31 Mar '09: daily, 10am–4pm. Closed 24–26 Dec & 1 Jan.
Admission: Free.
🔲 Wheelchair access (with assistance). 🅿 🔲 Dogs on leads.

©Lord Romsey

PORTCHESTER CASTLE ⌗

Portsmouth, Hampshire PO16 9QW

Tel/Fax: 02392 378291   www.english-heritage.org.uk/portchester

Owner: English Heritage   **Contact:** Visitor Operations Team

The rallying point of Henry V's expedition to Agincourt and the ruined palace of King Richard II. This grand castle has a history going back nearly 2,000 years and the most complete Roman walls in northern Europe. Exhibition telling the story of the castle and interactive audio tour.

Location: MAP 3:E6, OS196, Ref. SU625 046. On S side of Portchester off A27, M27/J11.

Open: 21 Mar–30 Sept: daily, 10am–6pm. 1 Oct–31 Mar '09: daily, 10am–4pm. Closed 24–26 Dec & 1 Jan.

Admission: Adult £4.20, Child £2.10, Conc. £3.40. Family £10.50. 15% discount for groups (11+). EH Members Free.

ℹ️ WCs. Exhibition. 🅿 ♿ Partial. 🅰 🅿 🚌 In grounds, on leads. ❀

PORTSMOUTH CATHEDRAL

Portsmouth, Hampshire PO1 2HH

Tel: 023 9282 3300   **Fax:** 023 9229 5480

E-mail: rosemary.fairfax@portsmouthcathedral.org.uk   **Contact:** Rosemary Fairfax

Maritime Cathedral founded in 12th century and finally completed in 1991. A member of the ship's crew of Henry VIII's flagship *Mary Rose* is buried in Navy Aisle.

Location: MAP 3:E6, OS Ref. SZ633 994. 1½ m from end of M275. Follow signs to Historic Ship and Old Portsmouth.

Open: 7.45am–6pm all year. Sun service: 8am, 9.30am, 11am, 6pm. Weekday: 6pm (Choral on Tues and Fris in term time).

Admission: Donation appreciated.

ST AGATHA'S CHURCH

MARKET WAY, PORTSMOUTH PO1 4AD

Tel: 02392 837050

Owner: St Agatha's Trust   **Contact:** Fr J Maunder (Tel/Fax: 01329 230330)

A grand Italianate basilica of 1894 enriched with marble, granite and carved stone. The apse contains Britain's largest sgraffito mural, by Heywood Sumner c1901. Fine furnishings, untouched by Vatican II, by Randoll Blacking, Sir Ninian Comper, Sir Walter Tapper, Martin Travers, Norman Shaw and others. Described by Pevsner as containing *"one of Portsmouth's few major works of art"*.

Location: MAP 3:D3, OS Ref. SU640 006. On route for Historic Ships. Near Cascades Centre car park.

Open: All year, Sats, 10am–4pm. Suns, 10am–2pm (High Mass 11am). Jun–Aug, Weds, 10.30am–3pm. Other times by appointment – 01329 230330.

Admission: No charge.

ℹ️ Available for hire – concerts, exhibitions & filming. Has featured in 'Casualty'.
🅿 ♿ Partial. WCs. 🍴 🅰 By arrangement. 🅿 Limited. ■ ✕ ❀

SANDHAM MEMORIAL CHAPEL ✿

BURGHCLERE, Nr NEWBURY, HAMPSHIRE RG20 9JT

Tel/Fax: 01635 278394   **E-mail:** sandham@nationaltrust.org.uk
www.nationaltrust.org.uk/Sandham

Owner: The National Trust   **Contact:** The Custodian

This red brick chapel was built in the 1920s for the artist Stanley Spencer to fill with paintings inspired by his experiences of the First World War. Influenced by Giotto's Arena Chapel in Padua, Spencer took five years to complete what is arguably his finest achievement. The Chapel has gardens and an orchard at the front of the property, and views over to Watership Down. Pictures best viewed on a bright day as no artificial lighting.

Location: MAP 3:D3, OS Ref. SU463 608. 4m S of Newbury, ½m E of A34, W end of Burghclere.

Open: 5–30 Mar, Wed–Sun & 1–31 Oct, Wed–Sun, 11am–3pm; 1 Nov–21 Dec, Sat & Sun, 11am–3pm; 2 Apr–28 Sept. Wed–Sun, 11am–5pm (inc BH Mon). Other times by prior appointment.

Admission: Adult £3.50, Child £1.75. NT Members free.

♿ Portable ramp for entrance. 🅰 By arrangement. ■ 🚌 In grounds, on leads. ❀

Highclere Castle – 3,000 year old Egyptian Wooden Coffin

© S.S.P.T.

STRATFIELD SAYE HOUSE 🏛
STRATFIELD SAYE, HAMPSHIRE RG7 2BZ
www.stratfield-saye.co.uk

Tel: 01256 882882 **Fax:** 01256 881466

Owner: The Duke of Wellington **Contact:** The Administrator

After the Duke of Wellington's victory against Napoleon at the Battle of Waterloo in 1815, the Duke chose Stratfield Saye as his country estate. The house provides a fascinating insight into how the 1st Duke lived and contains many of his possessions. It is still occupied by his descendents and is a family home rather than a museum. Over the last four years there has been an extensive programme of restoration and conservation. Of particular interest are many pieces of fine French furniture, porcelain and some rare examples of Print Rooms.

Location: MAP 3:E2, OS Ref. SU700 615. Equidistant from Reading (M4/J11) & Basingstoke (M3/J6) 1½m W of the A33.

Open: 20–24 Mar, (Easter) & 3–28, Jul: daily, 11.30am (Sats & Suns, 10.30am–3.30pm [last admission]).

Admission: Weekends: Adult £7.50, Child £5, OAP/Student £6.50. Weekdays: Adult £7, Child £4, OAP/Student £6. Groups by arrangement only.

⬜ ♿ WC. ⬛ ℹ Obligatory. 🅿 🚍 Guide dogs only.

TITCHFIELD ABBEY ⌗
Titchfield, Southampton, Hampshire PO15 5RA
Tel: 01329 842133 www.english-heritage.org.uk/titchfield

Owner: English Heritage **Contact:** The Titchfield Abbey Association

Remains of a 13th-century abbey overshadowed by the grand Tudor gatehouse. Reputedly some of Shakespeare's plays were performed here for the first time. Under local management of Titchfield Abbey Society.

Location: MAP 3:D6, OS Ref. SU542 067. ½m N of Titchfield off A27.

Open: 6 Apr–30 Sept: daily, 10am–5pm. 1 Oct–31 Mar '09: daily, 10am–4pm. Closed 24–26 Dec & 1 Jan. Guided tours Sats in Aug at 3pm.

Admission: Free.

♿ ℹ 🅿 🚍 Dogs on leads. ❋

©Patrick Lane

Hinton Ampner

©NTPL/Andrea Jones

THE VYNE ✿
SHERBORNE ST JOHN, BASINGSTOKE RG24 9HL
www.nationaltrust.org.uk

Tel: 01256 883858 **Infoline:** 01256 881337 **Fax:** 01256 881720

E-mail: thevyne@nationaltrust.org.uk

Owner: The National Trust **Contact:** The Property Manager

A 16th century house and estate and a treasure trove of history, set within beautiful gardens, with lake and woodland walks. Originally built as a great Tudor 'power house', The Vyne was visited by King Henry VIII on at least three occasions and was home to the Chute family for over 350 years. Dramatic improvements and changes have made The Vyne a fascinating microcosm of changing fads and fashions over five centuries. The house is filled with a vast indigenous collection of furniture, paintings, ornaments and *objets d'art*. The attractive gardens and grounds feature an ornamental lake, one of the earliest summer-houses in England and woodland walks. A newly developed wetlands area with new bird hide attracts a wide diversity of wildlife.

Location: MAP 3:E3, OS Ref. SU639 576. 4m N of Basingstoke between Bramley & Sherborne St John.

Open: House: 15 Mar–2 Nov; Sat & Sun; 11am–5pm, Mon–Wed, 1–5pm. Grounds, Shop & Restaurant: 2 Feb–9 Mar: Sat & Sun, 11am–5pm, 15 Mar–2 Nov; Mon–Wed, Sat & Sun; 11am–5pm. Shop & Restaurant: 6 Nov–21 Dec, Thur–Sun, 11am–3pm. Open Good Friday and BH Mon: 11am–5pm (inc. house). Guided tours of house for groups (25–50) by appointment only 17 Mar–29 Oct: Mon–Wed, 11am–12noon. During busy periods timed tickets will be issued for entry to house.

*Admission: House & Grounds: Adult £8.50, Child £4.25, Family £22. Grounds only: Adult £5.50, Child £2.75. Reduced rate when arriving by cycle or public transport (applies to house & grounds ticket only). *includes a voluntary 10% donation but visitors can choose to pay the standard prices displayed at the property and on the website. Groups £7.36.

ℹ No photography in house. ⬜ ♿ 🍴 ♿ ⬛ 🍴 ℹ 🅿 🚍 ❋ ♿

© Dean and Chapter, Winchester Cathedral

WINCHESTER CATHEDRAL
1 THE CLOSE, WINCHESTER SO23 9LS

www.winchester-cathedral.org.uk

Tel: 01962 857225 **Fax:** 01962 857201 **E-mail:** visits@winchester-cathedral.org.uk
Owner: The Dean and Chapter **Contact:** Group Visits Co-ordinator

Explore more than 1000 years of England's past. Walk in the footsteps of kings, saints, pilgrims, writers and artists in Europe's longest medieval Cathedral. Uncover the secrets of how a diver saved the Cathedral from collapse and learn why Jane Austen came to be buried in the nave. See the Winchester Bible, the finest of all the great 12th-century manuscripts, illuminated in gold and lapis lazuli, and tour the crypt to find Antony Gormley's sculpture *'Sound II'*. The Cathedral Café with its open-air terrace and Cathedral views has won awards for its architecture and food. The Cathedral Shop has a unique range of gifts and souvenirs, including CDs featuring the Catherdral Choir.

Location: MAP 3:D4, OS Ref. SU483 293. Winchester city centre.
Open: Daily 8.30am–6pm (5.30pm Sun). Times may vary for services and special events.
Admission: Adult £5, Conc. £4. Student/Language Schools £3. Conc. for booked groups.

◻ ⊤ ⅃ ▣ Licensed. ⅏ ⅋ ▣ ⊠ In grounds, on leads. ⊠ ⊟ Fairs and markets, concerts and theatre, lectures tours and even an ice rink! See website for details.

©NTLP

WINCHESTER CITY MILL ❁
BRIDGE STREET, WINCHESTER

www.nationaltrust.org.uk/winchestercitymill

Tel/Fax: 01962 870057 **E-mail:** winchestercitymill@nationaltrust.org.uk
Owner: The National Trust **Contact:** Anne Aldridge

Spanning the River Itchen and rebuilt in 1744 on an earlier medieval site, this corn mill has a chequered history. The machinery is completely restored making this building an unusual survivor of a working town mill. It has a delightful island garden and impressive mill races roaring through the building.

Location: MAP 3D:4, OS Ref. SU486 293. M3/J9 & 10. City Bridge near King Alfred's statue. 15 min walk from station.
Open: 16–24 Feb, daily. 5 Mar–24 Oct, Wed–Sun. 27 Oct–24 Dec, daily. All half terms and summer holidays, daily. 11am–5pm, last admission 4.30pm.
Admission: Adult £3.40, Child £1.70, Family (2+2) £8.50. NT & H & IoW WLT members Free.

◻ ⅋ By arrangement. ▣ Nearby public car park. ▣ ⊠

WOLVESEY CASTLE ⌗
College Street, Wolvesey, Winchester, Hampshire SO23 8NB
Tel: 02392 378291 www.english-heritage.org.uk/wolvesey
Owner: English Heritage **Contact:** Portchester Castle

The fortified palace of Wolvesey was the chief residence of the Bishops of Winchester and one of the greatest of all medieval buildings in England. Its extensive ruins still reflect the importance and immense wealth of the Bishops of Winchester, occupants of the richest seat in medieval England. Wolvesey Castle was frequently visited by medieval and Tudor monarchs and was the scene of the wedding feast of Philip of Spain and Mary Tudor in 1554.

Location: MAP 3:D4, OS Ref. SU484 291. ¾m SE of Winchester Cathedral, next to the Bishop's Palace; access from College Street.
Open: 6 Apr–30 Sept: daily, 10am–5pm. Guided tours: Aug, Suns, 2pm.
Admission: Free.

◻ ⅃ Grounds. ⊠ In grounds, on leads.

© NT Photographic Library All rights reserved DACS

Sandham Memorial Chapel

■ Owner
Mr & Mrs D Kendrick

■ Contact
Mrs M Kendrick
Boughton
Monchelsea Place
Boughton Monchelsea
Nr Maidstone
Kent ME17 4BU

Tel: 01622 743120
E-mail: mk@
boughtonplace.co.uk

■ Location
MAP 4:K3
OS Ref. TQ772 499

On B2163, 5½ m from
M20/J8 or 4½ m from
Maidstone via A229.

■ Opening Times
All year, except
24 Dec–4 Jan, by prior
arrangement only.

House & Garden
Not open to
individual visitors.

Group visits/ house tours:
(15–50),
Tues–Thur, 10am–4pm.

Private functions:
Mon–Fri, 9am–10pm.

Outdoor Event Site
365 days a year:
8am–11.30pm.

■ Admission
Gardens &
Guided House Tour
Adult   £5.50

Venue Hire
Prices on application

Day Delegate Rate
From £40

■ Special Events

July 6 (tbc)
Classic Car Show.

July

Open Air Theatre
Please telephone Hazlitt
Theatre for details. 01622
758611.

Conference/Function

ROOM	SIZE	MAX CAPACITY
Entrance Hall	25' x 19'	50 Theatre
Dining Room	31' x 19'	50 Dining
Drawing Room	28' x 19'	40 Reception
Courtyard Room	37' x 13'	60 Theatre

BOUGHTON MONCHELSEA PLACE
www.boughtonplace.co.uk

Boughton Monchelsea Place is a battlemented manor house dating from the 16th century, set in its own country estate just outside Maidstone, within easy reach of London and the channel ports. This Grade I listed building has always been privately owned and is still lived in as a family home.

From the lawns surrounding the property there are spectacular views over unspoilt Kent countryside, with the historic deer park in the foreground. A wicket gate leads from the grounds to the medieval church of St Peter, with its rose garden and ancient lych gate. At the rear of the house are to be found a pretty courtyard and walled gardens, while an extensive range of Tudor barns and outbuildings surround the old stableyard. Inside the house, rooms vary in character from Tudor through to Georgian Gothic; worthy of note are the fine Jacobean staircase and sundry examples of heraldic stained glass. Furnishings and paintings are mainly Victorian, with a few earlier pieces; the atmosphere is friendly and welcoming throughout.

The premises are licensed for Civil marriage and partnership ceremonies. In addition we welcome location work, group visits and all types of corporate, private and public functions, but please note times of availability. Use outside these hours is sometimes possible, subject to negotiation. All clients are guaranteed exclusive use of this prestigious venue.

i	Film location.
	By arrangement.
	By arrangement.
	By arrangement.

©NTPL/Ian Shaw

■ **Owner**
The National Trust

■ **Contact**
The Property Manager
Chartwell
Westerham
Kent TN16 1PS

Tel: 01732 866368
01732 868381
Fax: 01732 868193
E-mail: chartwell@
nationaltrust.org.uk

■ **Location**
MAP 19:F11
OS Ref. TQ455 515

2m S of Westerham,
forking left off B2026.

Bus: 246 from Bromley
South, 401 from
Sevenoaks, Buses4U from
Oxted (All services
Suns & BHs only).
Please check times.

■ **Opening Times**
15 March–29 June and
3 September–2 November
Wed–Sun & BHs

1 July–31 August
Tue–Sun & BHs
11am–5pm.

Last admission 4.15pm.

■ ***Admission**
House, Garden & Studio
Adult   £11.20
Child   £5.60
Family   £28.00

Pre-booked groups
(minimum 15)
Adult   £9.30
Child   £4.65

Garden & Studio only
Adult   £5.60
Child   £2.80
Family   £14.00

*includes a voluntary
donation but visitors can
choose to pay the standard
prices displayed at the
property and on the website.

CHARTWELL

www.nationaltrust.org.uk/chartwell

The family home of Sir Winston Churchill from 1924 until the end of his life. He said of Chartwell, simply '*I love the place – a day away from Chartwell is a day wasted*'. With magnificent views over the Weald of Kent it is not difficult to see why.

The rooms are left as they were in Sir Winston & Lady Churchill's lifetime with daily papers, fresh flowers grown from the garden and his famous cigars. Photographs and books evoke his career, interests and happy family life. Museum and exhibition rooms contain displays, sound recordings and superb collections of memorabilia, including gifts, uniforms and family photographs, and give a unique insight into Sir Winston's political career and personal life.

The garden studio contains Sir Winston's easel and paintbox, as well as many of his paintings. Terraced and water gardens descend to the lake, the gardens also include a golden rose walk, planted by Sir Winston and Lady Churchill's children on the occasion of their golden wedding anniversary, and the Marlborough Pavilion decorated with frescoes depicting the battle of Blenheim. Visitors can see the garden walls that Churchill built with his own hands, as well as the pond stocked with the golden orfe he loved to feed.

The Mulberry Room at the restaurant can be booked for meetings, conferences, lunches and dinners. Please telephone for details.

©NTPL/Andreas von Einsiedel

©NTPL/Ian Shaw

 Conference facilities.

 Partial. WC. Please telephone before visit.

 Licensed.

 By arrangement.

 In grounds, on leads.

■ Owner
The Denys Eyre Bower Bequest, Registered Charitable Trust

■ Contact
Chiddingstone Castle
Edenbridge
Kent TN8 7AD

Tel: 01892 870347

E-mail:
info@chiddingstonecastle.org

■ Location
MAP 19:G12
OS Ref. TQ497 452

10m from Tonbridge, Tunbridge Wells and Sevenoaks.
4m Edenbridge.
Accessible from A21 and M25/J5.

London 35m.

Bus: Enquiries: Tunbridge Wells TIC 01892 515675.

Rail: Tonbridge, Tunbridge Wells, Edenbridge then taxi. Penshurst then 2m walk.

Air: Gatwick 15m.

■ Opening Times
Please refer to website.

■ Admission
Please refer to website.

CHIDDINGSTONE CASTLE 🏛
www.chiddingstonecastle.org

0In 1803 Henry Streatfeild, Squire of Chiddingstone, intoxicated by the then current passion for medieval chivalry, embarked on the transformation of his ancient home into a fantasy castle. It would be the first major commission of young William Atkinson, which a contemporary guidebook predicted would be the '*fairest house*' in Kent. After five hectic years work ceased, leaving a random mix of old and new. The Establishment then was not impressed; today's visitors find the house enchanting.

In 1955 the now decrepit Castle was bought by the distinguished collector Denys Eyre Bower. He died in 1977, leaving his home and its rich collections to the Nation for the enjoyment of posterity. The place is now administered by a private Charitable Trust.

Chiddingstone Castle's fascinating array of Ancient Egyptian artefacts, Buddhist art, Japanese swords, armour and lacquer and a superb gathering of Royal Stuart portraits and mementoes celebrates twentieth-century collecting at its best.

The 35-acre landscaped park (a listed garden of Kent) is a haven for wildlife, providing idyllic walks.

ℹ️ Museum, weddings, business and private functions, scenic gardens and lake, picnics.

🍽 Available for special events. Wedding receptions.

♿ Partial (grounds unsuitable). WC.

🅿️ Ample for cars. Limited for coaches, please book.

We welcome visits from schools who wish to use the collections in connection with classroom work.

🐕 In grounds, on leads.

CHIDDINGSTONE

CASTLE

A MANOR FOR ALL SEASONS

An Idyllic Venue For Every Occasion

WEDDINGS • EDUCATIONAL WORKSHOPS • CABARET • PARTIES

■ Owner
Cobham Hall School

■ Contact
Mr N Powell
Bursar
Cobham Hall
Cobham
Kent DA12 3BL

Tel: 01474 823371
Fax: 01474 825904
E-mail: windiates@
cobhamhall.com

■ Location
MAP 4:K2
OS Ref. TQ683 689

Situated adjacent to the
A2/M2. ½m S of A2 4m
W of Strood. 8m E of
M25/J2 between
Gravesend & Rochester.

London 25m
Rochester 5m
Canterbury 30m

Rail: Meopham 3m
Gravesend 5m
Taxis at both stations.

Air: Gatwick 45 mins.
Heathrow 60 mins,
Stansted 50 mins.

■ Opening Times
19, 21, 23/24,
26 & 30 March;
2, 6, 8/9 April;
9, 13, 16, 20, 23,
27 & 30 July;
6, 10, 13, 17, 20, 24,
27 & 31 August.

Pre-booked Tours only
12–14 February;
25 & 27 March;
1, 3, 8 & 10 April;
8, 10, 15, 17, 22, 24,
29 & 31 July;
5, 7, 12, 14, 19, 21,
26 & 28 August.

House & Shop
2–5pm (5.30pm Shop).
Last tour at 4pm.

Garden
Closes at 6pm.

Dates could change,
please telephone to
confirm.

■ Admission
Adult	£4.50
Child (4–14yrs.)	£3.50
Conc.	£3.50

Gardens & Parkland
Self-guided tour   £2.50

Historical/Conservation tour of Grounds
(by arrangement)
Per person   £3.50

■ Special Events
July 13
Ellenor Foundation
Charity Walk

Conference/Function
ROOM	SIZE	MAX CAPACITY
Gilt Hall	41' x 34'	180
Wyatt Dining Rm	49' x 23'	135
Clifton Dining Rm	24' x 23'	75
Activities Centre	119' x 106'	300

COBHAM HALL
www.cobhamhall.com

Cobham Hall is now a leading Girls Boarding and Day School, and has been visited by several English monarchs from Elizabeth I to Edward VIII. Charles Dickens used regularly to walk through the grounds from his house in Higham to the Leather Bottle Public House in Cobham Village.

Cobham Hall is one of the largest, finest and most important houses in Kent, it is an outstanding beautiful red brick mansion in Elizabethan, Jacobean, Carolean and 18th century styles, it yields much interest to the students of art, architecture and history. The Elizabethan Wings were begun in 1584, whilst the central section, which contains the Gilt Hall, was wonderfully decorated by John Webb. Further rooms were decorated by James Wyatt in the 18th century.

In 1883 the Hon Ivo Bligh, later the 8th Earl of Darnley, led the victorious English cricket team against Australia bringing the Ashes home to Cobham.

Gardens
The Park was landscaped for the 4th Earl by Humphry Repton, and is now gradually being restored. The Gothic Dairy, Aviary and the Pump House are all being restored. The gardens are beautiful at all times of the year but especially delightful in the spring when the spring flowers are out in full bloom.

i Conferences, business or social functions, 150 acres of parkland for sports, corporate events, open air concerts, sports centre, indoor swimming pool, art studios, music wing, tennis courts, helicopter landing area. Filming and photography. No smoking.

In-house catering team for private, corporate hospitality and wedding receptions. (cap. 100).

House tour involves 2 staircases, ground floor access for w/chairs.

Cream teas 2–5pm on open days. Other meals by arrangement.

Obligatory guided tours; tour time 1½hrs. Tours also arranged outside standard opening times.

P Ample. Pre-booked coach groups are welcome any time.

Guide dogs only.

18 single and 18 double with bathroom. 22 single and 22 double without bathroom. Dormitory. Groups only.

DANSON HOUSE

www.dansonhouse.org.uk

In 1995 this Palladian villa by Robert Taylor was deemed the most significant building at risk in London. Following extensive restoration by English Heritage it has been returned to its former Georgian glory.

Completed in 1766, Danson was built for wealthy merchant Sir John Boyd. The house was designed to reflect its original purpose, that of a country house dedicated to entertainment. The sumptuous interior decoration tells stories that reveal the passion of Boyd for his wife and the love they shared.

The principal floor takes in the austere Entrance Hall that would have held Boyd's collection of souvenir sculpture from the Grand Tour. The exquisitely gilded Dining Room presents a set of wall paintings by Charles Pavillon. The octagonal Salon houses the only know portrait of Boyd in an original painting that has been reframed to the design of William Chambers. Chambers also made considerable changes to the house shortly after it was completed. The impressive Library is home to a George England organ, built for the house, and is still in working order. Further displays relating to the history of the house and its inhabitants can be found on the bedroom level.

The principal floor is licensed for Civil wedding ceremonies and can accommodate up to 65 guests. There is a programme of events throughout the whole year. Please telephone for details. Round off your visit with a light lunch and homemade cakes in the popular Breakfast Room, and indulge in our imaginatively stocked gift shop.

 Two.

 WCs.

Licenced.

 By prior arrangement. Please telephone 020 8298 6951.

 Limited for coaches. Parking here for The Red House see London section (15 mins walk).

■ Owner
English Heritage

■ Contact
Visitor Operations Team
Down House
Luxted Road
Downe
Kent BR6 7JT

Tel: 01689 859119
Fax: 01689 862755

■ Location
MAP 19:F9
OS Ref, TQ431 611

In Luxted Road, Downe,
off A21 near Biggin Hill.

Rail: From London
Victoria or Charing Cross.

Bus: Orpington
(& Bus R8) or Bromley
South (& Bus 146).
Buses R8 & 146
do not run on
Sundays or BHs.

■ Opening Times
21 March–30 June &
1 September–31 October:
Wed–Sun & BHs,
11am–5pm.
1 July–31 August: daily
11am–5pm.
1 November–
16 December: Wed–Sun,
11am–4pm.

■ Admission
Adult	£7.20
Child	£3.60
Conc.	£5.40
Family (2+3)	£18.00

EH Members Free.

Groups (11+)
15% discount

Tour leader and coach
driver have free entry.
1 extra place for every
20 additional people.

New for Spring, extended
tearoom and new shop.

Some building works may
be in progress 2007/8

THE HOME OF CHARLES DARWIN ▦

www.english-heritage.org.uk/darwinhouse

A visit to Down House is a fascinating journey of discovery for all the family. This was the family home of Charles Darwin for over 40 years and now you can explore it to the full.

See the actual armchair in which Darwin wrote 'On the Origin of Species', which shocked and then revolutionised the way we think about the origins of mankind. His study is much the same as it was in his lifetime and is filled with belongings that give you an intimate glimpse into both his studies and everyday life.

At Down House you will discover both sides of Darwin – the great thinker and the family man. Explore the family rooms where the furnishings have been painstakingly restored. An audio tour narrated by Sir David Attenborough will bring the house to life and increase your understanding of Darwin's revolutionary theory. Upstairs you will find state-of-the-art interpretation of the scientific significance of the house – especially designed to inspire a younger audience.

Outside, take the Sandwalk which he paced daily in search of inspiration, then stroll in lovely gardens. Complete your day by sampling the delicious selection of home-made cakes in the tea room.

ℹ	WCs.
🛍	
♿	
☕	Free.
🎧	
🅿	Limited for coaches.
🐕	Guide dogs only.
🎭	

©English Heritage Photo Library

DOVER CASTLE
AND THE SECRET WARTIME TUNNELS
www.english-heritage.org.uk/dovercastle

Owner
English Heritage

Contact
Visitor Operations Team
Dover Castle
Dover
Kent CT16 1HU

Tel: 01304 211067
Fax: 01304 214739

**Venue Hire and
Hospitality:**
Hospitality Manager
Tel: 01304 209889

Location
MAP 4:O4
OS Ref. TR325 419

Easy access from A2 and
M20. Well signed from
Dover centre and east
side of Dover.
2 hrs from
central London.

Rail: London Charing
Cross or Victoria
1½hrs.

Bus: 0870 6082608.

Opening Times
Summer
21 March–30 September:
Daily, 10am–6pm
(August opens 9.30am).
October:
Daily, 10am–5pm.

1 November–31 January:
Thur–Mon, 10am–4pm.
Closed 24–26 Dec & 1 Jan.

Last admission ½ hr
before closing.

NB. Keep closes at 5pm
on days when events are
booked.

*Admission
Adult	£10.30
Child	£5.20
Conc.	£8.20
Family (2+3)	£25.80

EH Members Free.
Charges may apply on
event days.

*Includes Secret Wartime
Tunnel tour.

Groups: 15% discount for
groups (11+). Free entry
for tour leader and coach
driver. One free place for
every additional 20 paying.

**Venue Hire and
Hospitality**
English Heritage offers
exclusive use of the Castle
Keep or Tunnels in the
evenings for receptions,
dinners, product launches
and themed banquets.

Journey deep into the White Cliffs of Dover and discover the top secret World War II tunnels. Through sight, sound and smells, relive the wartime drama of the underground hospital as a wounded Battle of Britain pilot is taken to the operating theatre in a bid to save his life. Discover how life would have been during the planning days of the Dunkirk evacuation and Operation Dynamo as you are led around the network of tunnels and casements housing the communications centre.

Above ground you can explore the magnificent medieval keep and inner bailey of King Henry II. Experience the exciting '1216 Siege' exhibition, and discover, through a dramatic light and sound presentation, how it must have felt to be a garrison soldier defending Dover Castle against the French King in 1216. See a reconstruction of the castle in preparation for a visit from Henry VIII and visit the hands-on exhibition explaining the travelling Tudor court.

Visit the evocative Princess of Wales' Royal Regiment Museum. There is also the Roman Lighthouse and Anglo-Saxon church to see as well as the intriguing 13th-century underground fortifications and medieval battlements. Enjoy magnificent views of the White Cliffs from Admiralty Lookout. The land train will help you around this huge site.

Throughout the summer there are many fun events taking place, bringing the castle alive through colourful enactments and living history.

©English Heritage Photo Library

WCs.

Two.

Exclusive private and corporate hire.
Tel: 01034 209889.

Lift for access to tunnels. Courtyard
and grounds, some very steep slopes.

3 restaurants, hot and cold food
and drinks.

Tour of tunnels: timed ticket system.
Last tour 1 hr before closing.

Ample.

Free visits available for schools.
Education centre. Pre-booking
essential.

Conference/Function

ROOM	MAX CAPACITY
The Castle Keep	standing 120 dining 90
Keep Yard Café	theatre-style 150
Secret Wartime Tunnels	standing 120 dining 80 theatre-style 80
Marquee on Palace Green	standing 400 dining 265

South East – England

■ Owner
Groombridge Asset Management

■ Contact
The Estate Office
Groombridge Place
Groombridge
Tunbridge Wells
Kent TN3 9QG

Tel: 01892 861444
Fax: 01892 863996
E-mail: office@
groombridge.co.uk

■ Location
MAP 4:J4
OS Ref. TQ534 375

Groombridge Place Gardens are located on the B2110 just off the A264. 4m SW of Tunbridge Wells and 9m E of East Grinstead.

Rail: London Charing Cross to Tunbridge Wells 55mins. (Taxis).

Air: Gatwick.

■ Opening Times
Summer
Gardens
21 March–8 November
Daily, 10am–5.30pm (or dusk if earlier).

The house is not open to visitors.

■ Admission
Adult	£8.95
Child* (3–12yrs)	£7.45
Senior	£7.45
Family (2+2)	£29.95

Groups (12+)
Adult	£7.25
Child/School (3–12yrs)	£5.50
Senior	£5.50/£6.25
Student	£6.25
Youth	£5.50

*Child under 3yrs Free.

■ Special Events
March 21–24
Easter Eggstravaganza.

July 20
Wings, Wheels and Steam.

August 3
Hot Air Balloons and Ferraris.

October 31 & 1 November
Halloween in the Spooky Gardens.

November 8
Spectacular Fireworks to Music.

GROOMBRIDGE PLACE GARDENS
www.groombridge.co.uk

There's magic and mystery, history and intrigue, romance and peace at this beautiful venue – which provides such an unusual combination of a traditional heritage garden with the excitement, challenge and contemporary landscaping of the ancient woodland – appealing to young and old alike.

First laid out in 1674 on a gentle, south-facing slope, the formal walled gardens are set against the romantic backdrop of a medieval moat, surrounding a classical Restoration manor house (not open to the public) and were designed as outside rooms. These award-winning gardens include magnificent herbaceous borders, the enchanting White Rose Garden with over 20 varieties of white roses, a Secret Garden with deep shade and cooling waters in a tiny hidden corner, Paradise Walk and Oriental Garden,

the Knot Garden and Nut Walk and the Drunken Garden with its crazy topiary. The gardens feature wonderful seasonal colour throughout spring, summer and autumn.

In complete contrast on a high hillside above the walled gardens and estate vineyard is the Enchanted Forest, where quirky and mysterious gardens have been developed in the ancient woodland by innovative designer, Ivan Hicks, to challenge the imagination. Children love the Dark Walk, Tree Fern Valley, Village of the Groms, the Serpent's Lair and the Mystic Pool, the Romany Camp, Double Spiral and the Giant Swings Walk. There are also Birds of Prey flying displays three times a day, a canal boat cruise to and from the Forest – plus a full programme of special events.

 Film location.

 Partial. WCs.

 Licensed.

 By arrangement.

 Limited for coaches.

 Guide dogs only.

HALL PLACE & GARDENS

www.hallplace.org.uk

■ Owner
Bexley Heritage Trust

■ Contact
Mrs Janet Hearn-Gillham
Hall Place & Gardens
Bourne Road
Bexley
Kent DA5 1PQ

Tel: 01322 526574
Fax: 01322 522921
E-mail:
info@hallplace.org.uk

■ Location
MAP 19:G8
OS Ref. TQ502 743

On the A2 less than
5m from the M25/J2
(London bound).

■ Opening Times
1 April–31 October:
Mon–Sat, 10am–5pm;
Sun & BHs, 11am–5pm.
1 Nov–31 Mar: Tue–Sat,
10am–4.15pm.

For house visits during
2008 please call in
advance as opening
subject to change due to
restoration.

■ Admission
Free. Charge made for
some Special Events.
Prearranged guided tours
(10+) £5.

A fine Grade I listed country house built in 1537 for Sir John Champneys, a wealthy merchant and former Lord Mayor of London. The house boasts a panelled Tudor Great Hall, overlooked by a minstrel's gallery, and various period rooms. The 17th century extension by Sir Robert Austen includes a vaulted Long Gallery and splendid Drawing Room with a fine plaster ceiling.

Managed by Bexley Heritage Trust, this beautiful estate of 65 hectares stands on the banks of the River Cray at Bexley. Surrounding the house are award winning formal gardens with magnificent topiary, enclosed gardens and inspirational herbaceous borders. In the former walled gardens there is a nursery selling plants grown in the Hall Place gardens, and a sub-tropical glasshouse where you can see ripening bananas in mid-winter.

The house closed in late 2007 for extensive restoration and will be re-opening in summer 2008: please phone or check the website for details. New displays will include an introduction to the house's history and exhibits on Tudor life, changing exhibitions from Bexley's extensive museum collection, as well as contemporary art exhibitions.

There is an extensive programme of events, art-based activities, concerts and theatre in the house and gardens. Several rooms are available to hire for meetings and events, including the Great Hall and Drawing Room, which are also licensed for civil wedding ceremonies. Bexley Heritage Trust offers an extensive education and outreach service and organised activities during the school holidays.

House, lift & WC.

Licensed.

By arrangement (10+).

Guide dogs only.

Owner
Hever Castle Ltd

Contact
Ann Watt
Hever Castle
Hever
Edenbridge
Kent TN8 7NG

Infoline: 01732 865224
Fax: 01732 866796
E-mail:
mail@HeverCastle.co.uk

Location
MAP 19:G12
OS Ref. TQ476 450

Exit M25/J5 & J6
M23/J10, 1½m S of
B2027 at Bough Beech,
3m SE of Edenbridge.

Rail: Hever Station 1m
(no taxis), Edenbridge
Town 3m (taxis).

Opening Times
Main Season
Easter–31 October
11am–5pm.
Last exit 6pm.

Winter
March, November and
December, please see
website for details.

Admission
Castle & Gardens
Adult   £11.50
Gardens only
Adult   £9.30
Concessions, child and
family tickets available.

Christmas Shop
& Restaurant
Free entry December

Groups (15+)
Available on request.

Pre-booked private guided
tours are available before
opening, during season.

HEVER CASTLE & GARDENS
www.hevercastle.co.uk

Hever Castle dates back to 1270, when the gatehouse, outer walls and the inner moat were first built. 200 years later the Bullen (or Boleyn) family added the comfortable Tudor manor house constructed within the walls. This was the childhood home of Anne Boleyn, Henry VIII's second wife and mother of Elizabeth I. There are many items relating to the Tudors, including two Books of Hours (prayer books) signed and inscribed by Anne Boleyn. The Castle was later given to Henry VIII's fourth wife, Anne of Cleves.

In 1903, the estate was bought by the American millionaire William Waldorf Astor, who became a British subject and the first Lord Astor of Hever. He invested an immense amount of time, money and imagination in restoring the castle and grounds. Master craftsmen were employed and the castle was filled with a fine collection of paintings, furniture and tapestries. The Miniature

Model Houses exhibition, a collection of 1/12 scale model houses, room views and gardens, depicts life in English Country Houses.

Gardens
Between 1904–8 over 30 acres of formal gardens were laid out and planted; these have now matured into one of the most beautiful gardens in England. The unique Italian Garden is a four acre walled garden containing a magnificent collection of statuary and sculpture. The glorious Edwardian Gardens include the Rose Garden and Tudor Garden, a traditional yew maze and a 110 metre herbaceous border. There are several water features including a water maze and a 35 acre lake with rowing boats. There is also an Adventure Play Area, the Hever Shop with an exquisite array of gifts, and a full programme of special events throughout the season including Jousting Tournaments and Falconry.

Conference/Function

ROOM	SIZE	MAX CAPACITY
Dining Hall	35' x 20'	70
Breakfast Rm	22' x 15'	12
Sitting Rm	24' x 20'	20
Pavilion	96' x 40'	250
Moat Restaurant	25' x 60'	75

ℹ Suitable for filming, conferences, corporate hospitality, weddings, product launches. Outdoor heated pool, tennis court and billiard room. No photography in house.

🛍 Gift, garden & book.

🍽 Exclusive use of Private Residence for Corporate Hospitality, Weddings and Golfing. Restaurants are also available for private functions and weddings.

♿ Access to gardens, ground floor only (no ramps into Castle), restaurants, gift, garden & book shops, and water maze. Wheelchairs available. WC.

🍴 Two licensed restaurants. Supper provided during open air theatre season. Pre-booked lunches and teas for groups.

🚶 Pre-booked tours in mornings. 1 Mar–23 Dec. Tour time 1 hr. Tours in French, German, Dutch, Italian and Spanish (min 20). Garden tours in English only (min 15).

🅿 Free admission and refreshment voucher for driver and courier. Please book, group rates for 15+.

🖼 Welcome (min 15). Private guided tours available (min 20). 1:6 ratio (up to 8 year olds; 1:10 9yrs+. Free preparatory visits for teachers during opening hours. Please book.

🐕 In grounds, on leads.

🔔

❄ Private Residence.

🏷 Call infoline: 01732 865224.

IGHTHAM MOTE 🌳

www.nationaltrust.org.uk/ighthammote

Beautiful moated manor house covering nearly 700 years of history from medieval times to the 1960s. Discover the stories and characters associated with the house from the first owners in 1320 to Charles Henry Robinson, the American businessman who bequeathed Ightham Mote to the National Trust in 1985.

Following the completion of the largest conservation project ever undertaken by the National Trust on a house of this age and fragility, it is now possible to enjoy the most extensive visitor route open since Ightham Mote's acquisition by the Trust. This includes the refurbished Great Hall and Jacobean staircase, along with the Old Chapel, Crypt, Tudor Chapel with painted ceiling, Drawing Room with Jacobean fireplace, frieze and 18th century hand-painted Chinese wallpaper, Victorian Billiards Room and the apartments of Mr Robinson. A special exhibition 'Conservation in Action' explains the project and gives insights into the techniques and skills used.

Extensive gardens with lakes and woodland walk. Surrounding 550 acre estate also provides many country walks including way-marked routes.

Free introductory talks, garden and tower tours. Varied events programme including children's events and lecture lunches through the season. Group and Educational Tours available, plus educational facility. For details please telephone: 01732 810378.

■ Owner
The National Trust

■ Contact
The Property Manager
Ightham Mote
Mote Road
Ivy Hatch
Sevenoaks
Kent TN15 0NT

Tel: 01732 810378
Info: 01732 811145
Fax: 01732 811029
E-mail: ighthammote@
nationaltrust.org.uk

■ Location
MAP 19:H11
OS Ref. TQ584 535

6m E of Sevenoaks off A25. 2½m S of Ightham off A227.

■ Opening Times
15 March–2 November:
Daily except Tues & Weds.

Gardens, Shop & Restaurant
10.30am–5pm
(last admission 4.30pm).

House
11am–5pm
(last admission 4.30pm).

Restaurant & Shop
winter opening times:
please call property.

■ *Admission
Adult	£9.85
Child	£4.95
Family	£24.65
Groups (booked)	
Adult	£8.35
Child	£4.20

*includes a voluntary donation but visitors can choose to pay the standard prices displayed at the property and on the website.

Ground floor. WC.

On leads, Estate only.

Owner
The National Trust

Contact
Property Manager
Knole
Sevenoaks
Kent TN15 0RP

Tel: 01732 462100
Info: 01732 450608
Fax: 01732 465528
E-mail: knole@
nationaltrust.org.uk

Location
MAP 19:H10
OS Ref. TQ532 543

M25/J5. 25m SE of
London. Just off A225 at
S end of High Street,
Sevenoaks.

Rail: ½hr from London
Charing Cross to
Sevenoaks.

Bus: Arriva 402 Tunbridge
Wells–Bromley North.

Opening Times
Park, Shop & Tearoom
1/2 & 8/9 March,
11am–4pm.

Great Hall
1/2 & 8/9 March,
11am–2pm

House
15 March–2 November:
Wed–Sun & BH Mons,
12 noon–4pm. Open
Tuesdays 29 Jul–2 Sept.
Last admission 3.30pm.

Premium guided tours for
pre-booked groups while
house is closed to public,
Wed, Fri & Sat, plus Thurs
in Aug, 11am. Please
telephone for further
information.

Garden
Weds throughout the
season, 11am–4pm
(last admission 3.30pm).

Shop & Tearoom
15 March–2 November:
Wed–Sun & BH Mons,
Open Tues 29 July–
2 Sept.10.30am–5pm.

**Christmas Shop &
Tearoom**
5 November–
21 December: Wed–Sun,
11am–4pm.

*Admission
House
Adult	£9.00
Child	£4.50
Family	£22.50

Groups (booked 15+)
Adult	£7.60
Child	£3.80

Garden
Adult	£2.20
Child	£1.10

NT members Free.

Parking £2.50

Park Free to pedestrians

*includes a voluntary
donation but visitors can
choose to pay the standard
prices displayed at the
property and on the website.

Knole ©NTPL

KNOLE

www.nationaltrust.org.uk/knole

Knole's fascinating historic links with Kings, Queens and the nobility, as well as its literary links with Vita Sackville-West and her friend Virginia Woolfe, make this one of the most intriguing houses in England. Thirteen superb state-rooms are laid out much as they were in the 18th century to impress visitors by the wealth and status of the Sackville family, who continue to live at Knole. The house includes Royal Stuart furniture, paintings by Gainsborough, Van Dyck and Reynolds as well as many 17th century tapestries.

The house inspired Vita Sackville-West, who was born at Knole, to write her best-selling novel "*The Edwardians*" and was also the setting for Virginia Woolf's famous novel "*Orlando*"

Knole is set at the heart of the only remaining medieval deer park in Kent, where Sika and Fallow deer still roam freely amongst ancient oak, beech and chestnut trees, as they have since the days of Henry VIII.

Relax in the original "Brew House" with a cup of tea or enjoy a delicious lunch before browsing through the well-stocked shop full of local produce, exquisite gifts and its large collection of books, including those by Vita Sackville-West, her son Nigel Nicolson, and Virginia Woolf.

Visit on a Wednesday and enjoy a leisurely stroll through Lord Sackville's private garden. The garden provides the most beautiful view of the house and allows visitors to observe the outside of the Orangery and the Chapel. Witness the changing seasons in the garden from early spring through to the late autumn.

©NTPL

Full range of NT goods and souvenirs of Knole.

Wheelchair access to Green Court, Stone Court and Great Hall. WC. Virtual reality tour of upstairs showrooms.

Serving morning coffee, lunch and teas. Also ice-creams and snacks in courtyard.

Guided tours for pre-booked groups, by arrangement. Short guides to the house available in French, Dutch & German.

Ample.

Welcome. Contact Education Officer.

Guide dogs only.

Park open all year to pedestrians.

Telephone for details.

LEEDS CASTLE

www.leeds-castle.com

■ **Owner**
Leeds Castle Foundation

■ **Contact**
Leeds Castle
Maidstone
Kent ME17 1PL

Tel: 01622 765400
Fax: 01622 735616

■ **Location**
MAP 4:L3
OS Ref. TQ835 533

From London to
A20/M20/J8, 40m, 1 hr.
7m E of Maidstone,
¼m S of A20.

Rail: Combined ticket
with South Eastern
Trains available, (train
and admission).
London–Bearsted.

Coach: Nat Express coach
and admission from
Victoria.

■ **Opening Times**
Summer
1 April–30 September
Daily, 10am–5pm (last
adm).

Winter
1 October–31 March
Daily, 10am–3pm
(last adm).

Castle & Grounds
Closed 25 December.
Please check with our
staff over possible
closures in July and for
the fireworks event in
November. Special private
tours for pre-booked
groups by appointment.

■ **Admission**
Castle, Park & Gardens
Individuals (valid 1 year)
Adult   £14.00
Child (4–15yrs)   £8.50
OAP/Student   £11.00
Visitor with disabilities
(1 carer Free)   £11.00
(2007 prices)

Group 15+
Adult   £11.00
Child (4–15yrs)   £7.50
OAP/Student   £10.50
Visitor with disabilities
(1 carer Free)   £10.50

A guidebook is published
in English, French,
Dutch, Spanish, Italian,
Russian, Japanese and
Mandarin.

Please check website
prior to your visit.

Set in 500 acres of beautiful parkland and gardens, Leeds Castle is one of the country's finest historic properties and is also one of the Treasure Houses of England.

A Norman fortress and a royal palace to the mediaeval and Tudor Kings and Queens of England, the development of Leeds Castle continued well into the 20th century. The last private owner, the Hon Olive, Lady Baillie, bought the castle in 1926, restored the castle and furnished its beautiful interiors.

The castle has a fine collection of paintings, tapestries and antiques and is also home to an unusual dog collar museum. The park and grounds include the colourful and quintessentially English Culpeper Garden, the delightful Wood Garden, and the terraced Lady Baillie Garden with its views over the tranquil Great Water. The Aviary houses approximately 100 rare and endangered species from around the world and next to the Vineyard can be discovered the Maze with its secret underground grotto. The Knights' Realm playground delights younger visitors and falconry shows add more interest.

A highly popular and successful programme of special events is arranged throughout the year, details of which can be found on the website.

ℹ️ Residential conferences, exhibitions, sporting days, clay shooting off site, laser shooting, falconry, field archery, golf, croquet and helipad. Talks can be arranged for horticultural, viticultural, historical and cultural groups.

🛍️ Corporate hospitality, large scale marquee events, wedding receptions, buffets and dinners.

♿ Land train for elderly/disabled, wheelchairs, wheelchair lift, special rates. WC.

☕ Restaurant, group lunch menus. Refreshment kiosks.

👤 Guides in rooms. French, Spanish, Dutch and German speaking guides.

🎧 For hire in English, French, Spanish, German and Japanese.

🅿️ Free parking.

📖 Workshops, outside normal opening hours, private tours. Teacher's resource pack and worksheets.

€

Conference/Function

ROOM	SIZE	MAX CAPACITY
Fairfax Hall	19.8 x 6.7m	200
Gate Tower	9.8 x 5.2m	70
Culpeper	6.3 x 5.3m	40
Terrace	8.9 x 15.4m	100
Castle Boardroom	9.7 x 4.8m	24
Castle Dining Rm	13.1 x 6.6m	60

Owner
Viscount De L'Isle

Contact
Ian Scott
Penshurst Place
Penshurst
Nr Tonbridge
Kent TN11 8DG

Tel: 01892 870307
Fax: 01892 870866
E-mail: enquiries
@penshurstplace.com

Location
MAP 19:H12
OS Ref. TQ527 438

From London M25/J5
then A21 to
Hildenborough, B2027
via Leigh; from Tunbridge
Wells A26, B2176.

Visitors entrance at SE
end of village,
S of the church.

Bus: Arriva 231, 233 from
Tunbridge Wells and
Edenbridge.

Rail: Charing Cross/
Waterloo–Hildenborough,
Tonbridge or Tunbridge
Wells; then bus or taxi.

Opening Times
1–16 March:
Sats & Suns only.
21 March–2 November
Daily.

House
Daily, 12 noon–4pm.

Grounds
Daily, 10.30am–6pm.

Shop
Open all year.

Winter
Open to Groups by
appointment only
(see Guided Tours).

Admission
House & Gardens
Adult	£8.50
Child*	£5.50
Family (2+2)	£23.00
Groups (15+)	
Adult	£7.00
Child	£4.00

Garden only
Adult	£7.00
Child*	£5.00
Family (2+2)	£20.00

Garden Season Ticket
£37.50

**Garden Family Season
Ticket** (2+2), additional
child £6.00 each. £60.00

House Tours
(pre-booked 15+)
Adult	£8.50
Child	£5.00

Garden Tours
(pre-booked 15+)
Adult	£8.50
Child	£5.00

House & Garden £12.00

*Aged 5–16yrs;
under 5s Free.

Conference/Function
ROOM	SIZE	MAX CAPACITY
Sunderland Room	45' x 18'	100
Baron's Hall	64' x 39'	250
Buttery	20' x 23'	50

©David Sellman/Penshurst Place

PENSHURST PLACE & GARDENS
www.penshurstplace.com

Penshurst Place is one of England's greatest family-owned stately homes with a history going back six and a half centuries.

In some ways time has stood still at Penshurst; the great House is still very much a medieval building with improvements and additions made over the centuries but without any substantial rebuilding. Its highlight is undoubtedly the medieval Baron's Hall, built in 1341, with its impressive 60ft-high chestnut-beamed roof.

A marvellous mix of paintings, tapestries and furniture from the 15th, 16th and 17th centuries can be seen throughout the House, including the helm carried in the state funeral procession to St Paul's Cathedral for the Elizabethan courtier and poet, Sir Philip Sidney, in 1587. This is now the family crest.

Gardens

The Gardens, first laid out in the 14th century, have been developed over successive years by the Sidney family who first came to Penshurst in 1552. A twenty-year restoration and re-planting programme undertaken by the 1st Viscount De L'Isle has ensured that they retain their historic splendour. He is commemorated with a new Arboretum, planted in 1991. The gardens are divided by a mile of yew hedges into "rooms", each planted to give a succession of colour as the seasons change. There is also a Venture Playground, Woodland Trail, Toy Museum and a Gift Shop.

A variety of events in the park and grounds take place throughout the season.

 Adventure playground & parkland & riverside walks. Product launches, garden parties, photography, filming, fashion shows, receptions, archery, clay pigeon shooting, falconry, parkland for hire. Conference facilities. No photography in house.

Private banqueting, wedding receptions.

Limited. Virtual tour of first floor of house, garden leaflet guide. Disabled and elderly may alight at private entrance. WC.

Licensed tearoom serving light lunches, cream teas and other refreshments. New 2 & 3 course dining menu available in the banqueting function room.

 Guided tours of House available by arrangement before the House opens to the public. Garden tours available 10.30am–4.30pm. Pre-booked freeflow (non-guided) visits available throughout opening hours.

Ample. Double decker buses to Park from village.

All year by appointment, discount rates, education room and packs.

Guide dogs only

SQUERRYES COURT 🏛

www.squerryes.co.uk

Squerryes Court is a beautiful 17th century manor house which has been the Warde family home since 1731. It is surrounded by 10 acres of attractive and historic gardens which include a lake, restored parterres and an 18th century dovecote. Squerryes is 22 miles from London and easily accessible from the M25. There are lovely views and peaceful surroundings. Visitors from far and wide come to enjoy the atmosphere of a house which is still lived in as a family home.

There is a fine collection of Old Master paintings from the Italian, 17th century Dutch and 18th century English schools, furniture,

porcelain and tapestries all acquired or commissioned by the family in the 18th century. General Wolfe of Quebec was a friend of the family and there are items connected with him in the Wolfe Room.

Gardens
These were laid out in the formal style but were re-landscaped in the mid 18th century. Some of the original features in the 1719 Badeslade print survive. The family have restored the formal garden using this print as a guide. The garden is lovely all year round with bulbs, wild flowers and woodland walks, azaleas, summer flowering herbaceous borders and roses.

Owner
John St A Warde Esq

Contact
Mrs P A White
Administrator
Squerryes Court
Westerham
Kent TN16 1SJ

Tel: 01959 562345
Fax: 01959 565949
E-mail: enquiries @squerryes.co.uk

Location
MAP 19:F11
OS Ref. TQ440 535

10 min from M25/J5 or 6 off A25, ½m W from centre of Westerham

London 1–1½ hrs.

Rail: Oxted Station 4m. Sevenoaks 6m.

Air: Gatwick, 30 mins.

Opening Times
Summer
Easter Sunday–
28 September
Wed, Sun & BH Mons.
12.30–5pm.
Last admission 4.30pm.

Grounds
11.30am–5pm
Last admission 4.30pm.

NB. Pre-booked groups welcome any day except Saturday.

Winter
October–31 March
Closed.

Admission
House & Garden
Adult	£6.50
Child (under 16yrs)	£3.50
Senior	£6.00
Family (2+2)	£13.50

Groups (20+)
Adult	£5.50
Child (under 16yrs)	£3.50

Wine Tasting
(inc. House & Garden)
Adult	£7.50

Garden only
Adult	£4.00
Child (under 16yrs)	£2.00
Senior	£3.50
Family (2+2)	£8.00

Groups (20+, booked)
Adult	£4.00
Child (under 16yrs)	£2.00

ℹ️ Suitable for conferences, product launches, filming, photography, outside events, garden parties. No photography in house. Picnics permitted in grounds.

🛍 Small.

💐

🍸 Wedding receptions (marquee).

♿ Limited access in house and garden. WCs.

☕ Lunches and light refreshments on open days. Licenced.

👣 For pre-booked groups (max 55), small additional charge. Tour time 1 hr. Wine tasting groups by arrangement 45 mins–1 hr. Additional charge.

🅿 Limited for coaches.

🐕 On leads, in grounds.

Conference/Function
ROOM	SIZE	MAX CAPACITY
Hall	32' x 32'	60
Old Library	20' x 25' 6"	40

■ Owner

Turkey Mill
Investments Ltd

■ Contact

Turkey Mill Events Ltd
The Events Office
Turkey Court
Turkey Mill
Ashford Road
Maidstone
Kent ME14 5PP

Tel: 01622 765511
Fax: 01622 765522
E-mail: events@
turkeymill.co.uk

■ Location

MAP 4:L3
OS Ref. TQ773 555

Turkey Mill is located
1½m from M20/J7
(follow the signs).

The entrance is off
the A20 ½m east of
Maidstone Town Centre.

■ Admission

Available for privately
booked functions only.

The Orangery and
Grounds are available all
year round for private
and corporate events.

TURKEY MILL

www.turkeymill.co.uk

Turkey Mill, in the heart of the Garden of England, in Kent's county town, Maidstone, represents and preserves the true and natural beauty of Kent itself. It is steeped in local history, originally a fulling mill, it was converted to paper making at the end of the 17th century. Under the ownership of James Whatman, father and son, it became world famous for producing the high-quality paper used by J M W Turner, Thomas Gainsborough and William Blake and for momentous documents including Napoleon's Will and the Peace Treaty with Japan at the end of the Second World War.

Since 1997, the current owners have created a spectacular venue for unforgettable events, maintaining the natural outstanding beauty of the landscape and adding those stylish features that capture modern comfort. The ultimate setting representing the best of "something old, something new".

Today, Turkey Mill is a business park and home to more than 60 companies. Alongside the business park are nine acres of award-winning landscaped parklands which include sweeping lawns, huge Wellingtonia Pines and Blue Cedars dating back over 400 years. A beautiful waterfall and lake, through which runs the River Len, make Turkey Mill a memorable venue for Weddings, Corporate and Private Events. The Orangery, completed in 2002, has been aesthetically designed to incorporate all the elements required for both comfort and grandeur.

The natural beauty of the water and grounds create a wonderfully tranquil atmosphere as well as unforgettable scenery. Photographic opportunities are endless throughout the grounds providing many wonderful backdrops for filming, photography and product launches. The discreet floodlighting brings the venue to life after dusk.

ℹ Film location.

🍸 Private and corporate events.

♿

🍴 Licensed.

🅿 80 spaces weekdays.
Unlimited weekends.

Conference/Function

ROOM	SIZE	MAX CAPACITY
The Orangery	82' x 30'	Dining 200 Dinner Dance 160 Theatre-style 200 (160 catered) Open block 38
The Whatman Room	23' x 19'	Theatre-style 40 (25 catered) Classroom-style 20 Open block 18

BEDGEBURY NATIONAL PINETUM & FOREST

Goudhurst, Cranbrook, Kent TN17 2SL
Tel: 01580 879820 **Fax:** 01580 212423
Owner: Forestry Commission **Contact:** Mark Clixby
Location: MAP 4:K4, OS Ref. TQ715 336 (gate on B2079). 7m E of Tunbridge Wells on A21, turn N on B2079 for 1m.
Open: All year: daily, 8am–8pm, Sept & Apr closes 7pm, Oct & May closes 6pm, Nov & Mar closes 5pm.
Admission: Car parking £6 per car, £20 per minibus, £30 per coach. Pay and Display.

BOUGHTON MONCHELSEA PLACE *See page 106 for full page entry.*

Goodnestone Park Gardens, Kent

BELMONT HOUSE & GARDENS 🏠
BELMONT PARK, THROWLEY, FAVERSHAM ME13 0HH
www.belmont-house.org

Tel: 01795 890202 **Fax:** 01795 890042 **E-mail:** belmontadmin@btconnect.com
Owner: Harris (Belmont) Charity **Contact:** Administrator

Belmont is an elegant 18th century house with views over the rolling Kentish North Downs. Its hidden gardens range from a Pinetum complete with grotto, a walled ornamental garden, a walled kitchen garden with Victorian greenhouse leading to a yew-lined walk to the family pets' graveyard.

Its very special collections echo its ownership by the Harris family since 1801 and include mementos of their travels and posts in India and Trinidad. The house was designed by Samuel Wyatt and includes many novel architectural details. In addition it has one of the most extensive collections of clocks in private hands in the country.

Location: MAP 4:M3, OS Ref. TQ986 564. 4½m SSW of Faversham, off A251.
Open: 31 Mar–30 Sept. House: Sats, Suns & BH Mons, 2–5pm (last tour 4pm accompanied only). Group tours weekdays by appointment. Pre-booked specialist clock tours last Sat of month, Apr–Sept. Gardens: Daily 10am–6pm (or dusk if earlier).
Admission: House & Garden: Please check website for prices.
ℹ No photography in house. ⬛ 🎁 🍴 ♿ Partial. WC. ☕ 🎫 Obligatory.
🅿 Limited for coaches. 🐕 In grounds on leads. ✳

CHART GUNPOWDER MILLS

Chart Mills, Faversham, Kent ME13 7SE
Tel: 01795 534542 **E-mail:** ticfaversham@btconnect.com
Owner: Swale Borough Council **Contact:** Peter Garner
Oldest gunpowder mill in the world. Supplied gunpowder to Nelson for the Battle of Trafalgar, and Wellington at Waterloo.
Location: MAP 4:M3, OS Ref. TQ615 015. M2/J6. W of town centre, access from Stonebridge Way or South Road.
Open: Apr–Oct: Sat, Sun & BHs, 2–5pm, or by arrangement.
Admission: Free.
⬛ 🅿

CHARTWELL 🌿 *See page 107 for full page entry.*

CHIDDINGSTONE CASTLE 🏠 *See pages 108/109 for double page entry.*

COBHAM HALL 🏠 *See page 110 for full page entry.*

DANSON HOUSE *See page 111 for full page entry.*

THE HOME OF CHARLES DARWIN ⊞ *See page 112 for full page entry.*

South East – England

English Heritage Photo Library: Skyscan Balloon Photography

DEAL CASTLE ⌗

VICTORIA ROAD, DEAL, KENT CT14 7BA

www.english-heritage.org.uk/dealcastle

Tel: 01304 372762 **Venue hire and Hospitality:** 01304 209889

Owner: English Heritage **Contact:** Visitor Operations Team

Crouching low and menacing, the huge, rounded bastions of this austere fort, built by Henry VIII, once carried 119 guns. A fascinating castle to explore, with long, dark passages, battlements and a huge basement. The interactive displays and exhibition give an interesting insight into the castle's history.

Location: MAP 4:O3, OS Ref. TR378 522. SE of Deal town centre.

Open: 21 Mar–30 Sept: daily, 10am–6pm (5pm Sats).

Admission: Adult £4.20, Child £2.10, Conc. £3.40. Family £10.50. EH Members free. Group discount available.

ⓘ WCs. ◻ ⊤ Exclusive private & corporate hospitality. ⬠ Restricted. ◯ Ⓟ Coach parking on main road. ⬚ Guide dogs only.

DODDINGTON PLACE GARDENS 🏠

Doddington, Nr Sittingbourne, Kent ME9 0BB

Tel: 01795 886101

Owner: Mr & Mrs Richard Oldfield **Contact:** Mrs Richard Oldfield

10 acres of landscaped gardens in an area of outstanding natural beauty.

Location: MAP 4:L3, OS Ref. TQ944 575. 4m N from A20 at Lenham or 5m SW from A2 at Ospringe, W of Faversham.

Open: Easter Sun–end Sept: Suns 2–5pm, BH Mons, 11am–5pm.

Admission: Adult £4, Child £1. Groups (10+) £3.50.

DOVER CASTLE AND THE ⌗ SECRET WARTIME TUNNELS

See page 113 for full page entry.

DYMCHURCH MARTELLO TOWER ⌗

Dymchurch, Kent TN29 0TJ

Tel: 01304 211067 **www.english-heritage.org.uk/dymchurch**

Owner: English Heritage **Contact:** Dover Castle

Built as one of 74 such towers to counter the threat of invasion by Napoleon, Dymchurch is perhaps the best example in the country. Fully restored, you can climb to the roof which is dominated by an original 24-pounder gun complete with traversing carriage.

Location: MAP 4:M4, OS189, Ref. TR102 294. In Dymchurch, access from High Street.

Open: Aug BH & Heritage Open Days, 6–9 Sept.

Admission: Free.

⬚

EASTBRIDGE HOSPITAL OF ST THOMAS

25 High Street, Canterbury, Kent CT1 2BD

Tel: 01227 471688 **Fax:** 01227 781641 **E-mail:** info@eastbridgehospital.org.uk

www.eastbridgehospital.org.uk **Contact:** The Bursar

Medieval pilgrims' hospital with 12th century undercroft, refectory and chapel.

Location: MAP 4:N3, OS189, Ref. TR148 579. S side of Canterbury High Street.

Open: All year (except Good Fri, Christmas Day & Boxing Day): Mon–Sat, 10am–4.45pm. Includes Greyfriars Franciscan Chapel, House & Garden. Easter Mon–end Sept: Mon–Sat, 2–4pm.

Admission: Adult £1, Child 50p, Conc. 75p.

Squerryes Court

visit hudsons guide online

©NTPL/Jerry Harpur

EMMETTS GARDEN ❧

IDE HILL, SEVENOAKS, KENT TN14 6AY

www.nationaltrust.org.uk/emmetts

Tel: 01732 750367/868381 (Chartwell office)   **Info:** 01732 751509
E-mail: emmetts@nationaltrust.org.uk
Owner: The National Trust
Contact: The Property Manager (Chartwell & Emmetts Garden, Mapleton Road, Westerham, Kent TN16 1PS)

Influenced by William Robinson, this charming and informal garden was laid out in the late 19th century, with many exotic and rare trees and shrubs from across the world. Wonderful views across the Weald of Kent – with the highest treetop in Kent. There are glorious shows of daffodils, bluebells, azaleas and rhododendrons, then acers and cornus in autumn, also a rose garden and rock garden.

Location: MAP 19:G11, OS Ref. TQ477 524. 1½m N of Ide Hill off B2042. M25/J5, then 4m.
Open: 15 Mar–1 Jun: Tue–Sun; 4–29 Jun: Wed–Sun, 2 Jul–2 Nov: Wed, Sat & Sun. Open BH Mons.
Admission: Adult £5.90 (£8 with Quebec House), Child £1.50, Family £13.30, Group Adult £4.45. Gift Aid.

Steep in places. WC. Buggy from car park to garden entrance. P By arrangement. In grounds, on leads.

FINCHCOCKS

GOUDHURST, KENT TN17 1HH

www.finchcocks.co.uk

Tel: 01580 211702   **Fax:** 01580 211007   **E-mail:** katrina@finchcocks.co.uk
Owner: Mr Richard Burnett   **Contact:** Mrs Katrina Burnett

In 1970 Finchcocks was acquired by Richard Burnett, leading exponent of the early piano, and it now contains his magnificent collection of over one hundred historical keyboard instruments: chamber organs, harpsichords, virginals, spinets and early pianos. Around 40 of these are restored to full concert condition and are played whenever the house is open to the public. The house, with its high ceilings and oak panelling, provides the perfect setting for music performed on period instruments, and Finchcocks is now a music centre of international repute. Many musical events take place here.

There is a fascinating collection of pictures and prints, mainly on musical themes, and a special exhibition on the theme of the 18th century pleasure gardens, which includes costumes and tableaux.

Finchcocks is a fine Georgian baroque manor noted for its outstanding brickwork, with a dramatic front elevation attributed to Thomas Archer. The present house was built in 1725 for barrister Edward Bathurst. Despite having changed hands many times, it has undergone remarkably little alteration and retains most of its original features. The

beautiful grounds, with their extensive views over parkland and hop gardens, include the fully restored walled garden, which provides a dramatic setting for special events.
Location: MAP 4:K4, OS Ref. TQ701 366. 1m S of A262, 2m W of Goudhurst. 5m from Cranbrook, 10m from Tunbridge Wells, 45m from London (1½ hrs). Rail: Marden 6m (no taxi), Paddock Wood 8m (taxi), Tunbridge Wells 10m (taxi).
Open: Easter–30 Sept: Suns & BH Mons, plus Wed & Thurs in Aug, 2–6pm. Groups & indivduals: Apr–Dec, by appointment. Closed Jan–Mar.
Admission: Adult £9, Child £5, Student £6. Garden only: Adult £2.50, Child 50p. Group (25+): Charge dependent on numbers and programme.

Music events, conferences, seminars, promotions, archery, ballooning, filming, television. Instruments for hire. No videos in house, photography by permission only. Private and corporate entertaining, weddings. Limited. WC. Suitable for visually handicapped. Licensed. Picnics permitted in grounds. Musical tours/recitals. Tour time: 2½–4 hrs. P Pre-booked groups (25–100) welcome from Apr–Oct. Opportunity to play instruments. Can be linked to special projects & National Curriculum syllabus. Music a speciality.

South East – England

GOODNESTONE PARK GARDENS

Goodnestone Park, Nr Wingham, Canterbury, Kent CT3 1PL
Tel/Fax: 01304 840107   **E-mail:** fitzwalter@btinternet.com
www.goodnestoneparkgardens.co.uk
Owner/Contact: The Lady FitzWalter

The garden is approximately 14 acres, set in 18th century parkland. A new gravel garden was planted in 2003. There are many fine trees, a woodland area and a large walled garden with a collection of old-fashioned roses, clematis and herbaceous plants. Jane Austen was a frequent visitor, her brother Edward having married a daughter of the house.

Location: MAP 4:N3, OS Ref. TR254 544. 8m ESE of Canterbury, 1½m E of B2046, at S end of village. The B2046 runs from the A2 to Wingham, the gardens are signposted from this road.
Open: 17 Feb–16 Mar: Suns, 12 noon–5pm. 19 Mar–6 June, Wed–Fri, 11am–5pm. Sats & Suns, 12 noon–5pm. 8 Jun–3 Oct, Tue–Fri, 11am–5pm, Suns 12 noon–5pm.
Admission: Adult £4.50, Child (6–16yrs) £1 (under 6 Free), OAP £4, Student £2.80, Groups (20+): Adult £4. Guided garden tours: £6.

THE GRANGE

St Augustine's Road, Ramsgate, Kent CT11 9NY
Tel: 01628 825925   **E-mail:** bookings@landmarktrust.org.uk
www.landmarktrust.org.uk
Owner/Contact: The Landmark Trust

Augustus Pugin built this house in 1843–4 to live in with his family. It was at The Grange that Pugin produced the designs for the interiors of the House of Lords and the Mediaeval Court at the Great Exhibition but he reserved some of his finest and most characteristic flourishes for his own home. The Landmark Trust, a building preservation charity, has undertaken a major restoration of the building which is now available for holidays all year round. Full details of The Grange and 184 other historic and architecturally important buildings are featured in the Landmark Trust Handbook (£11.50 refundable against a booking).

Location: MAP 4:O2, OS Ref: TR3764
Open: Available for holidays for up to 8 people throughout the year. Parts of the ground floor will be open to the general public by appointment on Wednesday afternoons and there are 8 Open Days a year. Contact the Landmark Trust for full details.
Admission: Free on Wednesday afternoons & Open Days.

GREAT COMP GARDEN

COMP LANE, PLATT, BOROUGH GREEN, KENT TN15 8QS

www.greatcomp.co.uk

Tel: 01732 886154
Owner: Great Comp Charitable Trust   **Contact:** Mr W Dyson

A skilfully designed 7 acre garden surrounding a fine, early 17th century manor. A maze of winding paths leads visitors through areas of different character; romantic ruins and statuary, tranquil woodland, sweeping lawns and colourful, exotic borders. Magnolias and azaleas are very much a feature of the spring. Salvias, dahlias, cannas and heleniums add fiery colours throughout the summer and autumn months. An annual garden show is held in August.

Location: MAP 4:K3, OS Ref. TQ635 567. 2m E of Borough Green, B2016 off A20. First right at Comp crossroads. ½m on left.
Open: 1 Apr–31 Oct: daily, 11am–5pm.
Admission: Adult £4.50, Child £1. Groups (20+) £4. Annual ticket: Adult £13.50, OAP £9. Family (2+4) £25.

Teas daily. Guide dogs only.

©Bexley Heritage Trust/Jarrold Publishing

Danson House Salon

GROOMBRIDGE PLACE GARDENS
See page 114 for full page entry.

HALL PLACE & GARDENS
See page 115 for full page entry.

HEVER CASTLE & GARDENS
See page 116 for full page entry.

THE HISTORIC DOCKYARD, CHATHAM

Chatham, Kent ME4 4TZ
Infoline: 01634 823807 **E-mail:** info@chdt.org.uk
Owner/Contact: Chatham Historic Dockyard Trust
Costumed guides bring this spectacular maritime heritage site alive! Discover over 400 years of maritime history as you explore the most complete dockyard of the age of sail to survive anywhere in the world and meet our custumed guides around the site. A great place to visit with family and friends!
Location: MAP 4:K2, OS Ref. TQ759 690. Signposted from M2/J1,3&4. From M2/J1&4 follow A289 to the Medway Tunnel. From M2/J3 follow the signs to Chatham, A229 then A230 and A231 and the brown tourist signs.
Open: 9 Feb–26 Oct: daily, 10am–4pm until 30 March, 10am–6pm thereafter. Nov: Sat & Sun only, 10am–4pm.
Admission: Adult £12.50, Child (5–15yrs) £7.50, Conc £10. Family (2+2) £32.50, Additional family child £5. Tickets valid for 12 months, terms and conditions apply.

HOLE PARK GARDENS
ROLVENDEN, CRANBROOK, KENT TN17 4JA

www.holepark.com

Tel: 01580 241344 / 241386 **Fax:** 01580 241882 **E-mail:** info@holepark.com
Owner/Contact: Edward Barham
A 15 acre garden with all year round interest, set in beautiful parkland with fine views. Trees, lawns and extensive yew hedges precisely cut are a feature. Walled garden with mixed borders, pools and water garden. Natural garden with bulbs, azaleas, rhododendrons and flowering shrubs. Bluebell walk and autumn colours a speciality.
Location: MAP 4:L4, OS Ref. TQ830 325. 1m W of Rolvenden on B2086 Cranbrook road.
Open: Bluebell Spectacular daily from 13 Apr–11 May: 11am–6pm. 23 Mar–29 Jun, Suns: 26 Mar–end Oct, Weds & Thur: BH Mons: 24 Mar, 5 & 26 May. Autumn Suns: 5, 12, 19 & 26 Oct. 2–6pm and by arrangement. Guided group visits available.
Admission: Adult £5, Child 50p. Group visits with conducted tour of the gardens by the owner or head gardener a speciality. Please contact us for details.
🕭 Suns, BHs & by arrangement. 🔲🖻🎬🎭 By arrangement. 🅿🖼 Car park only. 🍽 13 Apr–11 May: Bluebell Spectacular, 5, 12 & 19 Oct: Meet the Gardener, 2.30 prompt.

IGHTHAM MOTE
See page 117 for full page entry.

KNOLE
See page 118 for full page entry.

LEEDS CASTLE
See page 119 for full page entry.

LESNES ABBEY

Abbey Road, Abbey Wood, London DA17 5DL
Tel: 01322 526574
Owner: Bexley Council   **Contact:** Lynda Weaver
The Abbey was founded in 1178 by Richard de Lucy as penance for his involvement in events leading to the murder of Thomas à Becket. Today only the ruins remain.
Location: MAP 19:G7, OS Ref. TQ479 788. In public park on S side of Abbey Road (B213), 500yds E of Abbey Wood Station, ¾m N of A206 Woolwich–Erith Road.
Open: Any reasonable time.
Admission: Free.

LULLINGSTONE CASTLE

Lullingstone, Eynsford, Kent DA4 0JA
Tel: 01322 862114 **Fax:** 01322 862115 **E-mail:** info@lullingstonecastle.co.uk
www.lullingstonecastle.co.uk
Owner/Contact: Guy Hart Dyke Esq
Fine State rooms, family portraits and armour in beautiful grounds. The 15th century gatehouse was one of the first ever to be made of bricks. This is also the site for the World Garden of Plants and for Lullingstone's Parish Church of St Botolph. Opening 14 May 08, a fascinating new light and sound exhibition and coffee bar.
Location: MAP 19:G9, OS Ref. TQ530 644. 1m S Eynsford W side of A225. 600yds S of Roman Villa.
Open: Apr–Sept: Fris & Sats, House 2–5pm, Gardens 12 noon–5pm; Suns & BHs, 2–6pm. Booked groups by arrangement. Closed Good Fri.
Admission: Adult £6, Child £3, OAP £5.50, Family £15, Groups (20+): £8 pp plus £40 for a dedicated guide (Weds & Thurs only).
ℹ No interior photography. 🔲🎭🖻 Partial. 🍽 Teas at visitor centre, 1km. 🎬 By arrangement. 🅿 Limited for coaches. 🦮 Guide dogs only.

© English Heritage Photo Library

LULLINGSTONE ROMAN VILLA
LULLINGSTONE LANE, EYNSFORD, KENT DA4 0JA

www.english-heritage.org.uk/lullingstone

Tel: 01322 863467
Owner: English Heritage   **Contact:** Visitor Operations Team
Recognised as one of the most exciting archaeological finds of the century, the villa has splendid mosaic floors and one of the earliest private Christian chapels. Take the inclusive audio tour and discover how the prosperous Romans lived, worked and entertained themselves. Opening 13 May: a fascinating new light and sound exhibition and coffee bar.
Location: MAP 19:G9, OS Ref. TQ529 651. ½m SW of Eynsford off A225, M25/J3. Follow A20 towards Brands Hatch. 600yds N of Castle.
Open: 21 Mar–30 Sept: daily, 10am–6pm. 1 Oct–30 Nov & 1 Feb–20 Mar 2009: daily, 10am–4pm. 1 Dec–31 Jan: Wed–Sun, 10am–4pm. Closed 24–26 Dec & 1 Jan.
Admission: Adult £5.50, Child £2.80, Conc. £4.40. EH Members Free. Group discount available.
🔲🖻 Ground floor & grounds. WC. 🍽🔲🖼🎭🍽

Hever Castle

MAISON DIEU

Ospringe, Faversham, Kent

Tel: 01795 534542 **www.english-heritage.org.uk/maisondieu**

Owner: English Heritage **Contact:** The Faversham Society

This forerunner of today's hospitals remains largely as it was in the 16th century with exposed beams and an overhanging upper storey. It now displays Roman artefacts from nearby sites.

Location: MAP 4:M3, OS Ref. TR002 608. In Ospringe on A2, ½m W of Faversham.

Open: 6 Apr–31 Oct: Sats, Suns & BHs, 2–5pm. Group visits at other times by appointment.

Admission: Adult £1, Child 50p, Conc. 80p. EH Members Free. Group discount available.

WCs.

MILTON CHANTRY

New Tavern Fort Gardens, Gravesend, Kent

Tel: 01474 321520 **www.english-heritage.org.uk/miltonchantry**

Owner: English Heritage **Contact:** Gravesham Borough Council

A small 14th-century building which housed the chapel of the leper hospital and the chantry of the de Valence and Montechais families and later became a tavern.

Location: MAP 4:K2, OS Ref.TQ653 743. In New Tavern Fort Gardens ¼m E of Gravesend off A226.

Open: 21 Mar–30 Sept: Sats, Suns & BHs, 12 noon–5pm. Open by appointment outside these hours.

Admission: Free.

MOUNT EPHRAIM GARDENS

Hernhill, Faversham, Kent ME13 9TX

Tel: 01227 751496 **Fax:** 01227 750940

www.mountephraimgardens.co.uk

Owner: Mr & Mrs E S Dawes & Mrs M N Dawes **Contact:** Mrs L Dawes

In these enchanting 10 acres, terraces of fragrant roses lead to a small lake and woodland area. A new grass maze, Japanese-style rock garden, arboretum and many beautiful mature trees are other highlights. Peaceful, unspoilt atmosphere set in Kentish orchards.

Location: MAP 4:M3, OS Ref.TR065 598. In Hernhill village, 1m from end of M2. Signed from A2 & A299.

Open: Mid-Apr–end Sept: Weds, Thurs, Sats, Suns & BH Mons only, 11am–6pm. Groups Mar–end Oct, by arrangement.

Admission: Adult £4.50, Child (3–16) £2.50. Groups: £4.

By arrangement.

NURSTEAD COURT

Nurstead Church Lane, Meopham, Nr Gravesend, Kent DA13 9AD

Tel: 01474 812368 (guided tours); 01474 812121 (weddings & functions)

Fax: 01474 815133 **E-mail:** info@nursteadcourt.co.uk **www.nursteadcourt.co.uk**

Owner/Contact: Mrs S Edmeades-Stearns

Nurstead Court is a Grade I listed manor house built in 1320 of timber-framed, crown-posted construction, set in extensive gardens and parkland. The additional front part of the house was built in 1825. Licensed weddings are now held in the house with receptions and other functions in the garden marquee.

Location: MAP 4:K2, OS Ref. TQ642 685. Nurstead Church Lane is just off the A227 N of Meopham, 3m from Gravesend.

Open: Sept: Wed & Thur & 1/2 Oct, 2–5pm. All year round by arrangement.

Admission: Adult £5, Child £2.50, OAP/Student £4. Group (max 54): £4.

Weddings & functions catered for. Licensed. WCs. By arrangement.
Limited for coaches. On leads, in grounds.

OLD SOAR MANOR

Plaxtol, Borough Green, Kent TN15 0QX

Tel: 01732 810378 **Info Line:** 01732 811145

Owner: The National Trust **Contact:** The Property Manager

A solar chamber over a barrel-vaulted undercroft is all that remains of a late 13th century knight's dwelling of c1290 which stood until the 18th century.

Location: MAP 4:K3, OS Ref.TQ619 541. 1m E of Plaxtol.

Open: 7 Apr–28 Sept: daily except Fri, including BHs & Good Fri, 10am–6pm.

Admission: Free.

OWLETTS

The Street, Cobham, Gravesend, Kent DA12 3AP

Tel: 01372 453401 **Fax:** 01372 452023 **E-mail:** owletts@nationaltrust.org.uk

Owner: The National Trust **Contact:** The Property Manager

Former home of the architect Sir Herbert Baker. Highlights include an impressive Carolean staircase, plasterwork ceiling and large kitchen garden.

Location: MAP 4:K2, OS Ref. TQ669 686. 1m south of A2 at west end of village. Limited car parking at property. Parking nearby in Cobham village.

Open: 27 Mar–25 Oct: Thur & Sat, 2–5.30pm

Admission: Adult £3, Child £1.50, Family £7.50. Not suitable for groups.

PENSHURST PLACE & GARDENS

See page 120 for full page entry.

QUEBEC HOUSE ✻
WESTERHAM, KENT TN16 1TD

Tel: 01732 868381 (Chartwell office) **E-mail:** quebechouse@nationaltrust.org.uk
Owner: The National Trust **Contact:** Chartwell Office

This Grade I listed gabled house is situated in the centre of the beautiful village of Westerham. Many features of significant architectural and historical interest reflect its 16th century origins as well as changes made in the 18th and 20th centuries.

Quebec House was the childhood home of General James Wolfe, and rooms contain family and military memorabilia, prints and portraits. The Tudor Coach House contains an exhibition about the Battle of Quebec (1759) and the part played there by Wolfe, who led the British forces to victory over the French.

Location: MAP 19:F10, OS Ref. TQ449 541. At E end of village, on N side of A25, facing junction with B2026, Edenbridge Road.
Open: 15 Mar–2 Nov: House; Wed–Fri, 1–4.30pm; Sat & Sun, 1–5pm. Garden & Exhibition; Wed–Sun, 12 noon–5pm.
Admission: Adult £4, Child £1.50, Family (2+3) £9.50. Group: Adult £3.10. Joint ticket with Emmetts Garden £8.
🔾 Partial. WC. Please telephone before visit. 🅵 By arrangement.

Belmont House

QUEX MUSEUM, HOUSE & GARDENS, THE POWELL-COTTON COLLECTION

Quex Park, Birchington, Kent CT7 0BH

Tel: 01843 842168 **E-mail:** enquiries@quexmuseum.org **www.quexmuseum.org**
Owner: Trustees of Quex Museum, House & Gardens **Contact:** Julia Walton, Director

World-class collections in a Regency/Victorian country residence. Walled gardens.
Location: MAP 4:N2, OS Ref. TR308 683. ½m from Birchington Church via Park Lane.
Open: Mid-March–end Oct, Sun–Thurs, 11am–5pm. Winter: Suns only, 1–3.30pm.
Admission: Summer: Adult £7, Child, OAP, Disabled & Carer £5, Student £4, Family (2+3) £18. Winter: Adult £5, Child, OAP, Disabled & Carer £4, Family (2+3) £14.

RECULVER TOWERS & ROMAN FORT ⌗

Reculver, Herne Bay, Kent CT6 6SS

Tel: 01227 740676 **www.english-heritage.org.uk/reculver**
Owner: English Heritage **Contact:** Reculver Country Park

This 12th-century landmark of twin towers has guided sailors into the Thames estuary for seven centuries. Includes walls of a Roman fort, which were erected nearly 2,000 years ago.
Location: MAP 4:N2, OS Ref. TR228 693. At Reculver 3m E of Herne Bay by the seashore.
Open: Any reasonable time. External viewing only.
Admission: Free.
ⓘ WCs. 🔾 Long slope up from car park. 🅿 🖼 Dogs on leads. ✳

For unique **Civil wedding** venues see our index at the end of the book.

David Winston, Period Piano Company

RESTORATION HOUSE 🏠
17–19 CROW LANE, ROCHESTER, KENT ME1 1RF

www.restorationhouse.co.uk

Tel: 01634 848520 **Fax:** 01634 880058
E-mail: robert.tucker@restorationhouse.co.uk
Owner: R Tucker & J Wilmot **Contact:** Robert Tucker
Unique survival of an ancient city mansion deriving its name from the stay of Charles II on the eve of The Restoration. Beautiful interiors with exceptional early paintwork related to decorative scheme 'run up' for Charles' visit. The house also inspired Dickens to situate 'Miss Havisham' here.
'Interiors of rare historical resonance and poetry', *Country Life*. Fine English furniture and pictures (Mytens, Kneller, Dahl, Reynolds and several Gainsboroughs). Charming interlinked walled gardens of ingenious plan in a classic English style. A private gem. 'There is no finer pre-Civil war town house in England than this' – Simon Jenkins, *The Times*.

Location: MAP 4:K2, OS Ref. TQ744 683. Historic centre of Rochester, off High Street, opposite the Vines Park.
Open: 29 May–26 Sept: Thurs & Fris, plus Sat 31 May, 10am–5pm.
Admission: Adult £5.50 (includes 24 page illustrated guidebook), Child £2.75, Conc £4.50. Booked group (8+) tours: £6.50pp.
ℹ️ No stiletto heels. No photography in house. 🖼️ Garden by appointment.
▪️ 1st, 2nd & 4th Thurs in month & other days by arrangement.
🎨 By arrangement. 🅿️ None. 🐕 Guide dogs only.

RICHBOROUGH ROMAN FORT ⌗
Richborough, Sandwich, Kent CT13 9JW
Tel: 01304 612013 www.english-heritage.org.uk/richborough
Owner: English Heritage **Contact:** Visitor Operations Team
This fort and township date back to the Roman landing in AD43. The fortified walls and the massive foundations of a triumphal arch which stood over 80 feet high still survive. The inclusive audio tour and the museum give an insight into life in Richborough's heyday as a busy township.
Location: MAP 4:O3, OS Ref. TR324 602. 1½m NW of Sandwich off A257.
Open: Fort: 21 Mar–30 Sept: daily, 10am–6pm. Amphitheatre: any reasonable time, access across grazed land from footpath, please telephone for details.
Admission: Gardens: Adult £4.20, Child £2.10, Conc. £3.40. Family £10.50. EH Members Free. Group discount available.
ℹ️ Museum. 🖼️ 🖼️ Ground floor. 🖼️ 🅿️ 🐕 Guide dogs only.

RIVERHILL HOUSE 🏠
Sevenoaks, Kent TN15 0RR
Tel: 01732 458802/452557 **Fax:** 01732 458802 **E-mail:** jane@riverhillgarden.co.uk
Owner: The Rogers Family **Contact:** Mrs Rogers
Small country house built in 1714.
Location: MAP 4:J3, OS Ref. TQ541 522. 2m S of Sevenoaks on E side of A225.
Open: Garden: Easter–22June: Suns & BH weekends, 11am–5pm.
House: Easter–22June, open only to pre-booked groups of adults (20+).
Admission: Adult £3, Child 50p. Pre-booked groups: £5.50.

ROCHESTER CASTLE ⌗
The Lodge, Rochester-upon-Medway, Medway ME1 1SX
Tel: 01634 402276 www.english-heritage.org.uk/rochester
Owner: English Heritage (Managed by Medway Council)
Contact: Visitor Operations Team
Built in the 11th century. The keep is over 100 feet high and with walls 12 feet thick. Straegically placed astride the London Road, guarding an important crossing of the River Medway, this mighty fortress has a complex history of destruction and re-building.
Location: MAP 4:K2, OS Ref. TQ741 686. By Rochester Bridge. Follow A2 E from M2/J1 & M25/J2.
Open: 21 Mar–31 Oct: daily, 10am–6pm. 1 Nov–31 Mar '09: daily, 10am–4pm. Last adm. 45 mins before closing. Closed 24–25 Dec & 1 Jan. Group discount available.
Admission: Adult £4, Child/Conc £3, Family £11. EH Members Free.
ℹ️ WCs. 🖼️ 🖼️ 🐕 ❄️ 🖼️

ROCHESTER CATHEDRAL
Garth House, The Precinct, Rochester, Kent ME1 1SX
Tel: 01634 401301 **Fax:** 01634 401410 www.rochestercathedral.org
E-mail: visitsofficer@rochestercathedraluk.org
Rochester Cathedral has been a place of Christian worship since its foundation in 604AD. The present building is a blend of Norman and gothic architecture with a fine crypt and Romanesque façade. The first real fresco in an English Cathedral for 800 years is on view to the public.
Location: MAP 4:K2, OS Ref. TQ742 686. Signed from M20/J6 & A2/M2/J3. Best access from M2/J3.
Open: All year: 8.30am–5pm. Visiting may be restricted during services.
Admission: Suggested donation. Adult £3. Guided groups: £4, please book on above number. For special out-of-season rates see website. Separate prices for schools.
🖼️ 🖼️ 🖼️ 🎨 By arrangement. 🐕 🖼️ ❄️

ROMAN PAINTED HOUSE
New Street, Dover, Kent CT17 9AJ
Tel: 01304 203279
Owner: Dover Roman Painted House Trust **Contact:** Mr B Philp
Discovered in 1970. Built around 200AD as a hotel for official travellers. Impressive wall paintings, central heating systems and the Roman fort wall built through the house.
Location: MAP 4:N4, OS Ref. TR318 414. Dover town centre. E of York St.
Open: Apr–Sept: 10am–5pm, except Mons. Suns 2–5pm.
Admission: Adult £2, Students £1.60, Child/OAP 80p.

ST AUGUSTINE'S ABBEY ⌘

Longport, Canterbury, Kent CT1 1TF
Tel: 01227 767345   **www.english-heritage.org.uk/staugustine**
Owner: English Heritage   **Contact:** Visitor Operations Team
The abbey, founded by St Augustine in 598, is part of a World Heritage Site. Take the free interactive audio tour which gives a fascinating insight into the abbey's history and visit the museum displaying artefacts uncovered during archaeological excavations of the site.
Location: MAP 4:N3, OS Ref. TR155 578. In Canterbury ½m E of Cathedral Close.
Open: 21 Mar–30 Jun: Wed–Sun, 10am–5pm. Jul & Aug: daily, 10am–6pm. 1 Sept–31 Mar '09: Suns, 11am–5pm. Mons for educational groups by request. Closed 24–26 Dec & 1 Jan.
Admission: Adult £4.20, Child £2.10, Conc. £3.40. Family £10.50. 15% discount for groups (11+). EH Members Free.
🔲 ♿ Grounds. 📷 Free. 🅿 Nearby. 🐕 Guide dogs only. ❋

ST JOHN'S COMMANDERY ⌘

Densole, Swingfield, Kent
Tel: 01304 211067   **www.english-heritage.org.uk/southeast**
Owner: English Heritage   **Contact:** Dover Castle
A medieval chapel built by the Knights Hospitallers. It has a moulded plaster ceiling and a remarkable timber roof and was converted into a farmhouse in the 16th century.
Location: MAP 4:N4, OS Ref. TR232 440. 2m NE of Densole on minor road off A260.
Open: Any reasonable time for exterior viewing. Internal viewing by appointment only, please telephone.
Admission: Free.
🐕 ❋

For **corporate hospitality** venues see our special index at the end of the book.

ST JOHN'S JERUSALEM 🌿

Sutton-at-Hone, Dartford, Kent DA4 9HQ
Tel: 01732 810378   **Fax:** 01732 811029   **E-mail:** stjohnsjerusalem@nationaltrust.org.uk
Owner: The National Trust   **Contact:** Property Manager
The site of a former Knights Hospitaller Commandery chapel. See the garden, moated by the River Darent, and look inside one of the rooms.
Location: MAP 4:J2, OS Ref. TQ557 701. 3m south of Dartford at Sutton-at-Hone, on east side of A225. Turn into entrance gate near Balmoral Road; parking at end of drive.
Open: 2 Apr–24 Sept: Weds, 2–6pm. 1–29 Oct: Weds, 2–4pm.
Admission: Adult £2, Child £1, Family £5.

©NTPL

Emmetts Garden

SCOTNEY CASTLE 🌿
LAMBERHURST, TUNBRIDGE WELLS, KENT TN3 8JN

www.nationaltrust.org.uk/scotneycastle

Tel: 01892 893868   **Fax:** 01892 890110   **E-mail:** scotneycastle@nationaltrust.org.uk
Owner: The National Trust   **Contact:** Property Manager
Scotney Castle was home to the Hussey family from the late 18th century. In 1835 Edward Hussey III commissioned eminent architect Anthony Salvin, to design a new country house in an Elizabethan style. The celebrated gardens, designed around the ruins of a 14th century moated castle, feature spectacular displays of rhododendrons, azaleas and kalmia in spring, wisteria and roses rambling over the ruins in summer and trees and ferns providing rich colour in autumn. There are fine walks through the estate, with its parkland, woodland and hop farm and wonderful vistas and views. The house is opening in stages over the next five years, with the ground floor currently open to visitors.

Location: MAP 4:K4, OS Ref. TQ688 353. Signed off A21 1m S of Lamberhurst village.
Open: Garden & Shop: 1–9 Mar, Sat & Sun & 12 Mar–2 Nov, Wed–Sun, 11am–5.30pm. Garden & House also open 8 Nov–20 Dec, Sat/Sun, 11am–4pm. BH Mons, 11am–5.30pm. House: 12 Mar–2 Nov; Wed–Sun, 11am–5pm. BH Mons, 11am–5pm.
***Admission:** Garden & House: Adult £8.80, Child £4.40, Family £22. Garden only: Adult £6.60, Child £4.40, Family £22. NT members free. *includes a voluntary donation but visitors can choose to pay the standard prices displayed at the property and on the website.
🔲 ❖ ♿ Grounds (but steep parts). 🍴 🚻 🅿 🐕 ❋ 🎧

South East – England

©NTPL/Eric Crichton

SISSINGHURST CASTLE GARDEN ✄
SISSINGHURST, CRANBROOK, KENT TN17 2AB

www.nationaltrust.org.uk/sissinghurst

Tel: 01580 710700   **Infoline:** 01580 710701
E-mail: sissinghurst@nationaltrust.org.uk
Owner: The National Trust   **Contact:** The Administrator
One of the world's most celebrated gardens, the creation of Vita Sackville-West and her husband Sir Harold Nicolson. Developed around the surviving parts of an Elizabethan mansion with a central red-brick prospect tower, a series of small, enclosed compartments, intimate in scale and romantic in atmosphere, provide outstanding design and colour throughout the season. The study, where Vita worked, and library are also open to visitors.
Location: MAP 4:L4, OS Ref. TQ807 383. 2m NE of Cranbrook, 1m E of Sissinghurst village (A262).
Open: 15 Mar–2 Nov: Fri–Tues, including BHs & Good Fri, 11am–6.30pm; Sat, Sun, BHs & Good Fri, 10am–6.30pm. Last admission 1 hour before closing or dusk if earlier.
*Admission: Adult £9, Child £4.40, Family (2+3) £22.50, Groups £7.80. NT members Free. *includes a voluntary donation but visitors can choose to pay the standard prices displayed at the property and on the website.
🄲 🄵 🄳 WCs. 🄿 🄸 Licensed. 🄿 Ample, £2 per car (NT Members free). Limited for coaches. 🄷 Grounds only, on leads. Guide dogs only in Garden.

©NTPL/David Sellham

SMALLHYTHE PLACE ✄
TENTERDEN, KENT TN30 7NG

www.nationaltrust.org.uk/smallhytheplace

Tel: 01580 762334   **Fax:** 01580 762334
E-mail: smallhytheplace@nationaltrust.org.uk
Owner: The National Trust   **Contact:** Assistant Property Manager
This early 16th century half-timbered house was home to Shakespearean actress Ellen Terry from 1899 to 1928. The house contains many personal and theatrical mementoes, including her lavish costumes. The grounds include the barn theatre and beautiful cottage garden. Many events take place in the grounds and the theatre.
Location: MAP 4:L4, OS Ref. TQ893 300. 2m S of Tenterden on E side of the Rye road B2082.
Open: 1–9 Mar: Sats & Suns. 15 Mar–26 Oct: daily except Thur & Fri (open Good Fri), 11am–5pm, last admission 4.30pm.
Admission: Adult £5.25, Child £2.60, Family £13. Group £4.40.
ℹ No photography in house. 🄸 🄳 Ground floor only. 🄿 Limited. 🄷 On leads, in grounds. 🄲

SOUTH FORELAND LIGHTHOUSE ✄
THE FRONT, ST MARGARET'S BAY, Nr DOVER CT15 6HP

www.nationaltrust.org.uk/southforeland

Tel: 01304 852463   **Fax:** 01304 215484
E-mail: southforeland@nationaltrust.org.uk
Owner: The National Trust   **Contact:** Volunteer Co-ordinator
Distinctive and historical Victorian Lighthouse at St Margaret's Bay, part of the White Cliffs of Dover. Built to guide ships safely past Goodwin Sands, the lighthouse has the second highest light (above sea level) in the UK. Marconi and Faraday both used this lighthouse for their experimental work.
Location: MAP 4:O3, OS138 Ref. TR359 433. 2m walk from White Cliffs car park, 1m walk from St Margaret's Village, short walk from bus stop Diamond route 15.
Open: 14 Mar–3 Apr, 25 Apr–22 May, 6 Jun–17 Jul, 12–29 Sept, Fri–Mon, 11am–5.30pm. 4–24 Apr, 23 May–5 Jun, 18 Jul–11 Sept, 17–27 Oct, daily, 11am–5.30pm.
Admission: Adult £4, Child £2, Family £10. NT Members free.
🄲 Limited range of souvenirs. 🄷 In grounds only. 🄲

SQUERRYES COURT 🏛   *See page 121 for full page entry.*

STONEACRE ✄

Otham, Maidstone, Kent ME15 8RS
Tel/Fax: 01622 862871
Owner: The National Trust   **Contact:** The Tenant
A late 15th century yeoman's house, with great hall and crownpost, surrounded by harmonious garden, orchard and meadow.
Location: MAP 4:L3, OS Ref. TQ800 535. In narrow lane at N end of Otham village, 3m SE of Maidstone, 1m S of A20.
Open: 22 Mar–4 Oct: Sats & BH Mons, 11am–6pm (last admission 5pm).
Admission: Adult £3.50, Child £1.50, Family (2+3) £8.50. Groups £3.

TEMPLE MANOR ⌗

Strood, Rochester, Kent
Tel: 01634 718743   www.english-heritage.org.uk/templemanor
Owner: English Heritage   **Contact:** Medway Council
The 13th-century manor house of the Knights Templar which mainly provided accommodation for members of the order travelling between London and the continent.
Location: MAP 4:K2, OS Ref. TQ733 685. In Strood (Rochester) off A228.
Open: 21 Mar–31 Oct: Sats & Suns, 11am–3pm. For group visits, please telephone 01634 402267.
Admission: Free.
🄳 Grounds only. 🄿 🄷

For rare and unusual plants visit the **plant sales** index at the end of the book.

TONBRIDGE CASTLE

Castle Street, Tonbridge, Kent TN9 1BG

Tel: 01732 770929   **www.tonbridgecastle.org**

Owner: Tonbridge & Malling Borough Council   **Contact:** The Administrator

Location: MAP 19:H11, OS Ref. TQ588 466. 300 yds NW of the Medway Bridge at town centre.

Open: All year: Mon–Sat, 9am–4pm. Suns & BHs, 10.30am–4pm.

Admission: Gatehouse – Adult £6, Child/Conc. £3.50. Family £17 (max 2 adults). Admission includes audio tour. Last tour 1 hour before closing.

🔲 ✳

TURKEY MILL

See page 122 for full page entry.

UPNOR CASTLE ♯

Upnor, Kent ME2 4XG

Tel: 01634 718742   **www.english-heritage.org.uk/upnorcastle**

Owner: English Heritage   **Contact:** Medway Council

Well preserved 16th-century gun fort built to protect Queen Elizabeth I's warships. However in 1667 it failed to prevent the Dutch Navy which stormed up the Medway destroying half the English fleet.

Location: MAP 4:K2, OS Ref. TQ759 706. At Upnor, on unclassified road off A228. 2 miles NE of Strood.

Open: 21 Mar–30 Sept: daily 10am–6pm. Oct: daily, 10am–4pm. Last adm. 45 mins before closing.

Admission: Adult £4.50, Child/Conc £3.50, Family £12.50. EH Members Free. Group discount available.

ℹ WCs. 🔲 Grounds only. ▣ 🔲 🔲 On leads in restricted areas.

For **special events** held throughout the year, see the index at the end of the book.

Lullingstone Roman Villa

WALMER CASTLE AND GARDENS ♯

WALMER, DEAL, KENT CT14 7LJ

www.english-heritage.org.uk/walmer

Tel: 01304 364288   **Venue Hire and Hospitality:** 01304 209889

Owner: English Heritage   **Contact:** Visitor Operations Team

A Tudor fort transformed into an elegant stately home. The residence of the Lords Warden of the Cinque Ports, who have included HM The Queen Mother, Sir Winston Churchill and the Duke of Wellington. Take the inclusive audio tour and see the Duke's rooms where he died over 150 years ago. Beautiful gardens including the Queen Mother's Garden, The Broadwalk with its famous yew tree hedge, Kitchen Garden and Moat Garden. Lunches and cream teas available in the delightful Lord Warden's tearooms.

Location: MAP 4:O3, OS Ref. TR378 501. S of Walmer on A258. M20/J13 or M2 to Deal.

Open: 21 Mar–30 Sept: daily, 10am–6pm. 1 Oct–31 Mar: daily, 10am–4pm. Closed 13 Jul when Lord Warden is in residence.

Admission: Adult £6.50, Child £3.30, Conc. £5.20, Family £16.30. 15% discount for groups (11+). English Heritage members free.

ℹ WCs. 🔲 ⊤ Private & corporate hire. 🔲 Grounds. ▣ 🔲 🅿 🔲 Guide dogs only. ⬚

WESTENHANGER CASTLE AND BARNS
STONE STREET, WESTENHANGER, HYTHE, KENT CT21 4HX

www.westenhangercastle.co.uk

Tel: 01227 738223   **Fax:** 01227 738278   **E-mail:** grahamforge@btinternet.com
Owner: G Forge Ltd   **Contact:** Graham Forge

Westenhanger Castle was once a magnificent residence of great importance owned by Henry VIII and Elizabeth I. What remains today are romantic ruins which tell the story of its illustrious past. The monument has undergone several phases of English Heritage-assisted restoration work and retains many features within the ruins of the curtain wall including Tudor fireplaces and a stunning dovecote with 420 nesting boxes. The medieval barn adjoins an earlier accommodation base court and was built extravagantly with a hammerbeam roof. It has four wagon porches and was built astride a tributary of the East Stour river.

Location: MAP 4:M4, OS Ref. TR123 372. Leave M20/J11 towards Hythe. Turn right to Westenhanger village and left before station.

Open: 20 May–16 Sept, Tuesdays, 10am–4pm. Guided history tour groups by arrangement.

Admission: Adult £4, Child under 12yrs £2. Guided tour groups £6.50. Volunteer Friends half price.

⊤ ⬡ ▣ Licensed. ⒦ Obligatory. ⊞ Limited for coaches. ▣ ▣ On leads, in grounds. ▲ ❄ ♥

WHITE CLIFFS OF DOVER ✿
UPPER ROAD, LANGDON CLIFFS, Nr DOVER CT16 1HJ

www.nationaltrust.org.uk/whitecliffs

Tel: 01304 202756   **Fax:** 01304 215484
E-mail: whitecliffs@nationaltrust.org.uk
Owner: The National Trust   **Contact:** Visitor Services Manager

The Gateway to the White Cliffs is a Visitor Centre, Gift Shop and Coffee Shop with spectacular views across the English Channel. New interpretation gives visitors the opportunity to find out more about the formation of the cliffs, the importance of chalk grassland and the military history of the property.

Location: MAP 4:O3, OS138 Ref. TR336 422. Follow White Cliffs brown signs from roundabout 1 m NE of Dover at junction of A2/A258.

Open: All week, 1 Mar–31 Oct, 10am–5pm. 1 Nov–28 Feb, 11am–4pm.

Admission: Cars £2.50, Motorcycles & Blue Badge holders £1.50, Motor homes £3, Coaches £5, Season ticket £25. NT Members free.

▣⬡ Visitor centre, toilets and car parks. ▣ ⊞ ▣ ❄ ♥

WILLESBOROUGH WINDMILL

Mill Lane, Willesborough, Ashford, Kent TN24 0QG
Tel: 01233 661866

130 year old smock mill. Civil Wedding Licence.

Location: MAP 4:M4, OS Ref. TR031 421. Off A292 close to M20/J10. At E end of Ashford.

Open: Apr–end Sept; Sats, Suns & BH Mons, also Weds in Jul & Aug, 2–5pm or dusk if earlier.

Admission: Adult £3, Conc. £1.50. Groups 10% reduction by arrangement only.

Restoration House

■ Owner
The Baring Family

■ Contact
Nigel Baring
Ardington House
Wantage
Oxfordshire OX12 8QA

Tel: 01235 821566
Fax: 01235 821151
E-mail: info@ardingtonhouse.com

■ Location
MAP 3:D1
OS Ref. SU432 883

12m S of Oxford,
12m N of Newbury,
2½ m E of Wantage.

■ Opening Times
1 August–14 September,
daily **excluding
weekends and BHs**,
11am–2pm,
last entry at 1pm.
Guided tours at 12.30pm.

■ Admission
House & Gardens
Adult   £5.00
Child   Free

ARDINGTON HOUSE

www.ardingtonhouse.com

Just a few miles south of Oxford stands the hauntingly beautiful Ardington House. Surrounded by well-kept lawns, terraced gardens, peaceful paddocks, parkland and its own romantic island this Baroque house is the private home of the Barings. You will find it in the attractive village of Ardington, close to the Ridgeway on the edge of the Berkshire Downs.

Built by the Strong brothers in 1720 with typical Georgian symmetry, the House is also famous for its Imperial Staircase. Leading from the Hall, the staircase is considered by experts to be one of the finest examples in Britain.

Away from the crowds and the hustle of the workplace Ardington House provides a private and secluded setting. The calm, exclusive use environment allows for weddings, offsite board meetings, conferences and workshops utilising the splendid gardens and grounds. There is a heated outdoor swimming pool, tennis court, croquet lawn and trout river. Close by is the ancient Ridgeway Path, a popular place for walking or mountain biking.

Ardington House is licensed to hold Civil wedding ceremonies. Receptions can range from drinks and intimate dining in the house, to a full dinner and dance reception using marquees in the grounds.

Poet Laureate Sir John Betjeman wrote of the homeliness and warmth of Ardington House, and the rooms have seen many special occasions and important visitors in the past with this tradition being continued. The astonishing mixture of history, warmth and style you'll find at Ardington truly does place it in a class of its own.

ℹ	Conferences, product launches, films, weddings.
⍭	Lunches and teas by arrangement for groups.
⚘	By members of the family.
P	Free.
🐕	Guide dogs only.

Conference/Function

ROOM	MAX CAPACITY
Imperial Hall	
Theatre Style	80
U shape	30
Cabaret	40
Oak Room	
Theatre Style	40
U shape	20
Cabaret	30
Music Room	
Theatre Style	40
U shape	20
Cabaret	30

Owner
The Duke of Marlborough

Contact
Operations Director
Blenheim Palace
Woodstock OX20 1PX

Tel: 08700 602080
Fax: 01993 810570
E-mail: operations@
blenheimpalace.com

Location
MAP 7:A11
OS Ref. SP441 161

From London, M40, A44
(1½ hrs), 8m NW of
Oxford. London 63m
Birmingham 54m.

Air: Heathrow 60m.
Birmingham 50m.

Coach: From London
(Victoria) to Oxford.

Rail: Oxford Station.

Bus: No.20 from Oxford
Station, Gloucester
Green & Cornmarket.

Opening Times

16 February–
2 November, daily.
5 November–
14 December, Wed–Sun.

Palace and Formal Gardens
10.30am–5.30pm
(last admission 4.45pm).

Park
9am–6pm or dusk
during autumn and
winter months.

Open daily except for
one day in June,
November or December.

BLENHEIM PALACE

www.blenheimpalace.com

The state rooms of Blenheim Palace hold many treasures, from world famous tapestries to furniture, paintings, porcelain, clocks and sculptures. An unusually large collection of family portraits by great masters graces the walls. These include Joshua Reynolds' painting of the 4th Duke and family, a John Singer Sargent of the 9th Duke and family including Consuelo Vanderbilt, and a huge Clostermann of John Churchill, the 1st Duke, with his family. The collection of Chippendale and Boulle furniture is 'second to none in a historic home'.

The Palace, home of the 11th Duke of Marlborough and birthplace of Sir Winston Churchill, was built for John Churchill, 1st Duke of Marlborough by Sir John Vanbrugh between 1705 and 1722.

The original gardens were designed by Queen Anne's gardener Henry Wise, with later alterations by Lancelot 'Capability' Brown which included the creation of Blenheim's most outstanding feature, the lake. The French architect, Archille Duchene created the Italian Garden and the beautiful Water Terraces. The newly restored Secret Garden lies to the east of the Palace.

The combination of house, gardens and park was recognised as uniquely important when Blenheim was listed as a World Heritage Site in 1987.

A state-of-the-art visitor experience, 'Blenheim Palace: The Untold Story' is open in the heart of the Palace. Dramatic moments from the last 300 years of history at Blenheim Palace, as seen through the eyes of the servants, are brought to life through animatronic figures and innovative film and projection technology, .

The Pleasure Gardens area, which can be reached by miniature train, includes the Marlborough Maze, the Butterfly House and Adventure Playground, making it a great area for young children.

The Long Library

Conference/Function

ROOM	SIZE	MAX CAPACITY
Orangery		230
Marlborough Room		60
Saloon	50' x 30'	80
Great Hall		150
with Great Hall & Library		450
Library	180' x 30'	320
Oudenarde Room		20
Ramillies Room		15
Malplaquet Room		12
Spencer Churchill Room		30

Admission
Season Tickets available.

Palace, Garden & Park

Main Season:
16–24 Feb &
21 Mar–2 Nov
Adult	£16.50
Child*	£10.00
Conc.	£13.50
Family (2+2)	£44.00

Groups (15+)
Adult	£12.00
Child*	£6.60
Conc.	£10.50

Low Season:
25 Feb–20 Mar,
5 Nov–14 Dec (except
Mons & Tues)
Adult	£13.90
Child*	£7.70
Conc.	£11.30
Family (2+2)	£37.00

Groups (15+)
Adult	£10.25
Child*	£5.90
Conc.	£9.25

Gardens & Park

Main Season:
16–24 Feb &
21 Mar–2 Nov
Adult	£9.50
Child*	£4.80
Conc.	£7.30
Family	£24.50

Groups (15+)
Adult	£6.70
Child*	£3.20
Conc.	£5.50

Low Season:
25 Feb–20 Mar,
5 Nov–14 Dec (except
Mons & Tues)
Adult	£7.50
Child*	£2.65
Conc.	£5.30
Family	£18.00

Groups (15+)
Adult	£5.35
Child*	£1.95
Conc.	£4.25

*(5–16yrs)

Private tours by
appointment only,
prices on request.

ℹ️ Filming, product launches, activity days. No photography in house.

🏪 Four shops.

🍽️ Corporate Hospitality includes weddings, receptions, dinners, meetings and corporate events.

♿ Car Park for disabled, adapted toilets, disabled lift into Palace.

☕ 3 cafés.

🍴 Group enquiries welcome (up to 150). Menus on request.

🚶 Guided tours except Sundays, BHs and extremely busy days.

🅿️ Unlimited for cars and coaches.

🎓 Sandford Award holder since 1982. Teacher pre-visits welcome.

🐕 Dogs on leads in Park. Registered assistance dogs only in house and garden.

🔔 ❄️ 🎭 Full programme.

BROUGHTON CASTLE

www.broughtoncastle.com

Broughton Castle is essentially a family home lived in by Lord and Lady Saye & Sele and their family.

The original medieval Manor House, of which much remains today, was built in about 1300 by Sir John de Broughton. It stands on an island site surrounded by a 3 acre moat. The Castle was greatly enlarged between 1550 and 1600, at which time it was embellished with magnificent plaster ceilings, splendid panelling and fine fireplaces.

In the 17th century William, 8th Lord Saye & Sele, played a leading role in national affairs. He opposed Charles I's efforts to rule without Parliament and Broughton became a secret meeting place for the King's opponents.

During the Civil War William raised a regiment and he and his four sons all fought at the nearby Battle of Edgehill. After the battle the Castle was besieged and captured.

Arms and armour from the Civil War and other periods are displayed in the Great Hall. Visitors may also see the gatehouse, gardens and park together with the nearby 14th century Church of St Mary, in which there are many family tombs, memorials and hatchments.

Gardens

The garden area consists of mixed herbaceous and shrub borders containing many old roses. In addition, there is a formal walled garden with beds of roses surrounded by box hedging and lined by more mixed borders.

Owner
Lord Saye & Sele

Contact
Mrs J Hummer
Broughton Castle
Broughton
Nr Banbury
Oxfordshire OX15 5EB
Tel: 01295 276070
E-mail: info@broughton
castle.com

Location
MAP 7:A10
OS Ref. SP418 382

Broughton Castle is 2½m SW of Banbury Cross on the B4035, Shipston-on-Stour – Banbury Road. Easily accessible from Stratford-on-Avon, Warwick, Oxford, Burford and the Cotswolds. M40/J11.

Rail: From London/ Birmingham to Banbury.

Opening Times
Summer
Easter Sun & Mon,
1 May–15 September
Weds, Suns & BH Mons,
2–5pm.

Also Thurs in July and August, 2–5pm.

Groups welcome by appointment throughout the year.

Admission
Adult	£6.50
Child (5–15yrs)	£2.50
OAP/Student	£5.50

Groups (15–100)
Adult	£5.50
Child (5–15yrs)	£2.50
OAP/Student	£5.50

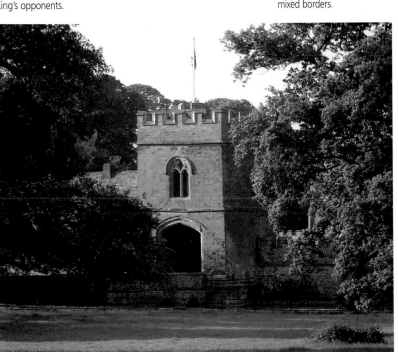

- Photography allowed in house.
- Partial.
- Teas on Open Days. Groups may book morning coffee, light lunches and afternoon teas.
- Available for booked groups.
- Limited.
- Guide dogs only in house. On leads in grounds.
- Open all year for groups.

STONOR 🏛

www.stonor.com

Stonor is one of the very few houses in England that has remained in the same family from the earliest records to the present day and has been home to The Lord and Lady Camoys and the Stonor family for 850 years. The history of the house inevitably contributes to the atmosphere, at once unpretentious yet grand. A façade of warm brick with Georgian windows conceals much older buildings dating back to the 12th Century and a 14th Century Catholic Chapel sits on the south east corner. Stonor nestles in a fold of the beautiful wooded Chiltern Hills and has breathtaking views of the surrounding park where Fallow deer have grazed since medieval times.

It contains many family portraits, old Master drawings and paintings, Renaissance bronzes and tapestries, along with rare furniture and a collection of modern ceramics.

St Edmund Campion sought refuge at Stonor during the Reformation and printed his famous pamphlet 'Ten Reasons' here, in secret, on a press installed in the roof space. A small exhibition celebrates his life and work.

Mass has been celebrated since medieval times in the Chapel and is sited close by a pagan stone prayer circle. The painted and stained glass windows were executed by Francis Eginton, and installed in 1797. The Chapel decoration is that of the earliest Gothic Revival, begun in 1759, with additions in 1797. The Stations of the Cross seen in the lobby, were carved by Jozef Janas, a Polish prisoner of war in World War II and given to Stonor by Graham Greene in 1956.

The gardens offer outstanding views of the Park and valley and are especially beautiful in May and June, containing fine displays of daffodils, irises, peonies, lavenders and roses along with other herbaceous plants and shrubs.

No photography in house.

Unsuitable for physically disabled.

Licensed.

For 20–60.

100yds away.

In Park on leads.

See website or telephone for details.

26A EAST ST HELEN STREET

Abingdon, Oxfordshire
Tel: 01865 242918 **E-mail:** info@oxfordpreservation.org.uk
www.oxfordpreservation.org.uk
Owner: Oxford Preservation Trust   **Contact:** Mrs Debbie Dance

One of best preserved examples of a 15th century dwelling in the area. Originally a Merchant's Hall House with later alterations, features include a remarkable domestic wall painting, an early oak ceiling, traceried windows and fireplaces.
Location: MAP 7:A12, OS Ref. SU497 969. 300 yards SSW of the market place and Town Hall.
Open: By prior appointment.
Admission: Free.

ARDINGTON HOUSE 🏠

See page 135 for full page entry.

ASHDOWN HOUSE ❦

Lambourn, Newbury RG17 8RE
Tel: 01793 762209   **E-mail:** ashdownhouse@nationaltrust.org.uk
www.nationaltrust.org.uk
Owner: The National Trust   **Contact:** Coleshill Estate Office
Location: MAP 3:C1, OS Ref. SU282 820. 3½m N of Lambourn, on W side of B4000.
Open: House & Garden: 2 Apr–29 Oct: Wed & Sat, 2–5pm. Admission by guided tour at 2.15, 3.15 & 4.15pm. Woodland: All year: daily except Fri, daylight hours.
Admission: House & garden: Adult £2.60, Child £1.30. Free to NT members. Woodland: Free.

BLENHEIM PALACE 🏠

See page 136 for full page entry.

BROOK COTTAGE

Well Lane, Alkerton, Nr Banbury OX15 6NL
Tel: 01295 670303/670590   **Fax:** 01295 730362
Owner/Contact: Mrs David Hodges
4 acre hillside garden. Roses, clematis, water gardens, colour co-ordinated borders, trees, shrubs.
Location: MAP 7:A10, OS Ref. SP378 428. 6m NW of Banbury, ½m off A422 Banbury to Stratford-upon-Avon road.
Open: Easter Mon–end Oct: Mon–Fri, 9am–6pm. Evenings, weekends and all group visits by appointment.
Admission: Adult £5, OAP £4, Child Free.

BROUGHTON CASTLE 🏠

See page 137 for full page entry.

BUSCOT OLD PARSONAGE ❦

Buscot, Faringdon, Oxfordshire SN7 8DQ
Tel: 01793 762209   **E-mail:** buscot@nationaltrust.org.uk
Owner: The National Trust   **Contact:** Coleshill Estate Office
An early 18th century house of Cotswold stone on the bank of the Thames with a small garden.
Location: MAP 6:P12, OS Ref. SU231 973. 2m from Lechlade, 4m N of Faringdon on A417.
Open: 2 Apr–29 Oct, Weds, 2–6pm by written appointment with tenant.
Admission: Adult £1.60, Child 80p, Family £4. Not suitable for groups. Free to NT members.
ℹ No WCs. ♿ Partial.

©NTPL/Thames and Chiltern

Part of the Harold Peto Water Garden

BUSCOT PARK ❦
BUSCOT, FARINGDON, OXFORDSHIRE SN7 8BU

www.buscotpark.com

Tel: Infoline 0845 345 3387 / Office 01367 240786   **Fax:** 01367 241794
E-mail: estbuscot@aol.com
Owner: The National Trust (Administered on their behalf by Lord Faringdon)
Contact: The Estate Office

The 18th century Palladian house contains the Faringdon Collection of fine paintings (including works by Murillo, Reynolds, Rossetti and the famous Briar Rose series by Burne-Jones) and furniture, with important pieces by Adam, Thomas Hope and others. The House is set in parkland, offering peaceful walks through water gardens and a well-stocked walled garden. A tearoom serves delicious home-made cream teas and cakes, and there is ample free parking.

Location: MAP 6:P12, OS Ref. SU239 973. Between Faringdon and Lechlade on A417.
Open: 21 Mar–30 Sep: Wed–Fri, 2–6pm (last entry to house 5pm). Also open BH Mons & Good Fri and weekends 22/23 Mar, 5/6 & 19/20 April, 3/4, 10/11 & 24/25 May; 14/15 & 28/29 Jun; 12/13 & 26/27 Jul; 9/10 & 23/24 Aug; 13/14 & 27/28 Sept. Grounds only: 21 Mar–30 Sept: Mon & Tue, 2–6pm. Tearoom: as House, 2.30–5.30pm.
Admission: House & Grounds: Adult £7.50, Child £3.75. Grounds only: Adult £5, Child £2.50. NT members Free. Groups must book in writing, or by fax or E-mail. Disabled visitors should book powered mobility vehicle in advance.
ℹ No photography in house. 🎭 Fully equipped theatre. ♿ Partial, tel for details.
🍴 BBQ lunches for groups by arrangement. 🅿 Ample for cars, 2 coach spaces.
🐕 May be exercised in overflow car park only.

CHASTLETON HOUSE

Chastleton, nr Moreton-in-Marsh, Oxfordshire GL56 0SU
Tel/Fax: 01608 674355 **Infoline:** 01494 755560
E-mail: chastleton@nationaltrust.org.uk
Owner: The National Trust **Contact:** The Custodian
One of England's finest and most complete Jacobean houses, dating from 1607. It is filled with a mixture of rare and everyday objects and the atmosphere of four hundred years of continuous occupation by one family. The gardens have a Jacobean layout and the rules of modern croquet were codified here.
Location: MAP 6:P10, OS Ref. SP248 291. 6m ENE of Stow-on-the-Wold. 1½ miles NW of A436. Approach only from A436 between the A44 (W of Chipping Norton) and Stow.
Open: 19 Mar–27 Sept: Wed–Sat, 1–5pm, last admission 4pm. 1 Oct–1 Nov: Wed–Sat, 1–4pm, last admission 3pm. Admission for all visitors (including NT members) by timed tickets booked in advance. Advanced bookings can be made until the day before your visit. Telephone 01608 674981.
Admission: Adult £7, Child £3.50, Family £17.50. Free to NT members.
Partial. **P** Coaches limited to 25 seat minibuses. Guide dogs only.

CHRIST CHURCH CATHEDRAL

The Sacristy, The Cathedral, Oxford OX1 1DP
Tel: 01865 276154
Contact: Tony Fox
12th century Norman Church, formerly an Augustinian monastery, given Cathedral status in 16th century by Henry VIII. Private tours available.
Location: MAP 7:A12, OS Ref. SP515 059. Just S of city centre, off St Aldates. Entry via Meadow Gate visitors' entrance on S side of college.
Open: Mon–Sat: 9am–5pm. Suns: 1–5pm (last entry 4.30pm) closed Christmas Day. Services: weekdays 7.20am, 6pm. Suns: 8am, 10am, 11.15am & 6pm. Areas of the college (especially the Great Hall & Cathedral) are closed at various times during the year. Please telephone to check before visit.
Admission: Adult £4.90, Child under 5 Free, Conc. £3.90, Family £9.80.

DEDDINGTON CASTLE

Deddington, Oxfordshire
Tel: 01424 775705 **www.english-heritage.org.uk/deddington**
Owner: English Heritage, managed by Deddington Parish Council
Contact: 1066 Battle Abbey
Extensive earthworks concealing the remains of a 12th century castle which was ruined as early as the 14th century.
Location: MAP 7:A10, OS Ref. SP472 316. S of B4031 on E side of Deddington, 17 miles N of Oxford on A423. 5 miles S of Banbury.
Open: Any reasonable time.
Admission: Free.
On leads.

DITCHLEY PARK

Enstone, Oxfordshire OX7 4ER
Tel: 01608 677346 **www.ditchley.co.uk**
Owner: Ditchley Foundation **Contact:** Brigadier Christopher Galloway
The most important house by James Gibbs, with magnificent interiors by William Kent and Henry Flitcroft. For three centuries the home of the Lee family, restored in the 1930s by Ronald and Nancy (Lancaster) Tree, it was frequently used at weekends by Sir Winston Churchill during World War II.
Location: MAP 7:A11, OS Ref. SP391 214. 2m NE from Charlbury. 13 miles NW of Oxford – 4 miles on from Woodstock (Blenheim Palace).
Open: Visits only by prior arrangement with the Bursar, weekdays preferred.
Admission: £6 per person (minimum charge £50).

Chastleton House

GREAT COXWELL BARN

Great Coxwell, Faringdon, Oxfordshire
Tel: 01793 762209 **E-mail:** greatcoxwellbarn@nationaltrust.org.uk
Owner: The National Trust **Contact:** Coleshill Estate Office
A 13th century monastic barn, stone built with stone tiled roof, which has an interesting timber construction.
Location: MAP 3:C1, OS Ref. SU269 940. 2m SW of Faringdon between A420 and B4019.
Open: All year: daily at reasonable hours.
Admission: £1.50. Free to NT members.

GREYS COURT

ROTHERFIELD GREYS, HENLEY-ON-THAMES, OXFORDSHIRE RG9 4PG
Infoline: 01494 755564 **Tel:** 01491 628529
E-mail: greyscourt@nationaltrust.org.uk
Owner: The National Trust **Contact:** The Custodian
Set amidst a series of walled gardens, in the remains of the courtyard walls and towers of a 14th century fortified house, discover the tranquility of Greys Court. A Tudor donkey wheel, well-house and an ice house are still intact, and the garden contains Archbishop's Maze, inspired by Archbishop Runcie's enthronement speech in 1980.
Location: MAP 3:E1, OS Ref. SU725 834. 3m W of Henley-on-Thames, E of B481.
Open: House closed for conservation, re-opening in April 2009. Garden & Tearoom: 22 Mar–27 Sept, Tue–Sat, 12 noon–5pm. Open BH Mons but closed Good Fri.
Admission: Garden only: £4.50, Child £2.25, Family £11.25. Coach parties must book in advance. Free to NT members.
Grounds partial. WCs. In car park only, on leads. Contact Custodian.

RICHARD JEFFERIES FARMHOUSE AND MUSEUM

Marlborough Road, Coate SN3 6AA
Tel: 01793 783040 **E-mail:** R.Jefferies_Society@tiscali.co.uk
Owner: Swindon Borough Council
Dating from the early 18th century, the Museum was the home of Richard Jefferies, nature writer, who is cited by historians as an authority upon agriculture and rural life in Victorian England. The main house is a Grade II listed building.
Location: Adjacent to the Sun Inn on Marlborough Road A4259 close to Coate Water Country Park.
Open: 1st and 3rd Sundays from May to end Sept 2–5pm. 2nd Wed throughout the year. 10am–4pm. Open at other times by request.
Admission: Free

KINGSTON BAGPUIZE HOUSE 🏛
ABINGDON, OXFORDSHIRE OX13 5AX
www.kingstonbagpuizehouse.org.uk

Tel: 01865 820259 **Fax:** 01865 821659 **E-mail:** virginiagrant@btinternet.com
Owner/Contact: Mrs Francis Grant

A family home, this beautiful house originally built in the 1660s was remodelled in the early 1700s in red brick with stone facings. It has a cantilevered staircase and panelled rooms with some good furniture and pictures. Set in mature parkland, the gardens, including shrub border and woodland garden, contain a notable collection of trees, shrubs, perennials and bulbs including snowdrops, planted for year round interest. A raised terrace walk leads to an 18th century panelled gazebo with views of the house and gardens, including a large herbaceous border and parkland. Licensed for Civil wedding ceremonies. Venue also available for wedding receptions, special events, corporate functions, product launches and filming. Facilities for small conferences.

Location: MAP 7:A12, OS Ref. SU408 981. In Kingston Bagpuize village, off A415 Abingdon to Witney road S of A415/A420 intersection. Abingdon 5m, Oxford 9m.

Open: House & Garden: 3, 10, 17, 24 Feb; 2, 16, 23/24 Mar; 6, 20 Apr; 4/5, 18, 25/26 May; 1/2, 15/16 Jun; 6/7, 20/21, Jul; 3/4, 17/18, 24/25 Aug; 7, 21 Sept. Gates open 2pm and close at 5.30pm. Last admission to house 3.50pm

Admission: House & Garden: Adult £5, Child (5–15) £2.50, (admission to house not recommended for children under 5yrs), Conc. £4.50. Gardens: £3 (child under 16yrs Free). Groups (20–80) by appointment throughout the year, prices on request.

ℹ️ No photography in house. Grounds. WC. Home-made cakes. Light meals for groups by appointment. P Obligatory

MAPLEDURHAM HOUSE & WATERMILL
MAPLEDURHAM, READING RG4 7TR
www.mapledurham.co.uk

Tel: 01189 723350 **Fax:** 01189 724016 **E-mail:** enquiries@mapledurham.co.uk
Owner: The Mapledurham Trust **Contact:** Mrs Lola Andrews

Late 16th century Elizabethan home of the Blount family. Original plaster ceilings, great oak staircase, fine collection of paintings and a private chapel in Strawberry Hill Gothick added in 1797. Interesting literary connections with Alexander Pope, Galsworthy's *Forsyte Saga* and Kenneth Grahame's *Wind in the Willows*. 15th century watermill fully restored producing flour and bran which is sold in the giftshop.

Location: MAP 3:E3, OS Ref. SU670 767. N of River Thames. 4m NW of Reading, 1½ m W of A4074.

Open: Easter–Sept: Sats, Suns & BHs, 2–5.30pm. Last admission 5pm. Midweek parties by arrangement only. Mapledurham Trust reserves the right to alter or amend opening times or prices without prior notification.

Admission: Please call 01189 723350 for details.

Grounds. WCs. P Guide dogs only. 10 holiday cottages (all year).

MILTON MANOR HOUSE
MILTON, ABINGDON, OXFORDSHIRE OX14 4EN

Tel: 01235 831287 **Fax:** 01235 862321
Owner: Anthony Mockler-Barrett Esq **Contact:** Alex Brakespear

Dreamily beautiful mellow brick house, traditionally designed by Inigo Jones. Celebrated Gothic library and Catholic chapel. Lived in by the family; pleasant relaxed and informal atmosphere. Park with fine old trees, stables, walled garden and woodland walk. Picnickers welcome.

Location: MAP 3:D1, OS Ref. SU485 924. Just off A34, village and house signposted, 9m S of Oxford, 15m N of Newbury. 3m from Abingdon and Didcot.

Open: Easter Sun & BH Mon, 4 May & BH Mon; then 25 May–10 June & 17–31 Aug. Guided tours of house: 2pm, 3pm & 4pm. For weddings/events etc. please write to the Administrator. Groups by arrangement throughout the year.

Admission: House & Gardens: Adult £8, Child £4. Garden & Grounds only: Adult £4, Child £2. Family tickets available for multiple visits throughout season. Garden & Grounds only (2+2): £40.

Grounds. Obligatory. P Free. Guide dogs only.

MINSTER LOVELL HALL & DOVECOTE ⚏

Witney, Oxfordshire
Tel: 01424 775705   www.english-heritage.org.uk/minsterlovell
Owner: English Heritage   **Contact:** 1066 Battle Abbey
The ruins of Lord Lovell's 15th century manor house stand in a lovely setting on the banks of the River Windrush.
Location: MAP 6:P11, OS Ref. SP325 113. Adjacent to Minster Lovell Church, ½mile NE of village. 3 miles W of Witney off A40.
Open: Any reasonable time. Dovecote – exterior only.
Admission: Free.
🐕 On leads. ✳

PRIORY COTTAGES ⚘

1 Mill Street, Steventon, Abingdon, Oxfordshire OX13 6SP
Tel: 01793 762209
Owner: The National Trust   **Contact:** Coleshill Estate Office
Former monastic buildings, converted into two houses. South Cottage contains the Great Hall of the original priory.
Location: MAP 3:D1, OS Ref. SU466 914. 4m S of Abingdon, on B4017 off A34 at Abingdon West or Milton interchange on corner of The Causeway and Mill Street, entrance in Mill Street.
Open: The Great Hall in South Cottage only: 4 Apr–26 Sept: Wed, 2–6pm, by written appointment with the tenant.
Admission: Adult £1.60, Child 80p, Family £4. Free to NT members.

ROUSHAM HOUSE
Nr STEEPLE ASTON, BICESTER, OXFORDSHIRE OX25 4QX
www.rousham.org

Tel: 01869 347110 / 07860 360407 **E-mail:** ccd@rousham.org
Owner/Contact: Charles Cottrell-Dormer Esq
Rousham represents the first stage of English landscape design and remains almost as William Kent (1685–1748) left it. One of the few gardens of this date to have escaped alteration. Includes Venus' Vale, Townesend's Building, seven-arched Praeneste, the Temple of the Mill and a sham ruin known as the 'Eyecatcher'. The house was built in 1635 by Sir Robert Dormer. Excellent location for fashion, advertising, photography etc.

Location: MAP 7:A10, OS Ref. SP477 242. E of A4260, 12m N of Oxford, S of B4030, 7m W of Bicester.
Open: Garden: All year: daily, 10am–4.30pm (last adm). House: Pre-booked groups, May–Sept.
Admission: Garden: £4. House: £4. No children under 15yrs.
♿ Partial. 🅿 🐕 ✳

RYCOTE CHAPEL ⚏

Rycote, Oxfordshire OX9 2PE
Tel: 01844 210210   www.english-heritage.org.uk/rycotechapel
Owner: English Heritage   **Contact:** Mr Taylor - Rycote Building Charitable Foundation
A 15th century chapel with exquisitely carved and painted woodwork. It has many intriguing features, including two roofed pews and a musicians' gallery.
Location: MAP 7:B12, OS165 Ref. SP667 046. 3 miles SW of Thame, off A329. 1½ miles NE of M40/J7.
Open: 21 Mar–30 Sept: Fri–Sun, 2–6pm. Times may change at short notice, please telephone for details.
Admission: Adult £3.50, Child £1.50, Conc. £2.50. Subject to change. (2007 prices.) EH Members Free.
🅿 🐕

STONOR 🏛
See page 138 for full page entry.

SWALCLIFFE BARN

Swalcliffe Village, Banbury, Oxfordshire
Tel: 01295 788278   **Contact:** Jeffrey Demmar
15th century half cruck barn, houses agricultural and trade vehicles which are part of the Oxford County Museum Services Collection. Exhibition of 2500 years' of Swalcliffe history.
Location: MAP 7:A10, OS Ref. SP378 378. 6m W of Banbury Cross on B4035.
Open: Easter–end Oct: Suns & BHs, 2–5pm.
Admission: Free.

THE COLLEGES OF OXFORD UNIVERSITY

For further details contact:
Oxford Information Centre,
15–16 Broad Street, Oxford OX1 3AS
Tel: +44 (0)1865 726871
Email: tic@oxford.gov.uk
Fax: +44 (0)1865 240261
www.visitoxford.org

All Souls' College
High Street
Tel: 01865 279379
Founder: Archbishop Henry Chichele 1438
Open: Mon–Fri, 2–4pm
            (4.30pm in summer)

Balliol College
Broad Street
Tel: 01865 277777
Founder: John de Balliol 1263
Open: Daily, 1–5pm (or dusk)

Brasenose College
Radcliffe Square
Tel: 01865 277830
Founder: William Smythe,
            Bishop of Lincoln 1509
Open: Daily, 10–11.30am (tour groups
            only) & 2–4.30pm
            (5pm in summer)

Christ Church
St. Aldates
Tel: 01865 286573
Founder: Cardinal Wolsey/Henry VIII 1546
Open: Mon–Sat, 9am–5.30pm;
            Sun, 1–5.30pm (last adm 1.30pm)

Corpus Christi College
Merton Street
Tel: 01865 276700
Founder: Bishop Richard Fox 1517
Open: Daily, 1.30–4.30pm

Exeter College
Turl Street
Tel: 01865 279600
Founder: Bishop Stapleden of Exeter 1314
Open: Daily, 2–5pm

Green College
Woodstock Road
Tel: 01865 274770
Founder: Dr Cecil Green 1979
Open: By appointment only

Harris Manchester College
Mansfield Road
Tel: 01865 271011
Founder: Lord Harris of Peckham 1996
Open: Chapel only: Mon–Fri,
            8.30am–5.30pm.
            Sat, 9am–12 noon

Hertford College
Catte Street
Tel: 01865 279400
Founder: TC Baring MP 1740
Open: Daily, 10am–noon & 2pm–dusk

Jesus College
Turl Street
Tel: 01865 279700
Founder: Dr Hugh Price
            (Queen Elizabeth I) 1571
Open: Daily, 2–4.30pm

Keble College
Parks Road
Tel: 01865 272727
Founder: Public money 1870
Open: Daily, 2–5pm

Kellogg College
Banbury Road
Tel: 01865 61200
Founder: Kellogg Foundation 1990
Open: Mon–Fri, 9am–5pm

Lady Margaret Hall
Norham Gardens
Tel: 01865 274300
Founder: Dame Elizabeth Wordsworth 1878
Open: Gardens: 10am–5pm

Linacre College
St Cross Road
Tel: 01865 271650
Founder: Oxford University 1962
Open: By appointment only

Lincoln College
Turl Street
Tel: 01865 279800
Founder: Bishop Richard Fleming
            of Lincoln 1427
Open: Mon–Sat, 2–5pm; Sun, 11am–5pm

Magdalen College
High Street
Tel: 01865 276000
Founder: William of Waynefleete 1458
Open: Oct–Jun: 1–6pm/dusk (whichever
            is the earlier) and Jul–Sept:
            12 noon–6pm

Mansfield College
Mansfield Road
Tel: 01865 270999
Founder: Free Churches 1995
Open: Mon–Fri, 9am–5pm

Merton College
Merton Street
Tel: 01865 276310
Founder: Walter de Merton 1264
Open: Mon–Fri, 2–4pm; Sat & Sun,
            10am–4pm

New College
New College Lane
Tel: 01865 279555
Founder: William of Wykeham,
            Bishop of Winchester 1379
Open: Daily, 11am–5pm (summer);
            2–4pm (winter)

Nuffield College
New Road
Tel: 01865 278500
Founder: William Morris
            (Lord Nuffield) 1937
Open: Daily, 9am–5pm

Oriel College
Oriel Square
Tel: 01865 276555
Founder: Edward II/Adam de Brome 1326
Open: By arrangement with TIC

Pembroke College
St Aldates
Tel: 01865 276444
Founder: James I 1624
Open: By appointment only

The Queen's College
High Street
Tel: 01865 279120
Founder: Robert de Eglesfield 1341
Open: By arrangement with TIC

Somerville College
Graduate House, Woodstock Road
Tel: 01865 270600
Founder: Association for the Education of
            Women 1879
Open: 2–5.30pm

St. Anne's College
56 Woodstock Road
Tel: 01865 274800
Founder: Association for the Education
            of Women 1878
Open: 9am–5pm

St. Antony's College
62 Woodstock Road
Tel: 01865 284700
Founder: M. Antonin Bess 1948
Open: By appointment only

St. Catherine's College
Manor Road
Tel: 01865 271700
Founder: Oxford University 1964
Open: 9am–5pm

St. Edmund Hall
Queens Lane
Tel: 01865 279000
Founder: St. Edmund Riche of
            Abingdon c.1278
Open: Mon–Sun, Term time,
            12 noon–4pm

St. Hilda's College
Cowley Place
Tel: 01865 276884
Founder: Miss Dorothea Beale 1893
Open: By appointment only

St. Hugh's College
St. Margarets Road
Tel: 01865 274900
Founder: Dame Elizabeth Wordsworth 1886
Open: 10am–4pm

St. John's College
St. Giles
Tel: 01865 277300
Founder: Sir Thomas White 1555
Open: 1–5pm (or dusk)

St. Peter's College
New Inn Hall Street
Tel: 01865 278900
Founder: Rev. Christopher Charvasse 1928
Open: 10am–5pm

Trinity College
Broad Street
Tel: 01865 279900
Founder: Sir Thomas Pope 1554–5
Open: Mon–Fri 10am–noon and 2–4pm.
            Sat & Sun in term, 2–4pm;
            Sat & Sun in vacation 10am–
            12 noon and 2–4pm

University College
High Street
Tel: 01865 276602
Founder: Archdeacon William of
            Durham 1249
Open: Contact College for details

Wadham College
Parks Road
Tel: 01865 277900
Founder: Nicholas & Dorothy
            Wadham 1610
Open: Term time: daily, 1–4.15pm.
            Vacation: daily, 10.30–11.45am
            & 1–4.15pm

Wolfson College
Linton Road
Tel: 01865 274100
Founder: Oxford University 1966
Open: Daylight hours

Worcester College
Worcester Street
Tel: 01865 278300
Founder: Sir Thomas Cookes 1714
Open: Daily, 2–5pm

Christchurch College, Oxford

This information is intended only as a guide. Times are subject to change due to functions, examinations, conferences, holidays, etc. You are advised to check in advance opening times and admission charges which may apply at some colleges, and at certain times of the year. Visitors wishing to gain admittance to the Colleges (meaning the Courts, not to the staircases and students' rooms) are advised to contact the Tourist Information Office. It should be noted that Halls normally close for lunch (12 noon–2pm) and many are not open during the afternoon. Chapels may be closed during services. Libraries are not normally open, and Gardens do not usually include the Fellows' garden. Visitors, and especially guided groups, should always call on the Porters Lodge first. Groups should always book in advance. Dogs, except guide dogs are not allowed in any colleges.

■ Owner
The National Trust

■ Contact
The Property Manager
Clandon Park &
Hatchlands Park
East Clandon
Guildford
Surrey GU4 7RT

Tel: 01483 222482
Fax: 01483 223176
E-mail: hatchlands@
nationaltrust.org.uk

■ Location
MAP 19:A11

Clandon
OS Ref. TQ042 512
At West Clandon
on the A247,
3m E of Guildford.

Rail: Clandon BR 1m.

Hatchlands
OS Ref. TQ063 516
E of East Clandon
on the A246 Guildford–
Leatherhead road.

Rail: Clandon BR
2½ m, Horsley 3m.

■ Opening Times
Clandon – House
16 March–2 November
Tue–Thur, Suns &
BH Mons, Good Fri
& Easter Sat
11am–4.30pm.

Garden
As house. 11am–5pm.

Museum
As house
12 noon–5pm.

Hatchlands – House
23 March–30 October
Tue–Thur,
Suns & BH Mon,
Fris in August.
2–5.30pm.

Park Walks
23 March–30 October
Daily 11am–6pm.

■ *Admission
Clandon
House/Grounds	£7.70
Child	£3.90
Family	£19.80
Pre-booked Groups	
Adult	£6.50

Hatchlands
House/Grounds	£6.60
Child	£3.30
Family	£17.00
Park Walks only	£3.50
Child	£1.80
Pre-booked Groups	
Adult	£5.60

Combined ticket
Adult	£11.00
Child	£5.50
Family	£30.00

*includes a voluntary
donation but visitors can
choose to pay the standard
prices displayed at the
property and on the website.

Conference/Function
ROOM	SIZE	MAX CAPACITY
Marble Hall Clandon Pk	40' x 40'	160 seated 200 standing

©NTPL Hatchlands Park

©NTPL Clandon Park

CLANDON PARK & HATCHLANDS PARK 🌿

www.nationaltrust.org.uk/clandonpark

Clandon Park & Hatchlands Park were built during the 18th century and are set amidst beautiful grounds. They are two of England's most outstanding country houses and are only five minutes' drive apart.

Clandon Park is a grand Palladian Mansion, built c1730 for the 2nd Lord Onslow by the Venetian architect Giacomo Leoni. Clandon's interior is the most complete of his work to survive and is notable for its magnificent two-storied, white Marble Hall.

The Onslows have been active in the country's political history, being the only family ever to have produced three Speakers of the House of Commons. The last of these, Arthur Onslow, held the post from 1727 for over 30 years. Activity was not restricted to England; at the end of the 19th century the 4th Earl of Onslow served as Governor of New Zealand, whereupon the Maori meeting house came to be in the gardens at Clandon Park.

There is also an intimate sunken Dutch garden, at its best in May and June and a stunning bulb field flowering in spring.

Displayed inside the house is a superb collection of 18th century furniture, textiles and one of the finest collections of porcelain, including Meissen *Commedia Dell' Arte* figures.

Hatchlands Park was built in 1756 for Admiral Boscawen, hero of the Battle of Louisburg, and contains the earliest recorded decorations in an English country house by Robert Adam, whose ceilings appropriately feature nautical motifs.

The rooms are hung with the Cobbe Collection of Old Master paintings and portraits. The house is also home to the Cobbe Collection of keyboard instruments, the world's largest group of early keyboard instruments owned or played by famous composers such as Purcell, JC Bach, Mozart, Liszt, Chopin, Mahler and Elgar.

Hatchlands is set in a beautiful 430-acre Repton park, with a variety of way-marked walks offering vistas of open parkland and idyllic views of the house. The woodlands are a haven for wildlife and there is a stunning Bluebell wood in May.

There are frequent concerts on the instruments on the collection (for more details please contact: The Cobbe Collection Trust, 01483 211474, www.cobbecollection.co.uk).

© David Mees

ℹ️	No photography.
🛍️	
⚭	For Clandon weddings and receptions tel: 01483 222502.
♿	WCs. Hatchlands suitable. Clandon please tel for details.
☕	Hatchlands: 01483 211120.
🍴	Licensed. Clandon: 01483 222502.
🚶	Clandon – by arrangement.
🖼️	Children's quizzes available.
🅿️	
🐕	Hatchlands Parkland only.
🔔	Clandon only.
📷	Tel: 01483 222482.

LOSELEY PARK 🏛

www.loseley-park.com

Loseley Park, built in 1562 by Sir William More to entertain Queen Elizabeth I, is a fine example of Elizabethan architecture – its mellow stone brought from the ruins of Waverley Abbey now over 850 years old. The house is set amid magnificent parkland grazed by the Loseley Jersey herd. Many visitors comment on the very friendly atmosphere of the house. It is a country house, the family home of descendants of the builder.

Furniture, paintings and artefacts have been collected by the family since Loseley was built, including panelling from Nonsuch Palace, English and European furniture, a unique chalk fireplace and porcelain from the East. However, with all the history, it is still a family home.

Loseley Park is a stunning wedding venue with ceremonies in the Great Hall and receptions in the 17th century Tithe Barn. There are also flexible facilities for corporate and private functions. Highly rated film location. Christian Cancer/Parkinson's Disease Help Centre.

Garden

A magnificent Cedar of Lebanon presides over the front lawn. Parkland adjoins the lawn and a small lake adds to the beauty of Front Park. Walled Garden: Based on a Gertrude Jekyll design, the five gardens include the award-winning rose garden containing over 1,000 bushes, a magnificent vine walk, herb garden, colourful fruit and flower garden and the serene white garden. Other features include an organic vegetable garden and moat walk. HDRA Seed Library plants.

ℹ️ Lakeside walk. Picnic area. Chapel. Hire of gardens and grounds for corporate and private events. All group visits to be booked in advance. Group garden tours available. Lectures on history of house and contents by arrangement. South East Tourism award winner 2006.

📷

✱

🍸 Corporate and private hire for special functions, conferences, meetings, wedding receptions. Marquees for hire.

♿ May alight at entrance to property. Access to all areas except house first floor. WCs.

☕ Courtyard Tea Room & Garden Marquee serving light lunches, snacks and cream teas.

🚶 House tour obligatory: 40 mins. Group Garden tours available.

🅿️ 150 cars, 6 coaches. Summer overflow car park.

🐕 Guide dogs only.

🔔 100 max.

❄️

🎭 Tel or see website for details.

Owner
Mr Michael More-Molyneux

Contact
Sue Grant
Events Office
Loseley Park
Guildford
Surrey GU3 1HS

Tel: 01483 304440
Tel Events: 01483 405119/120
Fax: 01483 302036
E-mail: enquiries @loseley-park.com

Location
MAP 3:G3
OS Ref. SU975 471

30m SW of London, leave A3 S of Guildford on to B3000. Signposted.

Bus: 1¼m from House.

Rail: Farncombe 1½m, Guildford 2m, Godalming 3m

Air: Heathrow 30m, Gatwick 30m.

Opening Times
Summer
Garden, Shop & Tearoom
May–September
Tues–Sun & BH Mons in May & August,
11am–5pm.

Loseley House
(guided tours)
May–August
Tues–Thurs,
Suns & BH Mons in May & August,
1–5pm.

All Year (Private Hire)
Tithe Barn, Chestnut Lodge, House, Garden Marquee, Walled Garden and Grounds. Civil ceremonies and receptions. Off-road 4x4 course and showground. Activity Days.

Admission
House & Gardens

Adult	£7.00
Child (5–16yrs)	£3.50
Conc.	£6.50
Child (under 5yrs)	Free
Family (2 + 3)	£17.50

Booked Groups (10+)
Adult	£6.00
Child (5–16yrs)	£3.00
Garden tours	£2.50pp

Garden & Grounds only
Adult	£4.00
Child (5–16yrs)	£2.00
Conc.	£3.50
Family (2 + 3)	£10.00

Booked Groups (10+)
Adult	£3.00
Child (5–16yrs)	£1.50
Garden tours	£2.50pp

Conference/Function

ROOM	SIZE	MAX CAPACITY
Tithe Barn	100' x 18'	180
Marquee sites available		up to 4,000
Great Hall	70' x 40'	80
Drawing Rm	40' x 30'	50
Chestnut Ldg	12.8' x 6.1'	50

■ Owner
Painshill Park Trust

■ Contact
Visitor Manager
Painshill Park
Portsmouth Road
Cobham
Surrey KT11 1JE

Tel: 01932 868113
Fax: 01932 868001
E-mail:
info@painshill.co.uk
education@painshill.co.uk

■ Location
MAP 19:B10
OS Ref. TQ099 605

M25/J10/A3 to London.
W of Cobham on A245.
Entrance 200 yds E of
A245/A307 roundabout.

Rail: Cobham/Stoke
d'Abernon 2m.

Bus: Surrey Parks &
Gardens Explorer Bus
Route 515/515A.

■ Opening Times
All year
March–October:
10.30am–6pm or dusk
(last entry 4.30pm),
November–February:
10.30am–4pm or dusk
(last entry 3pm).
Closed Christmas Day
and Boxing Day.

■ Admission
Adult	£6.60
Child (5–16)	£3.85
Conc.	£5.80
Family (2 adults, 4 children)	£22.00

Under 5s and disabled
carer free.
Season Tickets available.

Pre-booked
groups (10+)
Adult	£5.80
Child	£2.00

(optional guided tour
£1.00 per person). Free
entry and refreshments
for tour leader and
coach driver.

Grotto has limited
opening hours Sat, Sun
and Bank Holidays.
Opened for Groups by
prior arrangement.

PAINSHILL PARK 🏛
www.painshill.co.uk

Step into a 'living picture of paradise' when you discover 158 acres of authentically restored Georgian landscape, created by the Hon. Charles Hamilton between 1738 and 1773 as a Living Work of Art … As you stroll along the historic route you move from scene to scene through a series of unfolding vistas known as 'The Hamilton Landscapes'. The 18th century Grade I listed parkland has won the Europa Nostra Medal for exemplary restoration and is complete with a 14 acre lake, spectacular views across the Surrey downs, an amazing crystal Grotto, plus many more interesting and unusual follies.

From Snowdrops to Autumn colour the pleasure grounds and plantings have something to offer the visitor throughout the year. Enjoy exploring the American Roots exhibition which tells an amazing story of the 18th century craze for new and exciting exotic plants from outside the British Isles or discover the NCCPG John Bartram Heritage Plant Collection of North American Trees and Shrubs. Guided walks for pre-booked groups give a fascinating insight into Hamilton's vision and it's a great way to discover the pleasure grounds. Throughout the year there are fun-filled family and adult events, as well as entertaining talks covering a wide range of subjects.

We have a choice of children's birthday parties and a full educational programme which explores the nature, art, history and geography unique to our landscape. Painshill is available for location filming, photographic shoots and in the walled garden 'The Conservatory' is available for weddings and corporate or private hire.

i WCs. Filming, plays and photographic shoots.

Painshill Wine and Honey.

Private and Corporate Hospitality, Tel: 01932 584283, Email: events@painshillevents.co.uk, Website: www.painshillevents.co.uk.

WCs. Accessible route. Free pre-booked wheelchair loan and Buggy Tours (Cap. Max. 3).

Licensed. Picnic area.

By arrangement.

£2.50 pp. Free for Disabled person. English.

P Ample for Coaches (must book) and Cars.

By arrangement.

On leads.

All year – see website.

Conference/Function

ROOM	MAX CAPACITY
Abercorn and Small Courtyard	Standing 70 Seated 60 Theatre-style 60
Discovery Centre Rooms	Standing 50 Seated 40
The Conservatory in Walled Garden	Standing 400 Seated 320 Theatre-style 400

BOX HILL

The Old Fort, Box Hill Road, Box Hill, Tadworth KT20 7LB
Tel: 01306 885502 **Fax:** 01306 875030 **E-mail:** boxhill@nationaltrust.org.uk
www.nationaltrust.org.uk/northdowns
Owner: The National Trust   **Contact:** Head Warden
An outstanding area of woodland and chalk downland with magnificent views across the weald. Long famous as a destination for naturalists and excursions from London.
Location: MAP 19:C11, OS Ref. TQ171 519. 1m N of Dorking, 1½m S of Leatherhead on A24.
Open: Shop, Information Centre and Servery: All year, daily (except 25/26 Dec & 1 Jan), 11–5pm or dusk.
Admission: Countryside: Free. Car/coach park £3, NT members Free.

CLANDON PARK & HATCHLANDS PARK

See page 144 for full page entry.

Hampton Court Palace

CLAREMONT LANDSCAPE GARDEN

PORTSMOUTH ROAD, ESHER, SURREY KT10 9JG

www.nationaltrust.org.uk/claremont

Tel: 01372 467806 **Fax:** 01372 476420 **E-mail:** claremont@nationaltrust.org.uk
Owner: The National Trust   **Contact:** The Property Manager
One of the earliest surviving English landscape gardens, restored to its former glory. Begun by Sir John Vanbrugh and Charles Bridgeman before 1720, the garden was extended and naturalised by William Kent. 'Capability' Brown also made improvements. Features include a lake, island with pavilion, grotto, turf amphitheatre, viewpoints and avenues.

Location: MAP 19:B9, OS Ref. TQ128 632. On S edge of Esher, on E side of A307 (no access from Esher bypass).
Open: Jan–end Mar, Nov–end Dec: daily except Mons: 10am–5pm or sunset if earlier. Apr–end Oct: daily: 10am–6pm. Closed 25 Dec.
*Admission: Adult £5.80, Child £2.90. Family (2+2) £14.50 Groups (15+), £4.60. £1 tearoom voucher given if arriving by public transport. Coach groups must book; no coach groups on Suns. *includes a voluntary donation but visitors can choose to pay the standard prices displayed at the property and on the website.
Limited. WC. No dogs (Apr–Oct).

FARNHAM CASTLE

Farnham, Surrey GU9 0AG
Tel: 01252 721194 **Fax:** 01252 711283 **E-mail:** conf@farnhamcastle.com
Owner: The Church Commissioners **Contact:** Farnham Castle
Bishop's Palace built in Norman times by Henry of Blois. Tudor and Jacobean additions.
Location: MAP 3:F3, OS Ref. SU839 474. ½m N of Farnham town centre on A287.
Open: All year: Weds, Summer Sats & Suns (tel for details), 2–4pm except Christmas & New Year.
Admission: Adult £2.50, Child/Conc £1.50.

FARNHAM CASTLE KEEP

Castle Hill, Farnham, Surrey GU9 0JA
Tel: 01252 713393   **www.english-heritage.org.uk/farnham**
Owner: English Heritage **Contact:** Visitor Operations Team
The impressive motte, shell-keep, bailey wall and other defences of a castle founded in 1138 and redeveloped by Henry II after 1155. Long a residence of the wealthy Bishops of Winchester, the fortress itself was abandoned after Civil War service; later attendant buildings remain in private occupation.
Location: MAP 3:F3, OS Ref. SU837 473. ½m N of Farnham town centre on A287.
Open: Easter, May BHs, 1 Jul–31 Aug: Fri–Sun, 1–5pm. Guided tours: Aug, Suns, 2.30pm.
Admission: Adult £3, Child £1.50, Conc. £2.40. EH Members Free. Group discount available.
Ground floor & grounds. In grounds, on leads.

GODDARDS

Abinger Common, Dorking, Surrey RH5 6TH
Tel: 01628 825925 **E-mail:** bookings@landmarktrust.org.uk
www.landmarktrust.org.uk
Owner: The Lutyens Trust, leased to The Landmark Trust **Contact:** The Landmark Trust
Built by Sir Edwin Lutyens in 1898–1900 and enlarged by him in 1910. Garden by
Gertrude Jekyll. Given to the Lutyens Trust in 1991 and now managed and maintained
by the Landmark Trust, a building preservation charity who let it for holidays. The whole
house, apart from the library, is available for holidays. Full details of Goddards and 184
other historic and architecturally important buildings available for holidays are featured
in The Landmark Handbook (price £11.50 refundable against booking).
Location: MAP 19:B12, OS Ref. TQ120 450. 4½ m SW of Dorking on the village green in
Abinger Common. Signposted Abinger Common, Friday Street and Leith Hill from A25.
Open: Available for holidays for up to 12 people. Other visits strictly by appointment.
Must be booked in advance, including parking, which is very limited. Visits booked for
Weds afternoons from the Wed after Easter until the last Wed of Oct, between
2.30–5pm. Only those with pre-booked tickets will be admitted.
Admission: £3. Tickets available from Mrs Baker on 01306 730871, Mon–Fri, 9am &
6pm. Visitors will have access to part of the garden and house only.

Loseley Park

GREAT FOSTERS

Stroude Road, Egham, Surrey TW20 9UR
Tel: 01784 433822 **Fax:** 01784 472455 **E-mail:** enquiries@greatfosters.co.uk
www.greatfosters.co.uk
Owner: The Sutcliffe family **Contact:** Amanda Dougans
Grade II listed garden. Laid out in 1918 by W H Romaine-Walker in partnership with
G H Jenkins, incorporating earlier features. The site covers 50 acres and is associated
with a 16th century country house, reputed to be a former royal hunting lodge and
converted into an hotel by the owners in 1931. The main formal garden is surrounded
on three sides by a moat, thought to be of medieval origin, and is modelled on the
pattern of a Persian carpet. The garden also includes an amphitheatre, lake and a
sunken rose garden.
Location: MAP 3:G2, OS Ref. TQ015 694. M25 J/13, follow signs to Egham. Under
motorway bridge, first left at roundabout (The Avenue). Left at the mini roundabout into
Vicarage Rd. Right at next roundabout. Over M25, left into Stroude Rd. 500 yds on left.
Open: All year.
Admission: Free.

⊤ & Partial. WC. ☕ ⅋ Licensed. 🅿 🚲 Guide dogs only. 🏨 ▲ ❈

GUILDFORD HOUSE GALLERY

155 High Street, Guildford, Surrey GU1 3AJ
Tel/Fax: 01483 444742 (Guildford Borough Council) **www.guildfordhouse.co.uk**
Owner/Contact: Guildford Borough Council
A beautifully restored 17th century town house with a number of original features
including a finely carved staircase, panelled rooms and decorative plaster ceilings. A
varied temporary exhibition programme including paintings, photography and craft
work. Exhibition and events leaflet available. Lecture and workshop programme. Details
on application.
Location: MAP 3:G3, OS Ref. SU996 494. Central Guildford on High Street.
Open: All year, Tue–Sat, 10am–4.45pm.
Admission: Free.

⬜ ☕ ⅋ 🖊 Public car park nearby. 🅿 🚲 Guide dogs only. ❈ 🌀

©HRP 2007

HAMPTON COURT PALACE
HAMPTON COURT PALACE, SURREY KT8 9AU
www.hrp.org.uk

Tel: 0844 482 7777
Venue Hire and Corporate Hospitailty: 02031 666505
Owner/Contact: Historic Royal Palaces
The flamboyant Henry VIII is most associated with this majestic palace, which he
extended and developed in grand style after acquiring it from Cardinal Wolsey in the
1520s. He lavished money on fabulous tapestries and paintings, housed and fed a
huge court and pursued a succession of wives, political power and domination over
Rome. The Tudor buildings which remain are among the most important in
exisitence, but the elegance and romance of the palace owes much to the elegant
Baroque buildings commissioned by William and Mary at the end of the 17th
century. The palace is set in 60 acres of gardens, which include the famous Maze
and awe-inspiring Great Vine.

Location: MAP 19:B9, OS Ref. TQ155 686. From M25/J15 and A312, or M25/J12 and
A308, or M25/J10 and A307. Rail: From London Waterloo direct to Hampton Court
(32 mins).
Open: Mar–Oct: Daily, 10am–6pm (last admission 5.15pm). Nov–Feb: Daily,
10am–4.30pm (last admission 3.45pm). Closed 24–26 Dec.
Admission: Telephone Information Line for admission prices: 08444 827777. Advance
Ticket Sales:08444 827799. Group Bookings 08444 827770, Quote Hudson's.
ℹ️ Information Centre. No photography indoors. 🖾 ⊤
& Motorised buggies available at main entrance. WCs. ☕ ⅋ 🖊 🎧
🅿 Ample for cars, coach parking nearby. 🎦 Rates on request 0844 482 7777.
🚲 In grounds, on leads. Guide dogs only in Palace. ❈ 🌀

KEW GARDENS

Kew, Richmond, Surrey TW9 3AB

Tel: 020 8332 5655 **Fax:** 020 8332 5610 **E-mail:** info@kew.org **www.kew.org**
Contact: Visitor Information

Kew Gardens is a World Heritage Site. It is a mixture of stunning vistas, magnificent glasshouses and beautiful landscapes beside the River Thames. This once Royal residence represents nearly 250 years of historical gardens and today its 300 acres are home to over 40,000 types of plants from rainforest to desert. There is always something to see … as the seasons change so does Kew.

Location: MAP 19:C7, OS Ref. TQ188 776. A307. Junc. A307 & A205 (1m Chiswick roundabout M4).

Open: All year: daily (except 24/25 Dec) from 9.30am. Closing time varies according to the season. Please telephone for further information.

Admission: 1 Nov '07–31 Mar '08: Adults £12.25, From 1 Apr: £13. Concessions available. Child (under 17) Free. Discounts for groups (10+). School groups: Free.
⬜ 🍴 ♿ 🎦 Licensed. 🅿 Limited. ▣ 🐕 Guide dogs only. ⬛ ✳

KEW PALACE, HISTORIC ROYAL PALACES

Kew Gardens, Kew, Richmond, Surrey TW9 3AB

Tel: Group Bookings 020 8332 5648 **E-mail:** info@kew.org **www:hrp.org.uk**
Contact: Visitor Information 0844 482 7777

Kew Palace and Queen Charlotte's Cottage. The most intimate of the five royal palaces, Kew was built as a private house but became a royal residence between 1728 and 1818. Both the palace and the nearby Queen Charlotte's cottage, built in 1770, are most closely associated with King George III and his family. Discover their story.

Location: MAP 19:C7, OS Ref. TQ188 776.193. A307. Junc A307 & A205 (1m Chiswick roundabout M4).

Open: 21 Mar–28 Sept: daily, 10am–5pm, Last admission 4.15pm.

Admission: By joint ticket purchased through Kew Gardens.

LEITH HILL 🌿

Coldharbour, Surrey

Tel: 01306 711777 **Fax:** 01306 712153 **www.nationaltrust.org.uk/northdowns**
Owner: The National Trust **Contact:** Head Warden

The highest point in south-east England, crowned by an 18th century Gothic tower, from which there are magnificent views. The surrounding woodland contains ancient stands of hazel and oak, and there is a colourful display of rhododendrons in May–Jun.

Location: MAP 19:B12, OS Ref. TQ139 432. 1m SW of Coldharbour A29/B2126.

Open: Tower: To 29 Mar, Sat & Sun, 10.30am–3.30pm, 30 Mar–25 Oct: Fri–Sun, and Weds in Aug, 10am–5pm or dusk if earlier, 26 Oct–28 Mar 09: Sats & Suns, 10am–3.30pm. Open all BHs (closed 25 Dec). Last adm. 30 mins before closing. Wood & Estate: All year: daily.

Admission: Tower: £1, Child 50p. Rhododendron Wood: £2 per car. (2 circular nature trails with leaflet.) Last admission ½ hour prior to closing.
ℹ No vehicular access to summit. ♿ Partial. 🎦 When Tower open. 🎥 Guided walks.
🅿 Parking at foot of hill, ½m walk from Tower. 🐕 Not in picnic area or Tower. ✳

LOSELEY PARK 🏛   *See page 145 for full page entry.*

OAKHURST COTTAGE 🌿

HAMBLEDON, GODALMING, SURREY GU8 4HF

Tel: 01483 208477 **E-mail:** oakhurstcottage@nationaltrust.org.uk
Owner: The National Trust **Contact:** Winkworth Arboretum

A small 16th century timber-framed cottage, painted by both Helen Allingham and Myles Birket Foster, containing furniture and artefacts reflecting two or more centuries of continuing occupation. There is a delightful cottage garden and a small barn containing agricultural implements.

Location: MAP 3:G4, OS Ref. SU965 385. Hambledon, Surrey.

Open: 26 Mar–26 Oct: Weds, Thurs, Sats, Suns & BH Mons. Strictly by appointment, 2–5pm.

Admission: Adult £5, Child £3 (incl guided tour). No reduction for groups.
♿ Unsuitable. 🎥 Obligatory, by arrangement. 🅿 Limited. 🐕

PAINSHILL PARK 🏛   *See page 146 for full page entry.*

Titsey Place

©NTPL/Nick Meers

POLESDEN LACEY

GREAT BOOKHAM, Nr DORKING, SURREY RH5 6BD

www.nationaltrust.org.uk/polesdenlacey

Tel: 01372 452048 **Fax:** 01372 452023 **E-mail:** polesdenlacey@nationaltrust.org.uk
Owner: The National Trust   **Contact:** The Property Manager

Originally an elegant 1820s Regency villa in a magnificent landscape setting. The house was remodelled after 1906 by the Hon Mrs Ronald Greville, a well-known Edwardian hostess. Her collection of fine paintings, furniture, porcelain and silver are still displayed in the reception rooms and galleries. Extensive grounds (1,400 acre estate), walled rose garden, lawns and landscaped walks.

Location: MAP 19:B11, OS Ref. TQ136 522. 5m NW of Dorking, 2m S of Great Bookham, off A246.

Open: House: 15 Mar–28 Oct: Wed–Sun, & BH Mons, 11am–5pm. Grounds: All year: daily, 11am–5pm, (closes 4pm 29 Oct–28 Feb 2009). Closed 24 Dec–2 Jan 2009.

*Admission: House & Gardens: Adults £10.50, Child £5.50, Family £26.50, Group £8.90. Gardens only: Adult £6.50, Child £3.50, Family £16.50, Group £5.50. *includes a voluntary donation but visitors can choose to pay the standard prices displayed at the property and on the website.

◻ ▦ ♿ ⑪ Licensed. Ⓟ ▦ In grounds on leads. ❀ Grounds only.
♥ Tel: 01372 452048 for info.

RHS GARDEN WISLEY

Nr WOKING, SURREY GU23 6QB

www.rhs.org.uk

Tel: 01483 224234 **Fax:** 01483 211750
Owner/Contact: The Royal Horticultural Society

A garden to enjoy all year round with something to see for everyone. Wisley provides the visitor with ideas and inspiration and the benefit of experience from experts. Mixed borders, fruit and vegetables, spring bulbs, rock garden, arboetum, model gardens and glasshouse. The Wisley Plant Centre with plants for sale, The Wisley Shop with books and gifts and for refreshments the Café, Restaurant and Coffee Shop.

Location: MAP 19:A10, OS Ref. TQ066 583. On A3 N of Guildford nr. M25 J/10. Brown Signs.

Open: All year: daily (except Christmas Day), Mon–Fri, 10am–6pm (4.30pm Nov–Feb). Sat & Sun, 9am–6pm (4.30pm Nov–Feb). Last entry 1 hr before closing.

Admission: RHS Members: Free. Adult £8, Child (6–16yrs) £2, Child (under 6) Free. Groups (10+): Adult £6, Child £1.60.

◻ ▦ ♿ Wheelchairs available tel: 01483 211113 and special map. WC.
▦ ⑪ Licensed. Ⓕ By arrangement. ⌂ Ⓟ ▦
▦ Guide & Registered Support dogs only. ❀ ♥

visit hudsons guide online

RAMSTER GARDENS

Ramster, Chiddingfold, Surrey GU8 4SN
Tel: 01428 654167   **www.ramsterevents.com**
Owner/Contact: Mrs R Glaister

An idyllic, mature flowering shrub garden of 20 acres, with unusual and interesting plants. Spring colour changes from subtle daffodils and magnolias in April to the famous fiery display of rhododendrons, azaleas and bluebells in May, followed in June by the gentle pinks of climbing roses and cascades of primulas.
Location: MAP 3:G4, OS Ref. SU950 333. 1½ m S of Chiddingfold on A283.
Open: 4 Apr–22 Jun: daily. 10am–5pm.
Admission: Adult £5, Child (under 16) Free. Conc £4.50. Groups by arrangement.
🏵 ⅃ Partial. ☑🖼 On leads. ▲🖳

RUNNYMEDE 🌿

Egham, Surrey
Tel: 01784 432891   **Fax:** 01784 479007   **E-mail:** runnymede@nationaltrust.org.uk
www.nationaltrust.org.uk
Owner: The National Trust   **Contact:** The Head Warden

An historic area alongside the River Thames where, in 1215, King John sealed Magna Carta, an event commemorated by the American Bar Association Memorial. The John F Kennedy Memorial was erected in 1965 to commemorate his life. The Commonwealth Air Forces Memorial is situated overlooking Runnymede and commemorates over 20,000 airmen and women with no known grave who died during World War II. Also here are the Fairhaven Lodges, designed by Lutyens, which host a summer art gallery and tearoom all year.
Location: MAP 3:G2, OS Ref. TQ007 720. 2m W of Runnymede Bridge, on S side of A308, M25/J13.
Open: All year. Riverside Car park (grass): Apr–30 Sept: daily, 10am–7pm. Tearoom & car park (hard standing): daily, all year, 8.30am–5pm (later in Summer).
Admission: Fees payable for parking (NT members Free), fishing & mooring.
🖸 ⅃ Partial. ☑ 🎻 🅿 ❄ 🖳

THE SAVILL GARDEN   *See page 82 (Berkshire) for full page entry.*
(WINDSOR GREAT PARK, BERKSHIRE)

TITSEY PLACE & GARDENS
TITSEY PLACE, OXTED, SURREY RH8 0SD

www.titsey.org

Tel: 01273 715361   **Fax:** 01273 779783
E-mail: kate.moisson@struttandparker.co.uk
Owner: Trustees of the Titsey Foundation   **Contact:** Kate Moisson
Beautiful gardens incorporating formal lawns, rose garden, walled kitchen garden and 4 mile woodland walk and parkland. Titsey Place houses 4 stunning Canalettos and Porcelain Collection.
Location: MAP 19:F10, OS Ref. TQ406 553. 1 mile N of Limpsfield.
Open: mid May–end Sept: Weds & Suns, 1–5pm. Additionally Summer BHs. Gardens only Easter Mon.
Admission: House & Garden: Adult £6, Garden only £3.50. Child £1.
⅃ Partial. 🎻 Obligatory. ☑ 🅿 Limited for coaches. 🖼 Woods and park only.

©NTPL/D Sellman

©NTPL/D Sellman

WINKWORTH ARBORETUM 🌿
HASCOMBE ROAD, GODALMING, SURREY GU8 4AD

www.nationaltrust.org.uk/winkwortharboretum

Tel: 01483 208477   **Fax:** 01483 208252
E-mail: winkwortharboretum@nationaltrust.org.uk
Owner: The National Trust   **Contact:** Head Arborist
Established in the 20th century, the hillside arboretum now contains over 1,000 different shrubs and trees, many of them rare. The most impressive displays are in spring for bluebells and azaleas, and in autumn for colour and wildlife. New wetland area with boardwalk and circular route. In the summer it is an ideal place for family visits and a picnic.

Location: MAP 3:G4, OS Ref. SU990 412. Near Hascombe, 2m SE of Godalming on E side of B2130.
Open: All year round: daily during daylight hours. May be closed due to high winds. Boathouse: Apr–Nov.
*Admission: Adult £5.20, Child (5–16yrs) £2.60, Family (2+2) £13. Groups £4.40. Discounts for 15 or more. *includes a voluntary donation but visitors can choose to pay the standard prices displayed at the property and on the website.
🖸 ⅃ Limited. WC. ☑ 🖼 In grounds, on leads. ❄

■ **Owner**

Arundel Castle
Trustees Ltd

■ **Contact**

Bryan McDonald
Head of Opening
Arundel Castle
Arundel
West Sussex BN18 9AB

Tel: 01903 882173
Fax: 01903 884581
E-mail: bryan.mcdonald@
arundelcastle.org

■ **Location**

MAP 3:G6
OS Ref. TQ018 072

Central Arundel, N of A27
Brighton 40 mins,
Worthing 15 mins,
Chichester 15 mins.
From London A3 or A24,
1½ hrs.
M25 motorway, 30m.

Bus: Bus stop 100 yds.

Rail: Station ½m.

Air: Gatwick 25m.

■ **Opening Times**

21 March–2 November

Tuesday to Sunday
inclusive throughout the
season.

Closed on Mondays
(except Bank Holidays
and Mondays in August).

**Fitzalan Chapel,
Gardens & Grounds**
10am–5pm

Restaurant
10.30am – 4.30pm

Gift Shop
10.30am – 5pm

Castle Keep
11.00am – 4.30pm

Main Castle Rooms
12 noon – 5pm

Last entry 4pm

■ **Admission**

Summer
Adult	£13.00
Child (5–16yrs)	£7.50
Conc.	£10.50
Family (2+3 max)	£34.00
Bedrooms (when open)	
Adults	£2.00
Groups (20+)	
Adult	£11.00
Child (5–16yrs)	£6.00
Conc.	£9.00
Fitzalan Chapel, Castle Keep, Gardens & Grounds	£6.50

Winter
Closed.

ARUNDEL CASTLE

www.arundelcastle.org

A thousand years of history is waiting to be discovered at Arundel Castle in West Sussex. Dating from the 11th century, the Castle is both ancient fortification and stately home of the Dukes of Norfolk and Earls of Arundel.

Set high on a hill, this magnificent castle commands stunning views across the River Arun and out to sea. Climb the Keep, explore the battlements, wander in the grounds and recently restored Victorian gardens and relax in the garden of the 14th century Fitzalan Chapel.

In the 17th century during the English Civil War the Castle suffered extensive damage. The process of structural restoration began in earnest in the 18th century and continued up until 1900. The Castle was one of the first private residences to have electricity and central heating and had its own fire engine, which is still on view today.

Inside the Castle over 20 sumptuously furnished rooms may be visited including the breathtaking Barons' Hall with 16th century furniture, the Armoury with its fine collection of armour and weapory, and the magnificent Gothic library entirely fitted out in carved Honduras mahogany. There are works of art by Van Dyck, Gainsborough, Canaletto and Mytens, tapestries, clocks, and personal possessions of Mary Queen of Scots including the gold rosary that she carried to her execution.

There are special events throughout the season, including outdoor concerts, jousting, and medieval re-enactments.

New for 2008: The Earl's Garden, an exciting new garden based on early 17th century classical designs.

i No photography or video recording inside the Castle. Guidebooks in English, French & German.

& Many areas accessible. Visitors may alight at the Castle gates. Free parking in the allocated areas in the town car park. Passenger buggy available. WCs.

Licensed restaurant in Castle seats 140. Special rates for booked groups. Self-service. Serves home-made food, morning coffee, lunch or afternoon tea.

Pre-booked groups only. Tour time 1½–2 hrs. Tours available in Japanese.

P Ample in town car park. Coaches can park free in town coach park. Free admission and refreshment voucher for coach driver.

Items of particular interest include a Norman Motte & Keep, Armoury & Victorian bedrooms. Special rates for schoolchildren (aged 5–15) and teachers.

Registered Assistance Dogs only

※ For further information please visit our website, e-mail or telephone.

© NTPL/Rupert Truman

BATEMAN'S 🌿

www.nationaltrust.org.uk/batemans

■ Owner
The National Trust

■ Contact
The Administrator
Bateman's
Burwash
Etchingham
East Sussex TN19 7DS

Tel: 01435 882302
Fax: 01435 882811
E-mail: batemans@
nationaltrust.org.uk

■ Location
MAP 4:K5
OS Ref. TQ671 238

½ m S of Burwash
off A265.

Rail: Etchingham 3m,
then bus (twice daily).

Air: Gatwick 40m.

■ Opening Times
15 March–2 November:
Sat–Wed, Good Fri &
BH Mons, 11am–5pm.
Last admission 4.30pm.

■ *Admission
House & Garden
Adult   £7.20
Child   £3.60
Family (2+3)   £18.00
Groups   £5.60

*includes a voluntary
donation but visitors can
choose to pay the standard
prices displayed at the
property and on the website.

Built in 1634 and home to Rudyard Kipling for over 30 years, Bateman's lies in the richly wooded landscape of the Sussex Weald. Visit this Sussex sandstone manor house, built by a local ironmaster, where the famous writer lived from 1902 to 1936. See the rooms as they were in Kipling's day, including the study where the view inspired him to write some of his well-loved works including *Puck of Pook's Hill* and *Rewards and Fairies*. Find the mementoes of Kipling's time in India and illustrations from his famous Jungle Book tales of Mowgli, Baloo and Shere Khan.

Wander through the delightful Rose Garden with its pond and statues, with Mulberry and Herb gardens and discover the wild garden, through which flows the River Dudwell. Through the wild garden, you will find the Mill where you can watch corn being ground on most Saturday and Wednesday afternoons and one of the world's first water-driven turbines installed by Kipling to generate electricity for the house. In the garage, see a 1928 Rolls Royce, one of several owned by Kipling who was a keen early motorist.

Savour the peace and tranquillity of this beautiful property which Kipling described as '*A good and peaceable place*' and of which he said '*we have loved it, ever since our first sight of it …*'.

There is a picnic glade next to the car park, or you can enjoy morning coffee, a delicious lunch or afternoon tea in the licensed tearoom where there is special emphasis on using local produce. The well-stocked gift shop offers the largest collection of Kipling books in the area.

 Ground floor & grounds. WC. Computerised virtual tour of upper floors.

Licensed.

© NTPL/Geoffrey Frosh

■ **Owner**

The Charleston Trust

■ **Contact**

Visitor Manager
Charleston
Firle
Nr Lewes
East Sussex BN8 6LL

Tel: 01323 811265
Fax: 01323 811628
E-mail: info@charleston.
org.uk

■ **Location**

MAP 4:J6
OS Ref. TQ490 069

7m E of Lewes on A27
between Firle and
Selmeston.

■ **Opening Times**

19 March–2 November:
Wed–Sun & BH Mons.
Wed & Sat,
11.30am–6pm.
Thurs & Fri, 2–6pm
(July & August:
11.30am–6pm), guided
tours.
Sun & BH Mons, 2–6pm,
unguided.
(Last entry to the house
5pm.)

"Sisters" a specially
themed tour tracing the
lives of Vanessa Bell and
Virginia Woolf. Available
on most Fridays except in
July and August (1½ hr
tour length), it gives a
rare opportunity to see
the Kitchen and Vanessa
Bell's Studio.

■ **Admission**

House & Garden

Adult	£7.50
Children	£5.00
Disabled	£5.00
Family	£20.00
Conc. (Thur only)	£5.50
"Sisters" tour	£9.00

Garden only

Adults	£3.00
Children	£1.50

Group bookings tel:
01323 811626 for rates
and information.

CHARLESTON

www.charleston.org.uk

Charleston, a 17th century house in the heart of the beautiful Sussex countryside was, from 1916 the country retreat and home of the artists Vanessa Bell and Duncan Grant, and their unconventional household. From the moment they arrived they set out to embellish the house. Influenced by Post-Impressionists like Cézanne and Picasso they took painting beyond the canvas, decorating walls, doors and furniture, ceramics and textiles, and transforming the house itself into a work of art.

The walled garden was similarly transformed by the artists into a summer haven for playing and painting, filled with dazzling flowers, sculptures, mosaics and ponds. Charleston was also a country meeting place for Bloomsbury, the group of artists, writers and intellectuals that included Virginia and Leonard Woolf, John Maynard Keynes, E M Forster, Lytton Strachey, Roger Fry and

Clive Bell. Today, Charleston is the only complete example of the domestic decorative art of Bell and Grant anywhere in the world, its rooms encapsulating their pioneering, creative and bohemian life.

The Charleston Shop stocks a range of original ceramics, painted furniture, textiles, clothes and books relating to Charleston and to Bloomsbury. The Outer Studio Café provides light refreshment and the Charleston Gallery shows a changing programme of exhibitions.

The annual Charleston Festival is one of the UK's most successful independent literary events. Every May it presents a series of talks and lectures with an international cast of leading writers, performers and artists.

There is also an exciting programme of workshops, performances, walks, talks entertainments and celebrations available throughout the season.

ⓘ Filming and photography by arrangement.

♿ Partial. Access leaflet. WC.

Obligatory, except Sun and BH Mons.

Guide dogs only.

GOODWOOD HOUSE 🏛

www.goodwood.co.uk

Goodwood is one of the finest sporting estates in the world. At its heart lies Goodwood House, the ancestral home of the Dukes of Richmond and Gordon, direct descendants of King Charles II. Today, it is still lived in by the present Duke's son and heir, the Earl of March and Kinrara, with his wife and young family. Their home is open to the public on at least 60 days a year, the only house belonging to a son of Charles II that can be visited.

Set in the exquisitely decorated, gilded interiors of Goodwood House, the art collection is at museum level, with a magnificent collection of English paintings from the 17th and 18th centuries. These include the celebrated and glorious views of London by Canaletto, and magnificent horse paintings by George Stubbs. The rooms are filled with fine French and English furniture, Gobelins tapestries and Sèvres porcelain, all from the 18th century, as well as Regency furniture in the Egyptian Dining Room. Special works of art are regularly rotated and displayed. Arrangements to see the books can be made by written application to the Curator. (There is a special charge for these viewings.)

Items of especial Scottish interest will continue to be on display in 2008, explaining why the holder of the Dukedom of Gordon, by origin a Scottish title, lives in the south of England. Through paintings, watercolours, and *objets d'art* the story emerges of how three great Scottish dynasties became linked; those of the Royal House of Stuart, of Lennox, and finally, of Gordon.

Goodwood is not only a beautiful house to visit on an open day, with a relaxed and friendly atmosphere, but is also renowned for its entertaining. The House enjoys a reputation for excellence as a location for unforgettable weddings, parties and events. Goodwood's own organic farm, the largest in England, provides food for the table in the various restaurants on the estate. With internationally renowned horseracing and motor sport events, the finest Downland golf course in the UK, our own Aerodrome and hotel, Goodwood can offer an extraordinarily rich sporting experience.

5th Duke of Gordon by Sir Henry Raeburn

The Tapestry Drawing Room

 Conference facilities. No photography. Highly trained guides. Shell House optional extra on Connoisseurs' Days or by Group Appointment, or written request.

 Main shop at motor circuit.

 Obligatory.

P Ample.

 In grounds, on leads. Guide dogs only in house.

🔔 Civil Wedding Licence.

■ Owner

The Earl of March

■ Contact

Curator's PA
Goodwood House
Goodwood
Chichester
West Sussex PO18 0PX

Tel: 01243 755048
01243 755042 (Weddings)
Recorded Info:
01243 755040
Fax: 01243 755005
E-mail: curator
@goodwood.co.uk
or weddings@
goodwood.co.uk

■ Location

MAP 3:F6
OS Ref. SU888 088

3½m NE of Chichester. A3 from London then A286 or A285. M27/A27 from Portsmouth or Brighton.

Rail: Chichester 3½m Arundel 9m.

Air: Heathrow 1½ hrs Gatwick ¾ hr.

■ Opening Times

Summer
23 March–6 October:
Most Sundays and Mondays, 1–5pm.
(last entry 4pm).
3–31 August: Sun–Thurs, 1–5pm.

Please check Recorded Info 01243 755040.

Connoisseurs' Days
16 April, 7 & 14 May, 25 September & 22 October

Special tours for booked groups only.

Closures
Closed for special events: 18 May; 6/7 July (TBC); 13/14 July, Festival of Speed; 21 September, Goodwood Revival.

Please always check Recorded Info 01243 755040.

■ Admission

House
Adult	£8.50
Young Person (12–18yrs)	£4.00
Child (under 12yrs)	Free
Senior Citizen	£7.50
Family	£15.00

Booked Groups (20–200)	
Open Day (am)	£9.00
Open Day (pm)	£7.50
Connoisseur	£10.00

■ Special Events

Festival of Speed
Glorious Goodwood
Raceweek
Goodwood Revival

Please visit our website for up-to-date information.
www.goodwood.co.uk

■ Conference/Function

ROOM	SIZE	MAX CAPACITY
Ballroom	79' x 23'	180
11 other rooms also available		

■ Owner
Olivia Eller & The Great Dixter Charitable Trust

■ Contact
Perry Rodriguez
Northiam
Rye
East Sussex TN31 6PH

Tel: 01797 252878
Fax: 01797 252879
E-mail:
office@greatdixter.co.uk

■ Location
MAP 4:L5
OS Ref. TQ817 251.

Signposted off the A28 in Northiam.

■ Opening Times
21 March–26 October:
Tue–Sun, House 2–5pm.
Garden 11am–5pm.

■ Admission
House & Garden
Adult   £8.00
Child   £3.50

Gardens only
Adult   £6.50
Child   £3.00
Groups (25+) by appointment.

GREAT DIXTER HOUSE & GARDENS 🏛

www.greatdixter.co.uk

Great Dixter, built c1450, is the birthplace of the late Christopher Lloyd, gardening author. Its Great Hall is the largest medieval timber-framed hall in the country, restored and enlarged for Christopher's father (1910–12). The house was largely designed by the architect, Sir Edwin Lutyens, who added a 16th century house (moved from elsewhere) and knitted the buildings together with service accommodation and bedrooms above. The house retains most of the collections of furniture and other items put together by the Lloyds early in the 20th century, with some notable modern additions by Christopher.

The gardens feature a variety of topiary, pools, wild meadow areas and the famous Long Border and Exotic Garden. They featured regularly in "Country Life" from 1963, when Christopher was asked to contribute a series of weekly articles as a practical gardener – he never missed an issue in 42 years. There is a nursery on site which offers an array of unusual plants of the highest quality, many of which can be seen in the fabric of the gardens. Refreshments are available in the gift shop as well as tools, books and gifts.

The estate is not large (only 57 acres) but includes ancient woodlands, meadows and ponds which have been consistently managed on a traditional basis. Coppicing the woodlands, for example, has provided pea sticks for plant supports and timber for fencing and repairs to the buildings.

A Friends organisation has been set up. Friends enjoy invitations to events as well as a regular newsletter.

ⓘ No photography in House.

🌱 Obligatory.

🅿 Limited for coaches.

🐕 Guide dogs only.

LEONARDSLEE
LAKES & GARDENS
www.leonardslee.com

Leonardslee represents one of the largest and most spectacular woodland gardens in England, in a most magnificent setting, only a few miles from the M23. With over 200 acres (84 hectares), the valley is world famous for its spring display of azaleas and rhododendrons. Set alongside seven lakes, they provide superb views and magnificent reflections.

The exceptional "Beyond the Dolls House" exhibition boasts 140 ft of display and is a fascinating covered exhibition of Victorian life in miniature. Including a complete market town, shopping emporium, with working lift, and a superb Town House, it is one of the world's most detailed and fascinating models.

Leonardslee has been developed over 200 years, and since 1889 maintained by the Loder family. The famous *rhododendron loderi*, raised by Sir Edmund, blossoms in mid-May and the original plants

have grown into stunning trees. In Spring the fragrance of the rhododendrons and azaleas pervade the air throughout the valley. In early May the Rock Garden blossoms with a kaleidoscope of colour. Whilst the many plantings of *Kalmias*, *Cornus* and *Hydrangeas* bring colour to the valley over the summer months.

Ducks, geese, and swans swim on the lakes and huge carp can be seen basking under the surface. Wallabies, deer and other natural wildlife roam the parks. The wallabies have lived wild within the valley for over 100 years, and provide a useful environmentally-friendly mowing service.

The Loder collection of Victorian Motor cars is one of the country's most impressive of this era; all in working condition they show the development of the motor vehicle from 1890–1900.

Owner
The Loder Family

Contact
Tom Loder
Leonardslee Lakes &
Gardens
Lower Beeding
Horsham
West Sussex RH13 6PP

Tel: 01403 891212
Fax: 01403 891305
E-mail: info@
leonardsleegardens.com

Location
MAP 3:H4
OS Ref. TQ222 260

M23 to Handcross then
B2110 (signposted
Cowfold) for 4m.
From London:
1 hr 15 mins.

Rail: Horsham
Station 4½ m.

Bus: No. 17 from
Horsham and Brighton.

Opening Times
Summer
1 April–31 October
Daily 9.30am–6pm
Last admission 4.30pm

Winter
1 November–31 March
Closed (facilities available
for private functions)

Admission
26 April–1 June
Adult (Mon–Fri)   £8.00
(Sat/Sun & BHs)   £9.00

Other times
Adult   £6.50

Child (any time)   £4.00

Coach Parties (20+)
26 April–1 June
Adult (Mon–Fri)   £7.00
(Sat/Sun & BHs)   £8.00

Other times
Adult   £5.50

Child (any time)   £3.50

Special Events
May
Azaleas and
Rhododendron
flowering season

July 12/13
Craft Show

July 19/20
Model Boat Regatta

Aug 16/17
Model Boat Regatta

October
Autumn Colours

Behind the Dolls House – Victorian life in miniature

Splashes of colour in the rock garden

- Photography – landscape & fashion, film location.

- Restaurant available for private and corporate functions in the evenings and out of season.

- Unsuitable, due to natural valley slopes.

- Licenced self-service restaurant for hot lunches, tea, coffee & cakes.

- Ample. Average length of visit 3–5 hours.

€

Conference/Function

ROOM	MAX CAPACITY
Clock Tower	100
Garden Room	50

■ Owner

The National Trust

■ Contact

Nymans
Handcross
Haywards Heath
West Sussex
RH17 6EB

Tel: 01444 405250
Fax: 01444 400253
E-mail: nymans@
nationaltrust.org.uk

■ Location

MAP 4:I4
OS Ref. SU187:TQ265 294

At Handcross on B2114,
12 miles south of Gatwick,
just off London–Brighton
M23.

Bus: 273 Brighton–Crawley,
271 Haywards Heath–
Crawley.

Rail: Balcombe 4 miles;
Crawley 5 miles.

■ Opening Times

**Garden, Shop
& Restaurant**
All year: Wednesday–
Sunday, 10am–5pm,
closes 4pm
November–February.

House
19 March–2 November:
Wednesday–Sunday,
11am–4pm.

■ *Admission

House

Adult	£8.00
Child	£4.00
Family	£20.00
Booked Groups (15+)	£6.80

Half price admission
in Winter

NT members Free

*Includes a voluntary donation
but visitors can choose to pay
the standard prices displayed
at visitor reception and on the
website.

NYMANS 🌿

www.nationaltrust.org.uk

One of the great 20th century gardens with an important collectrion of rare plants, set around a romantic house and ruins in a beautiful wooded estate. Internationally known for its beauty and variety, the garden is the achievement of three generations of the Messel family and their Head Gardeners. The family sponsored great plant hunters, who explored far-off countries in search of wild and exotic plants, vastly adding to the plant collection: a tradition still continued today. The beautiful roses and flower borders make this a most delightful garden in spring and summer.

Much of the house was left in ruins after a fire in 1947, which now forms a romantic backdrop to the main lawn. Several family rooms survived the blaze and can be visited from March to the end of October; arranged as Anne, Countess of Rosse, neé Messel used them.

The garden lies along a ridge of the Sussex Weald at one of the highest points in the county, with wonderful views over the countryside toward the South Downs. There are 275 acres of natural woodland to explore, with marked walks that take in historic lakes, seasonal wild flowers and the tallest tree in Sussex. The Wild Garden is another hidden area worth exploring, where many rare plants have been growing untouched for over a century.

The garden should be visited throughout the changing seasons wih Rhododendron, Magnolia, Camellia and Azalea in spring, the renowned Summer Borders, the glorious colour of autumn and the scent of Daphne, the colour of Witch-hazel and the swathes of pure white Snowdrops in winter.

In Nymans woods only.

PASHLEY MANOR GARDENS

www.pashleymanorgardens.com

A winner of HHA/Christie's Garden of the Year Award. The gardens offer a sumptuous blend of romantic landscaping, imaginative plantings and fine old trees, fountains, springs and large ponds. This is a quintessential English garden of a very individual character with exceptional views to the surrounding valleyed fields. Many eras of English history are reflected here, typifying the tradition of the English Country House and its garden.

The gardens first opened in 1992 and were brought to their present splendour with the assistance of the eminent landscape architect, Anthony du Gard Pasley. A number of different gardens have been created within the 11 acres allowing the visitor to travel from blazing colour to cool creams, greens and golds.

The gardens are always evolving and never static; it is hoped that they will be inspirational yet restful to the first-time visitor and will never disappoint those who return regularly. Pashley prides itself on its delicious food. During warm weather, visitors can enjoy their refreshments on the terrace overlooking the moat or in the Jubilee Courtyard. Home-made soups, ploughman's lunches with pickles and patés, fresh salad from the garden (whenever possible), home-made scones and delicious cakes, filter coffee, specialist teas and fine wines are served from the Garden Room café. The gift shop caters for every taste … from postcards and local honey to traditional hand-painted ceramics and tapestry cushions. A selection of plants and shrubs, many of which grow at Pashley, are available for purchase.

Permanent exhibition and sale of sculpture and botanical art.

Excellent location for small corporate events and private parties.

■ Owner
Mr & Mrs
James A Sellick

■ Contact
Jenny Bigger
Pashley Manor
Ticehurst
Wadhurst
East Sussex TN5 7HE

Tel: 01580 200888
Fax: 01580 200102
E-mail: info@
pashleymanorgardens
.com

■ Location
MAP 4:K4
OS Ref. TQ707 291

On B2099 between A21 and Ticehurst Village.

■ Opening Times
3 April–30 September:
Tues, Weds, Thurs, Sat & BH Mons, 11am–5pm.

October: Garden only Mon–Fri, 10am–4pm.

■ Admission
Adult   £7.00
Children (6–16yrs) £5.00

Groups (20+)   £6.50

Coaches must book. Please telephone for details.

■ Special Events
25 April–5 May (inc.)
Tulip Festival

17–29 May (inc.)
Sculpture Fortnight

14/15 June
Special Rose Weekend

Mid July–Mid August
Lily Time

1–3 August
Lily Weekend

Tulip Time

© Ray Pearson

© David Dixon

'Mr Bennet's Daughter' by Philip Jackson

Partial.
Licensed.
By arrangement.
Guide dogs only.
Telephone for details.

South East – England

■ Owner
The National Trust

■ Contact
The Administration Office
Petworth House
Petworth
West Sussex GU28 0AE

Tel: 01798 342207
Info: 01798 343929
Fax: 01798 342963
E-mail: petworth@
nationaltrust.org.uk

■ Location
MAP 3:G5
OS Ref. SU976 218

In the centre of Petworth
town (approach roads
A272/A283/A285) Car
park signposted.

Rail: Pulborough 5¼m.

■ Opening Times
House
15 March–5 November.
Daily except Thur & Fri,
but open Good Fri,
11am–5pm.

Last admission to House
4.30pm.

Extra rooms shown on
Mon–Wed (closed BH
Mons).

Pleasure Ground
1–12 March for spring
bulbs and events,
11am–4pm.

15 March–5 November.
Saturday–Wednesday,
11am–6pm.

Park
All year: Daily,
8am–sunset.

Shop & Restaurant
1–12 March for
Mothering Sunday
lunches and events,
11am–4pm.

15 March–5 November.
Saturday–Wednesday,
11am–5pm.

■ *Admission
**House & Pleasure
Ground**
Adult	£9.50
Child (5–17yrs)	£4.80
Child (under 5yrs)	Free
Family (2+3)	£23.80

Groups (pre-booked 15+)
Adult	£7.50

Park Only   Free
Parking charge for non-
NT members.

Pleasure Ground
Adult	£3.80
Child (5–17yrs)	£1.90

NT Members Free.

*Includes a voluntary
donation but visitors can
choose to pay the standard
prices displayed at the
property and on the website.

PETWORTH HOUSE & PARK ❧

www.nationaltrust.org.uk/petworth

Petworth House is one of the finest houses in the care of the National Trust and is home to an art collection that rivals many London galleries. Assembled by one family over 350 years, it includes works by Turner, Van Dyck, Titian, Claude, Gainsborough, Bosch, Reynolds and William Blake.

The state rooms contain sculpture, furniture and porcelain of the highest quality and are complemented by the Victorian kitchens in the Servants' Quarters. The Carved Room contains some of Grinling Gibbons' finest limewood carvings.

Petworth House is also the home of Lord and Lady Egremont and extra family rooms are open on weekdays by kind permission of the family (not Bank Holidays).

Petworth Park is a 700 acre park landscaped by 'Capability' Brown and is open to the public all year free of charge. Spring and autumn are particularly breathtaking and the summer sunsets over the lake are spectacular.

©NTPL/Bill Batten

ℹ️ Events & Exhibitions throughout the year. Baby feeding and changing facilities, highchairs. Pushchairs admitted in house but no prams, please. No photography or mobile phones in house.

🛍️

☕ Contact Retail & Catering Manager on 01798 344975.

♿ Car park is 800 yards from house; there is a courtesy carriage available to take less able visitors to the House.

🍴 Licensed.

🚶 By arrangement with the Administration Office on variety of subjects.

🎧 Audio House Tours.

🅿️ 800 yards from house. Coach parties alight at Church Lodge entrance, coaches then park in NT car park. Coaches must book in advance.

🏫 Welcome. Must book. Teachers' pack available.

🐕 Assistance dogs only in House. Dogs in park only.

❄️

♿ Telephone for details.

©NTPL 2004/Lisa Barnard

SHEFFIELD PARK GARDEN

www.nationaltrust.org.uk/sheffieldpark

A magnificent 120 acre landscaped garden. The centrepiece of this internationally renowned, garden is the four lakes that mirror the unique planting and colour that each season brings. Displays of spring bulbs as the garden awakens, and a stunning exhibition of colour in May, of rhododendrons and the National Collection of Ghent Azaleas. Water lilies dress the lakes during the summer. Visitors to the garden during the summer months can enjoy a leisurely walk perhaps pausing to sit on a seat to enjoy the tranquil ambience. In the autumn the garden is transformed by trees planted specifically for their autumn colour including *Nyssa sylvatica, Amelanchier* and *Acer palmatum*. These and other fine specimen trees, particularly North American varieties, produce displays of gold, orange and crimson. The garden is open throughout the year and has something for all, whether a quiet stroll or a family gathering, allowing the children to participate in the many activities offered. Special Events run throughout the year – please telephone for details.

 Partial. WC.
 (not NT).
 By arrangement.

P

Assistance dogs only.

■ Owner
The National Trust

■ Contact
Jo Hopkins
Visitor Services &
Marketing Manager
Sheffield Park
East Sussex
TN22 3QX
Tel: 01825 790231
Fax: 01825 791264
E-mail: sheffieldpark@
nationaltrust.org.uk

■ Location
MAP 4:I5

OS Ref. TQ415 240

Midway between East Grinstead and Lewes, 5m NW of Uckfield on E side of A275.

■ Opening Times
2 February–2 March:
Sat & Sun,
10.30am–4pm.

4 March–4 May:
Tues–Sun,
10.30am–5.30pm.

5 May–1 June:
Daily,
10.30am–5.30pm.

3 June–5 October:
Tues–Sun,
10.30am–5.30pm.

6 October–2 November:
Daily,
10.30am–5.30pm.

4 November–
31 December, Tues–Sun
10.30am–4pm.

3–31 January 2009:
Sat–Sun,
10.30am–4pm.

Open BH Mons. Closed 23–26 December

Last admission 1 hour before closing or dusk if earlier.

■ *Admission
Adult	£7.30
Child	£3.65
Family	£18.25

Groups (15+ prebooked)
Adult	£6.20
Child	£3.10

Guided Tour   £2.00pp
(inc. NT members).
Must be prebooked.

NT, RHS Individual Members and Great British Heritage Pass holders Free.

Joint Ticket available with Bluebell Railway.

*includes a voluntary donation but visitors can choose to pay the standard prices displayed at the property and on the website.

©NTPL/Andrew Butler

ALFRISTON CLERGY HOUSE ⚜

THE TYE, ALFRISTON, POLEGATE, EAST SUSSEX BN26 5TL

Tel: 01323 870001 **Fax:** 01323 871318 **E-mail:** alfriston@nationaltrust.org.uk

Owner: The National Trust **Contact:** The Property Manager

Step back into the Middle Ages with a visit to this 14th century thatched Wealden 'Hall House'. Trace the history of this building which in 1896 was the first to be acquired by the National Trust. Discover what is used to make the floor in the Great Hall and visit the excellent shop. Explore the delightful cottage garden and savour the idyllic setting beside Alfriston's parish church, with stunning views across the meandering River Cuckmere. An intriguing variety of shops, pubs and restaurants in Alfriston village make this a wonderful day out.

Location: MAP 4:J6, OS Ref. TQ521 029. 4m NE of Seaford, just E of B2108.

Open: 1–9 Mar: Sats & Suns, 11am–4pm. 15 Mar–26 Oct: daily except Tue & Fri, 10am–5pm. 27 Oct–21 Dec: daily except Tue & Fri, 11am–4pm.

Admission: Adult £3.70, Child £1.85, Family (2+3) £9.20. Pre-booked groups £2.90.

ⓘ No WCs. 🅾 🅿 Parking in village car parks.

ANNE OF CLEVES HOUSE

52 SOUTHOVER HIGH STREET, LEWES, SUSSEX BN7 1JA

www.sussexpast.co.uk/anneofcleves

Tel: 01273 474610 **Fax:** 01273 486990 **E-mail:** anne@sussexpast.co.uk

Owner: Sussex Past **Contact:** Jamie Taylor

This lovely timber-framed house was once owned by Anne of Cleves. It now displays period furnishings, everyday domestic objects and tells the story of Lewes from 15th century to modern times, political revolutionary Tom Paine, the Lewes Bonfire traditions and the Wealden iron industry. The enclosed rear garden gives a feeling of stepping back into an earlier age.

Location: MAP 4:I5, OS198 Ref. TQ410 096. S of Lewes town centre, off A27/A275/A26.

Open: 1 Jan–29 Feb & 1 Nov–31 Dec: Tue–Sat, 10am–5pm. 1 Mar–31 Oct: Tue–Sat, 10am–5pm; Sun, Mon & BHs, 11am–5pm. Last adm. 4.30pm. Closed 24–26 Dec.

Admission: Adult £3.65, Child £1.70, Conc £3.25, Family (2+2) £9.85 & (1+4) £8.75, Disabled £1.75. Groups (15+): Adult £3.30, Child £1.70, Conc. £2.95. Combined ticket with Lewes Castle is also available.

🅾 🔧 By arrangement. 🅿 Limited (on road). 🔲 🔲 Guide dogs only. 🔺 ❄ ♿

ARUNDEL CASTLE
See page 152 for full page entry.

ARUNDEL CATHEDRAL

Parsons Hill, Arundel, Sussex BN18 9AY

Tel: 01903 882297 **Fax:** 01903 885335 **E-mail:** aruncath1@aol.com

Contact: Rev T Madeley

French Gothic Cathedral, church of the RC Diocese of Arundel and Brighton built by Henry, 15th Duke of Norfolk and opened 1873.

Location: MAP 3:G6, OS Ref. TQ015 072. Above junction of A27 and A284.

Open: Summer: 9am–6pm. Winter: 9am–dusk. Mon: Liturgy of the Word; Tues, Wed, Fri, Sat: Mass 10am; Thurs: Mass 8.30am (at Convent of Poor Clares, Crossbush); Sat: Vigil Mass 6.15pm (at Convent of Poor Clares, Crossbush); Sun: Masses 9.30am and 11.15am. Shop open in the summer, Mon–Fri, 10am–4pm and after services and on special occasions and otherwise on request.

Admission: Free.

BATEMAN'S ⚜
See page 153 for full page entry.

Great Dixter House & Gardens

visit hudsons guide online

1066 BATTLE OF HASTINGS ABBEY AND BATTLEFIELD ⌗

BATTLE, SUSSEX TN33 0AD

www.english-heritage.org.uk/1066

Tel: 01424 773792 **Fax:** 01424 775059

Owner: English Heritage   **Contact:** Visitor Operations Team

Visit the site of the 1066 Battle of Hastings. An inclusive interactive audio tour will lead you around the battlefield and to the exact spot where Harold fell. Explore the magnificent abbey ruins and gatehouse and enjoy our new visitor centre with interactive dispalys and auditorium.

Location: MAP 4:K5, OS Ref. TQ749 157. Top of Battle High Street. Turn off A2100 to Battle.

Open: 21 Mar–30 Sept: daily, 10am–6pm. 1 Oct–20 Mar 2009: daily 10am–4pm. Closed 24–26 Dec & 1 Jan.

Admission: Adult £6.50, Child £3.30, Conc. £5.20, Family £16.30. 15% discount for groups (11+). English Heritage members Free.

ℹ WCs. ▣ ♿ Ground floor & grounds. ▣ P Charge payable. ᐩ Inclusive. 🐕 In grounds, on leads. ✳ ♨

BAYHAM OLD ABBEY ⌗

Lamberhurst, Sussex TN3 8DE

Tel/Fax: 01892 890381   www.english-heritage.org.uk/bayhamoldabbey

Owner: English Heritage   **Contact:** Visitor Operations Team

These riverside ruins are of a house of 'white' canons, founded c.1208 and preserved in the 18th century, when its surroundings were landscaped to create its delightful setting. Rooms in the Georgian dower house are also open to the public.

Location: MAP 4:K4, OS Ref. TQ650 365. 1¾m W of Lamberhurst off B2169.

Open: 21 Mar–30 Sept: daily, 11am–5pm.

Admission: Adult £3.70, Child £1.90, Conc. £3. English Heritage Members Free. Group discount available.

▣ ♿ Grounds. WC. P 🐕 In grounds, on leads.

BIGNOR ROMAN VILLA

Bignor Lane, Bignor, Nr Pulborough, West Sussex RH20 1PH

Tel/Fax: 01798 869259   **E-mail:** t.r.tupper@farming.me.uk

Owner: Mr J R Tupper   **Contact:** John & Del Smith – Curators

One of the largest villas to be open to the public in Great Britain, with some of the finest mosaics all in situ and all under cover, including Medusa, Venus & Cupid Gladiators and Ganymede. Discovered in 1811 and open to the public since 1814. See the longest mosaic on display in Great Britain at 24 metres. Walk on original floors dating back to circa 350 AD. We have a small café and picnic area available.

Location: MAP 3:G5, OS Ref. SU987 146. 6m N of Arundel, 6m S of Pulborough A29. 7m S of Petworth A285.

Open: Mar & Apr: Tue–Sun & BHs, 10am–5pm; May & Oct: daily, 10am–5pm. Jun–Sept: daily, 10am–6pm.

Admission: Adult £4.60, Child £2, OAP £3.30. Groups (10+): Adult £3.70, Child £1.60, OAP £2.60. Guided tours (max 30 per tour) £30.

▣ ♿ Partial. ▣ 📷 By arrangement. P 🐕 ✕

Petworth House

©NTPL/D Sellman

BODIAM CASTLE ✄

BODIAM, NR ROBERTSBRIDGE, EAST SUSSEX TN32 5UA

www.nationaltrust.org.uk/bodiamcastle

Tel: 01580 830196 **Fax:** 01580 830398
E-mail: bodiamcastle@nationaltrust.org.uk
Owner: The National Trust   **Contact:** The Property Manager

Built in 1385 to defend the surrounding countryside and as a comfortable dwelling for a rich nobleman, Bodiam Castle is one of the finest examples of medieval architecture. The virtual completeness of its exterior makes it popular with adults, children and film crews alike. Inside, although a ruin, floors have been replaced in some of the towers and visitors can climb the spiral staircase to enjoy superb views of the Rother Valley and local steam trains from the battlements. Discover more of its intriguing past in the new introductory film, and wander in the peacefully romantic Castle grounds.

Location: MAP 4:K5, OS Ref. TQ782 256. 3m S of Hawkhurst, 2m E of A21 Hurst Green.

Open: 1 Jan–15 Feb: Sats & Suns, 10.30am–4pm. 16 Feb–31 Oct: daily including Good Fri, Easter Sat & Sun, 10.30am–6pm. 1 Nov–15 Feb 2009: Sats & Suns, 10.30am–4pm. Last admission to Castle 1 hour before closing or dusk if earlier.

*Admission: Adult £5.20, Child £2.60, Family (2+3) £13, Groups (15+) £4.40. Parking £2 per car. *Includes a voluntary donation but visitors can choose to pay the standard prices displayed at the property and on the website.

◻ ⬜ Ground floor & grounds. ⑪ ⯈ ■ Teacher & student packs & education base. ✳ ⬛

BOXGROVE PRIORY ⌗

Boxgrove, Chichester, Sussex

Tel: 01424 775705 www.english-heritage.org.uk/boxgrove

Owner: English Heritage   **Contact:** 1066 Battle Abbey

Remains of the Guest House, Chapter House and Church of this 12th-century priory, which was the cell of a French abbey until Richard II confirmed its independence in 1383.

Location: MAP 3:G6, OS Ref. SU908 076. N of Boxgrove, 4 miles E of Chichester on minor road N of A27.

Open: Any reasonable time.

Admission: Free.

⯈ 🐕 ✳

BRAMBER CASTLE ⌗

Bramber, Sussex

Tel: 01424 775705 www.english-heritage.org.uk/bramber

Owner: English Heritage   **Contact:** 1066 Battle Abbey

The remains of a Norman castle gatehouse, walls and earthworks in a splendid setting overlooking the Adur Valley.

Location: MAP 3:H5, OS Ref. TQ185 107. On W side of Bramber village NE of A283.

Open: Any reasonable time.

Admission: Free.

⯈ Limited. 🐕 On leads. ✳

CAMBER CASTLE ⌗

Camber, Nr Rye, East Sussex TN31 7RS

Tel: 01797 223862 www.english-heritage.org.uk/camber

Owner: English Heritage   **Contact:** Rye Harbour Nature Reserve

A fine example of one of many coastal fortresses built by Henry VIII to counter the threat of invasion during the 16th century. Monthly guided walks of Rye Nature Reserve including Camber Castle: telephone for details.

Location: MAP 4:L5, OS189, Ref. TQ922 185. Across fields off A259, 1 mile S of Rye off harbour road.

Open: 1 Jul–30 Sept: Sats & Suns, 2–5pm. Last admission 4.30pm. Opening times subject to change.

Admission: Adult £2, Accompanied children Free, Conc. £1. Friends of Rye Harbour Nature Reserve & EH Members Free. Group discount available. Prices subject to change.

🚫 Unsuitable. 🅕 By arrangement. ⯈ None. 🐕 Guide dogs only.

CHARLESTON

See page 154 for full page entry.

Charleston

For **accommodation** in the South East, see our special index at the end of the book.

CHICHESTER CATHEDRAL
CHICHESTER, W SUSSEX PO19 1PX

www.chichestercathedral.org.uk

Tel: 01243 782595 **Fax:** 01243 812499 **E-mail:** visitors@chichestercathedral.org.uk
Contact: Visitor Services Officer

In the heart of Chichester, this magnificent Cathedral has treasures ranging from medieval stone carvings to famous 20th century artworks. There is also a Treasury, regular exhibitions and free weekly lunchtime concerts. Guided tours daily and specialist tours are available (history, art, embroidery, stained glass, behind the scenes …). Superb new Cloisters Restaurant and Shop on site. The Cathedral does not charge for entry as we believe that this beautiful building should be available to all.

Location: MAP 3:F6, OS Ref. SU860 047. West Street, Chichester.
Open: Summer: 7.15am–7pm, Winter: 7.15am–6pm. Choral Evensong daily (except Wed) during term time.
Admission: Free entry. Donations greatly appreciated.
Private functions and conferences.

COWDRAY RUINS
COWDRAY PARK, MIDHURST, W SUSSEX GU29 9AL

www.cowdray.org.uk

Tel: 01730 810781   **E-mail:** info@cowdray.org.uk
Owner: Cowdray Heritage Trust   **Contact:** The Manager

As a major new attraction, Cowdray is one of the most important survivals of a Tudor nobleman's house. Set within the stunning 'Capability' Brown landscaped Cowdray Park, the house was partially destroyed by fire in 1793. Explore the Tudor Kitchens, Buck Hall, Chapel, Gatehouse, Vaulted Storeroom and Cellars, Visitor Centre and Shop.

Location: MAP 3:F5, OS Ref. TQ891 216. E outskirts of Midhurst on A272.
Open: 21 Mar–26 Oct: Wed–Sun & BH Mons, 10.30am–4pm (last admission). Groups at other times by arrangement.
Admission: Adult £5, Child (over 5yrs) £2.50, Conc. £4.50, Family £12. 10% discount for groups (10+).
Partial. WCs. By arrangement. None. Guide dogs only.

©David Dixon

CLINTON LODGE GARDEN
FLETCHING, E SUSSEX TN22 3ST

Tel/Fax: 01825 722952   **e-mail:** garden@clintonlodge.com
Owner/Contact: Lady Collum

Caroline house enlarged by the Earl of Sheffield for his daughter when she married Sir Henry Clinton, one of three generals at Waterloo. The 18th century façade is set in a tree lined lawn, flanked by a newly created canal and overlooking parkland. The 6 acre garden reflects periods of English gardening history and includes a knot garden, mediaeval style herb garden with camomile paths and turf seats, potager, wild flower garden, pre-Raphaelite inspired allée, pleached lime walks; garden of old roses, double blue, white and yellow herbaceous borders; orchard planted with crinums and many yew and beech hedges.

Location: MAP 4:I5, OS Ref. TQ428 238. In centre of village behind tall yew and holly hedge.
Open: NGS Days: 11 May. 8/9, 16, 23 & 29 Jun. 7 & 28 Jul. 4 Aug, 2–5.30pm.
Admission: NGS Days: £4 . Private groups by arrangement £6 .
WCs. Unsuitable. By arrangement. Limited. Guide dogs only.

DENMANS GARDEN

Denmans Lane, Fontwell, West Sussex BN18 0SU
Tel: 01243 542808   **Fax:** 01243 544064   **E-mail:** denmans@denmans-garden.co.uk
www.denmans-garden.co.uk
Owner: John Brookes & Michael Neve   **Contact:** Mrs Claudia Murphy

Beautiful 4 acre garden designed for year round interest – through use of form, colour and texture – the home of John Brookes MBE, renowned garden designer and writer. Beautiful plant centre and Les Routiers award-winning fully licensed Garden Café (Café of the Year 2005 London & South East).

Location: MAP 3:G6, OS197 Ref. SZ947 070. Off the A27 (westbound) between Chichester (6m) and Arundel (5m).
Open: Daily. Garden: 9am–5pm. Plant centre: 9am–5pm. Café: 10am–5pm. Nov–Feb: 9am–dusk. Closed 24–26 Dec & 1 Jan.
Admission: Adult £4.50, Child (4–16) £3, OAP £4.25, Family (2+2) £14. Pre-booked groups (15+) £4.
WC. Licensed. Licensed. Group menus on request. Guide dogs only.

Glynde Place

©Jeremy Whitaker

FIRLE PLACE

FIRLE, LEWES, EAST SUSSEX BN8 6LP

www.firleplace.co.uk

Tel: 01273 858307 (Enquiries)   **Events:** 01273 858567
Fax: 01273 858188   **Restaurant:** 01273 858307   **E-mail:** gage@firleplace.co.uk
Owner: The Rt Hon Viscount Gage

Firle Place is the home of the Gage family and has been for over 500 years. Set at the foot of the Sussex Downs within its own parkland, this unique house originally Tudor, was built of Caen stone, possibly from a monastery dissolved by Sir John Gage, friend of Henry VIII. Remodelled in the 18th century it is similar in appearance to that of a French château. The house contains a magnificent collection of Old Master paintings, fine English and European furniture and an impressive collection of Sèvres porcelain collected mainly by the 3rd Earl Cowper from Panshanger House, Hertfordshire.

Events: The Great Tudor Hall can, on occasion, be used for private dinners, with drinks on the Terrace or in the Billiard Room. A private tour of the house can be arranged. The paddock area is an ideal site for a marquee. The park can be used for larger events, using the house as a backdrop.

Restaurant: Enjoy the licensed restaurant and tea terrace with views over the garden for luncheon and cream teas.

Location: MAP 4:J6, OS Ref. TQ473 071. 4m S of Lewes on A27 Brighton / Eastbourne Road.

Open: Easter & BH Sun/Mon. Jun–Sept: Wed, Thur, Sun & BHs, 2–4.30pm. Dates and times subject to change without prior notice. Last admission 4.15pm. Garden Open Days: 27 Apr & 28 Sept.

Admission: Adult £6.50, Child £3, Conc. £5.50.

ℹ️ No photography in house. 🚻 Ground floor & restaurant. 🍴 Licensed. Tea Terrace. Wed & Thur. 🅿️ In grounds on leads.

FISHBOURNE ROMAN PALACE

SALTHILL ROAD, FISHBOURNE, CHICHESTER, SUSSEX PO19 3QR

www.sussexpast.co.uk/fishbourne

Tel: 01243 785859   **Fax:** 01243 539266   **E-mail:** adminfish@sussexpast.co.uk
Owner: Sussex Past   **Contact:** David Rudkin

See Britain's largest collection of *in situ* Roman Palace floor mosaics and garden, replanted using plants from that time. Everyday Roman objects found from the excavations are displayed in the museum gallery. Join a behind the scenes tour in the Collections Discovery Centre for an opportunity to handle artefacts. Free parking, café and gift shop plus special events.

Location: MAP 3:F6, OS Ref. SU837 057. 1½m W of Chichester in Fishbourne village off A27/A259. 5 minutes walk from Fishbourne railway station.

Open: Daily 21 Jan–Feb: 10am–4pm. Mar–Jul & Sept/Oct: 10am–5pm. Aug: 10am–6pm. 1 Nov–15 Dec: 10am–4pm. Weekends 20/21 & 27/28 Dec: 10am–4pm.

Admission: Adult £7, Child £3.70, Conc £6, Family (2+2) £17.90, Registered Disabled £5.50 (Carer Free).

By arrangement. 🅿️ Guide dogs only.

GLYNDE PLACE 🏛

GLYNDE, Nr LEWES, EAST SUSSEX BN8 6SX

www.glynde.co.uk

Tel/Fax: 01273 858224   **E-mail:** info@glynde.co.uk

Owners: Viscount & Viscountess Hampden   **Contact:** Sue Tester

Glynde Place is a magnificent example of Elizabethan architecture commanding exceptionally fine views of the South Downs. Amongst the collections of 400 years of family living can be seen 17th and 18th century portraits of the Trevors, furniture, embroidery and silver.

Location: MAP 4:J5, OS Ref. TQ456 093. Sign posted off of A27, 4m SE of Lewes at top of village. Rail: Glynde is on the London/Eastbourne and Brighton/Eastbourne mainline railway.

Open: May–Aug: Weds, Suns & BHs, 2–5pm (last tour 4pm). Garden & Tea Room: 12 noon–5pm. Private viewings by appointment.

Admission: House & Garden: Adult £6, Child (under 12yrs) Free, Conc. £5. CPRE 2 for 1. Groups (25+) by appointment.

🖼 🛇 🍴 🛇 🛇 🅿 Free. 🛇 Guide dogs only. 🛇

HAMMERWOOD PARK

EAST GRINSTEAD, SUSSEX RH19 3QE

www.hammerwoodpark.com

Tel: 01342 850594   **Fax:** 01342 850864   **E-mail:** latrobe@mistral.co.uk

Owner/Contact: David Pinnegar

Built in 1792 as an Apollo's hunting lodge by Benjamin Latrobe, architect of the Capitol and the White House, Washington DC. Owned by Led Zepplin in the 1970s, rescued from dereliction in 1982. Teas in the Organ Room; copy of the Parthenon frieze; and a derelict dining room still shocks the unwary. Guided tours (said by many to be the most interesting in Sussex) by the family. Also summer concerts.

Location: MAP 4:J4, OS Ref. TQ442 390. 3½ m E of East Grinstead on A264 to Tunbridge Wells, 1m W of Holtye.

Open: 1 June–end Sept: Wed, Sat & BH Mon, 2–5pm. Guided tour starts 2.05pm. Private groups: Easter–Jun. Coaches strictly by appointment. Small groups any time throughout the year by appointment.

Admission: House & Park: Adult £6, Child £2. Private viewing by arrangement.

ℹ Conferences. 🛇 🛇 🛇 Obligatory. 🛇 🛇 In grounds. 🛇 B&B. 🛇 🛇 €

GOODWOOD HOUSE 🏛   *See page 155 for full page entry.*

GREAT DIXTER HOUSE & GARDENS 🏛   *See page 156 for full page entry.*

Parham House & Gardens

GARDENS AND GROUNDS OF HERSTMONCEUX CASTLE

HAILSHAM, E SUSSEX BN27 1RN

www.herstmonceux-castle.com

Tel: 01323 833816   **Fax:** 01323 834499   **E-mail:** c_cullip@isc.queensu.ac.uk

Owner: Queen's University, Canada   **Contact:** C Cullip

This breathtaking 15th century moated Castle is set within 500 acres of parkland and gardens (including Elizabethan Garden) and is ideal for picnics and woodland walks. At Herstmonceux there is something for all the family.

Location: MAP 4:K5, OS Ref. TQ646 104. 2m S of Herstmonceux village (A271) by minor road. 10m WNW of Bexhill.

Open: 12 Apr–26 Oct (closed 2, 3 Aug & 25 Oct.): daily, 10am–6pm (last adm. 5pm). Closes 5pm from Oct.

Admission: Grounds & Gardens: Adults £5.50, Child under 15yrs & Students £3 (child under 5 Free), Conc. £4.50, Family £13. Group rates/bookings available.

ℹ Visitor Centre. 🛇 🛇 Limited for Castle Tour. 🛇 🛇 🅿 🛇 On leads. 🛇 🛇

David Sellman

HIGH BEECHES WOODLAND & WATER GARDENS
HIGH BEECHES, HANDCROSS, SUSSEX RH17 6HQ
www.highbeeches.com

Tel: 01444 400589 **Fax:** 01444 401543 **E-mail:** gardens@highbeeches.com
Owner: High Beeches Gardens Conservation Trust (Reg. Charity)
Contact: Sarah Bray
Explore 25 acres of magically beautiful, peaceful woodland and water gardens. Daffodils, bluebells, azaleas, naturalised gentians, autumn colours. Rippling streams, enchanting vistas. Four acres of natural wildflower meadows. Rare plants. Marked trails. Recommended by Christopher Lloyd. Enjoy lunches and teas in the tearoom and tea lawn in restored Victorian farm building.
Location: MAP 4:I4, OS Ref. TQ275 308. S side of B2110. 1m NE of Handcross.
Open: 21 Mar–31 Oct: daily except Weds, 1–5pm (last adm. 4.30pm). Coaches/ guided tours anytime, by appointment only.
Admission: Adult £5.50, Child (under 14yrs) Free. Concession for groups (20+). Guided tours for groups £10pp.

🔲 Partial. Tearoom fully accessible. 🍴 Licensed. 🎦 By arrangement. 🅿 🔲 🔲

HIGHDOWN GARDENS
Littlehampton Road, Goring-by-Sea, Worthing, Sussex BN12 6PE
Tel: 01903 501054
Owner: Worthing Borough Council **Contact:** Parks and Foreshore Manager
Unique gardens in disused chalk pit, begun in 1909.
Location: MAP 3:H6, OS Ref. TQ098 040. 3m WNW of Worthing on N side of A259, just W of the Goring roundabout.
Open: 1 Apr–30 Sept: daily, 10am–6pm. 1 Oct–30 Nov: Mon–Fri, 10am–4.30pm. 1 Dec–31 Jan: Mon–Fri, 10am–4pm.
Admission: Free.

LAMB HOUSE 🌿
West Street, Rye, Sussex TN31 7ES
Tel: 01580 762334 **Fax:** 01580 762334 **E-mail:** lambhouse@nationaltrust.org.uk
Owner: The National Trust
The beloved home of Henry James, where he wrote some of his best known novels including *The Wings of a Dove*. The house, with its pretty walled garden, has also been home to other literary names, including E F Benson and Rumer Godden.
Location: MAP 4:L5, OS Ref. TQ920 202. On West Street (facing west end of church).
Open: 20 Mar–25 Oct: Thurs & Sat, 2–6pm.
Admission: Adult £3.50, Child £1.80, Family £8.70. Group: £2.95.

LEONARDSLEE LAKES & GARDENS
See page 157 for full page entry.

For unique **Civil wedding** venues see our index at the end of the book.

LEWES CASTLE & BARBICAN HOUSE MUSEUM
169 HIGH STREET, LEWES, SUSSEX BN7 1YE
www.sussexpast.co.uk/lewescastle

Tel: 01273 486290 **Fax:** 01273 486990 **E-mail:** castle@sussexpast.co.uk
Owner: Sussex Past **Contact:** Dr Sally White
Lewes's imposing Norman castle offers magnificent views across the town and surrounding downland. Barbican House, towered over by the Barbican Gate, is home to an interesting museum of local history and archaeology. A superb scale model of Victorian Lewes provides the centrepiece of a 25 minute audio-visual presentation telling the story of the county town of Sussex.
Location: MAP 4:I5, OS198 Ref. TQ412 101. Lewes town centre off A27/A26/A275.
Open: Daily Tue–Sat: 10am–5.30pm; Sun, Mon & BHs, 11am–5.30pm (Closed Mons in Jan & 25/26 Dec). Castle closes at dusk in winter. Last admission 30 minutes prior to closing.
Admission: Adult £4.90, Child £2.55, Conc. £4.35, Disabled £2.45, Family (2+2) £13.55 or (1+4) £12.55. Groups (15+): Adult £4.40, Child £2.30, Conc £3.90., Disabled/Carer £2.20. Discounted joint ticket available with Anne of Cleves House.

🔲 🔲 Unsuitable. 🎦 By arrangement. 🔲 🔲 Guide dogs only. 🔲 🔲

MARLIPINS MUSEUM
HIGH STREET, SHOREHAM-BY-SEA, SUSSEX BN43 5DA
www.sussexpast.co.uk/marlipins

Tel: 01273 462994 or 01323 441279 **E-mail:** marlipins@sussexpast.co.uk
Owner: Sussex Past **Contact:** Helen Poole
Once a Customs House, it now holds artefacts from the long history of the Shoreham area and the maritime past plus a collection of local archaeological material from prehistoric to medieval times. In the upstairs gallery are displays on the local silent film industry and transport. A new extension hosts temporary visiting shows, activities and talks.
Location: MAP 3:H6, OS198 Ref. TQ214 051. Shoreham town centre on A259, W of Brighton.
Open: 1 May–1 Nov: Tue–Sat, 10.30am–4.30pm.
Admission: Adult £3, Child £1.75, Conc. £2.50. Groups (15+): Adult £2.70, Child £1.50, Conc. £2.25.

🔲 🔲 WC. 🎦 By arrangement. 🅿 None. 🔲 🔲 Guide dogs only. 🔲

MICHELHAM PRIORY 🏛
UPPER DICKER, HAILSHAM, SUSSEX BN27 3QS

www.sussexpast.co.uk/michelham

Tel: 01323 844224   **Fax:** 01323 844030   **E-mail:** adminmich@sussexpast.co.uk
Owner: Sussex Past   **Contact:** Chris Tuckett

Enter through the 14th-century gatehouse and wander through beautiful gardens or tour the historic house. Furniture and artefacts trace the property's religious origins and its development over 800 years to a grand country house. Explore the medieval watermill, working forge, rope museum and dramatic Elizabethan Great Barn. Plenty of free parking, restaurant and gift shop plus special events.

Location: MAP 4:J5, OS Ref. TQ557 093. 8m NW of Eastbourne off A22/A27. 2m W of Hailsham.

Open: 1 Mar–2 Nov: Tue–Sun & BH Mons & daily in Aug. 10.30am–4.30pm. Apr–Jul & Sept: 10.30am–5pm. Aug: Daily 10.30am–5.30pm.

Admission: Adult £6.25, Child £3.25, Conc £5.20, Family (2+2) £17.25, Registered disabled & carer £3.25 each. Groups (15+): Adult £5.30, Child £3. Conc. £4.90.
Special events: Adult £8, Child £5, Conc £6, Family (2+2) £23.50, Disabled £5.

🖵 🕭 🆃 🔄 🎧 🍴 Licensed. 🎥 By arrangement. 🅿 Ample for cars & coaches. ■ 🐕 Guide dogs only. ▲ ♿

MONK'S HOUSE 🌿

Rodmell, Lewes BN7 3HF
Tel: 01323 870001 (Property Office)
Owner: The National Trust   **Contact:** Property Office

A small weather-boarded house, the home of Leonard and Virginia Woolf until Leonard's death in 1969.

Location: MAP 4:I6, OS Ref. TQ421 064. 4 m E of Lewes, off former A275 in Rodmell village, near church.

Open: 2 Apr–29 Oct: Weds & Sats, 2–5.30pm. Last admission 5pm. Groups by arrangement with tenant.

Admission: Adult £3.50, Child £1.80, Family £8.70, Groups £2.90.

NYMAN'S 🌿   *See page 158 for full page entry.*

PALLANT HOUSE GALLERY

9 North Pallant, Chichester, West Sussex. PO19 1TJ
Tel: 01243 774557
Owner: Pallant House Gallery Trust   **Contact:** Reception

Museum of the Year 2007, Pallant House Gallery houses one of the best collections of modern British art in the world alongside an exciting programme of temporary exhibitions.

Location: MAP 3:F6, OS Ref. SU861 047. City centre, SE of the Cross.

Open: Tue–Sat: 10am–5pm (Thur: 10am–8pm. Sun & BH Mons: 12.30–5pm).

Admission: Adult £6.50, Child (6–15yrs): £2, Students £3.50.
Unemployed/Friends/Under 5s Free, Family (2 + 4): £15. Tue & Thur: 5–8pm, half price.

For **corporate hospitality** venues see our special index at the end of the book.

Glynde Place

PARHAM HOUSE & GARDENS 🏛

PARHAM PARK, STORRINGTON, Nr PULBOROUGH, WEST SUSSEX RH20 4HS

www.parhaminsussex.co.uk

Tel: 01903 742021 **Info Line:** 01903 744888 **Fax:** 01903 746557
Email: enquiries@parhaminsussex.co.uk
Owner: Parham Park Trust **Contact:** Richard Pailthorpe

One of the top twenty in Simon Jenkins's book *"England's Thousand Best Houses"*, Parham is one of the country's finest Elizabethan examples. Idyllically set in the heart of a 17th century deer park, below the South Downs, the house contains a particularly important collection of needlework, paintings and furniture. The spectacular Long Gallery is the third longest in England. The award winning gardens include a four acre walled garden with stunning herbaceous borders, greenhouse, orchard, potager and herbiary. All the flowers used in the house are home grown. Parham has always been

a much-loved family home. Now owned by a charitable trust, the house is lived in by Lady Emma Barnard, her husband James and their family.

Location: MAP 3: G5, OS Ref. TQ060 143. Midway between Pulborough & Storrington on A283. Equidistant from A24 &A29.

Open: 23 Mar–28 Sept. House: Wed, Thur, Sun & BH Mons from 2–5pm, also Aug, Tue & Fri. Gardens: Tue, Wed, Thu, Fri, Sun and BH Mons from 12noon–5pm.

Admission: Please contact property for details.

ⓘ No photography in house. 🄯 🛉 🚹 Partial. 🍴 Licensed. 🎫 By arrangement 🄯 🅿 🚻 🐾 In grounds, on leads. 🐶 Special charges may apply. Please contact property for details.

PASHLEY MANOR GARDENS 🏛 *See page 159 for full page entry.*

PETWORTH COTTAGE MUSEUM

346 High Street, Petworth, West Sussex GU28 0AU
Tel: 01798 342100 **E-mail:** stevensonguk@yahoo.co.uk
Owner: Petworth Cottage Trust **Contact:** Curator

Step into a Leconfield Estate Cottage furnished as if it were 1910. Lighting is by gas, heating by coal-fired range. The scullery has a stone sink and a copper for the weekly wash.

Location: MAP 3:G5

Open: Apr–Oct: Wed–Sun & BH Mons, 2–4.30pm.

Admission: Adult £2.50, Child (under 14yrs) 50p. Group visits by arrangement.

PETWORTH HOUSE & PARK 🌿 *See page 160 for full page entry.*

PEVENSEY CASTLE ⌗

Pevensey, Sussex BN24 5LE
Tel/Fax: 01323 762604 **www.english-heritage.org.uk/pevensey**
Owner: English Heritage **Contact:** Visitor Operations Team

Originally a 4th-century Roman fort, Pevensey was the place where William the Conqueror landed in 1066 and established his first stronghold. The Norman castle includes the remains of an unusual keep within the massive walls. An exhibition with artefacts found on site and an inclusive audio tour tells the story of the castle's 2,000 year history.

Location: MAP 4:K6, OS Ref. TQ645 048. In Pevensey off A259.

Open: 21 Mar–31 Oct: daily, 10am–6pm (4pm Oct). 1 Nov–31 Mar '09: Sats & Suns, 10am–4pm. Closed 24–26 Dec & 1 Jan.

Admission: Adult £4.20, Child £2.10, Conc. £3.40. Family £10.50. 15% discount for groups of 11+. EH Members free.

ⓘ WC. 🄯 🚹 Grounds. 🐾 🄯 Inclusive. 🅿 🚻 In grounds, on leads. 🕮

THE PRIEST HOUSE

NORTH LANE, WEST HOATHLY, SUSSEX RH19 4PP

www.sussexpast.co.uk/priest house

Tel: 01342 810479 **E-mail:** priest@sussexpast.co.uk
Owner: Sussex Past **Contact:** Antony Smith

The 15th century timber-framed hall house sits on the edge of Ashdown Forest in the picturesque Wealden village of West Hoathly. Celebrating 100 years as a museum in 2008, it now contains country furniture, ironwork, textiles and domestic objects and stands in a charming traditional cottage garden. Guided tours available.

Location: MAP 4:J4, OS187 Ref. TQ362 325. In triangle formed by Crawley, East Grinstead and Haywards Heath, 4m off A22, 6m off M23.

Open: 1 Mar–2 Nov: Tue–Sat & BHs plus Mons during Aug: 10.30am–5.30pm; Sun, 12 noon–5.30pm.

Admission: Adult £3.20, Child £1.60, Conc. £2.75. Disabled/Carer £1.60. Garden only £1. Groups (15+) Adult £2.90, Child £1.45, Conc. £2.50. Disabled/Carer £1.45.

🄯 🛉 🚹 Partial. 🎫 By arrangement. 🅿 Limited (on street). 🕮 🐾 In grounds, on leads.

ST MARY'S HOUSE & GARDENS 🏛
BRAMBER, WEST SUSSEX BN44 3WE
www.stmarysbramber.co.uk

Tel/Fax: 01903 816205 **E-mail:** info@stmarysbramber.co.uk
Owners: Mr Peter Thorogood MBE, Mary Thorogood and Mr Roger Linton MBE
This enchanting, medieval house is situated in the picturesque downland village of Bramber. The fine panelled interiors, including the unique Elizabethan 'Painted Room' with its intriguing *trompe l'oeil* murals, give an air of tranquillity and timelessness. Once the home of the real Algernon and Gwendolen brilliantly portrayed in Oscar Wilde's comedy, *The Importance of Being Earnest*, St Mary's has served as a location for a number of television series including the world-famous *Dr Who*. The formal gardens with amusing animal topiary include an exceptional example of the prehistoric 'Living Fossil' tree, *Gingko Biloba*, and a mysterious ivy-clad 'Monk's Walk'. In the Victorian 'Secret' Garden can be seen the fruit-wall and Rural Museum, Jubilee Rose Garden, Terracotta Garden, English Poetry Garden and woodland walk. St Mary's features in Simon Jenkins' book *England's Thousand Best Houses*, and was highly commended in the Tourism Excellence Awards. The garden, because of its literary connections, was nominated by *The Independent* as one of "Britain's 50 Best Gardens to Visit". St Mary's is a house of fascination and mystery. Many thousands of visitors have admired its picturesque charm and enjoyed its atmosphere of friendliness and welcome, qualities which make it a visit to remember.

Location: MAP 3:H6, OS Ref. TQ189 105. Bramber village off A283. From London 56m via M23/A23 or A24. Bus from Shoreham to Steyning, alight St Mary's, Bramber.
Open: May–end Sept: Suns, Thurs & BH Mons, 2–6pm. Last entry 5pm. Groups at other times by arrangement.
Admission: House & Gardens: Adult £6.50. Child £3. Conc. £6. Groups (25+) £6.
ℹ No photography in house. ◻ 🍴 ♿ Partial. 🍴 👤 Obligatory for groups (max 60). Visit time 2½hrs. 🅿 30 cars, 2 coaches. ◼ ✖ ▲ ♥

Arundel Castle

SACKVILLE COLLEGE
HIGH STREET, EAST GRINSTEAD, WEST SUSSEX RH19 3BX
www.sackville-college.co.uk

Tel: 01342 326561 **E-mail:** sackvillecollege@yahoo.com
Owner: Board of Trustees **Contact:** College Co-ordinator
Built in 1609 for Richard Sackville, Earl of Dorset, as an almshouse and overnight accommodation for the Sackville family. Feel the Jacobean period come alive in the enchanting quadrangle, the chapel, banqueting hall with fine hammerbeam roof and minstrel's gallery, the old common room and warden's study where "Good King Wenceslas" was composed. Chapel weddings by arrangement.
Location: MAP 4:I4, A22 to East Grinstead, College in High Street (town centre).
Open: 14 Jun–14 Sept: Wed–Sun, 2–5pm. Groups all year by arrangement.
Admission: Adult £3.50, Child £1. Groups: (10–60) no discount.
ℹ Large public car park adjacent to entrance. ◻ 🍴 T ♿ Partial.
👤 Obligatory. 🅿 Limited. ◼ ✖ Guide dogs only. ✽ By arrangement. ♥

SAINT HILL MANOR

SAINT HILL ROAD, EAST GRINSTEAD, WEST SUSSEX RH19 4JY

www.sainthillmanor.org.uk

Tel: 01342 326711 **Fax:** 01342 317057 **E-mail:** info@ hubbardfoundation.co.uk
Owner: Church of Scientology **Contact:** Liz Ostermann Saint Hill Manor
Built in 1792 by Gibbs Crawfurd, Saint Hill Manor is one of Sussex's finest sandstone buildings, with breathtaking views of unspoiled countryside. Impressive features include the magnificent black Spanish marble pillars added by the Maharajah of Jaipur, and the delightful 100-foot Monkey Mural, painted by Winston Churchill's nephew.
The final owner, author L Ron Hubbard, bought the Manor in 1959 and made it his family home, restoring much of the oak panelling and marble fireplaces. An impressive

collection of Mr. Hubbard's 590 published works is displayed in the library. There are 59 acres of grounds, lake and rose garden. Ideal for weddings and conferences.
Location: MAP 4:14, OS Ref. TQ383 359. 2 miles S of East Grinstead.
Open: All year. Guided tours of the house every afternoon 2–5 pm on the hour. Open in morning by arrangement. Gardens open all day.
Admission: Free of charge. Coach parties welcome, teas served.
⊤ ⊡ Teas available. 🎦 Obligatory. 🅿 ⊠ ❄ ⊠ 29 Feb: Group Visits Fair. 22 Jun: Open Air Theatre.

SHEFFIELD PARK GARDEN ❧

See page 161 for full page entry.

Stansted Park

©NTPL/Nadia Mackenzie

STANDEN ❧

EAST GRINSTEAD, WEST SUSSEX RH19 4NE

www.nationaltrust.org.uk/standen

Tel: 01342 323029 **Fax:** 01342 316424 **E-mail:** standen@nationaltrust.org.uk
Owner: The National Trust **Contact:** The Property Manager
Dating from the 1890s and containing original Morris & Co furnishings and decorations, Standen survives today as a remarkable testimony to the ideals of the Arts and Crafts Movement. The property was built as a family home by the influential architect Philip Webb and retains a warm, welcoming atmosphere. Details of Webb's designs can be found everywhere from the fireplaces to the original electric light fittings.
Location: MAP 4:I4, OS Ref. TQ389 356. 2m S of East Grinstead, signposted from B2110.
Open: House, Garden, Shop & Restaurant: 1–9 Mar: Sats & Suns, 11am–4.30pm. 15 Mar–2 Nov: Wed–Sun & BHs. 11am–4.30pm (last entry to house 4pm). Also Mons 21 Jul–31 Aug only. Garden, Shop & Restaurant: 8 Nov–21 Dec: Sats & Suns, 11am–3pm.
Admission: House & Garden: £7.80, Family £19.50. Garden only: £4.60. Groups £6.50 only if booked in advance. 1–9 March and 8 Nov–21 Dec: House & Garden £5.80, Family £14.50. Garden only £3.60.
⊡ ⊞ ⊤ ⊡ Partial. WC. 🍴 Licensed. 🅿 ▣ ⊠ In designated areas. ⊡

STANSTED PARK

STANSTED PARK, ROWLANDS CASTLE, HAMPSHIRE PO9 6DX

www.stanstedpark.co.uk

Tel: 023 9241 2265 **Fax:** 023 9241 3773 **E-mail:** enquiry@stanstedpark.co.uk
Owner: Stansted Park Foundation **Contact:** House and Events Manager

'One of the South's most beautiful stately homes'. The State Rooms and fully restored Servants' Quarters of Stansted House give the visitor a fascinating insight into the social history of an English Country House in its heyday in Edwardian times.

Location: MAP 3:F5, OS Ref. SU761 103. Follow brown heritage signs from A3 Rowlands Castle or A27 Havant. Rail: Mainline station, Havant.

Open: House & Chapel: Sun & Mon from Easter Sun–29 Sept: 1–4pm. House & Chapel closed during events. Jul & Aug: Sun–Wed. Tea Room & Garden Centre open all year. Restricted access to grounds on Sats and during events. Stansted Park Light Railway runs through Arboretum. Tel: 02392 413324 for timetable.

Admission: House, Grounds & Chapel: Adult £6, Child (5–15yrs) £3.50, Conc. £5, Family (2+3) £15. Groups/educational visits by arrangement.

Private & corporate hire. By arrangement. By arrangement. Guide dogs only. Grounds.

Raymond Woodham

UPPARK

SOUTH HARTING, PETERSFIELD GU31 5QR

www.nationaltrust.org.uk/uppark

Tel: 01730 825415 **Fax:** 01730 825873 **E-mail:** uppark@nationaltrust.org.uk
Owner: The National Trust **Contact:** Administrator

Marvel at the historic elegance of Uppark – with fine, late-Georgian interiors and collections of paintings, ceramics and textiles, extensive basement rooms, famous dolls house, Regency garden (stunning views to the sea), children's activities, award-winning shop and restaurant – there is everything for a perfect day out.

Location: MAP 3:F5, OS Ref 197 SU781 181. Between Petersfield & Chichester on B2146.

Open: 16 Mar–30 Oct: Sun–Thur; Grounds, Shop & Restaurant: 11.30am–5pm; House: 12.30–4.30pm. BH Suns, Mons & Good Friday, 11.30am–4.30pm. Print Room open 1st Mon of each month.

***Admission:** Adult £7.80, Child £3.90, Family £19.50, Groups (15+) must book: £6.60. *includes a voluntary donation but visitors can choose to pay the standard prices displayed at the property and on the website.

By arrangement.

WEALD & DOWNLAND OPEN AIR MUSEUM

Singleton, Chichester, Sussex PO18 0EU
Tel: 01243 811348 **www.wealddown.co.uk**

Over 45 original rescued historic buildings. Interiors and gardens through the ages. Plus traditional breed farm animals, all set in Sussex's beautiful South Downs.

Location: MAP 3:F5, OS Ref. SU876 127. 6m N of Chichester on A286. S of Singleton.

Open: Throughout the year, telephone or see website for details.

Admission: Adult £8.50, Child/Student £4.50, OAP £7.50. Family (2+3) £23.30. Group rates on request.

WEST DEAN GARDENS

WEST DEAN, CHICHESTER, WEST SUSSEX PO18 0QZ

www.westdean.org.uk

Tel: 01243 818210 **Fax:** 01243 811342 **E-mail:** gardens@westdean.org.uk
Owner: The Edward James Foundation **Contact:** Jim Buckland, Gardens Manager

A place of tranquillity and beauty in the rolling South Downs. West Dean features a restored walled kitchen garden with some of the finest Victorian glasshouses in the country, rustic summerhouses, a 300ft Edwardian pergola, ornamental borders and a pond contrast with over 200 varieties of carefully trained fruit trees, rows of vegetables and exotic produce behind glass. For the more active, a circular walk through a 49-acre arboretum offers breathtaking views of the estate and its fine flint house and parkland setting.

Location: MAP 3:F5, OS Ref. SU863 128. SE of A286 Midhurst Road, 6m N of Chichester, 7m S of Midhurst.

Open: Mar–Oct: daily, 10.30am–5pm (last adm 4.30pm). Nov–Feb: Wed–Sun, 10.30am–4pm.

Admission: Summer: Adult £6, Child £3, Family £15, Groups £5.50. Winter: Adult £3, Child £1.50, Family £7.50, Groups £2.75. Memberships: Single Season £22.50; Single Season and Guest £45; Family Season £50.

Licensed. Limited for coaches. By arrangement. Guide dogs only.

WILMINGTON PRIORY

Wilmington, Nr Eastbourne, East Sussex BN26 5SW
Tel: 01628 825925 **E-mail:** bookings@landmarktrust.org.uk
www.landmarktrust.org.uk
Owner: Leased to the Landmark Trust by Sussex Archaeological Society
Contact: The Landmark Trust

Founded by the Benedictines in the 11th century, the surviving, much altered buildings date largely from the 14th century. Managed and maintained by the Landmark Trust, which lets buildings for self-catering holidays. Full details of Wilmington Priory and 184 other historic and architecturally important buildings available for holidays are featured in The Landmark Handbook (price £11.50 refundable against booking), from The Landmark Trust, Shottesbrooke, Maidenhead, Berkshire, SL6 3SW.

Location: MAP 3:F5, OS Ref. TQ543 042. 600yds S of A27. 6m NW of Eastbourne.

Open: Available for self-catering holidays for up to 6 people throughout the year. Grounds, Ruins, Porch & Crypt: on 30 days between Apr–Oct. Whole property including interiors on 8 of these days. Contact the Landmark Trust for detailss.

Admission: Free entry on Open Days.

■ **Owner**

English Heritage

■ **Contact**

The House Administrator
Osborne House
Royal Apartments
East Cowes
Isle of Wight
PO32 6JX

Tel: 01983 200022
Fax: 01983 281380

Venue Hire and
Hospitality:
Tel: 01983 203055

■ **Location**

MAP 3:D6
OS Ref. SZ516 948

1 mile SE of East Cowes.

Ferry: Isle of Wight
ferry terminals.

Red Funnel, East Cowes
1½ miles
Tel: 02380 334010.

Wightlink, Fishbourne
4 miles
Tel: 0870 582 7744

■ **Opening Times**

21 March–30 September
Daily: 10am–6pm (House
closes 5pm).
Last admission 4pm.

October
Daily: 10am–4pm.

1 Nov–31 March 2009,
Wed–Sun: 10am–4pm.
Guided tours only.
Last tour 2.30pm.
Christmas Tour Season:
10 November–6 January.
Pre-booking essential on
01983 200022.

Closed 24–26 December
& 1 January.

Closes early 20/21 &
27/28 July & 6 Aug for
special events (House
3pm, Grounds 4pm).

■ **Admission**

House & Grounds
Adult   £10.00
Child (5–15yrs)   £5.00
Child under 5yrs   Free
Conc.   £8.00
Family (2+3)   £25.00

Grounds only
Adult   £6.00
Child (5–15yrs)   £3.00
Child under 5yrs   Free
Conc.   £4.80
Family (2+3)   £15.00

Groups (11+) 15%
discount. Tour leader and
driver have free entry.
1 extra free place for
every additional 20
paying. EH members free.

Conference/Function

ROOM	MAX CAPACITY
Durbar Hall	standing 80 seated 50
Upper Terrace	standing 250
Walled Gardens	standing 100
Marquee	Large scale events possible

© English Heritage Photo Library

OSBORNE HOUSE ▦

www.english-heritage.org.uk/osborne

Osborne House was the peaceful, rural retreat of Queen Victoria, Prince Albert and their family; they spent some of their happiest times here.

Step inside and marvel at the richness of the State Apartments including the Durbar Room with its lavish Indian décor. The Queen died at the house in 1901 and many of the rooms have been preserved almost unaltered ever since. The nursery bedroom remains just as it was in the 1870s when Queen Victoria's first grandchildren came to stay. Children were a constant feature of life at Osborne (Victoria and Albert had nine). Don't miss the Swiss Cottage, a charming chalet in the grounds built for teaching the royal children domestic skills.

Enjoy the beautiful gardens with their stunning views over the Solent and the fruit and flower Victorian Walled Garden.

ℹ️ WCs. Suitable for filming, concerts, drama. No photography in the House. Children's play area.

🛍️ Private and corporate hire.

♿ Wheelchairs available, access to house via ramp and first floor via lift. WC.

☕🍴 Hot drinks, light snacks & waiter service lunches in the stunning terrace restaurant.

🚶 Open from Nov–Mar for pre-booked guided tours only. These popular tours allow visitors to see the Royal Apartments and private rooms at a quieter time of the year, and in the company of one of our expert guides.

P Ample.

Visits free, please book. Education room available.

APPULDURCOMBE HOUSE ⌗

Wroxall, Shanklin, Isle of Wight
Tel: 01983 852484   www.english-heritage.org.uk/appuldurcombehouse
Owner: English Heritage   **Contact:** Mr & Mrs Owen
The bleached shell of a fine 18th-century Baroque style house standing in grounds landscaped by 'Capability' Brown. Once the grandest house on the Isle of Wight. An exhibition displays prints and photographs depicting the history of the house.
Location: MAP 3:D7, OS Ref. SZ543 800. ½mile W of Wroxall off B3327.
Open: 21 Mar–30 Sept: daily, 10am–4pm. Last entry 1hr before closing.
Admission: House: Adult £3.25, Child £2.25, Conc. £3, Family £10. EH members Free. Additional charge for the Falconry Centre. Group discount available.
◻ ⬛ **P** Limited. ⬛ In grounds, on leads. ⬛ Tel. for details.

BEMBRIDGE WINDMILL ⚘

High Street, Bembridge, Isle of Wight PO35 5SQ
Correspondence to: NT Office, Strawberry Lane, Mottistone,
Isle of Wight PO30 4EA
Tel: 01983 873945   www.nationaltrust.org.uk/isle of wight
Owner: The National Trust   **Contact:** The Custodian
Dating from around 1700, this is the only windmill to survive on the Island. Much of its original wooden machinery is still intact and there are spectacular views from the top.
Location: MAP 3:E7, OS Ref. SZ639 874. ½m S of Bembridge off B3395.
Open: 15 Mar–30 Jun & 1 Oct–2nd Nov daily except Mon, 1 Jul–30 Sept, daily, 10am–5pm, open Easter Mon & BH Mons.
Admission: Adult £2.50, Child £1.25, Family £6.25. Free to NT members. All school groups are conducted by a NT guide; special charges apply.
◻ ⬛ ⬛ By arrangement. **P** 100 yds. ⬛ ⬛ Guide dogs only.

BRIGHSTONE SHOP & MUSEUM ⚘

North St, Brighstone, Isle of Wight PO30 4AX
Tel: 01983 740689
Owner: The National Trust   **Contact:** The Manager
The traditional cottages contain a National Trust shop and Village Museum (run by Brighstone Museum Trust) depicting village life in the late 19th century.
Location: MAP 3:D7, OS Ref. SZ428 828. North Street, Brighstone, just off B3399.
Open: 2 Jan–20 Mar: Mon–Sat, 10am–1pm. 21 Mar–23 May: Mon–Sat, 10am–4pm. 24 May–27 Sept: Mon–Sat, 10am–5pm. Plus 25 May–28 Sept, Suns 12 noon–5pm, 29 Sept–21 Dec, Mon–Sat, 10am–4pm. 22 Dec–31 Jan, Mon–Sat 10am–1pm. Closed 25–28 Dec & 1 Jan.
Admission: Free.
⬛ Partial. ⬛

©Patrick Lane

The Needles

CARISBROOKE CASTLE ⌗
NEWPORT, ISLE OF WIGHT PO30 1XY

www.english-heritage.org.uk/carisbrooke

Tel: 01983 522107   **Fax:** 01983 528632
Owner: English Heritage   **Contact:** Visitor Operations Team
The island's royal fortress and prison of King Charles I before his execution in London in 1648. See the famous Carisbrooke donkeys treading the wheel in the Well House as donkeys would have done in the 18th century. Visit the on-site Carisbrooke Museum and enjoy an invigorating battlements walk. New from late Spring, the fascinating history of Carisbrooke Castle comes to life using dramatic film and interactive exhibits.
Location: MAP 3:E7, OS196 Ref. SZ486 877. Off the B3401, 1¼ miles SW of Newport.
Open: 21 Mar–30 Sept: daily, 10am–5pm. 1 Oct–31 Mar 2009: daily, 10am–4pm. Closed 24–26 Dec & 1 Jan.
Admission: Adult £6.50, Child £3.30, Conc. £5.20, Family (2+3) £16.30. 15% discount for groups (11+). EH Members Free.
ⓘ WCs. ◻ ⬛ ⬛ **P** ⬛ In grounds, on leads. ⬛ ⬛ Tel. for details.

MORTON MANOR

Brading, Isle of Wight PO36 0EP
Tel/Fax: 01983 406168   **E-mail:** mortonmanor-iow@amserve.com
Owner/Contact: Mr J A J Trzebski
Refurbished in the Georgian period. Magnificent gardens, vineyard and maize maze.
Location: MAP 3:E7, OS Ref. SZ603 863 (approx.). ¼m W of A3055 in Brading.
Open: Easter–end Oct: daily except Sats, 10am–5.30pm. Last admission 4.30pm.
Admission: Adult £5, Child £2.50, Conc. £4.50, Group (10+) £4.25.

MOTTISTONE MANOR GARDEN ⚘

Mottistone, Isle of Wight PO30 4ED
Tel: 01983 741302   www.nationaltrust.org.uk/isleofwight
Owner: The National Trust   **Contact:** The Gardener
This magical garden with colourful borders, shrub-filled banks and grassy terraces, is set in a sheltered valley with views to the sea and surrounds an Elizabethan manor house (tenanted). Family activity packs available plus delightful walks onto the Downs across the adjoining Mottistone Estate.
Location: MAP 3:D7, OS Ref. SZ406 838. Between Brighstone & Brook on B3399.
Open: 15 Mar–2 Nov: Sun–Thur, 11am–5.30pm. House: 26 May (BH) only: 2–5.30pm. Guided tours for NT members on that day 10am–12 noon.
*Admission: Garden: Adult £3.70, Child £1.90, Family £9.25. Free to NT members. Extra charges for house. *includes a voluntary donation but visitors can choose to pay the standard prices displayed at the property and on the website.
◻ ⬛ ⬛ Limited access for wheelchair users. ⬛ **P** ⬛ In grounds, on leads.

For rare and unusual plants visit the **plant sales** index at the end of the book.

NEEDLES OLD BATTERY & NEW BATTERY

Alum Bay, Totland, Isle of Wight PO39 0JH

Tel: 01983 754772 www.nationaltrust.org.uk/isleofwight

Owner: The National Trust **Contact:** The Fort Manager

Built in 1862 following the threat of a French invasion, this spectacularly sited fort contains exhibitions about its involvement in both World Wars. Two original gun barrels are displayed on the parade ground and a tunnel leads to a searchlight emplacement perched above the Needles Rocks. Family activity packs available. Rocket exhibition at Needles New Battery.

Location: MAP 3:C7, OS Ref. SZ300 848. Needles Headland W of Alum Bay (B3322).

Open: 15 Mar–30 Jun & 1 Sept–2 Nov, Tue–Sun & Easter Mon & May BH Mons; 1 Jul–31 Aug, daily, 10.30am–5pm. Tearoom also open 12 Jan–9 Mar & 8 Nov–14 Dec, Sat/Sun 11am–3pm. Closes in high winds; please telephone on day of visit to check. Needles New Battery open 15 Mar–2 Nov, Tues & Sats, 11am–4pm.

***Admission:** Adult £4.65, Child £2.35, Family £11.55. Free to NT members. Special charges for guided tours. Needles New Battery: Free. *includes a voluntary 10% donation but visitors can choose to pay the standard prices displayed at the property and on the website.

□ ⑤ Partial. ☞ ⓘ By appointment. ■ ⊞ In grounds, on leads.

NEWTOWN OLD TOWN HALL

Newtown, Isle of Wight PO30 4PA

Tel: 01983 531785 www.nationaltrust.org.uk/isleofwight

Owner: The National Trust **Contact:** The Custodian

A charming 17th century building that was once the focal point of the 'rotten borough' of Newtown. Regular art exhibitions.

Location: MAP 3:D7, OS Ref. SZ424 905. Between Newport and Yarmouth, 1m N of A3054.

Open: 15 Mar–29 Jun, 1 Sept–22 Oct: Sun, Mon & Wed; 30 Jun–31 Aug: Sun–Thur, 2–5pm. Open Good Fri & Easter Sat.

Admission: Adult £2, Child £1, Family £5. Free to NT members.

P Limited. ⊞ Guide dogs only.

NUNWELL HOUSE & GARDENS

Coach Lane, Brading, Isle of Wight PO36 0JQ

Tel: 01983 407240

Owner: Col & Mrs J A Aylmer **Contact:** Mrs J A Aylmer

Nunwell has been a family home for five centuries and reflects much architectural and Island history. King Charles I spent his last night of freedom here. Jacobean and Georgian wings. Finely furnished rooms. Lovely setting with Channel views and five acres of tranquil gardens including walled garden. Family military collections.

Location: MAP 3:E7, OS Ref. SZ595 874. 1m NW of Brading. 3m S of Ryde signed off A3055.

Open: 25/26 May & 30 Jun–3 Sept: Mon–Wed, 1–5pm. House tours: 2 & 3.30pm (extra tours when needed). Groups welcome by arrangement throughout the year.

Admission: Adult £5, Pair of Adults £9 (inc guide book), Child (under 10yrs) £1, OAP/Student £4. Garden only: Adult £2.50.

□ ⓘ Obligatory. P ⊞ Guide dogs only. ✳

OSBORNE HOUSE ⌗

See page 174 for full page entry.

YARMOUTH CASTLE ⌗

Quay Street, Yarmouth, Isle of Wight PO41 0PB

Tel: 01983 760678 www.english-heritage.org.uk/yarmouth

Owner: English Heritage **Contact:** Visitor Operations Team

This last addition to Henry VIII's coastal defences was completed in 1547 and is, unusually for its kind, square with a fine example of an angle bastion. It was garrisoned well into the 19th century. Fine views of the Solent and a new exhibition displaying artefacts.

Location: MAP 3:C7, OS Ref. SZ354 898. In Yarmouth adjacent to car ferry terminal.

Open: 21 Mar–30 Sept: Sun–Thurs, 11am–4pm.

Admission: Adult £3.50, Child £1.80, Conc. £2.80. EH Members Free. Group discount available.

□ ⑤ Ground floor. P None. ⊞ In grounds, on leads.

©Patrick Lane

Appuldurcombe House

Osborne House

©English Heritage Photo Library/Steve Cole

Saltram, Devon
©NTPL

South West

The moorlands of Devon and Cornwall are among the most dramatic in Britain, contrasting with the unspoilt beaches. The temperate climate means gardens (eg Abbotsbury Subtropical Gardens) can grow exotic plants that wouldn't survive in other parts of the country. Compare this with the bustling terraces of Georgian Bath, with its Pump Room and Fashion Museum.

Channel Islands

Cornwall

Devon

Dorset

Somerset

Wiltshire

Gloucestershire

■ Owner

The Seigneur de Sausmarez

■ Contact

Peter de Sausmarez
Sausmarez Manor
Guernsey
Channel Islands
GY4 6SG
Tel: 01481
235571/235655
Fax: 01481 235572
E-mail: sausmarezmanor
@cwgsy.net

■ Location

Map 3:D10

2m S of St Peter Port,
clearly signposted.

■ Opening Times

The Grounds:
Easter–End Oct
Daily: 10am–5pm

Guided tours of House
Easter–End Oct.
Mon–Thurs:
10.30 & 11.30am.
Additional 2pm tour
during high season.

■ Admission

There is no overall charge
for admission.

Sub Tropical Garden	£5.00
Sculpture Trail	£5.00
Pitch & Putt	£5.00
Putting	£2.00
House Tour	£6.90
Ghost Tour	£10.50
Train Rides	£2.00

Discounts for Children,
Students, OAPs &
Organised Groups.

SAUSMAREZ MANOR 🏛

www.sausmarezmanor.co.uk   www.artparks.co.uk

The home of the Seigneurs de Sausmarez since c1220 with a façade built at the bequest of the first Governor of New York.

An entrancing and entertaining half day encompassing something to interest everyone. The family have been explorers, inventors, diplomats, prelates, generals, admirals, privateers, politicians and governors etc, most of whom left their mark on the house, garden or the furniture.

The sub-tropical woodland garden is crammed with such exotics as banana trees, tree ferns, ginger, 300 plus camellias, lilies, myriads of bamboos, as well as the more commonplace hydrangeas, hostas etc. The RHS recommends the gardens to its own members.

The sculpture in the art park with its 200 or so pieces by artists from a dozen countries is the most comprehensive in Britain. The Magnolia Tree Art Gallery shows work by local and overseas artists and holds regular exhibitions. The pitch and put is a cruelly testing 500m 9 hole par 3. The Copper, Tin and Silversmith demonstrates his ancient skills in the large barn. The two lakes are a haven for ornamental wildfowl and some of the sculpture.

Sausmarez Manor is available for corporate hospitality functions and Civil weddings. It also offers guided tours, welcomes schools (has education programmes), and has a tearoom, café and gift shop.

There are concerts or plays on most Sunday afternoons in the summer and a Farmers' and Plantsmen's Market every other Saturday morning.

 Partial.

 Guided tours of House
Easter–Oct.

 Two holiday flats are available see
www.cottageguide.co.uk

€

National Trust/ Jon Hicks

COTEHELE

www.nationaltrust.org.uk

Cotehele, owned by the Edgcumbe family for nearly 600 years, is a fascinating and enchanting estate set on the steep wooded slopes of the River Tamar. Exploring Cotehele's many and various charms provides a full day out for the family and leaves everyone longing to return.

The steep valley garden contains exotic and tender plants which thrive in the mild climate. Remnants of an earlier age include a mediaeval stewpond and domed dovecote, a 15th-century chapel and 18th-century tower with fine views over the surrounding countryside. A series of more formal gardens, terraces, an orchard and a daffodil meadow surround Cotehele House.

One of the least altered medieval houses in the country, Cotehele is built in local granite, slate and sandstone. Inside the ancient rooms, unlit by electricity, is a fine collection of textiles, tapestries, armour and early dark oak furniture. The chapel contains the oldest working domestic clock in England, still in its original position.

A walk through the garden and along the river leads to the quay, a busy river port in Victorian times. The National Maritime Museum worked with the National Trust to set up a museum here which explains the vital role that the Tamar played in the local economy. As a living reminder, the restored Tamar sailing barge Shamrock (owned jointly by the Trust and the National Maritime Museum) is moored here.

A further walk through woodland along the Morden stream leads to the old estate corn mill which has been restored to working order.

This large estate with many footpaths offers a variety of woodland and countryside walks, opening up new views and hidden places. The Danescombe Valley, with its history of mining and milling, is of particular interest.

Owner
The National Trust

Contact
Toby Fox
Property Manager
Cotehele
St Dominick
Saltash, Cornwall
PL12 6TA

Tel: 01579 351346
Fax: 01579 351222
E-mail: cotehele@nationaltrust.org.uk

Location
MAP 1:H8
OS Ref. SX422 685

1m SW of Calstock by foot. 8m S of Tavistock, 4m E of Callington, 15m from Plymouth via the Tamar bridge at Saltash.

Trains: Limited service from Plymouth to Calstock (1¼m uphill).

Boats: Limited (tidal) service from Plymouth to Calstock Quay (Plymouth Boat Cruises).
Tel: 01752 822797

River ferry: Privately run from Calstock to Cotehele Quay.
Tel: 01822 833331

Buses: Western National (seasonal variations).
Tel: 01752 222666

Opening Times
House
15 March–2 November:
Daily except Fridays
(but open Good Friday),
11am–4.30pm
Last admission 30 mins before closing time.

Mill
15 March–2 November:
Daily 11am–5pm
(4.30pm from 1 October).

Garden
All year: Daily,
10.30am–dusk.

*Admission
House, Garden & Mill
Adult	£8.80
Family	£22.00
1-Adult Family	£13.20
Pre-booked Groups	£7.50

Garden & Mill only
Adult	£5.20
Family	£13.00
1-Adult Family	£7.80

Groups must book in advance with the Property Office.
No groups Suns or BHs.

NT members free.
You may join here.

*includes a voluntary donation but visitors can choose to pay the standard prices displayed at the property and on the website.

©NTPL/Jymn Lintell

ℹ️ No photography or large bags in house.

🏠 National Trust shop. Plant sales daily 17 Feb–23 Dec.

🌱

🍽 Available for up to 90 people.

♿ 4 wheelchairs at Reception (2 motorised). Hall & kitchen accessible. Ramps at house, restaurant and shop. Most of garden is steep with loose gravel. Riverside walks are flatter (from Cotehele Quay) & Edgcumbe Arms is accessible. WCs near house and at Quay. Parking near house & mill by arrangement.

☕

🍴 Barn restaurant daily (except Fri), 15 Mar–2 Nov, plus light refreshments from 17 Feb. Tel for details of pre-Christmas opening. At the Quay, Edgcumbe Arms offers light meals daily, 15 Mar–2 Nov. Both licensed.

🅿️ Near house and garden and at Cotehele Quay. No parking at Mill.

🧍 Groups (15+) must book with Property Office and receive a coach route (limited to two per day). No groups Suns & BH weekends. Visitors to house limited to 100 at any one time. Allow a full day to see estate.

🐕 Under control welcome only on woodland walks.

❄️ Tel for details of pre-Christmas opening of decorated hall.

■ Owner

The National Trust

■ Contact

Property Manager
Lanhydrock
Bodmin
Cornwall PL30 5AD

Tel: 01208 265950
Fax: 01208 265959
E-mail: lanhydrock@
nationaltrust.org.uk

■ Location

MAP 1:F8
OS Ref. SX085 636

2½ m SE of Bodmin,
follow signposts from
either A30, A38 or
B3268.

■ Opening Times

House:
15 March–2 November:
Daily except Mons
(but open BH Mons &
Mons in August)
11am–5.30pm.
October: 11am–5pm.
Last admission ½ hr
before closing.

Garden:
All year: Daily,
10am–6pm.
Charge levied from
9 February–2 November.

Plant Sales:
1–14 March:
Daily, 11am–4pm
15 March–30 September:
Daily, 11am–5.30pm.
1 Oct–2 November:
Daily, 11am–5pm.

Shop & Refreshments:
5 January–3 February:
Sat & Sun, 11am–4pm.
9 February–14 March,
3 Nov–24 December &
27–31 December:
Daily, 11am–4pm.
15 March–30 September:
Daily 11am–5.30pm
(refreshments open
10.30am).
1 Oct–2 November:
Daily, 11am–5pm
(refreshments open
10.30am).

■ *Admission

**House, Garden &
Grounds**

Adult	£9.90
Child	£4.95
Family	£24.75
1-Adult Family	£14.85
Groups	£8.40

**Garden &
Grounds only** £5.60

*includes a voluntary
donation but visitors can
choose to pay the standard
prices displayed at the
property and on the website.

LANHYDROCK ❦

www.nationaltrust.org.uk

Lanhydrock is the grandest and most welcoming house in Cornwall, set in a glorious landscape of gardens, parkland and woods overlooking the valley of the River Fowey.

The house dates back to the 17th century but much of it had to be rebuilt after a disastrous fire in 1881 destroyed all but the entrance porch and the north wing, which includes the magnificent Long Gallery with its extraordinary plaster ceiling depicting scenes from the Old Testament. A total of 50 rooms are on show today and together they reflect the entire spectrum of life in a rich and splendid Victorian household, from the many servants' bedrooms and the fascinating complex of kitchens, sculleries and larders to the nursery suite where the Agar-Robartes children lived, learned and played, and the grandeur of the dining room with its table laid and ready.

Surrounding the house on all sides are gardens ranging from formal Victorian parterres to the wooded higher garden where magnificent displays of magnolias, rhododendrons and camellias climb the hillside to merge with the oak and beech woods all around. A famous avenue of ancient beech and sycamore trees, the original entrance drive to the house, runs from the pinnacled 17th-century gatehouse down towards the medieval bridge across the Fowey at Respryn.

ⓘ No photography in house.

By arrangement.

Suitable. Braille guide. WC.

Licensed restaurant

In park, on leads. Guide dogs only in house.

Ⓟ Limited for coaches.

ANTONY HOUSE & GARDEN
& ANTONY WOODLAND GARDEN

TORPOINT, CORNWALL PL11 2QA

www.nationaltrust.org.uk

Antony House & Garden Tel: 01752 812191
Antony Woodland Garden Tel: 01752 814210
E-mail: antony@nationaltrust.org.uk
Antony House & Garden Owner: The National Trust
Antony Woodland Garden Owner: Carew Pole Garden Trust

Superb 18th-century house on the Lynher estuary, grounds landscaped by Repton. Formal garden with sculptures & National Collection of daylilies; woodland garden with magnolias, rhododendrons & National Collection of Camellia japonica.

Location: MAP 1:H9, OS Ref. SX418 564. 5m W of Plymouth via Torpoint car ferry, 2m NW of Torpoint.

Open: House & Garden: 24 Mar–30 Oct: Tue–Thur & BH Mons. Also Suns in June, July & Aug: 1.30–5.30pm. Shop & Restaurant as house, 12.30–5.30pm. Woodland Garden (not NT) 1 Mar–30 Oct: daily except Mon & Fri (open BH Mons), 11am–5.30pm.

Admission: House & Garden: £6, Child £3, Family £15, 1-Adult Family £9. Groups £5.10pp. NT Garden only: £3.10, Child £1.50. Woodland Garden: Adult £4.50, Child Free. (Free to NT members on days when the house is open.) Woodland Garden season ticket: £25. Joint Gardens-only tickets: Adult £5.20. Groups £4.20. Under 16s Free.

Braille guide.

BURNCOOSE NURSERIES & GARDEN

Gwennap, Redruth, Cornwall TR16 6BJ
Tel: 01209 860316   **Fax:** 01209 860011   **E-mail:** burncoose@eclipse.co.uk
www.burncoose.co.uk
Owner/Contact: C H Williams

The Nurseries are set in the 30 acre woodland gardens of Burncoose.

Location: MAP 1:D10, OS Ref. SW742 395. 2m SE of Redruth on main A393 Redruth to Falmouth road between the villages of Lanner and Ponsanooth.

Open: Mon–Sat: 9am–5pm, Suns, 11am–5pm. Gardens and Tearooms open all year (except Christmas Day).

Admission: Nurseries: Free. Gardens: Adult/Conc. £2. Child Free. Group conducted tours: £2.50 by arrangement.

Grounds. WCs. By arrangement. In grounds, on leads.

Pencarrow

BOCONNOC

THE ESTATE OFFICE, BOCONNOC, LOSTWITHIEL, CORNWALL PL22 0RG

www.boconnocenterprises.co.uk

Tel: 01208 872507   **Fax:** 01208 873836   **E-mail:** adgfortescue@btinternet.com
Owner/Contact: Anthony Fortescue Esq

Bought with the famous Pitt Diamond in 1717, Boconnoc remains one of Cornwall's best kept secrets. Home to three Prime Ministers, its unique combination of history, architecture, picturesque landscape and one of the great Cornish gardens created ideal film locations for Poldark and The Three Musketeers. King Charles I and the architect Sir John Soane played an influential part in Boconnoc's history. Groups visit the Boconnoc House restoration project, the gardens, church, Golden Jubilee lake walk, the Georgian Bath House and newly planted Pinetum. Ideal for weddings and receptions, private and corporate events, conferences, activities and holiday houses for long or short breaks.

Location: MAP 1:G8, OS Ref. 148 605. A38 Plymouth, Liskeard or from Bodmin to Dobwalls, then A390 to Middle Taphouse.

Open: House & Garden: 13, 20, 27 Apr; 4, 11, 18 & 25 May: Suns: 2–5pm. Visits in groups (15–255) by appointment all year.

Admission: House: £4, Garden £4.50. Child under 12yrs Free.

Conferences. Partial. By arrangement. In grounds, on leads. 10 doubles (8 ensuite).

9 Mar: Wedding Fair. 16 Mar: Regis Classic Tour. 5/6 Apr: Cornwall Garden Society Spring Flower Show. 14/15 May: Boconnoc Spring Fair. 24/25 May: Endurance Ride. 18–20 Jul: Boconnoc Steam Fair. 7 Oct: Red Cross Lecture & Demonstration.

CAERHAYS CASTLE & GARDEN 🏛

CAERHAYS, GORRAN, ST AUSTELL, CORNWALL PL26 6LY

www.caerhays.co.uk

Tel: 01872 501310   **Fax:** 01872 501870   **E-mail:** estateoffice@caerhays.co.uk
Owner: F J Williams Esq   **Contact:** Cheryl Kufel

One of the very few Nash built castles still left standing – situated within approximately 60 acres of informal woodland gardens created by J C Williams, who sponsored plant hunting expeditions to China at the turn of the century. As well as guided tours of the house from March to May visitors will see some of the magnificent selection of plants brought back by the intrepid plant hunters of the early 1900s these include not only the collection of magnolias but a wide range of rhododendrons and the camellias which Caerhays and the Williams familly are associated with worldwide.

Location: MAP 1:F9, OS Ref. SW972 415. S coast of Cornwall – between Mevagissey and Portloe. 9m SW of St Austell.

Open: House: 10 Mar–30 May: Mon–Fri only (including BHs), 12 noon–4pm, booking recommended. Gardens: 18 Feb–1 Jun: daily (including BHs), 10am–5pm (last admission 4pm).

Admission: House: £5.50. Gardens: £5.50. House & Gardens: £9.50. Guided group tours (15+) by Head Gardener, £6.50–by arrangement. Groups please contact Estate Office.

ℹ No photography in house. 📷 ♿ Partial. WC. 🍴 Licensed. 🎧 By arrangement. 🅿 🐕 In grounds, on leads.

CAERHAYS CASTLE – THE VEAN

THE ESTATE OFFICE, CAERHAYS CASTLE, GORRAN, ST AUSTELL, CORNWALL PL26 6TT

www.thevean.co.uk

Tel: 01872 501310   **Fax:** 01872 501870   **E-mail:** manager@thevean.eclipse.co.uk
Owner: Mrs Lizzy Williams   **Contact:** Sally Gammell

Staying at The Vean is like enjoying a house party where the owners have gone away for the weekend. The Vean is a luxury country house retreat, within the Caerhays Estate, that sleeps up to 16 people in its eight en-suite bedrooms. During the shooting season it is the shooting lodge for the guns at the Castle. The Vean is a restored former Georgian Rectory and is run with passion and a commitment to achieve the highest standards.

Location: MAP 1:F9, OS Ref. SW972 415. S coast of Cornwall – between Mevagissey and Portloe. 9m SW of St Austell.

Open: For private bookings only. Licensed for Civil weddings.

Admission: Contact property for details.

📷 ♿ 🎧 Conferences & corporate breaks. ♿ Partial. 🍴 Licensed. 🎧 By arrangement. 🅿 Ample for cars. 🐕 In grounds, on leads. 🛏 8 x en-suite. 🏠

CHYSAUSTER ANCIENT VILLAGE ⌗

Nr Newmill, Penzance, Cornwall TR20 8XA
Tel: 07831 757934 **www.english-heritage.org.uk/chysauster**
Owner: English Heritage **Contact:** Visitor Operations Team
On a windy hillside, overlooking the wild and spectacular coast, is this deserted Romano-Cornish village with a 'street' of eight well preserved houses, each comprising a number of rooms around an open court.
Location: MAP 1:C10, OS203 Ref. SW473 350. 2½m NW of Gulval off B3311.
Open: 21 Mar–31 Oct: daily, 10am–5pm (6pm Jul & Aug, 4pm Oct).
Admission: Adult £2.50, Child £1.30, Conc. £2. 15% discount for groups (11+). EH Members free.
ℹ WC. 🔲 🅿 No coaches. ♿ On leads.

COTEHELE ❦

See page 181 for full page entry.

GODOLPHIN ⚜

GODOLPHIN CROSS, HELSTON, CORNWALL TR13 9RE

www.nationaltrust.org.uk/godolphinhouse

Tel: 0844 800 1895 (information) **E-mail:** godolphin@nationaltrust.org.uk
Owner: The National Trust
One of Cornwall's most beautiful old houses at the heart of an historic estate, once the home of the illustrious Godolphin family. Centuries of benign neglect have given the place a haunting air of antiquity and peace, an atmosphere nurtured through the 20th century by the the Schofield family. Having bought Godolphin in 2007, the National Trust aims to continue its careful restoration. The garden is a rare survival from the 14th and 16th centuries and the estate has many fascinating walks.
Location: MAP 1:D10, OS Ref: SW602 318. On minor road from Godolphin Cross to Townshend. Some brown signs.
Open/Admission: Although the estate is open all year, details of opening arrangements for the house and garden had not been finalised at the time of going to print. Telephone for up-to-date information or visit website.
♿ 🅿 ◼ Estate only. ♿ On leads, on estate only. ♨

GLENDURGAN GARDEN ❦

MAWNAN SMITH, FALMOUTH, CORNWALL TR11 5JZ

www.nationaltrust.org.uk

Tel: 01326 250906 (opening hours) or 01872 862090 **Fax:** 01872 865808
E-mail: glendurgan@nationaltrust.org.uk
Owner: The National Trust
A valley of great beauty with fine trees, shrubs and water gardens. The laurel maze is an unusual and popular feature. The garden runs down to the tiny village of Durgan and its beach on the Helford River. Replica Victorian school room, rebuilt in 2002 in traditional thatch and cob to replace the 1876 original.
Location: MAP 1:D10, OS Ref. SW772 277. 4m SW of Falmouth, ½m SW of Mawnan Smith, on road to Helford Passage. 1m E of Trebah Garden. Accessible by ferry from Helford.
Open: 9 Feb–1 Nov: Tue–Sat, BH Mons & Mons in Aug, 10.30am–5.30pm. Last admission 4.30pm. Closed Good Friday.
***Admission:** Adult £6, Child £3, Family £15, 1-Adult Family £9. Booked groups: £5.10. *includes a voluntary donation but visitors can choose to pay the standard prices displayed at the property and on the website.
🔲 ♿ ♿ Unsuitable. ◼ ℹ By arrangement. 🅿 Limited for coaches. ♿

GODOLPHIN BLOWINGHOUSE

Blowinghouse Cottage, Godolphin Cross, Breage, Helston, Cornwall TR13 9RE
Tel: 01736 763218 **E-mail:** brian.portch@ndirect.co.uk
Owner/Contact: Mr & Mrs B J Portch
The Blowinghouse dates from the 16th century and was built as part of the Godolphin family tin mining works. The tin ingots weighed in excess of three hundredweight and were stamped with a cat's head that was the Godophin Mine logo.
Location: MAP 1:D10, OS Ref. SW508 521, Situated in the Godolphin Woods-National Trust opposite entrance to the Godolphin Manor House.
Open: 3 Aug, 9.30am–4.30pm. Other times by appointment.
Admission: Free.
♿ 🅿 Limited. ◼ ♿ In grounds, on leads.

THE JAPANESE GARDEN & BONSAI NURSERY

St Mawgan, Nr Newquay, Cornwall TR8 4ET
Tel: 01637 860116 **Fax:** 01637 860887 **E-mail:** rob@thebonsainursery.com
Owner/Contact: Mr & Mrs Hore
Authentic Japanese Garden set in 1½ acres.
Location: MAP 2:E8, OS Ref. SW873 660. Follow road signs from A3059 & B3276.
Open: Summer: Daily, 10am–6pm. Winter: 10am–5.30pm. Closed Christmas Day–New Year's Day.
Admission: Adult £3.50, Child £1.50. Groups (10+): £3.

KEN CARO GARDENS

Bicton, Nr Liskeard PL14 5RF
Tel: 01579 362446
Owner/Contact: Mr and Mrs K R Willcock
5 acre plantsman's garden with woods and picnic area. Total 12 acres.
Location: MAP 1:G8, OS Ref. SX313 692. 5m NE of of Liskeard. Follow brown sign off main A390 midway between Liskeard and Callington.
Open: 25 Feb–30 Sept: daily, 10am–6pm.
Admission: Adult £4.50, Child £1.

St Mawes

South West – England

LANHYDROCK ❧

See page 182 for full page entry.

LAUNCESTON CASTLE ♯

Castle Lodge, Launceston, Cornwall PL15 7DR
Tel: 01566 772365 **Fax:** 01566 772396
www.english-heritage.org.uk/launceston
Owner: English Heritage   **Contact:** Visitor Operations Team
Set on the motte of the original Norman castle and commanding the town and surrounding countryside. The shell keep and tower survive of this medieval castle which controlled the main route into Cornwall. An exhibition shows the early history.
Location: MAP 1:H7, OS201 Ref. SX330 846. In Launceston.
Open: 21 Mar–31 Oct: daily, 10am–5pm (6pm in Jul & Aug & 4pm in Oct).
Admission: Adult £2.50, Child £1.30, Conc. £2. 15% discount for groups (11+). EH members Free.
◻ ⌖ Grounds. 🅿 NCP adjacent. Limited. ■ 🐕 In grounds, on leads.

LAWRENCE HOUSE ❧

9 Castle Street, Launceston, Cornwall PL15 8BA
Tel: 01566 773277
Owner: The National Trust   **Contact:** The Custodian
A Georgian house given to the Trust to help preserve the character of the street, and now leased to Launceston Town Council as a museum and civic centre.
Location: MAP 1:H7, OS Ref. SX330 848. Launceston.
Open: 31 Mar–26 Sept: daily, except Sat & Sun, 10.30am–4.30pm. Other times by appointment.
Admission: Free, but contributions welcome.

For **accommodation** in the South West, see our special index at the end of the book.

MOUNT EDGCUMBE HOUSE & COUNTRY PARK

CREMYLL, TORPOINT, CORNWALL PL10 IHZ

www.mountedgcumbe.gov.uk

Tel: 01752 822236 **Fax:** 01752 822199 **E-mail:** mt.edgcumbe@plymouth.gov.uk
Owner: Cornwall County & Plymouth City Councils   **Contact:** Secretary
Former home of the Earls of Mount Edgcumbe. Miraculously the walls of the red stone Tudor House survived the bombs in 1941. Restored by the 6th Earl. Now beautifully furnished with family possessions. Set in historic 18th century gardens on the dramatic sea-girt Rame peninsula. Follies, forts; National camellia collection. Grade I listed gardens. Exhibitions and events. Winner of the RHS Britain in Bloom UK Public Park of the Year.
Location: MAP 1:H9, OS Ref. SX452 527. 10m W of Plymouth via Torpoint.
Open: House & Earl's Garden: 23 Mar–30 Sept: Sun–Thur, 11am–4.30pm. Group bookings by arrangement. Country Park: All year, daily, 8am–dusk.
Admission: House & Earl's Garden: Adult £5, Child (5–15) £2.50, Conc. £4, Family (2+2 or 1+3) £11.50. Groups (10+): Adult £4, Child £2.20. Park: Free.
◻ ♿ 🍽 ⌖ ♥ 🍴 Licensed. 🎦 By arrangement. 🅿 🐕 In grounds, on leads. ▲ ❊ ⚕

The Antiques Roadshow being recorded at Prideaux Place

visit hudsons guide online

PENCARROW 🏛

BODMIN, CORNWALL PL30 3AG

www.pencarrow.co.uk

Tel: 01208 841369   **Fax:** 01208 841722   **E-mail:** info@pencarrow.co.uk

Owner: Molesworth-St Aubyn family   **Contact:** Administrator

Still owned and lived in by the family. Georgian house and Grade II* listed gardens. Superb collection of pictures, furniture and porcelain. Marked walks through 50 acres of beautiful formal and woodland gardens, Victorian rockery, Italian garden, over 700 different varieties of rhododendrons, lake and ice house.

Location: MAP 1:F8, OS Ref. SX040 711. Between Bodmin and Wadebridge. 4m NW of Bodmin off A389 & B3266 at Washaway.

Open: House, Peacock Café & Craft Gallery: 23 Mar–Oct 19, Sun–Thur. House tours from 11.15am–3pm, Cafe & shop 11am–5pm. Gardens: 1 Mar–31 Oct: daily.

Admission: House & Garden: Adult £8, Child £4, Family £22. Garden only: Adult £4, Child £1. Groups (by arrangement): House & Garden: groups (20–30) £7, 31+ £6; Gardens only: groups (20–30) £3.50, 31+ £3. Discounts not normally available on Fri & Sat.

ℹ Craft centre, small children's play area, self-pick soft fruit. 🍴 🚉 By arrangement. 🔈 🍴 Licensed. 🍴 🔈 Obligatory. 🅿 🔲 🔲 Grounds only. 🔲 🔲 🔲

PINE LODGE GARDENS & NURSERY

Holmbush, St Austell, Cornwall PL25 3RQ

Tel: 01726 73500   **Fax:** 01726 77370   **E-mail:** garden@pine-lodge.co.uk

www.pine-lodge.co.uk

Owner/Contact: Mr & Mrs R H J Clemo

30 acres with over 6,000 plants all labelled. Herbaceous and shrub borders. Many water features, pinetum, arboretum, Japanese garden, wild flower meadow, lake with waterfowl and black swans. Plant hunting expeditions every year to gather seeds for our nursery which contain very unusual plants, many rare. The gardens were given a Highly Commended Award by the Cornwall Tourist Board for 2002. Plenty of seats in the gardens. There is a new 3 acre Winter Garden.

Location: MAP 1:F9, OS Ref. SX044 527. Signposted on A390.

Open: Daily, 10am–6pm, last ticket 5pm.

Admission: Adult £6.50, Child £3, OAP, £6, Groups £5.50.

ℹ WC. 🔲 🚉 🔈 🔈 🍴 🅿 🔲 🔲 🔲

©Godolphin

Godolphin

PENDENNIS CASTLE ⌗

FALMOUTH, CORNWALL TR11 4LP

www.english-heritage.org.uk/pendennis

Tel: 01326 316594   **Fax:** 01326 319911

Venue and Hire Hospitality: 01326 310106

Owner: English Heritage   **Contact:** Visitor Operations Team

Pendennis and its neighbour, St Mawes Castle, face each other across the mouth of the estuary of the River Fal. Built by Henry VIII in 16th century as protection against threat of attack and invasion from France. Extended and adapted over the years to meet the changing threats to national security from the French and Spanish and continued right through to World War II. It withstood five months of siege during the Civil War before becoming the penultimate Royalist Garrison to surrender on the mainland. Pendennis today stands as a landmark, with fine sea views and excellent site facilities including a hands-on discovery centre, exhibitions, a museum, guardhouse, shop and tearoom. Excellent special events venue.

Location: MAP 1:E10, OS Ref. SW824 318. On Pendennis Head.

Open: 21 Mar–30 Jun: daily, 10am–5pm (4pm Sats). Jul & Aug: daily, 10am–6pm (4pm Sats). Sept: daily 10am–5pm (4pm Sats), Oct/Nov–31 Mar: daily, 10am–4pm, (Nov–Mar, certain buildings by guided tour only, please telephone to check). Closed 24–26 Dec & 1 Jan. The Keep will close for 1hr at lunch on Sats when events are booked, please telephone to check.

Admission: Adult £5.50, Child £2.80, Conc. £4.40, Family £13.80. 15% discount for groups (11+). EH members Free.

ℹ WC. 🔲 🚉 🔈 Partial. 🔲 🅿 🔲 🔲 In grounds only. 🔲 0870 3331181 🔲 🔲 🔲 €

PRIDEAUX PLACE 🏛

PADSTOW, CORNWALL PL28 8RP

www.prideauxplace.co.uk

Tel: 01841 532411 **Fax:** 01841 532945 **E-mail:** office@prideauxplace.co.uk
Owner/Contact: Peter Prideaux-Brune Esq

Tucked away above the busy port of Padstow, the home of the Prideaux family for over 400 years, is surrounded by gardens and wooded grounds overlooking a deer park and the Camel estuary to the moors beyond. The house still retains its 'E' shape Elizabethan front and contains fine paintings and furniture. Now a major international film location, this family home is one of the brightest jewels in Cornwall's crown. The historic garden is undergoing major restoration work and offers some of the best views in the county. A cornucopia of Cornish history under one roof.

Location: MAP 1:E7, OS Ref. SW913 756. 5m from A39 Newquay/Wadebridge link road. Signposted by Historic House signs.

Open: Easter Sun–27 Apr, 11 May–9 Oct. Daily except Fris & Sats. Grounds & Tearoom: 12.30–5pm. House Tours: 1.30–4pm (last tour).

Admission: House & Grounds: Adult £7.50, Child £2. Grounds only: Adult £2, Child £1. Groups (15+) discounts apply.

🏛 ⊤ By arrangement. ♿ Ground floor & grounds. ◉ ⥣ Obligatory. 🅿
◼ By arrangement. 🐕 In grounds, on leads. ❋

RESTORMEL CASTLE ⌗

LOSTWITHIEL, CORNWALL PL22 0EE

www.english-heritage.org.uk/restormel

Tel: 01208 872687
Owner: English Heritage **Contact:** Visitor Operations Team

Perched on a high mound, surrounded by a deep moat, the huge circular keep of this splendid Norman castle survives in remarkably good condition. It is still possible to make out the ruins of Restormel's Keep Gate, Great Hall and even the kitchens and private rooms.

Location: MAP 1:F8, OS200 Ref. SX104 614. 1½m N of Lostwithiel off A390.
Open: 21 Mar–31 Oct: daily, 10am–5pm (6pm in Jul & Aug; 4pm in Oct).
Admission: Adult £2.50, Child £1.30, Conc. £2. 15% discount for groups (11+). EH Members free.

ℹ WC. 🏛 🅿 Limited for coaches. ◼ 🐕 In grounds, on leads.

ST CATHERINE'S CASTLE ⌗

Fowey, Cornwall
Tel: 01326 310109

Owner: English Heritage **Contact:** Visitor Operations Administrator

A small fort built by Henry VIII to defend Fowey harbour, with fine views of the coastline and river estuary.

Location: MAP 1:F9, OS200 Ref. SX118 508. 1½m SW of Fowey along footpath off A3082.
Open: Any reasonable time, daylight only.
Admission: Free.

🅿 🐕 ❋

Mount Edgcumbe – The Italian Garden

© English Heritage Photo Library

© English Heritage Photo Library

ST MAWES CASTLE ♯
ST MAWES, CORNWALL TR2 3AA
www.english-heritage.org.uk/stmawes

Tel/Fax: 01326 270526   **Venue Hire and Hospitality:** 01326 310106

Owner: English Heritage   **Contact:** Visitor Operations Team

The pretty fishing village of St Mawes is home to this castle. On the opposite headland to Pendennis Castle, St Mawes shares the task of watching over the mouth of the River Fal as it has done since Henry VIII built it as a defence against the French. With three huge circular bastions shaped like clover leaves, St Mawes was designed to cover every possible angle of approach. It is the finest example of Tudor military architecture. The castle offers views of St Mawes' little boat-filled harbour, the passenger ferry tracking across the Fal, and the splendid coastline which featured in the *Poldark* TV series. Also the start of some delightful walks along the coastal path.

Location: MAP 1:E10, OS204 Ref. SW842 328. W of St Mawes on A3078.

Open: 21 Mar–30 Sept: daily (except Sat), 10am–5pm (6pm Jul & Aug); 1–31 Oct: daily 10am–4pm. 1 Nov–31 Mar: Fri–Mon, 10am–4pm. (May close at 4pm on Suns & Fris for private events.) Closed 24–26 Dec & 1 Jan & 1–2pm in winter.

Admission: Adult £4, Child £2, Conc. £3.20. 15% discount for groups (11+). EH members Free.

⬚ ⊤ Private & corporate hire. ♿ Grounds. WC. ⬚ 🅿 Limited. ▣
🐾 Grounds only. ☎ 0870 3331181 ▲ ✳

©Trebah Garden Trust

Trebah Garden

ST MICHAEL'S MOUNT ✤
MARAZION, Nr PENZANCE, CORNWALL TR17 0HS
www.stmichaelsmount.co.uk   www.nationaltrust.org.uk

Tel: 01736 710507 (710265 tide information) **Fax:** 01736 719930

E-mail: mail@stmichaelsmount.co.uk

Owner: The National Trust   **Contact:** The Manor Office

This beautiful island set in Mount's Bay has become an icon for Cornwall, and in turn there are magnificent views when you reach its summit. There the church and castle, whose origins date from the 12th century, have at various times acted as a Benedictine priory, a place of pilgrimage, a fortress, a mansion house and now a magnet for visitors from all over the world. Following the Civil War, the island was acquired by the St Aubyn family who still live in the castle today.

Location: MAP 1:C10, OS Ref. SW515 300. 4m E of Penzance. At Marazion there is access on foot over causeway at low tide. In the main season, the property is reached at high tide by a short evocative boat trip. Please note many paths are steep and cobbled.

Open: Castle: 16 Mar–2 Nov: Sun–Fri, 10.30am–5pm (1 Jul–31 Aug, 10.30am–5.30pm). Last admission 45 mins before castle closing time, but allow plenty of time before this to reach the island. In winter, guided tours only, telephone in advance. Garden (not NT): May & Jun: Mon–Fri; Jul–Oct: Thur & Fri, 10.30am–5.30pm. Church Service: Whitsun–end Sept (also Christmas Day, Good Fri & Easter Sun): Sun, 11.15am. All visits subject to weather and tides.

Admission: Adult £6.60, Child (under 17) £3.30, Family £16.50, 1-Adult Family £9.60. Booked groups £5.60. Gardens (not NT) £3.

⬚ ✦ ▣ ⊓ ⊓ Tel for details. 🅿 On mainland (not NT.) ✳ Not permitted in the castle or garden.

© Trebah Garden Trust

TINTAGEL CASTLE ⌗
TINTAGEL, CORNWALL PL34 0HE
www.english-heritage.org.uk/tintagel

Tel/Fax: 01840 770328

Owner: English Heritage   **Contact:** Visitor Operations Team

The spectacular setting for the legendary castle of King Arthur on the wild and windswept Cornish coast. Clinging to the edge of the cliff face are the extensive ruins of a medieval royal castle, built by Richard, Earl of Cornwall, brother of Henry III. Also used as a Cornish stronghold by subsequent Earls of Cornwall. Despite extensive excavations since the 1930s, Tintagel Castle remains one of the most spectacular and romantic spots in the entire British Isles. Destined to remain a place of mystery and romance, Tintagel will always jealously guard its marvellous secrets. Relax in our newly refurbished tearoom from Summer 2008.

Location: MAP 1:F7, OS200 Ref. SX048 891. On Tintagel Head, ½m along uneven track from Tintagel.

Open: 21 Mar–31 Oct: daily, 10am–6pm (5pm in Oct). 1 Nov–31 Mar: daily, 10am–4pm. Closed 24–26 Dec & 1 Jan.

Admission: Adult £4.70, Child £2.40, Conc. £3.80. Family £11.80. 15% discount for groups (11+). EH members Free.

ⓘ WC. ▢ ▣ P No vehicles. Parking (not EH) in village only. ▦ ✳ ▦

TINTAGEL OLD POST OFFICE ⌘

Tintagel, Cornwall PL34 0DB

Tel: 01840 770024 or 01208 74281

Owner: The National Trust   **Contact:** The Custodian

One of the most characterful buildings in Cornwall, and a house of great antiquity, this small 14th-century yeoman farmhouse is full of charm and interest.

Location: MAP 1:F7, OS Ref. SX056 884. In the centre of Tintagel.

Open: 15 Mar–30 Sept: daily 11am–5.30pm. 1 Oct–2 Nov: daily, 11am–4pm. Last admission 30 mins before closing.

Admission: Adult £2.80, Child £1.40, Family £7, 1-Adult Family £4.20. Booked groups £2.40.

TREBAH GARDEN
MAWNAN SMITH, Nr FALMOUTH, CORNWALL TR11 5JZ
www.trebah-garden.co.uk

Tel: 01326 252200   **Fax:** 01326 250781   **E-mail:** mail@trebah-garden.co.uk

Owner: Trebah Garden Trust   **Contact:** V. Woodcroft

Steeply wooded 25 acre sub-tropical valley garden falls 200 feet from 18th century house to private beach on Helford River. Stream cascading over waterfalls through ponds full of Koi Carp and exotic water plants winds through 2 acres of blue and white hydrangeas and spills out over beach. Huge Australian tree ferns and palms mingle with shrubs of ever-changing colours and scent beneath over-arching canopy of 100 year old rhododendrons and magnolias. The striking Visitor Centre houses a garden shop, plant sales and stylish catering.

Location: MAP 1:D10, OS Ref. SW768 275. 4m SW of Falmouth, 1m SW of Mawnan Smith. Follow brown and white tourism signs from Treliever Cross roundabout at A39/A394 junction through Mawnan Smith to Trebah.

Open: All year: daily, 10.30am–5pm (last admission). Winter opening times may vary.

Admission: 1 Mar–31 Oct: Adult £7, Child (5–15yrs) £2. Disabled £3.50. Child under 5yrs Free, OAP £6. 1 Nov–28 Feb: Adult £3, Child (5–15yrs)/Disabled £1, Child under 5yrs Free, OAP £2.50. NT & RHS members: free entry 1 Nov–end Feb.

▢ ▣ ♿ Partial. ▣ ▥ ▨ By arrangement. P ▦ ▦ On leads. ✳

Boconnoc

TRELISSICK GARDEN 🌿
FEOCK, TRURO, CORNWALL TR3 6QL

www.nationaltrust.org.uk

Tel: 01872 862090 **Fax:** 01872 865808 **E-mail:** trelissick@nationaltrust.org.uk
Owner: The National Trust **Contact:** The Property Manager
A garden and estate of rare tranquil beauty with glorious maritime views over the Carrick Roads to Falmouth. The tender and exotic shrubs make this an attractive garden in all seasons. Extensive park and woodland walks beside the river. Art and Craft Gallery. Make your visit a really special day: travel to Trelissick by foot ferry from Truro, Falmouth and St Mawes by Fal River Links Partnerships Ferries, from April to September. Copeland Spode China on display in Trelissick House at 2pm on Thursdays, April to June, September and October, booking advisable 01872 864452.

Location: MAP 1:E10, OS Ref. SW837 396. 4m S of Truro on B3289 above King Harry Ferry.
Open: Garden, Shop, Restaurant, Gallery and Plant Sales: all year: daily, 10.30am–5.30pm. (11am–4pm, Nov–Jan). Closed 24–26 Dec & 1 Jan. Woodland Walks: All year: daily.
Admission: Adult £6.60, Child £3.30, Family £16.50, 1-Adult Family £9.90. Pre-arranged groups £5.60pp. Car Park £3 (refunded on admission). Garden & Copeland Spode China: £10.60 (NT members £4). Discounted rate for winter visits.
🅿 🚼 🍴 By arrangement. ♿ 🍴 🚻 By arrangement. 🅿 Limited for coaches.
🐕 In park on leads; only guide dogs in garden. ❄ ♿

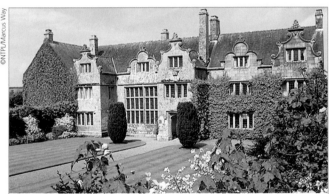

TRENGWAINTON GARDEN 🌿
PENZANCE, CORNWALL TR20 8RZ

www.nationaltrust.org.uk

Tel: 01736 363148 **Fax:** 01736 367762
Owner: The National Trust **Contact:** David Milne – The Property Manager
Intimate and closely linked to the picturesque stream running through its valley, the garden leads up to a terrace and summer houses with splendid views across Mount's Bay to the Lizard. The walled gardens contain many rare and unusual species which are difficult to grow in the open anywhere else in the country.
Location: MAP 1:B10, OS Ref. SW445 315. 2m NW of Penzance, ½m W of Heamoor on Penzance–Morvah road (B3312), ½ m off St. Just road (A3071).
Open: 10 Feb–2 Nov: Sun–Thur & Good Fri, 10.30am–5pm. Tearoom opens 10am. Last admission 15 mins before closing.
Admission: Adult £5.40, Child £2.70, Family £13.50, 1-Adult Family £8.20. Booked groups: £4.70. *includes a voluntary donation but visitors can choose to pay the standard prices displayed at the property and on the website.
🅿 🚼 ♿ Partial. ☕ Tea-house. 🚻 🐕 On leads (except in Tea-house garden).

TRERICE 🌿
KESTLE MILL, Nr NEWQUAY, CORNWALL TR8 4PG

www.nationaltrust.org.uk

Tel: 01637 875404 **Fax:** 01637 879300 **E-mail:** trerice@nationaltrust.org.uk
Owner: The National Trust **Contact:** David Milne – The Property Manager
Trerice is an architectural gem and something of a rarity – a small Elizabethan manor house hidden away in a web of narrow lanes and still somehow caught in the spirit of its age. An old Arundell house, it contains much fine furniture, ceramics, glasses and a wonderful clock collection. A small barn museum traces the development of the lawn mower. Several family activities. The garden has some unusual plants, an orchard with old varieties of south-west fruit trees and an experimental Tudor garden, developed in partnership with the local primary school.
Location: MAP 1:E8, OS Ref. SW841 585. 3m SE of Newquay via the A392 & A3058 (right at Kestle Mill). Or from A30–signs at Summercourt and Mitchell.
Open: 9 Mar–2 Nov: Daily except Sats, 11am–5pm. (Garden & tearoom 10.30am.) Tel for details of pre-Christmas opening.
*Admission: Adult £6.60, Child £3.30, Family £16.50, 1-Adult Family £9.90. Pre-arranged groups £5.60. Garden only: Adult £2.30, Child £1.10, Family £5.70, 1-Adult Family £3.40. Discounted pre-Christmas rates. *includes a voluntary donation but visitors can choose to pay the standard prices displayed at the property and on the website.
🅿 🚼 🍴 ♿ Braille & taped guides. WC. ☕ Licensed. 🐕 Guide dogs only. ▲ ♿

TREWITHEN 🏛

GRAMPOUND ROAD, TRURO, CORNWALL TR2 4DD

www.trewithengardens.co.uk

Tel: 01726 883647 **Fax:** 01726 882301
E-mail: gardens@trewithen-estate.demon.co.uk
Owner: A M J Galsworthy **Contact:** The Estate Office

Trewithen means 'house of the trees' and the name truly describes this fine early Georgian House in its splendid setting of wood and parkland. Country Life described the house as 'one of the outstanding West Country houses of the 18th century'. The gardens at Trewithen are outstanding and of international fame. It is now over 100 years since George Johnstone inherited and started developing the gardens which now contain a wide and rare collection of flowering shrubs. Some of the magnolias and rhododendron species in the garden are known throughout the world. They are one of two attractions in this county awarded three stars by Michelin. Viewing platforms and a Camera Obscura will be an additional interest to visitors.

Location: MAP 1:E9, OS Ref. SW914 476. S of A390 between Grampound and Probus villages. 7m WSW of St Austell.
Open: Gardens: 1 Mar–30 Sept: Mon–Sat, 10am–4.30pm. Suns in Mar–May only. House: Apr–Jul & Aug BH Mon, Mons & Tues, 2–4pm.
Admission: Mar–June: Adult £5 (groups 20+ £4.50), Child (5–15yrs) £1, Child under 5yrs Free. July–Sept: Adult £4.50 (groups 20+ £4), Child (5–15yrs) £1, Child under 5yrs Free. (2007 prices.)
ℹ No photography in house. 🅿 🖾 Partial. WC. 🖵 🅵 By arrangement.
🅿 Limited for coaches. 🐾 In grounds, on leads.

©NTPL/Peter Cade

St Michael's Mount

BICTON PARK BOTANICAL GARDENS
www.bictongardens.co.uk

■ **Owner**
Valerie Lister

■ **Contact**
Valerie Lister
Bicton Park
Botanical Gardens
East Budleigh
Budleigh Salterton
Devon
EX9 7BJ

Tel: 01395 568465
Fax: 01395 568374
E-mail: valerie@
bictongardens.co.uk

■ **Location**
MAP 2:L7
OS Ref. SY074 856

2m N of Budleigh
Salterton on B3178.

Follow the brown signs to
Bicton Park from M5/J30
at Exeter.

Rail: Exmouth 5mins,
Exeter St Davids 12m.

Air: Exeter Airport 5m.

■ **Opening Times**
Summer
10am–6pm.

Winter
10am–5pm.
Open all year except
Christmas Day &
Boxing Day.

■ **Admission**

Adult	£6.95
Child	£5.95
Conc	£5.95
Family (2+2)	£22.95

Groups (16-200)

Adult	£4.95
Child	£3.95
Conc.	£3.95

Children under 3yrs Free

Spanning three centuries of horticultural history, Bicton Park Botanical Gardens are set in the picturesque Otter Valley, near the coastal town of Budleigh Salterton and 10 miles south of Exeter.

The 63 acre park's oldest ornamental area is the Italian Garden, created in the axial style of Versailles landscaper Andre le Notre, c1735. By that time formal designs were becoming unfashionable in England, which may explain why the garden was located out of view of the manor house. Today, the full grandeur of the Italian Garden can be seen from the spacious restaurant in the classically styled Orangery, built at the beginning of the 19th century.

Bicton's high-domed Palm House, one of the world's most beautiful garden buildings, was the first of many developments between 1820 and 1850. Others included an important collection of conifers in the Pinetum, now the subject of a rare species conservation project, and St Mary's Church, where Queen Victoria worshipped.

A large museum reflects changes in agriculture and rural life generally over the past 200 years. The Grade I listed gardens, which are open all year, also feature a narrow-gauge railway which meanders through the garden on its 1½ mile track. Gift shop, garden centre, children's inside and outdoor play areas.

i	Children's inside & outdoor play areas.
	Garden Centre.
	WCs.
	Licensed.

	Licensed.
	By arrangement.
P	
	In grounds, on leads.

■ **Owner**

Hon John Rous

■ **Contact**

Visitor Centre
Clovelly
Nr Bideford
N Devon EX39 5TA

Tel: 01237 431781
Fax: 01237 431288

■ **Location**

MAP 1:H5
OS Ref. SS248 319

On A39 10 miles W of Bideford, 15 miles E of Bude. Turn off at 'Clovelly Cross' roundabout and follow signs to car park.

Air: Exeter & Plymouth Airport both 50 miles.

Rail: Barnstaple 19 miles.

Bus: from Bideford.

■ **Opening Times**

High season:
9am–6pm.

Low season:
10am–4.30pm.

■ **Admission**

The entrance fee covers parking and other facilities provided by Clovelly Estate. As well as admission to the audio-visual film, Fisherman's Cottage, and Kingsley Museum, your fee contributes to the ongoing maintenance of the village.

Adult	£5.50
Child (7–16yrs)	£3.50
Child (under 7yrs)	Free
Family (2+2)	£15.00
Group Rates (20+)	
Adult	£4.50
Child	£3.25

Prices correct at time of going to press.

■ **Special Events**

June
Literary celebration.

July
Clovelly Maritime Festival.

August
Lifeboat Day.

September
Lobster & Seafood Feast.

November
Clovelly Herring Festival.

CLOVELLY
www.clovelly.co.uk

From Elizabethan days until today, Clovelly Village has preserved its original atmosphere. The main traffic-free street, known as 'up-a-along' and 'down-a-long', tumbles its cobbled way down to the tiny harbour, which is protected by an ancient stone breakwater. It is a descent through flower-strewn cottages broken only by little passageways and winding lanes that lead off to offer the prospect of more picturesque treasures.

The New Inn, which is 400 years old, is halfway down the street, and another, the Red Lion, is right on the quayside. Both Inns have long histories and an atmosphere rarely found in the modern world. In addition you'll find the Visitor Centre, a range of gift shops, a café and an audio-visual theatre in which visitors are treated to a history of the village. Just below is the Stable Yard with a pottery and silk workshop. There are beautiful coastal and woodland walks.

Access is restricted to pedestrians only via the Visitor Centre with a Land Rover taxi service for those unable to walk.

i	Rubber soled, low heel shoes are recommended.
♿	Partial. Around the Visitor Centre.
☕	Licensed.
🍴	Licensed.
P	
🐕	On leads.
🛏	18 double, 1 single, all en suite.

A LA RONDE

SUMMER LANE, EXMOUTH, DEVON EX8 5BD

www.nationaltrust.org.uk

Tel: 01395 265514 **E-mail:** alaronde@nationaltrust.org.uk
Owner: The National Trust **Contact:** Assistant Property Manager

A unique 16-sided house built on the instructions of two spinster cousins, Jane and Mary Parminter, on their return from a grand tour of Europe. Completed c1796, the house contains many 18th-century contents and collections brought back by the Parminters. The fascinating interior decoration includes a feather frieze and shell-encrusted gallery which, due to its fragility, can be viewed fully by remote control on closed circuit television.

Location: MAP 2:L7, OS Ref. SY004 834. 2m N of Exmouth on A376.

Open: House: 15 Mar–2 Nov: daily except Thurs & Fri. 11am–5pm. Last admission ½ hour before closing. Shop & Grounds: 10.30am–5.30pm.

Admission: Adult £5.40, Child £2.70, Family £13.50, 1-Adult Family £8.10, Pre-booked Groups (15+) £4.60.

ARLINGTON COURT

Nr BARNSTAPLE, NORTH DEVON EX31 4LP

www.nationaltrust.org.uk

Tel: 01271 850296 **Fax:** 01271 851108
E-mail: arlingtoncourt@nationaltrust.org.uk
Owner: The National Trust **Contact:** Ana Chylak – Property Manager

The 3,000-acre estate lies in the wooded Yeo valley on the edge of Exmoor. The intimate Victorian house is full of treasures including model ships, pewter and shells; there are formal and informal gardens, a restored walled kitchen garden and extensive parkland, woodland and lakeside walks. The Victorian stable block and purpose built museum Wing houses the National Trust's Carriage Collection. Working stables provide carriage rides around the grounds.

Location: MAP 2:I4, OS180 Ref. SS611 405. 7m NE of Barnstaple on A39.

Open: House & Carriage Collection: 2 & 9 Mar, Sun, guided tours only, telephone to book. 16 Mar–2 Nov daily except Sat (open BH Sats), 11am–5pm. Last admission 4.30pm. Garden, shop, tearoom & Bat-cam, as house also Sats Jul & Aug and 7 Nov–21 Dec: Fri–Sun, 11am–4pm. Grounds open daily all year.

*Admission: House, Garden & Carriage Collection: Adult £7.80, Child £3.90, Family £19.50, 1-Adult family £11.70. Group £6.60. Garden & Carriage Collection only: Adult £5.60, Child £2.80. Sats during July & Aug: Adult £3, Child £1.50. Gardens only, Nov/Dec, Adult £2.50, Child Free. *includes a voluntary donation but visitors can choose to pay the standard prices displayed at the property and on the website.

Ground floor & grounds. WC. Licensed. Teachers' pack. In grounds & Carriage Collection, on leads.

ANDERTON HOUSE

Goodleigh, Devon EX32 7NR
Tel: 01628 825925 **E-mail:** bookings@landmarktrust.org.uk
www.landmarktrust.org.uk
Owner/Contact: The Landmark Trust

Anderton House is a Grade II* listed building of an exceptional modern design by Peter Aldington of Aldington and Craig. It was commissioned in 1969 as a family home and is highly evocative of its time, retaining the contemporary features and materials. Anderton House is cared for by The Landmark Trust, a building preservation charity who let it for holidays. Full details of Anderton House and 184 other historic and architecturally important buildings are featured in the Landmark Trust Handbook (price £11.50 refundable against a booking).

Location: MAP 2:I14, OS Ref. SS603 343. In village.

Open: Available for holidays for up to 5 people throughout the year. 2 Open Days a year. Other visits by appointment. Contact Landmark Trust for details.

Admission: Free on Open Days.

Buckland Abbey

BERRY POMEROY CASTLE

TOTNES, DEVON TQ9 6LJ

www.english-heritage.org.uk/berrypomeroy

Tel: 01803 866618
Owner: The Duke of Somerset **Contact:** Visitor Operations Team

A romantic late medieval castle, dramatically sited half-way up a wooded hillside, looking out over a deep ravine and stream. It is unusual in combining the remains of a large castle with a flamboyant courtier's mansion. Reputed to be one of the most haunted castles in the country.

Location: MAP 2:J8, OS202 Ref. SX839 623. 2½m E of Totnes off A385. Entrance gate ½m NE of Berry Pomeroy village, then ½m drive. Narrow approach, unsuitable for coaches.

Open: 21 Mar–31 Oct: daily, 10am–5pm (6pm in Jul & Aug; 4pm in Oct).

Admission: Adult £4, Child £2, Conc £3.20. 15% discount for groups (11+). EH members Free.

Ground floor & grounds. Not EH. No access for coaches.

BICTON PARK BOTANICAL GARDENS

See page 193 for full page entry.

BRADLEY MANOR 🌿

Newton Abbot, Devon TQ12 6BN
Tel: 01803 843235 **E-mail:** bradley@nationaltrust.org.uk
www.nationaltrust.org.uk
Owner: The National Trust

A delightful small medieval manor house set in woodland and meadows. Still lived in and managed by the donor family.
Location: MAP 2:K8, OS Ref. SX848 709. On Totnes road A381. ¾ m SW of Newton Abbot.
Open: 1 Apr–30 Sept: Tue–Thur, 2–5 pm. 1 Oct–31 Oct: Mon–Fri by appointment only. Last admission 4.30pm.
Admission: Adult £4, Child £2, no reduction for groups.
ℹ️ No WC. 🅿️ From 1.30pm. Not suitable for coaches.

BRANSCOMBE MANOR MILL, THE OLD BAKERY & FORGE 🌿

Branscombe, Seaton, Devon EX12 3DB
Tel: Manor Mill – 01392 881691   Old Bakery – 01297 680333   Forge – 01297 680481
www.nationaltrust.org.uk
Owner: The National Trust   **Contact:** NT Devon Office

Manor Mill, still in working order and recently restored, is a water-powered mill which probably supplied the flour for the bakery. There are regular working demonstrations. The Old Bakery was, until 1987, the last traditional working bakery in Devon. The old baking equipment has been preserved in the baking room and the rest of the building is now a tearoom. Information display in the outbuildings. The Forge opens regularly and ironwork is on sale - please telephone to check opening times.
Location: MAP 2:M7, OS Ref. SY198 887. In Branscombe ½ m S off A3052 by steep, narrow lane.
Open: Manor Mill: 23 Mar–26 Oct: Suns, 2–5pm; also Weds in Jul & Aug. The Old Bakery: 19 Mar–2 Nov, Wed–Sun, 11am–5pm. The Forge Open all year round.
Admission: Adult £2.60, Child £1.30. Manor Mill only.
🖼️ 📺

BUCKFAST ABBEY

Buckfastleigh, Devon TQ11 0EE
Tel: 01364 645500   **Fax:** 01364 643891   **E-mail:** education@buckfast.org.uk
Owner: Buckfast Abbey Trust   **Contact:** The Warden

The original monastery at Buckfast was formed during the reign of King Cnut in 1018.
Location: MAP 2:J8, OS Ref. SX741 674. ½m from A38 Plymouth – Exeter route.
Open: Church & Grounds: All year: 9am–7pm.
Admission: Free.

Branscombe Manor Mill

BUCKLAND ABBEY 🌿
YELVERTON, DEVON PL20 6EY

www.nationaltrust.org.uk

Tel: 01822 853607   **Fax:** 01822 855448
E-mail: bucklandabbey@nationaltrust.org.uk
Owner: The National Trust   **Contact:** Jon Cummins – Visitor Services Manager

The spirit of Sir Francis Drake is rekindled at his home with exhibitions of his courageous adventures and achievements throughout the world. One of the Trust's most interesting historical buildings and originally a 13th century monastery, the abbey was transformed into a family residence before Sir Francis bought it in 1581. Fascinating decorated plaster ceiling in Tudor Drake Chamber. Outside there are monastic farm buildings, craft workshops and country walks. Introductory film presentation. Beautiful Elizabethan garden now open. Letterbox Trail through Great North Wood.

Location: MAP 2:I8, OS201 Ref. SX487 667. 6m S of Tavistock; 11m N of Plymouth off A386. Bus: 55/56 from Yelverton (except Sun).
Open: 16 Feb–9 Mar: Sats & Suns only, 12.30–5pm (Abbey 2–5pm). 15 Mar–2 Nov: daily except Thurs, 10.30am–5.30pm (last adm. 4.45pm). 8 Nov–21 Dec: Fri–Sun only, 12 noon–4pm.
Admission: Abbey & Grounds: Adult £7.80, Child £3.90, Family £19.50, 1-Adult Family £11.70. Group (15+): Adult £6.60. Grounds only: Adult £4, Child £2.
ℹ️ No photography in house. 🖼️ 📷 📺 ♿ Ground floor & grounds. WC. 🍴 Licensed. 🍴 Licensed. 📷 By arrangement. ■ 🅿️ 🚌 Guide dogs only. ❋ 🐾

CADHAY 🏠
OTTERY ST MARY, DEVON EX11 1QT

www.cadhay.org.uk

Tel: 01404 812999 / 813511

Owner: Mr R Thistlethwayte   **Contact:** Jo Holloway / Jayne Lovell

Cadhay is approached by an avenue of lime-trees, and stands in an extensive garden, with herbaceous borders and yew hedges, with excellent views over the original medieval fish ponds. The main part of the house was built about 1550 by John Haydon who had married the de Cadhay heiress. He retained the Great Hall of an earlier house, of which the fine timber roof (about 1420–1460) can be seen. An Elizabethan Long Gallery was added by John's successor at the end of the 16th century, thereby forming a unique courtyard with statues of Sovereigns on each side, described by Sir Simon Jenkins as one of the 'Treasures of Devon'.

Location: MAP 2:L6, OS Ref. SY090 962. 1m NW of Ottery St Mary. From W take A30 and exit at Pattersons Cross, follow signs for Fairmile and then Cadhay. From E, exit at the Iron Bridge and follow signs as above.

Open: Late May BH. Sat–Mon. May–July: Fris; August: Fris & BH Sat–Mon. Sept: Fris, 2–5.30pm. Last tour 4.30pm.

Admission: Guided tours: Adult £6, Child £2. Gardens: Adults £2, Child £1.

⊡ ⊤ ⅗ Ground floor & grounds. ⬛ 𝒇 Obligatory. 🅿 🔁 Guide dogs only. ⊡ ⬛

RHS Garden Rosemoor

CASTLE DROGO 🌿
DREWSTEIGNTON, EXETER EX6 6PB

www.nationaltrust.org.uk

Tel: 01647 433306   **Fax:** 01647 433186   **E-mail:** castledrogo@nationaltrust.org.uk

Owner: The National Trust   **Contact:** David Bailey, Property Manager

Extraordinary granite and oak castle, designed by Sir Edwin Lutyens, which combines the comforts of the 20th century with the grandeur of a Baronial castle. Elegant dining and drawing rooms and fascinating kitchen and scullery. Terraced formal garden with colourful herbaceous borders and rose beds. Panoramic views over Dartmoor and delightful walks in the dramatic Teign Gorge.

Location: MAP 2:J7, OS191 Ref. SX721 900. 5m S of A30 Exeter–Okehampton road.

Open: Castle Drogo & Castle Tearoom 1/2 & 8/9 Mar, 11am–4pm. 15 Mar–2 Nov, daily except Tues, but open Tue 24 Mar–20 April, 26 May–1 Jun, 21 July–31 Aug, 26 Oct–2 Nov: 11am–5pm (4pm 26 Oct–2 Nov). For pre-Christmas opening tel for details. Last admission ½ hr before closing. Garden, Shop & Tearoom: open 10.30am.

*Admission: House & Garden: Adult £7.80, Child £3.90, Family £19.50, 1-Adult Family £11.70. Group: £6.60. Garden only: Adult £5, Child £2.75, Group £4.25. *includes a voluntary donation but visitors can choose to pay the standard prices displayed at the property and on the website.

⊡ ⅗ ⅗ 2 rooms in castle & grounds. WCs. ⬛ 𝒇 By arrangement. 🔁 Guide dogs only in certain areas. ✳

CHAMBERCOMBE MANOR

Ilfracombe, Devon EX34 9RJ
Tel: 01271 862624 **www.chambercombemanor.co.uk**
Owner: Chambercombe Trust **Contact:** Angela Powell

Guided tours of Norman Manor House which is mentioned in Domesday Book. Hear the legend of Chambercombe and visit Haunted Room. Set in 16 acres of woodland and landscaped gardens. Lady Jane Tea Rooms offering light lunches and cream teas.

Location: MAP 2:I3, OS Ref. SS539 461. East of Ilfracombe between A399 and B3230, follow brown historic house signs. Private car park at end of Chambercombe Lane.

Open: Easter–end Oct: Mon–Fri, 10.30am–5pm; Sun, 1–5pm. Last tour 4.30pm.

Admission: Adult £7, Child/Conc. £4, Family £22, under 5s free. Group (max 50) discount – apply to Manor.

ⓘ No photography in house. ♿ Partial. ▣🄵 Obligatory. 🅿 Limited for coaches.
▣▣ On leads, in grounds.

CLOVELLY

See page 194 for full page entry.

Bicton Park Botanical Gardens

COLETON FISHACRE ✖

BROWNSTONE ROAD, KINGSWEAR, DARTMOUTH TQ6 0EQ

www.nationaltrust.org.uk

Tel: 01803 752466 **Fax:** 01803 753017

E-mail: coletonfishacre@nationaltrust.org.uk

Owner: The National Trust **Contact:** Administrator

A 9 hectare property set in a stream-fed valley within the spectacular scenery of the South Devon coast. The Lutyens-style house with art deco-influenced interior was built in the 1920s for Rupert and Lady Dorothy D'Oyly Carte who created the delightful garden, planted with a wide range of rare and exotic plants giving year round interest.

Location: MAP 2:K9, OS202 Ref. SX910 508. 3m E of Kingswear, follow brown tourist signs.

Open: House, Garden & Tearoom: 15 Mar–2 Nov: Weds–Suns & BH Mons, & Mons 21 Jul–31 Aug, 10.30am–5pm. Last admission ½ hr before closing.

Admission: House & Garden: Adult £6.60, Child £3.30. Family £16.50, 1-Adult Family £9.90. Booked groups (15+): Adult £5.60, Child £2.85. Garden only: Adult £6.10, Child £3.10, Booked groups (15+) £5.

ⓘ No photography in house. ▣ ▣ ♿ Limited access. WC. ▣
🅿 Limited. Coaches must book. ✖ Assistance dogs only in garden.

Saltram

COMPTON CASTLE ❧

MARLDON, PAIGNTON TQ3 1TA

www.nationaltrust.org.uk

Tel: 01803 843235 **E-mail:** compton@nationaltrust.org.uk
Owner: The National Trust **Contact:** Administrator

Dramatic fortified manor house built by the Gilbert family between the 14th and 16th centuries. It has been the Gilberts' home for most of the last 600 years. Sir Humphrey Gilbert (1539-1583) was coloniser of Newfoundland and half-brother to Sir Walter Raleigh. There is a lovely rose garden and knot garden to complement the interior which includes great hall, solar, spiral staircases, old kitchen and chapel.

Location: MAP 2:K8, OS180 Ref. SX865 648. At Compton, 3m W of Torquay signed at Marldon. Coaches must approach from A381 Totnes Road at Ipplepen.
Open: 2 Apr–30 Oct: Mons, Weds & Thurs, 11am–5pm; last admission 4.30pm.
Admission: Adult £4, Child £2. Pre-arranged Groups Adult £3.40, Child £1.70.
🖸 🖲 (not NT) Castle Barton 01803 873314. 🚻 By arrangement.
🅿 Outside Castle or in Castle Barton Car Park. Coaches by appointment only.

CUSTOM HOUSE

The Quay, Exeter EX2 4AN

Tel: 01392 665521 **E-mail:** exeter.arch@exeter.gov.uk
Owner: Exeter City Council

The Custom House, located on Exeter's historic Quayside, was constructed from 1680–1682. It is the earliest substantial brick building in Exeter and was used by HM Customs and Excise until 1989. The building has an impressive sweeping staircase and spectacular ornamental plaster ceilings.

Location: MAP 2:K6, OS Ref. SX919 921. Exeter's historic Quayside.
Open: 1 Apr–31 Oct: Guided tour programme, telephone 01392 265203.
Admission: Free.
♿ Partial. 🚻 Obligatory. 🖲 🖾 Guide dogs only.

Hartland Abbey

CULVER HOUSE

LONGDOWN, EXETER, DEVON EX6 7BD

www.culver.biz

Tel: 01392 811885 **Fax:** 01392 811817 **E-mail:** info@culver.biz
Owner/Contact: Charles Eden Esq

Culver was built in 1836, but redesigned by the great Victorian architect, Alfred Waterhouse in a mock Tudor style. The distinctive interior of the house makes it a favoured location for functions and Culver was featured in BBC1's 'Down to Earth'. It has also been used by German and American film crews.

Location: MAP 2:J7, OS Ref. SX848 901. 5m W of Exeter on B3212.
Open: Not open to the public. Available for corporate hospitality.
Admission: Please telephone for booking details.
🖵

DARTMOUTH CASTLE ⊞

CASTLE ROAD, DARTMOUTH, DEVON TQ6 0JN

www.english-heritage.org.uk/dartmouth

Tel: 01803 833588 **Fax:** 01803 834445
Owner: English Heritage **Contact:** Visitor Operations Team

This brilliantly positioned defensive castle juts out into the narrow entrance to the Dart estuary, with the sea lapping at its foot. When begun in 1480s it was one of the most advanced fortifications in England, and was the first castle designed specifically with artillery in mind. For nearly 500 years it kept its defences up-to-date in preparation for war. Today the castle is in a remarkably good state of repair, along with excellent exhibitions, the history of the castle comes to life. A picnic spot of exceptional beauty.

Location: MAP 2:K9, OS202 Ref. SX887 503. 1m SE of Dartmouth off B3205, narrow approach road.
Open: 21 Mar–31 Oct: daily, 10am–5pm (6pm in Jul & Aug; 4pm in Oct). 1 Nov–31 Mar: Sat & Sun, 10am–4pm. Closed 24–26 Dec & 1 Jan.
Admission: Adult £4, Child £2, Conc. £3.20. 15% discount for groups (11+). EH members Free.
ℹ️ WC. 🖸 🖲 🅿 Limited (charged, not EH). 🖾 ✳

DOCTON MILL & GARDEN

Spekes Valley, Hartland, Devon EX39 6EA
Tel/Fax: 01237 441369
Owner/Contact: John Borrett
Garden for all seasons in 8 acres of sheltered wooded valley, plus working mill.
Location: MAP 1:G5, OS Ref. SS235 226. 3m Hartland Quay. 15m N of Bude. 3m W of A39, 3m S of Hartland.
Open: 1 Mar–31 Oct: 10am–6pm.
Admission: Adult £4, Child (under 16 yrs) Free, OAP £3.75.

DOWNES

Crediton, Devon EX17 3PL
Tel: 01392 439046 **Fax:** 01392 426183
Owner: Trustees of the Downes Estate Settlement **Contact:** Dianne Shirazian
Downes is a Palladian Mansion dating originally from 1692. As the former home of General Sir Redvers Buller, the house contains a large number of items relating to his military campaigns. The property is now predominantly a family home with elegant rooms hung with family portraits, and a striking main staircase.
Location: MAP 2:K6, OS Ref. SX852 997. Approx a mile from Crediton town centre.
Open: 24 Mar–17 Jun (and Aug BH Mon & Tues): Mons & Tues, guided tours 2.15 & 3.30pm. Easter–17 Jun open to groups (15+) at other times, by prior appointment.
Admission: Adult £5.50, Child (5–16yrs) £2.75, Child (under 5yrs) Free. Groups (15+) £5.
🎥 Obligatory.

THE ELIZABETHAN GARDENS

Plymouth Barbican Assoc. Ltd, New St, The Barbican, Plymouth PL1 2NA
Tel/Fax: 01822 611027/612983 **E-mail:** avdalo@dsi.pipex.com
Owner: Plymouth Barbican Association Limited **Contact:** Mr Anthony P Golding
Very small series of four enclosed gardens laid out in Elizabethan style in 1970.
Location: MAP 1:H8, OS Ref. SX477 544. 3 mins walk from Dartington Glass (a landmark building) on the Barbican.
Open: Mon–Sat, 9am–5pm. Closed Christmas.
Admission: Free.

EXETER CATHEDRAL

Exeter, Devon EX1 1HS
Tel: 01392 285983 (Visitors' Officer) **Fax:** 01392 285986
E-mail: visitors@exeter-cathedral.org.uk
Owner: Dean & Chapter of Exeter **Contact:** Visitors' Officer
Fine example of decorated gothic architecture. Longest unbroken stretch of gothic vaulting in the world.
Location: MAP 2:K6, OS Ref. SX921 925. Central to the City – between High Street and Southernhay. Groups may be set down in South Street.
Open: All year: Mon–Fri, 9.30am–6.30pm, Sats, 9am–5pm, Suns, 7.30am–6.30pm.
Admission: Donation requested of £3.50 per person. Charges apply to groups.

FINCH FOUNDRY

Sticklepath, Okehampton, Devon EX20 2NW
Tel: 01837 840046
Owner: The National Trust
19th-century water-powered forge, which produced agricultural and mining hand tools, holding regular demonstrations throughout the day.
Location: MAP 2:I6, OS Ref. SX641 940. 4m E of Okehampton off the A30.
Open: 15 Mar–2 Nov: Daily except Tue, 11am–5pm.
Admission: Adult £4, Child £2.
▣ ▣ 🅿 Not suitable for coaches. ▣ ▣ Except tearoom.

For **accommodation** in the South West, see our special index at the end of the book.

ESCOT

ESCOT PARK, OTTERY ST MARY, DEVON EX11 1LU
www.escot-devon.co.uk

Tel: 01404 822188 **Fax:** 01404 822903 **E-mail:** info@escot-devon.co.uk
Owner/Contact: Mr J-M Kennaway
House: an idyllic setting for weddings, conferences and product launches. **Gardens and Park:** 25 acres of gardens set within 220 acres of 'Capability' Brown parkland. Conservation activities within the park include water meadows restoration, studies on water voles and bats, resident beavers and even seahorses. The gardens are open to the public and feature a 4,000 beech-tree maze, wild boar, otters and birds of prey workshops and displays. Estate: 1200 privately owned acres of glorious East Devon – ideal as a film location, for musical festivals and other special events.
Location: MAP 2:L6, OS Ref. SY080 977 (gate). 9m E of Exeter on A30 at Fairmile.
Open: Gardens, Aquatic Centre, Restaurant & Gift Shop: open throughout the year as follows: Easter–31 Oct: daily, 10am–6pm. 1 Nov–Easter: daily, 10am–5pm except 25, 26 Dec.
Admission: Adult £5.95, Child £4.95, Child (under 3yrs) Free, Conc. £4.95, Family (2+2) £18.50. Booked groups (10+): Adult £5, Child/Conc. £3.50.
▣ 🎥 ▣ 🅵 Partial. ▣ Licensed. 🍴 Licensed. 🎥 By arrangement. 🅿 ▣
🐕 In grounds, on leads. ▲ ✳ ▣

FURSDON HOUSE 🏛

CADBURY, Nr THORVERTON, EXETER, DEVON EX5 5JS
www.fursdon.co.uk

Tel: 01392 860860 **Fax:** 01392 860126 **E-mail:** admin@fursdon.co.uk
Owner: Mr E D Fursdon **Contact:** Mrs C Fursdon
The Fursdons have lived here since the 13th century and the house, which was greatly modified in the 18th century, is at the heart of a small farming estate within a wooded and hilly landscape. Family memorabilia is displayed including a letter to Grace Fursdon from King Charles during the Civil War and there are fine examples of costume and textiles. The garden to the south flows naturally into the parkland beyond; to the west it slopes up to a walled and terraced area with mixed borders, roses and herbs. There are two private wings of the house for self-catering holiday accommodation.
Location: MAP 2:K6, OS Ref. SS922 046. 1½m S of A3072 between Tiverton & Crediton, 9m N of Exeter turning off A396 to Thorverton. Narrow lanes!
Open: House: BH Suns & Mons except Christmas. Jun–Aug, Suns & Weds. Guided tours at 2.30 & 3.30pm. Garden: as house 2–5pm. Groups by prior arrangement only.
Admission: House and Garden: Adult £6, Child (10–16yrs) £3, Child (under 10yrs) Free. Garden only: £3.
ℹ Conferences. No photography or video. 🅃 🅵 Partial. ▣ 🎥 Obligatory. 🅿
🐕 Guide dogs only. 🏠 Self-catering.

©NTPL/Hugh Palmer

GREENWAY ✤

GREENWAY ROAD, GALMPTON, CHURSTON FERRERS, DEVON TQ5 0ES

www.nationaltrust.org.uk

Tel: 01803 842382   **Greenway Quay Ferry Services:** 01803 844010

E-mail: greenway@nationaltrust.org.uk

Owner: The National Trust   **Contact:** Administrator

A glorious woodland garden, held on the edge of wildness and set on the banks of the River Dart; Greenway is one of Devon's best kept secrets. Renowned for rare half-hardy trees and shrubs and underplanted with native wild flowers, this peaceful haven has magnificent views and some challenging paths. Travel by river ferry from Dartmouth, Totnes or Torquay for a perfect day out.

Location: MAP 2:K8, OS Ref. SX876 548.

Open: 1 Mar–26 Oct: Wed–Sun, 10.30am–5pm (last admission 4.30pm).

Admission: Booked groups and visitors arriving on foot or by ferry: Adult £5, Child £2.50. Others (by car): Adult £6, Child £3.

⬜ 💺 🚻 ♿ Partial. WC. ◗ Licensed. 🍴 Licensed. 🎟 By arrangement. 🅿 1 midi size coach only. Groups must book. Please use river travel. 🐕

HALDON BELVEDERE/LAWRENCE CASTLE

Higher Ashton, Nr Dunchideock, Exeter, Devon EX6 7QY

Tel/Fax: 01392 833668   **E-mail:** enquiries@haldonbelvedere.co.uk

www.haldonbelvedere.co.uk

Owner: Devon Historic Building Trust   **Contact:** Ian Turner

18th century Grade II* listed triangular tower with circular turrets on each corner. Built in memory of Major General Stringer Lawrence, founder of the Indian Army. Restored in 1995 to illustrate the magnificence of its fine plasterwork, gothic windows, mahogany flooring and marble fireplaces. Breathtaking views of the surrounding Devon countryside.

Location: MAP 2:K7, OS Ref. SX875 861. 7m SW of Exeter. Exit A38 at Exeter racecourse for 2½m.

Open: Feb–Oct: Suns & BHs, 1.30–5.30pm.

Admission: Adult £2, Child Free.

🚻 ♿ Unsuitable. 🎟 By arrangement. 🅿 ▣ 🐕 In grounds, on leads. ▣ ▲

©NTPL / Stephen Robson

Knightshayes Court

HARTLAND ABBEY 🏛

HARTLAND, Nr BIDEFORD, N DEVON EX39 6DT

www.hartlandabbey.com

Tel: 01237 441264/234 or 01884 860225   **Fax:** 01237 441264/01884 861134

E-mail: ha_admin@btconnect.com

Owner: Sir Hugh Stucley Bt   **Contact:** The Administrator

Founded as an Augustinian Monastery in a beautiful valley leading to the Atlantic coast a mile's walk away, the Abbey was given by Henry VIII to the Sergeant of his Wine Cellar, whose descendants live here today. Remodelled in the 18th and 19th centuries, stunning architecture and decoration, important paintings, furniture, porcelain, early photographs, documents from 1160 and family memorabilia fascinate visitors. Winding paths, designed by Jekyll, make an enchanting walk through Woodland Gardens of bulbs, rhododendrons, azaleas, camellias and hydrangeas to the restored Bog Garden, Victorian Fernery and 18th century Walled Gardens; herbaceous, tender and rare plants including *echium pininana* and vegetables thrive here once again. Masses of bluebells and wildflowers in spring.

Peacocks, donkeys and black sheep. Popular film location including Jane Austen's '*Sense and Sensibility*' (BBC 2008) and Rosamunde Pilcher's '*The Shell Seekers*'. A stunning wedding venue. Holiday cottages. Snowdrop Sundays (10 & 17 Feb): lots of walks to areas normally closed.

Location: MAP 1:G5, OS Ref. SS240 249. 15m W of Bideford, 15m N of Bude off A39 between Hartland and Hartland Quay.

Open: House: 21 Mar–23 May: Wed/Thur, Sun & BHs; 26 May–5 Oct: Sun–Thurs, 2–5pm. Last adm. 4.30pm. Tearooms, Gardens & Grounds: daily except Sats, 12 noon–5pm.

Admission: House, Gardens & Grounds: Adult £8.50, Child (5–15ys) £2.50, Family £20. Groups (15+) £7.50, & (30+) £7. Gardens & Grounds only: Adult £4.50, Child (5–15ys) £1.50, Family £11.

⬜ 💺 🚻 Wedding receptions. ♿ Partial. WC. ◗ 🎟 By arrangement. 🅿 🐕 In grounds, on leads. ▣ ▲ 🐕 Snowdrop Sundays 10 & 17 Feb.

HEMYOCK CASTLE

Hemyock, Cullompton, Devon EX15 3RJ
Tel: 01823 680745 **www.hemyockcastle.co.uk**
Owner/Contact: Mrs Sheppard
Former medieval moated castle, displays show site's history as fortified manor house, castle and farm.
Location: MAP 2:L6, OS Ref. ST135 134. M5/J26, Wellington then 5m S over the Blackdown Hills.
Open: BH Mons 2–5pm. Other times by appointment. Groups & private parties welcome.
Admission: Adult £1, Child 50p. Group rates available.

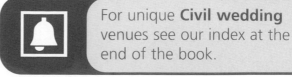

For unique **Civil wedding** venues see our index at the end of the book.

©NTPL/Phil Rider

©NTPL/Charlotte Eddington

KILLERTON

BROADCLYST, EXETER EX5 3LE

www.nationaltrust.org.uk

Tel: 01392 881345 **E-mail:** killerton@nationaltrust.org.uk
Owner: The National Trust **Contact:** Denise Melhuish – Assistant Property Manager
The spectacular hillside garden is beautiful throughout the year with spring flowering bulbs and shrubs, colourful herbaceous borders and fine trees. The garden is surrounded by parkland and woods offering lovely walks. The house is furnished as a family home and includes a costume collection dating from the 18th century in a series of period rooms and a Victorian laundry. New costume exhibition for 2008 'Recollections' – showing some of the gems of the Killerton costume collection, to mark 30 years of the collection being displayed to the public at Killerton.

Location: MAP 2:K6, OS Ref. SS977 001. Off Exeter – Cullompton Rd (B3181). M5 N'bound J30, M5 S'bound J28.
Open: House: 1–9 Mar, Sat & Sun, 2–4pm. 12 Mar–2 Nov: daily except Tue (Oct also closed Mon but open Mon ½ term); Aug: daily, 11am–5pm. Last entry ½ hour before closing. Garden & park: All year: daily, 10.30am–7pm or dusk.
*Admission: House & Garden: Adult £7.80, Child £3.90, Family £19.50, 1-Adult Family £11.70. Group £6.60. Garden only: Adult £5.70, Child £2.80. *includes a voluntary donation but visitors can choose to pay the standard prices displayed at the property and on the website.

Bookings required. Guide dogs only in house.

Devon Coastline near Hartland Abbey

© Hartland Abbey

KNIGHTSHAYES COURT
BOLHAM, TIVERTON, DEVON EX16 7RQ

www.nationaltrust.org.uk

Tel: 01884 254665 **E-mail:** knightshayes@nationaltrust.org.uk
Owner: The National Trust **Contact:** Penny Woollams – Property Manager
The striking Victorian gothic house is a rare survival of the work of William Burges with ornate patterns in many rooms. One of the finest gardens in Devon, mainly woodland and shrubs with something of interest throughout the seasons. Drifts of spring bulbs, summer flowering shrubs, pool garden and amusing animal topiary.
Location: MAP 2:K5, OS Ref. SS960 151. 2m N of Tiverton (A396) at Bolham.
Open: House: 16–24 Feb, daily except Fri, 1–9 Mar, Sat/Sun, 11am–4pm, 15 Mar–2 Nov,

daily except Fri (open Good Fri), 11am–5pm. Last adm. ½hr before closing. Garden as house, daily 11am–5pm. Shop/plant centre & restaurant as house plus limited opening Nov & Dec, tel for details.
*Admission: House & Garden: Adult £7.80, Child £3.90, Family £19.50, 1-Adult Family £11.70. Group £6.60. Garden only: Adult £6.20, Child £3.10. Group £5.20/£2.60. *includes a voluntary donation but visitors can choose to pay the standard prices displayed at the property and on the website.
Ground floor & grounds. WC. On leads in park.

LOUGHWOOD MEETING HOUSE

Dalwood, Axminster, Devon EX13 7DU
Tel: 01392 881691 **Fax:** 01392 881954
Owner: The National Trust **Contact:** National Trust Devon Office
Around 1653 the Baptist congregation of the nearby village of Kilmington constructed this simple thatched building dug into the hillside. It still contains the original box pews.
Location: MAP 2:M6, OS Ref. SY253993. 4m W of Axminster.
Open: All year, daily.
Admission: Free.
Pushchairs and baby carriers admitted. Steep slope from the car park. Ground floor only. Very narrow country lanes. No parking for coaches.

MARKER'S COTTAGE

Broadclyst, Exeter, Devon EX5 3HR
Tel: 01392 881345 (Killerton House for information)
Owner: The National Trust **Contact:** The Custodian
Thatched, medieval cob house containing a cross-passage screen decorated with a painting of St Andrew and his attributes.
Location: MAP 2:K6, OS Ref. SX985 973. ¼m E of B3181 in village of Broadclyst.
Open: 1 Apr–28 Oct: Sun–Tue, 2–5pm. Last entry ½ hour before closing.
Admission: Adult £2.60, Child £1.30. Joint ticket with Clyston Mill: Adult £4.20, Child £2.10.

MARWOOD HILL

Barnstaple, Devon EX31 4EB
Tel: 01271 342528 **Contact:** Patricia Stout
20 acre garden with 3 small lakes. Extensive collection of camellias, bog garden. National collection of astilbes.
Location: MAP 2:I4, OS Ref. SS545 375. 4m N of Barnstaple. ½m W of B3230. Signs off A361 Barnstaple – Braunton road.
Open: All year: 10am–5pm.
Admission: Adult £4.50, Child (under 12yrs) Free.

MORWELLHAM QUAY

Morwellham, Tavistock, Devon PL19 8JL
Tel: 01822 832766 **Fax:** 01822 833808
Owner: The Morwellham & Tamar Valley Trust **Contact:** Anthony Power
Award-winning visitor centre at historic river port.
Location: MAP 1:H8, OS Ref. SX446 697. Off A390 about 15 mins drive from Tavistock, Devon. 5m SW of Tavistock. 3m S of A390 at Gulworthy.
Open: Summer: daily, 10am–5.30pm, last adm. 3.30pm. Winter: daily, 10am–4.30pm, last adm. 2.30pm.
Admission: Adult £8.90, Child £6, OAP £7.80, Disabled £3.70, Family (2+2) £19.50. Group rate please apply for details. Usual concessions. Prices may be subject to change.

OKEHAMPTON CASTLE

Okehampton, Devon EX20 1JA
Tel: 01837 52844
www.english-heritage.org.uk/okehampton
Owner: English Heritage **Contact:** Visitor Operations Team
The ruins of the largest castle in Devon stand above a river surrounded by splendid woodland. There is still plenty to see, including the Norman motte and the jagged remains of the Keep. There is a picnic area and lovely woodland walks.
Location: MAP 2:I6, OS Ref. SX584 942. 1m SW of Okehampton town centre off A30 bypass.
Open: 21 Mar–30 Sept: daily, 10am–5pm (6pm in July & Aug).
Admission: Adult £3, Child £1.50, Conc. £2.40. 15% discount for groups (11+). EH members Free.
Access difficult for ambulant disabilities. Grounds. WC. In grounds, on leads.

©NTPL/Tony Murdoch

OLDWAY MANSION
TORQUAY ROAD, PAIGNTON, DEVON TQ3 2CR

Tel: 01803 207933 **E-mail:** fmhelpdesk@torbay.gov.uk
Owner: Torbay Council   **Contact:** Stuart Left

Oldway Mansion, one of the grandest houses in the Torbay, was built in 1874 for Isaac Singer, the American millionaire sewing machine manufacturer. It was one of Isaac's sons, Paris Singer, who took over residency in the mansion and who gave it its present form. A regular visitor to Oldway was Paris's mistress, Isadora Duncan. Modelled on the Palace of Versailles, Oldway Mansion is where visitors can see The Gallery, a miniature reproduction of the 'Hall of Mirrors' and the Ballroom. The formal gardens were originally laid out by Achille Duchêne, of Blenheim Palace fame.

Location: MAP 2:K8, OS Ref. SX888 615. Off W side of A3022.
Open: All year: Apr–Oct, daily, 9am–5pm. Nov–Mar, Mon–Sat, 9am–5pm.
Admission: Free.

⊤ ⅏ ▣ 𝒻 By arrangement. **P** Limited. ▣ ⊞ Guide dogs only. ⧆ ❄

OVERBECK'S ✾
SHARPITOR, SALCOMBE, SOUTH DEVON TQ8 8LW

www.nationaltrust.org.uk

Tel: 01548 842893 **E-mail:** overbecks@nationaltrust.org.uk
Owner: The National Trust   **Contact:** Property Manager

Elegant Edwardian house with diverse collections and luxuriant garden. The scientist Otto Overbeck lived here from 1928–37 and the museum containing his collections of curios and nautical artefacts has an intimate atmosphere. Some of Overbeck's inventions are on show, including the intriguing 'rejuvenator' machine. The house is set in 2¾ha (7acres) of beautiful exotic gardens with spectacular views over the Salcombe estuary. It enjoys a sheltered microclimate and so is home to many rare plants. There is also a secret room for children with dolls, tin soldiers, other toys and a ghost hunt.

Location: MAP 2:J10, OS Ref. SX728 374. 1½m SW of Salcombe. Signposted from Salcombe (single track lanes).
Open: House and shop: 15 Mar–30 Jun & 1 Sept–5 Oct: daily except Sat, 11am–5pm, 1 Jul–31 Aug: daily, 11am–5pm. 6 Oct–2 Nov: Sun–Thurs, 11am–5pm. Tearoom as house, 11am–4.15pm plus Sats & Suns 9–24 Feb, 11am–4pm. Garden: 1–24 Feb: daily, 25 Feb–14 Mar, Mon–Fri, 15 Mar–2 Nov, as house, all 10am–5pm. 3 Nov–31 Jan '09: Mon–Fri, 11am–4pm. Open Sats & BH Suns & Mons. Closed 24/25 Dec & 1 Jan.
Admission: Adult £6, Child £3, Family £15, 1-Adult Family £9. Groups £5.20.
ⓘ No photography in house. ▣ ⊞ ⅏ Partial. ▣ 𝒻 By arrangement. **P** Limited. Charge refunded on admission. ▣ ⊠ ❄

©NTPL/Stephen Robson

Knightshayes Court

POWDERHAM CASTLE 🏰
KENTON, Nr EXETER, DEVON EX6 8JQ
www.powderham.co.uk

Tel: 01626 890243   **Fax:** 01626 890729   **E-mail:** castle@powderham.co.uk
Owner: The Earl of Devon   **Contact:** Mrs Clare Crawshaw – General Manager
A splendid castle built in 1391 by Sir Philip Courtenay, remaining in the same family and currently home to the 18th Earl of Devon. Set in a tranquil deer park alongside the Exe estuary, its stunning location offers glorious views for miles around. A splendid Rose Garden terrace and walk through the Woodland Garden are very rewarding. Guided tours showcase the Castle's majestic rooms, stunning interiors and fine collection of treasures, while fascinating stories bring its intriguing history to life. The newly-restored Victorian kitchen offers an insight into domestic service at the Castle. The Victorian kitchen garden is now a children's play area with friendly animals.

Location: MAP 2:K7, OS Ref. SX965 832. 6m SW of Exeter, 4m S M5/J30. Access from A379 in Kenton village.
Open: 20 Mar– 2 Nov: Sun–Fri, 10am–5.30pm (last guided tour 4.30pm). Available for private hire all year.
Admission: Adult £8.50, Child (5–14yrs) £6.50, Senior £7.50, Family: £24. Groups (15+) special rates available.
ℹ️ Available for private hire all year round. ⬜ 🏷 🚂 ♿ Partial. WC. 🍽 Licensed.
🎬 Included. 1hr. 🅿 ◼ 🚌 Guide dogs only. ⬛ ⬛

RHS GARDEN ROSEMOOR
GREAT TORRINGTON, DEVON EX38 8PH
www.rhs.org.uk/rosemoor

Tel: 01805 624067   **Fax:** 01805 624717   **E-mail:** rosemooradmin@rhs.org.uk
Owner/Contact: The Royal Horticultural Society
An enchanting 65-acre garden offering year-round interest and something for all interests and tastes. Visit us for inspiration, tranquility or simply a marvellous day out. Shop, plant centre, restaurant and tearoom on site offering exciting gifts and a relaxing place to enjoy a delicious meal.
Location: MAP 2:I5, OS Ref. SS500 183. 1m S of Great Torrington on A3124.
Open: All year except Christmas Day; Apr–Sept: 10am–6pm. Oct–Mar: 10am–5pm.
Admission: Adult £6, Child (6–16yrs) £2, Child (under 6yrs) Free. Groups (10+) £5pp. Companion for disabled visitor Free. RHS member & 1 guest Free.
⬜ 🏷 ♿ 🍽 🍴 Licensed. 🎬 By arrangement. 🅿 🚌 Guide dogs only. ❄ ⬛

©English Heritage Photo Library

Dartmouth Castle

©NTPL/Rupert Truman

© NTPL/Joe Cornish

SALTRAM ※
PLYMPTON, PLYMOUTH, DEVON PL7 1UH

www.nationaltrust.org.uk

Tel: 01752 333500 **Fax:** 01752 336474 **E-mail:** saltram@nationaltrust.org.uk
Owner: The National Trust   **Contact:** Administrator

Saltram stands high above the River Plym in a rolling and wooded landscaped park that now provides precious green space on the outskirts of Plymouth. The house, with its magnificent decoration and original contents, was largely created between the 1740s and 1820s by three generations of the Parker family. It features some of Robert Adam's finest rooms, exquisite plasterwork ceilings, original Chinese wallpapers and an exceptional collection of paintings including many by Sir Joshua Reynolds and Angelica Kauffman. The garden is predominantly 19th-century and contains an orangery and several follies, as well as beautiful shrubberies and imposing specimen trees.

The shop and art gallery offer work for sale from contemporary local artists, and National Trust gifts. The Park Restaurant offers refreshments for its visitors. Corporate business and special functions are very welcome.

NB. A major project may necessitate disruption to house opening. Please telephone for details.

Location: MAP 2:I9, OS Ref. SX520 557. From A38, exit 3 miles north of Plymouth City Centre at Marsh Mill's roundabout. Take Plympton exit; continue in right hand lane to third set of traffic lights then turn right onto Cott Hill. At the top of the hill turn right into Merafield Road then right again after 200 yards.
Open: House: 21 Mar–2 Nov: daily except Fris (open Good Fri), 12 noon–4.30pm. Last admission to house 3.45pm. Garden: all year, daily (except Fri, open Good Fri), 11am–5pm (4pm Nov–Mar). Restaurant: all year, daily, 11am–5pm (4pm Nov–Mar). Tel for details of Christmas closure.
*Admission: House & Garden: Adult £8.80, Child £4.40, Family £22, 1–Adult Family £13.20. Groups (15+): £7.50. Garden only: Adult £4.40, Child £2.20. *includes a voluntary donation but visitors can choose to pay the standard prices displayed at the property and on the website.

⬛ ♿ ⛳ ⬛ WC. Braille guide. ⬛ ⬛ Licensed. ⬛ ⬛ **P**
🐕 On signed perimeter paths only, on leads. Guide dogs only in house & garden.
⬛ ⬛

SAND 🏛
SIDBURY, SIDMOUTH EX10 0QN

www.sandsidbury.co.uk

Tel: 01395 597230 **E-mail:** info@sandsidbury.co.uk
Contact: Mrs Stella Huyshe-Shires

Sand is one of East Devon's hidden gems. The beautiful valley garden extends to 6 acres and is the setting for the lived-in house, the 15th century Hall House, and the 17th century Summer House. The family, under whose unbroken ownership the property has remained since 1560, provide guided house tours.
Location: MAP 2:L7, OS Ref. SY146 925. Well signed, 400 yards off A375 between Honiton and Sidmouth.
Open: House: BH Suns & Mons, 23/24 Mar, 4/5 May, 25/26 May & 24/25 Aug: 2–6pm. Garden: 23 Mar–30 Sept: Sun–Tues, 2–6pm. Last admission to house & garden 5pm. Groups by appointment throughout the year.
Admission: House & Garden: Adult £6, Child/Student £1. Garden only: Adult £3, accompanied Child (under 16) Free.

ⓘ No photography in house. ♿ Partial. ⬛ ⬛ Obligatory. **P**
🐕 In grounds, on leads. ⬛ ⬛ Tel. for details.

SHUTE BARTON ※

Shute, Axminster, Devon EX13 7PT
Tel: 01297 34692 (tenant) www.nationaltrust.org.uk
Owner: The National Trust
One of the most important surviving non-fortified manor houses of the Middle Ages.
Location: MAP 2:M6, OS Ref. SY253 974. 3m SW of Axminster, 2m N of Colyton, 1m S of A35.
Open: 5 Apr–27 Sept: Weds & Sats, 2–5.30pm. Last admission 5pm. 1–29 Oct: Weds & Sats, 2–5pm. Last admission 4.30pm.
Admission: Adult £2.80, Child £1.40. No group reductions.

TAPELEY PARK & GARDENS

Instow, Bideford, Devon EX39 4NT
Tel: 01271 860897 **Fax:** 01271 342371
Owner: Tapeley Park Trust
Extensive gardens and park.
Location: MAP 1:H4, OS Ref. SS478 291. Between Bideford and Barnstaple near Instow. Follow brown tourist signs from the A39 onto B3233.
Open: Good Fri–end Oct: daily except Sats, 10am–5pm.
Admission: Adult £4, Child £2.50, OAP £3.50. Groups (5+): Adult £3.20, Child £2 (under 5s Free), OAP £2.80 (2007 prices).

©NTPL/Andreas Von Einsiedel

Arlington Court

TIVERTON CASTLE 🏰
TIVERTON, DEVON EX16 6RP

www.tivertoncastle.com

Tel: 01884 253200/255200 **Fax:** 01884 254200 **E-mail:** tiverton.castle@ukf.net
Owner: Mr and Mrs A K Gordon **Contact:** Mrs A Gordon
Celebrating 900 years since original construction, few buildings evoke such immediate feelings of history. Inside it looks like a fairytale castle, with romantic ruins, medieval towers and gatehouse, and later additions. Beautiful walled gardens, including working kitchen garden. Civil War Armoury – try some on – interesting furniture, pictures. Superb holiday apartments.
Location: MAP 2:K5, OS Ref. SS954 130. Just N of Tiverton town centre.
Open: Easter–end Oct: Sun, Thur, BH Mon, 2.30–5.30pm. Last admission 5pm. Open to groups (12+) by prior arrangement at any time.
Admission: Adult £5, Child (7–16yrs) £2, Child under 7 Free. Garden only: £1.50.
⬛ 🔲 Partial. 🔲 By arrangement. 🅿 🔲 🔲 🔲 4 Apartments. ✳

TORRE ABBEY
THE KING'S DRIVE, TORQUAY, DEVON TQ2 5JE

www.torre-abbey.org.uk

Tel: 01803 211211 **E-mail:** torre-abbey@torbay.gov.uk
Owner: Torbay Council **Contact:** Leslie Retallick
Torre Abbey was founded in 1196 as a monastery. It was turned into a country house, and was home to the Cary family from 1662–1930. The Abbey consists of Grade I and II listed buildings and a Scheduled Ancient Monument. It will open from July after extensive refurbishment.
Location: MAP 2:K8, OS Ref. SX906 638. On Torquay sea front, between station and town centre.
Open: 8 Jul onwards, daily from 10am. Please tel for exact dates and times.
Admission: Tel for details.
⬛ 🔲 🔲 WC. 🔲 🔲 By arrangement. 🅿 Limited. 🔲
🔲 In grounds, on leads. Guide dogs only in House. 🔲 ✳ 🔲

TOTNES CASTLE ⌗
Castle Street, Totnes, Devon TQ9 5NU
Tel/Fax: 01803 864406
www.english-heritage.org.uk/totnes
Owner: English Heritage **Contact:** Visitor Operations Team
By the North Gate of the hill town of Totnes you will find a superb motte and bailey castle, with splendid views across the roof tops and down to the River Dart. It is a symbol of lordly feudal life and a fine example of Norman fortification.
Location: MAP 2:J8, OS202 Ref. SX800 605. In Totnes, on hill overlooking the town. Access in Castle St off W end of High St.
Open: 21 Mar–31 Oct: daily 10am–5pm (6pm Jul–Aug, 4pm Oct).
Admission: Adult £2.50, Child £1.30, Conc. £2. 15% discount for groups (11+). EH members Free.
⬛ 🔲 Unsuitable. 🅿 Charged, 64 metres (70 yds), not EH. 🔲 🔲 In grounds, on leads.

Powderham Castle

South West – England

■ **Owner**
The Hon
Mrs Townshend DL

■ **Contact**
Shop Manager
Abbotsbury
Weymouth
Dorset DT3 4LA

Tel: 01305 871387
E-mail: info@abbotsbury-tourism.co.uk

■ **Location**
MAP 2:N7
OS Ref. SY564 851

Off A35 nr Dorchester, on B3157 between Weymouth & Bridport.

■ **Opening Times**
Mar–Nov: daily,
10am–6pm.

Winter: daily,
10am–4pm.
(Closed Christmas and New Year.)

Last admission
1 hr before closing.

■ **Admission**
Adult   £8.50
Child   £5.50
OAP   £8.00

©Steve Griffith/Curator

ABBOTSBURY SUBTROPICAL GARDENS

www.abbotsbury-tourism.co.uk   www.abbotsburyplantsales.co.uk

©Julien Lightfoot

Established in 1765 by the first Countess of Ilchester. Developed since then into a 20-acre Grade I listed, magnificent woodland valley garden.

World famous for its camellia groves, magnolias, rhododendron and hydrangea collections. In summer it is awash with colour.

Since the restoration after the great storm of 1990 many new and exotic plants have been introduced. The garden is now a mixture of formal and informal, with charming walled garden and spectacular woodland valley views.

Facilities include a Colonial Tea House for lunches, snacks and drinks, a plant centre and quality gift shop. Events such as Shakespeare and concerts are presented during the year. The floodlighting of the garden at the end of October should not be missed.

Voted "Our Favourite Garden" by readers of *The Daily Telegraph*.

 Plants also for sale online.

Partial.

Licensed.

 By arrangement.

 Free.

In grounds, on leads.

www.sky-mast.co.uk

■ **Owner**
Patrick Cooke Esq

■ **Contact**
Owen Davies or
Laura Dean
Athelhampton House
Dorchester DT2 7LG

Tel: 01305 848363
Fax: 01305 848135
E-mail: enquiry@
athelhampton.co.uk

■ **Location**
MAP 2:P6
OS Ref. SY771 942

Off A35 (T) at Puddletown
Northbrook junction, 5m E
of Dorchester.

Rail: Dorchester.

■ **Opening Times**
18 February–3 November:
Daily (except Fri & Sat).

November–February:
Sun only.

10.30am–5pm/dusk.
Last admission 4.30pm.

Coach House Restaurant
open as House & Gardens.
Sunday Carvery bookings
taken.

All facilities at
Athelhampton are available
for private hire outside our
normal opening hours.
We specialise in weddings
on Fridays and Saturdays
and dinners on any
evening. Please contact
Owen Davies, Manager.

Self catering cottage in the
grounds – see website or
telephone for details.

■ **Admission**
House & Gardens
Adult	£9.00
Child (under 16)	Free
Student/Disabled	£6.00
Senior	£8.50

Groups (12+)
Adult £7.00*

*£6.00 with pre-booked
catering order.

See our website for special
offers and up-to-date
admission charges.

■ **Special Events**
May 4
NCCPG Plant Sale

June 8–12
Flower Festival

August 7
Outdoor Theatre – Tess
of the d'Urbervilles
August 10
MG Owners' Day
August 25
Village Fete

ATHELHAMPTON HOUSE & GARDENS

www.athelhampton.co.uk

Athelhampton House and its Gardens have been in private ownership for over 500 years. Sir William Martyn was granted a licence by Henry VII to enclose 160 acres of deer park and to build the fortified manor. His Great Hall, with a roof of curved brace timbers and an oriel window with fine heraldic glass, is now one of the finest examples of Tudor architecture in the country. In 1891 Alfred Carte de Lafontaine (the then owner of Athelhampton) commissioned the building of the formal gardens. The wonderful architectural features of the gardens including the Great Court, pavilions, terrace and many ponds with fountains, are the masterpiece of Francis Inigo Thomas. They are carved from local Ham stone. Today 12 30ft high yew trees dominate the 'Pyramid Garden' and collections of tulips, roses, clematis and lilies can be seen. The Gardens have won the HHA 'Garden of the Year' Award and are Grade I listed. The River Piddle borders the estate and has a boarded walkway alongside, from which views take in the West Wing of the House and the 15th century Dovecote, complete with its colony of white fantail doves.

One of Dorset's treasures, the house contains a fine collection of furniture from Jacobean to Victorian periods. The second floor of the West Wing has been recently dedicated to an exhibition of paintings and sketches by the Russian artist, Marevna (1892–1984). The collection of her works, painted mainly in the Cubist style, includes some painted whilst she lived at Athelhampton during the 1940s and 50s.

The current owners, Patrick and Andrea Cooke, oversee the day-to-day running of the estate, including restoration projects and garden design. They can often be seen working with the gardening team or in the House, which is their home.

The Coach House contains all the facilities required for the comfort of daily visitors including a restaurant, gift shop and private room available for visiting groups. In addition to the normal opening hours, the House and Gardens can be opened by appointment for evening visits and dinners. Fridays and Saturdays are available for wedding ceremonies and/or receptions.

Great Hall

Mark Julian Wedding Photography www.markjulian.co.uk

	By arrangement.
	Partial. WC.
	Licensed.
	Licensed.
	By arrangement.
P	
	Guide dogs only.

Conference/Function

ROOM	SIZE	MAX CAPACITY
Coach House*		
Long Hall	13 x 6m	100
Conservatory*	16 x 11m	130
Main House*		
Great Hall	12 x 8m	70
Great* Chamber	10 x 6m	40
Garden Pavilions (2)	3 x 3m	6
*Licensed for Civil wedding ceremonies.		

■ **Owner**

Mark Roper Esq

■ **Contact**

Carolyn Clay
Forde Abbey
Chard
Somerset TA20 4LU

Tel: 01460 220231
E-mail:
info@fordeabbey.co.uk

■ **Location**

MAP 2:N6
OS Ref. ST358 041

Just off the B3167
4m SE of Chard.

■ **Opening Times**

House

18 March–31 October
Tue–Fri, Sun & BH Mons
12 noon–4pm.

Gardens

Daily all year:
10am–4.30pm.

■ **Admission**

For current admission
prices phone
01460 221290.

FORDE ABBEY & GARDENS 🏛

www.fordeabbey.co.uk

Forde Abbey is a treasure in an area already known for its outstanding beauty. More than 900 years of history is encapsulated in this elegant former Cistercian monastery and its 30 acres of award-winning gardens. In the peaceful solitude of its secluded position it is possible to imagine just how it looked to many of its previous owners: monks going about their daily round of work and prayer, prosperous Parliamentary gentlemen discussing the Cavalier threat, gifted philosophers debating the imponderable, elegant Victorian ladies fanning themselves by the fireside and country gentlemen going about their work on the estate.

Set on the banks of the River Axe, this magnificent home contains many treasures including the Mortlake Tapestries, woven from cartoons painted for the Sistine Chapel by Raphael. The intricacy of their original design is matched by the story behind these particular tapestries involving Civil war, rebellion and loyalty rewarded.

The beautiful gardens that surround the house date from the early 18th century, although much work has been done by the present occupiers. Highlights of the garden include: carpets of springtime bulbs, a magnificent Bog Garden, Beech House, summer borders, a working kitchen garden and the remarkable Centenary Fountain – the highest powered fountain in England. The garden has been described by Alan Titchmarsh as *"one of the greatest gardens of the West Country"*.

The Undercroft Restaurant serving morning coffee, lunches and cream teas (using produce from the garden, estate and local suppliers), together with the unique gift shop, plant centre and pottery exhibition will complete a perfect day out.

ℹ Available for wedding receptions. No photography in house.

♿ Partial.

☕ Licensed.

🍴 Licensed.

🚶 By arrangement.

🅿

🐕 On leads, in grounds.

KINGSTON LACY

www.nationaltrust.org.uk

Kingston Lacy House lies at the heart of the 8,500 acre Bankes Estate. Opened to the public nearly twenty years ago, the 'secret estate' is still only slowly revealing itself. Lying 1½ miles from Wimborne Minster and 9 miles from the market town of Blandford Forum on the B3082, Kingston Lacy is the gateway to true, rural Dorset.

As the home of the Bankes family for 300 years, Kingston Lacy replaced the original family seat of Corfe Castle and is now presented by the National Trust as it was in its Edwardian heyday. This elegant country mansion contains an outstanding collection of fine works of art, including a Titian, two Rubens and a Velázquez, as well as an unique group of Egyptian artefacts. Set in 32 acres of formal gardens, which include one of only two Egyptian obelisks in the UK (the other being Cleopatra's Needle), the house is surrounded by hundreds of

acres of park and woodland, crossed by way-marked walks and includes three child-friendly play areas.

In 2005 the restored Japanese Gardens opened for public viewing, part of a seven acre project funded by the Gordon Bulmer Charitable Trust, in the southern woodland shelter belt. In 2006 the magnificent Guido Reni detached fresco, "Separation of Night from Day", was remounted on the ceiling of the 18th century Library. The painting is unique and important, the only known example in England of the artist's fresco work, and a significant achievement of the Trust's conservation work at the property.

Events and activities occur throughout the year including concerts, outdoor theatre, walks, talks and a children's holiday club.

Garden only. Braille guide & Induction Loop system. WC. Less-abled access info: 01202 883402.

Licensed.

By arrangement.

P

On leads, in park & woodland walks only.

Tel: 01202 883402.

■ **Owner**
The National Trust

■ **Contact**
The Property Manager
Kingston Lacy
Wimborne Minster
Dorset BH21 4EA

Tel: 01202 883402 /
842913
(Sat & Sun 11am–5pm)
Fax: 01202 882402

Restaurant:
01202 889242

E-mail: kingstonlacy@
nationaltrust.org.uk

■ **Location**
MAP 3:A6
OS Ref. ST980 019

On B3082 – Blandford /
Wimborne road, 1½m NW
of Wimborne Minster.

Rail: Poole 8½m.

Bus: Wilts & Dorset
132/3, 182/3 from
Bournemouth, Poole,
alight Wimbourne
Square 2½m.

■ **Opening Times**
House
15 March–2 November
Wed–Sun, 11am–5pm.
Last admission 4pm.
(1hr to view the house
thoroughly.)

Garden & Park
15 March–2 November,
daily, 10.30am–6pm.
7 November–
21 December, Fri–Sun,
10.30am–4pm.
2 February–9 March
2008, Sat & Sun,
10.30am–4pm.

Shop & Restaurant
15 March–2 November,
daily, 10.30am–5.30pm.
7 November–
21 December, Fri–Sun,
10.30am–4pm.

2 February–9 March,
Sat & Sun, 10.30am–4pm.

Timed entry tickets may
be issued on BHs and
some weekends.

■ **Admission**
House & Gardens
Adult	£10.00
Child	£5.00
Family	£25.00

Groups
House & Gardens	£8.00
Child (under 15yrs)	£4.00

Park & Garden only
Adult	£5.00
Child	£2.50
Family	£12.50

ABBOTSBURY SUBTROPICAL GARDENS 🏛

See page 208 for full page entry.

ATHELHAMPTON HOUSE & GARDENS 🏛🏠

See page 209 for full page entry.

BROWNSEA ISLAND ✻

Poole Harbour, Dorset BH13 7EE
Tel: 01202 707744 **Fax:** 01202 701635 **E-mail:** brownseaisland@nationaltrust.org.uk
www.nationaltrust.org.uk/brownsea
Owner: The National Trust **Contact:** NT Office

Atmospheric island of heath and woodland with wide variety of wildlife. The island is dramatically located at the entrance to Poole harbour, offering spectacular views across to Studland and the Purbeck Hills. Its varied and colourful history includes use as a coastguard station, Victorian pottery, Edwardian country estate, daffodil farm, and as a decoy in the Second World War. In 1907 it was the site of Baden-Powell's experimental camp from which Scouting and Guiding evolved. Home to important populations of red squirrels and seabirds, the island provides a safe and relaxing place for walks and picnics, ideal for families to explore. 2007 sees the Centenary of Scouting – 100 years since the first experimental camp. There are events and celebrations planned throughout the year.
Location: MAP 3:A7, OS Ref. SZ032 878. In Poole Harbour. Boats run from Poole Quay and Sandbanks every 30 mins. There is also a service from Bournemouth and Swanage.
Open: 15 Mar–18 Jul, 1–27 Sept: daily, 10am–5pm. 19 Jul–31 Aug: daily 10am–6pm. 28 Sept–26 Oct: daily, 10am–4pm.
Admission: Adult £4.90, Child: £2.40, Family (2+2) £12.20. 1 Adult Family £7.30. Groups: Adult £4.20, Child £2.10, Group visits outside normal hours £3.60.
◻ ♿ Partial. ☕ 🚹 ■ ♨

CHETTLE HOUSE

Chettle, Blandford Forum, Dorset DT11 8DB
Tel: 01258 830858
Owner/Contact: Mr & Mrs Peter Bourke

A fine Queen Anne manor house designed by Thomas Archer and a fine example of English baroque architecture. The house features a basement with the typical north-south passage set just off centre with barrel-vaulted ceilings and a magnificent oak staircase. Newly restored interiors. The house is set in 5 acres of peaceful gardens.
Location: MAP 3:A5, OS Ref. ST952 132. 6m NE of Blandford NW of A354.
Open: Easter–Oct: 1st Sun in each month. Other times by appointment. Group guided tours by appointment.
Admission: Adult £4.50, Child Free (under 16yrs).
🎪 Wedding receptions and special events. ♿ Partial. ☕ 🚹 By appointment. ✖

CHURCH OF OUR LADY & ST IGNATIUS

North Chideock, Bridport, Dorset DT6 6LF
Tel: 01308 488348 **E-mail:** amyasmartelli40@hotmail.com
Owner: The Weld Family Trust **Contact:** Mrs G Martelli

The Church, dedicated to Our Lady Queen of Martyrs and St Ignatius, was built on the site of an exisitng chapel-barn in 1872 by Charles Weld of Chideock Manor. It is one of the gems of English Catholicism and is designed in the Italian Romanesque style. It is a pilgrimage centre of the Chideock martyrs who are depicted in portraits over the nave. 19th century wall paintings by the Weld family can be seen in the original barn-chapel (now priest's sacristry) by arrangement. The church is also a shrine to Our Lady and has been a centre of Catholicism since penal times. A Museum of village life is on view in the adjoining cloister.
Location: MAP 2:N6, OS Ref. SY419 937. A35 from Bridport into Chideock. Right at St Giles' Church. Continue towards North Chideock for ½m. The Church is on the right.
Open: All year: 10am–4pm.
Admission: Donations welcome.
♿ Moveable ramp in Church Porch. 🅿 Limited. ✖ ❋

Athelhampton, China

CLOUDS HILL ✻
WAREHAM, DORSET BH20 7NQ

www.nationaltrust.org.uk

Tel: 01929 405616
Owner: The National Trust **Contact:** The Custodian

A tiny isolated brick and tile cottage, bought in 1929 by T E Lawrence (Lawrence of Arabia) as a retreat. The austere rooms inside are much as he left them and reflect his complex personality and close links with the Middle East. An exhibition details Lawrence's extraordinary life.
Location: MAP 2:P6, OS Ref. SY824 909. 9m E of Dorchester, 1½m E of Waddock crossroads B3390.
Open: 20 Mar–26 Oct, Thurs–Sun & BH Mons, 12 noon–5pm or dusk if earlier; no electric light. Groups wishing to visit at other times must telephone in advance.
Admission: £4, Child £2
🚹 No WC. ♿ Braille guide. 🅿 No coaches. ■ Small groups.

CORFE CASTLE ✻
WAREHAM, DORSET BH20 5EZ

www.nationaltrust.org.uk

Tel: 01929 481294 **Fax:** 01929 477067 **E-mail:** corfecastle@nationaltrust.org.uk
Owner: The National Trust **Contact:** The Property Manager

One of Britain's most majestic ruins, the Castle controlled the gateway through the Purbeck Hills and had been an important stronghold since the time of William the Conqueror. Defended during the Civil War by the redoubtable Lady Bankes, the Castle fell to treachery from within and was substantially destroyed afterwards by the Parliamentarians. Many fine Norman and early English features remain. Visitor Centre at Castle View. Parts of Castle closed during 2008 for urgent conservation work. Please telephone property for details.
Location: MAP 3:A7, OS Ref. SY959 824. On A351 Wareham–Swanage Rd. NW of the village.
Open: All year: daily. Mar & Oct: 10am–5pm; Apr–Sept: 10am–6pm; Nov–Feb (Closed 25/26 Dec), 10am–4pm.
*Admission: Adult £5.60, Child £2.80, Family (2+3) £14, (1+3) £8.40. Groups: Adult £4.80, Child £2.40. *includes a voluntary donation but visitors can choose to pay the standard prices displayed at the property and on the website.
◻ ♿ Limited. Braille guide. WC. ☕ 🚹 ■ 🅿 On leads. ❋ ♨

©NTPL/Eric Crichton.

DEANS COURT 🏠
WIMBORNE, DORSET BH21 1EE

Tel: 01202 886116

Owner: Sir Michael & Lady Hanham   **Contact:** Wimborne Tourist Info Centre

13 peaceful acres. Specimen trees, lawns, borders, herb garden, long serpentine wall, kitchen and rose garden. Chemical-free produce usually for sale, also interesting herbaceous plants. Wholefood teas in garden or in Housekeeper's room (down steps).

Location: MAP 3:A6, OS Ref. SZ010 997. 2 mins walk S from centre of Wimborne Minster. Entrance signed from Deans Court Lane.

Open: 23/24 Mar, 25/26 May, 26/27 Jul, 24/25 Aug, 6/7 Sept: Suns, 2–6pm, BH Mons, 10am–6pm. House may be visited by prior written appointment, but not on garden open days.

Admission: Adult £4, Child under 16yrs Free, Senior Citizens £3. Groups by arrangement.

🌿 Garden produce sales. 🚐 🅿 Free in Garden. 🐕 Guide dogs only.

HARDY'S COTTAGE ✂
HIGHER BOCKHAMPTON, DORCHESTER, DORSET DT2 8QJ
www.nationaltrust.org.uk

Tel: 01305 262366

Owner/Contact: The National Trust

A small cob and thatch cottage where the novelist and poet Thomas Hardy was born in 1840, and from where he would walk to school every day in Dorchester, six miles away. It was built by his great-grandfather and is little altered. Since the family left the interior has been furnished by the Trust (see also Max Gate). His early novels *Under the Green Wood Tree* and *Far From the Madding Crowd* were written here. Charming cottage garden.

Location: MAP 2:P6, OS Ref. SY728 925. 3m NE of Dorchester, ½m S of A35. 10 mins walk through the woods from car park.

Open: 23 Mar–30 Oct: Sun–Thur, 11am–5pm.

Admission: Adult £3.50. No reduction for children.

ℹ No WC. 🚻 🚐 Partial. 🅿 No coach parking. ■🐕

EDMONDSHAM HOUSE & GARDENS 🏠

Cranborne, Wimborne, Dorset BH21 5RE

Tel: 01725 517207

Owner/Contact: Mrs Julia E Smith

Charming blend of Tudor and Georgian architecture with interesting contents. Organic walled garden, 6 acre garden with unusual trees and spring bulbs. 12th century church nearby.

Location: MAP 3:A5, OS Ref. SU062 116. Off B3081 between Cranborne and Verwood, NW from Ringwood 9m, Wimborne 9m.

Open: House & Gardens: All BH Mons & Weds in Apr & Oct 2–5pm. Gardens: Apr–Oct, Suns & Weds 2–5pm.

Admission: House & Garden: Adult £5, Child £1 (under 5yrs Free). Garden only: Adult £2.50, Child 50p. Garden Season Ticket (incl. children) £7. Groups by arrangement, teas for groups.

🌿 🚐 🅿 Pre-booked (max 50). 🅿 Obligatory. 🐕 Car park only. ▲ (max 50).

FORDE ABBEY & GARDENS 🏠   *See page 210 for full page entry.*

Dave Penman
Kingston Maurward Gardens

©NTPL / Joe Cornish
Brownsea Island

HIGHCLIFFE CASTLE 🏛

ROTHESAY DRIVE, HIGHCLIFFE-ON-SEA, CHRISTCHURCH BH23 4LE

www.highcliffecastle.co.uk

Tel: 01425 278807   **Fax:** 01425 280423   **E-mail:** enquiries@highcliffecastle.co.uk
Owner: Christchurch Borough Council   **Contact:** David Hopkins

Built in the 1830s for Lord Stuart de Rothesay in the Romantic/Picturesque style and incorporating French medieval stonework and stained glass. The rooms in this Grade I listed building remain mostly unrepaired and now house a Heritage Centre and Gift Shop. They also provide a unique setting for changing exhibitions, featuring local and national artists. Programme of concerts and outdoor events. The newly refurbished Dining Room opens for the first time in February. Also new is an internal Guided Tour incorporating the upper floors. Cliff-top grounds. Access to Christchurch Coastal Path.

Location: MAP 3:B6, OS Ref. SZ200 930. Off the A337 Lymington Road, between Christchurch and Highcliffe-on-Sea.
Open: 1 Feb–23 Dec: daily, 11am–5pm. Grounds: All year: daily from 7am. Access for coaches. Tearooms closed Christmas Day.
Admission: Adult £2.50, Child Free. Group (10+) rates available. Guided tours of unrestored areas (may be unsuitable for people with mobility problems – please ring for details): Adult £3.50, Child Free. Grounds: Free.

🖥 🍽 Wedding receptions. ♿ WC. 🖥 10am–5pm. 🚶 By arrangement.
🅿 Limited. Parking charge. 🍴 By arrangement. 🐕 In grounds, on leads. 🔺 ❋ ♨

HIGHER MELCOMBE

Melcombe Bingham, Dorchester, Dorset DT2 7PB
Tel: 01258 880251
Owner/Contact: Mr M C Woodhouse

Consists of the surviving wing of a 16th century house with its attached domestic chapel. A fine plaster ceiling and linenfold panelling. Conducted tours by owner.
Location: MAP 2:P6, OS Ref. ST749 024. 1km W of Melcombe Bingham.
Open: May–Sept by appointment.
Admission: Adult £2 (takings go to charity).
♿ Unsuitable. 🚶 By written appointment only. 🅿 Limited. 🐕 Guide dogs only.

KINGSTON LACY ❧

See page 211 for full page entry.

See page 211 for full page entry.

Athelhampton, The Great Chamber

Dave Penman

KINGSTON MAURWARD GARDEN

DORCHESTER, DORSET DT2 8PY

www.kmc.ac.uk/gardens

Tel: 01305 215003   **Fax:** 01305 215001   **E-mail:** events@kmc.ac.uk
Contact: Wendy Cunningham

Classical 18th century parkland setting, with majestic lawns sweeping down from the Grade I listed Georgian house to the lake. The Rainbow beds and beautiful herbaceous borders complement the series of 'rooms' within the formal Edwardian garden. National Collections of Penstemons and Salvias. Lakeside walks, animal park, shop, plant centre and refreshments.
Location: MAP 2:P7, OS Ref. SY713 911. 1m E of Dorchester. Roundabout off A35 by-pass.
Open: 2 Jan–22 Dec: daily, 10am–5.30pm or dusk if earlier.
Admission: Adult £5, Child £3 (under 3yrs Free), Family £15.50. Groups (10+): Adult £4.50. Guided tours (by arrangement) (12+): £5pp.

ℹ Conferences. 🖥 🍽 Wedding receptions. ♿ Partial. 🍷 Licensed.
🚶 By arrangement. 🅿 🖥 Guide dogs only. 🔺 ❋ ♨

©Patrick Cooke

KNOLL GARDENS & NURSERY

Stapehill Road, Hampreston, Wimborne BH21 7ND

Tel: 01202 873931 **Fax:** 01202 870842 **E-mail:** enquiries@knollgardens.co.uk

Owner: J & J Flude & N R Lucas **Contact:** Mr John Flude

Nationally acclaimed 6 acre gardens, with 6000+ named plants.

Location: MAP 3:B6, OS Ref. SU059 001. Between Wimborne & Ferndown. Exit A31 Canford Bottom roundabout, B3073 Hampreston. Signposted 1½m.

Open: May–Nov: Tue–Sun, 10am–5pm. Dec–Apr: Wed–Sat, 10am–4pm. Closed 21 Dec–31 Jan.

Admission: Adult £4.75, Child (5–15yrs) £3.25, Conc £4.25. RHS Free. Groups: Adult £3.75. Lower rates in low season.

LULWORTH CASTLE & PARK

WAREHAM, DORSET BH20 5QS

www.lulworth.com

Tel: 0845 4501054 **Fax:** 01929 400563 **E-mail:** office@lulworth.com

Owner: The Weld Estate

Surrounded by beautiful parkland with views of the Jurassic coast this 17th century hunting lodge was destroyed by fire in 1929 and has been restored by English Heritage. Steeped in history the Castle has remained in the same family since 1641. Features include a gallery on the Weld family, reconstructed kitchen, dairy and laundry rooms and a wine cellar. The Chapel is reputed to be one of the finest pieces of architecture in Dorset and houses an exhibition on vestments and recusant silver.

Location: MAP 3:A7, OS Ref. SY853 822. In E Lulworth off B3070, 3m NE of Lulworth Cove.

Open: Castle & Park: All year (but closed 24 & 25 Dec & 6–19 Jan) Sun–Fri. Open Easter Sat, 22 Mar & 9 Aug for Spirit of the Countryside Country Fair & some Sats for Special Events: 10.30am–6pm (closes 4pm autumn/winter). Entrance to Lulworth Castle House, the Weld family home, by appointment.

Admission: Castle: Adult £8, Child (4–15yrs) £4 (under 4yrs Free), Conc. £6, Family (2+3) £24, Family (1+3) £16. 10% discount for groups of 10+. Last admission 1 hour before closing. Prices may vary for special events including Summer Jousting Shows. Please see website or tel 0845 4501054 for details.

⬛ 🖼 Concerts, corporate & private hire/events by arrangement. ♿ Partial. WC. ⬛ Licensed. 🥢 By arrangement. ⬛ ⬛ 🅿 Free. Meal voucher & free access for coach drivers. 🐕 In grounds, on leads. 🛏 5 holiday cottages, tel: 01929 400100. ⬛❄⬛ See website.

MAPPERTON 🏛

BEAMINSTER, DORSET DT8 3NR

www.mapperton.com

Tel: 01308 862645 **Fax:** 01308 863348 **E-mail:** office@mapperton.com

Owner/Contact: The Earl & Countess of Sandwich

'The Nation's Finest Manor House' – *Country Life 2006.* Jacobean 1660s manor overlooking an Italianate upper garden with orangery, topiary and formal borders descending to fish ponds and shrub gardens. All Saints Church forms south wing opening to courtyard and stables. Area of Outstanding Natural Beauty with fine views of Dorset hills and woodlands.

Location: MAP 2:N6, OS Ref. SY503 997. 1m S of B3163, 2m NE of B3066, 2m SE Beaminster, 5m NE Bridport.

Open: House: 23 Jun–1 Aug: Mon–Fri, plus 26 May & 25 Aug, 2–4.30pm, last admission 4pm. Other times by appointment. Garden & All Saints Church: 1 Mar–31 Oct: daily (exc. Sat) 11am–5pm. Café: Mar–Sept: daily (exc. Sat) 11am–5.30pm, for lunch and tea.

Admission: Gardens: Adult £4.50, Child (under 18yrs) £2, under 5yrs Free. House: £4. Group tours by appointment.

⬛ 🌸 ♿ Partial. ⬛ Licensed. 🍽 🥢 By arrangement. ⬛ 🅿 Limited for coaches. 🐕 Guide dogs only. ⬛⬛

©NTPL

MAX GATE 🌿

ALINGTON AVENUE, DORCHESTER, DORSET DT1 2AB

www.thomas-hardy.connectfree.co.uk

Tel: 01305 262538 **E-mail:** maxgate@nationaltrust.org.uk

Owner: The National Trust **Contact:** The Tenant

Novelist and poet Thomas Hardy designed and lived in this house from 1885 until his death in 1928. Here he wrote *Tess of the d'Urbervilles, Jude the Obscure* and *The Mayor of Casterbridge*, as well as much of his poetry. The house contains several pieces of his furniture.

Location: MAP 2:P7, OS Ref. SY704 899. 1m E of Dorchester just N of the A352 to Wareham. From Dorchester follow A352 signs to the roundabout named Max Gate (at Jct. of A35 Dorchester bypass). Turn left and left again into cul-de-sac outside Max Gate.

Open: 26 Mar–29 Sept: Mons, Weds & Suns, 2–5pm. Only hall, dining, drawing rooms and garden open. Private visits, tours and seminars for schools, colleges and literary societies at other times by prior appointment with the tenants, Mr & Mrs Andrew Leah.

Admission: Adult £3, Child £1.50.

ℹ No WC. ♿ Partial. Braille guide. 🥢🅿⬛🐕

MILTON ABBEY CHURCH

Milton Abbas, Blandford, Dorset DT11 0BZ
Tel: 01258 880215
Owner: Diocese of Salisbury   **Contact:** Chris Fookes
Abbey church dating from 14th century.
Location: MAP 2:P6, OS Ref. ST798 024. 3½m N of A354. Between Dorchester/Blandford Road.
Open: Abbey Church: daily 10.30am–5pm. Groups by arrangement please.
Admission: By donation except Easter & mid-Jul–end Aug. Adult £2, Child Free.

MINTERNE GARDENS 🏛

MINTERNE MAGNA, Nr DORCHESTER, DORSET DT2 7AU

www.minterne.co.uk

Tel: 01300 341370   **Fax:** 01300 341747   **E-mail:** enquiries@minterne.co.uk
Owner/Contact: The Hon Henry & Mrs Digby
Landscaped in the manner of 'Capability' Brown in the 18th century, Minterne's unique garden has been described by Simon Jenkins as *'a corner of paradise.'* Wander peacefully through 20 wild woodland acres where magnolias, rhododendrons and eucryphias provide a new vista at each turn, with small lakes, streams and cascades. Minterne also hosts private house tours, dinners, seminars, weddings and events, ensuring that guests leave with cherished memories of those special occasions.
Location: MAP 2:O6, OS Ref. ST660 042. On A352 Dorchester/Sherborne Rd, 2m N of Cerne Abbas.
Open: 1 Mar–31 Oct: daily, 10am–6pm.
Admission: Adult £4, accompanied children Free.
🅣 🅖 Unsuitable. 🎦 By arrangement. 🅟 Free. Picnic tables in car park. 🐾 In grounds on leads. 🔺

PORTLAND CASTLE ⌗

CASTLETOWN, PORTLAND, WEYMOUTH, DORSET DT5 1AZ

www.english-heritage.org.uk/portland

Tel: 01305 820539   **Fax:** 01305 860853
Owner: English Heritage   **Contact:** Visitor Operations Staff
Discover one of Henry VIII's finest coastal fortresses. Perfectly preserved in a waterfront location overlooking Portland harbour, it is a marvellous place to visit for all the family whatever the weather. Explore the Tudor kitchen and gun platform, see ghostly sculptured figures from the past, enjoy the superb battlement views or picnic on the lawn in front of the Captain's House. An excellent audio tour, included in the admission charge, brings the castle's history and characters to life. Visit the 'Contemporary Heritage' Garden.
Location: MAP 2:O7, OS Ref. SY684 743. Overlooking Portland harbour.
Open: 21 Mar–31 Oct: daily, 10am–5pm (6pm Jul & Aug, 4pm Oct).
Admission: Adult £4, Child £2, Conc. £3.20. Family £10 .15% discount for groups (11+). EH members Free.
🅓🅣🅖 Captain's House & ground floor. WCs. 🖵 🏠 🅟 🍴 🔺 🐕

SANDFORD ORCAS MANOR HOUSE

Sandford Orcas, Sherborne, Dorset DT9 4SB
Tel: 01963 220206
Owner/Contact: Sir Mervyn Medlycott Bt
Tudor manor house with gatehouse, fine panelling, furniture, pictures. Terraced gardens with topiary and herb garden. Personal conducted tour by owner.
Location: MAP 2:O5, OS Ref. ST623 210. 2½m N of Sherborne, Dorset 4m S of A303 at Sparkford. Entrance next to church.
Open: Easter Mon, 10am–5pm. May & Jul–Sept: Suns & Mons, 2–5pm.
Admission: Adult £4, Child £2. Groups (10+): Adult £3, Child £1.50.
🅖 Unsuitable. 🎦 Obligatory. 🐾 In grounds, on leads.

Minterne

English Heritage Photo Library

© Ian Pollard

SHERBORNE CASTLE 🏰
SHERBORNE, DORSET DT9 5NR
www.sherbornecastle.com

Tel: 01935 813182   **Fax:** 01935 816727   **E-mail:** enquiries@sherbornecastle.com

Owner: Mr & Mrs John Wingfield Digby   **Contact:** Castle & Events Manager

Built by Sir Walter Raleigh in 1594, Sherborne Castle has been the home of the Digby family since 1617. Prince William of Orange was entertained here in 1688, and George III visited in 1789. Splendid interiors and collections of art, furniture and porcelain are on view in the Castle. Lancelot 'Capability' Brown created the lake in 1753 and gave Sherborne the very latest in landscape gardening, with magnificent vistas of the surrounding parklands. Today, some 30 acres of beautiful lakeside gardens and grounds are open for public viewing.

Location: MAP 2:O5, OS Ref. ST649 164. ¾m SE of Sherborne town centre. Follow brown signs from A30 or A352. ½m S of the Old Castle.

Open: Castle, Gardens, Shop & Tearoom: 22 Mar–30 Oct: daily except Mon & Fri (open BH Mons), 11am–4.30pm last admission. (Castle interior from 2pm Sats.) Groups (15+) by arrangement during normal opening hours.

Admission: Castle & Gardens: Adult £9, Child (0–15yrs) Free (max 4 per adult), Senior £8.50. Groups (15+): Adult/Senior £8, Child (0–15yrs) £3.50. Private views (15+): Adult/Senior £10.00, Child £5. Gardens only: Adult/Senior £4.50, Child (0–15yrs) Free (max 4 per adult), no concessions or group rates for gardens only.

⬜ ⬛ ♿ Partial. ⬛ Licensed. 🎫 By arrangement. ⬛ ⬛ In grounds, on leads. ⬛⬛

SHERBORNE OLD CASTLE ⊞
Castleton, Sherborne, Dorset DT9 3SA

Tel/Fax: 01935 812730

www.english-heritage.org.uk/sherborne

Owner: English Heritage   **Contact:** Visitor Operations Staff

The ruins of this early 12th century Castle are a testament to the 16 days it took Cromwell to capture it during the Civil War, after which it was abandoned. A gatehouse, some graceful arcading and decorative windows survive.

Location: MAP 2:O5, OS Ref. ST647 167. ½m E of Sherborne off B3145. ½m N of the 'new' 1594 Castle.

Open: 21 Mar–31 Oct: daily, 10am–5pm (6pm in Jul & Aug, 4pm in Oct).

Admission: Adult £2.50, Child £1.30, Conc. £2. 15% discount for groups of 11+. Joint ticket with Sherborne Castle grounds, £5.50. EH members Free.

⬜♿ Grounds. 🅿 Limited for cars. No coach parking. ⬛ ⬛

STOCK GAYLARD HOUSE
Stock Gaylard, Sturminster Newton, Dorset DT10 2BG

Tel: 01963 23215   **E-mail:** langmeadj@stockgaylard.com

www.stockgaylard.com

Owner: Mrs J Langmead   **Contact:** Mrs J Langmead

A Georgian house overlooking an ancient deer park with the parish church of St Barnabas in the garden. The grounds and principal rooms of the house are open to the public for 28 days a year.

Location: MAP 2:P5, OS Ref. ST722 130. 1 mile S of the junction of the A357 and the A3030 at the Lydlinch Common.

Open: 26 Apr–5 May, 22–30 Jun & 22–30 Sept, 2–5pm. Coaches by appointment only. Access to the Park by arrangement, please telephone for information.

Admission: Adult £5, Child £2.

🎫 🅿

©NTPL / Eric Crichton

Hardy's Cottage

WHITE MILL ⚜

Sturminster Marshall, Nr Wimborne, Dorset BH21 4BX
Tel: 01258 858051   **www.nationaltrust.org.uk**
Owner: The National Trust   **Contact:** The Custodian
Rebuilt in 1776 on a site marked as a mill in the Domesday Book, this substantial corn mill was extensively repaired in 1994 and still retains its original elm and applewood machinery (now too fragile to be operative).
Location: MAP 3:A6, OS Ref. ST958 006. On River Stour ½m NE of Sturminster Marshall. From the B3082 Blandford to Wimborne Rd, take road to Sturminster Marshall. Mill is 1m on right. Car park nearby.
Open: 22 Mar–2 Nov: Sats, Suns & BH Mons, 12 noon–5pm. Admission by guided tour only.
Admission: Adult £3, Child £2. Groups by arrangement.
ⓘ No WC. 🚷 Ground floor. 🚻 Obligatory. 🅿 ▣ ⊠ Under close control in grounds and car park.

WOLFETON HOUSE 🏛

Nr DORCHESTER, DORSET DT2 9QN

Tel: 01305 263500   **Fax:** 01305 265090
E-mail: kthimbleby@wolfeton.freeserve.co.uk
Owner: Capt N T L L T Thimbleby   **Contact:** The Steward
A fine mediaeval and Elizabethan manor house lying in the water-meadows near the confluence of the rivers Cerne and Frome. It was much embellished around 1580 and has splendid plaster ceilings, fireplaces and panelling of that date. To be seen are the Great Hall, Stairs and Chamber, Parlour, Dining Room, Chapel and Cyder House. The mediaeval Gatehouse has two unmatched and older towers. There are good pictures and furniture.
Location: MAP 2:O6, OS Ref. SY678 921. 1½m from Dorchester on the A37 towards Yeovil. Indicated by Historic House signs.
Open: June–end Sept: Mons, Weds & Thurs, 2–5pm. Groups by appointment throughout the year.
Admission: £6.
⊤ By arrangement. 🚷 Ground floor. ▣ By arrangement. 🚻 By arrangement. 🅿 ⊠ ✳

Deans Court

Kingston Lacy

©NTPL

BERKELEY CASTLE

www.berkeley-castle.com

Not many can boast of having their private house celebrated by Shakespeare nor of having held it in the possession of their family for nearly 850 years, nor having a King of England murdered within its walls, nor of having welcomed at their table the local vicar and Castle Chaplain, John Trevisa (1342–1402), reputed as one of the earliest translators of the Bible, nor of having a breach battered by Oliver Cromwell, which to this day it is forbidden by law to repair even if it was wished to do so. But such is the story of Berkeley.

This beautiful and historic Castle, begun in 1117, still remains the home of the famous family who gave their name to numerous locations all over the world, notably Berkeley Square in London, Berkeley Hundred in Virginia and Berkeley University in California. Scene of the brutal murder of Edward II in 1327 (visitors can see his

cell and nearby the dungeon) and besieged by Cromwell's troops in 1645, the Castle is steeped in history but twenty-four generations of Berkeleys have gradually transformed a Norman fortress into the lovely home it is today.

The State Apartments contain magnificent collections of furniture, rare paintings by primarily English and Dutch masters, and tapestries. Part of the world-famous Berkeley silver is on display in the Dining Room. Many other rooms are equally interesting including the Great Hall upon which site the Barons of the West Country met in 1215 before going to Runnymede to force King John to put his seal to the Magna Carta.

The Castle is surrounded by lovely terraced Elizabethan Gardens with a lily pond, Elizabeth I's bowling green, and sweeping lawns.

Owner
Mr R J G Berkeley

Contact
The Custodian
Berkeley Castle
Gloucestershire
GL13 9BQ

Tel: 01453 810332
Fax: 01453 512995
E-mail: info@berkeley-castle.com

Location
MAP 6:M12
OS Ref. ST685 990

SE side of Berkeley village. Midway between Bristol & Gloucester, 2m W off the A38.

From motorway M5/J14 (5m) or J13 (9m).

Opening Times
21 March–26 October: Suns only. May: also BH Weekends, June Sun only, July and August; daily, 11am–5.30pm, last entry at 4.30pm.

Special events throughout the year.

Admission
Global Ticket including Castle & Gardens

Adult	£7.50
Child (5–16yrs)	£4.50
Child (under 5s)	Free
OAP	£6.00
Family (2+2)	£21.00

Groups (25+ pre-booked)

Adult	£7.00
Child (5-16yrs)	£3.50
OAP	£5.50

Gardens only

Adult	£4.00
Child	£2.00

 Fashion shows and filming. No photography inside the Castle.

Wedding receptions and corporate entertainment.

Visitors may alight in the Outer Bailey.

Licensed. Serving lunches and home-made teas.

Free. Max. 120 people. Tour time: One hour. Evening groups by arrangement. Group visits must be booked.

Cars 150yds from Castle, 15 coaches 250yds away. Free.

Welcome. General and social history and architecture.

Conference/Function

ROOM	MAX CAPACITY
Great Hall	150
Long Drawing Rm	100

■ Owner

Mr David Lowsley-Williams

■ Contact

D Lowsley-Williams
or Caroline
Lowsley-Williams
Chavenage
Tetbury
Gloucestershire
GL8 8XP

Tel: 01666 502329
Fax: 01666 504696
E-mail: info@
chavenage.com

■ Location

MAP 3:A1
OS Ref. ST872 952

Less than 20m
from M4/J16/17 or 18.
1¾m NW of Tetbury
between the B4014 &
A4135. Signed from
Tetbury. Less than 15m
from M5/J13 or 14.
Signed from A46
(Stroud–Bath road).

Rail: Kemble Station 7m.

Taxi: SC Taxis
01666 504195.

Air: Bristol 35m.
Birmingham 70m.
Grass airstrip on farm.

■ Opening Times

Summer
May–September
Easter Sun, Mon
& BHs, 2–5pm.

Thurs & Suns 2–5pm.

NB. Will open on any day
and at other times by
prior arrangement for
groups.

Winter
October–March
By appointment only
for groups.

■ Admission

Tours are inclusive
in the following prices.

Summer
Adult   £6.00
Child (5–16 yrs)   £3.00

Concessions:
By prior arrangement,
concessions may be
given to groups of 40+
and also to disabled and
to exceptional cases.

Winter
Groups only:
Rates by arrangement.

© Skyscan

CHAVENAGE 🏛

www.chavenage.com

Chavenage is a wonderful Elizabethan house of mellow grey Cotswold stone and tiles which contains much of interest for the discerning visitor.

The approach aspect of Chavenage is virtually as it was left by Edward Stephens in 1576. Only two families have owned Chavenage; the present owners since 1891 and the Stephens family before them. A Colonel Nathaniel Stephens, MP for Gloucestershire during the Civil War was cursed for supporting Cromwell, giving rise to legends of weird happenings at Chavenage since that time.

Inside Chavenage there are many interesting rooms housing tapestries, fine furniture, pictures and many relics of the Cromwellian period. Of particular note are the Main Hall, where a contemporary screen forms a minstrels' gallery and two tapestry rooms where it is said Cromwell was lodged.

Recently Chavenage has been used as a location for TV and film productions including a Hercule Poirot story *The Mysterious Affair at Styles*, many episodes of the sequel to *Are you Being Served* now called *Grace & Favour*, a *Gotcha* for *The Noel Edmonds' House Party*, episodes of *The House of Elliot* and *Casualty*, in 1997/98 *Berkeley Square* and *Cider with Rosie* and in 2002 the US series *Relic Hunter III*. In 2005 it was one of the homes Jeremy Musson visited in the BBC's *The Curious House Guest*. Chavenage is the setting for the new BBC costume drama *Lark Rise to Candleford*.

Chavenage is especially suitable for those wishing an intimate, personal tour, usually conducted by the owner, or for groups wanting a change from large establishments. Meals for pre-arranged groups have proved hugely popular. It also provides a charming venue for small conferences and functions.

ⓘ	Suitable for filming, photography, corporate entertainment, activity days, seminars, receptions and product launches.
✳	Occasional.
🍸	Corporate entertaining. Private drinks parties, lunches, dinners, anniversary parties and wedding receptions.
♿	Partial. WC.
🍴	Lunches, teas, dinners and picnics by arrangement.
🚶	By owner. Large groups given a talk prior to viewing. Couriers/group leaders should arrange tour format prior to visit.
Ⓟ	Up to 100 cars. 2–3 coaches (by appointment). Coaches access from A46 (signposted) or from Tetbury via the B4014, enter the back gates for coach parking area.
▣	Chairs can be arranged for lecturing.
🐕	In grounds on leads. Guide dogs only in house.
❄	

Conference/Function

ROOM	SIZE	MAX CAPACITY
Ballroom	70' x 30'	120
Oak Room	25 'x 20'	30

©Jo Ward

SUDELEY CASTLE GARDENS & EXHIBITIONS

www.sudeleycastle.co.uk

Few historic houses can match Sudeley Castle's long, curious and fascinating history. Spanning a thousand years, the Castle has changed hands over a dozen times, has more than once been a Royal residence and has played host to at least six Kings and Queens of England, perhaps best known as the home of Queen Katherine Parr, who is entombed in St. Mary's Church in the Castle grounds.

Today the home of Lord and Lady Ashcombe, Henry and Mollie Dent-Brocklehurst and their respective families, on Tuesdays, Wednesdays & Thursdays the family's Castle Apartments are open for the Connoisseur Tour (see panel).

The Gardens bring to life the magic of the estate where Katherine Parr would have strolled alongside the tragic Lady Jane Grey. These award winning gardens are a delight throughout the seasons. Bold areas of planting surround the 15th century Tithe Barn, contrasting with intricate detail in the Knot Garden. Topiary features strongly throughout the famous Queen's Garden which is full of hundreds of varieties of roses with outstanding double hedges on two sides, sited on the original Tudor parterre.

The Pheasantry and Wildfowl area houses a collection of 15 rare and endangered species from around the world. Working closely with the World Pheasant Association, Sudeley is developing a programme of breeding and conservation for these beautiful and gloriously coloured birds.

Visitors can enjoy exhibitions featuring the fascinating collections of Emma Dent, the Victorian chatelaine of Sudeley. *Threads of Time – The Textile Treasures of Sudeley*, is a new exhibition of examples of textile techniques spanning 400 years, from a 17th century Stumpwork casket to delicate lace, sumptuous silk wall hangings and tapestry.

■ Owner
Lady Ashcombe,
Henry and Mollie
Dent-Brocklehurst

■ Contact
The Secretary
Sudeley Castle
Winchcombe
Gloucestershire
GL54 5JD

Tel: 01242 602308
Fax: 01242 602959
E-mail: enquiries@
sudeley.org.uk

■ Location
MAP 6:O10
OS Ref. SP032 277

8m NE of Cheltenham,
at Winchcombe
off B4632.

From Bristol or
Birmingham M5/J9.
Take A46 then B4077
towards Stow-on-the-
Wold.

Bus: Castleways to
Winchcombe.

Rail: Cheltenham
Station 8m.

Air: Birmingham or
Bristol 45m.

■ Opening Times
Summer
March–October: daily
10.30am–5.00pm

Winter
Groups by appointment.

■ Admission
Gardens & Exhibitions

Adults	£7.20
Children (5–15yrs)	£4.20
Conc.	£6.20
Family Ticket (2+2)	£20.80

Group rates available.

Castle Connoisseur Tours
£15 per person – only
available on Tuesdays,
Wednesdays and
Thursdays. Please call for
timings.

Details may be subject to
change – please ensure
you telephone or visit our
website for updated
information.

ℹ️ Photographs and filming by prior arrangement. Concerts, corporate events and conferences. Product launches and activity days. Sudeley reserves the right to close any area and to amend information as necessary.

🛍️

❄️

🍷 Corporate and private events, wedding receptions.

♿ Partial access to the grounds. WC.

Licensed.

🚶 Tours and talks by prior arrangement for groups and Connoisseur Tours of the Castle Apartments every Tuesday, Wednesday and Thursday.

🅿️ 1,000 cars. Meal vouchers, free access for coach drivers.

🚫🐕 11 holiday cottages for 2–5 occupants.

🛏️

🎭 A regular programme of events provide entertainment for the whole family. Find out more on the website or call for details.

Conference/Function

ROOM	MAX CAPACITY
Chandos Hall	60
Banqueting Hall + Pavilion	100
Marquee	Unlimited
Long Room	80
Library	50

© M B Paice

BATSFORD ARBORETUM
MORETON-IN-MARSH, GLOUCESTERSHIRE GL56 9QB
www.batsarb.co.uk

Tel: 01386 701441   **Fax:** 01386 701829
E-mail: arboretum@batsfordfoundation.co.uk
Owner: The Batsford Foundation   **Contact:** Mr Chris Pilling
56 acres of magical walks alongside tumbling streams and flower fringed ponds. Make a wish with the giant Buddha (*The Japanese Buddha of 'Heroic size'*) or visit the Hermit's Cave. From Snowdrop displays in Spring through to fiery Autumn colour. Peace and tranquillity, pure Cotswold magic!
Location: MAP 6:P10, OS Ref. SP180 338. 1 mile west of Moreton-in-Marsh on A44.
Open: All year, daily except Weds in Dec & Jan & Christmas Day.
Admission: Adult £6, Child (4–15 inc) £2. Conc. £5, Groups of 20 less 10%.
🖼 📷 ♿ Partial. 🍽 Licensed. 📷 By arrangement. 🅿 🖼 🖼 In grounds on leads. ✸

BOURTON HOUSE GARDEN 🏠
BOURTON-ON-THE-HILL GL56 9AE
www.bourtonhouse.com

Tel: 01386 700754   **Fax:** 01386 701081   **E-mail:** cd@bourtonhouse.com
Owner/Contact: Mr & Mrs Richard Paice
Exciting 3 acre garden surrounding a delightful 18th century Cotswold manor house and 16th century tithe barn. Featuring flamboyant borders, imaginative topiary, a unique shade house, a profusion of herbaceous and exotic plants and, not least, a myriad of magically planted pots.The mood is friendly and welcoming, the atmosphere tranquil yet inspiring. The garden … "positively fizzes with ideas". There are a further 7 of parkland where young trees progress apace. 'The Gallery' features contemporary art, craft and design in the tithe barn. Winner of the HHA/Christie's Garden Of The Year Award – 2006.
Location: MAP 6:P10, OS Ref. SP180 324. 1¾ m W of Moreton-in-Marsh on A44.
Open: 28 May–31 Aug: Wed–Fri; also 25/26 May & 24/25 Aug (BH Sun & Mon). Sept–Oct: Thur & Fri, 10am–5pm.
Admission: Adult £5.50, Conc. £5, Child Free.
🖼 📷 ♿ Partial. 🍽 📷 By arrangement. 🅿 Limited for coaches. ✸

BERKELEY CASTLE 🏠   *See page 219 for full page entry.*

BLACKFRIARS PRIORY ♯
Ladybellegate Street, Gloucester
Tel: 0117 9750700   www.english-heritage.org.uk/blackfriars
Owner: English Heritage   **Contact:** The South West Regional Office
A small Dominican priory church converted into a rich merchant's house at the Dissolution. Most of the original 13th century church remains, including a rare scissor-braced roof.
Location: MAP 6:N11, OS Ref. SO830 186. In Ladybellegate St, Gloucester, off Southgate Street and Blackfriars Walk.
Open: Access by guided tour only (Jul & Aug Suns 3pm). Heritage Open Days 8/9 Sept only, 12.30–3pm. Please contact the South West Regional Office.
Admission: Adult £3.50, Child/EH members £3.
📷 Obligatory. 🅿 Nearby, not EH, charged. ✸

CHAVENAGE 🏠   *See page 220 for full page entry.*

CHEDWORTH ROMAN VILLA ✤
Yanworth, Nr Cheltenham, Gloucestershire GL54 3LJ
Tel: 01242 890256   **Fax:** 01242 890909
E-mail: chedworth@nationaltrust.org.uk   www.nationaltrust.org.uk
Owner: The National Trust   **Contact:** The Property Manager
Discover one of the largest Romano-British sites in the country. Located within the beautiful Cotswolds scenery, a mile of walls survives along with several marvellous mosaics, two bathhouses, hypocausts, latrines and a water shrine. The site was first excavated in 1864 and retains a Victorian museum and atmosphere. A 15 minute introductory audio visual presentation is also available to visitors.
Location: MAP 6:O11, OS Ref. SP053 135. 3m NW of Fossebridge on Cirencester–Northleach road (A429) via Yanworth or from A436 via Withington. Coaches must approach from Fossebridge.
Open: 1–16 Mar: Tues–Sun, 11am–4pm. 18 Mar–2 Nov: Tues–Sun, 10am–5pm; 4–16 Nov: Tues–Sun, 10am–4pm. Open BH Mons. Shop open as Villa. Shop and reception close at above time.
*Admission: Adult £6.30, Child £3.70, Family (2+3) £16.30. Booked group tours (max 30 per guide): Schools £25, others £50. *includes a voluntary donation but visitors can choose to pay the standard prices displayed at the property and on the website.
🖼 ♿ Partial. WC. 📷 By arrangement. 🅿 📷 Adult £1.50, Child free.
🍽 By arrangement. ✸ ▾

For **corporate hospitality** venues see our special index at the end of the book.

©NTPL/Ian Shaw

DYRHAM PARK ✻

Nr BATH, GLOUCESTERSHIRE SN14 8ER

www.nationaltrust.org.uk

Tel: 01179 372501 **Fax:** 01179 371353 **E-mail:** dyrhampark@nationaltrust.org.uk

Owner: The National Trust   **Contact:** The Property Manager

Dyrham Park was built between 1691 and 1702 for William Blathwayt, William III's Secretary at War and Secretary of State. The rooms have changed little since they were furnished by Blathwayt and their contents are recorded in his housekeeper's inventory. Many fine textiles and paintings, as well as items of blue-and-white Delftware. Restored Victorian domestic rooms open, including kitchen, bells passage, bakehouse, larders, tenants' hall and Delft-tiled dairy.

Location: MAP 2:P2, OS Ref. ST743 757. 8m N of Bath, 12m E of Bristol. Approached from Bath Stroud road (A46), 2m S of Tormarton interchange with M4/J18.

Open: House: 14 Mar–2 Nov, Fri–Tue: 12 noon–5pm, last entry 1 hr before closing. Garden, Shop & Tearoom: 14 Mar–29 Jun, Fri–Tue, 11am–5pm. 30 Jun–31 Aug, daily, 11am–5pm. 1 Sept–2 Nov, Fri–Tue, 11am–5pm; 8 Nov–14 Dec, Sat & Sun 11am–4pm. 7 Feb–8 Mar 09, Sat & Sun 11am–4pm. Park: all year, daily except Christmas Day. Open BH Mons and Good Fri: 11 am–5pm.

***Admission:** Adult £10, Child £5, Family £25. Garden & Park only: Adult £4, Child £2, Family £8.90. Park only (on days when house & garden closed): Adult £2.60, Child £1.30, Family £5.80. *includes a voluntary donation but visitors can choose to pay the standard prices displayed at the property and on the website.

◻ ⬚ ⬚ Partial. No electric wheelchairs admitted. ⬚ Dates as garden. ⊞ Licensed. ⬚ Weekdays ⬚ House. ⬚ ⬚ ⬚ Only in dog-walking area. ⬚ ⬚

FRAMPTON COURT

FRAMPTON-ON-SEVERN, GLOUCESTERSHIRE GL2 7EU

www.framptoncourtestate.co.uk

Tel: 01452 740267 **Fax:** 01452 740698

E-mail: framptoncourt@framptoncourtestate.co.uk

Owner: Mr & Mrs Rollo Clifford   **Contact:** Jean Speed

Splendid Georgian family home of the Cliffords, who have lived in Frampton since the Norman Conquest. Built 1732, school of Vanbrugh, set in Grade I listed park and garden with fine views to extensive lake. Superb panelled interiors and period furniture. Also the famous 19th century "Frampton Flora" botanical watercolours. Principal bedrooms available for Bed and Breakfast.

Strawberry Hill Gothic Orangery with a Dutch ornamental canal is available for self catering holidays (tel: 01452 740698).

Location: MAP 6:M12, OS Ref. SO750 078. In Frampton, ¼ m SW of B4071, 3m NW of M5/J13.

Open: By arrangement for groups (10+).

Admission: House & Garden: £6.

ⓘ No photography in house. ⬚ Orangery walled garden. Pan Global Plants (tel: 01452 741641), rare plant nursery. ⬚ Small. ⬚ Garden only. ⬚ ⬚ Obligatory. ⬚ Coaches limited. ⬚ In grounds, on leads. ⬚ B&B contact Gillian Keightley on 01452 740267. Orangery tel: 01452 740698. ⬚

The Boudoir, Stanway House & Water Garden

FRAMPTON MANOR

Frampton-on-Severn, Gloucestershire GL2 7EP

Tel: 01452 740268 **Fax:** 01452 740698

Owner: Mr & Mrs Rollo Clifford   **Contact:** Mrs Rollo Clifford

Medieval/Elizabethan timber-framed manor house with walled garden. Reputed 12th century birthplace of 'Fair Rosamund' Clifford, mistress of King Henry II. Wool Barn c1560 and 16th century dovecote.

Location: MAP 6:M12, OS Ref. SO748 080. 3m M5/J13.

Open: House & Garden: open by appointment for groups (10+). Garden: 24 Apr–25 Jul: Thur & Fri, 2.30–5pm.

Admission: House, Garden & Wool Barn: £6. Garden only: £3. Wool Barn only £1.

ⓘ No photography inside. ⬚ Tearoom for groups. ⬚ Obligatory. ⬚ ⬚

GLOUCESTER CATHEDRAL

Chapter Office, College Green, Gloucester GL1 2LR

Tel: 01452 508211 **Fax:** 01452 300469

E-mail: lin@gloucestercathedral.org.uk www.gloucestercathedral.org.uk

Contact: Mrs L Henderson

Daily worship and rich musical tradition continue in this abbey church founded 1300 years ago. It has a Norman nave with massive cylindrical pillars, a magnificent east window with medieval glass and glorious fan-vaulted cloisters. You can also find the tombs of King Edward II and Robert, Duke of Normandy.

Location: MAP 6:M11, OS Ref. SO832 188. Off Westgate Street in central Gloucester.

Open: Daily, 8am until after Evensong. Groups must book via the Chapter Office.

Admission: £3 donation requested.

◻ ⬚ ⬚ Partial. WC. ⬚ ⬚ By arrangement. ⬚ ⬚ None. ⬚ In grounds, on leads. ⬚

HAILES ABBEY ⬚ ✻

Nr Winchcombe, Cheltenham, Gloucestershire GL54 5PB

Tel/Fax: 01242 602398 **E-mail:** customers@english-heritage.org.uk

www.english-heritage.org.uk/hailes

Owner: English Heritage & The National Trust   **Contact:** Visitor Operations Staff

Seventeen cloister arches and extensive excavated remains in lovely surroundings of an abbey founded by Richard, Earl of Cornwall, in 1246. There is a small museum and covered display area.

Location: MAP 6:O10, OS Ref. SP050 300. 2m NE of Winchcombe off B4632. ½m SE of B4632.

Open: 21 Mar–31 Oct: daily, 10am–5pm. (6pm in Jul & Aug, 4pm in Oct). Closed 1 Nov–31 Mar 09.

Admission: Adult £3.50, Child £1.80, Conc. £2.80. EH Members Free, NT members £1. Group discount available.

◻ ⬚ ⬚ Partial. WC. ⬚ ⬚ ⬚ In grounds, on leads. ⬚

GLOUCESTERSHIRE

Batsford Arboretum

HIDCOTE MANOR GARDEN 🌿

HIDCOTE BARTRIM, Nr CHIPPING CAMPDEN, GLOUCESTERSHIRE GL55 6LR

www.nationaltrust.org.uk

Tel: 01386 438333   **Fax:** 01386 438817   **E-mail:** hidcote@nationaltrust.org.uk
Owner: The National Trust   **Contact:** Visitor Services Manager
One of the most delightful gardens in England, created in the early 20th century by the great horticulturist Major Lawrence Johnston; a series of small gardens within the whole, separated by walls and hedges of different species; famous for rare shrubs, trees, herbaceous borders, 'old' roses and interesting plant species.
Location: MAP 6:O9, OS Ref. SP176 429. 4m NE of Chipping Campden, 1m E of B4632 off B4081. At Mickleton ¼ m E of Kiftsgate Court. Coaches are not permitted through Chipping Campden High Street.
Open: 15 Mar–1 Oct: Sat–Wed, 10am–6pm. Also Fris Jul & August. 2 Oct–2 Nov: Sat–Wed, 10am–5pm. Last admission 1hr before closing. Open Good Fri.
*Admission: Adult £8.50, Child £4.25, Family (2+3) £21.20. Groups (15+) Adult £7.70, Child £3.85. *includes a voluntary donation but visitors can choose to pay the standard prices displayed at the property and on the website.
🅿 ⚑ ♿ Limited. WC. ⬤ 🍴 Licensed. 🅿 ▦ ✖ 🎫 Send SAE for details.

HOLST BIRTHPLACE MUSEUM

4 CLARENCE ROAD, PITTVILLE, CHELTENHAM GL52 2AY

Tel: 01242 524846   **E-mail:** holstmuseum@btconnect.com
www.holstmuseum.org.uk
Owner: Holst Birthplace Trust   **Contact:** The Curator
Birthplace of Gustav Holst (1874–1934), composer of The Planets, containing his piano and personal memorabilia. Holst's music is played. The museum is also a fine period house showing the 'upstairs – downstairs' way of life in Regency and Victorian times, including a working kitchen, elegant drawing room and charming nursery.
Location: MAP 6:N11, OS163 Ref. SO955 237. 5mins walk from town centre, opposite Pittville Gates.
Open: Mid Feb–mid Dec: Tue–Sat, 10am–4pm. Except for booked groups or guided tours who are welcome by appointment.
Admission: Adult £3.50, Child/Conc. £3, Family (2+3) £8. Groups pay same prices unless having a guided tour (6–15): Adult £4.50, Conc. £3.50. Special rates for school groups on request.
ℹ Photography by prior permission only. 🅿 🍴 ♿ Partial. 🎫 By arrangement. 🅿 None. ▦ ⬤ Guide dogs only. 🎫 Tel. for details.

KELMSCOTT MANOR 🏛

KELMSCOTT, Nr LECHLADE, GLOUCESTERSHIRE GL7 3HJ

www.kelmscottmanor.org.uk

Tel: 01367 252486   **Fax:** 01367 253754   **E-mail:** admin@kelmscottmanor.co.uk
Owner: Society of Antiquaries of London   **Contact:** Jane Milne
Kelmscott Manor, a Grade I listed Tudor farmhouse adjacent to the River Thames, was William Morris' summer residence from 1871 until his death in 1896. Morris loved Kelmscott Manor, which seemed to him to have 'grown up out of the soil'. Its beautiful gardens with barns, dovecote, a meadow and stream provided a constant source of inspiration. The house, which is perhaps one of the most evocative of all the houses associated with Morris, contains an outstanding collection of the possessions and work of Morris, his family and associates, including furniture, original textiles, pictures, carpets and ceramics.
Location: MAP 6:P12, OS Ref. SU252 988. At SE end of the village, 2m due E of Lechlade, off the Lechlade – Faringdon Road.

Open: House & Garden: Weds, Apr–Sept, 11am–5pm (Ticket office open at 10.30am) Sats: 19 Apr, 17 May, 21 Jun, 5 & 19 Jul, 2 & 16 Aug, 20 Sept, 2–5pm (Ticket office open at 1.15pm). Last admission to the house 30 min prior to closing. No advance bookings on public open days. House has limited capacity; timed ticket system operates. Group Bookings: Thurs & Fri, must be booked in advance. Gardens: Jun–Sept, Thurs 2–5pm.
Admission: Adult £8.50, Child/Student £4.25. Gardens only: £2. Carer accompanying disabled person Free.
ℹ No photography in house. 🅿 ♿ Grounds. WCs. Parking on site.
⬤ Licensed. 🍴 Licensed. 🎫 By arrangement. 🅿 10 mins walk. Limited for coaches. ▦ ⬤ Guide dogs only. 🎫 See website www.24hourmuseum.org.uk.

KIFTSGATE COURT GARDENS 🏛

CHIPPING CAMPDEN, GLOUCESTERSHIRE GL55 6LN

www.kiftsgate.co.uk

Tel/Fax. 01386 438777 **E-mail:** info@kiftsgate.co.uk

Owner: Mr and Mrs J G Chambers **Contact:** Mr J G Chambers

Magnificently situated garden on the edge of the Cotswold escarpment with views towards the Malvern Hills. Many unusual shrubs and plants including tree peonies, abutilons, specie and old-fashioned roses. Winner HHA/Christie's Garden of the Year Award 2003.

Location: MAP 6:O9, OS Ref. SP173 430. 4m NE of Chipping Campden. ¼ m W of Hidcote Garden.

Open: Apr, Aug & Sept: Sun, Mon & Wed, 2–6pm. May, June & July: daily except Thurs & Fri, 12 noon–6pm. Coaches by appointment.

Admission: Adult: £6, Child £2. Groups (20+) £5.50.

◻ 🚻 ♿ 🅿 ✕

©NTPL/Matthew Antrobus

NEWARK PARK 🌡

OZLEWORTH, WOTTON-UNDER-EDGE, GLOUCESTERSHIRE GL12 7PZ

www.nationaltrust.org.uk

Tel/Fax: 01453 842644 **Infoline:** 01793 817666

E-mail: newarkpark@nationaltrust.org.uk

Owner: The National Trust **Contact:** Michael Claydon

A Tudor hunting lodge converted into a castellated country house by James Wyatt. An atmospheric house, set in spectacular countryside with outstanding views.

Location: MAP 2:P1, OS Ref172. ST786 934. 1½ m E of Wotton-under-Edge, 1¾ m S of Junction of A4135 & B4058, follow signs for Ozleworth, House signposted from main road.

Open: House & Garden: 19 Mar–29 May: Wed, Thurs & BH Mons; 1 Jun–2 Nov: Wed, Thur, Sat, Sun & BH Mons, 11am–5pm (last entry 4.30pm). Also open Easter: Good Fri–Mon, 11am–5pm.

Admission: Adult £5.60, Child £2.80, Family (2+3) £14.50. Groups by appointment. No reduction for groups.

ℹ No photography in house. ◻ ♿ Partial. ☞ ✗ By arrangement. 🅿 ▪
🐕 In grounds, on leads. ♿

©NTPL/Nadia MacKenzie

LODGE PARK & SHERBORNE ESTATE 🌡

ALDSWORTH, Nr CHELTENHAM, GLOUCESTERSHIRE GL54 3PP

www.nationaltrust.org.uk/lodgepark

Tel: 01451 844130 **Fax:** 01451 844131 **E-mail:** lodgepark@nationaltrust.org.uk

Owner: The National Trust **Contact:** The Visitor Services Manager

Lodge Park is a rare example of a grandstand, situated on the picturesque Sherborne Estate in the Cotswolds, Lodge Park was created in 1634 by John 'Crump' Dutton. Inspired by his passion for gambling and banqueting, it is a unique survival of a Grandstand, Deer Course and Park. It was the home of Charles Dutton, 7th Lord Sherborne, until 1983 when he bequeathed his family's estate to The National Trust. The interior of the grandstand has been reconstructed to its original form and is the first project of its kind undertaken by the Trust that relies totally on archaeological evidence. The park behind was designed by Charles Bridgeman in 1725. The Sherborne Estate is 1650ha (4000 acres) of rolling Cotswold countryside with sweeping views down to the River Windrush. Much of the village of Sherborne is owned by the Trust, including the post office, shop, school and the social club. There are walks for all ages around the estate, which include the restored and working water meadows.

Location: MAP 6:O11, OS Ref. SP146 123. 3m E of Northleach, approach only from A40. Bus: Swanbrook 853 Oxford-Gloucester, 1m walk from bus stop.

Open: Grandstand & Deer Park: 14 Mar–2 Nov: Fri–Sun, 11am–4pm.

Admission: Adult £5, Child £2.80, Family £12.50. Estate: Free.

ℹ Video shows during the day. 📹 Civil ceremonies only. ♿ Partial. 🅿 ▪
🐕 Dogs must be kept under close control. ▲ ♿

OLD CAMPDEN HOUSE

Church St, Chipping Campden, Gloucestershire GL55 6JG

Tel: 01628 825925 **E-mail:** bookings@landmarktrust.org.uk

www.landmarktrust.org.uk

Owner/Contact: The Landmark Trust

The site of Old Campden House, a Scheduled Ancient Monument, is owned and managed by the Landmark Trust, a building preservation charity. The main house was burnt to the ground during the Civil War but other buildings remain. The East and West Banqueting Houses and Almonry have been restored and are let for holidays throughout the year. Full details of Landmark's 184 historic and architecturally important buildings are featured in the Landmark Trust Handbook (price £11.50 refundable against first booking).

Location: MAP 6:O10, OS Ref. SP156 394. Next to St James's Church in Church Street.

Open: Available for holidays for up to 6 people (East Banqueting House) and 4 people (West Banqueting House and Almonry). Site open 30 days a year, with buildings open on 8 of these days. Other visits by appointment. Contact the Landmark Trust for dates.

Admission: Free on Open Days.

✕ ♿

The Gatehouse, Stanway House & Water Garden

OWLPEN MANOR 🏠
Nr ULEY, GLOUCESTERSHIRE GL11 5BZ

www.owlpen.com

Tel: 01453 860261 **Fax:** 01453 860819 **Restaurant:** 01453 860816
E-mail: sales@owlpen.com
Owner: Sir Nicholas and Lady Mander   **Contact:** Jayne Simmons
Romantic Tudor manor house, 1450–1616, with Cotswold Arts & Crafts
associations. Remote wooded valley setting, with 16th and 17th century formal
terraced gardens and magnificent yews. Contains unique painted cloth wall
hangings, family and Arts & Crafts collections. Mill (1726), Court House (1620);
licensed restaurant in medieval Cyder House. Victorian church. *"Owlpen – ah, what
a dream is there!"* – Vita Sackville-West.
Location: MAP 6:M12, OS Ref. ST801 984. 3m E of Dursley, 1m E of Uley, off B4066,
by Old Crown pub.
Open: May–Sept: Tue, Thurs & Sun, 2–5pm. Restaurant 12 noon–5pm.
Admission: Adult £5.50, Child (4–14yrs) £2.50, Family (2+4) £15.25. Gardens &
Grounds: Adult £3.50, Child £1.50. Group rates available.
🅣 🅖 Unsuitable. 🍴 Licensed. 🅿 🖼 Holiday cottages, all seasons, sleep 2–9.

PAINSWICK ROCOCO GARDEN 🏠
PAINSWICK, GLOUCESTERSHIRE GL6 6TH

www.rococogarden.org.uk

Tel: 01452 813204 **Fax:** 01452 814888 **E-mail:** info@rococogarden.org.uk
Owner: Painswick Rococo Garden Trust   **Contact:** P R Moir
Unique 18th century garden restoration situated in a hidden 6 acre Cotswold combe.
Charming contemporary buildings are juxtaposed with winding woodland walks and
formal vistas. Famous for its early spring show of snowdrops. Anniversary maze.
Location: MAP 6:N11, OS Ref. SO864 106. ½ m NW of village of Painswick on B4073.
Open: 10 Jan–31 Oct: daily, 11am–5pm.
Admission: Adult £5.50, Child £2.75, OAP £4.50. Family (2+2) £15.
Free introductory talk for pre-booked groups (20+).
🖸 🚻 🅖 Partial. WC. 🖙 Licensed. 🍴 🅿 🖼 🐕 In grounds, on leads. 🅐 ❋ 🅤

Hidcote Manor Garden

RODMARTON MANOR
CIRENCESTER, GLOUCESTERSHIRE GL7 6PF

www.rodmarton-manor.co.uk

Tel: 01285 841253 **Fax:** 01285 841298
E-mail: simon.biddulph1@btinternet.com
Owner: Mr & Mrs Simon Biddulph **Contact:** Simon Biddulph

A Cotswold Arts and Crafts house, one of the last great country houses to be built in the traditional way and containing beautiful furniture, ironwork, china and needlework specially made for the house. The large garden complements the house and contains many areas of great beauty and character including the magnificent herbaceous borders, topiary, roses, rockery and kitchen garden. Available as a film location and for small functions.

Location: MAP 6:N12, OS Ref. ST943 977. Off A433 between Cirencester and Tetbury.

Open: House & Garden: Easter Monday & May–Sept (Weds, Sats & BHs), 2–5pm (Not guided tours). Garden only, for snowdrops,: 10, 14 & 17 Feb: from 1.30pm. Groups please book. Individuals need not book. Guided tours of the house (last about 1hr) may be booked for groups (15+) at any time of year (minimum group charge of £105 applies). Groups (5+) may book guided or unguided tours of the garden at other times.
Admission: House & Garden: £7, Child (5–15yrs) £3.50. Garden only: £4, Child (5–15yrs) £1. Guided tour of Garden: Entry fee plus £40 per group.

ℹ Colour guidebook & postcards on sale. Available for filming. No photography in house. WCs in garden. ♿ Garden & ground floor. ☛ Most open days and groups by appointment. 🐾 By arrangement. 🅿 ■ 🚍 Guide dogs only. ✳

ST MARY'S CHURCH ⚏

Kempley, Gloucestershire
Tel: 0117 9750700 **www.english-heritage.org.uk/visits**
Owner: English Heritage **Contact:** The South West Regional Office

A delightful Norman church with superb wall paintings from the 12th–14th centuries which were only discovered beneath whitewash in 1871.

Location: MAP 6:M10, OS Ref. SO670 313. On minor road. 1½m SE of Much Marcle, A449.
Open: 1 Mar–31 Oct: daily, 10am–6pm. Telephone for winter appointments.
Admission: Free.

🚍

SEZINCOTE
MORETON-IN-MARSH, GLOUCESTERSHIRE GL56 9AW

www.sezincote.co.uk

Tel: 01386 700444
Owner/Contact: Dr E Peake

Exotic oriental water garden by Repton and Daniell. Large semi-circular orangery. House by S P Cockerell in Indian style was the inspiration for Brighton Pavilion.

Location: MAP 6:P10, OS Ref. SP183 324. 2½m SW of Moreton-in-Marsh. Turn W along A44 to Broadway and left into gateway just before Bourton-on-the-Hill (opposite the gate to Batsford Park, then 1m drive.

Open: Garden: Thurs, Fris & BH Mons, 2–6pm (dusk if earlier) throughout the year except Dec. House: Open as Garden but closed Oct–April. Groups at any time by written appointment.

Admission: House: Adult £8 (guided tour). Garden: Adult £5, Child £1.50 (under 5yrs Free).

♿ Gravel paths. 🐾 Obligatory. 🚍 Guide dogs only. ✳

David Brown/National Trust

Newark Park

©NTPL/Dominic Hamilton

SNOWSHILL MANOR ❧

SNOWSHILL, Nr BROADWAY, GLOUCESTERSHIRE   WR12 7JU

www.nationaltrust.org.uk

Tel: 01386 852410   **Fax:** 01386 842822   **E-mail:** snowshillmanor@nationaltrust.org.uk
Owner: The National Trust   **Contact:** The Property Manager
Snowshill Manor contains Charles Paget Wade's extraordinary collection of craftsmanship and design, including musical instruments, clocks, toys, bicycles, weavers' and spinners' tools and Japanese armour. Each room has something to interest or inspire the visitor. Run on organic principles, the intimate garden is laid out as a series of outdoor rooms, with terraces and ponds, and wonderful views across the Cotswold countryside. The Snowshill Costume Collection can be viewed by appointment only at Berrington Hall on Mondays and Tuesdays, please tel: 01568 613720.
Location: MAP 6:O10, OS Ref. SP096 339. 2½ m SW of Broadway, turning off the A44, at Broadway Green.

Open: House: 19 Mar–2 Nov: Wed–Sun & BH Mons, 12 noon–5pm. Last admission to the house 4.20pm. House is shown by timed ticket only. Garden, Shop & Restaurant: as House, 11am–5.30pm, also 8 Nov–14 Dec,12 noon–4pm.
*Admission: House, Gardens, Shop & Restaurant: Adult £8.10, Child £4.10, Family £20.60. Garden, Shop & Restaurant only: Adult £4.40, Child £2.20, Family £11.10. Visitors arriving by bicycle or on foot offered a voucher redeemable at Snowshill NT shop or tearoom. Coach & School groups by written appointment only. *includes a voluntary donation but visitors can choose to pay the standard prices displayed at the property and on the website.

▣ ♿ Partial. ⊤⊤ Licensed. ▣ ✖ ♥

STANWAY HOUSE & WATER GARDEN 🏛

STANWAY, CHELTENHAM, GLOS GL54 5PQ

www.stanwayfountain.co.uk

Tel: 01386 584528   **Fax:** 01386 584688   **E-mail:** stanwayhse@btconnect.com
Owner: Lord Neidpath   **Contact:** Debbie Lewis
"As perfect and pretty a Cotswold manor house as anyone is likely to see" (Fodor's Great Britain 1998 guidebook). Stanway's beautiful architecture, furniture, parkland and village are now complemented by the restored 18th century water garden and the magnificent fountain – 300 feet – making it the tallest garden fountain and gravity fountain in the world. Teas available. Beer for sale. Wedding reception venue.
Location: MAP 6:O10, OS Ref. SP061 323. N of Winchcombe, just off B4077.
Open: House & Garden: June–Aug: Tue & Thur, 2–5pm. Private tours by arrangement at other times.
Admission: Adult £6, Child £1.50, OAP £4.50. Garden only: Adult £4, Child £1, OAP £3.

ℹ Film & photographic location. ⊤ Wedding receptions. ▣ ⛾ 🎔 By arrangement.
Ⓟ 🚻 In grounds on leads. ❀

SUDELEY CASTLE GARDENS & EXHIBITIONS 🏛

See page 221 for full page entry.

TYTHE BARN

Tanhouse Farm, Churchend, Frampton-on-Severn, Gloucestershire GL2 7EH

Tel: 01452 741072   **E-mail:** tanhouse.farm@lineone.net

Owner/Contact: Michael Williams

Tythe Barn Grade II* c1650 recently restored in conjunction with English Heritage. Barn incorporating cow shed, the exceptional length and width of the timber framed structure upon a low stone plinth with box framing and undaubed wattle panels marks it out from other contemporary farm buildings.

Location: MAP 6:M12, OS Ref. SP014 206. Southern end of Frampton-on-Severn, close to church.

Open: By arrangement all year 10am–4pm.

Admission: Free.

🚹 Partial. 👷 By arrangement. 🅿 Limited. None for coaches. ✳

©NTPL/Stephen Robsc

WESTBURY COURT GARDEN 🌿

WESTBURY-ON-SEVERN, GLOUCESTERSHIRE GL14 1PD

www.nationaltrust.org.uk

Tel: 01452 760461   **E-mail:** westburycourt@nationaltrust.org.uk

Owner: The National Trust   **Contact:** The Head Gardener

A Dutch water garden with canals and yew hedges, laid out between 1696 and 1705; the earliest of its kind remaining in England. Restored in 1971 and planted with species dating from pre-1700 including apple, pear and plum trees.

Location: MAP 6:M11, OS Ref. SO718 138. 9m SW of Gloucester on A48.

Open: 12 Mar–30 Jun & 1 Sept–26 Oct: Wed–Sun, 10am–5pm. 1 Jul–31 Aug: daily, 10am–5pm. Open BH Mons. Other times of year by appointment.

***Admission:** Adult £4.50, Child £2.25, Family £11.60. *includes a voluntary donation but visitors can choose to pay the standard prices displayed at the property and on the website.

🖼 🚹 Grounds largely accessible. WCs. 🅿 🐕

WHITTINGTON COURT 🏛

Whittington, Cheltenham, Gloucestershire GL54 4HF

Tel: 01242 820556   **Fax:** 01242 820218

Owner: Mr & Mrs Jack Stringer   **Contact:** Mrs J Stringer

Elizabethan manor house. Family possessions including ceramics, antique and modern glass, fossils and fabrics.

Location: MAP 6:N11, OS Ref. SP014 206. 4m E of Cheltenham on N side of A40.

Open: 22 Mar–6 Apr & 9–25 Aug: 2–5pm.

Admission: Adult £5, Child £1, OAP £4.

🖼🅿

WOODCHESTER MANSION

NYMPSFIELD, STONEHOUSE, GLOUCESTERSHIRE GL10 3TS

www.woodchestermansion.org.uk

Tel: 01453 861541 **Fax:** 01453 861337 **E-mail:** office@woodchestermansion.org.uk

Owner: Woodchester Mansion Trust Ltd   **Contact:** Kate Lewington.

Location: MAP 6:M12, OS Ref. SO809 013. Near Nympsfield off the B4066 Stroud-Dursley road.

Hidden in a wooded valley near Stroud is one of the most intriguing houses in the country. Woodchester Mansion was started in the mid-1850s, but abandoned incomplete. It offers a unique insight into traditional building techniques. The Trust's repair programme includes courses in stone masonry and building conservation.

Open: Easter–Oct: Suns & 1st Sat of every month & BH weekends inc. Mon. Jul–Aug: Sat & Sun.

Admission: Adult £5.50, Child (under 14 yrs) Free, Conc £4.50. Group rates available.

🖼 ☕ 🎁 👷 Obligatory. 🅿 Limited. ▓ 🦮 Guide dogs only.

Frampton Court

■ **Owner**
The National Trust

■ **Contact**

For Room Hire
Mr Tom Deller
Room Hire Manager
Stall Street
Bath BA1 1LZ

Tel: 01225 477734
Fax: 01225 477476
E-mail: tom_deller@
bathnes.gov.uk

Museum Enquiries
Tel: 01225 477173
Fax: 01225 477743

■ **Location**
MAP 2:P2
OS Ref. ST750 648

Near centre of Bath,
10m from M4/J18.
Park & Ride or
public car park.

Rail: Great Western from
London Paddington
(regular service)
90 mins approx.

Air: Bristol airport
45 mins.

■ **Opening Times**
All Year, daily,
January/February &
November/December:
11am–4pm. March–
October: 11am–5pm.

Closed 25/26 December
Last exit 1hr after closing.

Special exhibitions
'1977', until
16 March, '17th century
gloves' ongoing, 'Fashion
and Bath' until end 2008.

■ **Admission**
Assembly Rooms Free

Museum of Fashion
Adult	£7.00
Child* (summer)	£5.00
Conc.	£6.00
Family (2+4)	£19.75

Groups (20+)
Adult	£5.75
Child* (summer)	£4.25
Child* (winter)	£3.80

**Joint Saver Ticket with
Roman Baths**
Adult	£14.00
Child*	£8.40
Conc.	£12.00
Family (2+4)	£39.00

Groups (20+)
Adult	£9.50
Child* (summer)	£6.10
Child* (winter)	£5.25

* Age 6–16yrs.
Child under 6yrs Free.

FASHION MUSEUM 🌿
& ASSEMBLY ROOMS

www.fashionmuseum.co.uk

The Assembly Rooms in Bath are open to the public daily (free of charge) and are also popular for dinners, dances, concerts, conferences and Civil weddings. Originally known as the Upper Rooms, they were designed by John Wood the Younger and opened in 1771. The magnificent interior consists of a splendid Ball Room, Tea Room and Card Room, connected by two fine octagonal rooms. This plan was perfect for 'assemblies', evening entertainments popular in the 18th century, which included dancing, music, card-playing and tea drinking. They are now owned by The National Trust and managed by Bath & North East Somerset Council, which runs a full conference service.

The building also houses the Fashion Museum, a world-class collection of contemporary and historical dress. See real examples of historic and up-to-the-minute fashions in new thematic displays, including day wear and evening wear, menswear and womenswear. There is a chance to try on replicas of corsets and crinolines and a special display of 17th century gloves, showing the skill and opulence of luxury goods 300 years ago. For the serious student of fashion, the reference library and study facilities are available by appointment.

There is a contemporary café, an extensive fashion bookshop and a fashion gift shop.

	i	Conference facilities.
	🏠	Extensive book & gift shops.
	♆	Corporate hospitality. Function facilities.
	♿	Suitable. WC.
	☕	
	🧍	Hourly. Individual guided tours by arrangement.
	🎧	English/Dutch/French/German/Italian/ Japanese/Spanish.
	P	Charlotte Street car park.
	📖	Teachers' pack.
	🐕	Guide dogs only.
	🔔	Civil Weddings/Receptions.
	❄	

Conference/Function

ROOM	SIZE	MAX CAPACITY
Ballroom	103' x 40'	500/310
Octagon	47' x 47'	120/120
Tea Room	58' x 40'	260/170
Card Room	59' x 18'	80/60

THE ROMAN BATHS & PUMP ROOM

www.romanbaths.co.uk

The first stop for any visitor to Bath is the Roman Baths surrounding the hot springs where the city began and which are still its heart. Here you'll see one of the country's finest ancient monuments – the great Roman temple and bathing complex built almost 2,000 years ago. Discover the everyday life of the Roman spa and see ancient treasures from the Temple of Sulis Minerva. A host of new interpretive methods for adults and children bring these spectacular buildings vividly to life and help visitors to understand the extensive remains.

The Grand Pump Room, overlooking the Spring, is the social heart of Bath. The elegant interior of 1795 is something every visitor to Bath should see. You can enjoy a glass of spa water drawn from the fountain, perhaps as an appetiser to a traditional Pump Room tea, morning coffee or lunch. The Pump Room Trio and resident pianists provide live music daily. The Roman Baths shop sells publications and gifts related to the site.

In the evening, the Pump Room is available for banquets, dances and concerts. Nothing could be more magical than a meal on the terrace which overlooks the Great Bath, or a pre-dinner drinks reception by torchlight around the Great Bath itself.

■ Owner
Bath & North East Somerset Council

■ Contact
For Room Hire
Mr Tom Deller
Stall Street
Bath BA1 1LZ
Tel: 01225 477734
Fax: 01225 477476
E-mail: tom_deller@ bathnes.gov.uk

For visits to Roman Baths
Tel: 01225 477785
Fax: 01225 477743

■ Location
MAP 2:P2
OS Ref. ST750 648

Centre of Bath, 10m from M4/J18. Park & Ride recommended.

Rail: Great Western from London Paddington, half hourly service, 1 hr 17 mins duration.

■ Opening Times
January–February: 9.30am–4.30pm.
March–June: 9am–5pm.
July–August: 9am–8pm.
September–October: 9am–5pm.
November–December: 9.30am–4.30pm.
Last exit 1 hour after closing.

Closed 25 & 26 December.

The Pump Room Trio plays 10am–12 noon Mon–Sat and 3–5pm Sunday. During the summer it also plays from 3–5pm, Mon–Sat. Resident pianists play at lunch-time.

■ Admission
Roman Baths

Adult	£10.50
Child (6–16yrs)	£7.00
Conc.	£9.00
Family (2+4)	£30.00

Groups (20+)

Adult	£7.80
Child* (summer)	£5.00
Child* (winter)	£4.75

Joint Saver Ticket with Fashion Museum

Adult	£14.00
Child*	£8.40
Conc.	£12.00
Family (2+4)	£39.00

Groups (20+)

Adult	£9.50
Child* (summer)	£6.10
Child* (winter)	£5.25

*Age 6–16yrs.
Child under 6yrs Free.

	Award-winning guide book in English, French and German.
	Extensive gift shop.
	Comprehensive service for private and corporate entertainment. The Assembly Rooms, Guildhall, Victoria Art Gallery and Pump Room are all available for private hire, contact the Pump Room.
	Free access to terrace. Restricted access to the Museum, special visits for disabled groups by appointment. People with special needs welcome, teaching sessions available.
	Pump Room coffees, lunches and teas, no reservation needed. Music by Pump Room Trio or pianist.
	Hourly. Private tours by appointment.
	English, French, German, Italian, Japanese, Spanish, Dutch, Mandarin.
	City centre car parks available.
	Teaching sessions available. Pre-booking necessary.
	Civil Weddings in two private rooms with photographs around the Great Bath.

Conference/Function

ROOM	SIZE	MAX CAPACITY
Ballroom	103' x 40'	500/310
Octagon	47' x 47'	120/120
Tea Room	58' x 40'	260/170
Card Room	59' x 18'	80/60

NO 1 ROYAL CRESCENT

BATH BA1 2LR

www.bath-preservation-trust.org.uk

Tel: 01225 428126   Fax: 01225 481850
E-mail: no1museum@bptrust.org.uk
Owner: Bath Preservation Trust   **Contact:** Victoria Barwell – Curator

Take a look inside a sumptuous piece of Bath's unmatched architectural heritage and revel in the opulence of grand Georgian life. The exquisitely restored and lavishly furnished house is the epitome of elegant 18th century living, and a unique museum shop completes the experience.

Location: MAP 2:P2, OS Ref. ST746 653. M4/J18. A46 to Bath. ¼m NW of city centre.
Open: Mid Feb–end Nov: Tues–Sun, 10.30am–5pm. BH Mons. Closes 4pm in Nov. Closed Good Fri. Last admission 30 mins before closing. Evening tours and other times by arrangement.
Admission: Adult £5, Child (5–16yrs) £2.50, Conc £4, Family £12. Groups: £3.
⊡⊤⊡ Unsuitable. ⊡⊡ The Royal Crescent & Bath centre. ▣

Glastonbury Abbey

THE AMERICAN MUSEUM & GARDENS

CLAVERTON MANOR, CLAVERTON HILL, BATH BA2 7BD

www.americanmuseum.org

Tel: 01225 460503   **Fax:** 01225 469160   **E-mail:** info@americanmuseum.org
Owner: The Trustees of the American Museum in Britain   **Contact:** Julian Blades

Claverton Manor was built in 1820 by Jeffry Wyattville. In the late 1950s it became the home of the American Museum in Britain. Inside the Manor there are 18 period rooms which show the development of American decorative arts from the 1680s to the 1860s. In addition there are galleries devoted to Folk Art, Native American Art, and our large collection of quilts and other textiles. The extensive grounds contain a replica of part of the garden at Mount Vernon, George Washington's house in Virginia, and an Arboretum of North American trees and shrubs. Light lunches and teas are available.

Location: MAP 2:P2, OS Ref. ST784 640. 2m SE of Bath city centre.
Open: 15 Mar–2 Nov: Tues–Sun (open BH Mons and Mons in Aug) 12noon–5pm. Last admission to museum 4pm. 22 Nov–14 Dec: Tues–Sun, 12 noon–4.30pm.
Admission: Adult £7.50, Child £4.00, Conc. £6.50. Groups (15–70): Adult £6.
⊡⊡⊤⊡ Partial. WC. ◼ Licensed. ⒳ By arrangement. ⊡ ▣
⊡ In grounds, on leads.⊡

©NTPL/Neil Campbell-Sharp

BARRINGTON COURT ✥
BARRINGTON, ILMINSTER, SOMERSET TA19 0NQ

www.nationaltrust.org.uk

Tel: 01460 241938   **Info:** 01460 242614
E-mail: barringtoncourt@nationaltrust.org.uk
Owner: The National Trust   **Contact:** Visitor Services Manager

The enchanting formal garden, influenced by Gertrude Jekyll, is laid out in a series of walled rooms, including the White Garden, the Rose and Iris Garden and the Lily Garden. The working Kitchen Garden has espaliered apple, pear and plum trees trained along high stone walls. The Tudor manor house was restored in the 1920s by the Lyle family. It is let to Stuart Interiors as showrooms with antique furniture for sale, thereby offering NT visitors a different kind of visit.

Location: MAP 2:N5, OS Ref. ST395 181. In Barrington village, 5m NE of Ilminster, on B3168.

Open: House, Garden & Shop: 1–31 Mar & 2 Oct–2 Nov: daily except Weds, 11am–4.30pm. 1 Apr–30 Sept: daily except Weds, 11am–5pm. 6–14 Dec: Sats & Suns, 11am–4pm. Restaurant: 1 Apr–30 Sept (weekdays: lunches only, weekends: lunch & teas), 1–30 Mar & 2 Oct–2 Nov: daily except Weds, 11am–4pm. 31 Mar–30 Sept: Mon, Tues, Thurs & Fri, 12 noon–3pm. Sats & Suns, 12 noon–5pm. 6–14 Dec: Sat & Suns, 11am–4pm. Beagles café: 29 Mar–30 Sept: daily except Weds, 11am–5pm. 4–26 Oct: Sat & Suns, 11am–4pm. NB. Café may close in poor weather (Oct).

*Admission: Adult £8.10, Child £3.50, Family (2+3) £19.70. Groups: £7. *includes a voluntary donation but visitors can choose to pay the standard prices displayed at the property and on the website.

⊡ 🅿 🔊 Grounds. WC. 🖵 🍴 Licensed. 🅿 🔲 🔄

For **accommodation** in the South West, see our special index at the end of the book.

BECKFORD'S TOWER & MUSEUM

Lansdown Road, Bath BA1 9BH
Tel: 01225 460705   **Fax:** 01225 481850   **E-mail:** beckford@bptrust.org.uk
Owner: Bath Preservation Trust   **Contact:** The Administrator
Built in 1827 for eccentric William Beckford and recently restored by Bath Preservation Trust. The tower is a striking feature of the Bath skyline.
Location: MAP 2:P2, OS Ref. ST735 676. Lansdown Road, 2m NNW of city centre.
Open: Easter weekend–end of Oct: Sats, Suns & BH Mons, 10.30am–5pm.
Admission: Adult £3, Child £1.50, Conc. £2, Family £8. BPT & NACF members: Free. Groups by arrangement.

BREAN DOWN ✥

Brean, North Somerset
Tel: 01934 844518   www.nationaltrust.org.uk
Owner: The National Trust   **Contact:** Property Manager
Brean Down, rich in wildlife and history, is one of the most striking landmarks of the Somerset coastline, extending 1½m into the Bristol Channel. A Palmerston Fort built in 1865 and then re-armed in World War II, provides a unique insight into Brean's past.
Location: MAP 2:M3, OS Ref. ST290 590. Between Weston-super-Mare and Burnham-on-Sea about 8m from M5/J22. Rail: Highbridge 5m.
Open: All year.
Admission: Free.
ℹ The cliffs are extremely steep. Please stay on the main paths and wear suitable footwear. ⊡ (Not NT.) 🔊 Partial. WC in café. 🖵 (Not NT.) 🎦 Guided walks. 🅿 🔲 🔲 On leads. ✳

THE BUILDING OF BATH MUSEUM

The Countess of Huntingdon's Chapel, The Vineyards, The Paragon, Bath BA1 5NA
Tel: 01225 333895   **Fax:** 01225 445473   **E-mail:** enquiries@bathmuseum.co.uk
Owner: Bath Preservation Trust   **Contact:** The Administrator
Discover the essence of life in Georgian Bath.
Location: MAP 2:P2, OS Ref. ST751 655. 5 mins walk from city centre. Bath M4/J18.
Open: 15 Feb–30 Nov: Tue–Sun & BH Mons, 10.30am–5pm (last adm. 4.30pm).
Admission: Adult £4, Child £2, Conc. £3.50. Groups: £3.

CLEEVE ABBEY ⌗

Washford, Nr Watchet, Somerset TA23 0PS
Tel: 01984 640377   **Fax:** 01984 641348
www.english-heritage.org.uk/cleeve
Owner: English Heritage   **Contact:** Visitor Operations Staff
There are few monastic sites where you will see such a complete set of cloister buildings, including the refectory with its magnificent timber roof. Built in the 13th century, this Cistercian abbey was saved from destruction at the Dissolution by being turned into a house and then a farm.
Location: MAP 2:L4, OS Ref. ST047 407. In Washford, ¼m S of A39.
Open: 21 Mar–30 Jun & Sept: daily, 10am–5pm. Jul & Aug: daily, 10am–6pm. Oct: daily, 10am–4pm. Closed 1 Nov–31 Mar 09.
Admission: Adult £3.50, Child £1.80, Conc. £2.80. 15% discount for groups (11+). EH Members free.
ℹ WC. ⊡ 🔊 Partial. 🅿 🔲 In grounds, on leads. 🔄

COLERIDGE COTTAGE ✥

35 Lime Street, Nether Stowey, Bridgwater, Somerset TA5 1NQ
Tel: 01278 732662   **E-mail:** coleridgecottage@nationaltrust.org.uk
Owner: The National Trust   **Contact:** The Custodian
The home of Samuel Taylor Coleridge for three years from 1797, with mementoes of the poet on display. It was here that he wrote *The Rime of the Ancient Mariner,* part of *Christabel, Frost at Midnight* and *Kubla Khan.*
Location: MAP 2:M4, OS Ref. ST191 399. At W end of Lime St, opposite the Ancient Mariner pub, 8m W of Bridgwater.
Open: 3 Apr–28 Sept: Thur–Sun, 2–5pm (open BH Mons).
Admission: Adult £3.90, Child £1.90, no reduction for groups, which must book.
ℹ No WC. 🔊 Braille guide. 🅿 500yds (not NT). 🔲

COMBE SYDENHAM COUNTRY PARK 🏠

Monksilver, Taunton, Somerset TA4 4JG
Tel: 0800 7838572
Owner: Theed Estates   **Contact:** John Burns
Built in 1580 on the site of a monastic settlement. Deer Park and woodland walks.
Location: MAP 2:L4, OS Ref. ST075 366. Monksilver.
Open: Country Park: Easter–end Sept. House: All year by appointment only.
Admission: Country Park & car park Free. House & Gardens £5pp. Tel for details.

©NTPL/ David Noton

Prior Park Landscape Garden

Courtesy of Marianne Majerus Garden Images

COTHAY MANOR & GARDENS

GREENHAM, WELLINGTON, SOMERSET TA21 0JR

www.cothaymanor.co.uk

Tel: 01823 672283 **Fax:** 01823 672345 **E-mail:** cothaymanor@btinternet.co.uk

Owner/Contact: Mr & Mrs Alastair Robb

The magical, romantic, gardens of Cothay surround what is said to be the most perfect example of a small classic medieval manor. Many garden rooms, each a garden in itself, are set off a 200yd yew walk. In addition there is a bog garden with azaleas, and drifts of primuli, fine trees, cottage garden, courtyards, and river walk. A plantsman's paradise. The manor is open to groups throughout the year.

Location: MAP 2:L5, OS Ref. ST085 212. From M5 W J/27, take A38 direction Wellington. 3½m left towards Greenham. From N/J26 take A38 direction Exeter. 3½m right towards Greenham (1½m). On LH corner at bottom of hill turn right. Cothay 1m, always keeping left.

Open: Garden: Easter–Sept: Weds, Thurs, Suns, & BHs, 2–6pm. Groups: Daily all season by appointment. House: Groups (20+) by appointment throughout the year.

Admission: Garden: Adult £4.50, Child (under 12yrs) £2.50.

ℹ️ No photography in house.

Andrew Lawson

CROWE HALL

Widcombe Hill, Bath, Somerset BA2 6AR

Tel: 01225 310322

Owner/Contact: John Barratt Esq

Ten acres of romantic hillside gardens. Victorian grotto, classical Bath villa with good 18th century furniture and paintings.

Location: MAP 2:P2, OS Ref. ST760 640. In Bath, 1m SE of city centre.

Open: Gardens only open 13 Apr, 11 May & 1 Jun, 2–6pm. House and Gardens by appointment.

Admission: House & Gardens: Adult £6. Gardens only: Adult £4, Child £1.

DODINGTON HALL

Nr Nether Stowey, Bridgwater, Somerset TA5 1LF

Tel: 01278 741400

Owner: Lady Gass **Contact:** P Quinn (occupier)

Small Tudor manor house on the lower slopes of the Quantocks. Great Hall with oak roof. Semi-formal garden with roses and shrubs.

Location: MAP 2:L4, OS Ref. ST172 405. ½m from A39, 11m N of Bridgwater, 7m E of Williton.

Open: 30 May–9 Jun, 2–5pm.

Admission: Donations to Dodington Church.

ℹ️ No inside photography. Unsuitable. P Limited. No coach parking.

Hestercombe Gardens

©NTPL/Nadia Mackenzie

DUNSTER CASTLE
DUNSTER, Nr MINEHEAD, SOMERSET TA24 6SL
www.nationaltrust.org.uk

Tel: 01643 821314 **Fax:** 01643 823000 **E-mail:** dunstercastle@nationaltrust.org.uk
Owner: The National Trust **Contact:** The Property Manager
Dramatically sited on a wooded hill, a castle has existed here since at least Norman times. The 15th century gatehouse survives, and the present building was remodelled in 1868–72 by Antony Salvin for the Luttrell family, who lived here for 600 years. The fine oak staircase and plasterwork of the 17th century house he adapted can still be seen. There is a sheltered terrace to the south which is home to palms, sub-tropical plant species, and a varied collection of citrus. The terraced gardens also house the National Collection of strawberry trees (arbutus) and there is a pleasant riverside walk beside the River Avill.
Location: MAP 2:K4, OS Ref. SS995 435. In Dunster, 3m SE of Minehead.
Open: Castle: 15 Mar–23 Jul: daily except Thur, 11am–4.30pm; 25 Jul–3 Sept: daily except Thur, 11am–5pm; 5 Sept–2 Nov: daily except Thur, 11am–4.30pm. Garden & Park: 1 Jan–14 Mar & 3 Nov–31 Dec: daily (closed 25/26 Dec), 11am–4pm. 15 Mar–2 Nov: 10am–5pm daily. Varied events programme, please telephone for full details. Major roof repairs will be undertaken in 2008. Property open as normal. Access to one or two rooms may be restricted. Please telephone for details.
*Admission: Castle, Garden & Park: Adult £8.60, Child £4.20, Family (2+3) £20.50. Groups (15+): £7. Garden & Park only: Adult £4.80, Child £2.20, Family £11.80. *includes a voluntary donation but visitors can choose to pay the standard prices displayed at the property and on the website.
🖾 🕭 🕭 Braille guide. 🎦 Out of hours by arrangement. 🅿 £2. 🔲
🐾 In park, on leads. 🐾 Tel for details (0870 2404068) or visit website.

DUNSTER WORKING WATERMILL
Mill Lane, Dunster, Nr Minehead, Somerset TA24 6SW
Tel: 01643 821759 www.nationaltrust.org.uk
Owner: The National Trust **Contact:** The Tenant
Built on the site of a mill mentioned in the Domesday Survey of 1086. The mill is a private business and all visitors, including NT members, are asked to pay the admission charge.
Location: MAP 2:K4, OS Ref. SS995 435. On River Avill, beneath Castle Tor, approach via Mill Lane or Castle gardens on foot.
Open: 21–24 Mar, Fri–Mon; 1 Apr–31 May daily except Fri; 1 Jun–3 Sept daily; 1–30 Oct daily except Fri, 11am–4.45pm.
Admission: Adult £3.25, Child £1.95, Senior Citizen £2.75, Family £8.
🖾 🕭 Ground floor. 🐾 🅿

ENGLISHCOMBE TITHE BARN
Rectory Farmhouse, Englishcombe, Bath BA2 9DU
Tel: 01225 425073 **E-mail:** jennie.walker@ukonline.co.uk
Owner/Contact: Mrs Jennie Walker
An early 14th century cruck-framed Tithe Barn built by Bath Abbey.
Location: MAP 2:P2, OS172 Ref. ST716 628. Adjacent to Englishcombe Village Church. 1m SW of Bath.
Open: BHs, 2–6pm. Other times by appointment or please knock at house. Closed 1 Dec–7 Jan.
Admission: Free.

FAIRFIELD
Stogursey, Bridgwater, Somerset TA5 1PU
Tel: 01722 555131 / 01278 732251
Owner: Lady Gass **Contact:** D W Barke FRICS
Elizabethan and medieval house. Occupied by the same family (Acland-Hoods and their ancestors) for over 800 years. Woodland garden. Views of Quantocks and the sea.
Location: MAP 2:L4, OS Ref. ST187 430. 11m W of Bridgwater, 8m E of Williton. From A39 Bridgwater/Minehead turn North. House 1m W of Stogursey on road to Stringston.
Open: 9 Apr–26 May & 4–20 Jun: Wed–Fri and May BHs. Guided house tours at 2.30 & 3.30pm. Groups at other times by arrangement. Garden open for NGS and other charities on dates advertised in Spring. Advisable to contact to confirm dates.
Admission: £4 in aid of Stogursey Church.
ⓘ No inside photography. 🕭🎦 Obligatory. 🅿 No coach parking.
🐾 Guide dogs only.

FARLEIGH HUNGERFORD CASTLE ⌗
Farleigh Hungerford, Bath, Somerset BA2 7RS
Tel/Fax: 01225 754026
www.english-heritage.org.uk/farleighhungerford
Owner: English Heritage **Contact:** Visitor Operations Staff
Extensive ruins of 14th century castle with a splendid chapel containing wall paintings, stained glass and the fine tomb of Sir Thomas Hungerford, builder of the castle.
Location: MAP 2:P3, OS173, ST801 577. In Farleigh Hungerford 3½m W of Trowbridge on A366.
Open: 21 Mar–31 Oct: daily, 10am–5pm (6pm in Jul & Aug, 4pm in Oct). 1 Nov–31 Mar: Sats & Suns, 10am–4pm. Closed 24–26 Dec & 1 Jan.
Admission: Adult £3.50, Child £1.80, Conc. £2.80. 15% discount for groups of 11+. EH Members free.
ⓘ WCs. 🖾 🕭 Grounds, Ground Floor & Virtual Reality Tour. 🅿 🔊
🐾 Guide dogs only. ❈ ❖

FASHION MUSEUM ⛋ & ASSEMBLY ROOMS

See page 230 for full page entry.

GATCOMBE COURT
Flax Bourton, Somerset BS48 3QT
Tel: 01275 393141 **Fax:** 01275 394274
Owner/Contact: Mrs Charles Clarke
A Somerset manor house, dating from early 13th century, which has evolved over the centuries since. It is on the site of a large Roman village, traces of which are apparent. Rose and herb garden. Described in Simon Jenkins' book, *England's Thousand Best Houses*.
Location: MAP 2:N2, OS Ref. ST525 698. 5m W of Bristol, N of the A370, between the villages of Long Ashton and Flax Bourton. Close to Tyntesfield.
Open: May–Auh: for groups of 15–40 people by appointment.
🕭 Unsuitable. 🎦 By arrangement. 🐾 🅿 🐾 ❈

THE GEORGIAN HOUSE
7 Great George Street, Bristol, Somerset BS1 5RR
Tel: 0117 921 1362
Owner: City of Bristol Museums & Art Gallery **Contact:** Karin Walton
Location: MAP 2:O2, OS172 ST582 730. Bristol.
Open: All year: Sat–Wed, 10am–5pm.
Admission: Free.

GLASTONBURY ABBEY

ABBEY GATEHOUSE, MAGDALENE STREET, GLASTONBURY BA6 9EL

www.glastonburyabbey.com

Tel: 01458 832267 **Fax:** 01458 836117 **E-mail:** info@glastonburyabbey.com
Owner: Glastonbury Abbey Estate **Contact:** Francis Thyer
"Unique", "Peaceful", "Such atmosphere", "A hidden gem". This is what some of our visitors say. Come and discover this wonderful place for yourself. From March to October hear, from our enactors, how the monks used to live and some of the history of this once great Abbey. See website for events. Outdoor Summer Café.
Location: MAP 2:N4, OS Ref. ST499 388. 50 yds from the Market Cross, in the centre of Glastonbury. M5/J23, then A39.
Open: Daily (except Christmas Day), 9.30am–6pm or dusk if earlier. Jun, Jul & Aug: opens 9am. Dec, Jan & Feb: opens 10am.
Admission: Adult £5, Child (5–15 yrs) £3, Conc. £4.50, Family (2+2) £14. Groups 10+ (booked): Adult £4.50, Child £2.50.

◻ ⬛ ⬛ Summer only. 🎫 🔲 🅿 ⬛ ⬛ ⬛ ⬛

HALSWELL HOUSE

HALSWELL PARK, GOATHURST, SOMERSET TA5 2DH

www.halswell.co.uk

Tel: 0845 204 1066 **E-mail:** info@halswell.co.uk
Owner: Grahame Bond **Contact:** Michael Coles
Halswell is a Grade I listed William & Mary mansion house with 20 suites/ bedrooms and six principal reception rooms for exclusive use for weddings, corporate events or private parties.
Nestling at the foot of the Quantock Hills with far reaching views to the Bristol Channel and over to Wales, this beautiful house has been restored to its former glory and is resplendent with period furniture, grand paintings and original features.
Location: MAP 2:M4, OS Ref. ST253 337. 5m from M5/J24. 4m SW of Bridgwater.
Open: Grounds all year. House by appointment only except during open days.
Admission: No admission charges but donations to charity encouraged.
⬛ ⬛ Partial. 🎫 By arrangement. 🅿 None for coaches. ⬛ ⬛ In grounds on leads.
⬛ 20 double, all en-suite. ⬛ ⬛

GLASTONBURY TOR ⬛

Nr Glastonbury, Somerset
Tel: 01985 843600 / 01934 844518
Owner: The National Trust **Contact:** The Regional Office
The dramatic and evocative Tor dominates the surrounding countryside and offers spectacular views over Somerset, Dorset and Wiltshire. At the summit of this very steep hill an excavation has revealed the plans of two superimposed churches of St Michael, of which only the 15th-century tower remains.
Location: MAP 2:N4, OS Ref. ST512 386. Signposted from Glastonbury town centre, from where seasonal park-and-ride (not NT) operates.
Open: All year.
Admission: Free.
🅿 Park & ride from town centre Apr–Sept. Also free at Rural Life Museum. Tel 01458 831197. ⬛ On leads only. ⬛

GLASTONBURY TRIBUNAL ⬛

Glastonbury High Street, Glastonbury, Somerset BA6 9DP
Tel: 01458 832954 www.english-heritage.org.uk/glastonbury
Owner: English Heritage **Contact:** The TIC Manager
A well preserved medieval town house, reputedly once used as the courthouse of Glastonbury Abbey. Now houses Glastonbury Tourist Information Centre.
Location: MAP 2:N4, OS182 Ref. ST499 390. In Glastonbury High Street.
Open: 21 Mar–30 Sept: daily, 10am–5pm (5.30pm Fri & Sat). Closed 25–26 Dec & 1 Jan.
Admission: TIC Free. Museum areas: Adult £2, Child/Conc £1.50. Senior £1. EH Members free. Group discount available.
⬛ Partial. 🅿 Charge. ⬛

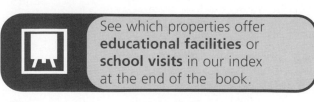
See which properties offer **educational facilities** or **school visits** in our index at the end of the book.

NTPL/ Magnus Rew
Dunster Castle

HESTERCOMBE GARDENS
CHEDDON FITZPAINE, TAUNTON, SOMERSET TA2 8LG

www.hestercombegardens.com

Tel: 01823 413923 **Fax:** 01823 413747
E-mail: info@hestercombegardens.com
Owner: Hestercombe Gardens Trust
Contact: The Gardens Office

Lose yourself in 40 acres of walks, streams and temples, vivid colours, formal terraces, woodlands, lakes, cascades and views that take your breath away. This is Hestercombe: a unique combination of three period gardens. The Georgian landscape garden was created in the 1750s by Copelstone Warre Bampfylde, whose vision was complemented by the addition of a Victorian terrace and shrubbery and the stunning Edwardian gardens designed by Sir Edwin Lutyens and Gertrude Jekyll. All once abandoned, now being faithfully restored to their former glory. Each garden has its own quality of tranquility, wonder and inspiration. Fabulous Courtyard Café and Restaurant, excellent shop, conference and business facilities, weddings, parties, year round events.

Location: MAP 2:M5, OS Ref. ST241 287. 4m NE from Taunton, 1m NW of Cheddon Fitzpaine.
Open: All year: daily, 10am–6pm (last admission 5pm). Groups & coach parties by arrangement.
Admission: Adult £7.50*, Conc. £6.95*, Student £4. Groups (20+) £6.10. Guided tour (20+): £8.80. *Prices include 2 children. Additional child £2.50.

▢ ▣ ⬚ ⊤ Partial. WC. ⬛ Licensed. ⑪ Licensed. ☒ By arrangement. ⅗ Limited for coaches. ⬚ On short leads ⬚ ⬚

THE HERSCHEL MUSEUM OF ASTRONOMY

19 New King Street, Bath BA1 2BL
Tel/Fax: 01225 446865 **E-mail:** herschelbpt@btconnect.com
Owner: The Herschel House Trust **Contact:** The Curator
Georgian town-house. Home to astronomer William Herschel and site of discovery of planet Uranus in 1781. Georgian garden. Audio tour. Star Vault Astronomy Auditorium.
Location: MAP 2:P2, OS Ref. ST750 648. Bath, Somerset.
Open: 1 Feb–15 Dec: daily except Weds, 1–5pm, Sats/Suns 11am–5pm. School visits and group bookings by arrangement.
Admission: Adult £4, Child £2.50, Full Time Student £3, OAP £3.50, Family £10.

HOLBURNE MUSEUM OF ART

Great Pulteney Street, Bath BA2 4DB
Tel: 01225 466669 **Fax:** 01225 333121
Owner: Trustees **Contact:** Katie Jenkins
This jewel in Bath's crown houses the treasures collected by Sir William Holburne: superb English and continental silver, porcelain, majolica, glass and Renaissance bronzes, and paintings by Turner, Guardi and Stubbs.
Location: MAP 2:P2, OS Ref. ST431 545. Via A4 or A431, follow brown signs.
Open: Mid Jan–Dec, please telephone for details.
Admission: Varies with exhibitions – telephone for details.

HOLNICOTE ESTATE ⅍

Selworthy, Minehead, Somerset TA24 8TJ
Tel: 01643 862452 **Fax:** 01643 863011 **E-mail:** holnicote@nationaltrust.org.uk
Owner: The National Trust **Contact:** The Estate Office
The Holnicote Estate covers 5042ha (12,500 acres) of Exmoor National Park. The Estate also covers 4 miles of coastline between Porlock Bay and Minehead. There are over 100 miles of footpaths to enjoy through the fields, woods, moors and villages.
Location: MAP 2:K3, OS Ref. SS920 469. Off A39 Minehead–Porlock, 3m W of Minehead. Station: Minehead 5m.
Open: Estate Office: All year: Mon–Fri, 9am–5pm. Estate: Daily, all year.
Admission: Free.

▢ ⬚ ⬛ (Not NT.) ⬚ ⬚

KENTSFORD

Washford, Watchet, Somerset TA23 0JD
Tel: 01984 631307
Owner: Wyndham Estate **Contact:** Mr R Dibble
Location: MAP 2:L4, OS Ref. ST058 426.
Open: House open only by written appointment with Mr R Dibble. Gardens: 6 Mar–28 Aug: Tues & BHs.
Admission: House: £3, Gardens: Free.
⬚ Gardens only. ⅗ Limited. ⬚ In grounds, on leads. ⬚

KING JOHN'S HUNTING LODGE ⅍

The Square, Axbridge, Somerset BS26 2AP
Tel: 01934 732012 www.nationaltrust.org.uk
Owner/Contact: The National Trust
An early Tudor merchant's house, extensively restored in 1971. Note: the property is run as a local history museum by Axbridge & District Museum Trust in co-operation with Sedgemoor District Council, County Museum's Service and Axbridge Archaeological & Local History Society.
Location: MAP 2:N3, OS Ref. ST431 545. In the Square, on corner of High Street, off A371.
Open: 21 Mar–30 Sept: Daily, 1–4pm.
Admission: Free. Donations welcome.
⬚ Ground floor. ⅗ ⬚ By arrangement.

LOWER SEVERALLS

Crewkerne, Somerset TA18 7NX
Tel: 01460 73234 **E-mail:** mary@lowerseveralls.co.uk
Owner/Contact: Mary Pring
2½ acre garden, developed over the last 25 years including herb garden, mixed borders and island beds with innovative features, ie a giant living dogwood basket and a wadi.
Location: MAP 2:N5, OS Ref. ST457 112. 1½m NE of Crewkerne, between A30 & A356.
Open: Mar–Sept: Tue & Wed & Fri & Sat, 10am–5pm. Closed Aug.
Admission: Adult £3.25, Child (under 16yrs) Free.

©NTPL/Nick Meers

LYTES CARY MANOR ✤
Nr CHARLTON MACKRELL, SOMERSET TA11 7HU

www.nationaltrust.org.uk

Tel: 01458 224471   **E-mail:** lytescarymanor@nationaltrust.org.uk
Owner: The National Trust   **Contact:** Visitor Services Manager
This charming manor house, with its 14th century chapel and 15th century Great Hall, was the former home of medieval herbalist Henry Lyte. In the 20th century it was rescued from dereliction by Sir Walter Jenner, who refurnished the interiors in period style. Its Arts & Crafts style garden is an intimate combination of outdoor rooms, topiary, statues and herbaceous borders.
Location: MAP 2:O5, OS Ref. ST529 269. 1m N of Ilchester bypass A303, signposted from Podimore roundabout at junction of A303. A37 take A372.
Open: 15 Mar–2 Nov: Sat–Wed, 11am–5pm. Closes dusk if earlier.
*Admission: Adult £7, Child £3.50. Family £17.50. Garden only: Adult £5, Child £2.50. *includes a voluntary donation but visitors can choose to pay the standard prices displayed at the property and on the website.
⚹ ⬜ Partial. Braille guide. ☐ 🔲 By arrangement. P Free. Small coaches only by arrangement. ⬜ On leads in car park & estate walks, only. ⬜ Estate. ⬜

MAUNSEL HOUSE
NORTH NEWTON, Nr TAUNTON, SOMERSET TA7 0BU

www.maunselhouse.co.uk

Tel: 01278 661076   **Fax:** 01278 661074   **E-mail:** info@maunselhouse.co.uk
Owner: Sir Benjamin Slade Bt   **Contact:** The Events Team
This imposing 13th century manor house offers the ideal location for wedding receptions, corporate events, private and garden parties, filming and family celebrations. The ancestral seat of the Slade family and home of the 7th baronet Sir Benjamin Slade, the house can boast such visitors as Geoffrey Chaucer, who wrote part of the *Canterbury Tales* whilst staying there. The beautiful grounds and spacious rooms provide both privacy and a unique atmosphere for any special event. Available for weekend/Christmas house parties, weddings, birthdays, dinner parties and conferences.
Location: MAP 2:M4, OS Ref. ST302 303. Bridgwater 4m, Bristol 20m, Taunton 7m, M5/J24, A38 to North Petherton. 2½m SE of A38 at North Petherton via North Newton.
Open: Coaches & groups welcome by appointment. Caravan rally field available.
🔲 Functions. ⬜ Partial. 🔲 P ⬜ In grounds, on leads. ⬜ ⬜ ⬜ ⬜

MILTON LODGE GARDENS 🏛
Old Bristol Road, Wells, Somerset BA5 3AQ
Tel: 01749 672168   www.miltonlodgegardens.co.uk
Owner/Contact: S Tudway Quilter Esq
"The great glory of the gardens of Milton Lodge is their position high up on the slopes of the Mendip Hills to the north of Wells ... with broad panoramas of Wells Cathedral and the Vale of Avalon", (Lanning Roper). Charming, mature, Grade II listed terraced garden dating from 1909. Replanned 1962 with mixed shrubs, herbaceous plants, old fashioned roses and ground cover; numerous climbers; old established yew hedges. Fine trees in garden and in 7-acre arboretum across old Bristol Road.
Location: MAP 2:O3, OS Ref. ST549 470. ½m N of Wells from A39. N up Old Bristol Road. Free car park first gate on left.
Open: Garden & Arboretum: Easter–end Oct: Tues, Weds, Suns & BHs, 2–5pm. Parties & coaches by prior arrangement.
Admission: Adult £4, Children under 14 Free.
☐ ⚹ ⬜ Unsuitable. ☐ P ⬜

©NTPL/Rupert Truman

MONTACUTE HOUSE ✤
MONTACUTE, SOMERSET TA15 6XP

www.nationaltrust.org.uk

Tel: 01935 823289   **Fax:** 01935 826921   **E-mail:** montacute@nationaltrust.org.uk
Owner: The National Trust   **Contact:** The Property Manager
A glittering Elizabethan house, adorned with elegant chimneys, carved parapets and other Renaissance features, including contemporary plasterwork, chimney pieces and heraldic glass. The magnificent state rooms, including a long gallery which is the largest of its type in England, are full of fine 17th and 18th century furniture and Elizabethan and Jacobean portraits from the National Portrait Gallery.
Location: MAP 2:N5, OS Ref. ST499 172. In Montacute village, 4m W of Yeovil, on S side of A3088, 3m E of A303.
Open: House: 15 Mar–2 Nov: daily except Tue, 11am–5pm. Garden: 1–14 Mar: Wed–Sun, 11am–4pm: 15 Mar–2 Nov: Wed–Mon, 11am–6pm, 5 Nov–1 Jan 09: Wed–Sun, 11am–4pm. Closes dusk if earlier.
*Admission: House, Park & Garden: Adult £9.50, Child £4.50, Family £23.50. Groups (15+): Adult £8.30. Garden only: Adult £5.70, Child £2.80. (5 Nov–31 Jan 09): Adult £2, Child £1. Group organisers please book in writing to House Manager with a SAE. *includes a voluntary donation but visitors can choose to pay the standard prices displayed at the property and on the website.
☐ ⚹ ⬜ Partial. Braille guide. WC. ☐ 🔲 Licensed. Christmas lunches in Dec (must book). P ⬜ In park, on leads. ⬜ ⬜

MUCHELNEY ABBEY ⌗
Muchelney, Langport, Somerset TA10 0DG
Tel: 01458 250664   **Fax:** 01458 253842   www.english-heritage.org.uk/muchelney
Owner: English Heritage   **Contact:** Visitor Operations Staff
Well-preserved ruins of the cloisters, with windows carved in golden stone, and abbot's lodging of the Benedictine abbey, which survived by being used as a farmhouse after the Dissolution. Tactile displays and interactive video.
Location: MAP 2:N5, OS193 Ref. ST428 248. In Muchelney 2m S of Langport.
Open: 21 Mar–31 Oct: daily 10am–5pm (6pm in Jul & Aug, 4pm in Oct).
Admission: Adult £3.50, Child £1.80, Conc. £2.80. 15% discount for groups (11+). EH Members free.
🔲 WCs.☐ ⚹ ⬜ Partial. P ⬜ ⬜

NUNNEY CASTLE ⌗

Nunney, Somerset
Tel: 0117 9750700   www.english-heritage.org.uk/nunneycastle
Owner: English Heritage   **Contact:** Visitor Operations Staff
A small 14th century moated castle with a distinctly French style. Its unusual design consists of a central block with large towers at the angles.
Location: MAP 2:P3, OS183 Ref. ST737 457. In Nunney 3½m SW of Frome, 1m N of the A361.
Open: Any reasonable time.
Admission: Free.

ORCHARD WYNDHAM

Williton, Taunton, Somerset TA4 4HH
Tel: 01984 632309   **Fax:** 01984 633526
Owner: Wyndham Estate   **Contact:** Wyndham Estate Office
English manor house. Family home for 700 years encapsulating continuous building and alteration from the 14th to the 20th century.
Location: MAP 2:L4, OS Ref. ST072 400. 1m from A39 at Williton.
Open: Telephone for details.
Admission: Telephone for details.
[i] Obligatory & pre-booked. [P] Limited. No coach parking. In grounds, on leads.

PRIEST'S HOUSE

Muchelney, Langport, Somerset TA10 0DQ
Tel. 01458 253771 (Tenant)   www.nationaltrust.org.uk
Owner: The National Trust   **Contact:** The Administrator
A late medieval hall house with large gothic windows, originally the residence of priests serving the parish church across the road. Lived-in and recently repaired.
Location: MAP 2:N5, OS Ref. ST429 250. 1m S of Langport.
Open: 16 Mar–28 Sept: Sun & Mon, 2–5pm. Admission by guided tour. Last tour commences at 5pm.
Admission: Adult £3.30, Child £1.60. Not suitable for groups.
[i] No WC.

PRIOR PARK LANDSCAPE GARDEN

RALPH ALLEN DRIVE, BATH BA2 5AH

www.nationaltrust.org.uk

Tel: 01225 833422   **E-mail:** priorpark@nationaltrust.org.uk
Owner: The National Trust   **Contact:** Visitor Services Manager
Beautiful and intimate 18th century landscape garden created by Bath entrepreneur Ralph Allen with advice from the poet Alexander Pope and 'Capability' Brown. Sweeping valley with magnificent views of the City of Bath, Palladian bridge and three lakes. The recently completed Wilderness Project, supported by the Heritage Lottery Fund, is the final phase of restoration of this sustainably managed garden. Access to the Bath Skyline Walk (NT) from the garden. Disabled parking only, telephone for a 'how to get there' leaflet. Prior Park College, a co-educational school, operates from the mansion (not NT).
Location: MAP 2:P2, OS Ref. ST760 633. Frequent bus service from City Centre. First 2, City Sightseeing Skyline open top tour bus. Pick up from railway station & Abbey. Tour bus half price to NT members.
Open: 1 Mar–31 Oct: Wed–Mon, 11am–5.30pm. 1 Nov–31 Jan 09: Sat & Sun, 11am–dusk. Last adm. 1 hr before closing. Closed 25/26 Dec & 1 Jan. Closes dusk if earlier than 5.30pm.
***Admission:** Adult: £5, Child £2.80, Family £12.80. *includes a voluntary donation but visitors can choose to pay the standard prices displayed at the property and on the website.
Grounds. WC. Braille guide. Hearing Loop. Mar–Oct Sat & Sun [i] By arrangement. Nov–Feb. Tel for details (0870 458 4000) or visit website.

Nunney Castle

ROBIN HOOD'S HUT

Halswell, Goathurst, Somerset TA5 2EW
Tel: 01628 825925   **E-mail:** bookings@landmarktrust.org.uk
www.landmarktrust.org.uk
Owner/Contact: The Landmark Trust
Robin Hood's Hut is an 18th century garden building with two distinct faces. On one side it is a small rustic cottage, with thatched roof and bark clad door while on the other is an elegant pavilion complete with umbrello (or stone canopy). In the 1740s, Charles Kemeys Tynte began to transform the landscape around Halswell House into one of the finest Georgian gardens in the south west. He built several follies including Robin Hood's Hut in 1767. It is cared for by The Landmark Trust, a building preservation charity who let it for holidays. Full details of Robin Hood's Hut and 184 other historic and architecturally important buildings are featured in the Landmark Trust Handbook (price £11.50 refundable against a booking).
Location: MAP 2:M4, OS Ref. ST255 333.
Open: Available for holidays for up to 2 people throughout the year. Other visits by appointment. Please contact the Landmark Trust for details.
Admission: Free on Open Days.

THE ROMAN BATHS & PUMP ROOM

See page 231 for full page entry

STEMBRIDGE TOWER MILL

High Ham, Somerset TA10 9DJ
Tel: 01935 823289   www.nationaltrust.org.uk
Owner: The National Trust   **Contact:** The Administrator
The last thatched windmill in England, dating from 1822 and in use until 1910.
Location: MAP 2:N4, OS Ref. ST432 305. 2m N of Langport, ½m E of High Ham.
Open: 15 Mar–2 Nov, daily 11am–5pm (outstide viewing only, please respect privacy of holiday tenants in cottage). To enter mill: Easter Mon, early May BH Mon and Aug BH Mon, 11am–5pm.
Admission: Adult £2.70, Child £1.60. Arrangements may be made for school groups on 01935 827767.
[i] No WC. [P] Limited.

For unique **Civil wedding** venues see our index at the end of the book.

STOKE-SUB-HAMDON PRIORY 🦋

North Street, Stoke-sub-Hamdon, Somerset TA4 6QP
Tel: 01935 823289 **www.nationaltrust.org.uk**
Owner/Contact: The National Trust
A complex of buildings, begun in the 14th century for the priests of the chantry of St Nicholas, which is now destroyed. The Great Hall is open to visitors.
Location: MAP 2:N4, OS Ref. ST473 174. ½m S of A303. 2m W of Montacute between Yeovil and Ilminster.
Open: 15 Mar–2 Nov: daily, 10am–6pm or dusk if earlier. Not suitable for coaches.
Admission: Free.
ℹ No WC. 🅿 Limited. 🖼

TINTINHULL GARDEN 🦋

Farm Street, Tintinhull, Somerset BA22 9PZ
Tel: 01935 823289 **E-mail:** tintinhull@nationaltrust.org.uk
www.nationaltrust.org.uk
Owner: The National Trust   **Contact:** The Head Gardener
A delightful formal garden, created in the 20th century around a 17th century manor house. Small pools, varied borders and secluded lawns are neatly enclosed within walls and clipped hedges and there is also an attractive kitchen garden.
Location: MAP 2:O5, OS Ref. ST503 198. 5m NW of Yeovil, ½m S of A303, on E outskirts of Tintinhull.
Open: 15 Mar–2 Nov: Wed–Sun (open BH Mon), 11am–5pm (Tearoom 11am–4.30pm) or dusk if earlier.
***Admission:** Adult £5.40, Child £2.80, Family £13.50. No reduction for groups. *includes a voluntary donation but visitors can choose to pay the standard prices displayed at the property and on the website.
♿ 🅻 Grounds. Braille guide. 🐕 🅿 Limited. 🖼 🖼

TREASURER'S HOUSE 🦋

Martock, Somerset TA12 6JL
Tel: 01935 825015 **www.nationaltrust.org.uk**
Owner/Contact: The National Trust
A small medieval house, recently refurbished by The Trust. The two-storey hall was completed in 1293 and the solar block is even earlier.
Location: MAP 2:N5, OS Ref. ST462 191. 1m NW of A303 between Ilminster and Ilchester.
Open: 16 Mar–28 Sept: Sun–Tue, 2–5pm. Only medieval hall, wall paintings and kitchen are shown.
Admission: Adult £3.30, Child £1.60. Not suitable for groups.
ℹ No WC. 🅿 Limited for cars. None for coaches & trailer caravans.

TYNTESFIELD 🦋

Wraxall, North Somerset BS48 1NT
Tel: 01275 461900   **E-mail:** tyntesfield@nationaltrust.org.uk
Owner/Contact: The National Trust
Situated on a ridge overlooking the beautiful Land Yeo Valley, Tyntesfield was inspired and remodelled by John Norton in c1864 for William Gibbs, a successful merchant. The mansion is an extraordinary Gothic Revival extravaganza and survives intact with an unrivalled collection of Victorian decorative arts, an insight into life below stairs and a sumptuously decorated private chapel. Its surrounding 200ha (500 acres) of land includes formal gardens and a wonderful walled kitchen garden. Tyntesfield was saved for the nation by the National Trust in June 2002 with funding from the National Heritage Memorial Fund, other heritage partners and a £3 million public appeal. The property is now one of the most exciting projects of the National Trust due to its innovative approach to giving access to the ongoing conservation. Visitors should expect to see building and conservation work in progress and access to parts of the estate will be restricted for health and safety reasons.
Location: MAP 2:N2, OS Ref. ST506 715. Off B3128.
Open: House & Chapel: 1/2 & 8/9 Mar, Sat & Sun, 11am–5pm; 15 Mar–2 Nov, Sat–Wed, 11am–5pm. Garden, Shop & Kiosk: 1–9 Mar, Sat & Sun, 10.30am–5.30pm, 15 Mar–2 Nov, Sat–Wed, 10.30am–5.30pm, 6–21 Dec, Sat & Sun 10am–5pm. Open Good Fri. Last admission to house 1 hr before closing.
***Admission:** House, Chapel & Gardens: Adult £10.40, Child £5.25, Family £26. Gardens & Chapel only: Adult £5.25, Child £2.60, Family £13.10. Groups by appointment. *includes a voluntary donation but visitors can choose to pay the standard prices displayed at the property and on the website.
🖥 ♿ 🅻 Partial. 🐕 ✗ By arrangement. 🅿 🖼 🎫

WELLS CATHEDRAL

Cathedral Green, Wells, Somerset BA5 2UE
Tel: 01749 674483   **Fax:** 01749 832210
Owner: The Chapter of Wells   **Contact:** Mr John Roberts
Fine medieval Cathedral. The West Front with its splendid array of statuary, the Quire with colourful embroideries and stained glass, Chapter House and 1392 astronomical clock should not be missed.
Location: MAP 2:O3, OS Ref. ST552 458. In Wells, 20m S from both Bath & Bristol.
Open: Apr–Sept: 7am–7pm; Oct–Mar: 7am–6pm.
Admission: Suggested donation: Adult £5.50, Child/Student £2.50, OAP £4. Photo permit £3.

© Andrew Lawson

Cothay Manor & Gardens

www.hudsonsguide.co.uk

BOWOOD HOUSE & GARDENS

www.bowood.org

Bowood is the family home of the Marquis and Marchioness of Lansdowne. Begun c1720 for the Bridgeman family, the house was purchased by the 2nd Earl of Shelburne in 1754 and completed soon afterwards. Part of the house was demolished in 1955, leaving a perfectly proportioned Georgian home, over half of which is open to visitors. Robert Adam's magnificent Diocletian wing contains a splendid library, the laboratory where Joseph Priestley discovered oxygen gas in 1774, the orangery, now a picture gallery, the Chapel and a sculpture gallery in which some of the famous Lansdowne Marbles are displayed.

Among the family treasures shown in the numerous exhibition rooms are Georgian costumes, including Lord Byron's Albanian dress; Victoriana; Indiana (the 5th Marquess was Viceroy 1888–94); and superb collections of watercolours, miniatures and jewellery.

The House is set in one of the most beautiful parks in England. Over 2,000 acres of gardens and grounds were landscaped by 'Capability' Brown between 1762 and 1768, and are embellished with a Doric temple, a cascade, a pinetum and an arboretum. The Rhododendron Gardens are open for six weeks from late April to early June. All the walks have seats.

i Receptions, film location, 2,000 acre park, 40 acre lake, 18-hole golf course and Country Club, open to all players holding a current handicap.

Visitors may alight at the House before parking. WCs.

Self-service snacks, teas etc.

¶¶ The Restaurant (waitress service, capacity 85). Groups that require lunch or tea should book in advance.

On request, groups can be given introductory talk, or for an extra charge, a guided tour. Tour time 1¼ hrs. Guide sheets in French, German, Dutch, Spanish & Japanese.

P 1,000 cars, unlimited for coaches, 400 yds from house. Allow 2–3 hrs to visit house, gardens and grounds.

Special guide books. Picnic areas. Adventure playground.

Working assistance dogs only.

Owner
The Marquis of Lansdowne

Contact
The Administrator
Bowood House and Gardens
Calne
Wiltshire SN11 0LZ
Tel: 01249 812102
Fax: 01249 821757
E-mail:
houseandgardens@ bowood.org

Location
MAP 3:A2
OS Ref. ST974 700

From London M4/J17, off the A4 in Derry Hill village, midway between Calne and Chippenham. Swindon 17m, Bristol 26m, Bath 16m.

Bus: to the gate, 1½ m through park to House

Rail: Chippenham Station 5m.

Taxi: AA Taxis, Chippenham 657777.

Opening Times
House & Garden
19 March–4 November.
Daily, 11am–6pm.
Last admission 5pm (or 1hr earlier after the autumn clock change).

Rhododendron Walks
Off the A342
Chippenham to Devizes road, midway between Derry Hill and Sandy Lane.

Open daily for 6 weeks during the flowering season, usually from late April to early June, 11am–6pm.

We recommend visitors telephone or visit the website to check the progress of the flowering season.

Admission
House & Garden
Adult	£8.00
Child (5–15yrs)	£6.50
Child (2–4yrs)	£4.50
Senior Citizen	£7.00
Family (2+2)	£25.00

Groups (20+)	
Adult	£7.00
Child (5–15yrs)	£5.50
Child (2–4yrs)	£3.50
Senior Citizen	£6.00

Rhododendron Walks
Adult	£5.25
Senior Citizen	£4.75

Season Tickets available, ask for details.

£1 discount if combined with a visit to the House on the same day.

■ Owner
J Methuen-Campbell Esq

■ Contact
Corsham Court
Corsham
Wiltshire
SN13 0BZ

Tel/Fax: 01249 701610

■ Location
MAP 3:A2
OS Ref. ST874 706

Corsham Court is
signposted from the
A4, approx. 4m W
of Chippenham.
From Edinburgh, A1,
M62, M6, M5, M4, 8 hrs.
From London, M4, 2¼ hrs.
From Chester, M6, M5,
M4, 4 hrs.

Motorway: M4/J17 9m.

Rail: Chippenham
Station 6m.

Taxi: 01249 715959.

■ Opening Times
Summer
20 March–30 September
Daily except Mons & Fris
but including BH Mons
2–5.30pm
Last admission 5pm.

Winter
1 October–19 March
Weekends only
2–4.30pm
Last admission 4pm.

Closed December.

NB: Open throughout the
year by appointment only
for groups of 15+.

For further details and
special viewings of the
the collection, see our
website.

■ Admission
House & Garden
Adult	£6.50
Child (5–15yrs)	£3.00
OAP	£5.00

Groups
(includes 1 hr guided tour)
Adult	£5.00

Garden only
Adult	£2.50
Child (5–15yrs)	£1.50
OAP	£2.00

CORSHAM COURT 🏛

www.corsham-court.co.uk

Corsham Court is an Elizabethan house of 1582 and was bought by Paul Methuen in the mid-18th century, to house a collection of 16th and 17th century Italian and Flemish master paintings and statuary. In the middle of the 19th century the house was enlarged to receive a second collection, purchased in Florence, principally of fashionable Italian masters and stone-inlaid furniture.

Paul Methuen (1723–95) was a great-grandson of Paul Methuen of Bradford-on-Avon and cousin of John Methuen, ambassador and negotiator of the Methuen Treaty of 1703 with Portugal which permitted export of British woollens to Portugal and allowed a preferential 33⅓ percent duty discount on Portuguese wines, bringing about a major change in British drinking habits.

The architects involved in the alterations to the house and park were Lancelot 'Capability' Brown in the 1760s, John Nash in 1800 and Thomas Bellamy in 1845–9. Brown set the style by retaining the Elizabethan Stables and Riding School, but rebuilding the Gateway, retaining the gabled Elizabethan stone front and doubling the gabled wings at either end and inside, by designing the East Wing as Stateroom Picture Galleries. Nash's work has now largely disappeared, but Bellamy's stands fast, notably in the Hall and Staircase.

The State Rooms, including the Music Room and Dining Room, provide the setting for the outstanding collection of over 150 paintings, statuary, bronzes and furniture. The collection includes work by such names as Chippendale, the Adam brothers, Van Dyck, Reni, Rosa, Rubens, Lippi, Reynolds, Romney and a pianoforte by Clementi.

Gardens
'Capability' Brown planned to include a lake, avenues and specimen trees such as the Oriental Plane now with a 200-yard perimeter. The gardens, designed not only by Brown but also by Repton, contain a ha-ha, herbaceous borders, secluded gardens, lawns, a rose garden, a lily pool, a stone bath house and the Bradford Porch.

ⓘ Souvenir desk. No umbrellas, no photography.

♿ Visitors may alight at the entrance to the property, before parking in the allocated areas.

🚶 Max 45. If requested the owner may meet the group. Bookings for morning tours are preferred. Tour time 1hr.

🅿 120 yards from the house. Coaches may park in Church Square. Coach parties must book in advance. No camper vans, no caravans.

◼ Available: rate negotiable. A guide will be provided.

🐕 Must be kept on leads in the garden.

❄

LONGLEAT

www.longleat.co.uk

■ **Owner**
Marquess of Bath

■ **Contact**
Longleat
Warminster
Wiltshire BA12 7NW
Tel: 01985 844400
Fax: 01985 844885
E-mail: enquiries@
longleat.co.uk
www.longleat.co.uk

■ **Location**
MAP 2:P4
OS Ref. ST809 430
Just off the A36 between
Bath–Salisbury (A362
Warminster–Frome). 2hrs
from London following
M3, A303, A36, A362 or
M4/J18, A46, A36.
Rail: Warminster (5m) on
Cardiff/Portsmouth line.
Westbury (12m) on
Paddington/Penzance line.
Taxis at Warminster &
Westbury Stations.
Air: Bristol 30m.

■ **Opening Times**
House
All year, daily (except
Christmas Day).
16 Feb–2 Nov:
10am–5pm (5.30pm on
Sats & Suns, BHs & State
school holidays). Rest of
year: 11am–3pm, guided
tours only. Guided tours
may be subject to change
– please tel. for info.
Safari Park
16–24 Feb & 15 Mar–
2 Nov, daily. 1–9 Mar,
Sats & Suns. 10am–4pm
(5pm on Sats & Suns,
BHs & State school
holidays).
Other attractions
16–24 Feb & 15 Mar–
2 Nov, daily; 1–9 Mar,
Sats & Suns, 11am–5pm.
(10.30am–5.30pm on
Sats & Suns, BHs & State
school holidays).
Note: last adm. may be
earlier Feb/Mar, Oct/Nov.

Set within 900 acres of 'Capability' Brown landscaped grounds, Longleat House is widely regarded as one of the best examples of high Elizabethan architecture in Britain and one of the most beautiful stately homes open to the public.

Visited by Elizabeth I in 1574, Longleat House was built by Sir John Thynne from 1568 and is the current home of the 7th Marquess of Bath, Alexander Thynn. Many treasures are included within. The fine collection of paintings ranges from English portraits dating from the 16th century to the present day, to Dutch landscapes and Italian Old Masters.

Inspired by various Italian palace interiors, including the Ducal Palace in Venice, the ceilings are renowned for their ornate paintings and abundance of gilt made by the firm of John Dibblee Crace in the 1870s and 1880s. The furniture collection includes English pieces from as early as the 16th century, 17th century chairs from the Coromandel coast of India, fine French furniture of the 17th and 18th centuries and a collection of major Italian pieces very unusual for an English country house.

The Murals in the private apartments in the West Wing have been painted by the present Marquess and are a fascinating and unique addition to the House. Incorporating a mixture of oil paints and sawdust, these private works of art offer a unique insight into Lord Bath's personality and beliefs. Mural Tours can be booked at the Front Desk of Longleat House on the day of your visit. They are subject to availability. Groups can enjoy a private tour of Longleat House or Gardens with a dedicated tour guide and a talk tailor-made to their interests, before enjoying a gourmet meal in Lord Bath's Banqueting suite.

Apart from the ancestral home, Longleat is a wonderland of attractions just waiting to be explored! The star of BBC's hugely popular Animal Park series invites you to discover some of the world's most magnificent animals in the UK's first Safari Park, get lost in the Longleat Hedge Maze, voyage on the Safari Boats, journey on the Longleat Railway and much, much more!

■ **Admission**
House & Grounds
Adult   £10.00
Child (3–14yrs)   £6.00
Senior (60yrs+)   £6.00

Longleat Passport
(see below)
Adult   £22.00
Child (3–14yrs)   £16.00
Senior (60yrs+)   £16.00

Groups (12+)
Adult   £15.40
Child (3–14yrs)   £11.20
Senior (60yrs+)   £11.20

Longleat Passport includes:
*Longleat House, Safari Park, Safari Boats,
Longleat Hedge Maze, Pets Corner, Adventure
Castle (including Blue Peter Maze)*, Longleat
Railway, Motion Simulator, Butterfly Garden,
Postman Pat Village*, Old Joe's Mine,
Grounds & Gardens. *under 14yrs only*

ⓘ Rooms in Longleat House can be hired for conferences, gala dinners and product launches. Extensive parkland for company fun days, car launches and fishing. Film location.

🍽 Wessex Pavilion (200 capacity). Cellar Café (capacity 80), licensed. Not open all year.

👟 Individuals & Groups (max 20; 15 for Murals). Booking essential.

🅿 Ample.

🎒 Welcome with 1 teacher free entry per 8 children. Talks and packs available on request. Booking essential. Education sheets.

🐕 In grounds, on leads.

🔔 Orangery.

❄ House only.

■ **Conference/Function**

ROOM	SIZE	MAX CAPACITY
Great Hall	8 x 13m	120
Banqueting Suite	2 x (7 x 10m)	50
Green Library	7 x 13m	70
Wessex Pavilion	13 x 12m	200

South West – England

©NTPL / Nick Meers

■ Owner
The National Trust

■ Contact
The Estate Office
Stourton
Nr Warminster
BA12 6QD

Tel: 01747 841152
Fax: 01747 842005
E-mail: stourhead@
nationaltrust.org.uk

■ Location
MAP 2:P4
OS Ref. ST780 340

At Stourton off the
B3092, 3m NW of A303
(Mere), 8m S of A361
(Frome).

Rail: Gillingham 6½m;
Bruton 7m.

Bus: South West Coaches
80 Frome to Stourhead
on Sat; First 58/0A.

■ Opening Times
House
15 Mar–2 Nov: Fri–Tue,
11.30am–4.30pm or dusk
if earlier. Last admission
4pm.

Garden
All year: daily,
9am–7pm or dusk if
earlier.

King Alfred's Tower
15 Mar–2 Nov: daily,
11.30am–4.30pm.
Last admission: 4pm.

Restaurant
All year, daily
(closed 25 December),
Mar & Oct: 10am–5pm;
Apr–Sept: 10am–5.30pm;
Nov–Feb: 10.30am–4pm.

Shop & Plant Centre
All year, daily,
(closed 25 December)
Mar & Oct: 10am–5pm;
Apr–Sept: 10am–6pm;
Nov–Feb: 10.30am–4pm.

Farm Shop
All year, daily, 1 Apr–
30 Sept: 10am–6pm,
1 Oct–31 Mar:
10am–(telephone for
closing times).

■ *Admission
House & Garden
Adult	£11.60
Child	£5.80
Family	£27.60
Groups (15+)	£10.50

House OR Garden
Adult	£7.00
Child	£3.80
Family	£16.60
Groups (15+)	£5.70

King Alfred's Tower
Adult	£2.60
Child	£1.40
Family	£6 .00
Groups (15+)	£2.10

NB. Groups must book.

*includes a voluntary
donation but visitors can
choose to pay the standard
prices displayed at the
property and on the website.

STOURHEAD

www.nationaltrust.org.uk

Often referred to as "Paradise", Stourhead is an exquisite example of an English landscape garden. It was once described by Horace Walpole as *'one of the most picturesque scenes in the world'*.

Visitors can discover the inspiration behind Henry Hoare II's world famous garden, laid out between 1741 and 1780, and enjoy breathtaking views all year round.

The garden is dotted with Classical temples including the Pantheon and the Temple of Apollo, which provide dramatic backdrops to the majestic lake, secluded valley and mature woodland replete with exotic trees.

Stourhead House is an 18th century Palladian Mansion home to the beautifully restored Pope's Cabinet, furniture by the younger Chippendale and a magnificent collection of paintings. It is situated at the top of the gardens surrounded by lawns and parkland.

The Stourhead Estate extends east to King Alfred's Tower, a triangular folly 2½ miles from the House which affords stunning views across three counties, and is the perfect place for picnics.

Visitors can also enjoy breathtaking walks across Whitesheet Hill's chalk downs, and explore open countryside where native wildlife, including woodland birds, badgers, deer and wildflowers, can be seen.

The Restaurant offers fresh new flavours and local produce, there is an extensive Gift Shop and Plant Centre, and there are many opportunities to get involved with Stourhead's exciting Events Programme.

The Estate also comprises The Spread Eagle Inn, First View Art Gallery and Stourhead Farm Shop (all non NT).

New in 2008: the Stourhead Explorer tour is an interactive tour of the gardens. The new Basement Exhibition area is opening in the House in Spring with 'Servants', and the recently restored Pope's Cabinet is available to view.

©NTPL/Stephen Robson

Wheelchair accessible. Designated parking. Transfer available in main season to house & garden entrances. Powered mobility vehicles, recommended route map available. WCs.

Refreshment kiosk in Spread Eagle Courtyard during summer.

Licensed.

Group tours, by arrangement.

1 Nov–18 Mar only; on short fixed leads. Not in the House or Alfred's Tower.

WILTON HOUSE 🏛

www.wiltonhouse.com

Wilton House has been the ancestral home of the Earl of Pembroke and his family for 460 years. In 1544 Henry VIII gave the Abbey and lands of Wilton to Sir William Herbert who had married Anne Parr, sister of Katherine, sixth wife of King Henry.

The Clock Tower, in the centre of the east front, is reminiscent of this part of the Tudor building which survived a fire in 1647. Inigo Jones and John Webb were responsible for the rebuilding of the house in the Palladian style, whilst further alterations were made by James Wyatt from 1801.

The chief architectural features are the magnificent 17th century state apartments (including the famous Single and Double Cube rooms) and the 19th century cloisters.

The house contains one of the finest art collections in Europe, with over 230 original paintings on display, including works by Van Dyck, Rubens, Joshua Reynolds and Brueghel. Also on show are Greek and Italian statuary, a lock of Queen Elizabeth I's hair, Napoleon's despatch case, and Florence Nightingale's sash.

The Old Riding School houses a dynamic introductory film (narrated by Anna Massey), the reconstructed Tudor kitchen and the Estate's Victorian laundry. The house is set in magnificent landscaped parkland, bordered by the River Nadder which is the setting for the majestic Palladian Bridge. The 17th Earl of Pembroke was a keen gardener who created four new gardens after succeeding to the title in 1969 including the North Forecourt Garden, Old English Rose Garden, Water and Cloister Gardens.

ℹ Film location, fashion shows, product launches, equestrian events, garden parties, antiques fairs, concerts, vehicle rallies. No photography in house. French, German, Spanish, Italian, Japanese and Dutch information.

🎁

🌷

🍷 Exclusive banquets.

♿ Visitors may alight at the entrance. WCs.

🍴 Licensed.

🚶 By arrangement. £6.

P 200 cars and 12 coaches. Free coach parking. Group rates (min 15), drivers' meal voucher.

▪ Teachers' handbook for National Curriculum. EFL students welcome. Free preparatory visit for group leaders.

🐕 Guide dogs only.

🔔

■ **Owner**
The Earl of Pembroke

■ **Contact**
The Estate Office
Wilton
Salisbury SP2 0BJ
Tel: 01722 746714
Fax: 01722 744447
E-mail: tourism@
wiltonhouse.com

■ **Location**
MAP 3:B4
OS Ref. SU099 311

3m W of Salisbury along the A36.

Rail: Salisbury Station 3m.

Bus: Every 10 mins from Salisbury, Mon–Sat.

Taxi: City Cabs 0800 888888.

■ **Opening Times**
Summer

House, Old Riding School, Exhibitions & Restaurant
21–24 March &
5 April–31 August:
Sun–Thurs & BH Sats;
1–28 September:
Tue–Thurs.
12 noon–5pm.
Last admission 4.15pm.

Grounds
21–24 March,
5 April–28 September,
daily, 11am–5.30pm.
Last admission 4.30pm.

Winter
Closed except for bespoke tours and private groups by prior arrangement.

■ **Admission**
Summer
House, Grounds, ORS and Exhibitions
Adult	£12.00
Child (5–15)	£6.50
Concession	£9.75
Family	£29.50

Groups (15+)
Adult	£10.00
Child	£5.00
Concession	£8.00

Guided Tour
Adult	£6.00
Schoolchildren	£4.50

Grounds
Adult	£5.00
Child (5–15)	£3.50
Family	£15.00

Membership
From £20.00

■ **Special Events**

29 February–2 March
Annual Antiques Fair

12 July
BSO Fireworks Concert

Conference/Function

ROOM	SIZE	MAX CAPACITY
Double cube	60' x 30'	150
Exhibition Centre	50' x 40'	140
Film Theatre	34" x 20"	67

South West – England

©NTPL/David Norton

©NTPL/Wessex region

AVEBURY MANOR & GARDEN, AVEBURY STONE CIRCLE ✤ ✣
& ALEXANDER KEILLER MUSEUM
AVEBURY, Nr MARLBOROUGH, WILTSHIRE SN8 1RF
www.nationaltrust.org.uk

Tel: 01672 539250   **E-mail:** avebury@nationaltrust.org.uk

Owner: The National Trust   **Contact:** The Visitor Services Manager

Avebury Manor & Garden: A much-altered house of monastic origin, the present buildings date from the early 16th century, with notable Queen Anne alterations and Edwardian renovation by Col Jenner. The garden comprises tranquil 'rooms', featuring topiary and a succession of seasonal colour and contrast. The Manor House is occupied and furnished by private tenants, who open a part of it to visitors. Due to restricted space, guided tours are in operation. Tours run every 40 mins from 2pm, last tour 4.40pm. Following prolonged wet weather it may be necessary to close the house and garden.

Avebury Stone Circle (above left): One of Britain's finest, most impressive circles stands proud amidst the rolling Wiltshire landscape, steeped in 6,000 years of history.

Alexander Keiller Museum Barn & Galleries: The investigation of Avebury Stone Circle was largely the work of archaeologist and 'marmalade' millionaire Alexander Keiller in the 1930s. He put together one of the most important prehistoric archeological collections, which can be seen in the Stables Gallery. The 'Story of the Stones', the people who strove to reveal the true significance of Avebury's Stone Circle and the development of the Avebury landscape, are depicted through interactive displays in the spectacular 17th century thatched threshing barn.

Location: MAP 3:B2, OS Ref. SU101 701 (Avebury Manor). OS Ref. SU102 699 (Stone Circle). OS Ref. SU100 699 (Alexander Keiller Museum). 7m W of Marlborough, 1m N of the A4 on A4361 & B4003.

Open: Avebury Manor: 1 Apr–28 Oct, 2–4.40pm, Sun–Tue. **Garden:** 31 Mar–28 Oct, 11am–5pm, Fri–Tue. **Stone Circle:** All Year. Usual facilities may not be available around summer solstice 17–22 Jun. **Alexander Keiller Museum Barn & Galleries** (above right): 1 Feb–31 Oct, daily, 10am–5pm; 1 Nov–31 Jan 2009; daily 10am–4pm.Closed 24–26 Dec. Barn Gallery may close in very cold temperatures.

Admission: Avebury Manor: House & Garden: Adult £4, Child £2. Garden only: Adult £3, Child £1.50. Stone Circle: Free. **Alexander Keiller Museum Barn & Galleries:** Adult £4.20, Child £2.10, Family (2+3) £10.50, Family (1+3) £7.50. Groups (15+): Adult £3.60, Child £1.80. Discount when arriving by public transport or cycle. EH members free.

⊡ Keiller Museum & Shop. ⓹ Avebury Manor: ground floor with assistance & grounds; Avebury: ground floor fully accessible. WCs. Braille guide.

⬤ Avebury, licensed. **P** £5 (pay & display). ▣

⬜ No dogs in house, guide dogs only in garden (Avebury Manor). On leads in Stone Circle. ✤ Stone Circle.

BOWOOD HOUSE & GARDENS ⌂   *See page 241 for full page entry.*

BRADFORD-ON-AVON TITHE BARN ✣

Bradford-on-Avon, Wiltshire

Tel: 0117 975 0700   **www.english-heritage.org.uk/bradford**

Owner: English Heritage   **Contact:** South West Regional Office

A magnificent medieval stone-built barn with a slate roof and wooden beamed interior.

Location: MAP 2:P2, OS Ref. ST824 604. ¼m S of town centre, off B3109.

Open: Daily, 10.30am–4pm. Closed 25 Dec.

Admission: Free.

⓹ **P** Charged. ▣ ✤

BROADLEAS GARDENS

Devizes, Wiltshire SN10 5JQ

Tel: 01380 722035

Owner: Broadleas Gardens Charitable Trust   **Contact:** Lady Anne Cowdray

10 acres full of interest, notably The Dell, where the sheltered site allows plantings of magnolias, camellias, rhododendrons and azaleas.

Location: MAP 3:A3, OS Ref. SU001 601. Signposted SW from town centre at S end of housing estate, (coaches must use this entrance) or 1m S of Devizes on W side of A360.

Open: Apr–Oct: Sun, Weds & Thurs, 2–6pm or by arrangement for groups.

Admission: Adult £5.50, Child (under 10yrs) £2, Groups (10+) £5.

CORSHAM COURT ⌂   *See page 242 for full page entry.*

GREAT CHALFIELD MANOR & GARDENS ✤

Nr Melksham, Wiltshire SN12 8NH

Tel: 01225 782239   **www.nationaltrust.org.uk**

Owner: The National Trust   **Contact:** The Tenant

Charming 15th century manor with Arts and Crafts gardens c1910. The manor sits between an upper moat, gatehouse and earlier parish church. Beautiful oriel windows and rooftop soldiers (c1480) adorn the house restored between 1905 and 1911 by Major R Fuller whose family live here and manage the property on behalf of the National Trust. Alfred Parsons designed the gardens, with walls, paths, terraces, gazebo and lily pond. There are large borders, lawn and roses surrounding a well. Grass paths offer romantic views across the spring fed fishpond which lies above the brook.

Location: MAP 3:A2, OS Ref. ST860 631. 3m SW of Melksham off B3107 via Broughton Gifford Common, sign for Atworth. Rail: Bradford-on-Avon 3m, Chippenham 10m.

Open: Manor (guided tours only): 30 Mar–2 Nov, Tue–Thur, 11.30am, 12.15pm, 2.15pm, 3pm & 3.45pm, Sun, 2.15pm, 3pm & 3.45pm. Garden: 30 Mar–2 Nov, Tue–Thur, 11am–5pm, Sun, 2–5pm. The tours take 45 mins and numbers are limited to 25. Visitors arriving during a tour can visit the adjoining parish church and garden first. Note: Group visits are welcome on Fri & Sat (not BHs) by written arrangement with the tenant Mrs Robert Floyd, charge applies. Organisers of coach parties should allow 2 hrs because of limit on numbers in the house.

Admission: Adult £6.40, Child £3.20, Family (2+2) £16.30. Groups £5.40, Child £2.70. Garden only: Adult £4.20 Child £2.10.

⓹ Ground floor with assistance. Limited access to Garden. WC. Ⓘ Obligatory. **P** Limited. ▣

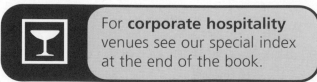

LONGLEAT 🏛   *See page 243 for full page entry.*

LYDIARD PARK
LYDIARD TREGOZE, SWINDON, WILTSHIRE SN5 3PA

www.lydiardpark.org.uk

Tel: 01793 770401   **Fax:** 01793 770968   **E-mail:** lydiardpark@swindon.gov.uk
Owner: Swindon Borough Council   **Contact:** The Keeper
Lydiard Park is the ancestral home of the Viscounts Bolingbroke. This beautifully restored Palladian house contains the family's furnishings and portraits, exceptional plasterwork, rare 17th century window and room devoted to the 18th century society artist Lady Diana Spencer. The faithfully restored 18th century ornamental Walled Garden is a beautiful and tranquil place to stroll, with seasonal displays of flowers and unique garden features. Exceptional monuments, including the Golden Cavalier, in the adjacent church.
Location: MAP 3:B1, OS Ref. SU104 848. 4m W of Swindon, 1½ m N of M4/J16.
Open: House: Tues–Sun, 11am–5pm (4pm Nov–Feb). Grounds: all day, closing at dusk. Victorian Christmas decorations in December.
Admission: Adult £3.50, Child £1.75, Senior Citizen £3. Pre-booked groups; Adult £3, Senior £2.50. Times and prices may change April 2008 – please telephone to confirm.
ℹ️ No photography in house. Open all year, but groups must book. By arrangement. In grounds on leads.

HAMPTWORTH LODGE 🏛
HAMPTWORTH, LANDFORD, SALISBURY, WILTSHIRE SP5 2EA

www.hamptworthestate.co.uk

Tel: 01794 390700   **Fax:** 01794 390644
E-mail: enquiries@hamptworthestate.co.uk
Contact: N D Anderson Esq/Miss K Anderson
Jacobean style manor house standing in mature deciduous woodland within the northern perimeter of the New Forest National Park. Grade II* with period furniture including clocks. The Great Hall has an unusual roof truss construction. There is a collection of prentice pieces and the Moffatt collection of contemporary copies. One room has late 17th century patterned wall hangings. Available for events.
Location: MAP 3:C5, OS Ref. SU227 195. 10m SE of Salisbury on road linking Downton on A338. (Salisbury to Ringwood road) to Landford on A36 (Salisbury to Southampton road).
Open: House and Garden: 17 Mar–21 May, Mons (closed 24 Mar & 5 May), Tues & Weds. 2.15–5.pm. Private groups and coaches by prior appointment.
Admission: Adult £5, Child (under 11yrs) Free. Gardens £1.
Ground floor & grounds. Obligatory.

LACOCK ABBEY, FOX TALBOT MUSEUM & VILLAGE
LACOCK, CHIPPENHAM, WILTSHIRE SN15 2LG

www.nationaltrust.org.uk

Tel: 01249 730459 (Visitor Reception)   **Fax:** 01249 730501 (Estate Office)
Owner: The National Trust   **Contact:** The Property Manager
Founded in 1232 and converted into a country house c1540, the fine medieval cloisters, sacristy, chapter house and monastic rooms of the abbey have survived largely intact. The handsome stable courtyard has half-timbered gables, a clockhouse, brewery and bakehouse. Victorian rose garden and a woodland garden boasting a fine display of spring flowers and magnificent trees. The Fox Talbot Museum commemorates William Fox Talbot, a previous resident of the Abbey and inventor of the modern photographic negative. The village has many limewashed half-timbered and stone houses, featured in the TV and film productions of *Pride & Prejudice*, *Moll Flanders*, *Emma* and the recent *Harry Potter* films.
Location: MAP 3:A2, OS Ref. ST919 684. In the village of Lacock, 3m N of Melksham, 3m S of Chippenham just E of A350.
Open: Museum: 23 Feb–2 Nov, Daily, 11am–5.30pm; 8 Nov–21 Dec & 3 Jan–15 Feb 09, Weekends only, 11am–4pm. Grounds & Cloisters: 1 Mar–2 Nov, daily, 11am–5.30pm. Abbey Rooms: 15 Mar–2 Nov, daily (closed Tue), 1–5.30pm. Shop: 23 Feb–14 Mar & 3 Nov–15 Feb 09, daily 11am–4pm; 15 Mar–2 Nov, daily, 10am–5.30pm.
Admission: Abbey Rooms, Museum, Cloisters & Grounds: Adult £10, Child £5, Family (2+2) £25.50. Groups: Adult £8.50, Child £4.30. **Abbey Rooms, Cloisters & Grounds:** Adult £8, Child £4, Family (2+2) £20.40. Groups: Adult £6.80, Child £3.40. **Museum, Cloisters & Grounds:** Adult £6, Child £3, Family (2+2) £15.30. Groups: Adult £5.20, Child £2.60.
Braille guides. By arrangement.

THE MERCHANT'S HOUSE
132 HIGH STREET, MARLBOROUGH, WILTSHIRE SN8 1HN

www.merchantshouse.co.uk

Tel/Fax: 01672 511491   **E-mail:** manager@merchantshousetrust.co.uk
Owner: Marlborough Town Council,
leased to The Merchant's House (Marlborough) Trust   **Contact:** Michael Gray
Situated in Marlborough's world-famous High Street, The Merchant's House is one of the finest middle-class houses in England. Its well-preserved Panelled Chamber was completed in 1656. Both the Dining Room and Great Staircase display recently uncovered 17th century wall paintings which have aroused much expert interest. Latest attraction is our 17th century formal garden.
Location: MAP 3:B2, OS Ref. SU188 691. N side of High Street, near Town Hall.
Open: Easter–end Sept: Fris & Sats, 11am–4pm. Booked groups at other times by appointment.
Admission: Adult £4, Child 50p. Booked groups (10-40): Adult £3, Child 50p.
ⓘ Photography only by arrangement. ⬚ ⬚ ⬚ Ⓟ Outside house, also in Hillier's Yard. ♿ Guide dogs only. ⬚

NEWHOUSE 🏛
REDLYNCH, SALISBURY, WILTSHIRE SP5 2NX

Tel: 01725 510055   **Fax:** 01725 510284
Owner: George & June Jeffreys   **Contact:** Mrs Jeffreys
A brick, Jacobean 'Trinity' House, c1609, with two Georgian wings and a basically Georgian interior. Home of the Eyre family since 1633.
Location: MAP 3:B5, OS184, SU218 214. 9m S of Salisbury between A36 & A338.
Open: 3 Mar–10 Apr, Mon–Fri & 25 Aug: 2–5pm.
Admission: Adult £3.50, Child £2.50, Conc. £3.50. Groups (15+): Adult £3, Child £2.50, Conc. £3.
ⓘ No photography in house, except at weddings. ⬚ ⬚ By arrangement. Ⓟ Limited for coaches. ♿ Guide dogs only. ⬚

NORRINGTON MANOR
Alvediston, Salisbury, Wiltshire SP5 5LL
Tel: 01722 780367   **Fax:** 01722 780667
Owner/Contact: Mrs S Sykes
Built in 1377 it has been altered and added to in every century since, with the exception of the 18th century. Only the hall and the 'undercroft' remain of the original. It is currently a family home and the Sykes are only the third family to own it.
Location: MAP 3:A5, OS Ref. ST966 237. Signposted to N of Berwick St John and Alvediston road (half way between the two villages).
Open: By appointment in writing.
Admission: A donation to the local churches is asked for.
♿ Unsuitable. ⬚ By arrangement. Ⓟ Limited for cars, none for coaches. ⬚ ⬚

©NTPL/Peter Cook

MOMPESSON HOUSE 🌿
THE CLOSE, SALISBURY, WILTSHIRE SP1 2EL

www.nationaltrust.org.uk

Tel: 01722 335659   **Infoline:** 01722 420980   **Fax:** 01722 321559
E-mail: mompessonhouse@nationaltrust.org.uk
Owner: The National Trust   **Contact:** The Property Manager
An elegant and spacious 18th century house in the Cathedral Close. Featured in the award-winning film Sense and Sensibility and with magnificent plasterwork and a fine oak staircase. As well as pieces of good quality period furniture the house also contains the Turnbull collection of 18th century drinking glasses. Outside, the delightful walled garden has a pergola and traditional herbaceous borders.
Location: MAP 3:B4, OS Ref. SU142 297. On N side of Choristers' Green in Cathedral Close, near High Street Gate.
Open: 15 Mar–2 Nov: Sat–Wed, 11am–5pm. Last admission 4.30pm. Open Good Fri.
*Admission: Adult £4.95, Child £2.45, Family (2+2) £12.40. Groups: £4.45. Garden only: £1. Reduced rate when arriving by public transport. *includes a voluntary donation but visitors can choose to pay the standard prices displayed at the property and on the website.
⬚ ♿ Ground floor & grounds. Braille guide. WC. ⬚ ⬚ By arrangement. ⬚ ⬚

The Merchant's House

OLD SARUM ⬚

CASTLE ROAD, SALISBURY, WILTSHIRE SP1 3SD

www.english-heritage.org.uk/oldsarum

Tel: 01722 335398 **Fax:** 01722 416037
E-mail: customers@english-heritage.org.uk
Owner: English Heritage   **Contact:** Visitor Operations Team

Built around 500BC by the Iron Age peoples, Old Sarum is the former site of the first cathedral and ancient city of Salisbury. A prehistoric hillfort in origin, Old Sarum was occupied by the Romans, the Saxons, and eventually the Normans who made it into one of their major strongholds, with a motte-and-bailey castle built at its centre. Old Sarum eventually grew into one of the most dramatic settlements in medieval England as castle, cathedral, bishop's palace and thriving township. When the new city we know as Salisbury was founded in the early 13th century the settlement faded away. With fine views of the surrounding countryside, Old Sarum is an excellent special events venue.

Location: MAP 3:B4, OS184, SU138 327. 2m N of Salisbury off A345.
Open: 21 Mar–30 Jun & Sept: daily, 10am–5pm. Jul & Aug: daily, 9am–6pm. Oct: daily, 10am–4pm. Nov–Feb: 11am–3pm, daily. Closed 24–26 Dec & 1 Jan.
Admission: Adult £3, Child £1.50, Conc. £2.40. 15% discount for groups (11+). EH Members Free.

ℹ WCs. ⬚ ⬚ Grounds. ⬚ Jul/Aug. **P** ⬚ Grounds, on leads. ⬚ ⬚

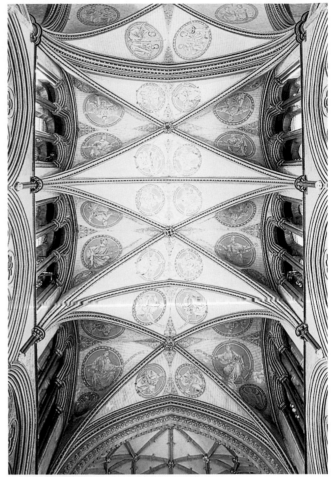

Salisbury Cathedral

OLD WARDOUR CASTLE ⬚

Nr TISBURY, WILTSHIRE SP3 6RR

www.english-heritage.org.uk/oldwardour

Tel/Fax: 01747 870487   **E-mail:** customers@english-heritage.org.uk
Owner: English Heritage   **Contact:** Visitor Operations Team

In a picture-book setting, the unusual hexagonal ruins of this 14th century castle stand on the edge of a beautiful lake, surrounded by landscaped grounds which include an elaborate rockwork grotto.

Location: MAP 3:A5, OS184, ST939 263. Off A30 2m SW of Tisbury.
Open: 21 Mar–31 Oct: daily, 10am–5pm (Jul & Aug, 6pm). Oct, 4pm). 1 Nov–31 Mar: Sats & Suns, 10am–4pm. Closed 24–26 Dec & 1 Jan.
Admission: Adult £3.50, Child £1.80, Conc. £2.80. Groups (11+): 15% discount. EH Members Free.

ℹ WCs. ⬚ ⬚ Grounds. ⬚ **P** ⬚ Grounds, on leads. ⬚ ⬚ ⬚

THE PETO GARDEN AT IFORD MANOR ⛪

BRADFORD-ON-AVON, WILTSHIRE BA15 2BA

www.ifordmanor.co.uk

Tel: 01225 863146   **Fax:** 01225 862364
Owner/Contact: Mrs E A J Cartwright-Hignett

This unique Grade I Italian-style garden is set on a romantic hillside beside the River Frome. Designed by the Edwardian architect Harold A Peto, who lived at Iford Manor from 1899–1933, the garden has terraces, a colonnade, cloister, casita, statuary, evergreen planting and magnificent rural views. Renowned for its tranquillity and peace, the Peto Garden won the 1998 HHA/Christie's *Garden of the Year* Award.

Location: MAP 2:P3, OS Ref. ST800 589. 7m SE of Bath via A36, signposted Iford. ½m SW of Bradford-on-Avon via Westwood on B3109.
Open: Apr & Oct: Suns only & Easter Mon, 2–5pm. May–Sept: Tue–Thur, Sats, Suns & BH Mons, 2–5pm. Children under 10yrs welcome weekdays only for safety reasons.
Admission: Adult £4.50, Conc, Students & Children £4. Groups (10+) welcome outside normal opening hours, by arrangement only, £5.

⬚ Partial. WCs. ⬚ Teas (May–Aug: Sats, Suns & BHs, 2.30–5pm). ⬚ By arrangement. **P** Limited for coaches. ⬚ On leads, in grounds.

© Steve Day

SALISBURY CATHEDRAL
33 THE CLOSE, SALISBURY SP1 2EJ

www.salisburycathedral.org.uk

Tel: 01722 555120 **Fax:** 01722 555116 **E-mail:** visitors@salcath.co.uk

Owner: The Dean & Chapter **Contact:** Visitor Services

In 2008, arguably Britain's finest 13th century gothic Cathedral is celebrating the 750th anniversary of the dedication of the completed Cathedral in 1258. Dates for some of the events to mark this occasion include:

25 April–30 September	Anniversary Exhibition in the Cloisters
26 April	Cathedral Open Day – including free entry to Salisbury & South Wiltshire Museum, The Rifles Museum and the garden of Mompesson House
4–5 May	Medieval Fair
17 May	Elgar's *Dream of Gerontius* Berlin Philharmonic Choir Salisbury Musical Society Chelsea Opera Group Orchestra
17–21 June	Flower Festival
5 July	A Vaughan Williams concert Salisbury Musical Society Salisbury Symphony Orchestra
End September	Major Anniversary Service

For more information on the 750th anniversary events please visit www.salisburycathedral.org.uk/750.php

Inside the Cathedral discover the best preserved original Magna Carta (AD 1215), and the oldest working clock (AD1386) in Europe. Boy and girl choristers sing daily services continuing a tradition of worship that dates back centuries.

Take a tower tour to explore Britain's tallest Spire and experience the breathtaking views down the length of the Nave and, from the top of the tower, out across Salisbury.

Location: MAP 3:B4, OS Ref. SU143 295. S of City. M3, A303, A30 from London or A36.

Open: All year daily: 7.15am–6.15pm.

Admission: Suggested donation: Adult £5, Child (5–17) £3, Conc. £4.25, Family (2+2) £12. Some 750 festival events require ticket purchase.

⬜ 🅣 ♿ 💺 Licensed. 🍴 🅕 By arrangement. 🅿 In city centre. ▣
🐕 In grounds, on leads. ❄ 💺

STOURHEAD ❧ *See page 244 for full page entry.*

STOURTON HOUSE FLOWER GARDEN

Stourton, Warminster, Wiltshire BA12 6QF

Tel: 01747 840417

Owner/Contact: Mrs E Bullivant

Four acres of peaceful, romantic, plantsman's garden. Rare daffodils, camellias, rhododendrons, roses, hydrangeas and wild flowers.

Location: MAP 2:P4, OS Ref. ST780 340. A303, 2m NW of Mere next to Stourhead car park. Follow blue signs.

Open: Apr–end Nov: Weds, Thurs, Suns, and BH Mons, 11am–6pm. Plants & dried flowers for sale during the winter on weekdays. Groups any day.

Admission: Adult £3.50, Child 50p.

WILTON HOUSE 🏛 *See page 245 for full page entry.*

© NTPL/Ian Shaw

Stourhead

STONEHENGE ⌗
AMESBURY, WILTSHIRE SP4 7DE
www.english-heritage.org.uk/stonehenge

Tel: 0870 3331181 (Customer Services)

Owner: English Heritage

The mystical and awe-inspiring stone circle at Stonehenge is one of the most famous prehistoric monuments in the world, designated by UNESCO as a World Heritage Site. Stonehenge's orientation on the rising and setting sun has always been one of its most remarkable features. Whether this was simply because the builders came from a sun-worshipping culture, or because – as some scholars have believed – the circle and its banks were part of a huge astronomical calendar, remains a mystery. Visitors to Stonehenge can discover the history and legends which surround this unique stone circle, which began over 5,000 years ago, with a complimentary three part audio tour available in 9 languages (subject to availability).

Location: MAP 3:B4, OS Ref. SU123 422. 2m W of Amesbury on junction of A303 and A344 / A360.

Open: 21 Mar–31 May: daily 9.30am–6pm. 1 Jun–31 Aug: daily, 9am–7pm. 1 Sept–15 Oct: daily, 9.30am–6pm. 16 Oct–15 Mar: daily, 9.30am–4pm. 26 Dec–1 Jan, 12 noon–4pm. Closed 24/25 Dec. Last recommended admission is ½ hr before advertised closing times and the site will be closed promptly 20 mins after the advertised closing times. Summer Solstice: 20–22 Jun, opening times may be amended.

Admission: Adult £6.50, Child £3.30, Conc £5.20, Family (2+3) £16.30. Groups (11+) 10% discount. NT/EH Members Free.

ℹ️ WCs. ▢ ♿ ♨ ☕ ♿ 🅿 ✖ ❀

The Library, Bowood House.

Eastern Region

East Anglia has magical coastal areas ranging from The Wash in Norfolk down to the Essex marshes. The half timbered houses in Suffolk villages such as Lavenham contrast with the Norfolk flint found further north. Among the major properties that welcome visitors are Sandringham, the country home of HM The Queen, Woburn Abbey and Hatfield House; but off the beaten track find time for Copped Hall or The Manor, Hemingford Grey.

Bedfordshire

Cambridgeshire

Essex

Hertfordshire

Norfolk

Suffolk

■ Owner:
The Duke and Duchess of Bedford & The Trustees of Bedford Estates

■ Contact
William Lash
Woburn Abbey
Woburn
Bedfordshire MK17 9WA

Tel: 01525 290333
Fax: 01525 290271
E-mail: admissions@ woburnabbey.co.uk

■ Location
MAP 7:D10
OS Ref. SP965 325

On A4012, midway between M1/J13, 3m, J14, 6m and the A5 (turn off at Hockliffe). London approx. 1hr by road (43m).

Rail: London Euston to Leighton Buzzard, Bletchley/Milton Keynes. Kings Cross Thameslink to Flitwick.

Air: Luton 14m. Heathrow 39m.

■ Opening Times
Woburn Abbey
15 March–28 September: daily, 11am–4pm (last entry).

Deer Park
All year: Daily 10am–5pm. (except 24–26 December).

Antiques Centre
All year: Daily 10am–5.30pm. (except 24–26 December).

■ Admission
Woburn Abbey, Grounds, Deer Park & Car Park
Please telephone for details. Group rates available. Reduced rates apply when Private Apartments are in use by the family.

WOBURN ABBEY
www.discoverwoburn.co.uk

Set in a beautiful 3,000 acre deer park, Woburn Abbey has been the home of the Russell Family for nearly 400 years, and is now occupied by the 15th Duke of Bedford and his family.

The Abbey houses one of the most important private art collections in the world, including paintings by Gainsborough, Reynolds, Van Dyck, Cuyp, and Canaletto, 21 of whose views hang in the Venetian Room.

The tour of the Abbey covers three floors, including the vaults, with 18th Century French and English furniture, silver and a wide range of porcelain on display. Amongst the highlights is the Sèvres dinner service presented to the 4th Duke by Louis XV of France.

The Deer Park is home to ten species of deer, including the Père David, descended from the Imperial Herd of China, which was saved from extinction at Woburn and is now the largest breeding herd of this species in the world. In 1985 the 14th Duke gave 22 Père David deer to the People's Republic of China and the herd is now well established in its natural environment and numbers several hundred.

Woburn Abbey is also noted for its excellent and unique Antiques Centre with over 70 dealers represented, housed behind original 18th century shop fronts and show cases, and has an enviable reputation for its in-house catering. Woburn Abbey specialises in banqueting, conferences, receptions and company days; and the Sculpture Gallery overlooking the Private Gardens provides a splendid setting for weddings and wedding receptions.

2008 will see a number of events in the Park including the 28th de Havilland Moth Club Fly-In, Craft Fairs and a variety of musical and theatrical performances.

i Suitable for fashion shows, product launches and company 'days out'. Use of parkland and garden. No photography in House.

Conferences, exhibitions, banqueting, luncheons, dinners in the Sculpture Gallery, Lantern & Long Harness rooms.

Group bookings in Sculpture Gallery. Flying Duchess Pavilion Coffee Shop.

Licensed.

£17.50, by arrangement, max 8. Tours in French, German & Italian available. Guide book available £5. Special interest tours can be arranged.

P

Please telephone for details.

In park on leads, and guide dogs in house.

Conference/Function

ROOM	SIZE	MAX CAPACITY
Sculpture Gallery	128' x 24'	300 / 250 (sit-down)
Lantern Rm	44' x 21'	60
Long Harness Room	35' x 21'	80

BUSHMEAD PRIORY ⌗

Colmworth, Bedford, Bedfordshire MK44 2LD
Tel: 01799 522842   **Regional Office:** 01223 582700
www.english-heritage.org.uk/bushmead
Owner: English Heritage   **Contact:** Visitor Operations Team
A rare survival of the medieval refectory of an Augustinian priory, with its original timber-framed roof almost intact and containing interesting wall paintings and stained glass.
Location: MAP 7:E9, OS Ref. TL115 607. On unclassified road near Colmworth; off B660, 2m S of Bolnhurst. 5m W of St. Neots (A1).
Open: 1 May–31 Aug. Pre-booked guided tours on first Sat of the month only, please call 01525 860000 to book.
Admission: Adult £5 Child £2.50, Conc. £4. Group discount. EH members Free.
ⓘ Picnickers welcome. 🅿 ⊠

CECIL HIGGINS ART GALLERY

Castle Lane, Bedford MK40 3RP
Tel: 01234 211222   **Fax:** 01234 327149   **E-mail:** chag@bedford.gov.uk
www.cecilhigginsartgallery.org
Owner: Bedford Borough Council & Trustees of Gallery   **Contact:** The Gallery
The Cecil Higgins Art Gallery is now closed for refurbishment and is due to re-open in 2009. Work on the adjoining Bedford Gallery and Hexagon building is due to be completed in 2008 providing additional space for exhibitions, events and corporate hospitality.
Location: MAP 7:E9, OS Ref. TL052 497. Centre of Bedford, just off The Embankment E of High St.
Open: Will re-open in 2009.
Admission: Free.
ⓘ Photography in house by arrangement. ▣ ⊤ By arrangement. ⬱
▣ Self-service coffee bar. ⌶ By arrangement. ■ ⊠ Guide dogs only. ✳ ⛉

DE GREY MAUSOLEUM ⌗

Flitton, Bedford, Bedfordshire
Tel: 01525 860094 (Key-keeper)
www.english-heritage.org.uk/degreymausoleum
Owner: English Heritage   **Contact:** Mrs Stimson
A remarkable treasure-house of sculpted tombs and monuments from the 16th to 19th centuries dedicated to the de Grey family of nearby Wrest Park.
Location: MAP 7:D10, OS Ref. TL059 359. Attached to the church on unclassified road 1½m W of A6 at Silsoe.
Open: Sats & Suns. Contact keyholder in advance: Mrs Stimson, 3 Highfield Rd, Flitton.
Admission: Free.
ⓘ Picnickers welcome.

HOUGHTON HOUSE ⌗

Ampthill, Bedford, Bedfordshire
Tel: 01223 582700 (Regional Office)
www.english-heritage.org.uk/houghton
Owner: English Heritage   **Contact:** East of England Regional Office
The shell of a 17th century mansion with magnificent views, reputedly the inspiration for the 'House Beautiful' in John Bunyan's *Pilgrim's Progress*. Built around 1615 for Mary, Dowager Countess of Pembroke, in a mixture of Jacobean and Classical styles: the ground floors of two Italianate loggias survive, possibly the work of Inigo Jones. Houghton House has recently undergone major conservation work. The greatly enhanced condition of the house will also be shortly augmented with a new interpretation scheme for the site.
Location: MAP 7:E9, OS Ref. TL039 394. 1m NE of Ampthill off A421, 8m S of Bedford.
Open: Any reasonable time.
Admission: Free.
ⓘ Picnickers welcome. 🅿 ⊠ ✳

MOGGERHANGER PARK

Park Road, Moggerhanger, Bedfordshire MK44 3RW
Tel: 01767 641007   **Fax:** 01767 641515
E-mail: enquiries@moggerhangerpark.com   **www.moggerhangerpark.com**
Owner: Moggerhanger House Preservation Trust   **Contact:** Mrs Jenny Cooper
Outstanding Georgian Grade I listed Country House, recently restored in keeping with the original design of architect, Sir John Soane and set in 33 acres of parkland originally landscaped by Humphry Repton. Moggerhanger House has 3 executive conference suites and 2 function rooms, making an ideal venue for conferences, promotions and corporate entertainment.
Location: MAP 7:E9, OS Ref. TL048 475. On A603, 3m from A1 at Sandy, 6m from Bedford.
Open: House Tours: Jun–Sept: Grounds, Tearooms & Visitors' Centre: All year.
Admission: Please telephone 01767 641007.
ⓘ No photography. No smoking. ▣ ⊤ ⬱ ▣ Licensed. 🍴 Licensed.
⌶ By arrangement. 🅿 Limited for coaches. ⊠ In grounds, on leads. ✳

SWISS GARDEN

Old Warden Park, Bedfordshire
Tel: 01767 627927   **www.shuttleworth.org**
Operated By: The Shuttleworth Trust
The Swiss Garden, Old Warden Park, Bedfordshire, created in the 1820s by Lord Ongley, is a late Regency garden and an outstanding example of the Swiss picturesque. The Swiss Cottage provides the main element for this unusual and atmospheric garden. It provides the principal aspect for a number of contrived vistas which lead the eye towards this attractive thatched structure. Interesting things to see in the garden are, a grotto and fernery, a thatched tree shelter, an Indian Pavilion, two ponds and many fine specimens of shrubs and conifers, plus some remarkable trees.
Location: MAP 7:E9, OS Ref. TL150 447. 1½m W of Biggleswade A1 roundabout, signposted from A1 and A600.
Open: Apr–Oct: 10am–5pm; Nov–Mar: 10am–4pm. Closed Christmas week.
Admission: Adult £5, Child Free, Conc. £4. Special rates for groups, tours & private hire.
✳ ⬱ ⊤ Catering. ▣ Refreshments adjacent. 🅿 ⊠ ▲ ✳

TURVEY HOUSE 🏛

Turvey, Bedfordshire MK43 8EL
Tel/Fax: 01234 881244   **E-mail:** danielhanbury@hotmail.com
Owner: The Hanbury Family   **Contact:** Daniel Hanbury
A neo-classical house set in picturesque parkland bordering the River Great Ouse. The principal rooms contain a fine collection of 18th and 19th century English and Continental furniture, pictures, porcelain, *objets d'art* and books. Walled Garden.
Location: MAP 7:D9, OS Ref. SP939520. Between Bedford and Northampton on A428.
Open: 5/6, 8, 20, 22, 24–26 & 29 May. 3, 5, 7/8 17, 19, 21/22 Jun. 1, 3, 5/6, 15, 17, 19/20, 29, 31 Jul. 25 Aug, 2–5pm.
Admission: Adult £5, Child £3.
ⓘ No photography in house. ⬱ Partial. ⌶ Obligatory.
🅿 Ample for cars, none for coaches. ⊠

WREST PARK ⌗

SILSOE, LUTON, BEDFORDSHIRE MK45 4HS

www.english-heritage.org.uk/wrest

Tel: 01525 860152
Owner: English Heritage   **Contact:** Visitor Operations Team
Over 90 acres of enchanting gardens originally laid out in the early 18th century, and inspired by the great gardens of Versailles and the Loire Valley in France. Marvel at the magnificent collection of stone and lead statuary, the Bath House and the vast Orangery, built by the Earl de Grey, and dream of days gone by. The gardens form a delightful backdrop to the house which is built in the style of an 18th century French château.
Location: MAP 7:E10, OS153, TL093 356. ¾m E of Silsoe off A6, 10m S of Bedford.
Open: 21 Mar–30 Jun, Sept & Oct: Sat, Sun & BHs, 10am–6pm (5pm in Oct). Jul & Aug: Thur–Mon, 10am–6pm. Last admission 1hr before closing.
Admission: Adult £4.90, Child £2.50, Conc. £3.90. Family £12.30. Group discounts. EH members Free.
ⓘ WCs. Picnickers welcome. Buggies available. ▣ ⬱ ▣ ⌂ 🅿 ⊠ On leads. ⛉

Drawing Room, Elton Hall

Dining Room, Elton Hall

©NTPL

ANGLESEY ABBEY, GARDENS & LODE MILL 🌿
LODE, CAMBRIDGE, CAMBRIDGESHIRE CB25 9EJ
www.nationaltrust.org.uk/angleseyabbey

Tel: 01223 810080   **Fax:** 01223 810088   **E-mail:** angleseyabbey@nationaltrust.org.uk
Owner: The National Trust   **Contact:** The Property Manager
Dating from 1600, the house, built on the site of an Augustinian priory, contains the famous Fairhaven collection of paintings and furniture. Surrounded by an outstanding 114 acre garden and arboretum, with a wonderful display of hyacinths in spring, magnificent herbaceous borders, a dahlia garden in summer, winter garden and woodland path. A watermill in full working order is demonstrated on the first and third Saturday each month. New visitor facilities fully opened for 2008.
Location: MAP 7:G8, OS Ref. TL533 622. 6m NE of Cambridge on B1102, signs from A14.

Open: Summer: House & Mill: 19 Mar–2 Nov: Wed–Sun & BH Mons: 1–5pm. Garden, Shop, Plant Centre & Restaurant: 19 Mar–2 Nov: Wed–Sun & BH Mons; 10.30am–5.30pm. Winter: Winter Garden, Shop, Plant Centre & Restaurant: 5 Nov–21 Dec & 31 Dec–28 Feb 09, Wed–Sun, 10.30am–4.30pm; Mill: Sat & Sun, 11am–3.30pm. Groups must book, no groups on BHs.
*Admission: Summer: House & Garden: Adult £9.25, Child £4.65. Groups: Adult £8.05, Child £4.05. Garden only: Adult £5.50, Child £2.75. Groups: Adult £4.55, Child £2.30. Winter (garden only): Adult £4.75, Child £2.40. Groups: Adult £4.15, Child £2.10.*includes a voluntary donation but visitors can choose to pay the standard prices displayed at the property and on the website.

🗔 🎫 ☂ 🗔 🦽 Partial. 🍴 Licensed. 🎦 🅿 🎠 ❄ 💷

©Nigel Luckhurst

CAMBRIDGE UNIVERSITY BOTANIC GARDEN
BATEMAN STREET, CAMBRIDGE CB2 1JF
www.botanic.cam.ac.uk

Tel: 01223 336265 **Fax:** 01223 336278   **E-mail:** enquiries@botanic.cam.ac.uk
Owner: University of Cambridge   **Contact:** Enquiries Desk
This 40 acre oasis of listed heritage landscape showcases over 8000 species, including alpines from every continent in the Rock Garden, nine National Collections, the finest collection of trees in the Eastern Region, the historic Systematic Beds, the Dry Garden, the renowned Winter Garden and tropical forest in the Glasshouses.
Location: MAP 7:G9, OS Ref. TL453 573. ¾m S of Cambridge city centre; entrance on Bateman Street off A1309 (Trumpington Rd). 10mins walk from railway station.
Open: 3 Jan–24 Dec: daily, 10am–6pm; closes 5pm in Autumn & Spring and 4pm in winter. Closed over Christmas and New Year, please telephone for details.
Admission: Adult £4, Child (under 16yrs) Free, Conc. £3.50. Groups must book. Please use Trumpington Park & Ride, now open daily, and alight Bateman Street stop.
🗔 🦽 🖐 🎦 By arrangement. 🅿 Street/Pay & Display. ▪ Schools must book.
🖐 Guide dogs only. ❄

OLIVER CROMWELL'S HOUSE
29 St Mary's Street, Ely, Cambridgeshire CB7 4HF
Tel: 01353 662062   **Fax:** 01353 668518   **E-mail:** tic@eastcambs.gov.uk
Owner: East Cambridgeshire District Council
The former home of the Lord Protector.
Location: MAP 7:G7, OS Ref. TL538 803. N of Cambridge, ¼m W of Ely Cathedral.
Open: 1 Nov–31 Mar: Sun–Fri, 11am–4pm; Sats, 10am–5pm. 1 Apr–31 Oct: daily, 10am–5.30pm.
Admission: Adult £4, Child £2.95, Conc. £3.60, Family (2+3) £12 (prices subject to change April 2008).

DENNY ABBEY & THE FARMLAND MUSEUM ⌗
Ely Road, Chittering, Waterbeach, Cambridgeshire CB25 9TQ
Tel: 01223 860489   www.english-heritage.org.uk/dennyabbey
Owner: English Heritage/Managed by the Farmland Museum Trust
Contact: Visitor Operations Team
What at first appears to be an attractive stone farmhouse is actually the remains of a 12th century Benedictine abbey which, at different times, also housed the Knights Templar and Franciscan nuns. Founded by the Countess of Pembroke. New family-friendly activities include hands-on interactives.
Location: MAP 7:G8, OS Ref. TL495 684. 6m N of Cambridge on the E side of the A10.
Open: 21 Mar–31 Oct: daily, 12 noon–5pm.
Admission: Abbey & Museum: Adult £4, Child £2, Child under 5 Free, Conc. £3, Family £10. Museum charge: EH Members/OVP £2.40.
ℹ️ Farmland museum. Picnickers welcome. WC. 🗔 🦽 🖐 Sat/Sun only. 🅿 🎠 On leads. 💷

DOCWRA'S MANOR GARDEN
Shepreth, Royston, Hertfordshire SG8 6PS
Tel: 01763 261473 **Information:** 01763 260677
Owner: Mrs Faith Raven   **Contact:** Peter Rocket
Extensive garden around building dating from the 18th century.
Location: MAP 7:F9, OS Ref. TL393 479. In Shepreth via A10 from Royston.
Open: All year: Weds & Fris, 10am–4pm & 1st Sun in month from Mar–Nov: 2–5pm.
Admission: £4.

ELTON HALL 🏛
Nr PETERBOROUGH PE8 6SH
www.eltonhall.com

Tel: 01832 280468 **Fax:** 01832 280584 **E-mail:** office@eltonhall.com

Owner: Sir William Proby Bt **Contact:** The Administrator

Sir Peter Proby rose to prominence during the reign of Elizabeth I and by the early 17th century had acquired the mills at Elton. His grandson, Sir Thomas, was the first member of the family to establish himself at Elton Hall and he built a charming Restoration house attached to medieval buildings. Succesive generations, who later became the Earls of Carysfort, have added to the house greatly, both in architecture and contents. The house has many fine paintings and furniture. The library is one of the finest in private hands and includes Henry VIII's prayer book. Since 1983 the garden has been energetically restored and includes finely clipped topiary, a stunning new flower garden, Millennium Orangery and Box Walk.

Location: MAP 7:E7, OS Ref. TL091 930. Close to A1 in the village of Elton, off A605 Peterborough – Oundle Road.

Open: 25/26 May; June: Weds. Jul & Aug: Wed, Thur, Sun & BH Mon, 2–5pm. Private groups by arrangement Apr–Sept.

Admission: House & Garden: £7.50, Conc. £6.50. Garden only: Adult £5, Conc. £4.50. Accompanied child under 16 Free.

ℹ️ No photography in house. 🔲♿ Garden suitable. ⬤ Obligatory. 🅿️
🦮 Guide dogs in gardens only.

ELY CATHEDRAL

The Chapter House, The College, Ely, Cambridgeshire CB7 4DL

Tel: 01353 667735 ext.261 **Fax:** 01353 665658

Contact: Sally-Ann Ford (Visits & Tours Manager)

A wonderful example of Romanesque architecture. Octagon and Lady Chapel are of special interest. Superb medieval domestic buildings surround the Cathedral. Stained Glass Museum. Brass rubbing. Octagon and West Tower tours peak season.

Location: MAP 7:G7, OS Ref. TL541 803. Via A10, 15m N of Cambridge City centre.

Open: Summer: 7am–7pm. Winter: Mon–Sat, 7.30am–6pm, Suns and week after Christmas, 7.30am–5pm. Sun services: 8.15am, 10.30am and 4pm. Weekday services: 7.40am, 8am, and 5.30pm (Thurs only also 12.10pm).

Admission: Adult £5.20, Child Free, Conc. £4.50. Discounts for groups of 15+. Separate rates for school visits.

✳️

© Patrick Lane

OCTAVIA HILL'S BIRTHPLACE HOUSE
8 SOUTH BRINK, WISBECH, CAMBRIDGESHIRE PE13 1JB
www.octaviahill.org

Tel/Fax: 01945 476358 **E-mail:** info@octaviahill.org

Owner: Octavia Hill Birthplace Museum Trust **Contact:** Mr Peter Clayton

A Grade II* listed Georgian house, in which Octavia Hill, social reformer and co-founder of the National Trust was born. Features for 2008 include a Victorian Chamber of Horrors, a history of social housing room, a National Trust room and one of Octavia's 'outdoor sitting rooms' in the 'secret' garden.

Location: MAP 7:G6, OS Ref. TF459 096. On S bank of River Nene, in Wisbech.

Open: 15 Mar–31 Oct, Mon–Wed, Sat & Sun, 1–4.30pm (last admission 4pm).

Admission: Adult £3.50, Child £1.50, Family (2+2) £8. Groups: max 25 (larger groups staggered entry). Conc. & NT members: £3.

🔲♿ WC. ⬤ By arrangement. 🅿️ 2 coach bays nearby. ⬛🦮 Guide dogs only.

Kimbolton Castle, Huntingdon

ISLAND HALL
GODMANCHESTER, CAMBRIDGESHIRE PE29 2BA
www.islandhall.com

Tel: (Groups) 01480 459676 (Individuals via Invitation to View) 01206 573948
E-mail: cvp@cvpdesigns.com
Owner: Mr Christopher & Lady Linda Vane Percy   **Contact:** Mr C Vane Percy
An important mid 18th century mansion of great charm, owned and restored by an award-winning interior designer. This family home has lovely Georgian rooms, with fine period detail, and interesting possessions relating to the owners' ancestors since their first occupation of the house in 1800. A tranquil riverside setting with formal gardens and ornamental island forming part of the grounds in an area of Best Landscape. Octavia Hill wrote *"This is the loveliest, dearest old house, I never was in such a one before."*
Location: MAP 7:F8, OS Ref. TL244 706. Centre of Godmanchester, Post Street next to free car park. 1m S of Huntingdon, 15m NW of Cambridge A14.
Open: Groups by arrangement: May–Jul & Sept. Individuals via Invitation to View.
Admission: Groups: (40+) Adult £5, (10–40) Adult £5.50. Under 20 persons, min charge £110 per group (sorry but no children under 13yrs).
🍴 Home made teas. ⊠

KIMBOLTON CASTLE
Kimbolton, Huntingdon, Cambridgeshire PE28 0EA
Tel: 01480 860505   **Fax:** 01480 861763
www.kimbolton.cambs.sch.uk/castlevisits.htm
Owner: Governors of Kimbolton School   **Contact:** Mrs N Butler
A late Stuart house, an adaptation of a 13th century fortified manor house, with evidence of Tudor modifications. The seat of the Earls and Dukes of Manchester 1615–1950, now a school. Katharine of Aragon died in the Queen's Room – the setting for a scene in Shakespeare's Henry VIII. 18th century rebuilding by Vanbrugh and Hawksmoor; Gatehouse by Robert Adam; the Pellegrini mural paintings on the Staircase, in the Chapel and in the Boudoir are the best examples in England of this gifted Venetian decorator. New Heritage Room.
Location: MAP 7:E8, OS Ref. TL101 676. 7m NW of St Neots on B645.
Open: 2 Mar & 2 Nov, 1–4pm.
Admission: Adult £4, Child £2, OAP £3. Groups by arrangement throughout the year, including evenings, special rates apply.
🅃 🅖 Unsuitable. 🍴 🎦 By arrangement. 🅿 🅱 🐕 On leads in grounds. 🔺 ❅

LONGTHORPE TOWER ⌗
Thorpe Rd, Longthorpe, Cambridgeshire PE1 1HA
Tel: 01799 522842   www.english-heritage.org.uk/longthorpe
Owner: English Heritage   **Contact:** Visitor Operations Team
The finest example of 14th century domestic wall paintings in northern Europe showing a variety of secular and sacred objects, including the Wheel of Life, the Nativity and King David. The Tower, with the Great Chamber that contains the paintings, is part of a fortified manor house. Special exhibitions are held on the upper floor.
Location: MAP 7:E6, OS Ref. TL163 983. 2m W of Peterborough just off A47.
Open: 1 May–31 Aug: Pre-booked guided tours only, please call 01799 522842.
Admission: Adult £5, Child £2.50, Conc. £4. Group discount. EH members Free.
ℹ️ Picnickers welcome. 🅾🅵 By arrangement. 🅿 None at site. ⊠

THE MANOR, HEMINGFORD GREY
HUNTINGDON, CAMBRIDGESHIRE PE28 9BN
www.greenknowe.co.uk

Tel: 01480 463134   **Fax:** 01480 465026   **E-mail:** diana_boston@hotmail.com
Owner: Mrs D S Boston   **Contact:** Diana Boston
Built about 1130 and one of the oldest continuously inhabited houses in Britain. Made famous as 'Green Knowe' by the author Lucy Boston. Her patchwork collection is also shown. Four acre garden, laid out by Lucy Boston, surrounded by moat, with topiary, old roses, award winning irises and herbaceous borders.
Location: MAP 7:F8, OS Ref. TL290 706. Off A14, 3m SE of Huntingdon. 12m NW of Cambridge. Access is by a small gate on the riverside footpath.
Open: House: All year (except May), to individuals or groups by prior arrangement. In May guided tours will be daily at 2pm (booking advisable). Garden: All year, daily, 11am–5pm (4pm in winter).
Admission: House: Adult £6, Child £2, OAP £4.50. Garden only: Adult £3–£1 (seasonal), Child Free.
ℹ️ No photography in house. 🅾 🍴 🍴 Locally, by arrangement. 🅵 Obligatory.
🅱 🅿 Disabled only. 🐕 In garden, on leads. ❅

Wimpole Hall

PECKOVER HOUSE & GARDEN ❧

NORTH BRINK, WISBECH, CAMBRIDGESHIRE PE13 1JR

www.nationaltrust.org.uk

Tel/Fax: 01945 583463 **E-mail:** peckover@nationaltrust.org.uk
Owner: The National Trust **Contact:** The Property Manager
A town house, built c1722 and renowned for its very fine plaster and wood rococo decoration. The outstanding 2 acre Victorian garden includes an orangery, summer-houses, roses, herbaceous borders, fernery, croquet lawn and Reed Barn Tearoom.
Location: MAP 7:G6, OS Ref. TF458 097. On N bank of River Nene, in Wisbech B1441.
Open: House, Garden, Shop & Tearoom: 15 Mar–2 Nov, Sat–Wed, 12 noon–5pm (House 1–4.30pm). Open Good Friday and 3/4 Jul for Wisbech Rose Fair.
Admission: Adult £5.50, Child £2.75, Family £14. Groups: £4.50.
🄿 👶 🍴 ♿ Partial. 🐕 🍴 🅿 Signposted. ✖ 🏠 🏠 🔻

PETERBOROUGH CATHEDRAL

Chapter Office, Minster Precincts, Peterborough PE1 1XS
Tel: 01733 355300 **Fax:** 01733 355316
E-mail: andrew.watson@peterborough-cathedral.org.uk
www.peterborough-cathedral.org.uk
Contact: Andrew Watson
'An undiscovered gem.' With magnificent Norman architecture a unique 13th century nave ceiling, the awe-inspiring West Front and burial places of two Queens to make your visit an unforgettable experience. Exhibitions tell the Cathedral's story. Tours by appointment, of the cathedral, tower, Deanery Garden or Precincts. Freshly prepared meals and snacks at Beckets Restaurant (advance bookings possible). Cathedral gift shop and Tourist Information Centre in Precincts. Business meeting facilities.
Location: MAP 7:E6, OS Ref. TL194 986. 4m E of A1, in City Centre.
Open: All year: Mon–Fri, 9am–6.30pm (restricted access after 5.30pm because of Evensong). Sat, 9am–5pm. Sun: services from 7.30am; visitors: 12 noon–5pm.
Admission: No fixed charge – donations are requested.
ℹ️ Visitors' Centre. 🄿 ♿ 🍴 🅵 By arrangement. 🅿 None. 🔳
🐕 Guide dogs only. 🌸

Cambridge University Botanic Garden

H Rice

WIMPOLE HALL & HOME FARM ❧

ARRINGTON, ROYSTON, CAMBRIDGESHIRE SG8 0BW

www.nationaltrust.org.uk   www.wimpole.org

Tel: 01223 206000 **Fax:** 01223 207838 **E-mail:** wimpolehall@nationaltrust.org.uk
Owner: The National Trust **Contact:** The Property Manager
Wimpole is a magnificent country house built in 18th century style with a colourful history of owners. The Hall is set in restored formal gardens with parterres and a walled garden. Home Farm is a working farm and is the largest rare breeds centre in East Anglia.
Location: MAP 7:F9, OS154. TL336 510. 8m SW of Cambridge (A603), 6m N of Royston (A1198).
Open: Hall: 15 Mar–29 Oct: Sat–Wed (open Good Fri & BH Mon); Aug: Sat–Thur (open BH Mons); 2, 8, 16 & 23 Nov, Suns only; 1–5pm, BH Mon, 11am–5pm, closes 4pm after 29 Oct. Garden: as Farm. Park: dawn–dusk. Farm: 15 Mar–29 Oct: Sat–Wed (open Good Fri & BH Mon); Aug: Sat–Thur & BH Mon; Nov–Mar 2009: Sat & Sun (open Feb half-term week); 15 Mar–29 Oct: 10.30am–5pm; 1 Nov–Mar 2009, 11am–4pm.
*Admission: Hall: Adult £8.40, Child £4.70. Joint ticket with Home Farm: Adult £12.60, Child £6.80, Family £33. Garden: £3.50. Group rates (not Suns or BH Mons). Farm: Adult £6.95, Child (3yrs & up) £4.70. Discount for NT members (not Suns or BH Mons). *includes a voluntary donation but visitors can choose to pay the standard prices displayed at the property and on the website.
🄿 👶 🍴 ♿ Partial. 🐕 🍴 Licensed. 🅵 By arrangement. 🅿 Limited for coaches. 🔳
🐕 In park, on leads. 🏠 🌸 🔻 Tel for details.

©NT/Fisheye Images

visit hudsons guide online

Christ's College
St Andrew's Street,
Cambridge CB2 3BU
Tel: 01223 334900
Website: www.christs.cam.ac.uk/admissn
Founder: Lady Margaret Beaufort
Founded: 1505

Churchill College
Madingley Road, Cambridge CB3 0DS
Tel: 01223 336000
Website: www.chu.cam.ac.uk
Founded: 1960

Clare College
Trinity Lane, Cambridge CB2 1TL
Tel: 01223 333200
Website: www.clare.cam.ac.uk
Founded: 1326

Clare Hall
Herschel Road, Cambridge CB3 9AL
Tel: 01223 332360
Website: www.clarehall.cam.ac.uk
Founded: 1965

Corpus Christi College
King's Parade, Cambridge CB2 1RH
Tel: 01223 338000
Website: www.corpus.cam.ac.uk
Founded: 1352

Darwin College
Silver Street, Cambridge CB3 9EU
Tel: 01223 335660
Website: www.dar.cam.ac.uk
Founded: 1964

Downing College
Regent Street, Cambridge CB2 1DQ
Tel: 01223 334800
Website: www.dow.cam.ac.uk
Founded: 1800

Emmanuel College
St Andrew's Street, Cambridge CB2 3AP
Tel: 01223 334200
Website: www.emma.cam.ac.uk
Founded: 1584

Fitzwilliam College
Huntingdon Road, Cambridge CB3 0DG
Tel: 01223 332000
Website: www.fitz.cam.ac.uk
Founded: 1966

Girton College
Huntingdon Road, Cambridge CB3 0JG
Tel: 01223 338999
Website: www.girton.cam.ac.uk
Founded: 1869

Gonville & Caius College
Trinity Street, Cambridge CB2 1TA
Tel: 01223 332400
Website: www.cai.cam.ac.uk
Founded: 1348

Homerton College
Hills Road, Cambridge CB2 2PH
Tel: 01223 507111
Website: www.homerton.cam.ac.uk
Founded: 1976

Hughes Hall
Wollaston Road, Cambridge CB1 2EW
Tel: 01223 334897
Website: www.hughes.cam.ac.uk
Founded: 1885

Jesus College
Jesus Lane, Cambridge CB5 8BL
Tel: 01223 339339
Website: www.jesus.cam.ac.uk
Founded: 1496

King's College
King's Parade, Cambridge CB2 1ST
Tel: 01223 331100
Website: www.kings.cam.ac.uk
Founded: 1441

Lucy Cavendish College
Lady Margaret Road, Cambs CB3 0BU
Tel: 01223 332190
Website: www.lucy-cav.cam.ac.uk
Founded: 1965

Magdalene College
Magdalene Street, Cambridge CB3 0AG
Tel: 01223 332100
Website: www.magd.cam.ac.uk
Founded: 1428

New Hall
Huntingdon Road, Cambridge CB3 0DF
Tel: 01223 762100
Website: www.newhall.cam.ac.uk
Founded: 1954

Newnham College
Grange Road, Cambridge CB3 9DF
Tel: 01223 335700
Website: www.newn.cam.ac.uk
Founded: 1871

Pembroke College
Trumpington Street, Cambs CB2 1RF
Tel: 01223 338100
Website: www.pem.cam.ac.uk
Founded: 1347

Peterhouse
Trumpington Street, Cambs CB2 1RD
Tel: 01223 338200
Website: www.pet.cam.ac.uk
Founder: The Bishop of Ely
Founded: 1284

Queens' College
Silver Street, Cambridge CB3 9ET
Tel: 01223 335511
Website: www.quns.cam.ac.uk
Founder: Margaret of Anjou,
Elizabeth Woodville
Founded: 1448

Ridley Hall
Ridley Hall Road, Cambridge CB3 9HG
Tel: 01223 741080
Website: www.ridley.cam.ac.uk
Founded: 1879

Robinson College
Grange Road, Cambridge CB3 9AN
Tel: 01223 339100
Website: www.robinson.cam.ac.uk
Founded: 1979

St Catherine's College
King's Parade, Cambs CB2 1RL
Tel: 01223 338300
Website: www.caths.cam.ac.uk
Founded: 1473

St Edmund's College
Mount Pleasant, Cambridge CB3 0BN
Tel: 01223 336086
Website: www.st-edmunds.cam.ac.uk
Founded: 1896

St John's College
St John's Street, Cambridge CB2 1TP
Tel: 01223 338600
Website: www.joh.cam.ac.uk
Founded: 1511

Selwyn College
Grange Road, Cambridge CB3 9DQ
Tel: 01223 335846
Website: www.sel.cam.ac.uk
Founded: 1882

Sidney Sussex College
Sidney Street, Cambridge CB2 3HU
Tel: 01223 338800
Website: www.sid.cam.ac.uk
Founded: 1596

Trinity College
Trinity Street, Cambridge CB2 1TQ
Tel: 01223 338400
Website: www.trin.cam.ac.uk
Founded: 1546

Trinity Hall
Trinity Lane, Cambridge CB2 1TJ
Tel: 01223 332500
Website: www.trinhall.cam.ac.uk
Founded: 1350

Wesley House
Jesus Lane, Cambridge CB5 8BJ
Tel: 01223 350127 / 367980
Website: www.wesley.cam.ac.uk

Wescott House
Jesus Lane, Cambridge CB5 8BP
Tel: 01223 741000
Website: www.ely.anglican.org/westcott

Westminster & Cheshunt
Madingley Road Cambridge CB3 0AA
Tel: 01223 741084
Website: www.westminstercollege.co.uk

Wolfson College
Grange Road, Cambridge CB3 9BB
Tel: 01223 335900
Website: www.wolfson.cam.ac.uk
Founded: 1965

Visitors wishing to gain admittance to the Colleges (meaning the Courts, not to the staircases & students' rooms) are advised to contact the Tourist Office for further information. It should be noted that Halls normally close for lunch (12–2pm) and many are not open during the afternoon. Chapels may be closed during services. Libraries are not normally open, and Gardens do not usually include the Fellows' garden. Visitors, and especially guided groups, should always call on the Porters Lodge first.

■ **Owner**

English Heritage

■ **Contact**

Visitor Operations Team
Audley End House
Audley End
Saffron Walden
Essex CB11 4JF

Tel: 01799 522842
Fax: 01799 521276

Venue Hire and
Hospitality:
Tel: 01799 529403

■ **Location**

MAP 7:G10
OS Ref. TL525 382

1m W of Saffron Walden
on B1383,
M11/J8 & J10.

Rail: Audley End 1¼ m.

■ **Opening Times**

House

21 March–30 September,
Wed–Sun, 11am–5pm
(Sat closes 3.30pm).
October, Wed–Sun
11am–4pm.

House (Guided Tours)

21 March–30 April
(except Easter) &
1 September–
31 October, Wed–Sun.
1 May–29 July, Wed–Fri.

Last admission 1 hr
before closing.

In some rooms, light
levels are reduced to
preserve vulnerable
textiles and other
collections. House may
have to close at 4.30pm
when events are booked.

**Gardens & Service
Wing***

21 March–23 December,
Wed–Sun, 10am–6pm
(closes 5pm Oct & 4pm
Nov & Dec).
* Service Wing opens
1 May.
Closed 24 December–
31 January.

■ **Admission**

House & Grounds

Adult	£10.50
Child (5–15yrs)	£5.30
Child (under 5yrs)	Free
Conc.	£8.40
Family (2+3)	£26.30

Grounds only

Adult	£5.50
Child (5–15yrs)	£2.80
Child (under 5yrs)	Free
Concessions	£4.40
Family (2+3)	£13.80

Groups
(11+) 15% discount.

EH Members free.

■ **Conference/Function**

ROOM	MAX CAPACITY
Grounds	Large scale events possible

English Heritage Photographic Library

AUDLEY END HOUSE & GARDENS

www.english-heritage.org.uk/audleyend

Audley End was a palace in all but name. Built by Thomas Howard, Earl of Suffolk, to entertain King James I. The King may have had his suspicions, for he never stayed there; in 1618 Howard was imprisoned and fined for embezzlement.

Charles II bought the property in 1668 for £50,000, but within a generation the house was gradually demolished, and by the 1750s it was about the size you see today. There are still over 30 magnificent rooms to see, each with period furnishings.

The house and its gardens, including a 19th century parterre and rose garden, are surrounded by an enchanting 18th century landscaped park laid out by 'Capability' Brown.

Visitors can also visit the working organic walled garden and purchase produce from its shop. Extending to nearly 10 acres the garden includes a 170ft long, five-bay vine house, built in 1802.

New for 2008: re-opening of the Audley End House Service Wing. Life behind the scenes for servants at Audley End during its Victorian heyday will be revealed from Spring 2008, as part of a major project to transform the great Service Wing of the house.

The scullery, dairy, meat and game larders, and laundries will be opened to the public for the first time and there will be 'activity days' when you will be able to see and hear from costumed interpreters.

English Heritage Photographic Library

i	Open air concerts and other events. WCs.
	Private and corporate hire.
	Ground floor and grounds.
	(Max 50).
	By arrangement for groups.
P	Coaches to book in advance. Free entry for coach drivers and tour guides. One additional place for every extra 20 people.
	School visits free if booked in advance. Contact the Administrator or tel 01223 582700 for bookings.
	On leads only.

BOURNE MILL

Bourne Road, Colchester, Essex CO2 8RT
Tel: 01206 572422 **www.nationaltrust.org.uk**
Owner: The National Trust **Contact:** The Custodian
Originally a fishing lodge built in 1591. It was later converted into a mill with a 4 acre mill pond. Much of the machinery, including the waterwheel, is intact.
Location: MAP 8:J11, OS Ref. TM006 238. 1m S of Colchester centre, in Bourne Road, off the Mersea Road B1025.
Open: June, Suns 2–5pm. July–August: Tues, Suns (& BH Mons), 2–5pm.
Admission: Adult £2.50, Child £1. No reduction for groups.
Guide dogs only.

BRENTWOOD CATHEDRAL

INGRAVE ROAD, BRENTWOOD, ESSEX CM15 8AT

Tel: 01277 232266 **E-mail:** bishop@dioceseofbrentwood.org
Owner: Diocese of Brentwood **Contact:** Rt Rev Thomas McMahon
The new (1991) Roman Catholic classical Cathedral Church of St Mary and St Helen incorporates part of the original Victorian church. Designed by distinguished classical architect Quinlan Terry with roundels by Raphael Maklouf. Architecturally, the inspiration is early Italian Renaissance crossed with the English Baroque of Christopher Wren. The north elevation consists of nine bays each divided by Doric pilasters. This is broken by a huge half-circular portico. The Kentish ragstone walls have a natural rustic look, which contrasts with the smooth Portland stone of the capitals and column bases. Inside is an arcade of Tuscan arches with central altar with the lantern above.
Location: MAP 4:J1, OS Ref. TQ596 938. A12 & M25/J28. Centre of Brentwood, opposite Brentwood School.
Open: All year, daily.
Admission: Free.
Limited. None for coaches.

CHELMSFORD CATHEDRAL

New Street, Chelmsford, Essex CM1 1TY
Tel: 01245 294489 **E-mail:** office@chelmsfordcathedral.org.uk
Contact: Mrs Bobby Harrington
15th century building became a Cathedral in 1914. Extended in 1920s, major refurbishment in 1980s and in 2000 with contemporary works of distinction and splendid new organs in 1994 and 1996.
Location: MAP 7:H12, OS Ref. TL708 070. In Chelmsford.
Open: Daily: 8am–5.30pm. Sun services: 8am, 9.30am, 11.15am and 6pm. Weekday services: 8.15am and 5.15pm daily. Holy Communion: Wed, 12.35pm & Thur, 10am. Tours by prior arrangement.
Admission: No charge but donation invited.

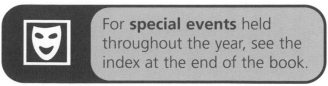

For **special events** held throughout the year, see the index at the end of the book.

COGGESHALL GRANGE BARN

Grange Hill, Coggeshall, Colchester, Essex CO6 1RE
Tel: 01376 562226 **www.nationaltrust.org.uk**
Owner: The National Trust **Contact:** The Custodian
One of the oldest surviving timber-framed barns in Europe, dating from around 1240, and originally part of a Cistercian Monastery. It was restored in the 1980s by the Coggeshall Grange Barn Trust, Braintree District Council and Essex County Council. Features a small collection of farm carts and wagons.
Location: MAP 8:I11, OS Ref. TL848 223. Signposted off A120 Coggeshall bypass. West side of the road southwards to Kelvedon.
Open: 23 Mar–12 Oct: Tues, Thurs, Suns & BH Mons, 2–5pm.
Admission: Adult £2.50, Child £1. Joint ticket with Paycocke's: Adult £4, Child £2.
Coaches must book. Guide dogs only.

COLCHESTER CASTLE MUSEUM

14 Ryegate Road, Colchester, Essex CO1 1YG
Tel: 01206 282939 **Fax:** 01206 282925
Owner: Colchester & Ipswich Museum Sevice **Contact:** Museum Resource Centre
The largest Norman Castle Keep in Europe with fine archaeological collections on show. Hands-on & interactive display brings history to life.
Location: MAP 8:J11, OS Ref. TL999 253. In Colchester town centre, off A12.
Open: All year: Mon–Sat, 10am–5pm, also Suns, 11am–5pm.
Admission: Adult £5.10, Child (5–15yrs)/Conc. £3.30. Child under 5yrs Free. Saver ticket: £13.30. Prices may increase from April 2008.

©Alan Cox

COPPED HALL

CROWN HILL, EPPING, ESSEX CM16 5HH

www.coppedhalltrust.org.uk

Tel: 020 7267 1679 **E-mail:** Coxalan1@aol.com
Owner: The Copped Hall Trust **Contact:** Alan Cox
Shell of 18th century Palladian mansion under restoration. Situated on ridge overlooking excellent landscaped park. Ancillary buildings including stables and small racquets court. Former elaborate gardens being rescued from abandonment. Large early 18th century walled garden – adjacent to site of 16th century mansion where 'A Midsummer Night's Dream' was first performed. Ideal film location.
Location: MAP 7:G12, OS Ref. TL433 016. 4m SW of Epping, N of M25.
Open: By appointment only for groups (20+) and events. Special open days.
Admission: Gardens £3.50. Part of Mansion and Stables £3.50, Child under 14yrs Free.
Partial. Obligatory. In grounds on leads. Concerts/plays.

FEERINGBURY MANOR

Coggeshall Road, Feering, Colchester, Essex CO5 9RB
Tel: 01376 561946
Owner/Contact: Mrs Giles Coode-Adams
Location: MAP 8:I11, OS Ref. TL864 215. 1¼m N of A12 between Feering & Coggeshall.
Open: From 1st Thur in Apr to last Fri in Jul: Thur & Fri only, 8am–4pm.
Admission: Adult £3, Child Free. In aid of National Gardens Scheme.

Rona Cox

GARDENS OF EASTON LODGE 🏛

WARWICK HOUSE, EASTON LODGE, LITTLE EASTON, GT DUNMOW CM6 2BB

www.eastonlodge.co.uk

Tel/Fax: 01371 876979 **E-mail:** enquiries@eastonlodge.co.uk

Contact: Jacquie Fanchette, Administrator

Historic gardens dating back over 400 years, their most renowned owner was the Countess of Warwick, "Darling Daisy", mistress of Edward VII. In 1903, leading Edwardian designer Harold Peto completed his stunning formal gardens here. Abandoned in 1950 after the demolition of the main house, the gardens were forgotten for nearly 45 years until 1993 when an ambitious restoration programme began. Today, the 23-acre Gardens offer an enchanting atmosphere as the splendour of a century ago is gently revealed. Further enhanced by inspired projects from the current custodians, visitors can imagine their past glories and enjoy their tranquil present.

Location: MAP 7:H11, OS Ref. TL593 240. 4m NW of Great Dunmow, off the B184 Dunmow to Thaxted road.

Open: Feb/Mar (snowdrops): daily. Easter–31 Oct: Fri–Sun & BHs, 12 noon–6pm or dusk if earlier. Groups at other times by appointment.

Admission: Adult £5, Child/Student (5–16yrs) £2.50, Conc. £4.50. Group (min 20 + 1 free): £4.20. Schools (20+) £2 per child, 1 teacher free per 10 children.

ℹ Exhibition & Study Centre in Dovecote. 🔲 🔲 🔲 Partial. WC. 🔲 Picnics. 🔲 By arrangement. 🅿 Limited for coaches. 🔲 🔲 In grounds on leads. 🔲 🔲 €

HARWICH REDOUBT FORT

Main Road, Harwich, Essex

Tel/Fax: 01255 503429   **E-mail:** info@harwich-society.co.uk

www.harwich-society.co.uk

Owner: The Harwich Society   **Contact:** Mr A Rutter

180ft diameter circular fort built in 1808 to defend the port against Napoleonic invasion. Being restored by Harwich Society and part is a museum. Eleven guns on battlements.

Location: MAP 8:K10, OS Ref. TM262 322. Rear of 29 Main Road.

Open: 1 May–31 Aug: daily, 10am–4pm. Sept–Apr: Suns only, 10am–4pm. Groups by appointment at any time.

Admission: Adult £2, Child Free (no unaccompanied children).

🔲 €

RHS Garden Hyde Hall

HYLANDS HOUSE & PARK

HYLANDS PARK, LONDON ROAD, CHELMSFORD CM2 8WQ

www.chelmsford.gov.uk/hylands

Tel: 01245 605500 **Fax:** 01245 605510

E-mail: hylands@chelmsford.gov.uk

Owner: Chelmsford Borough Council   **Contact:** Sarah Clements

Hylands House is a beautiful Grade II* listed building, set in 574 acres of historic landscaped parkland, partly designed by Humphry Repton. Built c1730, the original house was a Queen Anne style mansion. Subsequent owners modernised and enlarged the property, added East and West wings and a colonnaded portico, and covered the house in white stucco, which produced today's neo-classical house. Restoration was completed in 2005 and visitors can explore the spectacular rooms, ranging from the exquisitely gilded neo-baroque Banqueting Room and Drawing Room, restored to their early Victorian splendour, to the Georgian Dining Room. There are stunning views from the Repton Room to the Serpentine Lake. The Stables Centre (Grade II listed) incorporates a visitor centre, café and gift shop. Newly restored Pleasure Gardens. Group visits available by arrangement.

Location: MAP 7:H12, OS Ref. TL681 054. 2m SW of Chelmsford. Signposted on A414 from J15 of A12, near Chelmsford.

Open: House: Suns, Mons & BHs, 11am–6pm (Oct–Apr: Mons, 11am–4pm). Closed 25 Dec. Stables Centre: Daily.

Admission: Adult £3.50, accompanied children under 16 Free, Conc. £2.50. Groups: £3.60pp or £90 (whichever greater). Stables Centre Free.

ℹ Visitor Centre. No photography in house. 🔲 🔲 🔲 🔲 🔲 Sun & Mon. 🔲 🔲 By arrangement. 🅿 🔲 By arrangement. 🔲 In grounds. Guide dogs only in house. 🔲 🔲 🔲

INGATESTONE HALL 🏛
HALL LANE, INGATESTONE, ESSEX CM4 9NR

Tel: 01277 353010 **Fax:** 01245 248070

Owner: The Lord Petre **Contact:** The Administrator

16th century mansion, set in 11 acres of grounds (formal garden and wild walk), built by Sir William Petre, Secretary of State to four Tudor monarchs, which has remained in the hands of his family ever since. The two Priests' hiding places can be seen, as well as the furniture, portraits and family memorabilia accumulated over the centuries.

Location: MAP 7:H12, OS Ref. TQ653 986. Off A12 between Brentwood & Chelmsford. Take Station Lane at London end of Ingatestone High Street, cross level-crossing and continue for ¹/₂ m to SE.

Open: 22 Mar–28 Sept: Sats, Suns & BH Mons. Aug: Wed–Fri, 1–6pm.

Admission: Adult £4, Child £2 (under 5yrs Free), Conc. £3.50. 50p per head discount for groups (20+).

ℹ No photography in house. ⬚ 🖼 🍴 ♿ Partial. 🎦 🎓 By arrangement. 🅿 🚌 🐕 Guide dogs only. 🛡

MARKS HALL GARDENS AND ARBORETUM
COGGESHALL, ESSEX CO6 1TG

www.markshall.org.uk

Tel: 01376 563796

Owner: The Thomas Philips Price Trust **Contact:** Julia Fosker

In the Walled Garden five individual gardens and the longest double herbaceous border in East Anglia combine traditional and contemporary in a unique show of colourful planting. This garden is open to a lake on one side and on the opposite bank the Millennium Walk is planted to give colour, form and scent on the shortest days of the year. There is much to see in these 100 acres of gardens and Arboretum on every day of the year.

Location: MAP 8:I11, OS168 Ref. TQ840 252. Off B1024, 1¹/₂ m N of Coggeshall.

Open: Apr–Oct: Tues–Sun & BH Mons, 10.30am–5pm. Winter weekends, 10.30am–dusk.

Admission: Adult £3.20, Child £1, Conc. £2.90. Groups (10+): £2.

⬚ 🖼 🍴 ♿ Partial. WC. 🎦 🎓 By arrangement. 🅿 ❄

LAYER MARNEY TOWER 🏛
Nr COLCHESTER, ESSEX CO5 9US

www.layermarneytower.co.uk

Tel/Fax: 01206 330784 **E-mail:** info@layermarneytower.co.uk

Owner/Contact: Mr Nicholas Charrington

Built in the reign of Henry VIII, the tallest Tudor gatehouse in Great Britain. Lord Henry Marney clearly intended to rival Wolsey's building at Hampton Court, but he died before his masterpiece was finished. His son John died two years later, in 1525, and building work stopped. Layer Marney Tower has some of the finest terracotta work in the country, most probably executed by Flemish craftsmen trained by Italian masters. The terracotta is used on the battlements, windows, and most lavishly of all, on the tombs of Henry and John Marney. Visitors may climb the Tower, passing through the History Room, and enjoy the marvellous views of the Essex countryside. There are fine outbuildings, including the Long Gallery with its magnificent oak roof and the medieval barn which now houses some of the Home Farm's collection of farm machinery. Function rooms available for receptions, conferences and corporate days.

Location: MAP 8:J11, OS Ref. TL929 175. 7m SW of Colchester, signed off B1022.

Open: 20 Mar–28 Sept: Sun–Thur, 12 noon (11am on BHs)–5pm. Group visits/guided tours throughout the year by arrangement.

Admission: Adult £4.25, Child £2.75, Family £13. Groups (20+): Adult £4, Child £2.50. Guided tours (pre-booked) max 25 people £140. Schools by arrangement.

⬚ 🖼 🍴 ♿ Partial. WC. 🅿 🎓 By arrangement. 🚌 🐕 In grounds, on leads. 🛏 1 double, 2 single. 🍴 ❄ 🛡 On BHs.

MISTLEY TOWERS ⚜

Colchester, Essex

Tel: 01206 393884 / 01223 582700 (Regional Office)

www.english-heritage.org.uk/mistleytowers

Owner: English Heritage **Contact:** The Keykeeper (Mistley Quay Workshops)

The remains of one of only two churches designed by the great architect Robert Adam. Built in 1776. It was unusual in having towers at both the east and west ends.

Location: MAP 8:K10, OS Ref. TM116 320. On B1352, 1¹/₂m E of A137 at Lawford, 9m E of Colchester.

Open: Key available from Mistley Quay Workshops, 01206 393884.

Admission: Free.

ℹ Picnickers welcome. ♿ Grounds only. 🚌 Restricted areas.

SIR ALFRED MUNNINGS
ART MUSEUM
CASTLE HOUSE, CASTLE HILL, DEDHAM, ESSEX CO7 6AZ
www.siralfredmunnings.co.uk

Tel: 01206 322127 **Fax:** 01206 322127
Owner: Castle House Trust **Contact:** The Administrator
In 1959 Castle House was set up as an art museum and memorial to Sir Alfred Munnings. The house is a mixture of Tudor and Georgian periods restored and with original Munnings' furniture. Over 200 of Munnings' works are exhibited, representing his life's work. The house stands in spacious grounds with well maintained gardens. Visitors may also view his original studio where his working materials are displayed.
Location: MAP 8:K10, OS Ref. TM060 328. Approximately ¾m from the village centre on the corner of East Lane.
Open: Easter Sun–7 Oct. Sun, Wed & BH Mon. Also Thurs & Sats in Aug.
Admission: Adult £4, Child £1, Conc. £3.
🖾 🖾 Partial. WC. 🅿 🖾 In grounds, on leads.

RHS GARDEN HYDE HALL
BUCKHATCH LANE, RETTENDON, CHELMSFORD, ESSEX CM3 8ET
www.rhs.org.uk

Tel: 01245 400256 **Fax:** 01245 402100 **E-mail:** hydehall@rhs.org.uk
Owner: The Royal Horticultural Society **Contact:** Reception
A visit to the 360-acre estate at Hyde Hall is unforgettable in any season. The developed area of the garden, in excess of 24 acres, demonstrates an eclectic range of inspirational horticultural styles to be enjoyed by people of all ages and from all walks of life.
Location: MAP 8:I12, OS Ref. TQ782 995. SE of Chelmsford, signposted from A130.
Open: All year, daily (except Christmas Day) from 10am. Closing time varies between 4pm and 6pm. Last entry 1hr before closing. Please contact us for details.
Admission: Adult £5, Child (6–16yrs) £1.50, Child under 6, Companion/Carer of disabled person Free. RHS member and one guest Free. Pre-booked Groups (10+): £4.
🖾 🖾 🖾 Partial 🖾 Licensed 🖾 Licensed. 🅿 Limited for coaches 🖾
🖾 Guide dogs only. ❋

PAYCOCKE'S 🦋
West Street, Coggeshall, Colchester, Essex C06 1NS
Tel: 01376 561305 **www.nationaltrust.org.uk**
Owner: The National Trust **Contact:** The Tenant
A merchant's house, dating from about 1500, with unusually rich panelling and wood carving. A display of lace, for which Coggeshall was famous, is on show. Delightful cottage garden.
Location: MAP 8:I11, OS Ref. TL848 225. Signposted off A120.
Open: 23 Mar–12 Oct: Tues, Thurs, Suns & BH Mons, 2–5pm.
Admission: Adult £3, Child £1.50. Groups (10+) by prior arrangement, no reduction for groups. Joint ticket with Coggeshall Grange Barn: Adult £4, Child £2.
🖾 Access to ground floor and garden. 🅿 NT's at the Coggeshall Grange Barn.

PRIOR'S HALL BARN ♯
Widdington, Newport, Essex
Tel: 01233 582700 (Regional Office) **www.english-heritage.org.uk**
Owner: English Heritage **Contact:** East of England Regional Office
One of the finest surviving medieval barns in south-east England and representative of the group of aisled barns centred on north-west Essex.
Location: MAP 7:G10, OS Ref. TL538 319. In Widdington, on unclassified road 2m SE of Newport, off B1383.
Open: 21 Mar–30 Sept: Sats & Suns, 10am–6pm.
Admission: Free.
🖾 Picnickers welcome. 🖾 🖾

SALING HALL GARDEN
Great Saling, Braintree, Essex CM7 5DT
Tel: 01371 850 243 **Fax:** 01371 850 274
Owner/Contact: Hugh Johnson Esq
Twelve acres surrounding a 17th century house. Walled flower garden dated 1698. Many fine and rare trees and shrubs in glades and groves around five ponds, the subject and setting of "Trad's Diary" for the past 32 years in *The Garden* and *Gardening Illustrated*.
Location: MAP 7:H11, OS Ref. TL700 258. 6m NW of Braintree, 2m N of B1256.
Open: May, Jun & Jul: Weds, 2–5pm.
Admission: Adult £3, Child Free.
🖾 WCs. 🖾 Partial. 🅿 🖾 In grounds on leads.

TILBURY FORT ♯
No. 2 Office Block, The Fort, Tilbury, Essex RM18 7NR
Tel: 01375 858489 **www.english-heritage.org.uk/tilbury**
Owner: English Heritage **Contact:** Visitor Operations Team
The best and largest example of 17th century military engineering in England, commanding the Thames. Learn more about the fascinating history of Tilbury Fort with a new interpretation scheme in the North East Bastion magazine passages. See new graphic panels and displays, new reproduction lamps and two fully restored charging stations. There is also an interactive oral history programme to provide every visitor with a fascinating new insight to Tilbury.
Location: MAP 4:K2, OS Ref. TQ651 754. ½m E of Tilbury off A126. Near Port of Tilbury.
Open: 21 Mar–31 Oct: daily, 10am–5pm. 1 Nov–31 Mar '09: Thur–Mon, 10am–4pm. Closed 24–26 Dec & 1 Jan.
Admission: Adult £3.70, Child £1.90, Under 5s Free. Conc. £3, Family £9.30. EH Members/OVP Free. Group discount available.
🖾 Picnickers welcome. WCs. 🖾 🖾 Grounds only. 🖾 🅿 🖾 🖾 On leads. ❋

WALTHAM ABBEY GATEHOUSE & BRIDGE ♯
Waltham Abbey, Essex
Tel: 01992 702200 / 01223 582700 (Regional Office)
www.english-heritage.org.uk/waltham
Owner: English Heritage **Contact:** East of England Regional Office (01223 582700)
The late 14th century abbey gatehouse, part of the north range of the cloister and the medieval 'Harold's Bridge' of one of the great monastic foundations of the Middle Ages.
Location: MAP 7:G12, OS Ref. TL381 008. In Waltham Abbey off A112. Just NE of Abbey church.
Open: Any reasonable time.
Admission: Free.
🖾 Picnickers welcome. 🖾 Sensory trail guide. 🖾 On leads. ❋

Properties that **open all year** appear in the special index at the end of the book.

The South Front

HATFIELD HOUSE

www.hatfield-house.co.uk

Visit this stunning Jacobean house within an extensive Park. Home of the 7th Marquess of Salisbury and the Cecil family for 400 years, the house is steeped in Elizabethan and Victorian political history. Hatfield House has a fine collection of pictures, tapestries, furnishings and historic armour.

Delightful formal gardens, dating from 1611 when Robert Cecil employed John Tradescant the Elder to collect plants for the new scheme. The West garden includes scented garden, herb garden and knot garden. The adjoining wilderness areas are at their best in spring with masses of naturalised daffodils. The East garden's elegant parterres, topiary and rare plants are a delight for the gardening enthusiast and for those wishing to spend a quiet time in idyllic surroundings.

Within the gardens stands the surviving wing of The Royal Palace of Hatfield where Elizabeth I spent much of her childhood and held her first Council of State in November 1558. An oak tree marks the place where the young Princess Elizabeth first heard of her accession to the throne. Visitors can enjoy walking in the 1000 acres of park with woodland trails plus picnic areas and a children's play park.

The West Garden

The Marble Hall

i No photography in house. National Collection of model soldiers, 5m of marked trails, children's play area.

Weddings, functions: tel 01707 287080. Banquets held in the Old Palace: tel 01707 262055.

WCs. Parking next to house. Lift.

Seats 150. Pre-booked lunch and tea for groups 20+. Tel: 01707 262030.

Wed–Fri only. Group tours available in French, German, Italian, Spanish or Japanese by prior arrangement.

P Ample. Hardstanding for coaches.

Resource books, play area & nature trails. Living History days throughout the school year: tel 01707 287042. KS2 & 3 groups not permitted in house.

In grounds, on leads.

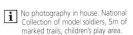

€

■ Owner
The 7th Marquess of Salisbury

■ Contact
Director – Visitors & Events
Hatfield House
Hatfield
Hertfordshire AL9 5NQ
Tel: 01707 287010
Fax: 01707 287033
E-mail: visitors@
hatfield-house.co.uk

■ Location
MAP 7:F11
OS Ref. TL 237 084
21m N of London, M25/J23 7m, A1(M)/J4, 2m.
Bus: Local services from St Albans and Hertford.
Rail: From Kings Cross every 30 mins. Station is opposite entrance to Park.
Air: Luton (30 mins). Stansted (45 mins).

■ Opening Times
22 Mar–end September
House
Wed–Sun & BHs.
12 noon–4pm. Guided tours Wed–Fri (not Aug).
Park, West Garden, Restaurant & Shop
Daily, 11am–5.30pm.
East Garden
Thurs only.
11am–5.30pm.

■ Admission
House, Park & West Garden
Adult	£10.00
Child (5–15yrs)	£4.50
Senior	£9.00
Family (2+4)	£26.00
Groups (20+) Adult	£8.50

Park & West Garden
Adult	£5.50
Child	£4.00

Park only
Adult	£2.50
Child (5–15yrs)	£1.50

East Garden
(Thursdays) £3.50 extra

RHS members free entry to Park & West Garden daily during open season, except during special events.

■ Special Events
May 8–11
Living Crafts.
June 21/22
Rose Weekend.
July 26
Battle Proms Concert.
Aug 1–3
Art in Clay.
Aug 15–17
Hatfield House Country Show.
Please see website for details of events programme.

Conference/Function

ROOM	SIZE	MAX CAPACITY
The Old Palace	112' x 33'	280
Riding School Conference Centre	100' x 40'	140

■ Owner

The Hon Henry Lytton
Cobbold

■ Contact

The Estate Office
Knebworth House
Knebworth
Hertfordshire SG3 6PY

Tel: 01438 812661
Fax: 01438 811908
E-mail: info@
knebworthhouse.com

■ Location

MAP 7:E11
OS Ref. TL230 208

Direct access off the
A1(M) J7 (Stevenage
South A602).
28m N of London.
15m N of M25/J23.

Rail: Stevenage Station
2m (from Kings Cross).

Air: Luton Airport 15m
Landing facilities.

Taxi: 01438 811122.

■ Opening Times

House, Park & Gardens
15/16 March, 12 April–
18 May, 7–22 June &
6–28 September:
Weekends and BHs.

21 March–6 April,
24 May–1 June &
28 June–3 September:
Daily.

**Park, Playground &
Gardens**
11am–5pm
(last adm. 4.15pm).

**House & Indian
Exhibition**
12 noon–5pm
(last adm. 4.15pm).

■ Admission

Including House
Adult	£9.50
Child*/Conc	£9.00

Family Day Ticket
(4 persons)	£33.00

Groups (20+)
Adult	£8.50
Child*/Conc	£8.00

Excluding House
All Persons	£7.50
Season Ticket	£34.00

Family Day Ticket
(4 persons)	£26.00

Groups (20+)
All persons	£6.50

House Supplements
Adults	£2.50
Child*/Conc	£2.00

*4–16 yrs, under 4s Free.

Conference/Function

ROOM	SIZE	MAX CAPACITY
Banqueting Hall	26' x 41'	80
Dining Parlour	21' x 38'	50
Library	32' x 21'	40
Manor Barn	70' x 25'	250
Lodge Barn	75' x 30'	150

KNEBWORTH HOUSE 🏛

www.knebworthhouse.com

Home of the Lytton family since 1490, and still a lived-in family house. Transformed in early Victorian times by Edward Bulwer-Lytton, the author, poet, dramatist and statesman, into the unique high gothic fantasy house of today, complete with turrets, griffins and gargoyles.

Historically home to Constance Lytton, the Suffragette, and her father, Robert Lytton, the Viceroy of India who proclaimed Queen Victoria Empress of India at the Great Delhi Durbar of 1877. Visited by Queen Elizabeth I, Charles Dickens and Sir Winston Churchill.

The interior contains various styles including the magnificent Jacobean Banqueting Hall, a unique example of the 17th century change in fashion from traditional English to Italian Palladian. The high gothic State Drawing Room by John Crace contrasts with the

Regency elegance of Mrs Bulwer-Lytton's bedroom and the 20th century designs of Sir Edwin Lutyens in the Entrance Hall, Dining Parlour and Library.

25 acres of beautiful gardens, simplified by Lutyens, including pollarded lime avenues, formal rose garden, maze, Gertrude Jekyll herb garden and newly designed Walled Garden. 250 acres of gracious parkland, with herds of red and sika deer, includes children's giant adventure playground and miniature railway. New Dino Trail with 72 life-size dinosaurs set grazing through the Wilderness Walk within the Formal Gardens. World famous for its huge open-air rock concerts, and used as a film location for *Batman*, *The Shooting Party*, *Wilde*, *Jane Eyre* and *The Canterville Ghost*, amongst others.

ℹ	Suitable for fashion shows, air displays, archery, shooting, equestrian events, cricket pitch, garden parties, shows, rallies, filming, helicopter landing. No pushchairs, photography, smoking or drinking in House.
🛍	
❄	
🍷	Indian Raj Evenings and Elizabethan Banquets with jousting. Full catering service.
♿	Partial. WCs. Parking. Ground floor accessible.
☕	Licensed tearoom. Special rates for advance bookings, menus on request.
🚶	Daily at 30 min intervals or at booked times including evenings. Tour time 1hr. Shorter tours by arrangement. Room Wardens on duty on busy weekends. Themed tours available.
P	Unlimited. Group visits must be booked in advance with Estate Office.
🎒	National Curriculum based school activity days.
🐕	Guide dogs only in House. Park, on leads.
🔔	Licensed Garden Gazebo & Manor Barn.
🎭	Telephone for details.

ASHRIDGE

Ringshall, Berkhamsted, Hertfordshire HP4 1LX

Tel: 01442 851227   **Fax:** 01442 850000   **E-mail:** ashridge@nationaltrust.org.uk

Owner: The National Trust   **Contact:** The Visitor Centre

The Ashridge Estate comprises over 1800ha of woodlands, commons and downland. At the northerly end of the Estate the Ivinghoe Hills are an outstanding area of chalk downland which supports a rich variety of plants and insects.

Location: MAP 7:D11 OS Ref. SP970 131. Between Northchurch & Ringshall, just off B4506.

Open: Visitor Centre & Shop: 15 Mar–21 Dec: daily, 12 noon–5pm. Monument: 15 Mar–26 Oct: Sats, Suns & BHs 12 noon–last admission 4.30pm. Tearoom: 15 Mar–21 Dec: daily, 10am–5pm.

Admission: Monument: £1.50, Child 70p. Free to NT members.

ℹ️ Visitor Centre. 📷 ♿ Vehicles available. 🍴 🅿 Limited for coaches. ▣

🐕 In grounds, on leads. ♿

BENINGTON LORDSHIP GARDENS

Stevenage, Hertfordshire SG2 7BS

Tel: 01438 869668   **Fax:** 01438 869622   **E-mail:** garden@beningtonlordship.co.uk

www.beningtonlordship.co.uk

Owner: Mr R R A Bott   **Contact:** Mr or Mrs R R A Bott

7 acre garden overlooking lakes in a timeless setting. Features include Norman keep and moat, Queen Anne manor house, James Pulham folly, formal rose garden, renowned herbaceous borders, walled vegetable garden, grass tennis court and verandah. Spectacular display of snowdrops in February. All location work welcome. Estate includes listed cottages, barns, buildings and airstrip.

Location: MAP 7:F11, OS Ref. TL296 236. In village of Benington next to the church. 4m E of Stevenage.

Open: Gardens only: Snowdrops: 2–24 Feb, daily, 12 noon–4pm. Easter & May BH weekends: Suns, 2–5pm. Mons, 12 noon–5pm. 28/29 Jun: Floral Festival, 12 noon–6pm. 24/25 Aug: Chilli Festival, 10am–5pm. By request all year, please telephone. Coaches must book.

Admission: Adult £4 (Suns in Feb £4.50), Child under 12 Free.

🎪 February. ♿ Unsuitable. 🍴 🅿 🐕 ♿

BERKHAMSTED CASTLE

Berkhamsted, St Albans, Hertfordshire

Tel: 01223 582700 (Regional Office)   **www.english-heritage.org.uk/berkhamsted**

Owner: English Heritage   **Contact:** East of England Regional Office

The extensive remains of a large 11th century motte and bailey castle which held a strategic position on the road to London.

Location: MAP 7:D12, OS Ref. SP996 083. Adjacent to Berkhamsted rail station.

Open: All year. Summer: daily, 10am–6pm; Winter: daily, 10am–4pm. Closed 25 Dec & 1 Jan.

Admission: Free.

ℹ️ Picnickers welcome. 🐕 ❄

CROMER WINDMILL

Ardeley, Stevenage, Hertfordshire SG2 7QA

Tel: 01279 843301

Owner: Hertfordshire Building Preservation Trust   **Contact:** Cristina Harrison

17th century Post Windmill restored to working order.

Location: MAP 7:F10, OS Ref. TL305 286. 4m NE of Stevenage on B1037. 1m SW of Cottered.

Open: 10 May–mid-Sept: Sun & BH Mons, 2nd & 4th Sat, 2.30–5pm.

Admission: Adult £2, Child 25p. Groups (10+) by arrangement: Adult £1, Child 25p.

FORGE MUSEUM & VICTORIAN COTTAGE GARDEN

High Street, Much Hadham, Hertfordshire SG10 6BS

Tel/Fax: 01279 843301   **E-mail:** cristinaharrison@btopenworld.com

Owner: The Hertfordshire Building Preservation Trust   **Contact:** The Curator

The garden reflects plants that would have been grown in 19th century.

Location: MAP 7:G11, OS Ref. TL428 195. Village centre.

Open: Closed for refurbishment until June. Please telephone for details.

THE GOLDEN PARSONAGE

GADDESDEN ROW, HEMEL HEMPSTEAD, HERTFORDSHIRE HP2 6HG

www.gaddesdenestate.co.uk

Tel: 01442 252421   **Fax:** 01442 231787   **E-mail:** nghalsey@gaddesdenestate.co.uk

Owner: Mr and Mrs Nicholas Halsey   **Contact:** Nicholas Halsey

An early 18th century house on an ancient site in the Chiltern Hills, The Golden Parsonage has been the family home of the Halseys for nearly 500 years. Beautifully set at the heart of a 1,900 acre estate, facilities are offered for coprorate team-building, marquee events, equestrian and sporting activities.

Location: MAP 7:E11, OS Ref. TL 051 125. 3m N of Hemel Hempstead off A4146. M1 J8 & J10, M25 J20, St Albans & Berkhamsted 15–20 minutes. Luton Airport ½hr.

Open: Open to small groups (max 15) by appointment only.

Admission: By arrangement.

🍴 ♿ Partial. 🎥 By arrangement. 🅿 Ample for cars, limited for coaches. 🐕 ❄ €

GORHAMBURY

St Albans, Hertfordshire AL3 6AH

Tel: 01727 854051   **Fax:** 01727 843675

Owner: The Earl of Verulam   **Contact:** The Administrator

Late 18th century house by Sir Robert Taylor. Family portraits from 15th–21st centuries.

Location: MAP 7:E11, OS Ref. TL114 078. 2m W of St Albans. Access via private drive off A4147 at St Albans.

Open: May–Sept: Thurs, 2–5pm (last entry 4.15pm).

Admission: House & Gardens: Adult £7, Child £4, Conc £5. Visitors join guided tours. Special groups by arrangement (Thurs mornings preferred).

♿ Partial. 🐕 🎥 Obligatory. 🅿

HATFIELD HOUSE

See page 267 for full page entry.

HERTFORD MUSEUM

18 Bull Plain, Hertford SG14 1DT

Tel: 01992 582686

Owner: Hertford Museums Trust   **Contact:** Helen Gurney

Local museum in 17th century house, altered by 18th century façade, with recreated Jacobean knot garden.

Location: MAP 7:F11, OS Ref. TL326 126. Town centre.

Open: Tue–Sat, 10am–5pm.

Admission: Free.

KNEBWORTH HOUSE

See page 268 for full page entry.

THE NATURAL HISTORY MUSEUM AT TRING

Akeman Street, Tring, Hertfordshire HP23 6AP
Tel: 020 7942 6171   **Fax:** 020 7942 6150
Owner: The Natural History Museum   **Contact:** General Organiser
The museum was opened to the public by Lord Rothschild in 1892. It houses his private natural history collection. Over 4,000 species of animal in a Victorian setting.
Location: MAP 7:D11, OS Ref. SP924 111. S end of Akeman Street, ¼m S of High Street.
Open: All year, daily: Mon–Sat, 10am–5pm, Suns, 2–5pm. Closed 24–26 Dec.
Admission: Free.

OLD GORHAMBURY HOUSE ♯

St Albans, Hertfordshire
Tel: 01223 582700 (Regional Office)   **www.english-heritage.org.uk/oldgorhambury**
Owner: English Heritage   **Contact:** East of England Regional Office
The decorated remains of this Elizabethan mansion, particularly the porch of the Great Hall, illustrate the impact of the Renaissance on English architecture.
Location: MAP 7:E11, OS Ref. TL110 077. On foot by permissive 2m path. By car, drive to Gorhambury Mansion and walk across the gardens.
Open: All year (except 1 Jun), any reasonable time.
Admission: Free.
ℹ️ Picnickers welcome. ✖ ✳

ST ALBANS CATHEDRAL

St Albans, Hertfordshire AL1 1BY
Tel: 01727 860780   **Fax:** 01727 850944   **E-mail:** mail@stalbanscathedral.org.uk
www.stalbanscathedral.org.uk
Owner: Dean and Chapter of St Albans   **Contact:** Susan Keeling, Visitors' Officer
Magnificent Norman abbey church built with recycled Roman bricks from the nearby city of Verulanium, the setting for the Shrine (1308) of Alban, Britain's first Christian martyr. Series of 12th–13th century wall paintings, painted Presbytery ceiling (1280), wooden watching loft (1400) and the tomb of Humphrey, Duke of Gloucester (1447).
Location: MAP 7:E12. OS Ref. TL145 071. Centre of St Albans.
Open: Daily, 9am–5.45pm.
Admission: Free, donations welcomed.
⬜ ♿ WCs. ⬛ Licenced. 💁 By prior arrangement. ✖ In grounds, on leads.

ST PAULS WALDEN BURY

Hitchin, Hertfordshire SG4 8BP
Tel/Fax: 01438 871218/341   **E-mail:** spw@boweslyon.demon.co.uk
Owner/Contact: S and C Bowes Lyon
Formal woodland garden, covering about 60 acres, laid out 1730. Long rides lined with clipped beech hedges lead to temples, statues, lake and ponds, and to an outdoor theatre. Seasonal displays of snowdrops, daffodils, irises, magnolias, rhododendrons, woodland paeonies, lilies and shrub roses. Wild flower areas. Grade I listed.
Location: MAP 7:E11, OS Ref. TL186 216. 30m N of London. 5m S of Hitchin on B651.
Open: Suns: 6 & 27 Apr, 18 May, 2–7pm. Other times by appointment.
Admission: Adult £3.50, Child 50p. Other times by appointment £6.
♿ ⬛ 🅿 ✖ On leads. €

SCOTT'S GROTTO

Ware, Hertfordshire S912 9SQ
Tel: 01920 464131
Owner: East Hertfordshire District Council   **Contact:** J Watson
One of the finest grottos in England built in the 1760s by Quaker Poet John Scott.
Location: MAP 7:F11, OS Ref. TL355 137. In Scotts Rd, S of the A119 Hertford Road.
Open: 1 Apr–30 Sept: Sat & BH Mon, 2–4.30pm. Also by appointment.
Admission: Suggested donation of £1 for adults. Children Free. Please bring a torch.

Ashridge, Berkhamsted

©NT Pl/Matthew Antrobus

SHAW'S CORNER ✂

AYOT ST LAWRENCE, WELWYN, HERTFORDSHIRE AL6 9BX

www.nationaltrust.org.uk

Tel/Fax: 01438 820307   **E-mail:** shawscorner@nationaltrust.org.uk
Owner: The National Trust   **Contact:** The House Manager
The fascinating home of playwright George Bernard Shaw until his death in 1950. The modest Edwardian villa contains many literary and personal relics, and the interior is still set out as it was in Shaw's lifetime. The garden, with its richly planted borders and views over the Hertfordshire countryside, contains the revolving summerhouse where Shaw retreated to write.
Location: MAP 7:E11, OS Ref. TL194 167. At SW end of village, 2m NE of

Wheathampstead, approximately 2m N from B653. A1(M)/J4, M1/J10.
Open: 15 Mar–2 Nov: Wed–Sun & BH Mons (open Good Fri), House: 1–5pm; Garden: 12 noon–5.30pm. Last admission to House & Garden 4.30pm. No large hand luggage inside house. Groups by prior appointment only.
Admission: Adult £4.95, Child £2.50, Family £12.40. Groups (15+ Adult £3.80, Child £1.90).
ℹ️ WC. 🚻 ♿ Partial, ground floor, no WC. 🅿 ⬛ ✖ Car park only.
📞 Tel 01438 829221 for details.

James Willis

HOLKHAM HALL 🏛

www.holkham.co.uk

This elegant Palladian style mansion, based on designs by William Kent, was built between 1734 and 1764 by Thomas Coke, the 1st Earl of Leicester, and is home to his descendants. It reflects Coke's natural appreciation of classical art, developed during his Grand Tour. Built from local, yellow brick, with its pedimented portico, square corner towers and side wings, it has been little altered over the years, and has been described by Sir Nikolaus Pevsner as "*The most classically correct house in Britain*".

"The Marble Hall" is a spectacular introduction to this vast and imposing house, with its 50ft pressed plaster dome ceiling and walls of English alabaster, not marble as its name implies. Stairs from the Hall lead to magnificent State rooms with superb collections of ancient statuary, original furniture, tapestries and paintings by Rubens, Van Dyck, Claude, Gaspar Poussin and Gainsborough.

On leaving the house, visitors enter the lavender-fringed Pottery Courtyard. Here the original stable block houses the Bygones Museum; a display of more than 4,000 items of domestic and agricultural memorabilia, ranging from working steam engines,

vintage cars and tractors to gramophones, craft tools and kitchenware. In the adjacent former brew house and malt house, the History of Farming Exhibition highlights how a great Estate such as Holkham works and has evolved, explaining Coke of Norfolk's role in the great Agricultural Revolution of the 18th century.

In the same courtyard, the elegant Gift Shop, once the former laundry for the Hall, offers a wide range of quality gifts, selected soft furnishings and souvenirs. Opposite, the light and airy Stables Café tempts visitors with delicious, local produce for a light snack, lunch or afternoon tea and Holkham's own, home made, mouth-watering ice cream.

Set in a 3,000 acre park with herd of fallow deer and mile-long lake, visitors can explore the park and wildlife with designated walks and a nature trail, or enjoy boat trips on the lake in the summer months. Outside the north gates to the park, Holkham Village, with its internationally-acclaimed hotel, fascinating shops, gallery, tearooms and beach, famous for the closing scenes of *Shakespeare in Love* and National Nature Reserve, offers more to discover.

Owner

The Earl of Leicester CBE

Contact

Marketing Manager
Laurane Herrieven
Holkham Estate Office
Wells-next-the-Sea
Norfolk NR23 1AB

Tel: 01328 710227
Fax: 01328 711707
E-mail: enquiries@
holkham.co.uk

Location

MAP 8:I4
OS Ref. TF885 428

From London 120m
Norwich 35m
King's Lynn 30m.

Rail: Norwich Station 35m
King's Lynn Station 30m.

Air: Norwich Airport 32m.

Opening Times

Hall & Museum
Easter Saturday, Sunday & Monday; May & August BHs, plus 1 June–30 September: Sun–Thu. 12 noon–5pm, last admission 4.30pm.

Hall Audio Tours
25 March–2 May, 6–23 & 27–31 May, 1–31 October. Sunday–Thursday. Two audio tours each day. First tour starts at 1pm and the second at 3pm prompt. Max 40 people each tour.

During the above dates the free History of Farming Exhibition will be open. The Bygones Museum will be closed.

The Libraries & Strangers' Wing form part of the private accommodation and are open at the family's discretion.

Terraces
1 June–30 September, Mon–Thurs (except BH Mondays), 12 noon–4.45pm.

The Stables Café & Gift Shop in the Park:
21 March–31 October (times vary). Closed Sats (except BH weekends) in Mar, Apr, May, Sep & Oct.

Admission

Hall
Adult	£7.00
Child (5–16yrs)	£3.50
May Audio Tour	
Adult	£9.00
Child (5–16yrs)	£4.50

Museum
Adult	£5.00
Child (5–16yrs)	£2.50

Hall & Museum
Adult	£10.00
Child (5–16yrs)	£5.00
Family (2+2)	£25.00
Acoustiguide Hire	£2.00

Groups (20+)10% discount

Private Guided Tours
£15.00

Boat trips on the lake:
Adult	£3.00
Child (5–16yrs)	£2.50

ℹ️	Grounds for shows, weddings, product launches, rallies and filming. Photography allowed in Hall. Central Ticket Office for admission & events tickets.	
🏬	Two Gift Shops & Gallery.	
🍽	Hall & Grounds.	
♿	Access to first floor in the Hall is suitable for most manual wheelchairs. Elsewhere, full disabled access.	
☕	Stables Café, licensed. Menus for pre-booked groups on request. Marsh Larder Tearooms in Holkham Village.	
🍴	The Victoria Hotel at Holkham and The Globe Inn, Wells-next-the-Sea.	
🎧	Acoustiguide £2.	

🚶	Private guided tours of Hall are available by arrangement when the Hall is not open to the public. Please tel for details.
🅿️	Unlimited for cars, 12+ coaches. Parking, admission, refreshments free to coach drivers.
🏛	Bygones Collection, History of Farming, three designated walks, nature trail and quiz.
🐕	No dogs in Hall, on leads in grounds.
🔔	Civil ceremonies available.
❄️	Deer Park, except Christmas Day, at no charge. Closed to vehicles at weekends November–Easter.
🎭	Outdoor Theatre Productions, Marble Hall & Open-Air Concerts.

■ **Owner**

H M The Queen

■ **Contact**

The Public Enterprises
Manager
The Estate Office
Sandringham
Norfolk PE35 6EN

Tel: 01553 612908
Fax: 01485 541571
E-mail: visits@
sandringhamestate.co.uk

■ **Location**

MAP 7:H5
OS Ref. TF695 287

8m NE of King's Lynn on
B1440 off A148.

Rail: King's Lynn.

Air: Norwich.

■ **Opening Times**

**House, Museum &
Gardens**
22 March–late July &
early Aug–26 Oct.

■ **Admission**

**House, Museum
& Gardens**

Adult	£9.00
Child (5–15yrs)	£5.00
Conc.	£7.00
Family	£23.00

Museum & Gardens

Adult	£6.00
Child (5–15yrs)	£3.50
Conc.	£5.00
Family	£15.50

Groups (20+):

Adult	£8.00
Child (5–15yrs)	£4.00
Conc.	£6.00

Conference/Function

ROOM	MAX CAPACITY
Restaurant	200
Tearoom	60

By gracious permission of HM Queen Elizabeth II

SANDRINGHAM

www.sandringhamestate.co.uk

Sandringham House is the charming country retreat of Her Majesty The Queen, hidden in the heart of 60 acres of beautiful wooded gardens. Still maintained in the style of Edward and Alexandra, Prince and Princess of Wales (later King Edward VII and Queen Alexandra), all the main ground floor rooms used by The Royal Family, full of their treasured ornaments, portraits and furniture, are open to the public.

More family possessions are displayed in the Museum housed in the old stables and coach houses, including vehicles ranging in date from the first car owned by a British monarch, a 1900 Daimler, to a half-scale Aston Martin used by Princes William and Harry. A display tells the mysterious tale of the Sandringham Company who fought and died at Gallipoli in 1915, and a photographic exhibition in the Museum shows the history of Sandringham House from 1870 to the present day.

The 60-acre gardens include the formal North Garden, the Stream Walk and Queen Alexandra's Summerhouse, perched above the lake; the formal planting of the Edwardian age has given way to great sweeping glades, bordered by splendid specimen trees and shrubs, to create an informal garden full of colour and interest throughout the year. Guided garden tours take place on Fridays and Saturdays. There are also 600 acres of the Country Park open to all, with tractor tours running daily; a free Land Train from within the entrance will carry passengers less able to walk through the gardens to the House and back.

By gracious permission of HM Queen Elizabeth II

The view from Queen Alexandra's Nest

ℹ️	No photography in house.
🛍️	
❀	Plant Centre.
ⓣ	Visitor Centre only.
♿	
☕	Licensed.

🍴	Licensed.
🚶	By arrangement. Private evening tours.
🅿️	Ample.
🐕	Guide dogs only.
🎭	

BINHAM PRIORY ⌘

Binham-on-Wells, Norfolk
Tel: 01328 830362 / 01223 582700 (Regional Office)
www.english-heritage.org.uk/binhampriory
Owner: English Heritage (Managed by Binham Parochial Church Council)
Contact: East of England Regional Office
Extensive remains of a Benedictine priory, of which the original nave of the church is still in use as the parish church, displaying a screen with medieval saints overpainted with Protestant texts.
Location: MAP 8:J4, OS Ref. TF982 399. ¼m NW of village of Binham-on-Wells, on road off B1388.
Open: Any reasonable time.
Admission: Free.
ⅈ Picnickers welcome. ✳

BIRCHAM WINDMILL

Snettisham Road, Great Bircham, Norfolk PE31 6SJ
Tel: 01485 578393
Owner/Contact: Mr & Mrs S Chalmers
One of the last remaining complete windmills. Tearoom, bakery, windmill museum, gift shop, cycle hire, regular events and holiday cottage.
Location: MAP 0:M, OS Ref. TF760 326. ¼m W of Bircham. N of the road to Snettisham.
Open: Easter–end Sept: Daily 10am–5pm.
Admission: Adult £3.50, Child £2, OAP £3.

For unique **Civil wedding** venues see our index at the end of the book.

BRADENHAM HALL GARDENS

Bradenham, Thetford, Norfolk IP25 7QP
Tel: 01362 687279/243   **Fax:** 01362 687669   **E-mail:** info@bradenhamhall.co.uk
www.bradenhamhall.co.uk
Owner: Chris & Panda Allhusen   **Contact:** Chris Allhusen
A plant-lover's garden for all seasons. The house and garden walls are covered with unusual climbers. Flower gardens, formal rose gardens, paved garden, herbaceous and shrub borders. Arboretum of over 800 different trees, all labelled. Traditional walled kitchen gardens, mixed borders, and two glasshouses. Massed daffodils in spring.
Location: MAP 8:J6, OS Ref. TF921 099. Off A47, 6m of Swaffham. 3m W of E Dereham. S on Dale Road, then S 2m to Bradenham.
Open: Apr–Sept: 2nd & 4th Suns of each month, 2–5.30pm. Groups by appointment at other times.
Admission: Adult £4, Child Free. Group discounts available.
ⅈ No commercial photography. House not open. ✦ ♿ Partial. ▣
✗ By arrangement. Ⓟ Ample. Limited for coaches. ♿ Guide dogs only.

BURGH CASTLE ⌘

Breydon Water, Great Yarmouth, Norfolk
Tel: 01223 582700 (Regional Office)   **www.english-heritage.org.uk/burghcastle**
Owner: English Heritage   **Contact:** East of England Regional Office
Impressive walls, with projecting bastions, of a Roman fort built in the late 3rd century as one of a chain to defend the coast against Saxon raiders.
Location: MAP 8:M6, OS Ref. TG475 046. At far W end of Breydon Water, on unclassified road 3m W of Great Yarmouth. SW of the church.
Open: Any reasonable time.
Admission: Free.
ⅈ Picnickers welcome. ♿ ✳

BLICKLING HALL ❧
BLICKLING, NORWICH, NORFOLK NR11 6NF

www.nationaltrust.org.uk

Tel: 01263 738030   **Fax:** 01263 738035   **E-mail:** blickling@nationaltrust.org.uk
Owner: The National Trust   **Contact:** The Property Manager
Built in the early 17th century and one of England's great Jacobean houses. Blickling is famed for its spectacular long gallery, superb library and fine collections of furniture, pictures and tapestries.
Location: MAP 8:K5, OS133 Ref. TG178 286. 1½m NW of Aylsham on B1354. Signposted off A140 Norwich (15m) to Cromer.
Open: House: 17 Mar–2 Nov: Wed–Sun & BH Mons, 11am–5pm. Also open Mons during local school holidays. Garden: Same days as house, 10.15am–5.15pm. 3 Nov–end Jan 2009: Thurs–Sun, 11am–4pm. Park & Woods: daily, dawn–dusk.
*Admission: Hall & Gardens: £9.10. Garden only: £6. Groups must book. *includes a voluntary donation but visitors can choose to pay the standard prices displayed at the property and on the website.
ⅈ Cycle hire available in Orchard, ring for details. ▣ Open as garden. ✦ ⊤
♿ Mostly suitable. ▣ ⅈ↑ Open as garden. Licensed. ✗ By arrangement. Ⓟ ▣
♿ In park, on leads. ▲ ✳ ♿

CAISTER CASTLE CAR COLLECTION

Caister-on-sea, Great Yarmouth, Norfolk NR30 5SN

Tel: 01572 787649

Owner/Contact: Mr J Hill

Large collection of historic motor vehicles from 1893 to recent. Moated Castle built by Sir John Falstaff in 1432. Car park free.

Location: MAP 8:M6, OS Ref. TG502 122. Take A1064 out of Caister-on-sea towards Filby, turn left at the end of the dual carriageway.

Open: Mid May–End Sept: Sun–Fri (closed Sats), 10am–4.30pm.

Admission: Contact property for details.

ⓘ No photography. Partial. WCs. 🅿

CASTLE ACRE PRIORY ⌗

Stocks Green, Castle Acre, King's Lynn, Norfolk PE32 2XD

Tel: 01760 755394 **www.english-heritage.org.uk/castleacre**

Owner: English Heritage **Contact:** Visitor Operations Team

Explore the romantic ruins of this 12th century Cluniac priory, set in the picturesque village of Castle Acre. The impressive Norman façade, splendid prior's lodgings and chapel, and delightful recreated medieval herb garden should not be missed.

Location: MAP 8:I5, OS Ref. TF814 148. ¼m W of village of Castle Acre, 5m N of Swaffham.

Open: 21 Mar–30 Sept: daily, 10am–6pm. 1 Oct–31 Mar '09: Thur–Mon, 10am–4pm. Closed 24–26 Dec & 1 Jan. EH Members/OVP free.

Admission: Adult £4.90, Child £2.50, Conc. £3.90. Family £12.30. Group discount available.

ⓘ Picnickers welcome. Ground floor & grounds. 🅿 On leads. ❋

CASTLE RISING CASTLE

CASTLE RISING, KING'S LYNN, NORFOLK PE31 6AH

Tel: 01553 631330 **Fax:** 01553 631724

Owner: Lord Howard **Contact:** The Custodian

Possibly the finest mid-12th century Keep left in England: it was built as a grand and elaborate palace. It was home to Queen Isabella, grandmother of the Black Prince. Still in surprisingly good condition, the Keep is surrounded by massive ramparts up to 120 feet high. Picnic area, adjacent tearoom. Free audio tour.

Location: MAP 7:H5, OS Ref. TF666 246. Located 4m NE of King's Lynn off A149.

Open: 1 Apr–1 Nov: daily, 10am–6pm. 2 Nov–31 Mar: Wed–Sun, 10am–4pm. Closed 24–26 Dec & 1 Jan.

Admission: Adult £4, Child £2.50, Conc. £3.30, Family £12. 15% discount for groups (11+). Prices include VAT.

ⓘ Picnic area. Grounds. WC. 🅿 ❋

Houghton Hall

FAIRHAVEN WOODLAND & WATER GARDEN

School Road, South Walsham NR13 6DZ

Tel/Fax: 01603 270449 **www.fairhavengarden.co.uk**

Owner: The Fairhaven Garden Trust **Contact:** Louise Rout, Manager

Delightful natural woodland and water garden with private broad in the beautiful Norfolk Broads. 3 miles of scenic paths. Boat trips on our private broad: April–end October. New sensory garden for visually and mobility impaired visitors.

Location: MAP 8:L6, OS Ref. TG368 134. 9m NE of Norwich. Signed on A47 at junction with B1140.

Open: Daily (except 25 Dec), 10am–5pm, also May–Aug: Wed & Thurs evenings until 9pm.

Admission: Adult £4.75, Child £2.25 (under 5yrs Free), Conc. £4.25. Group reductions.

🅿 ❋ Programme of events throughout the year. Telephone or visit website for information.

Oxburgh Hall

©NTPL/Matthew Antrobus

FELBRIGG HALL
FELBRIGG, NORWICH, NORFOLK NR11 8PR
www.nationaltrust.org.uk

Tel: 01263 837444 **Fax:** 01263 837032 **E-mail:** felbrigg@nationaltrust.org.uk
Owner: The National Trust **Contact:** The Property Manager
One of the finest 17th century country houses in East Anglia. The hall contains its original 18th century furniture and one of the largest collections of Grand Tour paintings by a single artist. The library is outstanding. The Walled Garden has been restored and features a series of pottager gardens, a working dovecote and the National Collection of Colchicums. The Park, through which there are way-marked walks, is well known for its magnificent and aged trees. There are also walks to the church and lake and through the 500 acres of woods.
Location: MAP 8:K4, OS133 Ref. TG193 394. Nr Felbrigg village, 2m SW of Cromer, entrance off B1436, signposted from A148 and A140.

Open: House: 1 Mar–2 Nov: daily except Thur & Fri, 11am–5pm. (Open Good Fri.) Gardens: 1 Mar–26 Oct: daily except Thur & Fri (open Good Fri), 11am–5pm. Some additional opening, please telephone property for details.
*Admission: House & Garden: Adult £7.90, Child £3.70, Family £19.50. Garden only: Adult £3.70, Child £1.60. Groups please telephone property to pre-book. *includes a voluntary donation but visitors can choose to pay the standard prices displayed at the property and on the website.
01263 837040. 01263 838237. Partial. Licensed. Licensed. By arrangement. In grounds, on leads. Tel 01263 837444 for details.

GREAT YARMOUTH ROW HOUSES & GREYFRIARS' CLOISTERS
South Quay, Great Yarmouth, Norfolk NR30 2RQ
Tel: 01493 857900 www.english-heritage.org.uk/greatyarmouth
Owner: English Heritage **Contact:** Visitor Operations Team
Two immaculately presented 17th century Row Houses, a type of building unique to Great Yarmouth. Row 111 House was almost destroyed by bombing in 1942/3 and contains items rescued from the rubble. Old Merchant's House boasts magnificent plaster-work ceilings and displays of local architectural fittings.
Location: MAP 8:M6, OS134, TG525 072. In Great Yarmouth, make for Historic South Quay, by riverside and dock, ½ m inland from beach. Follow signs to dock and south quay.
Open: 21 Mar–30 Sept: daily, 12 noon–5pm.
Admission: Adult £3.50. Child £1.80, Conc. £2.60. EH Members Free. Group discount available.
Picnickers welcome. Museum.

GRIME'S GRAVES
Lynford, Thetford, Norfolk IP26 5DE
Tel: 01842 810656
Owner: English Heritage **Contact:** Visitor Operations Team
www.english-heritage.org.uk/grimesgraves
These remarkable Neolithic flint mines, unique in England, comprise over 300 pits and shafts. The visitor can descend some 30 feet by ladder into one excavated shaft, and look along the radiating galleries, from where the flint used for making axes and knives was extracted.
Location: MAP 8:I7, OS 144, TL818 898. 7m NW of Thetford off A134.
Open: 21 Mar–30 Sept: daily, 10am–6pm. 1–31 Oct: Thu–Mon, 10am–5pm. Last visit to site 30 mins before close. No entry to the mines for children under 5 yrs. Closed 24 / 25 Dec and 1 Jan.
Admission: Adult £3, Child £1.50 (Child under 5yrs free), Conc. £2.40, Family £7.50. EH Members/OVP free. Group discount available.
Picnickers welcome. Exhibition area only. Restricted areas.

See which properties offer educational facilities or school visits in our index at the end of the book.

Holkham Hall

HOLKHAM HALL
See page 271 for full page entry.

HOUGHTON HALL

HOUGHTON, KING'S LYNN, NORFOLK PE31 6UE

www.houghtonhall.com

Tel: 01485 528569   **Fax:** 01485 528167   **E-mail:** enquiries@houghtonhall.com
Owner: The Marquess of Cholmondeley   **Contact:** Susan Cleaver

Houghton Hall is one of the finest examples of Palladian architecture in England. Built in the 18th century by Sir Robert Walpole, Britain's first prime minister. Original designs by James Gibbs & Colen Campbell, interior decoration by William Kent. The House has been restored to its former grandeur, containing many of its original furnishings. The spectacular 5-acre walled garden is divided into areas devoted to fruit and vegetables, elegant herbaceous borders, and a formal rose garden with over 150 varieties – full of colour throughout the summer. The unique Model Soldier Collection contains over 20,000 models arranged in various battle formations. Contemporary Sculptures in the Park.

Location: MAP 8:I5, OS Ref. TF792 287. 13m E of King's Lynn, 10m W of Fakenham 1½m N of A148.
Open: Easter Sun–28 Sept: Weds, Thurs, Suns & BH Mons. Walled Garden, Soldier Museum, Park, Restaurant & Gift Shop: 11am–5.30pm (last admission 5pm). House: 1.30–5pm (last admission 4.30pm).
Admission: Adult £8, Child (5–16) £3, Family (2+2) £20. Excluding House: Adult £5, Child £2. Family (2+2) £12. Group (20+) discounts available, please tel for details.
Licensed. Licensed. By arrangement. On leads, in grounds.

HOVETON HALL GARDENS

Wroxham, Norwich, Norfolk NR12 8RJ
Tel: 01603 782798   **Fax:** 01603 784564   **E-mail:** info@hovetonhallgardens.co.uk
Owner: Mr & Mrs Andrew Buxton   **Contact:** Mrs Buxton

15 acres of rhododendrons, azaleas, woodland and lakeside walks, walled herbaceous and vegetable gardens. The Hall (which is not open to the public) was built 1809–1812. Designs attributed to Humphry Repton.
Location: MAP 8:L5, OS Ref. TG314 202. 8m N of Norwich. 1½m NNE of Wroxham on A1151. Follow brown tourist signs.
Open: 23/24, & 30 Mar, 1 Apr–14 Sept: Wed–Fri, Sun & BH Mons, 10.30am–5pm.
Admission: Adult £5, Child (5–14yrs) £2, Wheelchair user and carers £2.50pp. Season Ticket: Single £13, Family £25.

Houghton Hall.

KIMBERLEY HALL

WYMONDHAM, NORFOLK NR18 0RT

www.kimberleyhall.co.uk

Tel/Fax: 01603 759447   **E-mail:** events@kimberleyhall.co.uk
Owner/Contact: R Buxton

Magnificent Queen Anne house built in 1712 by William Talman for Sir John Wodehouse, an ancestor of P G Wodehouse. Towers added after 1754 and wings connected to the main block by curved colonnades in 1835. Internal embellish-ments in 1770s include some very fine plasterwork by John Sanderson and a 'flying' spiral staircase beneath a coffered dome. The park, with its picturesque lake, ancient oak trees and walled gardens was laid out in 1762 by 'Capability' Brown.
Location: MAP 8:K6, OS Ref. TG091 048. 10m SW of Norwich, 3m from A11.
Open: House & Park not open to the public. Grounds, certain rooms and extensive cellars available for corporate hospitality and weddings (licensed for Civil ceremonies and partnerships) as well as product launches, film and fashion shoots. Tipis within walled garden available for hire.
Admission: Please telephone for details.

LETHERINGSETT WATERMILL

Riverside Road, Letheringsett, Holt, Norfolk NR25 7YD

Tel: 01263 713153 **E-mail:** watermill@ic24.net

Owner/Contact: M D Thurlow

Water-powered mill producing wholewheat flour from locally grown wheat. Built in 1802.

Location: MAP 8:J4, OS Ref. TG062 387. Riverside Road, Letheringsett, Holt, Norfolk.

Open: Whitsun–Oct: Mon–Fri, 10am–5pm, Sat 9am–1pm. Working demonstration, Tue–Fri, 2–4.30pm. Open to visitors from midday on weekdays. Oct–Whitsun: Mon–Fri, 9am–4pm. Sat, 9am–1pm. Not open on Bank Holidays. Winter working demonstration times: ring for details.

Admission: Adult £2.50, Child £1.50. When demonstrating: Adult £3.50, Child £2.50, OAP £3, Family (2+2) £10. Prices subject to change.

MANNINGTON GARDENS & COUNTRYSIDE

MANNINGTON HALL, NORWICH NR11 7BB

www.manningtongardens.co.uk

Tel: 01263 584175 **Fax:** 01263 761214

Owner: The Lord & Lady Walpole **Contact:** Lady Walpole

The gardens around this medieval moated manor house feature a wide variety of plants, trees and shrubs in many different settings. Throughout the gardens are thousands of roses especially classic varieties. The Heritage Rose and 20th Century Rose Gardens have roses in areas with designs reflecting their date of origin from the 15th century to the present day.

Location: MAP 8:K5, OS Ref. TG144 320. Signposted from Saxthorpe crossroads on the Norwich–Holt road B1149. 1½m W of Wolterton Hall.

Open: Gardens: May–Sept: Suns 12–5pm. Jun–Aug: Wed–Fri, 11am–5pm, and at other times by prior appointment. Walks: daily from 9am. Medieval Hall open by appointment. Grounds & Park open all year.

Admission: Adult £5, Child (under 16yrs) Free, Conc. £4. Groups by arrangement.

🔲🔲🔲🔲🔲 Grounds. WCs. 🔲 Licensed. 🔲 By arrangement. 🔲 £2 car park fee (walkers only). 🔲🔲 In park only. 🔲 Park. 🔲 €

NORWICH CASTLE MUSEUM & ART GALLERY

Norwich, Norfolk NR1 3JU

Tel: 01603 493625 **Fax:** 01603 493623 **E-mail:** museums@norfolk.gov.uk

Norman Castle Keep, housing displays of art, archaeology and natural history.

Location: MAP 8:K6, OS Ref. TG233 085. City centre.

Open: All year: Mon–Fri, 10am–4.30pm. Sat, 10am–5pm. Sun, 1–5pm. Closed 22–26 Dec & 1 Jan.

Admission: Adult £6.50, Child (4–16yrs) £4.75, Conc. £5.50. Subject to change Apr 2008.

OXBURGH HALL & ESTATE 🌿

OXBOROUGH, KING'S LYNN, NORFOLK PE33 9PS

www.nationaltrust.org.uk

Tel: 01366 328258 **Fax:** 01366 328066 **E-mail:** oxburghhall@nationaltrust.org.uk

Owner: The National Trust **Contact:** The Property Secretary

A moated manor house built in 1482 by the Bedingfeld family, who still live here. The rooms show the development from medieval austerity to Victorian comfort and include an accessible Priest's Hole and an outstanding display of embroidery by Mary Queen of Scots. The attractive gardens include a French parterre, kitchen garden and orchard and woodland walks.

Location: MAP 8:I6, OS143, TF742 012. At Oxborough, 7m SW of Swaffham on S side of Stoke Ferry road.

Open: House: 15 Mar–30 Jul & 1 Sept–2 Nov, Sat–Wed, 1–5pm (closes 4pm Oct); 1–31 Aug, daily 1–5pm; BH Mons & Good Fri, 11am–5pm. **Gatehouse:** 12 Jan–9 Mar, Sat & Sun 12 noon–3pm. Timed ticket tours only. **Garden, Shop & Tearoom:** 2 Feb–9 Mar & 8 Nov–21 Dec, Sat & Sun, 11am–4pm; 15 Mar–30 Jul & 1 Sept–1 Oct, 11am–5pm; 4 Oct–2 Nov, Sat & Sun 11am–4pm; 1–31 Aug, daily, 11am–5pm.

*****Admission: House & Garden:** Adult £7.10, Child £3.70, Family £19, Group; Adult £6, Child £3.10. Garden & Estate only: Adult £3.70, Child £2.10. Gatehouse & Garden: Adult £5.80, Child £2.95, Family £14.50. Out of hours group: Members £6.50, Non-members £9.50. Groups must book with SAE to the Property Secretary. *includes a voluntary 10% donation but visitors can choose to pay the standard prices displayed at the property and on the website.

🔲🔲🔲 Partial. 🔲🔲 Licensed. 🔲 By arrangement. 🔲🔲🔲🔲 Send SAE for details.

RAVENINGHAM GARDENS 🏛

RAVENINGHAM, NORWICH, NORFOLK NR14 6NS

www.raveningham.com

Tel: 01508 548152   **Fax:** 01508 548958
E-mail: info@raveningham.com
Owner: Sir Nicholas Bacon Bt   **Contact:** Mrs Janet Woodard

Superb herbaceous borders, 18th century walled kitchen garden, Victorian glasshouse, herb garden, Edwardian rose garden, contemporary sculptures, 14th century church and much more.

Location: MAP 8:L7, OS Ref. TM399 965. Between Norwich & Lowestoft off A146 then B1136.

Open: Easter–Aug BH: Mon–Fri, 11am–4pm (no teas). BH Suns & Mons, 2–5pm.

Admission: Adult £4, Child (under 16yrs) Free, OAP £3. Groups by prior arrangement.

🍽 Teas only on Suns & BH Mons. 🔟

SANDRINGHAM   *See page 272 for full page entry.*

See page 272 for full page entry.

ST GEORGE'S GUILDHALL 🌿

29 King Street, King's Lynn, Norfolk PE30 1HA
Tel: 01553 765565   www.west-norfolk.gov.uk
Owner: The National Trust   **Contact:** The Administrator

The largest surviving English medieval guildhall. The building is now converted into a theatre and arthouse cinema. Many interesting features survive.

Location: MAP 7:H5, OS132, TF616 202. On W side of King Street close to the Tuesday Market Place.

Open: Mon–Fri, 10am–2pm. Closed; Sat & Sun, Good Fri, BHs & 24 Dec–2 Jan. The Guildhall is not usually open on days when there are performances in the theatre. Please telephone box office 01553 764864 for details of opening dates and times.

Admission: Free.

🔲 🔇 Access to galleries. 🍽 🍴 Licensed. 🅿 Pay and Display 📷 ❄

SHERINGHAM PARK 🌿

Upper Sheringham, Norfolk NR26 8TL
Tel: 01263 820550   **E-mail:** sheringhampark@nationaltrust.org.uk
www.nationaltrust.org.uk
Owner: The National Trust   **Contact:** Visitor Centre

One of Humphry Repton's most outstanding achievements, the landscape park contains fine mature woodlands, and the large woodland garden is particularly famous for its spectacular show of rhododendrons and azaleas (mid May–June). There are stunning views of the coast and countryside from the viewing towers and many delightful waymarked walks. Programme of special events.

Location: MAP 8:K4, OS133, TG135 420. 2m SW of Sheringham, access for cars off A148 Cromer–Holt road; 5m W of Cromer, 6m E of Holt.

Open: Park open all year, daily, dawn–dusk.

Admission: Pay & Display: Cars £4 (NT members Free–display members' sticker in car). Coaches must book in advance.

🔲🔇 Partial. WC. 🍽 Easter–end Sept, daily. Sats/Suns all year. 🅿 Limited for coaches. 📷🐕 In grounds, on leads. ❄ 🛡

WALSINGHAM ABBEY GROUNDS & SHIREHALL MUSEUM 🏛

Little Walsingham, Norfolk NR22 6BP
Tel: 01328 820259   **Fax:** 01328 820098   **E-mail:** jackie@walsingham-estate.co.uk
Owner: Walsingham Estate Company   **Contact:** Estate Office

Set in the picturesque medieval village of Little Walsingham, a place of pilgrimage since the 11th century, the grounds contain the remains of the famous Augustinian Priory with attractive gardens and river walks. The Shirehall Museum includes a Georgian magistrates' court and displays on the history of Walsingham.

Location: MAP 8:J4, OS Ref. TF934 367. B1105 N from Fakenham–5m.

Open: 15 Mar–26 Oct: daily, 10am–4.30pm. Also daily during snowdrop season (February) 10am–4pm. (Closed 19 & 20 Jul). Abbey Grounds: many other times, please telephone for details.

Admission: Combined ticket: Adult £3, Conc. £2.

🔲 🔇 🔇 Partial. 🔟 By arrangement. 📷 🐕 In grounds, on leads. ❄ 🛡

WOLTERTON PARK 🏛

NORWICH, NORFOLK NR11 7LY

www.manningtongardens.co.uk

Tel: 01263 584175/768444   **Fax:** 01263 761214
Owner: The Lord and Lady Walpole   **Contact:** The Lady Walpole

18th century Hall. Historic park with lake.

Location: MAP 8:K5, OS Ref. TG164 317. Situated near Erpingham village, signposted from Norwich–Cromer Rd A140.

Open: Park: daily from 9am. Hall: 11 Apr–24 Oct: Fridays, 2–5pm (last entry 4pm) and by appointment.

Admission: £5. £2 car park fee only for walkers. (Groups by application: from £4.)

🔟🔇 Partial. WC. 🔟 🅿 📷 🐕 In park, on leads. 🏔 ❄ Park. 🛡 €

Houghton Hall.

THE ANCIENT HOUSE

Clare, Suffolk CO10 8NY

Tel: 01628 825925 **E-mail:** bookings@landmarktrust.org.uk

www.landmarktrust.org.uk

Owner: Leased to the Landmark Trust by Clare PC **Contact:** The Landmark Trust

A 14th century house extended in the 15th and 17th centuries, decorated with high relief pargetting. Half of the building is managed by the Landmark Trust, a building preservation charity who let it for holidays. The other half of the house is run as a museum. Full details of The Ancient House and 184 other historic buildings available for holidays are featured in The Landmark Handbook (price £11.50 refundable against booking).

Location: MAP 8:I9, OS Ref. TL769 454. Village centre, on A1092 8m WNW of Sudbury.

Open: House: Available for holidays for up to to 2 people throughout the year. 7 Open Days a year and at other times by appointment. Contact the Landmark Trust for details. Museum: Oct–May: Tue–Sat 9.30am–1pm & 2–5pm. Jun–Sep: Mon–Sat 9.30am–5pm, Sun 9.30am–1pm.

Admission: Free on Open Days.

BELCHAMP HALL

BELCHAMP WALTER, SUDBURY, SUFFOLK CO10 7AT

www.belchamphall.com

Tel: 01787 881961 **Fax:** 01787 466778

Owner/Contact: Mr C F V Raymond

Superb Queen Anne house on an estate belonging to the Raymond family since 1611. Historic portraits and period furniture. Suitable for corporate events and product launches, weddings in the church and receptions and as a film and television location. Gardens including a cherry avenue, follies, a sunken garden, walled garden and lake. Medieval church with 15th century wall paintings.

Location: MAP 8:I10, OS Ref. TL827 407. 5m SW of Sudbury, opposite Belchamp Walter Church.

Open: By appointment only: May–Sept: Tues and Thurs, 2.30–6pm.

Admission: Adult £10, Child £5. No reduction for groups.

ℹ No photography in house. Conference facilities. 🅃 🖵 By arrangement. 🅕 Obligatory. 🅿 🖼 Guide dogs only.

CHRISTCHURCH MANSION

Christchurch Park, Ipswich, Suffolk IP4 2BE

Tel: 01473 433554 **Fax:** 01473 433564

Owner/Contact: Ipswich Borough Council

A fine Tudor house set out as a museum.

Location: MAP 8:K9, OS Ref. TM165 450. Christchurch Park, near centre of Ipswich.

Open: All year: Tue–Sat, 10am–5pm (4pm in winter). Suns, 2.30–4pm. Also open BH Mons. Closed 24–26, 31 Dec/1 Jan & Good Fri.

Admission: Free.

EAST BERGHOLT PLACE GARDEN 'THE PLACE FOR PLANTS'

East Bergholt, Suffolk CO7 6UP

Tel/Fax: 01206 299224 **E-mail:** sales@placeforplants.co.uk

Owner: Mr & Mrs R L C Eley **Contact:** Sara Eley

Twenty acres of garden and arboretum originally laid out at the beginning of the last century by the present owner's great-grandfather. A wonderful collection of fine trees and shrubs, many of which are rarely seen growing in East Anglia and originate from the famous plant hunter George Forrest. Particularly beautiful in the spring when the rhododendrons, magnolias and camellias are in flower.

Location: MAP 8:K10, OS Ref. TM084 343. 2m E of A12 on B1070, Manningtree Rd, on the edge of East Bergholt.

Open: Mar–Sept: daily, 10am–5pm. Closed Easter Sun.

Admission: Adult £3, Child Free. (Proceeds to garden up-keep.)

🅟 Specialist Plant Centre in the Victorian walled garden. 🅕 By arrangement. 🖼 🖤

EUSTON HALL 🏛

ESTATE OFFICE, EUSTON, THETFORD, NORFOLK IP24 2QP

www.eustonhall.co.uk

Tel: 01842 766366 **Fax:** 01842 766764 **E-mail:** admin@euston-estate.co.uk

Owner: The Duke of Grafton **Contact:** Mrs L Campbell

Euston Hall has been home to the Dukes of Grafton for over 300 years. It contains a collection of paintings of the Court of Charles II by Van Dyck and Lely, also "Mares and Foals" by George Stubbs. The gardens were laid out by the diarist John Evelyn and his walk through the Pleasure Grounds can still be enjoyed today. The park and river layout was designed by William Kent and is considered one of his greatest works. The project was completed by 'Capability' Brown. The 18th century watermill has been restored recently. The church is one of only four country churches built during the reign of Charles II.

Location: MAP 8:J8, OS Ref. TL897 786. 12m N of Bury St Edmunds, on A1088. 2m E of A134.

Open: 19 Jun–18 Sept: Thurs only. Also 29 Jun, 13 Jul & 7 Sept: 2.30–5pm.

Admission: Adult £6, Child £2, OAP £5. Groups (12+): £5pp.

🖸 🅖 🖤 🖼

FLATFORD BRIDGE COTTAGE 🌿

Flatford, East Bergholt, Colchester, Essex CO7 6OL

Tel: 01206 298260 **Fax:** 01206 297212 **www.nationaltrust.org.uk**

Owner: The National Trust **Contact:** The Property Manager

Just upstream from Flatford Mill, the restored thatched cottage houses a display about John Constable, several of whose paintings depict this property. Facilities include a tearoom, shop, boat hire, an Information Centre and countryside walks.

Location: MAP 8:J10, OS Ref. TM077 332. On N bank of Stour, 1m S of East Bergholt B1070.

Open: Mar & Apr: Wed–Sun, 11am–5pm. May–end Sept: daily, 10.30am–5.30pm. Oct: daily, 11am–4pm. Nov & Dec: Wed–Sun, 11am–3.30pm. Jan & Feb: Sats & Suns only, 11am–3.30pm. Closed Christmas & New Year.

Admission: Guided walks (when guide available) £2.50, accompanied child Free.

🖸 🅖 Tea-room & shop. WC. 🖤 🅕 🖸 🅿 Charge applies. 🖼 Guide dogs only.

© English Heritage Photo Library

FRAMLINGHAM CASTLE ⌗
FRAMLINGHAM, SUFFOLK IP13 9BT

www.english-heritage.org.uk/framlingham

Tel: 01728 724189

Owner: English Heritage   **Contact:** Visitor Operations Team

A magnificent 12th century castle which, from the outside, looks almost the same as when it was built. From the continuous curtain wall linking 13 towers, there are excellent panoramic views of Framlingham and the charming reed-fringed Mere. From Spring 2008 visitors will be able to experience life at Framlingham Castle through the ages with a new introductory exhibition, themed trails and a variety of indoor and outdoor interactive games. Throughout its colourful history the castle has been a fortress, an Elizabethan prison, a poor house and a school. The many alterations over the years have led to a pleasing mixture of historic styles. Entry also includes access to the Lanman Trust's Museum of local history.

Location: MAP 8:L8, OS Ref. TM287 637. In Framlingham on B1116. NE of town centre.

Open: 21 Mar–30 Sept: daily, 10am–6pm. 1 Oct–31 Mar: Thur–Mon, 10am–4pm. Closed 24–26 Dec & 1 Jan. May close early if an event is booked. Please call to check.

Admission: Adult £5.50. Child £2.80, Children under 5 Free. Conc. £4.40, Family £13.80. EH Members/OVP Free. Group discount available.

ℹ Picnickers welcome. ▢ ♿ Ground floor & grounds. WCs. 🏠 🅿 🚌 ❄ ♿

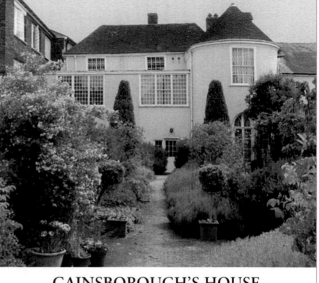

GAINSBOROUGH'S HOUSE
46 GAINSBOROUGH ST, SUDBURY, SUFFOLK CO10 2EU

www.gainsborough.org

Tel: 01787 372958   **Fax:** 01787 376991   **E-mail:** mail@gainsborough.org

Owner: Gainsborough's House Society   **Contact:** Rosemary Woodward

Birthplace of Thomas Gainsborough RA (1727–88). Historic house dating back to the 16th century with attractive walled garden. The outstanding collection is shown together with 18th century furniture and displays more of Gainsborough's work than any other gallery. Varied programme of exhibitions on both historic British and contemporary art.

Location: MAP 8:I10, OS Ref. TL872 413. 46 Gainsborough St, Sudbury town centre.

Open: All year: Mon–Sat, 10am–5pm. Closed: Suns, Good Fri and Christmas to New Year.

Admission: Adult £4, Child/Student £1.50, Conc £3.20, Family Ticket £9. Tues, 1–5pm: Free.

ℹ No photography. ▢ ♿ WCs. 🚌 🅿 None. ■ ❄

FRESTON TOWER

Nr Ipswich, Suffolk IP9 1AD

Tel: 01628 825925   **E-mail:** bookings@landmarktrust.org.uk

www.landmarktrust.org.uk

Owner/Contact: The Landmark Trust

An Elizabethan six-storey tower overlooking the estuary of the River Orwell. The tower was built in 1578 by a wealthy Ipswich merchant called Thomas Gooding, perhaps to celebrate the recent grant of his coat of arms. Freston Tower is cared for by The Landmark Trust, a building preservation charity who let it for holidays. Full details of Freston Tower and 184 other historic and architecturally important buildings are featured in the Landmark Trust Handbook (price £11.50 refundable against a booking).

Location: MAP 8:K9, OS Ref. TM177 397.

Open: Available for holidays for up to 4 people throughout the year. Please contact the Landmark Trust for details. Open Days on 8 days a year. Other visits by appointment.

Admission: Free on Open Days.

📷

HADLEIGH GUILDHALL

Hadleigh, Suffolk IP7 5DT

Tel: 01473 827752

Owner: Hadleigh Market Feoffment Charity   **Contact:** Jane Haylock

Fine timber framed guildhall, one of the least known medieval buildings in Suffolk.

Location: MAP 8:J9, OS Ref. TM025 425. S side of churchyard.

Open: mid Jun–end Sept: Building: Tues & Suns; Garden: Sun–Fri, 2–5pm.

Admission: Free. Donations welcome.

HAUGHLEY PARK 🏠

Stowmarket, Suffolk IP14 3JY

Tel: 01359 240701   **www.haughleyparkbarn.co.uk**

Owner/Contact: Mr & Mrs Robert Williams

Mellow red brick manor house of 1620 set in gardens, park and woodland. Original five-gabled east front, north wing re-built in Georgian style, 1820. 6 acres of well tended gardens including walled kitchen garden. 17th century brick and timber barn restored as meeting rooms. Woodland walks with bluebells (special Sun opening), lily-of-the-valley (May), rhododendrons and azaleas.

Location: MAP 8:J8, OS Ref. TM005 618. 4m W of Stowmarket signed off A14.

Open: Garden only: May–Sept: Tues & last Sun in Apr & 1st Sun in May, 2–5.30pm. Barn bookable for lectures, dinners, weddings etc (capacity 160).

Admission: Garden: £3. Child under 16 Free.

ℹ Picnics allowed. 🌸 Bluebell Sun. 🍴 ♿ 🚌 Bluebell Sun. 🅿 🚌 On leads only. ▲ ❄

Properties that **open all year** appear in the special index at the end of the book.

Helmingham Hall Gardens

HELMINGHAM HALL GARDENS 🏛
HELMINGHAM, SUFFOLK IP14 6EF

www.helmingham.com

Tel: 01473 890799   **Fax:** 01473 890776   **E-mail:** events@helmingham.com
Owner: The Lord & Lady Tollemache   **Contact:** Mrs Sarah Harris

The Tudor Hall, surrounded by its wide moat, is set in a 400 acre deer park. Two superb gardens, one surrounded by its own moat and walls extends to several acres and has wide herbaceous borders and an immaculate kitchen garden. The second enclosed within yew hedges, has a special rose garden with a herb and knot garden containing plants grown in England before 1750. Coach bookings welcome.

Location: MAP 8:K9, OS Ref. TM190 578. B1077, 9m N of Ipswich, 5m S of Debenham.
Open: Gardens only: 4 May–14 Sept: Suns & Weds, 2–6pm (25 May: 10.30am–4pm).
Admission: Adult £5, Child (5–15yrs) £3. Groups (30+) £4.50.

🄰 🄱 🅃 🄺 Grounds. WCs. 🄱 🄿 🄵 In grounds, on leads. 🄱 25 May: NCCPG Plant sale, 10am–4pm. 3 Aug: Festival of Classic & Sports Cars 10am–5pm, tel for details.

©NTPL/Rupert Truman

ICKWORTH HOUSE, PARK & GARDENS ❧
HORRINGER, BURY ST EDMUNDS IP29 5QE

www.nationaltrust.org.uk/ickworth

Tel: 01284 735270   **Fax:** 01284 735175   **E-mail:** ickworth@nationaltrust.org.uk
Owner: The National Trust   **Contact:** The Property Manager

One of the most unusual houses in East Anglia. The huge Rotunda of this 18th century Italianate house dominates the landscape. Inside are collections of Georgian silver, Regency furniture, Old Master paintings and family portraits.

Location: MAP 8:I9, OS155 Ref. TL816 611. In Horringer, 3m SW of Bury St Edmunds on W side of A143.
Open: House: 15 Mar–2 Nov: daily except Wed & Thur, 1–5pm, last admission 4.30pm (4pm in Oct). Garden: 2 Jan–14 Mar, daily, 11am–4pm. 15 Mar–2 Nov, daily, 10am–5pm. Park open all year dawn to dusk except Christmas Day.
*Admission: Adult £8.30, Child £3.30, Family (2+2) £19.80 (subsequent children £1.80). Park & Garden only (includes access to shop & restaurant): Adult £4.20, Child £1.10, Family (2+2) £9.50 (subsequent children 80p). Group discounts on pre-booked visits, no group discounts on Suns & BH Mons. *includes a voluntary donation but visitors can choose to pay the standard prices displayed at the property and on the website.

🄰 🄱 🄺 Partial. 🄱 🄸 Licensed. 🄵 By arrangement. 🄱 🄵 In park, on leads. 🄱

KENTWELL HALL & GARDENS 🏛
LONG MELFORD, SUFFOLK CO10 9BA

www.kentwell.co.uk

Tel: 01787 310207   **Fax:** 01787 379318   **E-mail:** info@kentwell.co.uk
Owner: Patrick Phillips Esq   **Contact:** The Estate Office

A beautiful mellow redbrick Tudor Mansion, surrounded by a broad moat, with rare service building of c1500. Interior 'improved' by Thomas Hopper in 1820s. Still a lived-in family home. Famed for the long-time, long term, ongoing restoration works. New for 2008: restored servants' quarters.

Gardens: Over 30 years' endeavour has resulted in gardens which are a joy in all seasons. Moats, massed spring bulbs, mature trees, delightful walled garden, with potager, herbs and ancient espaliered fruit trees. Much topiary including unique 'Pied Piper' story.

Re-Creations: Kentwell is renowned for its award-winning Re-Creations of Everyday Tudor Life. It also has occasional Re-Creations of WW2 Life. Re-Creations take place on selected weekends from April to October. Call or visit website for dates.

Corporate: House and upgraded 2500 sq ft Function Room for conferences, dinners, banquets of all sizes and Corporate Activity Days of originality.

Schools: Perhaps the biggest, most original and stimulating educational programme in the region enjoyed by about 20,000 schoolchildren each year.

Filming: Much used for medieval and Tudor periods for its wide range of perfectly equipped locations inside and out and access to Kentwell's 700 Tudors as extras.

Open-Air entertainments: 3 week summer season of opera, plays and concerts.

Location: MAP 8:I9, OS Ref. TL864 479. Off the A134. 4m N of Sudbury, 14m S of Bury St. Edmunds 1m NNW of Long Melford off A134.
Open: Feb–Oct. For full details see our website or e-mail info@kentwell.co.uk or telephone for leaflet.

ℹ No photography in house. 🄰 🅃 Conferences, dinners, Tudor feasts for groups of 40 or more. Car rallies. 🄺 🄱 Home-made food. 🄿 🄱 🄵 🄰 Including themed ceremonies. 🄱 Open-air theatre, opera and concert season Jul–Aug.

LANDGUARD FORT ⌗

Felixstowe, Suffolk
Tel: 07749 695523   www.english-heritage.org.uk/landguard
Owner: English Heritage   **Contact:** Visitor Operations Team
(Managed by Languard Fort Trust)
Impressive 18th century fort with later additions built on a site originally fortified by Henry VIII and in use until after World War II. Existing guided tours and audio tours of the fort will be supplemented by a DVD presentation of the site's history and by guided tours of the substantial outside batteries.
Location: MAP 8:L10, OS Ref. TM284 318. 1m S of Felixstowe town centre – follow brown tourist signs to Landguard Point and Nature Reserve from A14.
Open: 21 Mar–2 Nov: daily, 10am–5pm (6pm Jun–Sept). Last admission 1hr before closing. Telephone 07749 695523 for Battery & Group tour bookings.
Admission: Adult £3.50, Child £1, Conc. £2.50. Free entry for children under 5yrs and wheelchair users. No unaccompanied children. EH Members Free. Group discount available.
ℹ Picnickers welcome. ◻ ♿ P ♿ ♿ Contact David Morgan for details of tours of the outer batteries and charges for special events.

LEISTON ABBEY ⌗

Leiston, Suffolk
Tel: 01223 582700 (Regional Office)   www.english-heritage.org.uk/leiston
Owner: English Heritage   **Contact:** The East of England Regional Office
The remains of this abbey for Premonstratensian canons, including a restored chapel, are amongst the most extensive in Suffolk.
Location: MAP 8:M8, OS Ref. TM445 642. 1m N of Leiston off B1069.
Open: Any reasonable time.
Admission: Free.
ℹ Picnickers welcome. ♿ P ♿ ✽

For **accommodation** in the South West, see our special index at the end of the book.

© NTPL

LAVENHAM: THE GUILDHALL OF CORPUS CHRISTI ✣

THE MARKET PLACE, LAVENHAM, SUDBURY CO10 9QZ

www.nationaltrust.org.uk

Tel: 01787 247646   **E-mail:** lavenhamguildhall@nationaltrust.org.uk
Owner: The National Trust   **Contact:** The Property Manager
This splendid 16th century timber-framed building dominates the Market Place of the picturesque town of Lavenham with its many historic houses and wonderful church. Inside are exhibitions on local history, farming and industry, as well as the story of the medieval woollen cloth trade. There is also a walled garden with dye plants.
Location: MAP 8:J9, OS155, TL915 942. 6m NNE of Sudbury. Village centre. A1141 & B1071.
Open: 8–13 Mar, Wed–Sun,11am–4pm; 1 Apr–2 Nov, daily, 11am–5pm; 8–30 Nov, Sat & Sun, 11am–4pm. Open BH Mon, closed Good Fri. Parts of the building may be closed occasionally for community use.
Admission: Adult £4, Child £1.65. Family £9.65, Groups £3.25. School parties (by arrangement) £1 per child.
◻ ♿ Shop & tearoom. ♿

©NTPL/Fisheye Images

MELFORD HALL ✣

LONG MELFORD, SUDBURY, SUFFOLK CO10 9AA

www.nationaltrust.org.uk

Tel/Fax: 01787 379228   **Info:** 01787 376395
E-mail: melford@nationaltrust.org.uk
Owner: The National Trust   **Contact:** The House Manager
Set in the unspoilt villiage of Long Melford, the house has changed little externally since 1578 when Queen Elizabeth I was entertained here, and retains its original panelled banqueting hall. It has been the home of the Hyde Parker family since 1786. There is a Regency Library, Victorian bedrooms, good collections of furniture and porcelain and a small display of items connected with Beatrix Potter, who was related to the family. The garden contains some spectacular specimen trees and a banqueting house, and there is an attractive walk through the park.

Location: MAP 8:I9, OS Ref. TL867 462. In Long Melford off A134, 14m S of Bury St Edmunds, 3m N of Sudbury.
Open: 22–30 March, daily (except Tue), 5–27 Apr & 4–26 Oct, Sat & Sun only, 1 May–28 Sept, Wed–Sun, Open BH Mons. All 1.30–5pm.
Admission: Adult £5.80, Child (under 16yrs) £2.90, Family £14.50. Groups (15+): Adult £4.80, Child £2.40. Phone, e-mail or write with SAE to House Manager.
ℹ No photography in house. ◻ ♿ ♿ WC. ♿ P
♿ In car park & park walk only, on leads. ♿ Tel info line for details.

ORFORD CASTLE ⌗
ORFORD, WOODBRIDGE, SUFFOLK IP12 2ND

www.english-heritage.org.uk/orford

Tel: 01394 450472

Owner: English Heritage   **Contact:** Visitor Operations Team

An enchanting royal castle built by Henry II for coastal defence in the 12th century. A magnificent keep survives almost intact with three immense towers offering beautiful views over Orford Ness and the surrounding countryside. New Orford Museum housed in the Castle

Location: MAP 8:M9, OS169, TM419 499. In Orford on B1084, 20m NE of Ipswich.

Open: 21 Mar–30 Sept: daily, 10am–6pm. 1 Oct–31 Mar '09: Thur–Mon, 10am–4pm. Closed 24–26 Dec & 1 Jan.

Admission: Adult £4.90, Child £2.50, Under 5s Free, Conc. £3.90, Family £12.30. EH Members/OVP Free. Group discount available.

▢ ▢ P ⌧ ✱

OTLEY HALL
OTLEY, IPSWICH, SUFFOLK IP6 9PA

www.otleyhall.co.uk

Tel: 01473 890264   **Fax:** 01473 890803   **E-mail:** enquiries@otleyhall.co.uk

Owner: Dr Ian & Mrs Catherine Beaumont   **Contact:** Lucy Rudduck

A stunning medieval Moated Hall (Grade I) frequently described as "one of England's loveliest houses". Noted for its richly carved beams, superb linenfold panelling and 16th century wall paintings, Otley Hall was once the home of the Gosnold family and is still a family home. Bartholomew Gosnold voyaged to the New World in 1602 and named Cape Cod and Martha's Vineyard, (an account of the voyage is believed to have inspired Shakespeare's Tempest). Gosnold returned in 1607 and founded the Jamestown colony, the first English-speaking settlement in the US. The unique 10 acre gardens include historically accurate Tudor re-creations designed by Sylvia Landsberg (author of The Medieval Garden).and were voted among the top 10 gardens to visit in Great Britain.

Location: MAP 8:K9, OS Ref. TM207 563. 7m N of Ipswich, off the B1079.

Open: BH Suns (4 & 25 May, 24 Aug), 1–5pm. Afternoon teas available. Groups and individuals welcome all year by appointment for private guided tours.

Admission: BHs: Adult £5, Child £2.50.

▢ ▢ Partial. ▣ ⍰ By arrangement. P ▲ ✱ ♨

Somerleyton Hall

ST EDMUNDSBURY CATHEDRAL

Angel Hill, Bury St Edmunds, Suffolk IP33 1LS

Tel: 01284 754933   **Fax:** 01284 768655   **E-mail:** cathedral@burycathedral.fsnet.co.uk
www.stedscathedral.co.uk

Owner: The Church of England   **Contact:** Sarah Friswell

The striking Millennium Tower, completed on 2005, is the crowning glory of St Edmundsbury Cathedral. Built from English limestone, brick and lime mortar, the 150ft Lantern Tower, along with new chapels, cloisters and North Transept, completes nearly fifty years of development in a style never likely to be repeated.

Location: MAP 8:I8, OS Ref. TL857 642. Bury St Edmunds town centre.

Open: All year: daily 8.30am–6pm.

Admission: Donation invited.

▢ ▣ Partial. WC. ▣ ⍰ ▣ ✱

SAXTEAD GREEN POST MILL ⌗

Post Mill Bungalow, Saxtead Green, Woodbridge, Suffolk IP13 9QQ

Tel: 01728 685789   **www.english-heritage.org.uk/saxtead**

Owner: English Heritage   **Contact:** Visitor Operations Team

The finest example of a Suffolk Post Mill. Still in working order, you can climb the wooden stairs to the various floors, full of fascinating mill machinery. Ceased production in 1947.

Location: MAP 8:L8, OS Ref. TM253 645. 2½m NW of Framlingham on A1120.

Open: 21 Mar–29 Sept: Fri/Sat & BHs, 12 noon–5pm.

Admission: Adult £3.20, Child £1.60, Conc. £2.60. EH Members Free. Group discount available.

ℹ Picnickers welcome. Museum. ▢ ▢ ⍰

SOMERLEYTON HALL & GARDENS 🏛

SOMERLEYTON, LOWESTOFT, SUFFOLK NR32 5QQ

www.somerleyton.co.uk

Tel: 08712 224244 (office) **Fax:** 01502 732143
E-mail: enquiries@somerleyton.co.uk
Owner: Hon Hugh Crossley **Contact:** Cathy Hatt
Splendid early Victorian mansion built in Anglo-Italian style by John Thomas, with lavish architectural features, magnificent carved stonework and fine state rooms. Paintings by Landseer, Wright of Derby and Stanfield, wood carvings by Willcox of Warwick and Grinling Gibbons. Somerleyton's 12-acre gardens are justly renowned with beautiful borders, specimen trees and the 1846 yew hedge maze which ranks amongst the finest in the country. Special features include glasshouses by Paxton, 300ft pergola, walled garden, Vulliamy tower clock, Victorian ornamentation. Film location for BBC drama *The Lost Prince* (2002).

Location: MAP 8:M8, OS134 Ref. TM493 977. 5m NW of Lowestoft on B1074, 7m SW of Great Yarmouth off A143.
Open: 16 Mar–31 Aug: Thurs, Suns, & BHs, 1 Sept–30 Oct: Thurs & Suns, 2.30pm. Nov: Suns, Garden only. Gardens and Tearooms: 10am–5pm. Hall: 11.30am–4pm (guided tours only every half hour). Last tour 3.30pm. Please call or visit website to check.
Admission: Hall Tour & Gardens: Adult £8.25, Child (5–16yrs) £4.25, Conc. £7.25. Family £23, All day tours £25, Afternoon/evening tours £14. Groups: Adult £7.25, Child £3.25, Conc. £6.25. Gardens only: Adult £5, Child £3, Conc. £4. Groups: Adult £4.10, Child £2.10, Conc. £3.10. Season tickets: £24, Conc £9.
ℹ No photography in house. 📷 ❄ ⊤ Receptions/functions/conferences/weddings. ♿ ♨ 𝄞 Obligatory. 🅿 ■ ♨ 🔔 ❄

SOUTH ELMHAM HALL

ST CROSS, HARLESTON, NORFOLK IP20 0PZ

www.southelmham.co.uk   www.batemansbarn.co.uk

Tel: 01986 782526 **Fax:** 01986 782203 **E-mail:** enquiries@southelmham.co.uk
Owner/Contact: John Sanderson
A Grade I listed medieval manor house set inside moated enclosure. Originally built by the Bishop of Norwich around 1270. Much altered in the 16th century. Self guided trail through former deer park to South Elmham Minster, a ruined Norman chapel with Saxon origins.
Location: MAP 8:L7, OS30 Ref. TM778 324. Between Harleston and Bungay from the A143 take the B1062.
Open: Minster, Walks (Café: 1 May–30 Sept: Thurs, Fris & BH Mons). 1 Oct–30 Apr: Suns only, 10am–5pm. Hall: Guided tours only: 1 May–30 Sept: Thurs, 2pm, Sun & BH Mons, 3pm.
Admission: House: Adult £6.50, Child £3. Groups (15-50): Adult £4.50, Child £2.50. Walks (free).
⊤ ♿ WC. ♨ 🍴 𝄞 Obligatory. ■ 🅿 ♨ In grounds, on leads. 🛏 🔔 ❄ 🐾

SUTTON HOO 🌿

WOODBRIDGE, SUFFOLK IP12 3DJ

www.nationaltrust.org.uk/suttonhoo

Tel: 01394 389700 **Fax:** 01394 389702 **E-mail:** suttonhoo@nationaltrust.org.uk
Owner: The National Trust **Contact:** The Property Secretary
Anglo-Saxon royal burial site where priceless treasure was discovered in a ship grave in 1939. Site includes an exhibition hall, restaurant, shop, site walks and the famous burial mounds. Exhibition Summer 2008: Life and Death of a Kingdom: East Anglia 500–869AD.
Location: MAP 8:L9, OS Ref. TM288 487. Off B1083 Woodbridge to Bawdsey road. Follow signs from A12. Train ½m Melton.
Open: Exhibition Hall, shop & restaurant: 19 Mar–6 Apr, 21 May–1 Jun, 25 Jun–31 Aug & 22 Oct–2 Nov, daily, 10.30am–5pm; 7 Apr–20 May, 2–24 Jun, & 1 Sept–21 Oct, Wed–Sun, 10.30am–5pm, 3 Nov–31 Jan 09 Sat & Sun 11am–4pm. Open BH Mons.
***Admission:** Adult £6.20, Child £3.20. Family £15.70. Groups £5.50. Discount for visitors arriving by cycle or on foot. NT members free. *includes a voluntary donation but visitors can choose to pay the standard prices displayed at the property and on the website.
📷 ❄ ⊤ ♿ 🍽 Licensed. 🍴 Licensed. 𝄞 🅿 ■ ♨ In grounds, on leads. 🛏 ❄ 🐾 Programme of events, tel for details.

THE TIDE MILL

Woodbridge, Suffolk IP12 4SR

Tel: 01728 746959

Contact: Terina Booker

First recorded in 1170, now fully restored, machinery demonstrated at low tide. Ring for wheel turning times.

Location: MAP 8:L9, OS Ref. TM275 487. By riverside ¼m SE of Woodbridge town centre. 1¼m off A12.

Open: Easter & May–Sept: daily. Apr & Oct: Sats & Suns only, 11am–5pm.

Admission: Adult £2.50, Child Free, Conc. £1.50.

WYKEN HALL GARDENS

STANTON, BURY ST EDMUNDS, SUFFOLK IP31 2DW

www.wykenvineyards.co.uk

Tel: 01359 250287   **Fax:** 01359 253420

Owner: Sir Kenneth & Lady Carlisle   **Contact:** Mrs Storm Scott

Wyken is an Elizabethan manor house surrounded by a romantic, plantlovers' garden with maze, knot and herb garden and rose garden featuring old roses. A walk through ancient woodlands leads to award-winning Wyken Vineyards. The 16th century barn houses the Vineyard Restaurant featured in Michelin and Good Food Guides, and the Leaping Hare Country Store, described in *Country Living* as 'a model of what a shop should be.'

Location: MAP 8:J8, OS Ref. TL963 717. 9m NE of Bury St. Edmunds 1m E of A143. Follow brown tourist signs to Wyken Vineyards from Ixworth.

Open: 5 Jan–24 Dec: daily, 10am–6pm. Garden: 1 Apr–1 Oct: daily except Sat, 2–6pm. Open for dinner from 7pm Fri & Sat (advisable to book).

Admission: Gardens: Adult £3.50, Child (under 12yrs) Free, Conc. £3. Groups by appointment.

🖼 🎫 🛍 🍴 ♿ Suitable. WC. 🍴 Licensed. 🅿 🚻 In grounds, on leads. ✿

Sutton Hoo

Kentwell Hall & Gardens from the book *Historic Family Homes and Gardens from the Air*

YAXLEY HALL

YAXLEY, SUFFOLK IP23 8BY

www.yaxleyhall.com

Tel: 01379 788869   **E-mail:** enquiries@yaxleyhall.com

Owner: Dominic Richards   **Contact:** Richard Orton

Yaxley Hall is an intimate country house located on the Suffolk/Norfolk borders. It is a private home, which the owner makes available on a limited basis throughout the year. The property has been the subject of a recent thorough refurbishment including the reinstatement of a large Gothick window.

Location: MAP 8:K8, OS Ref. TM 125 736. Half way between Ipswich & Norwich on the A140, located on the opposite side of the road to the village of Yaxley.

Open: By appointment for weddings and groups only: All year.

Admission: Contact property for details.

🍴 🍴 Licensed. 🎫 Obligatory. 🅿 Limited. 🔲 🚻 Guide dogs only. 🔲 ✤ 🛡

Deene Park, Northamptonshire

East Midlands

This is a part of Britain that is sadly often overlooked, but merits further investigation. Visit Rockingham Castle, with its dramatic views over five counties. Further north, Chatsworth and Haddon Hall are two very different examples of stately homes. Contrast them with the charming manor house of Eyam Hall and the stunning gardens of Coton Manor.

Derbyshire

Leicestershire & Rutland

Lincolnshire

Northamptonshire

Nottinghamshire

■ Owner

Trustees of the Chatsworth Settlement. Home of the Devonshire family

■ Contact

Mr Simon Seligman
Chatsworth
Bakewell
Derbyshire DE45 1PP

Tel: 01246 582204
01246 565300
Fax: 01246 583536
E-mail: visit@
chatsworth.org

■ Location

MAP 6:P2
OS Ref. SK260 703

From London
3 hrs M1/J29,
signposted via
Chesterfield.

3m E of Bakewell,
off B6012,
10m W of Chesterfield.

Rail: Chesterfield
Station, 11m.

Bus: Chesterfield –
Baslow, 1½m.

■ Opening Times

House, garden and farmyard open daily, from 12 March to 23 December. The park is open every day.

■ Admission

The admission prices for the house, garden and farmyard are listed on our website at www.chatsworth.org, and discounted day tickets may be purchased from our on-line box office at the same web address.

CHATSWORTH

www.chatsworth.org

The home of the Duke and Duchess of Devonshire is one of the country's greatest Treasure Houses, renowned for the quality of its art, landscape and hospitality, and the warm welcome all visitors receive. Home of the Cavendish family since the 1550s, it has evolved through the centuries to reflect the tastes, passions and interests of succeeding generations, and today contains works of art that span 4000 years, from ancient Roman and Egyptian sculpture, and masterpieces by Rembrandt, Reynolds and Veronese, to work by outstanding modern artists, including Lucian Freud, Edmund de Waal, Sean Scully and David Nash. Among the many rooms on view are the five 17th century state apartments, recently re-presented to convey the original splendour of the 1st Duke's house. Special displays of rarely seen treasures in 2008 will mark the 400th anniversary of the death of Bess of Hardwick, who built the first house and founded the family dynasty. From early November, the house is redressed to celebrate Christmas, with spectacular decorations and lights.

The garden is famous for its rich history, historic and modern waterworks and sculptures, the Victorian rock garden and the maze. There are rose, cottage, kitchen and sensory gardens, and a new area opens to visitors in 2008, revealing a 300 year old waterfall, new site-specific sculptures and walks through a replanted arboretum of North American trees. Younger visitors enjoy the working farmyard and the woodland adventure playground and the 1,000 acre park is open for walks, picnics and play throughout the year. Chatsworth runs an exciting events programme every year, including International Horse Trials and the Country Fair, and we offer interesting tours and talks about the house, garden and works of art throughout the year. You can stay with us, in the wide range of comfortable holiday accommodation across the estate. The elegant gift and farm shops, and superb, seasonal home-made food will complete your visit.

ⓘ Farmyard & Adventure Playground. Guide book translations.

🛍

♿ Wheelchairs in part of the house, and welcome in garden (3 electric, 7 standard). WCs. Special leaflet.

🍽 Rooms available for conferences and private functions. Contact Head of Catering

🍴 Restaurant (max 300); home-made food. Menus on request.

🕴 Private tours of house or Greenhouses and Behind the Scenes Days, by arrangement only (extra charges apply). Groups please pre-book.

🎧 New adult and child audio tours, in English.

Ⓟ Cars 100 yds, Coaches 25 yds from house.

▣ Guided tours, packs, trails and school room. Free preliminary visit recommended.

🏠 Holiday cottages.

🔔

❄

Conference/Function

ROOM	SIZE	MAX CAPACITY
Hartington Rm.		70
Coffee Rm.		24

HADDON HALL

www.haddonhall.co.uk

Haddon Hall sits on a rocky outcrop above the River Wye close to the market town of Bakewell, looking much as is would have done in Tudor times. There has been a dwelling here since the 11th century but the house we see today dates mainly from the late 14th century with major additions in the following 200 years and some alterations in the early 17th century including the creation of the Long Gallery.

William the Conqueror's illegitimate son Peverel, and his descendants, held Haddon for 100 years before it passed to the Vernon family. In the late 16th century the estate passed through marriage to the Manners family, in whose possession it has remained ever since.

When the Dukedom of Rutland was conferred on the Manners family in 1703 they moved to Belvoir Castle, and Haddon was left deserted for 200 years. This was Haddon's saving grace as the Hall thus escaped the major architectural changes of the 18th and 19th centuries ready for the great restoration at the beginning of the 20th century by the 9th Duke of Rutland. Henry VIII's elder brother Arthur, who was a frequent guest of the Vernons, would be quite familiar with the house as it stands today.

Haddon Hall is a popular location for film and television productions. Recent films include *Pride & Prejudice* and the BBC dramatisation of *Jane Eyre*.

Gardens

Magnificent terraced gardens with over 150 varieties of rose and clematis, many over 70 years old, provide colour and scent throughout the summer.

■ **Owner**
Lord Edward Manners

■ **Contact**
Janet O'Sullivan
Estate Office
Haddon Hall
Bakewell
Derbyshire DE45 1LA

Tel: 01629 812855
Fax: 01629 814379
E-mail: info@
haddonhall.co.uk

■ **Location**
MAP 6:P2
OS Ref. SK234 663

From London 3 hrs
Sheffield ½ hr
Manchester 1 hr
Haddon is on the
E side of A6 1½m
S of Bakewell.
M1/J29.

Rail: Chesterfield
Station, 12m.

Bus: Chesterfield
Bakewell.

■ **Opening Times**
Summer
Easter: 20–25 March.
April & October:
Sat–Mon (inc 29/30 Mar).
May–September:
Daily, 12 noon–5pm
Last admission 4pm.

■ **Admission**
Summer

Adult	£8.50
Child (5–15yrs)	£4.50
Conc	£7.50
Family (2+3)	£22.00
Regular Visitor Pass	£15.50
Groups (15+)	
Adult	£7.50
Child (5–15yrs)	£3.50
Conc	£6.50

i	Haddon Hall is ideal as a film location due to its authentic and genuine architecture requiring little alteration. Suitable locations are also available on the Estate.
	Unsuitable, steep approach, varying levels of house.
	Self-service, licensed (max 75). Home-made food.
	Special tours £10.50pp for groups of 15, 7 days' notice.
P	Ample. 450 yds from house. £1 per car.
	Tours of the house bring alive Haddon Hall of old. Costume room also available, very popular!
	Guide dogs only.

East Midlands – England

■ Owner
The National Trust

■ Contact
Victoria Flanagan
Property Manager
Kedleston Hall
Derby DE22 5JH

Tel: 01332 842191
Fax: 01332 844059
Email: kedlestonhall@
nationaltrust.org.uk

■ Location
MAP 6:P4
OS ref. SK312 403

5 miles NW of Derby,
signposted from the
roundabout where the
A38 crosses A52 Derby
ring road

■ Opening Times
Hall
1 March–2 November:
Mon–Wed & Sat/Sun,
12noon–5pm

Garden
1 March–2 November:
daily, 10am–6pm

Park
All year daily 10am–6pm
(closes 4pm
November–March)

Shop & Restaurant
1 Mar–2 Nov, Mon–Wed
& Sat/Sun 11am–5pm;
24 Jul–29 Aug, Thu/Fri,
12 noon–4pm; 3 Nov–
27 Feb 09; Sat/Sun
11am–3pm.

Church
1 March–2 November,
Mon–Wed, Sat/Sun
11am–5pm.

Open Good Friday.
Park: Occasional day
restrictions may apply in
December & January
2009. Closed 25/26
December. Last entry into
Hall 4.15pm. A 25 minute
introductory tour of Hall
available at 11am.

■ *Admission
House & Garden
Adult	£8.50
Child	£4.20
Family	£21.50

Park & Garden
Adult	£3.80
Child	£1.90
Family	£9.60

Winter admission for Park
only, £4.00 per vehicle.

*includes a voluntary
donation but visitors can
choose to pay the standard
prices displayed at the
property and on the website.

Conference/Function
ROOM	SIZE	MAX CAPACITY
Caesars' Hall	40' x 60'	120 dining 150 reception 100 delegates theatre style
Saloon		Civil Weddings only – seats 110
Restaurant		90 dining split in 2 rooms

KEDLESTON HALL
www.nationaltrust.org.uk

Kedleston was built between 1759 and 1765 for the Curzon family who have lived in the area since the 12th century. The house boasts the most complete and least altered sequence of Robert Adam interiors in England, with the magnificent State rooms retaining much of their great collections of paintings and furniture. The Adam influence can also be seen across the 18th century pleasure grounds and 800 acre park. Since 1987 the National Trust has undertaken a programme of work to return these interiors to their original appearance so that visitors can re-live the experience of coming to see a 'palace of the arts'.

The Eastern Museum houses a remarkable collection by Lord Curzon when he was Viceroy of India (1899–1905).

Kedleston has a year wide programme of special events, please telephone for more details and to be sent an up-to-date programme or visit the website.

New for 2008
The trophy corridor, which traditionally displayed a collection of mounted heads and stuffed animals in cases, is being redisplayed for the first time since the 1990s and will be repainted to an historic colour scheme and re-interpreted. The state apartment also enters an exciting phase of complete restoration and visitors will see this in progress during the season. Kedleston is also available as a popular venue for corporate events and holds a licence for Civil wedding ceremonies in the Saloon on the state floor. Please ring the office on 01332 842191 for further details or to be sent an information pack.

Also available as a filming location.

Unfortunately no access to the State floor but visitors can access the ground floor rooms, which includes the Smoking Room where a virtual tour will enable visitors to experience the splendour of the State Rooms.

Must be booked in advance.

Dogs are permitted to all areas of the park apart from the Gardens and Long & Short Walk.

PAVILION GARDENS

www.paviliongardens.co.uk

The eminent Victorian landscape gardener Edward Milner's Pavilion Gardens nestle within the elegant setting of Victorian Buxton, a tranquil haven yet only a stone's throw from the busy shopping centre of the bustling market town.

The Pavilion is an impressive listed building dating from 1871. When first built it was likened to William Paxton's Crystal Palace (1851), and though parts have been changed over the years, it still evokes that same spirit of Victorian public recreational architecture. Indeed Paxton is remembered in the Pavilion's Paxton Suite, which is regularly used for a variety of concerts, functions and exhibitions.

The Pavilion boasts a wide range of spacious facilities including a large Restaurant, a Cafeteria and an upstairs Art Café. Here visitors can view and purchase the artwork of respected local artists in a relaxed environment, while enjoying superb views of the gardens.

The River Wye meanders through the 23 acres of beautiful landscaped gardens, a long-standing favourite with families and children. Buxton has been in the forefront of the revival of the ethos of the Victorian public park, and the gardens have recently been restored to the full splendour of Milner's original design, with its mix of formal and informal planting, its lawns and lakes, its leafy walks and beautifully restored wrought iron bridges.

The bandstand is a focal point on most summer Sunday afternoons, with plenty of seating available on the terrace promenade. There is also a colourful conservatory, with an impressive botanical display, linking the Pavilion complex with the glorious, Frank Matcham designed, Buxton Opera House.

■ Owner
High Peak Borough Council

■ Contact
Administration
Pavilion Gardens
St John's Road
Buxton
Derbyshire SK17 6XN

Tel: 01298 23114
Fax: 01298 27622
E-mail: paviliongardens@highpeak.gov.uk

■ Location
MAP 6:O2
OS Ref. SK055 734

Situated in the centre of Buxton in the Peak District, just off the A6, within easy reach of Manchester, Sheffield and the East Midlands.

Rail: Buxton station ½m.

■ Opening Times
Every day except Christmas Day.

Gardens always open.

Opens: 10am.

■ Admission
Free entry into building and gardens.

Many events and fairs are free entry, where entry charges occur the prices vary.

Special events
Antique & Collectors Fairs
Bailey's Decorative Arts Fair
Book Fairs
Buxton Festival & Fringe
Craft Fairs
Farmers Markets
Great Peak District Fair
H&H Classic Car Auctions
International Gilbert & Sullivan Festival
Plant and Garden Design Fairs
Record and CD Fairs
Regional Food fairs
Toy/Train Collectors Fairs
Trident Annual Antique Fair

Please see website for dates, times and prices.

- **i** Miniature train rides in gardens, crazy golf, excellent adventure playground and indoor swimming pool.
- Food and gift shop specialising in locally produced goods.
- Banquets, functions and conferences and wedding receptions.
- Partial.
- Art Café, Cafeteria (and famous Bradwell's ice cream.)
- Licensed. (Max 15). Menu on request.
- **P** Charge applies.
- In gardens on leads. Guide dogs only in Pavilion.
- Pavilion closed Christmas Day.

English Heritage Photo Library/Jonathan Bailey

BOLSOVER CASTLE ⌗
CASTLE STREET, BOLSOVER, DERBYSHIRE S44 6PR

www.english-heritage.org.uk/bolsover

Tel: 01246 822844

Owner: English Heritage   **Contact:** Visitor Operations Team

An enchanting and romantic spectacle, situated high on a wooded hilltop dominating the surrounding landscape. Built on the site of a Norman castle, this is largely an early 17th century mansion. Most delightful is the 'Little Castle', with intricate carvings, panelling and wall painting. See the restored interiors of the Little Castle including the only remaining copies of Titian's Caesar Paintings, and the Venus Fountain and statuary. There is also an impressive 17th century indoor Riding House built by the Duke of Newcastle. Enjoy the Visitor and Discovery Centre. Exciting recent interpretation scheme includes Audio/Visual and scale model of Little Castle. Also contemporary Visitor Centre with information about Bolsover town's development. Picnickers are welcome. (Bolsover is now available for Civil weddings, receptions and corporate hospitality.)

Location: MAP 7:A2, OS120, SK471 707. Signposted from M1/J29, 6m from Mansfield. In Bolsover 6m E of Chesterfield on A632.

Open: 21 Mar–30 Apr & Oct: Thur–Mon, 10am–5pm. 1 May–30 Sept: daily, 10am–6pm. 1 Nov–31 Mar '09: Thur–Mon, 10am–4pm. Closes 4pm Sats all year. Closed 24–26 Dec & 1 Jan. May close for 1hr if an event is booked, please call to check opening times.

Admission: Adult £7, Child £3.50, Conc. £5.60, Family £17.50. 15% discount for groups (11+). EH members Free.

ℹ Picnickers welcome. ⬛ Ⓣ ♿ Grounds. WC. ▣ Airconditioned café. 🐾
♫ Free with admission. Ⓟ ⬛ ✖ ⬛ ✳ 📹

©NTPL/Andreas von Einsiedel

CALKE ABBEY ❀
TICKNALL, DERBYSHIRE DE73 7LE

www.nationaltrust.org.uk

Tel: 01332 863822   **Fax:** 01332 865272   **E-mail:** calkeabbey@nationaltrust.org.uk

Owner: The National Trust   **Contact:** The Property Administrator

The house that time forgot, this baroque mansion, built 1701–3 for Sir John Harpur, is set in a landscaped park. Little restored, Calke is preserved by a programme of conservation as a graphic illustration of the English country house in decline; it contains the family's collection of natural history, a magnificent 18th century state bed and interiors that are virtually unchanged since the 1880s. Walled garden, pleasure grounds and orangery. Early 19th century Church. Historic parkland with Portland sheep and deer. Staunton Harold Church is nearby.

Location: MAP 7:A5, OS128, SK356 239. 10m S of Derby, on A514 at Ticknall between Swadlincote and Melbourne.

Open: House: 1–9 Mar, Sat & Sun; 15 Mar–2 Nov, Mon–Wed & Sat & Sun, 12.30–5pm Garden: 15 Mar–2 Nov, Mon–Wed & Sat & Sun, 3 Jul–5 Sept daily, 11am–5pm. Restaurant/shop: 5 Jan–12 Mar, Mon–Wed & Sat & Sun, 11am–4pm; 15 Mar–2 Nov Mon–Wed & Sat & Sun, 10.30am–5pm. 21 Mar–18 Apr, 3 Jul–5 Sept, daily 10.30am–5pm; 3 Nov–3 Dec, 5 Jan–Mar 09 Mon–Wed, Sat & Sun, 11am–4pm, 4–21 Dec, daily 11am–4pm. Coffee Shop Kiosk: 15 Mar–2 Nov, Thu–Sun, 26 Dec–4 Jan 09 Daily, 11am–4pm. Calke Park & National Nature Reserve, All year, Dawn–Dusk. House & Garden open Good Friday 21 Mar.

Admission: House & Garden, Adult £8.50, Child £4.20, Family £21.50. Garden only, Adult £5.30, Child £2.70, Family £13.30.

⬛ ✦ Ⓣ ♿ House. Braille guide. Wheelchairs. WCs. 🍴 Licensed. 🐾 By arrangement. Ⓟ ⬛ ✖ In park, on leads only. ✳ 📹

CARNFIELD HALL 🏛

South Normanton, Nr Alfreton, Derbyshire DE55 2BE
Tel: 01773 520084
Owner/Contact: J B Cartland
Unspoilt Elizabethan manor house. Panelled rooms and two Jacobean staircases. Since 1502 home of the Revell, Wilmot, Radford and Cartland families. 300 years of fascinating contents. Old walled garden and deer park in course of restoration.
Location: MAP 7:A3, OS Ref. SK425 561. 1½m W of M1/J28 on B6019. Alfreton Station 5 mins walk.
Open: Groups (8–25) by appointment.
Admission: £5. Evening visits £7.
ⓘ No photography in Hall. Park available for events. 🖼 Grounds.
▣ (Adjoining garden centre/café – in separate ownership.) 🅕 Obligatory.
🐕 In grounds, on leads only.

CATTON HALL 🏛

CATTON, WALTON-ON-TRENT, SOUTH DERBYSHIRE DE12 8LN
www.catton-hall.com

Tel: 01283 716311 **Fax:** 01283 712876 **E-mail:** kneilson@catton-hall.com
Owner/Contact: Robin & Katie Neilson
Catton, built in 1745, has been in the hands of the same family since 1405 and is still lived in by the Neilsons as their private home. This gives the house, with its original collection of 17th and 18th century portraits, pictures and antique furniture, a unique, relaxed and friendly atmosphere. With its spacious reception rooms, luxurious bedrooms and delicious food and wine, Catton is centrally located for residential or non-residential business meetings/seminars, product launches and team-building activities, as well as for accommodation for those visiting Birmingham, the NEC, the Belfry, the Potteries and Dukeries – or just for a weekend celebration of family and friends. The acres of parkland alongside the River Trent are ideal for all types of corporate and public events.
Location: MAP 6:P5, OS Ref. SK206 154. 2m E of A38 at Alrewas between Lichfield & Burton-on-Trent (8m from each). Birmingham NEC 20m.
Open: By prior arrangement all year for corporate hospitality, shooting parties, wedding receptions, private groups. Guided tours: 7 Apr–13 Oct, Mons only, 2pm prompt. (Groups 15+ all year by prior arrangement.)
ⓘ Conference facilities. 🍽 By arrangement. 🖼🅕 By arrangement for groups.
🛏 4 x four posters, 5 twin, all en-suite. ▣▣

CHATSWORTH

See page 288 for full page entry.

ELVASTON CASTLE COUNTRY PARK

Borrowash Road, Elvaston, Derbyshire DE72 3EP
Tel: 01332 571342 **Fax:** 01332 758751
Owner: Derbyshire County Council **Contact:** The Park Manager
200 acre park landscaped in 19th century by William Barron. Walled garden.
Location: MAP 7:A4, OS Ref. SK407 330. 5m SE of Derby, 2m from A6 or A52.
Open: Please contact park for details.
Admission: Park and Gardens Free. Car park: Midweek £1, weekends/BHs £1.50, Coaches £10.
🖼 Ground floor & grounds. WCs. ▣🅕 By arrangement. 🅿 🖼
🐕 In grounds, under close control. ✳

Bolsover Castle.

© English Heritage Photo Library/Jonathan Bailey

EYAM HALL 🏛

EYAM, HOPE VALLEY, DERBYSHIRE S32 5QW

www.eyamhall.co.uk

Tel: 01433 631976   **Fax:** 01433 631603   **E-mail:** info@eyamhall.co.uk
Owner: Mr R H V Wright   **Contact:** Mr J Wright

A lively guided tour is a feature of this small unspoilt manor house in the famous plague village of Eyam. Eyam Hall has been the home of the Wright family since 1671 and it retains the intimate atmosphere of a much loved family home. The tour includes tapestries, costumes, family portraits and anecdotes. The restoration of the beautiful walled garden is nearing completion and a visit forms part of the tour. A working Craft Centre in the historic farmyard houses craftspeople, shops and a licensed restaurant. Licensed for Civil wedding ceremonies, Eyam Hall is ideal for both intimate in-house and larger marquee receptions.

Location: MAP 6:P2, OS119, SK216 765. Approx 10m from Sheffield, Chesterfield and Buxton, Eyam is off the A623 between Chesterfield and Chapel-en-le-Frith. Eyam Hall is in the centre of the village past the church.
Open: House and Garden: Easter Week, 29 Jun–31 Aug: Wed, Thur, Sun & BH Mon, 12 noon–4pm. (Booked groups Easter–Oct.) Craft Centre: All year Tues–Sun.
Admission: House & Garden: Adult £6.25, Child £4, Conc. £5.75, Family: (2+4) £19. Group rates available.

ℹ️ Craft Centre, Free. 🅿 🍴 ♿ Partial. 🍴 Licensed. 📷 Obligatory. 🅿 Free. ▣
🐕 In grounds, on leads. Guide dogs only in house. ▣ ✳ ♿

HADDON HALL 🏛   *See page 289 for full page entry.*

 See which properties offer **educational facilities** or **school visits** in our index at the end of the book.

HARDSTOFT HERB GARDEN

Hall View Cottage, Hardstoft, Chesterfield, Derbyshire S45 8AH
Tel: 01246 854268
Owner: Mr Stephen Raynor/L M Raynor   **Contact:** Mr Stephen Raynor
Consists of two display gardens with information boards and well labelled plants.
Location: MAP 7:A3, OS Ref. SK436 633. On B6039 between Holmewood & Tibshelf, 3m from J29 on M1.
Open: Gardens, Nursery & Tearoom: 15 Mar–15 Sept: Wed–Sun, 10am–5pm. Closed Mon & Tue except Easter and BHs when open throughout.
Admission: Adult £1, Child Free.

Tissington Hall

©NTPL

©NTPL/Gerry Sweethman

HARDWICK HALL, GARDENS, PARK & STAINSBY MILL ❧
DOE LEA, CHESTERFIELD, DERBYSHIRE S44 5QJ

www.nationaltrust.org.uk

Tel: 01246 850430   **Fax:** 01246 858424   **Shop/Restaurant:** 01246 858409
E-mail: hardwickhall@nationaltrust.org.uk
Owner: The National Trust   **Contact:** The Property Manager
Hardwick Hall: A late 16th century 'prodigy house' designed by Robert Smythson for Bess of Hardwick. The house contains outstanding contemporary furniture, tapestries and needlework including pieces identified in an inventory of 1601; a needlework exhibition is on permanent display. Walled courtyards enclose fine gardens, orchards and a herb garden. The country park contains Whiteface Woodland sheep and Longhorn cattle. 2008 a year of special exhibitions and events commemorating the 400th anniversary of Bess of Hardwick's death.
Location: MAP 7:A3, OS120, SK456 651. 7½m NW of Mansfield, 9½m SE of Chesterfield: approach from M1/J29 via A6175.
Open: Hall: 1 Mar–2 Nov, Wed/Thu & Sat/Sun, 12noon–4.30pm. 6–21 Dec, Sat & Sun,11am–3pm; Hall Tours: 1 Mar–2 Nov, Wed–Sun, 11am–12 noon; Garden: 1 Mar–2 Nov, Wed–Sun, 11am–5.30pm, 6–21 Dec, 11am–3pm, Sat & Sun; Parkland gates: All year daily 8am–6pm.

Admission: House & Garden: Adults £9.50, Child £4.75, Family £23.75. Garden only: Adults £4.75, Child £2.30, Family £11.80.
Hardwick Estate – Stainsby Mill is an 18th century water-powered corn mill in working order. Flour for sale.
Open: 1 Mar–1 Jul, 5 Sept–2 Nov, Wed/Thu & Sat & Sun, 2 Jul–4 Sept, Wed–Sun, 10am–4pm; 6–21 Dec Sat & Sun 11am–3pm. Open BHs, Good Fri & 1 Jan 08.
Location: MAP 7:A3, OS120, SK455 653. From M1/J29 take A6175, signposted to Clay Cross then first left and left again to Stainsby Mill.
*Admission: Adult £3.15, Child £1.60, Family £7.90. No discounts for groups, suitable for school groups. For information send SAE to Property Manager at Hardwick Hall. *includes a voluntary donation but visitors can choose to pay the standard prices displayed at the property and on the website.

🔲 🔳 ♿ Garden, Hall: 3 display rooms only. 🍴 Licensed. 🐕 🅿 📷 🚐 In park, on leads. 🔺 🚾

© English Heritage Photo Library

HARDWICK OLD HALL ⌗
DOE LEA, NR CHESTERFIELD, DERBYSHIRE S44 5QJ

www.english-heritage.org.uk/hardwickoldhall

Tel: 01246 850431
Owner: National Trust, managed by English Heritage
Contact: Visitor Operations Team
This large ruined house, finished in 1591, still displays Bess of Hardwick's innovative planning and interesting decorative plasterwork. Graphics panels focus on the rich interiors Bess created. The views from the top floor over the country park and 'New' Hall are spectacular.
Location: MAP 7:A3, OS120, SK463 638. 7½m NW of Mansfield, 9½m SE of Chesterfield, off A6175, from M1/J29.
Open: 21 Mar–31 Oct: Wed, Thur, Sat & Sun, 11am–5.30pm (5pm Oct).
Admission: Adult £4, Child £2, Conc. £3.20, Family £10. 15% discount for groups (11+). NT members free, but small charge at events. EH members Free. Tickets for the New Hall (NT) and joint tickets for both properties available at extra cost.
ℹ️ Picnickers welcome. WC. 🔲 🔳 Free with admission. 🅿 🚐 On leads.

KEDLESTON HALL ❧

See page 290 for full page entry.

Chatsworth

MELBOURNE HALL & GARDENS 🏚
MELBOURNE, DERBYSHIRE DE73 8EN

www.melbournehall.com

Tel: 01332 862502 **Fax:** 01332 862263

Owner: Lord & Lady Ralph Kerr **Contact:** Mrs Gill Weston

This beautiful house of history, in its picturesque poolside setting, was once the home of Victorian Prime Minister William Lamb. The fine gardens, in the French formal style, contain Robert Bakewell's intricate wrought iron arbour and a fascinating yew tunnel. Upstairs rooms available to view by appointment.

Location: MAP 7:A5, OS Ref. SK389 249. 8m S of Derby. From London, exit M1/J24.

Open: Hall: Aug only (not first 3 Mons) 2–5pm. Last admission 4.15pm. Gardens: 1 Apr–30 Sept: Weds, Sats, Suns, BH Mons, 1.30–5.30pm. Additional open days possible in August, please telephone for details.

Admission: Hall: Adult £3.50, Child £2, OAP £3. Gardens: Adult £3.50, Child/OAP £2.50. Hall & Gardens: Adult £5.50, Child £3.50, OAP £4.50.

ℹ️ Crafts. No photography in house. 🖼 🅰 Partial. 🖼 🎦 Obligatory in house. 🅿 Limited. No coach parking. 🖼 Guide dogs only.

PAVILION GARDENS *See page 291 for full page entry.*

PEVERIL CASTLE ♯

Market Place, Castleton, Hope Valley S33 8WQ

Tel: 01433 620613   www.english-heritage.org.uk/peveril

Owner: English Heritage   **Contact:** Visitor Operations Team

There are breathtaking views of the Peak District from this castle, perched high above the pretty village of Castleton. The great square tower of Henry II stands almost to its original height. A walkway opens up new areas and views from the first floor of the Keep. Peveril Castle is one of the earliest Norman castles to be built in England. The new Peveril Castle Visitor Centre has displays which tell the story of Peveril as the focal point of the Royal Forest of the Peak as well as improved access and facilities.

Location: MAP 6:O2, OS110, SK150 827. S side of Castleton, 15m W of Sheffield on A6187.

Open: 21 Mar–31 Oct: daily, 10am–5pm (6pm May–Aug). 1 Nov–31 Mar '09: Thur–Mon, 10am–4pm. Closed 24–26 Dec & 1 Jan.

Admission: Adult £3.70, Child £1.90, Conc. £3, Family £9.30. 15% discount for groups (11+). EH members Free.

ℹ️ Picnickers welcome. WCs. 🖼 ▪ 🖼 ❄ 🖼

Peveril Castle

RENISHAW HALL GARDENS 🏚
SHEFFIELD, DERBYSHIRE S21 3WB

www.sitwell.co.uk

Tel: 01246 432310   **Fax:** 01246 430760   **E-mail:** info2@renishaw-hall.co.uk

Owner: Sir Reresby Sitwell Bt DL   **Contact:** The Administrator

Home of Sir Reresby and Lady Sitwell. Eight acres of Italian style formal gardens stand in 300 acres of mature parkland, encompassing statues, shaped yew hedges, herbaceous borders, a water garden and lakes. The Sitwell museum and art galleries are located in Georgian stables alongside craft workshops and Gallery café, furnished with contemporary art. The Rex Whistler meeting room is available for conferences and seminars. Beautiful camellias and carpets of daffodils in April. Separate children's garden featuring a maze and a willow tunnel. Reninshaw Hall is

available for exclusive hire as a film location. The Red Dining Room is available for Civil weddings.

Location: MAP 7:A2, OS Ref. SK435 786. On A6135 3m from M1/J30, equidistant from Sheffield and Chesterfield.

Open: 20 Mar–28 Sept: Thurs–Sun & BHs, 10.30am–4.30pm. Hall is not open to the general public, private groups (25+) only by prior arrangement. Hall tours may be booked.

Admission: Garden, Museum & Galleries: Adult £5, Conc. £4.20, Under 10s Free.

🖼 🖼 🖼 🅰 🖼 🎦 By arrangement. 🅿 🖼 In grounds, on leads. 🅰
🖼 Open every day for Bluebell Fortnight (24 Apr–11 May).

SUTTON SCARSDALE HALL ⌗

Chesterfield, Derbyshire
Tel: 01604 735400 (Regional Office)
www.english-heritage.org.uk/suttonscarsdale
Owner: English Heritage   **Contact:** The East Midlands Regional Office
The dramatic hilltop shell of a great early 18th century baroque mansion.
Location: MAP 7:A2, OS Ref. SK441 690. Between Chesterfield & Bolsover, 1½m S of Arkwright Town.
Open: All year, daily: 10am–4pm (6pm in summer). Closed 24–26 Dec & 1 Jan.
Admission: Free.
ℹ Picnickers welcome. 🅟 ❋

©English Heritage Photo Library

Bolsover Castle

TISSINGTON HALL 🏛
ASHBOURNE, DERBYSHIRE DE6 1RA
www.tissington-hall.com

Tel: 01335 352200 **Fax:** 01335 352201 **E-mail:** tissington.hall@btinternet.com
Owner/Contact: Sir Richard FitzHerbert Bt
Home of the FitzHerbert family for over 500 years. The Hall stands in a superbly maintained estate village, and contains wonderful panelling and fine old masters. A 10 acre garden and arboretum. Schools very welcome. Award-winning Old Coach House Tearoom, open Apr–Oct daily; Nov–Mar, Thurs–Sun, 11am–5pm for coffees, lunch and tea.

Location: MAP 6:P3, OS Ref. SK175 524. 4m N of Ashbourne off A515 towards Buxton.
Open: 24–28 Mar, 26–30 May, 22 Jul–22 Aug & BH Mon 25 Aug, 1.30–4pm.
Admission: Hall & Gardens: Adult £7.50, Child (10–16yrs) £4, Conc. £6.50. Group £7.50. Gardens only: Adult £3.50, Child £1, Conc. £3.50.
ℹ No photography in house. Partial. WCs at tearooms. Tearoom adjacent to Hall. Obligatory. 🅟 Limited. Guide dogs only.

Eyam Hall

■ Owner

Their Graces The Duke & Duchess of Rutland

■ Contact

Mary McKinlay
Castle Opening Office
Belvoir Castle
Grantham
Leicestershire NG32 1PE

Tel: 01476 871004
Fax: 01476 871018
E-mail: info@
belvoircastle.com

■ Location

MAP 7:C4
OS Ref. SK820 337

A1 from London 110m
Grantham Junction
York 100m. Leicester 30m
Grantham 7m.
Nottingham 20m.

Air: Nottingham
& Robin Hood Airports.
Helicopter Landing Pad.

Rail: Grantham Stn 7m

Bus: Melton Mowbray –
Vale of Belvoir via
Castle Car Park.

Taxi: Grantham Taxis
01476 563944 / 563988.

■ Opening Times

Summer
20 March–6 April, daily
and weekends in April.
May & June: daily except
Fris & Mons (open BH
Mons).
July & August: daily
except Fris.
September: Sats & Suns
11am–5pm.(Sats 4pm).

Winter
30 November–
7 December.
11am–5pm.
Last entry 4pm.

Groups welcome by
appointment.

■ Admission

Adult	£12.00
Child (5–16yrs)	£6.00
Conc.	£10.00
Family (2+3)	£32.00
Groups (15+)	
Adult	£8.50
Child (5–16yrs)	£4.70
Conc.	£7.50
School	£4.70
Grounds only	
Adult/Conc.	£6.00
Child (5–16yrs)	£2.00
Conc.	£5.00
Child (5–16yrs)	£15.00
Candlelit Tours per person	£29.50

Conference/Function

ROOM	SIZE	MAX CAPACITY
State Dining Room	52' x 31'	130
Regents Gallery	131' x 16'	220
Old Kitchen	45' x 22'	100
Ballroom		90
Guards Room		175
Stewards Restaurant		100

BELVOIR CASTLE

www.belvoircastle.com

Belvoir Castle, home of the Duke and Duchess of Rutland, commands a magnificent view over the Vale of Belvoir. The name Belvoir, meaning beautiful view, dates back to Norman times, when Robert de Todeni, Standard Bearer to William the Conqueror, built the first castle on this superb site. Destruction caused by two Civil Wars and by a catastrophic fire in 1816 have breached the continuity of Belvoir's history. The present building owes much to the inspiration and taste of Elizabeth, 5th Duchess of Rutland and was built after the fire.

Inside the Castle are notable art treasures including works by Poussin, Holbein, Rubens, and Reynolds, Gobelin and Mortlake tapestries, Chinese silks, furniture, fine porcelain and sculpture.

The Queen's Royal Lancers' Museum at Belvoir has a fascinating exhibition of the history of the Regiment, as well as a fine collection of weapons, uniforms and medals.

Gardens

A remarkable survival of English garden history that are being sensitively restored to their former glory. The Spring Gardens, opened to all day visitors in 2005, contain a collection of Victorian daffodils planted sympathetically with primroses and bluebells, against a background of rhododendrons and azaleas. There are also rare specimen trees, many the largest of their type in the British Isles.

Belvoir Castle is available for exclusive hire as a film location and for conferences, weddings and special events. It is also possible to put on events in conjunction with the open season.

ℹ️ Suitable for exhibitions, product launches, conferences, filming, photography welcomed (permit £2). Guide books £5.

🛍️

🍷 Banquets, private room available.

♿ Ground floor and restaurant accessible. Please telephone for advice. WC.

🍴 Licensed. Groups catered for (100 max).

🚶 Tue–Thur, twice daily. Tour time: 1¼ hrs. Specialist picture and costume tours.

🅿️ Ample. £1.50 per car at weekends & BH Mons. Coaches can take passengers to entrance by arrangement but should report to the main car park and ticket office on arrival.

📖 Guided tours. Teacher's pack. Education room. Picnic area and adventure playground.

🐕 Guide dogs only.

🔔

❄️

🎭 Belvoir Castle is a day out for all the family and hosts different events every weekend from jousting to medieval re-enactments. Tel for details.

■ Owner
Nicholas Fothergill Esq

■ Contact
Tim Bowie
Stanford Hall
Lutterworth
Leicestershire
LE17 6DH

Tel: 01788 860250
Fax: 01788 860870
E-mail: s.maughan@
stanfordhall.co.uk

■ Location
MAP 7:B7
OS Ref. SP587 793

M1/J18 6m, M1/J19
(from/to the N only) 2m,
M6 exit/access at
A14/M1(N)J 2m, A14 2m.
Follow Historic
House signs.

Rail: Rugby Stn 7½ m.

Air: Birmingham
Airport 27m.

Taxi: Fone-A-Car.
01788 543333.

■ Opening Times
Special two week easter
opening- Saturday
22 March to Sunday
6 April 2008. Also open
on selected days in
conjunction with park
events.
Please see our website or
telephone for details.

House open any day or
evening (except Saturdays)
for pre-booked groups.

■ Admission
House & Grounds

Adult	£6.00
Child (5–15yrs)	£2.50

Private Group Tours (20+)

Adult	£6.50
Child (5–15yrs)	£2.50

Grounds only

Adult	£3.50
Child (5–15yrs)	£1.50

STANFORD HALL

www.stanfordhall.co.uk

Stanford has been the home of the Cave family, ancestors of the present owner, since 1430. In the 1690s, Sir Roger Cave commissioned the Smiths of Warwick to pull down the old Manor House and build the present Hall, which is an excellent example of their work and of the William and Mary period.

As well as over 5000 books, the handsome Library contains many interesting manuscripts, the oldest dating from 1150. The splendid pink and gold Ballroom has a fine coved ceiling with four *trompe l'oeil* shell corners. Throughout the house are portraits of the family and examples of furniture and objects which they collected over the

centuries. There is also a collection of Royal Stuart portraits, previously belonging to the Cardinal Duke of York, the last of the male Royal Stuarts. An unusual collection of family costumes is displayed in the Old Dining Room, which also houses some early Tudor portraits and a fine Empire chandelier.

The Hall and Stables are set in an attractive Park on the banks of Shakespeare's Avon. There is a walled Rose Garden behind the Stables. An early ha-ha separates the North Lawn from the mile-long North Avenue.

Craft centre (most Suns). Corporate days, clay pigeon shoots, filming, photography, small conferences. Parkland, helicopter landing area, lecture room, Blüthner piano. Caravan site.

Lunches, dinners & wedding receptions.

Visitors may alight at the entrance. WC.

Teas, lunch & supper. Groups must book (70 max)

Tour time: ¾ hr in groups of approx 25.

1,000 cars and 6–8 coaches. Free meals for coach drivers, coach parking on gravel in front of house.

In Park, on leads.

Accomodation available.

Concerts/Theatre in the Ballroom or Park.

Conference/Function

ROOM	SIZE	MAX CAPACITY
Ballroom	39' x 26'	100
Old Dining Rm	30' x 20'	20
Crocodile Room	39' x 20'	60

ASHBY DE LA ZOUCH CASTLE ⌗

South Street, Ashby de la Zouch, Leicestershire LE65 1BR
Tel: 01530 413343   www.english-heritage.org.uk/asbydelazouche
Owner: English Heritage   **Contact:** Visitor Operations Team
The impressive ruins of this late medieval castle are dominated by a magnificent tower, over 80 feet high, which was split in two during the Civil War. Panoramic views. Explore the tunnel linking the kitchens to the Hastings Tower.
Location: MAP 7:A7, OS128, SK363 167. In Ashby de la Zouch, 12m S of Derby on A511. SE of town centre.
Open: 21 Mar–31 Oct: Thur–Mon, 10am–5pm. Jul & Aug: daily, 10am–6pm. 1 Nov–31 Mar '09: Thur–Mon, 10am–4pm. Closed 24–26 Dec & 1 Jan.
Admission: Adult £3.70, Child £1.90, Conc. £3, Family £9.30. 15% discount for groups (11+). EH Members free.
ⓘ Picnickers welcome. WC. ⌷ ⌷ Grounds. ⌷ Free with admission. **P** Restricted. ⌷ On leads. ⌷ ⌷

Exton Park

BELVOIR CASTLE 🏛

See page 298 for full page entry.

BRADGATE PARK & SWITHLAND WOOD COUNTRY PARK

Bradgate Park, Newtown Linford, Leics LE6 0HE
Tel: 0116 2362713
Owner: Bradgate Park Trust   **Contact:** M H Harrison
Includes the ruins of the brick medieval home of the Grey family and childhood home of Lady Jane Grey. Also has a medieval deer park.
Location: MAP 7:B6, OS Ref. SK534 102. 7m NW of Leicester, via Anstey & Newtown Linford. Country Park gates in Newtown Linford. 1¼ m walk to the ruins.
Open: All year during daylight hours.
Admission: No charge. Car parking charges.

DONINGTON-LE-HEATH MANOR HOUSE

Manor Road, Donington-le-Heath, Leicestershire LE67 2FW
Tel: 01530 831259 / 0116 2658326
Owner/Contact: Leicestershire County Council
Medieval manor c1280 with 16th–17th century alterations.
Location: MAP 7:A6, OS Ref. SK421 126. ½ m SSW of Coalville. 4½ m W of M1/J22, by A511.
Open: Mar–Nov: daily, 11am–4pm. Dec–Feb: Sat & Sun only, 11am–4pm. (Plus occasional weekdays. Tel for details.)
Admission: Free.

EXTON PARK

Exton, Oakham, Rutland LE15 8AN
Tel: 01572 812208 **Fax:** 01572 812473 www.extonpark.co.uk
E-mail: extonestate@btconnect.com
Owner/Contact: Viscount & Viscountess Campden
Attractive stone early 19th century mansion surrounded by sweeping lawns and magnificent trees. The ruins of the original Tudor house are in the garden. Exton has been the family home of the Noel family (Earls of Gainsborough) since 1613 and there are many family portraits. Exquisite mock-gothic 18th century fishing folly and dovecote, lakes, private roads and riding ring. Private Roman Catholic chapel by Buckler.
Location: MAP 7:D6, OS SK 922 114. In Exton village off A606 Oakham–Stamford Rd.
Open: By appointment only for group tours by owner.
Admission: Price on application.
ⓘ No photography. Filming, location shoots. Weddings in Chapel. Marquee receptions. ⌷ Partial. ⌷ Obligatory. **P** Ample. ⌷ Guide dogs only.

KIRBY MUXLOE CASTLE ⌗

Kirby Muxloe, Leicestershire LE9 9MD
Tel: 01162 386886   www.english-heritage.org.uk/kirbymuxloe
Owner: English Heritage   **Contact:** East of England Regional Office (01223 528700)
Picturesque, moated, brick built castle begun in 1480 by William Lord Hastings. Recently reopened after extensive conservation work.
Location: MAP 7:B6, OS140, SK524 046. 4m W of Leicester off B5380.
Open: 1 Jul–31 Aug: Sats & Suns, 10am–5pm.
Admission: Adult £3, Child £1.50, Conc. £2.40. EH Members free. Group discount available.
ⓘ Picnickers welcome. ⌷ **P**

LYDDINGTON BEDE HOUSE ⌗

Blue Coat Lane, Lyddington, Uppingham, Rutland LE15 9LZ
Tel: 01572 822438   www.english-heritage.org.uk/lyddington
Owner: English Heritage   **Contact:** Visitor Operations Team
Located in this picturesque 'Cotswold' village of honey coloured stone cottages and public houses lies the splendid former 'palace' of the powerful medieval Bishops of Lincoln. In the 1600s the building was converted into an almshouse.
Location: MAP 7:D6, OS141, SP875 970. In Lyddington, 6m N of Corby, 1m E of A6003.
Open: 21 Mar–31 Oct: Thur–Mon, 10am–5pm.
Admission: Adult £3.70, Child £1.90, Conc. £3, Family £9.30. 15% group discount (11+). EH Members free.
ⓘ Picnickers welcome. ⌷ ⌷ Ground floor only. **P** ⌷

OAKHAM CASTLE

Castle Lane (off Market Place), Oakham, Rutland LE15 6DF
Tel: 01572 758440   www.rutland.gov.uk/castle
Owner: Rutland County Council   **Contact:** Rutland County Museum
Exceptionally fine 12th century Great Hall, recognised as one of the finest examples of domestic Norman architecture in England. With contemporary musician sculptures, bailey earthworks and remains of earlier motte. The hall contains over 200 unique horseshoes forfeited by royalty and peers of the realm to the Lord of the Manor from Edward IV onwards.
Location: MAP 7:D6, OS Ref. SK862 088. Near town centre, E of the church. Off Market Place, Oakham.
Open: All year: Mon–Sat, 10.30am–1pm & 1.30–5pm; Sun, 2–4pm. Closed Good Fri, Christmas and New Year.
Admission: Free.
⌷ ⌷ Great Hall. **P** For disabled, on request. ⌷ ⌷ ⌷

STANFORD HALL 🏛

See page 299 for full page entry.

STAUNTON HAROLD CHURCH ⌘

Staunton Harold Church, Ashby-de-la-Zouch, Leicestershire
Tel: 01332 863822 **Fax:** 01332 865272   www.nationaltrust.org.uk
Owner: The National Trust   **Contact:** Regional Office
One of the very few churches to be built during the Commonwealth, erected by Sir Robert Shirley, an ardent Royalist. The interior retains its original 17th century cushions and hangings and includes fine panelling and painted ceilings.
Location: MAP 7:A5, OS Ref. SK379 208. 5m NE of Ashby-de-la-Zouch, W of B587.
Open: 5 Apr–2 Nov, Sat & Sun, 4 Jun–29 Aug, Wed–Sun, 1–4.30pm. Open Good Fri & BH Mpns.
Admission: £1 donation.
⌷ Partial. ⌷ At hall.

Properties that **open all year** appear in the special index at the end of the book.

BURGHLEY HOUSE

www.burghley.co.uk

Burghley House, home of the Cecil family for over 400 years, was built as a country seat during the latter part of the 16th century by Sir William Cecil, later Lord Burghley, principal adviser and Lord Treasurer to Queen Elizabeth.

The House was completed in 1587 and there have been few alterations to the architecture since that date thus making Burghley one of the finest examples of late Elizabethan design in England. The interior was remodelled in the late 17th century by John, 5th Earl of Exeter who was a collector of fine art on a huge scale, establishing the immense collection of art treasures at Burghley. Burghley is truly a 'Treasure House', containing one of the largest private collections of Italian art, unique examples of Chinese and Japanese porcelain and superb items of 18th century furniture. The remodelling work of the 17th century means that examples of the work of the principal artists

and craftsmen of the period are to be found at Burghley: Antonio Verrio, Grinling Gibbons and Louis Laguerre all made major contributions to the beautiful interiors.

Park and Gardens

The house is set in a 300-acre deer park landscaped by 'Capability' Brown. A lake was created by him and delightful avenues of mature trees feature largely in his design. The park is home to a large herd of Fallow deer, established in the 16th century. Opened in 2007, the Gardens of Surprise incorporates the existing Contemporary Sculpture Garden, containing many specimen trees and shrubs, and the new Elizabethan Garden, over an acre of yew mazes, revolving Caesars' heads and spurting fountains. The private gardens around the house are open in April for the display of spring bulbs.

i Suitable for a variety of events, large park, golf course, helicopter landing area, cricket pitch. No photography in house.

Visitors may alight at entrance. WC. Chair lift to Orangery Restaurant, house tour has two staircases one with chairlift.

Restaurant/tearoom. Groups can book in advance.

Available.

P Ample. Free refreshments for coach drivers.

Welcome. Guide provided.

No dogs in house. In park on leads.

Civil Wedding Licence.

■ Owner
Burghley House Preservation Trust Ltd

■ Contact
The House Manager
Burghley House
Stamford
Lincolnshire PE9 3JY

Tel: 01780 752451
Fax: 01780 480125
E-mail: burghley@burghley.co.uk

■ Location
MAP 7:E7
OS Ref. TF048 062

Burghley House is 1m SE of Stamford. From London, A1 2hrs.

Visitors entrance is on B1443.

Rail: London – Peterborough 1hr (GNER). Stamford Station 1½m, regular service to Peterborough.

Taxi: Direct Line: 01780 481481.

■ Opening Times
Summer
House & Gardens
21 March–30 October (closed 6 September):
Daily (Gardens only on Fridays), 11am–5pm, (last admission 4.30pm).

Winter
Orangery Restaurant & Gift Shop only
1 February–21 March
Wed–Sun, 11am–4pm.

South Gardens
April: Daily (except Fridays), 11am–4pm.

Park
All year. Admission is free except on event days.

■ Admission
House & Gardens
Adult	£10.90
Child (5–15yrs)	£5.40
Conc.	£9.50
Family	£28.00

Groups (20+)	
Adult	£9.00
School (up to 14yrs)	£5.40

Gardens of Surprise only
Adult	£6.30
Child (5–15yrs)	£3.00
Conc.	£5.30
Family	£16.00

We are a charitable trust, by paying an extra 10% we can claim back the tax paid on this and use it for the benefit of the house and collections.

Conference/Function

ROOM	SIZE	MAX CAPACITY
Great Hall	70' x 30'	150
Orangery	100' x 20'	120

■ Owner

Grimsthorpe and Drummond Castle Trust Ltd. A Registered Charity.

■ Contact

Ray Biggs
Grimsthorpe Estate Office
Grimsthorpe
Bourne, Lincolnshire
PE10 0LY

Tel: 01778 591205
Fax: 01778 591259
E-mail: ray@ grimsthorpe.co.uk

■ Location

MAP 7:D5
OS Ref. TF040 230

4m NW of Bourne on A151, 8m E of Colsterworth roundabout off A1.

■ Opening Times

Castle
April & May: Suns, Thurs & BH Mons.

June–September:
Sun–Thur.
1–4.30pm.

Park & Gardens
As Castle,
11am–6pm.

Groups: Apr–Sept: by arrangement.

■ Admission

Castle, Park & Garden
Adult	£9.00
Child	£3.50
Conc.	£8.00
Family (2+2)	£20.00

Park & Gardens
Adult	£4.00
Child	£2.00
Conc.	£3.50
Family (2+2)	£10.00

Special charges may be made for special events. Group rates on application.

GRIMSTHORPE CASTLE, 🏛
PARK & GARDENS

www.grimsthorpe.co.uk

Home of the Willoughby de Eresby family since 1516. Examples of 13th century architecture and building styles from the Tudor period. The dramatic 18th century North Front is Sir John Vanbrugh's last major work. State Rooms and picture galleries with magnificent contents including tapestries, furniture and paintings. Unusual collection of thrones, fabrics and objects from the old House of Lords, associated with the family's hereditary Office of Lord Great Chamberlain.

The Grounds and Gardens

3,000 acre landscaped park with lakes, ancient woods, woodland walk with all-weather footpath, adventure playground, red deer herd. Family cycle trail. Park tours in a vehicle with the Ranger.

Unusual ornamental vegetable garden and orchard, created in the 1960s by the Countess of Ancaster and John Fowler. Intricate parterres lined with box hedges. Herbaceous border with yew topiary framing views across to the lake. Woodland garden.

Groups can explore the park from the comfort of their coach by booking a one-hour, escorted park tour, with opportunities to discover more about the site of the Cistercian Abbey, the ancient deer parks and extensive series of early tree-lined avenues.

ℹ	No photography in house.
🛍	
🍽	Conferences (up to 40), inc catering.
♿	Partial. WC.
🍸	Licensed.
👤	Obligatory except Suns.
P	Ample.
🐾	
🐕	In grounds, on leads.
🎭	

AUBOURN HALL
LINCOLN LN5 9DZ

Tel: 01522 788224 **Fax:** 01522 788199 **E-mail:** aubournhall@btconnect.com
Owner: Mr & Mrs Christopher Nevile **Contact:** Ginny Lovell
Early 17th century house by John Smythson. Important staircase and panelled rooms. 10 acre garden.
Location: MAP 7:D3, OS Ref. SK928 628. 6m SW of Lincoln. 2m SE of A46.
Open: Garden: Open for Events, Groups and Garden visits. Please contact the property for details.
Admission: Please contact property for details.

BURGHLEY HOUSE

See page 301 for full page entry.

Easton Walled Gardens

For rare and unusual plants visit the **plant sales** index at the end of the book.

AYSCOUGHFEE HALL MUSEUM & GARDENS
CHURCHGATE, SPALDING, LINCOLNSHIRE PE11 2RA

www.ayscoughfee.org

Tel: 01775 764555 **E-mail:** museum@sholland.gov.uk
Owner: South Holland District Council **Contact:** Museum Manager
Ayscoughfee Hall, a magnificent Grade II* listed building, was built in the 1450s. The Hall is set in extensive landscaped grounds which include, amongst other impressive features, a memorial designed by. Edwin Lutyens. The building and gardens combined reflect the splendour of the Medieval, Georgian and Victorian ages.
The Hall has been fully restored and a number of important and rare features uncovered. The Museum explains the history of the Hall, and features the lives of the people who lived there and in the surrounding Fens.

Location: MAP 7:F5, OS Ref. TF249 223. E bank of the River Welland, 5 mins walk from Spalding town centre.
Open: Summer (Apr–Sep): Tue–Fri; 10.30am–5pm, Sat/Sun; 10am–4.30pm, BH Mon, 10.30am–4pm. Winter (Oct–Mar): Tue–Fri; 11.30am–4.30pm, Sat & Sun; 10am–4.30pm. BH Mons, 10.30am–4pm
Admission: Free.
WC. Guide dogs only.

BELTON HOUSE ❧
GRANTHAM, LINCOLNSHIRE NG32 2LS

www.nationaltrust.org.uk

Tel: 01476 566116   **Fax:** 01476 579071   **E-mail:** belton@nationaltrust.org.uk
Owner: The National Trust   **Contact:** The Property Manager

Belton, considered by many to be the perfect English Country House, with stunning interiors, fine silver and furniture collections and collection of Old Masters, also huge garden scenes by Melchior d'Hondecoeter acquired by the last Earl. The 17th century saloon in the centre of the house is panelled and decorated with intricate limewood carvings of the Grinling Gibbons school. The virtually unaltered north-facing chapel has a baroque plaster ceiling by Edward Gouge. Built in 1685–88, Belton offers a great day out whether you are looking for peace and tranquillity or lots to do. Magnificent formal gardens, Orangery, landscaped park with lakeside walk and adventure playground. Fine church (not NT) with family monuments. Winners of "Excellence in Tourism" and Sandford Heritage Education awards 2002.

Location: MAP 7:D4, OS Ref. SK929 395. 3m NE of Grantham on A607. Signed off the A1.

Open: House: 1–14 Mar, Sat/Sun, 12.30–4pm, 15 Mar–2 Nov, Wed–Sun, 12.30–5pm. Open BH Mons. Garden & Park: 2 Feb–14 Mar, Sat & Sun, 3 Nov–21 Dec, Fri–Sun, 26 Dec–4 Jan daily, 12 noon–4pm; 15 Mar–30 June, 8 Sept–2 Nov, Wed–Sun, 11am–5.30pm; 1 Jul–7 Sept, daily 10.30am–5.30pm. Closed 12 Jul.

*Admission: Adult £9.50, Child £5.50, Family £25; Garden, Park & Playground: Adult £7.50, Child £4.50, Family £20. Garden & Park (Winter), Adult £3.50, Child £2, *Includes a voluntary donation but visitors can choose to pay the standard prices displayed at the property and on the website.

ⓘ Adventure playground opens 15 Mar 08 ⬛ ♿ Partial. Please telephone for arrangements. 🍴 Licensed. 🅿 ⬛ ⬛ ⬛ ⬛

DODDINGTON HALL & GARDENS 🏛
LINCOLN LN6 4RU

www.doddingtonhall.com

Tel: 01522 694308   **Fax:** 01522 682584   **E-mail:** info@doddingtonhall.com
Owner: Mr & Mrs J J C Birch   **Contact:** The Estate Office

Romantic Smythson mansion which stands today as it was built in 1595 with its mellow walled gardens and gatehouse. Never sold since it was built, Doddington is still very much a family home and its contents reflect over 400 years of unbroken family occupation. There is an elegant Georgian interior with fine collections of porcelain, paintings and textiles. The five acres of beautiful gardens contain a superb layout of box-edged parterres filled with bearded Iris in midsummer, sumptuous borders that provide colour in all seasons, and a wild garden with a marvellous succession of spring bulbs and flowering shrubs set amongst mature trees. Exclusive private group visits with guided tours a speciality. Please call the Estate Office to discuss your requirements. Award winning facilities for disabled visitors, include sensory tours of house and gardens for the Visually Impaired; free use of electric buggy and panoramic tour of upper floors – please call for details. Free audioguides and children's activity trail. Civil weddings and receptions at Doddington Hall and in The Littlehouse next door. Newly resurrected working walled Kitchen Garden.

Farm shop with kitchen garden and local produce plus café serving delicious, seasonal and freshly cooked teas and lunches. Open Tue–Sun, reservations advisable for lunch.

Location: MAP 7:D2, OS Ref. SK900 710. 5m W of Lincoln on the B1190, signposted off the A46.

Open: Gardens only: 17 Feb–end April & Oct: Suns & BH Mons, 1–5pm. House & Gardens: May–Sept inclusive: Weds, Suns & BH Mons, 1–5pm (gardens open 12 noon).

Admission: House & Gardens: Adult £6, Child £3, Family £16. Gardens only: Adult £4, Child £2, Family £11, Season Ticket £15. 2 for 1 admission for disabled person and companion. Groups (20+): exclusive house-opening and private guided tour £7.50pp. Discount for pre-booked groups (20+) (self guided) on regular open days. RHS members Free.

ⓘ No photography in Hall. No stilettos. ⬛ 🍴 ♿ Gardens & ground floor. WC. 🅱
🍴 In farm shop & café. Groups must book. ⓕ By arrangement. 🅿 Free.
🅿 ⬛ ♿ Guide dogs only. ⬛ ⬛ Aug, Wed, Sun & BH Mon: Exhibition of Needlework: 'The English Walled Garden'.

© Fred Cholmeley

EASTON WALLED GARDENS

THE GARDEN OFFICE, EASTON, GRANTHAM, LINCOLNSHIRE NG33 5AP

www.eastonwalledgardens.co.uk

Tel: 01476 530063 **Fax:** 01476 530063 **E-mail:** info@eastonwalledgardens.co.uk

Owner: Sir Fred & Lady Cholmeley **Contact:** Maggie Dickinson

President Franklin Roosevelt described these gardens as a *'Dream of Nirvana … almost too good to be true'*. 50 years later, the house was pulled down and the gardens abandoned. 100 years later see the ongoing revival of these magnificent gardens. Funded privately and with the support of visitors, this garden experience is like no other. Alongside the recovery of these 400 year old gardens are: fantastic snowdrops, David Austin Roses, Daffodil and Iris Collections, a cut flower garden, cottage garden and pictorial meadow plantings. Teas and light lunches are served overlooking the garden. Groups can book out of hours if wished.

Location: MAP 7:D5, OS Ref. SK938 274. 1m from A1 (between Stamford and Grantham) N of the Colsterworth roundabout. Right onto B6403 and follow signs.

Open: 16–24 Feb for snowdrops: daily 11am–4pm; 21 Mar–28 Sept: BH Mons, Weds, Fris & Suns 11am–4pm. Sweet Pea Week 22–27 June: daily 11am–4pm. For other events and extended opening times please see our website.

Admission: Adult £4.75, Child £1. (Easter onwards.)

⬜ 🏛 🍴 ♿ Partial. WCs. ● ℹ By arrangement. 🅿 ⬛ 🐕 Guide dogs only. 🎫

FULBECK MANOR

Fulbeck, Grantham, Lincolnshire NG32 3JN

Tel: 01400 272231 **Fax:** 01400 273545 **E-mail:** fane@fulbeck.co.uk

Owner/Contact: Mr Julian Francis Fane

Built c1580. 400 years of Fane family portraits. Open by written appointment. Guided tours by owner approximately 1¼ hours. Tearooms at Craft Centre, 100 yards, for light lunches and teas.

Location: MAP 7:D3, OS Ref. SK947 505. 11m N of Grantham. 15m S of Lincoln on A607. Brown signs to Craft Centre & Tearooms and Stables.

Open: By written appointment.

Admission: Adult £6. Groups (10+) £5.

ℹ No photography. ♿ Partial. WCs. ● 🍴 ℹ Obligatory. 🅿 Ample for cars. Limited for coaches. 🐕 Guide dogs only. 🎫

GAINSBOROUGH OLD HALL ⬚

Parnell Street, Gainsborough, Lincolnshire DN21 2NB

Tel: 01427 612669 www.english-heritage.org.uk/gainsborough

Owner: English Heritage **Contact:** Visitor Operations Team

A large medieval manor house with a magnificent Great Hall and suites of rooms. A collection of historic furniture and a re-created medieval kitchen are on display.

Location: MAP 7:C1, OS121, SK815 895. In centre of Gainsborough, opposite library.

Open: 21 Mar–31 Oct: Mon–Sat, 10am–5pm, Sun 1–4.30pm. 1 Nov–31 Mar '09: Mon–Sat 10am–5pm. Closed 24–26 & 31 Dec/1 Jan.

Admission: Adult £3.80, Child (5–15yrs) £2.60, Child under 5yrs Free, Conc. £2.60, Family (2+3) £10. EH members free but there may be a small charge on event days. 15% group discounts (11+).

ℹ Picnickers welcome. WC. ♿ ● 🏠 🐕

GRIMSTHORPE CASTLE, 🏛 PARK & GARDENS

See page 302 for full page entry.

GUNBY HALL 🌿

Gunby, Spilsby, Lincolnshire PE23 5SS

Tel: 07870 758876 **Fax:** 01909 486377 www.nationaltrust.org.uk

Owner: The National Trust **Contact:** Dr & Mrs R M Ayres

A red brick house with stone dressings, built in 1700 and extended in 1870s. Within the house, there is good early 18th century wainscoting and a fine oak staircase, also English furniture and portraits by Reynolds. Also of interest is the contemporary stable block, a walled kitchen and flower garden, sweeping lawns and borders and an exhibition of Field Marshal Sir Archibald Montgomery-Massingberd's memorabilia. Gunby was reputedly Tennyson's 'haunt of ancient peace'.

Location: MAP 7:G2, OS122, TF466 672. 2½ m NW of Burgh Le Marsh, 7m W of Skegness On S side of A158 (access off roundabout).

Open: House & Garden: 4 Jun–27 Aug, Wed, 2–5pm. Garden only: 2 Apr–28 May, Wed, 2–5pm; 3 Jun–28 Aug, Tue–Thur, 2–5pm. 3–25 Sept, Wed/Thur, 2–5pm. The garden is also open on Tues & Thurs in Apr & May by written appointment to Dr & Mrs R M Ayres, at Gunby Hall.

Admission: Adult £6, Child £3, Family £14. Garden only: Adult £4, Child £2, Family £9.

♿ Grounds. 🐕 In grounds, on leads.

HECKINGTON WINDMILL

Hale Road, Heckington, Sleaford, Lincolnshire NG34 9JW

Tel: 01529 461919 **Contact:** Derek James

Britain's last surviving eight sail windmill. Now in full working order.

Location: MAP 7:E4, OS Ref. TF145 437. W side of B1394, S side of Heckington village.

Open: Contact property for details.

Admission: Ground floor & Shop: Free. Mill: Adult £1.50, Child 75p.

LEADENHAM HOUSE

Leadenham House, Lincolnshire LN5 0PU

Tel: 01400 273256 **Fax:** 01400 272237

Owner: Mr P Reeve **Contact:** Mr and Mrs P Reeve

Late eighteenth century house in park setting.

Location: MAP 7:D3, OS Ref. SK949 518. Entrance on A17 Leadenham bypass (between Newark and Sleaford).

Open: 5–9, 12–16, 19–23, 27–30 May, 22–26, 29/30 Sept & Spring & Aug BHs: all 2–5pm.

Admission: £3.50. Groups by prior arrangement only.

ℹ No photography. ♿ ℹ Obligatory. 🐕

LINCOLN CASTLE

Castle Hill, Lincoln LN1 3AA

Tel: 01522 511068 **E-mail:** lincoln_castle@lincolnshire.gov.uk

Contact: The Manager

Built by William the Conqueror in 1068. Informative exhibition of the 1215 Magna Carta.

Location: MAP 7:D2, OS Ref. SK975 718. Opposite west front of Lincoln Cathedral.

Open: Mon–Sats, 9.30am–5.30pm, Suns, 11am–5.30pm (Winter closes 4pm). Last admission 1hour before closing. Closed 24–26 & 31 Dec & 1 Jan.

Admission: Adult £3.90, Child (5–15), Conc. £2.60, Family (2+3) £10.40.

LINCOLN CATHEDRAL

Lincoln LN2 1PZ

Tel: 01522 561600 **Fax:** 01522 561634 **Contact:** Communications Office

One of the finest medieval buildings in Europe.

Location: MAP 7:D2, OS Ref. SK978 718. At the centre of Uphill, Lincoln.

Open: All year: Jun–Aug, 7.15am–8pm. Winter, 7.15am–6pm. Sun closing 6pm in Summer & 5pm in Winter. Tours of the floor, roof & tower available. Pre-booked groups welcome.

Admission: £4, Child (5–16yrs) £1, Child (under 5s) Free, Conc. £3, Family £10. Optional guided tours & photography Free. Audio guide £1. No charge on Sun or for services.

LINCOLN MEDIEVAL BISHOPS' PALACE ⌗

Minster Yard, Lincoln LN2 1PU
Tel: 01522 527468 **www.english-heritage.org.uk/lincoln**
Owner: English Heritage **Contact:** Visitor Operations Team
Constructed in the late 12th century, the medieval bishops' palace was once one of the most important buildings in England. Built on hillside terraces, it has views of the cathedral and the Roman, medieval and modern city. See a virtual tour of the Palace, explore the grounds and see the award winning Contemporary Heritage Garden and Vineyard (most northerly exposed vineyard in Europe).
Location: MAP 7:D2, OS121 Ref. SK981 717. S side of Lincoln Cathedral, in Lincoln.
Open: 21 Mar–31 Oct: daily, 10am–5pm (6pm Jul–Aug). 1 Nov–31 Mar '09: Thur–Mon, 10am–4pm. Closed 24–26 Dec & 1 Jan. Open daily for Lincoln Christmas Market.
Admission: Adult £4, Child £2, Conc. £3.20, Family £10. 15% discount for groups (11+). EH Members free.
ℹ Picnickers welcome. ⬚ ⬚ Ⓟ Limited disability parking only. ⬚ ✳ ⬚

MARSTON HALL

Marston, Grantham NG32 2HQ
Tel/Fax: 07812 356237 **E-mail:** johnthorold@aol.com
Owner/Contact: J R Thorold
The ancient home of the Thorold family. The building contains Norman, Plantaganet, Tudor and Georgian elements through to the modern day. Marston Hall is undergoing continuous restoration some of it which may be disruptive. Please telephone in advance of intended visits.
Location: MAP 7:D4, OS Ref. SK893 437. 5m N of Grantham and about 1m E of A1.
Open: 25–28 Feb, 15–18 Mar, 5–8 Apr, 5 & 26 May, 5–13 Jul, 25 Aug & 13–16 Sept: 1–6pm.
Admission: Adult £3.50, Child £1.50. Groups must book.
ℹ No photography.

SIBSEY TRADER WINDMILL ⌗

Sibsey, Boston, Lincolnshire PE22 0SY
Tel: 01205 750036 **www.english-heritage.org.uk/sibseytrader**
Owner: English Heritage **Contact:** The East Midlands Regional Office
An impressive old mill built in 1877, with its machinery and six sails still intact. Flour milled on the spot can be bought here. The award-winning tearoom sells produce made from the Mill's organic stoneground flour.
Location: MAP 7:F3, OS Ref. TF345 511. ½m W of village of Sibsey, off A16, 5m N of Boston.
Open: 21 Mar–30 Apr, Oct & Mar '09: Sat & BHs, 10am–6pm, Sun 11am–6pm. 1 May–30 Sept: Sat & BHs, 10am–6pm, Sun & Tue 11am–6pm. 1 Nov–29 Feb '09: Sats, 11am–5pm, (Mill only). Closed 24–26 Dec & 1 Jan.
Admission: Adult £2, Child £1 (under 5yrs Free), Conc. £1.50. Members OUP Free. EH Members free.
ℹ Picnickers welcome. WC. ♿ Exterior only. ⬚ Ⓟ ⬚

For unique **Civil wedding** venues see our index at the end of the book.

© NTPL / Andrew Butler

TATTERSHALL CASTLE ✤

TATTERSHALL, LINCOLN LN4 4LR
www.nationaltrust.org.uk

Tel: 01526 342543 **E-mail:** tattershallcastle@nationaltrust.org.uk
Owner: The National Trust **Contact:** The Property Manager
A vast fortified tower built c1440 for Ralph Cromwell, Lord Treasurer of England. The Castle is an important example of an early brick building, with a tower containing state apartments, rescued from dereliction and restored by Lord Curzon 1911–14. Four great chambers, with ancillary rooms, contain late gothic fireplaces and brick vaulting. There are tapestries and information displays in turret rooms.
Location: MAP 7:E3, OS122 Ref. TF209 575. On S side of A153, 15m NE of Sleaford, 10m SW of Horncastle.
Open: 1–14 Mar, 3 Nov–16 Dec, Sat & Sun, 12 noon–4pm; 15 Mar–1 Oct, Mon–Wed & Sat & Sun 11am–5.30pm; 4 Oct–2 Nov, Mon–Wed & Sat & Sun Nov, 11am–4pm.
*Admission: Adult £4.70, Child £2.50, Family £11.90. Group discounts. *includes a voluntary donation but visitors can choose to pay the standard prices displayed at the property and on the website.
♿ Ground floor. WC. ⬚ Free. ⬚ Car park only. ⬚

© NTPL / Nick Meers

WOOLSTHORPE MANOR ✤

23 NEWTON WAY, WOOLSTHORPE-BY-COLSTERWORTH, GRANTHAM NG33 5NR
www.nationaltrust.org.uk

Tel: 01476 860338 **Fax:** 01476 862826
E-mail: woolsthorpemanor@nationaltrust.org.uk
Owner: The National Trust **Contact:** The Property Manager
This modest 17th century manor house was the birthplace and family home of one of the world's most famous scientists. As a young man Isaac Newton developed his remarkable work about light and gravity here. Visit the famous apple tree, discover Newton's ideas in the hands-on Science Discovery Centre, explore the orchard and farm and enjoy the short film.
Location: MAP 7:D5, OS130 Ref. SK924 244. 7m S of Grantham, ½ m NW of Colsterworth, 1m W of A1.
Open: House & Grounds: 1–23 Mar, 4–26 Oct, Sat/Sun, 1–5pm; 26 Mar–29 Jun, 3–28 Sep Sept, Wed–Sun, 1–5pm. 2 Jul–31 Aug, Wed–Fri 1–5pm;
*Admission: Adult £5.50, Child £2.70, Family £13, no reduction for groups which must book in advance. *includes a voluntary donation but visitors can choose to pay the standard prices displayed at the property and on the website.
♿ Ground floor. Ⓟ Limited. ⬚ Car park only.

The Stable Block

ALTHORP

www.althorp.com

The history of Althorp is the history of a family. The Spencers have lived and died here for nearly five centuries and twenty generations.

Since the death of Diana, Princess of Wales, Althorp has become known across the world, but before that tragic event, connoisseurs had heard of this most classic of English stately homes on account of the magnificence of its contents and the beauty of its setting.

Next to the mansion at Althorp lies the honey-coloured stable block, a truly breathtaking building which at one time accommodated up to 100 horses and 40 grooms. The stables are now the setting for the Exhibition celebrating the life of Diana, Princess of Wales and honouring her memory after her death. The freshness and modernity of the facilities are a unique tribute to a woman who captivated the world in her all-too-brief existence.

All visitors are invited to view the House, Exhibition and Grounds as well as the Island in the Round Oval where Diana, Princess of Wales is laid to rest.

■ Owner
The Earl Spencer

■ Contact
Althorp
Northampton NN7 4HQ

Tel: 01604 770107
Fax: 01604 770042

Book online
www.althorp.com

E-mail: mail@althorp.com

■ Location
MAP 7:C9
OS Ref. SP682 652

From the M1/J16, 7m J18, 10m. Situated on A428 Northampton – Rugby. London on average 85 mins away.

Rail: 5m from Northampton station. 14m from Rugby station.

■ Opening Times
Summer
July and August, daily, 11am–5pm. (excluding 31 August.)

Last admission 4pm.

Winter Closed.

■ Admission
House & Garden
Contact for admission prices and group rates.

Carers accompanying visitors with disabilities are admitted free.

Please check website for up to date information.

The Picture Gallery

[i] Information leaflet issued to all ticket holders who book in advance. No indoor photography with still or video cameras.

Visitor Centre & ground floor of house accessible. WCs.

Café.

[P] Limited for coaches.

Guide dogs only.

■ Owner

His Grace The Duke of Buccleuch & Queensberry, KBE

■ Contact

Charles Lister
The Living
Landscape Trust
Boughton House
Kettering
Northamptonshire
NN14 1BJ

Tel: 01536 515731
Fax: 01536 417255
E-mail:
llt@boughtonhouse.org.uk

■ Location

MAP 7:D7
OS Ref. SP900 815

3m N of Kettering on A43/J7 from A14. Signposted through Geddington.

■ Opening Times

Summer
House
1 August–1 September
Daily, 2–5pm.
Last entry 4pm.
Self guided tour normally in operation, entry by guided tour only on Mons & Fris.

Grounds
1 May–31 July, daily, 1–5pm. Closed Saturdays.

1 August–1 September, daily, 1–5pm.

Winter
Daily by appointment throughout the year for educational groups – contact for details.

■ Admission

Summer
House & Grounds
Adult   £7.00
Child/Conc.   £6.00

Grounds
Adult   £1.50
Child/Conc.   £1.00

Wheelchair visitors Free. HHA Friends are admitted Free in August.

Winter
Group rates available – contact for further details.

BOUGHTON HOUSE 🏛

www.boughtonhouse.org.uk

Boughton House is the Northamptonshire home of the Dukes of Buccleuch and Queensberry and their Montagu ancestors since 1528. It is looked after by an educational charity, the Living Landscape Trust, established by the 9th Duke in 1986. The Trust's purpose is to foster understanding of the House and its heritage and the surrounding Boughton Estate, with which it has always been intimately linked. Amongst its priorities are conservation of the extremely fragile structure and contents, and gradual restoration of the outstanding designed landscape.

Boughton has been described as 'at once palace, manor house, and village' – its transformation at the end of the 17th century earned it the title of "The English Versailles." The House contains an exceptional fine art collection and is set in an early 18th century Designed Landscape which is currently under restoration.

For information on the group visits programme or education services, please contact The Living Landscape Trust.

Our website gives considerable information on Boughton House and the Living Landscape Trust, together with full details of our schools' educational facilities (Sandford Award winner 1988, 1993, 1998 and 2003).

"I never desired anything so earnestly as to go to Boughton to see my Lord, the Good Company and learning in its full lustre." Charles de Saint Evremond, the French soldier, poet and essayist writing in 1700 about the home of his good friend, Ralph Montagu.

ℹ Parkland available for film location and other events. Stableblock room contains 100 seats. No inside photography. No unaccompanied children. Browse our website for a 'virtual' tour of the house.

🛍

❄

♿ Access to ground floor and all facilities. Virtual tour of first floor.

☕ Tearoom seats 80, groups must book. Licensed.

🧑 By arrangement.

🅿

🎓 Heritage Education Trust Sandford Award winner 1988, 1993, 1998 & 2003. School groups Free.

🐕 No dogs in house and garden, welcome in Park on leads.

❊ By arrangement.

Conference/Function

ROOM	MAX CAPACITY
Lecture	100
Seminar Rm	25
Conference facilities available in stable block adjacent to House	

DEENE PARK 🏛

www.deenepark.com

A most interesting house, occupied and developed by the Brudenell family since 1514, from a mediaeval manor around a courtyard into a Tudor and Georgian mansion. Visitors see many rooms of different periods, providing an impressive yet intimate ambience of the family home of many generations. The most flamboyant member of the family to date was the 7th Earl of Cardigan, who led the charge of the Light Brigade at Balaklava and of whom there are many historic relics and pictures on view.

Mr Edmund Brudenell, the current owner, has taken considerable care in restoring the house after the Second World War. The gardens have also been improved during the last thirty years or so, with long, mixed borders of shrubs, old-fashioned roses and flowers, together with a parterre designed by David Hicks and long walks under fine old trees by the water. The car park beside the main lake is a good place for visitors to picnic.

■ Owner
E Brudenell Esq

■ Contact
The House Keeper
Deene Park
Corby
Northamptonshire
NN17 3EW

Tel: 01780 450278
or 01780 450223
Fax: 01780 450282
E-mail: admin@
deenepark.com

■ Location
MAP 7:D7
OS Ref. SP950 929

6m NE of Corby off A43.
From London via M1/J15
then A43, or via A1, A14,
A43 – 2 hrs.

From Birmingham via M6,
A14, A43, 90 mins.

Rail: Kettering Station
20 mins.

■ Opening Times
Summer
Open Suns & Mons of
Easter–August BH
weekends.
Also, June–August
Suns, 2–5pm

Open at all other times
by arrangement, including
pre-booked groups.

Winter
Gardens only
Suns 17 & 24 Feb:
11am–4pm for
snowdrops.
Refreshments available in
the Old Kitchen.

Otherwise House and
Gardens closed to casual
visitors. Open at all other
times by arrangement for
groups.

■ Admission
Public Open Days
House & Gardens
Adult   £7.50
Child (10–14yrs) £2.50
Conc.   £6.50

Gardens only
Adult   £5.00
Child (10–14yrs) £1.50

Groups (20+)
by arrangement:
Weekdays   £6.50
          (Min £130)
Weekends & BHs £7.00
          (Min £140)

*Child up to 10yrs free
with an accompanying
adult.

Winter
Groups visits only by prior
arrangement.

ⓘ Suitable for indoor and outdoor events, filming, specialist lectures on house, its contents, gardens and history. No photography in house.

🛍

🍷 Including buffets, lunches and dinners.

♿ Partial. Visitors may alight at the entrance, access to ground floor and garden. WC.

☕ Special rates for groups, bookings can be made in advance, menus on request.

🍴 By arrangement.

🚶 Tours inclusive of admittance, tour time 90 mins. Owner will meet groups if requested.

🅿 Unlimited for cars, space for 3 coaches 10 yds from house.

🐕 In car park only.

🏨 Residential conference facilities by arrangement.

❄

🎭

■ Conference/Function

ROOM	MAX CAPACITY
Great Hall	150
Tapestry Rm	75
East Room	18

■ Owner

The Kelmarsh Trust

■ Contact

Education & Heritage Manager
Kelmarsh Hall
Kelmarsh
Northamptonshire
NN6 9LY

Tel: 01604 686543
Fax: 01604 686437
E-mail: enquiries@ kelmarsh.com

■ Location

MAP 7:C7
OS Ref. SP736 795

⅓ m N of A14-A508 jct.

Rail & Bus:
Mkt Harborough

■ Opening Times

Guided House Tours
BH Suns and Mons, also Thursdays: From Easter– 28 September. 2–5pm. Check our website for additional events.

Gardens
Easter–28 September. BH Suns and Mons. Tue–Thu & Sun, Check our website to ensure the gardens are not closed for special events.

Croome Tours – Sundays
Available between 2–5pm on 3rd Sunday of each month, February–November. Check our website for details and any changes/additions to the programme.

■ Admission

House and Garden
Adult	£5.00
Child (5–12yrs)	£3.00
Conc.	£4.50

Gardens
Adult	£4.00
Child (5–12yrs)	£2.50
Conc.	£3.50

Croome Tours
Adult	£5.00
Child (5–12yrs)	£3.00
Conc.	£4.50

■ Special Events

February
Snowdrop Sunday

March
Country Fair

April
Tulip Week

May
Hardy Plant Fair

June
Norah Lindsay Day
Jazz Evening
Rose Week

September
Dahlia Week

November
Christmas Fair

See our website for details.

KELMARSH HALL 🏛

www.kelmarsh.com

Built in 1732 to a James Gibbs design, Kelmarsh Hall is surrounded by its working estate, grazed parkland and beautiful gardens. In 1928 Ronald and Nancy Tree rented the Palladian house from the Lancaster family and decorated the rooms in the manner that has become known as the English Country House style. In the 1950s she returned to Kelmarsh as Nancy Lancaster and continued to develop her style both in the house and in the gardens. Additional schemes and designs by Geoffrey Jellicoe and Norah Lindsay have created a remarkable garden including a stunning triangular walled garden. The cutting garden in the walled garden is particularly beautiful from August onwards. Gifted to the Kelmarsh Trust by the Lancaster family the house, gardens and estate are now available for study, group and general visits.

Croome Court in Worcestershire was home to the Earls of Coventry until 1948. Due to the foresight of the family much of the furniture and chattels, together with their original bills of sale, were retained. The collection was started by George William the 6th Earl of Coventry in 1763, and we are pleased to be working with the Croome Estate Trust to bring this fabulous collection of 18th century furniture, paintings and porcelain to Northamptonshire. Special Group Tours of the Hall, Garden & Croome Collection are available by arrangement.

ℹ	No photography in house.
✳	
🍸	Conferences & functions
♿	Partial. WC.
☕	Licensed.
👤	Obligatory.
🅿	
🚫	
🐕	In grounds, on leads.
🔔	
❄	For group visits.

LAMPORT HALL & GARDENS 🏛

www.lamporthall.co.uk

Home of the Isham family from 1560 to 1976. The 17th and 18th century façade is by John Webb and the Smiths of Warwick. The Hall contains an outstanding collection of furniture, china and paintings including portraits by Van Dyck, Kneller and Lely and other important works of art, many brought back from a Grand Tour in the 17th century. The Library contains books dating back to the 16th century and the Cabinet Room houses rare Italian cabinets. The first floor includes a replicated 17th century bedchamber and a photographic record of Sir Gyles Isham, a Hollywood actor, who initiated the restoration. Refreshments are served in the Victorian dining room. The gardens owe much to the 10th Baronet who, in the mid 19th century, created the famous rockery and populated it with the first garden gnomes. He also made a small Italian garden with a shell fountain, planted herbaceous borders and wisteria, which still thrives today. Other features include an 18th century box bower and a 17th century cockpit. The Lamport Hall Preservation Trust was formed in 1974 by Sir Gyles to complete the restoration work initiated by him. The final phase of this restoration work was completed in 2007.

ℹ	No photography in house, Available for filming.
🍴	Partial. WC.
☕	Licensed.
🚶	Obligatory other than Fair Days.
🅿	Limited for coaches.
🐕	In grounds, on leads.
❄	Groups only.
🎓	Telephone or visit website for History/Painting/Gardening study days.

■ Owner
Lamport Hall Trust

■ Contact
Executive Director
Lamport Hall
Northamptonshire
NN6 9HD

Tel: 01604 686272
Fax: 01604 686224
E-mail:
admin@lamporthall.co.uk

■ Location
MAP 7:C8
OS Ref. SP759 745.

Entrance on A508. 8m N of Northampton, 3m S of A14 J2.

Bus:
Limited Stagecoach from Northampton and Leicester.

■ Opening Times
House open for guided tours, 23 Mar–12 Oct: Suns, 2.30 & 3.15pm; 28 July–1 September: Mon–Fri, 2.30pm. Non-guided tours only on Fair Days: Antiques, Country Festival & Craft & Gift etc.

■ Admission
House & Garden,
Adult	£6.00
Child (5–16yrs)	£2.50
OAP	£5.50
Groups	£6.00
(Minimum £150.00)	

■ Special Events
March 23/24 Easter Sunday and Monday
Antiques and Collectors Fair

May 25/26 Spring Bank Holiday Sunday and Monday
Steam and Country Festival

June 20–22
Live music and theatre in the gardens

July 25–27
Live music and theatre in the gardens

August 24/25 Bank Holiday Sunday and Monday
Antiques and Collectors Fair

October 11/12
Gift and Craft Fair

Conference/Function

ROOM	SIZE	MAX CAPACITY
Victorian Dining Room	7.5 x 9.5m	80
High Room	5.9 x 9.2m	60
Oak Room	6.1 x 8.2m	70
Complete stable yard and buildings available for fairs, exhibitions, corporate use, etc.		

■ Owner
James Saunders Watson

■ Contact
Andrew Norman
Operations Manager
Rockingham Castle
Market Harborough
Leicestershire
LE16 8TH

Tel: 01536 770240
E-mail: estateoffice@
rockinghamcastle.com

■ Location
MAP 7:D7
OS Ref. SP867 913.

1m N of Corby on A6003.
9m E of Market
Harborough. 14m SW of
Stamford on A427.

■ Opening Times
Easter (23 March)–end
June: Suns & BH Mons.

July– end September:
Tues, Suns & BH Mon.

Grounds: 12 noon–5pm.

Castle opens at 1pm, last
entrance: 4.30pm.

■ Admission
House & Grounds
Adult	£8.50
Child (5–16yrs)	£5.00
OAP	£7.50
Family (2+2)	£22.00

Groups (20+) and school
parties can be
accommodated on most
days by arrangement.
Adult (on open days)	£7.50
Adult (private tour)	£9.50
Child (5–16yrs)	£4.00
Schoolchild*	£4.00

*1 Adult Free with every
15 children.

Grounds only
Including Gardens,
Salvin's Tower, Gift Shop
and Licensed Tea Room.

Adult or Child	£5.00

(Not available when
special events are held in
grounds.)

■ Special Events
March 23/24
Easter Egg Hunt, Family
Fun Quiz
& 'Animal Hunt'.

June 8
Jousting & Medieval
Living History Village

July 6
Falconry & Owl Day.

August 24/25
Vikings! Of Middle
England.

September 14
Kites Day

November 17–21
Christmas at Rockingham
Castle.

ROCKINGHAM CASTLE 🏛
www.rockinghamcastle.com

Rockingham Castle stands on the edge of an escarpment giving dramatic views over five counties and the Welland Valley below. Built by William the Conqueror, the Castle was a royal residence for 450 years. In the 16th century Henry VIII granted it to Edward Watson and for 450 years it has remained a family home. The predominantly Tudor building, within Norman walls, has architecture, furniture and works of art from practically every century including, unusually, a remarkable collection of 20th century pictures. Charles Dickens was a regular visitor to the Castle and based *Chesney Wolds* in *Bleak House* on Rockingham.

Surrounding the Castle are some 18 acres of gardens largely following the foot print of the medieval castle. The vast 400 year old "Elephant Hedge" bisects the formal 17th century terraced gardens. A circular yew hedge stands on the site of the mot and bailey and provides shelter for the Rose Garden. Surrounding the Rose Garden a three year project is underway to create a new garden with a series of new radial yew hedges and yew pillars providing vistas, walkways and seating within a series of garden 'rooms' that will contain deep borders of stunning herbaceous and shrub planting, each room being given a different character. Below the Castle is the beautiful 19th century Wild Garden replanted with advice from Kew Gardens during the early 1960s. Included in the gardens are many specimen trees and shrubs including the remarkable Handkerchief Tree.

- ℹ No photography in Castle.
- 🛍
- 🍸 Licensed.
- ☕ Partial. WC.
- ♿ By arrangement.
- 🎧
- 🅿
- 🐕 In grounds, on leads.
- 🔔
- 🎭

©NTPL/Andrew Butler

78 DERNGATE: THE CHARLES RENNIE MACKINTOSH HOUSE & GALLERIES

82 Derngate, Northampton NN1 1UH   www.78derngate.org.uk
Tel: 01604 603407   **Fax:** 01604 603408   **E-mail:** info@78derngate.org.uk
Owner: 78 Derngate Northampton Trust   **Contact:** House Manager
Charles Rennie Mackintosh, the renowned Scottish architect, artist and designer, transformed a typical terraced house into a startlingly modern home. It was his last major commission and his only work in England. Mackintosh's striking interiors have been painstakingly restored to their 1917 appearance.
Location: MAP 7:C9, OS Ref. SP759 603. In the heart of Northampton close to the rear of the Royal & Derngate Theatres. Follow Derngate out of the centre of town.
Open: 1 Feb 2008 until Christmas, Tues 1–5pm, Wed–Sun & BH Mons: 10.30am–5pm. Group and school bookings are also available.
Admission: Adult £5.50, Conc. £4.50. Family (2+2): £14. Groups (15+) £4pp.
ℹ️ No indoor photography. 🖼️⬜️♿ Partial. ♿🚻🅿️ None. ⬛️✖️♿

ALTHORP
See page 307 for full page entry.

BOUGHTON HOUSE 🏛️
See page 308 for full page entry.

Rockingham Castle

CANONS ASHBY 🌿
CANONS ASHBY, DAVENTRY, NORTHAMPTONSHIRE NN11 3SD

www.nationaltrust.org.uk

Tel: 01327 861900   **Fax:** 01327 861909   **E-mail:** canonsashby@nationaltrust.org.uk
Owner: The National Trust   **Contact:** The Property Manager
Home of the Dryden family since the 16th century, this Elizabethan manor house was built c1550, added to in the 1590s, and altered in the 1630s and c1710; largely unaltered since. Within the house, Elizabethan wall paintings and outstanding Jacobean plasterwork are of particular interest. A formal garden includes terraces, walls and gate piers of 1710. There is also a medieval priory church and a 70 acre park.
Location: Map 7:B9, OS Ref. SP577 506. Access from M40/J11, or M1/J16. Signposted from A5, 3m S of Weedon crossroads. Then 7m to SW.
Open: House: 1–14 March, Sat & Sun, 1–5pm, 6–21 Dec, Sat & Sun 12 noon–4pm, 15 Mar–30 Sept, Mon–Wed & Sat & Sun, 1–5pm & 1 Oct–2 Nov, 1–4pm. Gardens. Park & Church: 1–14 March, Sat & Sun, 11am–5.30pm, 8 Nov–21 Dec, 11am–4pm, 15 Mar–2 Nov, Mon–Wed & Sat & Sun, 11am–5.30pm, (closes 4.30pm in Oct).
***Admission:** Adult £7.50, Child £3.75, Family £18.75. Garden only: £2.75, Child £1.50. Winter grounds only, Adult £1.50, Child £0.75 *includes a voluntary donation but visitors can choose to pay the standard prices displayed at the property and on the website.
🖼️♿♿ Some steps. WC. ♿🅿️♿ In Home Paddock, on leads. ♿

COTON MANOR GARDEN
GUILSBOROUGH, NORTHAMPTONSHIRE NN6 8RQ

www.cotonmanor.co.uk

Tel: 01604 740219   **Fax:** 01604 740838
E-mail: pasleytyler@cotonmanor.co.uk
Owner: Ian & Susie Pasley-Tyler   **Contact:** Sarah Ball
Traditional English garden laid out on different levels surrounding a 17th century stone manor house. Many herbaceous borders, with extensive range of plants, old yew and holly hedges, rose garden, water garden and fine lawns set in 10 acres. Also wild flower meadow and bluebell wood.
Location: Map 7:B8, OS Ref. SP675 716. 9m NW of Northampton, between A5199 (formerly A50) and A428.
Open: Good Friday 21 Mar–27 Sep: Tue–Sat & BH weekends; also Suns Apr–May: 12 noon–5.30pm.
Admission: Adult £5, Child £2, Conc. £4.50. Groups: £4.50.
🖼️♿♿ Grounds. WC. 🍴♿♿ By arrangement. 🅿️✖️

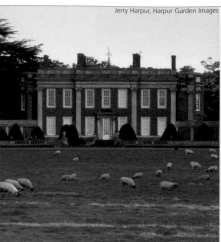
Jerry Harpur, Harpur Garden Images

COTTESBROOKE HALL & GARDENS 🏛
COTTESBROOKE, NORTHAMPTONSHIRE NN6 8PF
www.cottesbrookehall.co.uk

Tel: 01604 505808 **Fax:** 01604 505619 **E-mail:** enquiries@cottesbrooke.co.uk

Owner: Mr & Mrs A R Macdonald-Buchanan **Contact:** The Administrator

This magnificent Queen Anne house dating from 1702 is set in delightful rural Northamptonshire. Reputed to be the pattern for Jane Austen's *Mansfield Park*, the Hall's beauty is matched by the magnificence of the gardens and views and by the excellence of the picture, furniture and porcelain collections it houses. The Woolavington collection of sporting pictures at Cottesbrooke is possibly one of the finest of its type in Europe and includes paintings by Stubbs, Ben Marshall and many other artists renowned for works of this genre, from the mid 18th century to the present day. Portraits, bronzes, 18th century English and French furniture and fine porcelain are also among the treasures of Cottesbrooke Hall.

In the formal gardens huge 300-year-old cedars set off magnificent double herbaceous borders, pools and lily-ponds. In midsummer, visitors enjoy the splendid array of planters, a sight not to be missed. The Wild Garden is a short walk across the Park and is planted along the course of a stream with its small cascades and arched bridges. Previously winner of the HHA/Christie's *Garden of the Year* Award. Nominated as one of the best gardens in the world in "*1001 Gardens you must see before you die*".

Location: MAP 7:B8, OS Ref. SP711 739. 10m N of Northampton near Creaton on A5199 (formerly A50). Signed from Junction 1 on the A14.

Open: 1 May–end of Sept. May & Jun: Wed & Thur, 2–5.30pm. Jul–Sept: Thur, 2–5.30pm. Open BH Mons (May–Sept), 2–5.30pm.

Admission: House & Gardens: Adult £8, Child £3.50, Conc £6.50. Gardens only: Adult £5.50, Child £2.50, Conc £4.50. RHS members receive free access to gardens. Group & private bookings by arrangement.

ⓘ No photography in house. Filming & outside events. Unusual plants. Gardens. WC. Parking. Home-made cakes. Hall guided tours obligatory.

DEENE PARK 🏛

See page 309 for full page entry.

DRAYTON HOUSE

Lowick, Kettering NN14 3BB

Tel: 01832 731779

Owner: The Stopford Sackville family **Contact:** Bruce Bailey

A large house dating from c1300 which has never been let or sold. Splendid Baroque architechture and furnishings. Unique embroidered State bed of c1700. The house came into the ownership of the Sackville family in 1770 and the Dining Room has superb plasterwork of that period.

Location: MAP 7:D7, OS Ref. SP963 799, Lowick village is on A6116, from A14 (J12).

Open: For groups by written appointment only, Easter–end Sept, Tue–Thur.

Admission: £10 per head, with a minimum charge of £120.

ⓘ No photography inside the house. Unsuitable. By arrangement.

ELEANOR CROSS ⌗

Geddington, Kettering, Northamptonshire

Tel: 01604 735400 (Regional Office) www.english-heritage.org.uk/eleanorcross

Owner: English Heritage **Contact:** The East Midlands Regional Office

One of a series of famous crosses, of elegant sculpted design, erected by Edward I to mark the resting places of the body of his wife, Eleanor, when brought for burial from Harby in Nottinghamshire to Westminster Abbey in 1290.

Location: MAP 7:D7, OS Ref. SP896 830. In Geddington, off A43 between Kettering and Corby.

Open: Any reasonable time.

ⓘ Picnickers welcome.

See which properties offer **educational facilities** or **school visits** in our index at the end of the book.

HADDONSTONE SHOW GARDENS

The Forge House, Church Lane, East Haddon, Northampton NN6 8DB

Tel: 01604 770711 **Fax:** 01604 770027

E-mail: info@haddonstone.co.uk **www.haddonstone.co.uk**

Owner: Haddonstone Ltd **Contact:** Marketing Director

See Haddonstone's classic garden ornaments in the beautiful setting of the walled manor gardens including: urns, troughs, fountains, statuary, bird baths, sundials and balustrading – even an orangery. The garden is on different levels with shrub roses, conifers, clematis and climbers. The Jubilee garden features a pavilion, temple and Gothic grotto. As featured on BBC *Gardeners' World*.

Location: MAP 7:B8, OS Ref. SP667 682. 7m NW of Northampton off A428. Signposted.

Open: Mon–Fri, 9am–5.30pm. Closed weekends, BHs & Christmas period.

Admission: Free. Groups by appointment only. Not suitable for coach groups.

By arrangement. Limited. Guide dogs only.

KELMARSH HALL 🏛

See page 310 for full page entry.

Sulgrave Manor

HOLDENBY HOUSE 🏛
HOLDENBY, NORTHAMPTON NN6 8DJ

www.holdenby.com

Tel: 01604 770074   **Fax:** 01604 770962   **E-mail:** office@holdenby.com
Owner: James Lowther   **Contact:** Commercial Manager

Once the largest private house in England and subsequently the palace and prison of King Charles I, Holdenby has a special atmosphere all of its own. Its elegant rooms and acres of gardens and parkland make it a magnificent venue for corporate events, dinners and meetings, as well as an ideal location for films and TV. Visitors to the gardens can enjoy fascinating flying displays of birds from our famous Falconry Centre, while couples continue to choose Holdenby as an enchanting venue for weddings. Holdenby is five times winner of the Sandford Award for Heritage Education.

Location: MAP 7:B8, OS Ref. SP693 681. M1/J15a. 7m NW of Northampton off A428 & A5199.

Open: Gardens & Falconry: May–Aug, Suns & BH Mons 1–5pm. Gardens only: Apr & Sep, Suns 1–5pm. House: 24 Mar & 24/25 Aug and by appointment.

Admission: (with Falconry Centre) Adult £5, Child £3.50, Conc. £4.50, Family (2+2) £15; (Gardens only) Adult £3, Child £2, Conc. £2.50, Family (2+2) £8. Different prices on event days. Groups must book.

ⓘ Children's play area. 🖾 🐕 🍴 🔲 Partial. WC. ☕ Teas. (May–Aug). 🎭 By arrangement. 🅿 🚻 5 times Sandford Award Winner. 🐾 In grounds, on leads. 🔺

🎪 23/24 Mar, Victorian Easter. 24/25 Aug, Holdenby Food Show.

© English Heritage Photo Library

KIRBY HALL ⚏
DEENE, CORBY, NORTHAMPTONSHIRE NN17 3EN

www.english-heritage.org.uk/kirbyhall

Tel: 01536 203230
Owner: The Earl of Winchilsea & Nottingham (Managed by English Heritage)
Contact: Visitor Operations Team

Peaceful partial ruins of a large, stone-built Elizabethan mansion, begun in 1570 with 17th century alterations. The richly carved decoration is exceptional, full of amazing Renaissance detail. Fine gardens with topiary, home to peacocks. Jane Austen's *Mansfield Park* was filmed at Kirby Hall. Newly restored Elizabethan decorative schemes in the Great Hall, Billiard Room, Library and Best Bedchamber. Located in beautiful countryside close to both Rockingham Castle and Deene Park.

Location: MAP 7:D7 OS Ref. SP926 927. On unclassified road off A43, Corby to Stamford road, 4m NE of Corby. 2m W of Deene Park.

Open: 21 Mar–30 Jun: Thur–Mon, 10am–5pm. Jul & Aug: daily, 10am–6pm. 1 Sept–31 Mar '09: Thur–Mon, 10am–5pm (12noon–4pm Nov–Mar). Closed 24–26 Dec & 1 Jan.

Admission: Adult £4.90, Child £2.50, Conc. £3.90, Family £12.30. 15% discount for groups (11+). EH Members Free. May close early for private events. Please call to check.

ⓘ Picnickers welcome. WC. 🖾 🔲 Grounds, gardens & ground floor only. 🎧 Free with admission. 🅿 🚻 🐾 Restricted areas. ❄ 🎪

LAMPORT HALL & GARDENS 🏛

See page 311 for full page entry.

©NTPL/Paul Wakefield

LYVEDEN NEW BIELD ✤

Nr OUNDLE, PETERBOROUGH PE8 5AT

www.nationaltrust.org.uk

Tel: 01832 205358 **Fax:** 01832 205158
E-mail: lyvedennewbield@nationaltrust.org.uk
Owner: The National Trust   **Contact:** The Property Manager
An incomplete Elizabethan garden house and moated garden. Begun in 1595 by Sir Thomas Tresham to symbolise his Catholic faith, Lyveden remains virtually unaltered since work stopped when Tresham died in 1605. Fascinating Elizabethan architectural detail; remains of one of the oldest garden layouts; set amongst beautiful open countryside.
Location: MAP 7:D7, OS141, SP983 853. 4m SW of Oundle via A427, 3m E of Brigstock, off Harley Way. Access by foot along a ½m farm track.
Open: House & Garden: 1 Feb–1 Dec, Sat & Sun, 11am–4pm, 15 Mar–2 Nov, Wed–Sun, 10.30am–5pm. 1–30 Aug, daily 10.30am–5pm, BH Mons/Good Fri, 10.30am–5pm.
*Admission: Adult £4, Child Free. *includes a voluntary donation but visitors can choose to pay the standard prices displayed at the property and on the website.
P Limited. 🐕 On leads. ❊

NORTHAMPTON CATHEDRAL

Catholic Cathedral House, Primrose Hill, Northampton NN2 6AG
Tel: 01604 714556   **Contact:** Father J Udris
Partly 19th century Pugin.
Location: MAP 7:C9 , OS Ref. SP753 617. ¾m N of town centre on A508.
Open: Apply at house: Services: Sat 7pm; Sun 8.30am, 10.30am & 5.15pm; weekday 9.30am & 7pm.
Admission: Guided visits by prior application.

THE PREBENDAL MANOR

Nassington, Peterborough PE8 6QG
Tel: 01780 782575   **E-mail:** info@prebendal-manor.co.uk
www.prebendal-manor.co.uk
Owner/Contact: Mrs J Baile
Grade I listed, dating from the early 13th century, it retains many fine original medieval features and included in the visit are the 15th century dovecote, tithe barn museum and medieval fish ponds. Encompassing 6 acres are the largest 14th century re-created medieval gardens in Europe.
Location: MAP 7:E7, OS Ref. TL063 962. 6m N of Oundle, 9m W of Peterborough, 7m S of Stamford.
Open: Apr & Sept, Suns only, May–Aug, Sun & Wed, & BH Mon 2–5pm.
Admission: Adult £6, Child £3.50, OAP £5.50. Groups (20–50) outside normal opening times by arrangement.
ℹ No photography. T 🖼 Partial. 🍴 Home-made teas. P Limited. 🚹 ♿ Free. 🐕 Guide dogs only.

ROCKINGHAM CASTLE 🏛

See page 312 for full page entry.

RUSHTON TRIANGULAR LODGE ⌗

Rushton, Kettering, Northamptonshire NN14 1RP
Tel: 01536 710761   **www.english-heritage.org.uk/rushton**
Owner: English Heritage   **Contact:** Visitor Operations Team
This extraordinary building, completed in 1597, symbolises the Holy Trinity. It has three sides, 33 ft wide, three floors, trefoil windows and three triangular gables on each side.
Location: MAP 7:C7 OS141, SP830 831. 1m W of Rushton, on unclassified road 3m from Desborough on A6.
Open: 21 Mar–31 Oct: Thurs–Mon, 11am–4pm.
Admission: Adult £2.60, Child £1.30, Conc. £2.10. EH Members Free. Group discount available.
ℹ Picnickers welcome. 🎦 P Nearby lay-by. 🐕 Restricted areas.

Holdenby House

SOUTHWICK HALL 🏛

Nr Oundle, Peterborough PE8 5BL
Tel: 01832 274064   www.southwickhall.co.uk
Owner: Christopher Capron   **Contact:** G Bucknill
A family home since 1300, retaining medieval building dating from 1300, with Tudor rebuilding and 18th century additions. Exhibitions: Victorian and Edwardian Life, collections of agricultural and carpentry tools and local archaeological finds.
Location: MAP 7:E7, OS152, TL022 921. 3m N of Oundle, 4m E of Bulwick.
Open: BH Suns & Mons: 23,24 Mar; 4,5,25,26 May; 24,25 Aug: 2–5pm. Last admission 4.30pm. Groups at other times by arrangement.
Admission: House & Grounds: Adult £6, Child £2.50.
♿ Partial. WC. ☕ 🎦 By arrangement. 🅿 🐕 In grounds on leads.

STOKE PARK PAVILIONS

Stoke Bruerne, Towcester, Northamptonshire NN12 7RZ
Tel: 01604 862329 or 07768 230325
Owner/Contact: A S Chancellor Esq
The two Pavilions, dated c1630 and attributed to Inigo Jones, formed part of the first Palladian country house built in England by Sir Francis Crane. The central block, to which the Pavilions were linked by quadrant colonnades, was destroyed by fire in 1886. The grounds include extensive gardens and overlooks former parkland, now being restored.
Location: MAP 7:C10, OS Ref. SP740 488. 7m S of Northampton.
Open: Aug: daily, 3–6pm. Other times by appointment only.
Admission: Adult £3, Child £1.50.
♿ Grounds. 🅿 Limited. 🐕 In grounds, on leads.

SULGRAVE MANOR

MANOR ROAD, SULGRAVE, Nr BANBURY, OXFORDSHIRE OX17 2SD

www.sulgravemanor.org.uk

Tel: 01295 760205 **Fax:** 01295 768056 **E-mail:** enquiries@sulgravemanor.org.uk
Owner: The Sulgrave Manor Board **Contact:** Sulgrave Manor
A delightful 16th century Manor House that was the home of George Washington's ancestors. The Manor contains wonderful Tudor to Georgian furniture and artefacts, and the largest UK collection of George Washington memorabilia demonstrating the British contribution to the origins of the USA. The gardens were designed in the formal style by Sir Reginald Blomfield. There are herbaceous borders, fine topiary work, an orchard underplanted with thousands of daffodils and the knot garden with a sundial dating from 1579.
Sulgrave Manor is also home to The Herb Society who maintain the National Herb Garden and their Chelsea prize winning exhibit within the grounds. The Courtyard buildings house fine visitor/education/wedding and function facilities.

2008 is Sulgrave Manor's 'Year of the Garden' with an interesting range of additional events. See website for details.
Location: MAP 7:B9 OS Ref. 152, SP561 457. Off Banbury – Northampton road 5m from M40/J11. 15m from M1/J15A.
Open: 1 Apr–28 Oct: Sats/Sun, 12 noon–4pm (last entry). 1 May–31 Oct: Tue–Thu, 2–4pm (last entry). Open for booked groups on any day or evening throughout the year (except Jan). Access to house may be restricted during private wedding ceremonies.
Admission: All visitors on non-event days are taken round the Manor House on regularly organised guided tours.
ℹ No photography in house. 📷 🎫 🚻 ♿ Partial. ☕ 🎦 Obligatory. 🅿 🎦 🐕 ♿ ❄ ♿

Lyveden New Bield

WAKEFIELD LODGE

Potterspury, Northamptonshire NN12 7QX
Tel: 01327 811395 **Fax:** 01327 811051
Owner/Contact: Mrs J Richmond-Watson
Georgian hunting lodge with deer park.
Location: MAP 7:C10, OS Ref. SP739 425. 4m S of Towcester on A5. Take signs to farm shop for directions.
Open: House. 21 Apr–30 May: Mon–Fri (closed BHs), 12 noon–4pm. Appointments by telephone. Access walk open Apr & May.
Admission: £5.
ℹ No photography. 📷 ♿ Unsuitable. ☕ 🍴 🎦 Obligatory. 🅿 🐕 Guide dogs only.

Properties that **open all year** appear in the special index at the end of the book.

CARLTON HALL

Carlton-on-Trent, Nottinghamshire NG23 6LP

Tel: 01636 821421   **Fax:** 01636 821554

Owner/Contact: Lt Col & Mrs Vere-Laurie

Mid 18th century house by Joseph Pocklington of Newark. Stables attributed to Carr of York. Family home occupied by the same family since 1832.

Location: MAP 7:C3, OS Ref. SK799 640. 7m N of Newark off A1. Opposite the church.

Open: 1 Apr–30 Sept: Weds only, 2–5pm. Other dates and times by appointment.

Admission: Hall and Garden: £8. Groups (10+) £5pp.

Ⓣ Conferences. Ⓖ Unsuitable. Ⓚ Obligatory. Ⓜ In grounds, on leads. Guide dogs in house. ✳

Wollaton Hall Natural History Museum

©NTPL/Andrew Butler

CLUMBER PARK ✿

CLUMBER PARK, WORKSOP, NOTTINGHAMSHIRE S80 3AZ

www.nationaltrust.org.uk

Tel: 01909 544917   **Fax:** 01909 500721

Owner: The National Trust   **Contact:** Property Manager

Historic parkland with peaceful woods, open heath and rolling farmland around a serpentine lake.

Location: MAP 7:B2, OS120 Ref SK626 746. 4½m SE of Worksop, 6½m SW of Retford, just off A1/A57 via A614. 11m from M1/J30.

Open: Park: All year, daily, in daylight hours. Kitchen Garden: 29 Mar–28 Sept, daily 10am–5pm, closes 6pm Sat & Sun, 4–26 Oct, Sat & Sun 11am–4pm. Shop, Restaurant & Plant Sales: All year, daily 10am–5pm, closes 4pm Nov–Apr (6pm, Sat & Sun, Apr–Nov). Main facilities open BH Mons, closed 25 Dec. Chapel open as shop but closed 13 Jan–1 Apr for cleaning. Cycle hire open as shop except Oct–March, when open weekends & school holidays only. Interpretation centre open all year round.

Admission: Vehicle £4.80, Adult £2.75, Child Free.

▣ Ⓚ Ⓣ Ⓖ Partial. Wheelchairs available. Ⓦ Ⓟ Ⓜ Ⓜ In grounds on leads. ✳ ♨

HODSOCK PRIORY GARDENS

Blyth, Nr Worksop, Nottinghamshire S81 0TY

Tel: 01909 591204   www.snowdrops.co.uk

Owner: Sir Andrew & Lady Buchanan   **Contact:** George Buchanan

"A magical sight you will never forget". Myriads of flowers in the 5-acre garden plus a half mile walk through the woodland with sheets of snowdrops. Banks of *hellebores*, carpets of pink *cyclamen*, ribbons of golden *aconites*, blue *irises*, the red, orange, green, black and white stems of *Acers*, *Cornus* and *Willows* and the heady fragrance of *sarcococca*. There is a clearly marked trail, with plenty of seats. Shortcuts are signed for those who prefer a shorter walk.

Location: MAP 7:B1, OS Ref. SK612 853. W of B6045 Worksop/Blyth road, 1m SW of Blyth, less than 2m from A1.

Open: 1 Feb–2 Mar: Daily, 10am–4pm (last entry).

Admission: Adult £4.50, accompanied Child (6–16yrs) £1.

▣ Heritage shop. Ⓚ Ⓦ Ⓟ

HOLME PIERREPONT HALL 🏛

HOLME PIERREPONT, Nr NOTTINGHAM NG12 2LD

www.holmepierreponthall.com

Tel: 0115 933 2371

Owner: Mr & Mrs Robin Brackenbury   **Contact:** Robert Brackenbury

This charming late medieval manor house is set in 30 acres of Park and Gardens with regional furniture and family portraits. The Ball Room, Drawing Room and Long Gallery are available to hire for functions on an exclusive basis. Filming welcome.

Location: MAP 7:B4, OS Ref. SK628 392. 5m ESE of central Nottingham. Follow signs to the National Water Sports Centre and continue for 1½m.

Open: 4 Feb–19 Mar, Mon–Wed; also 10 Feb, 9 Mar, 13 Apr, 28 Sept: 2–5pm. Corporate, private and wedding venue. Functions at other times by arrangement. Groups by appointment all year.

Admission: Adult £5, Child £1.50. Gardens only £3.

ⓘ No photography or video recording in house when open to the public. Ⓣ Business and charity functions, wedding receptions, dinners, seminars and conferences. Ⓖ Please ring for details. Ⓜ In grounds on leads. ⬛ ✳ ♨

NEWARK TOWN HALL

Market Place, Newark, Nottinghamshire NG24 1DU
Tel: 01636 680333 **Fax:** 01636 680350
Owner: Newark Town Council   **Contact:** The Curator
A fine Georgian Grade I listed Town Hall containing a museum of the town's treasures. Disabled access – lift and WC.
Location: MAP 7:C3, OS Ref. SK570 395. Close to A46 and A1.
Open: All year: Mon–Sat, 11am–4pm. Closed BHs.
Admission: Free.

NEWSTEAD ABBEY HISTORIC HOUSE & GARDENS

Newstead Abbey Park, Nottinghamshire NG15 8NA
Tel: 01623 455900 **Fax:** 01623 455904 **www.newsteadabbey.org.uk**
Owner: Nottingham City Council   **Contact:** Gillian Crawley
Historic home of the poet, Lord Byron, set in extensive formal gardens and parkland of 300 acres. See Byron's private apartments, period rooms and the medieval cloisters. The West Front of the Priory Church is a stunning local landmark.
Location: MAP 7:B3, OS Ref. SK540 639. 12m N of Nottingham 1m W of the A60 Mansfield Rd.
Open: House: 1 Apr–30 Sept: 12 noon–5pm, last adm. 4pm. Grounds: All year: 9am–6pm or dusk except for the last Friday in November and 25 Dec.
Admission: House & Grounds: Adult £6, Child £2.50, Conc. £4, Family (2+3) £16. Groups (10+) £4. Grounds only: Adult £3, Child £1.50, Conc. £2.50, Family £8.50. Groups (10+) £2.50. (Oct–Mar: Adult £3, Child £1.50, Conc. £2.50). May be subject to change for 2008.

NOTTINGHAM CASTLE

Nottingham NG1 6EL
Tel: 0115 9153700 **Fax:** 0115 9153653 **E-mail:** castle@ncmg.org.uk
Owner: Nottingham City Council
17th century ducal mansion built on the site of the original medieval Castle, with spectacular views of the city. A vibrant museum and art gallery housing collections of paintings, silver, Wedgwood and armour, 15 centuries of Nottingham history plus exhibitions of contemporary and historical art. Tour the underground caves system. Special events take place throughout the year, please visit www.nottingham.gov.uk/enjoy.
Location: MAP 7:B4, OS Ref. SK569 395. Just SW of the city centre on hilltop.
Open: Daily, 10am–5pm (4pm during winter). Closed 24–26 Dec & 1 Jan.
Admission: Joint admission with The Museum of Nottingham Life at Brewhouse Yard, Adult £3.50, Child/Conc. £2. Family ticket £8 (2 adults and up to 3 children). May be subject to change for 2008.

Caves. Tel for details.

Holme Pierrepont Hall

PAPPLEWICK HALL

PAPPLEWICK, NOTTINGHAMSHIRE NG15 8FE

www.papplewickhall.co.uk

Tel: 0115 9632623 **E-mail:** godwinaust@aol.com
Owner/Contact: Mr & Mrs J R Godwin-Austen
A beautiful stone-built classical house, set in a park, with woodland garden laid out in the 18th century. The house is notable for its very fine plasterwork, and elegant staircase. Grade I listed.
Location: MAP 7:B3, OS Ref. SK548 518. Halfway between Nottingham & Mansfield, 3m E of M1/J27. A608 & A611 towards Hucknall. Then A6011 to Papplewick and B683 N for ½m.
Open: 1st, 3rd & 5th Wed in each month 2–5pm, and by appointment.
Admission: Adult £5. Groups (10+): £4.
No photography. Obligatory. Limited for coaches. In grounds on leads.

RUDDINGTON FRAMEWORK KNITTERS' MUSEUM

Chapel Street, Ruddington, Nottingham NG11 6HE
Tel: 0115 984 6914 **www.rfkm.org**
Owner: Framework Knitters' Charitable Trust
Contact: Kathy Powis
A unique collection of 19th century restored cottages and workshops arranged around a garden courtyard where a Victorian community of framework knitters lived and worked. Daily demonstrations on stocking frames and circular knitting machines. A former Primitive Methodist Chapel completes the site and houses a collection of hosiery spanning 200 years. A "Victorian Time Capsule".
Location: MAP 7:B4, OS Ref. SK571 329. 5 miles S of Nottingham.
Open: Apr–Dec: Wed–Sat & BHs 11am–4.30pm. Apr–Sep: Suns 1.30–4.30pm. Last admission 4pm.
Admission: Adults £3, Conc. £2. Family £6.
Partial, WC. By arrangement. Limited. In grounds, on leads.

RUFFORD ABBEY ⌗

Ollerton, Nottinghamshire NG22 9DF
Tel: 01623 822944 **www.english-heritage.org.uk/rufford**
Owner: English Heritage   **Contact:** Nottinghamshire County Council
The remains of a 17th century country house; built on the foundations of a 12th century Cistercian Abbey, set in Rufford Country Park.
Location: MAP 7:B3, OS120, SK645 646. 2m S of Ollerton off A614.
Open: All year daily, 10am–5pm. Closed 25 Dec. Call for full opening times and facilities.
Admission: Free – parking charge applies.
Picnickers welcome. WC.

See which properties offer **educational facilities** or **school visits** in our index at the end of the book.

THRUMPTON HALL

THRUMPTON, NOTTINGHAM NG11 0AX

www.thrumptonhall.com

Tel: 0795 855 6442 **E-mail:** lynn@thrumptonhall.com
Owner: Miranda Seymour **Contact:** Debbie Knox

Magnificent lakeside Jacobean house, built in 1607. Priest's hiding hole, carved Charles II staircase, panelled saloon, Byron memorabilia. Large lawns separated from landscaped park by ha-ha. Personal tours are led by family members. Dining room with capacity for 50 silver service or buffet for 100. Free access for coach drivers.

Location: MAP 7:A5, OS Ref. SK508 312. 7m S of Nottingham, 3m E M1/J24, 1m from A453, 4m from East Midlands Airport.

Open: By appointment throughout the year. Groups of (20+) 10.30am–6pm.

Admission: Adult £8, Child £3.50.

⬜ 🅃 Wedding receptions, conferences, events. ⬚ Ground floor & grounds. WC. 🅟 Unlimited. 🐕 In grounds on leads. ❋

UPTON HALL 🏛

Upton, Newark, Nottinghamshire NG23 5TE
Tel: 01636 813795 **Fax:** 01636 812258 www.bhi.co.uk
Owner: British Horological Institute **Contact:** The Museum Manager

A fine country house dating from the 16th century, but extensively altered in the 19th century, set within its own grounds. Since 1972, it has been the headquarters of the British Horological Institute and its fascinating museum containing a large historic collection of public and domestic clocks and watches.

Location: MAP 7:C3, OS Ref. SK735 544. A612 between Newark and Southwell.

Open: By appointment only.

Admission: £5pp.

🅃 Obligatory. 🅟 ❋

WINKBURN HALL

Winkburn, Newark, Nottinghamshire NG22 8PQ
Tel: 01636 636465 **Fax:** 01636 636717
Owner/Contact: Richard Craven-Smith-Milnes Esq

A fine William and Mary house.

Location: MAP 7:C3, OS Ref. SK711 584. 8m W of Newark 1m N of A617.

Open: Throughout the year by appointment only.

Admission: £6.

WOLLATON HALL, GARDENS & DEER PARK

Wollaton, Nottingham NG8 2AE
Tel: 0115 915 3900 **E-mail:** wollaton@ncmg.org.uk
www.wollatonhall.org.uk
Owner: Nottingham City Council **Contact:** The Manager

A beautiful 16th century Grade I listed building designed by Robert Smythson set in a 500 acre historic deer park, home to red and fallow deer. Featuring a Natural History Museum, Industrial Museum and the Yard Gallery, with constantly changing exhibitions. Visitors have a choice of a variety of walks. Events held regularly - please visit www.wollatonhall.org.uk for details.

Location: MAP 7:B4, OS Ref. SK532 392. Wollaton Park, Nottingham. 3m W of city centre.

Open: All year.

Admission: Free. Car parking charge of £2 per car applies. Admission payable for some events and tours.

⬜ 🅃 ⬚ 🍴 🏛 🅟 🐕 ❋ ♿

Hodsock Priory Gardens

Clumber Park
©NTPL

Little Malvern Court, Worcestershire
©Jerry Harpur

West Midlands

Shakespeare's birthplace of Stratford-upon-Avon justly receives thousands of visitors each year, but travel further west too, into the gloriously unspoilt counties of Herefordshire and Worcestershire. Surrounded by the Malvern Hills, the fairytale Eastnor Castle has something to interest all visitors, whilst Warwick Castle provides exciting living history to entertain all ages within its medieval walls.

Herefordshire

Shropshire

Staffordshire

Warwickshire

West Midlands

Worcestershire

■ **Owner**

The National Trust

■ **Contact**

The Property Manager
Berrington Hall
Nr Leominster
Herefordshire
HR6 0DW

Tel: 01568 615721
Fax: 01568 613263

Restaurant:
01568 610134

Shop:
01568 610529

Costume Curator:
01568 613720

E-mail: berrington
@nationaltrust.org.uk

■ **Location**

MAP 6:L8

OS137 SP510 637

3m N of Leominster, 7m
S of Ludlow on
W side of A49.

Rail: Leominster 4m.

■ **Opening Times**

House
1–16 March: Sats &
Suns. 17 March–
2 November: Sat–Wed
(open Good Fri), 1–5pm.
Last admission 4.30pm.

Garden
1–16 March: Sats &
Suns. 17 March–
2 November: Sat–Wed,
11am–5pm.
6 December–
21 December: Sats &
Suns, 12 noon–4.30pm.

Park Walk
17 Mar–2 November:
Sat–Wed, 11am–5pm
(closed 2/3 August).
6–21 December: Sats &
Suns, 12 noon–4.30pm.

Shop & Restaurant
As Garden.

■ ***Admission**

Adult	£6.50
Child (5–12yrs)	£3.25
Family (2+3)	£16.25

Groups (15–25)**

Adult	£5.60

Garden Ticket

Adult	£4.80
Child	£2.40

Joint Ticket
for Berrington &
Croft Castle   £9.50

**Groups must pre-
book. Two groups can
visit at a time.

Gift aid is not included in
group price.

*includes a voluntary
donation but visitors can
choose to pay the standard
prices displayed at the
property and on the website.

©NTPL

BERRINGTON HALL 🌿

www.nationaltrust.org.uk/berrington

Berrington Hall is the creation of Thomas Harley, the 3rd Earl of Oxford's remarkable son, who made a fortune from supplying pay and clothing to the British Army in America and became Lord Mayor of London in 1767 at the age of thirty-seven. The architect was the fashionable Henry Holland. The house is beautifully set above the wide valley of a tributary of the River Lugg, with views west and south to the Black Mountains and Brecon Beacons. This was the site chosen by 'Capability' Brown who created the lake with its artificial island. The rather plain neo-classical exterior with a central portico gives no clue to the lavishness of the interior. Plaster ceilings decorated in muted pastel colours adorn the principal rooms. Holland's masterpiece is the staircase hall rising to a central dome. The rooms are set off with a collection of French furniture, including pieces which belonged to the Comte de Flahault, natural son of Talleyrand, and Napoleon's step-daughter Hortense.

In the dining room, vast panoramic paintings of battles at sea, three of them by Thomas Luny, are a tribute to the distinguished Admiral Rodney.

ℹ️	No photography in the house. Groups by arrangement only.
♿	1 single seater batricar for use outdoors; pre-booking essential. Audio tours for the visually impaired.
☕	Licensed tearoom: open as house: 11am–5pm (4.30pm Oct–Dec).
🚶	By arrangement only. Tour time: 1 hr.
🅿️	Ample for cars. Parking for coaches limited; instructions given when booking is made.
	Children's guide. Play area in walled garden.
🐕	Guide dogs only.

EASTNOR CASTLE 🏛

www.eastnorcastle.com

In the style of a medieval Welsh-border fortress, Eastnor Castle was built in the early 19th century by John First Earl Somers and is a good example of the great Norman and Gothic revival in architecture of that time. The Castle is dramatically situated in a 5000 acre estate in the Malvern Hills and remains the family home of the Hervey-Bathursts, his direct descendants.

This fairytale home is as dramatic inside as it is outside. A vast, 60' high Hall leads to a series of State Rooms including a Gothic Drawing Room designed by Pugin, with its original furniture, and a Library in the style of the Italian Renaissance, with views across the Lake.

The Hervey-Bathursts have lovingly restored the interiors and many of the Castle's treasures which have been buried away in the cellars and attics since the Second World War – early Italian Fine Art, medieval armour, 17th century Venetian furniture, Flemish tapestries and paintings by Van Dyck, Reynolds, Romney and Watts and early photographs by Julia Margaret Cameron.

Gardens

Castellated terraces descend to a 21 acre lake with a restored lakeside walk. The arboretum holds a famous collection of mature specimen trees. There are spectacular views of the Malvern hills across a 300 acre deer park, once part of a mediaeval chase and now designated a Site of Special Scientific Interest.

ℹ️ Knight's maze, tree trail, children's adventure playground, junior assault course. Corporate events – off-road driving, country pursuits, outside adventure days, private dinners, exclusive hire, special events.

🎭 Exclusive use for weddings, private and corporate events. Product launches, TV and feature films, concerts and charity events.

♿ Wheelchair stairclimber to main State rooms. DVD tour of first floor rooms. Visitors may alight at the Castle. Priority parking.

☕ Snacks and lunches (open as Castle).

🍵 By arrangement, Mons & Tues all year, outside normal opening hours.

🅿️ Ample 10–200 yds from Castle. Coaches phone in advance to arrange parking & catering. Tearoom voucher for drivers/courier.

Guides available.

🐕 On leads in house and grounds.

🏠 Exclusive use accommodation.

🔔 See website for details.

■ Owner
Mr J Hervey-Bathurst

■ Contact
Portcullis Office
Eastnor Castle
Nr Ledbury
Herefordshire HR8 1RL

Tel: 01531 633160
Fax: 01531 631776
E-mail: enquiries@ eastnorcastle.com

■ Location
MAP 6:M10
OS Ref. SO735 368

2m SE of Ledbury on the A438 Tewkesbury road. Alternatively M50/J2 & from Ledbury take the A449/A438.

Tewkesbury 20 mins, Malvern 20 mins, Gloucester 25 mins, Hereford 25 mins, Worcester 30 mins, Cheltenham 30 mins, B'ham 1 hr, London 2¼ hrs.

Taxi: Richard James 07836 777196.

■ Opening Times
Easter 20–24 March: daily.
30 March–28 September:
Suns and BH Mons.
14 July–29 August: daily
(except Sats),
11am–4.30pm
(last admission 4pm).

■ Admission
Summer

Castle & Grounds
Adult	£8.00
Child (5–15yrs)	£5.00
OAP	£7.00
Family (2+3)	£21.00

Grounds only
Adult	£4.00
Child (5–15yrs)	£2.00
OAP	£3.00
Family (2+3)	£10.00

Groups (20+)
Guided	£10.00
Freeflow	£6.50
Schools	£5.50

Privilege Pass
Valid for 1 year and includes all Castle special events (apart from theatre productions)
Adult	£23.00
Child (5–15yrs)	£14.00
OAP	£20.00
Family (2+3)	£59.00

■ Special Events
See website for further details.

Conference/Function

ROOM	SIZE	MAX CAPACITY
Great Hall	16 x 8m	150
Dining Rm	11 x 7m	80
Gothic Rm	11 x 7m	80
Octagon Rm	9 x 9m	50

HEREFORDSHIRE

ABBEY DORE COURT GARDEN

Abbey Dore, Herefordshire HR2 0AD
Tel/Fax: 01981 240419
Owner/Contact: Mrs C L Ward

A peaceful 6 acre plant and bird lovers' garden with many contrasting areas. These include formal purple, gold and silver borders, an interesting walled garden, many herbaceous borders and a river walk leading to a further 5 acre meadow with unusual trees. Small nursery of herbaceous perennials.

Location: MAP 6:K10, OS Ref. SO387 309. 3 m W of A465 midway between Hereford and Abergavenny.

Open: Apr–Sept: Visitors welcome any day but must telephone first. Groups by arrangement.

Admission: Adult £3.50, Child £1.

BERRINGTON HALL ❧

See page 324 for full page entry.

BROCKHAMPTON ESTATE ❧

Bringsty, Nr Bromyard WR6 5TB
Tel: 01885 488099/482077   www.nationaltrust.org.uk/brockhampton
Owner: The National Trust   **Contact:** The Property Manager

Wood and parkland estate with waymarked walks including Lower Brockhampton, a 14th century moated manor house with timber framed gatehouse.

Location: MAP 6:L9, OS Ref. SO682 546. 2m E of Bromyard on A44.

Open: House: 1–16 Mar, Sat & Sun, 12 noon–4pm; 19–30 Mar, Wed–Sun & BH, 12 noon–4pm; 2 Apr–28 Sept, Wed–Sun, 12 noon–5pm; 1 Oct–2 Nov, Wed–Sun, 12 noon–4pm. Guided tours from 11am when house is open. Park and woodland walks: All year, dawn to dusk.

***Admission:** Park, House & Grounds: Adult £5.25, Child £2.60, Family £13. Park only: Adult £2.50, Child Free. *includes a voluntary donation but visitors can choose to pay the standard prices displayed at the property and on the website.

🚻 Partial. 🖤 🖤 Dogs in woodland walks, on leads. ❄ 🖤

CROFT CASTLE & PARKLAND ❧

Leominster, Herefordshire HR6 9PW
Tel: 01568 780246   **E-mail:** croftcastle@nationaltrust.org.uk
www.nationaltrust.org.uk
Owner: The National Trust   **Contact:** The Property Manager

Home of the Croft family since Domesday. Walls and corner towers date from 14th and 15th centuries, interior mainly 18th century.

Location: MAP 6:K8, OS Ref. SO455 655. 5m NW of Leominster, 9m SW of Ludlow, approach from B4362.

Open: House: 1–16 Mar: Sats & Suns, 1–5pm; 19 Mar–31 Oct: Wed–Sun, 1–5pm; 1 Nov–21 Dec: Sats & Suns, 1–4pm; 19 Mar–31 Oct. Taster tours in House, Wed–Sun, 11am–1pm. Gardens, Tearoom & Shop as House. Park: All year.

***Admission:** House & Garden: Adult £6.50, Child £3.25, Family £16, Group outside normal hours £11. Garden only: Adult £4, Child £2. Car park £3 (£2 reimbursement on entry, NT members Free). *includes a voluntary donation but visitors can choose to pay the standard prices displayed at the property and on the website. Gift Aid is not included in group prices.

🔲 ❄ 🖤 🚻 🅿

EASTNOR CASTLE 🏰

See page 325 for full page entry.

GOODRICH CASTLE ♯
ROSS-ON-WYE HR9 6HY
www.english-heritage.org.uk/goodrich

Tel: 01600 890538
Owner: English Heritage   **Contact:** Visitor Operations Team

This magnificent red sandstone castle is remarkably complete with a 12th century keep and extensive remains from 13th & 14th centuries. From the battlements there are fine views over the Wye Valley to Symonds Yat. Marvel at the maze of small rooms and the 'murder holes'.

Location: MAP 6:L11, OS162 Ref. SO577 200. 5m S of Ross-on-Wye, off A40.

Open: 21 Mar–31 Oct: daily, 10am–5pm (Jun–Aug 6pm). 1 Nov–29 Feb '09: Wed–Sun, 10am–4pm. Closed 24–26 Dec & 1 Jan.

Admission: Adult £5, Child £2.50, Conc. £4, Family £12.50. 15% discount for groups (11+). EH Members Free.

ℹ WC. 🔲 🔲 🅿 🖤 ❄ 🖤

Hergest Croft Gardens

HELLENS 🏠
MUCH MARCLE, LEDBURY, HEREFORDSHIRE HR8 2LY

Tel: 01531 660504

Owner: Pennington-Mellor-Munthe Charity Trust   **Contact:** The Administrator

Built as a monastery and then a stone fortress in 1292 by Mortimer, Earl of March, with Tudor, Jacobean and Stuart additions and lived in ever since by descendants of the original builder. Visited by the Black Prince, Bloody Mary and the 'family ghost'. Family paintings, relics and heirlooms from the Civil War and possessions of the Audleys, Walwyns and Whartons as well as Anne Boleyn. Also beautiful 17th century woodwork carved by the 'King's Carpenter', John Abel. All those historical stories incorporated into guided tours, revealing the loves and lives of those who lived and died here. Goods and chattels virtually unchanged.

Location: MAP 6:M10, OS Ref. SO661 332. Off A449 at Much Marcle. Ledbury 4m, Ross-on-Wye 4m.

Open: 23 Mar–1 Oct: Wed, Thur, Sun & BH Mons. Guided tours only at 2pm, 3pm & 4pm. Other times by arrangement with the Administrator throughout the year.

Admission: Adult £5, Child £2.50, OAP £4, Family £10.

ℹ️ No photography inside house. ▣ ⅃ Partial. ⒡ Obligatory. 🅿️
🖼 In grounds, on leads. ⏣

HEREFORD CATHEDRAL

Mappa Mundi and Chained Library Exhibition. Hereford HR1 2NG

Tel: 01432 374202 **Fax:** 01432 374220 **E-mail:** visits@herefordcathedral.org

Contact: The Visits Manager   **www: herefordcathedral.org**

Built on a place of worship used since Saxon times, Hereford Cathedral contains some of the finest examples of architecture from Norman times to the present day. The Mappa Mundi & Chained Library Exhibition houses the spectacular medieval map of the world and the Cathedral's unique Chained Library.

Location: MAP 6:L10, OS Ref. SO510 398. Hereford city centre on A49.

Open: Cathedral: Daily, 7.30am–Evensong. Exhibition: Easter–Oct: Mon–Sat, 10am–4.30pm. Nov–Easter: Mon–Sat, 10am–3.30pm. Sundays subject to change, please telephone to check before you visit.

Admission: Admission only for Mappa Mundi and Chained Library Exhibition: Adult £4.50, Child under 5yrs Free, Conc. £3.50. Family (2+3) £10.

▣ ⍾ ⅃ ▣ ⑪ ⒡ ▣ ✳ ⏣

HERGEST COURT

c/o Hergest Estate Office, Kington HR5 3EG

Tel: 01544 230160 **Fax:** 01544 232031 **E-mail:** gardens@hergest.co.uk

Owner/Contact: W L Banks

The ancient home of the Vaughans of Hergest, dating from the 13th century.

Location: MAP 6:J9, OS Ref. SO283 554. 1m W of Kington on unclassified road to Brilley.

Open: Strictly by appointment, with a month's notice, only through Estate Office.

Admission: Adult £5, Child £1.50. Groups: Adult £3.50, Child £1.

⅃ Unsuitable. 🅿️ Limited. 🖼 Guide dogs only. ✳

HERGEST CROFT GARDENS 🏠
KINGTON, HEREFORDSHIRE HR5 3EG

www.hergest.co.uk

Tel: 01544 230160 **Fax:** 01544 232031 **E-mail:** gardens@hergest.co.uk

Owner: W L Banks   **Contact:** Mrs Melanie Lloyd

From spring bulbs to autumn colour, Hergest Croft is a garden for all seasons. Four distinct gardens with over 4,000 rare shrubs and trees including 60 Champions are sure to delight everyone. Rhododendrons in Park Wood and Azaleas in the Azalea Garden are spectacular in spring. The large Kitchen Garden contains long colourful herbaceous borders, the Rose Garden, Spring Borders and unusual vegetables. Autumn colour is superb.

Location: MAP 6:J9, OS Ref. SO281 565. On W side of Kington. ½ m off A44, left at Rhayader end of bypass. Turn right and the car park is ½ m on right. Signposted from bypass.

Open: Mar: Sats & Suns. 21 Mar–2 Nov: daily, 12noon–5.30pm. Season tickets and groups by arrangement throughout the year. Winter by appointment.

Admission: Adult £5.50, Child (under 16yrs) Free. Pre-booked groups (20+) £4.50. Season ticket £20.

▣ ▣ Rare plants. ⅃ Partial. WCs. ▣ ⒡ By arrangement 🅿️
🖼 In grounds, on leads. ✳ ⏣

HEREFORDSHIRE

LANGSTONE COURT

Llangarron, Ross on Wye, Herefordshire HR9 6NR
Tel: 01989 770254
Owner/Contact: R M C Jones Esq
Mostly late 17th century house with older parts. Interesting staircases, panelling and ceilings.
Location: MAP 6:L11, OS Ref. SO534 221. Ross on Wye 5m, Llangarron 1m.
Open: 20 May–31 Aug: Wed & Thur, 11am–2.30pm, also spring & summer BHs.
Admission: Free.

LONGTOWN CASTLE ⌗

Abbey Dore, Herefordshire
Tel: 01926 852078   www.english-heritage.org.uk/longtowncastle
Owner: English Heritage   **Contact:** Visitor Operations Administrative Assistant
An unusual cylindrical keep, perched atop a large earthen motte, built c1200, with walls 15ft thick. There are magnificent views of the nearby Black Mountains.
Location: MAP 6:K10, OS161 Ref. SO321 291. 4m WSW of Abbey Dore.
Open: Any reasonable time.
Admission: Free.

🔄 ✳

OLD SUFTON

Mordiford, Hereford HR1 4EJ
Tel: 01432 870268/850328   **Fax:** 01432 850381   **E-mail:** jameshereford@aol.com
Owner: Trustees of Sufton Heritage Trust   **Contact:** Mr & Mrs J N Hereford
A 16th century manor house which was altered and remodelled in the 18th and 19th centuries and again in this century. The original home of the Hereford family (see Sufton Court) who have held the manor since the 12th century.
Location: MAP 6:L10, OS Ref. SO575 384. Mordiford, off B4224 Mordiford–Dormington road.
Open: By written appointment to Sufton Court or by fax.
Admission: Adult £3, Child 50p.
🔄 Partial. 📷 Obligatory. 🅿 ■ Small school groups. No special facilities. 🔄 ✳

ROTHERWAS CHAPEL ⌗

Hereford
Tel: 01926 852078   www.english-heritage.org.uk/rotherwas
Owner: English Heritage   **Contact:** Visitor Operations Administrative Assistant
This Roman Catholic chapel, dating from the 14th and 16th centuries, is testament to the past grandeur of the Bodenham family and features an interesting mid-Victorian side chapel and High Altar.
Location: MAP 6:L10, OS149 Ref. SO536 383. 1½m SE of Hereford 500yds N of B4399.
Open: Any reasonable time. Keykeeper at nearby filling station.
Admission: Free.

🔄 🅿 🔄 ✳

SUFTON COURT 🏛

Mordiford, Hereford HR1 4LU
Tel: 01432 870268/850328   **Fax:** 01432 850381   **E-mail:** jameshereford@aol.com
Owner: J N Hereford   **Contact:** Mr & Mrs J N Hereford
Sufton Court is a small Palladian mansion house. Built in 1788 by James Wyatt for James Hereford. The park was laid out by Humphrey Repton whose 'red book' still survives. The house stands above the rivers Wye and Lugg giving impressive views towards the mountains of Wales.
Location: MAP 6:L10, OS Ref. SO574 379. Mordiford, off B4224 on Mordiford–Dormington road.
Open: 13–26 May & 12–25 Aug: 2–5pm. Guided tours: 2, 3 and 4pm.
Admission: Adult £5, Child 50p.
🔄 📷 Obligatory. 🅿 Only small coaches. ■ Small school groups. No special facilities. 🔄 In grounds, on leads.

For **accommodation** in the West Midlands, see our special index at the end of the book.

Berrington Hall

©NTPL
Eastnor Castle

■ **Owner**
Mr & Mrs F Fisher

■ **Contact**
Mrs Ann E Fisher
Oakley Hall
Market Drayton
Shropshire TF9 4AG

Tel: 07799 114802
Fax: 01630 653282

■ **Location**
MAP 6:M4
OS Ref. SJ701 367

From London 3hrs:
M1, M6/J14, then A5013
to Eccleshall, turn right
at T-junction, 200 yards,
then left onto B5026.
Mucklestone is 1¾ m
from Loggerheads on
B5026. 3m NE of Market
Drayton N of the A53,
1½ m W of Mucklestone,
off B5145.

■ **Opening Times**
All Year
Not open to the public.
The house is available all
year round for private or
corporate events.

■ **Admission**
Please telephone for
details.

OAKLEY HALL

Oakley Hall is situated in magnificent countryside on the boundary of Shropshire and Staffordshire. The present Hall is a fine example of a Queen Anne mansion house and was built on the site of an older dwelling mentioned in the Domesday Survey of 1085. Oakley Hall was the home of the Chetwode family until it was finally sold in 1919.

Gardens

Set in 100 acres of rolling parkland, the Hall commands superb views over the surrounding countryside and the gardens include wild areas in addition to the more formal parts.

Oakley Hall is a privately owned family house and since it is not open to the general public it provides a perfect location for exclusive private or corporate functions. The main hall can accommodate 100 people comfortably and has excellent acoustics for concerts. Four double bedrooms are available for those attending functions. The secluded location and unspoilt landscape make Oakley an ideal setting for filming and photography.

The surrounding countryside is rich in historical associations. St Mary's Church at Mucklestone, in which parish the Hall stands, was erected in the 13th century and it was from the tower of this Church that Queen Margaret of Anjou observed the Battle of Blore Heath in 1459. This was a brilliant victory for the Yorkist faction in the Wars of the Roses and the blacksmith at Mucklestone was reputed to have shod the Queen's horse back to front in order to disguise her escape.

ℹ️ Concerts, conferences (see left for rooms available). Fashion shows, product launches, seminars, clay pigeon shooting, garden parties and filming. Grand piano, hard tennis court, croquet lawn, horse riding. No stiletto heels.

🍸 Wedding receptions, buffets, lunches and dinners can be arranged for large or small groups, using high quality local caterers.

♿ Visitors may alight at the entrance to the Hall, before parking in allocated areas. WCs.

🚶 By prior arrangement groups will be met and entertained by members of the Fisher family.

🅿️ 100 cars, 100 yds from the Hall.

🐾

🛏️ 4 double with baths.

🔔

❄️

Conference/Function

ROOM	SIZE	MAX CAPACITY
Hall	50' x 30'	100
Dining Rm	40' x 27'	60
Ballroom	40' x 27'	60

■ Owner

The Weston Park Foundation

■ Contact

Kate Thomas
Weston Park
Weston-under-Lizard
Nr Shifnal
Shropshire TF11 8LE

Tel: 01952 852100
Fax: 01952 850430
E-mail: enquiries@
weston-park.com

■ Location

MAP 6:N6
OS Ref. SJ808 107

Birmingham 40 mins.
Manchester 1 hr.
Motorway access
M6/J12 or M54/J3 and via
the M6 Toll road J11A.
House situated on A5 at
Weston-under-Lizard.

Rail: Nearest Railway
Stations:Wolverhampton,
Stafford or Telford.

Air: Birmingham,
West Midlands,
Manchester.

■ Opening Times

Easter Saturday, weekends
and Bank Holidays until
31 August and most days
during July and August.

■ Admission

House, Park & Gardens
Adult	£8.00
Child (3–14yrs)	£5.50
OAP	£7.00
Family (2+3 or 1+4)	£20.00

Groups
Adult	£6.00
Child (3–14yrs)	£5.00
OAP	£6.00

Park & Gardens
Adult	£5.00
Child (3–14yrs)	£3.00
OAP	£4.50

Groups
Adult	£4.00
Child (3–14yrs)	£3.00
OAP	£4.00

Privilege Pass
Adult	£20.00
Child (3–14yrs)	£15.00
OAP	£18.00
Family (2+3 or 1+4)	£55.00

NB. Visitors are advised
to telephone to confirm
opening times and
admission prices.

Conference/Function

ROOM	SIZE	MAX CAPACITY
Dining Rm	52' x 23'	90
Orangery	56'1" x 22'4"	120
Music Rm	55' x 17'	60
The Hayloft	32' x 22'	40
Doncaster	49' x 18'7"	80

South Side of the House

WESTON PARK

www.weston-park.com

Weston Park is a magnificent Stately Home and Parkland situated on the Staffordshire/Shropshire border. The former home of the Earls of Bradford, the Park is now held in trust for the nation by The Weston Park Foundation.

Built in 1671 by Lady Elizabeth Wilbraham, this warm and welcoming house boasts a superb collection of paintings, including work by Van Dyck, Gainsborough and Stubbs, furniture and *objéts d'art*, providing continued interest and enjoyment for all of its visitors.

Step outside to enjoy the 1,000 acres of glorious Parkland, take one of a variety of woodland and wildlife walks, all landscaped by the legendary 'Capability' Brown in the 18th century. Then browse through the Gift Shop before relaxing in The Stables Coffee Bar and Bistro Restaurant.

With the exciting Woodland Adventure Playground, Yew Hedge Maze, Orchard and Deer Park, as well as the Miniature Railway, there is so much for children to do.

Weston Park has a long-standing reputation for staging outstanding events. The exciting and varied programme of entertainment includes Music Festivals, Model Air Shows and Game Fairs.

The Tapestry Room

Formal Gardens

House available on a private use basis. Conferences, product launches, outdoor concerts and events, filming location. Helipad and airstrip. Sporting activities organised for private groups eg. clay pigeon shooting, archery, hovercrafts, rally driving. Interior photography by prior arrangement only.

Gift Shop.

Full event organisation service. Residential parties, special dinners, wedding receptions. Dine and stay arrangements in the house on selected dates.

House and part of the grounds. WCs.

Licensed.

The Stables Bar and Bistro Restaurant provide meals and snacks. Licensed.

By arrangement.

Ample 100 yds away. Private booked groups may park vehicles at front door.

Award-winning educational programme available during all academic terms. Private themed visits aligned with both National Curriculum and QCA targets.

In grounds, on leads.

Weston Park offers 28 delightful bedrooms with bathrooms (24 doubles & 4 singles) 17 en suite.

ACTON BURNELL CASTLE ⌗

Acton Burnell, Shrewsbury, Shropshire
Tel: 01926 852078   **www.english-heritage.org.uk/actonburnell**
Owner: English Heritage   **Contact:** Visitor Operations Administrative Assistant
The warm red sandstone shell of a fortified 13th century manor house.
Location: MAP 6:L6, OS126, SJ534 019. In Acton Burnell, on unclassified road 8m S of Shrewsbury.
Open: Any reasonable time.
Admission: Free.
 🔲 🔲 ✳

For **special events** held throughout the year, see the index at the end of the book.

giftaid it Some properties will be operating the Gift Aid on Entry scheme at their admission points. Where the scheme is operating, visitors are offered a choice between paying the standard admission price or paying the 'Gift Aid Admission' which includes a voluntary donation of at least 10%. Gift Aid Admissions enable the charity to reclaim tax on the whole amount paid* – an extra 28% – potentially a very significant boost to property funds. Money raised from paying visitors in this way will go towards restoration projects at the property and will be very welcome.

Where shown, the admission prices are inclusive of the 10% voluntary donation where properties are operating the Gift Aid on Entry scheme, but both the standard admission price and the Gift Aid Admission will be displayed at the property and on their website.

*Gift Aid donations must be supported by a valid Gift Aid declaration and a Gift Aid declaration can only cover donations made by an individual for him/herself or for him/herself and members of his/her family.

©NTPL/Richard Bifield

©NTPL/James Mortimer

ATTINGHAM PARK ❀
SHREWSBURY, SHROPSHIRE SY4 4TP

Infoline: 01743 708123   **Tel:** 01743 708162   **Fax:** 01743 708175
Owner: The National Trust   **Contact:** The Property Manager
Late 18th century house, sitting in 500 acres of wonderful parkland. Built for the 1st Lord Berwick, the Georgian house contains some beautiful Italian furniture and a large silver collection. Lord Berwick, and subsequently his two elder sons, had a passion for art and music and this is seen in the Picture Gallery with fine paintings and a Samuel Green organ, which is occasionally played for visitors' enjoyment during the season. Woodland walks along the River Tern and through the Deer Park take in picturesque views of the Wrekin and Shropshire Hills. Costumed guided tours of the House are on offer every day the house is open. Events planned for 2008 include Easter Egg Trail, Spring Plant Fair, Food Fayre, Apple Weekend & Frost Fair.

Location: MAP 6:L6, OS127, SJ837 083. 4m SE of Shrewsbury on N side of B4380 in Atcham village.
Open: 13 Mar–26 Oct (weekends only 1–9 Mar): daily (closed Wed), 1–5.30pm, last admission to house 4.30pm. Timed Taster tours only 11am–1pm. Park & Shop open daily all year (except Christmas Day) from 9am.
Admission: House & Grounds: Adult £7.40, Child £3.70, Family £18.50. Booked groups (15+): Adult £6.30, Child £2.75. Grounds only: Adult £4.20, Child £2.20. Family £10.40. Admission price includes voluntary Gift Aid donation. Gift Aid is not included in Group prices.
ⓘ No photography in house. 🔲 🔲 🔲 Licensed. 🎦 By arrangement. 🅿 🔲
🔲 In grounds on leads. ✳ 🔲

BENTHALL HALL ❀

Benthall, Nr Broseley, Shropshire TF12 5RX
Tel: 01952 882159
Owner: The National Trust   **Contact:** The Custodian
A 16th century stone house with mullioned windows and moulded brick chimneys.
Location: MAP 6:M6, OS Ref. SJ658 025. 1m NW of Broseley (B4375), 4m NE of Much Wenlock, 1m SW of Ironbridge.
Open: House & Garden: 25 Mar–25 Jun: Tues & Weds; 1 Jul–30 Sept: Tues, Weds & Suns, 2–5.30pm. Open BH Suns & Mons.
Admission: House & Garden: Adult: £5.10, Child: £2.50. Garden: Adults £3.15, Child £1.60. Groups outside normal times £6.30 (NT members £3.15).
🔲 Partial. Ground floor. WC. 🎦 By arrangement. 🅿 Limited.

© English Heritage Photo Library

Boscobel House & The Royal Oak, Brewood

English Heritage Photo Library

BOSCOBEL HOUSE & THE ROYAL OAK ⌗
BISHOP'S WOOD, BREWOOD, SHROPSHIRE ST19 9AR

www.english-heritage.org.uk/boscobel

Tel: 01902 850244

Owner: English Heritage   **Contact:** Visitor Operations Team

This 17th century hunting lodge was destined to play a part in Charles II's escape from the Roundheads. A descendant of the Royal Oak, which sheltered the fugitive future King from Cromwell's troops after the Battle of Worcester in 1651, still stands in the fields near Boscobel House. The timber-framed house where the King slept in a tiny 'sacred hole' has been fully restored and furnished in Victorian period and there are panelled rooms and secret hiding places. There is an exhibition in the house as well as the farmyard and smithy.

Location: MAP 6:N6, OS127, SJ838 082. On unclassified road between A41 & A5. 8m NW of Wolverhampton.

Open: 21 Mar–31 Oct: Wed–Sun & BH Mons, 10am–5pm. Last entry 1hr before closing.

Admission: Adult £5, Child £2.50, Conc. £4, Family £12.50. Grounds only: Adult £2.50, Child £1.30, Conc. £2. EH Members free. Group discount available.

🖻 🔄 Grounds. WC. 🐾 🇫 Obligatory. 🅿 ■ 🖼 🐾

BUILDWAS ABBEY ⌗

Iron Bridge, Telford, Shropshire TF8 7BW

Tel: 01952 433274   www.english-heritage.org.uk/buildwas

Owner: English Heritage   **Contact:** Visitor Operations Team

Extensive remains of a Cistercian abbey built in 1135, set beside the River Severn against a backdrop of wooded grounds. The remains include the church which is almost complete except for the roof.

Location: MAP 6:M6, OS127, SJ643 043. On S bank of River Severn on A4169, 2m W of Ironbridge.

Open: 21 Mar–30 Sept: Wed–Sun & BH Mons, 10am–5pm.

Admission: Adult £3, Child £1.50, Conc. £2.40. EH Members free. Group discount available.

🖻 🔄 🅿 🖼

CLUN CASTLE ⌗

Clun, Ludlow, Shropshire

Tel: 01926 852078   www.english-heritage.org.uk/cluncastle

Owner: English Heritage   **Contact:** Visitor Operations Administrative Assistant

Remains of a four-storey keep and other buildings of this border castle are set in outstanding countryside, near the Welsh border. Built in the 11th century.

Location: MAP 6:J7, OS137, SO299 809. In Clun, off A488, 18m W of Ludlow. 9m W of Craven Arms.

Open: Any reasonable time.

Admission: Free.

🖼 ❈

For unique **Civil wedding** venues see our index at the end of the book.

COLEHAM PUMPING STATION

Longden Coleham, Shrewsbury, Shropshire SY3 7DN

Tel: 01743 362947

E-mail: museums@shrewsbury.gov.uk   www.shrewsburymuseums.com

Owner: Shrewsbury & Atcham Borough Council   **Contact:** Mary White

Two Renshaw beam engines of 1901 now restored to steam by members of Shrewsbury Steam Trust.

Location: MAP 6:L6, OS Ref. SJ497 122. Shrewsbury town centre, near the River Severn.

Open: 27 Apr, 25 May, 22 Jun, 27 Jul, 13/14 Sept, 26 Oct, 10am–4pm. Other days by arrangement, telephone for details: 01743 361196.

Admission: Adult £1, Child 50p, Student £1.

🔄 Partial. 🇫 By arrangement. 🅿 No parking. ■ 🖼 Guide dogs only.

COMBERMERE ABBEY

Whitchurch, Shropshire SY13 4AJ

Tel: 01948 662880   **Fax:** 01948 871604

E-mail: estate@combermereabbey.co.uk   www.combermereabbey.co.uk

Owner: Mrs S Callander Beckett   **Contact:** Administrator

Combermere Abbey, originally a Cistercian monastery, remodelled as a Tudor manor house and in 1820 as a Gothic house, sits in a magnificent 1000 acre parkland designed by Webb, in front of a large natural mere. The Walled Gardens have been restored and a unique Fruit Tree Maze created. Tours can now include the gardens. Excellent accommodation is available on the Estate.

Location: MAP 6:L4, OS Ref. SJ590 440. 5m E of Whitchurch, off A530. Manchester, Liverpool and Birmingham airports 1hr.

Open: 25 Mar–22 May: Tues, Weds & Thurs only for tours, 12 noon, 2 & 4pm. Advance bookings necessary. Group visits (20–60) by arrangement. Available for corporate hospitality, meetings, location shoots, wedding and naming ceremonies. Please look at What's On/Abbey section on website for full events schedule.

Admission: On open days: Adult £5, Child (under 15yrs) £3. Group tours: £7.50–£10 per person inclusive of refreshments.

ℹ No photography. 🇹 🔄 Unsuitable. 🐾 By arrangement. 🇫 By arrangement. 🅿 Limited. 🎦 ⬛ ❈ For groups. 🐾

COUND HALL

Cound, Shropshire SY5 6AH

Tel: 01743 761721   **Fax:** 01743 761722

Owner: Mr & Mrs D R Waller   **Contact:** Mrs J Stephens

Queen Anne red brick Hall.

Location: MAP 6:L6, OS Ref. SJ560 053.

Open: 14–18 July, 10am–4pm.

Admission: Adult £4.50, Child £2.30, Conc. £3.40, Family £11.30.

ℹ No photography. 🅿 Limited. 🖼

Weston Park, Dining Room

©NTPL/Michael Caldwell

DUDMASTON ✤
QUATT, BRIDGNORTH, SHROPSHIRE WV15 6QN

Tel: 01746 780866 **Fax:** 01746 780744 **E-mail:** dudmaston@nationaltrust.org.uk
Owner: The National Trust **Contact:** The House & Visitor Services Manager
Late 17th century manor house. Contains furniture and china, Dutch flower paintings, watercolours, botanical art and modern pictures and sculpture, family and natural history. 9 acres of lakeside gardens and Dingle walk. Two estate walks 5½m and 3½m starting from Hampton Loade car park.
Location: MAP 6:M7, OS Ref. SO748 888. 4m SE of Bridgnorth on A442.
Open: House & Garden: 23 Mar–30 Sept, Tues, Weds, Suns & BH Mons, 2–5.30pm. Last admission to house 5pm. Garden: Mon–Wed, Suns & BH Mons, 12 noon–6pm.
*Admission: House & Garden: Adult £6.10, Child £3.05, Family £15.25, Group £5. Garden only: Adult £4.90, Child £2.45, Family £12.20. Free tours Mon afternoons (except BHs). *includes a voluntary donation but visitors can choose to pay the standard prices displayed at the property and on the website (group price does not include voluntary donation).
ℹ️ Countryside walks. 🖼️ ♿ 🛍️ 🎦 📷 🅿️
🐕 In parkland and estate, on leads, not garden. ♥

HAUGHMOND ABBEY ⌗

Upton Magna, Uffington, Shrewsbury, Shropshire SY4 4RW
Tel: 01743 709661 www.english-heritage.org.uk/haughmond
Owner: English Heritage **Contact:** Visitor Operations Team
Extensive remains of a 12th century Augustinian abbey, including the Chapter House which retains its late medieval timber ceiling, and including some fine medieval sculpture.
Location: MAP 6:L5, OS126, SJ542 152. 3m NE of Shrewsbury off B5062.
Open: 21 Mar–30 Sept: Wed–Sun & BH Mons, 10am–5pm.
Admission: Adult £3, Child £1.50, Conc. £2.40. EH Members free. Group discount available.
🖼️ ♿ 🅿️ 🐕

HAWKSTONE HALL & GARDENS

Marchamley, Shrewsbury SY4 5LG
Tel: 01630 685242 **Fax:** 01630 685565 **E-mail:** hawkhall@aol.com
Owner: The Redemptorists **Contact:** Guest Mistress
The secret jewel of Shropshire, 'home with a warm welcome', 'an experience of peace and beauty'. Set in the plains of north Shropshire, ancestral home of the Hill family 1556–1906.
Location: MAP 6:L5, OS Ref. SJ581 299. Entrance 1m N of Hodnet off A442.
Open: 14–31 Aug, 1–5pm.
Admission: Adult £5.50, Child £2. Group & Family concessions.
🖼️ 🍴 ♿ 🎦 📷 🅿️ 🐕

HODNET HALL GARDENS 🏛️

Hodnet, Market Drayton, Shropshire TF9 3NN
Tel: 01630 685786 **Fax:** 01630 685853
E-mail: secretary@heber-percy.freeserve.co.uk www.hodnethallgardens.org
Owner: Mr and the Hon Mrs A Heber-Percy **Contact:** Secretary
The 60+ acres are renowned as amongst the finest in the country. Forest trees provide a wonderful backdrop for formal gardens planted to give delight during every season, with extensive woodland walks amongst wild flowers and unusual flowering shrubs along the banks of a chain of ornamental pools.
Location: MAP 6:L5, OS Ref. SJ613 286. 12m NE of Shrewsbury on A53; M6/J15, M54/J3.
Open: 23/24 Mar; 18 & 25/26 May; 8, 15, 22 Jun; 13 Jul; 19 & 24/25 Aug; 14 Sept: 12 noon–5pm. Group bookings by appointment.
Admission: £4 per person.
🍴 For groups. 🅿️ 🖼️ Educational package linked to Key stages I & 2 of National Curriculum. 🐕 On leads.

IRON BRIDGE ⌗

Ironbridge, Shropshire
Tel: 0121 625 6820 www.english-heritage.org.uk/ironbridge
Owner: English Heritage **Contact:** Regional Head Office
The world's first iron bridge and Britain's best known industrial monument. Cast in Coalbrookdale by local ironmaster, Abraham Darby, it was erected across the River Severn in 1779. Iron Bridge is a World Heritage Site. Visit the recently refurbished Toll House on the Bridge, with interpretation displays.
Location: MAP 6:M6, OS127, SJ672 034. In Ironbridge, adjacent to A4169.
Open: Any reasonable time.
Admission: Free.
♿

LANGLEY CHAPEL ⌗

Acton Burnell, Shrewsbury, Shropshire
Tel: 0121 625 6820 (Regional Office) www.english-heritage.org.uk/langleychapel
Owner: English Heritage **Contact:** The West Midlands Regional Office
A delightful medieval chapel, standing alone in a field, with a complete set of early 17th century wooden fittings and furniture.
Location: MAP 6:L6, OS126, SJ538 001. 1½m S of Acton Burnell, on unclassified road 4m E of the A49, 9½m S of Shrewsbury.
Open: 1 Mar–31 Oct: daily, 10am–5pm; 1 Nov–29 Feb '09: daily, 10am–4pm.
Admission: Free.
🐕 ♿

LILLESHALL ABBEY ⌗

Oakengates, Shropshire
Tel: 01926 852078 www.english-heritage.org.uk/lilleshall
Owner: English Heritage **Contact:** Visitor Operations Administrative Assistant
Extensive ruins of an abbey of Augustinian canons including remains of the 12th and 13th century church and the cloister buildings. Surrounded by green lawns and ancient yew trees.
Location: MAP 6:M6, OS127, SJ738 142. On unclassified road off the A518, 4m N of Oakengates.
Open: 21 Mar–30 Sept: daily, 10am–5pm.
Admission: Free.
🐕

LONGNER HALL 🏛️

Uffington, Shrewsbury, Shropshire SY4 4TG
Tel: 01743 709215
Owner: Mr R L Burton **Contact:** Mrs R L Burton
Designed by John Nash in 1803, Longner Hall is a Tudor Gothic style house set in a park landscaped by Humphry Repton. The home of one family for over 700 years. Longner's principal rooms are adorned with plaster fan vaulting and stained glass.
Location: MAP 6:L6, OS Ref. SJ529 110. 4m SE of Shrewsbury on Uffington road, ¼m off B4380, Atcham.
Open: Apr–Sept: Tues & BH Mons, 2–5pm. Tours at 2pm & 3.30pm. Groups at any time by arrangement.
Admission: Adult £5, Child/OAP £3.
ℹ️ No photography in house. 🏠 ♿ Partial. 🎦 By arrangement for groups.
📷 Obligatory. 🅿️ Limited for coaches. 🖼️ By arrangement. 🐕 Guide dogs only. ♿

LUDLOW CASTLE
CASTLE SQUARE, LUDLOW, SHROPSHIRE SY8 1AY

www.ludlowcastle.com

Tel: 01584 873355 **E-mail:** hduce@ludlowcastle.com
Owner: The Earl of Powis & The Trustees of the Powis Estates
Contact: Helen J Duce (Custodian)
This magnificent ruin, the heart of Ludlow, a medieval market town, dates from 1086. Extended over the centuries to a fortified Royal Palace and seat of the government for the Council of Wales and the Marches; privately owned by the Earls of Powis since 1811. Castle House, newly renovated, is also open to the public. The Castle Tea Rooms serve fresh locally-sourced foods. The Beacon Rooms are available for corporate events, exhibitions and Civil weddings. Three self-catering holiday apartments (each for four persons), finished to the highest standards, are the ideal accommodation for a stay in Ludlow. Tel: 01584 873355/874465 for more details.

Location: MAP 6:L8, OS Ref. SO509 745. Shrewsbury 28m, Hereford 26m. A49 centre of Ludlow.
Open: Jan & Dec: Sat & Sun, 10am–4pm, Feb–Mar & Oct–Nov: daily, 10am–4pm. Apr–Sept: daily, 10am–5pm (7pm Aug). Daily 26 Dec–1 Jan. Last adm. 30mins before closing. Closed Christmas Day.
Admission: Adult £4.50, Child £2.50, Conc. £4, Family £12.50. 10% reduction for groups (10+).
◻ ⊤ ⅄ Partial. WCs ◼ Licensed. ⅋ Licensed. ⅋ By arrangement. ⌂ ⓟ None. ◼ ⛶ In grounds on leads. ⊞ Rated 4*–5* enjoyEngland.com ◪ ❊ ▿

MAWLEY HALL
CLEOBURY MORTIMER DY14 8PN

www.mawley.com

Tel: 020 7495 6702 **Fax:** 020 7409 1810 **E-mail:** administration@mawley.com
Owner: R Galliers-Pratt Esq **Contact:** Mrs R Sharp
Built in 1730 and attributed to Francis Smith of Warwick, Mawley is set in 18th century landscaped parkland with extensive gardens and walks down to the River Rea. Magnificent plasterwork and a fine collection of English and Continental furniture and porcelain.
Location: MAP 6:L8, OS137, SO688 753. 1m N of Cleobury Mortimer on the A4117 and 7m W of Bewdley.
Open: 14 Apr–17 Jul: Mons & Thurs, 3–5pm and throughout the year by appointment.
Admission: Adult £9, Child/OAP £6. Outside set opening dates and times all visitors £9.
⅋ By arrangement. ⓟ ◼ ⛶ In grounds, on leads. ❊

MORETON CORBET CASTLE ⌗

Moreton Corbet, Shrewsbury, Shropshire
Tel: 01926 852078 www.english-heritage.org.uk/moreton
Owner: English Heritage **Contact:** Visitor Operations Administrative Assistant
A ruined medieval castle with the substantial remains of a splendid Elizabethan mansion, captured in 1644 from Charles I's supporters by Parliamentary forces.
Location: MAP 6:L5, OS126, SJ561 231. In Moreton Corbet off B5063, 7m NE of Shrewsbury.
Open: Any reasonable time.
Admission: Free.
⅄ ⓟ ⛶ ❊

MORVILLE HALL ⚘

Bridgnorth, Shropshire WV16 5NB
Tel: 01746 780838
Owner: The National Trust **Contact:** Dr & Mrs C Douglas
An Elizabethan house of mellow stone, converted in the 18th century and set in attractive gardens.
Location: MAP 6:M7, OS Ref. SO668 940. Morville, on A458 3m W of Bridgnorth.
Open: By written appointment only with the tenants.
Admission: £3.50. NT members Free.

OAKLEY HALL

See page 329 for full page entry.

West Midlands – England

PREEN MANOR GARDENS

Church Preen, Church Stretton, Shropshire SY6 7LQ
Tel: 01694 771207
Owner/Contact: Mrs P Trevor-Jones
Six acre garden on site of Cluniac monastery, with walled, terraced, wild, water, kitchen and chess gardens. 12th century monastic church.
Location: MAP 6:L6, OS Ref. SO544 981. 10m SSE of Shrewsbury. 7m NE of Church Stretton, 6m SW of Much Wenlock.
Open: 30 Mar–29 May, & 5 Oct: 2–5pm. 26 Jun–24 Jul: 2–6pm. Groups by arrangement in Jun & Jul.
Admission: Adult £3.50, Child 50p.

SHIPTON HALL 🏠

Much Wenlock, Shropshire TF13 6JZ
Tel: 01746 785225 **Fax:** 01746 785125
Owner: Mr J N R Bishop **Contact:** Mrs M J Bishop
Built around 1587 by Richard Lutwyche who gave the house to his daughter Elizabeth on her marriage to Thomas Mytton. Shipton remained in the Mytton family for the next 300 years. The house has been described as *'an exquisite specimen of Elizabethan architecture set in a quaint old fashioned garden, the whole forming a picture which as regards both form and colour, satisfies the artistic sense of even the most fastidious'*. The Georgian additions by Thomas F Pritchard include some elegant rococo interior decorations. There is some noteworthy Tudor and Jacobean panelling. Family home. In addition to the house visitors are welcome to explore the gardens, the dovecote and the parish church which dates back to Saxon times.
Location: MAP 6:L7, OS Ref. SO563 918. 7m SW of Much Wenlock on B4378. 10m W of Bridgnorth.
Open: Easter–end Sept. Thurs, 2.30–5.30pm. Also Suns and Mons of BH, 2.30–5.30pm. Groups of 20+ at any time of day or year by prior arrangement.
Admission: Adult £5, Child (under 14yrs) £2.50. 10% Discount for groups (20+).
🚫 Unsuitable. 🍴 By arrangement for groups (20+). 🎟 Obligatory. 🐕 Guide dogs only.

SHREWSBURY ABBEY

Shrewsbury, Shropshire SY2 6BS
Tel: 01743 232723 **Fax:** 01743 240172
Contact: Gillian Keates
Benedictine Abbey founded in 1083, tomb of Roger de Montgomerie and remains of tomb of St Winefride, 7th century Welsh saint. The Abbey was part of the monastery and has also been a parish church since the 12th century.
Location: MAP 6:L6, OS Ref. SJ499 125. Signposted from Shrewsbury bypass (A5 and A49). 500yds E of town centre, across English Bridge.
Open: All year. Summer: 10am–4.30pm. Winter: 10.30am–3pm.
Admission: Donation. For guided tours, please contact Abbey.

SHREWSBURY CASTLE & THE SHROPSHIRE REGIMENTAL MUSEUM

Castle Street, Shrewsbury SY1 2AT
Tel: 01743 358516 **E-mail:** museums@shrewsbury.gov.uk
www.shrewsburymuseums.com
Owner: Shrewsbury & Atcham Borough Council **Contact:** Mary White
Norman Castle with 18th century work by Thomas Telford. Free admission to attractive floral grounds. The main hall houses The Shropshire Regimental Museum and displays on the history of the castle. Open-air theatre, music and events throughout the summer.
Location: MAP 6:L6, OS Ref. SJ495 128. Town centre, adjacent BR and bus stations.
Open: Main building & Museum: Late May BH–mid Sept: Mon–Sat, 10am–5pm; Suns, 10am–4pm. Winter: Please call for details. Grounds: Mon–Sat, 10am–5pm & Suns as above.
Admission: Museum: Adult £2.50, OAP £1.50, Shrewsbury residents, under 18s, Students & members of the regiments Free. Grounds: Free.
ℹ️ No photography. 📷 🚹 Partial. 🅿 None. 🍴 🐕 Guide dogs only. 🔺🚻

SHREWSBURY MUSEUM & ART GALLERY (ROWLEY'S HOUSE)

Barker Street, Shrewsbury, Shropshire SY1 1QH
Tel: 01743 361196 **E-mail:** museums@shrewsbury.gov.uk
www.shrewsburymuseums.com
Owner: Shrewsbury and Atcham Borough Council **Contact:** Mary White
Impressive timber-framed building and attached 17th century brick mansion with archaeology and natural history, geology, social history and special exhibitions, including contemporary art.
Location: OS Ref. SJ490 126.
Open: 1 Apr–25 May: Tue–Sat. 26 May–14 Sept: daily. Closed for rest of year as part of a major redevelopment project, but remains the headquarters of Shrewsbury Museums Service. Please telephone for opening times.
Admission: Free.
ℹ️ No photography. 📷 🚹 Ground floor only. 🅿 Adjacent public. 🍴 🐕 Guide dogs only. ❄

©English Heritage Photo Library

STOKESAY CASTLE ⌗

Nr CRAVEN ARMS, SHROPSHIRE SY7 9AH

www.english-heritage.org.uk/stokesay

Tel: 01588 672544
Owner: English Heritage **Contact:** Visitor Operations Team
This perfectly preserved example of a 13th century fortified manor house gives us a glimpse of the life and ambitions of a rich medieval merchant. Lawrence of Ludlow built this country house to impress the landed gentry. The magnificent Great Hall, almost untouched since medieval times, was used for feasting. The family's private quarters were in the bright, comfortable solar on the first floor. From the outside the castle forms a picturesque grouping of castle, parish church and timber-framed Jacobean gatehouse set in the rolling Shropshire countryside.
Location: MAP 6:K7, OS148, SO446 787. 7m NW of Ludlow off A49. 1m S of Craven Arms off A49.
Open: Mar, Apr, Sept & Oct: Wed–Sun & BH Mons, 10am–5pm. May & Jun: daily, 10am–5pm. Jul & Aug: daily, 10am–6pm. 1 Nov–29 Feb '09: Thur–Sun, 10am–4pm. Closed 24–26 Dec & 1 Jan.
Admission: Adult £5, Child £2.50, Conc. £4, Family £12.50. 15% discount for groups (11+). EH Members free.
📷 🚹 Great Hall & gardens. WC. 🍴 🅿 🐕 ❄ 🚻

© NTPL/James Mortimer
Attingham Park

STOKESAY COURT
ONIBURY, CRAVEN ARMS, SHROPSHIRE SY7 9BD
www.stokesaycourt.com

Tel: 01584 856238 **E-mail:** info@stokesaycourt.com

Owner/Contact: Ms Caroline Magnus

Unspoilt and undisturbed, Stokesay Court is an imposing late Victorian mansion with Jacobean style façade, magnificent interior and extensive grounds containing a grotto, woodland and interconnected pools. Set deep in the beautiful rolling green landscape of South Shropshire near Ludlow, the house and grounds were a primary location for the film *Atonement*.

Location: MAP 6:K7, OS148, SO444 786. A49 Between Ludlow and Craven Arms.

Open: Guided tours all year for booked groups (20+). Larger groups can be accommodated by arrangement. Also summer Suns for tours at 2.30pm (booking essential). Tours are usually taken by the owner.

Admission: Adult £12.50pp to include light refreshments (full catering service available on request).

ℹ️ No stilettos. No photography in house. ♿ Partial. WC. 🎥 📷 Obligatory. Ⓟ 🐾 Guide dogs only. ❋ ♨ €

©NTPL/Richard Bifield

SUNNYCROFT ❧
200 HOLYHEAD ROAD, WELLINGTON, TELFORD, SHROPSHIRE TF1 2DR

Tel: 01952 242884

Owner: The National Trust   **Contact:** The Custodian

Late Victorian gentleman's suburban villa. The grounds amount to a 'mini-estate', with pigsties, stables, kitchen garden, orchards, conservatory, flower garden and superb Wellingtonia avenue.

Location: MAP 6:M6, OS Ref. SJ652 109. M54 exit 7, follow B5061 towards Wellington.

Open: House & Garden: 14 Mar–26 Oct: Fri–Mon, 1–5pm. Open Good Fri and BH Mons. 13–21 Dec, Sat & Sun 1–5pm.

Admission: House & Garden: Adult £5.70, Child £2.80, Family £14.20. Garden only: Adult £3.60, Child £1.80, Family £9. Groups at other times £13 (NT Members £10).

♿ Ground Floor, Adapted WC. 📷 By arrangement. Ⓟ

WENLOCK GUILDHALL

Much Wenlock, Shropshire TF13 6AE

Tel: 01952 727509

Owner/Contact: Much Wenlock Town Council

16th century half-timbered building has an open-arcade market area.

Location: MAP 6:L6, OS Ref. SJ624 000. In centre of Much Wenlock, next to the church.

Open: 1 Apr–31 Oct: Mon–Sat, 10.30am–1pm & 2–4pm. Suns: 2–4pm.

Admission: Adult £1 (including guide), Child Free.

WENLOCK PRIORY ⌗

Much Wenlock, Shropshire TF13 6HS

Tel: 01952 727466 www.english-heritage.org.uk/wenlock

Owner: English Heritage   **Contact:** Visitor Operations Team

A prosperous, powerful priory at its peak in the Middle Ages. A great deal of the structure still survives in the form of high, romantic ruined walls and it is the resting place of St Milburga the first Abbess. A monastery was first founded at Wenlock in the 7th century, and little more is known of the site until the time of the Norman Conquest when it became a Cluniac monastery. These majestic ruins of the priory church are set in green lawns and topiary, and there are substantial remains of the early 13th century church and Norman Chapter House.

Location: MAP 6:L6, OS127, SJ625 001. In Much Wenlock.

Open: Mar, Apr, Sept & Oct: Wed–Sun & BH Mons, 10am–5pm. 1 May–31 Aug: daily, 10am–5pm. 1 Nov–29 Feb '09: Thur–Sun, 10am–4pm. Closed 24–26 Dec & 1 Jan.

Admission: Adult £3.50, Child £1.80, Conc. £2.80. EH Members free. Group discount available.

ℹ️ WC. 🖼️ 🔊 Ⓟ 🐾 ❋ ♨

WESTON PARK 🏛️   *See page 330 for full page entry.*

WOLLERTON OLD HALL GARDEN

Wollerton, Market Drayton, Shropshire TF9 3NA

Tel: 01630 685760   **Fax:** 01630 685583

Owner: Mr & Mrs J D Jenkins   **Contact:** Mrs Di Oakes

Four acre plantsman's garden created around a 16th century house (not open).

Location: MAP 6:L5, OS Ref. SJ623 296. 14m NE of Shrewsbury off A53 between Hodnet and Market Drayton.

Open: Easter Good Fri–end Sept: Fris, Suns & BHs, 12 noon–5pm. Groups (25+) by appointment at other times.

Admission: Adult £4.80, Child £1, Groups (25+) £4.50 (must book). RHS members Free Apr, May & Sept.

WROXETER ROMAN CITY ⌗

Wroxeter, Shrewsbury, Shropshire SY5 6PH

Tel: 01743 761330 www.english-heritage.org.uk/wroxeter

Owner: English Heritage   **Contact:** Visitor Operations Team

The part-excavated centre of the fourth largest city in Roman Britain, originally home to some 6,000 men and several hundred houses. Impressive remains of the 2nd century municipal baths. There is a site museum in which many finds are displayed, including those from recent work by Birmingham Field Archaeological Unit.

Location: MAP 6:L6, OS126, SJ565 087. At Wroxeter, 5m E of Shrewsbury, on B4380.

Open: 21 Mar–31 Oct: daily, 10am–5pm. 1 Nov–29 Feb: Wed–Sun, 10am–4pm. Closed 24–26 Dec & 1 Jan.

Admission: Adult £4.20, Child £2.10, Conc. £3.40, Family £10.50. EH Members free. Group discount available.

ℹ️ WC. 🖼️ ♿ 🔊 Ⓟ 🚽 🐾 ❋

Hodnet Hall Gardens

■ **Owner**
St Modwen Properties

■ **Contact**
Stone Road
Trentham
Staffordshire ST4 8AX

Tel: 01782 646646
Fax: 01782 644536
E-mail: shamilton@
trentham.co.uk

■ **Location**
MAP 6:N4
OS Ref. SJ864 408

5 minute drive M6/J15.
45 minutes from
Birmingham, Manchester,
Liverpool & Nottingham.

■ **Opening Times**
Summer
April–September: daily,
10am–6pm.

Grounds
October–March: daily,
10am–4pm.

The Italian Gardens are
open every day except
Christmas Day.

■ **Admission**
Summer
Adult   £6.50
Child   £5.50
Conc.   £6.00
Family (2+3)   £22.00
Groups (12+) from £5.00
Schools   £2.50

Winter
Adult   £5.00
Child   £3.50
Conc.   £4.50
Family (2+3)   £14.00
Groups (12+) from £4.00
Schools   £1.50

TRENTHAM GARDENS

www.trentham.co.uk

Described as the largest contemporary planting scheme in Europe. Utilising top designers Tom Stuart-Smith and Piet Oudolf, this is an iconic restoration, bringing such an important historic garden back to life with vast new plantings with in excess of 120,000 perennials and 200,000 spring bulbs, which will provide interest throughout the year.

The 10 acre Italian Gardens, planted by Tom Stuart-Smith, are now fully restored and the new plantings are well established. The new seven acre garden designed by Piet Oudolf consists of three distinct areas: a wetland meadow with beds of ornamental grasses, the floral prairie with winding paths running through the brightly coloured, tall perennial planting and, finally, two sculptured viewing mounds flanked either side by choice shrub borders.

The western side of the garden is full of activity with 12 show gardens offering a range of ideas for gardeners. The gardens include: 'The Winter Garden', 'Tropical Garden', a 'Pottager' with intimate beds of fruit and vegetables and the 'Sensory Garden' which is a garden to tantalise all the senses. "Barfuss Park" – Britain's first barefoot walk – has proved to be extremely popular as people exchange the comfort of their shoes and socks to experience the revitalising sensations of water, mud, sand, straw, and a range of other surfaces said to awaken the spirit. This year will see the opening of a brand new garden maze with its spiral viewing mound and sound pipes, allowing you to encourage those who have not yet found their way. With the action-packed adventure playground and woodland trails the garden as a whole provides interest for everyone.

Licensed.

By arrangement.

Guide dogs only.

STAFFORDSHIRE

THE ANCIENT HIGH HOUSE

Greengate Street, Stafford ST16 2JA
Tel: 01785 619131 **Fax:** 01785 619132 **E-mail:** ahh@staffordbc.gov.uk
www.staffordbc.gov.uk/heritage
Owner: Stafford Borough Council **Contact:** Mark Hartwell
Over four hundred years of history are waiting to be discovered within the walls of Stafford's Ancient High House – England's largest timber-framed town house and one of the finest Tudor buildings in the country. Now fully restored, the superb period room settings reflect its fascinating story.
Location: MAP 6:N5, OS Ref. SJ922 232. Town centre.
Open: All year: Tues–Sat, 10am–4pm.
Admission: Free. Check for events, charges may apply.
◻ ⬓ ⬓ Unsuitable. 🅵 By arrangement. ▣ School tours by arrangement.
🐾 Guide dogs only. ❀ ⬓

BIDDULPH GRANGE GARDEN ❧

GRANGE ROAD, BIDDULPH, STOKE-ON-TRENT ST8 7SD

Tel: 01782 517999 **Fax:** 01782 510624
Owner: The National Trust **Contact:** The Garden Office
E-mail: biddulphgrange@nationaltrust.org.uk
A rare and exciting survival of a High Victorian garden, restored by the National Trust. The garden is divided into a series of themed gardens within a garden, with a Chinese temple, Egyptian court, pinetum, dahlia walk, glen and many other settings. Difficult uneven levels, unsuitable for wheelchairs.
Location: MAP 6:N3, OS Ref. SJ891 592. E of A527, 3½m SE of Congleton, 8m N of Stoke-on-Trent.
Open: 1–9 Mar: Sat & Sun, 11am–4pm; 15 Mar–2 Nov, Wed–Sun & BH Mon, 11am–5pm or dusk; 8 Nov–21 Dec, Sat & Sun, 11am 3pm.
*Admission: 1 Mar–2 Nov; Adult £6.40, Child £3.20, Family £14.90, Groups £5. 8 Nov–21 Dec; Adult £2.40, Child £1.20, Family £5.60. New joint ticket with Little Moreton Hall, Cheshire; Adult £10.20, Child £5.10, Family £25. *includes a voluntary donation but visitors can choose to pay the standard prices displayed at the property and on the website. Gift Aid is not included in group prices.
◻ ⬓ ⬓ Unsuitable for wheelchairs and people with mobility problems. ▣
🐾 In car park, on leads. ⬓

CASTERNE HALL

Ilam, Nr Ashbourne, Derbyshire DE6 2BA
Tel: 01335 310489 **E-mail:** mail@casterne.co.uk **www.casterne.co.uk**
Owner/Contact: Charles & Susannah Hurt
Manor house in beautiful location, a seat of the Hurt family for 500 years.
Location: MAP 6:O3, OS Ref. SK123 523. Take first turning on left N of Ilam and continue past 'Casterne Farms only' sign.
Open: 1 May–11 Jun (closed 5 & 26 May): weekdays only. Tours at: 2 & 3pm.
Admission: £5.
Ⓣ ⬓ Partial. 🅵 Obligatory. 🅿 ▣ ▣ €

Dorothy Clive Garden, Staffordshire.

giftaid it Some properties will be operating the Gift Aid on Entry scheme at their admission points. Where the scheme is operating, visitors are offered a choice between paying the standard admission price or paying the 'Gift Aid Admission' which includes a voluntary donation of at least 10%. Gift Aid Admissions enable the charity to reclaim tax on the whole amount paid* – an extra 28% – potentially a very significant boost to property funds. Money raised from paying visitors in this way will go towards restoration projects at the property and will be very welcome.
Where shown, the admission prices are inclusive of the 10% voluntary donation where properties are operating the Gift Aid on Entry scheme, but both the standard admission price and the Gift Aid Admission will be displayed at the property and on their website.

*Gift Aid donations must be supported by a valid Gift Aid declaration and a Gift Aid declaration can only cover donations made by an individual for him/herself or for him/herself and members of his/her family.

The Ancient High House

CAVERSWALL CASTLE
CAVERSWALL, STAFFORDSHIRE ST11 9EA
www.caverswall-castle.co.uk

Tel: 01782 393239   **E-mail:** info@caverswall-castle.co.uk
Owner/ Contact: Robin Macdonald

Caverswall Castle is a 13th century jewel set in beautiful surroundings. Originally built in 1275 by Sir William-de-Caverswall and later rebuilt by the Mayor of Staffordshire in 1625, the Castle has a rich and diverse 700 year history. It has been a former nunnery, home of the Wedgwood family and survived the English Civil War. Approaching via a tree lined avenue, the Castle is naturally hidden by mature oaks and lyme trees, and is set in over 35 acres of private grounds, enjoying unique tranquillity. The Grade I Listed Castle has undergone complete restoration and is now available for private hire. The grand medieval and Jacobean architecture has been combined with modern luxuries, making it the perfect setting for special events. The romantically named bedroom suites are extremely spacious and beautifully furnished with four-poster beds and antique furniture. Each room has been individually decorated to reflect the character of the Castle, some of which have retained their original oak panelling. All of the bedrooms are en-suite with luxury modern bathrooms, including double showers and spa baths, with The Princess Suite having the additional benefit of a private sauna. A swimming pool, gym and spa are also located within the grounds. Caverswall Castle is only available on an exclusive basis, with a choice of packages to meet individual needs, be it for corporate events, as a wedding venue, romantic private dining, product launches, photo shoots or film locations.

Location: MAP 6:N4, OS SJ952 426. In the village of Caverswall, 1m from A50 and 10 minutes from M6 J15.

Open: Please contact property for details.

Admission: Please contact property for details.

⊤ ⬚ ⬚ ⊤⊤ Licensed. ⬚ By arrangement. ℗ ⬚ Guide dogs only. ⬚ ⬚ ⬚

CHILLINGTON HALL ⏂
CODSALL WOOD, WOLVERHAMPTON, STAFFORDSHIRE WV8 1RE
www.chillingtonhall.co.uk

Tel: 01902 850236   **Fax:** 01902 850768   **E-mail:** mrsplod@chillingtonhall.co.uk
Owner/Contact: Mr & Mrs J W Giffard

Home of the Giffards since 1178. Built during 18th century by Francis Smith of Warwick and John Soane. Park designed by 'Capability' Brown. Smith's Staircase, Soane's Saloon and the Pool (a lake of 70 acres) are splendid examples of the days of the Georgian landowner.

Location: MAP 6:N6, OS Ref. SJ864 067. 2m S of Brewood off A449. 4m NW of M54/J2.

Open: House: BH Suns & Mons (Easter, May & Aug) & July Suns. Aug, Wed–Fri & Suns, 2–5pm. Grounds: as House, also Suns Easter–end May. Last entry 4pm.

Admission: Adult £6, Child £3. Grounds only: half price.

⊤ ⬚ Partial. ⬚ Obligatory. ℗ ⬚ In grounds, on leads. €

THE DOROTHY CLIVE GARDEN

Willoughbridge, Market Drayton, Shropshire TF9 4EU
Tel: 01630 647237   **Fax:** 01630 647902   **E-mail:** info@dorothyclivegarden.co.uk
www.dorothyclivegarden.co.uk
Owner: Willoughbridge Garden Trust   **Contact:** Garden Office

The Dorothy Clive Garden accommodates a wide range of choice and unusual plants providing year round interest. Features include a quarry with spectacular waterfall, flower borders, a scree and water garden. Tearoom serving home-baked hot and cold snacks throughout the day.

Location: MAP 6:M4, OS Ref. SJ753 400. A51, 2m S of Woore, 3m from Bridgemere.

Open: 15 Mar–28 Sept: daily, 10am–5.30pm.

Admission: Adult £5, Child (11–16yrs) £1, (under 11yrs Free), OAP £4. Pre-booked Groups (20+) £4.

⬚ ⬚ ℗ ⬚ In grounds on leads.

Moseley Old Hall

STAFFORDSHIRE

ERASMUS DARWIN HOUSE 🏛

Beacon Street, Lichfield, Staffordshire WA13 7AD

www.erasmusdarwin.org

Tel: 01543 306260 **E-mail:** enquiries@erasmusdarwin.org

Owner: The Erasmus Darwin Foundation **Contact:** Alison Wallis

Grandfather of Charles Darwin and a founder member of the Lunar Society, Erasmus Darwin (1731–1802) was a leading doctor, scientist, inventor and poet. This elegant Georgian house was his home and contains an exhibition of his life, theories, and inventions. There is also an 18th century herb garden.

Location: MAP 6:P5, OS Ref. SK115 098. Situated at the West end of Lichfield Cathedral Close.

Open: All year. Please telephone for details and check our website.

Admission: Adult £2.50, Child/Conc. £2, Family £6. Groups (10–50) £2.

🖭 🚻 🖵 ⚗ ⚗ By arrangement. 🅟 Disabled only. ⬛ 🖼 Guide dogs only. ✳

THE HEATH HOUSE

Tean, Stoke-on-Trent, Staffordshire ST10 4HA

Tel: 01538 722212 / 01386 792110

E-mail: j-philips1@homecall.co.uk

Owner/Contact: Mr John Philips

The Heath House is an early Victorian mansion designed and built 1836–1840 in the Tudor style for John Burton Philips. The collection of paintings is a rare survival and has remained undisturbed since its acquisition. It is still a Philips family home. Large attractive formal garden.

Location: MAP 6:O4, OS Ref. SK030 392. A522 off A50 at Uttoxeter 5m W, at Lower Tean turn right.

Open: Easter Monday & August BH Mons & 26 May–8 Jun, Jul 23–5 Aug, 2.30–5pm. Please telephone in advance to confirm opening times.

Admission: £5. No Conc. No reductions for groups.

ⓘ No photography or video recording. ⚗ ⚗ Obligatory. 🅟
🖼 In grounds, on leads. 🔲

IZAAK WALTON'S COTTAGE

Worston Lane, Shallowford, Nr Stafford ST15 0PA

Tel/Fax: 01785 760278

E-mail: heritage@staffordbc.gov.uk **www.staffordbc.gov.uk/heritage**

Owner: Stafford Borough Council **Contact:** Mark Hartwell

Stafford's rural heritage is embodied in the charming 17th century cottage owned by the celebrated author of *The Compleat Angler*. Izaak Walton's Cottage gives a fascinating insight into the history of angling and the life of a writer whose work remains 'a unique celebration of the English countryside.'

Location: MAP 6:N5, OS Ref. SJ876 293. M6/J14, A5013 towards Eccleshall, signposted on A5013.

Open: May–Aug: Sat & Sun, 1–5pm.

Admission: Free. Check for events, charges may apply.

🖭 ⚗ Partial. WCs. ⬛ 🅟 Limited for cars. 🖼 Guide dogs only. 🔲

The Dorothy Clive Garden

MOSELEY OLD HALL ✣

FORDHOUSES, WOLVERHAMPTON WV10 7HY

Tel: 01902 782808 **E-mail:** moseleyoldhall@nationaltrust.org.uk

Owner: The National Trust **Contact:** The Property Manager

An Elizabethan timber-framed house encased in brick in 1870; with original interiors. Charles II hid here after the Battle of Worcester. The bed in which he slept is on view as well as the hiding place he used. An exhibition retells the story of the King's dramatic escape from Cromwell's troops, and there are optional, free guided tours. The garden has been reconstructed in 17th century style with formal box parterre, only 17th century plants are grown. The property is a Sandford Education Award Winner.

Location: MAP 6:N6, OS Ref. SJ932 044. 4m N of Wolverhampton between A449 and A46.

Open: 1 Mar–2 Nov: Sats, Suns, Weds, BH Mons & following Tues, (excluding Tues 6 May), 12 noon–5pm, BH Mons 11am–5pm. also 22 Jul–9 Sept, Tues, 12 noon–5pm. 9 Nov–21 Dec: Suns, 12–4pm (guided tours only), 23 Nov, 30 Nov & 7 Dec: Christmas activites. Last admission to the house 30 minutes before closing. Shop, Tearoom & Garden: Open 12 noon.

Admission: Adult £6, Child £3, Family £15. Groups (15+) £5pp (Weds £4.70). Private visits in closing times £7pp (Min £114). NT members free with valid membership card.

🖭 🚻 ⚗ Ground floor & grounds. WC. ⬛ Tearoom in 18th century barn. ⚗ 🅟 🖼
🖼 On leads. 🔲 🖼

©NTPL/Nic Meers

SANDON HALL

SANDON, STAFFORDSHIRE ST18 0BZ

www.sandonhall.co.uk

Tel/Fax: 01889 508004 **E-mail:** info@sandonhall.co.uk

Owner: The Earl of Harrowby **Contact:** Jon Guard

Sandon Hall, ancestral home of the Earls of Harrowby, is set in 400 acres of rolling parkland in the heart of Staffordshire. The impressive neo-Jacobean house contains numerous State Rooms as well as a family museum, which houses an array of different and unusual items. The Hall is an ideal setting for weddings, conferences and private parties, offering exclusivity in tranquil surroundings. The 50-acre formal gardens include many rare species and are particularly beautiful in May and autumn.

Location: MAP 6:N5, OS Ref. SJ957 287. 5m NE of Stafford on the A51, between Stone and Lichfield, easy access from M6/J14.

Open: All year for events, functions and for pre-booked visits to the museum and gardens. Evening tours by special arrangement.

Admission: Museum: Adult £4, Child £3, OAP £3.50. Gardens: Adult £1.50, Child £1, OAP £1. NB. Max group size 22 or 45 if combined Museum and Gardens.

⊤ ⬢ ⬛ Licensed. 🅧 Obligatory. 🅿 Limited for coaches. 🐾 In grounds, on leads. ⬛ ❄ ⬛

Biddulph Grange Garden

SHUGBOROUGH ESTATE ✿

MILFORD, STAFFORD ST17 0XB

www.shugborough.org.uk

Tel: 01889 881388 **Fax:** 01889 881323

E-mail: shugborough.promotions@staffordshire.gov.uk

Owner: The National Trust **Contact:** Sales and Marketing Office

Shugborough, The Complete Working Historic Estate, where the past comes to life. Shugborough is no ordinary stately home but a living, working experience of life as it was in the 1800s and 1900s.

Costumed living history characters welcome visitors and bring the past to life. Knead the dough for the servant's bread, admire and taste the sweets in the old fashioned sweet shop and grind flour in the watermill.

Set in 900 acres of picturesque parkland the elegant Mansion House, Victorian Servants' Quarters, homely Working Farm and Restored Walled Garden are preserved just as they were centuries ago.

Journey through the historic estate of Shugborough and discover a bygone era of our costumed living history characters bringing the past to life.

Location: MAP 6:N5, OS Ref. SJ992 225. 10mins from M6/J13 on A513 Stafford/Lichfield Rd.

Open: 14 Mar–31 Oct, daily 11am–5pm. Tearooms open 11am–4.30pm.

Admission: Adults £12, Child (under 5s Free) £7, Conc. £9.50, Family (2+3) £30, (1+1) £15, Group Rate £8.50. Parking £3. (National Trust Members consult handbook.)

⬛ ⊤ ⬢ ⬛ ⬛ 🅧 🅿 Limited for coaches. ⬛ 🐾 On leads. ⬛ ⬛

STAFFORDSHIRE

STAFFORD CASTLE & VISITOR CENTRE

Newport Road, Stafford ST16 1DJ
Tel/Fax: 01785 257698   **E-mail:** heritage@staffordbc.gov.uk
www.staffordbc.gov.uk/heritage
Owner: Stafford Borough Council   **Contact:** Mark Hartwell
Stafford Castle has dominated the Stafford landscape for over 900 years. William the Conqueror first built Stafford Castle as a fortress to subdue the local populace. The visitor centre – built in the style of a Norman guardhouse – features an audio-visual area that brings its turbulent past to life.
Location: MAP 6:N5, OS Ref. SJ904 220. On N side of A518, 1½m WSW of town centre.
Open: Apr–Oct: Tue–Sun, 10am–5pm (open BHs). Nov–Mar: Sat & Sun, 10am–4pm.
Admission: Free (admission charges may apply for events).
⚥ By arrangement. ✦

TRENTHAM GARDENS

See page 337 for full page entry

WALL ROMAN SITE (LETOCETUM) ✜ ✖

Watling Street, Nr Lichfield, Staffordshire WS14 0AW
Tel: 0121 625 6820   **www.english-heritage.org.uk/wallroman**
Owner: English Heritage   **Contact:** Regional Head Office
The remains of a staging post alongside Watling Street. Foundations of an Inn and a Bath House can be seen and there is a display of finds in the site museum.
Location: MAP 6:O6, OS139, SK098 066. Off A5 at Wall, nr Lichfield.
Open: Museum by appointment only. Please telephone for details.
Admission: Free.
Ⓟ ✖

For **accommodation** in the South West, see our special index at the end of the book.

WHITMORE HALL 🏛

WHITMORE, NEWCASTLE-UNDER-LYME ST5 5HW

Tel: 01782 680478 **Fax:** 01782 680906
Owner: Mr Guy Cavenagh-Mainwaring   **Contact:** Mr Michael Cavenagh-Thornhill
Whitmore Hall is a Grade I listed building, designated as a house of outstanding architectural and historical interest, and is a fine example of a small Carolinian manor house (1676), although parts of the hall date back to a much earlier period. The hall has beautifully proportioned light rooms, curving staircase and landing. There are some good family portraits to be seen with a continuous line, from 1624 to the present day. It has been the family seat, for over 900 years, of the Cavenagh-Mainwarings who are direct descendants of the original Norman owners. The interior of the hall has recently been refurbished and is in fine condition. The grounds include a beautiful home park with a lime avenue leading to the house, as well as landscaped gardens encompassing an early Victorian summer house. One of the outstanding features of Whitmore is the extremely rare example of a late Elizabethan stable block, the ground floor is part cobbled and has nine oak-carved stalls.
Location: MAP 6:M4, OS Ref. SJ811 413. On A53 Newcastle–Market Drayton Road, 3m from M6/J15.
Open: 1 May–31 Aug: Tues, Weds, 2–5pm (last tour 4.30pm).
Admission: Adult £4, Child 50p.
🛇 Ground floor & grounds.
▣ Afternoon teas for booked groups (15+), May–Aug. ⚥ Ⓟ ✖

Shugborough Estate

visit hudsons guide online

ARBURY HALL

Arbury Hall has been the seat of the Newdegate family for over 400 years and is the ancestral home of Viscount Daventry. This Tudor/Elizabethan House was gothicised by Sir Roger Newdegate in the 18th century and is regarded as the 'Gothic Gem' of the Midlands. The Hall contains a fine collection of both oriental and Chelsea porcelain, portraits by Lely, Reynolds, Devis and Romney and furniture by Chippendale and Hepplewhite. The principal rooms, with their soaring fan vaulted ceilings and plunging pendants and filigree tracery, stand as a most breathtaking and complete example of early Gothic Revival architecture and provide a unique and fascinating venue for corporate entertaining, product launches, receptions, fashion shoots and activity days. Exclusive use of this historic Hall, its gardens and parkland is offered to clients. The Hall stands in the middle of beautiful parkland with landscaped gardens of rolling lawns, lakes and winding wooded walks. Spring flowers are profuse and in June rhododendrons, azaleas and giant wisteria provide a beautiful environment for the visitor.

George Eliot, the novelist, was born on the estate and Arbury Hall and Sir Roger Newdegate were immortalised in her book 'Scenes of Clerical Life'.

■ **Owner**
The Viscount Daventry

■ **Contact**
Miss Brenda Newell
Arbury Hall
Nuneaton
Warwickshire CV10 7PT

Tel: 024 7638 2804
Fax: 024 7664 1147
E-mail: brenda.newell@arburyhall.net

■ **Location**
MAP 7:A7
OS Ref. SP335 893

London, M1, M6/J3
(A444 to Nuneaton),
2m SW of Nuneaton.
1m W of A444.

Chester A51, A34, M6
(from J14 to J3), 2½ hrs.
Nuneaton 10 mins.

London 2 hrs,
Birmingham ½ hr,
Coventry 20 mins.

Bus: Nuneaton 3m.

Rail: Nuneaton
Station 3m.

Air: Birmingham
International 17m.

■ **Opening Times**
All year
Tues, Weds & Thurs only,
for corporate events.

Pre-booked visits to the
Hall and Gardens for
groups of 25+ on Tues,
Weds & Thurs (until 4pm)
from Easter to the end of
September.

Hall & Gardens open
2–5pm on BH weekends
only (Suns & Mons)
Easter–September.

■ **Admission**
Summer
Hall & Gardens
Adult	£6.50
Child (up to 14 yrs)	£4.50
Family (2+2)	£18.00

Gardens Only
Adult	£5.00
Child (up to 14 yrs.)	£3.50

Groups (25+)
Adult	£6.50

ℹ Corporate hospitality, film location, small conferences, product launches and promotions, marquee functions, clay pigeon shooting, archery and other sporting activities, grand piano in Saloon, helicopter landing site. No cameras or video recorders indoors.

🛍 Exclusive lunches and dinners for corporate parties in dining room, max. 50, buffets 120.

♿ Visitors may alight at the Hall's main entrance. Parking in allocated areas. Ramp access to main hall.

☕ By arrangement for groups.

🚶 Obligatory. Tour time: 1hr.

🅿 200 cars and 3 coaches 250 yards from house. Follow tourist signs. Approach map available for coach drivers.

🎒 Welcome, must book. School room available.

🐕 In gardens on leads. Guide dogs only in house.

❄

🛡

Conference/Function

ROOM	SIZE	MAX CAPACITY
Dining Room	35' x 28'	120
Saloon	35' x 30'	70
Long Gallery	48' x 11'	40
Stables Tearooms	31' x 18'	80

■ **Owner**

The National Trust

■ **Contact**

The Estate Office
Baddesley Clinton
Rising Lane
Baddesley Clinton Village
Knowle
Solihull B93 0DQ

Tel: 01564 783294
Fax: 01564 782706
E-mail: baddesleyclinton@
nationaltrust.org.uk

■ **Location**
MAP 6:P8
OS Ref. SP199 715

¾ m W of A4141
Warwick/Birmingham
road at Chadwick End.

■ **Opening Times**
House
9 February–2 November:
Wed–Sun, Good Friday
& BH Mons, 11am–5pm.

Grounds
9 February–21 December:
Wed–Sun, Good Friday
& BH Mons.
9 February–2 November,
11am–5pm.
5 November–
21 December,
11am–4pm.

■ ***Admission**

Adult	£8.40
Child	£4.20
Family	£21.00
Groups	£6.50
Guided tours	
(out of hours)	£13.00

Grounds only

Adult	£4.20
Child	£2.10

**Combined Ticket with
Packwood House**

Adult	£12.00
Child	£6.00
Family	£30.00
Groups	£9.10

Gardens only

Adult	£6.30
Child	£3.15

*includes a voluntary
donation but visitors can
choose to pay the standard
prices displayed at the
property and on the website.
This does not apply to group
prices.

BADDESLEY CLINTON

www.nationaltrust.org.uk

Enjoy a day at Baddesley Clinton, the medieval moated manor house with hidden secrets! One of the most enchanting properties owned by the National Trust, Baddesley Clinton has seen little change since 1633 when Henry Ferrers 'the Antiquary' died. He was Squire at Baddesley for almost seventy years and remodelled the house over a long period of time, introducing much of the panelling and chimney pieces. Henry was proud of his ancestry and began the tradition at Baddesley of armorial glass, which has continued up to the present day. Henry let the house in the 1590s when it became a refuge for Jesuit priests, and hiding places, called 'priest's holes', created for their concealment, survive from this era.

Pictures painted by Rebecca, wife of Marmion Edward Ferrers, remain to show how the romantic character of Baddesley was enjoyed in the late 19th century when the family also recreated a sumptuously furnished Chapel.

The garden, which surrounds the house, incorporates many features including stewponds; a small lake (the 'Great Pool'); a walled garden with thatched summer house, and a lakeside walk with nature trail and wildflower meadow. Make a day of it! Complementary opening times and substantial discounts on joint ticket prices make a combined visit to Baddesley Clinton and Packwood House even more attractive, especially since both properties are only two miles apart.

Partial. WC.
Licensed.
By arrangement.

Guide dogs only.

PACKWOOD HOUSE

www.nationaltrust.org.uk

Packwood lies in the pleasantly wooded Forest of Arden and was, for many years, the home of the Fetherstons, who allowed Cromwell's General, Henry Ireton, to stay overnight before the Battle of Edgehill in 1642. There is also a tradition that Charles II was given refreshment at Packwood after his defeat at Worcester in 1651. Many of Packwood's interiors were designed in the 1920s and 30s in idealised Elizabethan or Jacobean styles for Graham Baron Ash. They offer a wonderful insight into the taste, rich decoration and way of life of a wealthy connoisseur in the period between the wars. Packwood still retains the intimate atmosphere of a real home, with lavishly furnished rooms containing French and Flemish tapestries and fine 17th & 18th century furniture. The oak panelled bedrooms with their sumptuous four-poster beds give you a glimpse of what it was like to stay the night as Baron Ash's guest. Queen Mary, another regal guest who took refreshment here, visited in August 1927. Look out for several reminders of that historic visit throughout the house.

The house is surrounded by its own delightful, tranquil grounds. A large flower garden complete with long terraced herbaceous borders, enclosed by red brick walls with a gazebo in each corner, is a blend of the traditional country house garden and the Carolean Garden of the Fetherstons. The famous 17th century Yew Garden is traditionally said to represent 'The Sermon on the Mount' and is a highly unusual and attractive feature. Make a day of it! Complementary opening times and substantial discounts on joint ticket prices make a combined visit to Packwood House and Baddesley Clinton even more attractive, especially since both properties are only two miles apart.

■ Owner
The National Trust

■ Contact
The Estate Office
Packwood House
Lapworth
Solihull B94 6AT

Tel: 01564 783294
Fax: 01564 782706
E-mail: packwood@
nationaltrust.org.uk

■ Location
MAP 6:O8
OS Ref. SP174 722

2m E of Hockley Heath
(on A3400), 11m SE of
central Birmingham.

■ Opening Times
House
9 February–2 November:
Wed–Sun, Good Friday &
BH Mons, 11am–5pm.

Garden
9 February–2 November:
Wed–Sun, Good Friday &
BH Mons, 11am–5pm.

Park & Woodland Walks
All year: daily.

■ *Admission

Adult	£7.30
Child	£3.65
Family	£18.25
Groups	£5.60
Guided tours	
(out of hours)	£11.20

Garden only

Adult	£4.20
Child	£2.10

Combined Ticket with Baddesley Clinton

Adult	£12.00
Child	£6.00
Family	£30.00
Groups	£9.10

Gardens only

Adult	£6.30
Child	£3.15

*includes a voluntary donation but visitors can choose to pay the standard prices displayed at the property and on the website. This does not apply to group prices.

Partial. WC.

By arrangement

Guide dogs only.

Parkland only.

■ **Owner**
The Marquess of Hertford

■ **Contact**
Ragley Hall
Alcester
Warwickshire B49 5NJ

Tel: 01789 762090
Fax: 01789 764791
E-mail: ragley@
ragleyhall.com

■ **Location**
MAP 6:O9
OS Ref. SP073 555

Off A46/A435 1m SW of
Alcester. From London
100m, M40 via Oxford
and Stratford-on-Avon.

Rail: Evesham Station 9m.

Air: Birmingham
International 20m.

Taxi: 007 Taxi
01789 414007

■ **Opening Times**
House & State Rooms
15 March–2 November:
Suns only, 11am–4pm.
(Open daily, except Sats in
school holidays.)

**Gardens, Park,
Adventure Wood &
Jerwood Sculpture Park**
15 March–2 November:
Sats & Suns, 11am–4pm.

Daily during School
Holidays:
20 March–6 April,
22 May–1 June &
17 July–31 August
23 October–2 November.

Winter:
2 November 2008–
March 2009: Closed.

■ **Admission**
**House, Garden, Park,
Adventure Playground
& Jerwood Sculpture
Park incl.**
Adult	£8.50
Child (5–16yrs)	£5.00
Conc.	£7.00
Family (2+3)	£27.00

Season Tickets:
Adult	£32.00
Child	£20.00
Family (2+3)	£90.00

RAGLEY HALL & GARDENS
www.ragleyhall.com

Ragley Hall, the family home of the Marquess and Marchioness of Hertford, was designed by Robert Hooke, the inventive genius, in 1680 and is one of the earliest and loveliest of England's great Palladian Houses. The perfect symmetry of the architecture of Ragley remains unchanged save for the spectacular portico by Wyatt added in 1780.

The majestic Great Hall, soaring two storeys high, is adorned with some of England's finest and most exquisite baroque plasterwork by James Gibbs, dated 1750.

Ragley houses a superb collection of 18th century and earlier paintings, china, and furniture and wonderful ceilings decorated with Grisaille panels and insets by Angelica Kauffman.

A most striking feature of Ragley is the breathtaking mural

"The Temptation" by Graham Rust in the south staircase hall, that was painted between 1969 and 1983.

Ragley is a working estate with more than 6000 acres of land. The house is set in 400 acres of picturesque parkland landscaped by Lancelot 'Capability' Brown and 27 acres of fascinating gardens including the enchanting rose garden, richly planted borders and mature woodland.

Near to the Hall the working stables, designed by James Gibbs in 1751, house a collection of carriages dating back to 1760 and equestrian equipment.

For children there is an exciting woodland adventure playground, 3D maze and an extensive lakeside play and picnic area, and for walkers the delightful woodland walk.

i	Product launches, dinners and activity days, film and photographic location, park, lake and picnic area, marquee. No photography or video in the house.
	Wedding ceremonies and receptions, private and corporate entertainment, conferences and seminars.
	Visitors may alight at entrance. Parking in allocated areas. WCs. Lifts. Coffee House & Restaurant on ground floor. Electric scooter for visiting the gardens may be available. Please enquire.
	Tearoom in the Park and Hooke's Coffee-House & Restaurant. Groups please book.
	By arrangement.
P	Coach drivers admitted free and receive info pack and voucher. Please advise of group visits.
	Teachers' packs and work modules available. Adventure Wood and Woodland Walk.
	In grounds, on leads.

■ **Conference/Function**

ROOM	SIZE	MAX CAPACITY
Great Hall	70' x 40'	150
Red Saloon	30' x 40'	40
Hertford	45' x 22'	60
Seymour	25' x 23'	30

Shakespeare's Birthplace

Hall's Croft

Anne Hathaway's Cottage

THE SHAKESPEARE HOUSES

www.shakespeare.org.uk

Step back in to Elizabethan England at the Shakespeare Houses, Stratford-Upon-Avon

Five beautifully preserved Tudor homes and gardens, all directly linked with William Shakespeare and his family. Each has a story to tell and together they provide a unique experience of the dramatist's life and times.

In Town: Shakespeare's Birthplace – this timber framed town house, where William Shakespeare was born, contains both original and replica artefacts depicting the house as Shakespeare would have known it. Period guides, dressed in replica Tudor clothing, welcome you to explore what life was like here in Tudor times. Stroll round the traditional English garden, which features many plants and herbs mentioned in Shakespeare's plays, and remember your visit with a purchase from the gift shop.

Nash's House & New Place – Nash's House is decorated with original Tudor furnishings and features an exhibition telling the remarkable story of *Shakespeare's Complete Works* as one of the best-loved books in the English language. Adjacent to Nash's House are the remaining foundations of New Place, where Shakespeare died, now preserved as a picturesque garden space.

Hall's Croft – visit the luxurious home of Shakespeare's daughter and her husband, Dr John Hall, an eminent physician. Explore the house's lavish and elegant rooms. Many exquisite furnishings and paintings of the period are on display, as well as a small exhibition of early medicine.

Out of Town: Anne Hathaway's Cottage – explore the romantic surroundings of this quintessential thatched country cottage where the young Shakespeare wooed his wife to be, Anne Hathaway, at her childhood home. Stroll round the award winning country cottage garden, which overflows with blooms, shrubs and traditional vegetables. Be inspired by Shakespeare's sonnets in the growing Willow Cabin and discover the Shakespeare Tree and Sculpture Garden and Elizabethan-style yew maze.

Mary Arden's – a charming farmhouse and childhood home of Shakespeare's mother, Mary Arden. Step back in time to the 1570s and experience what life was like for a farming household in Shakespeare's time at neighbouring Palmer's Farm. Watch the period interpreters, dressed in replica Tudor clothing, perform a wide range of activities from hand-milking sheep, cooking over an open fire, baking bread, dipping tallow candles … and much more.

Harvard House and the Museum of British Pewter – The Shakespeare Birthplace Trust also owns and cares for Harvard House, one of Stratford-upon-Avon's most striking Elizabethan houses. Discover pewter's fascinating history through the centuries, try your hand at decorative pewter, take a virtual reality tour and have fun in the Pewter Power young visitor's activity zone.

The Shakespeare Houses & Gardens are owned and cared for by the Shakespeare Birthplace Trust, which is an independent charity. Every admission to the Shakespeare Houses and purchase in the gift shops supports the work of the Shakespeare Birthplace Trust and preserves the houses and gardens for future generations.

Tudor life at Palmer's Farm

i	City Sightseeing guided bus tour service connecting the town houses with Anne Hathaway's Cottage and Mary Arden's House. No photography inside houses.
	Gifts are available at all five Shakespeare properties.
	Available, tel for details.
	WCs. Naturally difficult levels but much to enjoy at Mary Arden's, ground floor & gardens accessible. Virtual reality tour at Shakespeare's Birthplace & Anne Hathaway's Cottage. The gardens at Nash's House & New Place are also easily accessible.
	Available on site or close by.
	By special arrangement.
P	The Trust provides a free coach terminal for delivery and pick-up of groups, maximum stay 30 mins at Shakespeare's Birthplace. Parking at Anne Hathaway's Cottage and Mary Arden's.
	Available for all houses. For information 01789 201804.
	Guide dogs only.
	Hall's Croft

■ **Owner**
The Shakespeare Birthplace Trust

■ **Contact**
The Shakespeare Birthplace Trust
Henley Street
Stratford-upon-Avon
CV37 6QW
Tel: 01789 204016 (General enquiries)
Tel: 01789 201806/201836 (Group Visits)
01789 201808 (Special/Evening Visits).
Fax: 01789 263138
E-mail: info@shakespeare.org.uk
groups@shakespeare.org.uk

■ **Location**
MAP 6:P9
OS Refs:
Birthplace – SP201 552
New Place – SP201 548
Hall's Croft – SP200 546
Hathaway's – SP185 547
Arden's – SP166 582
Rail: Direct service from London (Marylebone)
2 hrs from London
45 mins from Birmingham by car.
4m from M40/J15 and well signed from all approaches.

■ **Opening Times**
Mid Season:
Apr–May & Sept–Oct.
Birthplace & Mary Arden's
Mon–Sun: 10am–5pm.
Hall's Croft & Nash's House & New Place
11am–5pm.
Anne Hathaway's
Mon–Sat: 9.30am–5pm.
Suns: 10am–5pm.
Summer Season:
Jun–Aug.
Birthplace & Anne Hathaway's
Mon–Sat: 9am–5pm.
Suns: 9.30am–5pm.
Hall's Croft & Nash's House & New Place
Mon–Sat: 9.30am–5pm.
Suns: 10am–5pm.
Mary Arden's
9.30am–5pm.
Winter Season:
Nov–Mar.
Birthplace & Anne Hathaway's House
Mon–Sat: 10am–4pm.
Suns: 10.30am–4pm.
(Anne Hathaway's 10am–4pm)
Hall's Croft & Nash's House & New Place
11am–4pm.
Closed 23–26 Dec.
All times are for admission to last entry.

■ **Admission**
Multiple house tickets for all five houses and the three in-town houses and single house tickets are available. Please telephone 01789 204016 for further information or visit www.shakespseare.org.uk

■ **Owner**

Stoneleigh Abbey Ltd

■ **Contact**

Enquiry Office
Stoneleigh Abbey
Kenilworth
Warwickshire CV8 2LF

Tel: 01926 858535
Fax: 01926 850724
E-mail: enquire
@stoneleighabbey.org

■ **Location**

MAP 6:P8
OS Ref. SP318 712

Off A46/B4115,
2m W of Kenilworth.
From London 100m,
M40 to Warwick.

Rail: Coventry station 5m,
Leamington Spa
station 5m.

Air: Birmingham
International 20m.

■ **Opening Times**

Good Fri–end October

Tue–Thur, Suns & BHs:
House tours at
11am, 1pm & 3pm.

Grounds: 10am–5pm.

■ **Admission**

House Tour & Grounds

Adult	£6.50
1 Child Free with each adult	
Additional Child	£3.00
OAP	£5.00

Discounts for Groups
(20+).

Jane Austen Tour

Sundays, 1pm	£6.50
Grounds only	£3.00
Parking	Free

Groups are welcome
during the published
opening times or at other
times by arrangement.
Please telephone.

Conference/Function

ROOM	SIZE	MAX CAPACITY
Saloon	14 x 9m	100
Gilt Hall	7 x 7m	60
Servants' Hall	14 x 8m	100
Riding School	12 x 33m	490
Conservatory	19 x 6m	100

STONELEIGH ABBEY

www.stoneleighabbey.org

Stoneleigh Abbey was founded in the reign of Henry II and after the Dissolution was granted to the Duke of Suffolk. The estate then passed into the ownership of the Leigh family who remained for 400 years. The estate is now managed by a charitable trust.

Visitors will experience a wealth of architectural styles spanning more than 800 years: the magnificent State rooms and chapel of the 18th century Baroque West Wing contain original pieces of furniture including a set of library chairs made by William Gomm in 1763; a medieval Gatehouse; the Gothic Revival-style Regency Stables. Jane Austen was a distant relative of the Leigh family and in her description of 'Sotherton' in *Mansfield Park* she recalls her stay at Stoneleigh

Abbey. Parts of *Northanger Abbey* also use Stoneleigh for inspiration.

The River Avon flows through the estate's 690 acres of grounds and parkland which displays the influences of Humphry Repton and other major landscape architects. In June 1858 Queen Victoria and Prince Albert visited Stoneleigh Abbey – during their stay Queen Victoria planted an oak tree. In 2003 HRH Prince Charles visited Stoneleigh to mark the completion of the restoration of the Abbey and during his visit he also planted an English oak tree.

Stoneleigh Abbey has been the subject of a major restoration programme funded by the Heritage Lottery Fund, English Heritage and the European Regional Development Fund.

ℹ Available for public and commercial hire.

House only. WCs.

Obligatory.

Schools welcome.

UPTON HOUSE & GARDENS ❧

www.nationaltrust.org.uk

Upton House stands less than a mile to the south of the battlefield of Edgehill and there has been a house on this site since the Middle Ages. The present house was built at the end of the 17th century and remodelled 1927–29 for the 2nd Viscount Bearsted.

He was a great collector of paintings, china and many other valuable works of art, and adapted the building to display them. The paintings include works by El Greco, Bruegel, Bosch, Canaletto, Guardi, Hogarth and Stubbs. The rooms provide an admirable setting for the china collection which includes Chelsea figures and superb examples of beautifully decorated Sèvres porcelain. The set of 17th century Brussels tapestries depict the Holy Roman Emperor Maximilian I's boar and stag hunts.

Artists and Shell Exhibition of Paintings and Posters commissioned by Shell for use in its publicity 1921–1949, while the 2nd Viscount Bearsted was chairman of the company, founded by his father.

Garden

The outstanding garden is of interest throughout the season with terraces descending into a deep valley from the main lawn. There are herbaceous borders, the national collection of asters, over an acre of kitchen garden, a water garden laid out in the 1930s and pools stocked with ornamental fish.

An 80-seat licensed restaurant in the grounds serves full lunches and afternoon teas. It is available for hire throughout the year for dinners, conferences and functions by arrangement.

■ Owner
The National Trust

■ Contact
The Visitor Services Manager
Upton House
Banbury
Oxfordshire OX15 6HT

Tel: 01295 670266
Fax: 01295 671144
E-mail: uptonhouse
@nationaltrust.org.uk

■ Location
MAP 7:A9
OS Ref. SP371 461

On A422, 7m NW of Banbury. 12m SE of Stratford-upon-Avon

Rail: Banbury Station, 7m.

■ Opening Times
Spring & Summer
1 March–2 November.

House, Garden, Restaurant & Shop: Sat–Wed & BHs: (Daily in Easter & Summer holidays). House by guided tour only, 11am–1pm. Last entry 4.30pm, 11am–5pm.

Winter
Garden, Restaurant & Shop: 3 November–21 December, Sat–Wed, 12 noon–4pm.
House (ground floor), 8 Nov–21 December, 12 noon–4pm, Sat & Sun.

■ *Admission
House & Garden
Adult	£8.50
Child	£4.20
Family	£21.00
Groups (15+)	£6.70

Garden only
Adult	£5.00
Child	£2.50
Family	£12.50
Groups (15+)	£4.25

House & Garden
3 Nov–21 Dec
Adult	£5.00
Child	£2.50
Family	£12.50

*includes a voluntary donation but visitors can choose to pay the standard prices displayed at the property and on the website. This does not apply to group prices.

■ Special Events
All Year
Art tours, historical re-enactments, concerts and other events, please send SAE or telephone.

'Picture in Focus' and 'Porcelain in Focus' displays for 2008. New all-weather route for garden.

ℹ️ Children's Trail. No indoor photography.

♿ Ground floor. Wheelchairs available. Virtual tour. WC. Motorised buggy to/from reception/lower garden on request.

🍴 Licensed.

🚶 Tour time 1½–2hrs. Groups (15+) must pre-book. Evening tours by written appointment (no reduction).

🅿️ 350 yds from House.

🐕 In car park, on leads.

■ Contact
Warwick Castle
Warwick CV34 4QU

Tel: 0870 442 2000
Fax: 0870 442 2394
E-mail:
customer.information
@warwick-castle.com

■ Location
MAP 6:P8
OS Ref. SP284 648

2m from M40/J15.
Birmingham 35 mins
Leeds 2 hrs 5 mins
London, 1 hr 30 mins
Vehicle entrance from
A429 ½ m SW of town
centre.

Rail: Intercity from
London Euston to
Coventry. Direct service
from Marylebone &
Paddington to Warwick.

■ Opening Times
All year, daily,
except 25 December
10am–6pm
(closes 5pm during
October–March).

■ Admission
Prices vary – see website
for details.

WARWICK CASTLE

www.warwick-castle.com

Bursting to the towers with tales of treachery and torture, passion and power and above all fascinating people, times and events, Warwick Castle is so much more than simply a castle. Experience preparations for battle, feel the weight of a sword and get a solider's eye view from beneath a battle helmet, see lavishly decorated State Rooms, watch as a household prepares for a Victorian party and discover how electricity was generated over 100 years ago to light up the castle.

With 60 acres of landscaped grounds and gardens, there is plenty to see outside as well as in. Wander around the beautiful Peacock Garden and enter the 18th century Conservatory, filled with an array of exotic plants. There is also the Victorian Rose Garden to explore.

See the world's largest Trebuchet, a mighty siege machine similar to a catapult, measuring 18 metres high, weighing in at 22 tonnes and capable of shooting missiles up to 300 metres.

Throughout the year there is a programme of fantastic special events including opportunities to see the trebuchet in action. Visit www.warwick-castle.com for further information.

i	Corporate events, receptions, Kingmaker's Feasts and Highwayman's Suppers. Guide books available in English, French, German, Japanese and Spanish.
	Three shops.
	Partial. WCs. Parking spaces in Stables Car Park. Telephone for details.
	Licensed. Ranging from cream teas to three-course hot meals. During the summer there is an open air barbecue and refreshment pavilion in the grounds (weather permitting).
	Licensed.
	For groups (pre-booked). Guides in most rooms.
P	Limited. A charge is made for car parking. Free coach parking, free admission and refreshment voucher for coach driver.
	Ideal location, being a superb example of military architecture dating back to the Norman Conquest and with elegant interiors up to Victorian times. Group rates apply. To qualify for group rates, groups must book in advance. Education packs available.
	Registered assistance dogs only.
	Seasonal entertainment and events – see website for details.

Conference/Function

ROOM	SIZE	MAX CAPACITY
Great Hall	61' x 34'	130
State Dining Room	40' x 25'	30
Undercroft	46' x 26'	120
Coach House	44' x 19'	80
Marquees		2000

CHARLECOTE PARK ⚜

WARWICK CV35 9ER

www.nationaltrust.org.uk

Tel: 01789 470277 **Fax:** 01789 470544 **Events (info & booking):** 07788 658495
E-mail: charlecote.park@nationaltrust.org.uk
Owner: The National Trust

Owned by the Lucy family since 1247, Sir Thomas Lucy built the house in 1558. Now, much altered, it is shown as it would have been a century ago, complete with Victorian kitchen, brewhouse and family carriages in the coach house. The formal gardens and informal parkland lie to the north and west of the house. Jacob Sheep were brought to Charlecote in 1756 by Sir Thomas Lucy. It is reputed that William Shakespeare was apprehended for poaching c1583 and Sir Thomas Lucy is said to be the basis of Justice Shallow in Shakespeare's *'Merry Wives of Windsor'*.

Location: MAP 6:P9, OS151, SP263 564. 1m W of Wellesbourne, 5m E of Stratford-upon-Avon.

Open: Please telephone or see our website for opening times, dates, and details of regular events and activities.

*Admission: NT members and those joining at Charlecote Park: Free. Adult £8.20, Child (5–16yrs) £4.10, Family £20. Garden & Grounds only: Adult £4.20, Child £2.10. *includes a voluntary donation but visitors can choose to pay the standard prices displayed at the property and on the website.

ℹ️ Children's play area. 🖼️ Ⓣ ⓺ 🖨️ 🍴 Licensed. 🎫 For booked groups.
Ⓟ Limited for coaches. ⬛ By arrangement. 🐕 On leads, in car park only. ♿

ARBURY HALL 🏛️   *See page 343 for full page entry.*

BADDESLEY CLINTON ⚜   *See page 344 for full page entry.*

Sculpture at Ragley Hall

COMPTON VERNEY

COMPTON VERNEY, WARWICKSHIRE CV35 9HZ

www.comptonverney.org.uk

Tel: 01926 645500 **Fax:** 01926 645501 **E-mail:** info@comptonverney.org.uk
Owner: Compton Verney House Trust   **Contact:** Ticketing Desk

Set in a restored 18th century Robert Adam mansion, Compton Verney offers a unique art gallery experience. Surrounded by 120 acres of 'Capability' Brown landscape, the gallery houses a diverse permanent collection, complemented by changing exhibitions, events and workshops. Call for details.

Location: MAP 7:A9, OS Ref. SP312 529. 9m E of Stratford-upon-Avon, 10 mins from M40/J12, on B4086 between Wellesbourne and Kineton.

Open: 15 Mar–14 Dec: Tues–Sun & BH Mons, 10am–5pm. Last entry to Gallery 4.30pm. Groups welcome, please book in advance.

Admission: Adult £7, Child (5–16yrs) £2, Conc. £6, Student £4, Family £16. Groups (15+): Adult £6.30, Conc. £4.50, group rate with tour, Adult £12, Conc. £10.

ℹ️ No photography in the Gallery. 🖼️ Ⓣ ⓺ 🖨️ Licensed. 🍴 Licensed. Ⓟ Ample.
⬛ 🐕 Assistance dogs only. ♿

©NTPL/Robert Morris

COUGHTON COURT ❧
ALCESTER, WARWICKSHIRE B49 5JA
www.nationaltrust.org.uk

Tel: 01789 400777 **Fax:** 01789 765544 **Visitor Information:** 01789 762435
E-mail: coughtoncourt@nationaltrust.org.uk
Contact: The National Trust

Coughton Court is one of England's finest Tudor houses. Home of the Throckmorton family since 1409, the house boasts fine collections of furniture, porcelain and family portraits and a fascinating exhibition of the Gunpowder Plot of 1605, with which the house has strong connections.

The family has created and developed the spectacular gardens over the past 12 years (see below for garden highlights).

Location: MAP 6:O9, OS Ref. SP080 604, Located on A435, 2m N of Alcester, 8m NW of Stratford-upon-Avon, 18m from Birmingham City Centre.

Open: House: 15 Mar–29 Jun; Wed–Sun, 1 Jul–31 Aug; Tue–Sun, 3–28 Sept, Wed–Sun, 4 Oct–2 Nov; Sat & Sun, 11am–5pm. Open BH Mons & Tues. Admission by timed ticket on very busy days. Closed Good Friday & 14 Jun & 6 Sept. Garden, Shop and Restaurant: As house, 11am–5.30pm. Walled Garden: As house, 11.30am–4.45pm.

*Admission: House & Garden: Adult £9.20, Child (5–16) £4.60, Family £23, Groups (15+) £7.30. Gardens only: Adult £6.40, Child (5–16) £3.20, Family £16, Groups (15+) £5. Walled Garden: NT members £2.50 (included in admission price for non-members). *includes a voluntary donation but visitors can choose to pay the standard prices displayed at the property and on the website. Not included in group prices.

ⓘ Children's trail. No indoor photography. 🚻 Ⓣ Private dinners can be provided by prior arrangement in restaurant. ♿ Ground floor of house, gardens & restaurant. WC. 🍴 Licensed. Capacity: 70 inside, Covered Courtyard 50. Ⓚ By arrangement. 🐕

COUGHTON COURT GARDENS 🏛
ALCESTER, WARWICKSHIRE B49 5JA
www.coughtoncourt.co.uk

Garden Tours: 01789 762542 **Fax:** 01789 764369
E-mail: office@throckmortons.co.uk
Contact: Throckmorton family

The beautiful 25 acres of grounds include a walled garden, lake, riverside walk, knot garden, colour-themed gardens, daffodils and fruit collections. The rose labyrinth boasts spectacular displays of roses and received an **"Award of Garden Excellence" from the World Federation of Rose Societies – a first for the UK.** Plants for sale are grown by the Family.

Location / Open / Admission: see above.

🚻 ♿ 🐕

©Coughton Court

©Coughton Court

FARNBOROUGH HALL 🌿
BANBURY, OXFORDSHIRE OX17 1DU

www.nationaltrust.org.uk

Tel: 01295 690002 (information line)

Owner: The National Trust

A classical stone house of the mid-18th century, the home of the Holbech family for 300 years. Collections include antiquities collected on the Grand Tour, whilst the interior plasterwork is some of the finest in the country. Superb Grade I listed grounds remain largely unchanged and include terraced walk with fine views, ornamented with temples.

Location: MAP 7:A9, OS151, SP430 490. 6m N of Banbury, ½ m W of A423.

Open: House, Garden & Terrace Walk: 2 Apr–27 Sept: Weds & Sats, 2–5.30pm. 4/5 May: Sun & Mon, 2–5.30pm. Last admission 5pm.

Admission: House, Garden & Terrace Walk: Adult £4.75, Child £2.40, Family £12. 🚹 House & grounds, but steep terrace walk. 🅿 🐕 In grounds, on leads.

THE HILLER GARDEN

Dunnington Heath Farm, Alcester, Warwickshire B49 5PD

Tel: 01789 491342 **Fax:** 01789 490439

Owner: A H Hiller & Son Ltd   **Contact:** Mr Jeff Soulsby

2 acre garden of unusual herbaceous plants and over 200 rose varieties.

Location: MAP 6:O9, OS Ref. SP066 539. 1½ m S of Ragley Hall on B4088 (formerly A435).

Open: All year: daily 9am–5pm.

Admission: Free.

The Stables at Stoneleigh Abbey

Honington Hall

HONINGTON HALL 🏛
SHIPSTON-ON-STOUR, WARWICKSHIRE CV36 5AA

Tel: 01608 661434 **Fax:** 01608 663717

Owner/Contact: Benjamin Wiggin Esq

This fine Caroline manor house was built in the early 1680s for Henry Parker in mellow brickwork, stone quoins and window dressings. Modified in 1751 when an octagonal saloon was inserted. The interior was also lavishly restored around this time and contains exceptional mid-Georgian plasterwork. Set in 15 acres of grounds.

Location: MAP 6:P9, OS Ref. SP261 427. 10m S of Stratford-upon-Avon. 1½ m N of Shipston-on-Stour. Take A3400 towards Stratford, then signed right to Honington.

Open: By appointment for groups (10+).

Admission: Telephone for details.

🚹 Obligatory. 🐕

KENILWORTH CASTLE
KENILWORTH, WARWICKSHIRE CV8 1NE

www.english-heritage.org.uk/kenilworth

Tel: 01926 864152

Owner: English Heritage   **Contact:** Visitor Operations Team

Kenilworth is the largest castle ruin in England, the former stronghold of great Lords and Kings. Its massive walls of warm red stone tower over the peaceful Warwickshire landscape. The Earl of Leicester entertained Queen Elizabeth I with 'Princely Pleasures' during her 19 day visit. He built a new wing for the Queen to lodge in and organised all manner of lavish and costly festivities. The Great Hall, where Gloriana dined with her courtiers, still stands and John of Gaunt's Hall is second only in width and grandeur to Westminster Hall. Climb to the top of the tower beside the hall and you will be rewarded by fine views over the rolling wooded countryside. The stunning Elizabethan Gatehouse has reopened with restored interiors and brand new exhibitions that chart the Castle's turbulent 900 year history and tell the story of a very royal romance.

Location: MAP 6:P8, OS140, SP278 723. In Kenilworth, off A452, W end of town.

Open: 21 Mar–31 Oct: daily, 10am–5pm (6pm Jun–Aug). 1 Nov–29 Feb '09, daily, 10am–4pm. Closed 24–26 Dec & 1 Jan. Gatehouse may close early on Saturdays for private events. Tearoom: Apr–Oct.

Admission: Adult £6.20, Child £3.10, Conc. £5, Family £15.50. 15% discount for groups (11+). EH Members Free.

ℹ WC. ▣ ⊤ ⛐ ⛟ ⛗ 🅿 ⛝ ⛞ ⛨ ❉ ♨

LORD LEYCESTER HOSPITAL
HIGH STREET, WARWICK CV34 4BH

www.lordleycester.com

Tel/Fax: 01926 491422

Owner: The Governors   **Contact:** The Master

This magnificent range of 14th century half-timbered buildings was adapted into almshouses by Robert Dudley, Earl of Leycester, in 1571. The Hospital still provides homes for ex-servicemen and their wives. The Guildhall, Great Hall, Chapel, Brethren's Kitchen and galleried Courtyard are still in everyday use. The Queen's Own Hussars regimental museum is here. The historic Master's Garden was featured in BBC TV's *Gardener's World*, and the hospital buildings in many productions including *"Dr Who"* and David Dimbleby's *"How We Built Britain"*.

Location: OS Ref. 280 648. 1m N of M40/J15 on the A429 in town centre.

Open: All year: Tue–Sun & BHs (except Good Fri & 25 Dec), 10am–5pm (4pm in winter). Garden: Apr–Sept: 10am–4.30pm.

Admission: Adult £4.90, Child £3.90, Conc. £4.40. Garden only £2. 5% discount for adult groups (20+).

▣ ⛊ ⊤ ⛐ Partial. ⛝ ⛱ ⛞ By arrangement. 🅿 Limited. ▣ ⛟ Guide dogs only. ❉

MIDDLETON HALL

Middleton, Tamworth, Staffordshire B78 2AE

Tel: 01827 283095   **Fax:** 01827 285717   **E-mail:** middletonhall@btconnect.com

Owner: Middleton Hall Trust   **Contact:** Carol Sullivan

Hall (1285–1824). Former home of Hugh Willoughby (Tudor explorer), Francis Willughby and John Ray (17th century naturalists).

Location: MAP 6:P6, OS Ref. SP193 982. A4091, S of Tamworth.

Open: Easter–25 Sept: Suns, 2–5pm, BH Mons, 11am–5pm.

Admission: Adult £2.50, OAP £1.50. BHs & Special Events: Adult £5, Child £1, OAP £3.50.

For **special events** held throughout the year, see the index at the end of the book.

HAGLEY HALL 🏛

www.hagleyhall.org

This elegant Palladian house, completed in 1760, contains some of the finest examples of Italian plasterwork. Hagley's rich rococo decoration is a remarkable tribute to the artistic achievement of great 18th century architects and designers. Hagley Hall was designed by Sanderson Miller and built for George, the First Lord Lyttelton, who was private secretary to The Prince of Wales in 1732, was made Lord of the Treasury in 1744 and Cofferer to the Royal Household in 1754. George was raised to the peerage in 1756 when he was created Baron of Frankley. The house is set in a 350-acre landscaped park and is the much loved, privately owned home of the 12th Viscount Cobham.

■ **Owner**
Viscount Cobham

■ **Contact**
Mrs Joyce Purnell
Hagley Hall
Hagley
Worcestershire
DY9 9LG

Tel: 01562 882408
Fax: 01562 882632
E-mail: joycepurnell@
hagleyhall.org

■ **Location**
MAP 6:N7
OS Ref. SO920 807

Easily accessible from all areas of the country. ¼m S of A456 at Hagley.

Close to the M42, M40, M6 and only 5m from M5/J3/J4.

Birmingham City Centre 12m.

Rail: Railway Station and the NEC 25 mins.

Air: Birmingham International Airport 25 mins.

■ **Opening Times**
House
7 January–29 February, daily, excluding Saturdays, 24–28 March, 26–30 May, 25–29 August, 2–5pm, guided tours.

Please telephone prior to visit to ensure the house is open.

Tearoom open during House Opening

■ **Admission**
Adult	£5.00
Child (5–14 yrs)	£2.00
Conc.	£2.50

ℹ Available on an exclusive basis for conferences, presentations, lunches, dinners, product launches, concerts, small wedding receptions, country sporting days, team-building activities, off-road driving and filming. Please tel for details.

🍸

♿ Visitors may alight at the entrance. No WC.

☕

🚶 Obligatory. Please book parties in advance, guided tour of house time: 1hr. Colour guidebook.

🅿 Unlimited for coaches and cars.

🎦 By arrangement.

🐕 Guide dogs only.

🔔

Conference/Function

ROOM	SIZE	MAX CAPACITY
Gallery	85' x 17'	120
Crimson Rm	23' x 31'	40
The Saloon	34' x 27'	70
Westcote	31' x 20'	60

BACK TO BACKS

55–63 HURST STREET, BIRMINGHAM B5 4TE

www.nationaltrust.org.uk

Tel: 0121 666 7671 (Booking line open Tues–Fri, 10am–4pm)
E-mail: backtobacks@nationaltrust.org.uk
Owner: The National Trust   **Contact:** House & Visitor Services Manager

Take an exciting step back into Birmingham's industrial past by visiting the last remaining courtyard of Back to Back houses in Birmingham. Visitors are taken back in time to the start of the 1840s when Court 15 was both a home and workplace for its many inhabitants. Four houses have been restored to reflect the different time periods and lives of the people who lived there. Experience the sights, sounds and smells of the 1930s sweetshop and see what life was like for George Saunders, a tailor from St Kitts, who came to live and work in Birmingham in the 1950s.

Location: MAP 6:O7, OS Ref. SP071 861. In the centre of Birmingham next to the Hippodrome Theatre, within easy walking distance of bus and railway stations.
Open: 2 Feb–23 Dec, Tues–Sun, 10am–5pm. Admission is by timed ticket and guided tour only. Advance booking strongly advised. Open BH Mons, closed following Tues. Please note: During term time property will normally be closed for use by school groups on Tues, Weds & Thurs mornings 10am–1pm. Closed 1–7 September.
*Admission: Adult £5.40, Child £2.70, Family £13.50. *includes a voluntary donation but visitors can choose to pay the standard prices displayed at the property and on the website.

▢ ⓘ Obligatory. ▧ ▨ ▦ ▩

THE BIRMINGHAM BOTANICAL GARDENS AND GLASSHOUSES

WESTBOURNE ROAD, EDGBASTON, BIRMINGHAM B15 3TR

www.birminghambotanicalgardens.org.uk

Tel: 0121 454 1860 **Fax:** 0121 454 7835
E-mail: admin@birminghambotanicalgardens.org.uk
Owner: Birmingham Botanical & Horticultural Society   **Contact:** Mrs L Keen

Tropical, Mediterranean and Arid Glasshouses contain a wide range of exotic and economic flora. 15 acres of beautiful gardens with the finest collection of plants in the Midlands. Home of the National Bonsai Collection. Children's adventure playground, aviaries, gallery and sculpture trail. An independent educational charity.

Location: MAP 7:N7, OS Ref. SP048 855. 2m W of city centre. Follow signs to Edgbaston then brown tourist signs.
Open: Daily: 9am–Dusk (7pm latest except pre-booked groups). Suns opening time 10am. Closed Christmas Day.
Admission: Adult £7, Conc. £4.50, Family £21. Groups (10+): Adult £6, Conc. £4.

▢ ▧ ▭ ▨ ▣ P ▦ ▩ Guide dogs only. ▲ ✳ ▩

CASTLE BROMWICH HALL GARDENS

Chester Road, Castle Bromwich, Birmingham B36 9BT
Tel/Fax: 0121 749 4100   **E-mail:** admin@cbhgt.org.uk
Owner: Castle Bromwich Hall & Gardens Trust   **Contact:** Sue Brain

A unique example of 17th and 18th century formal garden design within a 10 acre walled area, comprising historic plants, vegetables, herbs and fruit, with a 19th century holly maze.
Location: MAP 7:O7, OS Ref. SP142 898. Off B4114, 4m E of Birmingham city centre, 1m from M6/J5 (exit northbound only). Southbound M6/J6 and follow A38 & A452.
Open: 1 Apr–30 Sept: Tue–Thurs, 11am–4 30pm, Café & Shop 1.30–4.15pm. Sats, Suns & BH Mon 1.30–5.30pm, Café & Shop close 5.15pm. Fris 11am–3.30pm, Café & Shop closed. 1 Oct–31 Mar 2008: Tue–Fri, 11.30am–3.30pm, Café & Shop closed.
Admission: Summer: Adult £3.50, Child 50p, Concs. £3. Guided tours normally available. Winter: Adults £3, Child 50p. Includes printed tour guide.

COVENTRY CATHEDRAL

1 Hill Top, Coventry CV1 5AB
Tel: 024 7652 1200   **Fax:** 024 7652 1220
E-mail: information@coventrycathedral.org.uk
Owner: Dean & Canons of Coventry Cathedral   **Contact:** The Visits Secretary

The remains of the medieval Cathedral, bombed in 1940, stand beside the new Cathedral by Basil Spence, consecrated in 1962. Modern works of art include a huge tapestry by Graham Sutherland, a stained glass window by John Piper and a bronze sculpture by Epstein. 'Reconciliation' statue by Josefina de Vasconcellos.
Location: MAP 7:P7, OS Ref. SP336 790. City centre.
Open: Cathedral: All year: 9am–5pm. Groups must book in advance.
Admission: Free – donations welcomed.

HAGLEY HALL

See page 355 for full page entry.

KINVER EDGE AND THE ROCKHOUSES

Comer Road, Kinver, Nr Stourbridge, Staffordshire DY7 6HU
Tel: 01384 872553
Owner: The National Trust   **Contact:** The Custodian
The famous Holy Austin rockhouses, which were inhabited until the 1950s, have now been restored and are open to visitors at selected times.
Location: MAP 7:A8, OS Ref. SO836 836. 4m W of Stourbridge, 4m N of Kidderminster, 1½m W of A449.
Open: Kinver Edge: all year, daily. House grounds: 1 Feb–28 Feb 09; daily 10am–4pm. Open BH Mons. Upper Terrace & Rockhouses: 1 Mar–30 Nov, Sat & Sun, 2–4pm. Lower Rockhouses open for guided tours at other times (Mar–Nov) by prior arrangement with the Custodian.
Admission: Adult £2, Child £1, Family £5.

Properties that **open all year** appear in the special index at the end of the book.

WIGHTWICK MANOR

WIGHTWICK BANK, WOLVERHAMPTON, WEST MIDLANDS WV6 8EE

Tel: 01902 761400   **Fax:** 01902 764663
Owner: The National Trust   **Contact:** The Property Manager
Begun in 1887, the house is a notable example of the influence of William Morris, with many original Morris wallpapers and fabrics. Also of interest are pre-Raphaelite pictures, Kempe glass and De Morgan ware. The 17 acre Victorian/Edwardian garden designed by Thomas Mawson has formal beds, pergola, yew hedges, topiary and terraces, woodland and two pools.
Location: MAP 6:N6, OS Ref. SO869 985. 3m W of Wolverhampton, up Wightwick Bank (A454), beside the Mermaid Inn.
Open: 1 Mar–20 Dec: Wed–Sat, 11am–5pm (last entry 4.30pm). Admission by timed ticket. (Taster Tour: 11am–12.30pm, access limited.) Guided groups through ground floor, freeflow upstairs (min. tour time approx. 1 hr). Also open BH Suns & Mons and Suns in Aug, 11am–5pm (last entry 4.30pm) – ground floor only, no guided tours. Booked groups Tues. Garden: Wed–Sat, 11am–6pm; BH Suns & Mons & Suns in Aug, 11am–6pm.
***Admission:** Adult £7.90, Child £3.90. Garden only: £3.90, Child Free. *includes a voluntary donation but visitors can choose to pay the standard prices displayed at the property and on the website.
▢ ⅏ Ground floor & grounds. ☕ 🅿 400 yds. 🐕 In grounds, on leads.

SELLY MANOR

MAPLE ROAD, BOURNVILLE, WEST MIDLANDS B30 2AE

www.bvt.org.uk/sellymanor

Tel/Fax: 0121 472 0199   **E-mail:** sellymanor@bvt.org.uk
Owner: Bournville Village Trust   **Contact:** Gillian Ellis
A beautiful half-timbered manor house in the heart of the famous Bournville village. The house has been lived in since the 14th century and was rescued from demolition by George Cadbury. It houses furniture dating back several centuries and is surrounded by a delightful typical Tudor garden.
Location: MAP 6:O7, OS Ref. SP045 814. N side of Sycamore Road, just E of Linden Road (A4040). 4m SSW of City Centre.
Open: All year: Tue–Fri, 10am–5pm. Apr–Sept: Sats, Suns & BHs, 2–5pm. Closed Mons.
Admission: Adult £3.50, Child £1.50, Conc. £2, Family £9.
▢ ⅏ Partial. WC. 🎦 By arrangement. 🅿 Limited. ▣ 🐕 In grounds, on leads.
▲ ❄ ⌄

Birmingham Botanical Gardens

BROADWAY TOWER
BROADWAY, WORCESTERSHIRE WR12 7LB

www.broadwaytower.co.uk

Tel: 01386 852390 **Fax:** 01386 858038 **E-mail:** info@broadwaytower.co.uk
Owner: Broadway Tower Country Park Ltd **Contact:** Annette Gorton
Broadway Tower is a unique historic building on top of the Cotswold ridge, having been built by the 6th Earl of Coventry in the late 1790s. Its architecture, the fascinating views as well as its exhibitions on famous owners and occupants (including William Morris) make the Tower a "must" for all visitors to the Cotswolds. The Tower is surrounded by 35 acres of parkland, picnic/ BBQ facilities. A complete family day out.
Location: MAP 6:O10, OS Ref. SP115 362. ½m SW of the A44 Evesham to Oxford Rd. 1½m E of Broadway.
Open: 1 Apr–31 Oct: daily, 10.30am–5pm. Nov–Mar: Sats & Suns (weather permitting), 11am–3pm.
Admission: Adult £4, Child £2.50, Conc. £3.50. Family (2+2) £11. Group rate on request.

🖾 🖾 WC. 🖾 🍴 🅿 🖾 🖾 In grounds, on leads. 🖾

CROOME PARK 🌿
CROOME D'ABITOT, WORCESTERSHIRE WR8 9DW

www.nationaltrust.org.uk

Tel: 01905 371006 **Fax:** 01905 371090 **E-mail:** croomepark@nationaltrust.org.uk
Owner: The National Trust **Contact:** The Property Manager
Croome was 'Capability' Brown's first complete landscape, making his reputation and revolutionising garden design. Paths through the Pleasure Garden lead to the lake, river and meadows. The elegant park buildings are mostly by Robert Adam and James Wyatt. A 10 year restoration programme, completed in 2006, saw over 45,000 trees and shrubs replanted along with the restoring of statues and the dredging of the lake and river. Restoration of the park continues. A 1940s-style canteen is now open in a restored WWII building.
Location: MAP 6:N9, OS150, SO878 448. 3m E of Severn Stoke and 4m W of Pershore.
Open: Park & Church: 1–30 Mar, 3 Sept–26 Oct, Wed–Sun,10am–5.30pm; 31 Mar–31 Aug, daily, 10am–5.30pm; 1 Nov–21 Dec, Sat & Sun, 10am–4pm; 26 Dec–1 Jan 09, daily, 10am–4pm. Open BH Mons.
*Admission: Adult £4.80, Child (6–16) £2.40, Family £12. *includes a voluntary donation but visitors can choose to pay the standard prices displayed at the property and on the website.

🖾 🖾 🖾 🖾 🖾 🅿 🖾 🖾

 For **corporate hospitality** venues see our special index at the end of the book.

Witley Court

THE GREYFRIARS 🌿
WORCESTER WR1 2LZ

www.nationaltrust.org.uk

Tel: 01905 23571 **E-mail:** greyfriars@nationaltrust.org.uk
Owner: The National Trust **Contact:** The Custodian
Built about 1480 next to a Franciscan friary in the centre of medieval Worcester, this timber-framed house has 17th and late 18th century additions. It was rescued from demolition at the time of the Second World War and was carefully restored. The panelled rooms have noteworthy textiles and interesting furniture. An archway leads through to a delightful walled garden.
Location: MAP 6:N9, OS150, SO852 546. Friar Street, in centre of Worcester.
Open: 5 Mar–13 Dec: Wed–Sat (also Suns 2 Jul–31 Aug), 1–5pm. Open BH Mons.
*Admission: Adult £4.20, Child £2.10, Family £10.50. Booked Groups (8+) £3.10. *includes a voluntary donation but visitors can choose to pay the standard prices displayed at the property and on the website. This does not apply to group price.

🖾 🖾 🖾 Out of hours. 🖾 🖾

HANBURY HALL 🌿
DROITWICH, WORCESTERSHIRE WR9 7EA
www.nationaltrust.org.uk

Tel: 01527 821214 **Fax:** 01527 821251 **E-mail:** hanburyhall@nationaltrust.org.uk
Owner: The National Trust   **Contact:** The Property Manager
Completed in 1701, this homely William & Mary-style house is famed for its fine painted ceilings and staircase, and has other fascinating features including an orangery, ice house, pavilions and working mushroom house. The stunning 8 hectare (20 acre) garden, recreated in keeping with the period of the house, is surrounded by 160 hectares (395 acres) of parkland, with beautiful views over the surrounding countryside.
Location: MAP 6:N8, OS150, SO943 637. 4½m E of Droitwich, 4m SE M5/J5.

Open: 1–16 Mar: Sat & Sun; 17 Mar–29 Oct: Sat–Wed, 11am–5.30pm (House 1–5pm). Park/Tearoom/Shop only: 1 Nov–31 Jan, Sat & Sun, 11am–5.30pm. 26 Dec–1 Jan '09, daily, 11am–5.30pm. Garden, Tearoom & Shop: daily, Jul–Aug. (Tearoom & shop close at 5pm.)
*Admission: House & Garden: Adult £7.20, Child £3.60, Family £18. Garden & Park only: Adult £4.80, Child £2.40, Family £12. Park only (Nov–Dec): Adult £3, Child £1.50, Family £7.50. *includes a voluntary donation but visitors can choose to pay the standard prices displayed at the property and on the website.
▢ 🏵 🎫 ⬆ Partial. WC. 🐕 🍴 For pre-booked groups. 🅿 🚻 Guide dogs only. ▲ ▣

HARTLEBURY CASTLE
HARTLEBURY, Nr KIDDERMINSTER DY11 7XZ

Tel: 01299 250416 **Fax:** 01299 251890 **E-mail:** museum@worcestershire.gov.uk
Owner: The Church Commissioners   **Contact:** The County Museum
Hartlebury Castle has been home to the Bishops of Worcester for over a thousand years. The principal State Rooms – the medieval Great Hall and the Saloon – contain period furniture, fine plasterwork and episcopal portraits. In the Castle's North Wing the Worcestershire County Museum brings the county's past to life through a wide variety of exhibitions and a regular events programme.
Location: MAP 6:N8, OS Ref. SO389 710. N side of B4193, 2m E of Stourport, 4m S of Kidderminster.
Open: 1 Feb–23 Dec: Tue–Fri, 10am–5pm. Sat, Sun & BHs, 11am–5pm. Closed Mons (except BHs) & Good Friday.
Admission: Adults £4, Conc. £2, Family (2+2) £10. Children under 5yrs Free.
▢ 🎫 ⬆ 🐕 🍴 For pre-booked groups. 🅿 🚻 🚻 Guide dogs only. ▣

©NTPL/David Norton

Croome Park

HARVINGTON HALL 🏛
HARVINGTON, KIDDERMINSTER, WORCESTERSHIRE DY10 4LR
www.harvingtonhall.com

Tel: 01562 777846   **Fax:** 01562 777190
E-mail: harvingtonhall@btconnect.com
Owner: Roman Catholic Archdiocese of Birmingham   **Contact:** The Hall Manager
Harvington Hall is a moated, medieval and Elizabethan manor house. Many of the rooms still have their original Elizabethan wall paintings and the Hall contains the finest series of priest hides in the country. A full programme of events throughout the year including outdoor plays, craft fairs, living history weekends and a pilgrimage is available.

Location: MAP 6:N8, OS Ref. SO877 745. On minor road, ½ m NE of A450/A448 crossroads at Mustow Green. 3m SE of Kidderminster.
Open: Mar & Oct: Sats & Suns; Apr–Sept: Wed–Sun & BH Mons (closed Good Fri), 11.30am–5pm. Open throughout the year for pre-booked groups and schools. Occasionally the Hall may be closed for a private function.
Admission: Adult £5, Child £3.50, OAP £4.30, Family £14.50. Garden: £1.50.
◻ ▦ ▦ ▦ Partial. ▦ ▦ ▦ **P** Limited for coaches. ▦ ▦ Guide dogs only. ▦ ▦

HAWFORD DOVECOTE 🌿

Hawford, Worcestershire
Tel: 01527 821214   www.nationaltrust.org.uk
Owner: The National Trust   **Contact:** Property Manager
A 16th century half-timbered dovecote.
Location: MAP 6:N9, OS Ref. SO846 607. 3m N of Worcester, ½m E of A449.
Open: 1 Apr–31 Oct: daily, 9am–6pm or sunset if earlier. Other times by prior appointment.
Admission: £1.

LEIGH COURT BARN ⌗

Worcester
Tel: 01926 852078   www.english-heritage.org.uk/leighcourt
Owner: English Heritage   **Contact:** Visitor Operations Administrative Assistant
Magnificent 14th century timber-framed barn built for the monks of Pershore Abbey. It is the largest of its kind in Britain.
Location: MAP 6:M9, OS150 Ref. SO783 535. 5m W of Worcester on unclassified road off A4103.
Open: 21 Mar–30 Sept: Thur–Sun & BH Mons, 10am–5pm.
Admission: Free.
▦

Temple, Croome Park

LITTLE MALVERN COURT 🏛

Nr Malvern, Worcestershire WR14 4JN
Tel: 01684 892988   **Fax:** 01684 893057
Owner: Trustees of the late T M Berington   **Contact:** Mrs T M Berington
Prior's Hall, associated rooms and cells, c1480, of former Benedictine Monastery. Formerly attached to, and forming part of the Little Malvern Priory Church which may also be visited. It has an oak-framed roof, 5-bay double-collared roof, with two tiers of cusped windbraces. Library. Collections of religious vestments, embroideries and paintings. Gardens: 10 acres of former monastic grounds with spring bulbs, blossom, old fashioned roses and shrubs. Access to Hall only by flight of steps.
Location: MAP 6:M9, OS Ref. SO769 403. 3m S of Great Malvern on Upton-on-Severn Road (A4104).
Open: 16 Apr–17 Jul: Weds & Thurs, 2.15–5pm. 24 Mar & 5 May for NGS: 2–5pm. Last admission 4.30pm.
Admission: House & Garden: Adult £5.50, Child £2, Garden only: Adult £4.50, Child £1. Groups must book, max 35.
▦ Garden (partial). ▦ ▦

MADRESFIELD COURT

Madresfield, Malvern WR13 5AU
Tel: 01905 830680   **E-mail:** madrescourt@clara.co.uk
Owner: The Trustees of Madresfield Estate   **Contact:** Mrs Jane Facer
Elizabethan and Victorian house with medieval origins. Fine contents. Extensive gardens and arboretum.
Location: MAP 6:M9, OS Ref. SO809 474. 6m SW of Worcester. 1½ m SE of A449. 2m NE of Malvern.
Open: Guided tours: 9 Apr–31 Jul: mostly Wed & Thur, also Sats 19 Apr, 17 May, 21 Jun & 12 Jul: 10.45am & 2.30pm. Numbers are restricted and prior booking, by telephone to Mrs Jane Facer, is strongly recommended to avoid disappointment.
Admission: £9.
▦ Obligatory. ▦

ROSEDENE

Dodford, Worcestershire B61 9BU
Tel: 01527 821214 **www.nationaltrust.org.uk**
Owner: The National Trust **Contact:** Property Manager
Mid 19th century Chartist cottage with organic vegetable garden and orchard.
Location: MAP 6:N8, OS Ref. SO393 273. 3½ m NW of Bromsgrove off A448.
Open: 6 Apr–28 Sept, Sun only by pre-booked guide tour (telephone to book).
Admission: Adult £4, Child £2.

THE TUDOR HOUSE MUSEUM

16 Church Street, Upton-on-Severn, Worcestershire WR8 0HT
Tel: 01684 592447
Owner: Mrs Lavender Beard **Contact:** Mrs Wilkinson
Upton past and present, exhibits of local history.
Location: MAP 6:N10, OS Ref. SO852 406. Centre of Upton-on-Severn, 7m SE of Malvern by B4211.
Open: Apr–Oct: daily 2–5pm, inc BH. Winter: Suns only, 2–4pm. Groups by arrangement (out of hours if requested).
Admission: Adult £1, Conc. 50p, Family £2.

SPETCHLEY PARK GARDENS
SPETCHLEY PARK, WORCESTER WR5 1RS

www.spetchleygardens.co.uk

Tel: 01453 810303 **Fax:** 01453 511915 **E-mail:** hb@spetchleygardens.co.uk
Owner: Spetchley Gardens Charitable Trust **Contact:** Mr R J Berkeley
This lovely 30 acre private garden contains a large collection of trees, shrubs and plants, many rare or unusual. A garden full of secrets, every corner reveals some new vista, some treasure of the plant world. The exuberant planting and the peaceful walks make this an oasis of beauty, peace and quiet. Deer Park close by.
Location: MAP 6:N9, OS Ref. SO895 540. 3m E of Worcester on A44. Leave M5/J6/J7.
Open: 21 Mar–30 Sept: Wed–Sun & BHs, 11am–6pm. Oct: Sats & Suns, 11am–4pm. (last admission 1hr before closing).
Admission: Adult £6, Child (under 16yrs) Free. Groups (25+): Adult £5.50. Adult Season Ticket £25.

 Some properties will be operating the Gift Aid on Entry scheme at their admission points. Where the scheme is operating, visitors are offered a choice between paying the standard admission price or paying the 'Gift Aid Admission' which includes a voluntary donation of at least 10%. Gift Aid Admissions enable the charity to reclaim tax on the whole amount paid* - an extra 28% - potentially a very significant boost to property funds. Money raised from paying visitors in this way will go towards restoration projects at the property and will be very welcome.
Where shown, the admission prices are inclusive of the 10% voluntary donation where properties are operating the Gift Aid on Entry scheme, but both the standard admission price and the Gift Aid Admission will be displayed at the property and on their website.

*Gift Aid donations must be supported by a valid Gift Aid declaration and a Gift Aid declaration can only cover donations made by an individual for him/herself or for him/herself and members of his/her family.

English Heritage Photo Library

WITLEY COURT & GARDENS
GREAT WITLEY, WORCESTER WR6 6JT

www.english-heritage.org.uk/witleycourt

Tel: 01299 896636
Owner: English Heritage **Contact:** Visitor Operations Team
The spectacular ruins of a once great house. An earlier Jacobean manor house, converted in the 19th century into an Italianate mansion, with porticoes by John Nash. The adjoining church, by James Gibbs, has a remarkable 18th century baroque interior. The gardens, William Nesfield's 'Monster Work' were equally elaborate and contained immense fountains, which survive today. The largest is the Perseus and Andromeda Fountain which has been restored and now fires daily from April – October, contact the site for details and timings. The landscaped grounds, parterres, fountains and woodlands have recently been restored to their former glory. The Woodland Walks in the North Park include various species of tree and shrub acquired from all over the world.
Location: MAP 6:M8, OS150, SO769 649. 10m NW of Worcester off A443.
Open: 21 Mar–31 Oct: daily, 10am–5pm (Jun–Aug 6pm). 1 Nov–29 Feb '09: Wed–Sun, 10am–4pm. Closed 24–26 Dec & 1 Jan.
Admission: Adult £5.50, Child £2.80, OAP £4.40, Family £13.80. 15% discount for groups (11+). EH Members Free.
ⓘ Visitor welcome point. Grounds. WC.

Beningbrough Hall
©NTPL

Yorkshire and the Humber

York contains reminders of its medieval origins but is as well known for its elegant Jacobean and Georgian architecture. Within easy reach are grand palaces such as Castle Howard and Harewood House, but there are also more modest gems to be seen such as Sion Hill Hall, and the gardens at RHS Harlow Carr are amongst the finest in Britain.

■ Owner
Nick Lane Fox

■ Contact
The Estate Office
Bramham Park
Wetherby
West Yorkshire
LS23 6ND

Tel: 01937 846000
Fax: 01937 846007
E-mail: enquiries@
bramhampark.co.uk

■ Location
MAP 11:A10
OS Ref. SE410 416

A1/M1 1m,
Wetherby 5m,
Leeds 7m,
Harrogate 12m,
York 14m.

Rail: Leeds or York.

Bus: 770; Bus stop ½m.

Air: Leeds/Bradford 15m.

■ Opening Times
House
For groups of 10+ by
appointment only
(separate fee).

Gardens
1 April–30 September:
daily, 11.30am–4.30pm.
Closed 2–8 June &
11–29 August.

■ Admission
Gardens only
Adult   £4.00
Child (under 16yrs) £2.00
Child (under 5yrs)   Free
OAP.   £2.00

■ Special Events
June 5–8
Bramham International
Horse Trials.

August 22–24
Leeds Festival.

BRAMHAM PARK 🏛

www.bramhampark.co.uk

Bramham Park is the stunning family home of the Lane Fox family, who are direct descendants of Robert Benson, the founder of Bramham over 300 years ago. The gardens extend to some 66 acres and, with the Pleasure Grounds, extend to over 100 acres.

The focus at Bramham has always been the landscape (the house was merely built as a 'villa' from which to admire it). Inspiration for the design of the Garden at Bramham was French and formal, but the manner in which it was adapted to the national landscape is relaxed and entirely English. It is completely original and few other parks of this period survive; none on the scale and complexity of Bramham. It

is a rare and outstanding example of the formal style of the late 17th century and early 18th century.

Bramham is a garden of walks and vistas, architectural features and reflecting water. A broad vista stretches away at an angle from the house and a number of other *allées* have focal points – temples and vistas. This creates an experience of anticipation when walking around the grounds.

The house, gardens and surrounding parkland make an ideal venue for events, private dinners, corporate entertaining, product launches and filming.

Conference/Function

ROOM	SIZE	MAX CAPACITY
Gallery	80' x 20'	110
Hall	30' x 30'	50
North Room	27' x 48'	100
East Room	20' x 18'	14
Old Kitchen	22' x 23'	50

🍸
♿ Grounds. WC.
🅿
🐕 Dogs on leads.
🎭

BRODSWORTH HALL & GARDENS ⊞

www.english-heritage.org.uk/brodsworth

This once opulent Victorian Hall offers a fascinating insight into the changing fortunes of a previously wealthy Victorian family, with many original fixtures and fittings still in place.

The 15 acres of garden, a rare survival from the Victorian Age, have been replanted to their 1860s heyday. Against a backdrop of enchanting features like the summerhouse, pleasure grounds, fernery, pet cemetery and fountain centre-piece, the pathways wind through carpets of spring snowdrops, the dazzling laburnum arch, rainbows of period summer bedding and the seasonal delight of winter evergreens, all revealing the fashions and desires of the Victorian country gentry.

■ Owner
English Heritage

■ Contact
Visitor Operations Team
Brodsworth Hall
Brodsworth
Nr Doncaster
Yorkshire DN5 7XJ

Tel: 01302 724969
(infoline)
Fax: 01302 337165

■ Location
MAP 11:B12
OS Ref. SE506 070

In Brodsworth, 5m NW of Doncaster off A635. Use A1(M)/J37.

Rail: Doncaster.

■ Opening Times
Summer

House
21 March–30 September
Tue–Sun & BHs,
1–5pm.

October, Sats & Suns,
12 noon–4pm.

Gardens & Tearoom
21 March–31 October
Daily, 10am–5.30pm.

Winter

Gardens, Tearoom, Shop & Servants' Wing
21 March–31 October,
daily 10am–5.30pm.

1 November–31 March
Sats & Suns, 10am–4pm.

Closed 24–26 December & 1 January.

Last admission ½ hr before closing.

■ Admission*
House & Gardens
Adult   £8.50
Child (5–15yrs)   £4.30
Child (under 5yrs) Free
Conc.   £6.80

Groups (11+) 15% discount.

EH members Free

*Free admission for tour leaders and coach drivers.

Gardens only
Adult   £5.00
Child (5–15yrs)   £2.20
Child (under 5yrs) Free
Conc.   £4.00

ℹ Exhibitions about the family, the servants and the gardens. WCs.

🛍

♿ Most of house is accessible. WCs.

☕ Seating for 70.

🚶 Groups must book. Booked coach parties: 10am–1pm.

🅿 220 cars and 3 coaches. Free.

🏛 Education Centre. Free if booked in advance.

❌ / ❄ Gardens, Tearoom and Servants' Wing only.

🎭

■ Owner

The Hon Simon Howard

■ Contact

Visitor Services
Castle Howard
York, North Yorks
YO60 7DA

Tel: 01653 648333
Fax: 01653 648529
E-mail: house@
castlehoward.co.uk

■ Location

MAP 11:C8
OS Ref. SE716 701

Approaching from S, A64 to
Malton, on entering Malton,
take Castle Howard road via
Coneysthorpe village.
Or from A64 following signs
to Castle Howard via the
Carrmire Gate
9' wide by 10' high.

York 15m (20 mins), A64.
From London: M1/J32,
M18 to A1(M) to A64,
York/Scarborough Road,
3½ hrs.

Train: London Kings Cross
to York 1hr. 50 mins. York
to Malton Station 30 mins.

Bus: Service and tour buses
from York Station.

■ Opening Times

Summer
House: 1 March–
2 November &
29 November–21 December
Daily, 11am–4pm
(last admission).

Gardens: All year, daily
from 10am (closed
Christmas Day).

Stable Courtyard:
(Gift Shops, Farm Shop,
Chocolate Shop,
Plant Centre, Café):
All year, daily, 10am–5pm,
free admission.

Access to Pretty Wood
Pyramid 1 July–31 August.
Special tours to newly
restored rooms in the house
are available by
arrangement.
For more information please
contact Castle Howard
Estate Office
on 01653 648444.

■ Admission

Summer
House & Garden

Adult	£10.50
Child (4–16yrs)	£6.50
Under 4yrs	Free
Conc.	£9.50

Garden only

Adult	£8.00
Child (4–16yrs)	£5.00
Under 4yrs	Free
Conc.	£7.50

**Winter (when the house
is closed) Gardens only**

Adult	£4.00
Child (4–16yrs)	£2.00
Under 4yrs	Free
Conc.	£3.50

Conference/Function

ROOM	SIZE	MAX CAPACITY
Long Gallery	197' x 24'	280
Grecian Hall	40' x 40'	160

CASTLE HOWARD 🏛

www.castlehoward.co.uk

In a dramatic setting between two lakes with extensive gardens and impressive fountains, this 18th century Palace was designed by Sir John Vanbrugh in 1699. Undoubtedly the finest private residence in Yorkshire, it was built for Charles Howard, 3rd Earl of Carlisle, whose descendants still live here.

With its painted and gilded dome reaching 80ft into the Yorkshire sky, this impressive house has collections of antique furniture, porcelain and sculpture, while its fabulous collection of paintings is dominated by the famous Holbein portraits of Henry VIII and the Duke of Norfolk.

Designed on a heroic scale covering 1,000 acres. The gardens include memorable sights such as the Temple of the Four Winds and the Mausoleum, the New River Bridge and the restored waterworks of the South Lake, Cascade, Waterfall and Prince of Wales Fountain. The walled garden has collections of old and modern roses.

Ray Wood, acknowledged by the Royal Botanic Collection, Kew, as a *"rare botanical jewel"* has a unique collection of rare trees, shrubs, rhododendrons, magnolias and azaleas.

ℹ Outdoor tours, events, concerts, theatre, exhibitions, adventure playground, plant centre, farm shop, chocolate shop, gift & book shops. Gift fairs, product launches, garden parties, firework displays, banqueting and other events. Suitable for helicopter landing. Used as a film location. No photography in the House unless prior permission is granted.

🛍

❄

☂ Booked private parties and receptions, min. 25.

♿ Transport equipped for wheelchairs. Wheelchair lift in House to main floor. WCs.

☕ Four cafeterias (Stable Courtyard Café open all year).

🍴

👤 Guides posted throughout House. Private tours and lectures by arrangement covering architecture, history, art, collections, House including tours of recently refurbished rooms.

🅿 400 cars, 20 coaches.

▥ 1:10 teacher/pupil ratio required. KS2&3 education pack. Special interest: architecture, art, history, wildlife, horticulture.

🐕
🔔
❄
🛡

■ **Owner**
Doncaster Council

■ **Contact**
Cusworth Hall,
Museum and Park
Cusworth Lane
Doncaster
South Yorkshire
DN5 7TU

Tel: 01302 782342
E-mail: museum@
doncaster.gov.uk

■ **Location**
**MAP 10:P12,
OS Ref. SE547 039.**

2 miles north of
Doncaster, off the A638
Doncaster to Wakefield
Road. Signposted from
A1(J37) and A638.

Rail/Bus: 3 miles from
the Doncaster Transport
Interchange in the centre
of town. Regular Bus
sevices run to The Mallard
or Kempton Park Road
(Buses 42, 211 and 212).

■ **Opening Times**
All year, Mon–Fri
10.30am–5pm, Sat &
Sun, 1–5pm. Tearooms
open daily 10am–4pm.

■ **Admission**
Admission is free to the
Hall and Park. There is a
pay and display car park.

CUSWORTH HALL, MUSEUM & PARK

www.doncaster.gov.uk/cusworthhall

An imposing Grade I Georgian country house and home to extensive social history collections, which illustrate the way people lived, worked and entertained themselves over the last 200 years. Built by local mason and architect George Platt in 1740, the Hall was later altered and extended by James Paine.

Recently the Hall, Museum and Park have undergone a comprehensive £7.5 million restoration with the help of a £5 million grant from the Heritage Lottery Fund. Stunning ceiling paintings in the Italianate chapel were revealed and restored, having been hidden under layers of paint for 50 years. In addition, entire sections of the Hall, previously in too poor a state of repair to use, have been given

a new lease of life with the Great Kitchen, Bake House, Still Room and Laundry open to the public for the first time, giving a glimpse of what life was like 'below stairs'.

The extensive landscaped grounds provide a stunning setting for walks as well as a breathtaking backdrop to the Hall. They have been returned to their former glory with the replanting of over 20,000 trees, shrubs and plants and the reinstatement of a complex lake system, 18th century boat house and cascade.

Cusworth Hall, Museum and Park also hosts an exciting year-round programme of family events and seasonal activities.

ℹ Group visits are welcome, with coach parking available in the car park, please notify us of an intended visit.

🛍 The shop offers a range of distinctive gifts, from jewellery and china to traditional children's toys and books on a range of topics.

☕ Home-baked cakes and pastries, as well as a range of snacks, daily specials and ice cream.

🅿

🏛 An Education Suite is available for school parties and study groups.

🚶 By prior arrangement only.

♿ Level access to the Hall and much of the Park. The Hall has a lift and disabled toilet.

🐕 Dogs on leads are welcome throughout grounds. Guide dogs only in Hall.

❄
🎭

■ Owner
The National Trust

■ Contact
The National Trust
Fountains Abbey
and Studley Royal
Ripon
North Yorkshire
HG4 3DY

Tel: 01765 608888
E-mail: info@
fountainsabbey.org.uk

■ Location
MAP 10:P8
OS Ref. SE275 700

Abbey entrance:
4m W of Ripon off
B6265. 8m W of A1.

Rail: Harrogate 12m.

Bus: Regular
season service
tel: 0870 608 2608
for details.

■ Opening Times
March–October
Daily: 10am–5pm.

November–February
Daily: 10am–4pm.

Closed 24/25 December,
& Fridays from Nov–Jan.

Deer Park: All year,
daily during daylight
(closed 24/25 December).

■ *Admission

Adult	£7.90
Child† (5–16yrs)	£4.20
Family	£20.90
Groups (15+)	
Adult	£6.85
Child† (5–16yrs)	£3.70
Groups (31+)	
Adult	£6.30
Child† (5–16yrs)	£3.15

Group discount
applicable only with
prior booking.

Group visits and
disabled visitors, please
telephone in advance,
01765 643197.

*includes a voluntary
donation but visitors can
choose to pay the
standard prices displayed
at the property and on
the website. Does not
apply to group prices.
*NT, EH Members &
Under 5s Free.

The Abbey is owned by
the National Trust and
maintained by English
Heritage. St Mary's
Church is owned by
English Heritage and
managed by the
National Trust.

©NTPL/Matthew Antrobus

FOUNTAINS ABBEY & STUDLEY ROYAL

www.fountainsabbey.org.uk

One of the most remarkable sites in Europe, sheltered in a secluded valley, Fountains Abbey and Studley Royal, a World Heritage Site, encompasses the spectacular remains of a 12th century Cistercian abbey with one of the finest surviving monastic watermills in Britain, an Elizabethan mansion, and one of the best surviving examples of a Georgian green water garden. Elegant ornamental lakes, avenues, temples and cascades provide a succession of unforgettable eye-catching vistas in an atmosphere of peace and tranquillity. St Mary's Church, built by William Burges in the 19th century, provides a dramatic focal point to the medieval deer park with over 500 deer. Exhibitions in Fountains Hall, Swanley Grange and the Mill.

i Events held throughout the year. Exhibitions. Seminar facilities. Outdoor concerts, meetings, activity days, walks.

Two shops.

Dinners.

Free Batricars & wheelchairs, please book, tel. 01765 643185. 3-wheel Batricars not permitted due to terrain. Tours for visually impaired, please book. WC.

Groups please book, discounted rates. Licensed.

Licensed.

Free, but seasonal. Groups (please book on 01765 643197), please use Visitor Centre entrance.

Drivers must book groups.

P In grounds, on leads.

Fountains Hall, an Elizabethan Mansion is an ideal setting for weddings. For details or a Wedding pack tel: 01765 643198.

HAREWOOD HOUSE

www.harewood.org

Harewood House is the magnificent Yorkshire home of the Queen's cousin, the Earl of Harewood. Nestling in 'Capability' Brown landscaped surrounds, Harewood is one of the great Treasure Houses of England and is renowned for its magnificent architecture and outstanding art collections. Designed by John Carr and completed in 1772, the House features exquisite interiors by Robert Adam, was furnished throughout by Thomas Chippendale, contains world-class art collections, including watercolours by J M W Turner, who stayed at Harewood under the patronage of Edward Lascelles; family portraits by Gainsborough and Sir Joshua Reynolds; and Renaissance masterpieces.

Steeped in history, Royal Family memorabilia recalls Lord Harewood's mother, HRH Princess Mary, the Princess Royal, who lived at Harewood from 1929 until her death in 1965. A permanent exhibition, '*Below stairs: Harewood's Hidden Collections*', includes many items from throughout Princess Mary's life, as well as giving public access to previously unseen corridors and rooms, providing a fascinating glimpse into the hidden world of the servants' domain.

Harewood's stunning gardens enfold lakeside and woodland walks, a Rock Garden, Walled Garden and the restored Parterre Terrace. The Lakeside Bird Garden contains around 100 species of threatened and exotic birds as well as popular favourites, penguins and flamingos.

Throughout the season Harewood plays host to many special events, including concerts, craft festivals and car rallies, and features a programme of exhibitions within the House.

■ **Owner**
The Earl of Harewood

■ **Contact**
Harewood House Trust
Harewood
Leeds
West Yorkshire
LS17 9LG

Tel: 0113 2181010
Fax: 0113 2181002
E-mail: info@
harewood.org

■ **Location**
MAP 10:P10
OS Ref. SE311 446

A1 N or S to Wetherby. A659 via Collingham, Harewood is on A61 between Harrogate and Leeds. Easily reached from A1, M1, M62 and M18. Half an hour from York, 15 mins from centre of Leeds or Harrogate.

Rail: Leeds Station 7m.

Bus: No. 36 from Leeds or Harrogate.

■ **Opening Times**
House
March–October:
Daily, 11am–4pm.

Grounds
March–October:
Daily, 10am–6pm.

Please call for specific opening times.

■ **Admission**
All attractions*
Adult	£11.30
Child/Student	£6.50
OAP	£10.00
Family	£37.70

Bird Garden, Grounds, & Adventure Playground
Adult	£8.80
Child/Student	£5.90
OAP	£7.95
Family	£32.25

Groups (15+): please telephone for details.

*Prices are for Mon–Fri. Prices on weekends & BH Mons are slightly higher.

Prices vary depending on time of year, please check before visiting.

i Marquees can be accommodated, concerts and product launches. No photography in the House.

🛍️
❄️
🍸 Ideal for corporate entertaining including drinks receptions, buffets and wedding receptions. Specific rooms available.

♿ Visitors may alight at entrance. Parking in allocated areas. Most facilities accessible. Wheelchair available at House and Bird Garden. WC. Special concessions apply to disabled groups. Some steep inclines.

☕ Licensed.

🍽️ Licensed.

P Cars 400 yds from house. 50+ coaches 500 yds from house. Drivers to verify in advance.

👤 Lectures by arrangement. Daily free talks.

🎧 Audio tour of house available.

🏛️ Sandford Award for Education.

🐕 Dogs on leads in grounds, guide dogs only in house.

🔔
🎭

Conference/Function
ROOM	MAX CAPACITY
State Dining Room	32
Gallery	96
Courtyard	120

■ Owner

Mr Richard Compton

■ Contact

The Administrator
Newby Hall
Ripon
North Yorkshire
HG4 5AE

Tel: 01423 322583
Information Hotline:
0845 450 4068
Fax: 01423 324452
E-mail:
info@newbyhall.com

■ Location

MAP 11:A8
OS Ref. SE348 675

Midway between London
and Edinburgh, 4m W of
A1, towards Ripon. S of
Skelton 2m NW of (A1)
Boroughbridge.
4m SE of Ripon.

Taxi: Ripon Taxi Rank
01765 601283.

Bus: On Ripon–York
route.

■ Opening Times

Summer

House*
21 March–28 September.
April, May, June &
September:
Tues–Sun & BH Mons,
July–August: Daily
12 noon–5pm.
Last admission 4.30pm.
*Areas of the House can
be closed to the public
from time to time, please
check website for details.

Garden
Dates as House,
11am–5.30pm.
Last admission 5pm.

Winter
October–end March
Closed.

■ Admission

House & Garden
Adult	£10.20
Child/Disabled	£7.80
OAP	£9.20
Group (15+)	
Adult/Conc	£8.50
Child/Disabled	£6.50
Family (2+2)	£33.00
Family (2+3)	£36.00

Garden only
Adult	£7.20
Child/Disabled	£5.80
OAP	£6.20
Group (15+)	
Adult	£6.50
Child (4–16yrs)	£5.20
Family (2+2)	£24.00
Family (2+3)	£29.00

Conference/Function

ROOM	SIZE	MAX CAPACITY
Grantham Room	90' x 20'	200

NEWBY HALL & GARDENS

www.newbyhall.com

The home of Richard and Lucinda Compton, Newby Hall is one of England's renowned Adam houses. In the 1760s William Weddell, an ancestor of the Comptons, acquired a magnificent collection of Ancient Roman sculpture and Gobelins tapestries. He commissioned Robert Adam to alter the original Wren designed house and Thomas Chippendale to make furniture. The result is a perfect example of the Georgian 'Age of Elegance' with the atmosphere and ambience of a family home.

Gardens

25 acres of stunning award-winning gardens contain rare and beautiful shrubs and plants, including the National collection of the Genus Cornus (Dogwoods). Newby's famous double herbaceous borders, framed by great bastions of yew hedges, make the perfect walkway to the River Ure. Formal gardens such as the Autumn and Rose Garden, the tranquillity of Sylvia's Garden and a tropical garden make Newby an inspiring and exciting place to explore. Walking through the curved pergolas leads to the Victorian rock garden, which is an enchanting magical space for all ages. The gardens feature an exciting children's adventure garden and miniature railway. From 1st June there is an annual exhibition of contemporary sculptures in the mature woodland.

i Suitable for filming and for special events, craft and country fairs, vehicle rallies etc, promotions and lectures. No indoor photography. Allow a full day for viewing house and gardens.

Wedding receptions & special functions.

6 wheelchairs available. Access to ground floor of house and key areas in gardens. WC.

Garden restaurant, teas, hot and cold meals. Booked groups in Grantham Room. Menus/rates on request.

P Ample. Hard standing for coaches.

Welcome. Rates on request. Grantham Room for use as wet weather base subject to availability. Woodland discovery walk, adventure gardens and train rides on 10¼" gauge railway.

Guide dogs only.

 Globe Theatre, 1–3 August.

RIPLEY CASTLE

www.ripleycastle.co.uk

Ripley Castle has been the home of the Ingilby family for twenty-six generations and Sir Thomas and Lady Ingilby, together with their five children, continue the tradition. The guided tours are amusing and informative, following the lives and loves of one family for over 670 years and how they have been affected by events in English history. The Old Tower dates from 1555 and houses splendid armour, books, panelling and a Priest's Secret Hiding Place, together with fine paintings, china, furnishings and chandeliers collected by the family over the centuries.

The extensive Victorian Walled Gardens have been transformed and are a colourful delight through every season. In the Spring you can appreciate 150,000 flowering bulbs which create a blaze of colour through the woodland walks, and also the National Hyacinth Collection whose scent is breathtaking. The restored Hot Houses have an extensive tropical plant collection, and in the Kitchen Gardens you can see an extensive collection of rare vegetables from the Henry Doubleday Research Association.

Ripley village on the Castle's doorstep is a model estate village with individual charming shops, an art gallery, delicatessen and Farmyard Museum.

Owner
Sir Thomas Ingilby Bt

Contact
Tours: Jenny Carter
Meetings/Dinners:
Jill Robinson
Ripley Castle
Ripley, Harrogate
North Yorkshire
HG3 3AY

Tel: 01423 770152
Fax: 01423 771745
E-mail: enquiries@ ripleycastle.co.uk

Location
MAP 10:P9
OS Ref. SE283 605

W edge of village. Just off A61, 3 ½ m N of Harrogate, 8m S of Ripon. M1 18m S, M62 20m S.
Rail: London–Leeds/York 2hrs. Leeds/York–Harrogate 30mins.
Taxi: Blueline taxis Harrogate (01423) 503037.

Opening Times
Castle
Easter–end October: Daily.
November & March:
Tues, Thurs, Sat & Sun.
10.30am–3pm.
December–February:
Sats & Suns.
10.30am–3pm.
Gardens
All year, daily (except Christmas Day), 10am–5pm (winter 4.30pm).

Admission
All Year
Castle & Gardens
Adult	£7.50
Child (5–16yrs)	£4.50
Child under 5yrs	Free
OAP	£6.50
Groups (25+)	
Adult	£6.50
Child (5–16yrs)	£4.00

Gardens only
Adult	£5.00
Child (5–16yrs)	£3.00
OAP	£4.50
Groups (25+)	
Adult	£5.00
Child (5–16yrs)	£2.50
Child under 5yrs	Free

Special Events
June 5–8
Grand Summer Sale.

June 17–Jul 13
"Twelfth Night".

July 19
Last Night of the Proms.

 No photography inside Castle unless by prior written consent. Parkland for outdoor activities & concerts. Murder mystery weekends.

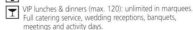 VIP lunches & dinners (max. 120): unlimited in marquees. Full catering service, wedding receptions, banquets, meetings and activity days.

 5/7 rooms accessible. Gardens accessible (not Tropical Collection). WCs. Parking 50 yds.

The Castle Tearooms (seats 54) in Castle courtyard. Licensed. Pub lunches or dinner at hotel (100 yds). Groups must book.

 Obligatory. Tour time 75 mins.

 290 cars – 300 yds from Castle entrance. Coach park 50 yds. Free.

Welcome by arrangement, between 10.30am–7.30pm.

Guide dogs only.

 Boar's Head Hotel (RAC***) 100 yds. Owned and managed by the estate.

Conference/Function

ROOM	SIZE	MAX CAPACITY
Morning Rm	27' x 22'	80
Large Drawing Rm	30' x 22'	80
Library	31' x 19'	70
Tower Rm	33' x 21'	70
Map Rm	19' x 14'	20
Dining Rm	23' x 19'	20
Long Gallery	19' x 6.5'	150
Amcotts Suite	10.2' x 6.6' 7.3' x 6'	120

■ Contact

Judith Parker
Skipton Castle
Skipton
North Yorkshire
BD23 1AW

Tel: 01756 792442
Fax: 01756 796100
E-mail: info@
skiptoncastle.co.uk

■ Location

MAP 10:O9
OS Ref. SD992 520

In the centre of
Skipton, at the N end
of High Street.

Skipton is 20m W of
Harrogate on the A59
and 26m NW of
Leeds on A65.

Rail: Regular services
from Leeds & Bradford.

■ Opening Times

All year
(closed 25 December)

Mon–Sat: 10am–6pm
Suns: 12 noon–6pm
(October–February 4pm).

■ Admission

Adult	£5.80
Child (0–4yrs)	Free
Child (5–17yrs)	£3.20
OAP	£5.20
Student (with ID)	£5.20
Family (2+3)	£17.90

Groups (15+)
Adult	£4.80
Child (0–17yrs)	£3.20

Includes illustrated tour
sheet in a choice of nine
languages, plus free
badge for children.

Groups welcome:
Guides available for
booked groups at no
extra charge.

SKIPTON CASTLE

www.skiptoncastle.co.uk

Guardian of the gateway to the Yorkshire Dales for over 900 years, this unique fortress is one of the most complete and well-preserved medieval castles in England. Standing on a 40-metre high crag, fully-roofed Skipton Castle was founded around 1090 by Robert de Romille, one of William the Conqueror's Barons, as a fortress in the dangerous northern reaches of the kingdom.

Owned by King Edward I and Edward II, from 1310 it became the stronghold of the Clifford Lords withstanding successive raids by marauding Scots. During the Civil War it was the last Royalist bastion in the North, yielding only after a three-year siege in 1645. 'Slighted' under the orders of Cromwell, the castle was skilfully restored by the redoubtable Lady Anne Clifford and today visitors can climb from the depths of the Dungeon to the top of the Watch Tower, and explore the Banqueting Hall, the Kitchens, the Bedchamber and even the Privy!

Every period has left its mark, from the Norman entrance and the

Medieval towers, to the beautiful Tudor courtyard with the great yew tree planted by Lady Anne in 1659. Here visitors can see the coat of arms of John Clifford, the infamous 'Bloody' Clifford of Shakespeare's Henry VI, who fought and died in the Wars of the Roses whereupon the castle was possessed by Richard III. Throughout the turbulent centuries of English history, the Clifford Lords fought at Bannockburn, at Agincourt and in the Wars of the Roses. The most famous of them all was George Clifford, 3rd Earl of Cumberland, Champion to Elizabeth I, Admiral against the Spanish Armada and conqueror of Puerto Rico in 1598.

In the castle grounds visitors can see the Tudor wing built as a royal wedding present for Lady Eleanor Brandon, niece of Henry VIII, the beautiful Shell Room decorated in the 1620s with shells and Jamaican coral and the ancient medieval chapel of St John the Evangelist. The Chapel Terrace, with its delightful picnic area, has fine views over the woods and Skipton's lively market town.

Unsuitable.

Tearoom. Indoor and outdoor picnic areas.

By arrangement.

Large public coach and car park off nearby High Street. Coach drivers' rest room at Castle.

Welcome. Guides available. Teachers free.

In grounds on leads.

372

ALDBOROUGH ROMAN SITE ⌗

Main Street, Aldborough, Boroughbridge, North Yorkshire YO51 9EP
Tel: 01423 322768
www.english-heritage.org.uk/aldborough
Owner: English Heritage   **Contact:** Visitor Operations Team
Aldborough succeeded Stanwick as the tribal capital of Britian's largest Roman tribe, the Brigantes. Parts of the town's defences, now lying in the peaceful surroundings of a Victorian arboretum, are clearly visible, along with two spectacular mosaic pavements, still in their original position.
Location: MAP 11:A8, OS Ref. SE405 662. Close to Boroughbridge off A1.
Open: 21 Mar–30 Sept: Sats & Suns & BHs, 11am–5pm.
Admission: Adult £3, Child £1.50, Conc. £2.40. 15% discount for groups (11+). EH members Free.
ℹ WC. ▢ ▣ ⬛

ASKE HALL ⛪

Richmond, North Yorkshire DL10 5HJ
Tel: 01748 822000   **Fax:** 01748 826611   **E-mail:** office@aske.co.uk
www.aske.co.uk
Owner: The Marquess of Zetland   **Contact:** The Secretary
A good, predominantly Georgian collection of paintings, furniture and porcelain in house which has been the seat of the Dundas family since 1763.
Location: MAP 10:P6, OS Ref. NZ179 035. 4m SW of A1 at Scotch Corner, 2m from the A66, on the B6274.
Open: 11/12 Sept (Heritage Open Days). Tours 10 & 11am & 12 noon, limited to 15 max. Booking advisable and ID will be required (passport, driving licence etc). For further details contact The Secretary.
Admission: Free.
🎫 Obligatory. 🅿 Limited. ⬛

BAGSHAW MUSEUM

Wilton Park, Batley, West Yorkshire WF17 0AS
Tel: 01924 326155   **Fax:** 01924 326164
Owner: Kirklees Culture & Leisure Services   **Contact:** Amanda Daley
A Victorian Gothic mansion set in Wilton Park.
Location: MAP10:P11, OS Ref. SE235 257. From M62/J27 follow A62 to Huddersfield. At Birstall, follow tourist signs.
Open: Closed for refurbishment, re-opening scheduled for Sept 2008.
Admission: Free.

BENINGBROUGH HALL & GARDENS ⛲

Beningbrough, North Yorkshire YO30 1DD
Tel: 01904 472027   **E-mail:** beningbrough@nationaltrust.org.uk
www.nationaltrust.org.uk
Owner: The National Trust   **Contact:** Visitor Services Manager
Imposing 18th century house with new interpretation galleries with the National Portrait Gallery.
Location: MAP 11:B9, OS Ref. SE516 586. 8m NW of York, 3m W of Shipton, 2m SE of Linton-on-Ouse, follow signposted route.
Open: House, Grounds, Shop & Restaurant: 1 Mar–30 Jun, 1 Sept–29 Oct: Sat–Wed, 11am–5.30pm. 1 Jul–31 Aug: daily except Thurs, 11am–5.30pm. Grounds, Shop & Restaurant: 2/3 & 23/24 Feb, 1 Nov–21 Dec: Sat & Sun, 11am–3.30pm. 9–17 Feb: daily except Thurs, 11am–3.30pm. Galleries: 2/3, 9–17 & 23–24 Feb, 1 Nov–21 Dec: times as grounds. Open Good Friday. Closed 27/28 Dec.
*Admission: Summer: Adult £8, Child £4, Family £18.50. Groups: £7, Child £3.50. Winter: Adult £5.30, Child £2.50, Family £11.60. *includes a voluntary donation but visitors can choose to pay the standard prices displayed at the property and on the website.
▢ ♿ ⬛ Lift to all floors. WC. 🍴 ▢ 🅿 Reduced rates for groups (15+), not Suns or BHs. ▣ ⬛ ⬛

BOLTON ABBEY

SKIPTON, NORTH YORKSHIRE BD23 6EX

www.boltonabbey.com

Tel: 01756 718009   **Fax:** 01756 710535   **E-mail:** tourism@boltonabbey.com
Owner: Chatsworth Settlement Trustees   **Contact:** Visitor Manager
Set in the heart of the Yorkshire Dales on the banks of the River Wharfe, this historic estate is the Yorkshire home of the Duke and Duchess of Devonshire and a magnet for visitors drawn to its breathtaking landscape and excellent facilities.
Explore the ruins of the Priory and discover a landscape full of history and legend. Wander along the woodland and riverside paths or cross the exposed heights of heather moorland. Enjoy local produce in the excellent restaurants, tea rooms and cafés. Indulge in a little retail therapy in the gift and food shops. Or simply relax and enjoy a picnic whilst the children play.

Location: MAP 10:O9, OS Ref. SE074 542. On B6160, N from the junction with A59 Skipton–Harrogate road, 23m from Leeds.
Open: All year from 9am.
Admission: £5.50 per vehicle or 50p per person for groups of 12 or more travelling in one vehicle.
▢ 🚻 ♿ ⬛ Licensed. 🍴 Licensed. 🎫 By arrangement. 🅿 ▣ ⬛ ⬛ Devonshire Arms Country House Hotel & Devonshire Fell Hotel nearby. ✳

BOLTON CASTLE 🏠
LEYBURN, NORTH YORKSHIRE DL8 4ET

www.boltoncastle.co.uk

Tel: 01969 623981 **Fax:** 01969 623332 **E-mail:** info@boltoncastle.co.uk
Owner: Lord Bolton **Contact:** Tom Orde-Powlett or Katie Gribble
Location: MAP 10:O7, OS Ref. SE034 918. Approx 6m W of Leyburn. 1m NW of Redmire.
A stunning mediaeval castle preserved in outstanding condition. Completed in 1399, its scars bear testament to over 600 years of history, including being besieged during the Civil War and Mary, Queen of Scots' imprisonment. There is a mediaeval garden, including herbs, roses, a vineyard and maze. The tearoom provides tea and cakes, as well as sandwiches and light lunches. Wedding ceremonies and receptions can be held here, as well as parties, corporate events and themed activity days for children.
Open: Mar–Oct daily, 10am–5pm. Please telephone for winter opening times.
Admission: Castle and Garden: Adults £6.50, Children £4.50, OAP £5. Family ticket £18. Garden only, £1.

🖼 ▼ Wedding receptions. ♿ Partial. ● 🅿 🖼 🖼 In grounds, on leads. 🔺 ❈

BRAMHAM PARK 🏠
See page 364 for full page entry.

BROCKFIELD HALL 🏠

Warthill, York YO19 5XJ
Tel: 01904 489362 **Fax:** 01904 488982 **E-mail:** simon@brockfieldhall.co.uk
www.brockfieldhall.co.uk
Owner: Mr & Mrs Simon Wood **Contact:** Simon Wood
A fine late Georgian house designed by Peter Atkinson, assistant to John Carr of York, for Benjamin Agar Esq. Begun in 1804, its outstanding feature is an oval entrance hall with a fine cantilevered stone staircase curving past an impressive Venetian window. It is the family home of Mr and Mrs Simon Wood. Mrs Wood is the daughter of the late Lord and of Lady Martin Fitzalan Howard. He was the brother of the 17th Duke of Norfolk and son of the late Baroness Beaumont of Carlton Towers, Selby. There are some interesting portraits of her old Roman Catholic family, the Stapletons, and some good English furniture. Permanent exhibition of paintings by Staithes Group Artists (by appointment outside August).
Location: MAP 11:C9, OS Ref. SE664 550. 5m E of York off A166 or A64.
Open: Aug: daily except Mons (open BH Mon), 1–4pm. Other times by appt.
Admission: Adult £5, Child £2.
ℹ No photography inside house. ♿ Partial. 🎭 By arrangement. 🅿
🖼 In grounds, on leads.

BRODSWORTH HALL ⌗
& GARDENS
See page 365 for full page entry.

For **accommodation** in Yorkshire, see our special index at the end of the book.

BRONTË PARSONAGE MUSEUM

Church St, Haworth, Keighley, West Yorkshire BD22 8DR
Tel: 01535 642323 **Fax:** 01535 647131 **E-mail:** bronte@bronte.org.uk
www.bronte.info
Owner: The Brontë Society **Contact:** The Administrator
Haworth Parsonage, with its moorland setting, was home and inspiration to the Brontës, the world's most famous literary family. This homely Georgian house still retains the atmosphere of the Brontës' time, along with displays of personal treasures. Come and experience the tragic, romantic and fascinating lives of this remarkable family.
Location: MAP 10:O10, OS Ref. SE029 373. 8m W of Bradford, 3m S of Keighley.
Open: Apr–Sept: 10am–5pm, Oct–Mar: 11am–4.30pm. Daily except 2–31 Jan & 24–27 Dec 2008.
Admission: Adult £5.50, Child (5–16yrs) £2.50, Conc. £4, Family £13. Discounts for booked groups.
🖼 ♿ Limited. 🖼 🖼 Guide dogs only. ❈ 🌀

Skipton Castle Gatehouse

visit hudsons guide online

BROUGHTON HALL
SKIPTON, YORKSHIRE BD23 3AE

www.broughtonhall.co.uk

Tel: 01756 799608 **Fax:** 01756 700357 **E-mail:** tempest@broughtonhall.co.uk
Owner: The Tempest Family **Contact:** The Estate Office
Home of the Tempest family since 1097, the Grade I Hall built in 1597 has fine Gillow furniture and family portraits. Set within 3,000 acres with parkland, Italianate gardens and stunning conservatory, it is an ideal venue for enterprise and living. Close by is the award-winning Broughton Hall Business Park, formed from the historic Estate buildings, home to 45 companies.
Location: MAP 10:N9, OS Ref. SD943 507. On A59, 2m W of Skipton.
Open: Group tours by arrangement.
Admission: £8.

BURTON CONSTABLE HALL 🏛
BURTON CONSTABLE, SKIRLAUGH, EAST YORKSHIRE HU11 4LN

www.burtonconstable.com

Tel: 01964 562400 **Fax:** 01964 563229 **Email:** helendewson@btconnect.com
Owner: Burton Constable Foundation **Contact:** Mrs Helen Dewson
One of the most fascinating country houses surviving with its historic collections, Burton Constable is a large Elizabethan mansion surrounded by extensive parkland. The interiors of faded splendour are filled with fine furniture, paintings and sculpture, a library of 5,000 books and a remarkable 18th century 'Cabinet of Curiosities'.
Location: MAP 11:E10 OS Ref TA 193 369. Beverley 14m, Hull 10m. Signed from Skirlaugh.
Open: 22 Mar–26 Oct & 22 Nov–7 Dec, Sat–Thur, 1–5pm. Grounds & Tearoom as house, 12.30–5pm. Last admission 4pm.
Admission: Hall & Grounds, Adult £5.50, Child £2.50, OAP £5, Family £12.50 Groups (15–60) £4.50. Connoisseur Study Visits, prices on request. Grounds only Adult £1.50, Child 75p.
ℹ️ No photography in house. 📷 ♿ WC. 🍽 🅿 ■ 🛏 In grounds on leads. ♿

BURTON AGNES HALL & GARDENS 🏛
DRIFFIELD, EAST YORKSHIRE YO25 4NB

www.burtonagnes.com

Tel: 01262 490324 **Fax:** 01262 490513
Owner: Burton Agnes Hall Preservation Trust Ltd **Contact:** Mr Simon Cunliffe-Lister
A lovely Elizabethan Hall containing treasures collected by the family over four centuries, from the original carving and plasterwork to modern and Impressionist paintings. The Hall is surrounded by lawns and topiary yew. The award-winning gardens contain a maze, potager, jungle garden, campanula collection and colour gardens incorporating giant game boards. Children's corner.
Location: MAP 11:E9, OS Ref. TA103 633. Off A614 between Driffield and Bridlington.
Open: Gardens, shops & café: 9 Feb (snowdrops)–20 Mar, daily, 11am–4pm. Hall & Gardens: 21 Mar–31 Oct, daily 11am–5pm. Christmas opening: 14 Nov–21 Dec, daily, 11am–5pm.
Admission: Hall & Gardens: Adult £6, Child £3, OAP £5.50. Gardens only: Adult £3, Child £1.50, OAP £2.75. 10% reduction for groups of 30+.
📷 Farm Shop. 🚻 ♿ Ground floor & grounds. 🍽 Café. Ice-cream parlour. 🅵 🅿 ■
🛏 In grounds, on leads. ♿

BYLAND ABBEY ⌗
Coxwold, Thirsk, North Yorkshire YO61 4BD

Tel: 01347 868614 **E-mail:** customers@english-heritage.org.uk
www.english-heritage.org.uk/yorkshire
Owner: English Heritage **Contact:** Visitor Operations Team
This beautiful ruin was once one of the great northern monasteries, second only to Rievaulx and Fountains. Its design, a mixture of Romanesque and Gothic, proclaimed the arrival of a new architectural style, which Byland pioneered. The Abbey's splendid collection of medieval floor tiles is a testament to its earlier magnificence.
Location: MAP 11:B8, OS Ref. SE549 789. 2m S of A170 between Thirsk and Helmsley, NE of Coxwold village.
Open: 21 Mar–31 Jul & Sept: Wed–Sun (Aug: daily), 11am–6pm.
Admission: Adult £3.50, Child £1.80, Conc. £2.80. 15% discount for groups (11+).
ℹ️ WC. ♿ 🅿 Limited. ■ 🛏 On leads.

CANNON HALL MUSEUM, PARK & GARDENS
Cawthorne, Barnsley, South Yorkshire S75 4AT

Tel: 01226 790270 **Fax:** 01226 792117 **E-mail:** cannonhall@barnsley.gov.uk
www.barnsley.gov.uk
Owner: Barnsley Metropolitan Borough Council **Contact:** The Museum Manager
Set in 70 acres of historic parkland and gardens, Cannon Hall now contains collections of fine furniture, old master paintings, stunning glassware and colourful pottery, much of which is displayed in period settings. Plus 'Charge', the Regimental museum of the 13th/18th Royal Hussars (QMO). Events and education programme and an ideal setting for conferences and Civil wedding ceremonies.
Location: MAP 10:P12, OS Ref. SE272 084. 6m NW of Barnsley of A635. M1/J38.
Open: Nov, Dec & Mar: Sun, 12 noon–4pm; closed Jan & Feb. Apr–Oct: Wed–Fri, 10.30am–5pm; Sat & Sun, 12 noon–5pm. Last admission 4.15pm for 5pm. Mon–Fri during school holidays. Open all year for weddings, school visits and corporate hospitality.
Admission: Free except for some events. Charge for car parking.
📷 🚻 ♿ Partial. WC. 🍽 Weekends & school holidays. 🅿 ■ 🅵 Pre-booked.
🛏 In grounds, on leads. ⬆ ✱ ♿

CASTLE HOWARD

See page 366 for full page entry.

CAWTHORNE VICTORIA JUBILEE MUSEUM

Taylor Hill, Cawthorne, Barnsley, South Yorkshire S75 4HQ
Tel: 01226 790545 / 790246
Owner: Cawthorne Village   **Contact:** Mrs Mary Herbert
A quaint and eccentric collection in a half-timbered building. Museum has a ramp and toilet for disabled visitors. School visits welcome.
Location: MAP 10:P12, OS Ref. SE285 080. 4m W of Barnsley, just off the A635.
Open: Palm Sun–end Oct: Sats, Suns & BH Mons, 2–5pm. Groups by appointment throughout the year.
Admission: Adult 50p, Child 20p.

CLIFFE CASTLE

Keighley, West Yorkshire BD20 6LH
Tel: 01535 618231
Owner: City of Bradford Metropolitan District Council   **Contact:** Daru Rooke
Victorian manufacturer's house of 1878 with tall tower and garden. Now a museum.
Location: MAP 10:O10, OS Ref. SE057 422. ¾ m NW of Keighley off the A629.
Open: All year: Tues–Sat & BH Mons, 10am–5pm. Suns, 12 noon–5pm. Closed 25/26 Dec.
Admission: Free.

CLIFFORD'S TOWER

Tower Street, York YO1 9SA
Tel: 01904 646940   **E-mail:** customers@english-heritage.org.uk
www.english-heritage.org.uk/yorkshire
Owner: English Heritage   **Contact:** Visitor Operations Team
Visit this proud symbol of the might of our medieval kings – originally built by William the Conqueror to subdue the rebellious north, it was rebuilt by Henry III in the 13th century. Fantastic panoramic views of York and the surrounding countryside from the top of the tower, show why it played such a key role in the control of northern England.
Location: MAP 21, OS Ref. SE 605 515. York city centre.
Open: 21 Mar–30 Sept: daily, 10am–6pm; Oct: daily, 10am–5pm. 1 Nov–31 Mar 2009: daily, 10am–4pm. Closed 24–26 Dec & 1 Jan.
Admission: Adult £3, Child £1.50, Conc. £2.40. Family ticket £7.50. 15% discount available for groups (11+).
Unsuitable. **P** Charged.

CONISBROUGH CASTLE

Castle Hill, Conisbrough, South Yorkshire DN12 3BU
Tel: 01709 863329   **E-mail:** customers@english-heritage.org.uk
www.english-heritage.org.uk/yorkshire
Owner: English Heritage   **Contact:** The Administrator
The white, cylindrical keep of this 12th century castle is a spectacular structure. Built of magnesian limestone, it is the only example of its kind in England, and was one of the inspirations for Sir Walter Scott's "Ivanhoe". Managed by The Ivanhoe Trust.
Location: MAP 7:A1, OS Ref. SK515 989. 4½m SW of Doncaster.
Open: 21 Mar–30 Sept: daily, 10am–5pm (last admission 4.20pm). 1 Oct–31 Mar 2009: Thur–Mon, 10am–4pm (last admission 3.20pm). Closed 24–26 Dec & 1 Jan.
Admission: Adult £4, Child £2, Conc. £3, Family £10.
Limited access. **P**

 Some properties will be operating the Gift Aid on Entry scheme at their admission points. Where the scheme is operating, visitors are offered a choice between paying the standard admission price or paying the 'Gift Aid Admission' which includes a voluntary donation of at least 10%. Gift Aid Admissions enable the charity to reclaim tax on the whole amount paid* - an extra 28% - potentially a very significant boost to property funds. Money raised from paying visitors in this way will go towards restoration projects at the property and will be very welcome.
Where shown, the admission prices are inclusive of the 10% voluntary donation where properties are operating the Gift Aid on Entry scheme, but both the standard admission price and the Gift Aid Admission will be displayed at the property and on their website.

*Gift Aid donations must be supported by a valid Gift Aid declaration and a Gift Aid declaration can only cover donations made by an individual for him/herself or for him/herself and members of his/her family.

CONSTABLE BURTON HALL GARDENS

LEYBURN, NORTH YORKSHIRE DL8 5LJ

www.constableburtongardens.co.uk

Tel: 01677 450428   **Fax:** 01677 450622
Owner/Contact: M C A Wyvill Esq
A delightful terraced woodland garden of lilies, ferns, hardy shrubs, roses and wild flowers, attached to a beautiful Palladian house designed by John Carr (not open). Garden trails and herbaceous borders. Stream garden with large architectural plants and reflection ponds. Impressive spring display of daffodils and tulips.
Location: MAP 10:P7, OS Ref. SE164 913. 3m E of Leyburn off the A684.
Open: Garden only: 24 Mar–28 Sept: daily, 9am–6pm.
Admission: Adult £3, Child (5–16yrs) 50p, OAP £2.50.
Partial, WC. Group tours of house & gardens by arrangement. **P** Limited for coaches. In grounds, on leads.

CUSWORTH HALL, MUSEUM & PARK

See page 367 for full page entry.

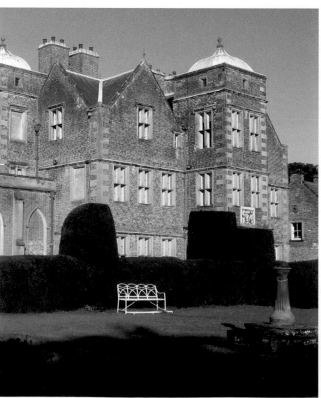

Kiplin Hall

Skyscan/William Cross

DUNCOMBE PARK 🏠
HELMSLEY, NORTH YORKSHIRE YO62 5EB

www.duncombepark.com

Tel: 01439 772625 **Fax:** 01439 771114 **E-mail:** liz@duncombepark.com
Owner/Contact: Lord & Lady Feversham

Lord and Lady Feversham's restored family home in the North York Moors National Park. Built on a virgin plateau overlooking Norman Castle and river valley, it is surrounded by 35 acres of beautiful 18th century landscaped gardens and 400 acres of parkland with national nature reserve and veteran trees.

Location: MAP 11:B7, OS Ref. SE604 830. Entrance just off Helmsley Market Square, signed off A170 Thirsk–Scarborough road.

Open: 23 Mar–26 Oct: Sun–Thur. House by guided tour only: 12.30, 1.30, 2.30 & 3.30pm. Gardens & Parkland Centre: 11am–5.30pm. Closed 11/12 & 16 Jun.

Admission: House & Gardens: Adult £7.25, Child (10–16yrs) £3.25, Conc. £5.50, Family (2+2) £15 Groups (15+): £5.25. Gardens & Parkland: Adult £4, Child (10–16yrs) £2, Conc £3.50. Groups (15+) £3. Parkland: Adult £2, Child (10–16yrs) £1. Season ticket: Adult £17.50, Family (2+2) £30.

ℹ️ Country walks, nature reserve, orienteering, conferences. 📷 🍴 Banqueting facilities. ♿ Partial. 🍴 Licensed. 👤 Obligatory. 🅿️ 🅿️ 🐕 In park on leads. ▲ 🛏️

EAST RIDDLESDEN HALL ✿
BRADFORD ROAD, KEIGHLEY, WEST YORKSHIRE BD20 5EL

www.nationaltrust.org.uk

Tel: 01535 607075 **E-mail:** eastriddlesden@nationaltrust.org.uk
Owner: The National Trust **Contact:** Visitor Services Manager

Homely 17th century merchant's house with beautiful embroideries and textiles, Yorkshire carved oak furniture and fine ceilings. Delightful garden with lavender and herbs. Also wild garden with old varieties of apple trees. Magnificent oak framed barn. Handling collection, children's play area. Costumed tours July and August. Events.

Location: MAP 10:O10, OS Ref. SE079 421. 1m NE of Keighley on S side of B6265 in Riddlesden. 50yds from Leeds/Liverpool Canal. Bus: Frequent services from Skipton, Bradford and Leeds. railway station at Keighley 2m.

Open: 15 Mar–2 Nov: Tue–Wed, Sat & Sun, Good Fri & BH Mons, plus Mons in Jul/Aug, 12 noon–5pm. Tearoom Suns from 11am.

Admission: Adult £5, Child £2.50, Family £11. Booked groups (15+): Adult £4.50, Child £2.25. £1 off when arriving by Keighley & District transport buses.

📷 🍴 ♿ Partial. 🍴 👤 By arrangement. 🅿️ 🅿️ Limited for coaches, please book. 🐕 In grounds, on leads. ▲ 🛏️

FAIRFAX HOUSE 🏠
FAIRFAX HOUSE, CASTLEGATE, YORK YO1 9RN
www.fairfaxhouse.co.uk

Tel: 01904 655543 **Fax:** 01904 652262 **E-mail:** peterbrown@fairfaxhouse.co.uk
Owner: York Civic Trust **Contact:** Mr Peter Brown

Fairfax House was acquired and fully restored by the York Civic Trust in 1983/84. The house, described as a classic architectural masterpiece of its age and certainly one of the finest townhouses in England, was saved from near collapse after considerable abuse and misuse this century, having been converted into a cinema and dance hall.

The richly decorated interior with its plasterwork, wood and wrought-iron, is now the home for a unique collection of Georgian furniture, clocks, paintings and porcelain. The Noel Terry Collection, gift of a former treasurer of the York Civic Trust, has been described by Christie's as one of the finest private collections formed in the 20th century. It enhances and complements the house and helps to create that

special 'lived-in' feeling, providing the basis for a series of set-piece period exhibitions which bring the house to life in a very tangible way.

Location: MAP 11:B9, OS Ref. SE605 515. In centre of York between Castle Museum and Jorvik Centre.

Open: 11 Feb–31 Dec, Mon–Thur: 11am –5pm. Fris: Guided tours only 11am and 2pm. Sats: 11am–5pm. Suns: 1.30–5pm. Last admission 4.30pm. Closed 1 Jan–10 Feb & 24–26 Dec.

Admission: Adult £5, Child Free with full paying adult, Conc. £4. Groups*: Adult £4, Child £1, Conc. £3.25 *Min payment 15 persons.

ℹ️ Suitable for filming. No photography in house. 📷 🍴 Max. 28 seated. Groups up to 50. ♿ Partial. 👤 🅿️ ✳️ 🛏️

FOUNTAINS ABBEY & STUDLEY ROYAL ❧

See page 368 for full page entry.

THE GEORGIAN THEATRE ROYAL

Victoria Road, Richmond, North Yorkshire DL10 4DW
Tel: 01748 823710   **Box Office:** 01748 825252
E-mail: admin@georgiantheatreroyal.co.uk
Owner: Georgian Theatre Royal Trust   **Contact:** Trish Hoines
The most complete Georgian playhouse in Britain. Built in 1788 by actor/manager, Samuel Butler and restored to its Georgian grandeur in 2003.
Location: MAP 10:P6, OS Ref. NZ174 013. 4m from the A1 (Scotch Corner) on the A6108.
Open: All year: Mon–Sat, 10am–7.30pm (5pm on non-performance nights, 4pm until curtain up on performance Suns). Guided tours: On the hour, 10am–4pm.
Admission: Donation £3.50. Child Free.

HAREWOOD HOUSE

See page 369 for full page entry.

HELMSLEY CASTLE ⌗
CASTLEGATE, HELMSLEY, NORTH YORKSHIRE YO62 5AB

www.english-heritage.org.uk/yorkshire

Tel: 01439 770442   **E-mail:** customers@english-heritage.org.uk
Owner: English Heritage   **Contact:** Visitor Operations Team
Originally a medieval castle, a Tudor mansion was added in the 1600s, before Cromwell's men blew up the great keep, slicing it in half. The changing fortunes of the castle over 900 years are explored in an audio tour and interactive displays, including original artefacts excavated from the site.
Location: MAP 11:B7, OS Ref. SE611 836. In Helmsley town.
Open: 21 Mar–31 Oct: daily, 10am–6pm (Oct 5pm). 1 Nov–28 Feb 2009: Thur–Mon, 10am–4pm. Closed 24–26 Dec & 1 Jan.
Admission: Adult £4, Child £2, Conc £3.20, Family £10. 15% discount for groups (11+).
ⅈ Tourist information located within Castle Visitor Centre. 🖨 ♿ 🔄 🅿 Charged.
🖼 🐕 Dogs welcome on leads. ✳ ✿

HELMSLEY WALLED GARDEN

Cleveland Way, Helmsley, North Yorkshire YO62 5AH
Tel/Fax: 01439 771427
Owner: Helmsley Walled Garden Ltd   **Contact:** Paul Radcliffe/Lindsay Tait
A 5 acre walled garden under restoration. Orchid house and vinery restored. Plant sales area and vegetarian café.
Location: MAP 11:B7, OS Ref. SE611 836. 25m N of York, 15m from Thirsk. In Helmsley follow signs to Cleveland Way.
Open: 1 Apr–31 Oct: daily, 10.30am–5pm. Nov–Mar: Sats/Suns, 12 noon–4pm.
Admission: Adult £4, Child Free, Conc. £3.

HOVINGHAM HALL
YORK, NORTH YORKSHIRE YO62 4LU

www.hovingham.co.uk

Tel: 01653 628771   **Fax:** 01653 628668   **E-mail:** office@hovingham.co.uk
Owner: William Worsley   **Contact:** Mrs Lamprey
This attractive Palladian family home, in its beautiful parkland setting, was designed and built by Thomas Worsley, Surveyor General to King George III. It is still lived in by his descendants and was the childhood home of Katharine Worsley, the Duchess of Kent. Hovingham Hall is unique in being entered through a huge riding school and features halls with vaulted ceilings and a beautiful collection of pictures and furniture. The house has attractive gardens with magnificent Yew hedges and the cricket ground in front of the house is reputed to be the oldest private cricket ground in England.
Location: MAP 11:C8, OS Ref. SE666 756. 18m N of York on Malton/Helmsley Road (B1257).
Open: 2 Jun–5 Jul, daily (closed Suns). 1.15–4.30pm (last tour 3.30pm).
Admission: Adult £6.50, Conc. £6, Child £3. Gardens only: £4.
ⅈ No photography in house. 🇹 ♿ Partial. 🍽 🎫 Obligatory. 🅿 Limited.
🦮 Guide dogs only.

JERVAULX ABBEY

Ripon, North Yorkshire HG4 4PH
Tel: 01677 460226 / 460391
Owner/Contact: Mr I S Burdon
Extensive ruins of a former Cistercian abbey.
Location: MAP 10:P7, OS Ref. SE169 858. Beside the A6108 Ripon–Leyburn road, 5m SE of Leyburn and 5m NW of Masham.
Open: Daily during daylight hours. Tearoom: Mar–1 Nov (all home baking, staff permitting).
Admission: Adult £2, Child £1.50 in honesty box at Abbey entrance.

York Gate Garden

KIPLIN HALL 🏛

KIPLIN, Nr SCORTON, RICHMOND, NORTH YORKSHIRE DL10 6AT

www.kiplinhall.co.uk   www.herriotdaysout.com

Tel/Fax: 01748 818178   **E-mail:** info@kiplinhall.co.uk

Owner: Kiplin Hall Trustees   **Contact:** The Administrator

A Grade I Listed Jacobean house built in 1620 by George Calvert, Secretary of State to James I, and founder of the State of Maryland, USA. Kiplin Hall is now furnished as a Victorian home with paintings and furniture collected over four centuries displayed in room settings. Visitors enjoy a uniquely relaxed tour of the Hall, freely wandering through the rooms and gardens which include topiary and rose gardens, woodland walk and lake. New exhibition for 2008: *'Images of Kiplin'*.

Location: MAP 11:A7, OS Ref. SE274 976. Signposted from Scorton–Northallerton road (B6271).

Open: Good Fri & Easter Sat, then Suns–Weds to 30 Sept, 2–5pm. Open at other times for group guided tours.

Admission: Adult £4.80, Child £2.80, Conc. £3.80. Family (2+3) £14. Groups (15–50) by arrangement.

🔲 🔲 Partial. 🔲 🔲 By arrangement. **P** 🔲 🔲 In grounds, on leads. Guide dogs only in house. 🔲 🔲

KIRKHAM PRIORY ⌗

Kirkham, Whitwell-on-the-Hill, North Yorkshire YO60 7JS

Tel: 01653 618768   **E-mail:** customers@english-heritage.org.uk

www.english-heritage.org.uk/yorkshire

Owner: English Heritage   **Contact:** Visitor Operations Team

The ruins of this Augustinian priory include a magnificent carved gatehouse, declaring to the world the Priory's association with the rich and powerful. However, the site also has more modern associations including a secret visit by the then Prime Minister Winston Churchill during the Second World War.

Location: MAP 11:C8, OS Ref. SE736 658. 5m SW of Malton on minor road off A64.

Open: 21 Mar–31 Jul & Sept: Thur–Mon, 10am–5pm. Aug: daily, 10am–5pm.

Admission: Adult £3, Child £1.50, Conc. £2.40. 15% discount for groups (11+).

ℹ️ WC. 🔲 🔲 **P** Limited. 🔲 🔲 On leads.

KNARESBOROUGH CASTLE & MUSEUM

Knaresborough, North Yorkshire HG5 8AS

Tel: 01423 556188   **Fax:** 01423 556130

Owner: Duchy of Lancaster   **Contact:** Diane Taylor

Ruins of 14th century castle standing high above the town. Local history museum housed in Tudor Courthouse. Gallery devoted to the Civil War.

Location: MAP 11:A9, OS Ref. SE349 569. 5m E of Harrogate, off A59.

Open: Good Friday–5 Oct: daily, 10.30am–5pm.

Admission: Adult £2.60, Child £1.50, OAP £1.60, Family £7.50, Groups (10+) £2.40

LEDSTON HALL

Hall Lane, Ledston, Castleford, West Yorkshire WF10 2BB

Tel: 01423 523423 Fax: 01423 521373   **E-mail:** james.hare@carterjonas.co.uk

Contact: James Hare

17th century mansion with some earlier work.

Location: MAP 11:A11, OS Ref. SE437 289. 2m N of Castleford, off A656.

Open: Exterior only: May–Aug: Mon–Fri, 9am–4pm. Other days by appointment.

Admission: Free.

LINDLEY MURRAY SUMMERHOUSE

The Mount School, Dalton Terrace, York YO24 4DD

Tel: 01904 667500   www.mountschoolyork.co.uk

Owner/Contact: The Mount School

Location: MAP 21, OS Ref. SE593 510. Dalton Terrace, York.

Open: By prior arrangement: Mon–Fri, 9am–4.30pm all the year (apart from BHs).

Admission: Free.

🔲 **P** 🔲 Guide dogs only. 🔲

LONGLEY OLD HALL

Longley, Huddersfield, West Yorkshire HD5 8LB

Tel: 01484 430852   **E-mail:** gallagher@longleyoldhall.co.uk

www.longleyoldhall.co.uk

Owner: Christine & Robin Gallagher   **Contact:** Christine Gallagher

This timber framed Grade II* manor house dates from the 14th century. It was owned by the Ramsden family, the former Lords of the Manors of Almondbury and Huddersfield, for over 400 years. It is included in Simon Jenkins' England's Thousand Best Houses.

Location: MAP 10:P11, OS Ref. SE154 150. 1½ m SE of Huddersfield towards Castle Hill, via Dog Kennel Bank.

Open: Easter and Summer BH weekends and 27–30 Dec for pre-booked guided tours. Group viewings by appointment (min 15, max 25 in winter and 50 in the summer; smaller groups by arrangement). Gardens open for Heritage Open Days 13/14 Sept.

Admission: £6 for open days, £10 for groups.

🔲 🔲 Unsuitable. 🔲 Obligatory. **P** Limited for coaches. 🔲 🔲

LOTHERTON HALL & GARDENS
ABERFORD, LEEDS, WEST YORKSHIRE LS25 3EB

www.leeds.gov.uk/lothertonhall

Tel: 0113 2813259   **E-mail:** lotherton@leeds.gov.uk

Owner: Leeds City Council   **Contact:** The Supervisor

Charming Edwardian country home rich in collections of paintings, furniture, silver, china, costume and oriental art. Beautiful formal, wildflower and wooded grounds, red deer park and one of the country's most impressive and important collections of rare and endangered birds.

Location: MAP 11:B10, OS92, SE450 360. 2½ m E of M1/J47 on B1217 the Towton Road.

Open: 1 Apr–31 Oct: Tue–Sat, 10am–5pm, Suns, 1–5pm. 1 Nov–31 Dec & Mar: Tue–Sat, 10am–4pm, Sun, 12 noon–4pm. Last adm. ¾ hr before closing. Closed Jan & Feb. Open BH Mons.

Admission: Adult £3, Child £1, Conc/Groups: £1.50. Car parking: £3.50 per day or £15 per year (including one year free admission to house for driver). Coach parking £20 per day.

🔲 🔲 🔲 **P** 🔲 🔲 🔲

For unique **Civil wedding** venues see our index at the end of the book.

MANSION HOUSE

ST HELEN'S SQUARE, YORK YO1 9QL

www.york.gov.uk/mansionhouse

Tel: 01904 552036 **Fax:** 01904 551052 **E-mail:** civicenquiries@york.gov.uk

Owner: City of York Council **Contact:** Richard Pollitt

The Mansion House is one of York's great historic treasures and the oldest surviving mayoral residence in the country. The beauiful simplicity of the hallway gives way to the magnificent grandeur of the stateroom. The extensive civic collection ranges from silver chamber pots to medieval ceremonial swords.

Location: MAP 21, SE601 518 situated in St Helen's Square, close to the post office and to York Minster.

Open: House tours: 11am & 2pm every Fri & Sat from Mar–Dec (no need to book in advance). Open all year for pre booked groups. For House, Silver & Connoisseur Tours, contact property for details.

Admission: House tours: Adult £5, Child (up to 16) Free, Conc £4. Pre-booked house tours 10% discount for groups 10+ (not Fri & Sat). *Silver Tour £7.95, *Connoisseur Tour £12.50. *Includes refreshments.

ⓘ No photography. 🔲 Ⓣ Ⓔ Ⓕ Obligatory. 🐕 Guide dogs only. ❄ ♿

MARKENFIELD HALL 🏛

Nr Ripon, North Yorkshire HG4 3AD

Tel: 01765 692303 **Fax:** 01765 607195

E-mail: info@markenfield.com **www.markenfield.com**

Owner: Lady Deirdre Curteis **Contact:** The Administrator

"This wonderfully little-altered building is the most complete surviving example of the meduim-sized 14th century country house in England" John Martin Robinson *The Architecture of Northern England.* Tucked privately away down a mile-long winding drive, Markenfield is one of the most astonishing and romantic of Yorkshire's medieval houses: fortified, completely moated, and still privately owned.

Location: MAP 10:P8, OS Ref. SE294 672. Access from W side of A61. 2½ miles S of the Ripon bypass.

Open: 4–17 May & 15–38 Jun: daily, 2–5pm. Groups all year round by appointment.

Admission: Adult £4, Conc £3. Booked groups (min charge £80).

Ⓣ Ⓕ Ⓟ 🅰 ♿

MIDDLEHAM CASTLE ♯

Castle Hill, Middleham, Leyburn, North Yorkshire DL8 4QR

Tel: 01969 623899 **E-mail:** customers@english-heritage.org.uk

www.english-heritage.org.uk/yorkshire

Owner: English Heritage **Contact:** Visitor Operations Team

This was the childhood and favourite home of Richard III, where he learnt the military skills and the courtly manners appropriate for a future king. The massive keep, one of the largest in England, was both a defensive building and a self-contained residence for the Lords of Middleham.

Location: MAP 10:O7, OS Ref. SE128 876. At Middleham, 2m S of Leyburn on A6108.

Open: 21 Mar–30 Sept: daily, 10am–6pm. 1 Oct–31 Mar 2009: Sat–Wed, 10am–4pm. Closed 24–26 Dec & 1 Jan.

Admission: Adult £4, Child £2, Conc. £3.20. 15% discount for groups (11+).

ⓘ Exhibition. 🔲 Ⓔ Partial. 🐕 In grounds, on leads. ❄ ♿

MOUNT GRACE PRIORY ♯

Staddlebridge, Nr Northallerton, North Yorkshire DL6 3JG

Tel: 01609 883494 **E-mail:** customers@english-heritage.org.uk

www.english-heritage.org.uk/yorkshire

Owner: English Heritage **Contact:** Visitor Operations Team

This 3-in-1 site is enchanting: the monastery ruins are the best-preserved of any in Britain; the manor house is a rare building of the Commonwealth period; and the gardens, re-modelled in the Arts & Crafts style, are a haven for the famous 'Priory Stoats'.

Location: MAP11:A7, OS Ref. SE449 985. 12m N of Thirsk, 7m NE of Northallerton on A19.

Open: 21 Mar–30 Sept: Thur–Mon, 10am–6pm. 1 Oct–31 Mar 2009: Thur–Sun, 10am –4pm. Closed 24–26 Dec & 1 Jan.

Admission: Adult £4, Child £2, Conc. £3.20, Family £10. 15% discount for groups (11+). NT Members Free, (except on event days).

ⓘ WCs. 🔲 Ⓔ Ⓟ 🅿 🐕 ❄ ♿

NATIONAL CENTRE FOR EARLY MUSIC

St Margaret's Church, Walmgate, York YO1 9TL

Tel: 01904 632220 **Fax:** 01904 612631 **E-mail:** info@ncem.co.uk **www.ncem.co.uk**

Owner: York Early Music Foundation **Contact:** Mrs G Baldwin

The National Centre for Early Music is based in the medieval church of St Margaret's York. The church boasts a 12th century Romanesque doorway and a 17th century brick tower of considerable note. The Centre hosts concerts, music education activities, conferences, recordings and events.

Location: MAP 21, OS Ref. SE609 515. Inside Walmgate Bar, within the city walls, on the E side of the city.

Open: Mon–Fri, 10am–4pm. Also by appointment. Access is necessarily restricted when events are taking place.

Admission: Free, donations welcome.

Ⓔ Ⓕ By arrangement. 🅿 Limited. No coaches. 🐕 Guide dogs only. 🔲 ❄ ♿

NEWBURGH PRIORY

COXWOLD, NORTH YORKSHIRE YO61 4AS

Tel: 01347 868435

Owner/Contact: Sir George Wombwell Bt

Originally 1145 with major alterations in 1568 and 1720, it has been the home of the Earls of Fauconberg and of the Wombwell family since 1538. Tomb of Oliver Cromwell (3rd daughter Mary married Viscount Fauconberg) is in the house. Extensive grounds contain a water garden, walled garden, topiary yews and woodland walks.

Location: MAP 11:B8, OS Ref. SE541 764. 4m E of A19, 18m N of York, ½ m E of Coxwold.

Open: 2 Apr–29 Jun: Wed & Sun & May BHs. House: 2.30–4.45pm. Garden: 2–6pm. Tours every ½ hour, take approximately 50–60mins. Booked groups by arrangement.

Admission: House & Grounds: Adult £5.50. Child £1.50. Gardens only: Adult £3, Child Free. Special tours of Private Apartment in addition to the above (Wed & Sun 9–23 Apr) £5pp.

ⓘ No photography in house. Ⓔ Partial. 🔲 Ⓕ Obligatory. 🅿 Limited for coaches. 🐕 In grounds, on leads. 🅰

NEWBY HALL & GARDENS 🏛 *See page 370 for full page entry.*

NORTON CONYERS

Nr RIPON, NORTH YORKSHIRE HG4 5EQ

Tel/Fax: 01765 640333 **E-mail:** norton.conyers@bronco.co.uk

Owner: Sir James and Lady Graham **Contact:** Lady Graham

Visited by Charlotte Brontë in 1839, Norton Conyers is an original of 'Thornfield Hall' in 'Jane Eyre', and a family legend was an inspiration for the mad Mrs Rochester. House and garden have a friendly, quiet and unspoilt atmosphere. They have been in the Grahams' possession for 384 years. Family pictures, furniture, costumes and ceramics on display. 18th century walled garden near house, with Orangery and herbaceous borders. Small plants sales area specialising in unusual hardy plants. Pick your own fruit in season.

Location: MAP 11:A8, OS Ref. SF319 763. 4m N of Ripon. 3½ m from the A1.

Open: House: Closed for repairs during first part of 2008, due to re-open mid-Jul; please call for details. Garden: 4/5 & 25/26 May; 8 Jun–11 Aug & 24/25 Aug: Sun & Mon; 2–5 Jul: daily. All 2–5pm; last admissions 4.40pm. Groups by appointment.

Admission: House: Adult £5.50, Child (under 16yrs) Free, OAP £4 (2007 prices). Garden: free, but donations are welcome. A charge is made when the garden is open for charity. National Gardens Scheme 8 Jun; Amnesty International 15 Jun.

ℹ No interior photography. No high-heeled shoes. 🖻 🖹 ♿ Partial. WC. ☻ Garden charity openings only. ⚡ By arrangement. 🅿 🖼 Dogs, other than guide dogs, are not allowed in the house and must be on a lead in the grounds. ▣

NOSTELL PRIORY & PARKLAND ✖

Doncaster Road, Wakefield, West Yorkshire WF4 1QE

Tel: 01924 863892 **E-mail:** nostellpriory@nationaltrust.org.uk

www.nationaltrust.org.uk

Owner: The National Trust **Contact:** Visitor Services Manager

Set in over 350 acres of parkland, Nostell Priory is one of Yorkshire's jewels. It is an architectural treasure by James Pane with later additions by Robert Adam, and an internationally renowned Chippendale Collection.

Location: MAP 11:A11, OS Ref. SE403 175. 6m SE of Wakefield, off A638.

Open: Parklands open daily, 9am–7pm. Priory: 15 Mar–2 Nov, Wed–Sun, 1–5pm, (last adm. 4.30pm). 6–14 Dec, daily, 12 noon–4pm. Open BH. Gardens Shop & Stables Tearoom: 1 Mar–2 Nov, Wed–Sun, 11am–5.30pm. 8–30 Nov, Sat & Sun, 11am–4.30pm. 6–14 Dec, daily, 11am–4.30pm.

*Admission: Parkland: Free. House & Garden: Adult £7.70, Child £3.85, Family (2+4) £18.50. Groups (15+) £6 (outside normal hours £12). Garden only: Adult £5, Child £2.50, Family Free. *Includes a voluntary donation but visitors can choose to pay the standard prices displayed at the property and on the website.

ℹ Baby facilities. 🖻 🖹 ♿ Partial. WC. ☻ ⚡ By arrangement. 🅿 🖼 🖼 In grounds, on leads. ▣ 🖩 Send SAE for details.

NUNNINGTON HALL ✖

Nunnington, North Yorkshire YO62 5UY

Tel: 01439 748283 **E-mail:** nunningtonhall@nationaltrust.org.uk

Owner: The National Trust **Contact:** The Property Manager

17th century manor house with magnificent oak-panelled hall, nursery, haunted room, and attics, with their fascinating Carlisle collection of miniature rooms fully furnished to reflect different periods.

Location: MAP 11:C8, OS Ref. SE670 795. In Ryedale, 4½ m SE of Helmsley, 1½ m N of B1257.

Open: Daily except Mons; 15 Mar–31 May & 1 Sep–2 Nov: 12 noon–5pm. 1 Jun–31 Aug: 12 noon–5.30pm. Tearoom & Garden 12 noon–5pm, House & shop 1–5pm, 1 June–31 Aug closes 5.30pm. Last adm. 30 min before closing. Open BH Mons.

*Admission: Adult £6, Child (under 17) £3, Family £15. Groups (15+) £5.20. National Trust Members Free. *includes a voluntary donation but visitors can choose to pay the standard prices displayed at the property and on the website.

🖻 ♿ Ground floor and grounds. WC. 🖼 🖼 Guide dogs only. ▣

ORMESBY HALL ✖

Ladgate Lane, Ormesby, Middlesbrough TS7 9AS

Tel: 01642 324188 **E-mail:** ormesbyhall@nationaltrust.org.uk

Owner: The National Trust **Contact:** Mr P Burton

A mid 18th century house with opulent decoration inside, including fine plasterwork by contemporary craftsmen.

Location: MAP 11:B6, OS Ref. NZ530 167. 3m SE of Middlesbrough.

Open: 15 Mar–2 Nov: daily, 1.30–5pm. Tearoom: as House.

*Admission: Adult £4.65, Child £3, Family £12.10. Groups (10+) £3.80pp, Child £2.50. Grounds Free. *includes a voluntary donation but visitors can choose to pay the standard prices displayed at the property and on the website.

🖻 ♿ Ground floor & grounds. WC. ☻

PARCEVALL HALL GARDENS

Skyreholme, Skipton, North Yorkshire BD23 6DE

Tel./Fax: 01756 720311 **E-mail:** info@parcevallhallgardens.co.uk

Owner: Walsingham College (Yorkshire Properties) Ltd.

Contact: Phillip Nelson (Head Gardener)

Location: MAP 10:O8, OS Ref. SE068 613. E side of Upper Wharfedale, 1½ m NE of Appletreewick. 12m NNW of Ilkley by B6160 and via Burnsall.

Open: 1 Apr–31 Oct: 10am–6pm.

Admission: Adult £5.50, Child £2.50.

PICKERING CASTLE ♯

Castlegate, Pickering, North Yorkshire YO18 7AX

Tel: 01751 474989 **E-mail:** customers@english-heritage.org.uk

www.english-heritage.org.uk/yorkshire

Owner: English Heritage **Contact:** Visitor Operations Team

An excellent example of a motte and bailey castle, built by William the Conqueror, with much of the original keep, towers and walls remaining, and offering superb views over North York Moors. It was used by a succession of medieval kings as a hunting lodge, holiday home and even stud farm.

Location: MAP 11:C7, OS Ref. SE998 845. In Pickering, 15m SW of Scarborough.

Open: 21 Mar–30 Sept: daily, 10am–6pm. Oct: Thur–Mon, 10am–4pm.

Admission: Adult £3.50, Child £1.80, Conc. £2.80, Family £8.80. 15% discount for groups (11+).

ℹ WCs. 🖻 ♿ Partial. 🅿 Limited. 🖼 🖼 In grounds, on leads. ▣

PLUMPTON ROCKS

Plumpton, Knaresborough, North Yorkshire HG5 8NA

Tel: 01289 386360 www.plumptonrocks.co.uk

Owner: Edward de Plumpton Hunter **Contact:** Robert de Plumpton Hunter

Grade II* listed garden extending to over 30 acres including an idyllic lake, dramatic millstone grit rock formation, romantic woodland walks winding through bluebells and rhododendrons. Declared by English Heritage to be of outstanding interest. Painted by Turner. Described by Queen Mary as 'Heaven on earth'.

Location: MAP 11:A9, OS Ref. SE355 535. Midway between Harrogate and Wetherby on the A661, 1m SE of A661 junction with the Harrogate southern bypass.

Open: Mar–Oct: Sat, Sun & BHs, 11am–6pm.

Admission: Adult £2, Child/OAP £1. (Subject to change 2008.)

♿ Unsuitable. 🅿 Limited for coaches. 🖼 🖼 In grounds, on leads.

Markenfield Hall

RHS GARDEN HARLOW CARR
CRAG LANE, HARROGATE, NORTH YORKSHIRE HG3 1QB

www.rhs.org.uk/harlowcarr

Tel: 01423 565418 **Fax:** 01423 530663 **E-mail:** harlowcarr@rhs.org.uk
Owner: Royal Horticultural Society **Contact:** Allison Mitchell / Alison Allan
One of Yorkshire's most relaxing yet inspiring gardens! Highlights of the beautiful garden include spectacular contemporary borders, Gardens Through Time, streamside garden, alpines, scented and kitchen gardens, woodland and wildflower meadow, extensive RHS Shop and Plant Centre, Betty's Café Tea Rooms and free parking. Events all year including children's activities.
Location: MAP 10:P9. OS Ref. SE285 543. 1½m W from town centre on B6162 Otley Road.
Open: Daily: 9.30am–6pm (4pm Nov–Feb). Last entry 1 hour before closing. Closed Christmas Day.
Admission: Adult £6.50, Child (6–16yrs) £2.20, Child (under 6yrs) Free. Groups (10+): £5.50. Groups must book in advance. RHS Members (+1 guest): Free.
🛈 Picnic area. 🔲 🔧 🔥 Partial. WC. 🔳 Licensed. 🍴 Licensed. 🎭 By arrangement. 🅿 🔳 🔳 Guide dogs only. 🔆 🔳

RICHMOND CASTLE ⌗
TOWER ST, RICHMOND, NORTH YORKSHIRE DL10 4QW

www.english-heritage.org.uk/yorkshire

Tel: 01748 822493 **E-mail:** customers@english-heritage.org.uk
Owner: English Heritage **Contact:** Visitor Operations Team
Built shortly after 1066 on a rocky promontory high above the River Swale, this is the best preserved castle of such scale and age in Britain. The magnificent keep, with breathtaking views, is reputed to be the place where the legendary King Arthur sleeps. An exhibition and contemporary garden reflect the castle's military history from the 11th to 20th century.
Location: MAP 10:P6, OS Ref. NZ172 007. In Richmond.
Open: 21 Mar–30 Sept: Thur–Mon, 10am–6pm. 1 Oct–31 Mar 2009: Thur–Mon, 10am–4pm. Closed 24–26 Dec & 1 Jan.
Admission: Adult £4, Child £2, Conc. £3.20 15% discount for groups (11+).
🛈 Interactive exhibition. WCs. 🔲 🔥 Partial. 🔳 🔳 In grounds, on leads. 🔆 🔳

RIEVAULX ABBEY ⌗
RIEVAULX, Nr HELMSLEY, NORTH YORKSHIRE YO62 5LB

www.english-heritage.org.uk/yorkshire

Tel: 01439 798228 **E-mail:** customers@english-heritage.org.uk
Owner: English Heritage **Contact:** Visitor Operations Team
Rievaulx was the first Cistercian Abbey to be founded in the North of England in the 12th century. Set in the Rye Valley, just a short drive from Helmsley, it is a place of beauty and calm. The atmospheric ruins were once home to the greatest spiritual writer of the Medieval Ages, St Aelred, who described it as *"everywhere peace, everywhere serenity, and a freedom from the tumult of the world"*.

A special exhibition, "The Work of God and Man", looks at the commercial activities of the monks and shows how religion blended with business.
Location: MAP 11:B7, OS Ref. SE577 850. 2¼m N of Helmsley on minor road off B1257.
Open: 21 Mar–30 Sept: daily, 10am–6pm). 1 Oct–31 Mar 2009: Thur–Mon, 10am–4pm (5pm Oct). Closed 24–26 Dec & 1 Jan.
Admission: Adult £5, Child £2.50, Conc. £4. 15% discount for groups (11+).
🛈 WCs. 🔲 🔧 🔥 Partial. 🔳 🔳 🅿 🔳 🔳 On leads. 🔆 🔳

RIEVAULX TERRACE & TEMPLES

Rievaulx, Helmsley, North Yorkshire YO62 5LJ
Tel: 01439 798340 (winter 01439 748283)
Owner: The National Trust **Contact:** The Property Manager
A ½m long grass-covered terrace and adjoining woodlands with vistas over Rievaulx Abbey and the Rye valley. There are two mid-18th century temples. Note: no access to the property Nov–end Mar.
Location: MAP 11:B7, OS Ref. SE579 848. 2½m NW of Helmsley on B1257. E of the Abbey.
Open: 15 Mar–30 Sept: daily, 11am–6pm, 1 Oct–2 Nov: 5pm. Last admission 1 hour before closing. Ionic Temple closed, 1–2pm.
*****Admission:** Adult £4.80, Child (under 17yrs) £2.60, Family (2+3) £12. Groups (15+): £4.15. NT Members Free. *includes a voluntary donation but visitors can choose to pay the standard prices displayed at the property and on the website.
⌂ ⌂ Grounds. Batricar available. ⌂ In grounds, on leads. ⌂

RIPLEY CASTLE

See page 371 for full page entry.

RIPON CATHEDRAL

Ripon, North Yorkshire HG4 1QR
Tel: 01765 604108 (information on tours etc.) **Contact:** Canon Keith Punshon
One of the oldest crypts in Europe (672). Marvellous choir stalls and misericords (500 years old). Almost every type of architecture. Treasury.
Location: MAP 10:P8, OS Ref. SE314 711. 5m W signposted off A1, 12m N of Harrogate.
Open: All year: 8am–6pm.
Admission: Donations: £3. Pre-booked guided tours available.

RIPON COURTHOUSE MUSEUM

Minster Road, Ripon HG4 1QS
Tel: 01765 690799 **E-mail:** info@riponmuseums.co.uk **www.riponmuseums.co.uk**
Owner: Ripon Museum Trust **Contact:** Penny Hartley (Museums Manager)
The Georgian Courthouse is virtually unchanged since opening in 1830. Stand in the dock and be sentenced, watch the AV presentation of cases heard in its opening session, explore the exhibition 'One Way to Botany Bay', illustrating the mass transportation of convicts to Australia. Featured in 'Heartbeat', as 'Ashfordley Magistrates Court'.
Location: MAP10:P8, OS Ref. SE314 711. Central Ripon, close to main coach/car park and bus station; beside the Cathedral and TIC.
Open: 21 Mar 26 Oct: daily, 1 4pm (school holidays 11am–4pm).
Admission: Adult £1.50 Child Free Conc £1, Family (1+4) £6/£5 (admission to the 3 Ripon Museums). Groups by arrangement.
⌂ ⌂ Partial. ⌂ By arrangement. ⌂ Ample for cars, limited for coaches. ⌂ ⌂ Guide dogs only.

RIPON PRISON & POLICE MUSEUM

St Marygate, Ripon HG4 1LX
Tel: 01765 690799 **E-mail:** info@riponmuseums.co.uk **www.riponmuseums.co.uk**
Owner: Ripon Museum Trust **Contact:** Penny Hartley (Museums Manager)
Sit in a prison cell, hear the door clang, imagine the harsh Victorian regime. Try on uniforms, turn the crank or work the treadmill. Trace policing history through the displays of uniforms and artefacts. Originally the Liberty Prison (1816–76), later the Police Station until 1956, this listed building remains little altered.
Location: MAP10:P8, OS Ref. SE314 711. Central Ripon, close to main coach/car park and bus station
Open: 21 Mar–26 Oct: daily, 1–4pm (school holidays 11am–4pm).
Admission: Adult £3.50, Child (7–15yrs) £1.50, Conc £3, Family (1+4) £6/£5 (admission to the 3 Ripon Museums). Groups by arrangement.
⌂ ⌂ By arrangement. ⌂ Ample for cars, limited for coaches. ⌂ ⌂ Guide dogs only.

RIPON WORKHOUSE MUSEUM

75 Allhallowgate, Ripon HG4 1LE
Tel: 01765 690799 **Email:** info@riponmuseums.co.uk **www.riponmuseums.co.uk**
Owner: Ripon Museum Trust **Contact:** Penny Hartley (Museums Manager)
Follow in the steps of the infirm, destitute and homeless, through the archway entrance to the Ripon Union Workhouse (1854). In the male vagrants' cell block, the grim atmosphere of Victorian treatment has been carefully recreated. Imagine being deloused in the ablution room, and eating gruel before being locked in at nightfall.
Location: MAP10:P8, OS Ref. SE314 711. Central Ripon, close to main coach/car park and bus station.
Open: 21 Mar–26 Oct: daily, 1–4pm (school holidays 11am–4pm).
Admission: Adult £2.50, Child (7–15yrs) £1, Conc £2, Family (1+4) £6/£5 (admission to the 3 Ripon Museums). Groups by arrangement.
⌂ ⌂ ⌂ By arrangement. ⌂ Ample for cars, limited for coaches. ⌂ ⌂ Guide dogs only.

ROCHE ABBEY

Maltby, Rotherham, South Yorkshire S66 8NW
Tel: 01709 812739 **E-mail:** customers@english-heritage.org.uk
www.english-heritage.org.uk/yorkshire
Owner: English Heritage **Contact:** Visitor Operations Team
Set in a beautiful, secluded valley landscaped by 'Capability' Brown in the 18th century, the early Gothic transepts of this 'miniature Fountains Abbey' still survive to their original height.
Location: MAP 7:B1, OS Ref. SK544 898. 1m S of Maltby off A634.
Open: 21 Mar–31 Jul & Sept: Thur–Sun, Aug daily, 11am–4pm.
Admission: Adult £3, Child £1.50, Conc. £2.40. 15% discount for groups (11+).
ⓘ WCs. ⌂ ⌂ Partial. ⌂ Limited. ⌂ ⌂ In grounds, on leads.

RYEDALE FOLK MUSEUM

Hutton le Hole, York, North Yorkshire YO62 6UA
Tel: 01751 417367 **E-mail:** info@ryedalefolkmuseum.co.uk
Owner: The Crosland Foundation
13 historic buildings showing the lives of ordinary folk from earliest times to the present day.
Location: MAP 11:C7, OS Ref. SE705 902. Follow signs from Hutton le Hole. 3m N of Kirkbymoorside.
Open: 20 Jan–18 Dec: 10am–5.30pm (last adm. 1 hour before dusk).
Admission: Adult £5, Child £3.50, Conc. £4.50. Family (2+2) £13.50. Season Ticket £30.

ST PETER'S CHURCH & BONES ALIVE! EXHIBITION

Beck Hill, Barton upon Humber DN18 5EX
Tel: 0870 333 1181 **E-mail:** customers@english-heritage.org.uk
www.english-heritage.org.uk/yorkshire
Owner: English Heritage **Contact:** Customer Services
With a history spanning a millennium, St Peter's is both an architectural and archaeological treasure. The thousand-year architecture includes a working Anglo-Saxon bell-tower and some surprising gargoyles. A major new exhibition opening May 2007 includes the UK's largest resource for historic bone analysis from excavations of 2800 burials dating back over 900 years. This reveals groundbreaking new insights into the diseases, diet, medicine and beliefs of our ancestors, and the forgotten objects that lay with the dead for centuries – clues to human dreams and beliefs.
Location: MAP 11:E11, OS Ref TA03 3219. In Barton upon Humber town centre.
Open: 21 Mar–30 Sept, Wed–Sun, 10am–5pm; Oct–31 Mar 2009, Sat–Mon, 10am–4pm. Closed 24-26 Dec & 1 Jan.
Admission: Adult £4, Child £2, Conc. £3.20.

Lady Georgiana's Bedroom, Castle Howard

SCAMPSTON HALL 🏛

Scampston, Malton, North Yorkshire YO17 8NG
www.scampston.co.uk
Tel: 01944 759111 **Fax:** 01944 758700 **E-mail:** info@scampston.co.uk
Owner: Sir Charles Legard Bt **Contact:** The Administrator

Scampston is among the best examples of the English country house, combining fine architecture with a wealth of art treasures and set in 18th century 'Capability' Brown parkland. The double award winning house was featured in 'Hidden Treasure Houses' on FIVE in 2006. Guided tours around this family home are often led by the owner. Restaurant, disabled facilities and shop in The Walled Garden (see separate entry).

Location: MAP 11:D8, OS Ref. SE865 755. 4m E of Malton, off A64.
Open: 23 May–22 Jun: daily (closed Mons except BHs), 1.30–5pm (last adm. 4pm).
Admission: House, Front Garden & Woodland Walk: Adult £6, Child (12–16yrs) £3, Child (11yrs & under) Free. Combined Ticket for House and Walled Garden: Adult £10, Child (12–16yrs) £6. Groups by appointment. HHA Members & Friends free admission to house only.

⚅ 🅿 ✖

THE WALLED GARDEN AT SCAMPSTON

SCAMPSTON HALL, MALTON, NORTH YORKSHIRE YO17 8NG

www.scampston.co.uk

Tel: 01944 759111 **Fax:** 01944 758700 **E-mail:** info@scampston.co.uk
Owner: Sir Charles Legard Bt **Contact:** The Administrator

A contemporary garden with striking perennial meadow planting, as well as traditional spring/autumn borders, created by internationally acclaimed designer and plantsman Piet Oudolf. Described in *The Times* as "a gem". The garden is complemented by an excellent restaurant. "It's bold and beautiful – a must if you are heading to Yorkshire" *Toparius*.

Location: MAP 11:D8, OS Ref. SE865 755. 4m E of Malton, off A64.
Open: 22 Mar–2 Nov: daily (closed Mons except BHs), 10am–5pm, last adm. 4.30pm.
Admission: Walled Garden: Adult £5, Child (12–16yrs) £3, Child (11yrs & under) Free, Senior £4.50. Front Garden & Woodland Walk £2.50 extra. Groups welcome by arrangement. See separate house listing for combined entry prices (23 May–22 Jun only).

⚅ T 🅂 ⚋ ⑪ 🅿 ✖

SCARBOROUGH CASTLE ⌗

CASTLE ROAD, SCARBOROUGH, NORTH YORKSHIRE YO11 1HY

www.english-heritage.org.uk/yorkshire

Tel: 01723 372451 **E-mail:** customers@english-heritage.org.uk
Owner: English Heritage **Contact:** Visitor Operations Team

This 12th century castle conceals over 2,500 years of history encompassing the Roman army, Saxon monks, Viking invaders, Civil War besiegers and even First World War German naval guns. With wonderful views over the East Coast and a new exhibition giving further insight into the Castle's fascinating history, including artefacts excavated from the site.

Location: MAP 11:E7, OS Ref. TA050 892. Castle Road, E of town centre.
Open: 21 Mar–30 Sept: daily, 10am–6pm. 1 Oct–31 Mar 2009: Thur–Mon, 10am–4pm (5pm Oct). Closed 24–26 Dec & 1 Jan.
Admission: Adult £4, Child £2, Conc. £3.20, Family £10. 15% discount for groups (11+).
ℹ WCs. 🅾 🅂 Partial. ⚋ 🅾 Inclusive. 🅿 ✖ In grounds, on leads. ⚅ 🆅

SHIBDEN HALL

Lister's Road, Halifax, West Yorkshire HX3 6XG
Tel: 01422 352246 **Fax:** 01422 348440 **Email:** shibden.hall@calderdale.gov.uk
www.calderdale.gov.uk
Owner: Calderdale MBC **Contact:** Valerie Stansfield

A half-timbered 15th century manor house, the home of Anne Lister, set in a newly restored historic landscaped park. Oak furniture, 17th century aisled barn containing carriages and a folk museum, make Shibden an intriguing place to visit.

Location: MAP 10:O11, OS Ref. SE106 257. 1½ m E of Halifax off A58.
Open: 1 Mar–30 Nov: Mon–Sat, 10am–5pm (last admission 4.30pm), Suns, 12 noon–5pm (last admission 4.30pm). Dec–Feb: Mon–Sat, 10am–4pm, Suns, 12 noon 4pm (last admission 3.30pm).
Admission: Adult £3.50, Child/Conc. £2.50, Family £10. Prices subject to change April 2008.

🅾 🅂 Ground floor & grounds. ⚋ ⚅ By arrangement. 🅿 🅿 ✖ In grounds on leads. ⚅

Newburgh Priory

SION HILL HALL 🏛

KIRBY WISKE, THIRSK, NORTH YORKSHIRE YO7 4EU

www.sionhillhall.co.uk

Tel: 01845 587206 **Fax:** 01845 587486 **E-mail:** sionhill@btconnect.com
Owner: H W Mawer Trust **Contact:** R M Mallaby
Sion Hill was designed in 1912 by the renowned York architect Walter H Brierley, 'the Lutyens of the North', receiving an award from the Royal Institute of British Architects as being of 'outstanding architectural merit'. The house is furnished with a fine collection of antique furniture, paintings ceramics and clocks.
Location: MAP 11:A7, OS Ref. SE373 844. 6m S of Northallerton off A167, signposted. 4m W of Thirsk, 6m E of A1 via A61.
Open: Jun–Sept: Weds only, 1–5pm, last entry 4pm. Also Easter Sun and BH Mons. Connoisseur tours at other times by arrangement (15 persons min.)
Admission: House: Adult £6, Child 12–16yrs, £3, Child under 12yrs £1, Conc. £5. Connoisseur Tours: £10. Grounds: £1.50.
♿ Partial. WC. 🎦 🅿

SLEDMERE HOUSE 🏛

SLEDMERE, DRIFFIELD, EAST YORKSHIRE YO25 3XG

www.sledmerehouse.com

Tel: 01377 236637 **Fax:** 01377 236560 **Email:** info@sledmerehouse.com
Owner: Sir Tatton Sykes Bt **Contact:** The House Secretary
Nestling high on the Yorkshire Wolds, Sledmere House is the home of Sir Tatton Sykes, 8th Baronet. Built in 1751 and enlarged by Sir Christopher Sykes, 2nd Baronet, in the 1780s. Sympathetically restored in the early 1900s after a serious fire. The house exudes 18th century elegance with each room containing decorative plasterwork by Joseph Rose Junior, and examples of work from the finest craftsmen of the period, including Chippendale, Hepplewhite and Sheraton. A tour of the house culminates in the magnificent Library which overlooks the 'Capability' Brown landscaped park. Award–winning Garden including Octagonal Walled Garden and Parterre, Wagoners' Military Museum, Children's Quiz, Picnic and Play Area, The Terrace Café and Gift Shop. Famous pipe organ played Wed & Sun, 1.30–3.30pm
Location: MAP 11:D9, OS Ref. SE931 648. Off the A166 between York & Bridlington. Scenic drive from York, Bridlington & Scarborough, 7 miles NW of Driffield.
Open: 21–24 Mar, 27 Apr–28 Sept, Tue–Fri & Sun, open BH Sats & Mons. House: 11am–3.30pm (last admission). Grounds, Shop & Café: 10am–5pm.
Admission: House & Gardens: Adult £6.50, Child £2.50, Conc. £6, Family £14 (2+2, 5–16) Groups (15+) £5. Gardens & Park: Adult £4, Child £1, RHS members £3.50 (Gardens & Grounds only).
ℹ No photography in house. 🖭 🚻 Licensed. 🎦 By arrangement: Garden Tour & Park, Estate & Outbuildings Tour. Tel for arrangements. 🅿 🎦
🐕 In grounds on leads. Guide dogs in house. 🎫

SKIPTON CASTLE   *See page 372 for full page entry.*

Bolton Abbey

STOCKELD PARK

WETHERBY, NORTH YORKSHIRE LS22 4AW

www.stockeldpark.co.uk

Tel: 01937 586101 **Fax:** 01937 580084
Owner: Mr and Mrs P G F Grant **Contact:** Mr P Grant
Stockeld is a beautifully proportioned Palladian villa designed by James Paine in 1763, featuring a magnificent cantilevered staircase in the central oval hall. The much loved home to the same family for 150 years, Stockeld houses a fine collection of 18th and 19th century furniture and paintings. The house is surrounded by stunning gardens of formal clipped hedges and topiary mixed with flowing herbaceous and shrub plantings. It is fringed by ancient woodland and set in over 100 acres of magnificent parkland in the midst of an extensive farming estate. A beautiful and fascinating house which is a popular location for filming and photography. Perfect parkland setting for exclusive outdoor activities.
Location: MAP 11:A9, OS Ref. SE376 497. York 12m, Harrogate 5m, Leeds 12m.
Open: Privately booked events only. Please contact the Estate Office: 01937 586101.
Admission: Prices on application.
🎦

SUTTON PARK 🏛

SUTTON-ON-THE-FOREST, NORTH YORKSHIRE YO61 1DP

www.statelyhome.co.uk

Tel: 01347 810249/811239 **Fax:** 01347 811251 **E-mail:** suttonpark@fsbdial.co.uk

Owner: Sir Reginald & Lady Sheffield **Contact:** Administrator

The Yorkshire home of Sir Reginald and Lady Sheffield. Charming example of early Georgian architecture. Magnificent plasterwork by Cortese. Rich collection of 18th century furniture, paintings, porcelain, needlework, beadwork. All put together with great style to make a most inviting house. Award winning gardens attract enthusiasts from home and abroad. Silver Yorkshire in Bloom 2007.

Location: MAP 11:B9, OS Ref. SE583 646. 8m N of York on B1363 York–Helmsley Road.

Open: House: Easter–Sept: Wed, Sun & BHs, 1.30–5pm (last tour 4.15pm). Gardens: Easter–Sept: daily, 11am–5pm. Tearoom: Easter–end Sept: Wed–Sun, 11am–5pm. Private groups any other day by appointment. House open Oct–Mar for private parties (15+) only.

Admission: House & Garden: Adult £6.50, Child £4, Conc. £5.50. Coaches £5.50. Private Groups (15+): £7. Gardens only: Adult £3.50, Child £1.50, Conc. £3. Coaches £3. Caravans: £7.50 per unit per night. Electric hookup: £9.50 per unit per night.

ℹ No photography. 🍽 Lunches & dinners in Dining Room. ♿ Partial. WCs. 🍰 Home-baked fayre. 👤 Obligatory. 🅿 Limited for coaches. 🔔

TEMPLE NEWSAM

LEEDS LS15 OAE

www.leeds.gov.uk/templenewsam

Tel: 0113 2647321 **E-mail:** temple.newsam@leeds.gov.uk

Owner: Leeds City Council **Contact:** Denise Lawson

One of the great country houses of England, this Tudor-Jacobean mansion was the birthplace of Lord Darnley, husband of Mary Queen of Scots and home to the Ingram family for 300 years. Rich in newly restored interiors, paintings, furniture (including Chippendale), textiles, silver and ceramics; an ever-changing exhibitions programme, audio-tours, family activities and children's trails are also on offer along with one of the largest working rare breed farms in Europe. Temple Newsam sits within 1500 acres of grand and beautiful 'Capability' Brown parkland with formal and wooded gardens as well as national plant collections.

Location: MAP 10:P10, OS Ref. SE358 321. 5m E of city centre, off A63 Selby Road. M1/J46.

Open: 27 Mar–30 Oct: Tue–Sun and BHs, House: 10.30am–5pm, Farm: 10am–5pm. 31 Oct–26 Mar: Tue–Sun and BHs. House: 10.30am–4pm. Farm, 10am–4pm. Last admission ¾ hour before closing. Estate open free, dawn to dusk.

Admission: House only: Adult £3.50, Child £2.50, Family £9. House and Home Farm: Adult £5, Child £3.50, Family £14, special rates for educational groups. Parking £3.50 (car), £20 (coach), annual parking pass £10.

🔲 🍽 ♿ 🍰 👤 🅿 ⬛ 🔳 💠

THORNTON ABBEY AND GATEHOUSE ⚑

Ulceby DN39 6TU

Tel: 0870 333 1181 **E-mail:** customers@english-heritage.org.uk

www.english-heritage.org.uk/yorkshire

Owner: English Heritage **Contact:** Customer Services

The enormous Gatehouse of Thornton Abbey is the finest surviving in Britain, its ornate facade trumpeting the prosperity of what was once one of the wealthiest Augustinian monasteries. But the Gatehouse has a darker side. Built and fortified in the nervous years following the Peasants' Revolt of 1381, it is thought to have protected the Abbey's treasures as well as the Abbot and his guests. A major restoration has opened locked doors and narrow passageways including the wall-walk. Now, for the first time, the Gatehouse will be opened to visitors in its entirety. In a new exhibition, explore the often turbulent lives of its former residents – and the wilder modern inhabitants of the Abbey ruins.

Location: MAP 11:E11, OS Map 284 Ref TA118 189. 18m NE of Scunthorpe on a road N of A160. 7m SE of Humber Bridge, on a road E of A1077.

Open: 21 Mar–30 Jun & Sept: Wed–Sun, Jul & Aug, daily, 10am–5pm. 1 Oct–31 Mar, Fri–Sun, 10am–4pm. Closed 24–26 Dec & 1 Jan.

Admission: Adult £4, Child £2, Conc. £3.20.

THORP PERROW ARBORETUM, WOODLAND GARDEN BIRDS OF PREY & MAMMAL CENTRE

Bedale, North Yorkshire DL8 2PR

Tel/Fax: 01677 425323 **E-mail:** enquiries@thorpperrow.com

www.thorpperrow.com

Owner: Sir John Ropner Bt **Contact:** Louise McNeill

85 acres of woodland walks. One of the largest collections of trees and shrubs in the north of England, including a 16th century spring wood and 19th century pinetum, and holds five National Collections – Ash, Lime, Walnut, Laburnum and Cotinus. The Bird of Prey and Mammal Centre is a captive breeding and conservation centre. Three flying demonstrations daily throughout the season.

Location: MAP 10:P7, OS Ref. SE258 851. Bedale–Ripon road, S of Bedale, 4m from Leeming Bar on A1.

Open: All year: dawn–dusk. Telephone for winter opening times.

Admission: Arboretum & Falcons: Adult £6.10, Child £3.30, OAP £4.80, Family (2+2) £18, (2+4) £24. Groups prices available (2007 prices).

ℹ Picnic area. Children's playground. 🔲 🍽 ♿ Partial. WCs. 🍷 Licensed. 👤 By arrangement. 🅿 Limited for coaches. ⬛ 🔳 In grounds, on leads. ❄ 💠

TREASURER'S HOUSE ※

Minster Yard, York, North Yorkshire YO1 7JL

Tel: 01904 624247 **E-mail:** treasurershouse@nationaltrust.org.uk

Owner: The National Trust **Contact:** The Property Manager

Named after the Treasurer of York Minster and built over a Roman road, the house is not all that it seems! Nestled behind the Minster, the size and splendour and contents of the house are a constant surprise to visitors – as are the famous ghost stories. Free trails for children and free access to the National Trust tearoom.

Location: MAP 21, OS Ref. SE604 523. The N side of York Minster. Entrance on Chapter House St.

Open: 15 Mar–2 Nov: daily except Fri, 11am–4.30pm. 3–30 Nov: daily except Fri, 11am–3.30pm. (Tearoom, ghost cellar, partial access to show rooms via themed tours.)

Admission: House: Adult £5.80, Child £2.90, Family £14.50. House & Cellar: Adult £8, Child £4.60, Groups: Adult £7.40, Child £4.40. Cellar: Adult £2.30, Child £1.80.

*includes a voluntary donation but visitors can choose to pay the standard prices displayed at the property and on the website.

🍽 ♿ Partial. WC. 🍷 Licensed. 🍴 Licensed. 🅿 None. ⬛ 🔳 In grounds, on leads. 🔔

WALCOT HALL

Nr Alkborough, North Lincolnshire DN15 9JT

Tel/Fax: 01724 720266 **E-mail:** WalcotHallEstate@gmail.com

www.WalcotHallEstate.com

Owner: Mr & Mrs Anthony Lane-Roberts **Contact:** Lucinda

Grade II listed Georgian hall built in 1726 with canted bays at either end and an imposing doric portico. Originally the family seat of Goulton-Constables. Set in glorious parkland in the North Lincolnshire countryside with five acres of beautifully landscaped gardens.

Location: MAP 11:D11, OS Ref. SE872 872. 15 mins SW of Humber Bridge & 15 mins N of M181. 45 mins from Robin Hood/Doncaster & Humberside international airports.

Open: Not open to the general public. Available for exclusive hire as a film location, corporate, weddings and special events.

🍽 🅿 🔔 💠

WASSAND HALL
SEATON, HULL, EAST YORKSHIRE HU11 5RJ

www.wassand.co.uk

Tel: 01964 534488   **Fax:** 01964 533334   **E-mail:** reorussell.wassand@tiscali.co.uk
Owner/Contact: R E O Russell – Resident Trustee

Fine Regency house 1815 by Thomas Cundy the Elder. Beautifully restored walled gardens, woodland walks, Parks and vistas over Hornsea Mere, part of the Estate since 1580. The Estate was purchased circa 1539 by Dame Joan Constable and has remained in the family to the present day, Mr Rupert Russell being the great nephew of the late Lady Strickland-Constable. The house contains a fine collection of 18/19th century paintings, English and Continental silver, furniture and porcelain. Wassand is very much a family home and retains a very friendly atmosphere. Homemade afternoon teas are served in the conservatory on Open Days.

Location: MAP 11:F9, OS Ref. TA174 460. On the B1244 Seaton–Hornsea road. Approximately 2m from Hornsea.

Open: 23–26 May; 5–9 & 20–24 Jun; 18/19 Jul; 20 Jul (Sunday afternoon concert – House not open); 1, 3, 4, 7–9 (evening concert of music and mirth), 10, 11 & 22–25 Aug.

Admission: Hall, all grounds & walks: Adult £5, Child (11–15yrs) £3. Hall: Adult £3, Child (11–15yrs) £1.50. Grounds & Garden: Adult £3, Child (11–15yrs) £1.50, Child under 10yrs Free.

  Limited.   By arrangement. **P** Ample for cars, limited for coaches. In grounds, on leads.

Scampston Hall

WENTWORTH CASTLE GARDENS

Lowe Lane, Stainborough, Barnsley, South Yorkshire S75 3ET
Tel: 01226 776040 **Fax:** 01226 776042
Owner: Wentworth Castle Trust   **Contact:** Richard Evans – Heritage Director
This historic 18th century parkland estate features over 26 listed monuments and a magnificent 60-acre pleasure garden open on selected days from spring to autumn.
Location: MAP 10:P12, OS Ref. SE320 034. 5 mins from M1/J37.
Open: All year daily: Apr–Sept 10am–5pm, Oct–Mar 10am–4pm.
Admission: Garden: Adult £3.95, Conc. £3.25 Guided tours £2 extra.

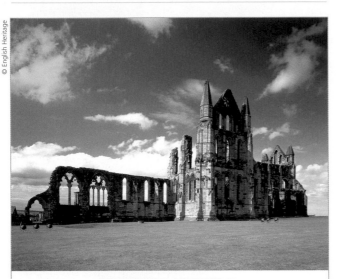

© English Heritage

WHITBY ABBEY ⌗
WHITBY, NORTH YORKSHIRE YO22 4JT

www.english-heritage.org.uk/whitbyabbey

Tel: 01947 603568
Owner: English Heritage   **Contact:** Visitor Operations Team
Since pre-history, successive generations have been drawn to this headland location. Founded by St Hilda in AD657, Whitby Abbey soon acquired great influence, before being ransacked by the invading Viking army. It was to be 200 years before the monastic tradition was revived, but yet again the Abbey was plundered, this time following the Dissolution. Inspired by detailed archaelogical investigation of the site, an interactive visitor centre recreates images of the Abbey over time and includes "Talking Heads" of personalities from the past.
Location: MAP 11:D6, OS Ref. NZ904 115. On cliff top E of Whitby.
Open: 21 Mar–30 Sept: daily, 10am–6pm. 1 Oct–31 Mar 2009: Thur–Mon, 10am–4pm. Closed 24–26 Dec & 1 Jan.
Admission: Adult £5, Child £2.50, Conc. £4, Family £12.50. 15% discounts for groups (11+). EH members Free.
ℹ WCs. ▣ ♿ Ground floor. ▣ Managed by the YHA. ▣ 🅿 Charged. ▣
🐕 In grounds, on leads. ▣ ▣

Red Wyverns at Skipton Castle

WILBERFORCE HOUSE

25 High Street, Hull, East Yorkshire HU1 1NQ
Tel: 01482 613902 **Fax:** 01482 613710
Owner: Hull City Council   **Contact:** S R Green
Birthplace of slavery abolitionist William Wilberforce. Reopened 2007 following £1.6 million redevelopment. Displays chart the history of slavery, the abolition campaign and slavery today.
Location: MAP 11:E11, OS Ref. TA102 286. High Street, Hull.
Open: Mon–Sat, 10am–5pm, Sun 1.30–4.30pm.
Admission: Free.

WORTLEY HALL

Wortley, Sheffield, South Yorkshire S35 7DB
Tel: 0114 2882100 **Fax:** 0114 2830695
Owner: Labour, Co-operative & Trade Union Movement   **Contact:** Marc Mallender
15 acres of formal Italianate gardens surrounded by 11 acres of informal pleasure grounds.
Location: MAP 6:P1, OS Ref. SK313 995. 10kms S of Barnsley in Wortley on A629.
Open: Gardens: Daily 10am–4pm. Specialist Plant Fairs 1 Jun & 24 Aug. Walk & Dine evenings.
Admission: Donation. Garden tours with Head Gardener for groups (15+) £2pp.

©John Whitaker

YORK GATE GARDEN
BACK CHURCH LANE, ADEL, LEEDS, WEST YORKSHIRE LS16 8DW

www.perennial.org.uk/yorkgate.html

Tel: 0113 2678240
Owner: Perennial   **Contact:** The Garden Co-ordinator
Inspirational one acre garden renowned for its outstanding design and exquisite detail. A series of smaller gardens, separated by hedges and stone walls, are linked by a succession of delightful vistas. One of many highlights is the famous herb garden with topiary and summerhouse.
Location: MAP 10:P10, OS Ref. 275 403. 2¼m SE of Bramhope. ½m E of A660.
Open: 23 Mar–28 Sept: Thur, Sun & BH Mons, 2–5pm. Also 5, 9, 17 & 25 Jun, 6.30–9pm.
Admission: Adult £3.50 (£2.50 Sept), Child (16yrs & under) Free.
Season Ticket £8.50.
ℹ Groups must book. ▣ ▣ Tea & Biscuits. ▣ By arrangement. 🅿 Limited.
🐕 Guide dogs only.

YORK MINSTER

Deangate, York YO1 7HH
Tel: 01904 557216 **Fax:** 01904 557218 **E-mail:** visitors@yorkminster.org
Owner: Dean and Chapter of York   **Contact:** Stephen Hemming
Large gothic church housing the largest collection of medieval stained glass in England.
Location: MAP 21, OS Ref. SE603 522. Centre of York.
Open: All year: Mon–Sat, 9.30am–5pm, Sun: 12 noon–3.45pm.
Admission: Adult £5.50, Child (under 16yrs) Free, Conc. £4.50. Groups: Adult £5, Child (under 16yrs) Free, Conc. £4.

visit hudsons guide online

Sledmere House

Holker Hall

North West

Cheshire has two strikingly different faces; the East, more industrial and more rugged where it adjoins the Peak District National Park, and the West, the flatter 'Cheshire Plain', more densely farmed and with easily recognisable red brick buildings. On the edge of the Lake District is Levens Hall and to the west is Muncaster Castle and its fascinating Owl Centre. For children, a visit to the Beatrix Potter Gallery is a must.

■ Owner
Mrs C J C Legh

■ Contact
Corporate Enquiries:
The Hunting Lodge
Adlington Hall
Macclesfield
Cheshire
SK10 4LF

Tel: 01625 827595
Fax: 01625 820797
E-mail: enquiries@
adlingtonhall.com

Hall Tours:
The Estate Office
Tel: 01625 829206

■ Location
MAP 6:N2
OS Ref. SJ905 804

5m N of
Macclesfield, A523,
13m S of Manchester.
London 178m.

Rail: Macclesfield
& Wilmslow
stations 5m.

Air: Manchester
Airport 8m.

■ Opening Times
July
Suns–Weds,
2–5pm.

■ Admission
Hall & Gardens
Adult	£7.00
Child	£3.00
Student	£3.00
Groups of 20+	£6.00

ADLINGTON HALL

www.adlingtonhall.com

Adlington Hall, the home of the Leghs of Adlington from 1315 to the present day, was built on the site of a Hunting Lodge which stood in the Forest of Macclesfield in 1040. Two oaks, part of the original building, remain with their roots in the ground and support the east end of the Great Hall, which was built between 1480 and 1505.

The Hall is a manor house, quadrangular in shape, and was once surrounded by a moat. Two sides of the Courtyard and the east wing were built in the typical 'Black and White' Cheshire style in 1581. The south front and west wing (containing the Drawing Room and Dining Room) were added between 1749 and 1757 and are built of red brick with a handsome stone portico with four Ionic columns on octagonal pedestals. Between the trees in the Great Hall stands an organ built by 'Father' Bernard Smith (c1670-80). Handel subsequently played on this instrument and, now fully restored, it is the largest 17th century organ in the country.

Gardens
The gardens were landscaped in the style of 'Capability' Brown in the middle of the 18th century. Visitors may walk round the 'wilderness' area; among the follies to be seen are 'Temple to Diana', a 'Shell Cottage', Chinese bridge and T'ing house. There is a fine yew walk and a lime avenue planted in 1688. An old-fashioned rose garden and yew maze have recently been planted. In this continually evolving garden, the 'Father Tiber' water garden was created in 2002. The Hunting Lodge is part of the converted Georgian Mews, a first floor conference and banqueting suite.

i — Suitable for corporate events, product launches, business meetings, conferences, concerts, fashion shows, garden parties, rallies, clay-pigeon shooting, filming and weddings.

— The Great Hall and Dining Room are available for corporate entertaining. Catering can be arranged.

— Visitors may alight at entrance to Hall. WCs.

— By arrangement.

P — For 100 cars and 4 coaches, 100 yds from Hall.

— By prior appointment.

Conference/Function
ROOM	SIZE	MAX CAPACITY
Great Hall	11 x 8m	80
Dining Rm	10.75 x 7m	80
Courtyard	27 x 17m	200
Hunting Lodge		130

visit hudsons guide online

ARLEY HALL & GARDENS 🏛

www.arleyhallandgardens.com

Owned by the same family for over 500 years, Arley is a delightful estate. The award-winning gardens, recently voted in the top 50 in Europe and in Britain's top 10, have been created gradually over 250 years with each generation of the family making its own contribution. The result is a garden of great atmosphere, interest and vitality, which blends strong elements of design from earlier centuries with modern ideas in both planting and design. Arley is, therefore, a wonderful example of the idea that the best gardens are living, changing works of art. Outstanding features are the renowned double herbaceous border (c1846), the Quercus Ilex and pleached Lime Avenues, Victorian Rootree, walled gardens, yew hedges and shrub rose collection. The family tradition continues today with the current Viscount Ashbrook, who over the last 30 years has created the less formal Grove and Woodland Walk, where 300 varieties of rhododendron grow amongst a collection of rare trees and shrubs in a delightful tranquil setting.

One of Cheshire's most charming stately homes, the Hall (Grade II*) was built by the present Viscount Ashbrook's great, great grandfather, Rowland Egerton-Warburton between 1832 and 1885 and is a fine example of the Victorian Jacobean style. Each room is given its own individual character by the elaborate plasterwork, wood panelling, family portraits and porcelain. From the grandeur of the Gallery to the intimacy of the Library the Hall exudes charm. The Emperor's Room was even home to Prince Louis Napoleon, later Napoleon III of France, in the winter of 1847–48.

Arley won the title of 2006 'Small Visitor Atraction of the Year' in the North West and is also a wonderful exclusive venue for weddings, corporate functions and private parties.

Owner
Viscount & Viscountess Ashbrook

Contact
The Estate Office
Arley
Nr Northwich
Cheshire CW9 6NA

Tel: 01565 777353
Fax: 01565 777465
E-mail: enquiries@
arleyhallandgardens.com

Location
MAP 6:M2
OS Ref. SJ675 809

5m W Knutsford,
5m from M6/J19 & 20
and M56/J9 & 10.

Opening Times
21 March–28 September & October weekends.

Gardens: Tuesday–Sunday & BHs, 11am–5pm.

Hall: Tues, Suns & BHs, 12noon–4.30pm.

Admission
Gardens, Grounds & Chapel:

Adult	£5.50
Child (5–16yrs)	£2.00
Senior	£5.00
Family	£13.00
Groups:	
Adult	£5.00
Senior	£4.50

Hall & Gardens

Adult	£8.00
Child (5–16yrs)	£3.00
Senior	£7.00
Family	£20.00
Groups:	
Adult	£6.50
Senior	£5.75

Season tickets

Individual	£25.00
Joint	£40.00
Family (2+2)	£58.00

Special Events
6 April
Spring Plant Fair

19/20 & 26/27 April
Bluebell Walks

17–18 May
Arley Horse Trials & Country Fair

28/29 June
Arley Garden Festival

25/26 October
Pumpkin Olympics

29 Nov–7 Dec
Christmas Floral Extravaganza

ℹ Suitable for weddings, corporate functions, product launches, conferences, filming, photography, concerts and fairs. Photography in Hall by permission only.

🛍 Open while the Garden is open.

🍽 Comprehensive set of menus available for entertaining in the Hall and Tudor Barn.

♿ Partial access to the Hall, full access to Gardens, WCs.

🍴 Licensed Tudor Barn Restaurant.

🚶 Welcomed by arrangement.

🅿

🐕 In the grounds on leads.

■ Owner
Mr & Mrs
Bromley-Davenport

■ Contact
Gwyneth Jones
Hall Manager
Capesthorne Hall
Siddington
Macclesfield
Cheshire SK11 9JY

Tel: 01625 861221
Fax: 01625 861619
E-mail: info@
capesthorne.com

■ Location
MAP 6:N2
OS Ref. SJ840 727

5m W of Macclesfield.
30 mins S of Manchester
on A34.
Near M6, M63 and M62.

Air: Manchester
International 20 mins.

Rail: Macclesfield 5m
(2 hrs from London).

Taxi: 01625 533464.

■ Opening Times
Summer
April–Oct
Suns, Mons & BHs.

Hall
1.30–4pm.
Last admission 3.30pm.

Gardens & Chapel
12 noon–5pm.

Groups welcome by
appointment.

Caravan Park also open
Easter–end October.

Corporate enquiries:
March–December.

■ Admission
Sundays & BHs only
Hall, Gardens & Chapel
Adult	£6.50
Child (5–16yrs)	£3.00
OAP	£5.50
Family*	£15.00

*Parents and children
aged up to 16yrs in the
same car.

Gardens & Chapel only
Adult	£4.00
Child (5–16yrs)	£2.00
OAP	£3.00

**Transfers from Gardens
& Chapel to Hall**
Adult/OAP	£3.50
Child (5–16yrs)	£1.50

**Mondays only: Hall,
Chapel & Gardens**
Car (up to 4 pass.)	£10.00
Additional person	£2.50
Minibus (up to 12 pass)	£25.00
Coach (up to 50 pass)	£50.00

Caravan Park
Up to 2 people £16.00pn
Over 2 people £20.00pn

15 Jul–30 Aug, inclusive
Up to 2 people £20.00pn
Over 2 people £25.00pn

CAPESTHORNE HALL 🏛
www.capesthorne.com

Capesthorne Hall, set in 100 acres of picturesque Cheshire parkland, has been touched by nearly 1,000 years of English history – Roman legions passed across it, titled Norman families hunted on it and, during the Civil War, a Royalist ancestress helped Charles II to escape after the Battle of Worcester. The Jacobean-style Hall has a fascinating collection of fine art, marble sculptures, furniture and tapestries. Originally designed by the Smiths of Warwick it was built between 1719 and 1732. It was altered by Blore in 1837 and partially rebuilt by Salvin in 1861 following a disastrous fire.

The present Squire is William Bromley-Davenport, Lord Lieutenant of Cheshire, whose ancestors have owned the estate since Domesday times when they were appointed custodians of the Royal Forest of Macclesfield.

In the grounds near the family Chapel the 18th century Italian Milanese Gates open onto the herbaceous borders and maples which line the beautiful lakeside gardens. But amid the natural spectacle and woodland walks, Capesthorne still offers glimpses of its man-made past … the remains of the Ice House, the Old Boat House and the curious Swallow Hole.

Facilities at the Hall can be hired for corporate occasions and family celebrations including Civil Wedding ceremonies.

ℹ️ Available for corporate functions, meetings, product launches, promotions, exhibitions, presentations, seminars, activity days, Civil Weddings and receptions, family celebrations, still photography, clay shooting, car rallies, garden parties, barbecues, concerts, antique, craft, country and game fairs. No photography in Hall.

🍸 Catering can be provided for groups (full menus on request). Function rooms available for wedding receptions, corporate hospitality, meetings and other special events. 'The Butler's Pantry' serves light refreshments.

♿ Compacted paths, ramps. WCs.

Guided tours available for pre-booked parties (except Sunday and Monday).

🅿️ 100 cars/20 coaches on hard-standing and unlimited in park, 50 yds from house.

🐕 Guide dogs in Hall. Under control in Park.

🔔

ADLINGTON HALL 🏠

See page 392 for full page entry.

ARLEY HALL AND GARDENS 🏠

See page 393 for full page entry.

BEESTON CASTLE ⌗

Chapel Lane, Beeston, Tarporley, Cheshire CW6 9TX
Tel: 01829 260464
www.english-heritage.org.uk/beestoncastle
Owner: English Heritage   **Contact:** Visitor Operations Team

Standing majestically on a sheer rocky crag, Beeston has perhaps the most stunning views of any castle in England. Its long history spans Bronze Age settlement to Iron Age hillfort, to impregnable royal fortress. This 4,000 year history is outlined in the "Castle of the Rock" exhibition.

Location: MAP 6:L3, OS Ref. SJ537 593. 11m SE of Chester on minor road off A49, or A41. 2m SW of Tarporley.
Open: 21 Mar–30 Sept: daily, 10am–6pm. 1 Oct–31 Mar: Thur–Mon, 10am–4pm. Closed 24–26 Dec & 1 Jan.
Admission: Adult £5, Child £2.50, Conc. £4. 15% discount for groups (11+). EH members Free.

ℹ️ Exhibition. WCs. 🔲 ♿ Unsuitable. 🅿️ ⬛ ⬛ In grounds on leads. ✳️ 🍴

CAPESTHORNE HALL 🏠

See page 394 for full page entry.

CHESTER CATHEDRAL

Werburgh Street, Chester, Cheshire
Tel: 01244 500958   **Fax:** 01244 341110   **E-mail:** fry@chestercathedral.com
Owner: Church of England   **Contact:** Nicholas Fry
Medieval monastic complex.
Location: MAP 6:K2, OS Ref. SJ406 665. Chester city centre.
Open: Mon–Sat: 9am–5pm. Sun 1–5pm.
Admission: Adult £4, Child (5–16) £1.50, Senior Citizens/Groups £3, Family Ticket £10.

CHESTER ROMAN AMPHITHEATRE ⌗

Vicars Lane, Chester, Cheshire
Tel: 01244 402466
www.english-heritage.org.uk/chester
Owner: Managed by English Heritage and Chester City Council
Contact: Chester City Council

The largest Roman amphitheatre in Britain. Excavations carried out over 2004/05 indicate that there were two stone-built amphitheatres, one very similar to those in Pompeii, emphasising the great importance of Chester during the Roman era.

Location: MAP 6:K2, OS Ref. SJ408 662. On Vicars Lane beyond Newgate, Chester.
Open: Any reasonable time.
Admission: Free.

♿ Partial ⬛ On leads. ✳️

CHOLMONDELEY CASTLE GARDEN 🏠
MALPAS, CHESHIRE SY14 8AH

Tel: 01829 720383   **Fax:** 01829 720877   **E-mail:** penny@cholmondeleycastle.co.uk
Owner: The Marchioness of Cholmondeley   **Contact:** The Secretary

Extensive ornamental gardens dominated by romantic Gothic Revival Castle built in 1801 of local sandstone. Visitors can enjoy the beautiful Temple Water Garden, Ruin Water Garden and memorial mosaic designed by Maggy Howarth. Rose garden and many mixed borders. Lakeside picnic area, children's play areas, rare breeds of farm animals, llamas, children's corner with rabbits, chickens and free flying aviary birds. Private chapel in the park.

Location: MAP 6:L3, OS Ref. SJ540 515. Off A41 Chester/Whitchurch Rd. & A49 Whitchurch/ Tarporley Road. 7m N of Whitchurch.
Open: Good Friday 21 Mar–Sun 28 Sep, Wed, Thur, Sun & BHs. Open for Autumn Tints, Sun 12 & 26 Oct, 11am–5pm. (The castle is only open to groups by prior arrangement on limited days).
Admission: Adult £5, Child £2, (reduction for groups to gardens of 25+).

🔲 🍴 🎫 ♿ Limited. WCs. ⬛ ⬛ In grounds on leads only.

DORFOLD HALL 🏛

ACTON, Nr NANTWICH, CHESHIRE CW5 8LD

Tel: 01270 625245 **Fax:** 01270 628723

Owner/Contact: Richard Roundell

Jacobean country house built in 1616 for Ralph Wilbraham. Family home of Mr & Mrs Richard Roundell. Beautiful plaster ceilings and oak panelling. Attractive woodland gardens and summer herbaceous borders.

Location: MAP 6:L3, OS Ref. SJ634 525. 1m W of Nantwich on the A534 Nantwich–Wrexham road.

Open: Apr–Oct: Tue only and BH Mons, 2–5pm.

Admission: Adult £5, Child £3.

🎫 Obligatory. 🅿 Limited. Narrow gates with low arch prevent coaches.
🐕 In grounds on leads.

GAWSWORTH HALL

MACCLESFIELD, CHESHIRE SK11 9RN

www.gawsworthhall.com

Tel: 01260 223456 **Fax:** 01260 223469 **E-mail:** gawsworthhall@btinternet.com

Owner: Mr and Mrs T Richards **Contact:** Mr T Richards

Fully lived-in Tudor half-timbered manor house with Tilting Ground. Former home of Mary Fitton, Maid of Honour at the Court of Queen Elizabeth I, and the supposed 'Dark Lady' of Shakespeare's sonnets. Pictures, sculpture and furniture. Open air theatre with covered grandstand – June, July and August, please telephone for details. Situated halfway between Macclesfield and Congleton in an idyllic setting close to the lovely medieval church.

Location: MAP 6:N2, OS Ref. SJ892 697. 3m S of Macclesfield on the A536 Congleton to Macclesfield road.

Open: 4 May–24 Sept: Sun–Wed and for Special Events & BHs. Jul–Aug: daily, 2–5pm.

Admission: Adult £6, Child £3. Groups (20+): £5.

🔲 🖥 🅿 🐕 Guide dogs in garden only. ▲ 🚻

DUNHAM MASSEY ✤

Altrincham, Cheshire WA14 4SJ

Tel: 0161 941 1025 **Fax:** 0161 929 7508

E-mail: dunhammassey@nationaltrust.org.uk **www.nationaltrust.org.uk**

Owner: The National Trust **Contact:** Property Manager

Originally an early Georgian house, Dunham Massey has sumptuous interiors with collections of walnut furniture, paintings and magnificent Huguenot silver. The richly planted garden contains waterside plantings, late flowering azaleas, an Orangery and Elizabethan mount. The surrounding deer park escaped the attentions of 18th century landscape gardeners and contains some notable specimen trees.

Location: MAP 6:M1, OS Ref. SJ735 874. 3m SW of Altrincham off A56. M6/J19. M56/J7. Station Altrincham (BR & Metro) 3m.

Open: House: 8 Mar–2 Nov: Sat–Wed, 12 noon–5pm (11am–5pm Good Fri, BH Sun & Mon). Garden: 8 Mar–2 Nov: daily, 11am–5.30pm. Last admission ½ hr before closing. Park open daily, all year.

***Admission:** House & Garden: Adult £8.50, Child £4.25, Family (2+3 max) £21.25. Garden only: Adult £6, Child £3, Family £15. Park entry: Car £4, Coach £10, Motorcycle £1. Groups should telephone for price details. *includes a voluntary 10% donation but visitors can choose to pay the standard prices displayed at the property and on the website.

ℹ No photography in house. 🔲 🎫 ♿ Partial. WC. Baticars. 🍴 Licensed.
🎫 Optional. No extra charge. 🅿 🖥 🐕 In grounds, on leads. ❄

HARE HILL ✤

Over Alderley, Macclesfield, Cheshire SK10 4QB

Tel: 01625 584412 (Countryside Office)

www.nationaltrust.org.uk

Owner: The National Trust **Contact:** The Countryside Office

A woodland garden surrounding a walled garden with pergola, rhododendrons, hollies and hostas. Parkland.

Location: MAP 6:N2, OS Ref. SJ875 765. Between Alderley Edge and Macclesfield (B5087). Turn off N onto Prestbury Road, continue for ¾m.

Open: 31 Mar–6 May, 2 Jun–1 Nov: Wed, Thur, Sat, Sun 10am–5pm. 7 May–1 Jun: daily 10am–5pm.

Admission: Adult £3.40, Child £1.70. Car park fee £1.90 (refundable on entry to garden). Groups by written appointment.

♿ Gravel paths – strong companion advisable. 🐕 On leads in park.

HOLMSTON HALL BARN

Little Budworth, Tarporley, Cheshire CW6 9AY

Tel: 01829 760366/07778 510287 **Fax:** 01829 760366

Owner/Contact: Mr Richard & Dr Yvonne Hopkins

Newly restored 15th century oak framed barn. Sandstone base and floors, with twelve exterior oak doors.

Location: MAP 6:L3, OS Ref. SJ607 626. Off A49. 2m from Eaton village.

Open: All year by appointment only.

Admission: Free.

❄

Beeston Castle

LITTLE MORETON HALL

Congleton, Cheshire CW12 4SD
Tel: 01260 272018 **www.nationaltrust.org.uk**
Owner: The National Trust   **Contact:** The Property Administrator
Begun in 1504 and completed 100 years later, Little Moreton Hall is regarded as the finest example of a timber-framed moated manor house in the country.
Location: MAP 6:N3, OS Ref. SJ833 589. 4m SW of Congleton on E side of A34.
Open: 1–16 Mar: Sat & Sun, 11.30am–4pm. 19 Mar–2 Nov: Wed–Sun & BH Mons, 11.30am–5pm. 8 Nov–21 Dec: Sat & Sun, 11.30am–4pm.
*Admission: Adult £6.40, Child £3.20, Family £14.90. Groups: £5.50 (must book). *includes a voluntary donation but visitors can choose to pay the standard prices displayed at the property and on the website.
🅿 📶 ⌖ Braille guide, wheelchair access to ground floor only. WCs. 🍽 ⏸ ⌖ ▦ 🐕 Car park only. ⌖

LYME PARK

Disley, Stockport, Cheshire SK12 2NX
Tel: 01663 762023 **Fax:** 01663 765035 **www.nationaltrust.org.uk**
Owner: The National Trust   **Contact:** The Property Manager
Originally Tudor, the House now resembles a fabulous Italianate palace. Inside there are incredible Mortlake tapestries, important collections of clocks, and beautifully furnished rooms. Colourful family history. Opulent Victorian garden with sunken parterre, Edwardian rose garden, Jekyll-style borders and Wyatt-designed Orangery. The moors and parkland are home to fallow and red deer.
Location: MAP 6:N2, OS Ref. SJ965 825. Off the A6 at Disley. 6½m SE of Stockport. M60 J1.
Open: House: 15 Mar–2 Nov: Fri–Tue, 11am–5pm, guided tours 11am–1pm, (last adm 4.30pm). Park: 1 Apr–12 Oct: daily, 8am–8.30pm; 12 Oct–31 Mar '09: 8am–6pm. Gardens: 15 Mar–2 Nov: daily, 11am–5pm (last adm 4.30pm); 1–9 Mar & 8 Nov–14 Dec: Sats & Suns only, 12noon–3pm.
*Admission: House & Garden: Adult £7.60, Child £3.80, Family £19. House only: Adult £5.60, Child £2.80. Garden only: Adult £4.80, Child £2.40. Park only: car £4.60, motorbike £2, coach £12, minibus £6. Booked coach groups Park admission Free. NT members Free. *includes a voluntary donation but visitors can choose to pay the standard prices displayed at the property and on the website.
ℹ No photography in house. 🅿 ⌖ Partial. WC. 🍽 ⏸ Licensed. ⌖ By arrangement. 🅿 ▦ 🐕 In park, close control. Guide dogs only in house & garden. ✳

NESS BOTANIC GARDENS

Ness, Neston, Cheshire CH64 4AY
Tel: 0151 353 0123 **Fax:** 0151 353 1004
Owner: University of Liverpool   **Contact:** Dr E J Sharples
New Visitor Centre opened in 2006. Leading garden in the North West for rhododendrons and azaleas.
Location: MAP 6:J2, OS Ref. SJ302 760 (village centre). Off A540. 10m NW of Chester. 1½m S of Neston.
Open: Mar–Oct: daily, 9.30am–5pm. Nov–Feb: 9.30am–4pm.
Admission: Adult £5.50, Conc £5, Child (5–16yrs) £2.50, Child (under 5yrs) Free., Family ticket (2+3) £13.50. 10% discount for groups. Please telephone for details.

NORTON PRIORY MUSEUM & GARDENS

Tudor Road, Manor Park, Runcorn WA7 1SX
Tel: 01928 569895 **E-mail:** info@nortonpriory.org www.nortonpriory.org
Owner/Contact: The Norton Priory Museum Trust
Discover the 800 year old priory range, excavated priory remains, museum gallery, the St Christopher statue – one of the great treasures of medieval Europe – exciting sculpture trail and award winning Walled Garden. Set in 38 acres of tranquil, woodland gardens, Norton Priory also has a coffee shop, retail area and temporary exhibitions gallery.
Location: MAP 6:K1, OS Ref. SJ545 835. 3m from M56/J11. 2m E of Runcorn.
Open: All year: daily, from 12 noon. Telephone for details.
Admission: Adult £5.20. Child/Conc. £3.70. Family £13.40. Groups £3.40, (as from Apr '08).
🅿 📶 ⌖ Wheelchairs, braille guide, audio tapes & WC. 🍽 ⌖ By arrangement. 🅿 ▦ 🐕 In grounds, on leads. ✳ ⌖

PEOVER HALL 🏛
OVER PEOVER, KNUTSFORD WA16 9HW

Tel: 01565 632358
Owner: Randle Brooks   **Contact:** I Shepherd
An Elizabethan house dating from 1585. Fine Carolean stables. Mainwaring Chapel, 18th century landscaped park. Large garden with topiary work, also walled and herb gardens.
Location: MAP 6:M2, OS Ref. SJ772 734. 4m S of Knutsford off A50 at Whipping Stocks Inn.
Open: May–Aug: Stables & Gardens, Mon & Thu except BHs, 2–5pm. Tours of the House at 2.30 & 3.30pm.
Admission: House, Stables & Gardens: Adult £5. Stables & Gardens only: Adult £4. Accompanied children free.
🍽 Mon & Thur. ⌖ Obligatory. ▦

Tatton Park

QUARRY BANK MILL & STYAL ESTATE
STYAL, WILMSLOW SK9 4LA

www.nationaltrust.org.uk

Tel: 01625 527468 **Fax:** 01625 539267
E-mail: quarrybankmill@nationaltrust.org.uk
Owner: The National Trust   **Contact:** Visitor Services Manager
Unique Georgian Cotton Mill with working machinery, daily demonstrations and fascinating living history. See the steam engines and mighty watermill in action. Experience the grim conditions in the Apprentice House. Enjoy the beautiful 300 acre Styal Estate.
Location: MAP 6:N1, OS Ref. SJ835 835. 1½m N of Wilmslow off B5166. 2½m from M56/J5. Styal Shuttle Bus, Airport 2½m.
Open: Mill: 1 Mar–31 Oct: daily, 11am–5pm, last adm. 4pm. 1 Nov–28 Feb '09: Wed–Sun, 11am–4pm, last adm. 3pm. Apprentice House: 1 Mar–31 Oct ; daily, 11am–5pm. 1 Nov–28 Feb 09: Wed–Sun, 11am–4pm. QBH Garden 1 Mar–31 Oct: daily, 11am–5pm.
*Admission: Estate: £3.50. Mill only: Adult £6.70, Child £3.70, Family (2+3) £17, Group 15+ £6.35. Mill & Apprentice House or Mill & QBH Garden (Mar–Oct): Adult £9.50, Child £4.80, Family (2+3) £22.70, Group (15+) £9. Garden only (Mar–Oct): Adult £5, Child £2.50, Family £12.50, Group 15+ £4.75. Garden upgrade (Mar–Oct): Adult £3.50, Child, £1.75, Family £8.75. *includes a voluntary 10% donation but visitors can choose to pay the standard prices displayed at the property and on the website.
☐ ⊤ ☐ Partial. ☞ ⊞ Licensed. ☒ By arrangement. ☐ ☐ ☐ In grounds on leads. ☒ ☒ ☒

RODE HALL 🏛
CHURCH LANE, SCHOLAR GREEN, CHESHIRE ST7 3QP

www.rodehall.co.uk

Tel: 01270 873237 **Fax:** 01270 882962
E-mail: richard.wilbra@btconnect.com
Owner/Contact: Sir Richard Baker Wilbraham Bt
The Wilbraham family have lived at Rode since 1669; the present house was constructed in two stages, the earlier two storey wing and stable block around 1705 and the main building was completed in 1752. Later alterations by Lewis Wyatt and Darcy Braddell were undertaken in 1812 and 1927 respectively. The house stands in a Repton landscape and the extensive gardens include a woodland garden, with a terraced rock garden and grotto, which has many species of rhododendrons, azaleas, hellebores and climbing roses following snowdrops and daffodils in the early spring. The formal rose garden was designed by W Nesfield in 1860; there is a large walled kitchen garden and a new Italian garden. The icehouse in the park has recently been restored.
Location: MAP 6:M3, OS Ref. SJ819 573. 5m SW of Congleton between the A34 and A50. Kidsgrove railway station 2m NW of Kidsgrove.
Open: 1 Apr–30 Sept: Weds & BHs and by appointment. Garden only: Tues & Thurs, 2–5pm. Snowdrop Walk: 2 Feb–2 March daily except Mons 12 noon–4pm.
Admission: House, Garden & Kitchen Garden: Adult £5, Conc £4. Garden & Kitchen Garden: Adult £3, Concession £2.50. Snowdrop Walk: £3.
☒ ☞ Home-made teas. ☒ ☐ ☐ On leads.

TABLEY HOUSE
KNUTSFORD, CHESHIRE WA16 0HB

www.tableyhouse.co.uk

Tel: 01565 750151 **Fax:** 01565 653230 **E-mail:** inquiries@tableyhouse.co.uk
Owner: The University of Manchester   **Contact:** The Assistant Administrator
The finest Palladian House in the North West, Tabley a Grade I listing, was designed by John Carr of York for the Leicester family. Set in landscaped parkland it contains the first collection of English paintings, including works of art by Turner, Reynolds, Lawrence and Lely. Furniture by Chippendale, Bullock and Gillow and fascinating family memorabilia adorn the rooms. Interesting Tea Room and 17th century Chapel adjoin.

Location: MAP 6:M2, OS Ref. SJ725 777. M6/J19, A556 S on to A5033. 2m W of Knutsford.
Open: House: Apr–end Oct: Thurs–Suns & BHs, 2–5pm. Tea Room: All year, Thurs–Suns & BHs, 12noon–5pm. Closed 24 Dec 2007–9 Jan 2008.
Admission: Adult £4. Child/Student £1.50. Groups by arrangement.
☐ ☐ Please telephone for easiest access. ☞ ☐ ☐ Civil Wedding Licence plus Civil Naming Ceremonies & Re-affirmation of Vows. ☒

TATTON PARK ※

KNUTSFORD, CHESHIRE WA16 6QN

www.tattonpark.org.uk

Tel: 01625 374400 **Info:** 01625 374435 **Fax:** 01625 374403

Owner: The National Trust (Managed by Cheshire County Council)

A stunning historic estate set in beautiful parkland. Over 1,000 acres of land are home to herds of red and fallow deer and provide the setting for the impressive Georgian Mansion designed by Wyatt. The Egerton family's collection of Gillow furniture, Baccarat glass, porcelain and paintings by Dutch and Italian artists are on display. The gardens extend over 50 acres and include Japanese, walled and formal gardens. The 1930s working farm includes rare breed animals and workshops. An extensive year-round events programme includes the Tatton Park Biennial (a new contemporary arts event) from May to Sep, RHS Flower Show and picnic concerts.

Location: MAP 6:M2, OS Ref. SJ745 815. From M56/J7 follow signs. From M6/J19, signed on A56 & A50.

Open: High (15 Mar–28 Sep). Low (30 Sept–20 Mar 2009). Parkland: High, Daily 10am–7pm. Low, Tue–Sun 11am–5pm. Gardens: High, Tue–Sun, 10am–6pm. Low, 11am–4pm. Farm: High, Tue–Sun 12noon–5pm, Low, Sats & Suns 11am–4pm. Old Hall open for pre-booked groups, educational tours and during certain events.

Admission: Per attraction: Adult £4, Child (4–15) £2, Family (2+3) £10. Inclusive ticket to all attractions attractions Adult £6, Child £3, Family £15 (NT members, see website/handbook). Park Entry: £4.50 per car (inc NT members). Coaches Free.

◻ ▦ ⊤ Dinners, dances, weddings and conferences. ◫ Partial. WCs. ◖
▯ Self-service. ⓘ By arrangement. ᴾ £4.50 per car (inc NT members), 200–300 yds. Meal vouchers for coach drivers. ◼ Please book. ◖ In grounds, on leads. ▲ ✳ ▨

WOODHEY CHAPEL

Faddiley, Nr Nantwich, Cheshire CW5 8JH

Tel: 01270 524215

Owner: The Trustees of Woodhey Chapel   **Contact:** Mr Robinson, The Curator
Small private chapel built in 1690, now restored.

Location: MAP 6:L3, OS Ref. SJ573 528. Proceeding W from Nantwich on A534, turn left 1m W of the Faddiley – Brindley villages onto narrow lane, keep ahead at next turn, at road end obtain key from farmhouse.

Open: Apr–Oct: Sats & BHs, 2–5pm, or apply for key at Woodhey Hall.

Admission: Donation box.

Arley Hall

giftaid it Some properties will be operating the Gift Aid on Entry scheme at their admission points. Where the scheme is operating, visitors are offered a choice between paying the standard admission price or paying the 'Gift Aid Admission' which includes a voluntary donation of at least 10%. Gift Aid Admissions enable the charity to reclaim tax on the whole amount paid* - an extra 28% - potentially a very significant boost to property funds. Money raised from paying visitors in this way will go towards restoration projects at the property and will be very welcome.

Where shown, the admission prices are inclusive of the 10% voluntary donation where properties are operating the Gift Aid on Entry scheme, but both the standard admission price and the Gift Aid Admission will be displayed at the property and on their website.

*Gift Aid donations must be supported by a valid Gift Aid declaration and a Gift Aid declaration can only cover donations made by an individual for him/herself or for him/herself and members of his/her family.

Lyme Park

■ **Owner**
Lakeland Arts Trust

■ **Contact**
Jeanette Edgar
Blackwell –
The Arts & Crafts House
Bowness on Windermere
Cumbria LA23 3JT

Tel: 01539 446139
Fax: 01539 488486
E-mail: info@
blackwell.org.uk

■ **Location**
MAP 10:K7
OS Ref. SD400 945

1½ m S of Bowness just
off the A5074 on
the B5360.

Rail: Windermere.

Air: Manchester.

■ **Opening Times**
5 February–31 December
Daily, 10.30am–5pm,
(4pm, Feb/Mar, Nov/Dec).

■ **Admission**
Adult £6.00
Gift Aid it for £6.60

All ages welcome.

BLACKWELL –
THE ARTS & CRAFTS HOUSE

www.blackwell.org.uk

Blackwell is a superb house situated in the Lake District, set on the hillside overlooking Lake Windermere. Completed in 1900, it is the largest and most important surviving example of work by architect Hugh Mackay Baillie Scott, and the only one of his buildings open to the public.

This treasure trove of Arts and Crafts design contains fine examples of stained glass, decorative oak panelling and intricate plasterwork, their designs inspired by Lakeland birds and local wild flowers and trees. Blackwell's wealth of original detail also includes William de Morgan tiled fireplaces. The house was designed for relaxation, and visitors can sit and enjoy the stunning views and garden terraces from its many window seats and inglenooks.

Blackwell's period rooms are furnished with Arts and Crafts furniture and decorative arts. They are complemented by a series of first-floor galleries, where regular exhibitions of historical applied arts and contemporary craft are held.

 No photography.
No mobile phones.

 Ground floor & part
of 1st floor. WCs.

 Licensed.

 By arrangement.

 Free for cars, coaches
by appointment.

 Service dogs only.

HOLKER HALL & GARDENS

www.holker-hall.co.uk

Holker is the family home of Lord and Lady Cavendish and you can discover the beauty and elegance of their home without the confines of ropes or barriers to restrict your viewing. Relax in 25 acres of National Award Winning Gardens and Parkland. Stroll through the formal gardens and thrill at the unique and rare treasures they offer. Treat yourself to a special lunch or afternoon tea in the Courtyard Restaurant or picnic in the grounds. Children will delight at the Adventure Playground. Unique gifts and speciality products, some hand selected by Lady Cavendish, are available in our Gift Shop. To complete your day the classic Lakeland Motor Museum, displays an extensive collection of transport and motoring memorabilia.

The year round interest begins with breathtaking early spring bulbs, followed by magnificent ancient Rhododendrons and innumerable Azaleas and Magnolias. From late Spring the borders begin filling with skilful palettes of colour. A voluptuous crescendo of colour in the herbaceous borders is accompanied by impressive summer plantings. Throughout the year the unique collection of trees and shrubs provide scent and interest including late summer flowering Eucryphias. The National Collection of Styracaceae and fragrant Rhododendrons are smothered in sweetly scented flowers in the summer. The formal gardens have splendidly sculptured Yew and box hedging and topiary trees and shrubs. In winter the woodland trees and shrubs have delightful architectural form. The colourful, twisted glades of Rhododendron trunks and the meadow and labyrinth are quite magical. The garden also is home to the huge Holker Lime, one of 50 of England's most magnificent trees, selected as part of Her Majesty's Jubilee celebrations.

Owner
Lord Cavendish of Furness

Contact
Sandy Kitching
Cark-in-Cartmel
Grange-over-Sands
Cumbria LA11 7PL

Tel: 01539 558328
E-mail: publicopening@ holker.co.uk

Location
MAP 10:K8
OS Ref. SD359 773

Close to Morecambe Bay, 5m W of Grange-over-Sands by B5277. From Kendal, A6, A590, B5277, B5278: 16m. Motorway: M6/J36.

Open
Hall:
16 March–2 November: daily (except Saturday), 11am–4pm.

Gardens:
3 February–23 December: daily (except Saturday), 10.30am–5.30pm.

Admission
House, Gardens & Motor Museum:
Adult	£11.50
Child	£6.50
Family	£32.00

Reduced rate for House or Gardens or Museum only. Discount for groups.

Special Events
30 May–1 June
Holker Festival 2008 Tickets can be booked through the website: www.holker-hall.co.uk

 No photography in house.

 Holker Food Hall – produce from the Estate.

Visitors alight at entrance. WCs.

Licensed.

 By arrangement.

 75 yds from Hall.

 In grounds, on leads (not formal gardens).

■ **Owner**

C H Bagot

■ **Contact**

Peter Milner
Levens Hall
Kendal
Cumbria LA8 0PD

Tel: 01539 560321
Fax: 01539 560669
E-mail: houseopening@
levenshall.co.uk

■ **Location**

MAP 10:L7
OS Ref. SD495 851

5m S of Kendal on the
A6. Exit M6/J36.

Rail: Oxenholme 5m.

Air: Manchester.

■ **Opening Times**

Summer
23 March–9 October
Sun–Thur
(closed Fris & Sats).

House: 12 noon–4.30pm
Last admission 4pm.

Gardens, Plant Centre,
Gift Shop & Tearoom:
10am–5pm.

Winter
Closed.

■ **Admission**

House & Gardens
Adult   £10.00
Child   £4.50
Family (2+3*)   £25.00

Groups (20+)
Adult   £8.50
Child   £4.00

Gardens
Adult   £7.00
Child   £3.50
Family (2+3*)   £19.00

Groups (20+)
Adult   £6.50
Child   £3.00
*Additional children at
group rate.

Evening Tours
House tours for pre-
arranged groups (20+/
min charge £220)
Mon–Thur   £11.00

Gardens guided tour by
the Head Gardener or his
Assistant for pre-
arranged groups (20+/
min charge £160)
Mon–Thur   £8.00

Morning Tours
House tours starting
between 10–10.30am
for pre-arranged groups
(20+/min charge £190)
                 £9.50

No admission charge for
gift shop, tearoom and
plant centre.

©Andrew Semple

LEVENS HALL

www.levenshall.co.uk

Levens Hall is an Elizabethan mansion built around a 13th century pele tower. The much loved home of the Bagot family, visitors comment on the warm and friendly atmosphere. Fine panelling and plasterwork, period furniture, Cordova leather wall coverings, paintings by Rubens, Lely and Cuyp, the earliest English patchwork and Wellingtoniana combine with other beautiful objects to form a fascinating collection.

The world famous Topiary Gardens were laid out by Monsieur Beaumont from 1694 and his design has remained largely unchanged to this day. Over 90 individual pieces of topiary, some over nine metres high, massive beech hedges and colourful seasonal bedding provide a magnificent visual impact.

On Sundays and Bank Holidays 'Bertha', a full size Showman's Engine, is in steam. Delicious home-made lunches and teas are available, together with the award-winning Levens beer 'Morocco Ale', in the Bellingham Buttery.

©Hal Bagot

ℹ️ No indoor photography.

🛍️

❀

♿ Partial. WC. Electric buggy hire. DVD of interior.

☕ Licensed.

🍴

🚶 By arrangement.

🅿️

🐕 Guide dogs only.

©Brian Sherwen

■ Owner
Mrs Phyllida
Gordon-Duff-Pennington

■ Contact
Peter Frost-Pennington
Muncaster Castle
Ravenglass
Cumbria CA18 1RQ

Tel: 01229 717614
Fax: 01229 717010
E-mail: info@
muncaster.co.uk

■ Location
MAP 10:J7
OS Ref. SD103 965

On the A595 1m S of
Ravenglass, 19m S of
Whitehaven.
From London 6 hrs,
Chester 2½ hrs, Edinburgh
3½ hrs, M6/J36, A590,
A595 (from S). M6/J40,
A66, A595 (from E).
Carlisle, A595 (from N).
Rail: Ravenglass
(on Barrow-in-Furness-
Carlisle Line) 1½ m.
Air: Manchester 2½ hrs.

■ Opening Times
Castle
10 February–20 March:
1–4pm. 21 March–
2 November:
12 noon–4.30pm.
Daily (closed Sat),
Gardens & Owl Centre
1–9 February &
3 November–
31 December: Daily
11am–4pm.
10 February–2 November:
Daily 10.30am–6pm
(or dusk if earlier).
'Meet the Birds'
10 February–2 November
Daily at 2.30pm.
'Heron Happy Hour'.
Daily at 4.30pm
(3.30pm winter).
Winter:
Castle closed. Open by
appointment for groups.
Darkest Muncaster
A Winter Evening of Magic
– see website for details.

MUNCASTER CASTLE
GARDENS, OWL CENTRE & MEADOWVOLE MAZE
www.muncaster.co.uk

Muncaster Castle, set in 77 acres of gardens with spectacular views of the Lakeland Fells, has been home to the Pennington family since at least 1208.

The Castle, complete with an impressive library, beautiful barrel-vaulted drawing room and exquisite dining room, is a treasure trove of paintings, silver, tapestries, and much more.

'Ghost tours' are possible by appointment, and up to 8 brave guests can book an overnight 'Ghost Sit' in the 'haunted' Tapestry Room.

The extensive, wild woodland gardens include glorious rhododendrons, camellias, azaleas, magnolias and many other interesting and rare trees and shrubs.

The World Owl Centre, HQ of the World Owl Trust, is home to one of the largest collections of these fascinating birds.

Most holiday and weekend evenings in winter (closed January),

Darkest Muncaster transforms the gardens with hundreds of multi-coloured lights, as well as music, sound and other special effects.

In the MeadowVole Maze visitors young and old help Max MeadowVole safely find his way home through this innovative, indoor attraction, with a strong conservation message. *Muncaster Interactive* gives visitors access to computers with games and quizzes, as well as facts and figures on the Castle, gardens, owls and the surrounding area.

Muncaster is the perfect place to entertain in style and frequently hosts weddings, dinner parties and similar family celebrations or corporate events.

Accommodation is available in the 4 star 'Coachman's Quarters' in the gardens of the Castle and in two houses on the wider estate or in the newly refurbished Pennington Hotel in Ravenglass.

■ Admission
**Castle, Gardens,
Owl Centre &
MeadowVole Maze**
Adult	£10.00
*Child (5–15yrs)	£7.00
Family (2+2)	£29.00

Groups
Adult	£8.50
*Child (5–15yrs)	£5.50

**Gardens, Owl Centre
& MeadowVole Maze**
Adult	£7.50
*Child (5–15yrs)	£5.50
Family (2+2)	£24.00

Groups
Adult	£6.50
*Child (5–15yrs)	£4.50
Under 5yrs	Free

Conference/Function
ROOM	MAX CAPACITY
Drawing Room	100
Dining Room	50
Family Dining Rm	60
Great Hall	100
Old Laundry	120
Library	48
Guard Room	30

©Brian Sherwen

ℹ️ Church. Garden parties, film location, clay pigeon shooting. No photography inside the Castle.

🛍️

🍽️ For wedding receptions, catering, & functions, tel: 01229 717614.

♿ By arrangement visitors can alight near Castle. Wheelchairs for loan. WCs. Audio tour tapes for partially sighted/those with learning difficulties. Allocated parking.

☕ Creeping Kate's Kitchen (licensed) (max 80) – full menu. Groups can book: 01229 717614 to qualify for discounts.

🚶 Private tours with a personal guide (family member possible) can be arranged at additional fee. Ghost Sits our speciality.

🎧 Individual audio tour (40mins) included in price.

🅿️ 500 cars 800 yds from House; coaches may park closer. Free.

📋 Guides available. Historical subjects, horticulture, conservation, owl tours.

🐕 In grounds, on leads.

ACORN BANK GARDEN & WATERMILL ✥

Temple Sowerby, Penrith, Cumbria CA10 1SP
Tel: 01768 361893   **E-mail:** acornbank@nationaltrust.org.uk
www.nationaltrust.org.uk
Owner: The National Trust   **Contact:** The Custodian
Seventeenth century walls enclose a herb garden with over 250 varieties of medicinal and culinary plants and orchards with traditional fruit trees surrounded by mixed borders. Beyond the walls, paths lead through woodland to a partially restored watermill. House not open.
Location: Gate: MAP 10:M5, OS Ref. NY612 281. Just N of Temple Sowerby, 6m E of Penrith just off A66.
Open: 15 Mar–2 Nov: daily except Mon and Tue, 10am–5pm. Last admission 4.30pm. Tearoom: 11am–4.30pm.
*****Admission:** Adult £3.80, Child £1.90, Family £9.50. *includes a voluntary 10% donation but visitors can choose to pay the standard prices displayed at the property and on the website.
⬛ ✥ ♿ WCs. ☕ 🐾 Woodland walks only.

BEATRIX POTTER GALLERY ✥

Main Street, Hawkshead, Cumbria LA22 0NS
Tel: 01539 436355   **Fax:** 01539 436187
E-mail: beatrixpottergallery@nationaltrust.org.uk   **www.nationaltrust.org.uk**
Owner: The National Trust   **Contact:** Ticket Office/House Steward
An annually changing exhibition of original watercolours and sketches by beloved children's author Beatrix Potter. *The Tale of Jemima Puddle-Duck* and *The Tale of Samuel Whiskers* feature for their 100th birthdays, along with displays on the film *Miss Potter*. The gallery was once the office of Beatrix Potter's husband, William Heelis. It is ideally matched with a visit to Beatrix Potter's house, Hill Top, two miles away. Quizzes for children.
Location: MAP 10:K7, OS Ref. SD352 982. 5m SSW of Ambleside. In the Square.
Open: 15 Mar–2 Nov: Sat–Thurs and Good Fri. Last admission 4pm. Admission is by timed ticket (incl. NT members). Daily quota, early sell outs possible. Shop: daily.
*****Admission:** Adult £4, Child £2, Family £10.00. No reduction for groups. Discount for Hill Top ticket holders. Group booking essential. *includes a voluntary donation but visitors can choose to pay the standard prices displayed at the property and on the website.
ℹ️ No photography inside. ⬛ 🐾 Assistance dogs only.

BLACKWELL –
THE ARTS & CRAFTS HOUSE

See page 400 for full page entry.

BRANTWOOD

Coniston, Cumbria LA21 8AD
Tel: 01539 441396   **Fax:** 01539 441263   **E-mail:** enquiries@brantwood.org.uk
www.brantwood.org.uk
Owner: The Brantwood Trust
Brantwood, the former home of John Ruskin, is the most beautifully situated house in the Lake District. Explore Brantwood's estate and gardens or experience contemporary art in the Severn Studio. Brantwood's bookshop, the Jumping Jenny restaurant and Coach House Craft Gallery combine for a perfect day out.
Location: MAP 10:K7, OS Ref. SD313 959. 2½m from Coniston village on the E side of Coniston Water.
Open: Mid Mar–mid Nov: daily, 11am–5.30pm. Mid Nov–mid Mar: Wed–Sun, 11am–4.30pm.
Admission: Adult £5.95, Child £1.20, Student £4.50, Family (2+3) £11.95. Garden only: Adult £4, Family (2+3) £8.50. Groups: Adult £4.95, Child £1.20, Student £3.50. Garden only: £3.50.
ℹ️ No photography in the house. ⬛ 🖼 ♿ Licensed. ☕ Licensed. 🍴 Licensed. ✍ By arrangement. 🅿 Ample. Limited for coaches. ⬛ 🐾 in grounds, on leads. 🛏 ✳

BROUGH CASTLE ⌗

Brough, Cumbria
Tel: 01228 591922
www.english-heritage.org.uk/broughcastle
Owner: English Heritage   **Contact:** Visitor Operations Manager
This ancient site dates back to Roman times. The 12th century keep replaced an earlier stronghold destroyed by the Scots in 1174.
Location: MAP 10:M6, OS Ref. NY791 141. 8m SE of Appleby S of A66. South part of the village.
Open: Any reasonable time.
Admission: Free.
🐾 On leads. 🅿 ✳

BROUGHAM CASTLE ⌗

Penrith, Cumbria CA10 2AA
Tel: 01768 862488
www.english-heritage.org.uk/broughamcastle
Owner: English Heritage   **Contact:** Visitor Operations Team
These impressive ruins on the banks of the River Eamont include an early 13th century keep and later buildings. You can climb to the top of the keep and survey the domain of its eccentric one-time owner Lady Anne Clifford. Exhibition about the Roman fort, medieval castle and Lady Anne Clifford.
Location: MAP 10:L5, OS Ref. NY537 290. 1½ m SE of Penrith, between A66 & B6262.
Open: 21 Mar–30 Sept: daily, 10am–5pm.
Admission: Adult £3, Child £1.50, Conc. £2.40. Family £7.50. 15% discount for groups (11+). EH members Free.
ℹ️ WCs. ⬛ ♿ Grounds. 🅿 Limited. ⬛ 🐾 In grounds, on leads. 🛏

© English Heritage Photo Library

CARLISLE CASTLE ⌗
CARLISLE, CUMBRIA CA3 8UR
www.english-heritage.org.uk/carlisle

Tel: 01228 591922
Owner: English Heritage   **Contact:** Visitor Operations Team
This impressive medieval castle, where Mary Queen of Scots was once imprisoned, has a long and tortuous history of warfare and family feuds. A portcullis hangs menacingly over the gatehouse passage, there is a maze of passages and chambers, endless staircases to lofty towers and you can walk the high ramparts for stunning views. There is also a medieval manor house in miniature: a suite of medieval rooms furnished as they might have been when used by the castle's former constable. The castle includes the King's Own Royal Border Regimental Museum.
Location: MAP 10:K3, OS Ref. NY396 562. In Carlisle town, at N end of city centre.
Open: 21 Mar–30 Sept: daily, 9.30am–5pm. 1 Oct–31 Mar '09: daily, 10am–4pm. Closed 24–26 Dec & 1 Jan.
Admission: Adult £4.50, Child £2.30, Conc £3.60. 15% discount for groups (11+). EH members Free.
⬛ ♿ Partial, wheelchairs available. ✍ By arrangement. 🅿 Disabled parking only. ⬛ 🐾 Dogs on leads. ✳ 🛏

Sizergh Castle

CARLISLE CATHEDRAL

Carlisle, Cumbria CA3 8TZ
Tel: 01228 548151 **Fax:** 01228 547049 **Contact:** Ms C Baines
Fine sandstone Cathedral, founded in 1122. Medieval stained glass.
Location: MAP 10:K3, OS Ref. NY399 559. Carlisle city centre, 2m from M6/J43.
Open: Mon–Sat: 7.40am–6.15pm, Suns, 7.40–5pm. Closes 4pm between Christmas Day & New Year. Sun services: 8am, 10.30am & 3pm. Weekday services: 8am, 5.30pm & a 12.30 service on Mons, Weds and Fris.
Admission: Donation.

CONISHEAD PRIORY & BUDDHIST TEMPLE

Ulverston, Cumbria LA12 9QQ
Tel: 01229 584029 **Fax:** 01229 580080 **E-mail:** visits@manjushri.org
www.manjushri.org
Owner: Manjushri Kadampa Meditation Centre **Contact:** Geoffrey Roe
Romantic gothic mansion with gardens and woodland walks to Morecambe Bay. Home to international Buddhist Centre and a unique Temple. Guided tours bring alive the spiritual and healing work at the Priory since 1160. Special features include huge reception rooms with decorative ceilings, a vaulted great hall, amazing stained glass windows, grand staircase and 177 feet long cloister corridor. Simon Jenkins says: '*There is no house in England like Conishead*'.
Location: MAP 10:K8, OS Ref. SD305 757. 2m S of Ulverston on A5087 Coast Road.
Open: Grounds open all year (except when closed for Buddhist festivals). Temple, guided tours, gift shop and tearoom Easter to Oct weekends and BHs 2–5pm. Please telephone for winter opening times.
Admission: Free. Guided Tours: Adult £2.50. Under 12yrs Free.

For unique **Civil wedding** venues see our index at the end of the book.

Holker Hall

DALEMAIN 🏛

PENRITH, CUMBRIA CA11 0HB

www.dalemain.com

Tel: 017684 86450 **Fax:** 017684 86223 **E-mail:** admin@dalemain.com
Owner: Robert Hasell-McCosh Esq **Contact:** Dawn Hurton – Estate Administrator
Dalemain is a fine mixture of mediaeval, Tudor and early Georgian architecture. The imposing Georgian façade strikes the visitor immediately but in the cobbled courtyard the atmosphere of the north country Tudor manor is secure. The present owner's family have lived at Dalemain since 1679 and have collected china, furniture and family portraits.
Delightful and fascinating 5 acre plantsman's gardens set against the picturesque splendour of the Lakeland Fells and Parkland. Richly planted herbaceous borders. Rose Walk with over 100 old-fashioned roses and ancient apple trees of named varieties. Magnificent Abies Cephalonica and Tulip Tree. Tudor Knot Garden. Wild Garden with profusion of flowering shrubs and wild flowers and in early summer the breathtaking display of blue Himalayan Poppies.

Location: MAP 10:L5, OS Ref. NY477 269. On A592 1m S of A66. 4m SW of Penrith. From London, M1, M6/J40: 5 hrs. From Edinburgh, A73, M74,M6/J40: 2½ hrs.
Open: Gardens & Tearoom: 5 Feb–20 Mar & 27 Oct–mid Dec:, Sun–Thur. 11am–4pm. House, Gardens, Tearoom & Gift Shop: 23 Mar–23 Oct, 10.30am–5pm. House opens 11.15am for first guided tour. Free flow in afternoons. Groups (10+) please book.
Admission: House & Garden: Adult £7.50, Accompanied Child Free. Gardens only: Adult £5, Accompanied Child Free. Group prices on application.
ℹ️ No photography in house. Moorings available on Ullswater. Visitors may drive into the Courtyard and alight near the gift shop. Electric scooter. WCs. Licensed. Groups must book for lunches/high teas. 1hr tours. German and French translations. Garden tour for groups extra. P 50 yds. Guide dogs in house only. No dogs in garden, allowed in grounds.

©The Wordsworth Trust

DOVE COTTAGE,
THE WORDSWORTH MUSEUM
& ART GALLERY
GRASMERE, CUMBRIA LA22 9SH

www.wordsworth.org.uk

Tel: 01539 435544 **Fax:** 01539 435748 **E-mail:** enquiries@wordsworth.org.uk
Owner: The Wordsworth Trust   **Contact:** Bookings Officer
Situated in the heart of the Lake District, Dove Cottage is the beautifully preserved home of William Wordsworth. Visitors can take a guided tour of the cottage then discover more about the poet at the award-winning Wordsworth Museum next door. On site café/restaurant and bookshop.
Location: MAP 10:K6, OS Ref. NY342 070. Immediately S of Grasmere village on A591. Main car/coach park next to Restaurant.
Open: All year: daily, 9.30am–5.30pm (last admission 5pm). Closed 24–26 Dec & early Jan–early Feb.
Admission: Adult £7.50, Child £4.50, Family tickets group rates available. Prices are subject to change without notice.
ℹ️ No photography. 📷 ♿ Partial. WC. ♿ 🍴 🎫 Obligatory for Dove Cottage. 🅿️ ♿ ♿ Guide dogs only. ✖ ♿

FELL FOOT PARK ✤

Newby Bridge, Cumbria LA12 8NN
Tel: 01539 531273 **Fax:** 01539 539926 **E-mail:** fellfootpark@nationaltrust.org.uk
Owner: The National Trust   **Contact:** Park Manager
Come and explore this lakeshore Victorian park on the edge of Windermere. A great place for the family, with boat hire, tearoom, play area, family activity sheets and wildlife room showing birds and bats who live around the park. Fantastic views of the Lakeland fells. Wonderful colour in spring.
Location: MAP 10:K7, OS Ref. SD381 869. S end of Lake Windermere on E shore, entrance from A592. Near Aquarium of the Lakes and Haverthwaite Steam Railway.
Open: Daily, 9am–5pm (except Christmas Day and Boxing Day). Shop & tearoom, 15 Mar–2 Nov, 11am–5pm.
Admission: Car park: Charge. NT Members Free parking. Coaches by arrangement.
📷 ♿ Partial. ♿ 🅿️ Charge. ♿ On leads. ✖ ♿

FURNESS ABBEY ⌘

Barrow-in-Furness, Cumbria LA13 0PJ
Tel: 01229 823420
www.english-heritage.org.uk/furness
Owner: English Heritage   **Contact:** Visitor Operations Staff
Hidden in a peaceful green valley are the beautiful red sandstone remains of the wealthy abbey founded in 1123 by Stephen, later King of England. This abbey first belonged to the Order of Savigny and later to the Cistercians. There is a museum and exhibition.
Location: MAP 10:J8, OS Ref. SD218 717. 1½m N of Barrow-in-Furness off A590.
Open: 21 Mar–30 Sept: daily, 10am–5pm. 1–31 Oct: Thur–Mon, 10am–4pm.
1 Nov–31 Mar '09: Thur–Sun, 10am–4pm. Closed 24–26 Dec & 1 Jan.
Admission: Adult £3.50, Child £1.80, Conc. £2.80. 15% discount for groups (11+).EH members Free.
ℹ️ WC. 📷 ♿ Grounds. 📷 Inclusive. 🅿️ ♿ ♿ In grounds, on leads. ✖ ♿

HARDKNOTT ROMAN FORT ⌘

Ravenglass, Cumbria
Tel: 0191 269 1200
www.english-heritage.org.uk/hardknottromanfort
Owner: English Heritage   **Contact:** The North East Regional Office
This fort, built between AD120 and 138, controlled the road from Ravenglass to Ambleside.
Location: MAP 10:J6, OS Ref. NY218 015. At the head of Eskdale. 9m NE of Ravenglass, at W end of Hardknott Pass.
Open: Any reasonable time. Access may be hazardous in winter.
Admission: Free.
🅿️ ♿ On leads. ✖

HERON CORN MILL & MUSEUM OF PAPERMAKING

Beetham Trust, Waterhouse Mills, Beetham, Milnthorpe LA7 7AR
Tel: 015395 65027 **Fax:** 015395 65033 **E-mail:** info@heronmill.org
Owner: Heron Corn Mill Beetham Trust   **Contact:** Audrey Steeley
A fascinating visitor attraction. An 18th century corn mill and museum of papermaking offers hand-made paper demonstrations and art workshops for visitors.
Location: MAP 10:L8, OS Ref. SD497 800. At Beetham. 1m S of Milnthorpe on the A6.
Open: Mar–Oct: daily except Mons (open BH Mons), 11am–5pm.
Admission: Please telephone for details. Redevelopment in progress causing some restrictions to visitors.

©NTPL/Tony West

HILL TOP ✤
NEAR SAWREY, AMBLESIDE, CUMBRIA LA22 0LF

www.nationaltrust.org.uk

Tel: 01539 436269 **Fax:** 01539 436811 **E-mail:** hilltop@nationaltrust.org.uk
Owner: The National Trust   **Contact:** Ticket Office/Administrator
Beatrix Potter wrote and illustrated many of her famous children's stories in this little 17th century house, which contains her furniture and china. There is a traditional cottage garden attached. A selection of the original illustrations may be seen at the Beatrix Potter Gallery in Hawkshead. Shop specialises in Beatrix Potter items.
Location: MAP 10:K7, OS Ref. SD370 955. 2m S of Hawkshead, in hamlet of Near Sawrey, behind the Tower Bank Arms.
Open: 15 Mar–2 Nov: Sat–Thur & Good Fri, 10.30am–4.30pm. Garden & Shop: 15 Mar–24 Dec, daily: Call for winter details. Admission by timed ticket (incl. NT members). Daily quota, early sell-outs possible. Group booking essential.
*Admission: Adult £5.40, Child £2.90, Family £14.50. No reduction for groups. Discount for Beatrix Potter Gallery ticket holders. Garden: Free on Fri. *includes a voluntary donation but visitors can choose to pay the standard prices displayed at the property and on the website.
ℹ️ No photography in house. 📷 ♿ Partial. 🅿️ None for coaches. ♿ Assistance dogs only. ♿

HOLEHIRD GARDENS

Patterdale Road, Windermere, Cumbria LA23 1NP
Tel: 01539 446008
Owner: Lakeland Horticultural Society   **Contact:** The Hon Secretary/Publicity Officer
Over 10 acres of hillside gardens overlooking Windermere, including a wide variety of plants, specimen trees and shrubs, extensive rock and heather gardens, a walled garden, alpine houses and herbaceous borders. The all year garden also is home to the national collections of Astilbe, Hydrangea and Polystichum ferns. Managed and maintained entirely by volunteers.
Location: MAP 10:K7, OS Ref. NY410 008. On A592, ¾m N of junction with A591. ½ m N of Windermere. 1m from Townend.
Open: All year: dawn till dusk. Groups strictly by arrangement. Reception: Apr–Oct, 10am–5pm.
Admission: Free. Donation appreciated (at least £3 suggested).

HOLKER HALL & GARDENS 🏛

See page 401 for full page entry.

Wordsworth House

HUTTON-IN-THE-FOREST 🏛
PENRITH, CUMBRIA CA11 9TH
www.hutton-in-the-forest.co.uk

Tel: 017684 84449   **Fax:** 017684 84571   **E-mail:** info@hutton-in-the-forest.co.uk
Owner: Lord Inglewood   **Contact:** Edward Thompson
The home of Lord Inglewood's family since 1605. Built around a medieval pele tower with 17th, 18th and 19th century additions. Fine collections of furniture, paintings, ceramics and tapestries. Outstanding grounds with terraces, topiary, walled garden, dovecote and woodland walk through magnificent specimen trees.
Location: MAP 10:L5, OS Ref. NY460 358. 6m NW of Penrith & 2½ m from M6/J41 on B5305.

Open: 20 Mar–6 Apr & 30 Apr–28 Sept. Sept: Weds, Thurs, Suns & BH Mons, 12.30–4pm (last entry). Tearoom: As house: 11am–4.30pm. Gardens & Grounds: 20 Mar–31 Oct, daily except Sats, 11am–5pm.
Admission: House, Gardens & Grounds: Adult £5.50, Child £3.50, Family £15. Gardens & Grounds: Adult £3.50, Child £1. (2007 prices.)
ℹ️ Picnic area. 🏪 Gift stall. 🍴 By arrangement. ♿ Partial. 🐕
🚶 Obligatory (except Jul/Aug & BHs). 🅿️ 🚌 🐕 On leads. 🐕

LANERCOST PRIORY ⌗

Brampton, Cumbria CA8 2HQ
Tel: 01697 73030
www.english-heritage.org.uk/lanercost
Owner: English Heritage   **Contact:** Visitor Operations Team
This Augustinian priory was founded c1166. The nave of the church, which is intact and in use as the local parish church, contrasts with the ruined chancel, transepts and priory buildings. Free audio tour.
Location: MAP 10:L3, OS Ref. NY556 637. 2m NE of Brampton. 1m N of Naworth Castle.
Open: 21 Mar–30 Sept: daily, 10am–5pm. 1–31 Oct: Thur–Mon, 10am–4pm. 3 Nov–16 Dec, Sats & Suns. 10am–4pm. Closed 24/25 Dec.
Admission: Adult £3, Child £1.50, Conc. £2.40, Family £7.50, Groups (11+): 15% discount. EH members Free.
📷 ♿ Ground floor. 🐕 Inclusive. 🅿️ Limited. 🚌 🐕 🐕

LEVENS HALL 🏛

See page 402 for full page entry.

For **accommodation** in the North West, see our special index at the end of the book.

©NTPL

MIREHOUSE
KESWICK, CUMBRIA CA12 4QE

www.mirehouse.com

Tel: 017687 72287   **E-mail:** info@mirehouse.com
Owner: James Fryer-Spedding   **Contact:** Janaki Spedding
Melvyn Bragg described Mirehouse as *'Manor from Heaven'*. Hunter Davies wrote *'Not to be missed'* and Simon Jenkins in *The Times* said *'It is the Lake District with its hand on its heart'*. Literary house linked with Tennyson and Wordsworth. Natural playgrounds and lakeside walk.
Location: MAP 10:J5, OS Ref. NY235 284. Beside A591, 3½ m N of Keswick. Good bus service.
Open: Apr–Oct: Gardens & Tearoom: daily, 10am–5.30pm. House: Suns & Weds (also Fris in Aug), 2–5pm (4.30pm last entry). Groups (20+) welcome by appointment.
Admission: House & Garden: Adult £5.60, Child £2.80, Family (2+4) £15.50. Gardens only: Adult £2.80, Child £1.40.
ℹ No photography in house. 🅱 🖵 🎦 By arrangement. 🅿 Limited. ▣
🐾 On leads only.

MUNCASTER CASTLE GARDENS, *See page 403 for full page entry.*
OWL CENTRE & MEADOW VOLE MAZE 🏠

PENRITH CASTLE ⌗

Penrith, Cumbria
Tel: 0161 242 1400
www.english-heritage.org.uk/penrith
Owner: English Heritage   **Contact:** The North West Regional Office
This mainly 15th century castle, set in a park on the edge of the town, was built to defend Penrith against repeated attacks by Scottish raiders.
Location: MAP 10:L5, OS Ref. NY513 299. Opposite Penrith railway station. W of the town centre. Fully visible from the street.
Open: Park: All year, daily: 7.30am–9pm (closes 4.30pm winter).
Admission: Free.
ℹ WC 🐾 On leads.

RYDAL MOUNT & GARDENS
RYDAL, CUMBRIA LA22 9LU

www.rydalmount.co.uk

Tel: 01539 433002   **Fax:** 01539 431738   **E-mail:** info@rydalmount.co.uk
Owner: Rydal Mount Trustees   **Contact:** Peter & Marian Elkington
Home of William Wordsworth – England's finest poet. Nestling in the beautiful fells between Lake Windermere and Rydal Water, lies the 'best loved family home' of William Wordsworth from 1813–1850. Experience the splendid historic home of Wordsworth's descendants; Enjoy the beautiful terraced gardens landscaped by the poet; Feel the peaceful relaxed 'romantic' atmosphere; The freedom of wandering through this 'spot of more perfect and enjoyable beauty' as wrote Dr Thomas Arnold.
Location: MAP 10:K6, OS Ref. NY364 063. 1½m N of Ambleside on A591 Grasmere Road.
Open: Mar–Oct: daily, 9.30am–5pm. Nov–Feb (closed Jan): daily except Tues, 10am–4pm. Garden & Tearoom: May–Sept.
Admission: House & Garden: Adult £5.50, Child £2, Conc. £4.50, Family £13. Garden only: £2.50. Free parking. Reciprocal discount ticket with Dove Cottage & Wordsworth House (on full paying admission only).
ℹ No inside photography. 🅾 🅱 Partial. 🎦 By arrangement. 🅿 Limited. ▣
🐾 In grounds, on leads. Guide dogs only in house. ✳

SIZERGH CASTLE & GARDEN 🦡

Sizergh, Nr Kendal, Cumbria LA8 8AE
Tel/Fax: 01539 560951   **E-mail:** sizergh@nationaltrust.org.uk
www.nationaltrust.org.uk
Owner: The National Trust   **Contact:** Property Administrator
This imposing house, at the gateway to the Lake District, stands proud in a rich and beautiful garden with a pond, a lake, an important collection of hardy ferns and a superb limestone rock garden. The estate is crossed with footpaths, giving stunning views over Morecambe Bay and the Lakeland hills. Still lived in by the Strickland family, Sizergh has many tales to tell, showing centuries-old portraits, fine furniture and ceramics collections alongside modern-day family photos – it certainly feels lived in! The exceptional wood panelling culminates in the Inlaid Chamber, previously at the Victoria & Albert, and returned here in 1999. Take time to explore the house and garden, sample fine local produce in our contempoary café: then follow one of our trail leaflets around the estate.
Location: MAP 10:L7, OS Ref. SD498 878. 3½m S of Kendal, NW of the A590 / A591 interchange.
Open: Castle: 17 Mar–2 Nov, daily except Fri & Sat, 1–5pm. Garden: daily except Fri & Sat, 11–5pm. Café & shop open 5 Jan–16 Mar, weekends 11–4pm, 17 Mar–2 Nov, daily except Fri & Sat, 11–5pm, 8 Nov–21 Dec, weekends, 11–4pm, daily Feb 08 half term.
*Admission: House & Garden: Adult £7.10, Child £3.60, Family £17.80 (1+3) £10.70. Garden only: Adult £4.70, Child £2.40, Groups tickets available. *includes a voluntary donation but visitors can choose to pay the standard prices displayed at the property and on the website.

STAGSHAW GARDEN ✤

Ambleside, Cumbria LA22 0HE
Tel/Fax: 015394 46027 **E-mail:** stagshaw@nationaltrust.org.uk
Owner: The National Trust

This woodland garden contains a fine collection of azaleas and rhododendrons, planted to give good blends of colour under thinned oaks on the hillside; also magnolias, camellias and embothriums. Adjacent to the woods are Skelghyll Woods which offer delightful walks and access to the fells beyond.

Location: MAP 10:K6, OS Ref. NY380 029. ½m S of Ambleside on A591. Ferry Waterhead ½m.

Open: 1 Apr–30 Jun: daily, 10am–6.30pm. Colours best Apr–Jun. Jul–end Oct: by appointment through the property office at St Catherines, Patterdale Road, Windermere LA23 1NH.

Admission: £2.50, by honesty box.

♿ Unsuitable. 🅿 Limited. ⊠

STOTT PARK BOBBIN MILL ⌗

Low Stott Park, Nr Newby Bridge, Cumbria LA12 8AX
Tel: 01539 531087

www.english-heritage.org.uk/stottpark

Owner: English Heritage **Contact:** Visitor Operations Team

When this working mill was built in 1835 it was typical of the many mills in the Lake District which grew up to supply the spinning and weaving industry in Lancashire but have since disappeared. A remarkable opportunity to see a demonstration of the machinery and techniques of the Industrial Revolution. Steam days: Tues–Thurs.

Location: MAP 10:K7, OS Ref. SD372 881. 1½m N of Newby Bridge off A590.

Open: 21 Mar–31 Oct: Mon–Fri, 11am–5pm (Steam days, Mon–Thurs). Last admission 1hr before closing.

Admission: Adult £4.20, Child £2.10, Conc. £3.40, Family £10.50. Groups: discount for groups (11+). EH members Free.

▣ ♿ Ground floor. WC. 🎧 Free. 🅿 ◾ ⊠

HELENA THOMPSON MUSEUM

Park End Road, Workington, Cumbria CA14 4DE
Tel: 01900 606155 **E-mail:** whghtm@hotmail.co.uk

Owner: Allerdale Borough Council **Contact:** Museum Manager

The museum is housed in a fine listed mid-Georgian building. Displays include pottery, silver, glass, furniture and dress collection.

Location: MAP 10:I5, OS Ref. NY007 286. Corner of A66, Ramsey Brow & Park End Road.

Open: All year: Tues–Sun, 1.30–4.30pm (Jul–Aug, 10.30am–4.30pm). Other times by arrangement.

Admission: Free.

Dalemain

TOWNEND ✤
TROUTBECK, WINDERMERE, CUMBRIA LA23 1LB

www.nationaltrust.org.uk

Tel: 01539 432628 **E-mail:** townend@nationaltrust.org.uk
Owner: The National Trust **Contact:** The Custodian

An exceptional relic of Lake District life during past centuries. Originally a 'statesman' (wealthy yeoman) farmer's house, built about 1626. Townend contains carved woodwork, books, papers, furniture and fascinating implements of the past which were accumulated by the Browne family who lived here from 1626 until 1943.

Location: MAP 10:K6, OS Ref. NY407 023. 3m SE of Ambleside at S end of Troutbeck village. 1m from Holehird, 3m N of Windermere.

Open: 15–30 Mar & 29 Oct–2 Nov: Wed–Sun, 1–4pm, 2 Apr–26 Oct: Wed–Sun, 1–5pm, Last admission ½ hour before closing.

*Admission: Adult £4.20, Child £2.10, Family £10.50. No reduction for groups which must be pre-booked. *includes a voluntary donation but visitors can choose to pay the standard prices displayed at the property and on the website.

♿ Unsuitable for wheelchairs. ⊠ ♨

WORDSWORTH HOUSE ✤

Main Street, Cockermouth, Cumbria CA13 9RX
Tel: 01900 824805 **Opening Info:** 01900 820884 **Fax:** 01900 820883
E-mail: wordsworthhouse@nationaltrust.org.uk **www.wordsworthhouse.org.uk**
Owner: The National Trust **Contact:** The Custodian

This Georgian town house was the birthplace of William Wordsworth. Imaginatively presented as the home of the Wordsworth family in the 1770s, the house offers a lively and participative visit with costumed living history. The garden, with terraced walk overlooking the River Derwent, has been restored to its 18th century appearance with vegetables, herbs, fruit and flowers.

Location: MAP 10:J5, OS Ref. NY118 307. Main Street, Cockermouth.

Open: 12 Mar–1 Nov: Mon–Sat, 11am–4.30pm. Last entry 4pm. Shop: 5 Mar–23 Dec: Mon–Sat, 10am–5pm and 2–26 Jan: Wed–Sat, 10am–4pm.

*Admission: Adult £5.60, Child £2.80, Family £14.50. Pre-booked groups (15+): Adult £4.90, Child £2.40. *includes a voluntary donation but visitors can choose to pay the standard prices displayed at the property and on the website.

ℹ No photography. ▣ ♿ Partial. WCs. 🎧 By arrangement only. ◾ ⊠ Guide dogs only.

For rare and unusual plants visit the **plant sales** index at the end of the book.

■ **Contact**

Mrs C S Reynolds
Leighton Hall
Carnforth
Lancashire LA5 9ST

Tel: 01524 734474
Fax: 01524 720357
E-mail: info@
leightonhall.co.uk

■ **Location**

MAP 10:L8
OS Ref. SD494 744

9m N of Lancaster,
10m S of Kendal,
3m N of Carnforth.
1½ m W of A6.
3m from M6/A6/J35,
signed from J35A.

Rail: Carnforth
Station 3m.

Bus: The Carnforth
Connect (line 1) bus from
Carnforth Railway Station
stops at the gates of
Leighton Hall
(info 01524 734311).

Air: Manchester
Airport 65m.

Taxi: Carnforth Radio
Taxis, 01524 732763.

■ **Opening Times**

Summer
May–September, Tue–Fri
(also BH Sun & Mon, Suns
in August) 2–5pm.

NB. Booked groups (25+)
at any time, all year by
arrangement.

Winter
1 October–30 April
Open to booked
groups (25+).

■ **Admission**

Summer
House, Garden & Birds
Adult   £6.00
Child (5-12yrs)   £4.00
Student/OAP   £5.00
Family (2+3)   £18.00

Groups (25+)
Adult   £4.50
Child (5-12yrs)   £3.50
Child under 5yrs, Free

Grounds only
(after 4.30pm)
Per person   £2.00

Winter
As above but groups by
appointment only.

Pre-booked Candlelit Tours
Nov–Jan.

Note: The owners reserve the
right to close or restrict access
to the house and grounds for
special events, or at any other
time without prior notice.

■ **Conference/Function**

ROOM	SIZE	MAX CAPACITY
Music Room	24' x 21'6"	80
Dining Rm		30
Other		80

LEIGHTON HALL

www.leightonhall.co.uk

Leighton Hall is one of the most beautifully sited houses in the British Isles, situated in a bowl of parkland, with the whole panorama of the Lakeland Fells rising behind. The Hall's neo-gothic façade was superimposed on an 18th century house, which, in turn, had been built on the ruins of the original medieval house. The present owner is descended from Adam d'Avranches who built the first house in 1246.

The whole house is, today, lived in by the Reynolds family whose emphasis is put on making visitors feel welcome in a family home. Mr Reynolds is also descended from the founder of Gillow and

Company of Lancaster. Connoisseurs of furniture will be particularly interested in the many 18th century Gillow pieces, some of which are unique. Fine pictures, clocks, silver and objéts d'art are also on display.

Gardens

The main garden has a continuous herbaceous border with rose covered walls, while the Walled Garden contains flowering shrubs, a herb garden, and an ornamental vegetable garden with a caterpillar maze. Beyond is the Woodland Walk where wild flowers abound from early spring.

 No photography in house.

Unusual plants for sale.

Product launches, conferences, seminars, filming, garden parties. Outdoor events include: overland driving, archery and clay pigeon shooting. Wedding receptions, buffets, lunches and dinners.

Partial. WC. Visitors may alight at the entrance to the Hall. Ground floor only.

Booking essential for group catering, menus on request.

Obligatory. By prior arrangement owner may meet groups. The 45 minute tour includes information on the property, its gardens and history. House tour time: 2 hrs.

Ample for cars and coaches.

School programme: all year round. Choice of Countryside Classroom, Victorian Leighton or Local History. Sandford Award for Heritage Education winner in 1983 and 1989.

In Park, on leads.

An unusual, but spectacular venue, Leighton Hall is a fairytale choice.

For booked groups & functions.

Visit website for details.

BLACKBURN CATHEDRAL

Cathedral Close, Blackburn, Lancashire BB1 5AA
Tel: 01254 503090 **Fax:** 01254 689666 **Contact:** Pauline Rowe
www.blackburncathedral.com
On an historic Saxon site in town centre. The 1826 Parish Church dedicated as the Cathedral in 1926 with new extensions to give a spacious and light interior. Of special interest is 'The Journey', a contemporary version of *The Stations of the Cross*, by Penny Warden commisioned by the Cathedral in 2005. The Cathedral is also noted for its outstanding music and significant contributions to the work of cultural understanding both locally and nationally.
Location: MAP 10:M11, OS Ref. SD684 280. 9m E of M6/J31, via A59 and A677. Town centre.
Open: Daily, 9am–5pm. Sun services: at 8am, 9am, 10.30am and 4pm. Catering: Tues–Sat, 10am–2.30pm.
Admission: Free. Donations invited.

BROWSHOLME HALL

Clitheroe, Lancashire BB7 3DE
Tel: 01254 827160 **E-mail:** rrp@browsholme.co.uk **www.browsholme.co.uk**
Owner/Contact: Robert Parker
Built in 1507 by Edmund Parker, 2007 is the 500th Anniversary of Browsholme Hall the ancestral Home of the Parker Family. This remarkable Tudor Hall has a major collection of oak furniture and portraits, arms and armour, stained glass and many unusual antiquities from the Civil war to a fragment of a Zeppelin. Browsholme, pronounced 'Brusom', lies in the Forest of Bowland, and is set in unspoilt parkland in the style of Capability Brown. The façade still retains the ' H' shape of the original house with later Queen Anne and Regency additions when the house was refurbished by Thomas Lister Parker a noted antiquarian and patron of artists such as Turner and Northcote.
Location: MAP 10:M10, OS Ref. SD683 452. 5m NW of Clitheroe off B6243.
Open: 24–31 May, 28 Jun–4 Jul, 15–31 Aug; Daily, 2–5pm except Mons (open BH Mons). Groups particularly welcome by appointment.
Admission: Adult £5, Child £1.50, OAP £4.50.

GAWTHORPE HALL

Padiham, Nr Burnley, Lancashire BB12 8UA
Tel: 01282 771004 **Fax:** 01282 776663 **E-mail:** gawthorpehall@nationaltrust.org.uk
Owner: The National Trust, managed by Lancashire County Council
Contact: Property Office
The house was built in 1600–05, and restored by Sir Charles Barry in the 1850s. Barry's designs have been re-created in the principal rooms. Gawthorpe was the home of the Shuttleworth family, and the Rachel Kay-Shuttleworth textile collections are on display in the house, private study by arrangement. Collection of portraits on loan from the National Portrait Gallery.
Location: MAP 10:N10, OS Ref. SD806 340. M65/J8. On E outskirts of Padiham, ¾ m to house on N of A671. Signed to Clitheroe, then signed from 2nd set of traffic lights.
Open: Hall & Tearoom: 21 Mar–30 Oct: daily except Mons & Fris, open Good Fri & BH Mons, 1–5pm. Last adm. 4.30pm. Garden: All year: daily, 10am–6pm.
Admission: Hall: Adult £4, Conc. £3, Child Free when accompanied by an adult. Prices subject to confirmation in 2008. Garden: Free. NT members Free, but charge to enter grounds may apply on special event days.
Please ring in advance. In grounds on leads.

HALL I'TH'WOOD

off Green Way, off Crompton Way, Bolton BL1 8UA
Tel: 01204 332370
Owner: Bolton Metropolitan Borough Council **Contact:** Liz Shaw
Late medieval manor house with 17/18th century furniture, paintings and decorative art.
Location: MAP 10:M12, OS Ref. SD724 116. 2m NNE of central Bolton. ¼m N of A58 ring road between A666 and A676 crossroads.
Open: Easter–31 Oct: Wed–Sun & BHs, 12 noon–5pm. Last adm. 4.15pm.
1 Nov–Easter '09: Sats & Suns, 12 noon–5pm. Last adm. 4.15pm.
Admission: Adult £2, Child/Conc. £1, Family £5.

Leighton Hall.

North West – England

Len Grant

HEATON PARK
PRESTWICH, MANCHESTER M25 2SW

www.heatonpark.org.uk

Tel: 0161 773 1085 **Fax** 0161 798 0107 **E-mail:** heatonpark@manchester.gov.uk
Owner: Manchester City Council **Contact:** Janet Kendall

Heaton Park has been in public ownership since 1902 when the 5th Earl of Wilton sold it to the Manchester Corporation. The landscape surrounding the house was designed by William Emes and modified by John Webb and has recently been restored in partnership with the HLF, together with four of the park's historic buildings. The magnificent James Wyatt house was built for Sir Thomas Egerton in 1772, and is one of Manchester's most impressive and important buildings. The principal rooms have been beautifully restored and are used to display furniture, paintings and other decorative arts appropriate to the late 18th century.

Location: MAP 6:N1, OS Ref. SD833 044. NW Manchester, close to M60/J19. Main entrance off St Margaret's Road, off Bury Old Road – A665.
Open: House: 22 Mar–31 Aug, Thur–Sun & BH Mons, 11am–5.30pm. Park: all year, daily, 8am–dusk.
Admission: Free.

ⓘ No photography in house, no dogs in buildings. ⬚ ⊤ ⬚ Partial. WCs. ⬚
ⓕ By arrangement. Ⓟ Ample for cars, but limited for coaches. ⬚
⬚ In grounds, on leads. ⬚ Double x 2. ⬚ ⬚

HOGHTON TOWER ⬚
HOGHTON, PRESTON, LANCASHIRE PR5 0SH

www.hoghtontower.co.uk

Tel: 01254 852986 **Fax:** 01254 852109 **E-mail:** mail@hoghtontower.co.uk
Owner: Sir Bernard de Hoghton Bt **Contact:** Office

Hoghton Tower, home of 14th Baronet, is one of the most dramatic looking houses in northern England. Three houses have occupied the hill site since 1100 with the present house re-built by Thomas Hoghton between 1560–1565. Rich and varied historical events including the Knighting of the Loin 'Sirloin' by James I in 1617.
Location: MAP 10:L11, OS Ref. SD622 264. M65/J3. Midway between Preston & Blackburn on A675.
Open: Jul, Aug & Sept: Mon–Thur, 11am–4pm. Suns, 1–5pm. BH Suns & Mons excluding Christmas & New Year. Group visits by appointment all year.
Admission: Gardens & House tours: Adult £6, Child/Conc. £5, Family £18. Gardens, Shop & Tearoom only: £3. Children under 5yrs Free. Private tours by arrangement (25+) £6, OAP £5.

⬚ ⊤ Conferences, wedding receptions. ⬚ Unsuitable. ⬚ ⓕ Obligatory. Ⓟ ⬚ ⬚

LEIGHTON HALL ⬚ *See page 410 for full page entry.*

MANCHESTER CATHEDRAL

Manchester M3 1SX

Tel: 0161 833 2220 **Fax:** 0161 839 6218 **www.manchestercathedral.co.uk**

In addition to regular worship and daily offices, there are frequent professional concerts, day schools, organ recitals, guided tours and brass-rubbing. The cathedral contains a wealth of beautiful carvings and has the widest medieval nave in Britain.
Location: MAP 6:N1, OS Ref. SJ838 988. Manchester.
Open: Daily. Visitor Centre: Mon–Sat, 10am–4.30pm.
Admission: Donations welcome.

ⓘ Visitor Centre. ⬚ ⬚

MARTHOLME

Great Harwood, Blackburn, Lancashire BB6 7UJ

Tel: 01254 886463
Owner: Mr & Mrs T H Codling **Contact:** Miss P M Codling

Part of medieval manor house with 17th century additions and Elizabethan gatehouse.
Location: MAP 10:M10, OS Ref. SD753 338. 2m NE of Great Harwood off A680 to Whalley.
Open: 2–11 & 23–26 May, 30 May–2 Jun, 22–31 Aug. Tours at 2pm & 4pm.
Admission: £5. Groups welcome by appointment.

---

visit hudsons guide online

RUFFORD OLD HALL

RUFFORD, Nr ORMSKIRK, LANCASHIRE L40 1SG

www.nationaltrust.org.uk

Tel: 01704 821254 **Fax:** 01704 823813 **Email:** ruffordoldhall@nationaltrust.org.uk
Owner: The National Trust **Contact:** The Property Manager
One of the finest 16th century buildings in Lancashire. The magnificent Great Hall contains an intricately carved movable screen and suits of armour, and is believed to have hosted Shakespeare. Collections of weapons, tapestries and oak furniture are found in the Carolean Wing and attractive gardens contain sculptures and topiary.
Location: MAP 10:L11, OS Ref. SD463 160. 7m N of Ormskirk, in Rufford village E of A59.
Open: 15 Mar–2 Nov: Mon–Wed, Sat, Sun. Also Garden, Shop & Restaurant 7 Nov–21 Dec: Fri–Sun, 12 noon–4pm), free entry to visitors except for special events. Grounds, Shop & Restaurant: 11am–5pm. House: 1–5pm. Last adm. 4.30pm.
Admission: House & Garden: Adult £5.70, Child £2.90, Family £14.30. Garden only: Adult £4, Child £2. Booked groups (15+): Adult £4.70, Child £2.40.
ⓘ No photography in house. Partial. Licensed. By arrangement. P Limited for coaches. In grounds, on leads.

SAMLESBURY HALL

Preston New Road, Samlesbury, Preston PR5 0UP

Tel: 01254 812010 **Fax:** 01254 812174
Owner: Samlesbury Hall Trust **Contact:** Mrs S Jones - Director
Built in 1325, the hall is an attractive black and white timbered manor house set in extensive grounds. Weddings and events welcome. Antiques and crafts all year.
Location: MAP 10:L11, OS Ref. SD623 305. N side of A677, 4m WNW of Blackburn.
Open: All year: daily except Sats: 11am–4.30pm.
Admission: Adult £3, Child £1. Free entry to Restaurant.

SMITHILLS HALL HISTORIC HOUSE

Smithills Dean Road, Bolton BL7 7NP

Tel: 01204 332377 **E-mail:** smithills@bolton.gov.uk
Owner: Bolton Metropolitan Borough Council **Contact:** Liz McNabb
14th century manor house with Tudor panelling. Stuart furniture. Stained glass.
Location: MAP 10:M12, OS Ref. SD699 119. 2m NW of central Bolton, ½m N of A58 ringroad.
Open: Apr–Oct: Tue–Fri & Sun, 12 noon–5pm. Last adm. 4pm. Nov–Mar: Fri & Sun, 12 noon–4pm. Last adm. 3pm. Open BH Mons: 12 noon–5pm.
Admission: Adult £3, Conc. £1.75, Family (2+3) £7.75.

TOWNELEY HALL ART GALLERY & MUSEUMS

Burnley BB11 3RQ

Tel: 01282 424213 **Fax:** 01282 436138 www.towneleyhall.org.uk
Owner: Burnley Borough Council **Contact:** Miss Susan Bourne
House dates from the 14th century with 17th and 19th century modifications. Collections include oak furniture, 18th and 19th century paintings. There is a Museum of Local History.
Location: MAP 10:N10, OS Ref. SD854 309. ½m SE of Burnley on E side of Todmorden Road (A671).
Open: All year: daily except Fris, 12 noon–5pm. Closed Christmas–New Year.
Admission: Small charge. Guided tours: Tues–Thur afternoons or as booked for groups.
WC.

TURTON TOWER

Tower Drive, Chapeltown Road, Turton BL7 0HG

Tel: 01204 852203 **Fax:** 01204 853759 **E-mail:** turtontower@mus.lancscc.gov.uk
Owner: The Trustees of Turton Tower (run by Lancashire County Museums Service)
Contact: Fiona Jenkins
Country house based on a medieval tower, extended in the 16th, 17th and 19th centuries.
Location: MAP 10:M11, OS Ref. SD733 153. On B6391, 4m N of Bolton.
Open: Mar, Apr & Nov, daily except Thurs & Fris, 12 noon–4pm. May–Sept, daily except Fris, 12 noon–5pm.
Admission: Adult £4, Child Free, Conc. £3.

WARTON OLD RECTORY

Warton, Carnforth, Lancashire

Tel: 0191 269 1200 www.english-heritage.org.uk/warton
Owner: English Heritage **Contact:** The North East Regional Office
A rare medieval stone house with remains of the hall, chambers and domestic offices.
Location: MAP 10:L8, OS Ref. SD499 723. At Warton, 1m N of Carnforth on minor road off A6.
Open: 21 Mar–30 Sept: daily, 10am–6pm. 1 Oct–31 Mar 09: daily 10am–4pm. Closed 24–26 Dec & 1 Jan.
Admission: Free.
On leads.

Rufford Old Hall

CROXTETH HALL & COUNTRY PARK

Liverpool, Merseyside L12 0HB

Tel: 0151 233 6910 **Fax:** 0151 228 2817

Owner: Liverpool City Council **Contact:** Mrs Irene Vickers

Ancestral home of the Molyneux family. 500 acres country park. Special events and attractions most weekends.

Location: MAP 6:K1, OS Ref. SJ408 943. 5m NE of Liverpool city centre.

Open: Parkland: daily throughout the year. Hall, Farm & Garden: Easter–Sept: daily, 10.30am–5pm. Telephone for exact dates.

Admission: Hall, Farm & Garden: Adult £4.70. Conc. £2.60 (subject to change from Easter 2008). Parkland: Free.

LIVERPOOL CATHEDRAL

Liverpool, Merseyside L1 7AZ

Tel: 0151 709 6271 **Fax:** 0151 702 7292

Owner: The Dean and Chapter **Contact:** Eryl Parry

Sir Giles Gilbert Scott's greatest creation. Built last century from local sandstone with superb glass, stonework and major works of art, it is the largest cathedral in Britain.

Location: MAP 6:K1, OS Ref. SJ354 893. Central Liverpool, ½m S of Lime Street Station.

Open: All year: daily, 8am–6pm. Sun services: 8am, 10.30am, 3pm, 4pm. Weekdays: 8am & 5.30pm, also 12.05pm on Fri. Sats: 8am & 3pm.

Admission: Donation. Lift to Tower and Embroidery Exhibition: £4.25 (concessions available). Family Ticket (2+3) £10. Opened 2007: *'The Great Space'* panoramic film and audio tours £4.75 (concessions, family ticket and combination ticket to include tower available).

LIVERPOOL METROPOLITAN CATHEDRAL OF CHRIST THE KING

Liverpool, Merseyside L3 5TQ

Tel: 0151 709 9222 **Fax:** 0151 708 7274 **E-mail:** enquiries@metcathedral.org.uk

www.liverpoolmetrocathedral.org.uk

Owner: Roman Catholic Archdiocese of Liverpool **Contact:** Canon Anthony O'Brien

Modern circular cathedral with spectacular glass by John Piper and numerous modern works of art. Extensive earlier crypt by Lutyens. Grade II* listed.

Location: MAP 6:K1, OS Ref. SJ356 903. Central Liverpool, ½m E of Lime Street Station.

Open: 8am–6pm (closes 5pm Suns in Winter). Sun services: 8.30am, 10am, 11am & 7pm. Weekday services: 8am, 12.15pm & 5.15pm. Sats, 9am & 6.30pm. Gift shop & Restaurant: Mon–Sat, 10am–5pm; Sun, 11am–4pm.

Admission: Donation.

🔲 🔲 ♿ Except crypt. WCs. 🔲 🍴 ⓘ By arrangement. 🅿 Ample for cars. 🔲 🐕 Guide dogs only.

MEOLS HALL 🏛

Churchtown, Southport, Merseyside PR9 7LZ

Tel: 01704 228326 **Fax:** 01704 507185 **E-mail:** events@meolshall.com

www.meolshall.com

Owner: The Hesketh Family **Contact:** Pamela Whelan

17th century house with subsequent additions. Interesting collection of pictures and furniture. Tithe Barn available for wedding ceremonies and receptions all year.

Location: MAP 10:K11, OS Ref. SD365 184. 3m NE of Southport town centre in Churchtown. SE of A565.

Open: 14 Aug–14 Sept: daily, 2–5pm.

Admission: Adult £4, Child £1. Groups only (25+) £10 (inclusive of full afternoon tea). ⓣ Wedding ceremonies and receptions now available in the Tithe Barn.

♿ 🔲 🅿 🔲 🔲

SPEKE HALL GARDEN & ESTATE 🌿

The Walk, Liverpool L24 1XD

Tel: 0151 427 7231 **Fax:** 0151 427 9860 **Info Line:** 08457 585702

www.nationaltrust.org.uk

Owner: The National Trust **Contact:** The Property Manager

One of the most famous half-timbered houses in the country.

Location: MAP 6:K1, OS Ref. SJ419 825. North bank of the Mersey, 6m SE of city centre. Follow signs for Liverpool John Lennon airport.

Open: House: 15 Mar–2 Nov: Wed–Sun, 1–5.30pm; 8 Nov–14 Dec: Sats & Suns only, 1–4.30pm. Grounds: 15 Mar–2 Nov: Tue–Sun, 11am–5.30pm; 4 Nov–31 Jan '09: Tue–Sun,11am–dusk. Home Farm/restaurant/shop: 15 Mar–13 July, Wed–Sun, 11am–5pm; 15 Jul–14 Sept: Tue–Sun, 11am–5pm; 17 Sept–2 Nov, Wed–Sun, 11am–5pm; 8 Nov–14 Dec :Sats & Suns only, 11–4.30pm. Open BH Mons closed 24–26 & 31 Dec & 1 Jan.

***Admission:** Adult £7.50, Child £3.80, Family £20.50. Grounds only: Adult £4.50, Child £2.50, Family £11.50. *includes a voluntary donation but visitors can choose to pay the standard prices displayed at the property and on the website.

World Her
LIVER

Liver Building
1908–11 Listed Grade I
The head offices of the Royal Liver Friendly Society were designed by Aubrey Thomas. It is notable as one of Britain's first multi-storey reinforced concrete framed buildings. The clock towers are mounted with copper Liver Birds which to many are the very identity of Liverpool.

Cunard Building
1913–1916 Grade II*
This substantial building was built as the offices of the Cunard Shipping Company to the designs of Willink and Thicknesse. Its proportions give it the form of an Italian palazzo. The portraits of races from around the world symbolise the global operations of the company.

Leeds and Liverpool Canal Locks
Circa 1848 Grade II
The canal had been in partial use since 1774 and was completed through to Leeds in 1816; a direct link to the docks was formed in 1848. The four locks were designed by Hartley, and are the only all-granite canal locks in the country. The brick viaduct carried the Liverpool and Bury Railway. The canal is being extended to the Albert Dock with its opening due in 2009.
www.britishwaterways.co.uk
/liverpoolcanallink/index.php

The Dock Wall
Its purpose was to control rather than prevent access from the town into the docks, and the monumental gateways with their heavy wooden gates sliding in iron guide rails effectively made the docks into a fortress-like stronghold. The design of the various gate piers demonstrates a fascinating progression from Foster's early classical style to Hartley's whimsical turrets.

St George's Hall
1840–55 Grade I
A design competition for a new musical venue for Liverpool was held and won by young architect Harvey Lonsdale Elmes. The Hall is built in Grecian style externally with a Roman interior. It contains the lavish Great Hall, with its Minton tiled floor and great organ, and the more intimate Small Concert Room, much visited by Charles Dickens. The Crown and Civil courts at either end were introduced following a further competition. The Hall re-opened in April 2007 following a £23m refurbishment to restore its concert room and create a Heritage visitor centre.

World Museum Liverpool and Central Library
1857–60 Grade II*
The completion of the magnificent new hall on St George's Plateau set the pattern for other civic projects on adjacent land. The Liverpool Improvements Act was passed and a competition was opened in 1855 for a new museum and public library. Local MP William Brown donated £6,000, and the street was renamed in his honour. The building is now home to the internationally important collections of World Museum Liverpool.

For further information visit

tage City
POOL

Port of Liverpool Building
Completed 1907   Grade II*
The domed head office of the Mersey Docks and Harbour Board was designed by Briggs, Wolstenholme and Thorneley in 1901. Features include cast iron gates and gate piers decorated with maritime symbols and lamp holders in the form of naval monuments.

George's Dock Tunnel Ventilation Building and Offices
1931–1934   Grade II
This stylised obelisk, reminiscent of ancient Egypt, was designed by Sir Basil Mott and J A Brodie, with Herbert J Rowse, to name the Mersey Road Tunnel. It has statues of Night and Day, symbols of the never-closing Mersey Tunnel and a black marble memorial to the workers who died in its construction.

Memorial to Heroes of the Engine Room (Titanic Memorial)
Circa 1916   Grade II
The memorial was originally intended to be for the engineers who stayed at their posts on 15th April 1912 when the Titanic sank. Its dedication was broadened to include all maritime engine room fatalities incurred during the performance of duty. The figures are naturalistic, the detail of their work-clothes being carefully studied.

Albert Dock's Warehouses
Albert Dock's warehouses form England's largest group of Grade I Listed Buildings. Jesse Hartley used well-established techniques adapted from textile mill methods. He introduced new solutions, such as the amazing stressed-skin iron roof. Raising of goods from the quaysides was performed with the first hydraulic cargo-handling installation. Today the dock is home to Tate Liverpool, Merseyside Maritime Museum and numerous bars and restaurants

Stanley Dock Warehouses
Stanley Dock opened in 1848, and between 1852–55 it was equipped with import warehouses. The complex includes: The North Stanley Warehouse 1852–5 Grade II*, The South Stanley Warehouse 1852–5 Grade II, The Stanley Dock Tobacco Warehouse The Hydraulic Tower 1852–55 Grade II, two entrances from Great Howard Street and two from Regent Road.

Liverpool Town Hall
Grade I
Liverpool's finest Georgian building, is the result of three building campaigns. The original design was by John Wood of Bath, and was built in 1749–54. Additions and alterations were designed by James Wyatt and carried out by the elder John Foster in 1789–92. Following a fire of 1795, it was reconstructed the work continuing until 1820.

India Building
1924–31   Grade II
This immense office block was built for the Blue Funnel Line and designed by Herbert J Rowse with Briggs, Wostenholme and Thorneley. It has stripped classical facades; Italian Renaissance detail is restricted to the top and bottom storeys. The building was badly damaged in the war, and restored under Rowse's supervision.

Martin's Building
1927–32   Grade II*
Originally Martin's Bank, designed by Rowse it is monumental and American influenced. The stylish top lit banking hall, with its Parisian jazz moderne fittings, survives well, as does the boardroom. Sculpture and carvings by Herbert Tyson Smith with Edmund Thompson and George Capstick celebrate maritime themes and commerce.

Oriel Chambers
1864   Grade I
Designed by Peter Ellis, the use of oriel windows was driven by a desire to provide good daylight. The oriels themselves are framed in the thinnest sections of iron. In its day, the building aroused much opposition. It is only recently that its futuristic qualities have become appreciated.

Bluecoat Chambers
Opened 1718   Grade I
Bluecoat Chambers was originally built as a charity school in 1717 in the Queen Anne style and in 1928 became one of the UK's first arts centres. The main is round headed with a broken pediment above containing a cartouche of the arms of Liverpool. To the rear is a landscaped garden. After a £12.5m refurbishment the building will reopen in early 2008, complete with a new wing. www.thebluecoat.org.uk

The Walker Art Gallery
Opened 1877   Grade II*
Known as the 'national gallery of the North', the Walker was designed by architects Sherlock and Vale and named after its principal benefactor, Alderman Sir Andrew Barclay Walker, at that time Lord Mayor of Liverpool. A classical portico is the centrepiece of the exterior, which includes friezes of scenes from the city's history, and is surmounted by a personification of Liverpool. www.liverpoolmuseums.org.uk /walker/

Croxteth Hall
Originally built in 1575, the Croxteth Hall you see today is an Edwardian Country house with beautiful surroundings including a country park. The Hall and its outbuilding are a Grade II* Listed Building, as are 3 other buildings; another 15 on the estate are Grade II. The ancestral home of the Molyneux family (Earls of Sefton) until 1972, it is two miles from Aintree racecourse, which the family had owned and developed. For more information please visit www.croxteth.co.uk

Sudley House
This Grade II late Regency/Victorian red Liverpool sandstone mansion, believed to be the work of Thomas Harrison, was completed in 1824 for Nicholas Robinson, Lord Mayor of Liverpool in 1828–9. Today Sudley House contains the only surviving Victorian merchant art collection in Britain still hanging in its original location. For more information visit www.sudleyhouse.org.uk

Speke Hall
Built in 1530 Speke Hall was central to a 2,500 acre farm until it passed to the National Trust in 1944. This Grade I listed half-timbered Tudor house is set on the banks of the River Mersey with extensive views across to the mountains of North Wales. The Hall's atmospheric interior spans many periods – from its fine Tudor Great Hall and priest hole, to smaller more intimate rooms furnished by Speke's Victorian occupants. For information visit www.nationaltrust.org.uk

Lowlands
Built by renowned Liverpool architect Thomas Haigh as his residence in 1846, Grade II-listed Lowlands (13 Haymans Green, West Derby, Liverpool L12 7JG) is the home of the West Derby Community Association. Italianate stucco-faced mansion set in rare city woodland garden. Lowlands hosts many public events and has function rooms available for hire. Re-opens autumn 2008 following conservation work and improvements.

Herterton House Gardens
©Andrew Lawson

North East

Rugged and Roman – the North East region of Britain offers the visitor a wealth of history going back to the Roman occupation. As well as visiting the magnificent fortress castles at Alnwick, Bamburgh and Chillingham, time should be set aside to explore properties such as Wallington, with its exceptional murals depicting Northumbrian history, and The Lady Waterford Murals at Ford, with its 1860 biblical murals.

Co. Durham

Northumberland

Tyne & Wear

■ Owner

The Bowes Museum
Charitable Trust

■ Contact

The Bowes Museum at
Barnard Castle
Co. Durham
DL12 8NP

Tel: 01833 690606
Fax: 01833 637163
E-mail: info@
thebowesmuseum.org.uk

■ Location

MAP 10:O6
OS Ref. NZ055 164

¼ m E of Market Place in
Barnard Castle,
just off A66, between A1
at Scotch Corner & M6.

■ Opening Times

All year, daily:
1 March–31 October,
10am–5pm.
1 November–29 February
10am–4pm.

Closed 25/26 December
& 1 January.

■ Admission

Adult*	£7.00
Child (under 16yrs)	Free
Conc.*	£6.00
Disabled carers	Free
Groups (12+)	
Adult	£6.00
Conc.	£5.00

*includes a voluntary
Gift Aid donation but
visitors can choose to
pay the standard prices
displayed at the property
and on the website.

THE BOWES MUSEUM

www.thebowesmuseum.org.uk

The Bowes Museum is a French style château nestling in the heart of the English countryside.

Purpose built in the 19th century by John and Joséphine Bowes, it was designed specifically as a museum to house their collections. The couple were avid collectors of beautiful works of art from the Middle Ages to their own time; the foundation of the Museum a natural progression of their shared passion.

Today the designated collection includes some of the best examples of European fine and decorative art in the UK, with works including Goya, Canaletto and El Greco.

The Bowes Museum possesses one of the largest collections of Spanish paintings in Britain. It also features the finest ceramics, furniture and textiles.

One of the most popular and entertaining pieces is the 230-year-old Silver Swan automaton, which is still played daily.

The wonderful story of the Museum is recounted as you wander around its treasures. A recent addition is the suite of Streatlam Galleries, which give visitors a taster of what to expect throughout the Museum.

The quality of the permanent collections is enhanced by an acclaimed exhibition programme. Major shows for 2008 include *Emile Gallé and the Origins of Art Nouveau*, until 20 January; and *Alfred Sisley: Impressionist Landscapes*, 17 May until 21 September.

The Museum also boasts Café Bowes, a gift shop, beautiful parkland and landscaped gardens, making it an excellent day out for all.

i	Film location.
	Palatial rooms and acres of parkland. Individual tailored packages for wedding or corporate functions.
	Access to most of the Museum including gift shop, café and WCs. Wheelchair facility is available. Signposted disabled parking and entrance.
	Licensed.
	By arrangement
P	Ample.
	In grounds. Guide dogs only in Museum.

RABY CASTLE

www.rabycastle.com

The magnificent Raby Castle has been home to Lord Barnard's family since 1626, when it was purchased by his ancestor, Sir Henry Vane the Elder, the eminent Statesman and Politician. The Castle was built mainly in the 14th Century by the Nevill family on a site of an earlier Manor House. The Nevills continued to live at Raby until 1569, when after the failure of the Rising of the North, the Castle and its land were forfeited to the Crown.

A particular highlight of the Castle is the magnificent Barons Hall (below), where 700 knights met to plot The Rising of the North. Architect John Carr raised the floor level by 3 metres when constructing a carriageway below in the Entrance Hall and later William Burn extended the room by 17 metres over his elaborate

Octagon Drawing Room. Today it houses an impressive Meissen bird collection. Other Raby treasures include fine furniture and artworks with paintings by Munnings, Reynolds, Van Dyck, Batoni, Teniers, Amigoni and Vernet.

There is a large Deer Park with two lakes and a beautiful walled garden with formal lawns, ancient yew hedges and ornamental pond. The 18th Century Stable block contains a horse-drawn carriage collection including the State Coach last used by the family for the Coronation of Edward VII in 1902. Parts of the Stables have been converted into a Gift Shop and Tearooms, where the former stalls have been incorporated to create an atmospheric setting.

Owner
The Lord Barnard

Contact
Clare Owen /
Katie Blundell
Raby Castle
Staindrop
Darlington
Co. Durham DL2 3AH

Tel: 01833 660202
Fax: 01833 660169
E-mail: admin@
rabycastle.com

Location
MAP 10:O5
OS Ref. NZ129 218

On A688, 1m N of Staindrop. 8m NE of Barnard Castle, 12m WNW of Darlington.

Rail: Darlington Station, 12m.

Air: Durham Tees Valley Airport, 20m.

Opening Times
Castle
Easter weekend, May, June & September, Sun–Wed. July & August: Daily except Sats. (Open BH Sats), 12.30–5pm.

Park & Gardens
As Castle, 11am–5.30pm.

Admission
Castle, Park & Gardens
Adult	£9.50
Child (5–16yrs)	£4.00
OAP/Student	£8.50
Family discounts available.	

Groups (12+)
Adult	£7.50
Child (5–16yrs)	£3.00

Park & Gardens
Adult	£5.00
Child (12–15yrs)	£3.00
Under 12s	Free
Conc.	£4.00

Groups (12+)
Adult	£3.50
Child (5–16yrs)	£2.50

Season Tickets available.

VIP Private Guided Tours (20+)*
(incl. reception, tea/coffee in entrance hall) Easter–Sept, Mon–Fri mornings.
£15.00

Standard Guided Tours (20+)*
(Easter–Sept, Mon–Fri.
Adult	£8.00

*Please book in advance.

Free RHS access to Park & Gardens.

 Film locations, product launches, corporate events, fairs and concerts. Raby Estates venison and game sold in tearooms. Soft fruit when in season. Lectures on Castle, its contents, gardens and history. No photography or video filming is permitted inside. Colour illustrated guidebook and DVD on sale. Christmas Shop in Stable Yard throughout December.

Partial. WC. Castle DVD viewing area.

Licensed.

By arrangement for groups (20+) or min charge. VIP & Standard Castle Tours available. Tour time 1½ hrs.

By arrangement (20+), weekday am. Primary & Junior £3.50; Secondary £4.

Guide dogs welcome. All dogs welcome in Park on leads.

Varied programme throughout the summer.

© Heritage House Group Ltd.

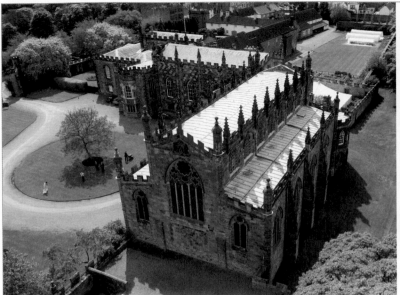

AUCKLAND CASTLE 🏛

BISHOP AUCKLAND, CO. DURHAM DL14 7NR

www.auckland-castle.co.uk

Tel: 01388 601627 **Fax:** 01388 609323 **E-mail:** info@auckland-castle.co.uk
Owner: Church Commissioners **Contact:** The Manager

Principal country residence of the Bishops of Durham since Norman times and now the official residence of the present day Bishops. The Chapel, reputedly one of the largest private chapels in Europe, was originally the 12th century banquet hall. Chapel and State Rooms including the Throne Room, Long Dining Room and King Charles Dining Room are open to the public. Access to the adjacent Bishop's Park with its 18th century Deer House.

Location: MAP 10:P5, OS Ref. NZ214 303. Bishop Auckland, N end of town centre.

Open: Easter Mon–end June: Suns & Mons, 2–5pm. Jul & Aug: Suns, 2–5pm, Mons & Weds, 11am–5pm, Sept: Suns & Mons 2–5pm. Last admission 4.30pm. The management reserves the right to close the castle to visitors. For events see website.

Admission: Adult £4, Child/Conc. £3. Child under 12yrs Free. Special openings for groups (25+).

ⓘ Exhibitions. No indoor photography. 📷 🔽 Wedding receptions, functions.
♿ Wheelchair access to chapel, ground floor. WC. Stairwalker available for upstairs State Rooms by prior arrangement. 🅰 🅿 ⏹ 🐕 Guide dogs only.

AUCKLAND CASTLE DEER HOUSE ⌗

Bishop Auckland, Durham
Tel: 0191 2691200
www.english-heritage.org.uk/aucklandcastle
Owner: English Heritage **Contact:** The Regional Office

A charming building erected in 1760 in the Park of the Bishops of Durham so that the deer could shelter and find food.

Location: MAP 10:P5, OS Ref. NZ216 304. In Bishop Auckland Park, just N of town centre on A68. About 500 yds N of the castle.

Open: Park: 21 Mar–30 Sept: daily, 10am–6pm 1 Oct–31 Mar: daily, 10am–4pm. Closed 24–26 Dec & 1 Jan.

Admission: Free.
🐕 On leads.

BARNARD CASTLE ⌗

Barnard Castle, Castle House, Durham DL12 8PR
Tel: 01833 638212
www.english-heritage.org.uk/barnardcastle
Owner: English Heritage **Contact:** Visitor Operations Team

The substantial remains of this large castle stand on a rugged escarpment overlooking the River Tees. Parts of the 14th century Great Hall and the cylindrical 12th century tower, built by the Baliol family can still be seen. Sensory garden.

Location: MAP 10:O5, OS92, NZ049 165. In Barnard Castle.

Open: 21 Mar–30 Sept: daily, 10am–6pm. 1–31 Oct: daily, 10am–4pm. 1 Nov–31 Mar: Thur–Mon, 10am–4pm. Closed 24–26 Dec & 1 Jan.

Admission: Adult £4, Child £2, Conc. £3.20. 15% discount for groups (11+). EH members Free.

ⓘ WCs in town. 📷 ♿ Grounds. 🐕 In grounds, on leads. ❄ ♿

BINCHESTER ROMAN FORT

Bishop Auckland, Co. Durham
Tel: 01388 663089 / 0191 3834212 (outside opening hours)
Owner: Durham County Council **Contact:** Deborah Anderson

Once the largest Roman fort in Co Durham, the heart of the site has been excavated.

Location: MAP 10:P5, OS92 Ref. NZ210 312. 1½ m N of Bishop Auckland, signposted from A690 Durham–Crook and from A688 Spennymoor–Bishop Auckland roads.

Open: Easter–30 Sept: daily, 11am–5pm.

Admission: Adult £2, Child/Conc. £1.

THE BOWES MUSEUM

See page 418 for full page entry.

CROOK HALL & GARDENS

Sidegate, Durham DH1 5SZ
Tel: 0191 3848028
Owner: Keith & Maggie Bell **Contact:** Mrs Maggie Bell

Medieval manor house set in rural landscape on the edge of Durham city.

Location: MAP 10:P4, OS Ref. NZ274 432. ½ m N of city centre.

Open: Easter weekend, 6 Mar–28 Sept: daily except Fri & Sat, 11am–5pm.

Admission: Adult £5.50, Conc. £5, Child. £4.50, Family £16.

Derwentcote Steel Furnace

Properties that **open all year** appear in the special index at the end of the book.

DERWENTCOTE STEEL FURNACE ⌗

Newcastle, Durham NE39 1BA
Tel: 0191 2691200 (Mon–Fri)
www.english-heritage.org.uk/derwentcote
Owner: English Heritage **Contact:** Regional Office
Built in the 18th century, it is the earliest and most complete authentic steel-making furnace to have survived.
Location: MAP 10:O3, OS Ref. NZ130 566. 10m SW of Newcastle N of the A694 between Rowland's Gill and Hamsterley.
Open: By arrangement.
Admission: Free.
🅿 ⌗ On leads in restricted areas.

DURHAM CASTLE

Palace Green, Durham DH1 3RW
Tel: 0191 3343800 **Fax:** 0191 3343801 **Contact:** Mrs Julie Marshall
Durham Castle, founded in the 1070s, with the Cathedral is a World Heritage Site.
Location: MAP 10:P4, OS Ref. NZ274 424. City centre, adjacent to Cathedral.
Open: Mar–Sept: 10am–12 noon & 2–4.30pm. Oct–Mar: Mon, Wed, Sat & Sun 2–4pm.
Admission: Adult £5, OAP £2.50, Family (2+2) £10. Guide book £2.50.

DURHAM CATHEDRAL

Durham DH1 3EH
Tel: 0191 3864266 **Fax:** 0191 3864267 **E-mail:** enquiries@durhamcathedral.co.uk
Contact: Miss A Heywood
A World Heritage Site. Norman architecture. Burial place of St Cuthbert and the Venerable Bede.
Location: MAP 10:P4, OS Ref. NZ274 422. Durham city centre.
Open: June–Aug: 9.30am–8pm. Open only for worship and private prayer: All year: Mon–Sat, 7.30am–9.30am and Suns, 7.45am–12.30pm. The Cathedral is closed to visitors during evening recitals and concerts. Visitors welcome Mon–Sat, 9.30–5pm, Suns 12.30–3.30pm.
Admission: Cathedral: Request a donation of min. £4. Tower: Adult £2.50, Child (under 16) £1.50, Family £7. Monk's Dormitory: Adult £1, Child 30p, Family £2.10. AV: Adult £1.10, Child 30p, Family £2.

EGGLESTONE ABBEY ⌗

Durham
Tel: 0191 2691200
www.english-heritage.org.uk/egglestone
Owner: English Heritage **Contact:** The Regional Office
Picturesque remains of a 12th-century abbey, located in a bend of the River Tees. Substantial parts of the church and abbey buildings remain.
Location: MAP 10:O6, OS Ref. NZ062 151. 1m S of Barnard Castle on minor road off B6277.
Open: Daily, 10am–6pm.
Admission: Free.
🅰 🅿 ⌗ On leads.

ESCOMB CHURCH

Escomb, Bishop Auckland DL14 7ST
Tel: 01388 602861
Owner: Church of England **Contact:** Mrs D Denham
Saxon church dating from the 7th century built of stone from Binchester Roman Fort.
Location: MAP 10:P5, OS Ref. NZ189 302. 3m W of Bishop Auckland.
Open: Summer: 9am–8pm. Winter: 9am–4pm. Key available from 26 Saxon Green, Escomb.
Admission: Free.

FINCHALE PRIORY ⌗

Finchdale Priory, Brasside, Newton Hall DH9 5SH
Tel: 0191 269 1200/386 3828
www.english-heritage.org.uk/finchale
Owner: English Heritage **Contact:** Regional Office
These beautiful 13th-century priory remains are located beside the curving River Wear.
Location: MAP 10:P4, OS Ref. NZ296 471. 3m NE of Durham.
Open: Telephone key keeper on 0191 386 3828.
Admission: Free.
ℹ WC. 🅲 ▣ (Not managed by EH.) 🅿 (charge) on S side of river. ⌗ On leads.

RABY CASTLE 📖 *See page 419 for full page entry.*

ROKEBY PARK
BARNARD CASTLE, CO. DURHAM DL12 9RZ

www.rokebypark.com

Tel: 01609 748612 **E-mail:** admin@rokebypark.com
An original and effective variant of the Palladian formula, Rokeby was built by Sir Thomas Robinson c1730. It was acquired by JS Morritt in 1769, in whose family it has remained ever since. Paintings and period furniture are on display, together with a unique collection of needlework pictures by Ann Morritt (d1797) and an unusual "Print Room". Known as the setting for Sir Walter Scott's ballad "Rokeby", there is a beautiful walk to the banks of the River Greta.
Location: MAP 10:O6, OS Ref NZ 080 142. 3m SE of Barnard Castle, N of A66.
Open: 5 May, 26 May–2 Sept: Mons & Tues, 2–5pm (last admission 4.30pm). Groups (Max 60) by appointment on any day during open months.
Admission: Adult £6.50. Children under 16 Free. Over 60s £5.50. Students £4. Groups £5.50 on open days, by arrangement other days.
ℹ No photography in house. 🅰 Ground floor only, no WC. 🎭 By arrangement.
⌗ 🅿

THE WEARDALE MUSEUM & HIGH HOUSE CHAPEL

Ireshopeburn, Co. Durham DL13 1EY
Tel: 01388 517433 **E-mail:** dtheatherington@ormail.co.uk
Contact: D T Heatherington
Small folk museum and historic chapel. Includes 1870 Weardale cottage room, John Wesley room and local history displays.
Location: MAP 10:N4, OS Ref. NZ872 385. Adjacent to 18th century Methodist Chapel.
Open: Easter & May–Sept: Wed–Sun & BH, 2–5pm. Aug: daily, 2–5pm.
Admission: Adult £1.50, Child 50p.

Heritage House Group Ltd

Raby Castle

■ Owner

His Grace the Duke of Northumberland

■ Contact

Alnwick Castle
Estate Office
Alnwick
Northumberland
NE66 1NQ

Tel: 01665 510777
Info: 01665 511100
Group bookings:
01665 510777
Fax: 01665 510876
E-mail: enquiries@
alnwickcastle.com

■ Location

MAP 14:M11
OS Ref. NU187 135

In Alnwick 1½ m
W of A1.
From London 6hrs,
Edinburgh 2hrs,
Chester 4hrs,
Newcastle 40mins
North Sea ferry
terminal 30mins.

Bus: From bus station
in Alnwick.

Rail: Alnmouth
Station 5m.
Kings Cross, London
3½hrs.

Air: Newcastle 40mins.

■ Opening Times

20 March–26 October
Daily, 10am–5pm.
State Rooms open
at 11am (last adm. to
State Rooms 4.30pm).

■ Admission

Adult	£9.50
Child (5–15yrs)	£4.50
Child (under 5yrs)	Free
Conc.	£8.00

Booked Groups
(14+, tel 01665 510777)

Adult	£7.00
Child	£2.50

Weekly & Season
Tickets available.

HHA members free
access to Castle only.

Conference/Function

ROOM	SIZE	MAX CAPACITY
The Guest Hall	100' x 30'	250

ALNWICK CASTLE

www.alnwickcastle.com

Set in a stunning landscape designed by 'Capability' Brown, Alnwick Castle was voted Best Large Visitor Attraction 2007 in the Enjoy England Awards for Excellence and is the family home of the Duke of Northumberland. Owned by his family since 1309, this beautiful castle, originally built to defend England from the Scots, now appeals to visitors of all ages from across the world.

Considered to be one of the finest castles in England, and known as the 'Windsor of the North', this has been the home of the Percy family for nearly 700 years. In the 1760s it was transformed from a fortification into a family home for the First Duke and Duchess. Today Alnwick Castle is an attraction of real significance, with lavish State Rooms, superb art treasures, fun activities and entertainment, all set in a beautiful landscape.

Visitors walking through the gates, set in massive stone walls, enter one of the most stunning castles in Europe. The Keep sits magnificently in the spacious grounds, with its medieval towers housing the castle's 14th century dungeon and the entrance to the remarkable State Rooms. The refurbished and restored dining room is worth a visit. Beautifully silked walls, a hand-woven carpet and intricate carved ceiling are among the delights. Important ceramics of the Meissen, Chelsea and Paris factories are impressively displayed in the china gallery.

Within the grounds are the museums and towers that tell the story of the Northumberland Fusiliers from 1674 to the present day, local archaeology of the area, the Percy Tenantry Volunteers and an exhibition on siege craft.

Adding to the magic of this castle is an interactive and fun activity area where children can enter the exciting and enchanting world of knights and dragons. They can learn how to become a Knight or Lady of Alnwick then take the ultimate challenge to win their spurs by facing the monster which rules the kingdom in Dragon's Quest.

ℹ Conference facilities, events, fairs and exhibitions. Film location hire. No photography inside the castle. No unaccompanied children.	☕ Coffee, light lunches and teas.
	🅿 Shared with Alnwick Gardens.
🛍	📖 Guidebook and worksheet, special rates for children and teachers.
🍸 Wedding receptions.	
♿ Partial. Parking.	🐕 Guide dogs only.

BAMBURGH CASTLE

www.bamburghcastle.com

Bamburgh Castle is the home of the Armstrong family. The earliest reference to Bamburgh shows the craggy citadel to have been a royal centre by AD 547. Recent archaeological excavation has revealed that the site has been occupied since prehistoric times.

The Norman Keep has been the stronghold for nearly nine centuries, but the remainder has twice been extensively restored, initially by Lord Crewe in the 1750s and subsequently by the 2nd Lord Armstrong at the beginning of the 20th century. This Castle was the first to succumb to artillery fire – that of Edward IV.

The public rooms contain many exhibits, including the loan collections of armour from The Board of Trustees, The Royal Armouries, Leeds, and other private sources, which complement the castle's armour. Porcelain, china, jade, furniture from many periods, oils, water-colours and a host of interesting items are all contained within one of the most important buildings of Britain's national heritage.

Views

The views from the ramparts are unsurpassed and take in Holy Island, the Farne Islands, one of Northumberland's finest beaches and, landwards, the Cheviot Hills.

 Filming. No photography in house.

 Limited access. WC.

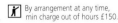 Tearooms for light refreshments. Groups can book.

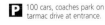 By arrangement at any time, min charge out of hours £150.

 100 cars, coaches park on tarmac drive at entrance.

 Welcome. Guide provided if requested, educational pack.

Guide dogs only.

Owner
Sir Humphry Wakefield Bt

Contact
Administrator
Chillingham Castle
Northumberland
NE66 5NJ

Tel: 01668 215359
Fax: 01668 215463
E-mail: enquiries@
chillingham-castle.com

Location
MAP 14:L11
OS Ref. NU062 258

45m N of Newcastle
between A697 & A1.
2m S of B6348
at Chatton.
6m SE of Wooler.

Rail: Alnmouth
or Berwick.

Opening Times
Summer
Easter
1 May–30 September
Closed Sats, Castle,
1–5pm, Grounds, Garden
& Tearoom, 12 noon–5pm.

Winter
October–April: Groups &
Coach Tours any time by
appointment. All function
activities available.

Admission
Summer

Adult	£6.75
Child (under 16yrs)	£3.00
Child (under 5yrs)	£1.00
Conc.	£5.50
Groups (10+)	
Per person	£6.00
Guide	£25.00

CHILLINGHAM CASTLE
www.chillingham-castle.com

Rated 4-star (amongst the top 100!) in Simon Jenkins' *England's Thousand Best Houses*. *The Independent*: First of *The 50 Best Castles in Britain & Ireland*.

This remarkable castle, the home of Sir Humphry Wakefield Bt, with its alarming dungeons has, as now and since the 1200s, been continuously owned by the family of the Earls Grey and their relations. You will see active restoration of complex masonry, metalwork and ornamental plaster as the great halls and state rooms are gradually brought back to life with tapestries, arms and armour as of old and even a torture chamber.

At first a 12th century stronghold, Chillingham became a fully fortified castle in the 14th century (see the original 1344 Licence to Crenellate). Wrapped in the nation's history it occupied a strategic position as a fortress during Northumberland's bloody border feuds, often besieged and at many times enjoying the patronage of royal visitors. In Tudor days there were additions but the underlying medieval character has always been retained. The 18th and 19th centuries saw decorative extravagances including the lake, garden and grounds laid out by Sir Jeffrey Wyatville, fresh from his triumphs at Windsor Castle. These contrast with the prehistoric Wild Cattle in the park beyond (a separate tour).

Gardens
With romantic grounds, the castle commands breathtaking views of the surrounding countryside. As you walk to the lake you will see, according to season, drifts of snowdrops, daffodils or bluebells and an astonishing display of rhododendrons. This emphasises the restrained formality of the Elizabethan topiary garden, with its intricately clipped hedges of box and yew. Lawns, the formal gardens and woodland walks are all fully open to the public.

Conference/Function

ROOM	MAX CAPACITY
King James I Room	
Great Hall	100
Minstrels' Hall	60
2 x Drawing Room	
Museum	
Tea Room	35
Lower Gallery	
Upper Gallery	

Corporate entertainment, lunches, drinks, dinners, wedding ceremonies and receptions.

Partial.

Booked meals for up to 100 people.

By arrangement.

 Avoid Lilburn route, coach parties welcome by prior arrangement. Limited for coaches.

Self catering apartments.

ESHOTT HALL
www.eshotthall.com

Owner
The Sanderson Family

Contact
Margaret Sanderson
Eshott Hall
Morpeth
Northumberland
NE65 9EN

Tel: (01670) 787777
Fax: (01670) 787999
E-mail:
thehall@eshott.co.uk

Location
MAP 14:M12

OS Ref NZ203 978

Almost equidistant between Morpeth and Alnwick, 1m E of the A1, 20m N of Newcastle-upon-Tyne.

Turn east off A1 trunk road about 6 miles north of Morpeth and 9 miles south of Alnwick at Eshott signpost. Unmarked Hall gates are approximately one mile down the country lane. Less than an hour's stunning coastal train journey from Edinburgh and about three hours from London, our local station, Alnmouth, is a taxi-ride away.

Rail: Newcastle 20m, Morpeth 8m, Alnmouth 5m.

Air: Newcastle International Airport ½hr drive.

Bus: Regular service.

Opening Times
All year for accommodation, exclusive use and groups by appointment.

Admission
The exclusive use of the house and grounds for events and activity days with no accommodation £500–£1500 (seasonal variations).

Accommodation rates:

Single with bath	£79.00
Double with bath	£128.00
Dinner	£33.00

This elegant country house has a 17th century core, much refashioned in the 19th century to include sumptuous 18th century plasterwork in the drawing room done by the same Italian stuccatori who worked at Alnwick Castle. Its setting at the heart of a secluded estate is a haven of peace and tranquillity. Red squirrels can still be seen and wildlife abounds. Wooded walks lead to open countryside with views towards the Cheviot Hills straddling the Scottish Border. The location is advantageous, being close to the Northumberland coast with some of the best beaches in Britain, an array of spectacular castles, and yet only 20 minutes north of the rejuvenated cultural centre of Newcastle and the vibrant lifestyle of its quayside.

Whilst still the private home of Margaret and Ho Sanderson, the 6th generation of the family to live here, the house has been adapted to provide superb facilities for weddings, business use and comfortable accommodation.

The house is offered for exclusive use, or as a place to stay, or both. Margaret Sanderson's design talents are evident in each of the individually styled and beautifully furnished bedrooms, with comfortable king-size beds and en suite bathrooms. Her lifetime experience of exclusive catering ensures that the most discerning tastes are rewarded. Organic fruit and vegetables are harvested in the walled garden.

It is an exceptional location for weddings and events and one of comparatively few such houses offering accommodation.

 Conferences, activity days, filming and photography, product launches, musical events, seminars, orienteering, training activity days, events, clay pigeon and game shooting, firework and laser shows, game and craft fairs, rope course. Non-smoking.

Exclusive dinners and weddings etc, prices and menus on request.

Level access and WC for disabled visitors.

Ample.

3 double with en suites, 3 twin with en suites.

Dining Room

Drawing Room

Library

Bedroom

Conference/Function

ROOM	SIZE	MAX CAPACITY
Reception hall	15'6"x 39'	50
Drawing Room	17'6"x 24'6"	30
Dining Room	17'6"x 24'6"	30
Ballroom	59'x 24'3"	140
Marquee	120'x 40'	500

ALNWICK CASTLE 🏛

See page 422 for full page entry.

Chipchase Castle

AYDON CASTLE ⌗

Corbridge, Northumberland NE45 5PJ
Tel: 01434 632450   **www.english-heritage.org.uk/aydoncastle**
Owner: English Heritage   **Contact:** Visitor Operations Team
One of the finest fortified manor houses in England, dating from the late 13th century. Its survival, intact, can be attributed to its conversion to a farmhouse in the 17th century.
Location: MAP 10:O3, OS Ref. NZ001 663. 1m NE of Corbridge, on minor road off B6321 or A68.
Open: 1 Apr–30 Sept: Thur–Mon, 10am–5pm.
Admission: Adult £3.50, Child £1.80, Conc. £2.80. 15% discount for groups (11+). EH Members free.
ⓘ WC. 🄳 🄳 Ground floor & grounds. 🄿 🖪 🖪 In grounds, on leads. 🄳

BAMBURGH CASTLE 🏛

See page 423 for full page entry.

BELSAY HALL, CASTLE & GARDENS ⌗
BELSAY, Nr PONTELAND, NORTHUMBERLAND NE20 0DX
www.english-heritage.org.uk/belsay

Tel: 01661 881636   **Fax:** 01661 881043
Owner: English Heritage   **Contact:** Visitor Operations Team
Belsay is one of the most remarkable estates in Northumberland's border country. The buildings, set amidst 30 acres of magnificent landscaped gardens, have been occupied by the same family for nearly 600 years. The gardens, created largely in the 19th century, are a fascinating mix of the formal and the informal with terraced gardens, a rhododendron garden, magnolia garden, mature woodland and even a winter garden. The buildings comprise a 14th century castle, a manor house and Belsay Hall, an internationally famous mansion designed by Sir Charles Monck in the 19th century in the style of classical buildings he had encountered during a tour of Greece.

Location: MAP 10:O2, OS87, NZ086 785. In Belsay 14m (22.4 km) NW of Newcastle on SW of A696. 7m NW of Ponteland. Nearest airport and station is Newcastle.
Open: 21 Mar–31 Oct: daily, 10am–5pm (4pm Oct). 1 Nov–31 Mar: Thur–Mon, 10am–4pm. Closed 24–26 Dec and 1 Jan.
Admission: Adult £6.50, Child £3.90, Conc. £5.20, Family £16.30. 15% discount for groups (11+). Different prices apply for Picture House Exhibition, see website for details. EH Members free.
🄳 🄳 🄣 🄳 Partial. WC. 🖪 During summer & weekends Apr–Oct. 🄿 🖪
🖪 In grounds, on leads. 🖪 🄳

BERWICK-UPON-TWEED BARRACKS & MAIN GUARD ⌗

The Parade, Berwick-upon-Tweed, Northumberland TD15 1DF
Tel: 01289 304493   **www.english-heritage.org.uk/berwickbarracks**
Owner: English Heritage   **Contact:** Visitor Operations Team
Among the earliest purpose built barracks, these have changed very little since 1717. They house an exhibition 'By Beat of Drum', which recreates scenes such as the barrack room from the life of the British infantryman, the Museum of the King's Own Scottish Borderers and the Borough Museum with fine art, local history exhibition and other collections.
Location: MAP 14:L9, OS Ref. NU001 531. On the Parade, off Church Street, Berwick town centre.
Open: Barracks: 21 Mar–30 Sept: Wed–Sun, 10am–5pm. Main Guard: Tel 01289 330430 for details.
Admission: Adult £3.50, Child £1.80, Conc. £2.80. 15% discount for groups (11+).
🄳 🄿 In town. 🖪 🖪 On leads. 🖪

Seaton Delaval Hall

BERWICK-UPON-TWEED CASTLE & RAMPARTS ⌗

Berwick-upon-Tweed, Northumberland
Tel: 0191 269 1200   www.english-heritage.org.uk/berwickcastle
Owner: English Heritage   **Contact:** The Regional Office
A remarkably complete system of town fortifications consisting of gateways, ramparts and projecting bastions built in the 16th century.
Location: MAP 14:L9, OS Ref. NT993 534. Surrounding Berwick town centre on N bank of River Tweed.
Open: Any reasonable time.
Admission: Free.
⊛

BRINKBURN PRIORY ⌗

Long Framlington, Morpeth, Northumberland NE65 8AR
Tel: 01665 570628   www.english-heritage.org.uk/brinkburn
Owner: English Heritage   **Contact:** Visitor Operations Staff
This late 12th century church is a fine example of early gothic architecture, almost perfectly preserved, and is set in a lovely spot beside the River Coquet.
Location: MAP 14:L12, OS Ref. NZ116 983. 4½ m SE of Rothbury off B6344 5m W of A1.
Open: 21 Mar–30 Sept: Thur–Mon, 11am–4pm.
Admission: Adult £3, Child £1.50, Conc. £2.40. 15% discount for groups (11+). EH Members free.
🄲 🅃 🄿 🔲 🔳 On leads. 🐕

CAPHEATON HALL

Newcastle-upon-Tyne NE19 2AB
Tel/Fax: 01830 530253
Owner/Contact: J Browne-Swinburne
Built for Sir John Swinburne in 1668 by Robert Trollope, an architect of great and original talent.
Location: MAP 10:O2, OS Ref. NZ038 805. 17m NW of Newcastle off A696.
Open: By written appointment only.
⊛

© English Heritage Photo Library.

CHESTERS ROMAN FORT & MUSEUM ⌗

CHOLLERFORD, Nr HEXHAM, NORTHUMBERLAND NE46 3EU

www.english-heritage.org.uk/chesters

Tel: 01434 681379
Owner: English Heritage   **Contact:** Visitor Operations Team
The best preserved example of a Roman cavalry fort in Britain, including remains of the bath house on the banks of the River North Tyne. The museum houses a fascinating collection of Roman sculpture and inscriptions.
Location: MAP 10:N2, OS87, NY913 701. ¼m W of Chollerford on B6318.
Open: 21 Mar–30 Sept: daily, 10am–4pm. 1 Oct–31 Mar: daily, 10am–4pm. Closed 24–26 Dec and 1 Jan.
Admission: Adult £4.50, Child £2.30, Conc. £3.60. 15% discount for groups (11+). EH Members free.
🄲 🅖 Grounds. WC. 🐕 Summer only. 🄿 🔲 🔳 In grounds, on leads. ⊛ 🐕

CHILLINGHAM CASTLE 🏰   *See page 424 for full page entry.*

CHIPCHASE CASTLE 🏰

Wark, Hexham, Northumberland NE48 3NT
Tel: 01434 230203   **Fax:** 01434 230740
Owner/Contact: Mrs P J Torday
The castle overlooks the River North Tyne and is set in formal and informal gardens. One walled garden is used as a nursery specialising in unusual perennial plants.
Location: MAP 10:N2, OS Ref. NY882 758. 10m NW of Hexham via A6079 to Chollerton. 2m SE of Wark.
Open: Castle: Easter–mid Oct. Tours by arrangement at other times.
Castle Gardens & Nursery: Easter–31 Jul, Thur–Sun & BH Mons, 10am–5pm.
Admission: Castle £6, Garden £4, concessions available. Nursery Free.
🅖 Unsuitable. 🄵 Obligatory for house only. 🔳

CORBRIDGE ROMAN TOWN ⌗

Corbridge, Northumberland NE45 5NT
Tel: 01434 632349   www.english-heritage.org.uk/corbridge
Owner: English Heritage   **Contact:** Visitor Operations Team
A fascinating series of excavated remains, including foundations of granaries with a grain ventilation system. From artefacts found, which can be seen in the site museum, we know a large settlement developed around this supply depot.
Location: MAP 10:N3, OS Ref. NY983 649. ½m NW of Corbridge on minor road, signposted for Corbridge Roman Site.
Open: 21 Mar–30 Sept: daily, 10am–5.30pm (last adm. 5pm). 1–31 Oct: daily, 10am–4pm. 1 Nov–31 Mar '09: Sat & Sun, 10am–4pm. Closed 24–26 Dec and 1 Jan.
Admission: Adult £4.50, Child £2.30, Conc. £3.60. 15% discount for groups (11+). EH Members free.
🄲 🅖 Partial. 🄰 Inclusive. 🄿 Limited for coaches. 🔲 🔳 In grounds, on leads. ⊛ 🐕

CRAGSIDE 🌿

Rothbury, Morpeth, Northumberland NE65 7PX
Tel: 01669 620333   www.nationaltrust.org.uk
Owner: The National Trust   **Contact:** Property Manager
Revolutionary home of Lord Armstrong, Victorian inventor and landscape genius, Cragside sits on a rocky crag high above the Debdon Burn. Crammed with ingenious gadgets, it was the first house in the world lit electrically. Armstrong constructed 5 lakes, one of Europe's largest rock gardens and planted over 7 million trees and shrubs. Today, this magnificent estate can be explored on foot and by car and provides one of the last shelters for the endangered red squirrel. Children will love the tall trees, tumbling streams, adventure play areas and labyrinth.
Location: MAP 14:L12, OS Ref. NU073 022. ½m NE of Rothbury on B6341.
Open: House: 15 Mar–5 Oct, daily except Mons (open BH Mons), 1–5.30pm (last admission 4.30pm). 7 Oct–2 Nov, daily except Mons, 1–4.30pm (last admission 3.30pm). Gardens, Estate, Restaurant & Shop 15 Mar–2 Nov, daily except Mons, 10.30am–5.30pm. 5 Nov–21 Dec, Wed–Sun, 11am–4pm.
*Admission: House, Gardens & Estate: Adult £12.10, Child (5–17 yrs) £6.10, Family (2+3) £29.20. Estate & Gardens: Adult £7.70, Child (5–17 yrs) £3.30, Family (2+3) £18.70. Groups (15+) £6. Gardens, Estate, Restaurant & Shop (House closed): Nov–Dec, Adult £3.85, Child (5–17 yrs) £1.80, Family (2+3) £8.80, Group (15+) £3.20. Debit/credit card payment at shop & restaurant only, not at admission point. *includes a voluntary donation but visitors can choose to pay the standard prices displayed at the property and on the website.
🄲 🅖 Partial. 🐕 🍴 🄿 🔲 🔳 In grounds, on leads. 🄰 🐕

DUNSTANBURGH CASTLE ⌗ 🌿

c/o Grieves Garage, Embleton, Northumberland NE66 3TT
Tel: 01665 576231   www.english-heritage.org.uk/dunstanburgh
Owner: The National Trust   **Guardian:** English Heritage
Contact: Visitor Operations Team
An easy, but bracing, coastal walk leads to the eerie skeleton of this wonderful 14th century castle sited on a basalt crag, rearing up more than 100 feet from the waves crashing on the rocks below. The surviving ruins include the large gatehouse, which later became the keep, and curtain walls.
Location: MAP 14:M11, OS75, NU257 219. 8m NE of Alnwick.
Open: 21 Mar–31 Oct: daily, 10am–5pm (4pm Oct). 1 Nov–31 Mar '09: Thur–Mon, 10am–4pm.
Admission: Adult £3.50, Child £1.80, Conc. £2.80. 15% discount for groups (11+). EH Members free.
🄿 None. 🔲 🔳 In grounds, on leads. ⊛

EDLINGHAM CASTLE ⊞

Edlingham, Alnwick, Northumberland
Tel: 0191 269 1200   www.english-heritage.org.uk/edlingham
Owner: English Heritage   **Contact:** The Regional Office
Set beside a splendid railway viaduct this complex ruin has defensive features spanning the 13th and 15th centuries.
Location: MAP 14:L11, OS Ref. NU116 092. At E end of Edlingham village, on minor road off B6341 6m SW of Alnwick.
Open: Any reasonable time.
Admission: Free.
🐕 In grounds, on leads. ❉

ESHOTT HALL

See page 425 for full page entry.

ETAL CASTLE ⊞

Cornhill-on-Tweed, Northumberland TD12 4TN
Tel: 01890 820332   www.english-heritage.org.uk/etalcastle
Owner: English Heritage   **Contact:** Visitor Operations Team
A 14th century castle located in the picturesque village of Etal. Award-winning exhibition about the castle, Border warfare and the Battle of Flodden.
Location: MAP 14:K10, OS75, NT925 393. In Etal village, 10m SW of Berwick.
Open: 21 Mar–30 Sept: daily, 11am–4.30pm.
Admission: Adult £3.50, Child £1.80, Conc. £2.80, Family £8.80. 15% discount for groups (11+). EH Members free.
ℹ WC in village. 🅿 ♿ Partial. WC. 🍽 Inclusive. 🅿 ■ 🐕 In grounds, on leads.

HERTERTON HOUSE GARDENS

Hartington, Cambo, Morpeth, Northumberland NE61 4BN
Tel: 01670 774278
Owner/Contact: C J "Frank" Lawley
One acre of formal garden in stone walls around a 16th century farmhouse, including a small topiary garden, physic garden, flower garden, fancy garden and gazebo.
Location: MAP 10:N1, OS Ref. NZ022 881. 2m N of Cambo, just off B6342, Signposted (brown).
Open: 1 Apr–30 Sept: Mons, Weds, Fri–Sun, 1.30–5.30pm.
Admission: Adult £3, Child (5–15yrs) £1.20. Groups by arrangement.
❉ ♿ Unsuitable. 🎦 By arrangement. 🅿 Limited for coaches.
■ Guided tours for adult students only. ❉

© English Heritage

Belsay Pillar Hall

English Heritage Photo Library

HOUSESTEADS ROMAN FORT ⊞ ⚘

Nr HAYDON BRIDGE, NORTHUMBERLAND NE47 6NN

www.english-heritage.org.uk/housesteads

Tel: 01434 344363
Owner: The National Trust   **Guardian:** English Heritage
Contact: Visitor Operations Team
Perched high on a ridge overlooking open moorland, this is the best known part of the Wall. The fort covers five acres and there are remains of many buildings, such as granaries, barrack blocks and gateways. A small exhibition displays altars, inscriptions and models.
Location: MAP 10:M3, OS Ref. NY790 687. 2m NE of Bardon Mill.
Open: 21 Mar–30 Sept: daily, 10am–6pm. 1 Oct–31 Mar 09: daily, 10am–4pm. Closed 24–26 Dec and 1 Jan.
Admission: Adult £4.50, Child £2.30, Conc. £3.60, Free entry to EH & NT members. Group discount available.
🅿 🅿 500 metres from site. Charge. ■ 🐕 In grounds, on leads. ❉

THE LADY WATERFORD HALL & MURALS

Ford, Berwick-upon-Tweed TD15 2QA
Tel: 01890 820503   **Fax:** 01890 820384
Owner: Ford & Etal Estates   **Contact:** Dorien Irving
Commissioned in 1860 the walls of this beautiful building are decorated with beautiful murals depicting Bible stories.
Location: MAP 14:K10, OS Ref. NT945 374. On the B6354, 9m from Berwick-upon-Tweed, midway between Newcastle-upon-Tyne and Edinburgh, close to the A697.
Open: 17 Mar–Oct: daily, 10.30am–12.30pm & 1.30–5.30pm. By arrangement with the caretaker during winter months. Note: the Hall may be closed on occasion for private functions. Please telephone prior to travelling.
Admission: Adult £2, Child 75p, Child (under 12yrs) Free, Conc. £1.50. Groups by arrangement. Prices subject to change.

LINDISFARNE CASTLE ⚘

Holy Island, Berwick-upon-Tweed, Northumberland TD15 2SH
Tel: 01289 389244   www.nationaltrust.org.uk
Owner: The National Trust   **Contact:** Property Manager
Built in 1550 to protect Holy Island harbour from attack, the castle was restored and converted into a private house for Edward Hudson by Sir Edwin Lutyens in 1903.
Location: MAP 14:L9, OS Ref. NU136 417. On Holy Island, ¾m E of village, 6m E of A1 across causeway. Usable at low tide.
Open: 16–24 Feb, 15 Mar–2 Nov: 10am–3pm, daily (closed Mons except BHs). Times vary, please telephone for details. 30 Dec–2 Jan '09, 10am–3pm, daily.
***Admission:** Adult £6, Child £3, Family £15. Garden only: Adult £1, Child Free. Out of hours group tours (20+) by arrangement £8pp, NT members £4.50. *includes a voluntary donation but visitors can choose to pay the standard prices displayed at the property and on the website.
🅿 NT Shop (in Main St). 🐕 In grounds, on leads.

See which properties offer **educational facilities** or **school visits** in our index at the end of the book.

visit hudsons guide online

© Mike Kipling

Lindisfarne Castle

© English Heritage Photo Library

LINDISFARNE PRIORY ⌗
HOLY ISLAND, NORTHUMBERLAND TD15 2RX

www.english-heritage.org.uk/lindisfarne

Tel: 01289 389200

Owner: English Heritage   **Contact:** Visitor Operations Team

The site of one of the most important early centres of Christianity in Anglo-Saxon England. St Cuthbert converted pagan Northumbria, and miracles occurring at his shrine established this 11th century priory as a major pilgrimage centre. The evocative ruins, with the decorated 'rainbow' arch curving dramatically across the nave of the church, are still the destination of pilgrims today. The story of Lindisfarne is told in an exhibition which gives an impression of life for the monks, including a reconstruction of a monk's cell. The Priory can only be reached at low tide.

Location: MAP 14:L9, OS Ref. NU126 417. On Holy Island, check tide times.

Open: 21 Mar–31 Oct daily, 9.30am–5pm (Oct 4pm), 1 Nov–31 Jan, Sat–Mon, 10am–2pm. Closed 24–26 Dec & 1 Jan.

Admission: Adult £4, Child £2, Conc. £3.20. 15% discount for groups (11+).

▢ ⌂ Partial. Disabled parking. **P** Charge. ▣ ⊞ Restricted. ✳ ⊽

NORHAM CASTLE ⌗

Norham, Northumberland TD15 2JY

Tel: 01289 304493   www.english-heritage.org.uk/norhamcastle

Owner: English Heritage   **Contact:** Visitor Operations Team

Set on a promontory in a curve of the River Tweed, this was one of the strongest of the Border castles, built c1160.

Location: MAP 14:K9, OS75, NT906 476. 6m SW of Berwick ,on minor road off B6470 (from A698).

Open: Admission is limited, please telephone for details.

Admission: Free.

⌂ Partial. ⊞ On leads.

PRESTON TOWER ⌂

Chathill, Northumberland NE67 5DH

Tel: 01665 589227

Owner/Contact: Major T Baker-Cresswell

The Tower was built by Sir Robert Harbottle in 1392 and is one of the few survivors of 78 pele towers listed in 1415. The tunnel vaulted rooms remain unaltered and provide a realistic picture of the grim way of life under the constant threat of "Border Reivers". Two rooms are furnished in contemporary style and there are displays of historic and local information. Visitors are welcome to walk in the grounds which contain a number of interesting trees and shrubs. A woodland walk to the natural spring from which water is now pumped up to the Tower for the house and cottages.

Location: MAP 14:M11, OS Ref. NU185 253. Follow Historic Property signs on A1 7m N of Alnwick.

Open: All year daily, 10am–6pm.

Admission: Adult £2, Child 50p, Conc. £1.50. Groups £1.50.

⌂ Grounds. ⊞ ✳

PRUDHOE CASTLE ⌗

Prudhoe, Northumberland NE42 6NA

Tel: 01661 833459   www.english-heritage.org.uk/prudhoecastle

Owner: English Heritage   **Contact:** Visitor Operations Team

Set on a wooded hillside overlooking the River Tyne are the extensive remains of this 12th century castle including a gatehouse, curtain wall and keep. Small exhibition and video presentation.

Location: MAP 10:O3, OS88 Ref. NZ091 634. In Prudhoe, on minor road off A695.

Open: 21 Mar–30 Sept: Thur–Mon, 10am–5pm.

Admission: Adult £3.50, Child £1.80, Conc. £2.80. 15% discount for groups (11+).

ℹ WC. ▢ ⌂ Partial. ⊽ **P** ▣ ⊞ In grounds, on leads. ⊽

SEATON DELAVAL HALL

SEATON SLUICE, WHITLEY BAY, NORTHUMBERLAND NE26 4QR

Tel: 0191 237 1493/0191 237 0786 **E-mail:** lordhastings@onetel.net.uk

Owner: Lord Hastings   **Contact:** Mrs Mills

The home of Lord and Lady Hastings, half a mile from Seaton Sluice, is the last and most sensational mansion designed by Sir John Vanbrugh, builder of Blenheim Palace and Castle Howard. It was erected 1718–1728 and comprises a high turreted block flanked by arcaded wings which form a vast forecourt. The centre block was gutted by fire in 1822, but was partially restored in 1862 and again in 1959–1962 and 1999–2000. The remarkable staircases are a visual delight, and the two surviving rooms are filled with family pictures and photographs and royal seals spanning three centuries as well as various archives. This building is used frequently for concerts and charitable functions. The East Wing contains immense stables in ashlar stone of breathtaking proportions. Nearby are the Coach House with farm and passenger vehicles, fully

documented, and the restored ice house with explanatory sketch and description. There are beautiful gardens described by gardening writers as '*a revelation and a delight*' and also as '*magical*' with herbaceous borders, rose garden, rhododendrons, azaleas, laburnum walk, statues, and a spectacular parterre by internationally famous Jim Russell, also a unique Norman Church.

Location: MAP 11:A2, OS Ref. NZ322 766. ½m from Seaton Sluice on A190, 3m from Whitley Bay.

Open: May & Aug BH Mons; Jun–Sept: Weds & Suns, 2–6pm.

Admission: Adult £4, Child £1, OAP £3.50, Student £2. Groups (20+): Adult £3, Child/Student £1.

Partial. WC. Free. In grounds, on leads.

Charlotte Karsemeijer

WALLINGTON

CAMBO, MORPETH, NORTHUMBERLAND NE61 4AR

www.nationaltrust.org.uk

Tel: 01670 773600 **E-mail:** wallington@nationaltrust.org.uk

Owner: The National Trust   **Contact:** The Estate Office

Dating from 1688, the much-loved home of the Trevelyan family contains magnificent rococo plasterwork, fine ceramics and a collection of dolls' houses. The Pre-Raphaelite Central Hall depicts floral wall paintings and a series of scenes of Northumbrian history by William Bell Scott.

There are extensive walks through a variety of lawns, shrubberies, lakes and woodland to the exuberant Walled Garden, which remain open throughout the year.

Location: MAP 10:O2, OS Ref. NZ030 843. Near Cambo, 6m NW of Belsay (A696).

Open: House: 15 Mar–30 Sep: daily, Wed–Mon, 1–5.30pm 1 Oct–2 Nov, 1–4.30pm. Restaurant & Shop: 1–15 Feb & 5 Nov–31 Jan '09, Wed–Sun; 10.30am–4.30pm, 16 Feb–30 Sep, 10.30am–5.30pm, daily, 1 Oct–2 Nov Wed–Mon 10.30am–4.30pm. Walled garden: 1 Feb–31 Mar & 1 Nov–31 Jan '09, daily, 10am–4pm, 1 Apr–30 Sep, daily, 10am–7pm, 1–31 Oct, daily 10am–6pm. Grounds open all year dawn–dusk.

*Admission: House, garden & grounds: Adult £9.25, Child £4.65, Family £23.10. Garden & grounds only: Adult £6.40, Child £3.20, Family £16. *includes a voluntary donation but visitors can choose to pay the standard prices displayed at the property and on the website.

Partial. By arrangement. In grounds on leads.

© English Heritage Photo Library

WARKWORTH CASTLE ⊞

WARKWORTH, ALNWICK, NORTHUMBERLAND NE65 0UJ

www.english-heritage.org.uk/warkworth

Tel: 01665 711423

Owner: English Heritage   **Contact:** Visitor Operations Team

The great towering keep of this 15th century castle, once the home of the mighty Percy family, dominates the town and River Coquet. Warkworth is one of the most outstanding examples of an aristocratic fortified residence. Upstream by boat from the castle lies Warkworth Hermitage, cutting into the rock of the river cliff (separate charge applies).

Location: MAP 14:M12, OS Ref. NU247 058. 7½m S of Alnwick on A1068.

Open: 21 Mar–31 Oct: daily, 10am–5pm (4pm Oct). 1 Nov–31 Mar '09: Sat–Mon, 10am–4pm. Closed 24–26 Dec and 1 Jan.

Admission: Castle: Adult £4, Child £2, Conc. £3.20, Family £10. 15% discount for groups (11+). EH Members free.

ⓘ WC. ▣ ⓖ Grounds. ⓐ Inclusive. ℗ ▣ ⊞ On leads. ✳ ⬚

WARKWORTH HERMITAGE ⊞

Warkworth, Northumberland

Tel: 01665 711423   **www.english-heritage.org.uk/warkworth**

Owner: English Heritage   **Contact:** Visitor Operations Team

Upstream by boat from the castle this curious hermitage cuts into the rock of the river cliff.

Location: MAP 14:M12, OS Ref. NU242 060. 7½ m SE of Alnwick on A1068.

Open: 21 Mar–30 Sept: Weds, Suns & BHs, 11am–5pm.

Admission: Adult £3, Child £1.50, Conc. £2.40. EH Members free. Group discount available.

▣ ⓖ Grounds. ℗ At Castle. ▣ ⊞ On leads.

TPL/Andreas Von Einsiedel

Cragside

Seaton Delaval Stables

ARBEIA ROMAN FORT

Baring Street, South Shields, Tyne & Wear NE33 2BB
Tel: 0191 456 1369 **Fax:** 0191 427 6862
Owner: South Tyneside Metropolitan Borough Council   **Contact:** The Curator
Managed by: Tyne & Wear Museums

More than 1,500 years on, the remains at Arbeia represent the most extensively excavated example of a military supply base anywhere in the Roman Empire. Museum includes weapons, jewellery and tombstones.
Location: MAP 11:A3, OS Ref. NZ365 679. Near town centre and Metro Station.
Open: Easter–Sept: Mon–Sat: 10am–5.30pm, Suns, 1–5pm. Open BH Mons. Oct–Easter: daily except Suns, 10am–3.30pm. Closed 25/26 Dec, 1 Jan & Good Friday.
Admission: Free, except for Time Quest Gallery: Adult £1.50, Child/Conc. £1.

BEDE'S WORLD MUSEUM

Church Bank, Jarrow, Tyne & Wear NE32 3DY
Tel: 0191 489 2106 **Fax:** 0191 428 2361 **E-mail:** visitor.info@bedesworld.co.uk
Managed by: Bede's World   **Contact:** Visitor Services

Discover the world of the Venerable Bede, who lived and worked at the monastery of Wearmouth-Jarrow 1300 years ago.
Location: MAP 11:A3, OS Ref. NZ339 652. Just off A19, S end of Tyne Tunnel. 300yds N of St Paul's.
Open: Apr–Oct: Mon–Sat, 10am–5.30pm, Suns, 12 noon–5.30pm. Nov–Mar: Mon–Sat, 10am–4.30pm, Suns, 12 noon–4.30pm. Open BH Mons, closed Good Fri. Tel for Christmas opening times.
Admission: Adult £4.50, Child/Conc. £3, Family (2+2) £10. Groups by arrangement.

BESSIE SURTEES HOUSE ♯

41–44 Sandhill, Newcastle, Tyne & Wear NE1 3JF
Tel: 0191 269 1200 **www.english-heritage.org.uk/bessiesurtees**
Owner: English Heritage   **Contact:** Reception

Two 16th and 17th century merchants' houses stand on the quayside near the Tyne Bridge. One is a rare example of Jacobean domestic architecture. 3 rooms open.
Location: MAP 10:P3, OS Ref. NZ252 638. Riverside. City centre.
Open: All year: Mon–Fri: 10am–4pm. Closed BHs & 24 Dec–3 Jan.
Admission: Free.
ⓘ WC. 🖾 🔲 🔲 On leads. ✺

GIBSIDE ✤

Nr Rowlands Gill, Burnopfield, Newcastle-upon-Tyne NE16 6BG
Tel: 01207 541820 **E-mail:** gibside@nationaltrust.org.uk **www.nationaltrust.org.uk**
Owner: The National Trust   **Contact:** The Property Manager

Gibside is one of the finest 18th century designed landscapes in the north of England. The Chapel was built to James Paine's design soon after 1760. Outstanding example of Georgian architecture approached along a terrace with an oak avenue. Walk along the River Derwent through woodland.
Location: MAP 10:P3, OS Ref. NZ172 583. 6m SW of Gateshead, 20m NW of Durham. Entrance on B6314 between Burnopfield and Rowlands Gill.
Open: 1 Feb–9 Mar: daily, 10am–4pm. 10 Mar–2 Nov: daily, 10am–6pm. 3 Nov–31 Jan 2009: daily, 10am–4pm. Chapel: 15 Mar–2 Nov, 11am–4.30pm. Stables: 1 Feb–9 Mar, 11am–3.30pm, 10 Mar–2 Nov, 11am–4.30pm. 3 Nov–31 Jan 2009: daily, 11am–3.30pm.
***Admission:** Adult £6, Child £3.50, Family (2+4) £17.50, Family (1+3) £12. Booked groups £4.70. *includes a voluntary donation but visitors can choose to pay the standard prices displayed at the property and on the website.
🖾 🔲 ⅁ Partial. 🖙 🔲 By arrangement. 🅿 Limited for coaches. 🔲 🔲 On leads, in grounds. 🔺 ✺ ⑊

Souter Lighthouse

NEWCASTLE CASTLE KEEP

CASTLE KEEP, CASTLE GARTH, NEWCASTLE-UPON-TYNE NE1 1RQ

www.museums.ncl.ac.uk/keep.

Tel: 01912 327938
Owner: Newcastle City Council   **Contact:** Paul MacDonald

The Castle Keep was built by Henry II between 1168–1178 and is one of the finest surviving examples of Norman Keep in the country. It stands within a site which also contains an early motte and bailey castle built by Robert Curthose, the son of William the Conqueror. It is managed by the Society of Antiquaries of Newcastle-upon-Tyne, the second oldest antiquarian society in the world.
Location: MAP 10:P3, OS Ref. NZ251 638. City centre between St Nicholas church and the High Level bridge.
Open: Apr–Sept, 9.30am–5.30pm; Oct–Mar, 9.30am–4.30pm. Last entry ½ hour before closing time. Closed: Good Friday, 25/26 Dec & 1 Jan 09.
Admission: Adult £1.50, Conc/Child 50p, Special rates for groups (12+).
🖾 ⅁ Partial. 🖙 By arrangement. 🅿 On street. 🔲 🔲 Guide dogs only. ✺

ST PAUL'S MONASTERY ♯

Jarrow, Tyne & Wear
Tel: 0191 489 7052 **www.english-heritage.org.uk/stpauls**
Owner: English Heritage   **Contact:** The Regional Office – 0191 269 1200

The home of the Venerable Bede in the 7th and 8th centuries, partly surviving as the chancel of the parish church. It has become one of the best understood Anglo-Saxon monastic sites.
Location: MAP 11:A3, OS Ref. NZ339 652. In Jarrow, on minor road N of A185. 300yds S of Bede's World.
Open: Any reasonable time.
Admission: Free.
🖾 ⅁ 🖙 🅿 🔲 ✺

Properties that **open all year** appear in the special index at the end of the book.

SEGEDUNUM ROMAN FORT, BATHS & MUSEUM

Buddle Street, Wallsend, NE28 6HR

Tel: 0191 236 9347 **Fax:** 0191 295 5858

Explore life on the Roman frontier as it was 1,800 years ago, at the most completely excavated fort on Hadrian's Wall. See reconstructions of a section of the Wall together with an impressive Roman military bath house building.

Location: MAP 11:A3, OS Ref. N2 301 660.

Open: 1 Apr–31 Oct: daily, 10am–5pm. 1 Nov–31 Mar: daily, 10am–3pm.

Admission: Adults £3.95, Child (16 and under) Free. Conc. £2.25. Groups: Adult £3.20, Conc. £1.80.

SOUTER LIGHTHOUSE ✻

Coast Road, Whitburn, Sunderland, Tyne & Wear SR6 7NH

Tel: 0191 529 3161 **E-mail:** souter@nationaltrust.org.uk

www.nationaltrust.org.uk

Owner: The National Trust **Contact:** The Property Manager

Dramatic red and white lighthouse tower on rugged coast. Built in 1871, the first to be powered by alternating electric current.

Location: MAP 11:A3, OS Ref. NZ408 641. 2½m S of South Shields on A183. 5m N of Sunderland.

Open: 15 Mar–2 Nov: daily except Fri (open Good Fri), 11am–5pm. Last adm 4.30pm.

*Admission: Adult £4.65, Child £3, Family £12.10. Booked Groups (10+): Adult £3.80, Child £2.50. NT members Free: membership available from shop. *includes a voluntary donation but visitors can choose to pay the standard prices displayed at the property and on the website.

◻ ⚥ Ⓣ ⬥ Partial. WCs. ● ⑪ ⒇ By arrangement. 🅿 ■ ↔ In grounds, on leads.

TYNEMOUTH PRIORY & CASTLE ⌗

North Pier, Tynemouth, Tyne & Wear NE30 4BZ

Tel: 0191 257 1090 **www.english-heritage.org.uk/tynemouth**

Owner: English Heritage **Contact:** Visitor Operations Team

The castle walls and gatehouse enclose the substantial remains of a Benedictine priory founded c1090 on a Saxon monastic site. Their strategic importance has made the castle and priory the target for attack for many centuries. In World War I, coastal batteries in the castle defended the mouth of the Tyne. Gun Battery: Access limited, ask staff for details.

Location: MAP 11:A2, OS Ref. NZ373 694. In Tynemouth near North Pier.

Open: 21 Mar–30 Sept: daily, 10am–5pm. 1 Oct–31 Mar '09: Thur–Mon, 10am–4pm. Closed 24–26 Dec & 1 Jan.

Admission: Adult £3.50, Child £1.80, Conc. £2.80, Family £8.80. 15% discount for groups (11+). EH Members free.

◻ Ⓣ ⬥ Grounds. ⒇ By arrangement. ■ ↔ In grounds, on leads. ❋ ⓥ

Gibside Chapel and Avenue

WASHINGTON OLD HALL ✻

The Avenue, Washington Village, Washington, Tyne & Wear NE38 7LE

Tel: 0191 416 6879 **E-mail:** washington.oldhall@nationaltrust.org.uk

www.nationaltrust.org.uk

Owner: The National Trust **Contact:** The Manager

Delightful 17th century house incorporating parts of the medieval home of George Washington's ancestors, their surname of "Washington" was taken from here. Furnished with Delftware, paintings and oak furniture. The knot and parterre gardens lead you to the tranquil wildflower nut orchard. This little gem is well worth a visit.

Location: MAP 11:A3, OS Ref. NZ312 566. In Washington on E side of The Avenue. 5m W of Sunderland (2m from A1), S of Tyne Tunnel, follow signs for Washington then A1231 – follow brown signs to Washington village. The Old Hall is on the avenue next to the church on the hill.

Open: House: 16 Mar–2 Nov: Sun–Wed, 11am–5pm. Garden: as house, 10am–5pm. Tearoom: as house, 11am–4pm. Open Good Fri & Easter Sat.

*Admission: Adult £4.65, Child £3, Family £12.10. Booked groups (10+): Adult £3.80, Child £2.50. NT Membership available from reception. *includes a voluntary donation but visitors can choose to pay the standard prices displayed at the property and on the website.

◻ Ⓣ Conferences. ⬥ Ground floor and grounds. ● ⒇ By arrangement. 🅿 Limited. ■ ↔ In grounds, on leads. ▲

Tynemouth Priory & Castle

Edinburgh Castle

Scotland

First time visitors to Scotland can only scratch the surface of its cultural and social history. Edinburgh Castle is, of course, Scotland's most famous castle but there are so many others which merit a visit: fairytale Dunrobin on the east coast, Dunvegan on the Isle of Skye and Cawdor, home of the Thanes of Cawdor from the 14th century.

■ Owner
His Grace the Duke of Roxburghe

■ Contact
Sarah Macdonald
Sales & Events
Organiser
Roxburghe Estates Office
Kelso
Roxburghshire
Scotland TD5 7SF

Tel: 01573 223333
Fax: 0845 2417190
E-mail: smacdonald@
floorscastle.com

■ Location
MAP 14:J10
OS Ref. NT711 347

From South A68, A698.

From North A68, A697/9
In Kelso follow signs.

Bus: Kelso Bus Station
1m.

Rail: Berwick 20m.

■ Opening Times
Summer
Easter 21–24 March.
1 May–31 October:
Daily: 11am–5pm.
Last admission 4.30pm.

Winter
November–March
Closed to the general
public, available for
events.

■ Admission
Summer
Adult	£7.00
Child* (5–16yrs)	£3.50
OAP/Student	£6.00
Family	£17.00

Groups (20+)
Adult	£5.50
Child* (5–16yrs)	£2.00
OAP/Student	£5.00

*Under 5yrs Free.

■ Special Events
Snowdrop Festival
Easter Eggstravaganza
Floors Castle Horse Trials
Massed Pipe Bands Day
Christmas Winter
Wonderland

Please check our website
for details.

Skyscan Photo Library

FLOORS CASTLE 🏛
www.floorscastle.com

Floors Castle, home of the Duke and Duchess of Roxburghe, is situated in the heart of the Scottish Border Country. It is reputedly the largest inhabited castle in Scotland. Designed by William Adam, who was both masterbuilder and architect, for the first Duke of Roxburghe, building started in 1721.

It was the present Duke's great-great-grand-father James, the 6th Duke, who embellished the plain Adam features of the building. In about 1849 Playfair, letting his imagination and talent run riot, transformed the castle, creating a multitude of spires and domes.

The apartments now display the outstanding collection of French 17th and 18th century furniture, magnificent tapestries, Chinese and European porcelain and many other fine works of art. Many of the treasures in the castle today were collected by Duchess May, American wife of the 8th Duke.

The castle has been seen on cinema screens worldwide in the film Greystoke, as the home of Tarzan, the Earl of Greystoke.

Gardens
The extensive parkland and gardens overlooking the River Tweed provide a variety of wooded walks. The garden centre and walled gardens contain splendid herbaceous borders and in the outer walled garden a parterre to commemorate the Millennium can be seen. An excellent children's playground and picnic area are very close to the castle.

ℹ Gala dinners, conferences, product launches, 4 x 4 driving, incentive groups, highland games and other promotional events. Extensive park, helicopter pad, fishing, clay pigeon and pheasant shooting. No photography inside the castle.

♿ Visitors may alight at the entrance. WC.

☕ Self-service, licensed, seats 125 opens 11am.

🅿 Unlimited for cars, 100 yds away, coach park 150 yds. Coaches can be driven to the entrance. Lunch or tea for coach drivers.

Welcome, guide provided. Playground facilities.

On leads, in grounds.

Conference/Function
ROOM	SIZE	MAX CAPACITY
Dining Rm	18m x 7m	150
Ballroom	21m x 8m	150

MANDERSTON

www.manderston.co.uk

■ Owner
The Lord Palmer

■ Contact
The Lord or Lady Palmer
Manderston
Duns
Berwickshire
Scotland TD11 3PP

Tel: 01361 883450
Secretary: 01361 882636
Fax: 01361 882010
E-mail: palmer@
manderston.co.uk

■ Location
MAP 14:K9
OS Ref. NT810 544

From Edinburgh
47m, 1hr.
1½ m E of Duns on
A6105.

Bus: 400 yds.

Rail: Berwick
Station 12m.

Taxi: Chirnside 818216.

Airport: Edinburgh or
Newcastle both
60m or 80 mins.

■ Opening Times
Summer
Mid-May–end September
Thurs & Sun, 1.30–5pm
Last entry 4.15pm.
Gardens: 11.30am–dusk.

BH Mons, late May
& late August. Gardens
open until dusk.

Groups welcome all year
by appointment.

Winter
September–May
Group visits welcome
by appointment.

■ Admission
House & Grounds
Adult   £8.00
Child (under 12yrs)   Free
Conc.   £8.00

Groups (15+)   £7.50
(£8.00 outside opening
days).

**Grounds only including
Stables & Marble Dairy**
£4.50

On days when the house
is closed to the public,
groups viewing by
appointment will have
personally conducted
tours. The Gift Shop will
be open. On these
occasions reduced party
rates (except for school
children) will not apply.
Group visits (15+) other
than open days are
£8.00pp. Snaffles
Tearoom open on Open
Days or by arrangement.

Manderston, together with its magnificent stables, stunning marble dairy and 56 acres of immaculate gardens, forms an ensemble which must be unique in Britain today.

The house was completely rebuilt between 1903 and 1905, with no expense spared. Visitors are able to see not only the sumptuous State rooms and bedrooms, decorated in the Adam manner, but also all the original domestic offices, in a truly 'upstairs downstairs' atmosphere. Manderston boasts a unique and recently restored silver staircase.

There is a special museum with a nostalgic display of valuable tins made by Huntly and Palmer from 1868 to the present day. Winner of the AA/NPI Bronze Award UK 1994.

Gardens
Outside, the magnificence continues and the combination of formal gardens and picturesque landscapes is a major attraction unique amongst Scottish houses. The stables, still in use, have been described by *Horse and Hound* as 'probably the finest in all the wide world'.

Manderston has often been used as a film location, most recently it was the star of Channel 4's '*The Edwardian Country House*'.

ℹ️ Corporate & incentives venue. Ideal retreat: business groups, think-tank weekends. Fashion shows, air displays, archery, clay pigeon shooting, equestrian events, garden parties, shows, rallies, filming, product launches and marathons. Two airstrips for light aircraft, approx 5m, grand piano, billiard table, pheasant shoots, sea angling, salmon fishing, stabling, cricket pitch, tennis court, lake. Nearby: 18-hole golf course, indoor swimming pool, squash court. No photography in house.

🛍️

🍽️ Available. Buffets, lunches and dinners. Wedding receptions.

♿ Special parking available outside the House.

🍰 Snaffles Tearoom – home made lunches, teas, cakes and tray bakes. Can be booked in advance, menus on request.

🧑‍🏫 Included. Available in French. Guides in rooms. If requested, the owner may meet groups. Tour time 1¼ hrs.

🅿️ 400 cars 125yds from house, 30 coaches 5yds from house. Appreciated if group fees are paid by one person.

🖼️ Welcome. Guide can be provided. Biscuit Tin Museum of particular interest.

🐕 Grounds only, on leads.

🛏️ 6 twin, 4 double.

❄️

Conference/Function

ROOM	SIZE	MAX CAPACITY
Dining Rm	22' x 35'	100
Ballroom	34' x 21'	150
Hall	22' x 38'	130
Drawing Rm	35' x 21'	150

■ Owner
Catherine Maxwell Stuart, 21st Lady of Traquair

■ Contact
Ms C Maxwell Stuart
Innerleithen
Peeblesshire EH44 6PW

Tel: 01896 830323
Fax: 01896 830639
E-mail: enquiries@ traquair.co.uk

■ Location
MAP 13:H10
OS Ref. NY330 354

On B709 near junction with A72. Edinburgh 1hr, Glasgow 1½ hrs, Carlisle 1½ hrs, Newcastle 1½ hrs.

■ Opening Times
March 21–24:
April: Sat/Sun
12 noon–5pm.
1 May–31 August: daily, 10.30am–5pm.
September: daily,
12 noon–5pm.
October: daily, November:
Sat/Sun, 11am–3pm.

Guided tours, conducted by an experienced guide or by the owner, may be arranged outside these hours for an additional charge. Groups may also book a free introductory talk.

Traquair Experiences
Lunches, dinners, receptions, coffee and shortbread, ale tastings and ghost tours may all be arranged during opening hours.

■ Admission
House & Grounds
Adult	£6.50
Child	£3.50
Senior	£6.00
Family(2+3)	£18.00

Groups (20+)
Adult	£5.80
Child	£2.80
Senior	£5.50

Grounds only
Adult	£3.50
Child	£2.50
Guide book	£3.75

■ Special Events
March 23
Easter Egg Extravaganza
May 24/25
Medieval Fayre
June 1
St Ronan's Tattoo
August 2/3
Traquair Fair
October 24–26
Halloween Experience
November 29/30
Christmas Opening

Conference/Function
ROOM	SIZE	MAX CAPACITY
Dining Room	33' x 16'	34 seated
Drawing Rm	27' x 24'	50/60 receptions

TRAQUAIR
www.traquair.co.uk

Traquair, situated amidst beautiful scenery and close by the River Tweed, is the oldest inhabited house in Scotland – visited by twenty-seven kings. Originally a Royal hunting lodge, it was owned by the Scottish Crown until 1478 when it passed to a branch of the Royal Stuart family whose descendants still live in the house today. Nearly ten centuries of Scottish political and domestic life can be traced from the collection of treasures in the house. It is particularly rich in associations with the Catholic Church in Scotland, Mary Queen of Scots and the Jacobite Risings.

Visitors are invited to enjoy the house, extensive grounds, maze, craft workshops, 1745 Cottage Restaurant and the famous Traquair House Brewery housed in the eighteenth century wing and producing the world famous Traquair House Ales.

Traquair is a unique piece of living history welcoming visitors from all over the world, providing a magical and romantic setting for weddings, hosting a wide range of summer events and a superb venue for corporate groups. You can even stay at Traquair House. There are three spacious double bedrooms furnished with antique furniture, canopied beds, private bathrooms and central heating. They are all available on a bed and breakfast basis.

 No photography in house.

 Exclusive lunches/dinners (max 30) in the Dining Room.

Licensed, self-service.

Home cooked meals (max 50) at 1745 Cottage Restaurant.

Apr & outside opening hours.

Coaches please book.

In grounds on leads.

3 en-suites. B&B.

AYTON CASTLE
AYTON, EYEMOUTH, BERWICKSHIRE TD14 5RD

Tel: 018907 81212   **Fax:** 018907 81550

Owner: D I Liddell-Grainger of Ayton   **Contact:** The Curator

Built in 1846 by the Mitchell-Innes family and designed by the architect James Gillespie Graham. Over the last ten years it has been fully restored and is now a family home. It is a unique restoration project and the quality of the original and restored workmanship is outstanding. The castle stands on an escarpment surrounded by mature woodlands containing many interesting trees and has been a film-making venue due to this magnificent setting.

Location: MAP 14:K8, OS Ref. NT920 610. 7m N of Berwick-on-Tweed on Route A1.

Open: 14 May–10 Sept: by telephone appointment.

Admission: Adult £3, Child (under 15yrs) Free.

⊤ ⅃ Partial. ⓕ Obligatory. ℙ ⊞ In grounds, on leads. ⊞

BOWHILL HOUSE & COUNTRY PARK
BOWHILL, SELKIRK TD7 5ET

Tel: 01750 22204   **Fax:** 01750 23893   **E-mail:** bht@buccleuch.com

Owner: His Grace the Duke of Buccleuch & Queensberry KBE

Contact: Buccleuch Heritage Trust

Rich history and beautiful landscape combine at the Scottish Borders home of the Duke of Buccleuch & Queensberry KBE providing an unique opportunity to enjoy culture and countryside at its best. Outstanding collection of art, silverware, porcelain and French furniture. Country Park with lochs, rivers and woodland walks.

Location: MAP 13:H10, OS Ref. NT426 278. 3m W of Selkirk off A708 Moffat Road, A68 from Newcastle, A7 from Carlisle or Edinburgh.

Open: House: 1–31 Jul, daily, 1–5pm. Country Park: Easter; May–Jun, Sats & Suns & BHs; Jul & Aug daily, 10am–5pm.

Admission: House & Country Park: Adult £7, Child (5–16yrs) £3, OAP £5. Country Park only: Adults £3, Child (under 5yrs) £2, Family tickets and group tickets available.

⊡ ⊞ ⊤ ⅃ WC. Wheelchair visitors free. ☑ Groups can book (special rates). Licensed. ⓕ For groups. Tour time 1¼ hrs. ℙ ☰ ⊞ On leads. ⊞ ☑

DAWYCK BOTANIC GARDEN
Stobo, Peeblesshire EH45 9JU

Tel: 01721 760254   **Fax:** 01721 760214   **E-mail:** dawyck@rbge.org.uk

Contact: The Curator

Renowned historic arboretum. Amongst mature specimen trees – some over 40 metres tall – are a variety of flowering trees, shrubs and herbaceous plants. Explore the world's first Cryptogamic Sanctuary and Reserve for 'non-flowering' plants.

Location: MAP 13:G10, OS Ref. NT168 352. 8m SW of Peebles on B712.

Open: Feb–Nov: daily, 10am–6pm (closes 4pm Feb & Nov, 5pm Mar & Oct). Last admission 1 hr before closing.

Admission: Adult £4, Child £1, Conc. £3.50, Family £9. Group discounts & membership programme available.

DRYBURGH ABBEY
St Boswells, Melrose

Tel: 01835 822381

Owner: Historic Scotland   **Contact:** The Steward

Remarkably complete ruins of Dryburgh Abbey.

Location: MAP 14:I10, OS Ref. NT591 317. 5m SE of Melrose off B6356. 1½ m N of St Boswells.

Open: 1 Apr–30 Sept: daily, 9.30am–5.30pm, last ticket 5pm. 1 Oct–31 Mar: daily, 9.30am–4.30pm, last ticket 4pm.

Admission: Adult £4.50, Child £2.25, Conc. £3.50 (2007 prices).

⊡ ⅃ Partial. ⓕ By arrangement. ℙ ☰ €

DUNS CASTLE
DUNS, BERWICKSHIRE TD11 3NW
www.dunscastle.co.uk

Tel: 01361 883211   **Fax:** 01361 882015   **E-mail:** info@dunscastle.co.uk

Owner: Alexander Hay of Duns   **Contact:** Natalie Scheff

This historical 1320 pele tower has been home to the Hay family since 1696, and the current owners Alexander and Aline Hay offer it as a welcoming venue for individuals, groups and corporate guests to enjoy. This beautiful castle maintains high standards of comfort while retaining all the character of its rich period interiors. Wonderful lakeside and parkland setting.

Location: MAP 14:J9, OS Ref. NT777 544. 10m off A1. Rail: Berwick station 16m. Airports: Newcastle & Edinburgh, 1 hr.

Open: Available all year by reservation for individuals, groups, parties, weddings and companies for day visits or residential stays, on an exclusive use basis. Not open to the general public.

Admission: Rates for private and corporate visits, wedding receptions and filming on application.

⊞ 4 x 4-poster, 4 x double, 3 x twin (all with bathrooms), 1 single plus 6 cottages in grounds. ⊞

For **corporate hospitality** venues see our special index at the end of the book.

FERNIEHIRST CASTLE
JEDBURGH, ROXBURGHSHIRE
TD8 6NX

Tel: 01835 862201
Fax: 01835 863992
Owner: The Ferniehirst Trust
Contact: Mrs J Fraser

Ferniehirst Castle – Scotland's Frontier Fortress. Ancestral home of the Kerr family. Restored (1984/1987) by the 12th Marquess of Lothian. Unrivalled 16th century Border architecture. Grand Apartment and Turret Library. A 16th century Chamber Oratory. The Kerr Chamber – Museum of Family History. A special tribute to Jedburgh's Protector to Mary Queen of Scots – Sir Thomas Kerr. Riverside walk by Jed Water. Archery Field opposite the Chapel where sheep of Viking origin still graze as they did four centuries ago.

Location:
MAP 14:J11, OS Ref. NT653 181. 2m S of Jedburgh on the A68.
Open: July: Tue–Sun, 11am–4pm. (Closed Mons.)
Admission: Adult £3.50, Child £1.50. Groups (max. 50) by prior arrangement (01835 862201).

🔲 ♿ Suitable. WCs.
👤 Guided tours only, groups by arrangement.
🅿 Ample for cars and coaches.
🐕 In grounds, on leads.

FLOORS CASTLE 🏛
See page 436 for full page entry.

HALLIWELL'S HOUSE MUSEUM

Halliwell's Close, Market Place, High Street, Selkirk
Tel: 01750 20096   **Fax:** 01750 23282
Owner: Scottish Borders Council   **Contact:** Brian Appleby
Re-creation of buildings, formerly used as a house and ironmonger's shop.
Location: MAP 14:I10, OS Ref. NT472 286. In Selkirk town centre.
Open: Apr–Sept: Mon–Sat, 10am–5pm, Sun, 10am–12 noon. Jul & Aug: Mon–Sat, 10am–5pm, Sun 10am–1pm. Oct: Mon–Sat, 10am–4pm. Sun, 10am–12 noon. Closed for Selkirk Common Riding. Please telephone in advance to confirm opening times.
Admission: Free.

HERMITAGE CASTLE 🏛

Liddesdale, Newcastleton
Tel: 01387 376222
Owner: In the care of Historic Scotland   **Contact:** The Steward
Eerie fortress at the heart of the bloodiest events in the history of the Borders. Mary Queen of Scots made her famous ride here to visit her future husband.
Location: MAP 10:L1, OS Ref. NY497 961. In Liddesdale 5½m NE of Newcastleton, B6399.
Open: 1 Apr–30 Sept: daily, 9.30am–5.30pm, last ticket 5pm.
Admission: Adult £3.50, Child £1.75, Conc. £2.80 (2007 prices).

🔲 🖼 🅿 🐕 €

THE HIRSEL GARDENS, COUNTRY PARK 🏛
& HOMESTEAD MUSEUM

Coldstream, Berwickshire TD12 4LP
Tel: 01573 224144   **Fax:** 01573 226313   **E-mail:** rogerdodd@btconnect.com
www.hirselcountrypark.co.uk
Owner: Lord Home of the Hirsel   **Contact:** Roger G Dodd
Wonderful spring flowers and rhododendrons. Homestead museum and crafts centre. The Cottage Tearoom. Displays of estate life and adaptation to modern farming.
Location: MAP 14:K10, OS Ref. NT838 393. Immediately W of Coldstream off A697.
Open: All year during daylight hours.
Admission: £2.50 per car, coaches by appointment.

🔲 🖼 ♿ WCs. 🅿 Limited for coaches. 🐕 In grounds, on leads. ❄

© The Mellerstain Trust

Mellerstain

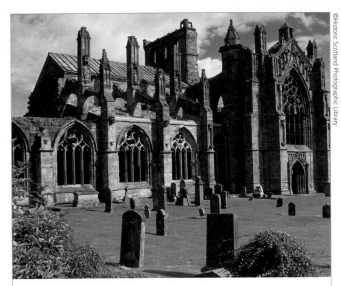

JEDBURGH ABBEY
4/5 ABBEY BRIDGEND, JEDBURGH TD8 6JQ

Tel: 01835 863925

Owner: In the care of Historic Scotland   **Contact:** The Steward

Founded by David I c1138 for Augustinian Canons. The church is mostly in the Romanesque and early Gothic styles and is remarkably complete. The award-winning visitor centre contains the priceless 12th century 'Jedburgh Comb' and other artefacts found during archaeological excavations.

Location: MAP 14:J11, OS Ref. NT650 205. In Jedburgh on the A68.

Open: Apr–Sept: daily, 9.30am–5.30pm. Oct–Mar: daily, 9.30am–4.30pm. Last ticket 30 mins before closing.

Admission: Adult £5, Child £2.50, Conc. £4 (2007 prices). 10% discount for groups (11+).

ℹ Picnic area. 🔲 ♿ Partial to visitor centre. WC. 🅿 🔲 ▣ Free when booked. 🐕 Guide dogs only. ✳

MANDERSTON 🏛   *See page 437 for full page entry.*

MELROSE ABBEY
MELROSE, ROXBURGHSHIRE TD6 9LG

Tel: 01896 822562

Owner: Historic Scotland   **Contact:** The Steward

The abbey was founded about 1136 by David I as a Cistercian abbey and at one time was probably the richest in Scotland. Richard II's English army largely destroyed it in 1385 but it was rebuilt and the surviving remains are mostly 14th century. Burial place of Robert the Bruce's heart. Local history displays.

Location: MAP 14:I10, OS Ref. NT549 342. In the centre of Melrose off the A68 or A7.

Open: Apr–Sept: daily, 9.30am–5.30pm. Oct–Mar: daily, 9.30am–4.30pm. Last ticket 30 mins before closing.

Admission: Adult £5, Child £2.50, Conc. £4 (2007 prices). 10% discount for groups (11+).

ℹ Picnic area. 🔲 ♿ Tape for visitors with learning difficulties. 🔲 🅿 ▣ Pre-booked visits free. 🐕 Guide dogs only. ✳ €

MERTOUN GARDENS 🏛

St Boswells, Melrose, Roxburghshire TD6 0EA

Tel: 01835 823236   **Fax:** 01835 822474   **E-mail:** mertounestatefarms@farming.co.uk

Owner: His Grace the Duke of Sutherland   **Contact:** Angela Dodds/Susan Murdoch

26 acres of beautiful grounds. Walled garden and well-preserved circular dovecote.

Location: MAP 14:J10, OS Ref. NT617 318. Entrance off B6404 2m NE of St Boswells.

Open: Apr–Sept: Fri–Mon, 2–6pm. Last admission 5.30pm.

Admission: Adult £2.50, Child 50p, OAP £1.50. Groups by arrangement: 10% reduction.

⌨ By arrangement. 🅿 🐕

MELLERSTAIN HOUSE 🏛
MELLERSTAIN, GORDON, BERWICKSHIRE TD3 6LG

www.mellerstain.com

Tel: 01573 410225   **Fax:** 01573 410636   **E-mail:** enquiries@mellerstain.com

Owner: The Earl of Haddington   **Contact:** The Administrator

One of Scotland's great Georgian houses and a unique example of the work of the Adam family; the two wings built in 1725 by William Adam, the large central block by his son, Robert 1770-78. Rooms contain fine plasterwork, colourful ceilings and marble fireplaces. The library is considered to be Robert Adam's finest creation. Many fine paintings and period furniture.

Location: MAP 14:J10, OS Ref. NT648 392. From Edinburgh A68 to Earlston, turn left 5m, signed.

Open: Easter weekend, 1 May–30 Jun & 1–30 Sept: Suns, Weds & BH Mons. 1 Jul–31 Aug: Sun, Mon, Wed & Thurs. Oct: Suns only. House: 12.30–5pm. Last ticket 4.15pm. Groups any time by appointment. Tearoom, shop & gardens: 11.30am–5pm.

Admission: Adult £6, Child (under 16yrs) with adult Free. Groups (20+) £5.50 (outside normal hours £6.50). Grounds only: £3.50.

ℹ No photography or video cameras. 🔲 🔲 🔲 ♿ Partial. ▣ Licensed. 🍴 Licensed. ⌨ By arrangement. 🅿 🐕 In grounds, on leads. Guide dogs only in house. 🎩

The Head Gardener's Cottage, Floors Castle

MONTEVIOT HOUSE GARDENS
JEDBURGH, ROXBURGHSHIRE TD8 6UQ
www.monteviot.com

Tel: 01835 830380 (mornings only) / 01835 830704 **Fax:** 01835 830288
Owner: The Marquis of Lothian **Contact:** The Administrator
The river garden planted with herbaceous shrub borders, has a beautiful view of the River Teviot. A semi-enclosed rose garden with a collection of hybrid teas, floribunda and shrub roses. The pinetum is full of unusual trees and nearby a water garden of islands is linked by bridges.
Location: MAP 14:J11, OS Ref. NT648 247. 3m N of Jedburgh. S side of B6400 (to Nisbet). 1m E of A68.
Open: House: 30 Jun–13 Jul: 12 noon–4.15pm. Garden: Apr–Oct: daily, 12 noon–5pm (last entry 4pm). Coach parties by prior arrangement.
Admission: House only: Adult £3. Garden: Adult £3.50. Under 16yrs Free.
Partial. Parking & WCs. By arrangement.

PAXTON HOUSE, GALLERY & COUNTRY PARK
BERWICK-UPON-TWEED TD15 1SZ
www.paxtonhouse.com

Tel: 01289 386291 **Fax:** 01289 386660 **E-mail:** info@paxtonhouse.com
Owner: The Paxton Trust **Contact:** The Director
Award winning Palladian country house built 1758 to the design of John Adam. 12 period rooms contain the finest collections of Chippendale and Regency furniture. Magnificent picture gallery and restored Georgian kitchen. Enjoy the grounds and gardens, riverside and woodland walks, red squirrel and salmon net fishing museum. Visit the shop, tearoom and the new Ellem Fishing Club exhibition, the oldest fishing club in the world.
Location: MAP 14:K9, OS Ref. NT931 520. 3m off the A1 Berwick-upon-Tweed bypass on B6461.
Open: Easter–31 Oct: House: 11am–5pm. Last house tour 4pm. Grounds: 10am–sunset. Open to groups/schools all year by appointment.
Admission: Adult £6, Child £3. Groups (pre-arranged, 12+). Adult £5, Child £2.50. Grounds only: Adult £3, Child £1.50.
No photography. Conferences, weddings. Partial. Licensed. Obligatory. In grounds, on leads.

OLD GALA HOUSE
Scott Crescent, Galashiels TD1 3JS
Tel: 01750 20096 **Fax:** 01750 23282
Owner: Scottish Borders Council
Dating from 1583, the former house of the Lairds of Gala. Particularly memorable is the painted ceiling dated 1635.
Location: MAP 14:I10, OS Ref. NT492 357. S of town centre, signed from A7.
Open: Apr, May & Sept: Tue–Sat, 10am–4pm. Jun–Aug: Mon–Sat, 10am–4pm, Sun, 1–4pm. Oct: Tue–Fri, 1–4pm, Sat, 10am–4pm.
Admission: Free.

SMAILHOLM TOWER
Smailholm, Kelso
Tel: 01573 460365
Owner: In the care of Historic Scotland **Contact:** The Steward
Set on a high rocky knoll this well preserved 16th century tower houses an exhibition of tapestries and costume dolls depicting characters from Sir Walter Scott's Minstrelsy of the Scottish Borders.
Location: MAP 14:J10, OS Ref. NT638 347. Nr Smailholm Village, 6m W of Kelso on B6937 then B6404.
Open: 1 Apr–30 Sept: daily, 9.30am–5.30pm. Oct: Sat–Wed, 9.30am–4.30pm. Nov–Mar: Sats & Suns only, 9.30am–4.30pm. Last tickets 30 mins before closing.
Admission: Adult £3.50, Child £1.75, Conc. £2.80 (2007 prices).

THIRLESTANE CASTLE
LAUDER, BERWICKSHIRE TD2 6RU
www.thirlestanecastle.co.uk

Tel: 01578 722430 **Fax:** 01578 722761 **E-mail:** admin@thirlestanecastle.co.uk
Owner: Thirlestane Castle Trust **Contact:** Ian Garner
Thirlestane Castle was the ancient seat of the Earls and Duke of Lauderdale and is still home to the Maitlands. Standing in beautiful Border countryside, Thirlestane has exquisite 17th century plasterwork ceilings, a fine portrait collection, historic toys, kitchens and country life exhibitions. Facilities include free parking, audio visual display, gift shop, café, adventure playground, and woodland picnic tables. Four star STB award; Registered Museum. The state rooms are available for banquets, dinners and receptions. Non-destructive events can be held in the grounds which overlook the Leader Valley and Lammermuir Hills.
Location: MAP 14:I9, OS Ref. NT540 473. Off A68 at Lauder, 28m S of Edinburgh.
Open: Easter: 21, 23 & 24 Mar; 30 Apr–29 June, Sun, Wed, Thur; 5 & 26 May; Jul & Aug: Sun–Thurs; 3–28 Sept Sun, Wed & Thurs; 10am–3pm (Grounds 5pm). Special opening at other times can be arranged for pre-booked groups with special rates. Minimum 20 people or £120.
Admission: Castle & Grounds: Adult £7.50, Child £5.50, Senior £6.50, Family (2+3) £20. Grounds only: Adult £3, Child £1.50. Group: Adult £6.50, Child £3.50. Friend or a Patron of Thirlestane Castle, ask for details. Check website for changes & prices.
Woodland walk, children's adventure playground, country life display area. Unsuitable. By arrangement. In grounds, on leads.

TRAQUAIR
See page 438 for full page entry.

DRUMLANRIG CASTLE 🏛

www.drumlanrig.com

Drumlanrig Castle, Gardens and Country Park, Dumfriesshire home of the Duke of Buccleuch and Queensberry KBE, was built between 1679 and 1691 by William Douglas, 1st Duke of Queensberry. Drumlanrig is rightly recognised as one of the first and most important buildings in the grand manner in Scottish domestic architecture. James Smith, who made the conversion from a 15th century castle, made a comparable transformation at Dalkeith a decade later.

The Castle, of local pink sandstone, offers superb views across Nithsdale. It houses a renowned art collection, cabinets made for Louis XIV's Versailles, relics of Bonnie Prince Charlie and a 300 year old silver chandelier.

The story of Sir James Douglas, killed in Spain while carrying out the last wish of Robert Bruce, pervades the Castle in the emblem of a winged heart. Douglas family historical exhibition. Other attractions include craft workshops, mountain bike trails and bike hire, Cycle Museum, working forge and adventure play area. The gardens, now being restored to the plan of 1738, include a plant centre and add to the overall effect. The fascination of Drumlanrig as a centre of art, beauty and history is complemented by its role in the Queensberry Estate, a model of dynamic and enlightened land management.

ℹ️ No photography inside the Castle.

🛍

✿

♿ Suitable. WC. Please enquire about facilities before visit.

☕ Licensed.

🍴 Snacks, lunches and teas during opening hours.

🏃

🅿 Adjacent to the Castle.

👶 Children's quiz and worksheets. Ranger-led activities, including woodlands and forestry. Adventure playground. School groups welcome throughout the year by arrangement.

🐕 In Country Park on leads.

❄

♨

■ Owner
His Grace the Duke of Buccleuch & Queensberry KBE

■ Contact
Claire Oram
Drumlanrig Castle
Thornhill
Dumfriesshire
DG3 4AQ

Tel: 01848 331555
Fax: 01848 331682
E-mail: bre@ drumlanrigcastle.org.uk

■ Location
MAP 13:E12
OS Ref. NX851 992

18m N of Dumfries, 3m NW of Thornhill off A76. 16m from M74 at Elvanfoot. Approx. 1½ hrs by road from Edinburgh, Glasgow and Carlisle.

■ Opening Times
Summer
Castle
21 March–31 August: daily, 11am–4pm (last tour).

Country Park, Gardens & Adventure Woodland
21 March–30 September: daily, 10am–5pm.

Winter
By appointment only.

■ Admission*
Castle and Country Park
Adult	£7.00
Child (5–15yrs)	£3.00
OAP/Student	£6.00
Family (2+4)	£24.50
Disabled in wheelchairs	Free

Pre-booked groups (20+)
Adult	£5.00
Child (5–15yrs)	£2.00

Outside normal opening times	£8.00

Country Park only
Adult	£4.00
OAP	£3.50
Child (5–15yrs)	£3.00
Family (2+4)	£19.00
Season Ticket	£25.00

*All visitors to the Castle must sign the visitor book as a condition of entry.

Conference/Function

ROOM	SIZE	MAX CAPACITY
Visitors' Centre	6m x 13m	50

ARDWELL GARDENS

Ardwell, Nr Stranraer, Dumfries and Galloway DG9 9LY

Tel: 01776 860227

Owner: Mr Francis Brewis   **Contact:** Mrs Terry Brewis

The gardens include a formal garden, wild garden and woodland.

Location: MAP 9:D4, OS Ref. NX102 455. A716 10m S of Stranraer.

Open: 1 Mar–30 Sept: daily, 10am–5pm.

Admission: Adult £3, Children under 14 free.

AUCHINLECK HOUSE

Ochiltree, Ayrshire

Tel: 01628 825925

E-mail: bookings@landmarktrust.org.uk   **www.landmarktrust.org.uk**

Owner/Contact: The Landmark Trust

One of the finest examples of an 18th century Scottish country house, the importance of which is further enhanced by its association with James Boswell, author of The Life of Samuel Johnson. The house has been restored by the Landmark Trust and is let for holidays for up to 13 people. Full details of Auchinleck House and 184 other historic and architecturally important buildings are featured in the Landmark Trust Handbook (price £11.50 refundable against booking).

Location: MAP 13:C11, OS Ref. NS507 230.

Open: Available for holidays for up to 13 people throughout the year. Parts of the house will be open to the public Easter–Oct: Wed afternoons. Grounds: dawn–dusk in the Spring & Summer season. Contact the Landmark Trust for details.

Admission: By appointment only. Tickets £3 from 01628 825920.

🐕 In grounds, on leads. ▣

BARGANY GARDENS

Girvan, Ayrshire KA26 9QL

Tel: 01465 871249   **Fax:** 01465 871282   **E-mail:** bargany@btinternet.com

Owner: Mr John Dalrymple Hamilton   **Contact:** Mrs Sally Anne Dalrymple Hamilton

Lily pond, rock garden and a fine collection of hard and softwood trees.

Location: MAP 9:E1, OS Ref. NX851 992. 18m N of Dumfries, 3m NW of Thornhill off A76. 16m from M74 at Elvanfoot.

Open: May: daily, 10am–5pm.

Admission: Adult: £2, Child Free. Buses by arrangement.

BRODICK CASTLE ♛

Isle of Arran KA27 8HY

Tel: 0131 243 9300

Owner: The National Trust for Scotland

Castle built on the site of a Viking fortress with interesting contents.

Location: MAP 12:P10, OS Ref. NX684 509. Off A711 /A755, in Kirkcudbright, at 12 High St.

BURNS' COTTAGE

Alloway, Ayrshire KA7 4PY

Tel: 01292 441215   **Fax:** 01292 441750

Contact: I Manson

Thatched cottage, birthplace of Robert Burns in 1759, with adjacent museum.

Location: OS Ref. NS335 190. 2m SW of Ayr. Two separate sites, 600yds apart.

Open: Apr–Sept: daily, 10am–5.30pm. Oct–Mar: daily, 10am–5pm. Closed 25/26 Dec & 1/2 Jan.

Admission: Adult £4, Child/OAP £2.50, Family £10.

Dean Castle Country Park

©Historic Scotland Photographic Library

CAERLAVEROCK CASTLE 🏛

GLENCAPLE, DUMFRIES DG1 4RU

Tel: 01387 770244

Owner: In the care of Historic Scotland   **Contact:** Valerie Bennett

One of the finest castles in Scotland on a triangular site surrounded by moats. Its most remarkable features are the twin-towered gatehouse and the Renaissance Nithsdale lodging. The site of two famous sieges. Exhibition with video presentation, children's park, replica siege engines and nature trail to site of earlier castle.

Location: MAP 10:I3, OS84 NY025 656. 8m S of Dumfries on the B725.

Open: Apr–Sept: daily, 9.30am–5.30pm; Oct–Mar: daily, 9.30am–4.30pm. Last ticket sold 30 mins before closing.

Admission: Adult £5, Child £2.50, Conc. £4 (2007 prices). 10% discount for groups (11+).

ℹ️ 🖻 ♿ Partial. WCs. ▣ 🅿 Limited for coaches. ■ Free if pre-booked.
🐕 In grounds, on leads. ✱ €

CARDONESS CASTLE 🏛

Gatehouse of Fleet

Tel: 01557 814427

Owner: In the care of Historic Scotland   **Contact:** The Steward

Well preserved ruin of a four storey tower house of 15th century standing on a rocky platform above the Water of Fleet. Ancient home of the McCullochs. Very fine fireplaces.

Location: MAP 9:G3, OS Ref. NX591 553. 1m SW of Gatehouse of Fleet, beside the A75.

Open: 1 Apr–30 Sept: daily, 9.30am–5.30pm. Last ticket 5pm. Oct: daily except Thurs & Fri; Nov–Mar: Sats & Suns only, 9.30am–4.30pm. Last ticket 4pm.

Admission: Adult £3.50, Child £1.75, Conc. £2.80 (2007 prices).

🖻 🅿 🐕 ✱ €

CASTLE KENNEDY & GARDENS

STAIR ESTATES, REPHAD, STRANRAER, DUMFRIES AND GALLOWAY DG9 8BX

www.castlekennedygardens.co.uk

Tel: 01776 702024 / 01581 400225 (Gardens) **Fax:** 01776 706248
E-mail: info@castlekennedygardens.co.uk
Owner/Contact: The Earl and Countess of Stair
Originally laid out in 1734, the gardens are located between two natural lochs, and extend to 75 acres of landscaped terraces and avenues. With the romantic 16th century Castle Kennedy overlooking a walled garden, these gardens are famous for their woodland walks, fine specimen trees, rhododendrons and tender exotic plants.
Location: MAP 9:D3, OS Ref. NX109 610. 5m E of Stranraer on A75.
Open: Feb & Mar: Sats & Suns. Easter–30 Sept: daily, 10am–5pm. Other times by appointment.
Admission: Adult £4, Child £1, OAP £3.

CASTLE OF ST JOHN

Stranraer, Dumfries and Galloway
Tel: 01776 705088 **Fax:** 01776 705835
Owner: Dumfries & Galloway Council **Contact:** John Picken
A much altered 16th century L-plan tower house, now a museum.
Location: MAP 9:D3, OS Ref. NX061 608. In Stranraer, towards centre, ¼m short of the harbour.
Open: The castle will be closed during 2008 to allow major Heritage Lottery-funded alterations to take place. Due to reopen for Easter 2009.
Admission: Free.

CRAIGDARROCH HOUSE

Moniaive, Dumfriesshire DG3 4JB
Tel: 01848 200202
Owner/Contact: Mrs Carin Sykes
Location: MAP 9:G1, OS Ref. NX741 909. S side of B729, 2m W of Moniaive, 19m WNW of Dumfries.
Open: Jul: daily, 2–4pm. Please note: no WCs.
Admission: £2.

CRAIGIEBURN GARDEN

Craigieburn House, Nr Moffat, Dumfriesshire DG10 9LF
Tel: 01683 221250
Owner/Contact: Janet Wheatcroft
A plantsman's garden with a huge range of rare and unusual plants surrounded by natural woodland.
Location: MAP 13:G12, OS Ref. NT117 053. NW side of A708 to Yarrow & Selkirk, 2½m E of Moffat.
Open: Easter–Oct: Tue–Sun.
Admission: Adult £2.50, Child Free (charges support Sherpa school in Nepal).

CROSSRAGUEL ABBEY

Maybole, Strathclyde
Tel: 01655 883113
Owner: In the care of Historic Scotland **Contact:** The Steward
Founded in the early 13th century by the Earl of Carrick. Remarkably complete remains include church, cloister, chapter house and much of the domestic premises.
Location: MAP 13:B11, OS Ref. NS275 083. 2m S of Maybole on the A77.
Open: 1 Apr–30 Sept: daily, 9.30am–5.30pm. Last ticket 5pm.
Admission: Adult £3.50, Child £1.75, Conc. £2.80 (2007 prices).

CULZEAN CASTLE

Maybole KA19 8LE
Tel: 0131 243 9300
Owner: The National Trust for Scotland
Romantic 18th century Robert Adam clifftop mansion.
Location: MAP 13:B11, OS Ref. NS240 100. 12m SW of Ayr, on A719, 4m W of Maybole.

DALGARVEN MILL MUSEUM

Dalgarven, Dalry Road, Nr Kilwinning, Ayrshire KA13 6PL
Tel/Fax: 01294 552448 **E-mail:** admin@dalgarvenmill.org.uk
Owner: Dalgarven Mill Trust **Contact:** The Administrator
Museum of Ayrshire Country Life and Costume.
Location: MAP 13:B9, OS Ref. NS295 460. On A737 2m from Kilwinning.
Open: All year: Summer: Easter–end Oct: Tue–Sat, 10am–5pm, Suns, 11am–5pm. Winter: Tue–Fri, 10am–4pm, Sat 10am–5pm, Sun, 11am–5pm.
Admission: Charges. Groups (10+) must book.

DEAN CASTLE COUNTRY PARK

Dean Road, Kilmarnock, East Ayrshire KA3 1XB
Tel: 01563 522702 **Fax:** 01563 572552
Owner: East Ayrshire Council **Contact:** Andrew Scott-Martin
Set in 200 acres of Country Park. Visits to castle by guided tour only.
Location: MAP 13:C10, OS Ref. NS437 395. Off A77. 1¼m NNE of town centre.
Open: Country Park: All year: dawn–dusk. Please telephone 01563 578155 for Castle opening details.
Admission: Free (group charge on application).

DRUMLANRIG CASTLE

See page 443 for full page entry.

DUNDRENNAN ABBEY

Kirkcudbright
Tel: 01557 500262
Owner: Historic Scotland **Contact:** The Steward
Mary Queen of Scots spent her last night on Scottish soil in this 12th century Cistercian abbey founded by David I. The abbey stands in a small and secluded valley.
Location: MAP 9:G4, OS Ref. NX749 4750. 6½ m SE of Kirkcudbright on the A711.
Open: 1 Apr–30 Sept: daily, 9.30am–5.30pm. Last ticket 5pm. Oct: Sat–Wed; Nov–Mar: Sats & Suns only, 9.30am–4.30pm. Last ticket 4pm.
Admission: Adult £3, Child £1.50, Conc. £2.50 (2007 prices).

GLENLUCE ABBEY

Glenluce
Tel: 01581 300541
Owner/Contact: In the care of Historic Scotland
A Cistercian abbey founded in 1190. Remains include a 16th century chapter house.
Location: MAP 9:D3, OS Ref. NX185 587. 2m NW of Glenluce village off the A75.
Open: 1 Apr–30 Sept: daily 9.30am–5.30pm. Last ticket 5pm. Oct: Closed Thurs/Fri. Nov–Mar: Sats & Suns only, 9.30am–4.30pm (closed Thurs & Fri). Last ticket 4pm.
Admission: Adult £3, Child £1.50, Conc. £2.50 (2007 prices).

GLENWHAN GARDENS

Dunragit, Stranraer, Wigtownshire DG9 8PH
Tel/Fax: 01581 400222   **Contact:** Tessa Knott
Beautiful 12 acre garden overlooking Luce Bay and the Mull of Galloway. Licensed tearoom, groups catered for.
Location: MAP 9:D3, OS Ref. NX150 580. N side of A75, 6m E of Stranraer.
Open: 1 Apr–30 Sept: daily, 10am–5pm or by appointment at other times.
Admission: Adult £4, Child £1.50, Conc. £3.50, Family £10. Honesty box runs until end of October.

Properties that **open all year** appear in the special index at the end of the book.

KELBURN CASTLE & COUNTRY CENTRE

FAIRLIE, BY LARGS, AYRSHIRE KA29 0BE

www.kelburncountrycentre.com

Country Park and Castle tours: Earl of Glasgow
Tel: 01475 568685   **Fax:** 01475 568121   **E-mail:** admin@kelburncountrycentre.com
Functions in the Castle: **Tel:** 01475 568204   **E-mail:** info@kelburncastle.com
Owner: The Earl of Glasgow
Kelburn is the home of the Earls of Glasgow and has been in the Boyle family for over 800 years. It is notable for its waterfalls, historic family gardens, romantic glen and unique trees. Recently the Castle has been the venue of a major and temporary art project. The Country Centre includes exhibitions, gift shop, licensed café, riding school, pottery workshop, falconry centre, full ranger service, stockade, new indoor playbarn, pet's corner and Scotland's most unusual attraction – The Secret Forest. The Castle is open for guided tours in July and August and available for weddings, conferences, dinner parties and other functions all the year round.
Location: MAP 13:B9, OS Ref NS210 580. A78 to Largs, 2m S of Largs.
Open: Country Centre: Easter–Oct: daily. Castle: July & Aug. Open by arrangement for groups at other times of the year.
Admission: Country Centre: Adult £7, Child/Conc. £4.50, Family £22. Groups (10+): Adult, £4.50, Conc. £3.50. Castle: £1.75 extra pp.
◻ ⊤ ⬇ Partial. ⬛ ⊤⊤ Licensed. ⎇ July & August. By arrangement at other times of the year. 🅿 ⬛ ⬛ In grounds on leads. ✳

LOGAN BOTANIC GARDEN

Port Logan, Stranraer, Dumfries & Galloway DG9 9ND
Tel: 01776 860231   **Fax:** 01776 860333   **E-mail:** logan@rbge.org.uk
Owner: Royal Botanic Garden Edinburgh   **Contact:** The Curator
Scotland's most exotic garden. Take a trip to the south west of Scotland and experience the southern hemisphere!
Location: MAP 9:D4, OS Ref. NX097 430. 14m S of Stranraer on B7065, off A716.
Open: 1 Mar–31 Oct: daily, 10am–5pm (Apr–Sept: closes 6pm).
Admission: Adult £4, Child £1, Conc. £3.50, Family (2+4) £9. Group discount and membership programme available.

MACLELLAN'S CASTLE

Kirkcudbright
Tel: 01557 331856
Owner: In the care of Historic Scotland   **Contact:** The Steward
Castellated mansion, built in 1577 using stone from an adjoining ruined monastery by the then provost. Elaborately planned with fine architectural details, it has been a ruin since 1752.
Location: MAP 9:G4, OS Ref. NX683 511. Centre of Kirkcudbright on the A711.
Open: 1 Apr–30 Sept: daily, 9.30am–5.30pm. Last ticket 5pm.
Admission: Adult £3.50, Child £1.75, Conc. £2.80 (2007 prices).
◻ ⬇ Partial. ⬛ ⬛ €

NEW ABBEY CORN MILL

New Abbey Village
Tel: 01387 850260
Owner: Historic Scotland   **Contact:** The Custodian
This carefully renovated 18th century water-powered oatmeal mill is in full working order and regular demonstrations are given for visitors in the summer.
Location: MAP 10:I3, OS Ref. NX962 663. 8m S of Dumfries on the A710. Close to Sweetheart Abbey.
Open: 1 Apr–30 Sept: daily, 9.30am–5.30pm. Last ticket 5pm. 1 Oct–31 Mar: Sat–Wed, 9.30am–4.30pm. Last ticket 4pm.
Admission: Adult £4, Child £2, Conc. £3 (2007 prices).
◻ ⬛ ✳ €

RAMMERSCALES

Lockerbie, Dumfriesshire DG11 1LD
Tel: 01387 810229   **Fax:** 01387 810940   **E-mail:** malcolm@rammerscales.co.uk
Owner/Contact: Mr M A Bell Macdonald
Georgian house, with extensive library and fine views over Annandale.
Location: MAP 10:I2, OS Ref. NY080 780. W side of B7020, 3m S of Lochmoben.
Open: Last week in Jul, 1st three weeks in Aug: daily (excluding Sat), 2–5pm. Bus tours by appointment.
Admission: Adult £5, Conc. £2.50.
⎇ 🅿 ⬛

SORN CASTLE

Ayrshire KA5 6HR
Tel: 01290 551555
Owner/Contact: Mrs R G McIntyre

Dating from the 14th century, the Castle stands on a cliff overlooking the River Ayr, surrounded by wooded grounds. It has been enlarged throughout the centuries, most recently in 1908. Sorn contains many fine Scottish paintings and artifacts.

Location: MAP 13:C10, OS Ref. NS555 265. 4m E of Mauchline on B743.
Open: 14 Jul–11 Aug: daily, 2–4pm and by appointment.
Admission: Adult £4.

SWEETHEART ABBEY

New Abbey Village
Tel: 01387 850397
Owner: In the care of Historic Scotland   **Contact:** The Steward

Cistercian abbey founded in 1273 by Devorgilla, in memory of her husband John Balliol. A principal feature is the well-preserved precinct wall enclosing 30 acres.

Location: MAP 10:I3, OS Ref. NX965 663. In New Abbey Village, on A710 8m S of Dumfries.
Open: 1 Apr–30 Sept: daily, 9.30am–5.30pm. Last ticket 5pm. 1 Oct–31 Mar: Sat–Wed, 9.30am–4.30pm. Last ticket 4pm.
Admission: Adult £3, Child £1.50, Conc. £2.50 (2007 prices).

THREAVE CASTLE

Castle Douglas
Tel: 07711 223101
Owner: The National Trust for Scotland   **Contact:** Historic Scotland

Built by Archibald the Grim in the late 14th century, early stronghold of the Black Douglases. Around its base is an artillery fortification built before 1455 when the castle was besieged by James II. Ring the bell and the custodian will come to ferry you over. Long walk to property. Owned by The National Trust for Scotland but under the guardianship of Historic Scotland.

Location: MAP 9:H3, OS Ref. NX739 623. 2m W of Castle Douglas on the A75.
Open: 1 Apr–30 Sept: daily, 9.30am to last outward sailing at 4.30pm.
Admission: Adult £4, Child £2, Conc. £3 (2007 prices). Charges include ferry trip.

WHITHORN PRIORY & MUSEUM

Whithorn
Tel: 01988 500508
Owner: In the care of Historic Scotland   **Contact:** The Project Manager

The site of the first Christian church in Scotland. Founded as 'Candida Casa' by St Ninian in the early 5th century it later became the cathedral church of Galloway. Visitors can now see the collection of early Christian carved crosses in a newly refurbished museum.

Location: MAP 9:F4, OS Ref. NX445 403. At Whithorn on the A746. 18m S of Newton Stewart.
Open: 1 Apr–31 Oct: daily, 10.30am–5pm.
Admission: Adult £3.50, Child £1.75, Conc. £2.50 (2007 prices). Joint ticket gives entry to Priory, Priory Museum and 'The Story of Whithorn'.

Historic Scotland

New Abbey Corn Mill

■ Owner
Hopetoun House
Preservation Trust

■ Contact
Piers de Salis
Hopetoun House
South Queensferry
Edinburgh
West Lothian EH30 9SL

Tel: 0131 331 2451
Fax: 0131 319 1885
E-mail: marketing@
hopetounhouse.com

■ Location
MAP 13:F7
OS Ref. NT089 790

2½m W of Forth Road
Bridge.

12m W of Edinburgh
(25 mins. drive).

34m E of Glasgow
(50 mins. drive).

■ Opening Times
Summer
21 March–28 September:
Daily, 10.30am–5pm.
Last admission 4pm.

Winter
By appointment only
for Groups (20+).

■ Admission
House & Grounds
Adult	£8.00
Child (5–16yrs)*	£4.25
Conc/Student	£7.00
Family (2+2)	£22.00
Additional Child	£3.00
Groups	£7.00

Grounds only
Adult	£3.70
Child (5–16yrs)*	£2.20
Conc/Student	£3.20
Family (2+2)	£10.00
Groups	£3.20

School Visits
Child	£5.50
Teachers	Free

*Under 5yrs Free.

Winter group rates on
request.

Admission to Tearoom
Free.

■ Special Events
July 29
Summer Fair

November 23–25
Christmas Fair

Conference/Function

ROOM	SIZE	MAX CAPACITY
Ballroom	92' x 35'	300
Tapestry Rm	37' x 24'	100
Red Drawing Rm	44' x 24'	100
State Dining Rm	39' x 23'	20
Stables	92' x 22'	200

HOPETOUN HOUSE 🏛

www.hopetounhouse.com

Hopetoun House is a unique gem of Europe's architectural heritage and undoubtedly 'Scotland's Finest Stately Home'. Situated on the shores of the Firth of Forth, it is one of the most splendid examples of the work of Scottish architects Sir William Bruce and William Adam. The interior of the house, with opulent gilding and classical motifs, reflects the aristocratic grandeur of the early 18th century, whilst its magnificent parkland has fine views across the Forth to the hills of Fife. The house is approached from the Royal Drive, used only by members of the Royal Family, notably King George IV in 1822 and Her Majesty Queen Elizabeth II in 1988.

Hopetoun is really two houses in one, the oldest part of the house was designed by Sir William Bruce and built between 1699 and 1707. It shows some of the finest examples in Scotland of carving, wainscotting and ceiling painting. In 1721 William Adam started enlarging the house by adding the magnificent façade, colonnades and grand State apartments which were the focus for social life and entertainment in the 18th century.

The house is set in 100 acres of rolling parkland including fine woodland walks, the red deer park, the spring garden with a profusion of wild flowers, and numerous picturesque picnic spots.

Hopetoun has been home of the Earls of Hopetoun, later created Marquesses of Linlithgow, since it was built in 1699 and in 1974 a charitable trust was created to preserve the house with its historic contents and surrounding landscape for the benefit of the public for all time.

ℹ Private functions, special events, antiques fairs, concerts, Scottish gala evenings, conferences, wedding ceremonies and receptions, grand piano, helicopter landing. No smoking or flash photography in house.

🍽 Receptions, gala dinners.

♿ Partial.

☕ Licensed.

👤 By arrangement.

🅿 Close to the house for cars and coaches. Book if possible, allow 1–2hrs for visit (min).

Special tours of house and/or grounds for different age/ interest groups.

🐕 No dogs in house, on leads in grounds.

❄

AMISFIELD MAINS

Nr Haddington, East Lothian EH41 3SA
Tel: 01875 870201   **Fax:** 01875 870620
Owner: Wemyss and March Estates Management Co Ltd   **Contact:** M Andrews
Georgian farmhouse with gothic barn and cottage.
Location: MAP 14:I8, OS Ref. NT526 755. Between Haddington and East Linton on A199.
Open: Exterior only: By appointment, Wemyss and March Estates Office, Longniddry, East Lothian EH32 0PY.
Admission: Please contact for details.

ARNISTON HOUSE 🏛
GOREBRIDGE, MIDLOTHIAN EH23 4RY

www.arniston-house.co.uk

Tel/Fax: 01875 830515   **E-mail:** arnistonhouse@btconnect.com
Owner: Mrs A Dundas-Bekker   **Contact:** Mrs H Dundas
Magnificent William Adam mansion started in 1726. Fine plasterwork, Scottish portraiture, period furniture and other fascinating contents. Beautiful country setting beloved by Sir Walter Scott.
Location: MAP 13:H9, OS Ref. NT326 595. Off B6372, 1m from A7, Temple direction.
Open: May & Jun: Tue & Wed; 1 Jul–14 Sept: Tue, Wed & Sun, guided tours at 2pm & 3.30pm. Pre-arranged groups (10–50) accepted all year.
Admission: Adult £5, Child £2, Conc. £4.
ℹ️ No inside photography. ♿ WC. 👤 Obligatory. 🅿 🚍 In grounds, on leads. ❄

BEANSTON

Nr Haddington, East Lothian EH41 3SB
Tel: 01875 870201   **Fax:** 01875 870620
Owner: Wemyss and March Estates Management Co Ltd   **Contact:** M Andrews
Georgian farmhouse with Georgian orangery.
Location: MAP 14:I8, OS Ref. NT546 763. Between Haddington and East Linton on A199.
Open: Exterior only: By appointment, Wemyss and March Estates Office, Longniddry, East Lothian EH32 0PY.
Admission: Please contact for details.

BLACKNESS CASTLE 🏛

Blackness
Tel: 01506 834807
Owner: In the care of Historic Scotland   **Contact:** The Steward
One of Scotland's most important strongholds. Built in the 14th century and massively strengthened in the 16th century as an artillery fortress, it has been a royal castle, prison armaments depot and film location for Hamlet. It was restored by the Office of Works in the 1920s. It stands on a promontory in the Firth of Forth.
Location: MAP 13:F7, OS Ref. NT055 803. 4m NE of Linlithgow on the Firth of Forth, off the A904.
Open: 1 Apr–30 Sept: daily, 9.30am–5.30pm. Last ticket 5pm. 1 Oct–31 Mar: 9.30am–4.30pm. Last ticket 4pm. Closed Thur & Fri in winter.
Admission: Adult £4, Child £2, Conc. £3 (2007 prices).
🖼 🛍 🅿 🚍 ❄ €

CRAIGMILLAR CASTLE 🏛

Edinburgh
Tel: 0131 661 4445
Owner: In the care of Historic Scotland   **Contact:** The Steward
Mary, Queen of Scots fled to Craigmillar after the murder of Rizzio. This handsome structure with courtyard and gardens covers an area of one and a quarter acres. Built around an L-plan tower house of the early 15th century including a range of private rooms linked to the hall of the old tower.
Location: MAP 13:H8, OS Ref. NT285 710. 2½m SE of Edinburgh off the A7.
Open: 1 Apr–30 Sept: daily, 9.30am–5.30pm. Last ticket 5pm. 1 Oct–31 Mar: daily, 9.30am–4.30pm. Last ticket 4pm. Closed Thur & Fri in winter.
Admission: Adult £4, Child £2, Conc. £3 (2007 prices).
🖼 🛍 🅿 ❄ €

CRICHTON CASTLE 🏛

Pathhead
Tel: 01875 320017
Owner: In the care of Historic Scotland   **Contact:** The Steward
A large and sophisticated castle with a spectacular façade of faceted stonework in an Italian style added by the Earl of Bothwell between 1581 and 1591 following a visit to Italy. Mary Queen of Scots attended a wedding here.
Location: MAP 13:H8, OS Ref. NT380 612. 2½m SSW of Pathhead off the A68.
Open: 1 Apr–30 Sept: daily, 9.30am–5.30pm, last ticket 5pm.
Admission: Adult £3.50, Child £1.75, Conc. £2.80 (2007 prices).
🅿 €

Gosford House

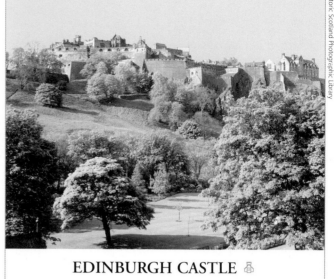

DIRLETON CASTLE & GARDEN

DIRLETON, EAST LOTHIAN EH39 5ER

Tel: 01620 850330

Owner: In the care of Historic Scotland **Contact:** The Steward

The oldest part of this romantic castle dates from the 13th century, when it was built by the De Vaux family. The renowned gardens, first laid out in the 16th century, now include a magnificent Arts and Crafts herbaceous border (the longest in the world) and a re-created Victorian Garden. In the picturesque village of Dirleton.

Location: MAP 14:I7, OS Ref. NT516 839. In Dirleton, 2m W of North Berwick on the A198.

Open: Apr–Sept: daily, 9.30am–5.30pm. Oct–Mar: daily, 9.30am–4.30pm. Last ticket 30 mins before closing.

Admission: Adult £4.50, Child £2.25, Conc. £3.50. 10% discount for groups (11+). (2007 prices).

🖻 🖾 Partial. 🅿 🔳 Free if booked. 🐾 ❄ €

EDINBURGH CASTLE

CASTLEHILL, EDINBURGH EH1 2NG

Tel: 0131 225 9846 **Fax:** 0131 220 4733

Owner: Historic Scotland **Contact:** The Stewards

Scotland's most famous castle, dominating the capital's skyline and giving stunning views of the city and countryside. Home to the Scottish crown jewels, the Stone of Destiny and Mons Meg. Other highlights include St Margaret's Chapel, the Great Hall and the Scottish National War Memorial.

Location: MAP 21, OS Ref. NT252 736. At the top of the Royal Mile in Edinburgh.

Open: Apr–Sept: daily, 9.30am–6pm. Oct–Mar: daily, 9.30am–5pm. Last ticket 45 mins before closing.

Admission: Adult £11, Child £5.50, Conc. £9. Pre-booked school visits available Free, except May–Aug. (2007 prices).

🖻 🍽 Private evening hire. 🖾 Partial. WCs. Courtesy vehicle. 🔳 🍴 Licensed. 🛈 🎧 In 6 languages. 🅿 (except Jun–Oct). 🔳 🐾 Guide dogs. ❄ €

DUNGLASS COLLEGIATE CHURCH

Cockburnspath

Tel: 0131 668 8600

Owner: In the care of Historic Scotland

Founded in 1450 for a college of canons by Sir Alexander Hume. A handsome cross-shaped building with vaulted nave, choir and transepts.

Location: MAP 14:J8, OS67 NT766 718. 1m NW of Cockburnspath. SW of A1.

Open: All year.

Admission: Free.

❄

THE GEORGIAN HOUSE

7 Charlotte Square, Edinburgh EH2 4DR

Tel: 0131 243 9300

Owner: The National Trust for Scotland

A good example of the neo-classical 'palace front'. Three floors are furnished as they would have been around 1796. There is an array of china and silver, pictures and furniture, gadgets and utensils.

Location: MAP 21, OS Ref. NT247 738. In Charlotte Square.

GLADSTONE'S LAND

477b Lawnmarket, Royal Mile, Edinburgh EH1 2NT

Tel: 0131 243 9300

Owner: The National Trust for Scotland

Gladstone's Land was the home of a prosperous Edinburgh merchant in the 17th century. Decorated and furnished to give visitors an impression of life in Edinburgh's Old Town some 300 years ago.

Location: MAP 21, OS Ref. NT255 736. In Edinburgh's Royal Mile, near the castle.

For **special events** held throughout the year, see the index at the end of the book.

Tantallon Castle

GOSFORD HOUSE 🏛
LONGNIDDRY, EAST LOTHIAN EH32 0PX

Tel: 01875 870201

Owner/Contact: The Earl of Wemyss

Though the core of the house is Robert Adam, the family home is in the South Wing built by William Young in 1890. This contains the celebrated Marble Hall and a fine collection of paintings and works of art. The house is set in extensive policies with an 18th century Pleasure Garden and Ponds. Greylag geese and swans abound.

Location: MAP 14:I7, OS Ref. NT453 786. Off A198 2m NE of Longniddry.

Open: 13 Jun–8 Aug: Fri–Sun, 2–5pm.

Admission: Adult £6, Child £1.

P ⊠ In grounds, on leads.

HAILES CASTLE 🏛

East Linton

Tel: 0131 668 8800

Owner: In the care of Historic Scotland

Beautifully-sited ruin incorporating a fortified manor of the 13th century. It was extended in the 14th and 15th centuries. There are two vaulted pit prisons.

Location: MAP 14:I8, OS Ref. NT575 758. 1½ m SW of East Linton. 4m E of Haddington. S of A1.

Open: All year.

Admission: Free.

P ✳

HARELAW FARMHOUSE

Nr Longniddry, East Lothian EH32 0PH

Tel: 01875 870201   **Fax:** 01875 870620

Owner: Wemyss and March Estates Management Co Ltd   **Contact:** M Andrews

Early 19th century 2-storey farmhouse built as an integral part of the steading. Dovecote over entrance arch.

Location: MAP 14:I8, OS Ref. NT450 766. Between Longniddry and Drem on B1377.

Open: Exteriors only: By appointment, Wemyss and March Estates Office, Longniddry, East Lothian EH32 0PY.

Admission: Please contact for details.

HOPETOUN HOUSE 🏛   *See page 448 for full page entry.*

HOUSE OF THE BINNS 🏛

Linlithgow, West Lothian EH49 7NA

Tel: 0131 243 9300

Owner: The National Trust for Scotland

17th century house, home of the Dalyells, one of Scotland's great families, since 1612.

Location: MAP 13:F7, OS Ref. NT051 786. Off A904, 15m W of Edinburgh. 3m E of Linlithgow.

GREYWALLS 🏛
MUIRFIELD, GULLANE, EAST LOTHIAN EH31 2EG

www.greywalls.co.uk

Tel: 01620 842144   **Fax:** 01620 842241   **E-mail:** hotel@greywalls.co.uk

Owner: Giles Weaver   **Contact:** Mrs Sue Prime

Stunning Edwardian Country House Hotel only 30 minutes from the centre of Edinburgh. Close to wonderful golf courses and beaches. Designed by Sir Edwin Lutyens with secluded walled gardens attributed to Gertrude Jekyll. Greywalls offers the delights of an award-winning menu and an excellent wine list in this charming and relaxed environment (non residents welcome).

Location: MAP 14:I7, OS Ref. NT490 835. Off A198, 5m W of North Berwick, 30 mins from Edinburgh.

Open: Mar–Dec inclusive.

⊤ ⊤⊤ P ⊠ ⊠

LENNOXLOVE HOUSE 🏛
HADDINGTON, EAST LOTHIAN EH41 4NZ

www.lennoxlove.com

Tel: 01620 823720   **Fax:** 01620 825112   **E-mail:** fraser-niven@lennoxlove.com

Owner: Lennoxlove House Ltd   **Contact:** Fraser Niven, Chief Executive

Service, Style and Seclusion. House to many of Scotland's finest artefacts, including the Death Mask of Mary, Queen of Scots, furniture and porcelain collected by the Douglas, Hamilton and Stewart families. Open to the public and available for events, the House lends itself perfectly to intimate parties offering 11 luxury suites for an overnight stay.

Location: MAP 14:I8, OS Ref. NT515 721. 18m E of Edinburgh, 1m S of Haddington.

Open: Easter–Oct: Weds, Thurs & Suns, 1.30–4pm. Guided tours.

⊤ ⨍ ⊠

LIBERTON HOUSE

73 Liberton Drive, Edinburgh EH16 6NP
Tel: 0131 467 7777 **Fax:** 0131 467 7774 **E-mail:** practice@grovesraines.com
Owner/Contact: Nicholas Groves-Raines
Built around 1600 for the Littles of Liberton, this harled L-plan house has been carefully restored by the current architect owner using original detailing and extensive restoration of the principal structure. Public access restricted to the Great Hall and Old Kitchen. The restored garden layout suggests the original and there is a late 17th century lectern doocot by the entrance drive.
Location: MAP 13:H8, OS Ref. NT267 694. 73 Liberton Drive, Edinburgh.
Open: 1 Mar–31 Oct: 10am–4.30pm, by prior appointment only.
Admission: Free.
♿ Unsuitable. **P** Limited. ♿

LINLITHGOW PALACE ♿

LINLITHGOW, WEST LOTHIAN EH49 7AL

Tel: 01506 842896
Owner: Historic Scotland **Contact:** The Steward
The magnificent remains of a great royal palace set in its own park and beside Linlithgow Loch. A favoured residence of the Stewart monarchs, James V and his daughter Mary, Queen of Scots were born here. Bonnie Prince Charlie stayed here during his bid to regain the British crown.
Location: MAP 13:F8, OS Ref. NT003 774. In the centre of Linlithgow off the M9.
Open: Apr–Sept: daily, 9.30am–5.30pm. Oct–Mar: Daily, 9.30am–4.30pm. Last ticket 30 mins before closing.
Admission: Adult £5, Child £2.50, Conc. £4. (2007 prices.) 10% discount for groups (11+).
♿ Picnic area. ♿ ♿ Private evening hire. ♿ Partial. ♿ Free if booked.
P Cars only. ♿ In grounds, on leads. ♿ ♿ €

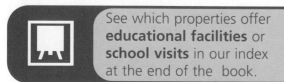

See which properties offer **educational facilities** or **school visits** in our index at the end of the book.

NEWLISTON ♿

Kirkliston, West Lothian EH29 9EB
Tel: 0131 333 3231
Owner/Contact: Mrs Caroline Maclachlan
Late Robert Adam house. 18th century designed landscape, rhododendrons, azaleas and water features. On Sundays there is a ride-on steam model railway from 2–5pm.
Location: MAP 13:G8, OS Ref. NT110 735. 8m W of Edinburgh, 3m S of Forth Road Bridge, off B800.
Open: 1 May–4 Jun: Wed–Sun, 2–6pm. Also by appointment.
Admission: Adult £3, Conc. £2.
♿ In grounds, on leads.

NIDDRY CASTLE

By Winchburgh, West Lothian EH52 6RP
Tel: 01506 891751
Owner/Contact: Richard Nairn
Niddry Castle is a late 15th/early 16th century L-plan tower built by George, 3rd Lord Seton. In 1676 it was sold to John Hope whose family lived there for around 30 years until Hopetoun House was built and the castle subsequently abandoned. It was ruined for almost 300 years until the mid-1980s when it was partially restored.
Location: MAP 13:F8, OS Ref. NT095 734. 1km S of Winchburgh, towards A89.
Open: 30 Aug–21 Sept, 27/28 Sept; Sat & Sun, 1.30–4.30pm; Mon–Thurs, 5–6pm; Fri, 3.30–5pm. Limited access to interior pending restoration.
Admission: Adult £2, Child £1.
♿ Unsuitable. **P** Limited. No coaches. ♿ Guide dogs only.

PALACE OF HOLYROODHOUSE

Edinburgh EH8 8DX
Tel: 0131 556 5100 **E-mail:** bookinginfo@royalcollection.org.uk
Owner: Official Residence of Her Majesty The Queen
Contact: Ticket Sales & Information Office
The Palace of Holyroodhouse, the official residence in Scotland of Her Majesty The Queen, stands at the end of Edinburgh's Royal Mile against the spectacular backdrop of Arthur's Seat. The Royal Apartments are used by The Queen for State ceremonies and official entertaining. They are finely decorated with magnificent works of art from the Royal Collection.
Location: MAP 21, OS Ref. NT269 739. Central Edinburgh, end of Royal Mile.
Open: Contact information office.
Admission: Contact information office.

Crichton Castle

PRESTON MILL

East Linton, East Lothian EH40 3DS
Tel: 0131 243 9300
Owner: The National Trust for Scotland   **Contact:** Property Manager
For centuries there has been a mill on this site and the present one operated commercially until 1957.
Location: MAP 14:I7, OS Ref. NT590 770. Off the A1, in East Linton, 23m E of Edinburgh.

RED ROW

Aberlady, East Lothian
Tel: 01875 870201   **Fax:** 01875 870620
Owner: Wemyss & March Estates Management Co Ltd   **Contact:** M Andrews
Terraced Cottages.
Location: MAP 14:I7, OS Ref. NT464 798. Main Street, Aberlady, East Lothian.
Open: Exterior only. By appointment, Wemyss & March Estates Office, Longniddry, East Lothian EH32 0PY.
Admission: Please contact for details.

ROYAL BOTANIC GARDEN EDINBURGH

20A Inverleith Row, Edinburgh EH3 5LR
Tel: 0131 552 7171   **Fax:** 0131 248 2901   **E-mail:** info@rbge.org.uk
Contact: Press Office
Scotland's premier garden. Discover the wonders of the plant kingdom in over 70 acres of beautifully landscaped grounds.
Location: MAP 21, OS Ref. NT249 751. Off A902, 1m N of city centre.
Open: Daily (except 25 Dec & 1 Jan): open 10am, closing: Nov–Feb: 4pm; Mar & Oct: 6pm; Apr–Sept: 7pm.
Admission: Free, with an admission charge on the Glasshouses.

ST MARY'S EPISCOPAL CATHEDRAL

Palmerston Place, Edinburgh EH12 5AW
Tel: 0131 225 6293   **Fax:** 0131 225 3181
Contact: Cathedral Secretary
Neo-gothic grandeur in the classical new town. Designed by G Gilbert Scott.
Location: MAP 21, OS Ref. NT241 735. 1/2 m W of west end of Princes Street.
Open: Mon–Fri, 7.30am–6pm; Sat & Sun, 7.30am–5pm. Sun services: 8am, 10.30am & 3.30pm. Services: Weekdays, 7.30am, 1.05pm & 5.30pm; Thurs, 11.30am, Sat, 7.30am.
Admission: Free.

SCOTTISH NATIONAL PORTRAIT GALLERY

1 Queen Street, Edinburgh EH2 1JD
Tel: 0131 624 6200
Unique visual history of Scotland.
Location: MAP 21, OS Ref. NT256 742. At E end of Queen Street, 300yds N of Princes Street.
Open: All year to permanent collection: daily, 10am–5pm (Thurs closes 7pm). Closed 25 & 26 Dec. Open 1 Jan, 12 noon–5pm.
Admission: Free. (There may be a charge for special exhibitions.)

©Historic Scotland Photographic Library

TANTALLON CASTLE
BY NORTH BERWICK, EAST LOTHIAN EH39 5PN

Tel: 01620 892727
Owner: In the care of Historic Scotland   **Contact:** The Steward
Set on the edge of the cliffs, looking out to the Bass Rock, this formidable castle was a stronghold of the powerful Douglas family. The castle has earthwork defences and a massive 80-foot high 14th century curtain wall. Interpretive displays include a replica gun.
Location: MAP 14:I7, OS67 NT595 850. 3m E of North Berwick off the A198.
Open: Apr–Sept: daily, 9.30am–5.30pm. Last ticket 5pm. Oct–Mar: Sat–Wed, 9.30am–4.30pm. Last ticket 4pm.
Admission: Adult £4.50, Child £2.25, Conc. £3.50. (2007 prices.) 10% discount for groups (11+).
ℹ Picnic area. ▣ ♿ Partial. ▤ ℙ ▦ Booked school visits free.
🐕 In grounds, on leads. ❄ €

TRINITY HOUSE MARITIME MUSEUM

99 Kirkgate, Edinburgh EH6 6BJ
Tel: 0131 554 3289
Owner: Historic Scotland
Contact: The Monument Manager
Tucked away in a side street within a few minutes' walk from the Royal Yacht Britannia, this fine Georgian mansion contains a treasure trove of maritime art and artefacts. Among them are paintings by Henry Raeburn, including a specially commissioned portrait of Admiral Duncan, victor of the 1797 Battle of Camperdown. The site has been home to the Incorporation of Masters and Mariners of Trinity House, Leith, since the Middle Ages. Many of the artefacts were given to Trinity House by Leith sailors who travelled to the remotest parts of the world in centuries gone by.
Location: MAP 13:G8, OS Ref. NT269 760, Kirkgate, Leith, Edinburgh.
Admission: Adult £4, Child £2, Conc £3 (2007 prices).
Open: Visits need to be prebooked by telephone.
ℙ

Dirleton Castle

BURRELL COLLECTION

Pollok Country Park, 2060 Pollokshaws Road, Glasgow G43 1AT

Tel: 0141 287 2550   **Fax:** 0141 287 2597

Owner: Glasgow Museums

An internationally renowned, outstanding collection of art.

Location: MAP 13:C8, OS Ref. NS555 622. Glasgow 15 min drive.

Open: All year: Mon–Thur & Sats, 10am–5pm, Fri & Sun, 11am–5pm. Closed 25/26 Dec, 31 Dec (pm) & 1/2 Jan.

Admission: Free. Small charge may apply for temporary exhibitions.

COLZIUM HOUSE & WALLED GARDEN

Colzium-Lennox Estate, off Stirling Road, Kilsyth G65 0RZ

Tel/Fax: 01236 828156

Owner: North Lanarkshire Council   **Contact:** John Whittaker

A walled garden with an extensive collection of conifers, rare shrubs and trees, curling pond, picnic tables, woodland walks.

Location: MAP 13:D7, OS Ref. NS722 786. Off A803 Banknock to Kirkintilloch Road. ½m E of Kilsyth.

Open: Walled Garden: Apr–Sept: daily, 12noon–7pm; Oct–Mar: Sats & Suns, 12 noon–4pm.

Admission: Free.

COREHOUSE

Lanark ML11 9TQ

Tel: 01555 663126

Owner: Colonel D A S Cranstoun of that Ilk TD   **Contact:** Estate Office

Designed by Sir Edward Blore and built in the 1820s, Corehouse is a pioneering example of the Tudor Architectural Revival in Scotland.

Location: MAP 13:E9, OS Ref. NS882 416. On S bank of the Clyde above the village of Kirkfieldbank.

Open: 3–21 May & 13–24 Sept: Sat–Wed. Guided tours: weekdays: 1 & 2pm, weekends: 2 & 3pm. Closed Thurs & Fri.

Admission: Adult £6, Child (under 14yrs)/OAP £3.

Obligatory.

CRAIGNETHAN CASTLE

Lanark, Strathclyde

Tel: 01555 860364

Owner: Historic Scotland   **Contact:** The Steward

In a picturesque setting overlooking the River Nethan and defended by a wide and deep ditch. The castle's defences include an unusual caponier, a stone vaulted artillery chamber, unique in Britain.

Location: MAP 13:E9, OS Ref. NS815 463. 5½m WNW of Lanark off the A72. ½m footpath to W.

Open: 1 Apr–30 Sept: daily, 9.30am–5.30pm. Oct: Sat–Wed; Nov–Mar: Sats & Suns only, 9.30am–4.30pm.

Admission: Adult £3.50, Child £1.75, Conc. £2.80 (2007 prices).

Picnic area. WC. €

GLASGOW CATHEDRAL

Castle Street, Glasgow

Tel: 0141 552 6891

Owner: Historic Scotland   **Contact:** The Steward

The only Scottish mainland medieval cathedral to have survived the Reformation complete. Built over the tomb of St Kentigern. Notable features in this splendid building are the elaborately vaulted crypt, the stone screen of the early 15th century and the unfinished Blackadder Aisle.

Location: MAP 13:D8, OS Ref. NS603 656. E end of city centre. In central Glasgow.

Open: 1 Apr–30 Sept: Mon–Sat, 9.30am–5.30pm, Sun 1–5.30pm. 1 Oct–31 Mar: Mon–Sat, 9.30am–4.30pm, Sun 1–4.30pm.

Admission: Free.

Partial.

For **special events** held throughout the year, see the index at the end of the book.

City Chambers, Glasgow

Glasgow & Clyde Valley Tourist Board

MOTHERWELL HERITAGE CENTRE

High Road, Motherwell ML1 3HU

Tel: 01698 251000

Owner: North Lanarkshire Council   **Contact:** The Manager

VisitScotland 4-star attraction. Technopolois multi-media display tells the story of the area from the Romans, through the days of heavy industry, to the present time. Exhibition gallery, shop and tower viewing platform. A local studies and family history research room has census, newspaper and other databases on-line. Staff assistance available.

Location: MAP 13:E9, OS Ref. NS750 570. In High Road, 200yds N of A723 (Hamilton Road).

Open: All year, 10am–5pm. Sun, 12 noon–5pm (closed 25/26 Dec & 1/2 Jan).

Admission: Free.

NEW LANARK WORLD HERITAGE SITE

New Lanark Mills, Lanark, S Lanarkshire ML11 9DB

Tel: 01555 661345   **Fax:** 01555 665738   **E-mail:** visit@newlanark.org

www.newlanark.org

Owner: New Lanark Conservation Trust   **Contact:** Trust Office

Surrounded by native woodlands and close to the famous Falls of Clyde, this cotton mill village was founded in 1785 and became famous as the site of Robert Owen's radical reforms. Now beautifully restored as both a living community and attraction, the fascinating history of the village is interpreted in an award-winning Visitor Centre. There is a Roof Garden and Viewing Platform giving panoramic views of the historic village and surrounding woodland. Accommodation is available in the New Lanark Mill Hotel and Waterhouses, a stunning conversion from an original 18th century mill. New Lanark is now a World Heritage Site.

Location: MAP 13:E9, OS Ref. NS880 426. 1m S of Lanark.

Open: All year: daily, 10.30am–5pm (11am–5pm Sept–May). Closed 25 Dec & 1 Jan.

Admission: Visitor Centre: Adult £5.95, Child/Conc. £4.95. Groups: 1 free/10 booked.

Conference facilities. Partial. WC. Visitor Centre wheelchair friendly. By arrangement. 5 min walk. In grounds, on leads. €

NEWARK CASTLE

Port Glasgow, Strathclyde

Tel: 01475 741858

Owner: In the care of Historic Scotland   **Contact:** The Steward

The oldest part of the castle is a tower built soon after 1478 with a detached gatehouse, by George Maxwell. The main part was added in 1597–99 in a most elegant style. Enlarged in the 16th century by his descendent, the wicked Patrick Maxwell who murdered two of his neighbours.

Location: MAP 13:B8, OS Ref. NS329 744. In Port Glasgow on the A8.

Open: 1 Apr–30 Sept: daily, 9.30am–5.30pm. Last ticket 5pm.

Admission: Adult £3.50, Child £1.75, Conc. £2.80 (2007 prices).

WC. €

POLLOK HOUSE

Pollok Country Park, Pollokshaws Road, Glasgow G43 1AT
Tel: 0131 243 9300
Owner: The National Trust for Scotland
The house contains an internationally famed collection of paintings as well as porcelain and furnishings appropriate to an Edwardian house.
Location: MAP 13:C8, OS Ref. NS550 616. In Pollok Country Park, off M77/J1, follow signs for Burrell Collection.

ST MARY'S EPISCOPAL CATHEDRAL

300 Great Western Road, Glasgow G4 9JB
Tel: 0141 339 6691   **Fax:** 0141 334 5669   **Email:** office@thecathedral.org.uk
Contact: The Office
Newly restored, fine Gothic Revival church by Sir George Gilbert Scott, with outstanding contemporary murals by Gwyneth Leech. Regular concerts and exhibitions.
Location: MAP 13:D8, OS Ref. NS578 669. ¼m after the Dumbarton A82 exit from M8 motorway.
Open: All year. Mon–Fri, 9.15–10am. Thur, 5.30–7.30pm. Sat, 9.30–10am.
Sun services: 8.30am, 10.30am & 6.30pm.
Admission: Free

SUMMERLEE INDUSTRIAL MUSEUM

Heritage Way, Coatbridge, North Lanarkshire ML5 1QD
Tel: 01236 638460
Owner: North Lanarkshire Council   **Contact:** The Manager
Summerlee, Scotland's museum of industrial life, is a VisitScotland 4-star attraction. It is based around the site of the former Summerlee Ironworks and a branch of the Monklands canal. The museum will be closed until the 2008 summer season for a major Heritage Lottery Fund supported redevelopment. On reopening, there will be new exhibits and displays, a new café, shop and meeting rooms and an interactive zone for children.
Location: MAP 13:D8, OS Ref. NS729 655. 600yds NW of Coatbridge town centre.
Open: Closed until Summer 2008 (please telephone for details).

THE TENEMENT HOUSE

145 Buccleuch Street, Glasgow G3 6QN
Tel: 0131 243 9300
Owner: The National Trust for Scotland
A typical Victorian tenement flat of 1892, and time capsule of the first half of the 20th century.
Location: MAP 13:D8, OS Ref. NS583 662. Garnethill (three streets N of Sauchiehall Street, near Charing Cross), Glasgow.

THE TOWER OF HALLBAR

Braidwood Road, Braidwood, Lanarkshire ML8 5RD
Tel: 0845 090 0194   **Fax:** 0845 090 0174   **E-mail:** enquiries@vivat.org.uk
www.vivat.org.uk
Owner/Contact: The Vivat Trust
A 16th century defensive tower and Bothy set in ancient orchards and meadowland. Converted into self-catering holiday accommodation by The Vivat Trust and furnished and decorated in keeping with its history. Hallbar sleeps up to seven people, including facilities for a disabled person and their carer.
Location: MAP 13:E9, OS Ref. NS842 471. S side of B7056 between Crossford Bridge & Braidwood.
Open: All year by appointment.
Admission: Free.
🖼 Partial. 🎦 By arrangement. 🅿 Limited. 🐾 In grounds, on leads.
🛏 3 single, 1 twin & 1 double. ❋

New Lanark World Heritage Site.

■ **Owner**

Blair Charitable Trust

■ **Contact**

Administration Office
Blair Castle
Blair Atholl
Pitlochry
Perthshire PH18 5TL

Tel: 01796 481207
Fax: 01796 481487
E-mail: office@
blair-castle.co.uk

■ **Location**

MAP 13:E3
OS Ref. NN880 660

From Edinburgh 80m,
M90 to Perth, A9,
follow signs for Blair
Castle, 1½ hrs.
Trunk Road A9 2m.

Bus: Bus stop 1m
in Blair Atholl.

Train: 1m, Blair Atholl
Euston-Inverness line.

Taxi: Elizabeth Yule,
01796 472290.

■ **Opening Times**

Summer
21 March–24 October
Daily, 9.30am–4.30pm
(Last admission).

Winter
Tuesday and Saturday
mornings and for groups
by arrangement.

■ **Admission**

House & Grounds
Adult	£7.90
Child (5–16yrs)	£4.90
Senior	£6.90
Student (with ID)	£6.50
Family	£20.50
Disabled	£2.60

Groups* (12+)
(Please book)
Adult	£6.10
Child(5–16yrs)	£4.60
Primary School	£3.50
Senior/Student	£6.10
Disabled	£2.30

Grounds only
(inc. Restaurant, Gift Shop
& WC)
Adult	£2.70
Child (5–16yrs)	£1.40
Senior/Student	£2.70
Family	£6.00
Disabled	Free
Scooter Hire	£3.50

Groups* (12+)
(Please book)
Adult	£2.30
Child (5–16yrs)	£1.30
Primary School	£1.30
Senior/Student	£2.30
Disabled	Free

*Group rates only apply
when all tickets bought
by the Driver, Courier or
Group leader at one time.
Contact us for winter
admission prices.

■ **Conference/Function**

ROOM	SIZE	MAX CAPACITY
Ballroom	88' x 36'	400 or 220 dining
State Dining Room	36' x 26'	150 or 16–50 dining
Banvie Hall	55' x 32'	150

BLAIR CASTLE 🏛

www.blair-castle.co.uk

Blair Castle has previously been the seat of the Earls and Dukes of Atholl for over 725 years. Its central location makes it easily accessible from all major Scottish centres in less than two hours.

The castle has known the splendour of Royal visitations, submitted to occupation by opposing forces on no less than four occasions and changed its architectural appearance to suit the taste of successive generations.

Today 30 rooms display fine furniture, paintings, arms, armour, china, costumes, lace and embroidery, and Jacobite relics.

The castle is also the home of the Atholl Highlanders, Europe's only remaining private army.

Gardens

Blair Castle is set in extensive and beautiful grounds. Hercules Garden is a walled garden of some 9 acres, which has recently been restored. Diana's Grove is a two acre plantation, which includes some of the tallest trees in the UK. A picnic area and a deer park are readily accessible from the car park and castle.

ℹ️ Equestrian events, Celtic nights, rallies, filming, highland and charity balls, piping championships, grand piano and resident piper. No smoking.

🛍️

🍷 Civil and religious weddings may be held in the castle and receptions for up to 220 guests can be held in the ballroom. Banquets, dinners and private functons are welcome.

♿ May alight at entrance. WC & wheelchair facilities. Limited mobility scooter available for hire.

🍴 Non-smoking. Seats up to 125. Private group lunches for up to 35 can be arranged in the Garry Room.

🚶 In English, German and French at no extra cost. Tour time 50mins (groups only). Illustrated guide books (English, German, French and Italian) £3.50. Special interest tours also available.

🅿️ 200 cars, 20 coaches. Coach drivers/couriers free, plus free meal and shop voucher, information pack.

🏞️ Nature walks, deer park, ranger service & pony trekking, children's play area.

🐕 Grounds only.

🏨 Within grounds.

❄️ Limited in winter.

❄️ Atholl Highlanders' parade 24 May. Event programme available on application.

visit hudsons guide online

■ **Owner**
Grimsthorpe &
Drummond Castle Trust

■ **Contact**
The Caretaker
Drummond Castle
Gardens
Muthill
Crieff
Perthshire PH7 4HZ

Tel: 01764 681433
Fax: 01764 681642
E-mail: thegardens@
drummondcastle.sol.co.uk

■ **Location**
MAP 13:E5
OS Ref. NN844 181

2m S of Crieff off the
A822.

■ **Opening Times**
Easter weekend,
1 May–31 October:
Daily, 1–6pm.
Last admission 5pm.

■ **Admission**
Adult   £4.00
Child   £1.50
Conc.   £3.00
Groups (20+)
                  10% discount.
Prices subject to change.

DRUMMOND CASTLE GARDENS 🏛

www.drummondcastlegardens.co.uk

Scotland's most important formal gardens, among the finest in Europe. A mile of beech-lined avenue leads to a formidable ridge top tower house. The magnificent Italianate parterre is revealed from a viewpoint at the top of the terrace, celebrating the saltaire and family heraldry that surrounds the famous multiplex sundial by John Milne, master mason to Charles I. First laid out in the early 17th century by John Drummond, 2nd Earl of Perth and renewed in the early 1950s by Phyllis Astor, Countess of Ancaster.

The gardens contain ancient yew hedges and two copper beech trees planted by Queen Victoria during her visit in 1842. Shrubberies are planted with many varieties of maple and other individual ornamental trees including purple-leaf oaks, whitebeam, weeping birch and a tulip tree, *Liriodendron tulipifera*. The tranquility of the gardens makes them the perfect setting to stroll amongst the well-manicured plantings or sit and absorb the atmosphere of this special place.

 Partial. Viewing platform. WC.

 By arrangement.

Ⓟ

 On leads.

■ Owner

The Earl of Strathmore & Kinghorne

■ Contact

Mr David Adams
General Manager
Estates Office
Glamis
by Forfar
Angus DD8 1RJ
Tel: 01307 840393
Fax: 01307 840733
E-mail: enquiries@
glamis-castle.co.uk

■ Location

MAP 13:H4
OS Ref. NO386 480

From Edinburgh M90,
A94, 81m.
From Forfar A94, 6m.
From Glasgow 93m.
Motorway: M90.

Rail: Dundee
Station 12m.

Air: Dundee
Airport 12m.

Taxi: K Cabs
01575 573744.

■ Opening Times

March–December
Daily, 10am–6pm.
Last admission 4.30pm.
(November–December,
11am–5pm. Last
admission 3pm.)

Extended opening
July–August.

Groups welcome. Out of
hours visits can also be
arranged.

■ Admission

Castle & Grounds

Adult	£8.00
Child (5–16yrs)	£5.00
OAP/Student	£7.00
Family	£22.50

Groups (20+)

Adult	£6.90
Child (5–16yrs)	£4.00
OAP/Student	£5.90

Grounds only

Adult	£4.00
Child/OAP/Student	£3.00

GLAMIS CASTLE

www.glamis-castle.co.uk

Glamis Castle is the family home of the Earls of Strathmore and Kinghorne and has been a royal residence since 1372. It was the childhood home of Her Majesty Queen Elizabeth The Queen Mother, the birthplace of Her Royal Highness The Princess Margaret and the legendary setting of Shakespeare's play *Macbeth*. Although the Castle is open to visitors it remains a family home, lived in and loved by the Strathmore family.

The Castle, a five-storey 'L' shaped tower block, was originally a royal hunting lodge. It was remodelled in the 17th century and is built of pink sandstone. It contains the Great Hall, with its magnificent plasterwork ceiling dated 1621, a beautiful family Chapel constructed inside the Castle in 1688, an 18th century billiard room housing what is left of the extensive library once at Glamis, a 19th century dining room containing family portraits and the Royal Apartments which have been used by Her Majesty Queen Elizabeth The Queen Mother.

The Castle stands in an extensive park, landscaped towards the end of the 18th century, and contains the beautiful Italian Garden and the Pinetum which reflect the peace and serenity of the Castle and grounds.

[i] Fashion shoots, archery, equestrian events, shows, rallies, filming, product launches, highland games, Royal memorials, Christmas programme of events Nov–Dec. Photography allowed during special events and private tours.

Shopping pavilion.

The State Rooms are available for grand dinners, lunches and wedding receptions.

Disabled visitors may alight at entrance. Those in wheelchairs will be unable to tour the castle but may visit exhibition room. Audio visual presentation. WC.

Morning coffees, light lunches, afternoon teas. Self-service, licensed restaurant.

All visits are guided, tour time 50–60 mins. Tours leave frequently throughout the day. Tours in French, German, Italian and Spanish by appointment at no additional cost. Three exhibitions.

P 500 cars and 20 coaches 200 yds from castle. Coach drivers and couriers admitted free and receive meal/refreshment voucher.

One teacher free for every 10 children. Nature trail, family exhibition rooms, dolls' house, play park. Glamis Heritage Education Centre in Glamis village. Children's guide book. Garden Trail.

In grounds, on leads.

By appointment Jan–Mar.

■ Conference/Function

ROOM	SIZE	MAX CAPACITY
Dining Room	84 sq.m	90
Restaurant	140 sq.m	100
16th century Kitchens		40

SCONE PALACE & GROUNDS 🏠

www.scone-palace.co.uk

Scone Palace is the home of the Earl and Countess of Mansfield and is built on the site of an ancient abbey. 1500 years ago it was the capital of the Pictish kingdom and the centre of the ancient Celtic church. In the intervening years, it has been the seat of the parliaments and crowning place of kings, including Macbeth, Robert the Bruce and Charles II. The State Rooms house a superb collection of *objets d'art*, including items of Marie Antoinette, bought by the 2nd Earl of Mansfield. Notable works of art are also on display, including paintings by Sir David Wilkie, Sir Joshua Reynolds, and Johann Zoffany. The Library boasts one of Scotland's finest collections of porcelain, including Sèvres, Ludwigsburg and Meissen, whilst the unique 'Vernis Martin' *papier mâché* may be viewed in the Long Gallery.

Gardens

The grounds of the Palace house magnificent collections of shrubs, with woodland walks through the Wild Garden containing David Douglas' original fir and the unique Murray Star Maze. There are Highland cattle and peacocks to admire and an adventure play area for children. The 100 acres of mature Policy Parks, flanked by the River Tay, are available for a variety of events, including corporate and private entertaining.

■ Owner

The Earl of Mansfield

■ Contact

The Administrator
Scone Palace
Perth PH2 6BD

Tel: 01738 552300
Fax: 01738 552588
E-mail: visits@
scone-palace.co.uk

■ Location

MAP 13:G5
OS Ref. NO114 266

From Edinburgh
Forth Bridge M90,
A93 1hr.

Bus: Regular buses from Perth.

Rail: Perth Station 3m.

Motorway: M90 from Edinburgh.

Taxi: 01738 636777.

■ Opening Times

Summer
21 March–31 October
Sun–Fri: 9.30am–5.45pm.
Last admission 5pm.

Sat: 9.30am–4.45pm.
Last admission 4pm.

Evening tours by appointment.

Winter by appointment
Grounds only.
11am–4pm.

■ Admission

Summer
Palace & Grounds
Adult	£8.00
Child (5–16yrs)	£5.00
Conc.	£7.00
Family	£24.00

Groups (20+)
Adult	£6.50
Child (5–16yrs)	£4.50
Conc.	£5.80

Grounds only
Adult	£4.50
Child (5–16yrs)	£3.00
Conc.	£4.00

Under 5s Free
Private Tour £45 supplement.

ℹ️ Receptions, fashion shows, war games, archery, clay pigeon shooting, equestrian events, garden parties, shows, rallies, filming, shooting, fishing, floodlit tattoos, product launches, highland games, parkland, cricket pitch, helicopter landing, croquet, racecourse, polo field, firework displays, adventure playground. No photography in state rooms.

🛍️ Gift shop & food shop.

🍸 Grand dinners in state rooms, buffets, receptions, wedding receptions, cocktail parties.

♿ All state rooms on one level, wheelchair access to restaurants. Stairlift in gift shop.

🍴 Licensed. Teas, lunches & dinners, can be booked, menus upon request, special rates for groups.

🚶 By arrangement. Guides in rooms, tour time 45 mins. French and German guides available by appointment.

🎧 Welcome.

🅿️ 300 cars and 15 coaches, groups please book, couriers and coach drivers free meal and admittance.

🐕 In grounds on leads.

❄️ Please telephone or see website for details.

Conference/Function

ROOM	SIZE	MAX CAPACITY
Long Gallery	140' x 20'	200
Queen Victoria's Rm	20' x 20'	20
Drawing Rm	48' x 25'	80

ABERDOUR CASTLE 🏛

Aberdour, Fife

Tel: 01383 860519

Owner: In the care of Historic Scotland   **Contact:** The Steward

A 14th century castle built by the Douglas family. The gallery on the first floor gives an idea of how it was furnished at the time. The castle has a 14th century tower extended in the 16th and 17th centuries, a delightful walled garden and a circular dovecote.

Location: MAP 13:G7, OS Ref. NT193 854. In Aberdour 5m E of the Forth Bridge on the A921.

Open: 1 Apr–30 Sept: daily, 9.30am–5.30pm, last ticket 5pm. 1 Oct–31 Mar: 9.30am–4.30pm, last ticket 4pm. Closed Thurs & Fri in winter.

Admission: Adult £4, Child £2, Conc. £3 (2007 prices).

ℹ️ Picnic area. WCs. ♿ WC. 🖼 🅿 ❖ €

ARBROATH ABBEY 🏛

Arbroath, Tayside

Tel: 01241 878756

Owner: In the care of Historic Scotland   **Contact:** The Steward

The substantial ruins of a Tironensian monastery, notably the gate house range and the abbot's house. Arbroath Abbey holds a very special place in Scottish history. Scotland's nobles swore their independence from England in the famous 'Declaration of Arbroath' in 1320. New visitor centre.

Location: MAP 14:J4, OS Ref. NO644 414. In Arbroath town centre on the A92.

Open: 1 Apr–30 Sept: daily 9.30am–5.30pm, last ticket 5pm. 1 Oct–31 Mar: daily, 9.30am–4.30 pm, last ticket 4pm.

Admission: Adult £4.50, Child £2.25, Conc. £3.50 (2007 prices).

ℹ️ WCs. 🖼 ♿ WC. 🅿 ❖ €

BALCARRES

Colinsburgh, Fife KY9 1HL

Tel: 01333 340520

Owner: Balcarres Trust   **Contact:** The Earl of Crawford

16th century tower house with 19th century additions by Burn and Bryce. Woodland and terraced gardens.

Location: MAP 14:I6, OS Ref. NO475 044. ½m N of Colinsburgh.

Open: Woodland & Gardens: 1–29 Feb & 1 Apr–28 Jun, 2–5pm. House not open except by written appointment and 1–21 Apr, excluding Sun.

Admission: Adult £6. Garden only: £3.50.

🖼 By arrangement.

BALGONIE CASTLE

Markinch, Fife KY7 6HQ

Tel: 01592 750119   **Fax:** 01592 753103   **E-mail:** sbalgonie@yahoo.co.uk

Owner/Contact: The Laird of Balgonie

14th century tower, additions to the building up to 1702. Still lived in by the family. 14th century chapel for weddings.

Location: MAP 13:H6, OS Ref. NO313 006. ½ m S of A911 Glenrothes–Leven road at Milton of Balgonie on to B921.

Open: All year: daily, 10am–5pm.

Admission: Adult £3, Child £1.50, OAP £2.

BALHOUSIE CASTLE (BLACK WATCH MUSEUM)

Hay Street, North Inch Park, Perth PH1 5HR

Tel: 0131 310 8530

Owner: MOD   **Contact:** Major Proctor

Regimental museum housed in the castle.

Location: MAP 13:G5, OS Ref. NO115 244. ½ m N of town centre, E of A9 road to Dunkeld.

Open: May–Sept: Mon–Sat, 10am–4.30pm. Oct–Apr: Mon–Fri, 10am–3.30pm. Closed 23 Dec–5 Jan & last Sat in Jun.

Admission: Free.

For **accommodation** in the Scotland, see our special index at the end of the book.

BRANKLYN GARDEN 🏵

Dundee Road, Perth PH2 7BB

Tel: 01738 625535

Owner: The National Trust for Scotland

Small garden with an impressive collection of rare and unusual plants.

Location: MAP 13:F5, OS Ref. NO125 225. On A85 at 116 Dundee Road, Perth.

BLAIR CASTLE 🏛

See page 456 for full page entry.

BRECHIN CASTLE

Brechin, Angus DD9 6SG

Tel: 01356 624566   **E-mail:** fay@dalhousieestates.co.uk

www.dalhousieestates.co.uk

Owner: Dalhousie Estates   **Contact:** Fay Clark

Dating from 1711 the Castle contains many family pictures and artefacts. Beautiful gardens.

Location: MAP 14:J3, OS Ref. NO593 602. Off A90 on A935.

Open: 3–11 May, 5–20 Jul: guided tours only, 2 & 3.15pm.

Admission: Adult £5. Child under 12yrs Free.

ℹ️ No photography. ♿ Unsuitable. 🖼 Obligatory. ❖

BROUGHTY CASTLE 🏛

Broughty Ferry, Dundee DD5 2TF

Tel: 01382 436916

Owner: Historic Scotland   **Contact:** The Monument Manager

A delightful castle originating from the 15th century and spectacularly positioned overlooking the Tay estuary. It was adapted over the centuries to reflect advances in warfare and defence. The castle withstood many assaults, and still has the scars from cannon balls to prove the point. By the 18th century it had fallen into ruin but was restored to use in the 1860s as part of the Crimean War effort. The castle houses a museum with fascinating displays on changing life, times and people of Broughty Ferry and about its wildlife, which is run by Dundee City Council.

Location: MAP 14:F4, OS Ref. NO464 304. On the shores of the River Tay at Broughty Ferry, Dundee off the A930.

Open: Tel for details or visit http://www.dundeecity.gov.uk/broughtycastle/main.htm.

Admission: Please telephone the site for details.

🖼 🅿

Edzell Castle & Garden

©Historic Scotland

CASTLE CAMPBELL ♥

Dollar Glen, Central District
Tel: 0131 243 9300
Owner: The National Trust for Scotland   **Contact:** Historic Scotland
Known as 'Castle Gloom' this spectacularly sited 15th century fortress was the lowland stronghold of the Campbells. Stunning views from the parapet walk.
Location: MAP 13:F6, OS Ref. NS961 993. At head of Dollar Glen, 10m E of Stirling on the A91.
❋

CHARLETON HOUSE

Colinsburgh, Leven, Fife KY9 1HG
Tel: 01333 340249 **Fax:** 01333 340583
Location: MAP 14:I6, OS Ref. NO464 036. Off A917. 1m NW of Colinsburgh. 3m NW of Elie.
Open: Sept: daily, 12 noon–3pm. Admission every ½hr with guided tours only.
Admission: £12.
🎦 Obligatory.

CORTACHY ESTATE

Cortachy, Kirriemuir, Angus DD8 4LX
Tel: 01575 570108 **Fax:** 01575 540400
E-mail: office@airlieestates.com **www.airlieestates.com**
Owner: Trustees of Airlie Estates   **Contact:** Estate Office
Countryside walks including access through woodlands to Airlie Monument on Tulloch Hill with spectacular views of the Angus Glens and Vale of Strathmore. Footpaths are waymarked and colour coded.
Location: MAP 13:H3, OS Ref. N0394 596. Off the B955 Glens Road from Kirriemuir.
Open: Woodland Walks: all year. Gardens: 21–24 Mar; 5 May & 12 May–1 Jun; 4 & 25 Aug: 10am–4pm, last admission 3.30pm. Castle not open.
Admission: Please contact estate office for details.
♿ Not suitable. 🅿 Limited. 🐕 ❋

CULROSS PALACE ♥

Tel: 0131 243 9300
Owner: The National Trust for Scotland   **Contact:** Property Manager
Relive the domestic life of the 16th and 17th centuries at this Royal Burgh fringed by the River Forth. Enjoy too the Palace, dating from 1597 and the medieval garden.
Location: MAP 13:F7, OS Ref. NS985 860. Off A985. 12m W of Forth Road Bridge and 4m E of Kincardine Bridge, Fife.

DRUMMOND CASTLE GARDENS 🏛 *See page 457 for full page entry.*

DUNFERMLINE ABBEY & PALACE 🏛

Dunfermline, Fife
Tel: 01383 739026
Owner: In the care of Historic Scotland   **Contact:** The Steward
The remains of the Benedictine abbey founded by Queen Margaret in the 11th century. The foundations of her church are under the 12th century Romanesque-style nave. Robert the Bruce was buried in the choir. Substantial parts of the abbey buildings remain, including the vast refectory.
Location: MAP 13:G7, OS Ref. NY090 873. In Dunfermline off the M90.
Open: All year 1 Apr–30 Sept: daily, 9.30am–5.30pm. 1 Oct–31 Mar: Mon–Sat, 9.30am–4.30pm. Closed Thurs pm, Fri and Sun.
Admission: Adult £3.50, Child £1.75, Conc. £2.80 (2007 prices).
ℹ️ 🖨 🐕 ❋ €

DUNNINALD 🏛

Montrose, Angus DD10 9TD
Tel: 01674 674842 **Fax:** 01674 674860 **www.dunninald.com**
Owner/Contact: J Stansfeld
This house, the third Dunninald built on the estate, was designed by James Gillespie Graham in the gothic Revival style, and was completed for Peter Arkley in 1824. It has a fine walled garden and is set in a planned landscape dating from 1740. It is a family home.
Location: MAP 14:J3, OS Ref. NO705 543 2m S of Montrose, between A92 and the sea.
Open: 26 Jun–27 Jul: Tue–Sun, 1–5pm. Garden: from 12 noon.
Admission: Adult £5, Child (under 12) Free, Conc. £4. Garden only: £2.50.
ℹ️ No photography in house. 🖨 ❋ ♿ Unsuitable. 🎦 Obligatory. 🅿 🐕
🐕 In grounds, on leads. €

The Maze at Scone Palace

EDZELL CASTLE AND GARDEN 🏛

Edzell, Angus
Tel: 01356 648631
Owner: In the care of Historic Scotland   **Contact:** The Steward
The beautiful walled garden at Edzell is one of Scotland's unique sights, created by Sir David Lindsay in 1604. The 'Pleasance' is a delightful formal garden with walls decorated with sculptured stone panels, flower boxes and niches for nesting birds. The fine tower house, now ruined, dates from the last years of the 15th century. Mary Queen of Scots held a council meeting in the castle in 1562 on her way north as her army marched against the Gordons.
Location: MAP 14:I2, OS Ref. NO585 691. At Edzell, 6m N of Brechin on B966. 1m W of village.
Open: 1 Apr–30 Sept: daily, 9.30am–5.30pm, last ticket 5pm. 1 Oct–31 Mar: daily, 9.30am–4.30pm, last ticket 4pm. Closed Thur and Fri in winter.
Admission: Adult £4.50, Child £2.25, Conc. £3.50 (2007 prices).
🖨 ♿ 🅿 🖨 🐕 ❋ ♥ €

ELCHO CASTLE 🏛

Perth
Tel: 01738 639998
Owner: In the care of Historic Scotland   **Contact:** The Steward
This handsome and complete fortified mansion of 16th century date has four projecting towers. The original wrought-iron grilles to protect the windows are still in place.
Location: MAP 13:G5, OS Ref. NO164 211. On the Tay, 3m SE of Perth.
Open: 1 Apr–30 Sept: daily, 9.30am–5.30pm, last ticket 5pm.
Admission: Adult £3, Child £1.50, Conc. £2.50 (2007 prices).
🖨 🅿 🐕 €

FALKLAND PALACE ♥

Falkland KY15 7BU
Tel: 0131 243 9300
Owner: The National Trust for Scotland
Built between 1502 and 1541, the Palace is a good example of Renaissance architecture. Surrounded by gardens, laid out in the 1950s.
Location: MAP 13:G6, OS Ref. NO253 075. A912, 11m N of Kirkcaldy.

GLAMIS CASTLE

See page 458 for full page entry.

GLENEAGLES

Auchterarder, Perthshire PH3 1PJ

Tel: 01764 682388

Owner: Gleneagles 1996 Trust   **Contact:** J Martin Haldane of Gleneagles

Gleneagles has been the home of the Haldane family since the 12th century. The 18th century pavilion is open to the public by written appointment.

Location: MAP 13:F6, OS Ref. NS931 088. ¾m S of A9 on A823. 2½m S of Auchterarder.

Open: By written appointment only.

HILL OF TARVIT MANSIONHOUSE

Cupar, Fife KY15 5PB

Tel: 0131 243 9300

Owner: The National Trust for Scotland

House rebuilt in 1906 by Sir Robert Lorimer, the renowned Scottish architect, for a Dundee industrialist, Mr F B Sharp.

Location: MAP 13:F6, OS Ref. NO379 118. Off A916, 2½m S of Cupar, Fife.

HOUSE OF DUN

Montrose, Angus DD10 9LQ

Tel: 0131 243 9300

Owner: The National Trust for Scotland

Georgian house, overlooking the Montrose Basin, designed by William Adam and built in 1730 for David Erskine, Lord Dun.

Location: OS Ref. NO670 599. 3m W Montrose on A935.

HUNTINGTOWER CASTLE

Perth

Tel: 01738 627231

Owner: In the care of Historic Scotland   **Contact:** The Steward

The splendid painted ceilings are especially noteworthy in this castle, once owned by the Ruthven family. Scene of a famous leap between two towers by a daughter of the house who was nearly caught in her lover's room. The two towers are still complete, one of 15th–16th century date, the other of 16th century origin. Now linked by a 17th century range.

Location: MAP 13:F5, OS Ref. NO084 252. 3m NW of Perth off the A85.

Open: 1 Apr–30 Sept: daily, 9.30am–5.30pm, last ticket 5pm. 1 Oct–31 Mar: 9.30am–4.30pm, last ticket 4pm. Closed Thur & Fri in winter.

Admission: Adult £4, Child £2, Conc. £3 (2007 prices).

By arrangement. €

INCHCOLM ABBEY

Inchcolm, Fife

Tel: 01383 823332

Owner: In the care of Historic Scotland   **Contact:** The Steward

Known as the 'Iona of the East'. This is the best preserved group of monastic buildings in Scotland, founded in 1123. Includes a 13th century octagonal chapter house.

Location: MAP 13:H7, OS Ref. NT190 826. On Inchcolm in the Firth of Forth. Reached by ferry from South Queensferry (30 mins), or Newhaven (45 mins). Tel. 0131 331 5000 for times/charges.

Open: 1 Apr–30 Sept: daily, 9.30am–5.30pm, last ticket 5pm.

Admission: Adult £4.50, Child £2.25, Conc. £3.50 (2007 prices). Additional charge for ferries.

Visitor Centre. €

For **accommodation** in Scotland, see our special index at the end of the book.

KELLIE CASTLE & GARDEN

Pittenweem, Fife KY10 2RF

Tel: 0131 243 9300

Owner: The National Trust for Scotland

Good example of domestic architecture in Lowland Scotland dates from the 14th century and was sympathetically restored by the Lorimer family in the late 19th century.

Location: MAP 14:I6, OS Ref. NO519 051. On B9171, 3m NW of Pittenweem, Fife.

LOCHLEVEN CASTLE

Loch Leven, Kinross

Tel: 07778 040483

Owner: In the care of Historic Scotland   **Contact:** The Steward

Mary Queen of Scots endured nearly a year of imprisonment in this 14th century tower before her dramatic escape in May 1568. During the First War of Independence it was held by the English, stormed by Wallace and visited by Bruce.

Location: MAP 13:G6, OS Ref. NO138 018. On island in Loch Leven reached by ferry from Kinross off the M90.

Open: Last sailing 4.30pm. Open summer only.

Admission: Adult £4.50, Child £2.25, Conc. £3.50 (2007 prices). Prices include ferry trip.

P €

MEGGINCH CASTLE GARDENS

ERROL, PERTHSHIRE PH2 7SW

Tel: 01821 642222   **Email:** catherine.herdman@gmail.com

Owner: Mr Giles & The Hon Mrs Herdman

15th century castle, 1,000 year old yews, flowered parterre, double walled kitchen garden, topiary, astrological garden, pagoda dovecote in courtyard. Part used as a location for the film *Rob Roy*.

Location: MAP 13:G5, OS Ref. NO241 245. 8m E of Perth on A90.

Open: By appointment.

Admission: Contact property for details.

Partial. By arrangement. Limited for coaches. In grounds, on leads.

MONZIE CASTLE

Crieff, Perthshire PH7 4HD

Tel: 01764 653110

Owner/Contact: Mrs C M M Crichton

Built in 1791. Destroyed by fire in 1908 and rebuilt and furnished by Sir Robert Lorimer.

Location: MAP 13:E5, OS Ref. NN873 244. 2m NE of Crieff.

Open: 10 May–8 Jun: daily, 2–5pm. By appointment at other times.

Admission: Adult £5, Child £1. Group rates available, contact property for details.

©Historic Scotland Photographic Library

ST ANDREWS CASTLE

THE SCORES, ST ANDREWS KY16 9AR

Tel: 01334 477196

Owner: Historic Scotland   **Contact:** David Eaton

This was the castle of the bishops of St Andrews and has a fascinating mine and counter-mine, rare examples of medieval siege techniques. There is also a bottle dungeon hollowed out of solid rock. Cardinal Beaton was murdered here and John Knox was sent to the galleys when the ensuing siege was lifted.

Location: MAP 14:I5, OS Ref. NO513 169. In St Andrews on the A91.

Open: Apr–Sept: daily, 9.30am–5.30pm. Oct–Mar: daily, 9.30am–4.30pm. Last ticket 30 mins before closing.

Admission: Adult £5, Child £2.50, Conc. £4 (2007 prices). 10% discount for groups (11+). Joint ticket with St Andrews Cathedral available.

ⓘ Visitor centre. ▣ ⬚ Partial. WCs. ⑤ By arrangement. ℙ On street. ▣ Free if booked. ⬛ Guide dogs. ✳ €

ST ANDREWS CATHEDRAL

St Andrews, Fife

Tel: 01334 472563

Owner: Historic Scotland   **Contact:** Alison Sullivan

The remains still give a vivid impression of the scale of what was once the largest cathedral in Scotland along with the associated domestic ranges of the priory.

Location: MAP 14:I5, OS Ref. NO514 167. In St Andrews.

Open: 1 Apr–30 Sept: daily, 9.30am–5.30pm, last ticket 4.45pm. 1 Oct–31 Mar: daily, 9.30am–4.30pm, last ticket 3.45pm.

Admission: Adult £4, Child £2, Conc. £3 (2007 prices). Joint entry ticket with St Andrews Castle available.

✳ €

SCONE PALACE & GROUNDS 🏛 *See page 459 for full page entry.*

STOBHALL 🏛

Stobhall, Cargill, Perthshire PH2 6DR

Tel: 01821 640332   **www.stobhall.com**

Owner: Viscount Strathallan

Original home of the Drummond chiefs from the 14th century. Romantic cluster of small-scale buildings around a courtyard in a magnificent situation overlooking the River Tay, surrounded by formal and woodland gardens. 17th century painted ceiling in Chapel depicts monarchs of Europe and North Africa on horse (or elephant) back.

Location: MAP 13:G4, OS Ref. NO132 343. 7m N of Perth on A93.

Open: 31 May–29 Jun: Tues–Sun, (closed Mons). Open by tour only. Tours at 2, 3 & 4pm of the Chapel, Drawing Room and Folly. Explore the garden at leisure after the tour. Library by prior appointment.

Admission: Adult £4, Child £2. Large group visits must be booked.

⬚ Partial. Please see website or ring for details. ⑤ Obligatory. ℙ Limited. Coaches please book.

STRATHTYRUM HOUSE & GARDENS

St Andrews, Fife

Tel: 01334 473600   **E-mail:** info@strathtyrumhouse.com

www.strathtyrumhouse.com

Owner: The Strathtyrum Trust   **Contact:** Cheryl Hanlon

Location: MAP 14:I5, OS Ref. NO490 172. Entrance from the St Andrews/Guardbridge Road which is signposted when open.

Open: 5–9 May, 2–6 Jun, 7–11 Jul, 4–8 Aug and 1–5 Sept: 2–4pm. Guided tours at 2 & 3pm.

Admission: Adult £5, Child £2.50.

⑤ 2pm and 3pm. ℙ Free. ⬛ Guide dogs only.

TULLIBOLE CASTLE

Crook of Devon, Kinross KY13 0QN

Tel: 01577 840236   **E-mail:** visit@tulbol.demon.co.uk

www.tulbol.demon.co.uk/visit.htm

Owner: Lord & Lady Moncreiff   **Contact:** Lord Moncreiff

Recognised as a classic example of the Scottish tower house. Completed in 1608, the Moncreiff family have lived here since 1747. The Castle is in a parkland setting with ornamental fishponds (moat), a roofless lectarn doocot, with a short walk to a 9th century graveyard and a ruined church.

Location: MAP 13:F6, OS Ref. NO540 888. Located on the B9097 1m E of Crook of Devon.

Open: Last week in Aug–30 Sept: Tue–Sun, 1–4pm. Admission every ½ hr with guided tours only.

Admission: Adult £3.50, Child/Conc. £2.50. Free as part of "Doors Open Day" (last weekend of Sept).

⬚ Unsuitable. ⑤ Obligatory. ℙ Ample for cars but limited for coaches. ▣ ⬛ Guide dogs only. ⛺ 1 x twin, 1 bed holiday cottage.

©Patrick Lane

Elcho Castle

■ Owner
Historic Scotland

■ Contact
The Steward
Argyll's Lodging
Castle Wynd
Stirling FK8 1EJ

Tel: 01786 431319
Fax: 01786 448194

■ Location
MAP 13:E7
OS Ref. NS793 938

At the top and on E side of Castle Wynd in Stirling. One way route from town centre from Albert Street.

Rail: Stirling.

Air: Edinburgh or Glasgow.

■ Opening Times
April–September
Daily, 9.30am–6pm.

October–March
Daily, 9.30am–5pm.

■ Admission
Adult	£4.50
Child*	£2.25
Conc**	£3.50

(2007 prices)

* up to 16 years. under 5yrs Free.

** (60+ & unemployed)

ARGYLL'S LODGING

This attractive townhouse, sitting at the foot of Stirling Castle, is decorated as it would have been during the 9th Earl of Argyll's occupation around 1680. Before coming into Historic Scotland's care the building was a youth hostel, but restoration revealed hidden secrets from the lodging's past. Perhaps the best of these was a section of 17th century *trompe l'oeil* panelling in the dining room, created by painter David McBeath.

Visitors to Argyll's Lodging might wonder at the highly decorated walls and rich materials and colours used but the restoration relied on a household inventory of 1680 found among the then Duchess's papers. But no matter how rich the decoration, it cannot match the colourful lives of Argyll Lodging's inhabitants.

The 9th Earl, Archibald Campbell, was sentenced to death for treason and imprisoned in Edinburgh Castle. However he escaped when his stepdaughter smuggled him out dressed as her page. Archibald escaped to Holland, but his stepdaughter was arrested and placed in public stocks – a major humiliation. He didn't cheat death a second time, however. Joining plots over the succession following Charles II's death, he was captured and beheaded in 1685.

An earlier inhabitant of Argyll's Lodging, Sir William Alexander, was tutor to James VI's son, Prince Henry and in 1621 he attempted to colonise Nova Scotia in Canada. Great wealth eluded him all his life, however, and he died a bankrupt in 1640, leading to the town council taking over the lodging and selling it to the Earl of Argyll in the 1660s.

i Interpretation scheme includes computer animations; joint ticket with Stirling Castle available.

Evening receptions/dinners.

Partial. No wheelchair access to upper floor.

P Ample parking for coaches and cars on Stirling Castle Esplanade.

Free pre-booked school visits scheme.

Guide dogs only.

Conference/Function

ROOM	SIZE	MAX CAPACITY
Laigh Hall	11 x 6m	60 for receptions
High Dining Room	11 x 6m	26 for dinner
Both rooms: 120 for receptions		

INVERARAY CASTLE

www.inveraray-castle.com

■ **Owner**
Duke of Argyll

■ **Contact**
Argyll Estate Office
Inveraray Castle
Inveraray
Argyll PA32 8XE

Tel: 01499 302203
Fax: 01499 302421
E-mail: enquiries@
inveraray-castle.com

■ **Location**
MAP 13:A6
OS Ref. NN100 090

From Edinburgh
2½–3hrs via Glasgow.

Just NE of Inveraray
on A83. W shore
of Loch Fyne.

Bus: Bus route stopping
point within ½m.

■ **Opening Times**
Summer
1 April–31 October:
Mon–Sat, 10am–5.45pm
Sun, 12 noon–5.45pm.
Last admission 5pm.

Winter
Closed.

■ **Admission**
House only
Adult   £6.80
Child (under 16yrs) £4.60
OAP/Student   £5.70
Family (2+2)   £19.00

Groups (20+)
              20% discount
Pre-booking available.

The ancient Royal Burgh of Inveraray lies about 60 miles north west of Glasgow by Loch Fyne in an area of spectacular natural beauty. The ruggedness of the highland scenery combines with the sheltered tidal loch, beside which nestles the present Castle built between 1745 and 1790.

The Castle is home to the Duke of Argyll, Head of the Clan Campbell, whose family have lived in Inveraray since the early 15th century. Designed by Roger Morris and decorated by Robert Mylne, the fairytale exterior belies the grandeur of its gracious interior. The Clerk of Works, William Adam, father of Robert and John, did much of the laying out of the present Royal Burgh, which is an unrivalled example of an early planned town.

Visitors enter the famous Armoury Hall containing some 1,300 pieces including Brown Bess muskets, Lochaber axes, 18th century Scottish broadswords, and can see preserved swords from the Battle of Culloden. The fine State Dining Room and Tapestry Drawing Room contain magnificent French tapestries made especially for the Castle, fabulous examples of Scottish, English and French furniture and a wealth of other works of art. The unique collection of china, silver and family artifacts spans the generations which are identified by a magnificent genealogical display in the Clan Room.

i No photography. Guide books in French, Italian, Japanese and German translations.

Visitors may alight at the entrance. 2 wheelchair ramps to castle. All main public rooms suitable but two long flights of stairs to the smaller rooms upstairs. WCs.

Seats up to 50. Licensed. Menus available on request. Groups book in advance. Tel: 01499 302112.

Available for up to 100 people at no additional cost. Groups please book. Tour time: 1 hr. Guided tour of castle garden: Fridays, May & un, 2pm.

P 100 cars. Separate coach park close to Castle.

£2.10 per child. A guide can be provided. Areas of interest include a nature walk.

In grounds, on leads. Guide dogs only inside Castle.

West Highlands & Islands, Loch Lomond, Stirling and Trossachs

ANGUS'S GARDEN

Barguillean, Taynuilt, Argyll, West Highlands PA35 1HY
Tel: 01866 822335   **Fax:** 01866 822539
Contact: Sean Honeyman
Memorial garden of peace, tranquillity and reconciliation.
Location: MAP 12:P5, OS Ref. NM978 289. 4m SW on Glen Lonan road from A85.
Open: All year: daily, 9am–5pm (dusk during summer months).
Admission: Adult £2, Child Free.

ARDENCRAIG GARDENS

Ardencraig, Rothesay, Isle of Bute, West Highlands PA20 9BP
Tel: 01700 505339   **Fax:** 01700 502492
Owner: Argyll and Bute Council   **Contact:** Allan Macdonald
Walled garden, greenhouses, aviaries. Woodland walk from Rothesay 1 mile (Skippers Wood.)
Location: MAP 13:A8, OS Ref. NS105 645. 2m from Rothesay.
Open: May–Sept: Mon–Fri, 10am–3.30pm, Sat & Sun, 1–4.30pm.
Admission: Free.

ARDKINGLAS ESTATE
CAIRNDOW, ARGYLL PA26 8BH
www.ardkinglas.com

Tel: 01499 600261   **Fax:** 01499 600241   **E-mail:** info@ardkinglas.com
Owner: David Sumsion   **Contact:** Jean Maskell
An oasis of beauty to explore and enjoy at the head of Loch Fyne. Add that special touch to your wedding celebrations by having your ceremony and/or reception here. See the fine gardens or holiday in the self catering "Butler's Quarters". Guided tours of house and gardens available.
Location: MAP 13:A6, OS Ref. NN175 104. Head of Loch Fyne, just off the A83 at Cairndow, 10m W of Arrochar. About 1hr from Glasgow.
Open: Woodland Garden & Woodland Trails: All year, dawn–dusk.
Admission: Garden – admission charge for adults.
◻ Tree shop. ⬚ ⬚ ⬚ Partial. ⬚ ⬚ By arrangement. **P** ⬚ In grounds, on leads. ⬚ €

ARGYLL'S LODGING ⬚

See page 464 for full page entry.

BALLOCH CASTLE COUNTRY PARK

Balloch, Dunbartonshire G83 8LX
Tel: 01389 737000
Contact: West Dunbartonshire Council
A 200 acre country park on the banks of Loch Lomond.
Location: MAP 13:C7, OS Ref. NS390 830. SE shore of Loch Lomond, off A82 for Balloch or A811 for Stirling.
Open: All year: dawn–dusk.
Admission: Free.

BENMORE BOTANIC GARDEN

Dunoon, Argyll PA23 8QU
Tel: 01369 706261   **Fax:** 01369 706369
Contact: The Curator
A botanical paradise. Enter the magnificent avenue of giant redwoods and follow trails through the Formal Garden and hillside woodlands with its spectacular outlook over the Holy Loch and the Eachaig Valley.
Location: MAP 12:P4, OS Ref. NS150 850. 7m N of Dunoon on A815.
Open: 1 Mar–31 Oct: daily, 10am–6pm. Closes 5pm in Mar & Oct.
Admission: Adult £3.50, Child £1, Conc. £3, Family £8. Group discounts available.

BONAWE IRON FURNACE ⬚

Taynuilt, Argyll
Tel: 01866 822432
Owner: In the care of Historic Scotland   **Contact:** The Steward
Founded in 1753 by Cumbrian iron masters this is the most complete remaining charcoal fuelled ironworks in Britain. Displays show how iron was once made here.
Location: MAP 12:P4, OS Ref. NN005 310. By the village of Taynuilt off the A85.
Open: 1 Apr–30 Sept: daily, 9.30am–5.30pm, last ticket 5pm.
Admission: Adult £4, Child £2, Conc. £3 (2007 prices).
◻ ⬚ **P** €

CASTLE STALKER

Portnacroish, Appin, Argyll PA38 4BA
Tel: 01631 730354   www.castlestalker.com
Owner: Mrs M Allward   **Contact:** Messrs R & A Allward
Early 15th century tower house and ancient seat of the Stewarts of Appin. Picturesquely set on a rocky islet approx 400 yds off the mainland on the shore of Loch Linnhe. Reputed to have been used by James IV as a hunting lodge. Garrisoned by Government troops during the 1745 rising. Restored from a ruin by the late Lt Col Stewart Allward following acquisition in 1965 and now retained by his family.
Location: MAP 12:P3, OS Ref. NM930 480. Approx. 20m N of Oban on the A828. On islet ¼m offshore.
Open: 12–16 & 19–23 May, 18–22 & 25–29 Aug, 8–12 Sept. Telephone for appointments. Times variable depending on tides and weather.
Admission: Adult £8, Child £4.
⬚ Not suitable for coach parties. ⬚ Unsuitable.

DOUNE CASTLE ⬚

Doune
Tel: 01786 841742
Owner: Earl of Moray (leased to Historic Scotland)   **Contact:** The Steward
A formidable 14th century courtyard castle, built for the Regent Albany. The striking keep-gatehouse combines domestic quarters including the splendid Lord's Hall with its carved oak screen, musicians' gallery and double fireplace.
Location: MAP 13:D6, OS Ref. NN720 020. In Doune, 8m S of Callander on the A84.
Open: 1 Apr–30 Sept: daily, 9.30am–5.30pm. 1 Oct–31 Mar: Mon–Wed, Sat & Sun, 9.30am–4.30pm, last admission 30 mins before closing.
Admission: Adult £4, Child £2, Conc. £3 (2007 prices).
◻ **P** ⬚ €

Kilchurn Castle

©Historic Scotland

DUART CASTLE 🏛
ISLE OF MULL, ARGYLL PA64 6AP
www.duartcastle.com

Tel: 01680 812309 or 01577 830311 **E-mail:** duart.guide@btinternet.com
Owner/Contact: Sir Lachlan Maclean Bt

Duart is a fortress, one of a line of castles stretching from Dunollie in the east to Mingary in the north, all guarding the Sound of Mull. The earliest part of the Castle was built in the 12th century, the keep was added in 1360 by the 5th Chief Lachlan Lubanach and the most recent alterations were completed in 1673. The Macleans were staunchly loyal to the Stuarts. After the rising of 1745 they lost Duart and their lands were forfeited. Sir Fitzroy Maclean, 25th Chief, restored the Castle in 1910. Duart remains the family home of the Chief of the Clan Maclean.

Location: MAP 12:O4, OS Ref. NM750 350. Off A849 on the east point of the Isle of Mull.
Open: Apr: Sun–Thurs, 11am–4pm. 1 May–12 Oct: daily, 10.30am–5.30pm. Shop: 1 May–5 Oct. Tearoom: Apr–5 Oct, as Castle.
Admission: Adult: £5, Child (3–14) £2.50, Conc. £4.50, Family (2+2) £12.50.
🔲 ⊤ ♿ Unsuitable. 🔲 🔲 By arrangement. 🅿 🐕 In grounds, on leads.

DUMBARTON CASTLE 🔔

Dumbarton, Strathclyde
Tel: 01389 732167
Owner: Historic Scotland   **Contact:** The Steward
Location: MAP 13:C8, OS Ref. NS401 744. 600yds S of A84 at E end of Dumbarton.
Open: 1 Apr–30 Sept: daily, 9.30am–5.30pm; 1 Oct–31 Mar: Sat–Wed, 9.30am–4.30pm, last ticket sold 45 mins before closing.
Admission: Adult £4, Child £2, Conc £3 (2007 prices).
🔲 ⊤ ♿ 🅿 🐕 ❄ 🔲 €

DUNBLANE CATHEDRAL 🔔

Dunblane
Tel: 01786 823388
Owner: Historic Scotland   **Contact:** The Steward

One of Scotland's noblest medieval churches. The lower part of the tower is Romanesque but the larger part of the building is of the 13th century. It was restored in 1889–93 by Sir Rowand Anderson.

Location: MAP 13:E6, OS Ref. NN782 015. In Dunblane.
Open: All year: Mon–Sat, 9.30am–5.30pm, Sun 2–5.30pm. Winter: Mon–Sat, 9.30am–4.30pm, Sun 2–4.30pm, last entry 30 mins before closing. Closed daily 12.30–1.30pm.
Admission: Free.
❄

©Historic Scotland Photographic Library

DUNSTAFFNAGE CASTLE 🔔
BY OBAN, ARGYLL PA37 1PZ

Tel: 01631 562465
Owner: In the care of Historic Scotland   **Contact:** The Steward

A very fine 13th century castle built on a rock with a great curtain wall. The castle's colourful history stretches across the Wars of Independence to the 1745 rising. The castle was briefly the prison of Flora Macdonald. Marvellous views from the top of the curtain wall. Close by are the remains of a chapel with beautiful architectural detail.

Location: MAP 12:P4, OS49 NM882 344. 3½m NE of Oban off A85.
Open: Apr–Sept: daily, 9.30am–5.30pm, last ticket 30 mins before closing. Oct–Mar: daily, 9.30am–4.30pm. Closed Thurs & Fri.
Admission: Adult £3.50, Child £1.75, Conc. £2.80 (2007 prices). 10% discount for groups (11+).
🔲 ♿ Partial. 🔲 By arrangement. 🅿 🔲 Free pre-booked school visits. 🐕 In grounds, on leads. ❄ €

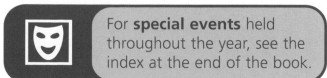

For **special events** held throughout the year, see the index at the end of the book.

THE HILL HOUSE

Upper Colquhoun Street, Helensburgh G84 9AJ
Tel: 0131 243 9300
Owner: The National Trust for Scotland
Charles Rennie Mackintosh set this 20th century masterpiece high on a hillside overlooking the Firth of Clyde. Mackintosh also designed furniture, fittings and decorative schemes to complement the house.
Location: MAP 13:B7, OS Ref. NS300 820. Off B832, between A82 & A814, 23m NW of Glasgow.

INCHMAHOME PRIORY

Port of Menteith
Tel: 01877 385294
Owner: In the care of Historic Scotland   **Contact:** The Steward
A beautifully situated Augustinian priory on an island in the Lake of Menteith founded in 1238 with much of the building surviving. The five year old Mary, Queen of Scots was sent here for safety in 1547.
Location: MAP 13:C6, OS Ref. NN574 005. On an island in Lake of Menteith. Reached by ferry from Port of Menteith, 4m E of Aberfoyle off A81.
Open: 1 Apr–30 Sept: daily, 9.30am–5.30pm, last outward sailing at 4.30pm.
Admission: Adult £4.50, Child £2.25, Conc. £3.50 (2007 prices). Charge includes ferry trip.

INVERARAY CASTLE

See page 465 for full page entry.

INVERARAY JAIL

Church Square, Inveraray, Argyll PA32 8TX
Tel: 01499 302381   **Fax:** 01499 302195   **E-mail:** info@inverarayjail.co.uk
www.inverarayjail.co.uk
Owner: Visitor Centres Ltd   **Contact:** Gavin Dick
A living 19th century prison! Uniformed prisoners and warders, life-like figures, imaginative exhibitions, sounds, smells and trials in progress, bring the 1820 courtroom and former county prison back to life. See the 'In Prison Today' exhibition, an original 'Black Maria' and 'Katie' the cow. Don't forget to bring your camera!
Location: MAP 13 A:6, OS Ref. NN100 090. Church Square, Inveraray, Argyll.
Open: Apr–Oct: 9.30am–6pm, last admission 5pm. Nov–Mar: 10am–5pm, last admission 4pm.
Admission: Adult £6.50, Child £3.25, OAP £4.30, Family £17.80. Groups (10+): Adult £5.20, OAP £3.45.

IONA ABBEY & NUNNERY

Iona, Argyll
Tel/Fax: 01681 700512   www.historic-scotland.gov.uk
Owner: In the care of Historic Scotland   **Contact:** The Steward
One of Scotland's most historic and venerated sites, Iona Abbey is a celebrated Christian centre and the burial place for many Scottish kings. The abbey and nunnery grounds house one of the most comprehensive collections of Christian carved stones in Scotland, dating from 600AD to the 1600s. Includes the Columba Centre, Fionnphort exhibition and giftshop.
Location: MAP 12:L5, OS Ref. NM270 240. Ferry service from Fionnphort, Mull.
Open: All year, depending on the ferries.
Admission: Adult £4.50, Child (under 16yrs) £2.25, Conc. £3.50 (2007 prices). Columba Centre, exhibition & giftshop: Free.
Partial. In grounds.

KILCHURN CASTLE

Loch Awe, Dalmally, Argyll
Tel: 01786 431323
Owner: In the care of Historic Scotland   **Contact:** The Steward
A square tower, built by Sir Colin Campbell of Glenorchy c1550, it was much enlarged in 1693 to give the building, now a ruin, its present picturesque outline. Spectacular views of Loch Awe.
Location: MAP 13:A5, OS Ref. NN133 276. At the NE end of Loch Awe, 2½ m W of Dalmally.
Open: Summer only, public access by boat, for times & prices contact: 01866 833333.
Admission: Please telephone for details.

MOUNT STUART
ISLE OF BUTE PA20 9LR

www.mountstuart.com

Tel: 01700 503877   **Fax:** 01700 505313   **E-mail:** contactus@mountstuart.com
Owner: Mount Stuart Trust   **Contact:** Laura McShane
Spectacular High Victorian gothic house, ancestral home of the Marquess of Bute. Splendid interiors, art collection and architectural detail. Set in 300 acres of stunning woodlands, mature Victorian pinetum, arboretum and exotic gardens.
Location: MAP 13:A9, OS Ref. NS100 600. SW coast of Scotland, 5m S of Rothesay. Local bus service to House, frequent ferry service from Wemyss Bay, Renfrewshire and Colintraive, Argyll.
Open: Easter & 1 May–30 Sept. Please telephone for detailed opening times.
Admission: Adult £8, Child £4, Conc. £6.50, Family £20. Groups (12+) discount available.
No photography. Licensed. Licensed. Obligatory. Ample. Guide dogs only.

ROTHESAY CASTLE

Rothesay, Isle of Bute
Tel: 01700 502691
Owner: In the care of Historic Scotland   **Contact:** The Steward
A favourite residence of the Stuart kings, this is a wonderful example of a 13th century circular castle of enclosure with 16th century forework containing the Great Hall. Attacked by Vikings in its earlier days.
Location: MAP 13:A8, OS Ref. NS088 646. In Rothesay, Isle of Bute. Ferry from Wemyss Bay on the A78.
Open: 1 Apr–30 Sept: daily, 9.30am–5.30pm, last ticket 5pm. 1 Oct–31 Mar: Sat–Wed, 9.30am–4.30pm, last ticket 4pm.
Admission: Adult £4, Child £2, Conc. £3 (2007 prices).
Partial. On leads.

ST BLANE'S CHURCH

Kingarth, Isle of Bute
Tel: 0131 668 8800
Owner: In the care of Historic Scotland
This 12th century Romanesque chapel stands on the site of a 12th century Celtic monastery.
Location: MAP 13:A9, OS Ref. NS090 570. At the S end of the Isle of Bute.
Open: All year: daily.
Admission: Free.

Properties that **open all year** appear in the special index at the end of the book.

visit hudsons guide online

©Historic Scotland Photographic Library

STIRLING CASTLE

CASTLE WYND, STIRLING FK8 1EJ

Tel: 01786 450000 **Fax:** 01786 464678

Owner: Historic Scotland

Stirling Castle has played a key role in Scottish history, dominating the north–south and east–west routes through Scotland. The battles of Stirling Bridge and Bannockburn were fought in its shadow and Mary, Queen of Scots lived here as a child. Renaissance architecture, restored Great Hall and tapestry weaving.

Location: MAP 13:E7, OS Ref. NS790 941. At the top of Castle Wynd in Stirling.

Open: Apr–Sept: 9.30am–6pm. Oct–Mar: 9.30am–5pm. Last ticket 45 mins before closing. Joint ticket available with Argyll's Lodging.

Admission: Adult £8.50, Child £4.25, Conc. £6.50 (2007 prices). 10% discount for groups (11+). Free booked school visits, except May–August.

i Picnic area. ◻ ⊤ Private hire. ♿ Partial. WC. 🍴 Licensed. 🎬 📷 🅿 ▮

🐕 Guide dogs only. ❋ ♥ €

TOROSAY CASTLE & GARDENS

CRAIGNURE, ISLE OF MULL PA65 6AY

www.torosay.com

Tel: 01680 812421 **Fax:** 01680 812470 **E-mail:** torosay@aol.com

Owner/Contact: Mr Chris James

Torosay Castle and Gardens set on the beautiful Island of Mull, was completed in 1858 by the eminent architect David Bryce in the Scottish baronial style, and is surrounded by 12 acres of spectacular gardens which offer a dramatic contrast between formal terraces, impressive statue walk and informal woodland, also rhododendron collection, alpine, walled, water and oriental gardens. The house offers family history, portraits, scrapbooks and antiques in an informal and relaxed atmosphere.

Location: MAP 12:O4, OS Ref. NM730 350. 1½m SE of Craignure by A849.

Open: House: Easter–31 Oct: daily, 10.30am–5pm. Gardens: All year: daily, 9am–7pm (dusk in winter).

Admission: Adult £6, Child £3.50, Conc. £5, Family £15.50.

i Children's adventure playground. ◻ 📷 ⊤ ♿ WC. 🍴 🅿 🏠 Holiday cottages.

❋ ♥ €

The King's Knot, Stirling Castle

ALTYRE ESTATE

Altyre Estate, Forres, Moray IV36 2SH

Tel: 01309 672265 **Fax:** 01309 672270 **E-mail:** office@altyre.com

Contact: Sir Alastair Gordon Cumming

Altyre Estate comprises architecturally interesting buildings including Italianate farm buildings, standing stones and access to areas of natural and ornithological interest. Altyre Estate may interest scientific groups, students, and the general public.

Location: MAP 16:P8, OS Ref. NJ028 552. Details given on appointment.

Open: Visitors are welcome by appointment on the first working day of Apr, May Jun, Jul & Aug.

Admission: Free.

ARBUTHNOTT HOUSE & GARDEN

Arbuthnott, Laurencekirk AB30 1PA

Tel: 01561 361226 **E-mail:** keith@arbuthnott.co.uk **www.arbuthnott.co.uk**

Owner: The Viscount of Arbuthnot **Contact:** The Master of Arbuthnott

Arbuthnott family home for 800 years with formal 17th century walled garden on unusually steep south facing slope. Well maintained grass terraces, herbaceous borders, shrubs and greenhouses.

Location: MAP 14:K2, OS Ref. NO796 751. Off B967 between A90 and A92, 25m S of Aberdeen.

Open: House: 6/7 Apr, 25/26 May, 27/28 Jul, 3/4 & 24/25 Aug and by arrangement. Guided tours: 2–5pm. Garden: All year: 9am–5pm.

Admission: House: £5. Garden: Adult £2.50, Child £1.

Ground floor. Obligatory.

BALFLUIG CASTLE

Alford, Aberdeenshire AB33 8EJ

Tel: 020 7624 3200

Owner/Contact: Mark Tennant of Balfluig

Small 16th century tower house in farmland, restored in 1967.

Location: OS Ref. NJ586 151. Alford, Aberdeenshire.

Open: Please write to M I Tennant Esq, 30 Abbey Gardens, London NW8 9AT. Occasionally let by the week for holidays. Graded *** by VisitScotland, see www.visitscotland.com

Unsuitable. 1 single, 4 double.

BALMORAL CASTLE (GROUNDS & EXHIBITIONS)

Balmoral, Ballater, Aberdeenshire AB35 5TB

Tel: 013397 42534 **Fax:** 013397 42034 **E-mail:** info@balmoralcastle.com

www.balmoralcastle.com

Owner: Her Majesty The Queen **Contact:** Garry Marsden

Scottish home to The Royal Family. Ballroom, grounds and exhibitions, large café seating 120, quality gift shop. Excellent for coaches and groups. Holiday cottages, salmon fishing, Land Rover safaris and activity holidays.

Location: MAP 13:G1, OS Ref. NO256 951. Off A93 between Ballater and Braemar. 50m W of Aberdeen.

Open: 1 Apr–31 Jul: daily, 10am–5pm, last admission 4.30pm. Nov & Dec: Guided tours available – ring for details.

Admission: Adult £7, Child £3, OAP £6, Family £15 (Audio tour included). Discounts for groups (20+).

BALVENIE CASTLE

Dufftown

Tel: 01340 820121

Owner: In the care of Historic Scotland **Contact:** The Steward

Picturesque ruins of 13th century moated stronghold originally owned by the Comyns. Visited by Edward I in 1304 and by Mary Queen of Scots in 1562. Occupied by Cumberland in 1746.

Location: MAP 17:B9, OS Ref. NJ326 408. At Dufftown on A941.

Open: 1 Apr–30 Sept: daily, 9.30am–5.30pm, last ticket 5pm.

Admission: Adult £3.50, Child £1.75, Conc. £2.80 (2007 prices).

€

For rare and unusual plants visit the **plant sales** index at the end of the book.

BRODIE CASTLE

Forres, Moray IV36 0TE

Tel: 0131 243 9300

Owner: The National Trust for Scotland

The lime harled building is a typical 'Z' plan tower house with ornate corbelled battlements and bartizans, with 17th & 19th century additions.

Location: MAP 16:P8, OS Ref. NH980 577. Off A96 4½m W of Forres and 24m E of Inverness.

CAIRNESS HOUSE

Lonmay, Fraserburgh, Aberdeenshire AB43 8XP

Tel/Fax: 01346 582078 **E-mail:** info@cairnesshouse.com

www:cairnesshouse.com

Owners: Mr J Soriano-Ruiz / Mr K H Khairallah **Contact:** Property Manager

Cairness is Scotland's most extraordinary neoclassical house. Forgotten and neglected for decades, it is being brought back to life in a major restoration and now has one of the finest collections of furniture and paintings in the North East. The exquisite interiors include the earliest Egyptian room in Britain.

Location: MAP 17:F8, OS Ref. NK038 609. Off A90, 4m SE of Fraserburgh, ¼m W of B9033 about 2m S of St Comb's.

Open: May, Jun, Sept: Weds & Suns 1–4pm (last admission). Jul & Aug: Mons, Weds, Fris & Suns, 11am–4pm (last admission). Tours of house and restoration works every hour on the hour. Groups and special visits at all other times by prior appointment.

Admission: Adult £7, OAP/Student £6.

No photography. No smoking. Obligatory. Limited.

CASTLE FRASER & GARDEN

Sauchen, Inverurie AB51 7LD

Tel: 0131 243 9300

Owner: The National Trust for Scotland

Begun in 1575, the two low wings contribute to the scale and magnificence of the towers rising above them, combining to make this the largest and most elaborate of the Scottish castles built on the 'Z' plan.

Location: MAP 17:D11, OS Ref. NJ723 125. Off A944, 4m N of Dunecht & 16m W of Aberdeen.

J Henderson.

Crathes Castle

CORGARFF CASTLE 🏛

Strathdon
Tel: 01975 651460
Owner: In the care of Historic Scotland   **Contact:** The Steward
A 16th century tower house converted into a barracks for Hanoverian troops in 1748.
Location: MAP 17:A11, OS Ref. NJ255 086. 8m W of Strathdon on A939. 14m NW of Ballater.
Open: 1 Apr–30 Sept: daily, 9.30am–5.30pm. 1 Oct–31 Mar: Sat & Sun, 9.30am–4.30pm. Last admission 30 mins before closing.
Admission: Adult £4.50, Child £2.25, Conc. £3.50 (2007 prices).
🅿 €

CRAIG CASTLE

Rhynie, Huntly, Aberdeenshire AB54 4LP
Tel: 01464 861705   **Fax:** 01464 861702
Owner: Mr A J Barlas   **Contact:** The Property Manager
The Castle is built round a courtyard and consists of a 16th century L-shaped Keep, a Georgian house (architect John Adam) and a 19th century addition (architect Archibald Simpson of Aberdeen). The Castle was a Gordon stronghold for 300 years. It has a very fine collection of coats-of-arms.
Location: MAP 17:C10, OS Ref. NJ472 259. 3m W of Rhynie and Lumsden on B9002.
Open: May–Sept: Wed & every 2nd weekend in each month, 2–5pm.
Admission: Adult £5, Child £1.
🖭 🖳 Unsuitable. 🎦 By arrangement. 🅿 Limited for coaches. 🐕 Guide dogs only.

CRAIGSTON CASTLE

Turriff, Aberdeenshire AB53 5PX
Tel: 01888 551228   **E-mail:** wu-gen01@craigston.co.uk
Owner: William Pratesi Urquhart   **Contact:** The Housekeeper
Built in 1607 by John Urquhart Tutor of Cromarty, Craigston bears the marks of a client's brief rather than an architect's whim, which seems to belong to that strange slightly Gothic world. Few changes have been made to its exterior in its 400 years. A sculpted balcony unique in Scottish architecture depicts a piper, two grinning knights and David and Goliath. The interior dates from the early 19th century. Remarkable carved oak panels of Scottish kings' biblical heroes, mounted in doors and shutters of the early 17th century.
Location: MAP 17:D8, OS Ref. NJ762 550. On B9105, 4½m NE of Turriff.
Open: 14 Jun–13 July: daily except Mons, 12 noon–3pm. Guided house tours: 12 noon, 1pm & 2pm. Groups by appointment throughout the year.
Admission: Adult £6, Child £2, Conc. £4. Groups: Adult £5, Child/School £1.
🖳 Unsuitable. 🎦 Obligatory. 🅿 🐕 In grounds on leads. 🅿

CRATHES CASTLE & GARDEN ♨

Banchory AB31 3QJ
Tel: 0131 243 9300
Owner: The National Trust for Scotland
The building of the castle began in 1553 and took 40 years to complete. Just over 300 years later, Sir James and Lady Burnett began developing the walled garden.
Location: MAP 17:D12, OS Ref. NO733 969: On A93, 3m E of Banchory and 15m W of Aberdeen.

CRUICKSHANK BOTANIC GARDEN

St Machar Drive, Aberdeen AB24 3UU
Tel: 01224 272704   **Fax:** 01224 272703
Owner: University of Aberdeen   **Contact:** R B Rutherford
Extensive collection of shrubs, herbaceous and alpine plants and trees. Rock and water gardens.
Location: MAP 17:E11, OS Ref. NJ938 084. In old Aberdeen. Entrance in the Chanonry.
Open: All year: Mon–Fri, 9am–4.30pm. Also May–Sept: Sat & Sun, 2–5pm.
Admission: Free.

DALLAS DHU DISTILLERY 🏛

Forres
Tel: 01309 676548
Owner: In the care of Historic Scotland   **Contact:** The Steward
A completely preserved time capsule of the distiller's craft. Wander at will through this fine old Victorian distillery then enjoy a dram. Visitor centre, shop and audio-visual theatre.
Location: MAP 16:P8, OS Ref. NJ035 566. 1m S of Forres off the A940.
Open: 1 Apr–30 Sept: daily, 9.30am–5.30pm, last ticket 5pm. 1 Oct–31 Mar: 9.30am–4.30pm, last ticket 4pm. Closed Thurs and Fri in winter.
Admission: Adult £5, Child £2.50, Conc. £4 (2007 prices).
ℹ Visitor centre. WC. 📷 🅿 €

DELGATIE CASTLE
TURRIFF, ABERDEENSHIRE AB53 5TD
www.delgatiecastle.com

Tel/Fax: 01888 563479   **E-mail:** jjohnson@delgatie-castle.freeserve.co.uk
Owner: Delgatie Castle Trust   **Contact:** Mrs Joan Johnson
"Best Visitor Experience" Award Winner. Dating from 1030 the Castle is steeped in Scottish history yet still has the atmosphere of a lived in home. It has some of the finest painted ceilings in Scotland, Mary Queen of Scots' bed-chamber, armour, Victorian clothes, fine furniture and paintings are displayed. Widest turnpike stair of its kind in Scotland. Clan Hay Centre. 17th best place in Britain for afternoon tea.
Location: MAP 17:D9, OS Ref. NJ754 506. Off A947 Aberdeen to Banff Road.
Open: Daily, 10am–5pm. Closed Christmas & New Year weeks.
Admission: Adult £5, Child/Conc. £4, Family £14. Groups (10+): £4.
ℹ No photography. 📷 🖭 🖳 Ground floor. WC. 🍴 Home-baking and lunches. 🎦 By arrangement. 🅿 🚌 🐕 🏠 6 x houses for self catering. 🅿

DRUM CASTLE & GARDEN ♨

Drumoak, by Banchory AB31 3EY
Tel: 0131 243 9300
Owner: The National Trust for Scotland
Owned for 653 years by one family, the Irvines. The combination over the years of a 13th century square tower, a very fine Jacobean mansion house and the additions of the Victorian lairds make Drum Castle unique among Scottish castles.
Location: MAP 17:D12, OS Ref. NJ796 004. Off A93, 3m W of Peterculter and 10m W of Aberdeen.

DRUMMUIR CASTLE

Drummuir, by Keith, Banffshire AB55 5JE
Tel: 01542 810332   **Fax:** 01542 810302
Owner: The Gordon-Duff Family   **Contact:** Alison Noakes
Castellated Victorian Gothic-style castle built in 1847 by Admiral Duff. 60ft high lantern tower with fine plasterwork. Family portraits, interesting artefacts and other paintings.
Location: MAP 17:B9, OS Ref. NJ372 442. Midway between Keith (5m) and Dufftown, off the B9014.
Open: 30 Aug–28 Sept: tours 2–5pm.
Admission: Adult £2, Child £1.50. Pre-arranged groups: Adult £2, Child £1.50.
🖳 🎦 Obligatory. 🅿 🐕 In grounds on leads.

DUFF HOUSE

Banff AB45 3SX
Tel: 01261 818181   **Fax:** 01261 818900
Contact: The Manager
One of the most imposing and palatial houses in Scotland, with a strong classical façade and a grand staircase leading to the main entrance.
Location: MAP 17:D8, OS Ref. NJ691 634. Banff. 47m NW of Aberdeen on A947.
Open: Apr–Oct: daily, 11am–5pm. Nov–Mar: Thur–Sun, 11am–4pm.
Admission: Adult £6, Conc. £5, Family £16. Groups (10+): £5. Free admission to shop, tearoom, grounds & woodland walks. (Prices may change April 2008.)

ELGIN CATHEDRAL

Elgin
Tel: 01343 547171
Owner: Historic Scotland **Contact:** The Steward
When entire this was perhaps the most beautiful of Scottish cathedrals, known as the Lantern of the North. 13th century, much modified after almost being destroyed in 1390 by Alexander Stewart, the infamous 'Wolf of Badenoch'. The octagonal chapterhouse is the finest in Scotland. You can see the bishop's home at Spynie Palace, 2m north of the town.
Location: MAP 17:A8, OS Ref. NJ223 630. In Elgin on the A96.
Open: 1 Apr–30 Sept: daily, 9.30am–5.30pm, last ticket 5pm. 1 Oct–31 Mar: daily, 9.30am–4.30pm, last ticket 4pm. Closed Thurs & Fri in winter.
Admission: Adult £4.50, Child £2.25, Conc. £3.50 (2007 prices). Joint entry ticket available with Spynie Palace.

FYVIE CASTLE

Turriff, Aberdeenshire AB53 8JS
Tel: 0131 243 9300
Owner: The National Trust for Scotland
The five towers of the castle bear witness to the five families who have owned it. Fyvie Castle has a fine wheel stair and a collection of arms and armour and paintings.
Location: MAP 17:D9, S Ref. NJ763 393. Off A947, 8m SE of Turriff, and 25m N of Aberdeen.

HADDO HOUSE

Tarves, Ellon, Aberdeenshire AB41 0ER
Tel: 0131 243 9300
Owner: The National Trust for Scotland
Designed by William Adam in 1731 for William, 2nd Earl of Aberdeen. Much of the interior is 'Adam Revival' carried out about 1880 for John, 7th Earl and 1st Marquess of Aberdeen and his Countess, Ishbel.
Location: MAP 17:E10, OS Ref. NJ868 348. Off B999, 4m N of Pitmedden, 10m NW of Ellon.

HUNTLY CASTLE

Huntly
Tel: 01466 793191
Owner: In the care of Historic Scotland **Contact:** The Steward
Known also as Strathbogie Castle, this glorious ruin stands in a beautiful setting on the banks of the River Deveron. Famed for its fine heraldic sculpture and inscribed stone friezes.
Location: MAP 17:C9, OS Ref. NJ532 407. In Huntly on the A96. N side of the town.
Open: 1 Apr–30 Sept: daily, 9.30am–5.30pm, last ticket 5pm. 1 Oct–31 Mar: 9.30am–4.30pm, last ticket 4pm. Closed Thurs & Fri in winter.
Admission: Adult £4.50, Child £2.25, Conc £3.50 (2007 prices).

Provost Skene's House

KILDRUMMY CASTLE

Alford, Aberdeenshire
Tel: 01975 571331
Owner: In the care of Historic Scotland **Contact:** The Steward
Though ruined, the best example in Scotland of a 13th century castle with a curtain wall, four round towers, hall and chapel of that date. The seat of the Earls of Mar, it was dismantled after the first Jacobite rising in 1715.
Location: MAP 17:C11, OS Ref. NJ455 164. 10m W of Alford on the A97. 16m SSW of Huntley.
Open: 1 Apr–30 Sept: daily, 9.30am–5.30pm, last ticket 5pm.
Admission: Adult £3.50, Child £1.75, Conc. £2.80 (2007 prices).

KILDRUMMY CASTLE GARDEN

Kildrummy, Aberdeenshire
Tel: 01975 571203 / 563451 **Contact:** Alastair J Laing
Ancient quarry, shrub and alpine gardens renowned for their interest and variety. Water gardens below ruined castle.
Location: MAP 17:C11, OS Ref. NJ455 164. On A97 off A944 10m SW of Alford. 16m SSW of Huntly.
Open: Apr–Oct: daily, 10am–5pm.
Admission: Adult £3.50, Child Free.

LEITH HALL

Huntly, Aberdeenshire AB54 4NQ
Tel: 0131 243 9300
Owner: The National Trust for Scotland **Contact:** The Property Manager
This mansion house, built around a courtyard was the home of the Leith family for almost 300 years.
Location: MAP 17:C10, OS Ref. NJ541 298. B9002, 1m W of Kennethmont, 7m S of Huntley.

LICKLEYHEAD CASTLE

Auchleven, Insch, Aberdeenshire AB52 6PN
Tel: 01651 821276
Owner: The Leslie family **Contact:** Mrs C Leslie
A beautifully restored Laird's Castle, Lickleyhead was built by the Leslies c1450 and extensively renovated in 1629 by John Forbes of Leslie, whose initials are carved above the entrance. It is an almost unspoilt example of the transformation from 'Chateau-fort' to 'Chateau-maison' and boasts many interesting architectural features.
Location: MAP 17:C10, OS Ref. NJ628 237. Auchleven is 2m S of Insch on B992. Twin pillars of castle entrance on left at foot of village.
Open: 1–10 May daily & 24 & 31 May: 21 Jun–6 Sept: Sats. 12 noon–2pm.
Admission: Free.
Unsuitable. Limited. No coaches. In grounds, on leads.

PITMEDDEN GARDEN

Ellon, Aberdeenshire AB41 0PD
Tel: 0131 243 9300
Owner: The National Trust for Scotland
The centrepiece of this property is the Great Garden which was originally laid out in 1675 by Sir Alexander Seton, 1st Baronet of Pitmedden.
Location: MAP 17:E10, OS Ref. NJ885 280. On A920 1m W of Pitmedden village & 14m N of Aberdeen.

PLUSCARDEN ABBEY

Nr Elgin, Moray IV30 8UA
Tel: 01343 890257 **Fax:** 01343 890258 **E-mail:** monks@pluscardenabbey.org
Contact: Brother Michael
Valliscaulian, founded 1230.
Location: MAP 17:A8, OS Ref. NJ142 576. On minor road 6m SW of Elgin. Follow B9010 for first mile.
Open: All year: 4.45am–8.30pm. Shop: 8.30am–5pm.
Admission: Free.

visit hudsons guide online

PROVOST SKENE'S HOUSE

Guestrow, off Broad Street, Aberdeen AB10 1AS

Tel: 01224 641086 **Fax:** 01224 632133

Owner: Aberdeen City Council   **Contact:** Christine Rew

Built in the 16th century, Provost Skene's House is one of Aberdeen's few remaining examples of early burgh architecture. Splendid room settings include a suite of Georgian rooms, an Edwardian nursery, magnificent 17th century plaster ceilings and wood panelling. The house also features an intriguing series of religious paintings in the Painted Gallery and changing fashions in the Costume Gallery.

Location: MAP 17:E11, OS Ref. NJ943 064. Aberdeen city centre, off Broad Street.

Open: Mon–Sat, 10am–5pm, Suns 1–4pm.

Admission: Free.

ST MACHAR'S CATHEDRAL TRANSEPTS

Old Aberdeen

Tel: 01667 460232

Owner: In the care of Historic Scotland

The nave and towers of the Cathedral remain in use as a church, and the ruined transepts are in care. In the south transept is the fine altar tomb of Bishop Dunbar (1514–32).

Location: MAP 17:E11, OS Ref. NJ939 088. In old Aberdeen. ½m N of King's College.

Admission: Free.

❄

SPYNIE PALACE ⚜

Elgin

Tel: 01343 546358

Owner: In the care of Historic Scotland   **Contact:** The Steward

Spynie Palace was the residence of the Bishops of Moray from the 14th century to 1686. The site is dominated by the massive tower built by Bishop David Stewart (1461–77) and affords spectacular views across Spynie Loch.

Location: MAP 17:A8, OS Ref. NJ231 659. 2m N of Elgin off the A941.

Open: 1 Apr–30 Sept: daily, 9.30am–5.30pm. 1 Oct–31 Mar: Sat & Sun, 9.30am–4.30pm. Last ticket 30 mins before closing.

Admission: Adult £3.50, Child £1.75, Conc. £2.80. Joint entry ticket with Elgin Cathedral: Adult £6, Child £3, Conc. £4 (2007 prices).

ℹ Picnic area. ⬚ ♿ WC. **P** ❄ €

TOLQUHON CASTLE ⚜

Aberdeenshire

Tel: 01651 851286

Owner: In the care of Historic Scotland   **Contact:** The Steward

Tolquhon was built for the Forbes family. The early 15th century tower was enlarged between 1584 and 1589 with a large mansion around the courtyard. Noted for its highly ornamented gatehouse and pleasance.

Location: MAP 17:E10, OS Ref. NJ874 286. 15m N of Aberdeen on the A920. 6m N of Ellon.

Open: 1 Apr–30 Sept: daily, 9.30am–5.30pm. 1 Oct–31 Mar: Sat & Sun, 9.30am–4.30pm. Last ticket 30 mins before closing.

Admission: Adult £3.50, Child £1.75, Conc. £2.80 (2007 prices).

ℹ Picnic area. ⬚ ♿ WC. **P** ❄ €

DAVID WELCH WINTER GARDENS – DUTHIE PARK

Polmuir Road, Aberdeen, Grampian Highlands AB11 7TH

Tel: 01224 585310 **Fax:** 01224 210532 **E-mail:** wintergardens@aberdeencity.gov.uk

www.aberdeencity.gov.uk

Owner: Aberdeen City Council   **Contact:** Alan Findlay

One of Europe's largest indoor gardens with many rare and exotic plants on show from all around the world.

Location: MAP 17:E11, OS Ref. NJ97 044. Just N of River Dee, 1m S of city centre.

Open: All year: daily from 9.30pm.

Admission: Free.

❄

Properties that **open all year** appear in the special index at the end of the book.

Duff House

■ Owner
The Dowager Countess Cawdor

■ Contact
The Administrator
David Broadfoot
Cawdor Castle
Nairn
Scotland IV12 5RD

Tel: 01667 404401
Fax: 01667 404674
E-mail: info@ cawdorcastle.com

■ Location
MAP 16:O9
OS Ref. NH850 500

From Edinburgh
A9, 3½ hrs,
Inverness 20 mins,
Nairn 10 mins.
Main road: A9, 14m.

Rail: Nairn
Station 5m.

Bus: Inverness to Nairn
bus route 200 yds.

Taxi: Cawdor Taxis
01667 404315.

Air: Inverness
Airport 5m.

■ Opening Times
Summer
1 May–12 October
Daily: 10am–5.30pm.
Last admission 5pm.

Winter
October–April
Groups by appointment,
admission prices on
application.

Auchindoune Garden
May–July: Tue & Thurs,
10am–4.30pm.

Otherwise by
appointment.

■ Admission
Summer
House & Garden
Adult	£7.90
Child (5–15yrs)	£4.90
OAP	£6.90
Student	£6.50
Family (2+5)	£24.00

Groups (20+)
Adult	£6.50
OAP/Student	£6.50
School Group (5–15yrs)	£4.00

Garden only
Per person	£4.00

RHS Access
Free admission to gardens
May, June, September &
October.

■ Special Events
June 7/8
Special Gardens
Weekend: Guided tours
of Gardens.

September 27
Living Food at Cawdor
Castle – A celebration of
organic food.

Conference/Function
ROOM	SIZE	MAX CAPACITY
Cawdor Hall		40

CAWDOR CASTLE
www.cawdorcastle.com

This splendid romantic castle, dating from the late 14th century, was built as a private fortress by the Thanes of Cawdor, and remains the home of the Cawdor family to this day. The ancient medieval tower was built around the legendary holly tree.

Although the house has evolved over 600 years, later additions, mainly of the 17th century, were all built in the Scottish vernacular style with slated roofs over walls and crow-stepped gables of mellow local stone. This style gives Cawdor a strong sense of unity, and the massive, severe exterior belies an intimate interior that gives the place a surprisingly personal, friendly atmosphere.

Good furniture, fine portraits and pictures, interesting objects and outstanding tapestries are arranged to please the family rather than to echo fashion or impress. Memories of Shakespeare's *Macbeth* give Cawdor an elusive, evocative quality that delights visitors.

Gardens
The flower garden also has a family feel to it, where plants are chosen out of affection rather than affectation. This is a lovely spot between spring and late summer. The walled garden has been restored with a holly maze, paradise garden, knot garden and thistle garden. The wild garden beside its stream leads into beautiful trails through spectacular mature mixed woodland, in which paths are helpfully marked and colour-coded. The Tibetan garden and traditional Scottish vegetable garden are at the Dower House at Auchindoune.

i 9 hole golf course, putting green, golf clubs for hire, Conferences, whisky tasting, musical entertainments, specialised garden visits. No photography, video taping or tripods inside.

Gift, book and wool shops.

Lunches, sherry or champagne receptions.

Visitors may alight at the entrance. WC. Only ground floor accessible.

Licensed Courtyard Restaurant, May–Oct, groups should book.

By arrangement.

P 250 cars and 25 coaches. Two weeks' notice for group catering, coach drivers/couriers free.

£4 per child. Room notes, quiz and answer sheet can be provided.

Guide dogs only.

DUNVEGAN CASTLE & GARDENS

www.dunvegancastle.com

■ **Owner**
Hugh Macleod of Macleod

■ **Contact**
The Administrator
Dunvegan Castle
Isle of Skye
Scotland IV55 8WF

Tel: 01470 521206
Fax: 01470 521205
Seal Tel: 01470 521500
E-mail: info@
dunvegancastle.com

■ **Location**
MAP 15:F9
OS Ref. NG250 480

1m N of village. NW corner of Skye.

From Inverness A82 to Invermoriston, A887 to Kyle of Lochalsh 82m. From Fort William A82 to Invergarry, A87 to Kyle of Lochalsh 76m.

Kyle of Lochalsh to Dunvegan 45m via Skye Bridge (toll).

Ferry: To the Isle of Skye, 'roll-on, roll-off', 30 minute crossing.

Rail: Inverness to Kyle of Lochalsh 3–4 trains per day – 45m.

Bus: Portree 25m, Kyle of Lochalsh 45m.

■ **Opening Times**
Summer
20 March–31 October
Daily: 10am–5.30pm.
Last admission 5pm.

Winter
1 November–mid March
Daily: 11am–4pm.
Last admission 3.30pm.

Closed Christmas Day, Boxing Day, New Year's Day and 2 January.

■ **Admission**
Summer
Castle & Gardens
Adult	£7.00
Child (5–15yrs)	£4.00
OAP/Student	£6.00
Groups (10+)	£6.00

Gardens only
Adult	£5.00
Child (5–15yrs)	£3.00
Senior/Student	£3.50

Seal Boats
Adult	£6.00
Child (5–12yrs)	£3.50
Child (under 5yrs)	£1.50

Winter
Adult	£5.00
Child (5–15yrs)	£2.50
Conc.	£3.50
Groups (10+)	£3.50

The Library

The Dining Room

Dunvegan is unique. It is the only Great House in the Western Isles of Scotland to have retained its family and its roof. It is the oldest home in the whole of Scotland continuously inhabited by the same family – the Chiefs of the Clan Macleod. A Castle placed on a rock by the sea – the curtain wall is dated before 1200 AD – its superb location recalls the Norse Empire of the Vikings, the ancestors of the Chiefs.

Dunvegan's continuing importance as a custodian of the Clan spirit is epitomised by the famous Fairy Flag, whose origins are shrouded in mystery but whose ability to protect both Chief and Clan is unquestioned. To enter Dunvegan is to arrive at a place whose history combines with legend to make a living reality.

Gardens

The gardens and grounds extend over some ten acres of woodland walks, peaceful formal lawns and a water garden dominated by two spectacular natural waterfalls. The temperate climate aids in producing a fine show of rhododendrons and azaleas, the chief glory of the garden in spring. One is always aware of the proximity of the sea and many garden walks finish at the Castle Jetty, from where traditional boats make regular trips to view the delightful Seal Colony.

Boat trips to seal colony. Pedigree Highland cattle. No photography in Castle.

Gift and craft shop.

Visitors may alight at entrance. WC.

Licensed restaurant, (cap. 70) special rates for groups, menus upon request. Tel: 01470 521310. Open late peak season for evening meals.

By appointment in English or Gaelic at no extra charge. If requested owner may meet groups, tour time 45mins.

120 cars and 10 coaches. Do not attempt to take passengers to Castle Jetty (long walk). If possible please book. Seal boat trip dependent upon weather.

Welcome by arrangement. Guide available on request.

In grounds only, on lead. Guide Dogs allowed in Castle.

4 self-catering units, 3 of which sleep 6 and 1 of which sleeps 7.

BALLINDALLOCH CASTLE

Ballindalloch, Banffshire AB37 9AX

Tel: 01807 500205 **Fax:** 01807 500210 **E-mail:** enquiries@ballindallochcastle.co.uk
www.ballindallochcastle.co.uk

Owner: Mr & Mrs Oliver Russell **Contact:** Mrs Clare Russell

Ballindalloch Castle is, first and foremost, a much-loved home, lived in by its original family, the MacPherson-Grants, since 1546. Filled with family memorabilia, including an important collection of 17th century Spanish paintings. Beautiful rock and rose gardens and river walks. The estate is home to the famous Aberdeen-Angus breed of cattle.

Location: MAP 17:A9, OS Ref. NJ178 366. 14 m NE of Grantown-on-Spey on A95. 22 m S of Elgin on A95.

Open: Good Fri–30 Sept: 10.30am–5pm. Closed Saturdays. Coaches outwith season by arrangement.

Admission: House & Grounds: Adult £7.50, Child (6–16) £4, Conc £6, Family (2+3) £18, Groups (20+) Adult £5, Child £2.50, Season Ticket £20. Grounds only: Adult £3.50, Child (6–16) £2, Conc £3, Season Ticket £10.

▣⬛& Ground floor and grounds only. WCs. ▆ ⬛ P ⬛ In dog walking area.

CASTLE LEOD

Strathpeffer IV14 9AA

Tel/Fax: 01997 421264 **E-mail:** cromartie@castle-leod.freeserve.co.uk

Owner/Contact: The Earl of Cromartie

Turreted 15th century tower house of rose-pink stone. Lived in by the Mackenzie family, chiefs of the clan, for 500 years and still very much a home where the family ensure a personal welcome. Magnificent setting below Ben Wyvis and amongst some of the finest trees in Scotland.

Location: MAP 16:M8, OS Ref. NH485 593. 1km E of Strathpeffer on the A834 Strathpeffer to Dingwall road.

Open: 24–27 Apr, 29 May–1 Jun, 25–29 Jun, 24–27 Jul, 28–31 Aug, 25–28 Sept: 2–5.30pm (last admission 4.45pm).

Admission: Adult £7, Child £2, Conc £5.

ⓘ No coaches. ⬛& Grounds only. WC. ⬛ By arrangement, all year. P No coach parking. ⬛ Guide dogs only. ⬛

CASTLE OF OLD WICK &

Wick

Tel: 01667 460232

Owner/Contact: Historic Scotland

Essential work to safeguard the future of Scotland's best-preserved Norse castle has been completed. Visitors can now enjoy visiting this dramatically located castle once again. One of the oldest keeps in Scotland, the castle is a simple square keep of at least three storeys. In addition to the tower the site contains the low-lying ruins of other buildings. These have never been excavated and are largely covered by turf in order to protect them from damage.

Location: MAP 17:B3, OS Ref. ND368 487. 1m S of Wick on Shore Road, E of A9.

Open: All year.

Admission: Free.

⬛

CAWDOR CASTLE ⬛

See page 474 for full page entry.

THE DOUNE OF ROTHIEMURCHUS ⬛

By Aviemore PH22 1QH

Tel: 01479 812345 **E-mail:** info@rothie.co.uk **www.rothiemurchus.net**

Owner: John Grant of Rothiemurchus, Lord Huntingtower

Contact: Rothiemurchus Centre

The family home of the Grants of Rothiemurchus was nearly lost as a ruin and has been under an ambitious repair programme since 1975. This exciting project may be visited on selected Mondays throughout the season and on other days by arrangement by email. Book with the Rothiemurchus Centre for a longer 2hr 'Highland Lady' tour which explores the haunts of Elizabeth Grant of Rothiemurchus, born 1797, author of Memoirs of a Highland Lady, who vividly described the Doune and its surroundings from the memories of her childhood.

Location: MAP 16:P11, OS Ref. NH900 100. 2m S of Aviemore on E bank of Spey river.

Open: House: selected Mons. Grounds: Apr–Aug: Mon, 10am–12.30pm & 2–4.30pm, also 1st Mon in the month during winter.

Admission: House only £2, Family £5. Tour (booking essential, 4+) £12.50pp. Group prices on application.

ⓘ Rothiemurchus Centre. ▣ ⬛ Obligatory. P Limited. ⬛ In grounds, on leads.

CASTLE OF MEY
THURSO, CAITHNESS KW14 8XH
www.castleofmey.org.uk

Tel: 01847 851473 **Fax:** 01847 851475 **E-mail:** castleofmey@totalise.co.uk
Owner: The Queen Elizabeth Castle of Mey Trust **Contact:** James Murray

The home of The Queen Mother in Caithness and the only property in Britain that she owned. She bought the Castle in 1952, saved it from becoming a ruin and developed the gardens. It became her ideal holiday home because of the beautiful surroundings and the privacy she was always given. Purpose-built Visitors' Centre with shop and tearoom and animal centre now open.

Location: MAP 17:B2, OS Ref. ND290 739. On A836 between Thurso and John O'Groats, just outside the village of Mey. 12m Thurso station, 18m Wick airport.

Open: 1 May–30 Sept: daily, 10.30am–4pm. Closed 31 Jul–12 Aug inc.

Admission: Adult £8, Child (16yrs and under) £3, Conc £7. Family £20. Booked groups (15+): £7. Gardens & grounds only: Adult £3, Conc £2.50.

ⓘ No photography in the Castle. ▣ ⬛& Partial. WCs. ▆ ⬛ By arrangement. P ⬛ ⬛ In grounds, on leads.

visit hudsons guide online

DUNROBIN CASTLE 🏰

GOLSPIE, SUTHERLAND KW10 6SF

www.highlandescape.com

Tel: 01408 633177 **Fax:** 01408 634081 **E-mail:** info@dunrobincastle.net
Owner: The Sutherland Trust **Contact:** Scott Morrison
Dates from the 13th century with additions in the 17th, 18th and 19th centuries. Wonderful furniture, paintings, library, ceremonial robes and memorabilia. Victorian museum in grounds with a fascinating collection including Pictish stones. Set in fine woodlands overlooking the sea. Magnificent formal gardens, one of few remaining French/Scottish formal parterres. Falconry display, telephone to confirm times.
Location: MAP 16:O6, OS Ref. NC850 010. 50m N of Inverness on A9. 1m NE of Golspie.
Open: 21 Mar–15 Oct: Mon–Sat, 10.30am–4.30pm, Sun, 12 noon–4.30pm. Jun, Jul & Aug daily, 10.30am–5.30pm, last admission ½ before closing.
Admission: Adult £7.50, Child £5, OAP/Student. £6.50, Family (2+2) £20. Booked groups: Adult £6, Child £4.70, OAP. £5.50.
🖼 🚻 ♿ Unsuitable for wheelchairs. 🍴 🍴 🎭 By arrangement. 🅿 ♿

DUNVEGAN CASTLE
& GARDENS 🏰

See page 475 for full page entry.

EILEAN DONAN CASTLE

Dornie, Kyle of Lochalsh, Wester Ross IV40 8DX
Tel: 01599 555202 **Fax:** 01599 555262 **E-mail:** eileandonan@btconnect.com
www.eileandonancastle.com **Contact:** David Win – Castle Keeper
A fortified site for eight hundred years, Eilean Donan now represents one of Scotland's most iconic images. Located at the point where three great sea lochs meet amidst stunning highland scenery on the main road to Skye. Spiritual home of Clan Macrae with century old links to Clan Mackenzie.
Location: MAP 16:J10, OS Ref. NG880 260. On A87 8m E of Skye Bridge.
Open: Apr–Oct: 10am–5pm.
Admission: Adult £4.95, Conc £3.95.

Ballindalloch Castle

FORT GEORGE 🏰

ARDERSIER BY INVERNESS IV1 2TD

Tel/Fax: 01667 460232
Owner: In the care of Historic Scotland **Contact:** Brian Ford
Built following the Battle of Culloden to subdue the Highlands, Fort George never saw a shot fired in anger. One of the most outstanding artillery fortifications in Europe with reconstructed barrack room displays. The Queen's Own Highlanders' Museum.
Location: MAP 16:O6, OS Ref. NH762 567. 11m NE of Inverness off the A96 by Ardersier.
Open: Apr–Sept: daily, 9.30am–6.30pm. Oct–Mar: daily, 9.30am–4.30pm. Last ticket sold 45 mins before closing.
Admission: Adult £6.50, Child £3.25, Conc. £5. 10% discount for groups (11+).
ℹ Picnic tables. 🖼 🍴 Private evening hire. ♿ Wheelchairs available. WCs.
🍴 🖼 🅿 ▪ Free if pre-booked. 🐕 In grounds, on leads. ✳ ♿ €

URQUHART CASTLE 🏰

DRUMNADROCHIT, LOCH NESS

Tel: 01456 450551
Owner: In the care of Historic Scotland **Contact:** Euan Fraser
The remains of one of the largest castles in Scotland dominate a rocky promontory on Loch Ness. Most of the existing buildings date from the 16th century. New visitor centre with original artefacts, audio-visual presentation, shop and café.
Location: MAP 16:M10, OS Ref. NH531 286. On Loch Ness, 1½m S of Drumnadrochit on A82.
Open: 1 Apr–30 Sept: daily, 9.30am–6pm. Last ticket 5.15pm. 1 Oct–31 Mar: daily, 9.30am–5pm. Last ticket 4.15pm.
Admission: Adult £6.50, Child £3.25, Conc £5 (2007 prices).
🖼 🍴 ♿ Partial. WCs. 🍴 🅿 🖼 ▪ Free if pre-booked. 🐕 Assistance dogs. ✳ €

BALFOUR CASTLE

Shapinsay, Orkney Islands KW17 2DY

Tel: 01856 711282 **Fax:** 01856 711283

Owner/Contact: Mrs Lidderdale

Built in 1848. Now a small private hotel specialising in house parties, weddings etc. A beautiful island escape.

Location: MAP 14, OS Ref. HY475 164 on Shapinsay Island, 3½m NNE of Kirkwall.

Open: May–Sept: Suns only, 2.15–5.30pm.

Admission: Admission includes boat fare, guided tour, gardens & afternoon tea. Bookings essential. Contact property for details.

BISHOP'S & EARL'S PALACES 👖

Kirkwall, Orkney

Tel: 01856 871918

Owner: In the care of Historic Scotland   **Contact:** The Steward

The Bishop's Palace is a 12th century hall-house with a round tower built by Bishop Reid in 1541–48. The adjacent Earl's Palace built in 1607 has been described as the most mature and accomplished piece of Renaissance architecture left in Scotland.

Location: MAP 14, Bishop's Palace: OS Ref. HY447 108. Earl's Palace: OS Ref. HY448 108. In Kirkwall on A960.

Open: 1 Apr–30 Sept: daily, 9.30am–5.30pm, last ticket 5pm.

Admission: Adult £3.50, Child £1.75, Conc. £2.80 (2007 prices). Joint entry ticket available for all the Orkney monuments.

€

BLACK HOUSE 👖

Arnol, Isle of Lewis

Tel: 01851 710395

Owner: In the care of Historic Scotland   **Contact:** The Steward

A traditional Lewis thatched house, fully furnished, complete with attached barn, byre and stockyard. A peat fire burns in the open hearth. New visitor centre open and restored 1920s croft house.

Location: MAP 15, OS Ref. NB320 500. In Arnol village, 11m NW of Stornoway on A858.

Open: 1 Apr–30 Sept: Mon–Sat, 9.30am–5.30pm, last ticket 5pm. 1 Oct–31 Mar: Mon–Sat, 9.30am–4.30pm, last ticket 4pm.

Admission: Adult £5, Child £2.50, Conc. £4. (2007 prices).

✳ €

BROCH OF GURNESS 👖

Aikerness, Orkney

Tel: 01856 751414

Owner: In the care of Historic Scotland   **Contact:** The Steward

Protected by three lines of ditch and rampart, the base of the broch is surrounded by Iron Age buildings.

Location: MAP 14, OS Ref. HY383 268. At Aikerness, about 14m NW of Kirkwall on A966.

Open: 1 Apr–30 Sept: daily, 9.30am–5.30pm, last ticket 5pm.

Admission: Adult £4.50, Child £2.25, Conc. £3.50 (2007 prices). Joint entry ticket available for all Orkney monuments.

€

CARRICK HOUSE

Carrick, Eday, Orkney KW17 2AB

Tel: 01857 622260

Owner: Mr & Mrs Joy   **Contact:** Mrs Rosemary Joy

17th century house built by John Stewart, Lord Kinclaven, Earl of Carrick younger brother of Patrick, 2nd Earl of Orkney in 1633. Scene of Pirate Gow's capture.

Location: MAP 14, OS Ref. NT227 773. N of island of Eday on minor roads W of B9063 just W of the shore of Calf Sound. Regular ferry service.

Open: Jun–Sept: occasional Suns by appointment only.

Admission: No fee. Donations to charity.

JARLSHOF PREHISTORIC & NORSE SETTLEMENT 👖

Shetland

Tel: 01950 460112

Owner: In the care of Historic Scotland   **Contact:** The Steward

Over 3 acres of remains spanning 3,000 years from the Stone Age. Oval-shaped Bronze Age houses, Iron Age broch and wheel houses. Viking long houses, medieval farmstead and 16th century laird's house.

Location: MAP 17, OS Ref. HY401 096. At Sumburgh Head, 22m S of Lerwick on the A970.

Open: 1 Apr–30 Sept: daily, 9.30am–5.30pm. Last ticket 30mins before closing.

Admission: Adult £4.50, Child £2.25, Conc. £3.50 (2007 prices).

€

Jarlshof Prehistoric and Norse Settlement

Ponies at St Ninian's, Shetland Islands

KISIMUL CASTLE

Castlebay, Isle of Barra HS9 5UZ
Tel: 01871 810313
Owner: In the care of Historic Scotland   **Contact:** The Monument Manager
The traditional seat of the chiefs of the clan Macneil, the castle stands on a rocky islet in a sea bay just off the island of Barra. It is the only significant surviving medieval castle in the Western Isles. Parts of Kisimul date back to the first half of the 1400s. The mighty curtain wall and strong tower helped fend off a series of attacks. It now makes a delightful place to visit and offers excellent views of the sea and the island.
Location: MAP 15 C:12. OS Ref. NL665 979. In Castlebay, Isle of Barra, five minute boat trip weather permitting.
Open: 1 Apr–30 Sept: daily, 9.30am–5.30pm.
Admission: Adult £4.50, Child £2.25, Conc. £3.50 (2007 prices). Includes boat trip.
🖾 €

MAESHOWE

Orkney
Tel: 01856 761606
Owner: In the care of Historic Scotland   **Contact:** The Steward
This world-famous tomb was built in Neolithic times, before 2700 BC. The large mound covers a stone-built passage and a burial chamber with cells in the walls. Runic inscriptions tell of how it was plundered of its treasures by Vikings.
Location: MAP 14, OS Ref. NY318 128. 9m W of Kirkwall on the A965.
Open: 1 Apr–30 Sept: daily, 9.30am–5.30pm. 1 Oct–31 Mar: daily, 9.30am–4.30pm.
Admission: Adult £5, Child £2.50, Conc. £4 (2007 prices). Joint entry ticket for all Orkney monuments available. Timed ticketing in place – please telephone for details, and to book. Admission and shop at nearby Tormiston Mill.
🖾 🛈 🅿 Limited. 🔀 ✳ €

RING OF BRODGAR STONE CIRCLE & HENGE

Stromness, Orkney
Tel: 01856 841815
Owner/Contact: In the care of Historic Scotland
A magnificent circle of upright stones with an enclosing ditch spanned by causeways. Of late Neolithic date.
Location: MAP 14, OS Ref. HY294 134. 5m NE of Stromness.
Open: All year.
Admission: Free.
✳

©Historic Scotland Photographic Library

SKARA BRAE & SKAILL HOUSE

SANDWICH, ORKNEY

Tel: 01856 841815
Owner: Historic Scotland/Major M R S Macrae   **Contact:** The Steward
Skara Brae is one of the best preserved groups of Stone Age houses in Western Europe. Built before the Pyramids, the houses contain stone furniture, hearths and drains. Visitor centre and replica house with joint admission with Skaill House – 17th century home of the laird who excavated Skara Brae.
Location: MAP 14, OS6 HY231 188. 19m NW of Kirkwall on the B9056.
Open: Apr–Sept: daily, 9.30am–5.30pm. Oct–Mar: daily, 9.30am–4.30pm. Last ticket 45 mins before closing.
Admission: Apr–Sept: Adult £6.50, Child £3.25, Conc. £5. Oct–Mar: Adult £5.50, Child £2.75, Conc. £4.50 (2007 prices). 10% discount for groups (11+). Joint ticket with other Orkney sites available.
🛈 Visitor centre. 🖾 ♿ Partial. WCs. 🍴 Licensed. 🅿
🐾 Free school visits when booked. 🐕 Guide dogs only. ✳ €

TANKERNESS HOUSE

Broad Street, Kirkwall, Orkney
Tel: 01856 873535   **Fax:** 01856 871560
Owner: Orkney Islands Council   **Contact:** Steve Callaghan
A fine vernacular 16th century town house contains The Orkney Museum.
Location: MAP 14, OS Ref. HY446 109. In Kirkwall opposite W end of cathedral.
Open: Oct–Apr: Mon–Sat, 10.30am–12.30pm & 1.30–5pm. May–Sept: Mon–Sat, 10.30am–5pm. Gardens always open. (2007 details.)
Admission: Free.

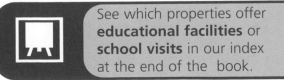

See which properties offer **educational facilities** or **school visits** in our index at the end of the book.

Castell Coch, South Wales
©CADW Welsh Historic Monuments Crown Copyright

Wales

The traditional border between Wales and England is Offa's Dyke, built by King Offa between 757 and 796AD. North Wales is a holiday area attracting lovers of coast and countryside alike. To the west lies Snowdon, a popular destination for climbers and walkers. To the east is a gentler landscape of moorlands, valleys and the hills of the Welsh Borders. Further south, the Gower Peninsula was the first place in Britain to be designated an Area of Outstanding Natural Beauty.

■ Owner
Paul and Victoria Humpherston

■ Contact
Paul Humpherston
The Hall at
Abbey-Cwm-Hir
Nr Llandrindod Wells
Powys LD1 6PH

Tel: 01597 851727
E-mail: info@
abbeycwmhir.com

■ Location
MAP 6:I8
OS Ref. SO054 711

7m NW of Llandrindod
Wells, 6m E of Rhayader,
turn for Abbey-Cwm-Hir
1 mile north of
Crossgates on the A483.

■ Opening Times
All year daily for pre-
booked tours only, at
10.30am, 2pm
and 7pm.

■ Admission
House Tour & Gardens
Adult   £13.00
Child (under 12) £5.00

Groups (10+) or
repeat visitors   £11.00

Gardens only
Adult   £5.00

■ Special Events
November 10 onwards
Each of the 52 rooms is
decorated for Christmas.

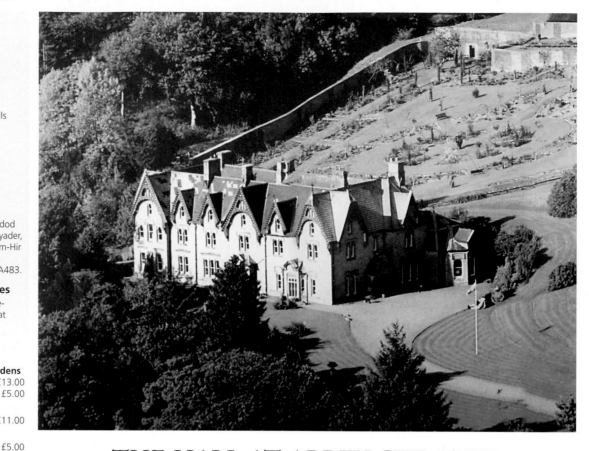

THE HALL AT ABBEY-CWM-HIR

www.abbeycwmhir.com

In a mid Wales setting of breathtaking beauty, history and romance, The Hall and its 12 landscaped acres overlook the ruins of the 12th century Cisterian 'Abbey of the Long Valley' in which Llewellyn the Last is buried and the church. It is Grade II* listed as one of Wales' finest examples of Victorian Gothic Revival architecture.

Having spent nine years restoring the house and the gardens, the owners now personally conduct unique tours of all 52 rooms in a true family atmosphere. The tours are not just about the architecture of an historic house. Visitors also experience stunning interior designs in all rooms, and items from a lifetime of collecting used as furnishings.

Each of the 52 rooms contain their original features. In the formal reception rooms and bedrooms these include 14 marble fireplaces; rococo and stained glass ceilings; gothic windows and shutters; and a Minton Hollins tiled floor.

In the former domestic rooms, features include 10 further iron fireplaces; original slate slab surfaces; and vaulted cellar ceilings.

The house bursts with interior design ideas. These include images hand-painted on to existing wallpapers; bathrooms themed to trains, castles and the 1930s; bedrooms themed to schooldays, the seaside and transport; the Arthurian room; and the eclectic Garden Room.

Overall collections include clocks and phonographs; signs and packaging; kitchen memorabilia and children's books in original bindings; china and vehicles; and The Abbey-Cwm-Hir Art and Photographic Collections.

The gardens (also listed) include a romantic walled garden; a lake and a waterfall; sweeping lawns and terraces; 4 courtyards; and some particularly fine mixed woodland.

Entrance Hallway

ⓘ Visitors are asked to remove outside shoes for the tour of the house, slippers can be provided.

🚻

♿ Partial.

☕ Licensed.

🍴 Licensed.

🚶 Obligatory.

🅿 Ample for cars, limited for coaches.

🐕 In grounds on leads.

❄

🎭

ABERCONWY HOUSE

Castle Street, Conwy LL32 8AY
Tel: 01492 592246 **Fax:** 01492 564818
Owner: The National Trust

Dating from the 14th century, this is the only medieval merchant's house in Conwy to have survived the turbulent history of this walled town for nearly six centuries. Furnished rooms and an audio-visual presentation show daily life from different periods in its history.

Location: MAP 5:H2, OS Ref. SH781 777. At junction of Castle Street and High Street.
Open: 21 Mar–2 Nov: Wed–Mon, 11am–5pm. Last adm. 30 mins before close. Shop: 1 Mar–31 Dec: daily (closed 25/26 Dec), 10am–5pm (5.30pm 25 Mar–29 Oct). Jan–Feb 2007: Wed–Sun, 11am–5pm. Suns open at 11am.
Admission: Adult £3, Child £1.50, Family (2+2) £7.50. Pre-booked groups (15+) Adult £2.50, Child £1. National Trust members Free.

ⓘ No indoor photography. ⬚ All year. ⒡ By arrangement. ⌂
🅿 In town car parks only. ▮ 🖼 Guide dogs only.

© CADW: Welsh Historic Monuments. Crown copyright

BEAUMARIS CASTLE ✚

BEAUMARIS, ANGLESEY LL58 8AP

www.cadw.wales.gov.uk

Tel: 01248 810361
Owner: In the care of Cadw **Contact:** The Custodian

The most technically perfect medieval castle in Britain, standing midway between Caernarfon and Conwy, commanding the old ferry crossing to Anglesey. A World Heritage Listed Site.

Location: MAP 5:G2, OS Ref. SH608 762. 5m NE of Menai Bridge (A5) by A545. 7m from Bangor.
Open: 1 Apr–31 May & Oct: daily, 9.30am–5pm. 1 Jun–30 Sept: daily, 9.30am–6pm. 1 Nov–31 Mar: Mon–Sat, 9.30am–4pm, Suns 11am–4pm.
Admission: Adult £3.50, Child (under 16 yrs)/Conc. £3, Child under 5yrs Free, Family (2+3) £10.

⬚ ♿ ⒡ 🅿 🖼 Guide dogs only. ✳

©NTPL/Nick Meers

Plas Newydd

BODELWYDDAN CASTLE

Bodelwyddan, Denbighshire LL18 5YA
Tel: 01745 584060 **Fax:** 01745 584563 **E-mail:** enquiries@bodelwyddan-castle.co.uk
www.bodelwyddan-castle.co.uk
Owner: Bodelwyddan Castle Trust **Contact:** Kevin Mason

Journey back in time as you tour this magnificently restored Victorian country house and view exquisite pieces from the National Portrait Gallery, Royal Academy and Victoria & Albert Museum. Explore 260 acres of parkland including formal gardens, woodland walks and WW1 practice trenches. Hands on Victorian Toys and Games Room. Exciting events and exhibition schedule. Café specialising in traditional, freshly prepared products.

Location: MAP 6:I2, OS Ref. SH999 749. Follow signs Junction 25 off A55 expressway. 2m W of St Asaph, opposite Marble Church.
Open: Easter–end Oct: daily except Fri, 10.30am–5pm. Aug: daily, 10.30am–5pm. Nov–Easter: Thurs, Sats & Suns, 10.30am–4.30pm. Last admission 30 mins before close. Visit website for details of Christmas and New Year opening.
Admission: Adult £5, Child (5–16yrs) £2 (under 4yrs free), Conc. £4.50, Disabled £3. Family (1+3) £10, (2+2) £12. Discounts for schools & groups. Season ticket available.

⬚ ⓣ ♿ Partial. WCs. ▮ ⒡ By arrangement. ⌂ Free. 🅿 ▮ 🖼 Assistance dogs only. ▲ ✳ ⊻

BODNANT GARDEN

Tal-y-Cafn, Colwyn Bay LL28 5RE
Tel: 01492 650460 **Fax:** 01492 650448 **E-mail:** office@bodnantgarden.co.uk
www.bodnantgarden.co.uk
Owner: The National Trust

Bodnant Garden is one of the finest gardens in the country not only for its magnificent collections of rhododendrons, camellias and magnolias but also for its idyllic setting above the River Conwy with extensive views of the Snowdonia range.

Location: MAP 5:H2, OS Ref. SH801 723. 8 miles S of Llandudno and Colwyn Bay, off A470. Signposted from A55, exit at Junction 19.
Open: 8 Mar–2 Nov: daily, 10am–5pm. Tearoom: as garden. Plant Centre: Daily, 10am–5pm.
Admission: Adult £7.20, Child £3.60. Groups (20+): Adult £5.50, Child £3.25. RHS members free.

⬚ ♿ ♿ Partial. WCs. ▮ 🅿 🖼 Guide dogs only.

BODRHYDDAN 🏛

Rhuddlan, Clwyd LL18 5SB
Tel: 01745 590414 **Fax:** 01745 590155 **E-mail:** bodrhyddan@hotmail.com
www.bodrhyddan.co.uk
Owner/Contact: Colonel The Lord Langford OBE DL

The home of Lord Langford and his family, Bodrhyddan is basically a 17th century house with 19th century additions by the famous architect, William Eden Nesfield, although traces of a 15th century semi-fortified Welsh farmhouse exist. The house has been in the hands of the same family since it was built over 500 years ago. There are notable pieces of armour, pictures, period furniture, a 3,000 year old mummy, a formal parterre, a woodland garden and attractive picnic areas. Bodrhyddan is a Grade I listing, making it one of few in Wales to remain in private hands.

Location: MAP 6:I2, OS Ref. SJ045 788. On the A5151 midway between Dyserth and Rhuddlan, 4m SE of Rhyl.
Open: Jun–Sept inclusive: Tues & Thurs, 2–5.30pm.
Admission: House & Gardens: Adult £5, Child £2.50 Gardens only: Adult £2, Child £1.
♿ Partial. ▮ ⒡ Obligatory. 🅿 ▲

BRYN BRAS CASTLE

Llanrug, Caernarfon, Gwynedd LL55 4RE
www.brynbrascastle.co.uk
Tel/Fax: 01286 870210 **E-mail:** holidays@brynbrascastle.co.uk
Owner: Mr & Mrs N E Gray-Parry **Contact:** Marita Gray-Parry

Built in the Neo-Romanesque style in c1830, on an earlier structure, and probably designed by Thomas Hopper, it stands in the Snowdonian Range. The tranquil garden includes a hill-walk with fine views of Mt Snowdon, Anglesey and the sea. Bryn Bras, a much loved home, offers a delightful selection of apartments for holidays for twos within the Grade II* listed castle. Many local restaurants, inns.

Location: MAP 5:F3, OS Ref. SH543 625. ½m off A4086 at Llanrug, 4½m E of Caernarfon.
Open: Only by appointment.
Admission: By arrangement. No children please.

🅿 🖼 🏠 Self-catering apartments for two within castle. ✳

CADW: Welsh Historic Monuments. Crown copyright

CAERNARFON CASTLE ✠
CASTLE DITCH, CAERNARFON LL55 2AY

www.cadw.wales.gov.uk

Tel: 01286 677617

Owner: In the care of Cadw   **Contact:** The Custodian

The most famous, and perhaps the most impressive castle in Wales. Taking nearly 50 years to build, it proved the costliest of Edward I's castles. A World Heritage Listed Site.

Location: MAP 5:F3, OS Ref. SH477 626. In Caernarfon, just W of town centre.

Open: 1 Apr–31 May & Oct: daily, 9.30am–5pm. 1 Jun–30 Sept: daily, 9.30am–6pm. 1 Nov–31 Mar: Mon–Sat, 9.30am–4pm, Suns 11am–4pm.

Admission: Adult £4.90, Child (under 16 yrs)/Conc. £4.50, Child under 5yrs Free, Family (2+3 all children under 16yrs) £15.

🖵 🅿 ♿ Guide dogs only. ✱

CHIRK CASTLE ❧

Chirk LL14 5AF

Tel: 01691 777701   **Fax:** 01691 774706   **E-mail:** chirkcastle@nationaltrust.org.uk

Owner: The National Trust

700 year old Chirk Castle, a magnificent marcher fortress, commands fine views over the surrounding countryside. Rectangular with a massive drum tower at each corner, the castle has beautiful formal gardens with clipped yews, roses and a variety of flowering shrubs. The dramatic dungeon is a reminder of the castle's turbulent history, whilst later occupants have left elegant state rooms, furniture, tapestries and portraits. The castle was sold for five thousand pounds to Sir Thomas Myddelton in 1595, and his descendants continue to live in part of the castle today.

Location: MAP 6:J4, OS Ref. SJ275 388. 8m S of Wrexham off A483, 2m from Chirk village.

Open: Castle & Shop: 2–10 Feb, Sat & Sun, 11am–4pm, 13–17 Feb, Wed–Sun; 11am–4pm, 15 Mar–30 Sept, Wed–Sun & BH Mons (+Tues Jul–Aug), 12 noon–5pm. 1 Oct–2 Nov, Weds–Sun, 11am–4pm, 6–14 Dec, Sat & Sun, 11am–5pm. Last admission ½hr before closing. Garden: as Castle, 10am–6pm (5pm in Oct), last admission 1hr before closing. Tearoom: as Castle, 10am–5pm (4pm in Oct). Shop: As Castle, 10am–6pm (5pm in Oct). NT shop as Castle, 11am–5pm (closes 4pm in Feb & Oct.) Home Farm & Estate: as Garden (not open Dec, closes 5pm in Oct).

*Admission: House & Garden: Adult £8.80, Child £4.40, Family £22. Pre-booked groups (15+): Adult £7.50, Child £3.75. Garden only: Adults £6.20, Child £3.10, Family £15.50. Pre-booked groups: Adult £5.20, Child £2.60. *includes a voluntary donation but visitors can choose to pay the standard prices displayed at the property and on the website.

ℹ No indoor photography. 🖵 ✱ ♿ 🖳 Licensed. 🎦 By arrangement. 🅿 ♿ ♿ Guide dogs only. ▲ 🛏

For **Civil wedding** venues in North Wales see our special index at the end of the book.

COCHWILLAN OLD HALL

Talybont, Bangor, Gwynedd LL57 3AZ

Tel: 01248 355853

Owner: R C H Douglas Pennant   **Contact:** Miss M D Monteith

A fine example of medieval architecture with the present house dating from about 1450. It was probably built by William Gryffydd who fought for Henry VII at Bosworth. Once owned in the 17th century by John Williams who became Archbishop of York. The house was restored from a barn in 1971.

Location: MAP 5:G2, OS Ref. SH606 695. 3½m SE of Bangor. 1m SE of Talybont off A55.

Open: By appointment.

Admission: Please telephone for details.

✱

Cadw: Welsh Historic Monuments. Crown Copyright

CONWY CASTLE ✠
CONWY LL32 8AY

www.cadw.wales.gov.uk

Tel: 01492 592358

Owner: In the care of Cadw   **Contact:** The Custodian

Taken together the castle and town walls are the most impressive of the fortresses built by Edward I, and remain the finest and most impressive in Britain. A World Heritage Listed Site.

Location: MAP 5:H2, OS Ref. SH783 774. Conwy by A55 or B5106.

Open: 1 Apr–31 May & Oct: daily, 9.30am–5pm. 1 Jun–30 Sept: daily, 9.30am–6pm. 1 Nov–31 Mar: Mon–Sat, 9.30am–4pm, Suns 11am–4pm.

Admission: Adult £4.50, Child (under 16yrs)/Conc. £4, Child under 5yrs Free, Family (2+3) £14. Joint ticket for entry to Conwy Castle and Plas Mawr: Adult £6.50, Conc. £5.50, Family (2+3) £18.50. (Prices subject to review Mar 2007.)

🖵 🎦 By arrangement. 🅿 ♿ Guide dogs only. ✱

CRICCIETH CASTLE ✠

Castle Street, Criccieth, Gwynedd LL52 0DP

Tel: 01766 522227   www.cadw.wales.gov.uk

Owner: In the care of Cadw   **Contact:** The Custodian

Overlooking Cardigan Bay, Criccieth Castle is the most striking of the fortresses built by the native Welsh Princes. Its inner defences are dominated by a powerful twin-towered gatehouse.

Location: MAP 5:F4, OS Ref. SH500 378. A497 to Criccieth from Porthmadog or Pwllheli.

Open: 1 Apr–31 May & Oct : daily, 10am–5pm. 1 Nov–31 Mar: Fri & Sat, 9.30am–4pm, Suns, 11am–4pm. (Open and unstaffed with no admission charge at all other times.) Closed 24–26 Dec & 1 Jan.

Admission: Adult £2.90, Child (under 16yrs)/Conc. £2.50, Child under 5yrs Free, Family (2+3 all children under 16yrs) £8.30.

🖵 🅿 ♿ Guide dogs only. ✱

DENBIGH CASTLE ✠

Denbigh, Clwyd

Tel: 01745 813385   **www.cadw.wales.gov.uk**

Owner: In the care of Cadw   **Contact:** The Custodian

Crowning the summit of a prominent outcrop dominating the Vale of Clwyd, the principal feature of this spectacular site is the great gatehouse dating back to the 11th century. Some of the walls can still be walked by visitors.

Location: MAP 6:I2, OS Ref. SJ052 658. Denbigh via A525, A543 or B5382.

Open: 1 Apr–30 Sept: Mon–Fri, 10am–5.30pm, Sats & Suns, 9.30am–5.30pm. (Open and unstaffed at all other times with no admission charge.)

Admission: Castle: Adult £2.90, Child (under 16yrs)/Conc. £2.50, Child under 5 yrs Free, Family (2+3 all children under 16yrs) £8.30.

🄰 🅿 ♿ Guide dogs only. ❋

DOLBELYDR

Trefnant, Denbighshire LL16 5AG

Tel: 01628 825925   **E-mail:** bookings@landmarktrust.org.uk

www.landmarktrust.org.uk

Owner/Contact: The Landmark Trust

A 16th century, Grade II* listed building, a fine example of a 16th century gentry house and has good claim to be the birthplace of the modern Welsh language. It was at Dolbelydr that Henry Salesbury wrote his Grammatica Britannica. Dolbelydr is cared for by The Landmark Trust, a building preservation charity who let it for holidays. Full details of Dolbelydr and 184 other historic and architecturally important buildings are featured in the Landmark Trust Handbook (£11.50 refundable against a booking).

Location: MAP 6:I2, OS Ref. SJ031 709.

Open: Available for holidays for max 6 people throughout the year. Open Days on 8 days throughout the year. Other visits by appointment. Contact the Landmark Trust for details.

Admission: Free on Open Days.

🖾

DOLWYDDELAN CASTLE ✠

Blaenau Ffestiniog, Gwynedd

Tel: 01690 750366   **www.cadw.wales.gov.uk**

Owner: In the care of Cadw   **Contact:** The Custodian

Standing proudly on a ridge, this stern building remains remarkably intact and visitors cannot fail to be impressed with the great solitary square tower, built by Llewelyn the Great in the early 13th century.

Location: MAP 5:G3, OS Ref. SH722 522. A470(T) Blaenau Ffestiniog to Betws-y-Coed, 1m W of Dolwyddelan.

Open: All year: Mon–Sat, 10am–6pm (1 Oct–31 Mar, 4pm), Suns 11am–4pm.

Admission: Adult £2.50, Child (5–16yrs)/Conc. £2, Child under 5 yrs Free, Family (2+3 all children under 16yrs) £7. Children under 16 must be accompanied by an adult. Prices vaild until 31 March 2008.

🅿 ♿ Guide dogs only. ❋

ERDDIG ⌘

Nr Wrexham LL13 0YT

Tel: 01978 355314   **Fax:** 01978 313333   **Info Line:** 01978 315151

Owner: The National Trust

One of the most fascinating houses in Britain, not least because of the unusually close relationship that existed between the family of the house and their servants. The beautiful and evocative range of outbuildings includes kitchen, laundry, bakehouse, stables, sawmill, smithy and joiner's shop, while the stunning state rooms display most of their original 18th & 19th century furniture and furnishings, including some exquisite Chinese wallpaper.

Location: MAP 6:K3, OS Ref. SJ326 482. 2m S of Wrexham.

Open: House: 15 mar–2 Nov, Sat–Wed (+Thur Jul–Aug), 12 noon–5pm (Mar & Oct closes 4pm). 8 Nov–21 Dec, Sat & Sun, 12 noon–4pm (Limited Access). Garden & Outbuildings: 9 Feb–9 Mar, Sat & Sun, 11am–4pm ; 15–31 Mar, Sat–Wed, 11am–5pm; 1 Apr–30 Jun, Sun–Wed, 11am–6pm; 1 Jul–31 Aug, Sat–Thur, 10am–6pm; 1–30 Sept, Sat–Wed, 11am–6pm; 1 Oct–2 Nov, Sat–Wed, 11am–5pm; 8 Nov–21 Dec, Sat & Sun, 11am–4pm.

*Admission: Adult £9.40, Child £4.70, Family (2+3) £23.50. Groups, Adult £7.20, Child £3.60. Garden & Outbuildings only: Adult £6, Child £3, Family £15. Groups, Adult £4.50, Child £2.25. NT members Free. *includes a voluntary donation but visitors can choose to pay the standard prices displayed at the property and on the website.

🄰 ❋ ♿ Partial. WCs. 🍴 Licensed. 🎞 AV presentation. 🅿 ■ ♿ Guide dogs only.

FFERM

Pontblyddyn, Mold, Flintshire

Tel: 01352 770204

Owner: The Executors of the late Dr M Jones Mortimer

Contact: Miss Miranda Kaufmann

17th century farmhouse. Viewing is limited to 7 persons at any one time. Prior booking is recommended. No toilets or refreshments.

Location: MAP 6:J3, OS Ref. SJ279 603. Access from A541 in Pontblyddyn, 3½m SE of Mold.

Open: 2nd Wed in every month, 2–5pm. Pre-booking is recommended.

Admission: £4.

⌘ ❋

GWYDIR CASTLE

LLANRWST, GWYNEDD LL26 0PN

www.gwydircastle.co.uk

Tel/Fax: 01492 641687   **E-mail:** info@gwydircastle.co.uk

Owner/Contact: Mr & Mrs Welford

Gwydir Castle is situated in the beautiful Conwy Valley and is set within a Grade I listed, 10 acre garden. Built by the illustrious Wynn family c1500, Gwydir is a fine example of a Tudor courtyard house, incorporating re-used medieval material from the dissolved Abbey of Maenan. Further additions date from c1600 and c1828. The important 1640s panelled Dining Room has now been reinstated, following its repatriation from the New York Metropolitan Museum.

Location: MAP 5:H3, OS Ref. SH795 610. ½m W of Llanrwst on B5106.

Open: 1 Mar–31 Oct: daily, 10am–4pm. Closed Mons & Sats (except BH weekends). Limited openings at other times. Please telephone for details.

Admission: Adult £4, Child £2, OAP £3.50. Group discount 10%.

🍴 ♿ Partial. ☕ By arrangement. 🎫 By arrangement. 🅿 ♿ 🛏 2 doubles. ▲

HAFOD

Hafod Estate Office, Pontrhydygroes, Ystrad-Meurig, Ceredigion SY25 6DX

Tel: 01974 282568   **Fax:** 01974 282579   **E-mail:** hafod.estate@forestry.gsi.gov.uk

www.hafod.org

Owner: Forestry Commission Wales   **Contact:** The Hafod Trust

Picturesque landscape, one of the most significant in Britain located in a remote valley and improved by Col Thomas Johnes 1780–1816. Ten miles of restored walks featuring cascades, bridges and wonderful views set in 500 acres of woodland and parkland. The epitome of the Picturesque and the Sublime.

Location: MAP 5:H7, OS Ref. SN768 736. 15 miles E of Aberystwyth near Devils Bridge, car park, off B4574.

Open: All year, daylight hours.

Admission: Free – guide book available at local shops or website.

♿ WC. 🎫 By arrangement. 🅿 ■ ♿ In grounds on leads. ❋

THE HALL AT ABBEY-CWM-HIR   *See page 482 for full page entry.*

HARLECH CASTLE ✛
Harlech LL46 2YH
Tel: 01766 780552   www.cadw.wales.gov.uk
Owner: In the care of Cadw   **Contact:** The Custodian
Set on a towering rock above Tremadog Bay, this seemingly impregnable fortress is the most dramatically sited of all the castles of Edward I. A World Heritage Listed Site.
Location: MAP 5:F4, OS Ref. SH581 312. Harlech, Gwynedd on A496 coast road.
Open: 1 Apr–31 May & Oct: daily, 9.30am–5pm. 1 Jun–30 Sept: daily, 9.30am–6pm. 1 Nov–31 Mar: Mon–Sat, 9.30am–4pm. Closed 24–26 Dec & 1 Jan.
Admission: Adult £3.50, Child (under 16yrs)/Conc. £3, Child under 5 yrs Free, Family (2+3 all children under 16yrs) £10. Children under 16 must be accompanied by an adult. Prices subject to review in March 2008.
⬛ 🅿 ♿ Guide dogs only. ✴

HARTSHEATH 🏠
Pontblyddyn, Mold, Flintshire
Tel/Fax: 01352 770204
Owner: The Executors of the late Dr M Jones Mortimer
Contact: Miss Miranda Kaufmann
18th and 19th century house set in parkland. Viewing is limited to 7 persons at any one time. Prior booking is recommended. No toilets or refreshments.
Location: MAP 6:J3, OS Ref. SJ287 602. Access from A5104, 3½m SE of Mold between Pontblyddyn and Penyffordd.
Open: 1st, 3rd & 5th Wed in every month, 2–5pm.
Admission: £4.
♿ ✴

ISCOYD PARK
Nr Whitchurch, Shropshire SY13 3AT
Owner/Contact: Mr P C Godsal
18th century Grade II* listed redbrick house in park.
Location: MAP 6:L4, OS Ref. SJ504 421. 2m W of Whitchurch on A525.
Open: By written appointment only.
🅃 ✴

PENRHYN CASTLE ⚜
Bangor LL57 4HN
Tel: 01248 353084   **Infoline:** 01248 371337   **Fax:** 01248 371281
Owner: The National Trust
This dramatic neo-Norman fantasy castle sits between Snowdonia and the Menai Strait. Built by Thomas Hopper between 1820 and 1845 for the wealthy Pennant family, who made their fortune from Jamaican sugar and Welsh slate. The castle is crammed with fascinating things such as a 1-ton slate bed made for Queen Victoria.
Location: MAP 5:G2, OS Ref. SH602 720. 1m E of Bangor, at Llandygai (J11, A55).
Open: Castle: 19 Mar–2 Nov, daily (except Tues), 12 noon–5pm. Grounds & Tearoom: as Castle. Shop & Museums: 19 Mar–2 Nov, daily (except Tues), 11am–5pm. Victorian kitchen, as Castle but last admission 4.45pm. Last audio tour 4pm.
Admission: Adult £9, Child £4.50, Family (2+2) £22.50. Pre-booked groups (15+) £7.50. Garden & Stableblock Exhibitions only: Adult £5.60, Child £2.80. Audio tour: £1 (including NT members). NT members Free.
⬛ 🎦 Licensed. 🍴 ⬛ ♿ Guide dogs only. ⬛

PLAS BRONDANW GARDENS 🏠
Plas Brondanw, Llanfrothen, Gwynedd LL48 6SW
Tel: 01743 241181/07880 766741
Owner: Trustees of the Second Portmeirion Foundation.
Italianate gardens with topiary.
Location: MAP 5:G4, OS Ref. SH618 423. 3m N of Penrhyndeudraeth off A4085, on Croesor Road.
Open: All year: daily, 9.30am–5.30pm. Coaches accepted, please book.
Admission: Adult £3, Subsequent adult £2pp, Child Free if accompanied by an adult.

For **special events** in North Wales see our special index at the end of the book.

Cadw: Welsh Historic Monuments. Crown Copyright

PLAS MAWR ✛
HIGH STREET, CONWY LL32 8EF
www.cadw.wales.gov.uk
Tel: 01492 580167
Owner: In the care of Cadw   **Contact:** The Custodian
The best preserved Elizabethan town house in Britain, the house reflects the status of its builder Robert Wynn. A fascinating and unique place allowing visitors to sample the lives of the Tudor gentry and their servants, Plas Mawr is famous for the quality and quantity of its decorative plasterwork.
Location: MAP 5:H2, OS Ref. SH781 776. Conwy by A55 or B5106 or A547.
Open: 1 Apr–31 May, Sept & Oct: Tues–Suns & BH Mons, 9.30am–5pm (4pm in Oct). 1 Jun–31 Aug: Tues–Suns & BH Mons, 9.30am–6pm.
Admission: Adult £4.90, Child (under 16yrs)/Conc. £4.50, Child under 5yrs Free, Family (2+3 all children under 16yrs) £15. Children under 16 must be accompanied by an adult. Joint ticket for entry to Conwy Castle and Plas Mawr: Adult £6.50, Conc. £5.50, Family (2+3) £18.50.
⬛ 🅿 Limited. ⬛ ♿ Guide dogs only.

PLAS NEWYDD ⚜
Llanfairpwll, Anglesey LL61 6DQ
Tel: 01248 714795   **Infoline:** 01248 715272   **Fax:** 01248 713673
Owner: The National Trust
Set amidst breathtaking beautiful scenery and with spectacular views of Snowdonia. Fine spring garden and Australasian arboretum with an understorey of shrubs and wildflowers. Summer terrace, and, later, massed hydrangeas and Autumn colour. A woodland walk gives access to a marine walk on the Menai Strait. Rhododendron garden open April–early June only. Elegant 18th century house by James Wyatt, famous for its association with Rex Whistler whose largest painting is here. Military museum contains relics of 1st Marquess of Anglesey and Battle of Waterloo. A historic cruise, a boat trip on the Menai Strait operates from the property weather and tides permitting (additional charge). 5 seater buggy to rhododendron garden and woodland walk.
Location: MAP 5:F2, OS Ref. SH521 696. 2m S of Llanfairpwll and A5.
Open: 1–12 Mar, 12 noon–4pm, Sat & Sun; 15–29 Oct, Sat–Wed & Good Fri. House, Coffee shop & Bookshop, 1–12 Mar, 11am–4pm; 15 Mar–29 Oct, 11am–5.30pm. Last admission 4.30pm. Shop & Dairy block tea-room: 1–12 Mar, 10.30am–4pm, Sat & Sun; 15 Mar–29 Oct, 10.30am–5.30pm, Sun–Wed; 1 Nov–14 Dec, 11am–4pm, Sat & Sun. Servants Hall tea-room and bookshop: 1–12 Mar, 11.30am–4pm, Sat & Sun; 15 Mar–29 Oct, 11.30am–4pm, Sun–Wed. Open Good Fri, Rhododendron garden, early Apr–early Jun, 11am–5.30pm.
Admission: House & Garden: Adult £7.00, Child £3.50 (under 5yrs free), Family (2+3) £17.50. Groups (15+) £6. Garden only: Adult £5, Child £2.50. NT members Free.
ℹ No indoor photography. ⬛ ♿ Partial. WCs. Minibus from car park to house. 🎦 Licensed. 🍴 🎫 By arrangement. 🅿 ⬛ ♿ Guide dogs only. ⬛

For **corporate hospitality** at unique venues in North Wales see our special index at the end of the book.

PLAS YN RHIW

Rhiw, Pwllheli LL53 8AB
Tel/Fax: 01758 780219
Owner: The National Trust
A small manor house, with garden and woodlands, overlooking the west shore of Porth Neigwl (Hell's Mouth Bay) on the Llyn Peninsula. The house is part medieval, with Tudor and Georgian additions, and the ornamental gardens have flowering trees and shrubs, divided by box hedges and grass paths, rising behind to the snowdrop wood.
Location: MAP 5:D5, OS Ref. SH237 282. 16m SW of Pwllheli, 3m S of the B4413 to Aberdaron. No access for coaches.
Open: 20 Mar–30 Apr: Thur–Sun, 12noon–5pm. May & Jun; Thurs–Mon, 12noon–5pm. Jul & Aug; Wed–Mon, 12 noon–5pm. Sept; Thurs–Mon, 12noon–5pm. 1 Oct–2 Nov; Thurs–Sun, 12noon–4pm. Garden & snowdrop wood open occasionally at weekends in Jan & Feb, tel for details.
Admission: Adult £3.60, Child £1.80, Family (2+3) £9. Groups: £3, Child £1.50.
Partial. WCs. By arrangement. Limited. Guide dogs only.

PORTMEIRION

Portmeirion, Gwynedd LL48 6ET
Tel: 01766 770000 **Fax:** 01766 771331 **E-mail:** enquiries@portmeirion-village.com
Owner: The Portmeirion Foundation **Contact:** Mr R Llywelyn
Built by Clough Williams-Ellis as an 'unashamedly romantic' village resort.
Location: MAP 5:F4, OS Ref. SH590 371. Off A487 at Minffordd between Penrhyndeudraeth and Porthmadog.
Open: All year: daily, 9.30am–5.30pm. Closed 25 Dec.
Admission: Adult £7, Child £3.50, Senior £5.50, Family (2+2) £17, prices are from Mar 08.

POWIS CASTLE & GARDEN

Nr Welshpool SY21 8RF
Tel: 01938 551929 **Infoline:** 01938 551944 **Fax:** 01938 554336
E-mail: powiscastle@nationaltrust.org.uk
Owner: The National Trust **Contact:** Visitor Services Manager
The world-famous garden, overhung with enormous clipped yew trees, shelters rare and tender plants in colourful herbaceous borders. Laid out under the influence of Italian and French styles, the garden retains its original lead statues and, an orangery on the terraces. Perched on a rock above the garden terraces, the medieval castle contains one of the finest collections of paintings and furniture in Wales.
Location: MAP 6:J6, OS Ref. SJ216 064. 1m W of Welshpool, car access on A483.
Open: Castle & Museum: 13 Mar–30 Jun; Thur–Mon, 1–5pm (Jul & Aug, Wed–Mon, 1–5pm); 1–21 Sept, 1–5pm; 25 Sept–2 Nov, 1–4pm). Shop & Restaurant: 1–9 Mar, Sat & Sun, 11am–4.30pm; 13 Mar–30 Jun, Thur–Mon, 11am–5.30pm; 2 Jul–31 Aug, Wed–Mon, 11am–5.30pm; 1–21 Sept, Thur–Mon, 11am–5.30pm; 25 Sept–2 Nov, Thur–Mon, 11am–5pm; 8 Nov–21 Dec, Sat & Sun, 10am–3pm. Garden: 1–9 Mar; Sats & Suns, 11am–4.30pm. 13 Mar–21 Sept; Thur–Mon (+ Wed Jul–Aug), 11am–5.30pm (25 Sept–2 Nov, 5pm). 8–29 Nov; 10am–3pm. Last entry 45 mins before closing.
*Admission: Castle & Garden: Adult £10.50, Child £5.25, Family (2+3) £26.25. Groups (15+ booked): £9. Garden only: Adult £7.50, Child £3.75, Family (2+3) £18.75. Groups (15+ booked): £6.40. No group rates on Suns or BHs. NT members & under 5s Free.*includes a voluntary donation but visitors can choose to pay the standard prices displayed at the property and on the website.
No indoor photography. Partial. Licensed. By arrangement. Limited for coaches. Guide dogs only.

RHUDDLAN CASTLE

Castle Gate, Castle Street, Rhuddlan LL18 5AD
Tel: 01745 590777 www.cadw.wales.gov.uk
Owner: In the care of Cadw **Contact:** The Custodian
Guarding the ancient ford of the River Clwyd, Rhuddlan was the strongest of Edward I's castles in North-East Wales. Linked to the sea by an astonishing deep water channel nearly 3 miles long, it still proclaims the innovative genius of its architect.
Location: MAP 6:I2, OS Ref. SJ025 779. SW end of Rhuddlan via A525 or A547.
Open: 1 Apr–30 Sept: daily, 10am–5pm.
Admission: Adult £2.90, Child (under 16yrs)/Conc. £2.50, Child under 5 yrs Free, Family (2+3 all children under 16yrs) £7.75. Children under 16 must be accompanied by an adult. Prices subject to review March 2008.
Guide dogs only.

RUG CHAPEL & LLANGAR CHURCH

c/o Coronation Cottage, Rug, Corwen LL21 9BT
Tel: 01490 412025 www.cadw.wales.gov.uk
Owner: In the care of Cadw **Contact:** The Custodian
Prettily set in a wooded landscape, Rug Chapel's exterior gives little hint of the wonders within. Nearby the attractive medieval Llangar Church still retains its charming early Georgian furnishings.
Location: Rug Chapel: MAP 6:I4, OS Ref. SJ065 439. Off A494, 1m N of Corwen. Llangar Church: MAP 6:I4, OS Ref. SJ064 423. Off B4401, 1m S of Corwen (obtain key at Rug).
Open: Rug 1 Apr–30 Sept: Wed–Sun (but open BH Mons & Tues), 10am–5pm. **Llangar** 1 Apr–30 Sept: Wed–Sun (but open BH Mons & Tues). Access is arranged daily at 2pm through Custodian at Rug Chapel; please telephone 01490 412025 for details.
Admission: Adult £3.50, Child (under 16yrs)/Conc. £3, Child under 5 yrs Free, Family (2+3 all children under 16yrs) £10. Children under 16 must be accompanied by an adult. Prices subject to review March 2008.
Guide dogs only.

ST ASAPH CATHEDRAL

St Asaph, Denbighshire LL17 0RL
Tel: 01745 583429 **Contact:** Cathedral Office www.stasaphcathedral.org.uk
The smallest ancient cathedral in Britain founded in 560AD. Memorial to Bishop William Morgan, translator of the Bible into Welsh. Wonderful stained glass windows and many interesting features. Venue for concerts and home of the annual North Wales International Music Festival.
Location: MAP 6:I2, OS Ref. SJ039 743. In St Asaph, S of A55.
Open: 9am–6pm. Sun services: 8am, 11am, 3.30pm. Morning Prayer: 9am.
By arrangement.

TOWER

Nercwys, Mold, Flintshire CH7 4EW
Tel: 01352 700220 **E-mail:** enquiries@towerwales.co.uk www.towerwales.co.uk
Owner/Contact: Charles Wynne-Eyton
This Grade I listed building is steeped in Welsh history and bears witness to the continuous warfare of the time. A fascinating place to visit or for overnight stays.
Location: MAP 6:J3, OS Ref. SJ240 620. 1m S of Mold.
Open: 3–8 May, 26 May–1 Jun, 9–25 Aug: 2–4.30pm. Groups also welcome at other times by appointment.
Admission: Adult £3, Child £2.

The Servants' Hall, Chirk Castle

TREWERN HALL

Trewern, Welshpool, Powys SY21 8DT

Tel: 01938 570243

Owner: Chapman Family   **Contact:** M Chapman

Trewern Hall is a Grade II* listed building standing in the Severn Valley. It has been described as *'one of the most handsome timber-framed houses surviving in the area'*. The porch contains a beam inscribed RF1610, though it seems likely that parts of the house are earlier. The property has been in the ownership of the Chapman family since 1918.

Location: MAP 6:J6 , OS Ref. SJ269 113. Off A458 Welshpool–Shrewsbury Road, 4m from Welshpool.

Opening: Last week in Apr, 1–31 May: Mon–Fri, 2–5pm.

Admission: Adult £2, Child/Conc. £1.

🔲 Unsuitable. 🅿 Limited. None for coaches. 🔳

TŶ MAWR WYBRNANT 🔳

Penmachno, Betws-y-Coed, Conwy LL25 0HJ

Tel: 01690 760213

Owner: The National Trust

Situated in the beautiful and secluded Wybrnant Valley, Tŷ Mawr was the birthplace of Bishop William Morgan, first translator of the entire Bible into Welsh. The house has been restored to its probable 16th-17th century appearance and houses a display of Welsh Bibles. A footpath leads from the house through woodland and the surrounding fields, which are traditionally managed.

Location: MAP 5:H3, OS Ref. SH770 524. From A5 3m S of Betws-y-Coed, take B4406 to Penmachno. House is 2½m NW of Penmachno by forest road.

Open: 20 Mar–2 Nov, Thur–Sun, 12 noon–5pm, last adm 4.30pm.

Admission: Adult £3, Child £1.50, Child under 5 yrs Free, Family £7.50. Children under 16 must be accompanied by an adult. Groups: Adult £2.50, Child £1.

🔲 Ground floor. 🅿 🔳 Guide dogs only.

VALLE CRUCIS ABBEY ✠

Llangollen, Clwyd

Tel: 01978 860326   www.cadw.wales.gov.uk

Owner: In the care of Cadw   **Contact:** The Custodian

Set in a beautiful valley location, Valle Crucis Abbey is the best preserved medieval monastery in North Wales, enhanced by the only surviving monastic fish pond in Wales.

Location: MAP 6:J4, OS Ref. SJ205 442. B5103 from A5, 2m NW of Llangollen, or A542 from Ruthin.

Open: 1 Apr–30 Sept: daily, 10am–5pm. Last adm. 4.30pm. Unstaffed with no admission charge during winter, generally between 10am–4pm.

Admission: Adult £2.50, Child (under 16yrs)/Conc. £2, Child under 5 yrs Free, Family (2+3 all children under 16yrs) £7. Under 16s must be accompanied by an adult. Prices subject to review Mar 2008.

🔲 🅿 🔳 Guide dogs only. 🔳

WERN ISAF

Penmaen Park, Llanfairfechan LL33 0RN

Tel: 01248 680437

Owner/Contact: Mrs P J Phillips

This Arts and Crafts house was built in 1900 by the architect H L North as his family home and it contains much of the original furniture and William Morris fabrics. It is situated in a woodland garden and is at its best in the Spring. It has extensive views over the Menai Straits and Conwy Bay. One of the most exceptional houses of its date and style in Wales.

Location: MAP 5:G2, OS Ref. SH685 75. Off A55 midway between Bangor and Conwy.

Open: 3–31 May: daily 1–4pm, except Tues.

Admission: Free.

For **educational facilities** or **school visits** in North Wales see our special index at the end of the book.

Bodelwyddan Castle

ABERCAMLAIS

Brecon, Powys LD3 8EY
Tel: 01874 636206 **Fax:** 01874 636964 **E-mail:** info@abercamlais.co.uk
www.abercamlais.co.uk
Owner/Contact: Mrs S Ballance

Splendid Grade I mansion dating from middle ages, altered extensively in early 18th century with 19th century additions, in extensive grounds beside the river Usk. Still in same family ownership and occupation since medieval times. Exceptional octagonal pigeon house, formerly a privy.

Location: MAP 6:I10, OS Ref. SN965 290. 5m W of Brecon on A40.
Open: Apr–Oct: by appointment.
Admission: Adult £5, Child Free.
ⓘ No photography in house. 🅰 🅵 Obligatory. 🅿 🖾

ABERDULAIS FALLS 🌿

Aberdulais, Vale of Neath SA10 8EU
Tel: 01639 636674 **Fax:** 01639 645069
Owner: The National Trust **Contact:** The Property Warden

For over 300 years this famous waterfall has provided the energy to drive the wheels of industry, from the first manufacture of copper in 1584 to present day remains of the tinplate works. It has also been visited by famous artists such as J M W Turner in 1796. The site today houses a unique hydro-electrical scheme which has been developed to harness the waters of the Dulais river.

Location: MAP 5:G12, OS Ref. SS772 995. On A4109, 3m NE of Neath. 4m from M4/J43, then A465.
Open: 2 Apr–2 Nov, Mon–Fri, 10am–5pm. 31 Mar–4 Nov, Sats & Suns, 11am–6pm. 9 Nov–23 Dec, Fri–Sun, 11am–4pm. Winter Opening: 12 Jan–29 Feb 2008, Sats & Suns, 11am–4pm.
*****Admission:** Adult £4, Child £2, Family £10. Groups (15+): Adult £3, Child £1.50. Children must be accompanied by an adult. *includes a voluntary donation but visitors can choose to pay the standard prices displayed at the property and on the website.
🖾 🍽 Light refreshments (Summer only). 🅿 Limited. 🔲

BLAENAVON IRONWORKS ✿

Nr Brecon Beacons National Park, Blaenavon, Gwent
Tel: 01495 792615 **Winter Bookings:** 01633 648082 **www.cadw.wales.gov.uk**
Owner: In the care of Cadw **Contact:** The Custodian

The famous ironworks at Blaenavon were a milestone in the history of the Industrial Revolution. Visitors can view much of the ongoing conservation work as well as 'Stack Square' – a rare survival of housing built for pioneer ironworkers. Part of a World Heritage Site.

Location: MAP 6:J11, OS Ref. SO248 092. Via A4043 follow signs to Big Pit Mining Museum and Blaenavon Ironworks. Abergavenny 8m. Pontypool 8m. From car park, cross road, then path to entrance gate.
Open: 1 Apr–31 Oct: Mon–Fri, 9:30am–4:30pm. Sat & Suns, 10am–4.30pm. For other times, telephone Torfaen County Borough Council, 01633 648081.
Admission: Adult £2.50, Child (under 16 yrs)/Conc. £2, Child under 5yrs free, Family (2+3, all children under 16yrs) £7. Under 16's must be accompanied by an adult.
🖾 🅰 Partial. 🅵 By arrangement. 🅿 🖾 Guide dogs only.

CAE HIR GARDENS

Cae Hir, Cribyn, Lampeter, Cardiganshire SA48 7NG
Tel: 01570 470839
Owner/Contact: Mr W Akkermans

This transformed 19th century smallholding offers a succession of pleasant surprises and shows a quite different approach to gardening.

Location: MAP 5:F9, OS Ref. SN521 520. NW on A482 from Lampeter, after 5m turn S on B4337. Cae Hir is 2m on left.
Open: Open daily, 1–6pm.
Admission: Adult £5, Child 50p, OAP £4.50. Free to RHS members.

For **Civil wedding** venues in South Wales see our special index at the end of the book.

ABERGLASNEY GARDENS
LLANGATHEN, CARMARTHENSHIRE SA32 8QH
www.aberglasney.org

Tel/Fax: 01558 668998 **E-mail:** info@aberglasney.org
Owner: Aberglasney Restoration Trust **Contact:** Booking Department

Aberglasney is one of the finest gardens in Wales and contains unique garden structures dating back to the beginning of the 17th century. The garden covers an area of 10 acres and includes three walled gardens. The plant collection is extensive and diverse, with collections of rare and unusual plants rarely seen in the UK. In the middle of the ruined courtyard of the mansion, a remarkable and exotic indoor garden has been created which won the best garden/construction award in 2006. The garden has been intentionally planted for year-round interest.

Location: MAP 5:F11, OS Ref. SN581 221. 4m W of Llandeilo. Follow signs from A40.
Open: All year: daily (except Christmas Day). Apr–Sept: 10am–6pm, last entry 5pm. Oct–Mar: 10.30am–4pm.
Admission: Adult £7, Child £4, Conc. £7, Booked groups (10+) Adult £6, Senior £6, Child £3.
🖾 🅵 🆃 🅰 🍽 Licensed. 🍴 Licensed. 🅵 🅿 Limited for coaches. 🔲 🖾 Guide dogs only.
🖾 ❋ ♿

CAERLEON ROMAN BATHS & AMPHITHEATRE ✠

High Street, Caerleon NP6 1AE
Tel: 01633 422518 www.cadw.wales.gov.uk
Owner: In the care of Cadw **Contact:** The Custodian
Caerleon is the most varied and fascinating Roman site in Britain – incorporating fortress and baths, well-preserved amphitheatre and a row of barrack blocks, the only examples currently visible in Europe.
Location: MAP 2:N1, OS Ref. ST340 905. 4m ENE of Newport by B4596 to Caerleon, M4/J25 (westbound), M4/J26 (eastbound).
Open: 1 Apr–31 Oct: daily, 9.30am–5pm. Last admission 4.30pm. 1 Nov–31 Mar: Mon–Sat, 9.30am–5pm. Sun 11am–4pm.
Admission: Adult £2.90, Child (under 16 yrs)/Conc. £2.50, Child under 5yrs Free, Family (2+3, all children under 16yrs) £8.30. Under 16's must be accompanied by an adult. (Prices subject to review March 2008.)
▣ ▣ ▣ Guide dogs only. ✳

CAERPHILLY CASTLE ✠

Caerphilly CF8 1JL
Tel: 029 2088 3143 www.cadw.wales.gov.uk
Owner: In the care of Cadw **Contact:** The Custodian
Often threatened, never taken, this vastly impressive castle is much the biggest in Wales. 'Red Gilbert' de Clare, Anglo-Norman Lord of Glamorgan, flooded a valley to create the 30 acre lake, setting his fortress on 3 artificial islands. Famous for its leaning tower, its fortifications are scarcely rivalled in Europe.
Location: MAP 2:L1, OS Ref. ST156 871. Centre of Caerphilly, A468 from Newport, A470, A469 from Cardiff.
Open: Summer 2007: 1 Apr–31 May, 9.30am–5pm; 1 June–30 Sept, 9.30am–6pm; daily. Winter 2007/08: Oct, daily, 9.30am–5pm; 1 Nov–31 Mar, Mon–Sat, 9.30am–4pm. Sun, 11am–4pm. Closed 24–26 Dec & 1 Jan.
Admission: Adults £3.50, Conc. £3, Family Ticket £10 (2 + 3, all children under 16 years). Children under 5 free. Under 16s must be accompanied by an adult.
▣ ▣ ▣ Limited. ▣ Guide dogs only. ▲✳

CALDICOT CASTLE & COUNTRY PARK

Church Road, Caldicot, Monmouthshire NP26 4HU
Tel: 01291 420241 **Fax:** 01291 435094
E-mail: caldicotcastle@monmouthshire.gov.uk www.caldicotcastle.co.uk
Owner: Monmouthshire County Council **Contact:** Castle Development Officer
Caldicot's magnificent castle is set in fifty acres of beautiful parkland. Founded by the Normans, developed in royal hands in the Middle Ages and restored as a Victorian home. Discover the Castle's past with an audio tour. Visitors can relax in tranquil gardens, explore medieval towers, discover children's activities and play giant chess.
Location: MAP 2:N1, OS Ref. ST487 887. From M4 take J23a and B4245 to Caldicot. From M48 take J2 and follow A48 & B4245. Castle signposted from B4245.
Open: Castle: Easter–Sept: daily, 11am–5pm. Active winter events programme, please telephone for winter opening times. Country Park: All year daily.
Admission: Adult £3.75, Child/Conc £2.50. Groups (10–100): Adult £3, Child/Conc £2.
▣ ▣ ▣ Partial. WCs. ▣ ▣ By arrangement. ▣ ▣ ▣ Free for formal educational visits. ▣ In Castle, on leads. ▲▣

CARDIFF CASTLE

Castle Street, Cardiff CF10 3RB
Tel: 029 2087 8100 **Fax:** 029 2023 1417
Owner: City and County of Cardiff **Contact:** Booking Office
2000 years of history, including Roman Walls, Norman Keep and Victorian interiors.
Location: MAP 2:M1, OS Ref. ST181 765. Cardiff city centre, signposted from M4.
Open: 1 Mar–31 Oct: daily, 9am–6pm. Tours 10am–5pm, last tour 4.50pm; 1 Nov–28 Feb: daily, 9.30am–5pm. Tours 10am–4pm, last tour 3.45pm. Closed 25/26 Dec & 1 Jan.
Admission: Full Tour: Adult £8.95, Child £6.35, OAP £7.50. Curator Tours: Adult/OAP £20.

CARMARTHEN CASTLE

Carmarthen, South Wales
Tel: 0126 7224923 **E-mail:** clgriffiths@carmarthenshire.gov.uk
Owner/Contact: The Conservation Department, Carmarthenshire County Council
The fortress, originally founded by Henry I in 1109, witnessed several fierce battles, notably in the 15th century when the Welsh hero Owain Glyndwr burnt the town and took the castle from the English.
Location: MAP 5:E11, OS Ref. SN413 200. In the town centre.
Open: Throughout the year.
Admission: Free.

CARREG CENNEN CASTLE ✠

Tir-y-Castell Farm, Llandeilo
Tel: 01558 822291 www.cadw.wales.gov.uk
Owner: In the care of Cadw **Contact:** The Custodian
Spectacularly crowning a remote crag 300 feet above the River Cennen, the castle is unmatched as a wildly romantic fortress sought out by artists and visitors alike. The climb from Rare Breeds Farm is rewarded by breathtaking views and the chance to explore intriguing caves beneath.
Location: MAP 5:G11, OS Ref. SN668 190. Minor roads from A483(T) to Trapp village. 5m SE of A40 at Llandeilo.
Open: 1 Apr–31 Oct: daily, 9.30am–6.30pm. 1 Nov–31 Mar, daily, 9.30am–4pm. Closed 25 Dec.
Admission: Adult £3.50, Child (under 16 yrs)/Conc. £3, Child under 5yrs Free, Family (2+3, all children under 16yrs) £10. Under 16's must be accompanied by an adult.
▣ ▣ ▣ ▣ ▣ Guide dogs only. ✳

CASTELL COCH ✠
TONGWYNLAIS, CARDIFF CF4 7JS
www.cadw.wales.gov.uk

Tel: 029 2081 0101
Owner: In the care of Cadw **Contact:** The Custodian
A fairytale castle in the woods, Castell Coch embodies a glorious Victorian dream of the Middle Ages. Designed by William Burges as a country retreat for the 3rd Lord Bute, every room and furnishing is brilliantly eccentric, including paintings of Aesop's fables on the drawing room walls.
Location: MAP 2:L1, OS Ref. ST131 826. M4/J32, A470 then signposted. 5m NW of Cardiff city centre.
Open: 1 Apr–31 May & Oct: daily, 9.30am–5pm. 1 Jun–30 Sept: daily, 9.30am–6pm. Nov–Mar: Mon–Sat, 9.30am–4pm, Sun 11am–4pm.
Admission: Adult £3.50, Child (under 16 yrs)/Conc. £3, Child under 5yrs Free, Family (2+3, all children under 16yrs) £10. Under 16's must be accompanied by an adult.
▣ ▣ ▣ ▣ ▣ ▣ Guide dogs only. ▲✳

CHEPSTOW CASTLE ✠

Chepstow, Gwent
Tel: 01291 624065 www.cadw.wales.gov.uk
Owner: In the care of Cadw **Contact:** The Custodian
This mighty fortress has guarded the route from England to South Wales for more than nine centuries. So powerful was this castle that it continued in use until 1690, being finally adapted for cannon and musket after an epic Civil War siege. This huge, complex, grandiosely sited castle deserves a lengthy visit.
Location: MAP 2:O1, OS Ref. ST533 941. Chepstow via A466, B4235 or A48. 1½m N of M48/J22.
Open: 1 Apr–31 May & Oct: daily, 9.30am–5pm. 1 Jun–30 Sept: daily, 9.30am–6pm. 1 Nov–31 Mar: Mon–Sat, 9.30am–4pm, Sun 11am–4pm.
Admission: Adult £3.50, Child (under 16 yrs)/Conc. £3, Child under 5yrs Free, Family (2+3, all children under 16yrs) £10. Under 16s must be accompanied by an adult.
▣ ▣ Partial. ▣ ▣ Guide dogs only. ✳

CILGERRAN CASTLE ♣ ⚒

Cardigan, Dyfed

Tel: 01239 615007   www.cadw.wales.gov.uk

Owner: In the care of Cadw   **Contact:** The Custodian

Perched high up on a rugged spur above the River Teifi, Cilgerran Castle is one of the most spectacularly sited fortresses in Wales. It dates from the 11th–13th centuries.

Location: MAP 5:D10, OS Ref. SN195 431. Main roads to Cilgerran from A478 and A484. 3½m SSE of Cardigan.

Open: 1 Apr–30 Sept: daily, 9.30am–6pm. Oct: daily, 9.30am–5pm. 1 Nov–31 Mar: daily, 9.30am–4pm. Closed 24–26 Dec & 1 Jan.

Admission: Adult £2.90, Child (under 16 yrs)/Conc. £2.50, Child under 5yrs Free, Child under 5yrs free, Family (2+3, all children under 16yrs) £8.30. Under 16's must be accompanied by an adult.

🖼 🅿 ♿ Guide dogs only. ✳

CLYNE GARDENS

Mill Lane, Blackpill, Swansea SA3 5BD

Tel: 01792 401737   **E-mail:** botanics@swansea.gov.uk

Owner: City and County of Swansea   **Contact:** Steve Hopkins

50 acre spring garden, large rhododendron collection, 4 national collections, extensive bog garden, native woodland.

Location: MAP 2:I1, OS Ref. SS614 906. S side of Mill Lane, 500yds W of A4067 Mumbles Road, 3m SW of Swansea.

Open: All year.

Admission: Free.

COLBY WOODLAND GARDEN ⚒

Amroth, Narbeth, Pembrokeshire SA67 8PP

Tel: 01834 811885   **Fax:** 01834 831766

Owner: The National Trust

This 3½ ha (8 acre) garden has a fine display of colour in spring, with rhododendrons, magnolias, azaleas and camellias, underplanted with bluebells. Later highlights are the summer hydrangeas and autumn foliage. Open and wooded pathways through the valley offer lovely walks.

Location: MAP 5:D12, OS Ref. SN155 080. ½m inland from Amroth beside Carmarthen Bay. Signs from A477.

*Admission: Adult £4.20, Child £2.10, Family £10.50. Groups (15+): Adult £3.60, Child £1.80. *includes a voluntary donation but visitors can choose to pay the standard prices displayed at the property and on the website.

ℹ Gallery events. 🖼 ♿

CORNWALL HOUSE 🏛

58 Monnow Street, Monmouth NP25 3EN

Tel/Fax: 01600 712031

Owner/Contact: Ms Jane Harvey

Town house, dating back to at least the 17th century. Red brick garden façade in Queen Anne style, dating from 1752. Street façade remodelled in Georgian style (date unknown). Many original features, including fine staircase. Delightful town garden with original walled kitchen garden.

Location: MAP 6:L11, OS Ref. SO506 127. Half way down main shopping street in Monmouth.

Open: 20–24 & 29/30 Mar, 5/6 & 26/27 April, 3–5 May, 23–25 & 30/31 Aug, 6/7, 13/14 & 20/21 Sept: 2–5pm.

Admission: Adult £4, Conc. £2.

♿ Grounds only. 📷 Obligatory. 🅿 Public car park nearby. ♿ Guide dogs only. €

CRESSELLY

Kilgetty, Pembrokeshire SA68 0SP

E-mail: hha@cresselly.com   www.cresselly.com

Owner/Contact: H D R Harrison-Allen Esq MFH

Home of the Allen family for 250 years. The house is of 1770 with matching wings of 1869 and contains good plasterwork and fittings of both periods. The Allens are of particular interest for their close association with the Wedgwood family of Etruria and a long tradition of foxhunting. Grade II listed holiday cottages nearby on river.

Location: MAP 5:C11, OS Ref. SN065 065. W of the A4075.

Open: 9–13, 16–20, 23–27 & 30 Jun; 1–4, 7–11 & 14–18 Jul: Mon–Fri, 10am–1pm. Guided tours only, on the hour. Coaches and at other times by arrangement.

Admission: Adult £4, no children under 12.

♿ Ground floor only. 📷 Obligatory. 🅿 Coaches by arrangement. ♿
🏠 Holiday cottages.

DINEFWR PARK AND CASTLE ⚒

Llandeilo SA19 6RT

Tel: 01558 823902   **Fax:** 01558 825925   **E-mail:** dinefwr@nationaltrust.org.uk

Owner: The National Trust   **Contact:** Janet Philpin, Property Administrator

Historic site including 12th century Welsh castle, magnificent parkland with historic deer park and Newton House.

Location: MAP 5:G11, OS Ref. SN625 225. On outskirts of Llandeilo.

Open: House & Park: 15 Mar–2 Nov, Daily, 11am–5pm. 7 Nov–21 Dec, Fri–Sun, 11am–5pm. Tearoom open daily all year.

*Admission: House & Park: Adult £6.30, Child £3.15, Family £15.75. Groups (15+) £5.35. *includes a voluntary donation but visitors can choose to pay the standard prices displayed at the property and on the website.

♿💷📷 By arrangement. 🅿 Limited for coaches. ♿♿ In grounds on leads.

The Judge's Lodging

DYFFRYN GARDENS AND ARBORETUM 🏛

ST NICHOLAS, Nr CARDIFF CF5 6SU

www.dyffryngardens.org.uk

Tel: 029 2059 3328 **Fax:** 029 2059 1966

Owner: Vale of Glamorgan Council **Contact:** Ms G Donovan

Dyffryn Gardens is a beautiful Grade I registered Edwardian garden, set in the heart of the Vale of Glamorgan countryside. The 55-acre gardens are the result of a unique collaboration between the eminent landscape architect, Thomas Mawson, and the passionate plant collector, Reginald Cory. The garden includes great lawns, herbaceous borders, many individual themed garden 'rooms' and a well established Arboretum including 11 champion trees. The magnificent gardens have been undergoing extensive restoration work with assistance from the Heritage Lottery Fund, including a striking Visitor Centre and tearooms. Ongoing work includes the Walled Garden and new glasshouses, which are due for completion this summer.

Location: MAP 2:L2, OS Ref. ST095 723. 3m NW of Barry, J33/M4. 1½m S of St Nicholas on A48.

Open: All year. For details please telephone 029 2059 3328.

Admission: Summer: Adult £6.50, Child £2.50. Conc. £4.50. Winter: Adult £3.50, Child £1.50. Conc. £2.50. Discount for groups (15+).

© Skyscan

FONMON CASTLE 🏛

FONMON, BARRY, VALE OF GLAMORGAN CF62 3ZN

Tel: 01446 710206 **Fax:** 01446 711687 **E-mail:** Fonmon_Castle@msn.com

Owner: Sir Brooke Boothby Bt **Contact:** Anne Broadway

Occupied as a home since the 13th century, this medieval castle has the most stunning Georgian interiors and is surrounded by extensive gardens. Available for weddings, dinners, corporate entertainment and multi-activity days.

Location: MAP 2:L2, OS Ref. ST047 681. 15m W of Cardiff, 1m W of Cardiff airport.

Open: 1 Apr–30 Sept: Tue & Wed, 2–5pm (last tour 4pm). Other times by appointment. Groups: by appointment.

Admission: Adult £5, Child Free.

ℹ Conferences. 🇹 By arrangement (up to 120). ♿ WC. 🅿 🐕 Guide dogs only. ▲ ❄

THE JUDGE'S LODGING

Broad Street, Presteigne, Powys LD8 2AD

Tel: 01544 260650 **Fax:** 01544 260652 **E-mail:** info@judgeslodging.org.uk

www.judgeslodging.org.uk

Owner: Powys County Council **Contact:** Gabrielle Rivers

Explore the fascinating world of the Victorian judges, their servants and felonious guests at this award-winning, totally hands-on historic house. From sumptuous judge's apartments to the gas-lit servants' quarters below, follow an 'eavesdropping' audio tour featuring actor Robert Hardy. Damp cells, vast courtroom and local history rooms included.

Location: MAP 6:K8, OS Ref. SO314 644. In town centre, off A44 and A4113. Easy reach from Herefordshire and mid-Wales.

Open: 1 Mar–31 Oct: daily, 10am–5pm. 1 Nov–22 Dec: Wed–Sun, 10am–4pm. Bookings by arrangement accepted all year.

Admission: Adult £5.25, Child £3.95, Conc. £4.75. Groups (10-80): Adult £4.75, Child/Conc. £4.25, Family £15.

◻ 🇹 ♿ Partial (access via lift). 🇽 By arrangement. ◻ 🅿 In town. ◾ 🐕 Guide dogs only. ▲ ❄

KIDWELLY CASTLE ✚

Kidwelly, West Glamorgan SA17 5BG

Tel: 01554 890104 **www.cadw.wales.gov.uk**

Owner: In the care of Cadw **Contact:** The Custodian

A chronicle in stone of medieval fortress technology this strong and splendid castle developed during more than three centuries of Anglo-Welsh warfare. The half-moon shape stems from the original 12th century stockaded fortress, defended by the River Gwendraeth on one side and a deep crescent-shaped ditch on the other.

Location: MAP 5:E12, OS Ref. SN409 070. Kidwelly via A484. Kidwelly Rail Station 1m.

Open: 1 Apr–31 May & Oct: daily, 9.30am–5pm. 1 Jun–30 Sept: daily, 9.30am–6pm. 1 Nov–31 Mar: Mon–Sat, 9.30am–4pm, Sun 11am–4pm. Closed 24–26 Dec & 1 Jan.

Admission: Adult £2.90, Child (under 16 yrs)/Conc. £2.50, Child under 5yrs Free, Family (2+3, all children under 16yrs) £8.30. Under 16's must be accompanied by an adult.

◻ ♿ 🇽 By arrangement. ◻ 🅿 🐕 Guide dogs only. ❄

LAMPHEY BISHOP'S PALACE ✛

Lamphey, Dyfed SA71 5NT
Tel: 01646 672224   www.cadw.wales.gov.uk
Owner: In the care of Cadw   **Contact:** The Custodian
Lamphey marks the place of the spectacular Bishop's Palace but it reached its height of greatness under Bishop Henry de Gower who raised the new Great Hall. Today the ruins of this comfortable retreat reflect the power enjoyed by the medieval bishops.
Location: MAP 5:C12, OS Ref. SN018 009. A4139 from Pembroke or Tenby. N of village (A4139).
Open: 1 Apr–31 Mar: daily, 10am–5pm (last admission 30 mins before closing).
Admission: Adult £2.90, Child (under 16 yrs)/Conc. £2.50, Child under 5yrs Free, Family (2+3, all children under 16yrs) £8.30. Under 16's must be accompanied by an adult.
◎ ⊡ 𝐏 ⇥ Guide dogs only. ✳

LAUGHARNE CASTLE ✛

King Street, Laugharne SA33 4SA
Tel: 01994 427906   www.cadw.wales.gov.uk
Owner: In the care of Cadw   **Contact:** The Custodian
Picturesque Laugharne Castle stands on a low ridge overlooking the wide Taf estuary, one of a string of fortresses controlling the ancient route along the South Wales coast.
Location: MAP 5:E11, OS Ref. SN303 107. 4m S of A48 at St Clears via A4066.
Open: 1 Apr–30 Sept: daily, 10am–5pm. The Monument is closed at all other times.
Admission: Adult £2.90, Child (under 16 yrs)/Conc. £2.50, Child under 5yrs Free, Family (2+3, all children under 16yrs) £8.30. Under 16's must be accompanied by an adult.
◎ 𝐏 ⇥ Guide dogs only

LLANCAIACH FAWR MANOR

Nelson, Treharris CF46 6ER
Tel: 01443 412248   **Fax:** 01443 412688
Owner: Caerphilly County Borough Council   **Contact:** The Administrator
Tudor fortified manor dating from 1530 with Stuart additions. Costumed guides.
Location: MAP 2:M1, OS Ref. ST114 967. S side of B4254, 1m N of A472 at Nelson.
Open: All year: daily, 10am–5pm. Last admission 1hour before closing. Nov–Feb: closed Mons. Closed Christmas week.
Admission: Adult £5.50, Child £4, Conc. £4.50, Family £16.50.

LLANERCHAERON ⚘

Ciliau Aeron, Nr Aberaeron, Ceredigion SA48 8DG
Tel: 01545 570200
Owner: The National Trust
This rare example of a self-sufficient 18th-century Welsh minor gentry estate has survived virtually unaltered. The Villa, designed in the 1790s, is the most complete example of the early work of John Nash. It has its own service courtyard with dairy, laundry. brewery and salting house, and walled kitchen gardens produce fruit, vegetables, herbs and plants, all on sale in season. The Home Farm complex has an impressive range of traditional and atmospheric outbuildings and is now a working organic farm with Welsh Black Cattle, Llanwenog Sheep and rare Welsh Pigs. Visitors can see farming activities in progress, such as lambing, shearing and hay-making.
Location: MAP 5:F8, OS Ref. SN480 602. 2½ miles East of Aberaeron off A482 / 2½ mile foot/cycle track from Aberaeron to property along old railway track.
Open: House: 15 Mar–20 Jul & 3 Sep–2 Nov, Wed–Sun; 22 Jul–31 Aug, Tues–Sun; 11.30am–4pm. Farm/Garden as House but 11am–5pm.
*****Admission:** Adult £6.70, Child £3.40, Family £16.80, Groups: Adult £5.80, Child £2.90.*includes a voluntary donation but visitors can choose to pay the standard prices displayed at the property and on the website.

LLANVIHANGEL COURT

Nr Abergavenny, Monmouthshire NP7 8DH
Tel: 01873 890217   **Fax:** 01873 890380   **E-mail:** djohnsonllanvihangel@hotmail.com
www.llanvihangel-court.co.uk
Owner/Contact: Julia Johnson
A Grade I Tudor Manor. The home in the 17th century of the Arnolds who built the imposing terraces and stone steps leading up to the house. The interior has a fine hall, unusual yew staircase and many 17th century moulded plaster ceilings. Delightful grounds. Includes 17th century features, notably Grade I stables.
Location: MAP 6:K11, OS Ref. SO433 139. 4m N of Abergavenny on A465.
Open: 2–12 May & 12–25 Aug, daily 2.30–5.30pm. Last tour 5pm.
Admission: Entry and guide, Adult £4.00, Child/Conc. £2.50.
ⓘ No inside photography. ⑤ Partial. 𝄐 𝐏 Limited. ⇥ On leads. ▲

Chepstow Castle

OXWICH CASTLE ♣

c/o Oxwich Castle Farm, Oxwich SA3 1NG
Tel: 01792 390359   www.cadw.wales.gov.uk
Owner: In the care of Cadw   **Contact:** The Custodian
Beautifully sited in the lovely Gower peninsula, Oxwich Castle is a striking testament to the pride and ambitions of the Mansel dynasty of Welsh gentry.
Location: MAP 2:I1, OS159 Ref. SS497 864. A4118, 11m SW of Swansea, in Oxwich village.
Open: 1 Apr–30 Sept: daily, 10am–5pm. The Monument is closed at all other times.
Admission: Adult £2.50, Child (under 16 yrs)/Conc. £2, Child under 5yrs Free, Family (2+3, all children under 16yrs) £7. Under 16's must be accompanied by an adult.
🄯 🅿 🗙 Guide dogs only.

PEMBROKE CASTLE

PEMBROKE SA71 4LA

www.pembrokecastle.co.uk

Tel: 01646 681510   **Fax:** 01646 622260   **E-mail:** info@pembrokecastle.co.uk
Owner: Trustees of Pembroke Castle   **Contact:** Mr D Ramsden
Pembroke Castle is situated within minutes of beaches and the breathtaking scenery of the Pembrokeshire Coastal National Park. This early Norman fortress, birthplace of the first Tudor King, houses many fascinating displays and exhibitions. Enjoy a picnic in the beautifully kept grounds, or on the roof of St. Anne's Bastion and take in the views along the estuary. Events every weekend in July and August.
Location: MAP 5:C12, OS Ref. SM983 016. W end of the main street in Pembroke.
Open: All year. 1 Apr–Sept: daily, 9.30am–6pm. Mar & Oct: daily, 10am–5pm. Nov–Feb: daily, 10am–4pm. Closed 24–26 Dec & 1 Jan. Cafe closed Dec–Jan. Brass rubbing centre open Summer months and all year by arrangement.
Admission: Adult £3.50, Child/Conc. £2.50, Family (2+2) £10. Groups (20+): Adult £3, OAP/Student £2.
🄯 🗙 🖵 Closed Dec & Jan. 🎦 End of May–Sept by arrangement. ▦
🗙 In grounds on leads. ❋ 🎗

Tudor Merchant's House

PICTON CASTLE 🏛

HAVERFORDWEST, PEMBROKESHIRE SA62 4AS

www.pictoncastle.co.uk

Tel/Fax: 01437 751326   **E-mail:** info@pictoncastle.co.uk
Owner: The Picton Castle Trust   **Contact:** Mr D Pryse Lloyd
Built in the 13th century by Sir John Wogan, his direct descendants still use the Castle as their family home. The medieval castle was modernised in the 1750s, above the undercroft and extended around 1790 with fine Georgian interiors. The 40 acres of woodland and walled gardens are part of The Royal Horticultural Society access scheme for beautiful gardens. There is a unique collection of rhododendrons and azaleas, mature trees, unusual shrubs, wild flowers, fern walk, fernery, maze, restored dewpond, a herb collection labelled with medicinal remedies and a children's nature trail. The Picton Gallery is used for nationally acclaimed exhibitions. Events include spring and autumn plant sales.
Location: MAP 5:C11, OS Ref. SN011 135. 4m E of Haverfordwest, just off A40.
Open: Easter–28 Sept: daily except Mon (open BH Mons), 10.30am–5pm. Entrance to Castle by guided tours only, between 11.30am–3.30pm. Winter opening – see website for details.
Admission: Castle, Garden & Gallery: Adult £5.95, Child £3, OAP £5.75. Garden & Gallery: Adult £4.95, Child £2.50, OAP £4.75. Groups (20+): reduced prices by prior arrangement.
ⓘ No indoor photography. 🄯 ♿ 🎦 🖵 🍴 Licensed. 🎦 Obligatory. 🅿
🗙 In grounds, on leads. ▲ 🎗

©NTPL/E/⬛ Pelham

RAGLAN CASTLE ♣

RAGLAN NP5 2BT

www.cadw.wales.gov.uk

Tel: 01291 690228
Owner: In the care of Cadw   **Contact:** The Custodian
Undoubtedly the finest late medieval fortress-palace in Britain, it was begun in the 1430s by Sir William ap Thomas who built the mighty 'Yellow Tower'. His son William Lord Herbert added a palatial mansion defended by a gatehouse and many towered walls. The high quality is still obvious today.
Location: MAP 6:K12, OS Ref. SO415 084. Raglan, NE of Raglan village off A40 (eastbound) and signposted.
Open: 14 Apr–31 May & Oct: daily, 9.30am–5pm. 1 Jun–30 Sept: daily, 9.30am–6pm. 1 Nov–31 Mar: Mon–Sat, 9.30am–4pm, Sun 11am–4pm.
Admission: Adult £2.90, Child (under 16 yrs)/Conc. £2.50, Child under 5yrs Free, Family (2+3, all children under 16yrs) £8.30. Under 16's must be accompanied by an adult.
🄯 🅿 🗙 Guide dogs only. ❋

ST DAVIDS BISHOP'S PALACE ✚

St Davids, Pembrokeshire SA62 6PE

Tel: 01437 720517   **www.cadw.wales.gov.uk**

Owner: In the care of Cadw   **Contact:** The Custodian

The city of St Davids boasts not only one of Britain's finest cathedrals but also the most impressive medieval palace in Wales. Built in the elaborate 'decorated' style of gothic architecture, the palace is lavishly encrusted with fine carving.

Location: MAP 5:B11, OS Ref. SM750 254. A487 to St Davids, minor road past the Cathedral.

Open: 1 Apr–31 May & Oct: daily, 9.30am–5pm. 1 Jun–30 Sept: daily, 9.30am–6pm. 1 Nov–31 Mar: Mon–Sat, 9.30am–4pm, Sun 11am–4pm.

Admission: Adult £2.90, Child (under 16 yrs)/Conc. £2.50, Child under 5yrs Free, Family (2+3, all children under 16yrs) £8.30. Under 16's must be accompanied by an adult.

🔲 ♿ Partial. 🅿 🚻 Guide dogs only. ✳

ST DAVIDS CATHEDRAL

St Davids, Pembrokeshire SA62 6QW

Tel: 01437 720691   **Fax:** 01437 721885

Contact: Mr R G Tarr

Over eight centuries old. Many unique and 'odd' features.

Location: MAP 5:B11, OS Ref. SM751 254. 5–10 mins walk from car/coach parks: signs for pedestrians.

Open: Daily: 8.30am–5.30pm. Sun: 12.30–5.30pm, may be closed for services in progress. Sun services: 8am, 9.30am, 11.15am & 6pm. Weekday services: 8am & 6pm. Weds extra service: 10am. (2007 details).

Admission: Donations. Guided tours (Adult £4, Child £1.20) must be booked.

ST FAGANS: NATIONAL HISTORY MUSEUM

St Fagans, Cardiff CF5 6XB

Tel: 029 2057 3500   **Fax:** 029 2057 3490

One of the world's best-loved open-air museums. Original buildings have been moved from all over Wales and re-erected at the Museum – these include a Victorian school, industrial ironworkers' cottages and a rural chapel. St Fagans Castle, an Elizabethan Manor House, also stands within the grounds.

Location: MAP 2:L2, OS Ref. ST118 772. 4m W of city centre, 1½ m N of A48, 2m S of M4/J33. Follow the brown signs (Museum of Welsh Life). Entrance drive is off A4232 (southbound only).

Open: All year: daily, 10am–5pm. Closed 24–26 Dec & 1 Jan.

Admission: Free.

STRATA FLORIDA ABBEY ✚

Ystrad Meurig, Pontrhydfendigaid SY25 6BT

Tel: 01974 831261   **www.cadw.wales.gov.uk**

Owner: In the care of Cadw   **Contact:** The Custodian

Remotely set in the green, kite-haunted Teifi Valley with the lonely Cambrian mountains as a backdrop, the ruined abbey has a wonderful doorway with Celtic spiral motifs and preserves a wealth of beautiful medieval tiles.

Location: MAP 5:H8, OS Ref. SN746 658. Minor road from Pontrhydfendigaid 14m SE of Aberystwyth by the B4340.

Open: 1 Apr–30 Sept: Wed–Sun, 10am–5pm. The Monument will be open and unstaffed on Mon & Tue (except BH Mons) between 1 Apr–30 Sept. Open at all other times generally between 10am–4pm, but unstaffed and with no admission charge.

Admission: Adult £2.90, Child (under 16 yrs)/Conc. £2.50, Child under 5yrs Free, Family (2+3, all children under 16yrs) £8.30. Under 16's must be accompanied by an adult.

🔲 ♿ 🅿 🚻 Guide dogs only. ✳

TINTERN ABBEY ✚

TINTERN NP6 6SE

www.cadw.wales.gov.uk

Tel: 01291 689251

Owner: In the care of Cadw   **Contact:** The Custodian

Tintern is the best preserved abbey in Wales and ranks among Britain's most beautiful historic sites. Elaborately decorated in 'gothic' architecture style this church stands almost complete to roof level. Turner sketched and painted here, while Wordsworth drew inspiration from the surroundings.

Location: MAP 6:L12, OS Ref. SO533 000. Tintern via A466, from M4/J23. Chepstow 6m.

Open: 1 Apr–31 May & Oct: daily, 9.30am–5pm. 1 Jun–30 Sept: daily, 9.30am–6pm. 1 Nov–31 Mar: Mon–Sat, 9.30am–4pm, Sun 11am–4pm.

Admission: Adult £3.50, Child (under 16 yrs)/Conc. £3, Child under 5yrs Free, Family (2+3, all children under 16yrs) £10. Under 16's must be accompanied by an adult.

🔲 ♿ 🔲 🅿 🚻 Guide dogs only. ✳

TREBERFYDD

Bwlch, Powys LD3 7PX

Tel: 01874 730205   **E-mail:** david.raikes@btinternet.com   **www.treberfydd.net**

Owner: David Raikes

Treberfydd is a Victorian country house, built in the Gothic style in 1847–50. The house was designed by J L Pearson, and the garden and grounds by W A Nesfield.

Location: MAP 6:I10, From A40 in Bwlch take road to Llangors, after ¼m turn left, follow lane for 2m until white gates and Treberfydd sign.

Open: 1–25 Aug. Guided tours of the House: 2 & 4pm, telephone or e-mail to secure a place on a tour. Grounds: 2–6pm.

Admission: House: Adult £3.50 (inc. tour), Child (under 12yrs) Free. Grounds only: £2.

♿ Partial. 🎦 Obligatory. 🅿 Limited. None for coaches. 🚻 On leads, in grounds.

TREBINSHWN

Nr Brecon, Powys LD3 7PX

Tel: 01874 730653   **Fax:** 01874 730843

Owner/Contact: R Watson

16th century mid-sized manor house. Extensively rebuilt 1780. Fine courtyard and walled garden.

Location: MAP 6:I10, OS Ref. SO136 242. 1½m NW of Bwlch.

Open: Easter–31 Aug: Mon–Tue, 10am–4.30pm.

Admission: Free.

🅿

For rare and unusual plants visit the **plant sales** index at the end of the book.

TREDEGAR HOUSE & PARK 🏛

NEWPORT, SOUTH WALES NP1 9YW

Tel: 01633 815880 **Fax:** 01633 815895 **E-mail:** tredegar.house@newport.gov.uk
Owner: Newport City Council **Contact:** The Manager

South Wales' finest country house, ancestral home of the Morgan family. Parts of a medieval house remain, but Tredegar owes its reputation to lavish rebuilding in the 17th century. Visitors have a lively and entertaining tour through 30 rooms, including glittering State Rooms and 'below stairs'. Set in 90 acres of parkland with formal gardens. Winner of Best Public Park and Garden in Great Britain 1997. Craft workshops.

Location: MAP 2:M1, OS Ref. ST290 852. M4/J28 signposted. From London 2½hrs, from Cardiff 20 mins. 2m SW of Newport town centre.

Open: Easter–Sept: Wed–Sun & BHs, 11am–4pm. Evening tours & groups by appointment. Oct–Mar: Groups only by appointment.

Admission: Adult £5.60, Child Free (when accompanied by paying adult), Conc. £4.10. Discount for Newport Leisure card holders. (2007 prices.)

ℹ️ Conferences. No photography in house. 🖼 🔲 🔲 Partial. WC. 🔲 🔲 Obligatory. 🅿 🔲 🔲 In grounds, on leads. 🔲 🔲

TREOWEN 🏛

Wonastow, Nr Monmouth NP25 4DL

Tel/Fax: 01600 712031 **E-mail:** john.wheelock@virgin.net **www.treowen.co.uk**
Owner: R A & J P Wheelock **Contact:** John Wheelock

Early 17th century mansion built to double pile plan with magnificent well-stair to four storeys.

Location: MAP 6:L11, OS Ref. SO461 111. 3m WSW of Monmouth.

Open: May, Jun, Aug & Sept: Fri, 10am–4pm. Also 12/13, 19/20 & 26/27 April; 13/14 & 20/21 Sept: 2–5pm. HHA Friends Free on Fri only.

Admission: £5 (£3 if appointment made). Groups by appointment only.

🔲 🔲 Entire house let, self-catering. Sleeps 25+. 🔲

TRETOWER COURT & CASTLE ♣

Tretower, Crickhowell NP8 2RF

Tel: 01874 730279 **www.cadw.wales.gov.uk**
Owner: In the care of Cadw **Contact:** The Custodian

A fine fortress and an outstanding medieval manor house, Tretower Court and Castle range around a galleried courtyard, now further enhanced by a beautiful recreated medieval garden.

Location: MAP 6:J11, OS Ref. SO187 212. Signposted in Tretower Village, off A479, 3m NW of Crickhowell.

Open: Mar & Oct: Tues–Sun, 10am–4pm (5pm, Apr–Sept). Both Monuments closed at all other times.

Admission: Adult £2.90, Child (under 16 yrs)/Conc. £2.50, Child under 5yrs Free, Family (2+3, all children under 16yrs) £8.30. Under 16's must be accompanied by an adult.

🖼 🖼 🅿 🔲 Guide dogs only.

For **Civil wedding** venues in South Wales see our special index at the end of the book.

TUDOR MERCHANT'S HOUSE 🔲

Quay Hill, Tenby SA70 7BX

Tel/Fax: 01834 842279
Owner: The National Trust **Contact:** The Custodian

A late 15th century town house, characteristic of the area at the time when Tenby was a thriving trading port. The house is furnished to recreate family life from the Tudor period onwards. There is access to the small herb garden, weather permitting.

Location: MAP 5:D12, OS Ref. SN135 004. Tenby. W of alley from NE corner of town centre square.

Open: 17 Mar–2 Nov: daily (closed Sats, except BH weekends), 11am–5pm.

Admission: Adult £2.70, Child £1.30, Family £6.70. Groups: Adult £2.30, Child £1.15.

ℹ️ No indoor photography. 🅿 No parking. 🔲 🔲 Guide dogs only.

TYTHEGSTON COURT

Tythegston, Bridgend CF32 0NE

E-mail: cknight@tythegston.com **www.tythegston.com**
Owner/Contact: C Knight

Location: MAP 2:K1, OS Ref. SS857 789. 2m E of Porthcawl on Glamorgan coast.

Open: By written appointment (no telephone calls please).

Admission: Adult £10, Child £2.50, Conc. £5.

🔲 🔲 Partial. 🔲 Obligatory. 🅿 Limited. No coaches. 🔲 Guide dogs only.

USK CASTLE

Usk, Monmouthshire NP5 1SD

Tel: 01291 672563 **E-mail:** info@uskcastle.co.uk **www.uskcastle.com**
Owner/Contact: J H L Humphreys

Romantic, ruined castle overlooking the picturesque town of Usk. Inner and outer baileys, towers and earthwork defences. Surrounded by enchanting gardens (open under NGS) incorporating The Castle House, the former medieval gatehouse.

Location: MAP 6:K12, OS Ref. SO376 011. Up narrow lane off Monmouth road in Usk, opposite fire station.

Open: Castle ruins: daily, 11am–5pm. Groups by appointment. Gardens: private visits welcome & groups by arrangement. House: Jun & BHs: 2–5pm (closed 28/29 Jun), small groups & guided tours only.

Admission: Castle ruins: Adult £2, Child Free. Gardens: Adult £4. House: Adult £6, Child £3.

🔲 🔲 Partial. 🔲 By arrangement. 🅿 No coaches. 🔲 🔲 In grounds, on leads. 🔲

WEOBLEY CASTLE ♣

Weobley Castle Farm, Llanrhidian SA3 1HB

Tel: 01792 390012 **www.cadw.wales.gov.uk**
Owner: In the care of Cadw **Contact:** The Custodian

Perched above the wild northern coast of the beautiful Gower peninsula, Weobley Castle was the home of the Knightly de Bere family. Its rooms include a fine hall and private chamber as well as numerous 'garderobes' or toilets and an early Tudor porch block.

Location: MAP 2:I1, OS Ref. SN477 928. B4271 or B4295 to Llanrhidian Village, then minor road for 1½m.

Open: 1 Apr–31 Oct: daily, 9.30am–6pm (5pm, Nov–Mar).

Admission: Adult £2.50, Child (under 16 yrs)/Conc. £2, Child under 5yrs Free, Family (2+3, all children under 16yrs) £7. Under 16's must be accompanied by an adult.

🖼 🅿 🔲 Guide dogs only. 🔲

WHITE CASTLE ♣

Llantillio Crossenny, Gwent

Tel: 01600 780380 **www.cadw.wales.gov.uk**
Owner: In the care of Cadw **Contact:** The Custodian

With its high walls and round towers reflected in the still waters of its moat, White Castle is the ideal medieval fortress. It was rebuilt in the mid-13th century by the future King Edward I to counter a threat from Prince Llywelyn the Last.

Location: MAP 6:K11, OS Ref. SO380 167. By minor road 2m NW from B4233 at A7 Llantillio Crossenny. 8m ENE of Abergavenny.

Open: 1 Apr–30 Sept: Wed–Sun, 10am–5pm. The Monument will be open and unstaffed on Mon & Tue (except BH Mons). Open at all other times generally between 10am–4pm, but unstaffed and with no admission charge.

Admission: Adult £2.50, Child (under 16 yrs)/Conc. £2, Child under 5yrs Free, Family (2+3, all children under 16yrs) £7. Under 16's must be accompanied by an adult.

🖼 🅿 🔲 Guide dogs only. 🔲

Llanerchaeron.

Mount Stewart
©NTPL/Joe Cornish

Ireland

Visitors come largely to enjoy the countryside and what it has to offer. Fishing (both river and sea) and golf are two of the most popular attractions. There are many heritage properties both in private ownership and owned by the National Trust for Ireland that have fascinating histories, among them Mount Stewart, once the home of Lord Castlereagh.

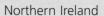

ANTRIM CASTLE GARDENS

Randalstown Road, Antrim BT41 4LH
Tel: 028 9448 1338 **Fax:** 028 9448 1344 **E-mail:** clotworthyarts@antrim.gov.uk
Owner: Antrim Borough Council   **Contact:** Philip Magennis
Situated adjacent to Antrim Town, the Sixmilewater River and Lough Neagh's shore, these 17th century Anglo-Dutch water gardens are maintained in a manner authentic to the period. The gardens comprise of ornamental canals, round pond, ancient motte and a parterre garden planted with 17th century plants – many with culinary or medicinal uses. An interpretative display introducing the history of the gardens and the process of their restoration is located in the reception of Clotworthy Arts Centre.
Location: MAP 18:O3, OS Ref. J186 850. Outside Antrim town centre off A26 on A6.
Open: All year: Mon–Fri, 9.30am–9.30pm (dusk if earlier). Sats, 10am–5pm. Jul & Aug: also open Suns, 2–5pm.
Admission: Free. Charge for guided group tours (by arrangement only).
▣ ▣ ⟦ᴕ⟧ ✳

ARDRESS HOUSE ✄

64 Ardress Road, Portadown, Co Armagh BT62 1SQ
Tel 028 8778 4753 **Fax:** 028 3885 1236 **E-mail:** ardress@nationaltrust.org.uk
www.ntni.org.uk
Owner: The National Trust   **Contact:** The Custodian
Nestled in the apple orchards of Armagh, Ardress is a 17th century house with elegant 18th century decoration. On display is the 1799 table made for the Speaker of the Irish Parliament upon which King George V signed the Constitution of Northern Ireland on 22 June 1921.
Location: MAP 18:N4, OS Ref. H912 561. On B28, 5m from Moy, 5m from Portadown, 3m from M1/J13.
Open: 17 Mar–30 Sept: Sats, Suns & BH/PHs, 2–6pm. My Lady's Mile: all year dawn–dusk.
***Admission:** House tour: Adult £4, Child £2, Family £10. Groups £3.10 (outside normal hours £5.10). *includes a voluntary donation but visitors can choose to pay the standard prices displayed at the property and on the website.
▣ 𝄐 Ground floor. WC. ⟦ᴕ⟧ Obligatory. ℗ ⊞ On leads.

THE ARGORY ✄

Moy, Dungannon, Co Tyrone BT71 6NA
Tel: 028 8778 4753 **Fax:** 028 8778 9598
E-mail: argory@nationaltrust.org.uk **www.ntni.org.uk**
Owner: The National Trust   **Contact:** The Property Manager
The Argory was built in the 1820s on a hill and has wonderful views over the gardens and 320 acre wooded riverside estate. This former home of the McGeough-Bond family has a splendid stable yard with horse carriages, harness room, acetylene gas plant and laundry.
Location: MAP 18:N4, OS Ref. H871 577. On Derrycaw road, 4m from Moy, 3m from M1/J13 or J14 (coaches J13).
Open: House: Closed for conservation work until March 2008. Grounds: 1 Oct–30 Apr: daily, 10am–4pm; 1 May–30 Sept: daily, 10am–7pm (2–7pm on Event Days). Tearoom & Shop: 17 Mar–30 Jun & Sept: Sats/Suns & BH/PHs, (Jul & Aug: daily).
***Admission:** Car £3, Minibus £15, Coach £20, Motorcycle £1.50. *includes a voluntary donation but visitors can choose to pay the standard prices displayed at the property and on the website.
▣ 🅣 𝄐 Ground floor. WC. ▣ ⟦ᴕ⟧ Obligatory. ℗ ⊞ On leads. ▲

©NTPL/Andreas Von Einsiedel

Castle Ward

BALLYWALTER PARK 🏛

BALLYWALTER, NEWTOWNARDS, CO DOWN BT22 2PP
www.ballywalterpark.com

Tel: 028 4275 8264 **Fax:** 028 4275 8818 **E-mail:** enq@dunleath-estates.co.uk
Owner: The Lord and Lady Dunleath
Contact: Mrs Sharon Graham, The Estate Office
Ballywalter Park was built, in the Italianate Palazzo style, between 1846 and 1852 by Sir Charles Lanyon for the present owner's great, great, great, grandfather Andrew Mulholland. A single-storey Gentlemen's wing, comprising Billiard Room, Smoking Room and Conservatory, was added in 1870 for Andrew's son, John Mulholland, later 1st Baron Dunleath. Further Edwardian additions were made by W J Fennell. The house has a fine collection of original furniture and paintings, complemented by contemporary pieces added by the present owner. The house has undergone major conservation works over the past 20 years with the Billiard and Smoking Rooms being restored in 2003/4. Access to the Conservatory is likely to be restricted in 2008/9 due to major works being undertaken.
Location: MAP 18:P3, OS Ref. J610 723. Off A2 on unclassified road, 1 km S of Ballywalter village.
Open: By prior appointment only; please contact The Estate Office.
Admission: House or Gardens: £6. House & Gardens: £10. Groups (max 50): £6.
ℹ No photography indoors. ▣ Pick-your-own, Jun–Aug. 🅣
▣ By prior arrangement. ⟦ᴕ⟧ Obligatory. ℗ ⊞ ▣ Tel for details. €

BARONS COURT

Newtownstewart, Omagh, Co Tyrone BT78 4EZ
Tel: 028 8166 1683 **Fax:** 028 8166 2059 **E-mail:** info@barons-court.com
www.barons-court.com
Contact: The Agent
The home of the Duke and Duchess of Abercorn, Barons Court was built between 1779 and 1782, and subsequently extensively remodelled by John Soane (1791), William and Richard Morrison (1819–1841), Sir Albert Richardson (1947–49) and David Hicks (1975–76).
Location: MAP 18:M3, OS Ref. H236 382. 5km SW of Newtownstewart.
Open: By appointment only.
Admission: Adult £7. Groups max. 50.
𝄐 Partial. WCs. ⟦ᴕ⟧ By arrangement. ℗ ▣ ⊠ ✳ €

CASTLE COOLE ✄

Enniskillen, Co Fermanagh BT74 6JY
Tel: 028 6632 2690 **Fax:** 028 6632 5665 **E-mail:** castlecoole@nationaltrust.org.uk
www.ntni.org.uk
Owner: The National Trust   **Contact:** The Property Manager
Surrounded by its stunning landscape park on the edge of Enniskillen, this majestic 18th century home of the Earls of Belmore, designed by James Wyatt, was created to impress. The surrounding wooded landscape park sloping down to Lough Coole is ideal for long walks.
Location: MAP 18:L4, OS Ref. H245 436. On A4, 1.5m from Enniskillen on A4, Belfast–Enniskillen road.
Open: House: 17–19 Mar, 1–6pm. 1 Apr–28 May: Sats, Suns & BH/PHs 1–6pm (6–15 Apr: daily). Jun: daily (except Thurs), 1–6pm. Jul & Aug: daily 12 noon–6pm. Sept: Sats & Suns, 1–6pm. Grounds: 1 Apr–30 Sept, daily, 10am–8pm, 1 Oct–31 Mar: daily, 10am–4pm.
***Admission:** House Tour & Grounds: Adult £5, Child £2.20, Family £12.20. Groups: £3.90 (outside normal hours £5).*includes a voluntary donation but visitors can choose to pay the standard prices displayed at the property and on the website.
▣ 🅣 𝄐 Partial. WC. ▣ ⟦ᴕ⟧ ℗ ⊞ In grounds, on leads. ▲ ✳

Castle Coole

CASTLE WARD & STRANGFORD LOUGH WILDLIFE CENTRE 🦋

Strangford, Downpatrick, Co Down BT30 7LS
Tel: 028 4488 1204   **Fax:** 028 4488 1729   **E-mail:** castleward@nationaltrust.org.uk
www.ntni.org.uk
Owner: The National Trust   **Contact:** The Property Manager
Situated in a stunning location within an 820 acre walled demesne overlooking Strangford Lough, the lawns rise up to the unique 18th century house and its Gothic façade. This fascinating house features both Gothic and Classical styles of architectural treatment, internally and externally.
Location: MAP 18:P4, OS Ref. J573 498. On A25, 7m from Downpatrick and 1½m from Strangford.
Open: House: 17–19 Mar, 1 Apr–30 Jun: Sats, Suns & BH/PHs (6–15 Apr: daily), Jul & Aug: daily, Sept: Sats & Suns, 1–6pm. Grounds: All year: daily, 10am–4pm (8pm Apr–Sept).
*Admission: Grounds, Wildlife Centre & House Tour: Adult £6.50, Child £3, Family £16. Groups: £6.50. Grounds & Wildlife Centre: Adult £4.50, Child £2, Family £10.50, Groups £3.10. *includes a voluntary donation but visitors can choose to pay the standard prices displayed at the property and on the website.
🖼 🎕 🗲 Ground floor & grounds. ☕ 🛈 Obligatory. 🅿 🖾 In grounds, on leads.
🖾 Caravan park, holiday cottages, basecamp. 🔺 ✳

CROM 🦋

Newtownbutler, Co Fermanagh BT92 8AP
Tel/Fax: 028 6773 8118 (Visitor Centre) 028 6773 8174 (Estate)
E-mail: crom@nationaltrust.org.uk   **www.ntni.org.uk**
Owner: The National Trust   **Contact:** The Visitor Facilities Manager
Crom is one of Ireland's most important nature conservation areas. It is set in 770 hectares of romantic and tranquil islands, woodland and ruins on the shores of Upper Lough Erne.
Location: MAP 18:M4, OS Ref. H359 246. 3m from A34, well signposted from Newtownbutler. Jetty at Visitor Centre.
Open: Grounds: 17 Mar–1 Jun & Sept: daily, 10am–6pm; 2 Jun–31 Aug: daily, 10am–7pm. Visitor Centre: 17 Mar–29 Apr: Sats, Suns & BH/PHs, 10am–6pm (6–15 Apr: daily); 1 May–9 Sept: daily, 10am–6pm. 15–30 Sept: Sats & Suns, 10am–6pm.
*Admission: Demesne & Visitor Centre: Car/Boat £5.50. Minibus £15, Coach £19, Motorcycle £2.20. *includes a voluntary donation but visitors can choose to pay the standard prices displayed at the property and on the website.
🎕 ☕ 🅿 🖾 7 x 4-star holiday cottages & play-area. 🔺

THE CROWN BAR 🦋

46 Great Victoria Street, Belfast BT2 7BA
Tel: 028 9027 9901
Belfast has many watering holes but none quite like The Crown! Rich in colour and design, it is famous for its special atmosphere, gas lamps, cosy snugs, fine ales and wines, and delicious lunch-time cuisine. The most famous pub in Belfast and one of the finest high-Victorian gin palaces in the UK, with an ornate interior of brightly-coloured tiles, carvings and glass. Wonderfully atmospheric setting in which to down a pint.
Location: MAP 18:O3, OS Ref. J336 736. Central Belfast.
Open: Mon–Sat: 11.30am–11pm, Sun: 12.30–10pm.
Admission: Free.
🍴 ✳

DERRYMORE 🦋

Bessbrook, Newry, Co Armagh BT35 7EF
Tel: 028 8778 4753   **Fax:** 028 8778 9598   **E-mail:** derrymore@nationaltrust.org.uk
www.ntni.org.uk
Owner: The National Trust
An elegant late 18th century thatched cottage, built by Isaac Corry, who represented Newry in the Irish House of Commons. Park laid out in the style of 'Capability' Brown.
Location: MAP 18:O5, OS Ref. J059 276. On A25, 2m from Newry on road to Camlough.
Open: Grounds: May–Sep: daily, 10am–7pm. Oct–Apr: daily, 10am–4pm.
*Admission: Treaty Room Tour: Adult £3.50, Child £1.70, Family £8.50. *includes a voluntary donation but visitors can choose to pay the standard prices displayed at the property and on the website.
🅿 🖾 On leads.

DIVIS & THE BLACK MOUNTAIN 🦋

12 Divis Road, Hannahstown, Belfast BT17 0NG
Tel: 028 9082 5434   **Fax:** 028 9082 5065   **E-mail:** divis@nationaltrust.org.uk
With spectacular panoramic views over Belfast, Divis and the Black Mountain is a haven for those seeking the wild countryside experience. On a clear day there are views of Strangford Lough, the Mournes and the Sperrins, as well as Scotland and Donegal.
Location: MAP 18:O3, OS Ref. J265 740. Access from Divis Road, off Upper Springfield Road. Signed from M1 Kennedy Way roundabout.
Open: All year.
Admission: Free
✳

FLORENCE COURT 🦋

Enniskillen, Co Fermanagh BT92 1DB
Tel: 028 6634 8249   **Fax:** 028 6634 8873   **E-mail:** florencecourt@nationaltrust.org.uk
www.ntni.org.uk
Owner: The National Trust   **Contact:** The Property Manager
Florence Court is a fine mid-18th century house and estate set against the stunning backdrop of the Cuilcagh Mountains. House tour includes service quarters popular with all ages. Beautiful walled garden and lots of walks in grounds.
Location: MAP 18:L4, OS Ref. H178 347. 8m SW of Enniskillen via A4 and then A32 to Swanlinbar.
Open: House: 17–19 Mar: 1 Apr–28 May: Sats, Suns & BH/PHs (6–15 Apr: daily). Jun: daily except Tues, 1–6pm; Jul & Aug: daily, 12 noon–6pm. Sept: Sats & Suns, 1–6pm. Grounds: All year, daily, 10am–4pm (8pm Apr–Sept).
*Admission: House tour: Adult £5, Child £2.20, Family £12.20. Groups: £3.90 (outside normal hours £5). Grounds only: Car £3.50, Minibus £16.50, Coach £22. *includes a voluntary donation but visitors can choose to pay the standard prices displayed at the property and on the website.
🖼 🎕 🗲 Ground floor. WC. ☕ 🛈 Obligatory. 🅿 🖾 In grounds, on leads.
🖾 Holiday cottage. 🔺

GIANT'S CAUSEWAY 🦋

North Coast Office, 60 Causeway Road, Bushmills BT57 8SU
Tel: 028 2073 1582 / 2972   **Fax:** 028 2073 2963
E-mail: giantscauseway@nationaltrust.org.uk
The Giant's Causeway, renowned for its polygonal columns of layered basalt, is the only World Heritage Site in Northern Ireland. Resulting from a volcanic eruption 60 million years ago, this is the focal point of a designated Area of Outstanding Natural Beauty and has attracted visitors for centuries. It harbours a wealth of local and natural history. Geology, flora and fauna of international importance. Beautiful coastal path extends 11 miles to the Carrick-a-Rede rope bridge with wonderful views and coastal scenery.
Location: MAP 18:O1, OS Ref. C952 452. Off A2 Bushmills to Ballintoy road.
Open: Stones & North Antrim Coastal Path: all year. NT Shop & Tea Room: all year but closed 25 & 26 December. For opening times please contact property directly.
Admission: Specialist guided tours: Adult: £3.50 Child: £2.25. Outside of hours: £4.50. Car park charge (inc NT members). *includes a voluntary donation but visitors can choose to pay the standard prices displayed at the property and on the website.
🛈 Suitable for picnics. 🖼 🎕 🗲 ☕ 🛈 For groups (15+), must be booked. 🅿 Charge. 🖾 On leads 🐾

GRAY'S PRINTING PRESS 🦋

49 Main Street, Strabane, Co Tyrone BT82 8AU
Tel: 028 7188 0055   **E-mail:** grays@nationaltrust.org.uk   **www.ntni.org.uk**
Owner: The National Trust   **Contact:** The Administrator
An icon of Strabane's 18th century reputation as Ireland's capital of publishing, a local museum with a fine collection of print presses. Fascinating guided tours, demonstrations and audio-visual displays.
Location: MAP 18:M2, OS Ref. H345 976. in the centre of Strabane.
Open: 7 Apr–26 May & 1–29 Sept: Sats, 2–5pm; 2–30 Jun: Tue–Sat, 2–5pm; 3 Jul–31 Aug: Tue–Sat, 11am–5pm.
Admission: Press Tour: Adult £3, Child £2, Family £8. Group £2.30 (outside normal hours £4). *includes a voluntary donation but visitors can choose to pay the standard prices displayed at the property and on the website.
🛈 🏠

HEZLETT HOUSE

107 Sea Road, Castlerock, Coleraine, Co Londonderry BT51 4TW
Tel/Fax: 028 8778 4753 **E-mail:** downhillcastle@nationaltrust.org.uk
www.ntni.org.uk
Owner: The National Trust   **Contact:** The Custodian
Charming 17th century thatched house with 19th century furnishings. One of only a few pre-18th century Irish buildings still surviving.
Location: MAP 18:N1, OS Ref. C773 356. 5m W of Coleraine on Coleraine–Downhill coast road, A2.
Open: Contact the property for visiting times..
*Admission: House Tour: Adult £3, Child £2, Family £8. Groups £2.30. (£4 outside normal hours.) *includes a voluntary donation but visitors can choose to pay the standard prices displayed at the property and on the website.
Ground floor. Obligatory. In grounds, on leads.

KILLYLEAGH CASTLE

Killyleagh, Downpatrick, Co Down BT30 9QA
Tel/Fax: 028 4482 8261 **E-mail:** gatehouses@killyleagh.plus.com
www.killyleaghcastle.com
Owner/Contact: Mrs G Rowan-Hamilton
Oldest occupied castle in Ireland. Self-catering towers available to sleep 4–15. Swimming pool and tennis court available by arrangement. Access to garden.
Location: MAP 18:P4, OS Ref. J523 529. At the end of the High Street.
Open: By arrangement. Groups (30–50): by appointment.
Admission: Adult £3.50, Child £2. Groups: Adult £2.50, Child £1.50.
No photography in house. Wedding receptions. Unsuitable. Obligatory.

LARCHFIELD ESTATE BARN & GARDENS

375 Upper Ballynahinch Road, Lisburn, Co Antrim BT27 6XL
Tel: 02892 638 025 **E-mail:** enquiries@larchfieldestae.co.uk
www.larchfieldestate.co.uk
Owner: Mr & Mrs G Mackie   **Contact:** Gavin Mackie
Just 20 minutes from Belfast City are the converted barns and spectacular walled gardens at Larchfield Estate. A stunning location year round, this venue offers exclusive use for private parties, weddings and corporate events. A private estate, viewings are strictly by appointment only.
Location: MAP 18:O4, OSNI J301 592. 4 Miles S of Lisburn, on the upper Ballynahinch Road, 10m SW of Belfast.
Open: Not open to general public. Weddings, events and conferences only.
Partial. WCs.

MOUNT STEWART

Newtonards, Co Down BT22 2AD
Tel: 028 4278 8387 **Fax:** 028 4278 8569 **E-mail:** mountstewart@nationaltrust.org.uk
Owner: The National Trust   **Contact:** The Property Manager
Home of the Londonderry family since the early 18th century, Mount Stewart was Lord Castlereagh's house and played host to many prominent political figures. The magnificent gardens planted in the 1920s have made Mount Stewart famous and earned it a World Heritage Site nomination.
Location: MAP 18:P3, OS Ref. J556 703. On A20, 5m from Newtownards on the Portaferry road.
Open: House: 10 Mar–29 Apr: Sats, Suns & BH/PHs (6–15 Apr: daily), 12 noon–6pm; 2 May–30 Jun: daily (except Tues in May), 1–6pm (12 noon–6pm Sats & Suns); 1 Jul–30 Sept: daily 12 noon–6pm (except Tues in Sept); 6–28 Oct: Sats & Suns, 12 noon–6pm. Lakeside Gardens: All year, daily, 10am–sunset. Formal Gardens: 10–31 Mar: Sats, Suns & BH/PHs, 10am–4pm; 1 Apr–31 Oct: daily, 10am–8pm (6pm in Apr & Oct). Temple of the Winds: 1 Apr–28 Oct: Suns & BH/PHs, 2–5pm.
*Admission: House Tour, Gardens & Temple of Winds: Adult £6.50, Child £3, Family £16. Group: £5 (outside normal hours £6.50). Gardens only: Adult £5, Child £2.50, Family £12.50. Group: £4. *includes a voluntary donation but visitors can choose to pay the standard prices displayed at the property and on the website.
Obligatory. In grounds, on leads. Lakeside area. €

MUSSENDEN TEMPLE & DOWNHILL DEMESNE

North Coast Office, 60 Causeway Road, Bushmills BT57 8SU
Tel/Fax: 028 2073 1582 **E-mail:** downhilldemesne@nationaltrust.org.uk
www.ntni.org.uk
Owner: The National Trust
Set on a stunning and wild headland with fabulous views over Ireland's north coast is the landscaped demesne of Downhill.
Location: MAP 18:N1, OS Ref. C757 357. 1m W of Castlerock.
Open: Grounds: Dawn to dusk all year.
Admission: Contact property for admission rates.
On leads.

PATTERSON'S SPADE MILL

751 Antrim Road, Templepatrick BT39 0AP
Tel: 028 9443 3619 **Fax:** 028 9443 9713 **E-mail:** pattersons@nationaltrust.org.uk
Owner: The National Trust
Listen to the hammers, smell the grit, feel the heat and witness the thrill of the only surviving water-driven spade mill in Ireland. Visitors can watch as red-hot billets of steel are removed from the forge and fashioned into spades using the mill's massive trip hammer.
Location: MAP 18:O3, OS Ref. J263 852. 2m NE of Templepatrick on A6. M2/J4.
Open: 17–19 & 24/25 Mar: 2–6pm; 1 Apr–28 May: Sats, Suns & BH/PHs (6–15 Apr: daily); 1 Jun–31 Aug: daily (except Tues), 2–6pm; Sept & 6–14 Oct: Sats & Suns, 2–6pm. Last admission 1 hour prior to closing.
*Admission: Adult £4.30, Child £2.50, Family £11.10, Group £3.30, Group outside normal hours £5. *includes a voluntary donation but visitors can choose to pay the standard prices displayed at the property and on the website.
Suitable for picnics. In grounds, on leads.

ROWALLANE GARDEN

Saintfield, Ballynahinch, Co Down BT24 7LH
Tel: 028 9751 0721 **Fax:** 028 9751 1242 **E-mail:** rowallane@nationaltrust.org.uk
www.ntni.org.uk
Owner: The National Trust   **Contact:** Head Gardener
Rowallane is an enchanting garden enclosed within a demesne landscape of some 21 hectares, planted with an outstanding collection of trees, shrubs and other plants from many parts of the world, creating a beautiful display of form and colour throughout the year.
Location: MAP 18:P4, OS Ref. J405 585. On A7, 1m from Saintfield on road to Downpatrick.
Open: 14 Apr–16 Sept: daily, 10am–8pm; 17 Sept–11 Apr (2008): daily, 10am–4pm. Closed 25/26 Dec & 1 Jan.
*Admission: Adult £4.50, Child £2, Family £11, Group £3.50. Group outside normal hours £5. *includes a voluntary donation but visitors can choose to pay the standard prices displayed at the property and on the website.
Grounds. WC. Apr–Aug. In grounds, on leads.

SEAFORDE GARDENS

Seaforde, Co Down BT30 8PG
Tel: 028 44811 225 **Fax:** 028 44811 370 **E-mail:** plants@seafordegardens.com
www.seafordegardens.com
Owner/Contact: Patrick Forde
18th century walled garden and adjoining pleasure grounds, containing many rare and beautiful trees and shrubs; many of them tender. There are huge rhododendrons and the National Collection of Eucryphias. The oldest maze in Ireland is in the centre of the walled garden, which can be viewed from the Mogul Tower. The tropical butterfly house contains hundreds of beautiful highly coloured butterflies; also a collection of parrots, insects and reptiles. The nursery garden contains many interesting plants for sale.
Location: MAP 18:P4, OS Ref. J401 433. 20m S of Belfast on the main road to Newcastle.
Open: Easter–end Sept: Mon–Sat, 10am–5pm; Suns, 1–6pm. Gardens only: Oct–Mar: Mon–Fri, 10am–5pm.
Admission: Butterfly House or Gardens: Adult £3.50, Child £2.30. Groups (10+): Adult £3, Child £1.80. Butterfly House & Gardens: Adult £6, Child £4. Groups: Adult £5, Child £3.50, Family (2+2) £16. RHS members Free access: Apr–Jun.
By arrangement. €

Properties that **open all year** appear in the special index at the end of the book.

SPRINGHILL HOUSE & COSTUME COLLECTION �

20 Springhill Road, Moneymore, Co Londonderry BT45 7NQ
Tel/Fax: 028 8674 8210 **E-mail:** springhill@nationaltrust.org.uk **www.ntni.org.uk**
Owner: The National Trust   **Contact:** The Property Manager

Described as 'one of the prettiest houses in Ulster'. A charming plantation house with portraits, furniture and decorative arts that bring to life the many generations of Lenox-Conynghams who lived here from 1680. The old laundry houses one of Springhill's most popular attractions, the Costume Collection with some exceptionally fine 18th to 20th century pieces.

Location: MAP 18:N3, OS Ref. H845 819. 1m from Moneymore on B18 to Coagh, 5m from Cookstown.

Open: 17 Mar–30 Jun: Sats, Suns & BH/PHs (6–15 Apr, daily); 1 Jul–31 Aug: daily; Sept: Sats & Suns, 1–6pm.

*Admission: House & Costume Collection Tour: Adult £4.80, Child £2.50, Family £12.10. Group £3.70 (outside normal hours £5.50). *includes a voluntary donation but visitors can choose to pay the standard prices displayed at the property and on the website.

🔲 🔳 ⬛ Partial. WC. ⬛ ⬛ 🅿 🔲 In grounds, on leads. 🔲

TEMPLETOWN MAUSOLEUM ⚲

Templepatrick, Antrim BT39
Tel: 028 9082 5870

The mausoleum or monumental tomb was erected in 1789 by the Hon Sarah Upton to the Rt Hon Arthur Upton and displays some of Robert Adam's best classical work which is chaste, crisp and elegant. Given to the National Trust in 1965 by William Henderson Smith and Sir Robin Kinahan, it stands in the graveyard of Castle Upton. Castle Upton is privately owned and not open to the public.

Location: MAP 18:P4, OS Ref. J225 855. At Templepatrick on the Belfast-Antrim Road.

Open: All year.

Admission: Free access. Please contact Belfast Properties Office for further information.

WELLBROOK BEETLING MILL ⚲

20 Wellbrook Road, Corkhill, Co. Tyrone BT80 9RY
Tel: 028 8674 8210/8675 1735 **E-mail:** wellbrook@nationaltrust.org.uk
www.ntni.org.uk
Owner: The National Trust   **Contact:** The Custodian

If you come to the mill when there is a flax pulling you will find a hive of industry and when the beetling engines are running their thunder fills the valley. There are hands-on demonstrations of the linen process, led by costumed guides, original hammer machinery, used to beat a sheen into the cloth, lovely walks and picnic opportunities by the Ballinderry River. A truly unique experience.

Location: MAP 18:N3, OS Ref. H750 792. 4m from Cookstown, following signs from A505 Cookstown–Omagh road.

Open: 17 Mar–30 Jun: Sats, Suns & BH/PHs (6–15 Apr, daily); 1 Jul–31 Aug: daily; Sept: Sats & Suns; 2–6pm.

*Admission: Mill Tour: Adult £3.50, Child £2, Family £9. Group: £2.70 (outside normal hours £4.10).*includes a voluntary donation but visitors can choose to pay the standard prices displayed at the property and on the website.

🔲 🅿

For rare and unusual plants visit the **plant sales** index at the end of the book.

Mussenden Temple on Ireland's North Coast

Opening Arrangements
at properties grant-aided by English Heritage

ENGLISH HERITAGE

I am very pleased to introduce this year's list of opening arrangements at properties grant-aided by English Heritage. The extent of public access varies from one property to another. The size of the building or garden, their nature and function are all taken into account. Some buildings, such as town halls, museums or railway stations, are of course open regularly. For other properties, especially those which are family homes or work places, access may need to be arranged in a way that also recognises the vulnerability of the building or the needs of those who live or work in it. Usually this will mean opening by arrangement or on an agreed number of days each year. This is made clear by each entry.

Some properties are open by written arrangement only. In most cases you should still be able to make initial contact by telephone, but you will be asked to confirm your visit in writing. This is to confirm the seriousness of your interest just as you would for example when making a hotel booking. It also provides a form of identification, enabling owners to feel more confident about inviting strangers into their house.

Over half the properties are open free, but we give details of admission charges where appropriate. There is also a brief description of each property, information on parking and access for people with disabilities.

It has always been a condition of grant-aid from English Heritage that the public should have a right to see the buildings to whose repair they have contributed. We therefore welcome feedback from visitors on the quality of their visit to grant-aided properties. In particular, please let us know if you are unable to gain access to any of the buildings on the list on the days or at the times specified, or if you have difficulty in making an appointment to visit and do not receive a satisfactory explanation from the owner. Please contact English Heritage Customer Services at PO Box 569, Swindon SN2 2YP (telephone: 0870 3331181; e-mail: customers@english-heritage.org.uk).

Information about public access is also included on our website (www.english-heritage.org.uk). The website is updated regularly to include new properties, any subsequent changes that have been notified to us or any corrections. We suggest that you consult our website for up-to-date information before visiting. If long journeys or special requirements are involved, we strongly recommend that you telephone the properties in advance, even if no appointment is required.

Finally, may I use this introduction to thank all those owners with whom we work, their support for the access arrangements has been hugely encouraging. That the public can enjoy a visit to a grant-aided property is not only good in itself, it demonstrates that the historic environment is in a very real sense a common wealth, part of the richness and diversity that makes the English landscape – both urban and rural – so special. It also illustrates how crucially important the private owner is in maintaining that quality and distinctiveness.

I very much hope you enjoy the sites and properties you find in this list – from the famous to the many lesser-known treasures. They are all worth a visit – I hope we have helped you to find, and enjoy, them.

Lord Bruce-Lockhart
Chairman

BEDFORDSHIRE

MOGGERHANGER HOUSE

Moggerhanger, Sandy, Bedfordshire MK44 3RW
Grade I listed Country House. 18th century core, refurbished by Sir John Soane 1790–99 for Godfrey Thornton and further altered by Soane for Thornton's son, Stephen between 1806 and 1811. Set in 33 acre parkland originally landscaped by Humphry Repton.
www.moggerhangerpark.com
Grant Recipient: Harvest Vision Ltd
Access Contact: Mrs Jenny Cooper
T: 01767 641007   **F:** 01767 641515
E-mail: enquiries@moggerhangerpark.com
Open: Mid June–mid September: daily, guided tours at 12 noon and 2.30pm. Tea room and grounds throughout the year.
Heritage Open Days: Yes
P Spaces: 50.
& Full. WC for the disabled. Guide Dogs allowed.
£ **Adult:** £6.00. **Child:** Free. **Other:** £5.00 (concessions).

OLD WARDEN PARK

Old Warden, nr. Biggleswade, Bedfordshire SG18 9EA
Built in 1872 by Joseph Shuttleworth in a Jacobean design by Henry Clutton. Still housing original Gillows furniture oak panelling and carvings, and a collection of 18th century paintings. The park was laid out by landscape architect Edward Milner.
www.shuttleworth.org
Grant Recipient: The Shuttleworth Trust
Access Contact: Ms Amanda McBrayne
T: 01767 627972   **F:** 01767 627976
Open: To the exterior of the building daily between May and September 9–5pm. Access to the interior by arrangement. Occasionally the site will be closed for private events, please call in advance: 01767 627972.
Heritage Open Days: No
P Spaces: 15.
& Partial. Ramps and lifts available. WC for the disabled. Guide Dogs allowed.
£ Free, except on event days.

BERKSHIRE

BASILDON PARK

Lower Basildon, Reading, Berkshire RG8 9NR
Designed in the 18th century by Carr of York and set in parkland in the Thames Valley. Rich interiors with fine plasterwork. Small flower garden, pleasure ground and woodland walks.
www.nationaltrust.org.uk
Grant Recipient: The National Trust
Access Contact: Property Manager
T: 01189 843040   **F:** 01189 767370
E-mail: basildonpark@nationaltrust.org.uk
Open: House: 15 March to 26 October: daily except Mondays and Tuesdays (but open pm Bank Holiday Mondays and Good Friday), 12–5pm. Park, garden and woodland walks: as house, 11–5pm. Property closes at 4pm on 15/16 and 17 August for concerts. 10–14 December: Wednesday, Thursday, Saturday and Sunday, 12–4pm, Friday, 12–7pm.
Heritage Open Days: Yes
P Car park 400 metres from property.
& Partial. Wheelchair access to ground floor and garden, ramp available. Stairs with handrail to other floors. WC for the disabled. Guide Dogs allowed.
£ **Adult:** £6.60 (house), £3.30 (park & garden only). **Child:** £3.30 (house), £1.65 (park & garden only). **Other:** Family: £16.50 (house), £8.25 (park & garden only). Free to National Trust members.

WELFORD PARK

Welford, Newbury, Berkshire RG20 8HU
Red brick country house c1652 and remodelled in 1702, when a third storey was added and the front façade was decorated with Ionic columns. Other alterations were made in the Victorian period.
www.welfordpark.co.uk
Grant Recipient: Mr J H L Puxley
Access Contact: Mr J H L Puxley
T: 01488 608691   **F:** 01488 657896
E-mail: pamela@welfordpark.co.uk
Open: 2–27 June (except Sundays) and 30 June–4 July: to the exterior only 11am–5pm. Interior of house (4 principal rooms) by prior arrangement only.

Heritage Open Days: No
P Spaces: 40. 80 more spaces within ¼ mile walk.
& Full. No WC for the disabled. Guide Dogs allowed.
£ **Adult:** £5.00 (for interior of house). Free entry to garden and grounds, except on occasional charity days.
Child: Free. **Other:** £5.00 (for interior of house). Free entry to garden and grounds, except on occasional charity days.

BRISTOL

29 QUEEN SQUARE RAILINGS

Bristol BS1 4ND
Fronted by repaired, grant-aided railings, 29 Queen Square is an early Georgian town house, 1709–11, listed Grade II*. One of the few surviving original houses in Queen Square which was laid out in 1699 and has claim to be the largest square in England.
Grant Recipient: The Queen Square Partnership
Access Contact: Ms Kate Difford
T: 0117 975 0700
E-mail: southwest@english-heritage.org.uk
Open: Access to the exterior at all reasonable times to view the railings from the pavement.
Heritage Open Days: No
P Paid parking in Queen Square and car park in The Grove (behind 29 Queen Square).
& Full. No WC for the disabled. Guide Dogs allowed.
£ No

ARNOS VALE CEMETERY

Bath Road, Bristol BS4 3EW
Forty five acre burial grounds together with exterior of three Grade II* listed buildings and other listed structures. West Lodge also Grade II*, now fully restored.
www.arnosvale.org.uk
Grant Recipient: Arnos Vale Cemetery Trust & Bristol City Council
Access Contact: Mr Richard Smith
T: 0117 971 9117   **F:** 0117 971 5505
E-mail: richard@arnosvale.org.uk
Open: Cemetery: March–September: Monday–Saturday 9am–5pm, Sunday and Public Holidays 10am–5pm; October to February: Monday–Saturday 9am–4.30pm, Sunday and Public Holidays 10am–4.30pm, or dusk whichever is earlier. West Lodge Visitor Centre: Monday–Friday (except Bank Holidays) same as Cemetery opening times; Saturday 10am–1.00pm. Sundays and Bank Holidays: closed.
Heritage Open Days: Yes
P Spaces: 50. There may be reduced parking during 2008 due to major restoration works.
& Partial. Lower level Arcadian Garden area accessed from Bath Road. No WC for the disabled. Guide Dogs allowed.
£ No

BRITISH EMPIRE AND COMMONWEALTH MUSEUM

Clock Tower Yard, Temple Meads, Bristol BS1 6QH
Museum housed in world's earliest surviving railway terminus, which was completed in 1840 and was originally part of the Great Western Railway designed by I.K. Brunel. Over 220ft long with timber and iron roof spans of 72ft, this Grade I listed building has been nominated as a World Heritage Site. Contains the Passenger shed and the adjoining former Engine and Carriage shed.
www.empiremuseum.co.uk
Grant Recipient: Empire Museum Ltd
Access Contact: Ms Anne Lineen
T: 0117 925 4980   **F:** 0117 925 4983
E-mail: anne.lineen@empiremuseum.co.uk
Open: Daily, 10am–5pm (except 22–26 December). Access to exterior is unrestricted.
Heritage Open Days: No
P Spaces: 15. Additional parking in Station car park.
& Full. WC for the disabled. Guide Dogs allowed.
£ **Adult:** £7.95 (subject to change). **Child:** £3.95 (subject to change). **Other:** £6.95 (subject to change). Free annual pass available on payment of admission.

LORD MAYOR'S CHAPEL

College Green, Bristol BS1 5TB
13th century church with 16th century floor of Spanish tiles in the Poyntz Chapel and a collection of stained glass. The only church in England that is owned, maintained and run by a City Council.

Grant Recipient: Bristol City Council
Access Contact: Mr Alan F Canterbury
T: 0117 929 4350   **F:** 0117 929 4350
Open: Wednesday–Saturday 10am–12pm and 1–4pm. Sunday service 11am.
Heritage Open Days: Yes
P On-street parking and multi-storey car park behind Council House and Trenchard Street.
& No wheelchair access. No WC for the disabled. Guide Dogs allowed.
£ No

ROYAL WEST OF ENGLAND ACADEMY

Queen's Road, Clifton, Bristol BS8 1PX
Bristol's first Art Gallery, founded in 1844, Grade II* listed and a registered museum. A fine interior housing five naturally lit art galleries, a new commercial gallery and a permanent fine art collection.
www.rwa.org.uk
Grant Recipient: Royal West of England Academy
Access Contact: Mrs Dee Smart
T: 0117 9735129   **F:** 0117 9237874
E-mail: info@rwa.org.uk
Open: Monday–Saturday 10am–5.30pm, Sunday 2–5pm. Bank Holidays 11am–4pm. Closed 25 December–3 January and Easter Day. Open Doors Day 8 September.
Heritage Open Days: Yes
P Parking for Disabled Badge Holders only (5 spaces).
& Partial. Wheelchair access to New Gallery on ground floor and Main Galleries accessible by lift. Fedden Gallery not accessible. WCs fitted with handrails. Guide Dogs allowed.
£ **Adult:** £4.00. **Child:** Free (under 16s). **Other:** £2.50 (students/senior citizens).

BUCKINGHAMSHIRE

CLIVEDEN MANSION & CLOCK TOWER

Cliveden, Taplow, Maidenhead, Buckinghamshire SL6 0JA
Built by Charles Barry in 1851, once lived in by Lady Astor now let as an hotel. Series of gardens, each with its own character, featuring roses, topiary, water gardens, a formal parterre, informal vistas, woodland and riverside walks.
www.nationaltrust.org.uk
Grant Recipient: The National Trust
Access Contact: Property Manager
T: 01628 605069   **F:** 01628 669461
E-mail: cliveden@nationaltrust.org.uk
Open: House (main ground floor rooms) and Octagon Temple: 1 April–31 October, Thursday and Sunday 3–5.30pm. Estate and garden: 1 March–21 December, daily 11am–5.30pm (closes at 4pm from 27 October).
Heritage Open Days: Yes
P Spaces: 300. Woodlands car park: open all year, daily 11am–5.30pm (closes at 4pm November–March). Overflow car park with 1000 spaces available.
& Partial. Wheelchair access to ground floor of house and wheelchair route in grounds. WC for the disabled. Guide Dogs allowed.
£ **Adult:** £1.00 extra (house), £7.50 (grounds), £3.00 (woodlands). **Child:** 50p extra (house), £3.70 (grounds), £1.50 (woodlands). **Other:** £18.70 (family: grounds), £7.50 (family: woodlands). Free to NT Members.

HALL BARN GOTHIC TEMPLE

Beaconsfield, Buckinghamshire HP9 2SG
Garden building in existence by 1740 but possibly c1725 and by Colen Campbell. Gothic Revival style hexagonal-shaped garden building. Situated in landscaped garden, laid out in 1680s.
Grant Recipient: 5th Baron Burnham's Will Trust
Access Contact: J A C Read
T: 01494 673 020
Open: By written application to Mrs Farncombe, Hall Barn, Windsor End, Beaconsfield, Buckinghamshire HP9 2SG.
Heritage Open Days: No
P Spaces: 10.
& Full. No WC for the disabled. Guide Dogs allowed.
£ No

STOWE HOUSE

Buckingham, Buckinghamshire MK18 5EH
Mansion built in 1680 and greatly altered and enlarged in the 18th century, surrounded by important 18th century gardens which are owned by the National Trust (see entry for Stowe Landscape Gardens). House and gardens

variously worked on by Vanbrugh, Gibbs, Kent and Leoni and is one of the most complete neo-classical estates in Europe. The House is now occupied by the Preservation Trust's tenant, Stowe School.

www.shpt.org
Grant Recipient: The Stowe House Preservation Trust
Access Contact: Ms Anna McEvoy
T: 01280 818229 (Mon–Fri)   **F:** 01280 818186
E-mail: amcevoy@stowe.co.uk
Open: School holidays: Wednesday–Sunday 12 noon–5pm (last admission 4pm), tours at 2pm; July and August: Friday and Saturday tours at 11am only. Term time: Wednesday–Sunday tours at 2pm. Group visits (15 plus) by arrangement throughout the year. Please check opening arrangements before visiting (tel: 01280 818229 or 01280 818166 for 24 hour info line, or website: www.shpt.org).
Heritage Open Days: No
P Spaces: 520. Free parking. 20 spaces adjacent to site, 500 spaces 500 yards away.
Full. WC for the disabled. Guide Dogs allowed.
£ Adult: £4.00. **Child:** £2.50. **Other:** £3.00 (National Trust members), £3.50 (groups).

STOWE LANDSCAPE GARDENS

Buckingham, Buckinghamshire MK18 5EH
Extensive and complex pleasure grounds and park around a country mansion. Begun late 17th century but substantially developed in the 18th and 19th centuries by, among others, Charles Bridgeman, Sir John Vanbrugh, James Gibbs, William Kent and Lancelot 'Capability' Brown (Brown was originally head gardener here before leaving to set up his own landscape practice). The park and gardens contain over 30 buildings, many of great architectural importance. Stowe was supremely influential on the English landscape garden during the 18th century.
www.nationaltrust.org.uk
Grant Recipient: The National Trust
Access Contact: Property Manager
T: 01280 822850   **F:** 01280 822437
E-mail: stowegarden@nationaltrust.org.uk
Open: 5 January–2 March and 8 November–1 February: Saturday and Sunday 10.30am–4pm (last admission 3pm); 5 March–2 November: daily, except Monday and Tuesday 10.30am–5.30pm (last admission 4pm). Open Bank Holiday Mondays and closed 24 May. Contact property for Christmas opening arrangements.
Heritage Open Days: Yes
P Spaces: 100.
Partial. Self-drive battery cars available. Uneven surfaces, map of accessible areas available. WC for the disabled. Guide Dogs allowed.
£ Adult: £6.90. **Child:** £3.50. **Other:** £17.10 (family). Free for National Trust members.

WIDMERE FARM CHAPEL

Widmere, nr. Marlow, Buckinghamshire SL7 3DF
Chapel attached to farmhouse, early 13th century with traces of 14th century windows and later alterations, listed Grade II*. 11th or 12th century crypt and medieval roof.
Grant Recipient: Mr G J White
Access Contact: Mr G J White
T: 01628 484204
Open: Access by prior arrangement.
Heritage Open Days: No
P Spaces: 6.
No wheelchair access. No WC for the disabled. No Guide Dogs allowed.
£ No

CAMBRIDGESHIRE

ELTON HALL

Elton, nr. Peterborough, Cambridgeshire PE8 6SH
Grade I historic building and country house. Late 15th century gatehouse and chapel built by Sapcote family. Main entrance façade built by Sir Thomas Proby in the 17th century and remodelled by Henry Ashton for 3rd Earl of Carysfort in the 19th century. South Garden façade built between 1789 and 1812 in Gothic style.
www.eltonhall.com
Grant Recipient: Sir William Proby Bt
Access Contact: Sir William Proby Bt
T: 01832 280468   **F:** 01832 280584
E-mail: whp@eltonhall.com
Open: 25 and 26 May; June: Wednesdays; July and August: Wednesdays, Thursdays and Sundays plus August Bank Holiday Monday, 2–5pm. Private groups by

arrangement April–October.
Heritage Open Days: No
P Spaces: 500. Parking 300 metres from the Hall.
Partial. Full wheelchair access to garden. Access to house is difficult. Please telephone 01832 280468. WC for the disabled. Guide Dogs allowed.
£ Adult: £7.50 (house), £5.00 (garden). **Child:** Free if accompanied by an adult. **Other:** Concessions: £6.50 (house), £4.50 (garden).

MINSTER PRECINCTS

Peterborough Cathedral, Peterborough, Cambridgeshire PE1 1XS
The Minster Precincts incorporate many remains from the medieval monastery of which the Cathedral church was a part. These include the richly decorated 13th century arcades of the former infirmary, the originally 13th century Little Prior's Gate and the 15th century Table Hall.
www.peterborough-cathedral.org.uk
Grant Recipient: The Dean & Chapter of Peterborough Cathedral
Access Contact: The Chapter of Peterborough Cathedral
T: 01733 355300   **F:** 01733 355316
E-mail: a.watson@peterborough-cathedral.org.uk
Open: All year, exterior only.
Heritage Open Days: Yes
P Spaces: 2. Disabled parking only. City centre car parks (nearest 5 minute walk).
Full. WC for the disabled in Cathedral restaurant, Tourist Information Centre and Cathedral Education Centre. Guide Dogs allowed.
£ Adult: £3.50 (guided tour). **Child: Other:** £2.50 (concession guided tour), £1.50 (school visit guided tour). Otherwise, donations welcome from Cathedral visitors.

SULEHAY HOUSE

32 Old Market, Wisbech, Cambridgeshire PE13 1NF
Grade II* town house, built 1723, with fine original staircase.
Grant Recipient: Cambridgeshire Historic Buildings Preservation Trust
Access Contact: Richard Miers
T: 01945 461 873
Open: By prior arrangement.
Heritage Open Days: Yes
P No
No wheelchair access. No WC for the disabled. Guide Dogs allowed.
£ No

THE MANOR

Hemingford Grey, Huntingdon, Cambridgeshire PE28 9BN
Built c1130 and one of the oldest continuously inhabited houses in Britain. Made famous as Green Knowe by the author Lucy Boston. Her patchwork collection is also shown. Four acre garden, laid out by Lucy Boston and surrounded by moat, with topiary, irises, old roses and herbaceous borders.
www.greenknowe.co.uk
Grant Recipient: Mrs Diana Boston
Access Contact: Mrs Diana Boston
T: 01480 463134   **F:** 01480 465026
E-mail: diana_boston@hotmail.com
Open: House: all year (except May) to individuals or groups by prior arrangement; May: guided tours daily at 2pm (booking advisable). Garden: all year, daily 11am–5pm (4pm in winter).
Heritage Open Days: No
P Spaces: 2. Parking for the disabled only adjacent to property.
Partial. Wheelchair access to garden and dining room only. WC for the disabled. Guide Dogs allowed.
£ Adult: £6.00, £3–£1 (garden only) seasonal price variations. **Child:** £2.00, free (garden only). **Other:** £4.50, £3–£1 (garden only) seasonal price variations.

THE OLD PALACE

Sue Ryder Care, Palace Green, Ely, Cambridgeshire CB7 4EW
Grade I listed building formerly a bishops palace opposite cathedral, with an Elizabethan promenading gallery, bishops chapel and monks' room. Two acre garden contains the oldest plane tree in Europe. Used as a neurological centre for the physically disabled.
www.suerydercare.org/theoldpalace
Grant Recipient: The Sue Ryder Care

Access Contact: Mr Martin Russell
T: 01353 667686   **F:** 01353 669425
E-mail: martin.russell@suerydercareely.org.uk
Open: By prior arrangement for access to the Long Gallery and Chapel. Gardens: open during the Open Gardens Scheme May–June. Other events held throughout the year, contact Mr Russell for details.
Heritage Open Days: No
P Nearest car park: St Mary's Street and Barton Road.
Partial. Wheelchair access to garden and Long Gallery. WC for the disabled. Guide Dogs allowed.
£ Charge made on garden open days only: adult £3.00, child 50p.

CHESHIRE

ADLINGTON HALL

Mill Lane, Adlington, Macclesfield, Cheshire SK10 4LF
Tudor/Elizabethan/Georgian manor house built around a Medieval hunting lodge. The Great Hall houses a 17th century organ, the most important of its type in the country, once played by Handel.
www.adlingtonhall.com
Grant Recipient: Mrs C J C Legh
Access Contact: Mrs Camilla J C Legh
T: 01625 829 206   **F:** 01625 828 756
E-mail: camilla@adlingtonhall.com
Open: July: Sunday–Wednesday 2–5pm. Open to groups on weekdays throughout the year by prior arrangement.
Heritage Open Days: No
P Spaces: 100. Ample areas for parking at North front and East front.
Partial. Wheelchair access to ground floor and some areas of gardens. WC for the disabled. Guide Dogs allowed.
£ Adult: £7.00 (house & gardens), £4.00 (gardens only). **Child:** £3.00 (house & gardens), free (gardens only). **Other:** £6.00 (groups).

BACHE HOUSE FARM

Chester Road, Hurleston, Nantwich, Cheshire CW5 6BO
A timber-framed house with slate roof dating from 17th century with an 18th century extension. The house is a four square house with two gables at the rear. The interior shows timbers in the house walls and an oak staircase.
Grant Recipient: Mr P R Posnett
Access Contact: Mr P R Posnett
T: 01829 260251
Open: By prior arrangement at all reasonable times.
Heritage Open Days: No
P Spaces: 10.
No wheelchair access. No WC for the disabled. No Guide Dogs allowed.
£ No

BELMONT HALL

Great Budworth, Northwich, Cheshire CW9 6HN
Country house, built 1755, initial design by James Gibbs, with fine plasterwork interiors. Set in parkland. Now a private day school with family apartments in the East Wing. Also accessible is surrounding farmland, woods and medieval moat.
Grant Recipient: The Trustees of Belmont Hall
Access Contact: Mr R C Leigh
T: 01606 891235   **F:** 01606 892349
E-mail: asmleigh@hotmail.com
Open: Guided tours during the school holidays and on weekends by prior arrangement with the Estate Manager, Belmont Hall, Great Budworth, Northwich, Cheshire CW9 6HN (tel: 01606 891235). Please note: the property and adjacent area are also open by way of a Countryside Stewardship Educational Access Agreement for schools as well as adult parties.
Heritage Open Days: No
P Spaces: 100. Unlimited free parking on site.
No wheelchair access. No WC for the disabled. Guide Dogs allowed.
£ Adult: £5.00.

BRAMALL HALL

Bramall Park, Stockport, Cheshire SK7 3NX
Black and white timber-framed manor house, set in 70 acres of parkland, dating back to the 14th century, with several subsequent renovations (many during the Victorian period). Contains 14th century wall paintings, an Elizabethan plaster ceiling and Victorian kitchen and

servants quarters.

www.bramallhall.org.uk

Grant Recipient: Stockport Metropolitan Borough Council

Access Contact: Ms Caroline Egan

T: 0845 833 0974   **F:** 0161 486 6959

E-mail: bramall.hall@stockport.gov.uk

Open: Guided Tours only: 1 April–30 September:
Sunday–Thursday 1–5pm, Friday–Saturday 1–4pm. Bank
Holidays 11am–5pm. 1 October–1 January:
Tuesday–Sunday 1–4pm; 2 January–31 March: weekends
only 1–4pm. Last entry 1 hour before closing. Hourly tours
begin at 1.15pm, 2.15pm, 3.15pm and 4.15pm (if open).

Heritage Open Days: Yes

🅿 Spaces: 60. Pay parking.

♿ Partial. Wheelchair access to ground floor only. WC for
the disabled. Guide Dogs allowed.

£ **Adult:** £3.95. **Child:** £3.00. **Other:** £3.00
(concessions).

CAPESTHORNE HALL

Macclesfield, Cheshire SK11 9JY

Jacobean style hall with a collection of fine art, sculpture,
furniture, tapestry and antiques from Europe, America and
the Far East. The Hall dates from 1719 when it was
originally designed by the Smith's of Warwick. Altered in
1837 by Blore and rebuilt by Salvin in 1861 following a
disastrous fire.

www.capesthorne.com

Grant Recipient: Mr William Arthur Bromley-Davenport

Access Contact: Mrs Gwyneth Jones

T: 01625 861221   **F:** 01625 861619

E-mail: info@capesthorne.com

Open: April–October: Sunday, Monday and Bank Holidays.
Gardens and Chapel 12 noon–5pm, Hall from 1.30–4pm
(last admission 3.30pm). Parties on other days by
arrangement.

Heritage Open Days: No

🅿 Spaces: 2000. 80 parking spaces in the car park and
remainder in park.

♿ Partial. Wheelchair access to ground floor and butler's
pantry. WC for the disabled. Guide Dogs allowed.

£ **Adult:** £6.50 (Sundays & Bank Holidays), £4.00
(garden & chapel only). **Child:** £3.00 (5–18 yrs), £2.00
(garden & chapel only). **Other:** £5.50 (senior citizen),
£3.00 (senior citizen: garden & chapel), £15 (family). Mon
only: £10 (car: 4 people) £25 (minibus) £50 (coach).

HIGHFIELDS

Audlem, nr. Crewe, Cheshire CW3 0DT

Small half-timbered manor house dating back to c1600.

Grant Recipient: Mr J B Baker

Access Contact: Mrs Susan Baker

T: 01630 655479

Open: Guided tour of hall, drawing room, dining room,
parlour, bedrooms and gardens by prior written
arrangement.

Heritage Open Days: No

🅿 Spaces: 20.

♿ Partial. Wheelchair access to ground floor only. WC for
the disabled with assistance (down 2 steps). No WC for
the disabled. Guide Dogs allowed.

£ **Adult:** £5.00. **Child:** £2.50. **Other:** £5.00.

RODE HALL

Church Lane, Scholar Green, Cheshire ST7 3QP

Country house built early–mid 18th century, with later
alterations. Set in a parkland designed by Repton. Home to
the Wilbraham family since 1669.

www.rodehall.co.uk

Grant Recipient: Sir Richard Baker Wilbraham Bt

Access Contact: Sir Richard Baker Wilbraham Bt

T: 01270 873237   **F:** 01270 882962

E-mail: richard.wilbra@btconnect.com

Open: Hall and Gardens: 1 April–30 September,
Wednesdays and Bank Holidays (closed Good Friday)
2–5pm. Gardens only: Tuesdays and Thursdays 2–5pm.
Snowdrop Walks: February, daily except Mondays
12–4pm.

Heritage Open Days: No

🅿 Spaces: 200. Parking for the disabled available
adjacent to entrance by arrangement.

♿ Partial. Wheelchair access with assistance to ground
floor. WC for the disabled. Guide Dogs allowed.

£ **Adult:** £5.00 (house & garden), £3.00 (garden only).
Child: £4.00 over 12s (house & garden), £2.50 (garden
only). **Other:** £4.00 (house & garden, senior citizens),
£2.50 (garden only).

ST CHAD'S CHURCH TOWER

Wybunbury, Nantwich, Cheshire CW5 7NA

Grade II* listed 15th or 16th century church tower, rest of
church demolished in 1977. 96ft high and containing six
restored bells, spiral staircase, charity boards, monuments
and affords panoramic views over the South Cheshire
plain. Bells are rung every Thursday evening, for weddings
on request and by visiting bell teams.

www.wybunbury.org.uk

Grant Recipient: Wybunbury Tower Preservation Trust

Access Contact: Mrs D Lockhart

T: 01270 841481

Open: Saturday 7 June 'Fig Pie Wakes' (local race and
festival) 1–5pm. Heritage Open Days 11am–4pm. At other
times by prior arrangement with Mrs D Lockhart (tel:
01270 841481) or Mr John Colbert (tel: 01270 841158).

Heritage Open Days: Yes

🅿 Spaces: 20. Limited parking at rear of Swan Hotel in
Village.

♿ Partial. Wheelchair access to ground floor only. No WC
for the disabled. Guide Dogs allowed.

£ **Adult:** £2.00. **Child:** £1.00.

THE CAGE

Lyme Park, Disley, Stockport, Cheshire SK12 2NX

Early 18th century hunting tower within the 1400 acre
medieval deer park of Lyme Park.

www.nationaltrust.org.uk

Grant Recipient: The National Trust

Access Contact: Mr Philip Burt

T: 01663 762023   **F:** 01663 765035

E-mail: lymepark@nationaltrust.org.uk

Open: The Cage: April–October, second and fourth
Saturday and Sunday of each month, 1–4pm. Hall: 15
March–2 November, daily except Wednesday and
Thursday, 11–5pm. Garden: 15 March–2 November, daily,
11am–5pm; 8 November–21 December: weekends,
12–3pm. Park: 1 April–12 October, daily, 8am–8.30pm; 13
October–31 January 2009: daily, 8am–6pm.

Heritage Open Days: No

🅿 Spaces: 1000. Park entry £4.60 per car.

♿ Partial. Wheelchair access to garden, first floor of
house, parts of park, shop and restaurant. WC for the
disabled. Guide Dogs allowed.

£ **Adult:** Free (The Cage only), £7.60 (house & garden).
Child: Free (The Cage only), £3.80 (house & garden).
Other: National Trust members free.

CORNWALL

CAERHAYS CASTLE & GARDENS

Gorran, St Austell, Cornwall PL26 6LY

Built by John Nash in 1808. Set in 60 acres of informal
woodland gardens created by J C Williams, who sponsored
plant hunting expeditions to China at the turn of the 19th
century.

www.caerhays.co.uk

Grant Recipient: The Trustees of Charles Williams
(Caerhays Estate)

Access Contact: Mrs Cheryl Kufel

T: 01872 501144/501310   **F:** 01872 501870

E-mail: estateoffice@caerhays.co.uk

Open: House: 10 March–30 May (including Bank
Holidays), Monday–Friday 12–4pm. Conducted tours every
45 minutes. Gardens: 18 February–1 June, daily 10am to
5pm (last entry 4pm).

Heritage Open Days: No

🅿 Spaces: 500.

♿ Partial. Limited wheelchair access to gardens (area
around castle). Access to ground floor of castle with
assistance, please telephone 01872 501144 or 01872
501310 in advance to check. WC for the disabled. Guide
Dogs allowed.

£ **Adult:** £9.50 (garden & house), £5.50 (house tour
only), £5.50 (gardens). **Child:** £3.50 (garden & house),
£2.50 (house tour only), £2.50 (gardens). Under 5s free.
Other: £5.00 (groups 15+, house tour), £6.50 (groups,
garden tour), £4.00 (groups, garden without tour).

COTEHELE

St Dominick, Saltash, Cornwall PL12 6TA

Cotehele, situated on the west bank of the River Tamar,
was built mainly between 1485–1627. Home of the
Edgcumbe family for centuries. Its granite and slatestone
walls contain intimate chambers adorned with tapestries,
original furniture and armour.

www.nationaltrust.org.uk

Grant Recipient: The National Trust

Access Contact: Mr Toby Fox

T: 01579 351346   **F:** 01579 351222

E-mail: cotehele@nationaltrust.org.uk

Open: House and restaurant: 17 March–2 November daily
except Friday (but open Good Friday) 11am–4pm. Mill: 17
March–2 November daily except Friday (but open Fridays in
July and August) 11–5.30pm; 1 July–31 August open daily;
11 September–30 September daily except Friday 1–5pm;
11–31 October daily except Friday 1–5.30pm. Garden:
daily all year 10.30am–dusk.

Heritage Open Days: No

🅿 Spaces: 100. Parking space available for pre-booked
coaches.

♿ Partial. Wheelchair access to house (hall, kitchen and
Edgcumbe Room only), garden, area around house,
restaurant and shop. Ramps available. Woodland walks:
some paths accessible. WC for the disabled. Guide Dogs
allowed.

£ **Adult:** £8.40 (house, garden & mill). £5.00 (garden &
mill). **Child:** £4.20 (house, garden & mill), £2.50 (garden &
mill). **Other:** Family: house, garden & mill: 1 adult £12.60,
2 adults £21.00. Family: garden & mill: 1 adult £7.40, 2
adults £12.50. £7.40 (pre-booked groups).

CULLACOTT FARMHOUSE

Werrington, Launceston, Cornwall PL15 8NH

Grade I listed medieval hall house, built in the 1480s as a
long house, and extended 1579. Contains wall paintings
of fictive tapestry, Tudor arms, St James of Compostella
and remains of representation of St George and the
Dragon. Extensively restored 1995–7 but still retains many
original features. Now used as holiday accommodation.

www.cullacottholidays.co.uk

Grant Recipient: Mr & Mrs J Cole

Access Contact: J Cole

T: 01566 772631

E-mail: cullacott@btinternet.com

Open: By prior arrangement.

Heritage Open Days: No

🅿 Spaces: 20.

♿ Partial. Wheelchair access to Great Hall, through
passage. WC for the disabled. Guide Dogs allowed.

£ **Adult:** £2.50. **Child:** Free.

PORTH-EN-ALLS LODGE

Prussia Cove, St Hilary, Cornwall TR20 9BA

Originally a chauffeur's lodge, built c1910–1914 and
designed by Philip Tilden. It is built into the cliff and sits in
close proximity to the main house. The Chauffeur's lodge
is one of a number of historic houses on the Porth-en-Alls
Estate.

www.prussiacove.com

Grant Recipient: Trustees of Porth-en-Alls Estate

Access Contact: Mr P Tunstall-Behrens

T: 01736 762 014   **F:** 01736 762 014

E-mail: penapc@dial.pipex.com

Open: Available as self-catering holiday lets throughout
the year. Members of the public may view the property by
arrangement, but only if it is unoccupied at the time. Most
Fridays throughout the year 11am–3pm and other days
out of season.

Heritage Open Days: No

🅿 Spaces: 50. Public car park approximately 0.5 miles
from the Lodge, off the A394 (near Rosudgeon village).

♿ Wheelchair access to the lodge is very difficult. No WC
for the disabled. Guide Dogs allowed.

£ Charges apply.

TREGREHAN

Par, Cornwall PL24 2SLJ

Mid 19th century gardens and pleasure grounds designed
by W A Nesfield together with significant 19th and 20th
century plant collections. Concentrating on genera from
warm temperate regions. An important green gene bank
of known source plants. 1846 glasshouse range in walled
garden. Set in 18th and 19th century parkland.

www.tregrehan.org
Grant Recipient: Mr T C Hudson
Access Contact: Mr T C Hudson
T: 01726 814 389   **F:** 01726 814389
E-mail: greengene@tregrehan.org
Open: Mid March–end of May: Wednesday–Sunday and Bank Holidays, 10.30am–5pm. June–end August: Wednesdays only, 2–5pm.
Heritage Open Days: No
P Spaces: 50.
⌖ Partial. Wheelchair access to 10 acres of garden. WC for the disabled. Guide Dogs allowed.
£ Adult: £4.50. **Child:** Free.

CUMBRIA

CROWN AND NISI PRIUS COURT

The Courts, English Street, Carlisle, Cumbria CA3 8NA
Former Crown Court in Carlisle situated at southern entrance to the city. One of a pair of sandstone towers built in the early 19th century as replicas of the medieval bastion. The towers were built to house the civil and criminal courts, used until the 1980s.
Grant Recipient: Cumbria Crown Court
Access Contact: Mr Mike Telfer
T: 01228 606116
Open: Guided Tours July and August Monday–Friday 1.30pm and 3pm (excluding August Bank Holiday Monday).
Heritage Open Days: Yes
P Town centre car parks.
⌖ Partial. Wheelchair access to Grand Jury Room, Court No.2 and Public Area Crown Court Room. WC for the disabled. Guide Dogs allowed.
£ Adult: £3.00. **Child:** £2.00 (age 5–15). **Other:** £2.50.

DIXON'S CHIMNEY

Shaddongate, Carlisle, Cumbria CA2 5TZ
270ft chimney, formerly part of Shaddongate Mill. Built in 1836 by Peter Dixon. At its original height of 306ft the chimney was the tallest cotton mill chimney to have been constructed. Structural problems meant that the decorative stone capping had to be removed in the 1950s.
Grant Recipient: Carlisle City Council
Access Contact: Mr Peter Messenger
T: 01228 871195   **F:** 01228 817199
E-mail: PeterMe@carlisle-city.gov.uk
Open: Chimney can be viewed from Shaddongate and Junction Street.
Heritage Open Days: Yes
P No
⌖ No wheelchair access. No WC for the disabled. No Guide Dogs allowed.
£ No

DRAWDYKES CASTLE

Brampton Old Road, Carlisle, Cumbria CA6 4QE
Pele tower, probably 14th century, converted to house 1676 by William Thackery and John Aglionby. Original tower with Classical Revival facade. Grade II* listed.
Grant Recipient: Mr J M Milbourn
Access Contact: Mr J M Milbourn
T: 01228 525 804
Open: By prior arrangement.
Heritage Open Days: No
P No
⌖ No wheelchair access. No WC for the disabled. No Guide Dogs allowed.
£ No

KIRKBY HALL WALLPAINTINGS

Kirkby-in-Furness, Cumbria LA17 7UX
Wall paintings are in Chapel in the west wing of a private residence, accessible only by use of a loft ladder and through a trap door above the dairy passage. Wall paintings in red ochre and black consisting of panels with stylised trees, animals and birds with texts above of the Lord's Prayer, Creed, Ten Commandments and Galations 5, 16–21 from the Great Bible of 1541.
Grant Recipient: Holker Estates Company Ltd
Access Contact: Duncan Peake or Andrew Thomas
T: 015395 58313   **F:** 015395 58966
E-mail: estateoffice@holker.co.uk
Open: January–31 October: by prior written arrangement with the Holker Estate Office, Cark-in-Cartmel, Grange-over-Sands, Cumbria LA11 7PH. Please note that access to

the wall paintings is by the use of a loft ladder and through a trap door.
Heritage Open Days: No
P Spaces: 3.
⌖ No wheelchair access. No WC for the disabled. No Guide Dogs allowed.
£ No

LEVENS HALL

Kendal, Cumbria LA8 0PD
Elizabethan house built around a 13th century pele tower, containing fine furniture, panelling, plasterwork and an art collection. The gardens, which include much topiary, were laid out in the late 17th century by Monsieur Beaumont for Colonel James Grahme and are of national importance.
www.levenshall.co.uk
Grant Recipient: Mr C H Bagot
Access Contact: Mr PE Milner
T: 01539 560321   **F:** 01539 560669
E-mail: houseopening@levenshall.co.uk
Open: House: 23 March–9 October, Sunday–Thursday 12 noon–4.30pm (last admission 4pm). Garden: as house 10am–5pm. Admission prices are under review at time of publication, please check with Mr Milner at the Estate Office for current information.
Heritage Open Days: No
P Spaces: 80.
⌖ House unsuitable for wheelchair users due to stairs and narrow doorways but all other facilities (topiary garden, plant centre, gift shop, and tea room) are accessible. A DVD tour of the House is available in the Buttery during opening hours. A mobility buggy is available for hire. No WC for the disabled. No Guide Dogs allowed.
£ Prices for 2008 under review.

MUNCASTER CASTLE

Ravenglass, Cumbria CA18 1RQ
Large house incorporating medieval fortified tower, remodelled by Anthony Salvin for the 4th Lord Muncaster in 1862–66. Ancestral home of the Pennington family for 800 years containing a panelled Hall and octagonal library. Headquarters of the World Owl Trust. Woodland garden, Lakeland setting. World-famous rhododendrons, camellias and magnolias with a terrace walk along the edge of the Esk valley.
www.muncaster.co.uk
Grant Recipient: Mrs P R Gordon-Duff-Pennington
Access Contact: Mrs Iona Frost-Pennington
T: 01229 717614   **F:** 01229 717010
E-mail: info@muncaster.co.uk
Open: Castle: 10 February–20 March, 1–4pm; 21 March–2 November: 12 noon–4:30 pm, Sunday to Friday (closed Saturday). Gardens, Owl Centre and Maze open daily 1–9 February 11am–4pm, 10 February–2 November, 10.30 am–6pm (or dusk if earlier) 3 November–31 December, 11am–4pm.
Heritage Open Days: No
P Spaces: 150.
⌖ Partial. Wheelchair access to ground floor of Castle only but other attractions and facilities accessible. The hilly nature of the site can create access difficulties so please ask for further information on arrival. WC for the disabled. Guide Dogs allowed.
£ Adult: £10.00 (Castle, gardens, owls & maze), £7.00 (gardens, owls & maze). **Child:** £7.00 (Castle, gardens, owls & maze), £5.50 (gardens, owls & maze). Under 5s free. **Other:** £29.00 (family: Castle, gardens, owls & maze), £24.00 (family: gardens, owls & maze).

PERCY HOUSE

38–42 Market Place, Cockermouth, Cumbria CA13 9NG
Built in 1598 by Henry Pery the 9th Earl of Northumberland. Many of the original features of the building still remain, including carved plaster ceiling, Percy coat of arms, Tudor fireplace, oak plank and muslin screen and flag stone and oak floors.
www.percyhouse.co.uk
Grant Recipient: Mr R E Banks
Access Contact: Mr R E Banks
T: 01900 85643/ 07710 800973   **F:** 01900 85543
E-mail: banksrothersyke@aol.com
Open: Monday–Saturday 10am–5pm.
Heritage Open Days: Yes
P Spaces: 150. On street parking in Market Place and public car park off Market Place.
⌖ Partial. Wheelchair access to ground floor only. WC for

the disabled available in public toilets in nearby car park. Guide Dogs allowed.
£ No

PRIOR'S TOWER

The Abbey, Carlisle, Cumbria CA3 8TZ
This Grade I listed three storey pele tower type building was constructed c1500. It formed part of the Prior's Lodgings and until relatively recently was part of the Deanery. Of special interest is the magnificent ceiling of 45 hand-painted panels dating from c1510 and associated with Prior Senhouse.
Grant Recipient: The Chapter of Carlisle Cathedral
Access Contact: Mr T I S Burns
T: 01228 548151   **F:** 01228 547049
E-mail: office@carlislecathedral.org.uk
Open: By prior arrangement with Mr T I S Burns, The Chapter of Carlisle Cathedral, 7 The Abbey, Carlisle, Cumbria CA3 8TZ.
Heritage Open Days: Yes
P Parking in nearby City centre car parks. 2 parking spaces for the disabled in Cathedral grounds.
⌖ No wheelchair access. WC for the disabled is nearby (approx. 100 yards). Guide Dogs allowed.
£ No

RYDAL HALL MAWSON GARDENS

Rydal, Ambleside, Cumbria LA22 9LX
Formal Italianate gardens designed by Thomas Mawson in 1911set in 34 acres. The gardens have been restored over a two year period returning them to their former glory. The gardens include an informal woodland garden, leading to a 17th century viewing station/summerhouse, fine herbaceous planting, community vegetable garden, orchard and apiary.
www.rydalhall.org
Grant Recipient: Church of England/Carlisle Diocesan Board of Finance
Access Contact: Mr Jonathon Green
T: 01539 432050   **F:** 01539 434887
E-mail: mail@rydalhall.org
Open: Daily 10am–4pm.
Heritage Open Days: No
P Spaces: 40.
⌖ Partial. Most garden paths are accessible for wheelchairs. WC for the disabled. Guide Dogs allowed.
£ No

SCALEBY CASTLE

Scaleby, Carlisle, Cumbria CA6 4LN
Medieval ruins of Scaleby Castle which is a Scheduled Ancient Monument.
Grant Recipient: Lord Henley
Access Contact: Smiths Gore
T: 01228 527586   **F:** 01228 520802
E-mail: charles.baker@smithsgore.co.uk
Open: By prior written arrangement with the owner's agents Smiths Gore, 64 Warwick Road, Carlisle CA1 1DR
Heritage Open Days: No
P Spaces: 10.
⌖ Partial. All areas viewable but no wheelchair access to internal parts of the monument. No WC for the disabled. Guide Dogs allowed.
£ No

SIZERGH CASTLE

nr. Kendal, Cumbria LA8 8AE
Sizergh Castle has been the home of the Strickland family for over 760 years. Its core is the 14th century tower, later extended and containing some fine Elizabethan carved wooden chimney-pieces and inlaid chamber. The Castle is surrounded by gardens, including a rock garden.
www.nationaltrust.org.uk
Grant Recipient: The National Trust
Access Contact: Ms Fiona Clark, Property Manager
T: 01539 560 951
E-mail: sizergh@nationaltrust.org.uk
Open: Castle: 17 March–2 November, daily except Friday and Saturday, 1–5pm. Garden: 17 March–2 November, daily except Friday and Saturday, 11–5pm. Closed Good Friday. Cafe/Shop: 17 March–2 November, daily except Friday and Saturday, 11am–5pm.
Heritage Open Days: No
P Spaces: 130. Space for 6 coaches.

& Partial. Wheelchair access to Castle Lower Hall and garden gravel paths only. WC for the disabled. Guide Dogs allowed.

£ **Adult:** £7.10, £4.70 (garden only). **Child:** £3.60, £2.40 (garden only). **Other:** £17.80 (family), £6.00 per person (pre-booked parties, minimum 15 persons, not Bank Holidays).

SMARDALE GILL VIADUCT

Kirkby Stephen, Cumbria
Disused rail viaduct, built 1860–1 by Sir Thomas Bouch for the South Durham and Lancashire Union Railway. 550ft long with 14 arches, 90 ft high, spanning Scandal Beck at Smardale Gill, a National Nature Reserve. A well-preserved example of a large viaduct on this line.
www.nvt.org.uk
Grant Recipient: The Trustees of the Northern Viaduct Trust
Access Contact: Mr G J Biddle
T: 01539 560993
Open: All year, access by footpaths only from Newbiggin-on-Lune or Smardale. Path along former railway.
Heritage Open Days: No
P Spaces: 8. Parking at Smardale. Cumbria Wildlife Trust car park 1½ miles.
& Partial. Wheelchair access from Smardale only. No WC for the disabled. Guide Dogs allowed.
£ No

DERBYSHIRE

ASSEMBLY ROOMS

The Crescent, Buxton, Derbyshire SK17 6BH
The Crescent was designed by John Carr of York and built by the Fifth Duke of Devonshire between 1780–89. It provided hotels, lodgings and a suite of elaborately decorated Assembly Rooms. The front elevation of three storeys is dominated by Doric pilasters over a continuous rusticated ground floor arcade.
Grant Recipient: Derbyshire County Council
Access Contact: Mr Allan Morrison
T: 01629 580 000 X3351   **F:** 01629 585 507
E-mail: allan.morrison@derbyshire.gov.uk
Open: Exterior accessible from public highway. No interior access until refurbishment works completed, other than special agreement. Renovation works are likely to be in progress during 2008.
Heritage Open Days: No
P Spaces: 20. On-street pay and display parking available.
& No wheelchair access. No WC for the disabled. No Guide Dogs allowed.
£ No

BARLBOROUGH HALL

Barlborough, Chesterfield, Derbyshire S43 4TL
Built by Sir Francis Rhodes in the 1580s, the Hall is square in plan and stands on a high basement with a small internal courtyard to provide light. Contains Great Chamber, now a chapel, bearing a date of 1584 on the overmantel whilst the porch is dated 1583. Now a private school.
Grant Recipient: The Governors of Barlborough Hall School
Access Contact: Mr C F A Bogie
T: 01246 435138   **F:** 01246 435090
Open: By prior arrangement only 20 March–14 April, 25 May–15 June, 8 July–3 September and most weekends throughout the year. External visits (without guide) any evening after 6pm at weekend.
Heritage Open Days: No
P Spaces: 50.
& No wheelchair access. No WC for the disabled. Guide Dogs allowed.
£ No

BENNERLEY VIADUCT

Erewash Valley, Ilkeston, Derbyshire
Disused railway viaduct over the Erewash valley, c1878–9, and approximately 500 yards long with 15 piers. It is one of two remaining wrought iron lattice-girder bridges in the British Isles.
Grant Recipient: Railway Paths Ltd
Access Contact: Mr Simon Ballantine
T: 01548 550 331   **F:** 01548 550 331
E-mail: simonb@sustrans.org.uk

Open: There is access to the viaduct by a public footpath running underneath it, but the deck itself is inaccessible.
Heritage Open Days: No
P No
& No wheelchair access. No WC for the disabled. No Guide Dogs allowed.
£ No

CALKE ABBEY

Ticknall, Derbyshire DE73 1LE
Baroque mansion, built 1701–3 for Sir John Harpur and set in a landscaped park. Little restored, Calke is preserved by a programme of conservation as a graphic illustration of the English house in decline. It contains the natural history collection of the Harpur Crewe family, an 18th century state bed and interiors that are essentially unchanged since the 1880s.
www.nationaltrust.org.uk
Grant Recipient: The National Trust
Access Contact: Property Manager
T: 01332 863822   **F:** 01332 865272
E-mail: calkeabbey@nationaltrust.org.uk
Open: House: 1, 2, 8 and 9 March: 12.30–5pm, 15 March–2 November: daily except Thursday and Friday, 12.30–5pm. Garden and Church: 15 March–2 November: daily except Thursday and Friday, 11am–5pm; 3 July–5 September: daily, 11am–5pm. House and Garden open Good Friday 21 March. Park: All year dawn–dusk.
Heritage Open Days: No
P Spaces: 75.
& Partial. Wheelchair access to ground floor of house, stables, shop and restaurant. Garden and park partly accessible. WC for the disabled. Guide Dogs allowed.
£ **Adult:** £8.50, £5.30 (garden only). **Child:** £4.20, £2.70 (garden only). **Other:** £21.50 (family) £13.30 (family: garden only). Admission price includes voluntary gift aid donation.

CATTON HALL

Catton, Walton-on-Trent, Derbyshire DE12 8LN
Country house built c1741 by Smith of Warwick for Christopher Horton. Property owned by the same family since 1405. Contains an interesting collection of 17th and 18th century pictures, including Royal and Family portraits; also Byron and Napoleon memorabilia. Gardens, which run down to the River Trent, include a family chapel.
www.catton-hall.com
Grant Recipient: Mr R Neilson
Access Contact: Mrs C Neilson
T: 01283 716311   **F:** 01283 712876
E-mail: kneilson@catton-hall.com
Open: 7 April–13 October: including tour of the house, chapel and gardens every Monday at 2pm. Group tours (15 or more) at any time of year by prior arrangement.
Heritage Open Days: Yes
P Spaces: 200. Unlimited parking available.
& Partial. Wheelchair access by separate entrance to all ground floor rooms. No WC for the disabled. Guide Dogs allowed.
£ **Adult:** £4.50. **Child: Other:** £3.50 (concessions).

CROMFORD MILL

Mill Lane, Cromford, nr. Matlock, Derbyshire DE4 3RQ
Grade I listed mill complex established by Sir Richard Arkwright in 1771. The world's first successful water powered cotton spinning mill situated in the Derwent Valley Mills World Heritage Site. Currently being conserved by the Arkwright Society, an educational charity. The Mill is permanently home to five shops and a restaurant.
www.arkwrightsociety.org.uk
Grant Recipient: The Arkwright Society
Access Contact: Mrs Sarah McLeod
T: 01629 823256   **F:** 01629 824297
E-mail: smcleod@arkwrightsociety.org.uk
Open: Daily, 9am–5pm, closed on Christmas Day. Free entry to main site, charges for guided tours.
Heritage Open Days: No
P Spaces: 100.
& Partial. Wheelchair access to shops, lavatories and restaurant. WC for the disabled. Guide Dogs allowed.
£ **Adult:** £2.00 (guided tour). **Child:** £1.50 (guided tour).
Other: £1.50 (guided tour).

DEVONSHIRE ROYAL HOSPITAL

1 Devonshire Road, Buxton, Derbyshire SK17 6LX
Originally built as stables to service the adjacent Crescent, converted to a hospital in 1859. Central feature is a large circular colonnade capped with a spectacular dome added, along with the clock tower, in 1880. Listed Grade II*. Converted to and opened as the University of Derby Buxton campus in 2006.
www.derby.ac.uk/buxton
Grant Recipient: University of Derby
Access Contact: Professor Michael Gunn, Provice Chancellor
T: 01332 594682
Open: University working site open throughout the year during normal working hours.
Heritage Open Days: No
P Spaces: 30. Access needs to be pre-arranged.
& Full. WC for the disabled. Guide Dogs allowed.
£ No

HARDWICK HALL AND STABLEYARD COTTAGES

Doe Lea, Chesterfield, Derbyshire S44 5QJ
A late 16th century 'prodigy house' designed by Robert Smythson for Bess of Hardwick. Contains an outstanding collection of 16th century furniture, tapestries and needlework. Walled courtyards enclosed gardens, orchards and herb garden. The Hall's environs include the late 16th century stableyard cottages, some of which have been converted to holiday cottages.
www.nationaltrust.org.uk
Grant Recipient: The National Trust
Access Contact: Property Manager
T: 01246 850430   **F:** 01246 858424
E-mail: hardwickhall@nationaltrust.org.uk
Open: 1 March–2 November: daily except Monday, Tuesday and Friday tours 11am – 12 noon, open 12 noon–4.30pm; 6 December–21 December: Saturday and Sunday 12 noon–4.30pm. Garden: 1 March–2 November, Wednesday–Sunday, 11am–5.30pm; 6–21 December Saturday and Sunday 11am–5.30 pm. Parkland: daily 8am–6pm. The stableyard cottages are available to rent throughout the year and the public can view the cottages by prior arrangement with the access contact.
Heritage Open Days: Yes
P Spaces: 200.
& Partial. Wheelchair access to ground floor with audio guide. WC for the disabled in main car park. Guide Dogs allowed.
£ **Adult:** £9.50, £4.75 (garden only). **Child:** £4.75, £2.30 (garden only). **Other:** £23.75 (family), £11.80 (garden only). Admission price includes voluntary gift aid donation.

KEDLESTON HALL

Derby, Derbyshire DE22 5JH
A classical Palladian mansion built 1759–65 for the Curzon family and little altered since. Robert Adam interior with state rooms retaining their collection of paintings and original furniture. The Eastern museum houses a range of objects collected by Lord Curzon when Viceroy of India (1899–1905). Set in 800 acres of parkland and 18th century pleasure ground, garden and woodland walks.
www.nationaltrust.org.uk
Grant Recipient: The National Trust
Access Contact: Property Manager
T: 01332 842191   **F:** 01332 844059
E-mail: kedlestonhall@nationaltrust.org.uk
Open: House: 1 March–2 November: daily except Thursday and Friday, 12 noon–5pm. Garden: 1 March–2 November: daily 10am–6pm. Park: 1 March–2 November: 10am–6pm, 3 November–27 February 2009: 10am–4pm (occasional day restrictions may apply in December and January 2009).
Heritage Open Days: No
P Spaces: 60. Winter admission for park only, parking charge of £2.70.
& Partial. Wheelchair access to ground floor of house via stair-climber, garden, restaurant and shop. WC for the disabled. Guide Dogs allowed.
£ **Adult:** £8.50 £3.80 (park & garden only). **Child:** £4.20, £1.90 (park & garden only). **Other:** £20.00 (family), £9.60 (park & garden only). Admission price includes voluntary gift aid donation.

MASSON MILLS (SIR RICHARD ARKWRIGHT'S)

Derby Road, Matlock Bath, Derbyshire DE4 3PY
Sir Richard Arkwright's 1783 showpiece Masson Mills are the finest surviving example of one of Arkwright's cotton mills. The "Masson Mill pattern" of design was an important influence in nascent British and American mill development. Museum with historic working textile machinery. Part of the Derwent Valley Mills World Heritage Site.
www.massonmills.co.uk
Grant Recipient: Mara Securities Ltd
Access Contact: Museum Reception
T: 01629 581001   **F:** 01629 581001
Open: All year except Christmas Day and Easter Day: Monday–Friday 10am–4pm, Saturday 11am–5pm and Sunday 11am–4pm.
Heritage Open Days: No
P Spaces: 200.
& Partial. WC for the disabled. No Guide Dogs allowed.
£ **Adult:** £2.50. **Child:** £1.50. **Other:** £2.00 (school groups £1.00 per child).

SACHEVERELL-BATEMAN MAUSOLEUM

Churchyard of St Matthew's Church, Church Lane, Morley, Derbyshire
A Grade II* listed small rectangular mausoleum built in red sandstone designed in the Perpendicular Revival style by GF Bodley, in 1897. It contains a marble sarcophagus with a cut-glass cross incorporated in its lid, stained glass, a painted panelled roof and a framed memorial inscription written on vellum.
www.mausolea-monuments.org.uk
Grant Recipient: Mausolea & Monuments Trust
Access Contact: Miss Sheila Randall
T: 0115 875 8393
E-mail: se.randall@ntlworld.com
Open: When events are taking place in the Church (advertised locally). At other times by prior arrangement with Miss Sheila Randall (116 Kenilworth Drive, Kirk Hallam, Ilkeston, Derbyshire DE7 4EW. Tel: 0115 875 8393).
Heritage Open Days: No
P Spaces: 20.
& Full. Access for wheelchairs across churchyard but no designated path. No WC for the disabled. Guide Dogs allowed.
£ No

ST ANN'S HOTEL

The Crescent, Buxton, Derbyshire SK17 6BH
The Crescent was designed by John Carr of York and built by the Fifth Duke of Devonshire between 1780–89. It provided hotels, lodgings and a suite of elaborately decorated Assembly Rooms. The front elevation of three storeys is dominated by Doric pilasters over a continuous rusticated ground floor arcade.
Grant Recipient: High Peak Borough Council
Access Contact: Mr Richard Tuffrey
T: 01457 851653   **F:** 01457 860290
E-mail: richard.tuffrey@highpeak.gov.uk
Open: Exterior accessible from public highway. No interior access until refurbishment works completed.
Heritage Open Days: No
P On-street parking available.
& No wheelchair access. No WC for the disabled. No Guide Dogs allowed
£ No

SUDBURY HALL

Sudbury, Ashbourne, Derbyshire DE6 5HT
17th century house with rich interior decoration including wood carvings by Laguerre. The Great Staircase (c1676) with white-painted balustrade with luxuriantly carved foliage by Edward Pierce, is one of the finest staircases of its date in an English house. 19th century service wing houses the National Trust Museum of Childhood.
www.nationaltrust.org.uk
Grant Recipient: The National Trust
Access Contact: Property Manager
T: 01283 585305   **F:** 01283 585139
E-mail: sudburyhall@nationaltrust.org.uk
Open: Hall: 21 March–2 November: Wednesday–Sunday (but open Bank Holiday Mondays), 1–5pm. Schools and tours 11am–1pm. Museum: 21 March (provisional)–27 July: Wednesday–Sunday 10.30am–5pm; 28 July–7 September: daily 11am–5pm; 10 September–2 November: Wednesday–Sunday 10.30am–5pm;

8 November–21 December: weekends only. Grounds: 15 March–21 December: daily 10.30am–5pm.
Heritage Open Days: No
P Spaces: 100. Car park is a short distance from the Hall; six-seater volunteer driven buggy available.
& Partial. Wheelchair access to lake, tea room and shop. Ground floor access to museum. Access to Hall difficult–please contact the Property Manager in advance. WC for the disabled. Guide Dogs allowed.
£ **Adult:** £6.80. **Child:** £3.40, under 3s free. **Other:** £17.00 (family). Admission price includes voluntary gift aid donation.

TISSINGTON HALL

Tissington, Ashbourne, Derbyshire DE6 1RA
Grade II* listed Jacobean manor house altered in the 18th century and extended in the 20th. Contains fine furniture, pictures and interesting early 17th century panelling. Home of the FitzHerbert family for over 500 years.
www.tissington-hall.com
Grant Recipient: Sir Richard FitzHerbert Bt
Access Contact: Sir Richard FitzHerbert Bt
T: 01335 352200   **F:** 01335 352201
E-mail: tisshall@dircon.co.uk
Open: 24–28 March, 26–30 May: Monday–Friday; 22 July–22 August: Tuesday–Friday. Bank Holiday Monday 25 August: 1.30–4pm.
Heritage Open Days: Yes
P Spaces: 100.
& Partial. Wheelchair access to gardens and various rooms. Guide dogs: by arrangement. WC for the disabled. Guide Dogs allowed.
£ **Adult:** £7.50 (house & garden), £3.50 (garden). **Child:** £4.00 age 10–16 (house & garden), £1.00 (garden). **Other:** £6.50 (house & garden), £3.50 (garden).

DEVON

21 THE MINT

Exeter, Devon EX4 3BL
The refectory range of St Nicholas Priory, converted into a substantial town house in the Elizabethan period and later into tenements. Features include medieval arch-braced roof, traces of the Norman priory and later Elizabethan panelling. Restored, now dwellings and meeting room with courtyard garden planted to represent the Tudor period.
www.ehbt.org.uk
Grant Recipient: Exeter Historic Buildings Trust
Access Contact: Ms Katharine Chant
T: 01392 436000 / 496653   **F:** 01392 496653
E-mail: enquiries@ehbt.org.uk
Open: House and meeting room: 24, 25, 26 May; 2 and 13 July, Heritage Open Days (11–14 September), 11am–4pm. Meeting room: every Monday throughout the year, 2–4pm (except Bank Holidays). Also open for Redcoat guided tour 'Catacomb and The Mint' starting from Cathedral Close, March–October every Wednesday and Friday, 2pm.
Heritage Open Days: Yes
P Car parks in Exeter.
& Partial. Wheelchair access to ground floor and courtyard garden only. No WC for the disabled. Guide Dogs allowed.
£ No

ANDERTON HOUSE/RIGG SIDE

Goodleigh, North Devon, Devon
Anderton House also known as Rigg Side. 1970–1 to the designs of Peter Aldington and John Craig for Mr and Mrs Anderton. The inspiration for its profile is taken from the longhouses of Devon. Timber frame, forming a two-row grid of double posts and beams with a tent roof, set half proud of concrete block walls and glazed clerestory and stained tiled gabled roof. Timber linings and ceilings internally, with tiled floors. Its sliding doors give views of the Devon countryside.
www.landmarktrust.org.uk
Grant Recipient: The Landmark Trust
Access Contact: Mrs Victoria O'Keeffe
T: 01628 825920   **F:** 01628 825417
E-mail: vokeeffe@landmarktrust.org.uk
Open: The Landmark Trust is an independent charity, which rescues small buildings of historic or architectural importance from decay or unsympathetic improvement. Landmark's aim is to promote the enjoyment of these historic buildings by making them available to stay in for holidays. Anderton House can be rented by anyone, at all

times of the year, for periods ranging from a weekend to three weeks. Bookings can be made by telephoning the Booking Office on 01628 825925. As the building is in full-time use for holiday accommodation, it is not normally open to the public. However, the public can view the building by prior arrangement by telephoning the access contact (Victoria O'Keeffe on 01628 825920) to make an appointment. Potential visitors will be asked to write to confirm the details of their visit.
Heritage Open Days: Yes
P Parking at local playing fields.
& Partial. Wheelchair access to kitchen, bedrooms and dining room. No WC for the disabled. Guide Dogs allowed.
£ No

AYSHFORD CHAPEL

Ayshford, Burlescombe, Devon
Grade I listed private medieval chapel with a simple medieval screen. Distinctive stained glass of 1848 and 17th century monuments to the Ashford family.
www.friendsoffriendlesschurches.org.uk
Grant Recipient: Friends of Friendless Churches
Access Contact: Mr & Mrs Kelland
T: 01884 820271
Open: At any reasonable time. Keyholder lives nearby.
Heritage Open Days: Yes
P Spaces: 2. On-street parking
& Partial. Wheelchair access possible with assistance: access to church through field and up one step. No WC for the disabled. No Guide Dogs allowed.
£ No

DARTINGTON HALL

Dartington, Totnes, Devon TQ9 6EL
Medieval mansion and courtyard built 1388–1399 by John Holland, Earl of Huntingdon and later Duke of Exeter, half brother to Richard II. Set in a landscaped garden and surrounded by a 1200 acre estate. The Champernowne family owned Dartington for 400 years before selling the estate to Leonard and Dorothy Elmhirst who founded the Dartington Hall Trust.
www.dartington.org
Grant Recipient: The Dartington Hall Trust
Access Contact: Mrs J McConville
T: 01803 847002   **F:** 01803 847007
E-mail: trust@dartington.org.
Open: Throughout the year for courses, events and activities. The Hall, courtyard and gardens are accessible for external viewing all year. Access to the interior by prior arrangement. Coach parties by prior arrangement only.
Heritage Open Days: Yes
P Spaces: 250.
& Partial. Wheelchair access to Great Hall, courtyard and top garden paths. No WC for the disabled. Guide Dogs allowed.
£ Some activities have an entry fee.

EXETER CUSTOM HOUSE

The Quay, Exeter, Devon EX1 1NN
Located on the historic quayside, the Custom House was constructed in 1680–1 and is the earliest purpose-built customs house in Britain. Contains many original fittings and three exceptionally ornamental plaster ceilings by John Abbot of Frithelstock (amongst the finest such work of this date in the south west).
www.exeter.gov.uk/visiting/attractions
Grant Recipient: Exeter City Council
Access Contact: Tourism Promotion Officer
T: 01392 265204   **F:** 01392 265625
E-mail: tourismpr@exeter.gov.uk
Open: Guided tours from May–September: Weekends. Times to be confirmed.
Heritage Open Days: Yes
P Spaces: 400. Cathedral and Quay car park (75 metres). 5 public spaces for the disabled in front of Custom House.
& Partial. Wheelchair access to ground floor stair area only. WC for the disabled in car park. No WC for the disabled. Guide Dogs allowed.
£ No

FINCH FOUNDRY

Sticklepath, Okehampton, Devon EX20 2NW
19th century water-powered forge, which produced agricultural and mining hand tools. Still in working order with regular demonstrations. The foundry has three water-wheels driving the huge tilt hammer and grindstone.

www.nationaltrust.org.uk
Grant Recipient: The National Trust
Access Contact: Mr Roger Boney
T: 01837 840046
E-mail: finchfoundry@nationaltrust.org.uk
Open: 15 March–2 November: daily except Tuesday 11am–5pm. Tea room/shop as Foundry.
Heritage Open Days: Yes
P Spaces: 50. Access to car park is narrow and unsuitable for coaches and wide vehicles.
S Partial. Wheelchair access to museum and workshop is difficult. Foundry can be viewed through shop window. No WC for the disabled. Guide Dogs allowed.
£ **Adult:** £4.00. **Child:** £2.00.

LAWRENCE CASTLE HALDON BELVEDERE

Higher Ashton, nr. Dunchideock, Exeter, Devon EX6 7QY
Grade II* listed building built in 1788 as the centrepiece to a 11,600 acre estate. Stands 244 metres above sea level overlooking the cathedral city of Exeter, the Exe estuary and the surrounding countryside. Contains a spiral staircase and miniature ballroom.
www.haldonbelvedere.co.uk
Grant Recipient: Devon Historic Buildings Trust
Access Contact: Mr Ian Turner
T: 01392 833668   **F:** 01392 833668
E-mail: turner@haldonbelvedere.co.uk
Open: 3 February–26 October: Sundays and Bank Holidays 1.30–5.30pm. At other times by prior arrangement. Grounds open all year.
Heritage Open Days: No
P Spaces: 15. Parking for the disabled adjacent to building.
S Partial. Wheelchair access to ground floor only. WC for the disabled. Guide Dogs allowed.
£ **Adult:** £2.00. **Child:** Free. **Other:** Free for wheelchair bound visitors.

LYNTON TOWN HALL

Lee Road, Lynton, Devon EX35 6HT
Grade II* listed Town Hall. Cornerstone laid 1898, opened by the donor Sir George Newnes, 15 August 1900. Neo-Tudor design with Art Nouveau details. In use as Town Hall and community facility.
www.lyntonandlynmouth.org.uk/towncouncil
Grant Recipient: Lynton & Lynmouth Town Council
Access Contact: Mr Dwyer
T: 01598 752384   **F:** 01598 752677
E-mail: ltc@northdevon.gov.uk
Open: Monday–Friday, 9.30–11.00am. Other times by arrangement.
Heritage Open Days: No
P No
S Partial. No WC for the disabled. Guide Dogs allowed.
£ No

MERCHANT'S HOUSE

8 Fore Street, Cullompton, Devon EX15 1JL
Formerly a merchant's town house. 17th century, three storey half timbered, with cob and stone mix, lime plastered under gable-end slate roof. The house appears to conform to merchant-house plan type with shop and storage on ground floor with main rooms on the first floor. Decorative, dentilled frieze. Jettied with oriel windows and early crown glass.
Grant Recipient: Mr & Mrs J Rusalen
Access Contact: Mr & Mrs J Rusalen
T: 01884 34704
Open: Access to the exterior only whilst building work in progress, please check the English Heritage website or with the access contact for current information.
Heritage Open Days: No
P Parking in town centre car parks.
S No wheelchair access. No WC for the disabled. No Guide Dogs allowed.
£ No

OLD QUAY HEAD

The Quay, Ilfracombe, Devon EX34 9EQ
Grade II* listed quay originally constructed early in the 16th century by William Bourchier, Lord Fitzwarren. The Quay was paved with stone in the 18th century and extended further in the 19th. This extension is marked by a commemorative stone plaque at its southern end. The Quay separates the inner harbour basin from the outer harbour.

Grant Recipient: North Devon District Council
Access Contact: Lieutenant Commander R Lawson
T: 01271 862108   **F:** 01271 862 108
E-mail: harbour_master@northdevon.gov.uk
Open: At all times.
Heritage Open Days: No
P Spaces: 144. Charges apply. Places for disabled available.
S Full. WC for the disabled immediately adjacent to the Old Quay Head. WC for the disabled. Guide Dogs allowed.
£ No

SALEM CHAPEL

East Budleigh, Budleigh Salterton, Devon EX9 7EF
Dating from 1719, built as a Presbyterian Chapel which later became congregational. Three galleries and school room added later in 1836 when the façade was re-designed.
www.hct.org.uk
Grant Recipient: Historic Chapels Trust
Access Contact: Mrs Kathy Moyle
T: 01395 445 236
Open: At any reasonable time by prior arrangement with the key holder, Kathy Moyle, 4 Collins Park, East Budleigh, Budleigh Salterton, Devon EX9 7EG. Occasional events during the summer; please check the Historic Chapels Trust website or contact the key holder for further information.
Heritage Open Days: Yes
P 2 parking spaces for the disabled, otherwise public parking close by.
S Partial. Wheelchair access to ground floor only. WC for the disabled. Guide Dogs allowed.
£ Donations invited.

SALTRAM HOUSE

Plympton, Plymouth, Devon PL7 1UH
A remarkable survival of a George II mansion, complete with its original contents and set in a landscaped park. Robert Adam worked here on two occasions to create the state rooms and produced what are claimed to be the finest such rooms in Devon. These show his development as a designer, from using the conventional Rococo, to the low-relief kind of Neo-Classical detail that became his hallmark and with which he broke new ground in interior design.
www.nationaltrust.org.uk
Grant Recipient: The National Trust
Access Contact: Carol Murrin
T: 01752 333500   **F:** 01752 336474
E-mail: saltram@nationaltrust.org.uk
Open: House: 21 March–2 November daily except Friday (but open Good Friday), 12 noon–4.30pm. Garden: 1 February–20 March daily except Friday (but open Good Friday), 11am–4pm; 21 March–2 November daily except Friday, 11am–5pm; 3 November–31 January daily except Friday, 11am–4pm.
Heritage Open Days: No
P Spaces: 2500. Parking 500 metres from house, 30 marked spaces on tarmac, remainder on grass.
S Partial. Wheelchair access to ground floor. WC for the disabled. Guide Dogs allowed.
£ **Adult:** £8.80 (house & garden), £4.40 (garden only). **Child:** £4.40 (house & garden), £2.20 (garden only). Under 5s free. **Other:** £13.20 (family: 1 adult), £22.00 (family: 2 adults). £7.50 (groups 15+).

SMEATON'S TOWER

The Hoe, Plymouth, Devon PL1 2NZ
Re-sited upper part of the former Eddystone Lighthouse. Built 1759 by John Smeaton, erected here on new base in 1882. Circular tapered tower of painted granite with octagonal lantern. When this lighthouse was first constructed it was considered to be an important technical achievement.
www.plymouthmuseum.gov.uk
Grant Recipient: Plymouth City Museum & Art Gallery
Access Contact: Mr Mark Tosdevin
T: 01752 304774   **F:** 01752 304775
E-mail: museum@plymouth.gov.uk
Open: 1 April–30 September: Tuesday–Friday 10am–12 noon, 1pm–4:30pm, Saturday and Bank Holiday Mondays 10am–12 noon, 1pm–4pm. October 1–March 31: Tuesday–Saturday and Bank Holiday Mondays 10am–12 noon, 1pm–3pm.
Heritage Open Days: Yes

P Spaces: 40. On-street parking.
S No wheelchair access. No WC for the disabled. No Guide Dogs allowed.
£ **Adult:** £2.00. **Child:** £1.00 (Under 5s free). **Other:** £4.80 (Family up to 2 adults & 3 children). Group rates available. Blue Badge guides & school groups (England, under 16s) free.

SOUTH MOLTON TOWN HALL AND PANNIER MARKET

South Molton, Devon EX36 3AB
Guild Hall, dating from 1743 and Grade I listed. Incorporates Court Room, Old Assembly Room and Mayors Parlour with Museum on ground floor. Adjacent to Pannier Market and New Assembly Room.
Grant Recipient: South Molton Town Council
Access Contact: Mr Malcolm Gingell
T: 01769 572501   **F:** 01769 574008
E-mail: smtc@northdevon.gov.uk
Open: Museum: March–October: Monday, Tuesday, Thursday and Saturday. All other rooms used for meetings and functions as and when required. Constable Room rented by Devon County Council.
Heritage Open Days: No
P Parking available in Pannier Market except Thursdays and Saturdays.
S Partial. Wheelchair access to all areas except Court Room, Mayors Parlour and Old Assembly Room. WC for the disabled. Guide Dogs allowed.
£ No

DORSET

HIGHCLIFFE CASTLE

Rothesay Drive, Highcliffe-on-Sea, Christchurch, Dorset BH23 4LE
Cliff-top mansion built in the 1830s by Charles Stuart. Constructed in the romantic, picturesque style, much of its stonework is medieval coming from France. Exterior has been restored, interior houses changing exhibitions and the 16th century stained glass Jesse window. Gift shop and tea rooms on site with 14 acre cliff-top park.
www.highcliffecastle.co.uk
Grant Recipient: Christchurch Borough Council
Access Contact: Mr David Hopkins
T: 01425 278807   **F:** 01425 280423
E-mail: d.hopkins@christchurch.gov.uk
Open: 1 February–23 December: daily 11 am–5pm. Also some evenings for special events. Tea rooms open all year 10am–late afternoon. Grounds all year from 7am.
Heritage Open Days: Yes
P Spaces: 120. Charged parking in Council car park with additional parking in Highcliffe Village (1 mile from Castle).
S Partial. Wheelchair access to all ground floor rooms and toilet facilities for the disabled at the site. Guide Dogs allowed.
£ **Adult:** £2.50 (from 1 February 2008). **Child:** Free. **Other:** HHA/Season ticket holders free.

DURHAM

CROXDALE HALL

Durham DH6 5JP
18th century re-casing of an earlier Tudor building, containing comfortably furnished mid-Georgian rooms with Rococo ceilings. There is also a private chapel in the north elevation, walled gardens, a quarter-of-a-mile long terrace, an orangery and lakes which date from the mid-18th century.
Grant Recipient: The Trustees of Captain GM Salvin's 1983 Settlement
Access Contact: Mr W H T Salvin
T: 01833 690100   **F:** 01833 637004
E-mail: williamsalvin@whtsalvin@aol.com
Open: By prior arrangement on Tuesdays and Wednesdays from first Tuesday in May to second Wednesday in July, 10am–1pm.
Heritage Open Days: Yes
P Spaces: 20.
S Partial. WC for the disabled. No Guide Dogs allowed.
£ **Adult:** £7.50. **Child:** Free (under 16s).

DURHAM CASTLE

Palace Green, Durham DH1 3RW
Dating from 1072, the Castle was the seat of the Prince Bishops until 1832. Together with the Cathedral, the Castle is a World Heritage site. It now houses University College, the Foundation College of Durham University, and is a conference, banqueting and holiday centre in vacations.
www.durhamcastle.com
Grant Recipient: University of Durham
Access Contact: University of Durham
T: 0191 334 3800
Open: University vacations: tours normally at 10 and 11am, 12 noon, 2, 3 and 4pm; term times: tours normally at 2, 3 and 4pm. Times may vary subject to events and functions, please phone the Castle Porter (tel: 0191 334 3800) in advance to confirm and for term dates, or check the website for term dates.
Heritage Open Days: Yes
P Parking in city car parks.
🚻 Partial. Wheelchair access to courtyard only. WC for the disabled inaccessible to wheelchairs. Guide Dogs allowed.
£ **Adult:** £5.00, £4.50 (group rate 10+). **Child:** £3.50 (3–14), £3.00 (group rate 10+). **Other:** £3.50 (concessions), £12.00 (family).

HAMSTEELS HALL

Hamsteels Lane, Quebec, Durham DH7 9RS
Early 18th century farmhouse with 19th century alterations. Panelled window shutters, ground-floor room with full early 18th century panelling; similar panelling and cupboards in first-floor room. Good quality dogleg stair with turned balusters.
www.hamsteelshall.co.uk
Grant Recipient: Mr G F Whitfield
Access Contact: Mrs June Whitfield
T: 01207 520 388   **F:** 01207 520 388
E-mail: june@hamsteelshall.co.uk
Open: By prior arrangement.
Heritage Open Days: No
P Spaces: 8.
🚻 Partial. Wheelchair access to dining room and front parlour only. No WC for the disabled. No Guide Dogs allowed.
£ No

HARDWICK PARK BONO RETIRO

Sedgefield, Durham TS21 2EH
The gothic style Bono Retiro (a place of pleasant retirement) is one of a number of garden buildings set around a 17 acre lake in Hardwick Park. The 18th century landscape park and structures are being restored by Durham Country Council. The Bono Retiro has been consolidated as a ruin.
Grant Recipient: Durham County Council
Access Contact: Mr Darryl Cox
T: 0191 3835508
Open: Daily, dawn to dusk, when the park is open.
Heritage Open Days: No
P Spaces: 200. Car park adjacent to the Park.
🚻 Partial. Most of the park has paths suitable for wheelchairs. WC for the disabled. Guide Dogs allowed.
£ No

LOW BUTTERBY FARMHOUSE

Croxdale & Hett, Durham DH6 5JN
Stone built farmhouse constructed on medieval site incorporating elements of 17th, 18th and 19th century phases of development.
Grant Recipient: The Trustees of Captain GM Salvin's 1983 Settlement
Access Contact: Mr W H T Salvin
T: 01833 690100   **F:** 01833 637004
E-mail: williamsalvin@whtsalvin@aol.com
Open: By prior written or telephone arrangement with Mr W H T Salvin, The Estate Office, Egglestone Abbey, Barnard Castle, Co. Durham DL12 9TN.
Heritage Open Days: Yes
P Spaces: 2.
🚻 Partial. Limited wheelchair access with assistance (some changes in floor level). No WC for the disabled. No Guide Dogs allowed.
£ No

RABY CASTLE

PO Box 50, Staindrop, Darlington, Durham DL2 3AY
Medieval castle, built in the 14th century. Once the seat of the Nevills, it has been home to Lord Barnard's family since 1626. Contains collections of art, fine furniture and highly decorated interiors. Also has a deer park, gardens, carriage collection and woodland adventure playground.
www.rabycastle.com
Grant Recipient: Lord Barnard TD
Access Contact: Ms Katie Blundell
T: 01833 660888/660202   **F:** 01833 660169
E-mail: admin@rabycastle.com
Open: Easter and Bank Holiday weekends, Saturday–Monday; May, June and September: Sunday–Wednesday; July and August: daily except Saturday. Castle open 12.30–5pm. Garden and park 11am–5.30pm. Educational visits and private guided tours including tea/coffee reception (groups 20+) available weekday mornings from Easter to the end of September by prior arrangement.
Heritage Open Days: No
P Spaces: 500.
🚻 Partial. Limited wheelchair access to lower floor with assistance (3 steps to entrance and some internal steps to be negotiated). 3 wheelchairs available. WC for the disabled. Guide Dogs allowed.
£ **Adult:** £9.00 (castle, park & gardens), £5.00 (park & gardens). **Child:** Age 5–15: £4.00 (castle, park & gardens), Age 12–15: £3.50 (park & gardens) under 12's free. **Other:** £8.00 (castle, park & gardens), £3.50 (park & gardens), £25 (family), £15.00, £7.50 & £10.00 (season ticket park & gardens). Group rates available.

RECTORY FARM BARN

Hall Walks, Easington, Peterlee, Durham SR8 3BS
Barn, possibly 13th century with extensive alterations. May originally have been an oratory connected with Seaton Holme. Limestone rubble construction; first floor contains medieval windows. Purchased by Groundwork in 1997 and recently renovated. Listed Grade II*.
Grant Recipient: Groundwork East Durham
Access Contact: Mr Peter Richards
T: 0191 5273333   **F:** 0191 5273665
E-mail: peter.richards@groundwork.org.uk
Open: Access to the exterior all year, Monday to Friday 9am–5pm.
Heritage Open Days: Yes
P Spaces: 10.
🚻 Full. WC for the disabled. Guide Dogs allowed.
£ No

SHOTLEY HALL

Shotley Bridge, Consett, Durham DH8 9TE
Grade II* listed building designed in 1862 by Edward Robson in a Gothic style. Exceptionally complete and unaltered interior with stained glass tiles and interior elements designed by Edward Burne-Jones and made by William Morris.
Grant Recipient: Mr Martell
Access Contact: A Martell
T: 01207 582285
E-mail: lallamartell@kreme.co.uk
Open: 1 May–1 June: daily except Sundays 10am to 4pm. It is advisable to telephone the Hall before visiting. By prior appointment only at other times between 1 April and 30 September to scholars, researchers and enthusiasts of William Morris and Edward Burne-Jones.
Heritage Open Days: No
P Spaces: 5.
🚻 Partial. Wheelchair access to ground floor only. No WC for the disabled. Guide Dogs allowed.
£ No

UNTHANK HALL

Stanhope, Durham DL13 2PQ
Jacobean farmhouse dating from 1520s. Many original features still remain.
Grant Recipient: Alan Morton
Access Contact: Mr Alan Morton
T: 01388 526025
E-mail: alanunthank@aol.com
Open: 7, 14, 21 and 28 January; 4 and 11 February; 3, 10 and 17 March; 5, 12 and 19 May; 9, 16 and 23 June; 8, 15 and 22 September; 6, 13, 20 and 27 October; 10, 17, and 24 November; 1, 8 and 15 December: 10am–3pm.
Heritage Open Days: No

P Parking by river.
🚻 No wheelchair access. No WC for the disabled. No Guide Dogs allowed.
£ No

EAST RIDING OF YORKSHIRE

CONSTABLE MAUSOLEUM

Halsham, nr. Kingston-upon-Hull, East Riding of Yorkshire
The Constable Mausoleum was commissioned by Edward Constable in 1792, built by Atkinson and York and completed in 1802 at a cost of £3,300. It comprises a central domed rotunda of stone, internally lined with black marble and surrounded by heraldic shields. The external raised and railed podium is part of a vaulted ceiling to the crypt below, in which various generation of the Constable family are interned.
Grant Recipient: Mr John Chichester-Constable
Access Contact: Mr John Chichester-Constable
T: 01964 562316   **F:** 01964 563283
E-mail: info@burtonconstable.co.uk
Open: By prior written arrangement with Mr John Chichester-Constable, South Wing–Estate Office, Burton Constable Hall, nr Kingston-upon-Hull, East Riding of Yorkshire HU11 4LN.
Heritage Open Days: No
P Spaces: 1. On street parking.
🚻 No wheelchair access. WC for the disabled at Halsham Arms approximately 300 metres. No Guide Dogs allowed.
£ No

MAISTER HOUSE

160 High Street, Hull,
East Riding of Yorkshire HU1 1NL
Rebuilt in 1743 during Hull's heyday as an affluent trading centre, this house is a typical but rare survivor of a merchant's residence of that period. The restrained exterior belies the spectacular plasterwork staircase inside. The house is now let as offices.
www.maisterhouse@nationaltrust.org.uk
Grant Recipient: The National Trust
Access Contact: Property Manager
T: 0173 870423
Open: Daily except Saturday and Sunday (closed Good Friday and all Bank Holidays) 10am–4pm. Access is to entrance hall and staircase only. Unsuitable for groups.
Heritage Open Days: No
P No
🚻 No wheelchair access. No WC for the disabled. Guide Dogs allowed.
£ Donations welcome.

EAST SUSSEX

DE LA WARR PAVILION

The Marina, Bexhill-on-Sea, East Sussex TN40 1DP
Built in 1935 by architects Erich Mendholson and Serge Chermayeff was the first welded steel-framed building in this country. Its circular staircase and sweeping sea views make it unique as an iconic building of the Modernist movement.
www.dlwp.com
Grant Recipient: De La Warr Pavilion Trust
Access Contact: Ms Emma Morris
T: 01424 229100   **F:** 01424 229101
E-mail: info@dlwp.com
Open: Daily, 10am–6pm. Closed Christmas Day.
Heritage Open Days: No
P Spaces: 100. Pay car park.
🚻 Full. WC for the disabled. Guide Dogs allowed.
£ No

GLYNDE PLACE

Glynde, nr. Lewes, East Sussex BN8 6SX
Elizabethan manor house built in 1589 from local flint and stone from Normandy, then extensively added on to in the 18th century. Contains a collection of Old Masters, family portraits, furniture, embroidery and silver belonging to the family who have lived there for over 400 years.
Grant Recipient: Viscount Hampden
Access Contact: Viscount Hampden
T: 01273 858224   **F:** 01273 858224
E-mail: info@glyndeplace.co.uk
Open: May: Sundays and Bank Holidays; June–August: Sundays, Wednesdays and Bank Holidays 2–5pm (last admission 4.45pm). House open at other times by prior

arrangement. Admission prices for groups if booked in advance. Refreshments available.
Heritage Open Days: No
P Spaces: 150.
& Partial. Wheelchair access to tea room and gardens. WC for the disabled. Guide Dogs allowed.
£ **Adult:** £6.00 **Child:** £3.00. **Other:** £4.50 (groups of 25+ on open days), £7.50 (groups of 25+ at other times).

GREAT DIXTER HOUSE & GARDENS

Northiam, nr. Rye, East Sussex TN31 6PH
Original medieval hall house built c1450 comprising three rooms, the Great Hall, Parlour and Solar. Bought by Nathanial Lloyd in 1910 who employed Lutyens to restore and extend the property. A Yeoman's hall, originally located in Benenden, was dismantled and re-erected at Great Dixter.
www.greatdixter.co.uk
Grant Recipient: Ms O Eller
Access Contact: Mr Perry Rodriguez
T: 01797 252878 ext 2　**F:** 01797 252879
E-mail: office@greatdixter.co.uk
Open: 1 May–30 September: Tuesday–Sunday 2pm–5pm. Gardens open from 11am.
Heritage Open Days: No
P Spaces: 100.
& Partial. Wheelchair access to most areas. Map of routes available. WC for the disabled. Guide Dogs allowed.
£ **Adult:** £7.50 (house and garden), £6.00 (garden only). **Child:** £3.00 (house and garden), £2.50 (garden only).

LAMB HOUSE (COROMANDEL LACQUER PANELS)

3 Chapel Hill, Lewes, East Sussex, BN7 2BB
The incised lacquer panels in the study of Lamb House are a unique surviving example of imported late 17th century Chinese lacquer work that remains as decorative wall panelling. Recently restored.
Grant Recipient: Professor Paul Benjamin
Access Contact: Professor Paul Benjamin
T: 01273 475657
E-mail: p.r.benjamin@sussex.ac.uk
Open: Weekends only by prior telephone or e-mail arrangement.
Heritage Open Days: Yes
P On-street parking.
& Partial. Steps to front door. Wheelchair access to ground floor only. No WC for the disabled. No Guide Dogs allowed.
£ No

ROTUNDA TEMPLE

Brightling Park, nr. Rotherbridge, East Sussex
Built c1812 as an eye-catcher by Sir Robert Smirke for John Fuller, wealthy philanthropist and eccentric. Small circular building with colonnade and dome: the centre-piece of Brightling Park.
Grant Recipient: Mr H C Grissell
Access Contact: Mr H C Grissell
T: 01424 838207　**F:** 01424 838467
E-mail: henrygrissell@hotmail.com
Open: By prior arrangement only. Otherwise Temple can be viewed from public footpaths and other permitted access routes through the Park.
Heritage Open Days: No
P Parking in surrounding roads.
& No wheelchair access. No WC for the disabled. Guide Dogs allowed.
£ No

ST MARY-IN-THE-CASTLE

Pelham Crescent, Hastings, East Sussex TN34 3AF
Built in 1828, architect Joseph Kay, forming an integral part of the design of Pelham Crescent. The Church has a horseshoe-shaped auditorium with gallery and is now used as an arts centre and a place of worship on Sundays.
www.stmaryinthecastle.co.uk
Grant Recipient: Friends of St Mary in the Castle
Access Contact: Ms Kenroy Jones
T: 01424 446999
E-mail: smic2007@aol.com
Open: Arts activities run throughout the year. At other times by prior arrangement.
Heritage Open Days: No
P Spaces: 400. Pay and Display parking opposite.
& Full. WC for the disabled. Guide Dogs allowed.
£ **Adult:** £2.00. **Child:** £1.00.

THE DOVECOTE

Alciston, East Sussex BN8 6NS
14th century dovecote of flint facings with green sand stone dressings on a chalk rubble core with chalk blocks and nesting boxes internally.
www.firleplace.co.uk
Grant Recipient: Trustees of the Firle Estate Settlement
Access Contact: Mr Jamie Evans-Freke
T: 01273 858567　**F:** 01273 858570
E-mail: jamie@firleplace.co.uk
Open: Access to the dovecote is by prior arrangement with the Estate Office.
Heritage Open Days: No
P No
& Partial. No WC for the disabled. Guide Dogs allowed.
£ No

THE FLUSHING INN

4 Market Street, Rye, East Sussex TN31 7LA
15th century timber-framed building, now a restaurant, with large recently restored 16th century wall painting.
www.theflushinginn.com
Grant Recipient: Mr Flynn
Access Contact: Mr Flynn
T: 01797 223292　**F:** 01797 229748
E-mail: j.e.flynn@btconnect.com
Open: Restaurant open Wednesday–Sunday for lunches and dinners, Mondays lunch only and Tuesdays closed. Closed first two weeks in January and June. Unless dining, visiting to view the Fresco is restricted to 10.30am–12 noon.
Heritage Open Days: No
P Parking on-street but restricted to 1 hour, otherwise public parking elsewhere in Rye.
& Partial. Wheelchair access to Fresco with assistance (entrance steps to be negotiated). No WC for the disabled. Guide Dogs allowed.
£ No

THE ROYAL PAVILION

Brighton, East Sussex BN1 1EE
Former seaside residence of George IV in Indian style with Chinese-inspired interiors. Originally a neo-classical villa by Henry Holland was built on the site in 1787, but this was subsequently replaced by the current John Nash building constructed between 1815–23.
www.royalpavilion.org.uk
Grant Recipient: Brighton & Hove City Council
Access Contact: Mr Andrew Barlow
T: 01273 292746　**F:** 01273 292871
E-mail: andrew.barlow@brighton-hove.gov.uk
Open: April–September: daily, 9.30am–5.45pm (last admission 5pm). October–March, daily 10am–5.15pm (last admission 4.30pm). Closed 25 and 26 December. Admission charges are valid until 31 March 2008, for rates after that date please check the English Heritage website or with the Royal Pavilion for current information.
Heritage Open Days: No
P NCP car park on Church Street. Parking for the disabled is available in the grounds of the Pavilion by prior arrangement.
& Partial. Wheelchair access to ground floor only, reduced rate of admission. WC for the disabled. Guide Dogs allowed.
£ **Adult:** £7.70, £3.70 (local residents, Oct–Feb only). Prices valid until 31.3.08. **Child:** £5.10 under 16 (Oct–Feb, local residents free with paying adult). Prices valid until 31.3.08. **Other:** £5.90 (seniors/students/unemployed), £20.50 (family of 2 adults, 2 children), £12.80 (1 adult, 2 children). Prices valid until 31.3.08.

WINDMILL HILL WINDMILL

Herstmonceux, Hailsham, East Sussex BN27 4RT
Grade II* listed, dating from 1815, the second tallest and largest post mill in body size. The mill last worked by wind in 1894 and has recently been authentically restored.
www.windmillhillwindmill.co.uk
Grant Recipient: Windmill Hill Windmill Trust
Access Contact: Mrs B Frost
T: 01323 833033　**F:** 01323 833744
E-mail: admin@windmillhillwindmill.co.uk
Open: All year: First and third Sunday of the month and Bank Holidays 2.30–5pm. School parties and groups by prior arrangement.
Heritage Open Days: Yes

P Spaces: 4.
& Partial. Wheelchair access to visitor centre. Film enables full visitor experience without climbing long ladder to mill body. WC for the disabled. Guide Dogs allowed.
£ No

ESSEX

HARWICH REDOUBT FORT

behind 29 Main Road, Harwich, Essex CO12 3LT
180ft diameter circular fort commanding the harbour entrance built in 1808 to defend the port against a Napoleonic invasion. Surrounded by a dry moat, there are 11 guns on the battlements. 18 casemates which originally sheltered 300 troops in siege conditions now house a series of small museums.
www.harwich-society.co.uk
Grant Recipient: The Harwich Society
Access Contact: Mr A Rutter
T: 01255 503429　**F:** 01255 503429
E-mail: info@harwich-society.co.uk
Open: 1 May–31 August: daily 10am–4pm. Rest of year: Sundays only 10am–4pm.
Heritage Open Days: Yes
P Parking for the disabled only (4 spaces).
& No wheelchair access. No WC for the disabled. Guide Dogs allowed.
£ **Adult:** £2.00. **Child:** Accompanied children free. **Other:** £2.00.

JOHN WEBB'S WINDMILL

Fishmarket Street, Thaxted, Essex CM6 2PG
Brick tower mill built in 1804 consisting of five floors. Has been fully restored as a working mill. On two floors there is a museum of rural and domestic bygones. There is also a small picture gallery of early photographs of the mill and the surrounding countryside.
Grant Recipient: Thaxted Parish Council
Access Contact: Mr L A Farren
T: 01371 830285　**F:** 01371 830285
Open: May–September: Saturday–Sunday and Bank Holidays 2–6pm. Groups during weekdays by special arrangement. For further information please contact Mr L A Farren, Borough Hill, Bolford Street, Thaxted, Essex CM6 2PY.
Heritage Open Days: Yes
P Spaces: 80. Public parking in Thaxted.
& Partial. Wheelchair access to ground floor only. WC for the disabled in public car park in Margaret Street. Guide Dogs allowed.
£ Donations welcome.

OLD FRIENDS MEETING HOUSE

High Street, Stebbing, Essex CM6 3SG
The Stebbing Meeting House is the earliest Quaker meeting House in Essex. Built c1674 it is a particularly fine and complete example of an early Quaker meeting house and its historical importance is recognised by its Grade II* listing.
Grant Recipient: The Trustees of the Old Friends Meeting House
Access Contact: Mrs A Newbrook
T: 01371 856464
E-mail: jnewbrook@aol.com
Open: By prior telephone or written arrangement with Mrs A Newbrook, 7 Oakfield, Stebbing, Essex CM6 3SX (tel: 01371 856464).
Heritage Open Days: Yes
P Spaces: 10.
& Partial. Wheelchair access to ground floor. WC for the disabled. Guide Dogs allowed.
£ No

THE GREAT DUNMOW MALTINGS

Mill Lane, Great Dunmow, Essex CM6 1BD
Grade II* maltings complex (listed as Boyes Croft Maltings, White Street), early 16th century and later, timber-framed and plastered, part weatherboarding and brick. The building exhibits the entire floor malting process whilst the Great Dunmow Museum Society occupies the ground floor with displays of local history. The first floor is available for community use.
www.greatdunmowmaltings.co.uk
Grant Recipient: Great Dunmow Maltings Preservation Trust
Access Contact: Mrs B A Ball
T: 01371 872097　**F:** 01371 872097

E-mail: bball_barnston@yahoo.co.uk
Open: All year: Saturday, Sunday and Bank Holidays
11am–4pm. Groups at any reasonable time by prior
arrangement. Closed over Christmas/New Year holiday
week.
Heritage Open Days: Yes
P Spaces: 100. Public car park nearby (pay and display,
free on Sundays and Bank Holidays).
Full. WC for the disabled. Guide Dogs allowed.
£ Adult: £1.00. Child: 50p. Other: 50p (senior citizens).

GLOUCESTERSHIRE

ACTON COURT

**Latteridge Road, Iron Acton, South Gloucestershire
BS37 9TJ**
Seat of the Poyntzes, an influential courtier family who
occupied the house until 1680 when it was converted into
a farm house. A Tudor range, constructed in 1535 to
accommodate King Henry VIII and Queen Anne B oleyn
survives along with part of the North range. The rooms are
unfurnished but contain important traces of original
decoration.
www.actoncourt.com
Grant Recipient: Rosehill Corporation
Access Contact: Ms Lisa Kopper
T: 01454 228224   **F:** 01454 227256
E-mail: actonct@dircon.co.uk or info@actoncourt.com
Open: Guided tours and events 17 June–24 August.
Closed Mondays. Pre-booking essential. Ring information
line for details 01454 228 224.
Heritage Open Days: No
P Spaces: 40.
Partial. WC for the disabled. Guide Dogs allowed.
£ Adult: £5.00. Child: £4.00. Other: £4.00 (senior
citizens & the disabled), £100 (exclusive group tours
maximum 25). Special events priced separately.

CHASTLETON HOUSE

**Chastleton, Moreton-in-Marsh, Gloucestershire GL56
0SU**
Jacobean house filled with a mixture of rare and everyday
objects, furniture and textiles collected since 1612.
Continually occupied for 400 years by the same family.
Emphasis lies on conservation rather than restoration.
www.nationaltrust.org.uk
Grant Recipient: The National Trust
Access Contact: The Custodian
T: 01608 674355   **F:** 01608 674355
E-mail: chastleton@nationaltrust.org.uk
Open: 26 March–30 September: Wednesday–Saturday
1–5pm (last admission 4pm); 1 October–1 November:
Wednesday–Saturday 1–4pm (last admission 3pm). Visitor
numbers limited, pre-booking advised (Telephone 01608
674981 Monday–Friday 10am–2pm). Groups by written
arrangement with the Custodian.
Heritage Open Days: No
P Spaces: 50.
Partial. Wheelchair access to ground floor with
assistance and parts of garden only. WC for the disabled.
Guide Dogs allowed.
£ Adult: £7.00. Child: £3.50. Other: £17.50 (family),
Private View £7.50 (£2.50 NT members).

CHAVENAGE

Tetbury, Gloucestershire GL8 8XP
Elizabethan Manor House (c1576), contains tapestry
rooms, furniture and relics from the Cromwellian Period.
Has been the home of only two families since the time of
Elizabeth I. Used as a location for television and film
productions.
www.chavenage.com
Grant Recipient: Trustees of the Chavenage Settlement
Access Contact: Miss Caroline Lowsley-Williams
T: 01666 502329   **F:** 01453 836778
E-mail: info@chavenage.com
Open: May–September: Thursday, Sunday and Bank
Holidays plus Easter Sunday and Monday 2–5pm. Groups
at other times by prior arrangement.
Heritage Open Days: Yes
P Spaces: 40.
Partial. Wheelchair access to ground floor only. Parking
for the disabled near front door. WC for the disabled.
Guide Dogs allowed.
£ Adult: £6.00. Child: £3.00.

DEER PARK

Cirencester Park, Cirencester, Gloucestershire
The Deer Park is part of a much larger landscaped area. It
has recently been landscaped to remove concrete bases
and roadways of World War II military hospitals, reinstating
the original landscape designed in the 1700s by the First
Earl and Alexander Pope.
Grant Recipient: Bathurst Estate
Access Contact: Mr Allsop
T: 01285 653135   **F:** 01285 656291
Open: All year: daily, 8am–5pm.
Heritage Open Days: No
P Car parking in the town and limited parking in Cecily
Hill (short stay).
Partial. Wheelchair access available but may be uneven
due to unsurfaced tracks which may be rough or wet.
Guide dogs should be accompanied due to farm hazards.
WC for the disabled in the town. Guide Dogs allowed.
£ No

DYRHAM PARK

Dyrham, nr. Bath, Gloucestershire SN14 8ER
17th century house set within an ancient deer park,
woodlands and formal garden. The house was furnished in
the Dutch style and still has many original contents
including paintings, ceramics, furniture and 17th century
tapestries. The Victorian domestic rooms include the
kitchen, larder, bakehouse, dairy and tenants hall.
www.nationaltrust.org.uk
Grant Recipient: The National Trust
Access Contact: Visitor Services Manager
T: 01179 372501   **F:** 01179 371353
E-mail: dyrhampark@nationaltrust.org.uk
Open: House: 14 March–2 November, daily except
Wednesday and Thursday 11am–5pm (last admission to
house 4pm). Garden: as for house 11am–5pm or dusk if
earlier. Park: all year (closed 25 December) 11am–5.30pm
or dusk if earlier. Bank Holiday Mondays and Good Friday
11am–5pm.
Heritage Open Days: Yes
P Spaces: 250. Free shuttle bus from car park to house.
Partial. Wheelchair access to all but four upstairs
rooms. A photograph album of these rooms is available.
WC for the disabled. Guide Dogs allowed.
£ Adult: £10.00 (House, park & garden), £4.00 (park &
garden), £2.60 (garden only). Child: £5.00 (House, park &
garden), £2.00 (park & garden), £1.30 (garden only).
Other: Family: £25.00 (House, park & garden), £8.90
(park & garden), £5.80 (garden only).

ELMORE COURT ENTRANCE GATES

Elmore, Gloucestershire GL2 3NT
Early 18th century carriage and pedestrian gateway, with
19th century flanking walls. By William Edney, blacksmith
of Bristol for Sir John Guise at Rendcomb. Gateway was
removed from Rendcomb and re-erected here in early 19th
century.
Grant Recipient: Trustees of the Elmore Court Estate
Access Contact: Trustees of the Elmore Court Estate
T: 01452 720293   **F:** 01452 724166
E-mail: ans@gladesfestival.com
Open: Visible at all times from public highway.
Heritage Open Days: No
P Spaces: 5. Off-road parking on forecourt in front of
gates.
Full. No WC for the disabled. Guide Dogs allowed.
£ No

FRAMPTON MANOR BARN (THE WOOL BARN,
MANOR FARM)

**The Green, Frampton-on-Severn, Gloucestershire GL2
7EP**
Grade I listed timber framed barn built c1560. Re-used
worked stones in ashlar plinth wall were found during
repair works.
www.framptoncourtestate.co.uk
Grant Recipient: Mr P R H Clifford
Access Contact: Mr P R H Clifford
T: 01452 740698   **F:** 01452 740698
E-mail: clifford@framptoncourt.wanadoo.co.uk
Open: During normal office hours (8.30am–4.30pm
Monday–Friday). Other times by arrangement.
Heritage Open Days: No
P Spaces: 30.
Full. WC for the disabled. Guide Dogs allowed.
£ Adult: £1.00. Child: Free (special rates for school
parties). Other: Free.

STANCOMBE PARK TEMPLE

Dursley, Gloucestershire GL11 6AU
One in a series of buildings in the folly gardens at
Stancombe Park, in the form of a Greek temple. Built in
approximately 1815.
www.thetemple.info
Grant Recipient: Mr N D Barlow
Access Contact: Mrs G T Barlow
T: 01453 542815
E-mail: nicb@nicbarlow.com
Open: All year by prior telephone arrangement. To the
exterior only during Heritage Open Days.
Heritage Open Days: Yes
P Spaces: 20. Limited parking at the site (4 cars)
No wheelchair access. No WC for the disabled. Guide
Dogs allowed.
£ Adult: £3.00 (charity donation for visits to garden). No
charge is made for anyone specifically wishing to see the
temple only.

STANLEY MILL

**King's Stanley, Stonehouse,
Gloucestershire GL10 3HQ**
Built 1813, with large addition c1825, of Flemish bond red
brick with ashlar dressings and Welsh slate roof. Early
example of fireproof construction (which survived a major
fire in 1884).
Grant Recipient: Stanley Mills Ltd
Access Contact: Mr Mark Griffiths/ Jill May
T: 01453 821800   **F:** 01453 791 167
E-mail: jill@marlings.co.uk
Open: By prior written arrangement as the Mill is used by
various manufacturing companies.
Heritage Open Days: No
P Spaces: 30. By prior written arrangement as the Mill is
used by various manufacturing companies.
No wheelchair access. No WC for the disabled. No
Guide Dogs allowed.
£ No

TANHOUSE FARM TITHE BARN

Frampton-on-Severn, Gloucestershire GL2 7EH
17th century Tithe Barn with cattle Byre.
Grant Recipient: M R & C R Williams
Access Contact: M R & C A Williams
T: 01452 741 072
E-mail: tanhouse.farm@lineone.net
Open: All year by prior arrangement with M R or C R
Williams (tel: 01452 741072).
Heritage Open Days: Yes
P Spaces: 20. Parking within 100 metres.
Partial. Wheelchair access to main areas. No WC for
the disabled. Guide Dogs allowed.
£ No

WEST BANQUETING HOUSE

Chipping Campden, Gloucestershire
The West Banqueting House stands opposite the East
Banqueting House across a broad terrace. It is elaborately
decorated with spiral chimney stacks, finials and strapwork
parapets.
www.landmarktrust.org.uk
Grant Recipient: The Landmark Trust
Access Contact: Mrs Victoria O'Keeffe
T: 01628 825920   **F:** 01628 825417
E-mail: vokeeffe@landmarktrust.org.uk
Open: The Landmark Trust is an independent charity,
which rescues small buildings of historic or architectural
importance from decay or unsympathetic improvement.
Landmark's aim is to promote the enjoyment of these
historic buildings by making them available to stay in for
holidays. West Banqueting House can be rented by
anyone, at all times of the year, for periods ranging from a
weekend to three weeks. Bookings can be made by
telephoning the Booking Office on 01628 825925. The
public can also view the building on eight Open Days
throughout the year (dates to be set) or by prior
arrangement; telephone the access contact Victoria
O'Keeffe on 01628 825920 to make an appointment.
Potential visitors will be asked to write to confirm the
details of their visit.
Heritage Open Days: No
P Parking available in town only.
No wheelchair access. No WC for the disabled. Guide
Dogs allowed.
£ No

WOODCHESTER PARK MANSION

Nympsfield, Stonehouse, Gloucestershire GL10 3TS
Grade I listed Victorian mansion, abandoned incomplete in 1870. One of the most remarkable houses of its period and uniquely exhibiting its construction process. Set in a large landscaped park (possibly by 'Capability' Brown). The building is also a Site of Special Scientific Interest housing two nationally important populations of endangered bats.
www.woodchestermansion.org.uk
Grant Recipient: Woodchester Mansion Trust
Access Contact: Ms Kate Lewington
T: 01453 861541   **F:** 01453 861337
E-mail: office@woodchestermansion.org.uk
Open: Easter–End of October: every Sunday, first Saturday in month and Bank Holiday weekends; July–August: Saturday and Sunday, and 21 March, 11am–5.00pm (last admission to house at 4.00pm). Groups and private visits by prior arrangement.
Heritage Open Days: No
P Spaces: 60. Parking is 1 mile from Mansion, access via woodland walk. Minibus service available.
♿ Partial. Wheelchair access to ground floor only. No WC for the disabled. Guide Dogs allowed.
£ Adult: £5.50. **Child:** Free with parents. **Other:** £4.50 (English Heritage & National Trust members, senior citizens & NUS card holders).

GREATER MANCHESTER

1830 WAREHOUSE

The Museum of Science & Industry, Liverpool Road, Castlefield, Manchester, Greater Manchester M3 4FP
Former railway warehouse, c1830, originally part of the Liverpool Road Railway Station (the oldest surviving passenger railway station in the world) which was the terminus of the Liverpool and Manchester Railway built by George Stephenson and his son Robert. Now part of The Museum of Science and Industry.
www.musi.org.uk
Grant Recipient: The Museum of Science & Industry
Access Contact: Mr Robin Holgate
T: 0161 832 2244   **F:** 0161 606 0186
E-mail: collections@msim.org.uk
Open: Daily (except 24, 25 and 26 December and 1 January) 10am–5pm.
Heritage Open Days: No
P Spaces: 50.
♿ Full. WC for the disabled. Guide Dogs allowed.
£ Free entry to all to main museum building. Charge for special exhibitions.

FORMER CHURCH OF ST BENEDICT

Bennett Street, West Gorton, Manchester M12 5ND
Former church, built 1880 and the most original designed by JS Crowther. Includes notable stained glass and vestry furnishings. Now an indoor climbing centre with café and shop.
Grant Recipient: Manchester Climbing Centre Ltd
Access Contact: Mr John Dunne
T: 07798 857138   **F:** 0161 2307049
E-mail: info@manchesterclimbingcentre.com
Open: All year: Monday to Friday, 10am–10pm. Saturday, Sunday and Bank Holidays: 10 am–6pm.
Heritage Open Days: Yes
P Spaces: 20.
♿ Partial. Wheelchair access to main hall but not to café. WC for the disabled. Guide Dogs allowed.
£ No

HALL I' TH' WOOD MUSEUM

Green Way, Bolton, Greater Manchester BL1 8UA
Grade I listed manor house, early 16th century, where Samuel Crompton invented and built his spinning mule in 1779. Part of the Hall is timber-framed and shows the development of a house in the 16th and 17th centuries. Now a museum.
www.boltonmuseums.org.uk
Grant Recipient: Bolton Council
Access Contact: Mrs Elizabeth McNab
T: 01204 332370   **F:** 01204 332215
E-mail: museum.hallithwood@bolton.gov.uk
Open: 8 January–9 April: Saturday and Sunday 12 noon–5pm; 12 April–30 October: Wednesday–Sunday 112 noon–5pm (last admission 4.15pm); 31 October–end March 2008: Saturday and Sunday 12 noon–5pm (last admission 4.15pm).
Heritage Open Days: No

P Spaces: 10.
♿ No wheelchair access. No WC for the disabled. No Guide Dogs allowed.
£ Adult: £2.00. **Child:** £1.00 (under 5 free).
Other: Family £5.00 (2 adults & 2 children).

STAIRCASE HOUSE

30a/31 Market Place, Stockport, Greater Manchester SK1 3XE
Timber framed town house. Dating from 1460, enlarged in 16th and 17th centuries and altered in 18th, 19th and 20th centuries. Early panelled rooms and an important 17th century caged newel staircase from which the house takes its name. Damaged by fire, but restored by Stockport Council. Interpretation charts the history of the house and its evaluation to WWII. The house is fully interactive with visitors invited to touch all objects and furniture.
www.staircasehouse.org.uk
Grant Recipient: Stockport Metropolitan Borough Council
Access Contact: Mr Scott Manton
T: 0161 480 1460   **F:** 0161 474 0312
E-mail: scott.manton@stockport.gov.uk
Open: Daily: Monday–Friday, 12pm–5pm; Saturday and Sunday, 10am–5pm. Closed Christmas Day, Boxing Day and New Years Day.
Heritage Open Days: Yes
P Town centre car parks and street parking.
♿ Full. WC for the disabled. Guide Dogs allowed.
£ Adult: £3.95. **Child:** Free (under 5s) £2.95 (age 5–15).
Other: £2.95 (senior citizens), £12.00 (family), £2.00 with leisure key.

VICTORIA BATHS

Hathersage Road, Manchester, Greater Manchester M13 0FE
An ornate and complete municipal swimming pool complex built 1903–1906, with 2 pools, Turkish and Russian Bath suite, Aeratone and extensive stained glass and tile work. Restoration Phase 1, comprising external and structural restoration to front of building has taken place.
www.victoriabaths.org.uk
Grant Recipient: The Manchester Victoria Baths Trust
Access Contact: Ms Gill Wright
T: 0161 224 2020   **F:** 0161 224 0707
E-mail: info@victoriabaths.org.uk
Open: April–October: first Sunday in each month 12–4pm. Additional opening days include Heritage Open Days in September. At other times by prior arrangement with the Manchester Victoria Baths Trust, Studio 20, Longsight Business Park, Hamilton Road, Longsight, Manchester M13 0PD (tel: 0161 224 2020). Group visits welcome.
Heritage Open Days: Yes
P Telephone for details as adjacent car park is being redeveloped.
♿ Partial. Wheelchair access to ground floor with assistance. Most of the building can be seen from the ground floor. No WC for the disabled. Guide Dogs allowed.
£ Adult: £1.00. **Child:** Free.

HAMPSHIRE

AVINGTON PARK

Winchester, Hampshire SO21 1DB
Palladian mansion dating back to the 11th century, enlarged in 1670 by the addition of two wings and a classical Portico surmounted by three statues. Visited by Charles II and George IV. Has highly decorated State rooms and a Georgian church in the grounds.
www.avingtonpark.co.uk
Grant Recipient: Mrs Sarah Bullen
Access Contact: Mrs Sarah Bullen
T: 01962 779260   **F:** 01962 779202
E-mail: enquiries@avingtonpark.co.uk
Open: May–September: Sundays and Bank Holidays and Mondays in August 2.30–5.30pm. Group booking and other times by prior arrangement.
Heritage Open Days: Yes
P Spaces: 150.
♿ Partial. Wheelchair access to ground floor only. Church with assistance (one step to interior). WC for the disabled. Guide Dogs allowed.
£ Adult: £4.50. **Child:** £2.00.

BOATHOUSE NO. 6

Portsmouth Naval Base, Portsmouth PO1 3LJ
Large Victorian naval boathouse constructed 1845. Designed by Captain James Beatson of the Royal Engineers, it is one of the first examples of a brick building constructed around a metal frame. Its massive cast iron beams are inscribed with their load-bearing capacity.
www.actionstations.org
Grant Recipient: Portsmouth Naval Base Property Trust
Access Contact: Mr Mark Meacher
T: 023 9282 0921   **F:** 023 9286 2437
E-mail: mm@pnbpt.com
Open: All year except Christmas Eve, Christmas Day and Boxing Day 10am–5.30pm (April–October) and 10am–5pm (November–March). Groups by prior arrangement.
Heritage Open Days: Yes
P Spaces: 150. Additional parking 500 metres from the site.
♿ Full. WC for the disabled. Guide Dogs allowed.
£ Adult: £11.50. **Child:** £9.00. **Other:** £32.00 (family).

CALSHOT (ACTIVITIES SUNDERLAND SOPWITH HANGAR AND SCHNEIDER HANGER)

Calshot, Fawley, Hampshire SO45 1BR
Part of the most outstanding group of early aircraft structures of this type in Britain and the largest hangar built for use by fixed-wing aircraft during World War 1. Now an activities centre.
www.calshot.com
Grant Recipient: Hampshire County Council
Access Contact: Mr Phil Quill
T: 023 8089 2077   **F:** 023 8082 1267
E-mail: phil.quil@hants.gov.uk
Open: Daily except Christmas Day, Boxing Day and New Year's Day: 8.30am–5pm.
Heritage Open Days: No
P Spaces: 150. Ample free parking on-site.
♿ Full. WC for the disabled. Guide Dogs allowed.
£ No

HIGHCLERE CASTLE & PARK

Highclere, Newbury, Hampshire RG20 9RN
Early Victorian mansion rebuilt by Sir Charles Barry in 1842, surrounded by 'Capability' Brown parkland with numerous listed follies including Heavens Gate, an 18th century eye-catching hill-top landscape feature and The Temple, c1760, altered by Barry in mid 19th century, a regular classical circular structure. Family home of the 8th Earl and Countess of Carnarvon.
www.highclerecastle.co.uk
Grant Recipient: Executors of the 7th Earl of Carnarvon & Lord Carnarvon
Access Contact: Mr Alec Tompson
T: 01223 236996   **F:** 01223 3234859
E-mail: agent@hwdean.co.uk
Open: 23 March–10 April: Sunday–Thursday; 4, 5, 26 and 27 May, 1 July–31 August: Sunday–Thursday: 11am–4.30pm. Last admission 3.30pm. Temple: permissive path on days when Castle is open. At all other times by prior arrangement with Estate Office, Highclere Park (Tel: 01635 255401). All opening times are provisional and visitors are recommended to confirm opening times with the Estate Office before travelling.
Heritage Open Days: No
P Spaces: 200. Unlimited parking.
♿ Partial. Wheelchair access to ground floor only. WC for the disabled. Guide Dogs allowed.
£ Adult: £8.00 (provisional). **Child:** £4.00 (provisional). **Other:** £7.00 (concession, provisional).

HOUGHTON LODGE GARDENS

Stockbridge, Hampshire SO20 6LQ
Landscaped pleasure grounds and a park laid out c1800 with views from higher ground over informal landscape (Grade II*) surrounding the 18th century Cottage Ornee (Grade II*). Chalk cob walls enclose ancient espaliers, greenhouses and herb garden. Formal topiary 'Peacock' Garden, snorting topiary dragon and wild flowers. A popular TV Film location. 14 acres of Meadow Walks through river valley.
www.houghtonlodge.co.uk
Grant Recipient: Captain M W Busk
Access Contact: Capt. M W Busk
T: 01264 810502   **F:** 01264 810063
E-mail: info@houghtonlodge.co.uk
Open: 1 March–30 October: daily 10am–5pm. Wednesdays by appointment.

Opening arrangements at properties grant-aided by English Heritage

Heritage Open Days: No
Ⓟ Spaces: 100.
♿ Partial. WC for the disabled. Guide Dogs allowed.
£ **Adult:** £5.00. **Child:** Free. **Other:** £4.50 (group rate).

ST MICHAEL'S ABBEY

Farnborough, Hampshire GU14 7NQ
Grade I listed church and Imperial Mausoleum crypt of Napoleon III and his family. Abbey Church also built for the Empress Eugenie so the monks could act as custodians of the tombs. Initially a Benedictine priory, raised to Abbey status in 1903.
www.farnboroughabbey.org
Grant Recipient: Empress Eugenie Memorial Trust
Access Contact: Fr Magnus Wilson
T: 01252 894211/546105   **F:** 01252 372822
E-mail: abbot@farnboroughabbey.org
Open: Saturdays and Public Holidays guided tours at 3.30pm. Contact Fr Magnus Wilson, Bursar, or Fr D C Brogan, Abbot, for further information.
Heritage Open Days: No
Ⓟ Spaces: 10.
♿ No wheelchair access. No WC for the disabled. No Guide Dogs allowed.
£ No

THE VYNE

Sherborne St John, Basingstoke, Hampshire RG24 9HL
Built in the early 16th century for Henry VIII's Lord Chamberlain. The house acquired a classical portico mid 17th century (the first of its kind in England). Tudor chapel with Renaissance glass, Palladian staircase, old panelling and fine furniture. Grounds, containing wild garden, lakes and woodland walks.
www.nationaltrust.org.uk
Grant Recipient: The National Trust
Access Contact: The Property Manager
T: 01256 883858   **F:** 01256 881720
E-mail: thevyne@nationaltrust.org.uk
Open: House: 15 March–2 November: daily except Thursday and Friday (but open Good Friday and Bank Holidays) Saturday and Sunday 11am–5pm, Monday–Wednesday 1–5pm (11am–12pm pre-booked groups only for guided tours). Grounds: 2 February–9 March, weekends only 11am–5pm; 15 March–2 November, as house 11am–5pm.
Heritage Open Days: Yes
Ⓟ Car park (with capacity for 140 cars and 3 coaches) located 450 metres from house (buggy service subject to volunteer availability). Disabled drivers will be able to park by house by prior arrangement.
♿ Partial. Wheelchair access to ground floor, stairs to other floors. No WC for the disabled. No Guide Dogs allowed.
£ **Adult:** £8.50, £5.50 (grounds only). **Child:** £4.25, £2.75 (grounds only). **Other:** £22.00 (family). Free to National Trust members.

WHITCHURCH SILK MILL

28 Winchester Street, Whitchurch, Hampshire RG28 7AL
Grade II* watermill built c1800 and has been in continuous use as a silk weaving mill since the 1820s. Now a working museum, the winding, warping and weaving machinery installed between 1890 and 1927 produces silks to order for theatrical costume, historic houses, fashion and artworks.
www.whitchurchsilkmill.org.uk
Grant Recipient: Hampshire Buildings Preservation Trust
Access Contact: General Manager
T: 01256 892065   **F:** 01256 893882
E-mail: silkmill@btinternet.com
Open: Mill and shop: Tuesday–Sunday 10.30am–5pm (last admission 4.15pm). Mill and shop closed Mondays (except Bank Holidays) and between Christmas and New Year.
Heritage Open Days: Yes
Ⓟ Spaces: 20. Adjacent to Mill and additional parking in the town.
♿ Partial. Wheelchair access to ground floor, shop and gardens. Stair lift to first floor and two steps to tea room. WC for the disabled. Guide Dogs allowed.
£ **Adult:** £3.50. **Child:** £1.75. **Other:** £3.00, £8.75 (family).

HEREFORDSHIRE

EASTNOR CASTLE

nr. Ledbury, Herefordshire HR8 1RL
Norman-style castellated mansion set in the western slopes of the Malvern Hills. Constructed 1812–1820 and designed by Sir Robert Smirke, the castle has 15 state and other rooms fully-furnished and open to visitors. The decoration includes tapestries, paintings, armour and a drawing room by Augustus Pugin.
www.eastnorcastle.com
Grant Recipient: Mr J Hervey-Bathurst
Access Contact: Mr S Foster
T: 01531 633160   **F:** 01531 631776
E-mail: enquiries@eastnorcastle.com
Open: Easter–end September: Sundays and Bank Holiday Mondays 11am–5pm. 17 July–31 August: Sunday–Friday 11am–5pm.
Heritage Open Days: Yes
Ⓟ Spaces: 150.
♿ Partial. Wheelchair access to grounds and ground and first floor with assistance (always available). WC for the disabled. Guide Dogs allowed.
£ **Adult:** £7.50. **Child:** £4.50. **Other:** £6.50 (senior citizens).

HERGEST COURT

Kington, Herefordshire HR5 3EG
House dates back to 1267 and was the ancestral home of the Clanvowe and Vaughan families. It is an unusual example of a fortified manor in the Welsh Marches. It has literary associations with Sir John Clanvowe and Lewis Glyn Cothi.
Grant Recipient: Mr W L Banks
Access Contact: Messrs W L Banks & R Banks
T: 01544 230160   **F:** 01544 232031
E-mail: gardens@hergest.co.uk
Open: By prior arrangement with the Hergest Estate Office, Kington, Herefordshire HR5 3EG. Bookings by phone or fax with five days' notice.
Heritage Open Days: No
Ⓟ Spaces: 5.
♿ Partial. Wheelchair access to ground floor only. No WC for the disabled. Guide Dogs allowed.
£ **Adult:** £5.00. **Child:** Free. **Other:** £3.50 (groups).

THE WATERWORKS MUSEUM–HEREFORD (FORMERLY BROOMY HILL PUMPING STATION)

Broomy Hill, Hereford, Herefordshire HR4 0LJ
Set in the Victorian water pumping station of Hereford with working pumping engines telling the story of drinking water. Oldest triple-expansion steam engine working in Britain plus beam, gas and diesel engines and overshot waterwheel.
www.waterworksmuseum.org.uk
Grant Recipient: Herefordshire Waterworks Museum Ltd
Access Contact: Dr Noel Meeke
T: 01600 890 118   **F:** 01600 890 009
E-mail: info@waterworksmuseum.org.uk
Open: Easter–October: every Tuesday 11am–4pm. Engines working on second and last Sundays in month. Plus Easter, Spring and August Bank Holidays 1–4pm.
Heritage Open Days: Yes
Ⓟ Spaces: 30. Additional 50 spaces nearby, disabled parking in courtyard. Space for one full size coach.
♿ Full. WC for the disabled. Guide Dogs allowed.
£ **Adult:** £3.00. **Child:** £1.00. **Other:** £2.00 (senior citizens).

WILTON CASTLE

Bridstow, nr. Ross on Wye, Herefordshire HR9 6AD
12th century castle, partly demolished for 16th century house which in turn became ruinous. A dry moat surrounds restored curtain walls which include three fortified accommodation towers.
www.wiltoncastle.co.uk
Grant Recipient: Mr & Mrs A K Parslow
Access Contact: A K Parslow
T: 07836 386317   **F:** 01985 212217
E-mail: sue@Wiltoncastle.co.uk
Open: 24 April, 5 May, 22 June and 3 August: 11am–6pm.
Heritage Open Days: No
Ⓟ Spaces: 25.
♿ Partial. Wheelchair access throughout (except towers). WC for the disabled. Guide Dogs allowed.
£ **Adult:** £3.50. **Child:** £1.75. **Other:** English Heritage members free.

HERTFORDSHIRE

ALL SAINTS PASTORAL CENTRE

Shenley Lane, London Colney, St Albans, Hertfordshire AL2 1AF
Grade II* listed building, designed by architect Leonard Stokes. Chapel begun in 1927 by Ninian Comper and finished in 1964 by his son Sebastian Comper.
www.allsaintspc.org.uk
Grant Recipient: Diocese of Westminster
Access Contact: Mr Alan Johnstone
T: 01727 829306   **F:** 01 727 822 880
E-mail: conf.office@allsaintspc.org.uk
Open: Daily, 9am–5pm, except last week of December.
Heritage Open Days: No
Ⓟ Spaces: 130.
♿ Full. WC for the disabled. Guide Dogs allowed.
£ No

BERKHAMSTED TOWN HALL

196 High Street, Berkhamsted, Hertfordshire HP4 3AP
Berkhamsted Town Hall and Market House, built in 1859, also housed the Mechanics' Institute. It has a gothic façade and retains much of the original stonework. There are three rooms: the Great Hall, Clock Room, Sessions Hall. In the Great Hall many of the original features have been preserved, including the fireplace and barrel vaulted ceiling.
www.berkhamstedtownhall.com
Grant Recipient: Berkhamsted Town Hall Trust
Access Contact: Mr Ian Hall
T: 01442 862288
E-mail: bthtmanager@tiscali.co.uk
Open: Monday–Friday 10am–1pm. At other times the Town Hall is let for functions. Additional opening by arrangement with the Town Hall Manager (tel: 01442 862288).
Heritage Open Days: Yes
Ⓟ Parking in nearby public car parks.
♿ Full. WC for the disabled. Guide Dogs allowed.
£ No

BRIDGEWATER MONUMENT

Ashbridge Estate, Aldbury, Hertfordshire HP4 1LT
The monument was erected in 1832 to commemorate the Duke of Bridgewater. It is the focal point of Ashridge Estate which runs across the borders of Hertfordshire and Buckinghamshire along the main ridge of the Chilterns.
www.nationaltrust.org.uk
Grant Recipient: The National Trust
Access Contact: The National Trust
T: 01494 528051   **F:** 01494 463310
Open: Monument: 15 March–26 October: Saturday, Sunday and Bank Holiday Mondays 12 noon–5pm. Monday–Friday by prior arrangement, weather permitting. Estate: open all year. Visitor Centre: 15 March–21 December, daily Monday–Friday 12–5pm. Saturday, Sunday, Bank Holiday Mondays and Good Friday 12 noon–5pm.
Heritage Open Days: Yes
Ⓟ Spaces: 100.
♿ Partial. Wheelchair access to monument area, monument drive and visitor centre. Map of accessible route available. WC for the disabled. Guide Dogs allowed.
£ **Adult:** £1.50. **Child:** 70p. **Other:** Free to National Trust members.

CROMER WINDMILL

Ardeley, Stevenage, Hertfordshire SG2 7QA
Grade II* postmill dated 1674, last surviving postmill in Hertfordshire. Restored to working order (but not actually working). Houses displays about Hertfordshire's lost windmills, television and video display on the history of Cromer Mill and audio sound effects of a working mill.
www.hertsmuseums.org.uk
Grant Recipient: Hertfordshire Building Preservation Trust
Access Contact: Ms Cristina Harrison
T: 01279 843301/07949 577760   **F:** 01279 843301
E-mail: cristinaharrison@btopenworld.com
Open: 12 May–9 September, open Saturday before National Mill Day, i.e. second Sunday in May. Thereafter Sundays and Bank Holidays, and second and fourth Saturdays, until Heritage Open Days, 2.30–5pm. 30 minute video available for schools and other groups. Guided tours. Special parties by prior arrangement with Ms Cristina Harrison, The Forge Museum, High Street, Much Hadham, Hertfordshire SG10 6BS. Refreshments available.

Heritage Open Days: Yes
ℙ Spaces: 20.
♿ Partial. Access to The Roundhouse of the mill with video display showing upper levels. No WC for the disabled. Guide Dogs allowed.
£ **Adult:** £1.50 **Child:** 25p

FOLLY ARCH

Hawkshead Road, Little Heath, Potters Bar, Hertfordshire EN6 1NN
Grade II* listed gateway and folly, once the entrance to Gobions estate. Circa 1740 for Sir Jeremy Sambrooke, probably by James Gibbs. Red brick with large round-headed arch and thin square turrets.
Grant Recipient: Mr R J Nicholas
Access Contact: Mr and Mrs Nicholas
T: 01707 663553
E-mail: robnic@mac.com
Open: The Arch is on the boundary between public open space and a private garden and can be viewed from public ground at any time.
Heritage Open Days: No
ℙ On-street parking.
♿ Full. No WC for the disabled Guide Dogs allowed.
£ No

KNEBWORTH HOUSE

Knebworth, nr. Stevenage, Hertfordshire SG3 6PY
Originally a Tudor manor house, rebuilt in gothic style in 1843. Contains rooms in various styles, which include a Jacobean banqueting hall. Set in 250 acres of parkland with 25 acres of formal gardens. Home of the Lytton family since 1490.
www.knebworthhouse.com
Grant Recipient: Knebworth House Education & Preservation Trust
Access Contact: Mrs Christine Smith
T: 01438 812661   **F:** 01438 811908
E-mail: info@knebworthhouse.com
Open: Daily: 21 March–6 April, 24 May–1 June, 30 June–2 September. Weekends and Bank Holidays: 15–16 March, 12 April–18 May, 7–29 June, 6–28 September. Gardens, Park and Playground: 11.00am–5.30pm. House: 12 noon–5pm (last admission 4.15pm).
Heritage Open Days: No
ℙ Spaces: 75. 50–75 parking spaces on gravel, unlimited space on grass.
♿ Partial. Wheelchair access to ground floor of house only. Gravel paths around gardens and house but level route from car park to house entrance. WC for the disabled. Guide Dogs allowed.
£ **Adult:** £9.50 (£8.50 group) **Child:** £9.00 (£8.00 group) **Other:** £9.00 (senior citizens, £8.00 group).

THE OLD CHURCH TOWER OF ALL SAINTS

Chapel Lane, Long Marston, Hertfordshire HP23 4QT
Grade II* listed 15th century tower set in small churchyard with ancient yew trees. The only remnant of a Chapel of Ease dating back to the 12th century, the rest of the church was demolished in 1883.
Grant Recipient: Tring PCC Tower Conservation
Access Contact: Dr Noakes
T: 01296 660 072
Open: Exterior (churchyard) open at all times. Interior by prior arrangement and under supervision only.
Herita ge Open Days: No
ℙ Parking in nearby village, 200 metre walk.
♿ Partial. Wheelchair access to churchyard only. No WC for the disabled. Guide Dogs allowed.
£ No

WOODHALL PARK

Watton-at-Stone, Hertfordshire SG14 3NF
Country house, now a school. Designed and built by Thomas Leverton in 1785 in neo-Classical style. Normally associated with London houses, this is one of his few country houses. Highly decorated interiors which include the Print Room with walls covered in engraved paper, reproductions of paintings with frames, ribbons, chains, busts, candelabra and piers with vases.
Grant Recipient: The Trustees of R M Abel Smith 1991 Settlement

Access Contact: The Trustees of R M Abel Smith 1991 Settlement
T: 01920 830286   **F:** 01920 830162
E-mail: rmas@woodhallestate.co.uk
Open: At all reasonable times, preferably school holidays, by prior arrangement with the Trustees.
Heritage Open Days: No
ℙ Spaces: 30. Parking limited to 10 spaces during school terms.
♿ Partial. Wheelchair access to ground floor only. No WC for the disabled. Guide Dogs allowed.
£ No

KENT

ABBEY FARM BARNS–MINOR AND MAJOR BARNS

Faversham, Swale, Kent ME13 7BL
Monastic timber-framed, weatherboarding-clad barns. The two barns are amongst the few surviving buildings of Faversham Abbey. The larger, Major Barn, dates from circa 1500 with some early 19th century alterations and is listed Grade II*. The smaller, Minor Barn, dates from circa 1350 and is listed Grade I. In use as a working sawmill.
Grant Recipient: Mr Robin Dane
Access Contact: Robin Dane
T: 01795 537062
E-mail: robin.dane@favershamjoinery.co.uk
Open: 5, 6, 12, 13, 19, 20, 26 and 27 June, 13 and 14 September 12 noon–4pm.
Heritage Open Days: No
ℙ Spaces: 10. Not suitable for children under 14 as building is in use as a working sawmill.
♿ Partial. Guide dogs not admitted when workshop is operating. No WC for the disabled.
£ **Adult:** £2.00. **Child:** Free. **Other:** £1.50 (over 65).

ALL SAINTS REDUNDANT CHURCH

Waldershare, Dover, Kent
Redundant Norman church with later chapels containing examples of classical funerary monuments, Victorian murals and stained glass. Still a consecrated building although not used for regular worship.
www.visitchurches.org.uk
Grant Recipient: Diocese of Canterbury
Access Contact: Mr John Vigar
T: 07884 436649
E-mail: jvigar@tcct.org.uk
Open: All year: daily, 10.30am–3.30pm.
Heritage Open Days: No
ℙ Spaces: 4.
♿ Partial. Assistance needed at lychgate, thereafter church is accessible. No WC for the disabled. Guide Dogs allowed.
£ No

THE ARCHBISHOPS' PALACE

Mill Street, Maidstone, Kent ME15 6YE
14th century Palace built by the Archbishops of Canterbury. Much altered and extended over the centuries, the interior contains 16th century panelling and fine wood or stone fireplaces. Now used as Kent County Council's Register Office.
www.tour-maidstone.com
Grant Recipient: Mr John Williams, Maidstone Borough Council
Access Contact: Mr Christopher Finch
T: 01622 602720   **F:** 01622 602586
E-mail: christopherfinch@maidstone.gov.uk
Open: Throughout the year for weddings and at other times by prior arrangement with the Registrar.
Heritage Open Days: Yes
ℙ Spaces: 100. Public parking in town centre car parks (pay and display).
♿ Partial. Wheelchair access to ground floor via lift. WC for the disabled. Guide Dogs allowed.
£ No

AYLESFORD PRIORY

The Friars, Aylesford, Kent ME20 7BX
Home of a community of Carmelite Friars and a popular centre of pilgrimage. Chapels contain modern religious art created by Adam Kossowski and other notable artists.
www.thefriars.org.uk
Grant Recipient: The Carmelite Friars
Access Contact: Rev. Father Prior
T: 01622 717272   **F:** 01622 715575
E-mail: fkemsley@carmelnet.org

Open: At all times.
Heritage Open Days: Yes
ℙ Spaces: 1500.
♿ Full. WC for the disabled. Guide Dogs allowed.
£ No

BARN AT HOWBURY FARM

Moat Lane, Slade Green, Kent DA8 2NE
Jacobean tithe barn standing to the west of Howbury Moat House. Queen post timber roof. In agricultural use. Situated in an urban area of Bexley.
Grant Recipient: Trustees of The Russell Stoneham Estate
Access Contact: Mr C Stoneham
T: 01322 333111   **F:** 01322 330347
E-mail: russellstoneham@aol.com
Open: By prior arrangement throughout the year, plus London Open House weekend. Warden present Saturday, 15 August, 8am–6pm.
Heritage Open Days: Yes
ℙ Spaces: 10.
♿ Full. No WC for the disabled. Guide Dogs allowed.
£ No

CHURCH HOUSE

72 High Street, Edenbridge, Kent TN8 5AR
Late 14th century timber-framed farmhouse, Tudor additions include fireplace and 18th century brick frontage. Now houses the Eden Valley Museum which illustrates economic and social changes during the 14th to 20th centuries.
www.evmt.org.uk
Grant Recipient: Edenbridge Town Council
Access Contact: Mrs Jane Higgs
T: 01732 868102   **F:** 01732 867866
E-mail: curator@evmt.org.uk
Open: February–December (until Christmas): Wednesday and Friday 2–4.30pm, Thursday and Saturday 10am–4.30pm; April–September: Sundays 2–4.30pm. Closed Good Friday and Easter Sunday.
Heritage Open Days: No
ℙ Spaces: 150. Free parking in town centre car park, 200 yards from House.
♿ Partial. Wheelchair access to ground floor only (visual computer link to upstairs). WC for the disabled. Guide Dogs allowed.
£ Except for out of hours pre-arranged visits.

COBHAM HALL AND DAIRY

Cobham, Kent DA12 3BL
Gothic-style dairy in grounds of Cobham Hall, built by James Wyatt c1790.
www.cobhamhall.com
Grant Recipient: Cobham Hall Heritage Trust
Access Contact: Mr N G Powell
T: 01474 823371   **F:** 01474 825904
E-mail: enquiries@cobhamhall.com
Open: Easter–July / August: Hall open Wednesday and Sunday, 2–5pm (last tour 4.30pm). Please telephone to confirm opening times. At other times (and coach parties) by prior arrangement. Self-guided tour of Gardens and Parkland (historical/conservation tour by prior arrangement).
Heritage Open Days: No
ℙ Spaces: 100.
♿ Partial. Wheelchair access to ground floor, manual assistance required for first floor access. WC for the disabled. Guide Dogs allowed.
£ **Adult:** £4.50. **Child:** £3.50. **Other:** £3.50 (senior citizens & groups).

DOVER TOWN HALL

Biggin Street, Dover, Kent CT16 1DL
The Town Hall incorporates the remains of a medieval hospital, 14th century chapel tower, 19th century prison, town hall and assembly rooms. The Maison Dieu Hall of c1325 was originally part of a hospital founded by Hubert de Burgh in the early 13th century. The Town Hall designed by Victorian Gothic architect William Burges was built in 1881 on the site of the hospital.
Grant Recipient: Dover District Council
Access Contact: Mr Steve Davis
T: 01843 296111 (Admin)
E-mail: dover@leisureforce.co.uk
Open: Normally open during the week for functions and other bookings. Open on Wednesdays throughout the year. Guided tours can be arranged.
Heritage Open Days: No

P Parking at the rear of the building.
  Full. WC for the disabled. Guide Dogs allowed.
£ No

THE GRANGE

St Augustine's Road, Ramsgate, Kent CT11 9PA
The Grange is a Grade I listed building that was designed and lived in by Augustus Pugin, an influential 19th century architect. The building fell into a state of severe disrepair in the 1990s and was acquired and restored by the Landmark Trust.
www.landmarktrust.org.uk
Grant Recipient: The Landmark Trust
Access Contact: Mrs Victoria O'Keeffe
T: 01628 825920   **F:** 01628 825417
E-mail: vokeeffe@landmarktrust.org.uk
Open: The Landmark Trust is an independent charity, which rescues small buildings of historic or architectural importance from decay or unsympathetic improvement. Landmark's aim is to promote the enjoyment of these historic buildings by making them available to stay in for holidays. The Grange can be rented by anyone, at all times of the year, for periods ranging from a weekend to three weeks. Bookings can be made by telephoning the Booking Office on 01628 825925. As the building is in full-time use for holiday accommodation, it is not normally open to the public. However, the public can view the building by prior arrangement by telephoning the access contact (Victoria O'Keeffe on 01628 825920) to make an appointment. Potential visitors will be asked to write to confirm the details of their visit. In addition, the main rooms will be open every Wednesday afternoon by appointment. There is a small exhibition in the Cartoon Room (a separate building next to The Grange) which provides information about the building, its history and the Pugin family. Open on Wednesday afternoons (2–4pm), on Open Days and by appointment.
Heritage Open Days: Yes
P Parking on Royal Esplanade nearby.
  Partial. Wheelchair access to ground floor. WC for disabled. Guide Dogs allowed.
£ No

HERNE WINDMILL

Mill Lane, Herne Bay, Kent CT6 7DR
Kentish smock mill built 1789, worked by wind until 1952 and then by electricity until 1980. Bought by Kent County Council in 1985, which carried out some restoration. Now managed by Friends of Herne Mill on behalf of the County Council. Much of the original machinery is in place, some is run for demonstration and the sails used when the wind conditions permit.
www.kentwindmills.co.uk
Grant Recipient: Kent County Council
Access Contact: Mr Ken Cole
T: 01227 361326
Open: Easter–end September: Sunday and Bank Holidays, plus Thursdays in August, 2–5pm. National Mills Weekend, Saturday and Sunday, 2–5pm. For further information contact Ken Cole, Secretary, Friends of Herne Mill (tel: 01227 361326) or John Fishpool (Chairman, tel: 01227 366863).
Heritage Open Days: Yes
P Spaces: 6. Six parking spaces in Mill grounds. Free on-street parking (Windmill Road).
  Partial. Wheelchair and guide dog access to ground floor of Mill and meeting room. WC for the disabled. Guide Dogs allowed.
£ **Adult:** £1.00. **Child:** 25p (accompanied by an adult).

IGHTHAM MOTE

Ivy Hatch, Sevenoaks, Kent TN15 0NT
Moated manor house covering nearly 700 years of history from medieval times to 1960s. Extended visitor route now includes the refurbished north-west quarter with Tudor Chapel, Billiards Room and Drawing Room, south west quarter and apartments of Charles Henry Robinson, the American donor of Ightham Mote to the National Trust. Interpretation displays and special exhibition featuring conservation in action.
www.nationaltrust.org.uk/ighthammote
Grant Recipient: The National Trust
Access Contact: Property Manager
T: 01732 810378   **F:** 01732 811 029
E-mail: ighthammote@nationaltrust.org.uk
Open: 15 March–2 November, daily except Tuesday and Saturday. House, 11am–5pm; Garden, Shop and

Restaurant 10.30am–5pm. (last entry 4.30pm). Estate open all year dawn–dusk.
Heritage Open Days: Yes
P Spaces: 420.
  Partial. Wheelchair access to ground floor with assistance and part of the exterior only. WC for the disabled. Guide Dogs allowed.
£ **Adult:** £9.85. **Child:** £4.95. **Other:** £24.65 (family), £8.35 (groups).

KNOLE CARTOON GALLERY

Sevenoaks, Kent TN15 0RP
The largest private house in England, Knole is a fine example of late medieval architecture. It has been the home of the Sackville family since 1603. The Cartoon Gallery contains six large copies of Raphael's cartoons. It includes carved grotesque decoration and a fine plasterwork ceiling.
www.nationaltrust.org.uk/knole
Grant Recipient: The National Trust
Access Contact: The Property Manager
T: 01732 462100   **F:** 01732 465528
E-mail: knole@nationaltrust.org.uk
Open: 15 March–2 November: Wednesday–Sunday, 12–4pm (last admission 3.30pm); 29 July–2 September: daily, except Monday, 12–4pm (last admission 3.30pm).
Heritage Open Days: Yes
P Spaces: 200.£2.50 per car. National Trust members free. Parking for the disabled 50 yards from house.
  Partial. Wheelchair access to the Great Hall, shop and tea room, but not the Cartoon Gallery. Virtual reality tour available. WC for the disabled. No Guide Dogs allowed.
£ **Adult:** £9.00. **Child:** £4.40. **Other:** £22.50 (family). Free to NT members.

PROVENDER

Provender Lane, Faversham, Swale, Kent ME13 0ST
A grade II* listed timber framed country house dating from 14th century with later additions. The north east range has been restored. Further restoration work is in progress.
Grant Recipient: Princess Olga Romanoff
Access Contact: Princess Olga Romanoff
T: 01795 521300
Open: By prior arrangement until restoration work completed, please check the English Heritage website or with the access contact for opening arrangements.
Heritage Open Days: No
P Spaces: 20.
  Partial. Wheelchair access to the entrance hall, dining room, and ground floor of north east range. No WC for the disabled. Guide Dogs allowed.
£ **Adult:** Will depend on extent of completed restoration work, but will be £10.00. **Child:** £7.50 (full-time school children). Free (12 years and under). **Other:** Concessions: senior citizens and students.

LANCASHIRE

BROWSHOLME HALL

nr. Clitheroe, Lancashire BB7 3DE
Browsholme Hall, pronounced 'Brewsom', was built in 1507 and the ancestral home of the Parker Family who have lived there since it was built. Listed Grade I. The house contains a collection of oak furniture, portraits and stained glass.
www.browsholme.co.uk
Grant Recipient: Mr R R Parker
Access Contact: Mr Robert Redmayne Parker
T: 01254 826719
E-mail: rrp@browsholme.co.uk
Open: 24–31 May; 28 June–4 July (except Mondays); 15–31 August (except Mondays, but including Bank Holiday Monday) 2–5pm.
Heritage Open Days: No
P Spaces: 30.
  Partial. Wheelchair access to ground floor. WC for the disabled. Guide Dogs allowed.
£ **Adult:** £5.00 (provisional). **Child:** £1.50 (provisional). **Other:** £4.50 (senior citizens & groups), £2.50 (grounds only).

GAWTHORPE HALL

Padiham, nr. Burnley, Lancashire BB12 8UA
An Elizabethan property in the heart of industrial Lancashire. Restored and refurbished in the mid 19th century by Sir Charles Barry. There are many notable paintings on display loaned to the National Trust by the National Portrait Gallery, and a collection of needlework, assembled by the last family member to live there, Rachel Kay-Shuttleworth.
www.nationaltrust.org.uk
Grant Recipient: The National Trust
Access Contact: Property Manager
T: 01282 771004   **F:** 01282 770178
E-mail: gawthorpehall@nationaltrust.org.uk
Open: Hall: 1 April–28 October, daily except Monday and Friday (but open Good Friday and Bank Holiday Mondays), 1–5pm. Garden: all year, 10am–6pm.
Heritage Open Days: No
P Spaces: 50.
  Partial. Wheelchair access to garden only. WC for the disabled. Guide Dogs allowed.
£ **Adult:** £4.00 (provisional). **Child:** Free when accompanied by an adult. **Other:** £1.50 (concessions), garden free (provisional).

INDIA MILL CHIMNEY

Bolton Road, Darwen, Blackburn, Lancashire BB3 1AE
Chimney, 1867, built as part of cotton spinning mill. Brick with ashlar base. Square section, 300 feet high, in the style of an Italian campanile. Rests on foundation stone said to have been the largest single block quarried since Cleopatra's Needle. Listed Grade II*.
www.indiamill.com
Grant Recipient: Brookhouse Managed Properties Ltd
Access Contact: Ms Pamela Blackwell
T: 01254 777 788   **F:** 01254 777 799
E-mail: pam.blackwell@indiamill.com
Open: Chimney visible from public highway (no interior access).
Heritage Open Days: No
P On-street parking.
  Full. No WC for the disabled. Guide Dogs allowed.
£ No

LEIGHTON HALL

Carnforth, Lancashire LA5 9ST
Country House, 1765, probably by Richard Gillow, with earlier remains. Gothic south-east front early 19th century, possibly by Thomas Harrison. Tower at west end of the façade 1870 by Paley and Austin. Ancestral home of the Gillow family with fine furniture, paintings and objects d'art.
www.leightonhall.co.uk
Grant Recipient: Mr Richard Reynolds
Access Contact: Richard Reynolds
T: 01524 734474   **F:** 01524 720357
E-mail: leightonhall@yahoo.co.uk
Open: May–September: Tuesday–Friday (also Bank Holiday Sundays and Mondays), 2–5pm. August only: Tuesday–Friday and Sunday (also Bank Holiday Monday), 2–5pm. Groups of 25+ all year by prior arrangement. The owner reserves the right to close or restrict access to the Hall and grounds for special events (please see website for up to date information).
Heritage Open Days: No
P Spaces: 100.
  Partial. Wheelchair access to ground floor, shop and tea rooms. WC for the disabled. Guide Dogs allowed.
£ **Adult:** £6.00. **Child:** £4.00 (age 5-12). **Other:** £5.00 (senior citizen/student), £18.00 (family), £4.50 (adult group of 25+), £3.50 (child group).

QUEEN STREET MILL

Harle Syke, Burnley, Lancashire BB10 2HX
Built in 1894, containing much of its original 19th century equipment including over 300 Lancashire looms and steam engine, which are demonstrated at intervals throughout each working day.
www.lancsmuseums.gov.uk
Grant Recipient: Lancashire County Council
Access Contact: Ms Catherine Pearson, Assistant Keeper
T: 01282 412555   **F:** 01282 430220
E-mail: queenstreet.mill@mus.lancscc.gov.uk
Open: March and November: Tuesday–Thursday, 12–4pm; April and October: Tuesday–Friday, 12–5pm; May–September: Tuesday–Saturday,12–5pm. Open Sunday and Mondays on Bank Holiday weekends only. Closed December, January and February.

Heritage Open Days: Yes
P Spaces: 40. Free parking.
占 Full. WC for the disabled. Guide Dogs allowed.
£ Adult: £3.00. Child: Free if accompanied. Other: £2.00 (concessions).

SAMLESBURY HALL

Preston New Road, Samlesbury, Preston, Lancashire PR5 0UP
Built in 1325, the hall is a black and white timbered manor house set in extensive grounds. Independently owned and administered since 1925 by The Samlesbury Hall Trust whose primary aim is to maintain and preserve the property for the enjoyment and pleasure of the public. Currently open to the public as a historic, educational, craft, design and antique centre.
www.samlesburyhall.co.uk
Grant Recipient: Samlesbury Hall Trust
Access Contact: Ms Sharon Jones
T: 01254 812010/01254 812229   **F:** 01254 812174
E-mail: enquiries@samlesburyhall.co.uk
Open: Daily except Saturdays, 11am–4.30pm. Open Bank Holidays. For Christmas closing times please contact the Hall.
Heritage Open Days: No
P Spaces: 70. Additional parking for 100 cars in overflow car park.
占 Partial. Wheelchair access to ground floor of historical part of Hall. WC for the disabled. Guide Dogs allowed.
£ Adult: £3.00. Child: £1.00 (ages 4–16).

STONYHURST COLLEGE

Stonyhurst, Clitheroe, Lancashire BB7 9PZ
16th century manor house, now home to a Catholic independent co-educational boarding and day school. Contains dormitories, library, chapels, school-rooms and historical apartments.
www.stonyhurst.ac.uk
Grant Recipient: Stonyhurst College
Access Contact: Miss Frances Ahearne
T: 01254 826345   **F:** 01254 827040
E-mail: domestic-bursar@stonyhurst.ac.uk
Open: House: 21 July–25 August daily (except Friday), plus August Bank Holiday Monday, 1–4.30pm. Gardens: 1 July–25 August daily (except Friday), plus August Bank Holiday Monday, 1–4.30pm. Coach parties by prior arrangement.
Heritage Open Days: No
P Spaces: 200.
占 Partial. WC for the disabled. Guide Dogs allowed.
£ Adult: £6.00. Child: £5.00. Other: £5.50 (concessions).

TODMORDEN UNITARIAN CHURCH

Honey Hole Road, Todmorden, Lancashire OL14 6LE
Grade I church with a large wooded burial ground and ornamental gardens designed by John Gibson, 1865–69. Victorian Gothic style with tall tower and spire. Detached smaller burial ground nearby and listed lodge in churchyard. Lavish interior with highly decorated fittings and furnishings. One of the most elaborate Non conformist churches of the High Gothic Revival.
www.hct.org.uk
Grant Recipient: Historic Chapels Trust
Access Contact: Mr Rob Goldthorpe
T: 01706 815648
E-mail: rob.goldthorpe@btinternet.com
Open: At all reasonable times by application to the key holder, Mary Clear, 5–6 Cockpit, Longfield Road, Todmorden, Lancashire OL14 6LY or by calling at the caretaker's house, Todmorden Lodge, at the entrance to the churchyard.
Heritage Open Days: Yes
P Parking in local car park.
占 Full. WC for the disabled. Guide Dogs allowed.
£ Donations invited.

WEST DERBY COURTHOUSE

Almonds Green, Liverpool L12 5HP
Mid 17th century sandstone Courthouse. Its interior, lit by four mullioned windows contains original court furniture such as stewards and jury benches as well as muniment cupboards for rolls of parchment documents produced by the Manor and Hundred Courts.
www.croxteth.co.uk
Grant Recipient: Liverpool City Council
Access Contact: Ms Irene Vickers

T: 0151 233 6910   **F:** 0151 228 2817
E-mail: croxtethcountrypark@liverpool.gov.uk
Open: 1 April–31 October: Sundays, 2–4pm. All other times by prior arrangement, seven days notice required.
Heritage Open Days: Yes
P On-street parking nearby.
占 No wheelchair access. No WC for the disabled. Guide Dogs allowed.
£ No

LEICESTERSHIRE

BELVOIR CASTLE RIDING RING

Grantham, Leicestershire NG32 1PD
Grade II* listed circular exercise ring for horses, circa 1819. Constructed of colour washed brick. Timber superstructure and slate roof over curved rafters. It is 3 metres (12 feet) wide, enclosing central space of 6.5 metres (20 feet) in diameter, with two doorways access from the stable yard. The building forms part of the intact stable block. The ring is probably the earliest free-standing structure of its kind in England.
www.belvoircastle.com
Grant Recipient: The Duke of Rutland
Access Contact: Mr Tim Stansby
T: 01476 870262   **F:** 01476 870443
Open: 1 May–31 August: Wednesday, 11am–5pm to view the exterior of the riding ring. Access to the interior is also permitted on this day by request at the Estate Office. Access at other times by prior arrangement.
Heritage Open Days: No
P Two parking spaces at the ring.
占 Partial. Exterior only. No WC for the disabled. Guide Dogs allowed.
£ Adult: £12.00 (castle & gardens), £6.00 (gardens) – charge to view ring included in entrance fee on specified Weds), £2.50 at other times. Child: £6.00 (castle & gardens), £2.00 (gardens), £2.50 at other times for age 16+.

REARSBY PACKHORSE BRIDGE

Rearsby, Leicestershire LE7 4YE
Low narrow medieval bridge, perhaps 16th century, comprising seven arches of random granite masonry and brick coping. On the upstream side there are four cutwaters, three of granite and one of brick. The bridge has recently been restored.
Grant Recipient: Leicestershire County Council
Access Contact: Mr C Waterfield
T: 0116 265 7167   **F:** 0116 265 7135
E-mail: cwaterfield@leics.gov.uk
Open: At all times: in use as a public highway.
Heritage Open Days: No
P In use as a public highway.
占 Full. No WC for the disabled. Guide Dogs allowed.
£ No

SIR JOHN MOORE'S SCHOOL

Top Street, Appleby Magna, Swadlincote, Leicestershire DE12 7AH
Grade I listed school, built 1697, based on designs by Sir Christopher Wren.
www.sirjohnmoore.org.uk
Grant Recipient: Trustees of Sir John Moore's Foundation
Access Contact: Mrs D Morris
T: 01530 273629
E-mail: deana@sirjohnmoore.org.uk
Open: Throughout the year for events and activities. Group and school visits by prior arrangement.
Heritage Open Days: No
P Spaces: 50.
占 Partial. Wheelchair access to ground floor and telecentre gardens. WC for the disabled. Guide Dogs allowed.
£ £3.00 per person (for group visits). Some activities and events have a fee.

LINCOLNSHIRE

3/3A VICARS COURT

Lincoln, Lincolnshire LN2 1PT
Former priests' vicars lodgings, now 2 houses. Begun late 13th century by Bishop Sutton and completed c1309. Altered 15th century, re-roofed and altered late 16th, 17th, 18th and 19th centuries.
Grant Recipient: Dean & Chapter of Lincoln Cathedral
Access Contact: Mrs Carol Heidschuster

T: 01522 527637   **F:** 01522 575688
E-mail: worksmanager@lincolncathedral.com
Open: By prior written arrangement with the Works Manager, Lincoln Cathedral, 28 Eastgate, Lincoln LN2 4AA.
Heritage Open Days: No
P No
占 No wheelchair access. No WC for the disabled. Guide Dogs allowed.
£ No

ARABELLA AUFRERE TEMPLE

Brocklesby Park, Grimsby, Lincolnshire DN41 8PN
Garden Temple of ashlar and red brick with coupled doric columns on either side of a central arch leading to a rear chamber. Built c1787 and attributed to James Wyatt. Inscription above inner door: "Dedicated by veneration and affection to the memory of Arabella Aufrere."
Grant Recipient: The Earl of Yarborough
Access Contact: Mr H A Rayment
T: 01469 560214   **F:** 01469 561346
E-mail: office@brocklesby.co.uk
Open: 1 April–31 August: viewable from permissive paths through Mausoleum Woods at all reasonable times.
Heritage Open Days: No
P Spaces: 10. Free parking in village or walks car park, _ mile from site.
占 No wheelchair access. No WC for the disabled. Guide Dogs allowed.
£ No

BROCKLESBY MAUSOLEUM

Brocklesby Park, Grimsby, Lincolnshire DN41 8PN
Family Mausoleum designed by James Wyatt and built between 1787 and 1794 by Charles Anderson Pelham, who subsequently became Lord Yarborough, as a memorial to his wife Sophia who died at the age of 33. The classical design is based on the Temples of Vesta at Rome and Tivoli.
Grant Recipient: The Earl of Yarborough
Access Contact: Mr H A Rayment
T: 01469 560214   **F:** 01469 561346
E-mail: office@brocklesby.co.uk
Open: Exterior: 1 April–31 August: viewable from permissive paths through Mausoleum Woods at all reasonable times. Interior (excluding private crypt) by prior arrangement with the Estate Office. Admission charge for interior.
Heritage Open Days: No
P Spaces: 10. Free parking in village or walks car park, 0.25 mile from site.
占 No wheelchair access. No WC for the disabled. No Guide Dogs allowed.
£ Adult: £2.00 (charge for interior). Child: £2.00 (charge for interior). Other: £2.00 (charge for interior).

BURGHLEY HOUSE

Stamford, Lincolnshire PE9 3JY
Large country house built by William Cecil, Lord High Treasurer of England, between 1555 and 1587, and still lived in by descendants of his family. Eighteen State Rooms, many decorated by Antonio Verrio in the 17th century, housing a collection of artworks including 17th century Italian paintings, Japanese ceramics, European porcelain and wood carvings by Grinling Gibbons and his followers. There are also four State Beds, English and continental furniture, and tapestries and textiles. 'Capability' Brown parkland.
www.burghley.co.uk
Grant Recipient: Burghley House Preservation Trust Ltd
Access Contact: Mr Philip Gompertz
T: 01780 761 974   **F:** 01780 480125
E-mail: philip.gompertz@burghley.co.uk
Open: 21 March–30 October: daily (except Fridays and 6 September) 11am–4.30pm. Guided tours available at certain times.
Heritage Open Days: No
P Spaces: 500. Parking for the disabled available close to visitors' entrance.
占 Full. Please telephone the Property Manager for information on wheelchair access. WC for the disabled. Guide Dogs allowed.
£ Adult: £10.90. Child: £5.40. Other: £9.50 (senior citizens & students), £9.00 (per person for groups 20+), £28.00 (family).

FYDELL HOUSE GATES, PIERS AND RAILINGS

South Street, Boston, Lincolnshire PE21 6HU
Fronted by renewed, grant-aided gate, gate piers and railings, Fydell House was built in 1726 with minor 19th century alterations. Example of a small 18th century stately home. It contains links between Boston England and Boston Mass and houses the Fydell House Centre Ltd, a provider of educational and cultural facilities.
Grant Recipient: Boston Preservation Trust Ltd
Access Contact: Mr Ronald Ernest Coley
T: 01205 351520
Open: Access to the exterior at all reasonable times. Open throughout the year (except Bank Holidays) but in term-time access to rooms is limited.
Heritage Open Days: No
P Public car park nearby.
Full. WC for the disabled. Guide Dogs allowed.
£ No

HARLAXTON MANOR RAILWAY TUNNEL

Harlaxton, Grantham, Lincolnshire NG32 1AG
Curved brick viaduct with buttresses and slate roof containing a narrow gauge railway for supplying the service courtyard of Harlaxton Manor. The entrance vestibule has at the north end two 3-bay arcades with heavily rusticated round arches adorned with enormous ashlar trophies. Constructed between 1838–1844. The Elizabethan, Revival style Manor is now a university.
www.ueharlax.ac.uk
Grant Recipient: University of Evansville-Harlaxton College
Access Contact: Mr Ian Welsh
T: 01476 403000   **F:** 01476 403030
E-mail: iwelsh@ueharlax.ac.uk
Open: Guided tours (for approx. 20 plus) by prior arrangement. 10 August 11am–5pm open house.
Heritage Open Days: Yes
P Spaces: 150.
Full. WC for the disabled. Guide Dogs allowed.
£ Adult: £6.00. Child: £3.00. Other: £4.50 (concessions), £8.00 (guided tours, including refreshments).

KYME TOWER

Manor Farm, South Kyme, Lincoln, Lincolnshire LN4 4JN
23.5m high tower with one storey and a stair turret. Remainder of a fortified medieval manor house, built on the site of an Augustinian priory, itself built on an Anglo-Saxon religious establishment. There are also visible earthworks of the former moat and fishponds.
Grant Recipient: The Crown Estate Commissioners
Access Contact: Mr W B Lamyman
T: 01526 860603
Open: By prior telephone arrangement with Mr W B Lamyman of Manor Farm (tel: 01526 860603). At least one week's notice required.
Heritage Open Days: No
P Spaces: 3.
No wheelchair access. No WC for the disabled. No Guide Dogs allowed.
£ No

LINCOLN CASTLE

Castle Hill, Lincoln, Lincolnshire LN1 3AA
Lincoln Castle was begun by William the Conqueror in 1068. For 900 years the castle has been used as a court and prison. Many original features still stand and the wall walks provide magnificent views of the cathedral, city and surrounding countryside.
www.lincolnshire.gov.uk/lincolncastle
Grant Recipient: Lincolnshire County Council
Access Contact: Mr Peter Allen
T: 01522 511068   **F:** 01522 512150
E-mail: allenp@lincolnshire.gov.uk
Open: Monday–Saturday: 9.30am–5.30pm. Sunday 11am–5.30pm. Winter closing at 4pm. Also closed 24–26 December, 31 December and 1 January.
Heritage Open Days: No
P Paid parking available in the Castle / Cathedral area.
Partial. Wheelchair access to grounds, Magna Carta exhibition, audio visual presentation, Victorian Prison Experience and café. WC for the disabled. Guide Dogs allowed.
£ Adult: £3.90. Child: £2.60 (under 5s free). Other: £2.60 (concessions), £10.40 (family).

MONKSTHORPE CHAPEL

Spilsby, East Lindsey, Lincolnshire
Resembling a brick barn, this remote chapel with outdoor baptistery was used by local Baptists as a secluded place of worship and is one of the two best surviving examples in England. It was substantially altered to its present appearance in the early 19th century.
Grant Recipient: The National Trust
Access Contact: The National Trust
Open: 5 April, 3 May, 7 June, 5 July (craft fair), 2 August, 6 September. Services at 3pm on 19 April, 17 May, 21 June, 19 July,16 August, 20 September, 11 October, 13 December. At other times access by key obtained from Gunby Hall, (£10.00 returnable deposit). Please contact The National Trust East Midlands Regional Office (Tel: 01909 486411) for further details.
Heritage Open Days: No
P No
No wheelchair access. No WC for the disabled. No Guide Dogs allowed.
£ No

MOULTON WINDMILL

High Street, Moulton, Spalding, Lincolnshire PE12 6QB
Grade I listed tower mill. Built circa 1822 in brown brick by Robert King. Eight storeys plus basement, this was the tallest windmill in the country when built. Almost all the internal machinery survives intact.
Grant Recipient: Moulton Windmill Project Ltd.
Access Contact: Mrs J Prescott
T: 01775 724929
Open: All year: Thursday–Sunday, 10am–4pm; Monday–Wednesday by prior arrangement.
Heritage Open Days: Yes
P Spaces: 12. Secure area for bicycles.
Partial. Wheelchair access to first two floors, granary, tea rooms, mill shop, interpretation centre and working stones on first floor. WC for the disabled. Guide Dogs allowed.
£ Adult: £4.00. Child: £2.00. Other: £2.95 (concessions).

ST PETER

Sotby, Lincolnshire
Grade II* listed church dating from early 12th and 13th centuries.
Grant Recipient: Mr B F Cotton
Access Contact: Ms Sandra Meakin
T: 01507 343662 (evenings)
Open: Key available by prior arrangement with Sandra Meakin, Chapel Cottage, Moor Lane, Sotby, Lincolnshire (Tel: 01507 343662).
Heritage Open Days: No
P Roadside parking.
Partial. Grass entry to building and small step. No WC for the disabled. Guide Dogs allowed.
£ No

TATTERSHALL CASTLE

Tattershall, Lincoln, Lincolnshire LN4 4LR
A vast fortified and moated red-brick tower, built c1440 for Ralph Cromwell, Treasurer of England. The building was rescued from becoming derelict by Lord Curzon 1911–14 and contains four great chambers with enormous Gothic fireplaces, tapestries and brick vaulting. Gatehouse with museum room.
www.nationaltrust.org.uk
Grant Recipient: The National Trust
Access Contact: Property Manager
T: 01526 342543   **F:** 01526 342543
E-mail: tattershallcastle@nationaltrust.org.uk
Open: 1 March–14 March and 3 November–16 December: Saturday and Sunday 12 noon–4pm; 15 March–1 October: Saturday–Wednesday and Good Friday 11am–5.30pm; 4 October–2 November: Saturday–Wednesday 11am–4pm. Castle opens at 1pm on Saturdays with weddings except during July and August.
Heritage Open Days: No
P Spaces: 40.
Partial. Wheelchair access to ground floor via ramp. Photograph album of inaccessible parts of Castle. WC for the disabled. Guide Dogs allowed.
£ Adult: £4.70. Child: £2.50. Other: £11.90 (family). Admission price includes voluntary gift aid donation.

WESTGATE HOUSE

Westgate, Louth, Lincolnshire LN11 9YQ
Grade II* Georgian town house in brick and stone, with 1775 neo-classical additions and proto-Regency remodelling c1799 on the Westgate façade. Interior contains fine plasterwork, mahogany doors, Carrara fireplaces and other fine details. Used as a school 1937–1980s but now in course of restoration as a residence by the present owners, after dereliction.
Grant Recipient: Professor P Byrne
Access Contact: Professor Byrne & Mrs Byrne
T: 01507 354388
E-mail: peterbyrnewestgate@keme.co.uk
Open: Ground floor only. Guided visits between 11.30am–4pm, by prior arrangement. Evening group visits for societies, etc., by prior arrangement throughout the year.
Heritage Open Days: Yes
P Spaces: 6. Public parking in town centre (5 minutes walk).
Partial. Wheelchair access by prior arrangement only. No WC for the disabled. Guide Dogs allowed.
£ Adult: £3.00. Child: Free (when accompanied by an adult). Other: Evening group visits: £5.00 per person (maximum 30) including wine and canapés.

LONDON

19 PRINCELET STREET

London E1 6QH
Grade II* listed terraced house, 1719 by Samuel Worrall, builder; adapted and extended as a synagogue 1870 by a Mr Hudson for the Loyal United Friends Friendly Society. The house retains a wealth of original features and exemplifies the special history of Spitalfields, whose character has been marked by successive waves of immigrants. The upper portions retain associations with the Huguenot silk industry, whilst the rear extension is the best surviving small-scale Jewish prayer hall or 'shtiebl' once distinctive in the area.
www.19princeletstreet.org.uk
Grant Recipient: Spitalfields Centre
Access Contact: Ms Paramjit Kaur
T: 020 7247 5352   **F:** 020 7375 1490
E-mail: office@19princeletstreet.org.uk
Open: By prior arrangement. Open days in May, June and September (dates to be set), please check the website or with the access contact for current information.
London Open House: Yes
P On-street parking.
Partial. Wheelchair access to ground floor and synagogue. No WC for the disabled. Guide Dogs allowed.
£ Adult: £2.00 (minimum donation requested per person for group visits). Free open days. Child: £1.00 (minimum donation requested per person for group visits). Free open days.

BENJAMIN FRANKLIN'S HOUSE

36 Craven Street, London WC2N 5NF
A 1730s terraced house with c1792 alterations. Part of the Craven family's 18th century development of their Brewhouse estate, laid out by Flitcroft. Listed Graded I for historical associations, retaining a majority of original features (central staircase; lathing; 18th century panelling; stoves; windows; fittings; beams; brick, etc) 'unimproved' over time. The world's only remaining home of the diplomat, scientist, inventor, writer, and philosopher Benjamin Franklin. The house is a museum and educational facility.
www.benjaminfranklinhouse.org
Grant Recipient: Friends of Benjamin Franklin House
Access Contact: Dr Marcia Balisciano
T: 020 7839 2006   **F:** 020 7930 9124
E-mail: info@benjaminfranklinhouse.org
Open: All year: Wednesday–Sunday 10.30am–5.30pm.
London Open House: No
P No
No wheelchair access. No WC for the disabled. Guide Dogs allowed.
£ Adult: £7.00. Child: Free.

BRIXTON ACADEMY

211 Stockwell Road, Lambeth, London SW9 9SL
Built in 1929 as the largest of the four "Astoria" theatres. Retains many original features including elaborate presenium arch over stage and art deco interior. Presently used as a music venue.

www.brixton-academy.co.uk
Grant Recipient: McKenzie Group Ltd (Ex Magstack Ltd)
Access Contact: Mr Nigel Downs
T: 020 7787 3150   **F:** 020 7738 4427
E-mail: nigel@brixton-academy.co.uk
Open: Academy Open Day: 15 September, 10am–4pm. Performances throughout the year.
London Open House: Yes
P Spaces: 300. NCP car park located on Popes Road. Restricted parking around Brixton Academy. Not open Sundays.
♿ Partial. Wheelchair access to ground floor and auditorium. WC for the disabled. Guide Dogs allowed.
£ Charge applies to events at the venue.

BROMLEY HALL

Gillender Street, Tower Hamlets, London E14 6RN
A rare surviving 15th century house and one of the oldest brick built houses in London. Tree ring analysis has established that the Hall was constructed around 1485 and it retains features from all periods dating back to Tudor times. The house has been used as a private residence, calico printing works and offices. The building now provides the new home for the London Voluntary Sector Training Consortium.
www.leasideregeneration.com
Grant Recipient: Leaside Regeneration
Access Contact: Mr John Hills/ Ms Helen James
T: 0845 262 0846   **F:** 0845 262 0847
E-mail: jhills@leasideregeneration.co.uk
Open: By prior arrangement during working hours.
London Open House: Yes
P Spaces: 4.
♿ Partial. Wheelchair access to ground floor only. WC for the disabled. Guide Dogs allowed.
£ No

BRUNSWICK SQUARE GARDENS

Brunswick Square, London WC1
A public park originally part of the grounds of the Foundling Hospital, founded by Sir Thomas Coram.
www.camden.gov.uk
Grant Recipient: London Borough of Camden
Access Contact: Mr Martin Stanton
T: 020 7974 1693   **F:** 020 7974 1543
E-mail: martin.stanton@camden.gov.uk
Open: From 7.30am until dusk throughout the year.
London Open House: No
P On-street parking.
♿ Full. No WC for the disabled. Guide Dogs allowed.
£ No

BUILDING 40, ROYAL MILITARY ACADEMY

Woolwich, London SE18 6ST
Building 40 is a Grade II* listed building on the historic Royal Arsenal site. Constructed in 1718 and 1723 of red brown stock brick with a slate roof, attributed to Nicholas Hawsmoor. One of four buildings now housing the Royal Artillery Museum called Firepower.
www.firepower.org.uk
Grant Recipient: Royal Artillery Museums Ltd
Access Contact: Mrs Eileen Noon
T: 020 8855 7755   **F:** 020 88557100
E-mail: eileen@firepower.org.uk
Open: Building 40: used for corporate events and temporary exhibitions. Museum: Wednesday–Sunday 10:30am–5pm, closed Monday and Tuesday.
London Open House: Yes
P Spaces: 400.
♿ Partial. Wheelchair access through the rear of the building to the ground floor only. WC for the disabled. Guide Dogs allowed.
£ **Adult:** £5.00. **Child:** £2.50. **Other:** £12.00 (Family), £4.50 (Concessions).

CATHEDRAL FOOTBRIDGE

Borough High Street, Southwark, London SE1 9DA
Victorian footbridge providing access from Borough High Street to the Cathedral churchyard.
www.southwark.anglican.org/cathedral
Grant Recipient: Dean and Chapter of Southwark Cathedral
Access Contact: Mr Matthew Knight
T: 020 7367 6726   **F:** 020 7367 6725
E-mail: matthew.knight@southwark.anglican.org
Open: Daily: 7.30am–6.30pm. Closes Christmas Day at 1pm.

London Open House: Yes
P No
♿ Partial. Wheelchair access to footbridge but steps down to churchyard. Step-free access available via Borough Market. WC for the disabled. Guide Dogs allowed.
£ No

CHURCH OF THE HOSPITAL OF ST JOHN AND ST ELIZABETH

60 Grove End Road, London NW8 9NH
Built in 1864 and designed by George Goldie, a leading Catholic architect of the day in the Italian Baroque style.
Grant Recipient: Trustees for the Hospital Church
Access Contact: Ms Christine Malcolmson, Matron
T: 0207 806 4000 (ext.4294)   **F:** 0207 806 4001
E-mail: christine.malcolmson@hje.org.uk
Open: At all times.
London Open House: No
P Public Car park.
♿ Partial. Wheelchair access is via the balconies on the first floor. WC for the disabled. Guide Dogs allowed.
£ No

COLLEGE OF ARMS

Queen Victoria Street, London EC4V 4BT
Built in 1670s/1680s to the design of Francis Sandford and Morris Emmett to house the Heralds' offices, on the site of their earlier building, Derby Place, which was destroyed in the Great Fire of 1666. The principal room is Earl Marshal's Court, which is two floors high with gallery, panelling and throne. New record room added 1842 and portico and terrace in 1867.
www.college-of-arms.gov.uk
Grant Recipient: College of Arms
Access Contact: The Bursar
T: 020 7248 2762   **F:** 020 7248 6448
E-mail: enquiries@college-of-arms.gov.uk
Open: Earl Marshal's Court only: all year (except Public Holidays and State and Special Occasions), Monday–Friday 10am–4pm. Group tours of Record Room (max 20) and lecture in evenings after 6pm by prior arrangement with Officer-in -Waiting (tel. 020 7248 2762).
London Open House: Yes
P National Car Park nearby.
♿ No wheelchair access. No WC for the disabled. Guide Dogs allowed.
£ No

CROSSNESS BEAM ENGINE HOUSE

Abbey Wood, London SE2 9AQ
Grade I listed beam engine house, opened 1865, engineer Joseph Bazalgette. Constructed in the Romanesque style. The interior includes important ornamental cast ironwork and four original beam engines by James Watt and Co.
www.crossness.org.uk
Grant Recipient: Crossness Engines Trust
Access Contact: Mr Mike Jones
T: 020 8311 3711
E-mail: mike@jones86.freeserve.co.uk
Open: Steaming days: 27 April, 15 June, 27 July, 21 September (London Open House) and 19 October, 10.30am–4.30pm. A free bus service will operate between Abbey Wood rail station and Crossness Pumping Station on all steaming days, at approx 30 minute intervals. The first minibus leaves Abbey Wood station at 10.20am. Tours at other times by prior arrangement. Building work anticipated in 2008, please see website or telephone the site office (tel: 020 8311 3711–open Tuesdays and Sundays) to check.
London Open House: Yes
P Spaces: 50.
♿ Partial. Video link to areas not accessible by wheelchairs (beam floor and basement). No WC for the disabled. Guide Dogs allowed.
£ **Adult:** £4.00, £5.00 (steaming days). Free (London Open House).

DISSENTERS' CHAPEL

Kensal Green Cemetery, Harrow Road, London W10 4RA
Grade II* listed building within Grade II* Registered cemetery. Cemetery dates from 1832 and is London's oldest. The Chapel was designed in Greek Revival style by John Griffith in 1834. It is now used by the Friends of Kensal Green Cemetery as a headquarters, exhibition space and art gallery and as a centre for their guided walks, lectures and special events.

www.hct.org.uk or www.kensalgreen.co.uk
Grant Recipient: Historic Chapels Trust
Access Contact: Mr Henry Vivian-Neal
T: 020 8960 1030
E-mail: henry.vivianneal@btinternet.com
Open: Cemetery: daily: Dissenters' Chapel: Sunday afternoons and at other times by prior arrangement. Guided tours of chapels and cemetery for modest charge, also tours of the Catacombs 1st and 3rd Sunday in every month.
London Open House: Yes
P Parking in adjacent streets, parking for the disabled in cemetery.
♿ Full. WC for the disabled. Guide Dogs allowed.
£ £5.00 (donation requested for guided tours only).

DR JOHNSON'S HOUSE

17 Gough Square, London EC4A 3DE
Fine 18th century town house in the heart of the City of London. Here Dr Johnson compiled his dictionary (published 1755). Original staircase and woodwork throughout and collection of prints, paintings and Johnson memorabilia.
www.drjohnsonshouse.org
Grant Recipient: Dr Johnson's House Trust
Access Contact: The Curator, Dr Johnson's House Trust
T: 020 7353 3745   **F:** 020 7353 3745
E-mail: curator@drjohnsonshouse.org
Open: Monday–Saturday: May–September 11am–5.30pm, October–April 11am–5pm. Closed Sundays and Bank Holidays.
London Open House: Yes
P 2 parking bays for the disabled. On-street meter parking.
♿ No wheelchair access. WC for the disabled. Guide Dogs allowed.
£ **Adult:** £4.50. **Child:** £1.50. **Other:** £3.50 (student/senior citizens).

DULWICH COLLEGE

College Road, Dulwich, London SE21 7LD
Dulwich College was founded in 1619; the main buildings date from 1866–70 by the younger Charles Barry and are listed Grade II*. Three blocks lined by arcades in ornate Northern Italian Renaissance style. Close to Dulwich Village.
www.enterprise.dulwich.org.uk
Grant Recipient: Dulwich College
Access Contact: Ms Julia Field
T: 020 8299 9284   **F:** 020 8299 9296
E-mail: fieldjg@dulwich.org.uk
Open: Exterior visible from South Circular. Interior by prior arrangement with the Enterprise Manager
London Open House: Yes
P Spaces: 50. 200 parking spaces during school holidays.
♿ Partial. Wheelchair access with assistance (a few steps at entrance). WC for the disabled. Guide Dogs allowed.
£ **Adult:** £5.50, £7.50 (tour and archives). **Child:** £5.50, £7.50 (tour and archives). **Other:** £5.50, £7.50 (tour and archives).

FULHAM PALACE STABLEYARD WALL

Bishop's Avenue, London SW6
Home to the Bishops of London for over a thousand years to 1973. The two storey medieval west court is red brick with terracotta roof tiles. The mainly three storey Georgian east court is brown and yellow brick with parapets and slate roofs. Set in historic grounds near the river.
www.fulhampalace.org
Grant Recipient: London Borough of Hammersmith & Fulham
Access Contact: Dr Scott Cooper
T: 020 7736 3233   **F:** 020 7751 0164
E-mail: scott.cooper@lbhf.gov.uk
Open: The Palace grounds are open daily throughout the year during daylight hours.
London Open House: Yes
P Parking available for the disabled, otherwise pay parking on Bishop's Avenue, next to Palace.
♿ Partial. Prior notice is desirable for wheelchair users wishing to visit the ground floor rooms to enable the ramp to be installed. Gardens accessible. WC for the disabled. Guide Dogs allowed.
£ No

GARRICK'S TEMPLE

Hampton Court Road, Hampton, London TW12 2EN
The actor-manager David Garrick built the Temple in 1756 to celebrate the genius of William Shakespeare. The Temple was restored between 1997–1999 and now houses an exhibition of Garrick's acting career and life at Hampton, while the grounds have been landscaped to echo their original 18th century layout.
www.garricktemple.org.uk
Grant Recipient: London Borough of Richmond-upon-Thames
Access Contact: Mark De Novellis
T: 020 8831 6000   **F:** 020 8744 0501
E-mail: m.denovellis@richmond.gov.uk
Open: Temple: Beginning of April–end of September, Sundays 2–5pm. Also pre-arranged visits for small groups throughout the year (tel: 020 8831 6000). Lawn: open all year 7.30am–dusk.
London Open House: Yes
P Public parking in various locations near the Temple and large car park in Molesey Hurst from where Temple access is via Ferry which runs all day throughout the summer.
♿ Partial. Wheelchair access to lawn gardens only. WC for the disabled. Guide Dogs allowed.
£ No

HACKNEY EMPIRE

291 Mare Street, London E8 1EJ
Hackney Empire, designed and built by Frank Matcham in 1901, is one of the finest surviving variety theatres in Britain. Restoration and renovation completed 2004, providing modern facilities and access for all.
www.hackneyempire.co.uk
Grant Recipient: Hackney Empire Ltd
Access Contact: Mr S Thomsett
T: 020 8510 4500   **F:** 020 8510 4530
E-mail: info@hackneyempire.co.uk
Open: Performances throughout the year.
London Open House: Yes
P On-street parking.
♿ Full. WC for the disabled. Guide Dogs allowed.
£ Charges are made for performances and some organised tours.

HEADSTONE MANOR

Headstone Manor Recreation Ground, Pinner View, Harrow, London HA2 6PH
Grade I listed timber framed Manor House, surrounded by a water filled moat. Earliest parts date from 1310, with numerous extensions and adaptations through to 18th century. Original residence of Archbishops of Canterbury until the Reformation.
www.harrow.gov.uk
Grant Recipient: London Borough of Harrow
Access Contact: The Museum Manager
T: 020 8861 2626/ 020 8863 6720
Open: 1 April–30 September: Saturdays and Sundays for guided tours 2–3pm. Guided tours for groups throughout the year.
London Open House: Yes
P Spaces: 50. Parking for disabled badge holders only adjacent to property.
♿ Partial. WC for the disabled in adjacent tithe barn. Wheelchair access to some exterior parts and ground floor with assistance. Guide Dogs allowed.
£ **Adult:** £3.00. **Child:** Free.

HIGHPOINT

North Hill, Highgate, London N6 4BA
Two blocks of flats built in 1935 and 1938 by Lubetkin and Tecton. Constructed of reinforced concrete with decorative features.
Grant Recipient: Mantra Ltd
Access Contact: Mr Stephen Ellman
T: 020 7702 0701   **F:** 020 7480 7999
E-mail: Stephen.Ellman@rendallandrittner.co.uk
Open: By prior arrangement with Mr Stephen Ellman of Rendall and Rittner Limited, Gun Court, 70 Wapping Lane, London E1W 2RF.
London Open House: Yes
P No
♿ No wheelchair access. No WC for the disabled. Guide Dogs allowed.
£ No

HIMALAYA PALACE CINEMA (FORMERLY LIBERTY CINEMA)

14 South Road, Southall, London UB1 1RT
Former cinema, later market hall. 1928. An early work by George Coles; the only known example of cinema built in the Chinese style. Street elevation faced with coloured glazed tiles with red pantiled pagoda roofs. Interior badly fire damaged. Repaired and returned to use as a three screen cinema showing Bollywood, Tamil, Telugu and Afghanistan movies.
www.himalayapalacecinema.co.uk
Grant Recipient: Himalaya Carpets Ltd
Access Contact: Mr S Pandher
T: 020 8574 6193   **F:** 020 8574 2317
E-mail: himalayacarpets@tiscali.co.uk
Open: Daily, 10.30am–11.30pm. Non-public areas by prior arrangement.
London Open House: Yes
P Council car park at rear of cinema.
♿ Full. WC for the disabled. No Guide Dogs allowed.
£ **Adult:** £3.95 (before 2pm), £5.95 other times.
Child: £4.95 (all times). **Other:** £4.95 (senior citizens).

KEW BRIDGE STEAM MUSEUM

Kew Bridge Pumping Station, Green Dragon Lane, Brentford, London TW8 0EN
19th century Victorian waterworks with original steam pumping engines which are operated every weekend. "Water for Life" gallery exploring 2000 years of London's water.
www.kbsm.org
Grant Recipient: Kew Bridge Engines Trust & Water Supply Museum Ltd.
Access Contact: Kew Bridge Engines Trust & Water Supply Museum Ltd
T: 020 8568 4757   **F:** 020 8569 9978
E-mail: info@kbsm.org
Open: Daily (except Mondays) 11am–5pm. Closed Good Friday and Christmas. Contact the Museum or website for up-to-date information.
London Open House: No
P Spaces: 45.
♿ Partial. Wheelchair access to all areas except upper floors of Pump Houses. WC for the disabled. Guide Dogs allowed.
£ **Adult:** £5.00 (weekdays), £7.00 (weekends,) £8.00 (Cornish weekend). **Child:** Free. **Other:** £4.00 (weekdays), £6.00 (weekends), £7.00 (Cornish weekends).

LANDMARK ARTS CENTRE

Ferry Road, Teddington, London TW11 9NN
Grade II* former church, c1889, in French-Gothic style by architect William Niven. A number of intended architectural features were never in the end built, due to insufficient funds (hence the incomplete flying buttresses for example). Redundant as a church in 1977. Following renovation now used as an Arts Centre with a variety of arts events, classes and private events.
www.landmarkartscentre.org
Grant Recipient: London Diocesan Fund
Access Contact: Mr Graham Watson
T: 020 8614 8036   **F:** 020 8614 8080
E-mail: grahamgwatson@aol.com
Open: Normally open Monday–Friday 10am–5pm (shorter hours at weekends when public events are held), visitors are advised to contact the Arts Centre Manager at the Landmark Arts Centre (tel: 020 8977 7558, fax: 020 8977 4830, email: info@landmarkartscentre.org) to check. Visits at other times by prior arrangement with the Arts Centre Manager, subject to staff availability.
London Open House: No
P Spaces: 4. Additional on-street parking nearby.
♿ Full. WC for the disabled. Guide Dogs allowed.
£ Admission charges for some public events.

MAPPIN TERRACE CAFÉ

London Zoo, Regents Park, London NW1 4RY
The café was designed by John James Joass and built between 1914–20. It was funded by John Newton Mappin. It is a single story red-brick building with a pantiled roof. It is characterised by paired Tuscan columns, French windows, bracketed eaves and pavilion towers at three angles.
Grant Recipient: Zoological Society of London
Access Contact: Ms Philippa Roberts
T: 020 7449 6226   **F:** 020 7586 6177
E-mail: philippa.roberts@zsl.org

Open: On view to visitors to London Zoo which is open daily except 25 December.
London Open House: No
P Spaces: 300. Car park £10.00 and 250 yards away.
♿ Full. Guide dogs are housed and a personal guide provided. WC for the disabled. No Guide Dogs allowed.
£ **Adult:** £14.50. **Child:** £11.00 (under 3s free). **Other:** £13.00 (concessions).

ORLEANS HOUSE GALLERY

Riverside, Twickenham, London TW1 3DJ
Orleans House Gallery comprises the Octagon Room (1721) with its fine Baroque interior, and the surviving wing/Orangery of the 18th century Orleans House, the rest having been demolished in 1926. Overlooking the Thames and residing in preserved natural woodland, the Gallery presents a programme of temporary exhibitions, organises educational projects/activities and is responsible for the Richmond Borough Art Collection.
www.richmond.gov.uk/orleanshouse
Grant Recipient: London Borough of Richmond-upon-Thames
Access Contact: Mr Mark De Novellis
T: 020 8831 6000   **F:** 020 8744 0501
E-mail: m.denovellis@richmond.gov.uk
Open: All year: Tuesday–Saturday 1–5.30pm. Sundays 2–5.30pm. October–March, closes 4.30pm. Grounds open every day from 9am until dusk. For Bank Holiday and Christmas opening hours please call in advance.
London Open House: Yes
P Spaces: 60.
♿ Partial. Wheelchair access to ground floor only. WC for the disabled. Guide Dogs allowed.
£ No

PITZHANGER MANOR HOUSE AND GALLERY

Walpole Park, Mattock Lane, London W5 5EQ
Pitzhanger Manor House is set in Walpole Park, Ealing and was owned and rebuilt by architect and surveyor Sir John Soane (1753–1837). Much of the house has been restored to its early 19th century style. Pitzhanger Manor Gallery opened in 1996 in a 1940s extension and exhibitions of professional contemporary art in all media are shown in both the House and Gallery.
www.ealing.gov.uk/pmgalleryandhouse
Grant Recipient: London Borough of Ealing
Access Contact: Ms Helen Walker
T: 020 8567 1227   **F:** 020 8567 0596
E-mail: pmgallery&house@ealing.gov.uk
Open: Tuesday–Friday 1pm–5pm, Saturday 11am–5pm. Summer Sunday openings (ring for details). Closed Bank Holidays, Christmas and Easter.
London Open House: Yes
P Parking meters in Mattock Lane.
♿ Partial. Access for certain types of wheelchair only with assistance (domestic lift and some steps), please phone in advance for further information. WC for the disabled. Guide Dogs allowed.
£ No

PRIORY CHURCH OF THE ORDER OF ST JOHN

St John's Square, Clerkenwell, London EC1M
Remains of the Priory Church of the Knights Hospitallers' London headquarters, including choir and 12th century crypt. Museum in adjacent St John's Gate presents information on the Order of St John and conducts guided tours.
www.sja.org.uk/museum
Grant Recipient: The Order of St John of Jerusalem
Access Contact: Ms Pamela Willis
T: 020 7324 4071   **F:** 020 7336 0587
E-mail: museum@nhq.sja.org.uk
Open: Guided tours: Tuesday, Friday and Saturday 11am and 2.30pm. Other days and times by arrangement with the Museum.
London Open House: Yes
P Metered parking available in St John's Square.
♿ Partial. Wheelchair ramp for access to Church but not the crypt. WC for the disabled at St John's Gate. WC for the disabled. Guide Dogs allowed.
£ Donations requested for guided tours.

RED HOUSE

Red House Lane, Bexley DA6 8JF
Commissioned by William Morris, designed and built in 1859 by his friend and colleague, architect Philip Webb. Strongly influenced by Gothic medieval architecture and constructed with an emphasis on natural materials. Interior almost unaltered with numerous original features, including some items of fixed cupboards, settle and other furnishings designed by Morris and Webb, as well as wall paintings and stained glass by Edward Burne-Jones.
www.nationaltrust.org.uk
Grant Recipient: The National Trust
Access Contact: The Custodian
T: 020 8304 9878
E-mail: redhouse@nationaltrust.org.uk
Open: 1 March–21 December: Wednesday–Sunday. Admission by pre-booked guided tours (tel: 020 8304 9878, Tuesday–Saturday 9.30am–1.30pm). Limited free flow entry after 3.30pm. Last entry 4.15pm.
London Open House: Yes
🅿 Limited pre-booked parking for the disabled. Additional parking at Danson Park (1 mile). Parking charge at weekends and Bank Holidays.
♿ Partial. Wheelchair access to shop only. No WC for the disabled. Guide Dogs allowed.
💷 **Adult:** £6.60. **Child:** £3.30. **Other:** £16.50 (family). Free to NT members.

RICHMOND WEIR AND LOCK

Riverside, Richmond-upon-Thames, London
The lock and weir are important examples in the history of hydraulic engineering. Constructed in 1894 to control river levels between Richmond and Teddington at half-tide level, the weir was engineered to ensure that the river remained navigable at all times. Operated and maintained by the Port of London Authority since its establishment in 1909, the machinery was designed and built by Ransomes and Rapier.
www.portoflondon.co.uk
Grant Recipient: Port of London Authority
Access Contact: Mr James Trimmer
T: 01474 562200   **F:** 01474 562398
E-mail: james.trimmer@pola.co.uk
Open: The lock and weir are open at all times for passage by river except for 3 weeks in November/December for major maintenance undertaken by the Port of London Authority. The footbridge over the lock is open 6.30am–9.30pm British Summer Time and 6.30am–7.30pm GMT.
London Open House: Yes
🅿 No
♿ No wheelchair access. No WC for the disabled. No Guide Dogs allowed.
💷 No

ST ANDREWS OLD CHURCH

Old Church Lane, Kingsbury, Brent, London
Possibly of Saxon origin, now of 15th century appearance with 19th century restoration work. Considered to be the oldest building in Brent. Contains brasses and memorials to well-known local families dating from the 16th to the 19th centuries.
Grant Recipient: The Churches Conservation Trust
Access Contact: Ms Chloe Cockerill
T: 020 7213 0660   **F:** 020 7213 0678
Open: 28 May (Welsh Harp Day) and London Open House, at other times by prior arrangement.
London Open House: Yes
🅿 On-street parking.
♿ Full. No WC for the disabled. Guide Dogs allowed.
💷 No

ST ETHELBURGA'S CENTRE FOR RECONCILIATION AND PEACE

78 Bishopgate, London EC2N 4AG
Church of St Ethelburga the Virgin built in the late 14th and early 15th centuries. Devastated by a terrorist bomb in April 1993 and re-opened in November 2002, after restoration, for use as a Centre for Reconciliation and Peace.
www.stethelburgas.org
Grant Recipient: St Ethelburga's Centre for Reconciliation & Peace
Access Contact: Mr Simon Keyes
T: 020 7496 1610   **F:** 020 7638 1440
E-mail: enquiries@stethelburgas.org
Open: Every Friday 11am–3pm. Groups may visit at other times by arrangement. Details of services, public lectures and other events available from the website or by telephone.
London Open House: Yes
🅿 No
♿ Full. WC for the disabled. Guide Dogs allowed.
💷 No

ST GEORGE'S GERMAN LUTHERAN CHURCH

55 Alie Street, London E1 8EB
Oldest surviving German church in England from 1763 with mostly original furnishings including box pews on ground floor and in balconies. Double-decker central pulpit with sounding board set behind altar rails. 19th century Walcker organ.
Grant Recipient: Historic Chapels Trust
Access Contact: Dr Jennifer Freeman
T: 020 7481 0533   **F:** 020 7488 3756
E-mail: chapels@hct.org.uk
Open: By prior arrangement.
London Open House: Yes
🅿 Multi-storey car park to rear and on-street parking.
♿ Partial. Wheelchair access to ground floor. WC for the disabled. Guide Dogs allowed.
💷 Donations invited.

ST MATTHIAS OLD CHURCH COMMUNITY CENTRE

113 Poplar High Street, Poplar, London E14 0AE
Built by in 1650–54 by the East India Company, St Matthias Old Church is the oldest building in Docklands. Declared redundant in 1977, the building became derelict. In 1990 the building was restored and is now used as a community arts/cultural centre.
Grant Recipient: London Diocesan Fund
Access Contact: Mr Nizam Uddin
T: 020 7987 0459   **F:** 020 7531 9973
E-mail: niz_68@hotmail.com
Open: Monday–Friday: 10am–3pm.
London Open House: Yes
🅿 Car park for limited number of cars.
♿ Full. WC for the disabled. Guide Dogs allowed.
💷 No

ST PAUL'S STEINER PROJECT

1 St Paul's Road, London N1 2QH
Grade II* listed church, 1826–28 by Sir Charles Barry. Perpendicular in style. Converted to a 'cradle to grave' education and cultural centre, including a Steiner school, multi use community performance space, adult education and information centre.
www.stpaulssteinerproject.org
Grant Recipient: St Paul's Steiner Project
Access Contact: Ms Jane Gerhard
T: 020 7226 4454   **F:** 102 7226 2062
E-mail: st.pauls.school@btinternet.com
Open: Weekdays: 22 January, 4 March, 22 April, 10 June, 23 September and 18 November. At other times by prior arrangement with 2 days notice. Weekends and evenings: as per events at the Nave: see www.thenave.org.
London Open House: No
🅿 Pay and display
♿ Partial. Wheelchair access to ground floor. WC for the disabled. Guide Dogs allowed.
💷 No

THE HOUSE MILL

Three Mill Lane, Bromley-by-Bow, London E3 3DU
Industrial water mill, originally built 1776 as part of a distillery. Contains four floors with remains of un-restored machinery, four water wheels and gearing. Originally had 12 pairs of millstones and has unique survival of Fairbairn-style "silent millstone machinery".
www.HouseMill.org.uk
Grant Recipient: River Lea Tidal Mill Trust
Access Contact: Miss Beverley Charters
T: 0208 980 4626   **F:** 0208 980 0725
E-mail: RLTMT@bcos.demon.co.uk
Open: Sunday of National Mills Week, Heritage Open Days and first Sunday of each month April–December: 11am–4pm. Other Sundays May–October: 1–4pm. Groups by prior arrangement with Miss Beverley Charters.
London Open House: Yes
🅿 Car park nearby.
♿ Full. WC for the disabled. Guide Dogs allowed.
💷 **Adult:** £3.00. **Child:** Free. **Other:** £1.50.

THE QUEEN'S CHAPEL OF THE SAVOY

Savoy Hill, Strand, London WC2R 0DA
Originally part of a hospital founded in 1512 by Henry VII. Rebuilt by Robert Smirke after a fire in 1864, from which time the ceiling covered with heraldic emblems dates. Recently restored.
Grant Recipient: Duchy of Lancaster
Access Contact: Mr Phillip Chancellor
T: 020 7836 7221
E-mail: pdc46@mailcity.com
Open: All year except August and September: Tuesday–Friday 11.30am–3.30pm; Sunday for Morning Service only. Closed the week after Christmas Day and the week after Easter Day.
London Open House: No
🅿 No
♿ Full. No WC for the disabled. Guide Dogs allowed.
💷 No

THE ROUND CHAPEL (CLAPTON PARK UNITED REFORMED CHURCH)

1d Glenarm Road, London E5 0LY
Grade II* listed United Reformed Church, c1871. Horseshoe-shaped plan with roof and gallery supported by iron pillars. Detailed columns form a continuous iron arcade at roof level with latticework effects. Contemporary pulpit with double flight of stairs, organ and organ case.
www.hhbt.org.uk
Grant Recipient: Hackney Historic Buildings Trust
Access Contact: Miss Beliz Tecirli
T: 020 8525 0706/ 02089860029   **F:** 020 8986 0029
E-mail: beliz@hhbt.org.uk
Open: Many public/community events take place in the Round Chapel which the public can attend; it is also available to hire for private events, otherwise access by prior arrangement.
London Open House: Yes
🅿 Spaces: 3.
♿ Partial. Wheelchair access to ground floor only. WC for the disabled. Guide Dogs allowed.
💷 No

THE ROUNDHOUSE

Chalk Farm Road, London NW1 8EH
The Roundhouse is a grade II* listed engine maintenance and turning shed built in 1846 for the London and North Western railway. By the 1860s engines had become too long to be turned and stored there so it was leased to W&A Gilbey Ltd as a liquor store until its conversion into a theatre in the 1960s. The Roundhouse re-opened in 2006 and houses an international performance venue and creative centre for young people, The Roundhouse Studios.
www.roundhouse.org.uk
Grant Recipient: The Roundhouse Trust
Access Contact: Ms Emily Hahn, Development Manager
T: 020 7424 9991   **F:** 020 7424 9992
E-mail: info@roundhouse.org.uk
Open: All year, excluding some public holidays.
London Open House: No
🅿 7 spaces for disabled parking only.
♿ Full. WC for the disabled. Guide Dogs allowed.
💷 Charges apply for most events.

WAPPING HYDRAULIC POWER PUMPING STATION

Wapping Wall, London E1W 3ST
The Wapping Hydraulic Power Station was built by the London Hydraulic Power Company in 1890. One of the five London Stations of its kind, it harnessed Thames water to provide power throughout the central London area. The showcase building of the LHPC, it was used as a model for power stations in Argentina, Australia, New York and Europe. Now houses an art gallery and restaurant.
www.thewappingproject.com
Grant Recipient: Women's Playhouse Trust
Access Contact: Women's Playhouse Trust
T: 020 7680 2080   **F:** 020 7680 2081
E-mail: jules@thewappingproject.com
Open: Throughout the year (except 23 December–4 January): Monday–Friday: 12 noon–Midnight, Saturday 10am–Midnight and Sunday 10am–6pm.
London Open House: No
🅿 Spaces: 30.
♿ Full. WC for the disabled. Guide Dogs allowed.
💷 No

WHITECHAPEL ART GALLERY

Whitechapel High Street, London E1 7QX
Grade II* listed Arts and Crafts building constructed in the late 1890s by C H Townsend. Occupied by the Whitechapel Art Gallery, which was founded in 1901 by the Revd Canon Barnett 'to bring great art to the people of the East End'.
www.whitechapel.org
Grant Recipient: Trustees of the Whitechapel Art Gallery
Access Contact: Mr Tom Wilcox
T: 020 7522 7865   **F:** 020 7377 1685
E-mail: TomWilcox@whitechapel.org
Open: All year: Wednesday–Sunday 11am–6pm, Thursday 11am–9pm. Various exhibitions (5–6 per year).
London Open House: No
P Paid parking in Spreadeagle Yard to the left of the gallery off Whitechapel High Street.
♿ Full. WC for the disabled. Guide Dogs allowed.
£ One exhibition per year will have entrance fee.

WILTONS MUSIC HALL

Graces Alley, Tower Hamlets, London E1 8JB
The world's oldest surviving grand Victorian music hall listed Grade II*. John Wilton built the theatre behind his public house 'The Prince of Denmark' in 1858, in Graces Alley and it continued as a music hall until 1884. Hall open for regular performances, shows and private events.
www.wiltons.org.uk
Grant Recipient: Wiltons Music Hall Trust
Access Contact: Ms Frances Mayhew, Director
T: 020 7702 9555   **F:** 0871 2532424
E-mail: info@wiltons.org.uk
Open: Monday–Friday for pre-booked guided tours only. Other public performances and private events, and two open weekends a year.
London Open House: No
P On-street parking (parking meters) and two public car parks (5 minutes walk).
♿ Full. Wheelchair access to ground floor and auditorium. WC for the disabled. Guide Dogs allowed.
£ £5.00 (guided tour).

MERSEYSIDE

FORMBY HALL

Southport Old Road, Formby, Merseyside L37 0AB
Built c1620 with 18th century extensions and later alterations.
Grant Recipient: Mr Michael McComb
Access Contact: Mr Michael McComb
T: 01704 878 999   **F:** 01704 572 436
Open: Access to the exterior by prior arrangement with Mr McComb, 8 Victoria Road, Formby, Liverpool L37 7AG. Tel: 01704 878 999.
Heritage Open Days: No
P Spaces: 1.
♿ No wheelchair access. No WC for the disabled. No Guide Dogs allowed.
£ No

GRAND ENTRANCE

Birkenhead Park, Park Road North, Birkenhead, Wirral, Merseyside CH41 4HD
Grand triple entrance archway to Birkenhead Park, with two-storey lodges on either side. Dated 1847, by L.Hornblower and J.Robertson for Sir Joseph Paxton. Full-height coupled Ionic columns which also continue across the flanking lodges. Balustraded parapet. Listed Grade II*.
www.wirral.gov.uk
Grant Recipient: Wirral Metropolitan Borough Council
Access Contact: Mr Martin McCoy, Parks Manager
T: 0151 652 5197   **F:** 0151 652 4521
E-mail: martinmccoy@wirral.gov.uk
Open: March–September: Wednesday, tour 2–3pm; Heritage Open Days (11–14 September). At other times by prior arrangement.
Heritage Open Days: Yes
P Spaces: 20. Additional parking in parkland.
♿ Partial. Entrance arches accessible but not internal buildings. WC for the disabled at Birkenhead Park Pavilion and cafeteria. Guide Dogs allowed.
£ No

LIVERPOOL COLLEGIATE APARTMENTS

Shaw Street, Liverpool, Merseyside L6 1NR
Grade II* former school built 1843 of red sandstone in Tudor Gothic style, gutted by fire and now converted into residential block.
Grant Recipient: Urban Splash Ltd
Access Contact: Mr Bill Maynard
T: 0161 839 2999   **F:** 0161 839 8999
E-mail: billmaynard@urbansplash.co.uk
Open: Exterior only, visible from Shaw Street.
Heritage Open Days: No
P No
♿ Full. No WC for the disabled. No Guide Dogs allowed.
£ No

SEFTON PARK

Liverpool, Merseyside L18 3JD
108 hectare public park, designed in 1867, the first to introduce French influence to the design of parks through the designer Edouard André who had worked on the design of major Parisian parks. Sefton Park is Grade II* registered and contains several listed statues and other features. The Grade II* listed Palm House, 1896 by Mackenzie and Moncur, is an octagonal iron frame structure which appears as 3 domed roofs, one above the other.
www.palmhouse.org.uk
Grant Recipient: Liverpool City Council
Access Contact: Ms Emma Reid
T: 0151 726 9304   **F:** 0151 726 2419
E-mail: info@palmhouse.org.uk
Open: Park open at all times. Palm House: 1 April–31 October: Monday–Saturday 10.30am–5pm, Sunday 10.30am–4pm, may be closed on Tuesdays and Thursdays and from 4pm for events; 1 November–31 March: Monday–Sunday 10.30am–4pm, may be closed on Tuesdays and Thursdays for events. The Trust reserves the right to shut the Palm House on other occasions and will endeavour to give as much notice as possible on the website and information line (tel: 0151 726 2415).
Heritage Open Days: Yes
P On-street parking available on edge of park.
♿ Full. No WC for the disabled. Guide Dogs allowed.
£ No

THE ARCHES

136 High Street, Newton-le-Willows, Merseyside WA12
Early 19th century entrance archway with flanking buildings. Originally at Haydock Lodge a mile away and rebuilt on the present site in 1840 as a centre piece of Newton's revived market. Later, the entrance to Randall's Nurseries, now a restaurant. The archway has been glazed to form the entrance lobby to the restaurant. Listed Grade II*.
Grant Recipient: Mr Bahman Rashidi
Access Contact: Mr Bahman Rashidi
T: 07855 824269   **F:** 0161 4488900
E-mail: bahmancasatapas@hotmail.com
Open: Daily, 9am–10pm.
Heritage Open Days: No
P Spaces: 4.
♿ Full. WC for the disabled. Guide Dogs allowed.
£ No

WALLASEY UNITARIAN CHURCH

Manor Road, Liscard, Wallasey, Merseyside CH44 1BU
Arts and Crafts chapel interior dating from 1899 with fittings by Bernard Sleigh and craftsmen associated with Bromsgrove Guild.
www.hct.org.uk
Grant Recipient: Historic Chapels Trust
Access Contact: Mr Terry Edgar
T: 0151 639 9707
E-mail: terryedgar@hotmail.com
Open: At all reasonable times by prior arrangement with key holder, Terry Edgar, 5 Mere Lane, Wallasey Village, Wirral CH45 3HY.
Heritage Open Days: Yes
P Restricted on-street parking.
♿ Full. WC for the disabled. Guide Dogs allowed.
£ Donations invited.

NORFOLK

15 ST MARTIN AT PALACE PLAIN (NORFOLK ACRO)

Norwich, Norfolk NR3 1RW
Medieval former church, now housing the Norfolk Association for the Care and Resettlement of Offenders. Has a fine 16th century tomb for Lady Elizabeth Calthorpe.
Grant Recipient: Norwich Historic Churches Trust
Access Contact: Ms Amanda Payne
T: 01603 763555   **F:** 01603 230524
E-mail: amanda@norfolkacro.org
Open: By prior written arrangement.
Heritage Open Days: No
P In city centre car parks.
♿ Partial. Wheelchair access to ground floor only, by prior arrangement. WC for the disabled. Guide Dogs allowed.
£ No

FELBRIGG HALL

Felbrigg, Norwich, Norfolk NR11 8PR
17th century house containing its original 18th century furniture and paintings. The walled garden has been restored and features a working dovecote, small orchard and the national collection of Colchicum. The park is renowned for its fine and aged trees.
www.nationaltrust.org.uk
Grant Recipient: The National Trust
Access Contact: Property Manager
T: 01263 837444   **F:** 01263 837032
E-mail: felbrigg@nationaltrust.org.uk
Open: House: 3 March–2 November: Saturday–Wednesday 11am–5pm. Garden: 3 March–26 October: Saturday–Wednesday, 26 May–1 June, 21 July–31 August, 27–2 November: daily 11am–5pm. 27–31 December: Saturday–Wednesday 11am–4pm. Open Bank Holidays and Good Friday. Estate walks: All year, dawn to dusk.
Heritage Open Days: No
P Spaces: 200. Separate parking for disabled and drop-off point.
♿ Partial. Wheelchair access to ground floor, photograph album of first floor. Garden, shop and bookshop (ramp), tea room and restaurant accessible. WC for the disabled. Guide Dogs allowed.
£ **Adult:** £7.50 (house), £3.50 (garden). **Child:** £3.50 (house), £1.50 (garden). **Other:** £18.50 (family). Groups: £6.50 (adult), £3.00 (child).

HOLKHAM HALL VINERY

Wells-next-the-Sea, Norfolk NR23 1AB
Range of late 19th century Glasshouses. Six houses in the range, four of which have been repaired.
www.holkham.co.uk
Grant Recipient: Coke Estates Ltd
Access Contact: Mr Richard Gledson
T: 01328 710227   **F:** 01328 711707
E-mail: enquiries@holkham.co.uk
Open: The walled gardens are not currently open to the public. Access to view the glasshouses by appointment only.
Heritage Open Days: No
P Spaces: 25.
♿ No wheelchair access. No WC for the disabled. No Guide Dogs allowed.
£ No

NELSON'S MONUMENT

Great Yarmouth, Norfolk
Grade I listed monument, also knows as Norfolk Pillar. 1817–19 by William Wilkins. The first monument in England to Admiral Lord Nelson (Nelson's Column in Trafalgar Square is 1840–43). Consists of a fluted Greek Doric column on a square pedestal standing on a raised plinth. The column is surmounted by a figure of Britannia in fibreglass standing on a disc supported by Caryatid figures. The figures were of Coade stone when built, replaced in concrete in 1896 and finally in fibreglass during the restoration of 1982–4. Fully restored for the bicentenary celebrations in 2005.
www.nelsonsmonument.org.uk
Grant Recipient: Norfolk Historic Buildings Trust
Access Contact: Mr Colin Smith
T: 01603 629048   **F:** 01603 629048
E-mail: nfkhisbuildtrust@btconnect.com
Open: Exterior can be viewed at all times. The interior and tower are open on 10 days throughout the year (dates to

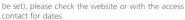

be set), please check the website or with the access contact for dates.
Heritage Open Days: No
🅿 On-street parking.
♿ Partial. Wheelchair access to exterior only. No WC for the disabled. Guide Dogs allowed.
💷 £7.50 (open days only).

OLD HALL

Norwich Road, South Burlingham, Norfolk NR13 4EY
Small Elizabethan manor house with a painted stucco fireplace, painted stucco mermaids and scrollwork on the front porch, and a long gallery of hunting scenes in grisaille, c1600.
Grant Recipient: Mr P Scupham
Access Contact: Mr P Scupham
T: 01493 750804
E-mail: margaret@moonshinecat.fsnet.co.uk
Open: By prior telephone arrangement with Mr P Scupham or Ms M Steward. No access for guide dogs to the Long Gallery.
Heritage Open Days: Yes
🅿 Spaces: 8. 12 extra parking spaces available in small attached meadow.
♿ Partial. Wheelchair access to ground floor and garden, painted gallery inaccessible. No WC for the disabled. Guide Dogs allowed.
💷 No

RUINED CHURCH OF ST PETER

Wiggenhall St Peter with Wigge, Norfolk
Former parish church, largely 15th century, now ruined. South aisle was demolished in 1840.
Grant Recipient: Wiggenhall St Peter PCC
Access Contact: Mrs A Yeoman
T: 01553 617518
Open: To the exterior at all reasonable times.
Heritage Open Days: No
🅿 Spaces: 2.
♿ No wheelchair access. No WC for the disabled. No Guide Dogs allowed.
💷 No

ST BENET'S ABBEY

Horning, Norfolk
Site of the medieval abbey beside the River Bure. Parts of the gatehouse remain attached to an 18th century brick windmill. Within the whole monastic precinct are the foundations of the abbey church, monastic fishponds and other earthworks, all surrounded by a precinct boundary ditch.
www.norfarchtrust.org.uk
Grant Recipient: Norfolk Archaeological Trust
Access Contact: Norfolk Archaeological Trust
T: 01362 667 043   **F:** 01362 667225
E-mail: peterwm@hotmail.com
Open: At all times.
Heritage Open Days: No
🅿 Spaces: 4.
♿ No wheelchair access. No WC for the disabled. Guide Dogs allowed.
💷 No

ST BENET'S LEVEL MILL

Ludham, Norfolk
Typical example of a Broadland drainage mill with tapering red brick tower, white boat shaped cap, sails and fantail. Built in 18th century and altered over the years, it became redundant in the 1940s. Ground and first floors accessible. Information boards on site.
Grant Recipient: Crown Estates Commissioners
Access Contact: Mrs Alison Ritchie
T: 01692 678232
E-mail: alison@ludhamhall.co.uk
Open: Second Sunday in May and first Sunday in August. At other times by prior arrangement with Mrs Alison Ritchie at Hall Farm, Ludham, Great Yarmouth, Norfolk NR29 5NU (tel: 01692 678232) or Mrs Jenny Scaff, Carter Jonas, 6–8 Hills Road, Cambridge CB2 1NH (tel: 01223 346628).
Heritage Open Days: Yes
🅿 No
♿ No wheelchair access. Guide dog access possible to ground floor only. No WC for the disabled.
💷 No

ST CLEMENT

Colegate, Norwich, Norfolk NR3 1BQ
15th century church, now a pastoral care and counselling centre. Has a slender tower decorated with lozenges of flushwork (patterns made from flint and stone).
Grant Recipient: Norwich Historic Churches Trust
Access Contact: Rev. Reverend Jack Burton
T: 01603 622747
Open: Daily 10am–4pm (sometimes longer). Occasionally closed when steward on leave.
Heritage Open Days: Yes
🅿 In city centre car parks.
♿ Partial. Wheelchair access to Nave at street level. No WC for the disabled. Guide Dogs allowed.
💷 No

ST LAWRENCE

The Street, South Walsham, Norfolk NR13 6DQ
Medieval church destroyed by fire and rebuilt in 1832 as a parish church and used for worship until c1890. Formerly redundant but now re-licensed for worship. Now houses St Lawrence Centre for Training and the Arts, open to the public and used for exhibitions, classes and concerts. Access to Sacristans Garden.
www.st-lawrence.org.uk
Grant Recipient: South Walsham Parochial Church Council
Access Contact: Mrs Caroline Linsdell
T: 01603 270522
Open: Daily 9am–6pm or dusk in winter.
Heritage Open Days: No
🅿 Spaces: 8.
♿ Full. WC for the disabled. Guide Dogs allowed.
💷 No

ST MARGARET-DE-WESTWICK

St Benedict's Street, Norwich, Norfolk
Medieval church, now redundant. Used for art exhibitions.
www.norwichchurches.co.uk
Grant Recipient: Norwich Historic Churches Trust
Access Contact: Ms Jane Jones
T: 07867 801 995
E-mail: norhistch.trust@btinternet.com
Open: By prior arrangement with Jane Jones (tel: 07867 801 995). Also open for art exhibitions during the summer months and limited exhibitions during winter months.
Heritage Open Days: Yes
🅿 No
♿ Full. No WC for the disabled. Guide Dogs allowed.
💷 No

ST MARTIN AT OAK

Oak Street, Norwich, Norfolk
15th century former church, now redundant.
www.norwichchurches.co.uk
Grant Recipient: Norwich Historic Churches Trust
Access Contact: Mrs J Jones
T: 07867 801995   **F:** 01603 722008
E-mail: norhistch.trust@btinternet.com
Open: By arrangement with the tenant. Please telephone 07867 801995 for details.
Heritage Open Days: Yes
🅿 Parking meters in St Martin Lane and city centre car parks.
♿ No wheelchair access. No WC for the disabled. No Guide Dogs allowed.
💷 No

ST MARY

Fordham, Downham Market, Norfolk
Medieval aisleless church in rural landscape, now redundant. Listed Grade II*.
Grant Recipient: Fordham St Mary Preservation Trust
Access Contact: Mr Robert Bateson
T: 01366 388399   **F:** 01366 385859
E-mail: bateson@rannerlow.co.uk
Open: By prior arrangement or key may be available from farm opposite church.
Heritage Open Days: No
🅿 Spaces: 12.
♿ No wheelchair access. No WC for the disabled. No Guide Dogs allowed.
💷 No

ST PETER AND ST PAUL

Tunstall, Norfolk
Origins of church date to early years of 14th century as evidenced by double piscinas in chancel. Ruined tower and nave never rebuilt.
Grant Recipient: Tunstall (Norfolk) Church Preservation Trust
Access Contact: The Secretary
T: 01493 700279   **F:** 01493 700279
Open: Normally all year. If locked, it is due to severe weather. Key available at the Manor House in Tunstall.
Heritage Open Days: No
🅿 Spaces: 6.
♿ Full. Wheelchair access is across uneven path. No WC for the disabled. Guide Dogs allowed.
💷 No

THE DEANERY

56 The Close, Norwich, Norfolk NR1 4EG
13th century with later additions, originally the Prior's lodgings. It remains the residence of the Dean of Norwich. The interior is closed to the public.
www.cathedral.org.uk
Grant Recipient: The Chapter of Norwich Cathedral
Access Contact: The Chapter Steward
T: 01603 218300   **F:** 01603 766032
E-mail: chapter@cathedral.org.uk
Open: Exterior visible from The Close which is open to visitors during daylight hours throughout the year.
Heritage Open Days: No
🅿 No
♿ Full. No WC for the disabled. No Guide Dogs allowed.
💷 No

THURNE DYKE DRAINAGE MILL

Thurne Staithe, Thurne, Norfolk NR29 3BU
Broadland drainage mill c1820 with classic 'hained' appearance and turbine pump. Originally 2 storey tapering circular whitewashed brick tower but raised to 3 storeys in mid 19th century, with timber weatherboarded boat shaped cap, sails and fan.
www.norfolkwindmills.co.uk
Grant Recipient: Norfolk Windmills Trust
Access Contact: Mrs Amanda Rix
T: 01603 222705   **F:** 01603 224413
E-mail: amanda.rix@norfolk.gov.uk
Open: April–September: second and forth Sunday of each month; National Mills weekend (second weekend in May) 2–5pm and at other times by arrangement.
Heritage Open Days: No
🅿 Spaces: 4. Parking at parish staithe, approx. 100 yards. Pub also allows parking for visitors.
♿ No wheelchair access. No WC for the disabled. No Guide Dogs allowed.
💷 Donations invited.

WAXHAM GREAT BARN

Sea Palling, Norfolk NR1 2DH
Grade I listed barn, 1570s–80s, with later additions. Flint with ashlar dressings and thatched roof. Much of its fabric is re-used material from dissolved monasteries.
Grant Recipient: Norfolk County Council
Access Contact: Mrs Helen Wiggins
T: 01603 222705   **F:** 01603 224413
E-mail: helen.wiggins@norfolk.gov.uk
Open: Provisional: 5 May–28 October, daily 10.30am–4.30pm. Visitors should ring nearer the time to confirm opening times.
Heritage Open Days: No
🅿 Spaces: 100. Free parking.
♿ Partial. Wheelchair access with assistance (gravel path from car park to Barn). WC for the disabled. Guide Dogs allowed.
💷 Adult: £3.00. Child: Free. Other: £2.50 Concessions.

NORTH YORKSHIRE

AISKEW WATER CORNMILL

Bedale, North Yorkshire DL8 1AW
Grade II* watermill, late 18th and early 19th century. Sold in 1918 in a major dispersal of estate properties. Roof and main structure restored. Restoration of interior with original wooden machinery is planned.
www.farmattraction.co.uk
Grant Recipient: David Clark
Access Contact: Messrs Jared, Duncan & Carol Clark
T: 01677 422125   **F:** 01677 425205

E-mail: enquiries@farmattraction.co.uk
Open: Access to the exterior at all reasonable times. Guided tours available by prior arrangement.
Heritage Open Days: Yes
P Spaces: 40.
Full. WC for the disabled. Guide Dogs allowed.
£ No

BENINGBROUGH HALL

Beningbrough, North Yorkshire Y030 1DD
Country house, c1716, contains an impressive Baroque interior exhibiting over one hundred 18th century portraits in partnership with the National Portrait Gallery. A very high standard of craftsmanship is displayed throughout, most of the original work surviving with extremely fine woodcarving and other ornate decoration, and an unusual central corridor running the full length of the house. There is a fully equipped Victorian laundry and walled garden.
www.nationaltrust.org.uk
Grant Recipient: The National Trust
Access Contact: Property Manager
T: 01904 472027   **F:** 01904 470002
E-mail: beningbrough@nationaltrust.org.uk
Open: House: 1 March–30 June: daily except Thursday and Friday; 1 July–31 August: daily except Thursday; 1 September–26 October: daily except Thursday and Friday, 11am–3.30pm. Grounds and shop: 1 March–30 June: daily except Thursday and Friday 11am–5.30pm; 1 July–31 August: daily except Thursday and Friday 11am–5.30pm; 1 September–26 October: daily except Thursday and Friday 11am–5.30pm; 1 November–21 December: Monday to Friday 11am–3.30pm. Restaurant: as grounds.
Heritage Open Days: No
P Spaces: 250.
Partial. Wheelchairs available on all floors, as well as seating. Steps to entrance with handrail or lift available as well as alternative entrance. Access to ground floor and stairs with handrail or lift to other floors. WC for the disabled. Guide Dogs allowed.
£ **Adult:** £8.80 (house & grounds). **Child:** £4.00 (house & grounds). **Other:** £18.50 (Family: 2 Adults & 3 Children/1 Adult & 4 Children). Group: £6.50 (adult), £4.00 (child). Reduced rate when arriving by cycle.

CASTLE HOWARD

York, North Yorkshire YO60 7DA
Large stately home dating from the beginning of the 18th century and designed by Sir John Vanbrugh. Situated in 10,000 acres of landscaped grounds, which includes numerous monuments.
www.castlehoward.co.uk
Grant Recipient: The Hon. Simon Howard, Castle Howard Estate Ltd
Access Contact: Hon Simon Howard
T: 01653 648444   **F:** 01653 648529
E-mail: sh@cashow.net
Open: 1 March–5 November: daily, 11am–4.00pm (grounds only from 10am); November–mid-March: grounds open most days but please telephone for confirmation in November, December and January. Access to interior of Temple of the Four Winds by prior arrangement only.
Heritage Open Days: No
P Spaces: 300.
Partial. Wheelchair access to all but chapel and first floor of exhibition wing. WC for the disabled. Guide Dogs allowed.
£ **Adult:** £10.50 (provisional) **Child:** £6.50 (provisional) **Other:** £9.00 (provisional).

DUNCOMBE PARK

Helmsley, York, North Yorkshire YO62 5EB
Recently restored family home of Lord and Lady Feversham. Originally built in 1713 and then rebuilt after a fire in 1879 largely to the original design. Early 18th century gardens.
www.duncombepark.com
Grant Recipient: Lord Feversham
Access Contact: Duncombe Park Estate Office
T: 01439 770213   **F:** 01439 771114
E-mail: liz@duncombepark.com
Open: 23 March–26 October: Sunday–Thursday. Closed 11,12 and 16 June. House: Guided tours hourly 12.30pm–3.30pm lasting 1¼ hours. Garden: 11am–5.30pm (last admission to gardens and parkland 4.30pm). Special Events throughout the year. Duncombe Park reserve the right to alter opening arrangements without prior notice–please telephone to check.

Heritage Open Days: No
P Spaces: 200.
Partial. Wheelchair access to ground and first floor only. WC for the disabled. Guide Dogs allowed.
£ **Adult:** £7.25 (house & gardens), £4.00 (gardens & parkland), £2.00 (parkland). **Child:** £3.25 (10–16, house & garden), £2.00 (10–16, gardens & garden), £1.00 (10–16, parkland). **Other:** £5.50 (concessions, house & garden), £15.00 (family, house & garden), £5.25 (groups, house & garden), £30.00 (family season ticket).

FOUNTAINS HALL

Ripon, North Yorkshire HG4 3DY
Elizabethan mansion, built between 1589 and 1604 for Stephen Proctor. Three rooms; the Stone Hall, the Arkell Room, and the Reading Room, all unfurnished, are open to the public. The conservation of a fourth room, the Great Chamber, has been completed. This upper room features an ornate chimney piece depicting the Biblical story of the Judgement of Solomon. The mansion is situated within a World Heritage Site which also includes the ruins of a 12th century Cistercian Abbey, monastic water mill and Georgian water garden.
www.fountainsabbey.org.uk
Grant Recipient: The National Trust
Access Contact: Property Manager
T: 01765 608888   **F:** 01765 601002
E-mail: fountainenquiries@nationaltrust.org.uk
Open: As part of the Fountain's Abbey and Studley Royal Estate. 1 March–31 October: daily 10am–5pm; 1 November–31 January 2009 daily (except Thursday), 10am–4pm. Estate closed 24, 25 December and Fridays in January, November and December. Deer Park: open all year, dawn to dusk.
Heritage Open Days: Yes
P Spaces: 1200.
Full. WC for the disabled. Guide Dogs allowed.
£ **Adult:** £7.90. **Child:** £4.20. **Other:** £20.00 (family). £6.50 (adult, groups 15–30), £3.50 (child, groups 15–30). £6.00 (adult, groups 31+), £3.00 (child, 31+). English Heritage Members free.

GIGGLESWICK SCHOOL CHAPEL

Giggleswick, Settle, North Yorkshire BD24 0DE
Built 1897–1901 by T G Jackson for Walter Morrison as a gift to the school to commemorate the Diamond Jubilee of Queen Victoria. Constructed of Gothic banded rockfaced millstone grit sandstone and limestone, with lead hipped roof to nave and copper covered terracotta dome to chancel. Contains Italian grafitto work throughout.
www.giggleswick.org.uk
Grant Recipient: The Governors of Giggleswick School
Access Contact: The Bursar and Clerk to the Governors
T: 01729 893000/893012   **F:** 01729 893150
E-mail: bursar@giggleswick.org.uk
Open: Monday–Friday 9am–5pm, closed Bank Holidays. Other times by arrangement. Visitors must report to reception to obtain the key to the Chapel.
Heritage Open Days: Yes
P Spaces: 40.
Partial. Wheelchair access to ground floor only. WC for the disabled in main school premises. WC for the disabled. No Guide Dogs allowed.
£ No

HOVINGHAM HALL

Hovingham, York, North Yorkshire YO62 4LU
Palladian house built c1760 by Thomas Worsley to his own design. Unique entry through huge riding school. Extensive gardens in a parkland setting. The private cricket ground in front of the house is reported to be the oldest in England.
www.hovingham.co.uk
Grant Recipient: Mr William Worsley
Access Contact: Mrs Kathryn Lamprey
T: 01653 628771   **F:** 01653 628668
E-mail: office @hovingham.co.uk
Open: 2 June–5 July: Monday–Saturday, 1.15–4.30pm (closed Sunday). Last tour 3.30pm.
Heritage Open Days: No
P Spaces: 80.
Partial. Wheelchair access to ground floor. WC for the disabled in adjacent village hall. WC for the disabled. Guide Dogs allowed.
£ **Adult:** £6.50. **Child:** £3.00. **Other:** £6.00 (concessions), £4.00 (gardens).

JERVAULX ABBEY

Ripon, North Yorkshire HG4 4PH
Ruins of Cistercian Abbey moved to this site in 1156, built of sandstone ashlar in Early English style. Remains of nave, transepts and choir, with a cloister on the south side of the nave, flanked by a chapter house to the east and a kitchen and dorter to the south.
Grant Recipient: Mr Ian Burdon
Access Contact: Mr Ian Burdon
T: 01677 460391/01677 460226
E-mail: ba123@btopenworld.com
Open: At any reasonable time throughout the year.
Heritage Open Days: No
P Spaces: 55.
Partial. Wheelchair access to church, infirmary, frater and cloisters. Uneven terrain and steps on other parts of site. WC for the disabled. Guide Dogs allowed.
£ **Adult:** £2.00 (honesty box). **Child:** £1.50 (honesty box).

MARKENFIELD HALL

Ripon, North Yorkshire HG4 3AD
Fortified moated manor house, built 1310–23 for John de Markenfield (Chancellor of the Exchequer to Edward II), with further additions and alterations in the 16th, 18th and 19th centuries. Restored 1981–4 and 2001–3.
www.markenfield.com
Grant Recipient: Lady Deirdre Curteis
Access Contact: Mrs Sarah Robson
T: 01765 692303   **F:** 01765 607195
E-mail: info@markenfield.com
Open: 4–17 May and 15–28 June: 2–5pm (last entry 4.30pm). Groups with guided tour by appointment all year round.
Heritage Open Days: No
P Spaces: 25.
Partial. Wheelchair access to ground floor only. No WC for the disabled. Guide Dogs allowed.
£ **Adult:** £4.00. **Child:** £3.00. **Other:** £3.00 (senior citizens), £80.00 (minimum charge groups out of opening times).

MOWBRAY POINT

The Ruin, Hackfall, Harrogate, North Yorkshire
Folly, built c1750, standing in the Grade I registered remains of the 18th century garden at Hackfall. It is a small pavilion above a steep wooded gorge.
www.landmarktrust.org.uk
Grant Recipient: The Landmark Trust
Access Contact: Mrs Victoria O'Keeffe
T: 01628 825920   **F:** 01628 825417
E-mail: vokeeffe@landmarktrust.org.uk
Open: The Landmark Trust is an independent charity, which rescues small buildings of historic or architectural importance from decay or unsympathetic improvement. Landmark's aim is to promote the enjoyment of these historic buildings by making them available to stay in for holidays. Mowbray Point can be rented by anyone, at all times of the year, for periods ranging from a weekend to three weeks. Bookings can be made by telephoning the Booking Office on 01628 825925. As the building is in full-time use for holiday accommodation, it is not normally open to the public. However, the public have access to and across the terrace all year 11am–4pm and to the interior by prior arrangement by telephoning the access contact (Victoria O'Keeffe on 01628 825920) to make an appointment. Potential visitors will be asked to write to confirm the details of their visit.
Heritage Open Days: Yes
P Spaces: 2.
No wheelchair access. No WC for the disabled. Guide Dogs allowed.
£ No

NATIONAL CENTRE FOR EARLY MUSIC

St Margaret's Church, Walmgate, York, North Yorkshire YO1 9TL
14th century church with highly decorated 12th century Romanesque doorway (removed from chapel of the ruined hospital of St Nicholas, probably during 1684–5 rebuilding of church (orange-red brick tower of same date) occasioned by Civil War damage). Now houses the National Centre for Early Music and used for concerts, music educational activities, conferences, recordings and events.
www.ncem.co.uk
Grant Recipient: York Early Music Foundation
Access Contact: Mrs G Baldwin

T: 01904 632220   **F:** 01904 612631
E-mail: info@ncem.co.uk
Open: All year: Monday–Friday 10am–4pm. Also by prior arrangement. Access is necessarily restricted when events are taking place.
Heritage Open Days: No
P Spaces: 9. 2 parking places for the disabled.
& Full. WC for the disabled. Guide Dogs allowed.
£ No

NORTON CONYERS

nr. Ripon, North Yorkshire HG4 5EQ
Medieval house with Stuart and Georgian additions. Listed Grade II*. Family pictures, furniture and costumes. Visited by Charlotte Bronte in 1839; a family legend of a mad woman confined in an attic room contributed towards the mad Mrs Rochester in 'Jane Eyre' and the house was a model for 'Thornfield Hall'. Located within the walled garden to the west of the house, the 18th century Orangery is a five bay arcaded sandstone building, flanked by Victorian glasshouses. The Orangery is listed Grade II.
Grant Recipient: Sir James Graham Bt
Access Contact: Sir James Graham Bt
T: 01765 640333   **F:** 01765 640333
E-mail: norton.conyers@bronco.co.uk
Open: Garden and Orangery: 4 and 5 May, 25 and 26 May: Sundays and Mondays; 8 June–11 August: daily, 2–5 July, 24 and 25 August: 2–5pm (last admission 4.40pm). House: building work will be taking place during the first part of 2008. The house should be open from mid July. Please telephone to check the house is open before visiting.
Heritage Open Days: No
P Spaces: 60. Free car park approx. 50 metres from the house; disabled parking available near front door by arrangement.
& Partial. Wheelchair access to ground floor of house only. Some gravelled paths in garden may be difficult. WC for the disabled. Guide Dogs allowed.
£ **Adult:** House: to be arranged. Garden: charge is made on charity open days. At other times, donations are welcome. **Child:** Free (16 and under).

RIBBLEHEAD VIADUCT

Ribblehead, North Yorkshire
Railway viaduct, 1870–74, rockfaced stone and brick. 104 feet high at highest point. Largest and most impressive of the viaducts of the Settle–Carlisle line of the Midland Railway.
Grant Recipient: British Rail
Access Contact: Mr Simon Brooks
T: 0161 880 3139   **F:** 0161 880 3433
E-mail: simon.brooks@networkrail.co.uk
Open: Viewing from ground level only. Strictly no access from Network Rail property.
Heritage Open Days: No
P On-street parking in Cave.
& No wheelchair access. No WC for the disabled. No Guide Dogs allowed.
£ No

SCAMPSTON HALL

Scampston, Malton, North Yorkshire, YO17 8NG
Late 17th century country house, extensively remodelled in 1801 by Thomas Leverton. Contains Regency interiors and an art collection. Set in a parkland designed by 'Capability' Brown with 10 acres of lakes and a Palladian bridge.
www.scampston.co.uk
Grant Recipient: Sir Charles Legard Bt
Access Contact: Sir Charles Legard Bt
T: 01944 759111   **F:** 01944 758700
E-mail: info@scampton.co.uk
Open: 23 May–22 June (closed Mondays), 1.30–5.00pm. Last admission 4pm.
Heritage Open Days: No
P Spaces: 50.
& Partial. Wheelchair access to ground floor only. WC for the disabled. Guide Dogs allowed.
£ **Adult:** £6.00 (house, garden & park). **Child:** £3.00 (age 12–16). Free for 11 & under.

ST MARY'S CHURCH STAIRS

Whitby, North Yorkshire
Flight of steps originally built of wood in 14th century, replaced in stone now largely 18th and 19th century. Flight of 199 stone steps leading up to the parish church. Listed Grade I.
www.whitbyparish.org.uk
Grant Recipient: PCC of St Mary's Whitby
Access Contact: Canon David Smith

T: 01947 606578   **F:** 01974 602798
E-mail: whitbyparishoffice@biscit.co.uk
Open: At all times.
Heritage Open Days: No
P Pay and display parking.
& Partial. Wheelchair access for viewing only. WC for the disabled in the church. Guide Dogs allowed.
£ No

ST PAULINUS

Brough Park, Richmond, North Yorkshire DL10 7PJ
Catholic neo-Gothic chapel designed by Bonomi with priest's accommodation and school room in undercroft.
Grant Recipient: Mr Greville Worthington
Access Contact: Mr Greville Worthington
T: 01748 812127
E-mail: grev@saintpaulinus.co.uk
Open: By prior arrangement.
Heritage Open Days: No
P Spaces: 2.
& Partial. Wheelchair access to downstairs. No WC for the disabled. Guide Dogs allowed.
£ No

ST SAVIOUR'S CHURCH (DIG)

St Saviourgate, York, North Yorkshire YO1 8NN
Church on site by late 11th century, present building dates from the 15th and extensively remodelled in 1845. Refurbished 2005/06 as DIG–an archaeological centre introducing the visitor to exploration, scientific study and conservation.
www.digyork.co.uk or www.yorkarchaeology.co.uk
Grant Recipient: York Archaeological Trust
Access Contact: Mrs Christine McDonnell
T: 01904 654324 /619264   **F:** 01904 671756
E-mail: cmcdonnell@yorkarchaeology.co.uk
Open: By prior arrangement (tel: 01904 543403). Or alternatively archaeological centre all year: daily 10am–5pm.
Heritage Open Days: Yes
P Public car park adjacent and street parking for the disabled.
& Full. WC for the disabled. Guide Dogs allowed.
£ **Adult:** £5.50. **Child:** £5.00 (under 5s free). **Other:** £16.00 (family), £19.60 (family of five). Carers/enablers free when helping disabled person.

THOMPSON MAUSOLEUM

Little Ouseburn Churchyard, Little Ouseburn, North Yorkshire YO26 9TS
18th century mausoleum in magnesian limestone. It is a rotunda encircled by 13 Tuscan columns, above which a frieze and cornice support a plain drum and ribbed domed roof. Listed Grade II*. Built for the use of the Thompson family of Kirby Hall.
Grant Recipient: Little Ouseburn Mausoleum Ltd
Access Contact: Mr H Hibbs
T: 01423 330414
E-mail: helier@talktalk.net
Open: Always available to view from the outside, interior visible through a replica of the original wrought iron gate. Access to interior by arrangement. Contact Mr Hibbs, Little Ouseburn Mausoleum Ltd, Hilltop Cottage, Little Ouseburn, North Yorks YO26 9TD (tel: 01423 330414).
Heritage Open Days: Yes
P Spaces: 8.
& Partial. Wheelchair access with assistance (gravel path and grass). No WC for the disabled. Guide Dogs allowed.
£ No

THORPE PREBEND HOUSE

High St. Agnesgate, Ripon, North Yorkshire HG4 1QR
Late medieval house with 17th century alterations. Restored 2002–4 to form a heritage interpretation centre for the region. The house also has facilities for small scale public events and meetings.
Grant Recipient: Chapter of Ripon Cathedral
Access Contact: The Administrator
T: 01765 603462/ 01765 609076
E-mail: ianhorsford@riponcathedral .org.uk
Open: April–end of October: daily except Sunday, 10.30am–4pm. Occasionally closed for special events, please telephone to check before visiting.
Heritage Open Days: No
P Parking available for the disabled.
& Full. WC for the disabled. Guide Dogs allowed.
£ **Adult:** £2.00. **Child:** £1.00. **Other:** £1.00 (students).

TRINITY CHURCH TOWER

Market Place, Richmond, North Yorkshire DL10 4QN
Church clock tower to the former castle church, now in the centre of Richmond Market Place.
Grant Recipient: Richmond Town Council
Access Contact: Richmond Town Council
Open: Access to the exterior at all times from Richmond Market Place.
Heritage Open Days: No
P Spaces: 120.
& Full. WC for the disabled available in Town Hall opposite. Guide Dogs allowed.
£ No

NORTHAMPTONSHIRE

BOUGHTON PARK

Boughton, Northamptonshire NN16 9UP
Extensive remains of formal gardens of late 17th and early 18th century around a country house rebuilt at the same time, set in a park developed from a late medieval deer park. Beyond the park are avenues and rides, also part of the landscape of the late 17th and early 18th centuries. The grant aided Lily pool is approximately 100 metres south of the House.
www.boughtonhouse.org.uk
Grant Recipient: Boughton Estates Ltd
Access Contact: Mr Christopher B Sparrow MRICS
T: 01536 482308   **F:** 01536 410 452
E-mail: csparrow@boughtonestate.co.uk
Open: 1 May–1 September, daily (except Fridays in May–July) 1–5pm.
Heritage Open Days: No
P Spaces: 100.
& Partial. Wheelchair access to ground floor fully accessible, first floor viewable on virtual tour in gift shop. No WC for the disabled. Guide Dogs allowed.
£ **Adult:** £1.50 (grounds), £7.00 (house and grounds). **Child:** £1.00 (grounds), £6.00 (house and grounds). **Other:** £1.00 (grounds), £6.00 (house and grounds).

HARROWDEN HALL GARDEN STATUES

Wellingborough, Northamptonshire NN9 5AD
Early 18th century Harrowden Hall retains its surprisingly unaltered contemporary garden containing a number of garden features, including statues by the Dutch sculptor Van Nost, of which one has recently been repaired.
Grant Recipient: Wellingborough Golf Club
Access Contact: Mr David Waite
T: 01933 677234   **F:** 01933 679379
E-mail: secretary@wellingboroughgolfclub.com
Open: 27 March to 2 October: Mondays.
Heritage Open Days: No
P Spaces: 100.
& Full. WC for the disabled. Guide Dogs allowed.
£ No

LAXTON HALL

Corby, Northamptonshire NN17 3AU
Stone built 18th century manor house, enlarged and modified in 19th century and set in 60 acres of parkland. Stable block by Repton. Formerly a boys school, now a residential home for elderly Poles.
Grant Recipient: Polish Benevolent Housing Association Ltd
Access Contact: Sister Teresa Sabok
T: 01780 444 292   **F:** 01780 444 574
E-mail: Teresa@pbfgroup.co.uk
Open: By prior written arrangement with Sister Teresa at Laxton Hall.
Heritage Open Days: No
P Spaces: 10.
& Partial. Wheelchair access to ground floor only. WC for the disabled. Guide Dogs allowed.
£ No

NORTHUMBERLAND

ALNWICK TOWN HALL

Market Place, Alnwick, Northumberland NE66 1HS
Situated in Alnwick Market Place. Property includes the Hall, the Freemens' Council Room and the Clock Tower. The 18th century building houses the Freemen's Shields and various items of Freemen's History.
Grant Recipient: The Freemens' Common Council
Access Contact: Mr Dennis Nixon, Clerk to the Freemen
T: 01665 603 517   **F:** 01665 603 517

Open: To the exterior at all times and to the interior by prior arrangement.
Heritage Open Days: Yes
P No
♿ No wheelchair access. No WC for the disabled. No Guide Dogs allowed.
£ No

BRIZLEE TOWER

Hulne Park, Alnwick, Northumberland NE66 1NQ
Elaborate Gothick style ornamental tower, dated 1781. An important landscape feature; built as a viewing platform for the 1st Duke of Northumberland. Listed Grade I.
Grant Recipient: Duke of Northumberland
Access Contact: The Estate Office
T: 01665 510777   **F:** 01665 510876
E-mail: enquiries@alnwick castle.co
Open: Access to the exterior when the park is open, daily 9am–5pm. Further public access under review at time of publication, please check the English Heritage website or with the access contact for current information.
Heritage Open Days: Yes
P Roadside parking, 3km from the Tower.
♿ No wheelchair access. No WC for the disabled. No Guide Dogs allowed.
£ No

COANWOOD FRIENDS MEETING HOUSE

Coanwood nr. Haltwhistle, Northumberland NE49
Built in 1760, remaining relatively unchanged. Located in a remote valley south of Hadrian's Wall.
www.hct.org.uk
Grant Recipient: Historic Chapels Trust
Access Contact: Dr Jennifer Freeman
T: 020 7481 0533   **F:** 020 7488 3756
E-mail: chapels@hct.org.uk
Open: At all reasonable times.
Heritage Open Days: Yes
P Spaces: 20.
♿ Full. No WC for the disabled. Guide Dogs allowed.
£ Donations invited.

GRACE DARLING MONUMENT

St Aidans Churchyard, Bamburgh, Berwick-upon-Tweed, Northumberland NE69 7AE
Grade II* listed churchyard memorial of 1842. Designed by Anthony Salvin in Gothic Revival style. The tomb was repaired in 1885 by Frederick Wilson, when a new effigy was carved by C R Smith in Portland stone. (The original is in the church). Rectangular base bearing life-size effigy. Surrounded by railings with spear-head finials. Grace Darling became a national heroine following the wreck of the steamship Forfarshire on the Farne Islands in September 1838 when she and her father, the keeper of the Longstone Lighthouse, rowed out and rescued 9 survivors.
Grant Recipient: Grace Darling Memorial Trust
Access Contact: Ms Christine Bell
T: 01668 214183
Open: At all reasonable times.
Heritage Open Days: No
P Spaces: 200. Parking in village car park.
♿ Full. No WC for the disabled. Guide Dogs allowed.
£ No

HEXHAM MOOT HALL

Market Place, Hexham, Northumberland NE46 1XD
Built c1400 and used as a home, office and court for the Archbishop of York's bailiff who administered Hexhamshire from the Hall. The former stores on the ground floor are now an art gallery, the first floor courtroom houses Tynedale Council's Museum offices and the second floor hall is used for community activities.
Grant Recipient: Tynedale District Council
Access Contact: Ms Lynn Turner
T: 01434 652346
E-mail: lynn.turner@tynedale.gov.uk
Open: Art Gallery: opening dates to be to be confirmed, please check the English Heritage website or with the access contact for current information. Courtroom and second floor hall open for community activities.
Heritage Open Days: No
P No
♿ No wheelchair access. WC for the disabled. Guide Dogs allowed.
£ No

LAMBLEY VIADUCT

Lambley, Tynedale, Northumberland
17 arch stone viaduct, 100ft high and 1650ft long, spanning the South Tyne river. Originally carried single track, now used as a footpath.
www.npht.com
Grant Recipient: British Rail Property Board/North Pennines Heritage Trust
Access Contact: Mr David Flush, Chief Executive
T: 01434 382 294   **F:** 01434 382 294
E-mail: trust@npht.com
Open: At all times as part of the South Tyne Trail between Featherstone Park and Alston.
Heritage Open Days: No
P Spaces: 30.
♿ Full. No WC for the disabled. Guide Dogs allowed.
£ No

LINDISFARNE CASTLE

Holy Island, Berwick-upon-Tweed, Northumberland TD15 2SH
Built in 1550 to protect Holy Island harbour from attack, the castle was converted into a private house for Edward Hudson by Sir Edwin Luytens in 1903. Small walled garden was designed by Gertrude Jekyll. 19th century lime kilns in field by the castle.
www.nationaltrust.org.uk
Grant Recipient: The National Trust
Access Contact: Property Manager
T: 01289 389244   **F:** 01289 389349
E-mail: lindisfarne@nationaltrust.org.uk
Open: Castle: 16–24 February: daily 10am–3pm. 15 March–2 November: Tuesday–Sunday, times vary. 30 December–2 January 2009: Wednesday–Friday, 10.30am–3pm. Garden: all year 10am–dusk.
Heritage Open Days: No
P Local authority car park 1 mile from site.
♿ No wheelchair access. No WC for the disabled. Guide Dogs allowed.
£ **Adult:** £5.40 (castle), £1.00 (garden only). **Child:** £2.70. **Other:** £13.50 (family), £4.50 (NT members), £8.00 (groups 20+, out-of-hours by prior arrangement).

LITTLE HARLE TOWER

Kirkwhelpington, Newcastle-upon-Tyne, Northumberland NE19 2PD
Medieval tower with 17th century range and a Victorian wing which contains a recently restored 1740s drawing room. It has been one family's home since 1830 though part is now let.
Grant Recipient: Mr J P P Anderson
Access Contact: Mr Simon Rowarth
T: 01434 609000   **F:** 01434 606900
E-mail: simon.rowarth@youngscs.com
Open: By prior arrangement (at least two weeks notice required) with Mr Simon Rowarth of Youngs, 3 Wentworth Place, Hexham, Northumberland NE46 1XB.
Heritage Open Days: No
P Spaces: 6.
♿ Partial. Wheelchair access to the ground floor only. No WC for the disabled. Guide Dogs allowed.
£ Donations to the church requested.

MITFORD HALL CAMELLIA HOUSE

Morpeth, Northumberland NE61 3PZ
East wing and conservatory of country house built c1820 by John Dobson, detached from main house by demolition of north-east wing in the 20th century. The conservatory houses a superb specimen of a red flowering camellia dating to c1826.
Grant Recipient: Shepherd Offshore plc
Access Contact: Mr B Shepherd
T: 01670 512602 or 0191 2629614   **F:** 0191 2639872
Open: By prior written arrangement during the summer.
Heritage Open Days: No
P Spaces: 3.
♿ Full. Wheelchair access by prior arrangement. Ordinary toilet on site may be accessible for some disabled persons, please contact Hall for further information. Guide Dogs allowed.
£ No

NETHERWITTON HALL

Morpeth, Northumberland NE61 4NW
Grade I listed mansion house built c1685 by Robert Trollope for Sir Nicholas Thornton. Access to main ground floor rooms and external elevations. Built as a family home and remains the current family home.
Grant Recipient: Mr J H T Trevelyan
Access Contact: Mr J H T Trevelyan
T: 01670 772 249   **F:** 01670 772 510
Open: By prior arrangement at least 24 hours in advance. 30 April–26 May and 2–12 June: Monday–Friday 11am–2pm by compulsory tour. Groups at other times by prior arrangement.
Heritage Open Days: No
P Spaces: 20.
♿ Full. Use of ramps up external steps. WC for the disabled available at village hall. Guide Dogs allowed.
£ **Adult:** £5.00. **Child:** £1.00.

SEATON DELAVAL HALL

Seaton Sluice, Whitley Bay, Northumberland NE26 4QR
Country house, 1718–29 by Sir John Vanbrugh for Admiral George Delaval. Listed Grade I. The house comprises a centre block between two arcaded pedimented wings. In 1822 the centre block was gutted by fire and was partially restored in 1862–63, and again in 1959–62 and 1999–2000. Extensive gardens with statues and also a Norman church.
Grant Recipient: The Lord Hastings
Access Contact: Mrs Mills
T: 0191 2371493
E-mail: lordhastings@onetel.com
Open: 1 June–30 September: May and August Bank Holiday Mondays, Wednesdays and Sundays 2–6pm.
Heritage Open Days: No
P Spaces: 50.
♿ Partial. Wheelchair access to stables, tea room, coach house, ice house, Norman church and gardens. WC for the disabled. Guide Dogs allowed.
£ **Adult:** £4.00. **Child:** £1.00. **Other:** £3.50 (senior citizens), £1.00 (students), £3.00 (groups 20+ adults).

ST CUTHBERT'S CHAPEL

Farne Islands, Northumberland
St Cuthbert's Chapel was completed in 1370. By the early 19th century it was in a ruinous condition. Restored in 1840 by Archdeacon Thorp it includes some fine 17th century woodwork from Durham Cathedral and a memorial to Grace Darling. Remains of an original window.
www.nationaltrust.org.uk
Grant Recipient: The National Trust
Access Contact: Mr John Walton
T: 01665 720651   **F:** 01665 720651
E-mail: john.walton@nationaltrust.org.uk
Open: 1–30 April and 1 August–30 September: daily 10.30am–6pm; 1 May–31 July (breeding season) daily Staple Island 10.30am–1.30pm, Inner Farne 1.30–5pm.
Heritage Open Days: No
P Public parking in Seahouses (nearest mainland village).
♿ Inner Farne is accessible for wheelchairs (telephone the Property Manager in advance). Staple Island is not accessible. WC for the disabled on Inner Farne. Guide dogs are allowed on boat but not on islands.
£ **Adult:** £5.60 (breeding season), £4.60 (outside breeding season). **Child:** £2.80 (breeding season), £2.30 (outside breeding season). **Other:** £2.80 (booked school parties, breeding season, per island), £2.30 (outside breeding season, per island). Admission fees do not include boatmen's charges.

ST MICHAEL'S PANT

Alnwick, Northumberland
St Michael's Pant (drinking fountain) was built in 1765 by Matthew Mills, designed by Mr Bell. St Michael and Dragon (the symbol of the Town) on top of an octagonal drum, gargoyle for the water spout with large square trough which measures approximately ten square metres. Listed Grade II*.
Grant Recipient: The Freemen of Alnwick
Access Contact: Mr D Nixon
T: 01665 603517   **F:** 01665 603517
Open: To the exterior at all times.
Heritage Open Days: Yes
P No
♿ Full. No WC for the disabled. Guide Dogs allowed.
£ No

SWINBURNE CASTLE

Hexham, Northumberland NE48 4DQ
Kitchen range 1600–1650, incorporating earlier fabric and with later alterations, stands at right angles to the footprint of the now demolished (1966) mid 18th century house which stood on the site of the medieval castle. East (laundry) wing 1770, restored in 2000. Orangery early 19th century.
Grant Recipient: Trustees of R W Murphy
Access Contact: Major Major R P Murphy
T: 01434 681610
Open: 1–4, 7–11, 14–18, 21–25, 28–30 April; 1–2, 5–6 May; 25 August: 12 noon–4.30pm.
Heritage Open Days: No
P Spaces: 6.
& Partial. Wheelchair access to East Wing ground floor only. No WC for the disabled. No Guide Dogs allowed.
£ No

THE TOWER

Elsdon, Northumberland NE19 1AA
14th century Tower House, residence of the Rector until 1961 and originally used as a refuge from the Border Reivers. Fine example of a medieval tower house and listed Grade I.
Grant Recipient: Dr J F Wollaston
Access Contact: Dr J F Wollaston
F: 01830 520904
Open: 1 April–30 October: by previously arranged guided visit, weekends only.
Heritage Open Days: No
P Spaces: 30.
& No wheelchair access. No WC for the disabled. Guide Dogs allowed.
£ Adult: £5.00.

VINDOLANDA ROMAN FORT

Bardon Mill, Hexham, Northumberland, NE47 7NJ
Roman Fort and civilian settlement in central sector of Hadrian's Wall with active excavation and education programmes. The site is owned and administered by the Vindolanda Charitable Trust and has an on-site museum, with full visitor services, reconstructed Roman buildings and gardens.
www.vindolanda.com
Grant Recipient: Vindolanda Trust
Access Contact: Mrs Patricia Birley
T: 01434 344277   **F:** 01434 344060
E-mail: info@vindolanda.com
Open: 14 February–14 November. February–March and October–November: daily 10am–5pm; April–September: daily 10am–6pm. Winter opening to be decided.
Heritage Open Days: No
P Spaces: 60. Coach parking available on-site.
& Partial. Wheelchair access to parts of the archaeological site and all of the museums, gardens and open air museum. WC for the disabled. Guide Dogs allowed.
£ Adult: £4.95 (provisional) (10% reduction for EH members). **Child:** £3.00 (provisional) (10% reduction for EH members). **Other:** £4.10 (provisional) (10% reduction for EH members).

WALLINGTON HALL & CLOCK TOWER

Cambo, Morpeth, Northumberland NE61 4AR
Dating from 1688, the house was home to many generations of the Blackett and Trevelyan family. Contains Rococo plasterwork, fine ceramics, paintings and a doll's house collection. Pre-Raphaelite central hall with scenes from Northumbrian history. Hall, Clock Tower and stable buildings set among lawns, lakes and woodland with walled garden.
www.nationaltrust.org.uk
Grant Recipient: The National Trust
Access Contact: Property Manager
T: 01670 773967   **F:** 01670 774420
E-mail: wallington@nationaltrust.org.uk
Open: House: daily (except Tuesday), 15 March–30 September 1–5.30pm; 10 October–2 November 1–4.30pm. Walled garden: daily, 1 February–31 March 10am–4pm; 1 April–30 September 10am–7pm; 1–31 October 10am–6pm; 1 November–31 January 10am–4pm. Grounds: daily in daylight hours.
Heritage Open Days: No
P Spaces: 500.
& Partial. Lift to first floor for visitors with mobility problems. WC for the disabled. Guide Dogs allowed.

£ Adult: £9.25 house & gardens), £6.40 (gardens only). **Child:** £4.65 (house & gardens), £3.20 (gardens only). **Other:** £23.10 (family, house & gardens), £16.40 (family, gardens only), £6.80 (groups 15+ house & gardens), £4.70 (groups 15+ gardens only).

NOTTINGHAMSHIRE

CHURCH OF ST MARY

New Road, Colston Bassett, Rushcliffe, Nottinghamshire NG12 3FP
Grade I listed and scheduled monument dating from 1130, now ruined in isolated hill-top position. Former parish church of Colston Bassett set in an open graveyard.
Grant Recipient: P.C.C. of St John the Divine.
Access Contact: Rev. Rev E B Gamble
T: 0115 989 3172
E-mail: brongamble@hotmail.com
Open: Access at all times.
Heritage Open Days: No
P Spaces: 7. Additional unlimited on street parking on New Road.
& Full. No WC for the disabled. Guide Dogs allowed.
£ No

KILN WAREHOUSE

Mather Road, Newark, Nottinghamshire NG24 1FB
Grade II* former warehouse. Early example of the use of massed concrete construction. Interior completely destroyed by fire in the early 1990s, the exterior walls have been restored and warehouse converted into offices.
Grant Recipient: British Waterways Midlands & South West
Access Contact: Sang Leong
T: 01636 675707
Open: The exterior walls for which the property is notable can be viewed without arrangement. Access to the internal courtyard is by prior arrangement with Sang Leong, British Waterways (tel: 01636 675707).
Heritage Open Days: No
P Parking is available on adjacent land.
& Full. WC for the disabled. Guide Dogs allowed.
£ No

PLEASLEY COLLIERY

Pit Lane, Pleasley, nr. Mansfield, Nottinghamshire
Victorian winding engine house and associated buildings. Engine house contains two steam winding engines under restoration, one turns on electronic motor and work to dismantle the second engine has started.
Grant Recipient: Pleasley Pit Trust
Access Contact: Mr Peter Chambers
T: 01623 811231
E-mail: peter-chambers@tiscoli.co.uk
Open: All year: Thursdays 10am–1pm and Sundays 9am–3pm. Open weekend 6th and 7th September (provisional). Group visits by prior arrangement.
Heritage Open Days: No
P Spaces: 50. Free parking.
& No wheelchair access. No WC for the disabled. No Guide Dogs allowed.
£ No

OXFORDSHIRE

ASTON MARTIN HERITAGE TRUST

Drayton St Leonard, Wallingford, Oxfordshire OX10 7BG
15th century tithe barn, 6 bays. Constructed of elm with hipped roof. Listed Grade II*.
www.amheritrust.org
Grant Recipient: Aston Martin Owners Club
Access Contact: Mr Robert Ellis
T: 01865 400414   **F:** 01865 400200
E-mail: secretary@amheritrust.org
Open: Wednesday afternoons 2–5pm. At other times by prior arrangement.
Heritage Open Days: No
P Spaces: 30.
& Partial. Wheelchair access to ground floor only. WC for the disabled. Guide Dogs allowed.
£ No

BAPTIST CHAPEL

Shifford Road, Cote, Oxfordshire OX18 2EG
Built around 1739–40 on earlier site and enlarged in 1756.
www.hct.org.uk
Grant Recipient: Historic Chapels Trust
Access Contact: Mr Peter Wilson
T: 01993 850 901
E-mail: peterwilson@tourpartnership.com
Open: At all reasonable times by prior arrangement with key holder, Peter Wilson, San Marino, Cote, Oxon OX18 2EG.
Heritage Open Days: Yes
P Spaces: 20. On-street parking.
& Full. WC for the disabled. Guide Dogs allowed.
£ Donations invited.

BLENHEIM PALACE & PARK

Woodstock, Oxfordshire OX20 1PX
Ancestral home of the Dukes of Marlborough and birthplace of Winston Churchill. Built between 1705–22 for John Churchill, the 1st Duke, in recognition of his victory at the Battle of Blenheim in 1704. Designed by Sir John Vanbrugh, the house contains in its many state rooms a collection of paintings, furniture, bronzes and the Marlborough Victories tapestries. A five-room Churchill Exhibition includes his birth room. 'Capability' Brown park and gardens.
www.blenheimpalace.com
Grant Recipient: Duke of Marlborough
Access Contact: Mrs Heather Carter
T: 01993 810531   **F:** 01993 810580
E-mail: hcarter@blenheimpalace.com
Open: Palace: 16 February–14 December, daily 10.30am–5.30pm (last admission 4.45pm). November and December closed Monday and Tuesday. Park: daily (except Christmas Day) 9am–6pm (last admission 4.45pm).
Heritage Open Days: No
P Spaces: 10000.
& Partial. Some rough terrain in the park. WC for the disabled. Guide Dogs allowed.
£ Adult: £13.90 off peak, £16.50 peak. **Child:** £7.70 off peak, £10.00 peak. **Other:** £11.30 off peak, £13.80 (senior citizens).

CHANTRY HOUSE

St Mary the Virgin, Hart Street, Henley on Thames, Oxfordshire
Grade I listed 14th–15th century, three storey timber framed building with exposed interior timbering and early leaded glazing.
Grant Recipient: PCC of St Mary the Virgin
Access Contact: Mr M Parish Secretary
T: 01491 577340   **F:** 01491 571827
Open: June, July and August: Saturdays 2–5pm. At other times by prior telephone arrangement (tel: 01491 577340).
Heritage Open Days: No
P No
& Partial. Wheelchair access to middle floor only. WC for the disabled. Guide Dogs allowed.
£ No

CORNBURY PARK

Charlbury, Oxford, Oxfordshire OX7 3EH
400 acre deer park adjacent to Wychwood Forest containing newly restored/replanted beech avenues, ancient English oak trees and several ancient monuments.
www.cornburypark.co.uk
Grant Recipient: The Lord Rotherwick
Access Contact: The Lord Rotherwick
T: 01608 811276   **F:** 01608 811252
E-mail: estate@cpark.co.uk
Open: 1 March–31 October: Tuesdays and Thursdays 10am–4pm. Please note that a permit is required for access to the Park; permit must be applied for in advance. Organised educational access walks for groups by prior arrangement.
Heritage Open Days: No
P Spaces: 20.
& No wheelchair access. No WC for the disabled. No Guide Dogs allowed.
£ No

CULHAM MANOR DOVECOTE

The Green, Culham, Oxfordshire OX14 4LZ
Dovecote constructed from brick and stone, with a date stone above the door of 1685. Reputed to be the second largest dovecote in England, formed of two large cells each with an entry lantern for dove access. In total, it has over 3,000 nesting boxes.
Grant Recipient: Mr James Wilson MacDonald
Access Contact: Mr James Wilson MacDonald
T: 01235 527009   **F:** 01865 744520
E-mail: wil.mac@virgin.net
Open: By prior arrangement (telephone: evenings, fax/E-mail: anytime).
Heritage Open Days: No
P Spaces: 20. On Green by Church.
No wheelchair access. No WC for the disabled. Guide Dogs allowed.
£ No

FARNBOROUGH HALL

Farnborough, Banbury, Oxfordshire OX17 1DU
Mid-18th century honey-coloured stone built home of the Holbech family for over 300 years, contains impressive plasterwork. Set in grounds with 18th century temples, a terrace walk and an obelisk.
www.nationaltrust.org.uk
Grant Recipient: The National Trust
Access Contact: Mrs Julie Smith
T: 01295 670266   **F:** 01295 671144
E-mail: julie.smith@nationaltrust.org.uk
Open: House and garden: 2 April–27 September, Wednesday and Saturday 2–5.30pm; 4–5 May: Sunday and Monday 2–5.30pm.
Heritage Open Days: No
P Spaces: 10. Additional free parking, 200 yards.
Partial. Wheelchair access to ground floor of house and garden. Terrace walk may be difficult as it is very steep. No WC for the disabled. Guide Dogs allowed.
£ **Adult:** £4.75. **Child:** £2.40. **Other:** £11.90.

FREEMAN MAUSOLEUM

St Mary's Churchyard, Fawley, nr Henley-on-Thames, Oxfordshire RG9 6HZ
Built in 1752 for the Freeman family who owned the Fawley Estate. Design by John Freeman based on the mausoleum of Cecilia Metella on the Appian Way in Rome, which he visited while on his Grand Tour. It contains 30 coffin slots with 12 being filled by the Freemans before they sold the Estate in 1850.
Grant Recipient: St Mary's Parochial Church Council
Access Contact: Mrs Dorothea Giddy
T: 01491 572686
Open: By prior arrangement with Churchwarden, Mrs D Giddy (tel: 01491 572686).
Heritage Open Days: No
P Spaces: 10. On-street parking adjacent to church.
Full. No WC for the disabled. Guide Dogs allowed.
£ No

MARTYRS' MEMORIAL

St. Giles, Oxford, Oxfordshire OX1
Erected in 1841–3 and designed by Sir George Gilbert Scott, in commemoration of Protestant martyrs, Archbishop Cranmer, Bishops Ridley and Latimer who were burnt to death in 1555 and 1556. The memorial is hexagonal in plan and takes the form of a steeple of three stages reaching a height of 21 metres.
Grant Recipient: Oxford City Council
Access Contact: Mr Nick Worlledge
T: 01865 252147   **F:** 01865 252144
E-mail: nworlledge@oxford.gov.uk
Open: Accessible at all times.
Heritage Open Days: No
P No
Full. No WC for the disabled. Guide Dogs allowed.
£ No

SHOTOVER PARK GOTHIC TEMPLE

Wheatley, Oxfordshire OX33 1QS
Early 18th century garden folly. The Gothic Temple/eyecatcher (designer unknown) lies east of the house at the end of a long canal vista. Has a battlemented gable with a central pinnacle and a rose-window, below which is an open loggia of three pointed arches.
Grant Recipient: Shotover Estate Company
Access Contact: Sir Beville Stanier Bt
T: 07778 305419   **F:** 01865 875838

E-mail: BDStonier@aol.com
Open: Access to Temple at all reasonable times (lies close to public rights of way).
Heritage Open Days: No
P Spaces: 50. Parking for a few cars on the drive near the Gothic Temple, otherwise other arrangements can be made in advance with Sir Beville Stanier on 07778 305419.
Partial. Wheelchair access to the Gothic Temple with assistance. No WC for the disabled. Guide Dogs allowed.
£ No

SWALCLIFFE TITHE BARN

Shipston Road, Swalcliffe, nr. Banbury, Oxfordshire OX15 5DR
15th century barn built for the Rectorial Manor of Swalcliffe by New College, who owned the Manor. Constructed between 1400 and 1409, much of the medieval timber half-cruck roof remains intact. It is now a museum operated by Oxfordshire Museums Service for the display storage of agricultural and trade vehicles.
www.oxfordshire.gov.uk
Grant Recipient: Oxfordshire Historic Building Trust Ltd
Access Contact: Mr Carol Anderson
T: 01993 814105   **F:** 01993 813239
E-mail: carol.anderson@oxfordshire.gov.uk
Open: Easter–end of September: Sunday and Bank Holidays, 2–5pm. At other times by prior arrangement (contact Carol Anderson tel: 01993 814105).
Heritage Open Days: No
P Spaces: 10.
Full. WC for the disabled. Guide Dogs allowed.
£ No

REDCAR AND CLEVELAND

MARSKE HALL

Marske by the Sea, Redcar and Cleveland TS11 6AA
Country house built by Sir William Pennyman in 1625. 2 storeys with 3-storey projecting towers in a 9-bay range forming a symmetrical front approx. 115ft long. Altered in the late 19th and 20th centuries. Varied uses during 20th century include as quarters for the Royal Flying Corps in WWI, Army quarters in WWII, school 1948–58 and since 1963 a Cheshire Foundation nursing home.
Grant Recipient: Teesside Cheshire Homes
Access Contact: Mrs Sue O'Brien
T: 01642 482672   **F:** 01642 759973
E-mail: marske@ney.leonard-cheshire.org.uk
Open: Hall by prior arrangement only. Grounds open to public at all fund raising events such as the Summer Fete (one Saturday in June).
Heritage Open Days: No
P Spaces: 20.
Full. WC for the disabled. Guide Dogs allowed.
£ No

ORMESBY HALL

Church Lane, Ormesby, Middlesbrough, Redcar and Cleveland TS7 9AS
A mid-18th century Palladian mansion, notable for its fine plasterwork and carved wood decoration. The Victorian laundry and kitchen with scullery and game larder are interesting. 18th century stable block, attributed to Carr of York, is leased to the Cleveland Mounted Police. Large model railway and garden with holly walk.
www.nationaltrust.org.uk
Grant Recipient: The National Trust
Access Contact: Property Manager
T: 01642 324188   **F:** 01642 300937
E-mail: ormesbyhall@nationaltrust.org.uk
Open: Hall: 15 March–2 November, Saturdays and Sundays only (and Bank Holiday Mondays and good Friday) 1.30–5pm (last admission 4.30pm). Tea room: as Hall 12.30–5pm.
Heritage Open Days: No
P Spaces: 200. Car park 100 metres from House.
Partial. Wheelchair access to ground floor of Hall (shallow step at entrance), shop, tea room and garden. No WC for the disabled. Guide Dogs allowed.
£ **Adult:** £4.40. **Child:** £2.80. **Other:** £11.50 (family), £3.50 (groups).

SHROPSHIRE

2/3 MILK STREET

Shrewsbury, Shropshire SY1 1SZ
Timber-framed two and a half storey building dating from the 15th century with later alterations and additions. Medieval shop front to rear. Still a shop.
Grant Recipient: Mr M J Cockle
Access Contact: Mr H Carter
T: 01743 276633   **F:** 01743 242140
E-mail: htc@pooks.co.uk
Open: Ground floor shop open 6 days a week all year. Monday–Saturday 9.30am–5.30pm. Upper floor flats can be visited only by prior arrangement with Mr H Carter, Pooks, 26 Claremont Hill, Shrewsbury, Shropshire SY1 1RE.
Heritage Open Days: No
P No
Partial. Wheelchair access to ground floor only. No WC for the disabled. Guide Dogs allowed.
£ No

ATTINGHAM PARK

Atcham, Shrewsbury, Shropshire SY4 4TP
Built 1785 by George Steuart for the 1st Lord Berwick, with a picture gallery by John Nash. Contains Regency interiors, Italian neo-classical furniture and Grand Tour paintings. Park landscaped by Humphry Repton in 1797.
www.nationaltrust.org.uk
Grant Recipient: The National Trust
Access Contact: The Property Manager
T: 01743 708162/708123   **F:** 01743 708155
E-mail: attingham@nationaltrust.org.uk
Open: House: 1–9 March, Saturday and Sunday 1–4pm; 13 March–26 October, Friday–Wednesday, 1–5.30pm; 27 October 2 November daily except Wednesday 1–4pm. Guided tours from 11am. Park: Open daily 9 am–6pm or dusk if earlier. Closed Christmas Day.
Heritage Open Days: No
P Spaces: 150.
Partial. Wheelchair access: to lower ground and ground floors only (house), drives and paths (grounds), and shop. Improved tea room access planned for 2008. WC for the disabled. Guide Dogs allowed.
£ **Adult:** £7.40 (house & grounds) £4.20 (park & grounds). **Child:** £3.70 (house & grounds) £2.20 (park & grounds). **Other:** £18.50 (family: house & grounds), £10.40 (family: grounds only), £6.30 (booked parties 15+).

BENTHALL HALL

Broseley, Shropshire TF12 5RX
16th century stone house situated on a plateau above the gorge of the River Severn, with mullioned and transomed windows, carved oak staircase, decorated plaster ceilings and oak panelling. Also has a restored plantsman's garden, old kitchen garden and a Restoration church.
www.nationaltrust.org.uk
Grant Recipient: The National Trust
Access Contact: The Custodian
T: 01952 882159
E-mail: benthall@nationaltrust.org.uk
Open: 25 March–25 June: Tuesday and Wednesday 2–5.30pm; 1 July–30 September: Tuesday, Wednesday and Sunday 2–5.30pm. Open Bank Holiday Sundays and Mondays. Groups by prior arrangement with the custodian.
Heritage Open Days: No
P Spaces: 50.
Partial. Wheelchair access to ground floor of Hall and part of garden only. No WC for the disabled. Guide Dogs allowed.
£ **Adult:** £5.10. **Child:** £2.50. **Other:** Admission price includes voluntary gift aid donation.

BROSELEY PIPEWORKS

King Street, Broseley, Shropshire TF8 7AW
19th century clay pipe factory comprising a three storey factory range, bottle kiln, workers cottage and school room. Contents include pipe-making machinery and collection of smoking pipes. Main rooms contain the original equipment installed in the 1880s and used until the site was abandoned at the end of the 1950s.
www.ironbridge.org.uk
Grant Recipient: Ironbridge Gorge Museum Trust
Access Contact: Mr Michael Vanns, Curator
T: 01952 884 391   **F:** 01952 884 391
E-mail: tic@ironbridge.org.uk
Open: Late May–end of October: 1–5pm.

Heritage Open Days: No
P Spaces: 10. Overflow car park at adjacent site for 20.
♿ Partial. Wheelchair access to ground floor and yard. WC for the disabled. Guide Dogs allowed.
£ Adult: £3.95 (provisional). **Child:** £2.50 (provisional).
Other: £2.95 (senior citizens provisional).

CASTLE HOUSE

Castle Square, Ludlow, Shropshire SY8 1AY
Grade II* listed house within Ludlow Castle. Probably 14th–15th century with late 16th to early 17th century additions. Late 18th century railings and gate. Interior includes decorative plaster ceilings and pendants; fireplaces with fireback and imported 16th–19th century panelling.
www.ludlowcastle.com
Grant Recipient: Powis Castle Estate
Access Contact: Mr Tom Till
T: 01938 552554   **F:** 01938 556617
Open: As part of Ludlow Castle the house is open January and December: Saturday and Sunday 10am–4pm; February, March, October and November: daily 10 am–4pm; April–July: daily 10 am–5pm; August: daily 10 am–7pm. September: daily 10 am–5pm. Closed Christmas Day.
Heritage Open Days: No
P Town square parking nearby and on-street meter parking.
♿ Full. WC for the disabled. Guide Dogs allowed.
£ No

COMBERMERE ABBEY

Whitchurch, Shropshire SY13 4AJ
Originally founded in 1133 as a Cistercian Abbey, and it has now evolved into a complex medieval and 16th century building with extensive pasteboard Gothic enveloping dating from the early 19th century.
www.combermereabbey.co.uk
Grant Recipient: Mrs S Callander Beckett
Access Contact: Mrs Sarah Callander Beckett
T: 01948 662880   **F:** 01948 871 604
E-mail: estate@combermereabbey.co.uk
Open: 25 March–22 May: Tuesday, Wednesday and Thursday afternoon, guided tours only at midday, 2pm and 4pm. Please telephone in advance. Plus Heritage Open Days in September.
Heritage Open Days: Yes
P Spaces: 50.Weather dependent.
♿ No wheelchair access. No WC for the disabled. Guide Dogs allowed.
£ Adult: £5.00. **Child:** £3.00 (16 and under).

DORTER HOUSE

15 Barrow Street, Much Wenlock, Shropshire TF13 6EN
A detached portion of the former Wenlock Priory Guesten hall, comprising solar chamber and ground floor service accommodation, of early 14th century origin. Some medieval window openings exist. Converted to residential use.
Grant Recipient: Mr and Mrs L de Wet
Access Contact: Mr & Mrs L de Wet
T: 01952 727911
Open: Access to exterior only, 12–16 May and 15–19 September (inclusive) 12 noon–4pm.
Heritage Open Days: No
P Spaces: 35. Public car park off Barrow Street, within 200 meters of Dorter House.
♿ No wheelchair access. No WC for the disabled. Guide Dogs allowed.
£ Adult: £1.00. **Child:** £1.00. **Other:** £1.00.

JACKFIELD TILE MUSEUM & FACTORY

Jackfield, Telford, Shropshire TF8 7LJ
Home to the Craven Dunnill factory, where decorative tiles were mass-produced from 1874 until just after the Second World War. Surviving example of a purpose-built Victorian tile factory and continues to manufacture products today.
www.ironbridge.org.uk
Grant Recipient: Ironbridge Gorge Museum Trust
Access Contact: Mr Michael Vanns, Curatorr
T: 01952 884 391   **F:** 01952 884 391
E-mail: tic@ironbridge.org.uk
Open: Daily, 10am–5pm. Closed 24 and 25 December and 1 January 2008.
Heritage Open Days: No
P Spaces: 30. Free car park.

♿ Full. WC for the disabled. Guide Dogs allowed.
£ Adult: £5.95 (provisional). **Child:** £4.25 (provisional).
Other: £4.60 (senior citizens, provisional).

JOHN ROSE BUILDING

High Street, Coalport, Telford, Shropshire TF8 7HT
A range of china painting workshops, centre part dating from late 18th century, outer wings rebuilt early 20th century. Restored and converted to a Youth Hostel, craft workshops and shop. Main entrance is paved with mosaic celebrating the amalgamation of Coalport, Swansea and Nantgarw brands. Coalbrookdale cast iron windows of large dimension line both major elevations.
www.ironbridge.org.uk
Grant Recipient: Ironbridge Gorge Museum Trust
Access Contact: Ms Cath Young
T: 01952 588 755   **F:** 01952 588 722
E-mail: tic@ironbridge.org.uk
Open: Access to exterior at all times. This is a working Youth Hostel and access to interior by prior telephone arrangement.
Heritage Open Days: No
P Spaces: 65. Museum car park.
♿ Partial. Youth Hostel: wheelchair access to ground and first floor (stair lift) with WC and shower facilities for the disabled. China Museum: majority accessible, visiting guide available on arrival. Guide Dogs allowed.
£ No

LANGLEY GATEHOUSE

Acton Burnell, Shropshire SY5 7PE
This gatehouse has two quite different faces: one is of plain dressed stone; the other, which once looked inwards to long demolished Langley Hall, is timber-framed. It was probably used for the Steward or important guests. It was rescued from a point of near collapse and shows repair work of an exemplary quality.
www.landmarktrust.org.uk
Grant Recipient: The Landmark Trust
Access Contact: Mrs Victoria O'Keeffe
T: 01628 825920   **F:** 01628 825417
E-mail: vokeeffe@landmarktrust.org.uk
Open: The Landmark Trust is an independent charity, which rescues small buildings of historic or architectural importance from decay or unsympathetic improvement. Landmark's aim is to promote the enjoyment of these historic buildings by making them available to stay in for holidays. Langley Gatehouse can be rented by anyone, at all times of the year, for periods ranging from a weekend to three weeks. Bookings can be made by telephoning the Booking Office on 01628 825925. As the building is in full-time use for holiday accommodation, it is not normally open to the public. However, the public can view the building by prior arrangement by telephoning the access contact (Vicky O'Keeffe on 01628 825920) to make an appointment. Potential visitors will be asked to write to confirm the details of their visit.
Heritage Open Days: No
P Spaces: 2.
♿ No wheelchair access. No WC for the disabled. Guide Dogs allowed.
£ No

LOTON HALL

Alberbury, Shropshire SY5 9AJ
Country house, c1670, but extensively altered and enlarged in the early 18th and 19th centuries. Set in parkland which includes the ruins of the early 13th century Alberbury Castle. Home of the Leighton family since the 14th century.
Grant Recipient: Sir Michael Leighton
Access Contact: Mr Mark Williams
T: 01691 655334   **F:** 01691 657798
Open: House: 7 January–10 April, Mondays and Thursdays by guided tour only at 10am or 12 noon. Garden and castle can also be viewed at the same times.
Heritage Open Days: No
P Spaces: 30. Access for coaches via back drive.
♿ Partial. Wheelchair access to ground floor only. 5 steps at front door–ramp can be put in place for wheelchair access. No WC for the disabled. Guide Dogs allowed.
£ Adult: £5.00. **Child:** Free. **Other:** £5.00 (senior citizens).

OLD MARKET HALL

The Square, Shrewsbury, Shropshire SY1 1HJ
Old market hall and court house, dated 1596 and listed Grade I. Recently repaired and refurbished to accommodate a Film and Digital Media Centre, including auditorium and café/bar.
www.oldmarkethall.co.uk
Grant Recipient: Shrewsbury & Atcham Borough Council
Access Contact: Mr David Jack
T: 01743 281250   **F:** 01743 281283
E-mail: davidjack@musichall.co.uk
Open: Daily, 10am–11pm. Auditorium closed to public when film being screened. Current screening times: Monday–Sunday evening films. Matinee films on most days.
Heritage Open Days: Yes
P No
♿ Full. WC for the disabled. Guide Dogs allowed.
£ Charges for performances only (Adult £5.00, Child £4.00).

THE LYTH

Ellesmere, Shropshire SY12 0HR
Grade II* listed small country house, c1820, with minor later additions. Cast-iron verandah with trellised supports, one of the earliest and largest examples in the country. Birthplace of E and D Jebb, founders of Save the Children.
Grant Recipient: Mr L R Jebb
Access Contact: Mr L R Jebb
T: 01691 622339   **F:** 01691 624134
Open: To the exterior: 30 March, 18 May, 21 September, 12 October 2–6pm. At other times by arrangement with Mr Lionel Jebb.
Heritage Open Days: No
P Spaces: 40.
♿ Full. No WC for the disabled. Guide Dogs allowed.
£ Adult: £2.00 (charity donation for visits to garden).
Child: £1.00 (charity donation for visits to garden).

THE OLD MANSION

St Mary's Street, Shrewsbury, Shropshire SY1 1UQ
Early 17th century house with original staircase. The building was renovated in 1997 and now provides 4 bedroom suites for the Prince Rupert Hotel.
Grant Recipient: Mr A Humphreys
Access Contact: Michael Matthews
T: 01743 499 955   **F:** 01743 357 306
E-mail: post@prince-rupert-hotel.co.uk
Open: By prior arrangement with the Prince Rupert Hotel (tel: 01743 499 955).
Heritage Open Days: No
P No
♿ Partial. Access to ground floor via external entrance, to first floor via Prince Rupert Hotel. WC for the disabled on ground floor of hotel. Guide Dogs allowed.
£ No

YEATON PEVEREY HALL

Yeaton Peverey, Shrewsbury, Shropshire SY4 3AT
Mock Jacobean country house, 1890–2 by Aston Webb. Previously a school, now reinstated as a family home. Principal rooms on the ground floor open to visitors.
Grant Recipient: Mr Martin Ebelis
Access Contact: Mr Martin Ebelis
T: 01743 851185   **F:** 01743 851186
E-mail: mae@earlstone.co.uk
Open: By prior arrangement with written confirmation or introduction through known contact.
Heritage Open Days: No
P Spaces: 6. Parking adjacent to the property for the disabled.
♿ Full. No WC for the disabled. Guide Dogs allowed.
£ Adult: £5.00. **Child:** £2.00. **Other:** £5.00.

SOMERSET

BATH ASSEMBLY ROOMS

Bennett Street, Bath, Somerset BA1 2QH
Built in 1771 by John Wood the Younger, now owned by the National Trust and administered by Bath and North East Somerset District Council. Each of the rooms has a complete set of original chandeliers. The Fashion Museum is located on the lower ground floor.
www.fashionmuseum.co.uk
Grant Recipient: Bath City Council/National Trust
Access Contact: Mr Iain Johnston

T: 01225 477752
E-mail: iain_johnston@bathnes.gov.uk
Open: Daily: January, February, November and December 11am–5pm; March–October 11am–6pm when not in use for pre-booked functions. Last admission is one hour before closing. Telephone in advance (01225 477789) to check availability. There are no pre-booked functions during the day during August. Closed Christmas Day and Boxing Day.
Heritage Open Days: No
P On-street car parking (pay and display).
& Full. WC for the disabled. Guide Dogs allowed.
£ But charge for Museum of Costume.

CHARD GUILDHALL

Fore Street, Chard, Somerset TA20 2PP
Grade II* listed building dating to 1834. Former Corn Exchange and Guildhall, now Town Hall.
www.chard.gov.uk
Grant Recipient: Chard Town Council
Access Contact: Guildhall Manager
T: 01460 260 371 **F:** 01460 260 372
E-mail: sandra.hutchings@chard.gov.uk
Open: Public events throughout the year. Also available for hire and the Tourist Information Centre is based in the Guildhall. Access at any other time by prior arrangement.
Heritage Open Days: No
P No
& Full. WC for the disabled. Guide Dogs allowed.
£ No

CLEVEDON PIER

The Beach, Clevedon, Somerset BS21 7QU
Pier with attached toll house built c1860s to serve steamers bound for South Wales. Wrought and cast iron structure and shelters consisting of eight 100ft arched spans leading to a landing stage. The exceptionally slender spans are constructed from riveted broad-gauge railway track as designed by W H Barlow for the Great Western Railway. Scottish baronial style toll house contains shop and art gallery. Pier restored in 1999 after partial collapse 30 years earlier and is one of only two Grade I listed piers. This pier is of outstanding importance for its delicate engineering and the relationship of pier to landward buildings, which creates an exceptionally picturesque ensemble.
www.clevedonpier.com
Grant Recipient: The Clevedon Pier and Heritage Trust
Access Contact: Mrs Linda Strong
T: 01275 878846 **F:** 01275 790077
E-mail: clevedonpier@zoom.co.uk
Open: All year except Christmas Day: daily; 30 March–26 October 10am–5pm; 27 October–29 March 2009 10am–4pm. Please check opening times prior to visit.
Heritage Open Days: No
P Car parking on seafront.
& Partial. No wheelchair access to art gallery. No WC for the disabled. No Guide Dogs allowed.
£ **Adult:** £1.50. **Child:** 75p. **Other:** £1.00 (concession).

ENGLISHCOMBE TITHE BARN

Rectory Farmhouse, Englishcombe, Bath, Somerset BA2 9DU
Early 14th century cruck framed tithe barn. Recently restored with new crucks, masonry and straw lining to the roof, and filigree windows unblocked. There are masons and other markings on the walls.
Grant Recipient: Mrs Jennie Walker
Access Contact: Mrs Jennie Walker
T: 01225 425073
E-mail: jennie.walker@ukonline.co.uk
Open: Bank Holidays 2–6pm; all other times by arrangement with Mrs Walker (tel: 01225 425073). Closed 18 December 2007–1 March 2008.
Heritage Open Days: Yes
P Spaces: 34.
& Full. WC for the disabled. Guide Dogs allowed.
£ Donations invited.

FAIRFIELD

Stogursey, nr. Bridgwater, Somerset TA5 1PU
Elizabethan and medieval house and Grade II* listed. Undergoing repairs. Occupied by the same family (Acland-Hoods and their ancestors) for over 800 years. Woodland garden with views of the Quantocks and the sea.
Grant Recipient: Lady Gass
Access Contact: Mr D W Barke

T: 01722 555131 or 01278 732251
Open: House: 9 April–26 May and 4–20 June: Wednesday, Thursday, Friday and Bank Holiday Mondays by guided tour at 2.30pm and 3.30pm. Groups at other times by prior arrangement. Garden: open for NGS and other charities on dates advertised in Spring. No inside photography. No dogs except Guide Dogs.
Heritage Open Days: No
P Spaces: 30. No parking for coaches.
& Full. WC for the disabled. Guide Dogs allowed.
£ **Adult:** £4.00. **Child:** £1.00. **Other:** Admission charges in aid of Stogursey Church.

FORDE ABBEY

Chard, Somerset TA20 4LU
Cistercian monastery founded in 1140 and dissolved in 1539 when the church was demolished. The monks quarters were converted in 1640 into an Italian style "palazzo" by Sir Edmund Prideaux. Interior has plaster ceilings and Mortlake tapestries.
www.fordeabbey.co.uk
Grant Recipient: Trustees of the Roper Settlement
Access Contact: Mrs Clay
T: 01460 220231
E-mail: info@fordeabbey.co.uk
Open: Gardens: daily, 10am–4.30pm. House: April–October; Tuesday–Friday, Sunday and Bank Holidays 12 noon–4pm.
Heritage Open Days: No
P Spaces: 500.
& Partial. Wheelchair access to ground floor and garden. WC for the disabled. Guide Dogs allowed.
£ **Adult:** £8.80 (provisional). **Child:** Free. **Other:** £8.20 (senior citizen, provisional).

GREAT HOUSE FARM

Theale, Wedmore, Somerset BS28 4SJ
17th century farmhouse with Welsh slate roof, oak doors and some original diamond paned windows. Inside is a carved well staircase with two murals on the walls. There are four servants rooms at the top, three of which are dark and occupied by Lesser Horseshoe bats.
Grant Recipient: Mr A R Millard
Access Contact: Mr A R Millard
T: 01934 713133
Open: April–August: Tuesdays and Thursdays 2–6pm by prior telephone arrangement.
Heritage Open Days: No
P Spaces: 6.
& No wheelchair access. No WC for the disabled. Guide Dogs allowed.
£ **Adult:** £2.00. **Child:** Free. **Other:** £1.00 (senior citizens).

HALL FARM HIGH BARN

Stogumber, Taunton, Somerset TA4 3TQ
17th century, Grade II* listed building, with seven bays of red local sandstone rubble with jointed cruck roof. South wall supported by four buttresses but there are none on the North wall. There are blocked windows on the South wall and two stub walls extend north. Lines of joist holes were provided for internal flooring and the two main entrances were to the north and south.
Grant Recipient: CM & R Hayes
Access Contact: CM & R Hayes
T: 01984 656321
Open: By prior arrangement with CM & R Hayes at Hall Farm.
Heritage Open Days: No
P Spaces: 4.
& Full. No WC for the disabled. Guide Dogs allowed.
£ No

HIGHER FLAX MILLS (JOHN BOYD TEXTILES LTD)

Torbay Road, Castle Cary, Somerset BA7 7DY
Listed Grade II*, Higher Flax Mills is one of the largest and unusually complete examples of an integrated rope and twine works in the West Country, a significant regional industry in the 19th century. Part of the site is used by John Boyd Textiles, Horsehair fabric manufacturer, established in 1837 and still using the original looms of 1870. The company is unique in being the only horsehair weaving factory in the world that uses power looms.
www.johnboydtextiles.co.uk
Grant Recipient: South Somerset District Council
Access Contact: John Boyd Textiles Ltd
T: 01963 350 451 **F:** 01963 351 078

E-mail: enquiries@johnboydtextiles.co.uk
Open: By prior arrangement only: Monday–Friday, 8am–5pm.
Heritage Open Days: No
P Spaces: 7.
& Partial. WC for the disabled. Guide Dogs allowed.
£ By prior arrangement only: Monday–Friday, 8am–5pm.

LANCIN FARMHOUSE

Wambrook, Chard, Somerset TA20 3EG
14th century farmhouse with old oak beams, fireplaces with the original smoking thatch, flagstone floors and breadoven.
Grant Recipient: Mr S J Smith
Access Contact: Mrs R A Smith
T: 01460 62290
Open: 21and 28 April, 15 and 22 May, 11and 18 June, 7 and 14 July: 9.30am–3pm. Any other day by prior telephone arrangement.
Heritage Open Days: No
P Spaces: 5.
& No wheelchair access. No WC for the disabled. No Guide Dogs allowed.
£ **Adult:** £2.00.

PRIOR PARK COLLEGE OLD GYMNASIUM

Ralph Allen Drive, Bath, Somerset BA2 5AH
Built for Ralph Allen in the mid-18th century as an early and successful demonstration of the quality of Bath stone. The Old Gymnasium is part of the mid-19th century additions to adapt the property as a Catholic seminary for Bishop Baines. Now a boarding and day school.
www.priorpark.co.uk
Grant Recipient: Governors of Prior Park College
Access Contact: C J Freeman
T: 01225 837491 **F:** 01225 835753
E-mail: bursar@priorpark.co.uk
Open: 21–25 August: daily 10.30am–4pm. Group tours during school holidays, otherwise by prior arrangement. Please telephone in advance.
Heritage Open Days: No
P Spaces: 50.
& Full. Limited by slope of the ground. WC for the disabled in school theatre nearby. Guide Dogs allowed.
£ No

ROWLANDS MILL

Rowlands, Ilminster, Somerset TA19 9LE
Grade II* stone and brick 3-storey millhouse and machinery, c1620, with a mill pond, mill race, overshooting wheel and waterfall. The millhouse is now a holiday let but the machinery has separate access and is in working condition.
Grant Recipient: Mr P G H Speke
Access Contact: Mr P G H Speke
T: 01460 52623 **F:** 01460 52623
Open: Millhouse Fridays and machinery Monday–Friday 10am–4pm by prior written arrangement (at least 1 week's notice required). Heritage Open Days machinery only unless a Friday, then whole building.
Heritage Open Days: Yes
P Spaces: 7.
& Partial. Wheelchair access to ground floor only. WC for the disabled at Rowlands House nearby. Guide Dogs allowed.
£ **Adult:** £3.00. **Child:** Free.

ST ANDREWS

Stogursey, Somerset
Benedictine priory church, now parish church. Listed Grade I.
Grant Recipient: St Andrews PCC, Church of England
Access Contact: Mr D J Mott
T: 01984 632670
Open: Daily during daylight hours.
Heritage Open Days: No
P Spaces: 6.
& Partial. Wheelchair access to most areas except the High Altar, ramp available on request. No WC for the disabled. Guide Dogs allowed.
£ No

ST GEORGE'S BRISTOL

Great George Street, Bristol, Somerset BS1 5RR
Grade II* listed Georgian former church, c1821–3, by Robert Smirke in Greek Revival style, now 550 seater concert hall. A Waterloo church, built as a chapel-of-ease to Cathedral of St Augustine, and converted to a concert hall in 1987. The crypt now houses a café and art gallery.

www.stgeorgesbristol.co.uk
Grant Recipient: St George's Bristol
Access Contact: Ms Jillian Wilson
T: 0117 929 4929   **F:** 0117 927 6537
E-mail: j.wilson@stgeorgesbristol.co.uk
Open: For seasonal concert programmes–mainly evenings, some lunchtimes and Sunday afternoons, contact Box Office on 0845 40 24 001 for brochure. Free access to crypt and art gallery from 1 hour before concerts. Tours can be arranged if dates comply with events schedule.
Heritage Open Days: No
P Spaces: 3.
♿ Partial. Wheelchair access via Charlotte Street. The auditorium stalls, crypt, café, gallery and Box Office are accessible but preferable if you ring in advance as entry is not straightforward. WC for the disabled. Guide Dogs allowed.
£ Tickets required for concerts.

SOUTH YORKSHIRE

HICKLETON HALL

Hickleton, South Yorkshire DN5 7BB
Georgian Mansion, Grade II* listed, built in the 1740s to a design by James Paine with later additions. The interior is noted for its plasterwork ceilings. Set in 15 acres of formal gardens laid out in the early 1900s, the Hall is now a residential care home.
Grant Recipient: Sue Ryder Care
Access Contact: The Administrator
T: 01709 892070   **F:** 01709 890140
Open: By prior arrangement with the administrator at Sue Ryder Care, Monday–Friday 2–4pm.
Heritage Open Days: No
P Parking available.
♿ Partial. Wheelchair access to Hall only; no access to gardens. WC for the disabled. Guide Dogs allowed.
£ No

THE LYCEUM THEATRE

Tudor Square, Sheffield, South Yorkshire S1 1DA
Grade II* listed theatre built 1897. The only surviving example of the work of WGR Sprague outside London. Its special features include a domed corner tower, a lavish Rococo auditorium (1097 seats) and a proscenium arch with a rare open-work valance in gilded plasterwork. A notable example of a theatre of the period, with a largely unaltered interior.
www.sheffieldtheatres.co.uk
Grant Recipient: The Lyceum Theatre Trust
Access Contact: Ms Angela Galvin, Chief Executive
T: 0114 249 5999   **F:** 0114 249 6003
E-mail: info@sheffieldtheatres.co.uk
Open: Performances throughout the year. 21 scheduled backstage tours per year. All tours commence at 10.30am. Group guided tours by prior arrangement. Contact the Box Office (tel: 0114 249 6000) or check the website for further information.
Heritage Open Days: No
P Spaces: 600. National Car Park adjacent to the theatre.
♿ Partial. Wheelchair access to all areas except two private entertaining rooms. WC for the disabled. Guide Dogs allowed.
£ **Adult:** £3.00 (backstage tour). **Child: Other:** Admission charge for performances.

STAFFORDSHIRE

10 THE CLOSE

Lichfield, Staffordshire WS13 7LD
Early 15th century timber-framed house, originally one-up one-down and part of a five-dwelling range in the Vicar's Close. Notable doors and solid tread staircase remains in attic.
Grant Recipient: Dean & Chapter of Lichfield Cathedral
Access Contact: Chief Officer
T: 01543 306100   **F:** 01543 306109
E-mail: enquiries@lichfield-cathedral.org
Open: By prior written arrangement with Cathedral Chapter Office.
Heritage Open Days: No
P Public car parks nearby.
♿ No wheelchair access. No WC for the disabled. Guide Dogs allowed.
£ No

BARLASTON HALL

Barlaston, nr. Stoke-on-Trent, Staffordshire ST12 9AT
Mid-18th century Palladian villa attributed to Sir Robert Taylor, with public rooms containing some fine examples of 18th century plasterwork. Extensively restored during the 1990s.
Grant Recipient: Mr James Hall
Access Contact: Mr James Hall
F: 01782 372391
E-mail: wadey54@mac.com
Open: 6 March–11 September: Tuesdays 2–5pm. No groups.
Heritage Open Days: No
P Spaces: 3.
♿ No wheelchair access. No WC for the disabled. No Guide Dogs allowed.
£ **Adult:** £2.50. **Child:** £1.50. **Other:** No charge for Historic Houses Association members.

BIDDULPH GRANGE GARDEN

Biddulph, Staffordshire ST8 7SD
Garden with series of connected compartments designed to display specimens from James Bateman's extensive and wide ranging plant collection. Visitors are taken on a miniature tour of the world featuring the Egyptian court, China, a Scottish glen, as well as a pinetum and rock areas.
www.nationaltrust.org.uk
Grant Recipient: The National Trust
Access Contact: Property Manager
T: 01782 517999   **F:** 01782 510624
E-mail: biddulphgrange@nationaltrust.org.uk
Open: 15 March–2 November: Wednesday–Sunday 11.30am–5pm (High Season). 1–9 March: Saturday and Sunday 11am–4pm, 8 November–21 December: Saturday and Sunday 11am–3pm (Low Season).
Heritage Open Days: No
P Spaces: 100.
♿ Partial. Wheelchair access to Lime Avenue, Lake, Pinetum, Cheshire Cottage, Egypt and East Terrace. Steps and undulating terrain throughout the garden. WC for the disabled. Guide Dogs allowed.
£ **Adult:** £6.40 (High Season), £2.40 (Low Season). **Child:** £3.20 (High Season), £1.20 (Low Season). **Other:** £14.90 (family, High Season), £5.60 (family, Low Season).

BISHTON HALL DORIC SCREEN

Woseley Bridge, Staffordshire ST17 0XN
1840s screen with a summerhouse at the centre, in the form of a Greek Doric temple, with flanking porticos and terrace. Listed Grade II*. The screen might have been built to screen the gardens from the nearby Trent Valley Railway Line, which was built in 1845–7.
Grant Recipient: St Bede's School Limited
Access Contact: The Administrator
T: 01889 881277   **F:** 01889 882749
E-mail: admin@saintbedes.com
Open: 31 March–4 April, 7–11 April, 14–18 and 21–25 July, 1–5 September, 15–17 December: 10am–2pm. Please report to the School Office on arrival.
Heritage Open Days: No
P Spaces: 5.
♿ Partial. Steps up to the screen. No WC for the disabled. No Guide Dogs allowed.
£ No

CASTERNE HALL

Ilam, Ashbourne, Derbyshire DE6 2BA
Casterne Hall is a Grade II* manor house. The house was rebuilt in 1730, with a classic Georgian front and incorporating a 17th century and medieval back. Home of the Hurt family since the 16th century.
www.casterne.co.uk
Grant Recipient: Mr Charles Hurt
Access Contact: Mr Charles Hurt
T: 01335 310 489
E-mail: mail@casterne.co.uk
Open: 1 May–11 June: weekday afternoons. Tours at 2pm and 3pm. Closed on 5 and 26 May.
Heritage Open Days: No
P Spaces: 20.
♿ Partial. Wheelchair access to ground floor only. No WC for the disabled. Guide Dogs allowed.
£ **Adult:** £5.00.

CHEDDLETON FLINT MILL

Cheddleton, Leek, nr. Stoke-on-Trent, Staffordshire ST13 7HL
18th century complex for grinding flint comprising two working watermills. South Mill modified in 19th century and now contains displays relating to the pottery industry.
www.ex.ac.uk/~akoutram/cheddleton-mill

Grant Recipient: Cheddleton Flint Mill Industrial Heritage Trust
Access Contact: Mr E E Royle, MBE
T: 01782 502907
Open: April–September (including Bank Holidays), Saturday–Sunday 1pm–5pm. Weekdays by arrangement (tel: 01782 502907).
Heritage Open Days: No
P Spaces: 16.
♿ Partial. Wheelchair access to ground floor only. WC for the disabled. Guide Dogs allowed.
£ No

CHILLINGTON HALL

Codsall Wood, nr. Wolverhampton, Staffordshire WV8 1RE
House by Sir John Soane with earlier wing by Francis Smith (1724). Home of the Giffard family for over 800 years. Extensive grounds with gardens landscaped by Capability Brown.
www.chillingtonhall.co.uk
Grant Recipient: Mr J W Giffard
Access Contact: Mr J W Giffard
T: 01902 850236   **F:** 01902 850 768
E-mail: mrsplod@chillingtonhall.co.uk
Open: Hall: Easter, May and August Bank Holiday Sunday and Monday. July: Sundays. August: Wednesday, Thursday, Friday and Sunday 2–5pm (last admission 4pm). Parties at other times by prior arrangement. Grounds only: Easter–1 June: Sundays only.
Heritage Open Days: No
P Spaces: 100. Unlimited parking.
♿ Full. WC for the disabled. Guide Dogs allowed.
£ **Adult:** £6.00, (£3.00 grounds only). **Child:** £3.00. **Other:** Free to HHA members.

CLAYMILLS PUMPING ENGINES

The Victorian Pumping Station, Meadow Lane, Stretton, Burton-on-Trent, Staffordshire DE13 0DA
Large Victorian steam-operated sewage pumping station built in 1885. Four beam engines housed in two Italianate engine houses, two operational on steaming weekends. Boiler house with range of five Lancashire boilers, large Victorian steam-operated workshop with blacksmith's forge, steam hammer, and steam driven machinery. 1930s dynamo house with very early D.C. generating equipment, earliest dynamo 1889 (all operational). The site houses the largest number of steam engines in Britain still working in their original state (23).
www.claymills.org.uk
Grant Recipient: Severn Trent Water Ltd
Access Contact: Mr Roy Barratt
T: 01283 534960   **F:** 07092 275534
E-mail: webmaster@claymills.org.uk
Open: Every Thursday and Saturday for static viewing. Guided tours available. Easter 23 and 24 March, early May Bank Holiday 4 and 5 May, end of May Bank Holiday 25 and 26 May, 24 and 25 August, 13 and 14 September, 18 and 19 October, 27 and 28 December.
Heritage Open Days: No
P Spaces: 100. Parking for the disabled adjacent to site. Parking available for 1 coach.
♿ Partial. Wheelchair access to ground floor (engine house, boiler house, workshop, & refreshment area). Interactive video link to Engine House. WC for the disabled. Guide Dogs allowed.
£ **Adult: Child: Other:** Charges apply on steaming days, at other times donation invited.

CLIFTON HALL

Clifton Campville, Staffordshire B79 0BE
Small country house built in 1705, perhaps by Francis Smith of Warwick for Sir Charles Pye. Two monumental wings flanking a courtyard, the intention being to link them with a central main building which was never constructed. This strange history explains why the Hall unusually developed out of what would have been the servants wing.
Grant Recipient: Mr Richard Blunt
Access Contact: Mr Richard Blunt
T: 01827 373681   **F:** 01827 373111
E-mail: richard@richardblunt.com
Open: By prior arrangement only, any weekday 9am–5pm all year.
Heritage Open Days: No
P Spaces: 10.
♿ Full. No WC for the disabled. Guide Dogs allowed.
£ **Adult:** £5.00. **Child:** £2.00. **Other:** £2.00.

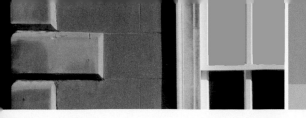

HAMSTALL HALL

Hamstall Ridware, Staffordshire WS15 3RS
Small scheduled ancient monument known as 'The Porch', with stone balcony, now restored and two stone fireplaces. Restored oak doors and windows. Some carvings on the stone balcony. Interior is made up of two rooms.
Grant Recipient: Mr and Mrs Shore
Access Contact: Mr and Mrs Shore
T: 0121 382 6540 office hrs only
Open: By prior arrangement with Mr and Mrs Shore.
Heritage Open Days: No
P No
& No wheelchair access. No WC for the disabled. No Guide Dogs allowed.
£ No

MALTHOUSE

Malthouse Road, Alton, Staffordshire ST10 4AG
Rare underground malthouse. Brick vaulted cellars and network of tunnels. Listed Grade II*. Used to produce malt for brewing from late 17th century.
enquiries@the-malthouse.com
Grant Recipient: Mr Owen John Venables
Access Contact: Mr Owen John Venables
T: 01538 703 273
E-mail: enquiries@the-malthouse.com
Open: April, May, June, July, September and October: every Saturday; Heritage Open Days in September (Thursday to Sunday), 12 noon–4pm (last admittance at 3.30pm).
Heritage Open Days: Yes
P On-street parking.
& No wheelchair access. No WC for the disabled. Guide Dogs allowed.
£ No

MIDDLEPORT POTTERY

Port Street, Middleport, Stoke on Trent, Staffordshire ST6 3PE
Grade II* listed pottery works built 1888–9 in brick and terracotta. The site includes a Burgundy bottle oven, the largest now standing in Stoke-on-Trent. In use by Burleigh–a family pottery business established in 1851 and still manufacturing using Victorian methods and machinery.
www.burleigh.co.uk
Grant Recipient: Burgess Dorling & Leigh
Access Contact: Mrs Rosemary Dorling
T: 01782 577 866   **F:** 01782 575 529
E-mail: sales@burleigh.co.uk
Open: All year: Wednesdays 10am guided tour only, except during Potters holidays (usually last week of June, first week of July, last week of August and 2 weeks over Easter). At all other times by prior arrangement. Due to hazardous nature of the site, minimum age for children is 10 years.
Heritage Open Days: No
P Spaces: 6. Weekday parking, 6 spaces. Weekend parking, 24 spaces. Additional on street parking available.
& Partial. Wheelchair access to shop only. No WC for the disabled. Guide Dogs allowed.
£ Adult: £5.00.

SHUGBOROUGH

Milford, Stafford, Staffordshire ST17 0XB
The present house was begun c1695. Between 1760 and 1770 it was enlarged and refashioned by James "Athenian" Stuart and again partly remodelled by Samuel Wyatt at end of 18th century. The interior is particularly notable for its plaster work and other decorations. Ancestral home of the Earls of Lichfield. Houses the Staffordshire County Museum, Georgian working farm and Rare Livestock Breed project.
www.shugborough.org.uk
Grant Recipient: The National Trust
Access Contact: Ms Louise Jones, Marketing Manager
T: 01889 881388   **F:** 01889 881323
E-mail: shugborough.promotions@staffordshire.gov.uk
Open: Estate open 14 March–24 October, daily 11am–5pm (last admission 4.30pm). Tours for groups throughout the year, daily 10.30am. Evening tours also available.
Heritage Open Days: No
P Spaces: 250.
& Partial. Wheelchair access to ground floor of house and museum only. WC for the disabled. Guide Dogs allowed.
£ Adult: £10.00. Child: £6.00. Other: £25.00 (family), £8.00 (concessions), Free to house for NT members.

SINAI HOUSE

Shobnall Road, Burton on Trent, Staffordshire DE14 2BB
Timber-framed E-shaped house, two-thirds derelict, on moated hill-top site, dating from the 13th century. House built variously during 15th, 16th and 17th centuries with later additions, including wall paintings and carpenters marks. 18th century bridge and plunge pool in the grounds.
Grant Recipient: Ms C A Newton
Access Contact: Ms C A Newton
T: 01283 544161/01283 840732   **F:** 01283 841054
E-mail: knewton@brookesvernons.co.uk
Kate@brookesandro.net
Open: By prior arrangement only. Minimum of one week's notice required.
Heritage Open Days: No
P Spaces: 10.
& Partial. Temporary ramps to internal steps can be arranged. No WC for the disabled. Guide Dogs allowed.
£ Donations requested.

TRENTHAM MAUSOLEUM

Stone Road, Trentham, Stoke on Trent
Built circa 1808 in a neo-Egyptian style, designed by Charles Heathcote Tatham. Monumental exterior. Stone vaulted ceiling inside. Erected for the Marquis of Stafford, later Duke of Sutherland. All tombs of the Sutherland family have been removed. Listed Grade I.
Grant Recipient: Stoke on Trent City Council
Access Contact: Mr Richard Marsland
T: 01782 232154
E-mail: heritage@stoke.gov.uk
Open: To the exterior at all reasonable times and to the interior by prior arrangement.
Heritage Open Days: Yes
P On-street parking.
& Partial. Wheelchair access to exterior unrestricted on flat land. Access to interior is restricted by two steps to entrance. No WC for the disabled. No Guide Dogs allowed.
£ No

SUFFOLK

ABBEY FARM BARN

Snape, Saxmundham, Suffolk IP17 1RQ
Grade II* listed Aisled barn. Circa 1300. Built by resident monks living in adjacent Priory (no remains standing above ground). Refurbished and still used by farmer for storage.
Grant Recipient: Mr & Mrs Raynor
Access Contact: Mr and Mrs Raynor
T: 01728 688088   **F:** 01728 688989
E-mail: thecartshed@hotmail.com
Open: By prior arrangement.
Heritage Open Days: No
P Spaces: 10.
& Full. No WC for the disabled. Guide Dogs allowed.
£ No

BARDWELL WINDMILL

School Lane, Bardwell, Suffolk IP31 1AD
Grade II* listed tower mill, under restoration. Circa 1830; a beam in the cap frame bears the date 1823. Ground floor and 3 upper floors, with tarred red brick tower. Machinery largely intact. Sails being built on the premises. Two pairs of over-driven millstones a flour sifter and underground driving shaft in adjacent out building.
Grant Recipient: Messrs Jonathan & David Wheeler & Ms Susan Wooster
Access Contact: Messrs Jonathan & David Wheeler & Ms Susan Wooster
T: 01359 251331/07887 912624
E-mail: jwheeler@wheeler-steam.co.uk
Open: Daily (except Christmas and New Year), 10am–4pm. Advisable to telephone before visiting to check open.
Heritage Open Days: Yes
P On-street parking.
& Partial. Wheelchair access to exterior. No WC for the disabled. Guide Dogs allowed.
£ Donations welcome.

CHRISTCHURCH MANSION

Christchurch Park, Soane Street, Ipswich, Suffolk IP4 2BE
16th century red brick mansion with some blue brick diapering, set in fine parkland in the centre of town. The Mansion and its collections trace the lives of the three wealthy families who made it their home. Paintings, English domestic furniture, kitchen and servants' area.
www.colchestermuseums.org.uk
Grant Recipient: Ipswich Borough Council
Access Contact: Mr Peter Berridge
T: 01473 433 543   **F:** 01473 433558
E-mail: peter.berridge@colchester.gov.uk
Open: Daily, all year 10am–5pm. For further information please contact Peter Berridge, or the Mansion (Tel: 01473 433554 fax: 01473 433558)
Heritage Open Days: No
P Public parking within 400 metres. Parking for the disabled adjacent to the Mansion.
& Partial. Wheelchair access to most of ground floor and Wolsey Art Gallery. WC for the disabled. Guide Dogs allowed.
£ No

CULFORD SCHOOL IRON BRIDGE

Culford, Bury St Edmunds, Suffolk IP28 6TX
Constructed for the second Marquis Cornwallis in the late 1790s by Samuel Wyatt, brother of James, to a design patented by Wyatt. The bridge, in Culford Park, is one of the earliest surviving bridges with an unmodified cast-iron structure, being the earliest known example with hollow ribs.
Grant Recipient: Methodist Colleges and Schools
Access Contact: Michael Woolley
T: 01284 729318   **F:** 01284 729077
E-mail: bursar@culford.co.uk
Open: Access to the iron bridge and Culford Park is available at any time throughout the year.
Heritage Open Days: No
P No
& Partial. Access for the disabled may be difficult as over grass and rough track. Toilet facilities are only available when Culford School is open and ramps in place. Guide Dogs allowed.
£ No

FRESTON TOWER

Freston, Babergh, Suffolk IP9 1AD
Elizabethan six-storey tower built in 1578 by Thomas Gooding, an Ipswich Merchant, to demonstrate his wealth and status and probably used as a look-out tower. Overlooks the estuary of the River Orwell.
www.landmarktrust.org.uk
Grant Recipient: The Landmark Trust
Access Contact: Mrs Victoria O'Keeffe
T: 01628 825920   **F:** 01628 825417
E-mail: vokeeffe@landmarktrust.org.uk
Open: The Landmark Trust is an independent charity, which rescues small buildings of historic or architectural importance from decay or unsympathetic improvement. Landmark's aim is to promote the enjoyment of these historic buildings by making them available to stay in for holidays. Freston Tower can be rented by anyone, at all times of the year, for periods ranging from a weekend to three weeks. Bookings can be made by telephoning the Booking Office on 01628 825925. The public can also view the building on eight Open Days throughout the year (dates to be set) or by prior arrangement; telephone the access contact Victoria O'Keeffe on 01628 825920 to make an appointment. Potential visitors will be asked to write to confirm the details of their visit.
Heritage Open Days: No
P Spaces: 2.
& No wheelchair access. No WC for the disabled. Guide Dogs allowed.
£ No

FRISTON MILL

Friston, Suffolk IP17 1NW
A Suffolk post windmill, one of the tallest of its type built in Britain. Built in 1812 and operational until 1956. Listed Grade II*. In a semi-derelict condition but many of the original components can still be seen. Suffolk once had 250 mills. Today there are fewer than a dozen.
Grant Recipient: Mr Piers Hartley
Access Contact: Mr Piers Hartley
T: 01728 688 650

E-mail: piersh@rtley.com
Open: By prior arrangement. Due to building being in a semi-derelict state, it may not be suitable for people with mobility difficulties and very young children. Sensible footwear essential.
Heritage Open Days: No
P No
No wheelchair access. No WC for the disabled. No Guide Dogs allowed.
£ No

ICKWORTH HOUSE

Park and Garden, Horringer, Bury St Edmunds, Suffolk IP29 5QE
The Earl of Bristol created this eccentric house, with its central rotunda and curved corridors, in 1795 to display his collections. These include paintings by Titian, Gainsborough and Velazquez and a Georgian silver collection. The house is surrounded by an Italianate garden set in a 'Capability' Brown park with woodland walks, deer enclosure, vineyard, Georgian summerhouse, church, canal and lake.
www.nationaltrust.org.uk
Grant Recipient: The National Trust
Access Contact: Property Manager
T: 01284 735270   **F:** 01284 735175
E-mail: ickworth@nationaltrust.org.uk
Open: House and Gardens: 15 March–30 September: Friday–Tuesday 1–5pm (gardens open 10am); 1 October–2 November: Friday–Tuesday 1–4.30pm (gardens open at 11am–4pm). Park open daily 8am–8pm (closes dusk if earlier). Park and Gardens open daily during half term, Easter and summer holidays, closed 25 and 27 December.
Heritage Open Days: No
P Spaces: 200.
Partial. Wheelchair access to House: ramped access (restricted access in House for large powered vehicles/chairs); lift to first floor; stair-lift to basement (shop and restaurant) suitable for wheelchair users able to transfer; wheelchair on each floor. Garden largely accessible, some changes of level, gravel drive and paths. West Wing: all floors accessible. Separate parking in visitor car park (200 yards). WC for the disabled. Guide Dogs allowed.
£ **Adult:** £7.50 (House & garden), £3.50 (garden). **Child:** £3.00 (House & garden), £1.00 (garden). **Other:** £18.00 (family, house & garden), £8.00 (family, garden).

MORETON HALL

Mount Road, Bury St Edmunds, Suffolk IP32 7BJ
White brick residence designed by Robert Adam in 1773 for Dr. Symonds, noted Cambridge professor and author. The design was inspired by the ruins of Emperor Diocletian's palace and many of the original Adam features remain on the ground and first floors. It is now the home of Moreton Hall Preparatory School.
www.moretonhall.net
Grant Recipient: Moreton Hall School Trust Ltd
Access Contact: Ms Doreen Young
T: 01284 753 532   **F:** 01284 769 197
E-mail: office@moretonhall.net
Open: By prior arrangement at any reasonable time, plus the Saturday of Heritage Open Days weekend.
Heritage Open Days: Yes
P Spaces: 20. Free parking.
Partial. Wheelchair access to ground floor only. WC for the disabled. Guide Dogs allowed.
£ No

RUINED CHURCH TOWER

Fornham St Genevieve, St Edmundsbury, Suffolk
Only the tower remains of the 15th century church. Church destroyed by fire in 1782.
Grant Recipient: Rossfleet Investments Ltd
Access Contact: Mr Steve Stuteley
T: 01953 717176   **F:** 01953 717173
Open: By prior arrangement with Steve Stuteley (Rossfleet Investments, Manor Farm, Bridgham, Norfolk).
Heritage Open Days: No
P No
No wheelchair access. No WC for the disabled. Guide Dogs allowed.
£ No

SOMERLEYTON HALL & GARDENS

Somerleyton, Lowestoft, Suffolk NR32 5QQ
Early Victorian stately home, built in Anglo-Italian style for Sir Morton Peto by John Thomas upon former Jacobean mansion. Contains fine furnishings, paintings, ornate carved stonework and wood carving, and state rooms. Set in twelve acres of historic gardens including a yew hedge maze.
www.somerleyton.co.uk
Grant Recipient: The Rt Hon Lord Somerleyton GCVO
Access Contact: Mrs C Hatt
T: 01502 734901   **F:** 01502 732143
E-mail: enquiries@somerleyton.co.uk
Open: House: 16 March–30th October, Thursday, Sunday and Bank Holidays plus Tuesday and Wednesday in July and August, 11.30 am–3.30. Half hourly guided tours. Gardens 10am–5pm. 1–30 November (Sundays): Gardens only, 10 am–5 pm.
Heritage Open Days: No
P Spaces: 200.
Full. WC for the disabled. Guide Dogs allowed.
£ **Adult:** £4.85 (gardens only), £8.25 (Hall & gardens). **Child:** £2.85 (gardens only), £4.25 (Hall & gardens). **Other:** Over 60's : £3.85 (gardens only), £7.25 (Hall & gardens).

WALTON OLD HALL

Felixstowe, Suffolk
Remains of 13th century Manor House built by the Bigod family c1292.
Grant Recipient: Suffolk Coastal District Council
Access Contact: Mrs Chris Robinson
T: 01394 444 518   **F:** 01394 385 100
E-mail: chris.robinson@suffolkcoastal.gov.uk
Open: Monday–Friday, 8am–4pm. At all other times by prior arrangement.
Heritage Open Days: No
P On-street parking.
Partial. Wheelchair access to all areas but grass surfaces may limit access in poor weather conditions. No WC for the disabled. Guide Dogs allowed.
£ No

SURREY

CLANDON PARK

West Clandon, Guildford, Surrey GU4 7RQ
Palladian mansion, built c1730 by Venetian architect Giacomo Leoni with a two-storeyed Marble Hall, collection of 18th century furniture, porcelain, textiles, carpets, the Ivo Forde Meissen collection of Italian comedy figures and a series of Mortlake tapestries. Grounds contain grotto, sunken Dutch garden, Maori Meeting House and Museum of the Queen's Royal Surrey Regiment.
www.nationaltrust.org.uk
Grant Recipient: The National Trust
Access Contact: Property Manager
T: 01483 222482   **F:** 01483 223479
E-mail: clandonpark@nationaltrust.org.uk
Open: House: 16 March–2 November, daily except Monday, Friday and Saturday (but open Good Friday, Easter Saturday and Bank Holiday Mondays) 11am–4.30pm (last admission 4pm). Museum: as house 12 noon–5pm. Garden: as house 11am–5pm.
Heritage Open Days: No
P Spaces: 200.
Partial. Lift provides access to all areas of the house open to the public, some restrictions apply; please telephone for details. Grounds partially accessible, with some slopes and uneven terrain. WC for the disabled. Guide Dogs allowed.
£ **Adult:** £7.70. **Child:** £3.90. **Other:** £19.80 (family), £6.50 (groups).

GREAT HALL

Virginia Park, Christchurch Road, Virginia Water, Surrey GU25 4BH
By W H Crossland for Thomas Holloway and opened 1884. Built of red brick with Portland stone dressings and slate roofs in Franco-Flemish Gothic style. Formerly part of the Royal Holloway Sanatorium.
Grant Recipient: Virginia Park Management Co Ltd
Access Contact: Ms Liz Adams
T: 01344 845276   **F:** 01344 842428
E-mail: virginia.park@btinternet.com
Open: Entrance Hall, Staircase and Great Hall of former Sanatorium: 13 and 24 February, 19 and 23 March, 9, 20 and 23 April, 11, 25 and 28 May, 15,18 and 22 June, 9, 20 and 23 July, 6, 17 and 20 August, 10, 21 ad 24 September, 8, 19 and 22 October, 23 and 26 November, 10am–4pm.
Heritage Open Days: No
P Parking for the disabled only. Public car park nearby at Virginia Water Station.
Partial. Wheelchair access with assistance (steps into building to be negotiated). Downstairs entrance Hall but not the Great Hall (no lift). Key required from security for access to WC for the disabled. Guide Dogs allowed.
£ No

IVY CONDUIT

Holy Cross Preparatory School, George Road, Kingston, Surrey KT2 7NU
Conduit house built c1514, part of an elaborate water system built in 16th century to provide water to Hampton Court Palace situated over 5km away. Scheduled Ancient Monument.
Grant Recipient: Holy Cross Preparatory School
Access Contact: Mr Michael Harrison
T: 020 8942 0729   **F:** 020 8336 0764
E-mail: michael@holycrossprep.co.uk
Open: By prior arrangement on weekdays, with 24 hours notice.
Heritage Open Days: No
P Spaces: 20.
Partial. Steep gradient through gardens, about 150m from car park. No WC for the disabled. Guide Dogs allowed.
£ No

PAINSHILL PARK

Portsmouth Road, Cobham, Surrey KT11 1JE
Restored Grade I Registered 18th century landscape garden of 158 acres, created by Charles Hamilton between 1738 and 1773. Contains a Gothic temple, Chinese bridge, ruined abbey, Turkish tent, crystal grotto, vineyard and 14 acre serpentine lake fed by a large waterwheel. Europa Nostra medal winner for 'Exemplary Restoration'.
www.painshill.co.uk
Grant Recipient: Painshill Park Trust Ltd
Access Contact: Miss Sarah AM Hallett
T: 01932 868113   **F:** 01932 868001
E-mail: info@painshill.co.uk
Open: March–October: 10.30am–6pm (last admission 4.30pm) or dusk if earlier; November–February: 10.30am–4pm (last admission 3pm) or dusk if earlier. Closed Christmas Day and Boxing Day. Guided tours by prior arrangement at additional cost of £1.00 per person.
Heritage Open Days: No
P Spaces: 400. Parking for 15 coaches.
Partial. Wheelchair access to most of the site, apart from the Grotto and Alpine Valley. Wheelchairs and electric buggies available on request. Pre-book one week in advance. WC for the disabled. Guide Dogs allowed.
£ **Adult:** £6.60. **Child:** £3.85 (under 5s free). **Other:** £5.80 (concessions); £22.00 (family–2 adults and 4 children); Group £5.80 (adult).

TYNE AND WEAR

GIBSIDE CHAPEL, ORANGERY AND STABLES

Gibside, nr. Rowlands Gill, Burnopfield, Tyne & Wear NE16 6BG
Palladian chapel, 1760–69 and completed 1812; designed by James Paine for George Bowes, MP and coal owner. Palladian style stables built 1746 by Daniel Garrett. The Orangery, built 1771-5, is one tall storey with seven bays. Situated south-west of Gibside Hall, overlooking the River Derwent.
www.nationaltrust.org.uk
Grant Recipient: The National Trust
Access Contact: Visitor Services Manager
T: 01207 542255   **F:** 01207 542255
E-mail: gibside@nationaltrust.org.uk
Open: Chapel: daily, 15 March–2 November 11am–4.30pm. Stables: daily, 1 February–9 March 11am–3.30pm; 10 March–2 November 11am–4.30pm; 3 November–31 January 2009 11am–3.30pm. Orangery: daily, 10 March–2 November 10am–6pm; 3 November–31 January 2009 10am–4.30pm. Chapel, Stables and Orangery closed 22–26 December and 29 December–2 January 2009.
Heritage Open Days: Yes
P Spaces: 500. Limited coach parking
Full. WC for the disabled. Guide Dogs allowed.
£ **Adult:** £6.00. **Child:** £3.50. **Other:** £17.50 (family).

FREEMASONS HALL

Queen Street East, Sunderland, Tyne and Wear SR1 2HT
Grade I listed oldest purpose-built Masonic meeting place in the world, c1785. Contains an ornate Lodge Room which remains virtually unaltered with elaborate thrones from 1735. Also has a cellar is in its original condition and the last remaining example of a Donaldson organ which was specially constructed for the building in 1785.
Grant Recipient: Queen Street Masonic Temple Ltd
Access Contact: Mr Colin Meddes
T: 0191 522 0115   **F:** 0191 522 0115
E-mail: colinmeddes@tiscali.co.uk
Open: Guided tours throughout the year by prior arrangement. Heritage Open Days Sunday 11am–3pm.
Heritage Open Days: Yes
P Spaces: 80.
Full.Five external steps to main entrance: guides available to assist wheelchair users. Access ramp for the disabled due to be installed. WC for the disabled. Guide Dogs allowed.
£ No

HIGH LEVEL BRIDGE

linking Newcastle & Gateshead, Tyne and Wear
Grade I listed railway and road bridge of ashlar and cast iron, 1849, designed by Robert Stephenson. One of the finest pieces of architectural iron work in the world.
Grant Recipient: Network Rail
Access Contact: Mr Richard Bell
T: 01904389 876   **F:** 01904 389 802
E-mail: richard.bell@networkrail.co.uk
Open: Best viewed from adjacent riverbanks or via access road/footpath under bridge. Also may be viewed from the footways which cross the lower deck of the bridge. Access to the lower deck is not available until May 2008 as major refurbishment will be taking place. No access to the upper deck of the bridge.
Heritage Open Days: No
P On-street parking.
Partial. Footways across the lower deck of the bridge are accessible for wheelchairs but the lower deck is not available until May 2008 due to major refurbishment. No WC for the disabled. Guide Dogs allowed.
£ No

THEATRE ROYAL

100 Grey Street, Newcastle-upon-Tyne, Tyne and Wear NE1 6BR
Victorian theatre opened in 1837, rebuilt in 1899 by Frank Matcham in a richly-ornamented style. Classical façade with rare Hanoverian coat of arms. Traditional 4-tier 1,294 seat auditorium hosting annual programme of touring productions and international companies.
www.theatreroyal.co.uk
Grant Recipient: Newcastle Theatre Royal Trust Ltd
Access Contact: Mr Philip Bernays
T: 0191 232 0997   **F:** 0191 261 1906
E-mail: philip.bernays@theatreroyal.co.uk
Open: Regular tours available depending on production schedule, contact theatre on 08448 112121 for details. Regular public programme except Sundays. Café and Foyer: Monday–Saturday from 10am.
Heritage Open Days: No
P Public car parks in city centre.
Partial. Wheelchair access to foyer, cafe and stalls. WC for the disabled. Guide Dogs allowed.
£ **Adult:** £3.50 (tours, some free). **Child:** £3.50 (tours, some free).

WARWICKSHIRE

CHARLECOTE PARK

Wellesbourne, Warwick, Warwickshire CV35 9ER
Owned by the Lucy family since 1247, Sir Thomas built the house in 1558. Now much altered, it is shown as it would have been a century ago. The balustraded formal garden gives onto a deer park landscaped by 'Capability' Brown.
www.nationaltrust.org.uk
Grant Recipient: The National Trust
Access Contact: Glen Sutton, Property Manager
T: 01789 470277   **F:** 01789 470544
E-mail: charlecote.park@nationaltrust.org.uk
Open: House: 1 March–28 October, Friday–Tuesday 12 noon–5pm; 6–21 December, Saturday and Sunday 12 noon–4pm. House Tours: Friday–Tuesday 11 am–12 noon. Gardens: 2–24 February 10.30 am–4pm, 1 March–28

October 10.30 am–6pm, 31 October–31 January 2009 10.30 am–4pm.
Heritage Open Days: Yes
P Spaces: 200. Overflow car park available.
Partial. Wheelchair access to ground floor of house, restaurant and shop. WC for the disabled. Guide Dogs allowed.
£ **Adult:** £8.20. **Child:** £4.10. **Other:** £20.00 (family), 7.00 (group).

LORD LEYCESTER HOSPITAL

High Street, Warwick, Warwickshire CV34 4BH
14th century chantry chapel, Great Hall, galleried courtyard and Guildhall. Acquired by Robert Dudley, Earl of Leicester in 1571 as a home for his old soldiers. Still operating as a home for ex-servicemen.
www.lordleycester.com
Grant Recipient: Patron & Governors of Lord Leycester Hospital
Access Contact: Lieut. Colonel G F Lesinski
T: 01926 491422
E-mail: lordleycester@btinternet.com
Open: Tuesday–Sunday 10am–4pm (winter), 10am–5pm (summer), plus Bank Holiday Mondays. Closed Good Friday and Christmas Day.
Heritage Open Days: No
P Spaces: 10.
Partial. Wheelchair access to ground floor only. WC for the disabled. Guide Dogs allowed.
£ **Adult:** £4.90, £2.00 (garden only). **Child:** £3.90. **Other:** £4.40, £2.00 (garden only).

RAGLEY HALL

Alcester, Warwickshire B49 5NJ
Family home of the Marquess and Marchioness of Hertford. Built in 1680 to a design by Robert Hooke in the Palladian style, with portico added by Wyatt in 1780. Contents include baroque plasterwork by James Gibb, family portraits by Sir Joshua Reynolds and a mural by Graham Rust completed in 1983. Surrounding park designed by 'Capability' Brown.
www.ragleyhall.com
Grant Recipient: Hugh Edward Conway Seymour The 8th Marquess of Hertford & Earl of Yarmouth
Access Contact: Mr Tom Sherstone
T: 01789 762090   **F:** 01789 764791
E-mail: tomshepstone@ragleyhall.com
Open: State Rooms: 16 March–2 November: Sunday during school term time, and everyday except Saturday during school holidays.Times and dates may vary subject to events and functions, please phone 01789 762 090 to confirm. Park and gardens: Saturdays and Sundays during school term time, and every day during school holidays, 10 am–6pm (last admission 4.30pm).
Heritage Open Days: No
P Spaces: 4000.
Partial. Wheelchair access via lift to first floor. WC for the disabled. Guide Dogs allowed.
£ **Adult:** £8.50. **Child:** £5.00 (age 5–16). **Other:** £7.00 (seniors & Orange/Blue Badge), £27.00 (family). Groups 20+ POA (adult/seniors, child).

STONELEIGH ABBEY

Kenilworth, Warwickshire CV8 2LF
16th century house built on site and incorporating remains of Cistercian Abbey founded in 1155. West wing designed by Francis Smith of Warwick between 1714–26 and northern wing reconstructed in 19th century by Charles S Smith of Warwick. South wing c1820. West wing contains a range of State Apartments. Also has restored Regency riding stables, 19th century conservatory and Humphrey Repton landscaped riverside gardens.
www.stoneleighabbey.org
Grant Recipient: Stoneleigh Abbey Preservation Trust (1996) Ltd
Access Contact: Estate Office
T: 01926 858535   **F:** 01926 850274
E-mail: enquire@stoneleighabbey.org
Open: Good Friday–end of October: Tuesday, Wednesday, Thursday and Sunday, plus Bank Holidays. Opening arrangements may change, please check with the Preservation Trust for current information.
Heritage Open Days: No
P Spaces: 400.
Full. WC for the disabled. Guide Dogs allowed.
£ **Adult:** £6.50. **Child:** £3.00. **Other:** £5.00 (senior citizens), £3.00 grounds only.

WEST MIDLANDS

MOLINEUX HOTEL

Whitmore Hill, Wolverhampton, West Midlands WV1 1RY
Grade II* listed house of c1720 with mid 18th century additions. Used as an hotel from 1860 onwards. Vacant since 1979 and acquired by Wolverhampton City Council in 2004. The first stage of repairs was undertaken during 2004–5. Restoration and conversion to house the City's Archives and Local Studies service started in May 2007 and will run until September 2008.
www.wolverhampton.gov.uk
Grant Recipient: Wolverhampton City Council
Access Contact: Mr Nigel Brown
T: 01902 556 556   **F:** 01902 555 637
E-mail: nigel.brown@wolverhampton.gov.uk
Open: Guided tours for groups by prior arrangement (subject to building work due to be completed September 2008). Heritage open days subject to completion of building work.
Heritage Open Days: Yes
P Limited parking available evenings and most weekends.
Partial. Wheelchair access to ground floor and most of the site. Full access by lift will be available to the Archives. WC for the disabled. Guide Dogs allowed.
£ No

PERROTT'S FOLLY

Waterworks Road, Edgbaston, Birmingham, West Midlands. B16 9BD
Built in 1758 by John Perrott as folly adjacent to his house (long demolished). The tower or folly is 94 feet high with circular stair tower attached. In 1884 the Birmingham glass-maker and meteorologist Abraham Follet Osler began using the building for weather observations. As the Edgbaston Observatory it became part of one of the world's first regular weather forecasting services–keeping up that work until 1979, at which time it fell into disuse. First phase of repair completed.
Grant Recipient: The Perrott's Folly Company
Access Contact: Mr Dennis Minnis
T: 0121 454 4152
E-mail: dennis.minnis@linone.net
Open: By prior arrangement. Contact telephone number on gate.
Heritage Open Days: Yes
P Unrestricted on-street parking close by.
No wheelchair access. No WC for the disabled. No Guide Dogs allowed.
£ No

RED HOUSE GLASSCONE

Wordsley, Stourbridge, West Midlands DY8 4AZ
Built around 1790, the Cone was used for the manufacture of glass until 1936 and is now one of only four left in the Country. Reaching 100ft into the sky, the Cone enclosed a furnace where glass was made for 140 years. In its 200 year history, the site has remained virtually unaltered and therefore provides an interesting insight into the history and tradition of glassmaking. Glassmaking and exhibitions tell the story of glassmaking in the area and the history of the glassworks.
www.dudley.gov.uk/redhousecone
Grant Recipient: Dudley Metropolitan Borough Council
Access Contact: Ms Sarah Hall
T: 01384 812752   **F:** 01384 812751
E-mail: sarah.hall@dudley.gov.uk
Open: January–31 March: daily 10am–4pm. 1 April–31 October: Monday–Saturday 10am–5pm, Sunday 10am–4pm.
Heritage Open Days: Yes
P Spaces: 40. 2 parking bays for the disabled.
Partial. Full wheelchair access to the Cone, glassmaking area and all display areas. Lift to upper floor and galleries. Some studios are inaccessible. WC for the disabled. Guide Dogs allowed.
£ Free audio guide.

ST JAMES

Great Packington, Meriden, nr. Coventry, West Midlands CV7 7HF
Red brick building with four domes topped by finials in neo-classical style. Built to celebrate the return to sanity of King George III. The organ was designed by Handel for his librettist, Charles Jennens, who was the cousin of the 4th

Earl of Aylesford, who built the church.
Grant Recipient: St James Great Packington Trust
Access Contact: Packington Estate Office
T: 01676 522020   **F:** 01676 523399
E-mail: jameschurch@packingtonestate.co.uk
Open: Monday–Friday 9am–5pm: key can be obtained from the Estate Office at Packington Hall, preferably by phoning in advance (01676 522020). At other times by prior arrangement with Lord Guernsey (tel: 01676 522274).
Heritage Open Days: No
P Spaces: 10.
 Partial. Wheelchair access with assistance (entrance steps and heavy door to be negotiated). No WC for the disabled. Guide Dogs allowed.
£ Donations towards restoration welcomed.

THE BIG HOUSE
44 Church Street, Oldbury, West Midlands B69 3DE
Grade II* 3-storey house dating from c1730. Originally with agricultural land and later the house and officers of a solicitor in 1857 when the land was sold. Restored and reopened in 2002 as Civic offices.
www.sandwell.gov.uk
Grant Recipient: Sandwell Metropolitan Borough Council
Access Contact: Civic Affairs Officer
T: 0121 569 3041   **F:** 0121 569 3050
E-mail: ann_oneill@sandwell.gov.uk
Open: By arrangement with the Mayor's office via the Civic Affairs officer (tel: 0121 569 3041). The Mayor will also hold 'Open House' at various times throughout the year.
Heritage Open Days: No
P Market Street Public Car Park (30 spaces). Parking for the disabled (4 spaces) adjacent to property.
 Full. WC for the disabled. Guide Dogs allowed.
£ No

WIGHTWICK MANOR
Wightwick Bank, Wolverhampton, West Midlands WV6 8EE
Built 1887, the house is a notable example of a late Victorian manor house. Contains original William Morris wallpapers and fabrics, Pre-Raphaelite paintings, Kempe glass and de Morgan ware. Also has a 17 acre Victorian/Edwardian garden designed by Thomas Mawson.
www.nationaltrust.org.uk
Grant Recipient: The National Trust
Access Contact: Property Manager
T: 01902 761400/01902 760100   **F:** 01902 764663
E-mail: wightwickmanor@nationaltrust.org.uk
Open: By guided tour only 1 March–20 December: Wednesday, Thursday, Friday and Saturday (also Bank Holiday Sunday and Monday to ground floor only) 12.30–5pm. Taster tours 11am–12.30 pm. Also open days Sundays in August 12.30–5pm. Admission by timed ticket issued from 11am at Visitor Reception. Other days by prior arrangement. Garden: Wednesday–Saturday and Bank Holiday Sunday and Monday 11am–6pm. First Thursday and Saturday of each month: no guided tours, free flow only.
Heritage Open Days: Yes
P Spaces: 50. For coach parking please telephone 01902 760100.
 Partial. Wheelchair access to ground floor only, two steps. WC for the disabled. Guide Dogs allowed.
£ Adult: £7.90, £3.90 (garden only). Admission price includes voluntary gift aid donation. Child: £3.90 (children free for garden only). Other: £3.90 (students), £20.00 (family).

WEST SUSSEX

HIGH BEECHES WOODLAND AND WATER GARDENS
High Beeches, Handcross, Haywards Heath, West Sussex RH17 6HQ
Twenty five acre garden with woodland, open glades, natural wildflower meadows and water gardens. Many rare plants to be seen in all seasons. National collection of Stewartia Trees. Tree and walking trails. Restaurant in restored Victorian farm buildings and tea room/garden.
www.highbeeches.com
Grant Recipient: The Trustees of High Beeches Gardens Conservation Trust
Access Contact: Mrs Sarah Bray
T: 01444 400589   **F:** 01444 401543
E-mail: gardens@highbeeches.com

Open: 21 March–31 October: 1–5pm (last admission 4.30pm), closed Wednesdays. All coaches and Guided Tours by prior arrangement. Tea room open all year except Wednesdays.
Heritage Open Days: No
P Spaces: 100. Free parking, coaches by prior arrangement, disabled parking adjacent to tea room.
 Partial. Wheelchair access to tea room and tea garden only. WC for the disabled. Guide Dogs allowed.
£ Adult: £5.50. Child: Free. Other: Concessions for groups. Guided tours £10.00 per person.

OUSE VALLEY VIADUCT
Balcombe, West Sussex
The most important surviving architectural feature of the original layout of the London–Brighton railway, the grade II* Ouse Valley Viaduct has 37 circular arches, is 492 yards long and 92 feet high. Designed by John Rastrick with stonework accredited to David Mocatta, it is known for its pierced piers, ornate limestone parapets and pavilions. Built 1839–1841.
Grant Recipient: Railtrack plc (now Network Rail)
Access Contact: Network Rail
Open: Public access at all times on the footpath running underneath the viaduct. It is possible to view the viaduct from Borde Hill Lane without walking across the field.
Heritage Open Days: No
P Limited on-street parking.
 No wheelchair access. Wheelchair users can view viaduct form Borde Hill Lane. No WC for the disabled. No Guide Dogs allowed.
£ No

PARHAM HOUSE
Parham Park, Storrington, nr. Pulborough, West Sussex RH20 4HS
Dating from 1577, Parham is listed Grade I and is one of the country's finest examples of an Elizabethan House. From the panelled Great Hall to the Long Gallery, the house contains an important collection of paintings, furniture and needlework.
www.parhaminsussex.co.uk
Grant Recipient: Parham Park Ltd
Access Contact: Mr Richard Pailthorpe, General Manager
T: 01903 742021   **F:** 01903 743260
E-mail: pat@parhaminsussex.co.uk
Open: Easter–End of September: Wednesday, Thursday, Sunday and Bank Holiday Mondays. Tuesdays and Fridays during August (also Saturday 7 July). Gardens open at 12 noon, house at 2pm with last entry at 4.30pm.
Heritage Open Days: No
P Spaces: 300. Parking for the disabled close to the house.
 Partial. Wheelchair access to ground floor only by prior arrangement, there is a reduced admission charge for wheelchair users and carers. Free loan of recorded tour tape. WC for the disabled. Guide Dogs allowed.
£ Adult: £7.50 (provisional). Child: £3.50 (age 5–15) (provisional). Other: £6.50 (senior citizens), £15.50 (family) (provisional).

PETWORTH HOUSE
Petworth, West Sussex GU28 0AE
Late 17th century mansion in 'Capability' Brown landscaped park. The house contains the Trust's largest collection of pictures including Turners and Van Dycks, as well as sculpture, furniture and Grinling Gibbons' carvings. Also there are the Servants' Quarters with interesting kitchens and other service rooms. Extra rooms open Monday, Tuesday and Wednesday afternoon by kind permission of Lord and Lady Egremont.
www.nationaltrust.org.uk/petworth
Grant Recipient: The National Trust
Access Contact: Property Manager
T: 01798 342207   **F:** 01798 342963
E-mail: petworth@nationaltrust.org.uk
Open: House and Servants' Quarters: 15 March–5 November, daily except Thursday and Friday (but open Good Friday), 11am–5pm (last admission to house 4.30pm). Extra rooms shown weekday afternoons (but not Bank Holiday Mondays) as follows: Monday: White and Gold Room and White Library; Tuesday and Wednesday: three bedrooms on first floor. Park: All year, daily and afternoons of open-air concerts in July.
Heritage Open Days: Yes
P Spaces: 150. Car park for house and park on A283, 800 yards from property.

 Partial. Wheelchair access to ground floor of house, shop and tea room. WC for the disabled. Guide Dogs allowed.
£ Adult: £9.50. Child: £4.80. Other: £23.80 family), £7.50 (booked groups of 15+).

SHIPLEY WINDMILL
Shipley, nr. Horsham, West Sussex RH13 8PL
Grade II* listed smock mill with five floors, built 1879 and restored in 1990 to full working order. Once owned by the Sussex writer and poet, Hilaire Belloc, who lived nearby. The milling process is demonstrated on open days for the benefit of visitors.
www.shipleywindmill.org.uk
Grant Recipient: Shipley Windmill Charitable Trust
Access Contact: Ms Penny Murray
T: 01243 777830   **F:** 01243 777952
E-mail: penny.murray@westsussex.gov.uk
Open: April–October: first, second and third Sunday of each month, plus Bank Holiday Mondays. Also National Mills Day, Shipley Festival (May) and the Sunday of the Heritage Open Days weekend.
Heritage Open Days: Yes
P Spaces: 10.
 Partial. Wheelchair access to ground floor of mill and engine shed. No WC for the disabled. No Guide Dogs allowed.
£ Adult: £3.00. Child: £2.00. Other: £2.00 (senior citizens).

ST HUGH'S CHARTERHOUSE
Henfield Road, Partridge Green, Horsham, West Sussex RH13 8EB
Large monastery covering 10 acres. One large cloister of over 100 square yards comprising 34 four-room hermitages where the monks live. The fore part is a smaller cloister about 200ft square which contains the cells of the Brothers and their work places. There is also a large church, library, refectory, Brothers Chapel and other monastic buildings. The large quad encloses a cemetery. The spire is 203ft high and has a five-bell chime.
www.parkminster.org.uk
Grant Recipient: St Hugh's Charterhouse
Access Contact: Mr John Babeau
T: 01403 864231   **F:** 01403 864231
Open: By prior arrangement, with due respect for the rules of the Charterhouse monastery. For further details please contact the monastery.
Heritage Open Days: No
P Spaces: 20.
 Partial. Wheelchair access to ground level only. No WC for the disabled. Guide Dogs allowed.
£ No

WEST YORKSHIRE

BRAMHAM PARK LEAD LADS TEMPLE
Wetherby, West Yorkshire LS23 6ND
Park folly, in the form of an open temple in the classical style, built in the 1750s by local craftsmen on the instructions of Harriet Benson (about a mile from the house in woodland called Black Fen, close to a public footpath). The 'Lead Lads' were classical lead figures that stood on the three small blocks at the apex and base of the front pediment, and were lost to vandals many years ago.
www.bramhampark.co.uk
Grant Recipient: Trustees of the Bramham Settled Estate
Access Contact: The Estate Office
T: 01937 846000   **F:** 01937 846007
E-mail: enquiries@bramhampark.co.uk
Open: 1 April–30 September. Closed 2–8 June and 11–30 August.
Heritage Open Days: No
P Spaces: 50. £2.50 (senior citizens). No charge made for visitors via the footpath but charge made for visitors to the house and gardens.
 Partial. WC for the disabled is not on site, but in visitors car park via footpath (1 mile). Guide Dogs allowed.
£ Adult: £4.50. Child: £2.50 (under 5s free). Other: £2.50 (senior citizens). No charge made for visitors via the footpath but charge made for visitors to the house and gardens.

CROSSLEY PAVILION

The People's Park, King Cross Road, Halifax, West Yorkshire HX1 1EB
Grade II* listed building, designed by Sir Joseph Paxton and constructed in 1857. Contains seating and a statue of the park's benefactor, Sir Francis Crossley (1860), by Joseph Durham. Four gargoyle fountains supply pools flanking each side of the pavilion, set on formal terrace, balustrades and steps.
www.calderdale.gov.uk/tourism/parks/peoples.html
Grant Recipient: Calderdale Metropolitan Borough Council
Access Contact: People's Park Development Officer
T: 01422 323824   **F:** 01422 323824
Open: Park: daily 8am–dusk. Pavilion: visits by prior arrangement with Calderdale Metropolitan Borough Council Leisure Services, 25 Bedford Street North, Halifax, West Yorkshire HX1 5BH. Public toilets open during park hours. Information Centre open by prior arrangement as above.
Heritage Open Days: Yes
🅿 On-street parking in Park Road (up to 30 spaces). Limited spaces in adjacent college.
♿ Partial. There is one step into the pavilion, otherwise full wheelchair access. WC for the disabled. Guide Dogs allowed.
£ No

FARFIELD FRIENDS MEETING HOUSE

off Bolton Road, Addingham, nr. Ilkley, West Yorkshire LS29
Land for burial ground purchased in 1666, followed by construction of Meeting House in 1669. A simple single cell building with rubblestone walls, mullioned windows, stone-slated roof and stone-flagged floor. Contains loose benches and an oak minister's stand of an unusual panelled design with turned balusters.
www.hct.org.uk
Grant Recipient: Historic Chapels Trust
Access Contact: Barry Cody
T: 01756 710587
Open: At all reasonable times by application to key holders Mr and Mrs Barry Cody, Riverview Cottage, Farfield, nr Addingham, West Yorks LS29 0RQ. Burial ground open for viewing and picnics.
Heritage Open Days: No
🅿 Spaces: 2.
♿ No wheelchair access. No WC for the disabled. Guide Dogs allowed.
£ Donations invited.

HAREWOOD HOUSE

Harewood, Leeds, West Yorkshire LS17 9LQ
Designed in neo-classical style by John Carr and completed in 1772. Contains Adam interiors, Chippendale furniture, an art collection and museum. Home of the Earl and Countess of Harewood.
www.harewood.org
Grant Recipient: The Trustees of Harewood House Trust Ltd
Access Contact: Mr Mick Stanley, Head of Collections
T: 0113 218 1010   **F:** 0113 218 1002
E-mail: mick.stanley@harewood.org
Open: Daily 15 March–2 November. Grounds and Bird Garden open 10am–6pm (last admission 4pm). House 11am–4.30pm (last admission 4pm). Grounds close at 6pm. Grounds and Bird Garden also open weekends between 8 November and 14 December. Guide dogs are not allowed in the Bird Garden but a free sound guide is available for the partially sighted visitor and a minder for the dog.
Heritage Open Days: Yes
🅿 Spaces: 200. Unlimited overflow parking on grass.
♿ Full. WC for the disabled. Guide Dogs allowed.
£ Adult: £14.50. Child: £9.00. Other: £13.50 (senior), £49.00 (family), season tickets & concessions for disabled groups, 50% reduction for arrivals by public transport, students free Wednesday.

HUDDERSFIELD STATION

St George's Square, Huddersfield, West Yorkshire HD1 1JF
Designed by J P Pritchett of York and built by local builder Joseph Kaye using local ashlar sandstone, the station is the oldest of the seven Grade I listed station buildings in use for railway passengers having opened on 3 August 1847. When the foundation stone was laid the year before a public holiday was declared and church bells were rung from dawn till dusk. The grandeur of the station is the result of it having been built at the joint expense of the Huddersfield and Manchester Rail and Canal Company and the Manchester and Leeds Railway Company.
Grant Recipient: Kirkless Metropolitan Council
Access Contact: Head of Design & Property Service
T: 01484 226174   **F:** 01484 226086
E-mail: matthew.newton@kirklees.gov.uk
Open: Operational building open to the public every day except Christmas Day and Boxing Day. Please note that the building may also be closed on other days specified by Network Rail or other railway operators.
Heritage Open Days: Yes
🅿 Spaces: 20. One hour stay maximum in station car park. Pay and display car park.
♿ Full. Full wheelchair access to main buildings. Access with assistance to inner platforms. No WC for the disabled. Guide Dogs allowed.
£ No

NATIONAL COAL MINING MUSEUM FOR ENGLAND

Caphouse Colliery, New Road, Wakefield, West Yorkshire WF4 4RH
A colliery complex dating back to the 18th century with an underground tour into authentic coal workings and major galleries covering social history, science and technology within mining. Most of the historic buildings are open to the public. Facilities include a research library, restaurant, shop and education services.
www.ncm.org.uk
Grant Recipient: The National Coal Mining Museum for England Trust Ltd
Access Contact: Dr M Faull
T: 01924 848806   **F:** 01924 840694
E-mail: info@ncm.org.uk
Open: All year: daily, 10am–5pm except 24–26 December and 1 January.
Heritage Open Days: Yes
🅿 Spaces: 200.
♿ Partial. Wheelchair access to all galleries and historic buildings and underground (limited tour) but not the screens. WC for the disabled. Guide Dogs allowed but not permitted underground.
£ No

NOSTELL PRIORY

Doncaster Road, Nostell, Wakefield, West Yorkshire WF4 1QE
Country house, c1736–1750, by James Paine for Sir Rowland Winn 4th baronet. Later Robert Adam was commissioned to complete the State Rooms. On display is a collection of Chippendale furniture, designed especially for the house, an art collection with works by Pieter Breughel the Younger and Angelica Kauffmann, an 18th century dolls house, complete with its original fittings and Chippendale furniture and an un-restored 18th century Muniments Room. Other attractions include lakeside walks, historic park, family croquet, giant chess set and open day for cabinets.
www.nationaltrust.org.uk
Grant Recipient: The National Trust
Access Contact: Property Manager
T: 01924 863892   **F:** 01924 866846
E-mail: nostellpriory@nationaltrust.org.uk
Open: House: 15 March–2 November, daily except Monday and Tuesday (open Good Friday and Bank Holidays) 1–5pm; 6 December–14 December: daily 12 noon–4pm. Grounds, shop and tea room: 1 March–2 November, 11am–5.30pm, daily (except Monday and Tuesday); 8–30 November, Saturday and Sunday, 11am–4.30 pm; 6–14 December, daily 11am–4.30pm.
Heritage Open Days: No
🅿 Spaces: 700. Parking £2.00, refundable on purchase of House or Garden ticket.
♿ Partial. Wheelchair access to ground floor of house with lift to first floor, tea room, children's playground and shop. No WC for the disabled. Guide Dogs allowed.
£ Adult: £7.20. Child: £3.60. Other: £17.50 (family).

PONTEFRACTE OLD TOWN HALL AND ASSEMBLY ROOMS

Bridge Street, Pontefract, West Yorkshire WF8 1PG
Grade II and II* Listed buildings. Old Town Hall built in 1785 and designed by Bernard Hartley. Assembly Rooms later added in 1882 and designed by Perkin and Bulmer. Currently used for productions, concerts and dance.

Grant Recipient: Wakefield Metropolitan District Council
Access Contact: Mrs Olive Rendell
T: 01924 305 573   **F:** 01924 306 963
E-mail: orendell@wakefield.gov.uk
Open: Monday–Thursday 9–11.30am. Friday 9–10.30am. All other times by prior arrangement.
Heritage Open Days: Yes
🅿 Car park nearby, disabled parking adjacent to property.
♿ Full. WC for the disabled. Guide Dogs allowed.
£ No

TEMPLE NEWSAM HOUSE

Leeds Museums and Galleries, Leeds, West Yorkshire LS15 0AE
Tudor-Jacobean mansion in 1200 acre park. Birthplace of Henry Lord Darnley, husband of Mary Queen of Scots, and later the home of the Ingram family, Viscounts Irwin. Over 30 fully restored rooms open to the public with pre-eminent collections of paintings, furniture, metalwork, ceramics, textiles and wallpapers.
www.leeds.gov.co.uk/templenewsam
Grant Recipient: Leeds City Council
Access Contact: Mr Anthony Wells-Cole
T: 0113 264 7321   **F:** 0113 260 2285
E-mail: temple.newsam@leeds.gov.uk
Open: January–December: daily except Monday (open Bank Holiday Mondays), 10.30am–5.00pm (4pm in winter). Last admission 45 minutes before closing. Closed Christmas Day, Boxing Day and New Year's Day.
Heritage Open Days: Yes
🅿 Spaces: 200.
♿ Partial. Wheelchair access to all public areas except the first floor of the south wing. WC for the disabled. Guide Dogs allowed.
£ Adult: £3.50 (includes audio tour). Child: £2.50 (5–16). Free (under 5). Other: £9.00 (family) Admission charges subject to change. Leeds Card holders free.

THE ROUNDHOUSE

Wellington Road, Leeds, West Yorkshire LS12 1DR
Grade II* railway roundhouse built in 1847 for the Leeds and Thirsk Railway by Thomas Granger. In full use by the North-Eastern Railway until 1904, now home to Leeds Commercial Van and Truck Hire.
farnborough Hall
Grant Recipient: Wellbridge Properties Ltd
Access Contact: Mr J D Miller
T: 0113 2435964   **F:** 0113 246 1142
E-mail: sales@leedscommercial.co.uk
Open: By prior written arrangement with the occupiers, Leeds Commercial, who manage the property as a working garage, or call in during office hours.
Heritage Open Days: Yes
🅿 Spaces: 100. Free parking.
♿ Full. WC for the disabled. Guide Dogs allowed.
£ No

WILTSHIRE

AVONCLIFFE AQUEDUCT

Kennet & Avon Canal, Westwood, Wiltshire
19th century limestone aqueduct carrying the Kennet and Avon Canal over the River Avon and the railway line. The canal towpath crosses alongside the canal providing a foot link to Bradford-on-Avon or Bath.
www.britishwaterways.co.uk/southwest
Grant Recipient: British Waterways
Access Contact: Mrs Tina Martin Botham
T: 01452 318000   **F:** 01452 318076
E-mail: tina.martin@britishwaterways.co.uk
Open: At all times.
Heritage Open Days: No
🅿 Spaces: 12.
♿ Partial. Wheelchair access to top of aqueduct from the small car park beside the canal. No WC for the disabled. Guide Dogs allowed.
£ No

BARTON GRANGE FARM WEST BARN

Bradford on Avon, Wiltshire
Part of Barton Farm, once a grange of Shaftesbury Abbey (the richest nunnery in England), which includes the adjacent 14th century Tithe Barn. The West Barn was destroyed by fire in 1982 but has subsequently been rebuilt by the Preservation Trust and is now used as an 'Interpretation Centre' and as a Community Hall.
www.bradfordheritage.co.uk/PAGES/project.htm
Grant Recipient: Bradford on Avon Preservation Trust

Limited
Access Contact: Mr Chris Penny
T: 01225 866551
E-mail: christiangdpenny@tiscali.co.uk
Open: May–September: weekends and Bank Holidays 12 noon–4pm. Also open at other times throughout the year, please check with Mr Penny for further details.
Heritage Open Days: Yes
P Pay parking (15 spaces) near the site. Pay parking (200 spaces) at railway station.
Partial. Wheelchair access to main building but not galleries. Entrance pathways are loose gravel. WC for the disabled. Guide Dogs allowed.
£ No

HEMINGSBY

56 The Close, Salisbury, Wiltshire SP1 2EL
14th century canonical residence with spacious 18th century rooms and medieval Great Hall. Contains 15th century linenfold panelling. Large and interesting garden. Home of Canon William Fideon, a Greek scholar who escaped from Constantinople in 1453, and Canon Edward Powell, advocate of Catherine of Aragon and later hanged for denying the Act of Supremacy.
Grant Recipient: The Dean & Chapter of Salisbury Cathedral
Access Contact: Mr Peter Edds
T: 01722 555115   **F:** 01722 555140
E-mail: p.edds@salcath.co.uk
Open: By prior arrangement only. Exterior can be viewed at all times.
Heritage Open Days: No
P No
No wheelchair access. No WC for the disabled. Guide Dogs allowed.
£ Donations invited.

LACOCK ABBEY

Lacock, nr. Chippenham, Wiltshire SN15 2LG
Founded in 1232 and converted into a country house c1540, the fine medieval cloisters, sacristy, chapter house and monastic rooms of the Abbey have survived largely intact. The handsome 16th century stable courtyard has half timbered gables, a clockhouse, brewery and bakehouse. Victorian woodland garden. Former residents include William Fox Talbot 'the father of modern photography' and the Abbey now houses the Fox Talbot Museum.
www.nationaltrust.org.uk
Grant Recipient: The National Trust
Access Contact: Property Manager
T: 01249 730459   **F:** 01249 730501
E-mail: lacockabbey@nationaltrust.org.uk
Open: Abbey: 15 March–2 November, daily 1–5.30pm (closed Tuesdays and Good Friday). Museum, cloisters and garden: 23 February–2 November, daily 11am–5.30pm (closed Good Friday). Museum also open 8 November–21 December and 3 January–15 February 11am–4pm.
Heritage Open Days: Yes
P Spaces: 300.
Partial. Wheelchair access to Abbey is difficult as four sets of stairs. Garden, cloisters and museum are accessible (non-wheelchair stair lift in museum). Limited parking in Abbey courtyard by arrangement. WC for the disabled at Red Lion car park, High Street, and abbey courtyard, RADAR lock. Guide Dogs allowed.
£ **Adult:** £10.00 (Abbey, museum, cloisters & garden), £8 (Abbey,cloisters & garden), £6.00 (garden, cloisters & museum). **Child:** £5.00 (Abbey, museum, cloisters & garden), £4.00 (Abbey, cloisters & garden), £3.00 (garden, cloisters & museum). **Other:** £25.50 (family: Abbey, museum, cloisters & garden), £20.40 (family: Abbey, cloisters & garden), £15.30 (family: garden, cloisters & museum). Group rates.

LADY MARGARET HUNGERFORD ALMSHOUSES

Pound Pill, Corsham, Wiltshire SN13 9HT
Fine complex of Grade I listed 17th Almshouses, Schoolroom, Warden's House and Stables. Schoolroom with original 17th century furniture and Exhibition Room. Recently restored. Lady Margaret Hungerford founded the Almshouses for the care of six poor people and the schoolroom for educating poor children. Arms of the foundress are well displayed.
Grant Recipient: Trustees Of The Lady Margaret Hunderford Charity
Access Contact: Mr R L Tonge
T: 01225 742471   **F:** 01225 742471
E-mail: rtonge@northwilts.gov.uk

Open: 4 April–30 September: Tuesday, Wednesday, Friday and Saturday 1.30–4.00pm; October, November, February and March: Saturdays 1.30pm–4.00pm. Closed December and January and Bank Holidays. Groups welcome by appointment.
Heritage Open Days: No
P Spaces: 100. Parking in the town within 100 yards.
Partial. Wheelchair access to ground floor only. WC for the disabled. Guide Dogs allowed.
£ **Adult:** £2.00. **Child:** 50p. **Other:** £1.75 (senior citizens and concession).

LARMER TREE GARDENS

nr Tollard Royal, Salisbury, Wiltshire SP5 5PY
Created by General Pitt Rivers in 1880 as a pleasure grounds for 'public enlightenment and entertainment', the Larmer Tree Gardens are set high on the Cranbourne Chase providing exceptional views of the surrounding countryside. One of the most unusual gardens in England containing an extraordinary collection of colonial and oriental buildings, a Roman Temple and an Open Air Theatre.
www.larmertree.co.uk
Grant Recipient: Trustees of MALF Pitt-Rivers No. 1 Discretionary Settlement
Access Contact: Estate Secretary
T: 01725 516225   **F:** 01725 516321
E-mail: enquiries@larmertree.co.uk
Open: Summer opening: Easter Sunday–End of September: Sunday–Thursday 11am–5pm. Closed July, Fridays and Saturdays for private hire. Winter opening: October, November, February and March: Monday–Friday 11am–4pm. Tea rooms: Sundays and Bank Holidays. Please check website to confirm opening arrangements.
Heritage Open Days: No
P Spaces: 500.
Partial. Wheelchair access to the sunken dell is difficult. WC for the disabled. Guide Dogs allowed.
£ **Adult:** £3.75. **Child:** £2.50 (over 5 yrs). **Other:** £3.00 (Admission charges apply on Sundays only, other times donations invited).

OLD BISHOP'S PALACE

Salisbury Cathedral School, 1 The Close, Salisbury, Wiltshire SP1 2EQ
13th century building, much altered over the centuries, with 13th century undercroft, Georgian drawing room and a chapel.
www.salisburycathedralschool.com
Grant Recipient: Salisbury Diocesan Board of Finance
Access Contact: Mr Neil Parsons
T: 01722 555302   **F:** 01722 410910
E-mail: bursar@salisburycathedralschool.com
Open: Guided tours on 10 days in July and August. Details can be obtained from the Visitors' Office at Salisbury Cathedral (tel: Fiona Nelder: 01722 555124).
Heritage Open Days: No
P No
No wheelchair access. There is a WC for the disabled in the cloister (100 yards). WC for the disabled. No Guide Dogs allowed.
£ **Adult:** £2.50.

SALISBURY CATHEDRAL EDUCATION CENTRE (WREN HALL)

56c The Close, Salisbury, Wiltshire SP1 2EL
Originally north wing of adjacent Braybrook House, early 18th century. Former choristers' school (founded 13th century). Many of the original fixtures and fittings are still present. Items of particular interest are the teacher's and head teacher's desks, original wood panelling and various photographs and artefacts from the history of the schoolroom.
www.salisburycathedral.org.uk/education.php
Grant Recipient: The Dean & Chapter of Salisbury Cathedral
Access Contact: Mr Peter Edds
T: 01722 555115   **F:** 01722 555 140
E-mail: p.edds@salcath.co.uk
Open: By prior arrangement.
Heritage Open Days: No
P As part of Close parking arrangements for members of the public.
No wheelchair access. WC for the disabled available within the Close. Guide Dogs allowed.
£ No

THE CLOISTERS

Iford Manor, Bradford-on-Avon, Wiltshire BA15 2BA
Small stone-built cloister in gardens of Manor, completed 1914 by Harold Peto and based on 13th century Italian style. Interesting early contents. Used for concerts and opera evenings during the summer.
www.ifordmanor.co.uk
Grant Recipient: Mrs E Cartwright-Hignett
Access Contact: Mrs E Cartwright-Hignett
T: 01225 863146   **F:** 01225 862364
E-mail: ifordmanor@countryside.uk.net
Open: Gardens only: April and October, Sundays and Easter Monday 2–5pm; May–September, daily (except Mondays and Fridays), 2–5pm. Children under 10 not encouraged at weekends. Coaches and groups by prior arrangement only outside normal opening hours. Teas available at weekends May–August.
Heritage Open Days: No
P Spaces: 100. Free parking.
Partial. Wheelchair access by prior arrangement to Cloisters and part of the gardens. WC for the disabled. Guide Dogs allowed.
£ **Adult:** £4.50. **Child:** £4.00 (10–16, under 10 free). **Other:** £4.00 (concessions).

WILTON HOUSE

Wilton, Salisbury, Wiltshire SP2 0BJ
Ancestral home of the Earls of Pembroke for over 450 years, rebuilt by Inigo Jones and John Webb in the Palladian style with further alterations by James Wyatt c1801. Contains 17th century state rooms and an art collection including works by Van Dyck, Rubens, Joshua Reynolds and Brueghel. Surrounded by landscaped parkland.
www.wiltonhouse.com
Grant Recipient: Wilton House Charitable Trust
Access Contact: Mr Chris Rolfe
T: 01722 746720   **F:** 01722 744447
E-mail: tourism@wiltonhouse.com
Open: House: 21–24 March, 5 April–31 August: Sunday–Thursday; 1–28 September: Tuesday–Thursday, 12 noon–5pm (last admission 4.30pm). House closed on Saturdays except bank holiday weekends. Grounds: 5 April–28 September: 11am–5.30pm.
Heritage Open Days: Yes
P Spaces: 200.
Full. WC for the disabled. Guide Dogs allowed.
£ **Adult:** £12.00. **Child:** £6.50. **Other:** £9.75 (senior citizens), £29.50 (family); Group rates on application.

WORCESTERSHIRE

ABBERLEY HALL CLOCK TOWER

Great Witley, Worcester, Worcestershire, WR6 6DD
Victorian folly, built 1883–4, by J P St Aubyn in a fantastic mixture of 13th and 14th century Gothic styles. 161ft tall, it can be seen from six counties.
Grant Recipient: Abberley Hall Ltd
Access Contact: Mr John G W Walker
T: 01299 896275   **F:** 01299 896875
E-mail: johnwalker@abberleyhall.co.uk
Open: 17 and 18 July; other times by prior arrangement.
Heritage Open Days: No
P Spaces: 20.
No wheelchair access. No WC for the disabled. No Guide Dogs allowed.
£ **Adult:** £3.00. **Child:** £1.50.

HANBURY HALL

School Road, Hanbury, Droitwich, Worcestershire WR9 7EA
Built in 1701, this William and Mary-style house contains painted ceilings and staircase. It has an orangery, ice house and Moorish gazebos. The re-created 18th century garden is surrounded by parkland and has a parterre, wilderness, fruit garden, open grove and bowling green pavilions. The recently redecorated Long Gallery houses an exhibition of the Vernon family and the history of Hanbury Hall. Original 17th century panelling to the study.
www.nationaltrust.org.uk
Grant Recipient: The National Trust
Access Contact: Property Manager
T: 01527 821214   **F:** 01527 821251
E-mail: hanburyhall@nationaltrust.org.uk
Open: House: 1–16 March, Saturday and Sunday; 17 March–29 October, Saturday–Wednesday 1–5pm. Garden, grounds, tea room, Long Gallery and shop: 1–16 March, Saturday and Sunday; 17 March–29 October,

Saturday–Wednesday (except July and August, 21 March–3 April, 24–1 June May, 25 October–2 November, daily 11am–5.30pm); 1 November–1 March 2009, Saturday and Sunday 11am–5.30pm.
Heritage Open Days: No
[P] Spaces: 150. Car parking 200 metres from house. Buggy transfer available.
[&] Partial. Wheelchair access to ground floor, gardens, tea room and shop. WC for the disabled. Guide Dogs allowed.
[£] **Adult:** £7.20, £4.80 (garden only). **Child:** £3.60, £2.40 (garden only). **Other:** £18.00 (family), £6.00 (group) Admission price includes voluntary gift aid donation.

HAWFORD GRANGE DOVECOTE

Hawford, Worcestershire
16th century dovecote.
Grant Recipient: National Trust
Access Contact: Property Manager
T: 01527 821 214
Open: All year: daily, 9am–6pm.
Heritage Open Days: No
[P] Spaces: 3.
[&] Partial. View from exterior. No WC for the disabled. Guide Dogs allowed.
[£] **Adult:** £1.00.

HOPTON COURT CONSERVATORY

Cleobury Mortimer, Kidderminster, Worcestershire DY14 0EF
Grade II* listed conservatory, c1830, of cast iron with a rounded archway leading to a rear room roofed with curved glass. Two rooms either side, one housing the boiler beneath to supply heat by way of cast iron grilles running around the floor of the interior.
www.hoptoncourt.co.uk
Grant Recipient: Mr C R D Woodward
Access Contact: Mr Christopher Woodward
T: 01299 270734   **F:** 01299 271132
E-mail: info@hoptoncourt.co.uk
Open: Weekends of 10/11 May and 30/31 August 10am–4.30pm. At other times by prior arrangement.
Heritage Open Days: No
[P] Spaces: 150.
[&] Full. WC for the disabled. Guide Dogs allowed.
[£] **Adult:** £3.50.

LOWER BROCKHAMPTON

Bringsty, Worcestershire WR6 5UH
A late 14th century moated manor house with a detached half-timbered 15th century gatehouse. Also, the ruins of a 12th century chapel. Woodland walks.
www.nationaltrust.org.uk
Grant Recipient: The National Trust
Access Contact: Property Manager
T: 01885 488099   **F:** 01885 482151
E-mail: brockhampton@nationaltrust.org.uk
Open: House: 1–16 March, Saturday and Sunday (open Bank Holiday Mondays and Good Friday) 12 noon–4pm; 19 March–2 November: Wednesday–Sunday 12 noon–5pm (until 4pm in October and November) and Bank Holiday 12–5pm.
Heritage Open Days: Yes
[P] Spaces: 60. Parking for the disabled near house. Car parking free when visiting house.
[&] Partial. WC for the disabled in estate car park. Guide Dogs allowed.
[£] **Adult:** £5.25 (admission price includes voluntary gift aid donation). **Child:** £2.60. **Other:** £13.00 (family) £3.50 (15+groups) £2.00 (park only).

ST MICHAEL'S RUINED NAVE AND WEST TOWER

Abberley, Worcestershire
Ruins of tower, nave (both 12th century) and south aisle (c1260). Walls standing approximately 4ft high with many surviving features from Medieval church. 12th century chancel and south chapel, c1260, repaired in 1908 and still used for services.
Grant Recipient: Abberley Parochial Church Council
Access Contact: Mrs M A Nott
T: 01299 896392
Open: At all times.
Heritage Open Days: Yes
[P] Spaces: 7. Also parking at Manor Arms Hotel.
[&] Full wheelchair access to ruins but assistance required to visit interior of church. No WC for the disabled. Guide Dogs allowed.
[£] Donations welcome (place in Green Box).

WALKER HALL

Market Square, Evesham, Worcestershire WR11 4RW
16th century timber-framed building adjoining Norman gateway, much altered. In the late 19th century the floor was removed and it became an open hall. In 1999 it was repaired and refitted to form offices (first floor) and a retail unit (ground floor).
Grant Recipient: Saggers & Rhodes
Access Contact: Messrs Saggers & Rhodes
T: 01386 446623   **F:** 01386 48215
E-mail: wds@ricsonline.org
Open: Access to interior by prior arrangement only.
Heritage Open Days: No
[P] Spaces: 500. Parking in town centre car parks.
[&] Partial. Wheelchair and guide dog access to ground floor only. WC for the disabled. Guide Dogs allowed.
[£] Charitable donation only.

WHITBOURNE HALL AND PALM HOUSE

Whitbourne, Worcester, Worcestershire WR6 5SE
Victorian Greek Revival style country house with large palm house built later (circa 1865–77) in the space between main block and service wing. The south front has an imposing Ionic portico. The main hall, with Maw and Co. mosaic tiled floor, is lit entirely by glazed blue-glass ceiling and surrounded by a gallery accessed by a white marble staircase with limestone balustrade.
www.whitbournehall.co.uk
Grant Recipient: Whitbourne Hall Community Ltd
Access Contact: Ms H D Colley
T: 01886 821165
E-mail: heatherdcolley@aol.com
Open: 27 April: 2pm–6pm; 5, 12, 19, 26 May, 2, 9, 16, 23 and 30 June: 11am–4pm.
Heritage Open Days: No
[P] Spaces: 100. Parking around the House.
[&] Partial. Wheelchair access to part of the garden. Mobile ramp available for access to the house (three steps). No WC for the disabled. Guide Dogs allowed.
[£] **Adult:** £3.00. **Child:** £1.50. **Other:** £5.00 (adult, April open day) £2.50 (child, April open day) Includes special attractions.

Heritage Open Days: an annual event over four days in September (11–14) which aims to increase opportunities for access to properties outside London which are predominantly inaccessible to the general public or usually charge an admission fee. English Heritage funds the Civic Trust to co-ordinate Heritage Open Days.

London Open House: a similar annual event, co-ordinated by London Open House, for buildings in the Capital over one weekend in September (20/21).

Information carried in this section is based on that supplied by English Heritage. Every effort has been made to ensure that the information given is accurate and while believed to be at the time of going to press, opening times, entrance charges and facilities available at properties may be changed at the discretion of the owners.
If long journeys are involved, visitors are advised to telephone the property to ensure the opening times are as published.

H Historic Places to Stay

Auchen Castle Hotel

Jewel of the Scottish Borders

Welcome

**Auchen Castle Hotel
Beattock
Near Moffat
Dumfriesshire
DG10 9SH
Scotland**

**Tel: 01683 300 407
Fax: 01683 300 727
E-mail: reception
@auchencastle.com**

Auchen Castle is set in forty acres of perfectly manicured gardens with dramatic panoramic views. The former home of Sir William Younger dates back to the thirteenth century and still retains many of its original features. Our private loch and on-site Falconry Centre all contribute to our unique and atmospheric venue.

Whether you wish a romantic hideaway accommodation break in Scotland or a Scottish Castle Wedding – we should be your venue of choice.

Accommodation at the Four Star Auchen Castle Hotel in Scotland includes 25 bedrooms, of these 15 are feature bedrooms within the original castle. The feature rooms and honeymoon suites have Champagne stocked mini bars, wide screen televisions, DVD players and mini hi-fis. Auchen Castle Hotel has various rooms with 4 poster beds, one of which is an exact replica of the bed used by Anne Boleyn at her ancestral home. The 10 Auchen Castle Lodge rooms are family sized and have fabulous views over the private trout loch.

The award winning Auchen Castle Hotel restaurant enjoys an excellent reputation for the cuisine prepared by one of the Worlds' Master Chefs. In addition, the restaurant team are very attentive and trained to deliver the very best of service.

There are extensive Conference & Event facilities, a range of Bedrooms to suit any business needs and onsite Car Parking. It is conveniently located just off Junction 15 on the M74, just an hour away from both Glasgow & Edinburgh and forty minutes from Carlisle.

www.auchencastlehotel.co.uk

The Castle of Brecon Hotel

In the heart of the Brecon Beacons

The Castle at Brecon is an hotel of charm and character, built around the walls and tower of Brecon Castle. It is located right in the centre of the Georgian City of Brecon, but still with extensive grounds and beautiful views all around to the Brecon Beacon mountains.

With 30 comfortable bedrooms and an excellent restaurant and bar, this is a fine base for enjoying the Brecon Beacons. Four function rooms (for 10 up to 160) are ideal for weddings, meetings, conferences, dinners and banquets.

The Castle at Brecon
The Castle Square
Brecon
Wales LD3 9DB
Tel. +44 (0)1874 624611
Fax. +44 (0)1874 623737

www.breconcastle.co.uk

Experience Coombe Abbey Hotel

Originally a 12th Century Cistercian Abbey Hotel nestling in England's historic heartland in Warwickshire, Coombe Abbey Hotel has been restored to its former glory. Set within 500 acres of breathtaking parkland, majestically overlooking a moat, the hotel boasts a stunning garden that was designed by Lancelot 'Capability' Brown in 1771.

We invite you to visit and stay at this truly unique and inspirational venue and to complete your experience by booking one of our Special Packages or Events.

Luxurious Accommodation

Coombe Abbey Hotel is home to 83 individually designed bedchambers, each one filled with special touches. Choose from Crown, Feature and Grand Feature bedchambers, including the Lady Craven Suite. The Lady Craven Suite got its name from Elizabeth Craven, widow of Sir William Craven, (Lord Mayor of London from 1610 - 1611, one of the richest men in his day). She purchased Coombe Abbey and the Craven family remained as owners for 300 years.

Special Packages

Explore all that Coombe Abbey Hotel and Warwickshire have to offer during your visit and book a Special Package. Please call or visit our website for latest availability.

'No Ordinary Shakespeare Experience'

Includes an exclusive tour of Shakespeare's houses, a one night stay at Coombe Abbey Hotel and a private dinner where a speaker from the Shakespeare group will share their knowledge, telling tales of Shakespeare and the gunpowder plot and the Coombe Abbey connection.

Become a 'Baron of Coombe'

As a 'Baron of Coombe' you can enjoy a one night stay including dinner, breakfast and champagne. You will also receive exclusive offers and incentives worthy of your new title.

Come live like Lordes and Ladyes at 'Mediaeval Memories'

Includes a one night stay with entry to a Mediaeval Banquet, and one night's dinner in the sumptuous surroundings of the restaurant.

Also at Coombe Abbey Hotel:

Beautiful Weddings, Inspirational Conference Facilities, Corporate Entertainment, Exquisite Fine Dining.

Nearby Facilities:

Coombe Abbey Park, Birmingham NEC, Stratford upon Avon, Coventry Cathedral, Shakespeare Theatre, Warwick Castle.

Events

Coombe Abbey Hotel hosts an array of exciting special events throughout the year. Attend a special Event during your stay and ensure a memorable experience. Please call or visit our website for latest availability.

Mediaeval Banquets

Armed only with a dagger and a bib you will be served four courses of delicious food whilst maids fill your goblets with mead and wine and entertain you with song, and dance. Held most Friday and Saturday evenings.

Murder Mystery Evenings

Step back in time and enjoy watching the murder mystery unfold at our renowned Murder Mystery Dinner.

Christmas and New Year's Eve Events

We have an exciting programme of Christmas and New Year's Eve dinners, party nights, family lunches and banquets for all to enjoy.

The Midlands is rich with places to go, things to do and attractions to visit, and Coombe Abbey Hotel is a perfect base from which to explore all that this exciting region has to offer.

COOMBE ABBEY
no ordinary hotel

Coombe Abbey Hotel Brinklow Road Binley Warwickshire England CV3 2AB
T: + 44 (0) 2476 450 450 E: reservations@coombeabbey.com www.coombeabbey.com

Experience Lumley Castle Hotel

Standing proud for more than 600 years, Lumley Castle Hotel dominates the County Durham landscape. Surrounded by beautiful parklands overlooking the River Wear and Durham County Cricket Ground, Lumley Castle is a magnificent monument to a bygone age of chivalry and honour.

Lumley Castle Hotel takes its name from Sir Ralph Lumley who converted the building in the late 14th Century from the manor house built by his ancestors into the magnificent castle it is today.

We invite you to visit and stay at this historical venue and to complete your experience by booking one of our unique Special Packages or Events.

Luxurious Accommodation
Lumley Castle Hotel is home to 73 individually designed bedchambers, each one filled with special touches. Choose from Courtyard, Castle and Feature bedchambers and the remarkable King James Suite. The King James Suite is located in the chapel of the castle and is where his Royal Highness King James I once slept.

Special Packages
Explore all that Lumley Castle Hotel and the North East have to offer during your visit and book a Special Package. Please call or visit our website for latest availability.

Become a 'Knight of Lumley'
As a Knight of Lumley you can enjoy a one night stay including dinner, breakfast and champagne. You will also receive discount vouchers for future accommodation, dining and banquets at Lumley Castle Hotel.

Come live like Lords and Ladies
Includes a two night stay, one night at an award winning Elizabethan Banquet, and one night's dinner in the sumptuous surroundings of the Black Knight restaurant.

Discover the North East
Includes champagne on arrival, a one or two night stay, one night's dinner in the Black Knight restaurant and entrance tickets to the Beamish Open Air Museum or the award winning Alnwick Gardens.

Also at Lumley Castle Hotel:
Beautiful Weddings, Inspirational Conference Facilities, Corporate Entertainment, Exquisite Fine Dining.

Nearby Facilities:
Chester le Street Golf Club, Durham County Cricket Ground, Durham City & Cathedral, Beamish Museum, Gateshead Metro Centre.

Events
Lumley Castle Hotel hosts an array of exciting special events throughout the year. Attend a special Event during your stay and ensure a memorable experience. Please call or visit our website for latest availability.

Elizabethan Banquets
Step straight into the pages of Elizabethan history and savour a unique atmosphere that has been centuries in the making. A feast of fine food, wine, mead and entertainment awaits. Held most Friday and Saturday evenings.

Murder Mystery Evenings
Can you solve the crime of the last century? Includes a reception drink, three-course dinner and of course, murder!

Christmas and New Year's Eve Events
We have an exciting programme of Christmas and New Year's Eve dinners, party nights, family lunches and banquets for all to enjoy.

Located near to Durham, Newcastle and Sunderland, Lumley Castle Hotel is the perfect location from which to explore the North East of England.

LUMLEY CASTLE
no ordinary hotel

Lumley Castle Hotel Chester-le-Street County Durham England DH3 4NX
T: + 44 (0) 191 389 1111 E: reservations@lumleycastle.com www.lumleycastle.com

LORDS *of the* MANOR

Hidden in a timeless corner of the Cotswolds nestles a haven of tranquility. The Lords of the Manor was originally a 17th century rectory but despite now giving guests the ultimate in luxury and indulgence, this award-winning hotel still retains all the charm and mystery of its former life.

The Lords of the Manor, Upper Slaughter, Gloucestershire GL54 2JD
Tel: 01451 820 243   Fax: 01451 820 696   Email: reservations@lordsofthemanor.com   www.lordsofthemanor.com

*The*FEATHERS

The Feathers, a 17th century Country townhouse hotel in the heart of historic Woodstock, a minute's walk from gates of Blenheim Palace and also an ideal touring base for Stowe Gardens and Waddesdon Manor. Relax in the atmosphere of The Feathers – roaring log fires, an aperitif in the Bistro, a Cognac in the study, a warm friendly and relaxing environment complemented by a highly acclaimed Restaurant serving the finest Modern British food and twenty individually furnished and decorated bedrooms.

The Feathers, Market Street,
Woodstock, Oxfordshire OX20 1SX

Tel: 0845 365 2491
E-mail: enquiries@feathers.co.uk
Web: www.feathers.co.uk

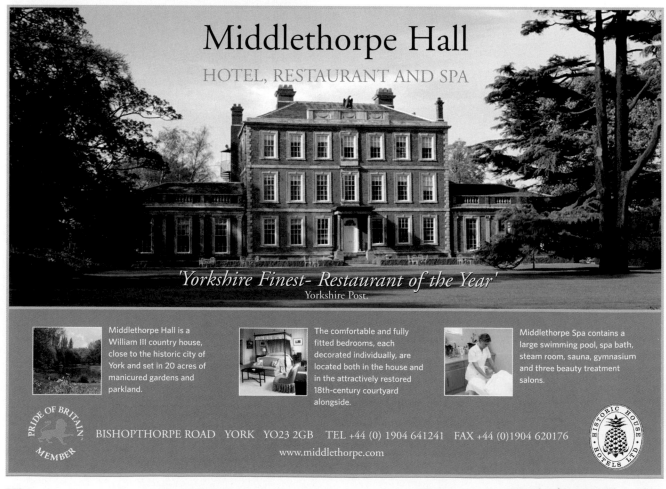

The Old Rectory, Suffolk

The Old Rectory is a listed building dating from the 16th century standing in mainly walled grounds, a feature of which are the rose beds and various mature trees. The house is well situated to explore East Anglia being on the Suffolk/Norfolk border 12 miles from Bury St Edmunds and 8 miles from the market town of Diss. Cambridge, Ipswich and Norwich are within easy reach.

The house is beautifully furnished. Many period features add to the charm of this lovely stylish family home. The luxurious bedrooms have en suite bathrooms.

Sarah is a trained cook and Bobby, who has travelled extensively, offers an interesting and varied wine list. Together they delight in entertaining guests in their beautifully restored home.

Bobby and Sarah Llewellyn
The Old Rectory
Hopton, Suffolk
IP22 2QX

Tel: 01953 688135
Fax: 01953 681686
E-mail: llewellyn.hopton@btinternet.com
Web: www.theoldrectoryhopton.com

Brills Farm, Lincolnshire

Brills Farm enjoys a commanding position on top of one of the few hills in Lincolnshire and is part of a working arable and livestock farm, owned and run by the family. Whilst the décor and furnishings in this restored Georgian house reflect the age of the property, concessions have been made to modern-day living with the welcome addition of central heating!

In this much loved family home, the old sits comfortably with the new in beautifully stylish bedrooms. Spectacular views can be enjoyed from the cosy beds and in individually designed, period-style bathrooms, guests find ultra modern power showers, gleaming baths and plenty of hot water.

Charlie & Sophie White
Brills Farm
Brills Hill
Norton Disney
Lincoln
Lincs LN6 9JN

Tel: 01636 892311
E-mail: admin@brillsfarm-bedandbreakfast.co.uk
Web: www.brillsfarm-bedandbreakfast.co.uk

Church Farm House, Norfolk

The house is a thatched Grade II listed Norfolk farmhouse dating from the mid-16th century, lovingly and sympathetically brought up to modern standards. The mature garden features a rose arbour and a rockery with a waterfall. Guests can enjoy the sun-filled patio, the swing under the old walnut tree, or read by the inglenook fireplace.

Hosts Richard and Georgia Bassett are American music teachers who came to England for a brief stay … over 20 years ago. Their extensive travels influence both décor and cooking at Church Farm House. Recent retirement from teaching allows

more time for gardening, walking with Bella the dog, and the cooking and entertaining they both enjoy.

Richard and Georgia Bassett
Church Farm House
North Lopham
Diss, Norfolk
IP22 2LP

Tel: 01379 687270
Fax: 01379 687270
E-mail: hosts@bassetts.demon.co.uk
Web: www.churchfarmhouse.org

West Farm, Devon

Only 20 paces from the sea West Farm, built in 1600 and Grade II listed, is one of the oldest houses in what is reputedly England's most ancient fishing port. A high wall and unpretentious façade belie the lovely 'secret' garden and luxurious home that lie within. Gail's food and hospitality are of local renown and meals are served 'al fresco' in the beautiful enclosed courtyard, weather permitting. Please bring your own wine.

Appledore, with its long history of fishing, shipbuilding and smuggling is still unspoilt, and a wonderful place to explore. The north Devon coast is an Area of Outstanding Natural Beauty, a

must for walkers and nature lovers. Dartmoor and Exmoor are within easy reach and the Royal North Devon Golf Club is one mile away.

Gail Sparkes
West Farm
Irsha St, Appledore
Nr Bideford
North Devon
EX39 1RY

Tel: 01237 425269
E-mail: westfarm@appledore-devon.co.uk
Web: www.appledore-devon.co.uk

Treverbyn Vean, Cornwall

This listed, neo-Gothic manor house is of great architectural and historical importance. During the war it was acquired by Lord Beaverbrook who met here with Churchill and Montgomery when devising their war plans. The house stands high above the beautiful wooded Glynn valley, enjoying the peace and tranquillity of pine woodlands, bordered by the rivers Fowey and Loveny.

The unique combination of work by architects George Gilbert Scott and William Burges has created a breathtaking and yet fabulously welcoming home. On warm evenings, drinks are served on the long terrace overlooking the woods or in the hall.

Feel totally pampered in large, comfortable, centrally-heated bedrooms with views through leaded windows and glorious en suite bathrooms with Victorian roll top baths and many original features.

Anthony & Carolyn Hindley
The West Wing
Treverbyn Vean Manor
Two Watersfoot, Liskeard, Cornwall
PL14 6HN

Tel : 01579 326105
E-mail: ahindley@mac.com
Web: www.treverbynvean.co.uk

The Old Vicarage, Derbyshire

Step inside this classical Victorian vicarage and you will instantly appreciate its warm and relaxing atmosphere. The central hall, with its original Minton tiles partially covered with antique rugs, boasts galleried stairs and landing. The well proportioned sitting and dining room are tastefully decorated with antiques, original paintings and comfortable soft furnishings. Here, log fires blaze in the marble fireplace during winter months.

Upstairs, the restful bedrooms have lovely aspects – the twin room having pleasant views over the garden and into the valley beyond, and the double looking toward the historic 12th century church, often floodlit at night.

Arranged on three levels, the large garden features a well planted rockery with small shrubs and alpines, extensive lawns and a peaceful summerhouse, which guests are welcome to use.

Pauline & Roger Litchfield
The Old Vicarage, Horsley Road
Horsley, Derbyshire
DE21 5BR

Tel : 01332 880656
E-mail: litchfield@litchfieldr.freeserve.co.uk

Lywood House, Sussex

This Yeoman's home, dating from the 17th century, situated in rolling Sussex countryside is set in its own delightful gardens with excellent views. The house is beautifully decorated and the drawing room and dining room are set aside for the use of guests. There is an attractive swimming pool.

Cleone is a professional cook and delights in trying new recipes. There is plenty to do and see – the gardens of Wakehurst Place(5 mins), Sheffield Park (15 mins) and Nymans (20 mins) being close by. The South of England Showground is on the doorstep.

The historic towns of Lewes and Brighton are within easy driving distance. Excellent rail services from Haywards Heath (met by arrangement) and convenient for Gatwick airport (25 mins). Glyndebourne is only 35 minutes away.

Max & Cleone Pengelley
Lywood House
Ardingly
West Sussex
RH17 6SW

Tel: 01444 892369
Fax: 01444 892291
E-mail: staying@lywoodhouse.com
Web: www.lywoodhouse.com

Higher Huxley Hall, Chester

Descend from the hamlet of Huxley and the Hall emerges across the river valley with a sandstone, cobbled drive lined with a pleached hornbeam hedge, below which lies a carpet of snowdrops, primroses and cowslips in Spring.

Parts of this historical 13th century manor house complement beautiful Elizabethan additions which now dominate, such as the low beams and an exquisite oak staircase leading up to guest 'bedchambers' which are luxurious en-suite rooms, with views out to three castles or towards the purple Welsh Mountains

Extensive gardens boast red breasted geese atop a calm natural pond, a large aviary of exotic Chinese golden pheasants and secluded seats from which to enjoy magnificent views. There is a 40 foot indoor swimming pool open in the Summer months only

Pauline and Jeremy Marks
Higher Huxley Hall
Red Lane, Huxley, Chester
CH3 9BZ

Tel: 01829 781484
E-mail: wl@huxleyhall.co.uk
Web: www.huxleyhall.co.uk

Lawrence House, Yorkshire

Lawrence House is a Georgian Grade II listed house on the edge of the village of Studley Roger, which is two miles from the market and cathedral town of Ripon. Two acres of fine garden adjoins the historic Studley Royal deer park and Fountains Abbey.

The Yorkshire Dales, Harrogate and York are all within easy driving distance. Lawrence House is beautifully furnished with many antiques and fine pictures, and in the winter months the house is filled with roaring log fires. The bedrooms, with views over open countryside are spacious and beautifully furnished. The bathrooms are pretty and luxurious.

John has been in the wine trade for many years. Harriet has had her own interior decorating business. She enjoys producing delicious and interesting dinners.

John & Harriet Highley
Lawrence House
Studley Roger
Ripon
North Yorkshire
HG4 3AY

Tel: 01765 600947
Fax: 01765 609297
E-mail: john@lawrence-house.co.uk
Web: www.lawrence-house.co.uk

Woodhayes, Devon

Woodhayes has a commanding view of the Otter Valley which Daniel Defoe once noted to be 'The finest landscape in the world'. This small estate, providing enjoyable walks, includes 150 acres of wood and pasture land and an acre of carefully tended garden. Honiton, only a mile away, is a thriving market town and centre for antiques and has excellent shops.

The setting is idyllic for this classical listed Georgian house with superb views from all the windows. The farm and vegetable garden provide much of the produce which Christy, a talented and imaginative cook, converts into the most delicious cuisine,

eaten with your hosts in the pre-18th century dining room hung with family portraits. The family's history is evident everywhere in this friendly house.

Noel and Christy Page-Turner
Woodhayes
Honiton
Devon
EX14 4TP

Tel: 01404 42011
Fax: 01404 42011
E-mail: cmpt@inweb.co.uk

Great Weddington, Kent

Two ancient, Oriental plane trees stand guard at the entrance to the drive and a majestic Holm Oak dominates the lawn at Great Weddington, a Regency Grade II listed country house, built around 1835, sitting in spendour in a beautiful English country garden.

Kate and Neil love welcoming guests to their home. Trained at Constance Spry, Kate is one of the resident flower arrangers at Canterbury Cathedral and is also a keen gardener Neil, after many years in the steel industry, runs his own business – a mail order Audio Book Library.

He also plays golf at Sandwich and tries to improve his bridge during the winter.

Kate and Neil Gunn
Great Weddington
Ash
Canterbury
Kent
CT3 2AR

Tel: 01304 813407 or 01304 812531
Fax: 01304 812531
E-mail: traveltale@aol.com
Web: www.greatweddington.co.uk

Sirelands, Cumbria

Situated in a quiet unsung corner of Cumbria, Sirelands is a beautiful sheltered and peaceful Cumbrian cottage dating from about 1730, overlooking the North Pennines, yet only 10 minutes from the nearest M6 junction at Carlisle.

Guests enjoy this relaxing home with home baked afternoon tea, served in front of the open fire or in the summerhouse, depending on the season. The drawing room and guest rooms are decorated in a traditional style and have views of the secluded two acre garden with a tranquil pond and stream, which is home to rare red squirrels and brimming with rhododendrons in late Spring.

David and Angela have farmed here since 1962 and have derived enormous pleasure from developing Sirelands and entertaining guests there.

David and Angela Carr
Sirelands
Heads Nook
Brampton
Cumbria
CA8 9BT

Tel: 01228 670389
E-mail: carr_sirelands@btinternet.com

Indexes

Plant Sales — 554

Properties and gardens offering collections of rare and unusual plants not generally available.

Corporate Hospitality — 557

Properties able to accommodate corporate functions, wedding receptions and events.

Education — 561

Properties providing facilities for schools / educational groups.

Accommodation — 566

Historic properties which offer accommodation - from basic comfort to ultimate luxury.

Civil Wedding Venues — 568

Places where the ceremony itself can take place and may also provide facilities for reception.

Open All Year — 571

Properties and/or their grounds included in this list are open for all or most of the year.

Special Events — 577

Historical re-enactments, festivals, country & craft fairs, concerts, fireworks, car & steam rallies.

RHS Partner Gardens — 584

Properties in Hudsons that offer free garden access at specified times to RHS Members

Plant Sales

Properties where plants are offered for sale.

ENGLAND

LONDON

SOUTH EAST

SOUTH WEST

EASTERN REGION

EAST MIDLANDS

WEST MIDLANDS

YORKSHIRE & THE HUMBER

Bourton House Garden, Gloucestershire

Corporate Hospitality

Properties which are able to accommodate corporate functions, wedding receptions and events. Some properties specialise in corporate hospitality and are open, only rarely, if ever, to day visitors. Others do both. See entry for details.

ENGLAND

LONDON

SOUTH EAST

SCOTLAND

WALES

NORTH WALES

SOUTH WALES

NORTHERN IRELAND

Beaulieu, Hampshire

Education

The properties listed below provide special facilities for schools' groups. The range of these services varies, so it is vital that you contact the property directly when preparing to arrange a school trip. English Heritage offers free admission for pre-booked educational groups. For a free teacher's information pack: e-mail: education@english-heritage.org.uk or visit the website www.english-heritage.org.uk/education

ENGLAND

LONDON

SOUTH EAST

EAST MIDLANDS

WEST MIDLANDS

YORKSHIRE & THE HUMBER

WALES

NORTH WALES

SOUTH WALES

NORTHERN IRELAND

© Ripon Museums

Accommodation

Accommodation for individuals in historic hotels or Wolsey Lodges (private homes) is listed on page 543. The historic properties listed below are not hotels. Their inclusion indicates that accommodation can be arranged, often for groups only. The type and standard of rooms offered vary widely – from the luxurious to the utilitarian. Full details can be obtained from each individual property.

ENGLAND

SOUTH EAST

SOUTH WEST

EASTERN REGION

EAST MIDLANDS

WEST MIDLANDS

Weston Park, Shropshire

The Blue Room at Traquair, Borders

visit hudsons guide online

An English Heritage cottage interior

Civil Wedding Venues

Places at which the marriage or Civil partnership ceremonies can take place – many will also be able to provide facilities for wedding receptions.

Full details about each property are available in the regional listings. There are numerous other properties included within *Hudson's* which do not have a Civil Wedding Licence but which can accommodate wedding receptions. In Scotland religious wedding ceremonies can take place anywhere, subject to the Minister being prepared to perform them.

ENGLAND

LONDON

SOUTH EAST

SOUTH WEST

Caverswall Castle, Staffordshire
©Perrot Photography

Open All Year

Properties included in this list are open to some extent for all or most of the year.
See individual entries for details.

ENGLAND

LONDON

SOUTH EAST

SOUTH WEST

YORKSHIRE & THE HUMBER

NORTH WEST

NORTH EAST

SCOTLAND

WALES

NORTH WALES

SOUTH WALES

NORTHERN IRELAND

Exbury Gardens, Hampshire

visit hudsons guide online

Special Events

This is merely a selection of special events being staged in 2008 – more information can be obtained from individual property websites – for quick access to these sites visit: www.hudsonsguide.co.uk

FEBRUARY

9–17

Blenheim Palace, Oxfordshire
Living History Interpretation.

29

Saint Hill Manor, Sussex
Group Visits Fair.

29

Wilton House, Wiltshire
Annual Antiques Fair.

MARCH

1–2

Wilton House, Wiltshire
Annual Antiques Fair.

9

Boconnoc, Cornwall
Wedding Fair.

16

Boconnoc, Cornwall
The Regis Classic Tour.

21–24

Blenheim Palace, Oxfordshire
Great Blenheim Palace Easter Egg
Challenge.

21–24

Groombridge Place Gardens, Kent
Easter Eggstravaganza.

23

Traquair, Borders
Easter Egg Extravaganza.

23–24

Holdenby House, Northamptonshire
Victorian Easter.

23–24

Lamport Hall, Northamptonshire
Antiques & Collectors Fair.

23–24

Rockingham Castle, Northamptonshire
Easter Egg Hunt, Family Fun Quiz and
'Animal Hunt'.

24

Chenies Manor House,
Buckinghamshire
Easter Fun for Children.

APRIL

5–6

Boconnoc, Cornwall
Cornwall Garden Society Spring Flower
Show.

6

Arley Hall & Gardens, Cheshire
Spring Plant Fair.

Groombridge Place Gardens, Kent

13–30

Hole Park Gardens, Kent
Bluebell Spectacular.

19–20

Arley Hall & Gardens, Cheshire
Bluebell Walks.

25–30

Pashley Manor Gardens, Sussex
Tulip Festival.

26

Salisbury Cathedral, Wiltshire
Cathedral Open Day, including free
entry to Salisbury & South Wiltshire
Museum, The Rifles Museum, and the
garden of Mompesson House.

26–27

Arley Hall & Gardens, Cheshire
Bluebell Walks.

27

Beaulieu, Hampshire
Boatjumble & Boatworld.

MAY

1–5

Pashley Manor Gardens, Sussex
Tulip Festival.

1–11

Hole Park Gardens, Kent
Bluebell Spectacular.

4

Athelhampton House & Gardens,
Dorset
NCCPG Plant Sale.

4–5

Salisbury Cathedral, Wiltshire
Medieval Fair.

5

Chenies Manor House,
Buckinghamshire
Tulip Festival.

5–7

Rockingham Castle, Northamptonshire
Call to Arms History Fair.

8–11

Hatfield House, Hertfordshire
Living Crafts.

14–15

Boconnoc, Cornwall
Boconnoc Spring Fair.

17

Salisbury Cathedral, Wiltshire
Elgar's "Dream of Gerontius" – Berlin
Philharmonic Choir, Salisbury Musical
Society, Chelsea Opera Group
Orchestra.

17–18

Arley Hall & Gardens, Cheshire
Arley Horse Trials & Country Fair.

17–18

Beaulieu, Hampshire
Spring Motormart & Autojumble.

17–29

Pashley Manor Gardens, Sussex
Sculpture Fortnight.

'Mr Bennet's Daughter' by Philip Jackson, Pashley Manor, Sussex
©Ray Pearson

24

Blair Castle, Perthshire/Fife
Atholl Highlanders' Parade.

24–25

Boconnoc, Cornwall
Endurance Ride.

24–25

Traquair, Borders
Medieval Fayre.

25

Helmingham Hall Gardens, Suffolk
NCCPG Plant Sale, 10.30am-4pm.

25–26

Lamport Hall, Northamptonshire
Steam and Country Festival.

26

Chenies Manor House,
Buckinghamshire
Special Entertainment.

30

Holker Hall & Gardens, Cumbria
Holker Festival.

JUNE

1

Holker Hall & Gardens, Cumbria
Holker Festival.

1

Stonor, Oxfordshire
VW Owners' Rally.

1

Traquair, Borders
St Ronan's Tattoo.

5-8

Bramham Park, Yorkshire
Bramham International Horse Trials.

5–8

Ripley Castle, Yorkshire
Grand Summer Sale.

7–8

Blenheim Palace, Oxfordshire
The Blenheim Triathlon.

7–8

Cawdor Castle, Highlands & Skye
Special Gardens Weekend: guided tours
of the gardens.

8

Norton Conyers, Yorkshire
Garden open for NGS.

8

Rockingham Castle, Northamptonshire
Jousting & Medieval Living History
Village.

8–12

Athelhampton House & Gardens,
Dorset
Flower Festival.

14–15

Pashley Manor Gardens, Sussex
Special Rose Weekend.

14–15

Rockingham Castle, Northamptonshire
People, Pets & Family Fun Day.

15

Norton Conyers, Yorkshire
Garden open for Amnesty International.

17–21

Salisbury Cathedral, Wiltshire
Flower Festival.

Exbury Gardens & Steam Railway, Hampshire

17–30

Ripley Castle, Yorkshire
"Twelfth Night".

20–22

Lamport Hall & Gardens,
Northamptonshire
Live music and theatre in the gardens.

21–22

Hatfield House, Hertfordshire
Rose Weekend.

22

Saint Hill Manor, Sussex
Open Air Theatre.

28–29

Arley Hall & Gardens, Cheshire
Arley Garden Festival.

28–29

Beaulieu, Hampshire
Motorcycle World.

28–29

Benington Lordship Gardens,
Hertfordshire
Floral Festival, 12 noon-6pm.

JULY

1–13

Ripley Castle, Yorkshire
"Twelfth Night".

3–4

Peckover House & Garden,
Cambridgeshire
Wisbech Rose Fair.

5

Salisbury Cathedral, Wiltshire
A Vaughan Williams concert – Salisbury
Musical Society, Salisbury Symphony
Orchestra.

6

Rockingham Castle, Northamptonshire
Falconry & Owl Day.

12

Wilton House, Wiltshire
BSO Fireworks Concert.

12–13

Leonardslee Lakes & Gardens, Sussex
Craft Show.

13

Cobham Hall, Kent
Ellenor Foundation Charity Walk.

18–20

Boconnoc, Cornwall
Boconnoc Steam Fair.

19

Blenheim Palace, Oxfordshire
Battle Proms Concert (evening event).

19

Ripley Castle, Yorkshire
Last Night of the Proms.

Historical Re-enactment ©English Heritage Photo Library

19–20

Leonardslee Lakes & Gardens, Sussex
Model Boat Regatta.

20

Chenies Manor House,
Buckinghamshire
Plant & Garden Fair (the Manor opens
at 2pm). Rare and exceptional plants,
topiary and trees from specialist
nurseries. Gardening advice, sculpture
and garden furniture.

20

Groombridge Place Gardens, Kent
Wings, Wheels and Steam.

25–27

Blenheim Palace, Oxfordshire
The CLA Game Fair.

25–27

Lamport Hall & Gardens,
Northamptonshire
Live music and theatre in the gardens.

26

Hatfield House, Hertfordshire
Battle Proms Concert.

29

Hopetoun House, Edinburgh City, Coast
& Countryside
Summer Fair.

AUGUST

1

Stonor, Oxfordshire
Jazz Concert in the Park.

1–3

Hatfield House, Hertfordshire
Art in Clay.

1–3

Newby Hall & Gardens, Yorkshire
Globe Theatre.

1–3

Pashley Manor Gardens, Sussex
Lily Weekend.

2

Stonor, Oxfordshire
Classic Concert in the Park.

2–3

Traquair, Borders
Traquair Fair.

3

Groombridge Place Gardens, Kent
Hot Air Balloons and Ferraris.

3

Helmingham Hall Gardens, Suffolk
Festival of Classic & Sports Cars,
10am–5pm.

7

Athelhampton House & Gardens,
Dorset
Outdoor Theatre, "Tess of the
d'Urbervilles".

Skipton Castle, Yorkshire

7

Cobham Hall, Kent
Summer Stroll at 7pm (guidebook tour and glass of wine, £5pp – please telephone to book).

7–10

Rockingham Castle, Northamptonshire
Steam & Country Show in the Park.

10

Athelhampton House & Gardens, Dorset
MG Owners Day.

15–17

Hatfield House, Hertfordshire
Hatfield House Country Show.

16–17

Leonardslee Lakes & Gardens, Sussex
Model Boat Regatta.

22–24

Bramham Park, Yorkshire
Leeds Festival.

22–25

Stonor, Oxfordshire
Chilterns Craft Fair.

23–25

Blenheim Palace, Oxfordshire
Living Heritage Craft Fair.

24–25

Benington Lordship Gardens, Hertfordshire
Chilli Festival, 10am-5pm.

24–25

Holdenby House, Northamptonshire
Holdenby Food Show.

24–25

Lamport Hall, Northamptonshire
Antiques & Collectors Fair.

24–25

Rockingham Castle, Northamptonshire
Vikings! Of Middle England.

25

Athelhampton House & Gardens, Dorset
Village Fete.

25

Chenies Manor House, Buckinghamshire
Special Entertainment.

SEPTEMBER

11–14

Blenheim Palace, Oxfordshire
Blenheim International Horse Trials (different admission prices apply).

13–14

Beaulieu, Hampshire
International Autojumble.

14

Rockingham Castle, Northamptonshire
Kites Day.

27

Cawdor Castle, Highlands & Skye
Living Food at Cawdor Castle – a celebration of organic food.

OCTOBER

5

Hole Park Gardens, Kent
Meet the Gardener, 2.30pm.

7

Boconnoc, Cornwall
Red Cross Lecture & Demonstration.

Kite Festival at Raby Castle, Co Durham

11–12

Lamport Hall & Gardens,
Northamptonshire
Gift and Craft Fair.

12

Hole Park Gardens, Kent
Meet the Gardener, 2.30pm.

16–26

Blenheim Palace, Oxfordshire
Living History Interpretation.

19

Hole Park Gardens, Kent
Meet the Gardener, 2.30pm.

24–26

Traquair, Borders
Halloween Experience.

25

Beaulieu, Hampshire
Fireworks Spectacular.

25–26

Arley Hall & Gardens, Cheshire
Pumpkin Olympics.

31

Groombridge Place Gardens, Kent
Halloween in the Spooky Gardens.

NOVEMBER

1

Groombridge Place Gardens, Kent
Halloween in the Spooky Gardens.

8

Groombridge Place Gardens, Kent
Spectacular Fireworks to Music.

8–30

Blenheim Palace, Oxfordshire
'Christmas at Blenheim Palace'.

17–21

Rockingham Castle, Northamptonshire
Christmas at Rockingham Castle.

23–25

Hopetoun House, Edinburgh City, Coast
& Countryside
Christmas Fair.

26–29

Belvoir Castle, Leicestershire & Rutland
Belvoir by Candlelight.

29–30

Arley Hall & Gardens, Cheshire
Christmas Floral Extravaganza.

29–30

Traquair, Borders
Christmas Opening.

DECEMBER

1–7

Arley Hall & Gardens, Cheshire
Christmas Floral Extravaganza.

1–7

Blenheim Palace, Oxfordshire
'Christmas at Blenheim Palace'.

Fantastic Fireworks at Highclere Castle and Gardens, Hampshire

RHS Partner Gardens

Properties in Hudsons that offer free garden access at specified times to RHS Members

York Gate Garden

GARDEN	FREE ACCESS DATES FOR 2007
Abbotsbury Subtropical Gardens	Oct - Feb
Aberglasney Gardens	Jan-Mar and 8-31 Dec
Anglesey Abbey Gardens	When open (gardens only)
Arley Hall & Gardens	Apr-May & Sept-Oct (gardens only and not special event days)
Bedgebury National Pinetum	Mon-Fri when open (not weekends and Bank Holidays)
Belvoir Castle	Apr-Jul, Mon-Sat (excluding Mons and Bank Holidays)
Benington Lordship Gardens	2-10 Feb and May Bank Holiday (Sun 2-5pm, Mon 12-5pm)
Bicton Park Botanical Gardens	Jan-Feb & Nov (excl. train rides)
Blenheim Palace Park & Gardens	16 Feb - 23 May (excl. Easter) & 1 Oct – 14 Dec (gardens only)
Bodnant Garden	When open
Branklyn Gardens	When open
Broadleas Gardens	When open (excluding NGS days)
Burton Agnes Hall	When open
Cae Hir Gardens	When open
Caerhays Castle Garden	18 Feb - 16 Mar
Cambo Gardens	Jan, Mar-Jun and Sept-Dec
Cawdor Castle & Gardens	May - Jun & Sept - Oct (gardens only)
Cholmondeley Castle Garden	June
Corsham Court Gardens	When open (gardens only) excl. NGS days 6 Apr and 8 Jun
Cottesbrooke Hall & Gardens	When open (gardens only) excl. special event days.
Coughton Court	When open (gardens only) excl. special event days.
Dalemain	1-30 Apr, 1-30 Sept and 1-20 Oct (gardens only)
Docton Mill & Garden	Saturdays 1 Mar - 31 Oct inclusive
Doddington Hall	When open
The Dorothy Clive Garden	Jul - Aug
Drummond Castle	May, Sept and Oct
Duncombe Park	When open (not special event days)
Dunrobin Castle Gardens	When open
Dyffryn Gardens	When open (except special event days)
East Bergholt Place Garden	When open (except Sundays)
Elton Hall	May-Jul (gardens only)
Exbury Gardens	8-31 Mar and Sept
Fairhaven Woodland & Water Garden	Feb - Apr & Oct
Floors Castle Gardens	When open (gardens only)
Forde Abbey & Gardens	Jan-Feb & Oct - Feb (gardens only)
Furzey Gardens	Mar - Oct
Glen Chantry	Every Saturday when open (excl. group visits)
Glenwhan Garden	Aug-Sept and 1-30 Oct by appointment
Goodnestone Park Gardens	Apr - May & Sept (gardens only, not special event days)
Grimsthorpe Castle	Apr, May & Sept
Harewood House	Mar - 30 Jun (excl. special event days and bank holidays)
Harmony Garden	When open
Hatfield House & Gardens	When open (except major event days)
Hergest Croft	1 Mar- 30 Apr and 1 Jul-30 Sept
Hestercombe Gardens	Oct – Mar inclusive
Hill of Tarvit Mansionhouse & Garden	When open (gardens only)

Parham House & Gardens

Holker Hall & Gardens

Hestercombe Gardens

Royal Horticultural Society

Holker Hall & Gardens	When open (gardens only) excl. special event days
Houghton Hall	June (gardens only)
Kellie Castle & Garden	When open
Kelmarsh Hall	When open (except special event days)
Kingston Maurward Garden	When open (except special event days)
Leith Hall and Garden	When open
Loseley Park	May & Sept (garden only) except NGS days, 6 May & 2 Sept
Mannington Gardens	When open (gardens only, not special event days)
Mapperton Gardens	When open
Muncaster Castle Garden	1 Jul - 2 Nov
National Botanic Garden of Wales, The	Jan - Mar & Oct - Dec
Newby Hall & Gardens	Apr, May & Sept (gardens only, not special event days)
Nymans	When open
Painswick Rococo Garden	When open
Parcevall Hall Gardens	Apr- May
Parham House and Gardens	When open (except 12-13 Jul for special event)
Penshurst Place & Gardens	When open
Picton Castle	Apr – Sept, gardens only (except special event days)
Plas Brondanw Gardens	When open
Portmeirion	When open
Raby Castle	When open
Ragley Hall	When open (gardens only, not special event days)
Renishaw Hall	When open (except special event days)
Ripley Castle	When open (not special event days)
Rode Hall	When open
Ryton Organic Gardens	When open (except special event days)
Sandringham	When open (gardens only)
Sausmarez Manor	First week of every month when open
Scone Palace & Grounds	When open
Seaforde Gardens	Apr - Jun (gardens only)
Sheffield Park Garden	When open (not special event days)
Syon Park	When open (gardens only, not special event days)
Tapeley Park	8 Jun - 8 Jul
Tatton Park	When open (gardens only)
Thorp Perrow Arboretum	Mon - Fri when open (not BHs and special event days)
Threave Garden & Estate	Apr - May & Sept - Oct
Torosay Castle & Gardens	When open
Trebah Garden	1 Jan- 31 Mar and 1 Nov- 31 Jan '09
Trewithen Gardens	Jul - Sept
Waddesdon Manor	Mar & Sept - Oct
Wentworth Castle Gardens	When open (not special event days)
West Dean	Jan-Mar and Nov-Dec (except special event days)
Westonbirt Arboretum	When open except 18-25 Aug and 1-31 Oct
Wilton House	When open
Wollerton Old Hall Garden	Mar-Apr & Sept
Wyken Hall Gardens	When open
Yalding Organic Gardens	When open
York Gate Garden	Apr-May and Sept

York Gate Garden

The RHS, the UK's leading gardening charity

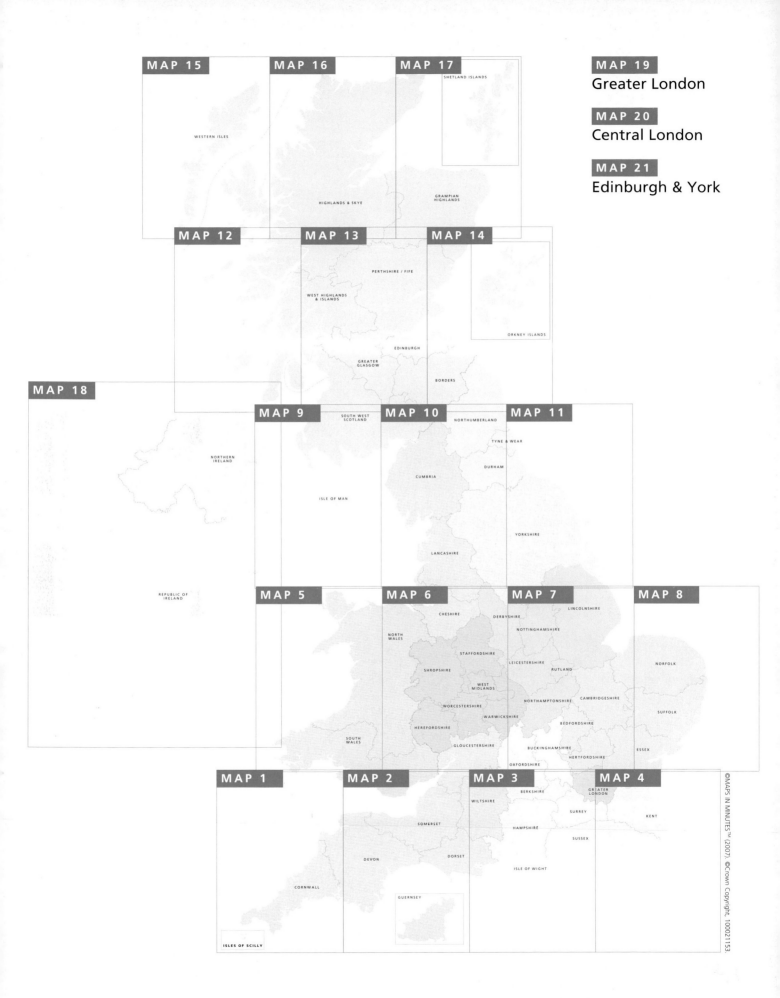

MAP 15

MAP 16

MAP 17

SHETLAND ISLANDS

MAP 19
Greater London

MAP 20
Central London

MAP 21
Edinburgh & York

WESTERN ISLES

GRAMPIAN
HIGHLANDS

HIGHLANDS & SKYE

MAP 12

MAP 13

MAP 14

PERTHSHIRE / FIFE

WEST HIGHLANDS
& ISLANDS

ORKNEY ISLANDS

EDINBURGH

GREATER
GLASGOW

BORDERS

MAP 18

MAP 9

SOUTH WEST
SCOTLAND

MAP 10

NORTHUMBERLAND

MAP 11

TYNE & WEAR

NORTHERN
IRELAND

DURHAM

CUMBRIA

ISLE OF MAN

YORKSHIRE

REPUBLIC OF
IRELAND

LANCASHIRE

MAP 5

MAP 6

CHESHIRE

DERBYSHIRE

MAP 7

LINCOLNSHIRE

MAP 8

NOTTINGHAMSHIRE

NORTH
WALES

STAFFORDSHIRE

LEICESTERSHIRE

NORFOLK

SHROPSHIRE

RUTLAND

WEST
MIDLANDS

CAMBRIDGESHIRE

NORTHAMPTONSHIRE

SUFFOLK

WORCESTERSHIRE

WARWICKSHIRE

BEDFORDSHIRE

HEREFORDSHIRE

BUCKINGHAMSHIRE

ESSEX

SOUTH
WALES

GLOUCESTERSHIRE

HERTFORDSHIRE

OXFORDSHIRE

MAP 1

MAP 2

MAP 3

BERKSHIRE

MAP 4

GREATER
LONDON

WILTSHIRE

SURREY

KENT

SOMERSET

HAMPSHIRE

SUSSEX

DEVON

DORSET

CORNWALL

ISLE OF WIGHT

GUERNSEY

ISLES OF SCILLY

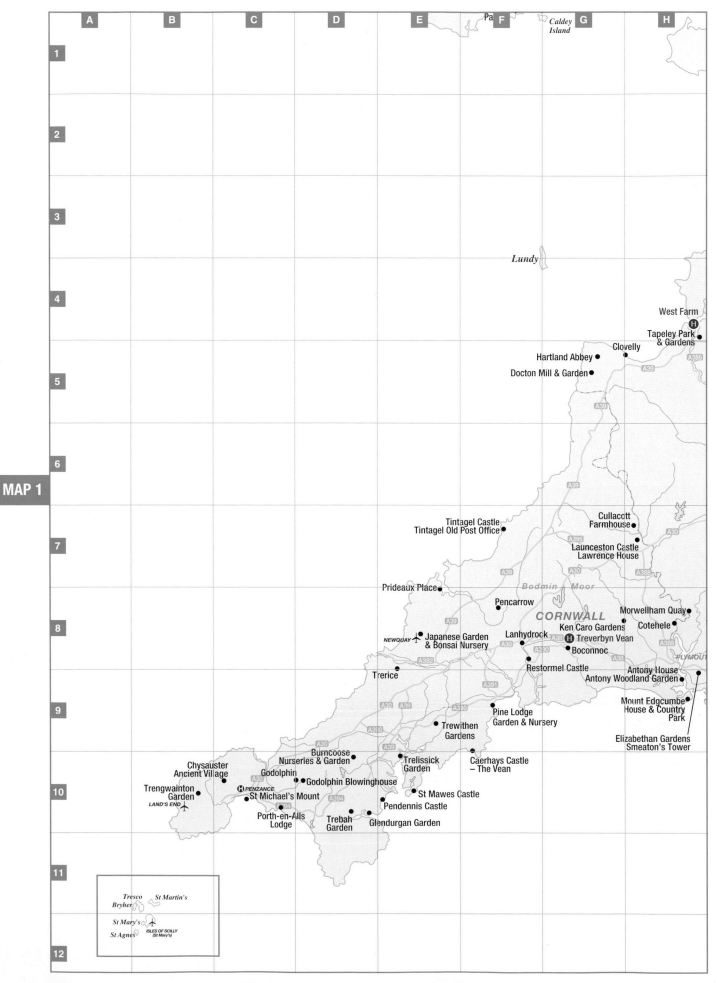

MAP 1

Pa... Caldey Island

Lundy

A B C D E F G H

1
2
3
4
5
6
7
8
9
10
11
12

West Farm
Tapeley Park & Gardens
Clovelly
Hartland Abbey •
Docton Mill & Garden •

Tintagel Castle
Tintagel Old Post Office •

Cullacott Farmhouse •

Launceston Castle
Lawrence House

Bodmin Moor

Prideaux Place •

Pencarrow •

CORNWALL

Morwellham Quay •
Cotehele •

NEWQUAY
Japanese Garden & Bonsai Nursery •
Lanhydrock •
Ken Caro Gardens •
Treverbyn Vean
Boconnoc •

Trerice •

Restormel Castle •

Antony House
Antony Woodland Garden

Pine Lodge Garden & Nursery •

Mount Edgcumbe House & Country Park

Trewithen Gardens •

Elizabethan Gardens
Smeaton's Tower

Burncoose Nurseries & Garden •

Trelissick Garden •

Caerhays Castle – The Vean •

Chysauster Ancient Village •

Godolphin •

Godolphin Blowinghouse •

Trengwainton Garden •

PENZANCE
St Michael's Mount •

LAND'S END

St Mawes Castle •
Pendennis Castle •

Porth-en-Alls Lodge •

Trebah Garden •

Glendurgan Garden •

Tresco
Bryher
St Martin's
St Mary's
St Agnes
ISLES OF SCILLY (St Mary's)

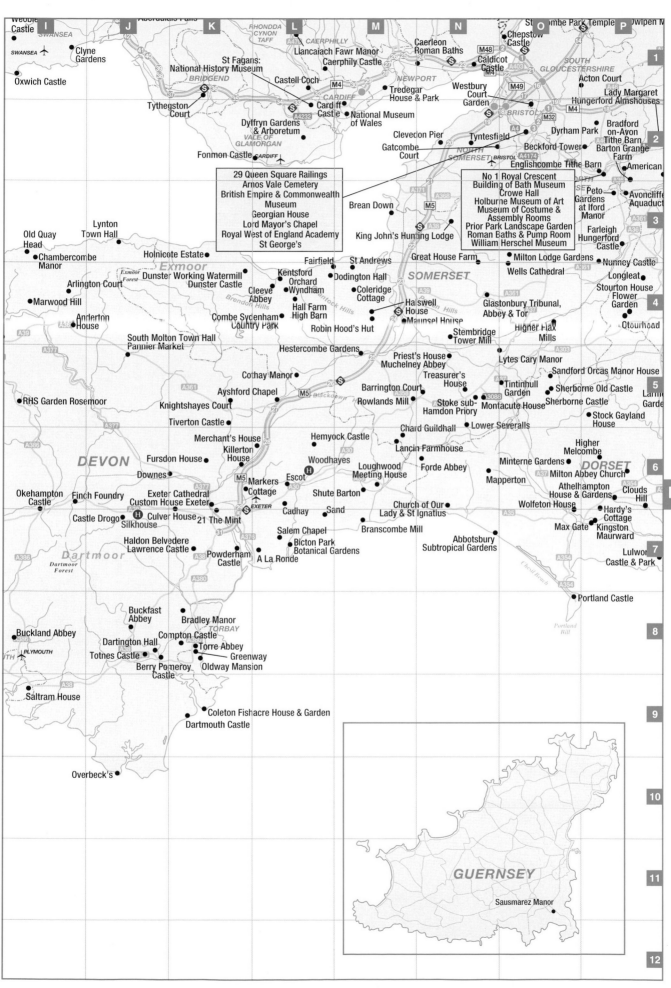

Weoble
Castle

I

SWANSEA ✈

SWANSEA

Clyne
Gardens

Oxwich Castle

Aberdulais Falls

J

K

St Fagans:
National History Museum

BRIDGEND

Castell Coch

Tythegston
Court

Dyffryn Gardens
& Arboretum

VALE OF
GLAMORGAN

Fonmon Castle

RHONDDA
CYNON
TAFF

CAERPHILLY

Llancaiach Fawr Manor

Caerphily Castle

M4

CARDIFF

Cardiff
Castle

A4232

National Museum
of Wales

Tredegar
House & Park

L

M

Caerleon
Roman Baths

NEWPORT

Westbury
Court
Garden

Clevedon Pier

Gatcombe
Court

NORTH
SOMERSET

N

M48

Caldicot
Castle

M4

M49

BRISTOL

M32

BRISTOL ✈

St

Chepstow
Castle

O

SOUTH
GLOUCESTERSHIRE

Acton Court

Dyrham Park

Beckford Tower

Combe Park Temple

P

wlpen M

Lady Margaret
Hungerford Almshouses

Bradford
on-Avon
Tithe Barn

Barton Grange
Farm

American

Englishcombe Tithe Barn

1

2

29 Queen Square Railings
Arnos Vale Cemetery
British Empire & Commonwealth
Museum
Georgian House
Lord Mayor's Chapel
Royal West of England Academy
St George's

Brean Down

King John's Hunting Lodge

No 1 Royal Crescent
Building of Bath Museum
Crowe Hall
Holburne Museum of Art
Museum of Costume &
Assembly Rooms
Prior Park Landscape Garden
Roman Baths & Pump Room
William Herschel Museum

Peto
Gardens
at Iford
Manor

Avoncliffe
Aqueduct

Farleigh
Hungerford
Castle

3

Old Quay
Head

Lynton
Town Hall

Chambercombe
Manor

Arlington Court

Marwood Hill

Anderton
House

RHS Garden Rosemoor

Holnicote Estate

Exmoor
Forest

Dunster Working Watermill
Dunster Castle

Cleeve
Abbey

Combe Sydenham
Country Park

South Molton Town Hall
Pannier Market

Kentsford
Orchard
Wyndham

Hall Farm
High Barn

Exmoor

Fairfield

Dodington Hall

St Andrews

Coleridge
Cottage

Halswell
House

Robin Hood's Hut

Hestercombe Gardens

Great House Farm

SOMERSET

Maunsel House

A39

Milton Lodge Gardens

Wells Cathedral

Glastonbury Tribunal,
Abbey & Tor

Stembridge
Tower Mill

Higher Flax
Mills

Nunney Castle

Longleat

Stourton House
Flower
Garden

Otourhoad

4

Cothay Manor

Ayshford Chapel

Knightshayes Court

Tiverton Castle

M5

Blackdown

Barrington Court

Rowlands Mill

Priest's House
Muchelney Abbey

Treasurer's
House

Stoke sub-
Hamdon Priory

Montacute House

Tintinhull
Garden

Sherborne Old Castle

Sherborne Castle

Lytes Cary Manor

Sandford Orcas Manor House

Stock Gayland
House

Larri
Gard

5

DEVON

Merchant's House

Killerton
House

Fursdon House

Downes

Okehampton
Castle

Finch Foundry

Castle Drogo

Silkhouse

Haldon Belvedere
Lawrence Castle

Dartmoor
Forest

Dartmoor

A386

Hemyock Castle

Woodhayes

Escot

Markers
Cottage

Exeter Cathedral
Custom House Exeter

Culver House

21 The Mint

EXETER

Cadhay

Salem Chapel

Bicton Park
Botanical Gardens

Powderham
Castle

A La Ronde

Shute Barton

Sand

Loughwood
Meeting House

Forde Abbey

Church of Our
Lady & St Ignatius

Branscombe Mill

Lancin Farmhouse

Lower Severalls

Chard Guildhall

Mapperton

Minterne Gardens

Higher
Melcombe

Milton Abbey Church

Athelhampton
House & Gardens

Wolfeton House

DORSET

Clouds
Hill

Hardy's
Cottage

Abbotsbury
Subtropical Gardens

Max Gate

Kingston
Maurward

Lulwor
Castle & Park

6

7

Ched Reach

Portland Castle

Buckfast
Abbey

Buckland Abbey

PLYMOUTH

Dartington Hall

Totnes Castle

Berry Pomeroy
Castle

Bradley Manor

TORBAY

Compton Castle

Torre Abbey

Greenway

Oldway Mansion

Portland
Bill

8

Saltram House

Coleton Fishacre House & Garden

Dartmouth Castle

9

Overbeck's

GUERNSEY

Sausmarez Manor

10

11

MAP 2

12

589

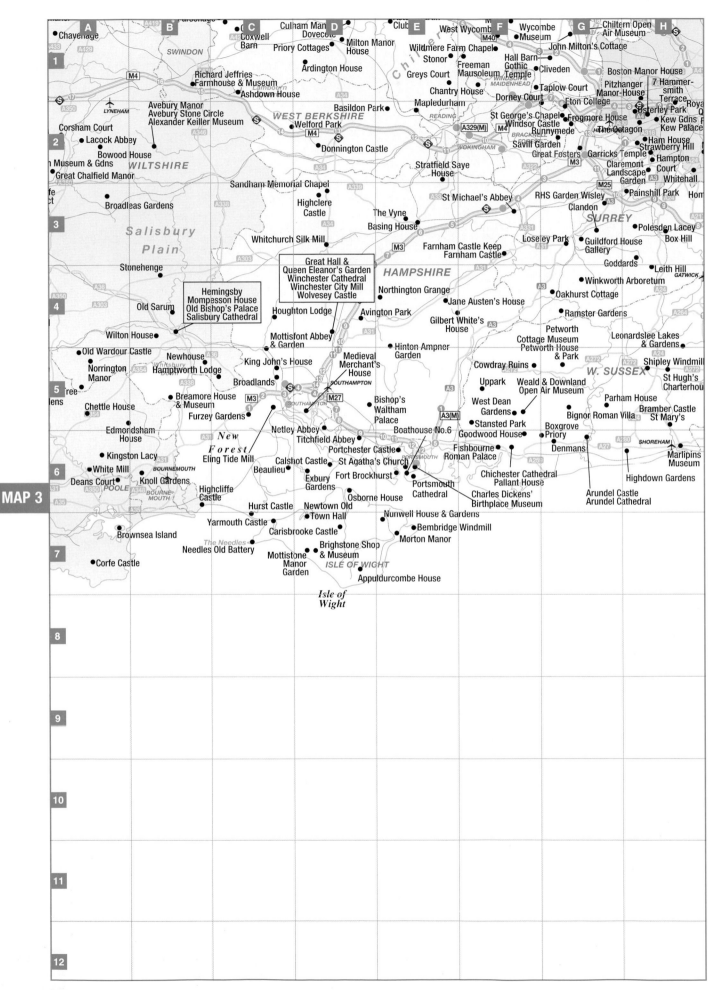

MAP 3

590

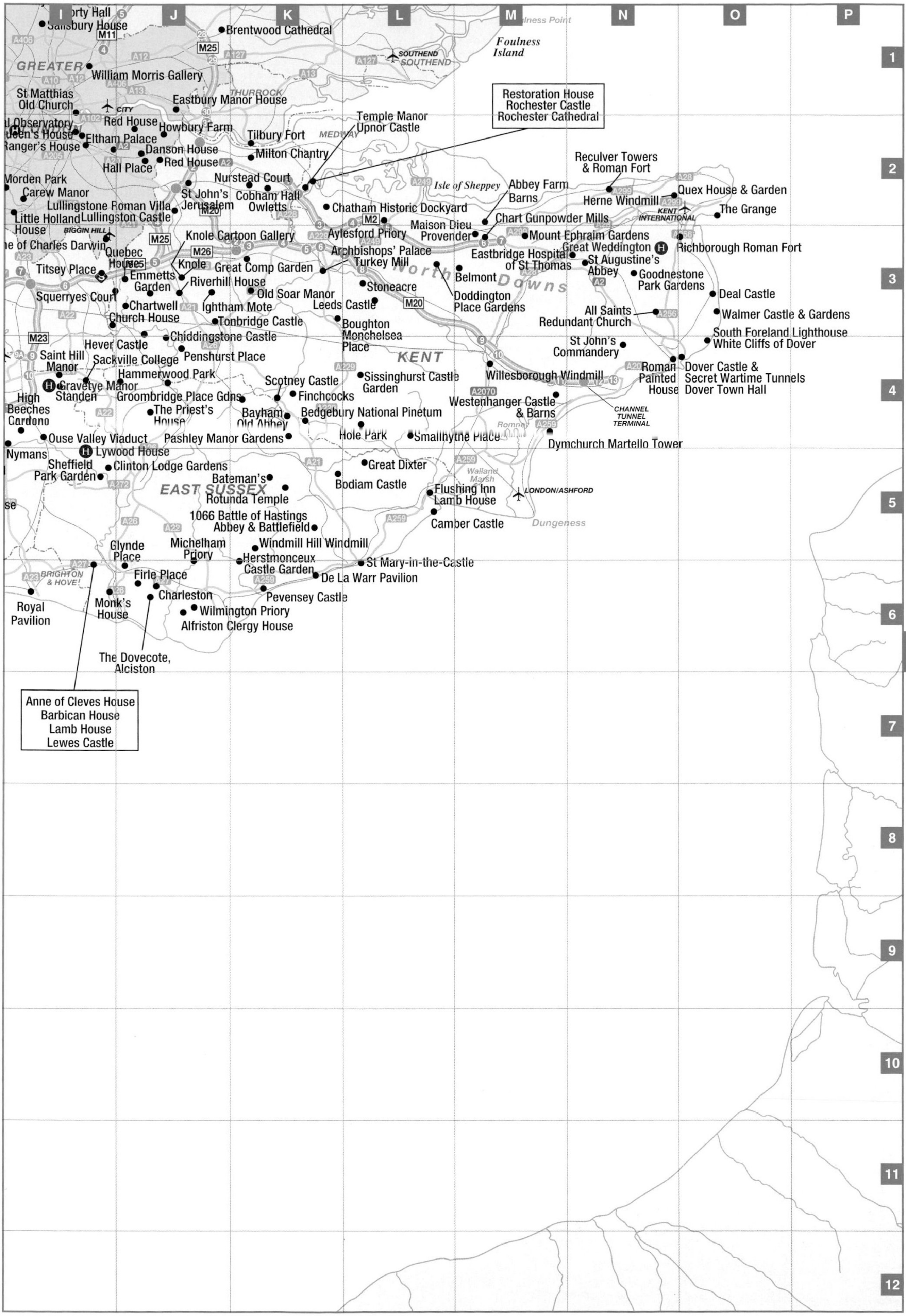

I J K L M N O P

1

Forty Hall
Salisbury House
M11
Brentwood Cathedral
GREATER
M25
Foulness Island
Southend/Southend
Inness Point

William Morris Gallery
THURROCK
2
St Matthias Old Church
Eastbury Manor House
CITY
A13
Red House
Howbury Farm
Tilbury Fort
Temple Manor
Upnor Castle
MEDWAY
Restoration House
Rochester Castle
Rochester Cathedral
Reculver Towers & Roman Fort
Quex House & Garden
Observatory
Queen's House
Eltham Palace
Danson House
Red House
Milton Chantry
Isle of Sheppey
Abbey Farm Barns
Herne Windmill
KENT INTERNATIONAL
The Grange
Ranger's House
Hall Place
Nurstead Court
St John's Jerusalem
Cobham Hall
Owletts
Chatham Historic Dockyard
M2
Chart Gunpowder Mills
Mount Ephraim Gardens
Great Weddington
Richborough Roman Fort
Morden Park
Carew Manor
Lullingstone Roman Villa
Little Holland House
Lullingston Castle
BIGGIN HILL
Knole Cartoon Gallery
Aylesford Priory
Maison Dieu
Provender
Archbishops' Palace
Turkey Mill
Eastbridge Hospital of St Thomas
Belmont
St Augustine's Abbey
Goodnestone Park Gardens
Deal Castle

3
Home of Charles Darwin
Quebec House
M25
M26
Knole
Great Comp Garden
Emmetts Garden
Riverhill House
Old Soar Manor
Stoneacre
Leeds Castle
North Downs
Doddington Place Gardens
All Saints Redundant Church
St John's Commandery
Walmer Castle & Gardens
South Foreland Lighthouse
White Cliffs of Dover
Titsey Place
Squerryes Court
Chartwell
Church House
Ightham Mote
Tonbridge Castle
Boughton Monchelsea Place
M20
Willesborough Windmill
Roman Painted House
Dover Castle & Secret Wartime Tunnels
Dover Town Hall

4
M23
Saint Hill Manor
Hever Castle
Sackville College
Chiddingstone Castle
Penshurst Place
KENT
Westenhanger Castle & Barns
CHANNEL TUNNEL TERMINAL
Gravetye Manor
Standen
Hammerwood Park
Groombridge Place Gdns
Scotney Castle
Finchcocks
Sissinghurst Castle Garden
High Beeches
Cardono
The Priest's House
Bayham Old Abbey
Bedgebury National Pinetum
Hole Park
Smallhythe Place
Dymchurch Martello Tower
Ouse Valley Viaduct
Pashley Manor Gardens
Nymans
Lywood House
Great Dixter
Walland Marsh
LONDON/ASHFORD

5
Sheffield Park Garden
Clinton Lodge Gardens
Bateman's
Bodiam Castle
Flushing Inn
Lamb House
Camber Castle
Dungeness
EAST SUSSEX
Rotunda Temple
1066 Battle of Hastings Abbey & Battlefield

6
Glynde Place
Michelham Priory
Windmill Hill Windmill
Firle Place
Herstmonceux Castle Garden
St Mary-in-the-Castle
De La Warr Pavilion
BRIGHTON & HOVE
Charleston
Wilmington Priory
Pevensey Castle
Royal Pavilion
Monk's House
Alfriston Clergy House

The Dovecote, Alciston

Anne of Cleves House
Barbican House
Lamb House
Lewes Castle

MAP 4

7

8

9

10

11

12

591

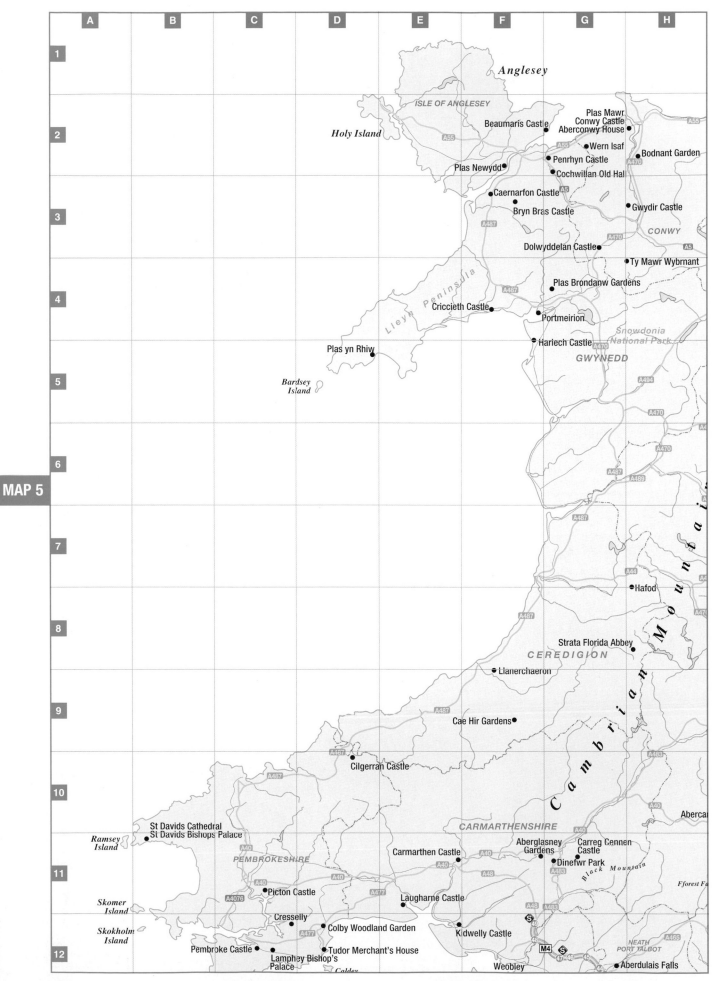

MAP 5

Anglesey

ISLE OF ANGLESEY

Holy Island

Plas Mawr
Conwy Castle
Beaumaris Castle
Aberconwy House
Wern Isaf
Bodnant Garden
Penrhyn Castle
Plas Newydd
Cochwillan Old Hall
Caernarfon Castle
Gwydir Castle
Bryn Bras Castle
CONWY
Dolwyddelan Castle
Ty Mawr Wybrnant
Plas Brondanw Gardens
Lleyn Peninsula
Criccieth Castle
Portmeirion
Snowdonia
National Park
Harlech Castle
Plas yn Rhiw
GWYNEDD
Bardsey
Island
Hafod
Strata Florida Abbey
CEREDIGION
Llanerchaeron
Cae Hir Gardens
Cilgerran Castle
CARMARTHENSHIRE
St Davids Cathedral
St Davids Bishops Palace
Ramsey
Island
Aberglasney
Gardens
Carreg Cennen
Castle
PEMBROKESHIRE
Carmarthen Castle
Dinefwr Park
Black Mountain
Fforest Fa
Picton Castle
Skomer
Island
Laugharne Castle
Cresselly
Skokholm
Island
Colby Woodland Garden
Kidwelly Castle
Pembroke Castle
NEATH
PORT TALBOT
Tudor Merchant's House
Aberdulais Falls
Lamphey Bishop's
Palace
Weobley
Caldey

Cambrian Mountains

592

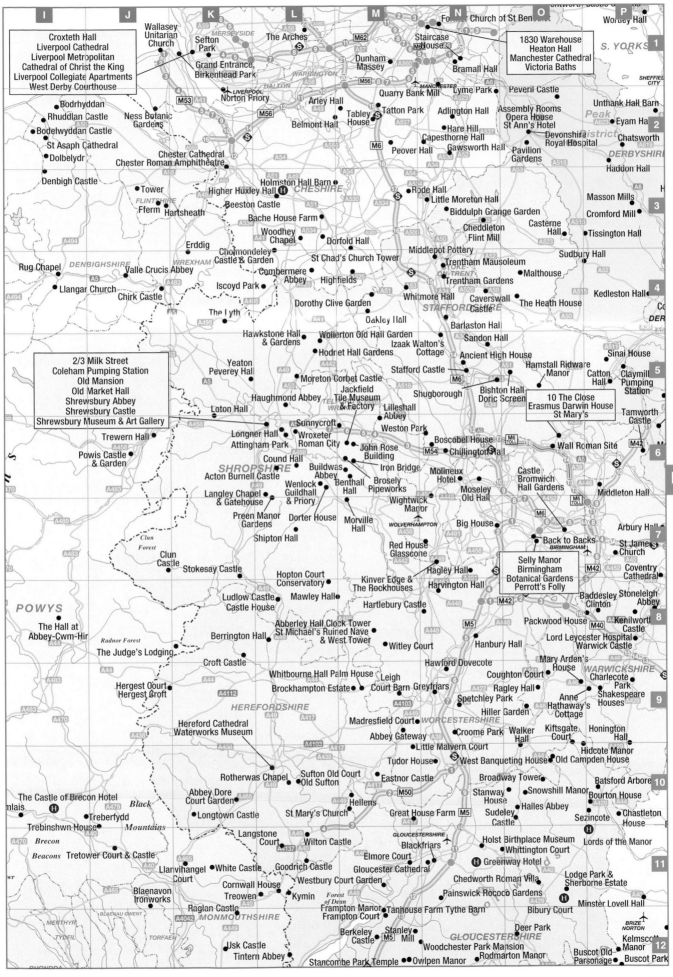

MAP 6

Croxteth Hall
Liverpool Cathedral
Liverpool Metropolitan
Cathedral of Christ the King
Liverpool Collegiate Apartments
West Derby Courthouse

1830 Warehouse
Heaton Hall
Manchester Cathedral
Victoria Baths

2/3 Milk Street
Coleham Pumping Station
Old Mansion
Old Market Hall
Shrewsbury Abbey
Shrewsbury Castle
Shrewsbury Museum & Art Gallery

10 The Close
Erasmus Darwin House
St Mary's

Selly Manor
Birmingham
Botanical Gardens
Perrott's Folly

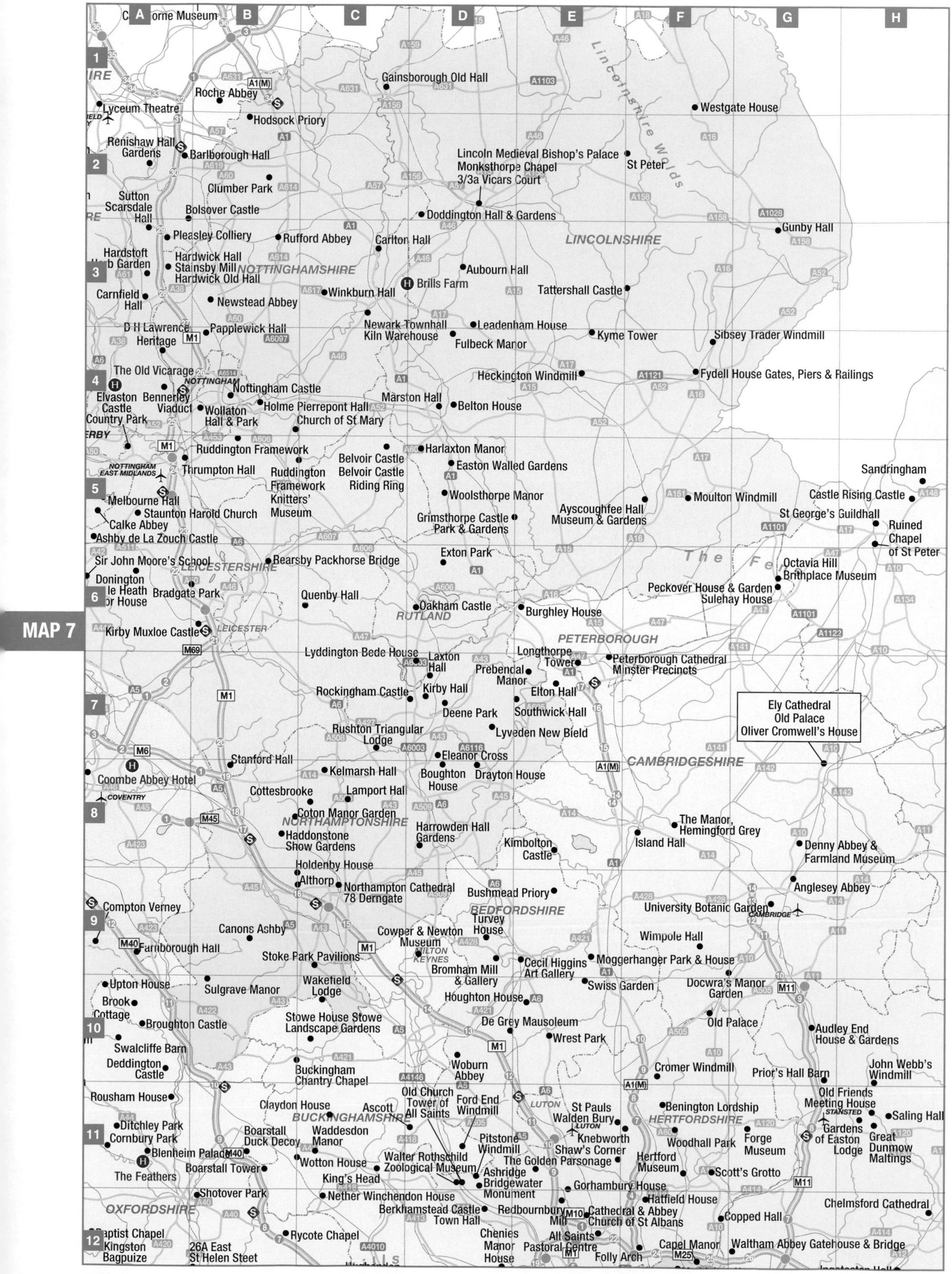

MAP 7

Grid columns: A B C D E F G H
Grid rows: 1–12

Lincolnshire Wolds

C... orne Museum

1
Gainsborough Old Hall
Westgate House
Roche Abbey
Lyceum Theatre
Hodsock Priory

2
Renishaw Hall Gardens
Barlborough Hall
Lincoln Medieval Bishop's Palace
Monksthorpe Chapel
3/3a Vicars Court
St Peter
Clumber Park
Sutton Scarsdale Hall
Bolsover Castle
Doddington Hall & Gardens
LINCOLNSHIRE
Gunby Hall

3
Pleasley Colliery
Rufford Abbey
Carlton Hall
Hardstoft Herb Garden
Hardwick Hall
Stainsby Mill
Hardwick Old Hall
NOTTINGHAMSHIRE
Aubourn Hall
Brills Farm
Tattershall Castle
Carnfield Hall
Newstead Abbey
Winkburn Hall

4
D H Lawrence Heritage
Papplewick Hall
Newark Townhall
Kiln Warehouse
Leadenham House
Fulbeck Manor
Kyme Tower
Sibsey Trader Windmill
The Old Vicarage
NOTTINGHAM
Heckington Windmill
Fydell House Gates, Piers & Railings
Elvaston Castle Country Park
Bennerley Viaduct
Nottingham Castle
Wollaton Hall & Park
Holme Pierrepont Hall
Church of St Mary
Marston Hall
Belton House
DERBY

5
Ruddington Framework
Harlaxton Manor
NOTTINGHAM EAST MIDLANDS
Thrumpton Hall
Ruddington Framework Knitters' Museum
Belvoir Castle
Belvoir Castle Riding Ring
Easton Walled Gardens
Woolsthorpe Manor
Sandringham
Castle Rising Castle
Melbourne Hall
Staunton Harold Church
Calke Abbey
Ashby de La Zouch Castle
Grimsthorpe Castle Park & Gardens
Ayscoughfee Hall Museum & Gardens
Moulton Windmill
St George's Guildhall
Ruined Chapel of St Peter

6
Sir John Moore's School
Bearsby Packhorse Bridge
Exton Park
The Fens
Octavia Hill Birthplace Museum
Donington le Heath Manor House
LEICESTERSHIRE
Quenby Hall
Peckover House & Garden
Sulehay House
Bradgate Park
Oakham Castle
Burghley House
RUTLAND
LEICESTER
Kirby Muxloe Castle
PETERBOROUGH

7
Lyddington Bede House
Laxton Hall
Longthorpe Tower
Peterborough Cathedral Minster Precincts
Prebendal Manor
Rockingham Castle
Kirby Hall
Elton Hall
Deene Park
Southwick Hall
Ely Cathedral
Old Palace
Oliver Cromwell's House
Stanford Hall
Rushton Triangular Lodge
Lyveden New Bield
CAMBRIDGESHIRE

8
Coombe Abbey Hotel
Eleanor Cross
Kelmarsh Hall
Boughton House
Drayton House
COVENTRY
Cottesbrooke
Lamport Hall
The Manor, Hemingford Grey
Denny Abbey & Farmland Museum
NORTHAMPTONSHIRE
Coton Manor Garden
Harrowden Hall Gardens
Island Hall
Anglesey Abbey
Haddonstone Show Gardens
Kimbolton Castle

9
Holdenby House
Althorp
University Botanic Garden
CAMBRIDGE
Compton Verney
Northampton Cathedral
78 Derngate
Bushmead Priory
BEDFORDSHIRE
Turvey House
Wimpole Hall
Canons Ashby
MILTON KEYNES
Cowper & Newton Museum
Moggerhanger Park & House
Farnborough Hall
Stoke Park Pavilions
Bromham Mill
Cecil Higgins Art Gallery
Swiss Garden
Docwra's Manor Garden

10
Upton House
Sulgrave Manor
Wakefield Lodge
Houghton House
Old Palace
Brook Cottage
Broughton Castle
Stowe House Stowe Landscape Gardens
De Grey Mausoleum
Wrest Park
Cromer Windmill
Audley End House & Gardens
Swalcliffe Barn
Deddington Castle
Buckingham Chantry Chapel
Woburn Abbey
John Webb's Windmill
Rousham House
Claydon House
Old Church Tower of All Saints
Ford End Windmill
LUTON
St Pauls Walden Bury
Benington Lordship
Prior's Hall Barn
Old Friends Meeting House
STANSTED
Saling Hall

11
Ditchley Park
Cornbury Park
Boarstall Duck Decoy
Ascott
Pitstone Windmill
Knebworth
Shaw's Corner
Woodhall Park
Forge Museum
Gardens of Easton Lodge
Great Dunmow Maltings
Blenheim Palace
Waddesdon Manor
Walter Rothschild Zoological Museum
The Golden Parsonage
Hertford Museum
Scott's Grotto
The Feathers
Boarstall Tower
Wotton House
King's Head
Ashridge
Bridgewater Monument
Gorhambury House
Hatfield House

12
...Baptist Chapel
Kingston Bagpuize
26A East St Helen Street
Shotover Park
Nether Winchendon House
Berkhamstead Castle Town Hall
Chenies Manor House
Redbournbury Mill
All Saints Pastoral Centre
Cathedral & Abbey Church of St Albans
Capel Manor
Chelmsford Cathedral
Copped Hall
Waltham Abbey Gatehouse & Bridge
Rycote Chapel
Folly Arch
OXFORDSHIRE
BUCKINGHAMSHIRE
HERTFORDSHIRE

I J K L M N O P

1
2
3
4
5

MAP 8

6
7
8
9
10
11
12

Holkham Hall●
Binham Priory●
Sheringham Park
Walsingham Abbey Grounds
●Felbrigg Hall
Letheringsett Watermill
●Bircham Windmill

The Deanery
Norwich Castle Museum
Old Meeting House
St Margaret-de-Westwick
St Martin at Oak
St Martin at Palace

Mannington Gardens
●Waxham Great Barn
Houghton Hall●
●Wolterton Park
Blickling Hall●
Hoveton Hall Gardens●
St Benet's Level Mill●
●Thurne Dyke Drainage Mill
Castle Acre Priory●
NORWICH
St Benet's Abbey
●Caister Castle Car Collection
Fairhaven Woodland & Water Gardens
NORFOLK
●Nelson's Monument
●Great Yarmouth Row Houses
Bradenham Hall Gardens●
Old Hall●
St Peter & St Paul
The Broads
●Berney Arms Windmill
Kimberley Hall●
●Burgh Castle

Raveningham Gardens
●Somerleyton Hall

●Grime's Graves

St Clement●
Ⓗ Church Farm House
Ⓗ The Old Rectory
South Elmham Hall

Euston Hall●
●Bardwell Windmill ●Yaxley Hall
Culford School Iron Bridge
Ruined Church Tower
●Wyken Hall Gardens
St Edmundsbury Cathedral
Saxtead Green Post Mill
Framlingham Castle
Moreton Hall●
SUFFOLK
●Leiston Abbey
Ickworth House & Park
Haughley Park●
Helmingham Hall Gardens●
●Otley Hall
●Friston Mill
Abbey Farm Barn
Kentwell Hall●
Lavenham Guildhall
Sutton Hoo●
Hadleigh Guildhall
●Orford Castle
Ancient House
●Melford Hall
The Tide Mill●
Orford Ness
Freston Tower●
Christchurch Mansion
●Gainsborough's House
Belchamp Hall●
East Bergholt Place●
●Sir Alfred Munnings Art Museum
●Walton Old Hall
Flatford Bridge Cottage●
●Landguard Fort
Mistley Towers●
Harwich Redoubt Fort
Marks Hall Gardens & Aboretum
Feeringbury Manor
The Naze
Colchester Castle Museum
Coggeshall Grange Barn & Paycocke's
Bourne Mill
ESSEX
●Layer Marney Tower

St Mary●
●RHS Garden Hyde Hall

A148 A1065 A47 A1074 A11 A140 A143 A12 A1117 A146 A134 A1066 A14 A131 A120 A133

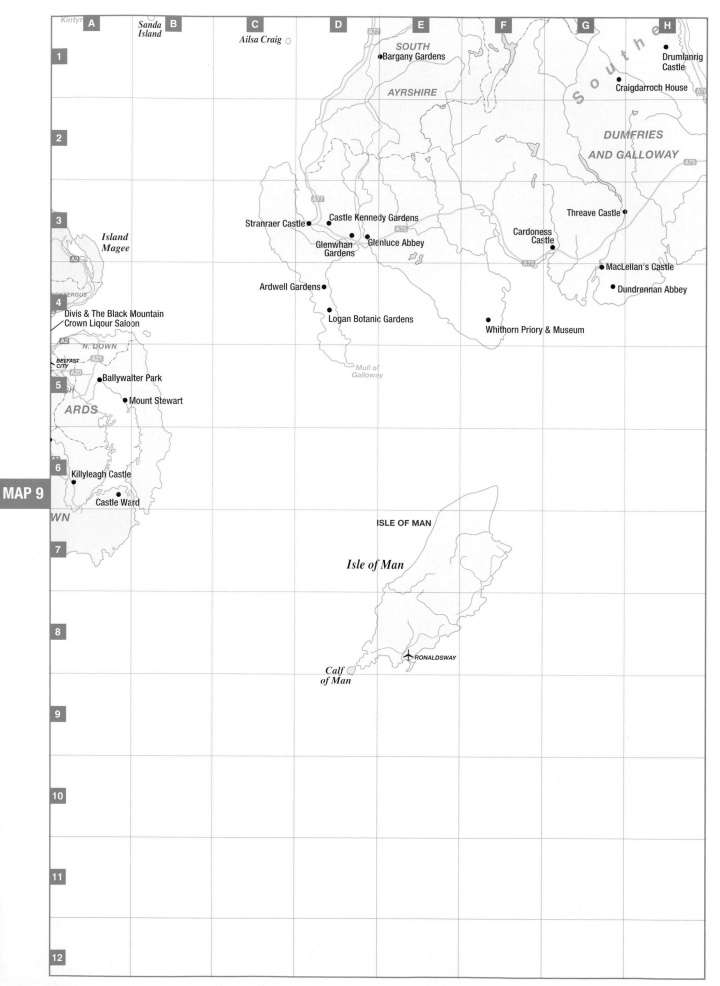

MAP 9

A · B · C · D · E · F · G · H

1
2
3
4
5
6
7
8
9
10
11
12

Kintyr

Sanda
Island

Ailsa Craig ○

SOUTH
● Bargany Gardens

AYRSHIRE

South

Drumlanrig
Castle ●

● Craigdarroch House

DUMFRIES

AND GALLOWAY

A75

Threave Castle ●

Cardoness
Castle
●

● MacLellan's Castle

● Dundrennan Abbey

Stranraer Castle ● ● Castle Kennedy Gardens

Glenwhan
Gardens

● Glenluce Abbey
A77
A75
A75

Island
Magee
A2

CARRICKFERGUS

Ardwell Gardens ●

● Logan Botanic Gardens

Whithorn Priory & Museum
●

Divis & The Black Mountain
Crown Liqour Saloon

A2
N. DOWN
A21
BELFAST
CITY
A20
AGH

Mull of
Galloway

ARDS

● Ballywalter Park

● Mount Stewart

A7

DOWN

● Killyleagh Castle

● Castle Ward

ISLE OF MAN

Isle of Man

RONALDSWAY ✈

*Calf
of Man*

596

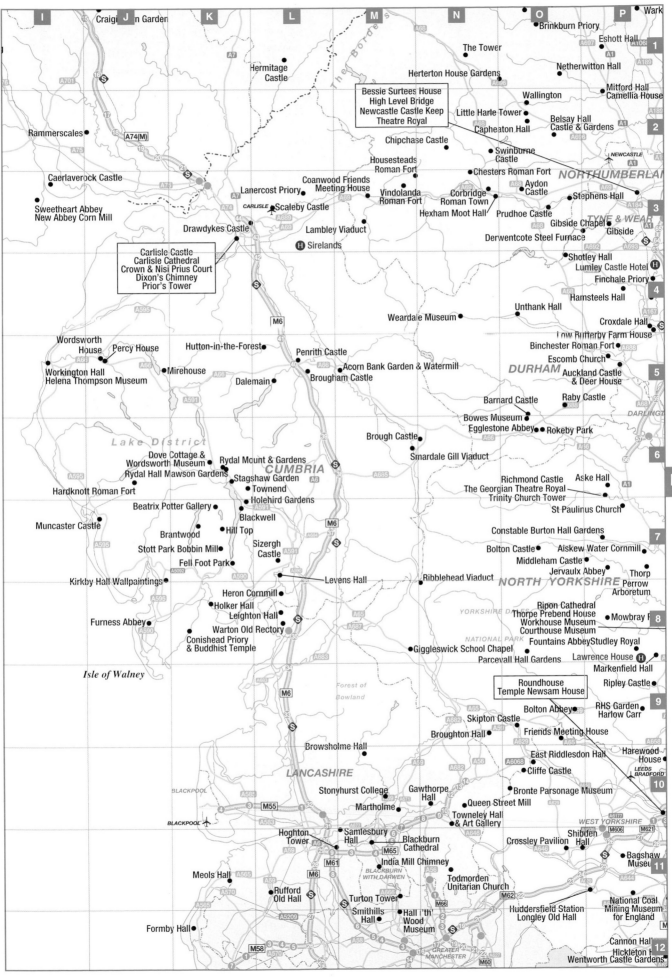

Craigi n Garden

Wark
Brinkburn Priory
Eshott Hall

Hermitage Castle

The Tower
Netherwitton Hall

Herterton House Gardens
Mitford Hall
Camellia House

Bessie Surtees House
High Level Bridge
Newcastle Castle Keep
Theatre Royal

Wallington

Little Harle Tower
Capheaton Hall
Belsay Hall
Castle & Gardens

Rammerscales

Chipchase Castle
Swinburne
Castle

Housesteads
Roman Fort
Chesters Roman Fort
NORTHUMBERLAN

Caerlaverock Castle
Coanwood Friends
Meeting House
Lanercost Priory
Vindolanda
Roman Fort
Corbridge
Roman Town
Aydon
Castle
Stephens Hall

TYNE & WEAR

Sweetheart Abbey
New Abbey Corn Mill
CARLISLE Scaleby Castle
Hexham Moot Hall
Prudhoe Castle
Gibside Chapel
Gibside

Drawdykes Castle
Lambley Viaduct
Derwentcote Steel Furnace

Sirelands
Shotley Hall
Lumley Castle Hotel

Carlisle Castle
Carlisle Cathedral
Crown & Nisi Prius Court
Dixon's Chimney
Prior's Tower
Finchale Priory

Hamsteels Hall

Weardale Museum
Unthank Hall
Croxdale Hall

Low Butterby Farm House
Binchester Roman Fort

Wordsworth
House
Percy House
Hutton-in-the-Forest
Penrith Castle
Escomb Church
Auckland Castle
& Deer House

Workington Hall
Helena Thompson Museum
Mirehouse
Acorn Bank Garden & Watermill
Brougham Castle
DURHAM

Dalemain
Barnard Castle
Raby Castle

Bowes Museum
Egglestone Abbey
Rokeby Park
DARLINGT

Lake District
Brough Castle
Smardale Gill Viaduct

Dove Cottage &
Wordsworth Museum
Rydal Mount & Gardens
CUMBRIA
Richmond Castle
Aske Hall

Rydal Hall Mawson Gardens
Stagshaw Garden
The Georgian Theatre Royal
Trinity Church Tower
St Paulinus Church

Hardknott Roman Fort
Townend
Holehird Gardens
Constable Burton Hall Gardens

Beatrix Potter Gallery
Blackwell
Bolton Castle
Aiskew Water Cornmill

Muncaster Castle
Hill Top
Middleham Castle

Brantwood
Jervaulx Abbey
Thorp

Stott Park Bobbin Mill
Sizergh
Castle
NORTH YORKSHIRE
Perrow
Arboretum

Kirkby Hall Wallpaintings
Fell Foot Park
Ribblehead Viaduct
YORKSHIRE D
Ripon Cathedral
Thorpe Prebend House
Mowbray

Heron Cornmill
Levens Hall
Workhouse Museum
Courthouse Museum

Holker Hall
Leighton Hall
NATIONAL PARK
Fountains Abbey Studley Royal

Furness Abbey
Warton Old Rectory
Giggleswick School Chapel
Lawrence House

Conishead Priory
& Buddhist Temple
Parcevall Hall Gardens
Markenfield Hall

Isle of Walney
Roundhouse
Temple Newsam House
Ripley Castle

Bolton Abbey
RHS Garden
Harlow Carr

Forest of
Bowland
Skipton Castle
Friends Meeting House

Browsholme Hall
Broughton Hall
East Riddlesden Hall
Harewood
House

LANCASHIRE
Cliffe Castle
LEEDS
BRADFORD

BLACKPOOL
Stonyhurst College
Gawthorpe
Hall
Bronte Parsonage Museum

Martholme
Queen Street Mill
WEST YORKSHIRE

BLACKPOOL
Hoghton
Tower
Samlesbury
Hall
Towneley Hall
& Art Gallery
Shibden
Hall

Meols Hall
Blackburn
Cathedral
Crossley Pavilion
Bagshaw
Muse

India Mill Chimney
BLACKBURN
WITH DARWEN
Todmorden
Unitarian Church

Rufford
Old Hall
Turton Tower
National Coal
Mining Museum
for England

Formby Hall
Smithills
Hall
Hall 'th'
Wood
Museum
Huddersfield Station
Longley Old Hall

GREATER
MANCHESTER
Cannon Hall
Hickleton
Wentworth Castle Gardens

MAP 10

597

MAP 11

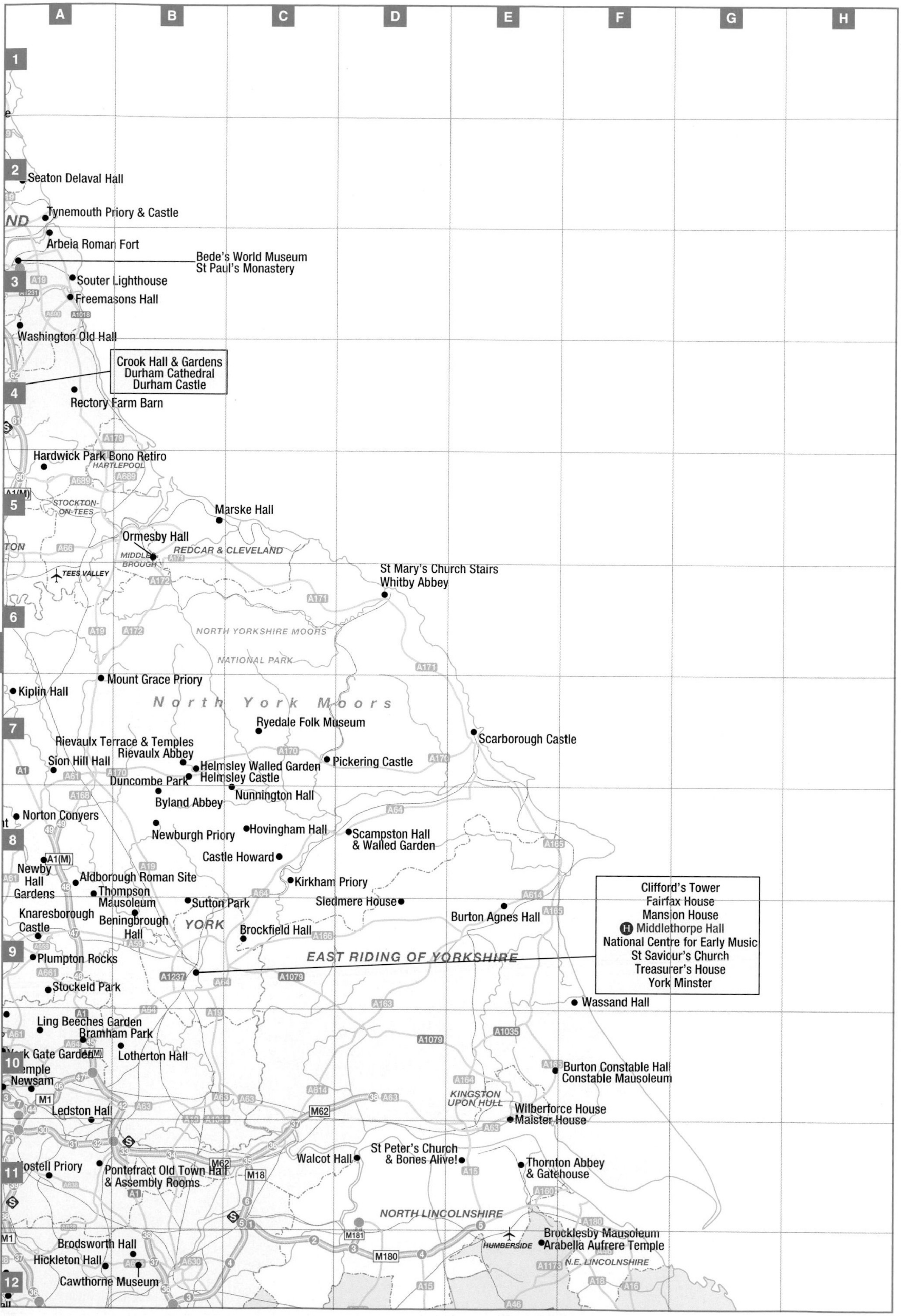
A
B
C
D
E
F
G
H
1
2
3
4
5
6
7
8
9
10
11
12
Seaton Delaval Hall
Tynemouth Priory & Castle
Arbeia Roman Fort
Bede's World Museum
St Paul's Monastery
Souter Lighthouse
Freemasons Hall
Washington Old Hall
Crook Hall & Gardens
Durham Cathedral
Durham Castle
Rectory Farm Barn
Hardwick Park Bono Retiro
HARTLEPOOL
STOCKTON-ON-TEES
Marske Hall
Ormesby Hall
MIDDLESBROUGH
REDCAR & CLEVELAND
TEES VALLEY
St Mary's Church Stairs
Whitby Abbey
NORTH YORKSHIRE MOORS
NATIONAL PARK
Mount Grace Priory
Kiplin Hall
North York Moors
Ryedale Folk Museum
Scarborough Castle
Rievaulx Terrace & Temples
Rievaulx Abbey
Sion Hill Hall
Helmsley Walled Garden
Helmsley Castle
Pickering Castle
Duncombe Park
Nunnington Hall
Byland Abbey
Norton Conyers
Newburgh Priory
Hovingham Hall
Scampston Hall & Walled Garden
Castle Howard
Newby Hall Gardens
Aldborough Roman Site
Thompson Mausoleum
Kirkham Priory
Sutton Park
Sledmere House
Burton Agnes Hall
Knaresborough Castle
Beningbrough Hall
YORK
Brockfield Hall
Clifford's Tower
Fairfax House
Mansion House
Middlethorpe Hall
National Centre for Early Music
St Saviour's Church
Treasurer's House
York Minster
EAST RIDING OF YORKSHIRE
Plumpton Rocks
Stockeld Park
Wassand Hall
Ling Beeches Garden
Bramham Park
York Gate Garden
Lotherton Hall
Temple Newsam
Burton Constable Hall
Constable Mausoleum
KINGSTON UPON HULL
Ledston Hall
Wilberforce House
Maister House
St Peter's Church & Bones Alive!
Walcot Hall
Thornton Abbey & Gatehouse
Nostell Priory
Pontefract Old Town Hall & Assembly Rooms
NORTH LINCOLNSHIRE
HUMBERSIDE
Brocklesby Mausoleum
Arabella Aufrere Temple
N.E. LINCOLNSHIRE
Brodsworth Hall
Hickleton Hall
Cawthorne Museum
A1(M)
A19
A66
A171
A172
A170
A64
A165
A614
A1079
A1237
A59
A61
A1
M1
M62
M18
M180
M181
A63
A15
A46
A1035
A163
A164
A166
A689
A179
A1018
A690
A168
A661
A160
A1173
A180
A18
A16
A630
A628
A639
A1041

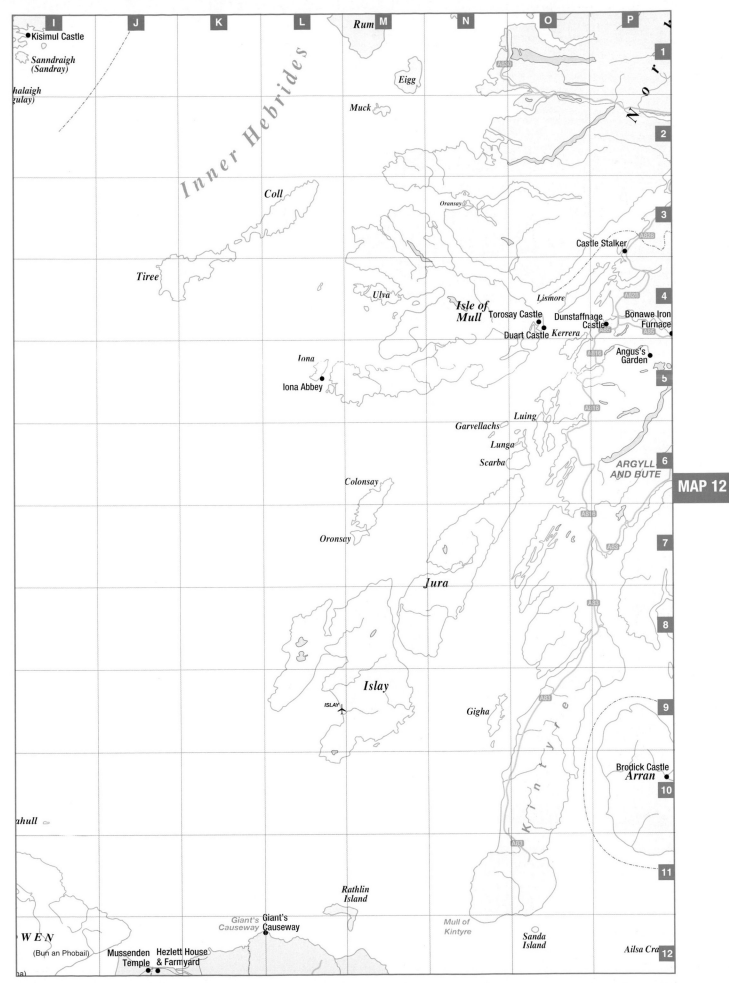

I
● Kisimul Castle

J

K

L

Rum M

N

O

P

Sanndraigh
(Sandray)

Eigg

halaigh
gulay)

Muck

2

Inner Hebrides

Coll

Oransay

3

Castle Stalker ●

Tiree

Ulva

Lismore

A828

A82B 4

Isle of
Mull Torosay Castle ● Dunstaffnage
Castle ● Bonawe Iron
Furnace ●
Duart Castle ● *Kerrera* A85 A85

A816

Angus's
Garden ●

Iona

5

Iona Abbey ●

Luing

Garvellachs

A816

Lunga

Scarba

ARGYLL
AND BUTE 6

Colonsay

A816 MAP 12

7

Oronsay

A83

Jura

8

Islay

ISLAY ✈

9

Gigha

A83

Brodick Castle ●
Arran

10

A83

11

Rathlin
Island

ahull

Mull of
Kintyre

W E N

(Bun an Phobail)

Giant's
Causeway

Giant's
Causeway ●

Mussenden Hezlett House
Temple & Farmyard ●

Sanda
Island

Ailsa Cra 12

ha)

599

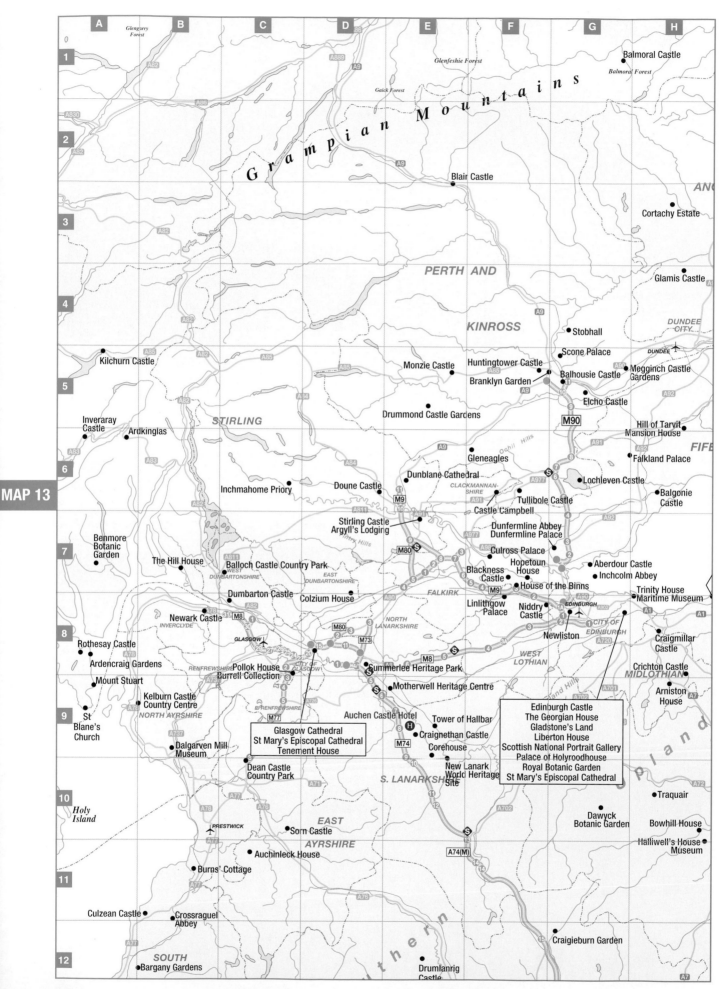

MAP 13

600

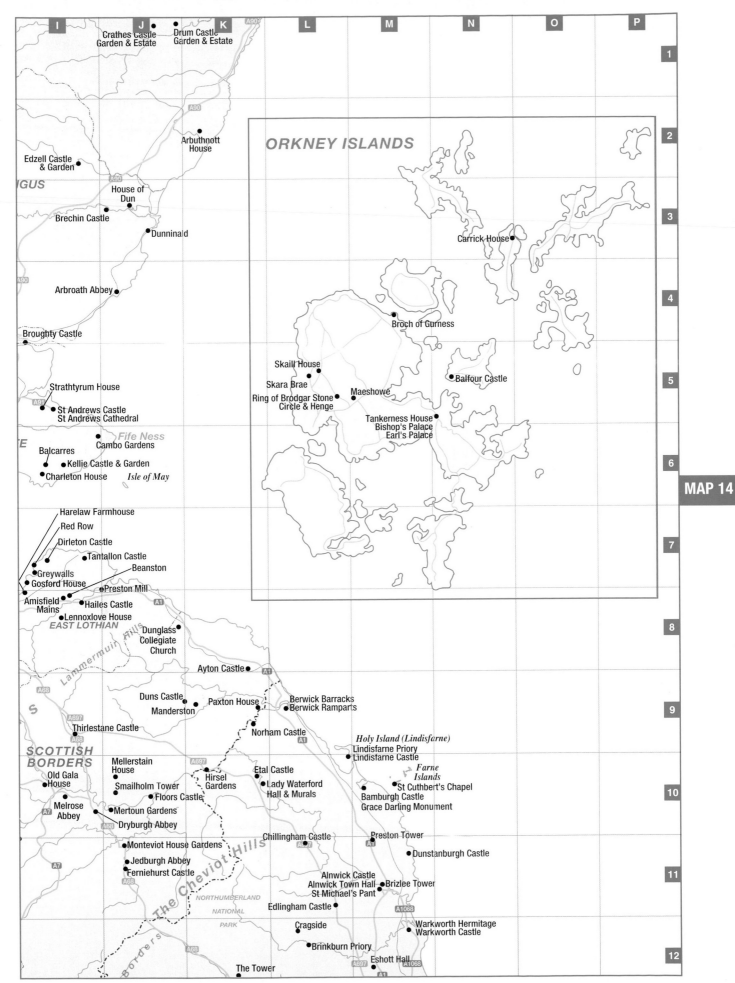

I **J** **K** **L** **M** **N** **O** **P**

1

Crathes Castle
Garden & Estate

Drum Castle
Garden & Estate

ORKNEY ISLANDS

2

Arbuthnott
House

Edzell Castle
& Garden

GUS

House of
Dun

3

Brechin Castle

Dunninald

Carrick House

Arbroath Abbey

4

Broch of Gurness

Broughty Castle

5

Skaill House

Balfour Castle

Strathyrum House

Skara Brae

Maeshowe

St Andrews Castle
St Andrews Cathedral

Ring of Brodgar Stone
Circle & Henge

Fife Ness

Cambo Gardens

Tankerness House
Bishop's Palace
Earl's Palace

E

Balcarres

Kellie Castle & Garden

6

Charleton House

Isle of May

MAP 14

Harelaw Farmhouse

7

Red Row

Dirleton Castle

Tantallon Castle

Beanston

Greywalls

Gosford House

Preston Mill

Amisfield
Mains

Hailes Castle

8

Lennoxlove House

EAST LOTHIAN

Dunglass
Collegiate
Church

Lammermuir Hills

Ayton Castle

Duns Castle

Berwick Barracks

9

Manderston

Paxton House

Berwick Ramparts

Thirlestane Castle

Norham Castle

Holy Island (Lindisfarne)
Lindisfarne Priory
Lindisfarne Castle

*SCOTTISH
BORDERS*

Mellerstain
House

*Farne
Islands*

Old Gala
House

Smailholm Tower

Hirsel
Gardens

Etal Castle

St Cuthbert's Chapel

10

Melrose
Abbey

Floors Castle

Lady Waterford
Hall & Murals

Bamburgh Castle
Grace Darling Monument

Mertoun Gardens

Dryburgh Abbey

Chillingham Castle

Preston Tower

Monteviot House Gardens

Dunstanburgh Castle

Jedburgh Abbey

11

Ferniehurst Castle

Alnwick Castle
Alnwick Town Hall
St Michael's Pant

Brizlee Tower

NORTHUMBERLAND

Edlingham Castle

NATIONAL

Cragside

Warkworth Hermitage
Warkworth Castle

PARK

The Cheviot Hills

Brinkburn Priory

12

Borders

The Tower

Eshott Hall

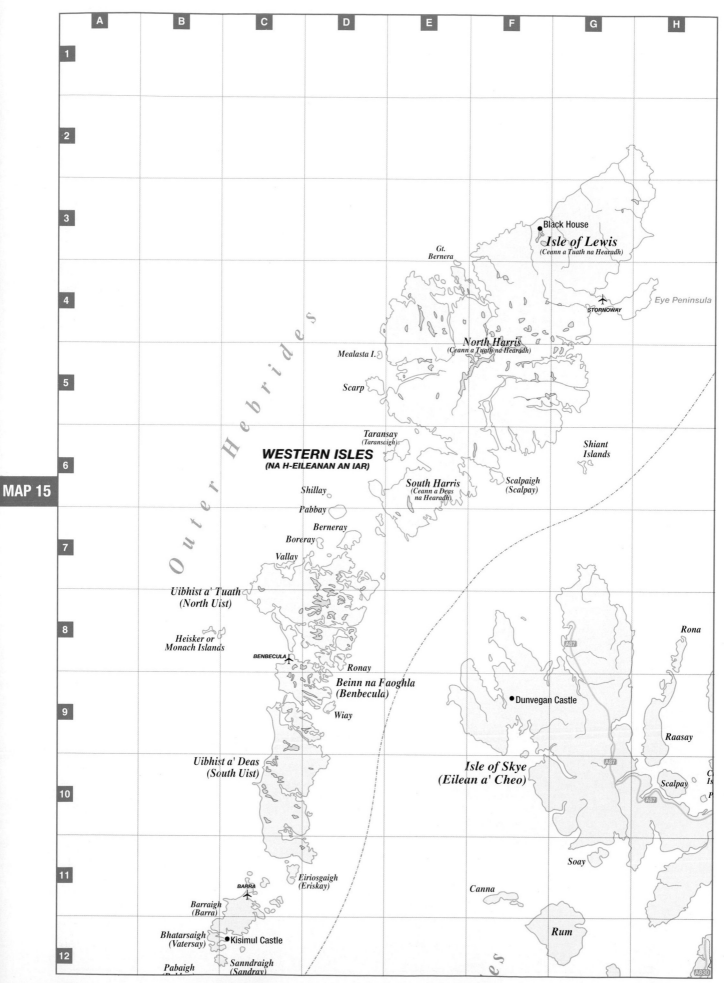

MAP 15

A **B** **C** **D** **E** **F** **G** **H**

1

2

3

• Black House

Isle of Lewis
(Ceann a Tuath na Hearadh)

Gt.
Bernera

4

✈
STORNOWAY

Eye Peninsula

North Harris
(Ceann a Tuath na Hearadh)

Mealasta I.

5

Scarp

Taransay
(Taransaigh)

Shiant
Islands

6

WESTERN ISLES
(NA H-EILEANAN AN IAR)

South Harris
(Ceann a Deas
na Hearadh)

Scalpaigh
(Scalpay)

Shillay

Pabbay

Berneray

Boreray

7

Vallay

Uibhist a' Tuath
(North Uist)

8

Heisker or
Monach Islands

BENBECULA ✈

Ronay

Rona

Beinn na Faoghla
(Benbecula)

• Dunvegan Castle

9

Wiay

Raasay

Uibhist a' Deas
(South Uist)

Isle of Skye
(Eilean a' Cheo)

Scalpay

10

Soay

11

Eiriosgaigh
(Eriskay)

Canna

BARRA ✈

Barraigh
(Barra)

Rum

Bhatarsaigh
(Vatersay)

• Kisimul Castle

12

Pabaigh

Sanndraigh
(Sandray)

O u t e r   H e b r i d e s

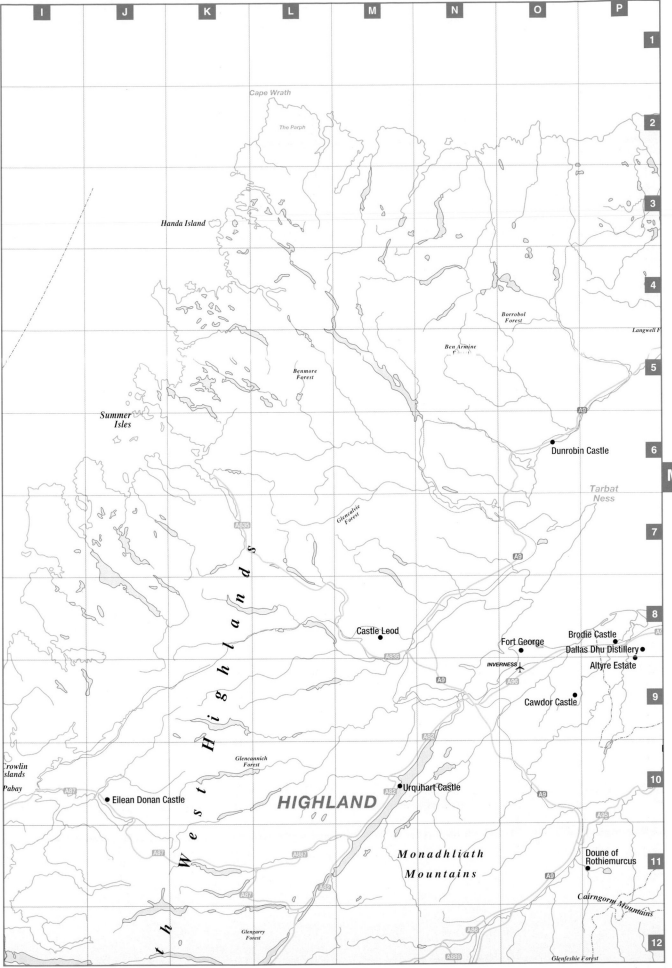

I J K L M N O P

1

Cape Wrath

2

The Parph

3

Handa Island

4

Borrobol
Forest

Langwell F

Ben Armine

5

A9

Benmore
Forest

Summer
Isles

Dunrobin Castle

6

MAP 16

Tarbat
Ness

Glencalvie
Forest

A835

7

A9

8

Castle Leod

Brodie Castle

A8

Fort George

Dallas Dhu Distillery

A835

Altyre Estate

INVERNESS ✈

A96

9

A9

Cawdor Castle

A82

Glencannich
Forest

Crowlin
Islands

10

Pabay

A87

Urquhart Castle

A82

A95

Eilean Donan Castle

HIGHLAND

A887

Monadhliath

A87

A82

Mountains

Doune of
Rothiemurcus

11

A9

Cairngorm Mountains

A87

Glengarry
Forest

A86

A889

Glenfeshie Forest

12

603

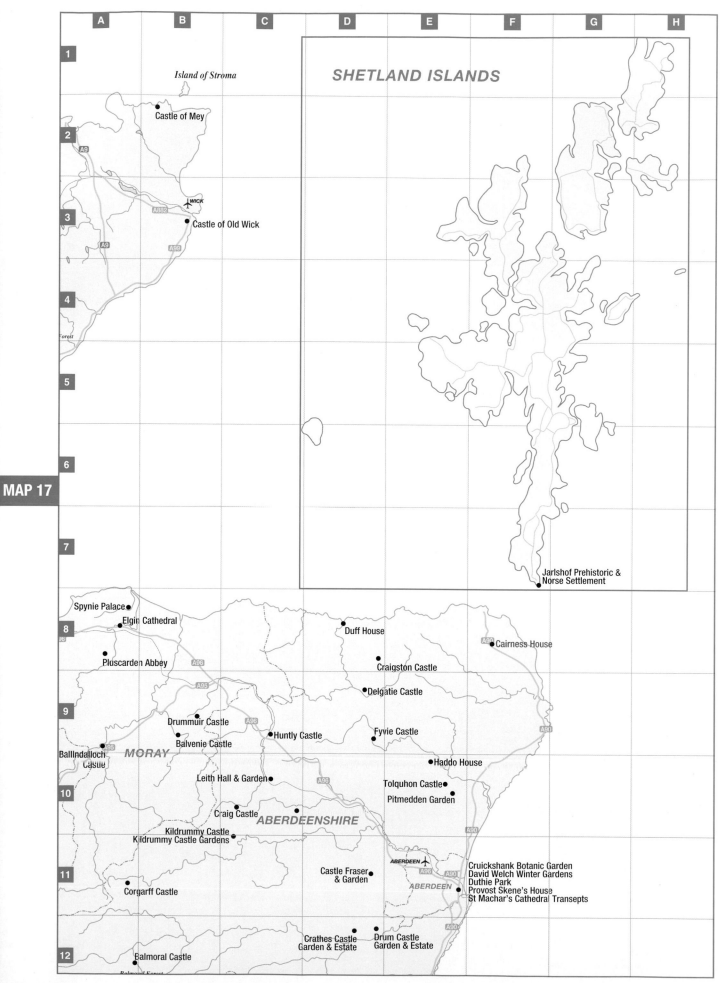

MAP 17

SHETLAND ISLANDS

Island of Stroma

● Castle of Mey

WICK

● Castle of Old Wick

Jarlshof Prehistoric &
Norse Settlement ●

Spynie Palace ●
● Elgin Cathedral

Duff House ●

Cairness House ●

● Pluscarden Abbey

Craigston Castle ●

● Delgatie Castle

● Drummuir Castle

● Huntly Castle

Fyvie Castle ●

● Balvenie Castle

MORAY

Haddo House ●

Ballindalloch
Castle ●

Leith Hall & Garden ●

Tolquhon Castle ●
Pitmedden Garden ●

● Craig Castle

ABERDEENSHIRE

ABERDEEN

Kildrummy Castle ●
Kildrummy Castle Gardens

Cruickshank Botanic Garden
David Welch Winter Gardens
Duthie Park
Provost Skene's House
St Machar's Cathedral Transepts

● Corgarff Castle

Castle Fraser
& Garden ●

ABERDEEN

Crathes Castle
Garden & Estate ●

Drum Castle
Garden & Estate ●

● Balmoral Castle

Balmoral Forest

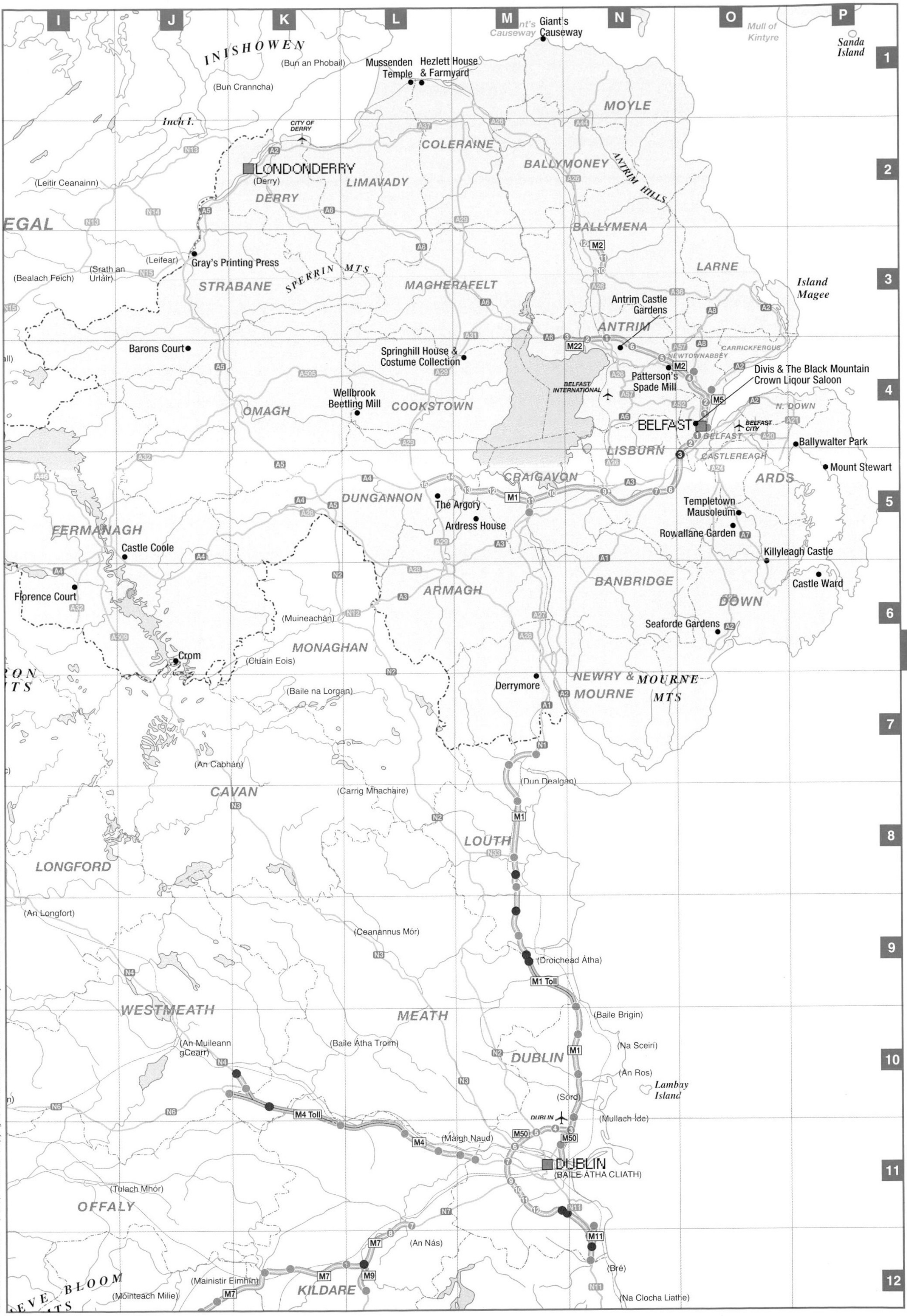

INISHOWEN
(Bun an Phobail)
(Bun Cranncha)

Giant's Causeway
Giant's Causeway

Mull of Kintyre

Sanda Island

Mussenden Temple
Hezlett House & Farmyard

MOYLE

Inch I.

CITY OF DERRY

COLERAINE

BALLYMONEY

ANTRIM HILLS

Island Magee

(Leitir Ceanainn)

LONDONDERRY
(Derry)

DERRY

LIMAVADY

BALLYMENA

LARNE

EGAL

(Bealach Feich)
(Srath an Urláir)

(Leifear)
Gray's Printing Press

STRABANE
SPERRIN MTS

MAGHERAFELT

CARRICKFERGUS

Antrim Castle Gardens

ANTRIM

NEWTOWNABBEY

Divis & The Black Mountain
Crown Liqour Saloon

Barons Court

Springhill House & Costume Collection

BELFAST INTERNATIONAL

Patterson's Spade Mill

Wellbrook Beetling Mill

OMAGH

COOKSTOWN

BELFAST

BELFAST CITY

N. DOWN

Ballywalter Park

LISBURN

CASTLEREAGH

ARDS

Mount Stewart

FERMANAGH

Castle Coole

DUNGANNON

The Argory
Ardress House

CRAIGAVON

Templetown Mausoleum

Rowallane Garden

Killyleagh Castle

Florence Court

ARMAGH

BANBRIDGE

DOWN

Castle Ward

Crom

(Muineachán)

MONAGHAN

(Cluain Eois)

Seaforde Gardens

MAP 18

(Baile na Lorgan)

Derrymore

NEWRY & MOURNE
MOURNE MTS

(An Cabhán)

CAVAN

(Carrig Mhachaire)

(Dun Dealgan)

LOUTH

LONGFORD

(An Longfort)

(Ceanannus Mór)

(Droichead Átha)

M1 Toll

WESTMEATH

MEATH

(Baile Brigin)

(An Muileann gCearr)

(Baile Átha Troim)

(Na Sceirí)

DUBLIN

(An Ros)

Lambay Island

M4 Toll

M4

(Máigh Nuad)

(Sord)

DUBLIN

(Mullach Íde)

M50

DUBLIN
(BAILE ÁTHA CLIATH)

(Tulach Mhór)

OFFALY

(An Nás)

M7

(Bré)

SLEVE BLOOM

(Mainistir Eimhín)

(Móinteach Milic)

KILDARE

(Na Clocha Liatha)

©MAPS IN MINUTES™ (2007). ©Crown Copyright, 100021153 & Ordnance Survey Northern Ireland 2007 Permit No. NI 1675.

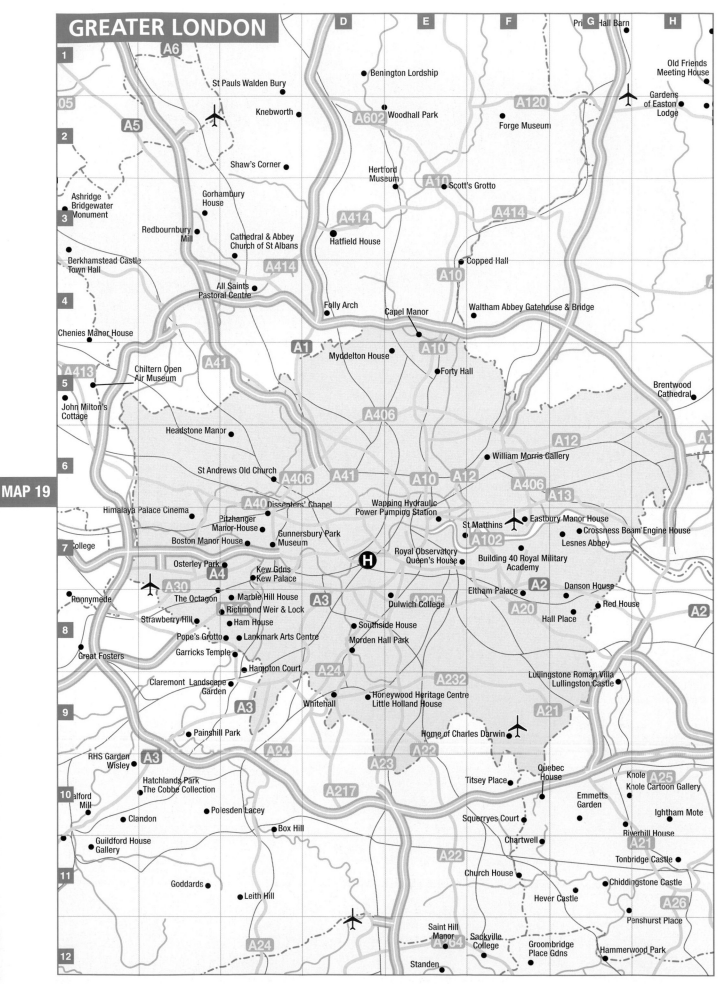

GREATER LONDON

MAP 19

A6

A5

A120

D · E · F · G · H

Benington Lordship

St Pauls Walden Bury

Knebworth

Woodhall Park

Forge Museum

Old Friends
Meeting House

Gardens
of Easton
Lodge

A602

Shaw's Corner

Hertford
Museum

Scott's Grotto

A10

Ashridge
Bridgewater
Monument

Gorhambury
House

A414

A414

Redbournbury
Mill

Cathedral & Abbey
Church of St Albans

Hatfield House

Berkhamstead Castle
Town Hall

A414

Copped Hall

A1

All Saints
Pastoral Centre

Folly Arch

Capel Manor

Waltham Abbey Gatehouse & Bridge

A10

Chenies Manor House

A41

Myddelton House

A10

A413

Chiltern Open
Air Museum

Forty Hall

Brentwood
Cathedral

John Milton's
Cottage

A406

Headstone Manor

A1

A12

William Morris Gallery

St Andrews Old Church

A406

A41

A10

A12

A406

A13

Himalaya Palace Cinema

A40

Dissenters' Chapel

Wapping Hydraulic
Power Pumping Station

St Matthins

Eastbury Manor House

Crossness Beam Engine House

Pitzhanger
Manor-House

Gunnersbury Park
Museum

A102

Lesnes Abbey

College

Boston Manor House

Royal Observatory
Queen's House

Building 40 Royal Military
Academy

Osterley Park

A4

Kew Gdns
Kew Palace

H

A2

Danson House

A30

The Octagon

Marble Hill House

A3

Dulwich College

A205

Eltham Palace

Red House

A2

Runnymede

Richmond Weir & Lock

Strawberry Hill

Ham House

Southside House

A20

Hall Place

Great Fosters

Pope's Grotto

Lankmark Arts Centre

Morden Hall Park

Lullingstone Roman Villa
Lullingston Castle

Garricks Temple

Hampton Court

A24

A232

Honeywood Heritage Centre
Little Holland House

A21

Claremont Landscape
Garden

Whitehall

A3

Painshill Park

A22

Home of Charles Darwin

A23

Quebec
House

Knole
A25

RHS Garden
Wisley

A3

Titsey Place

Knole Cartoon Gallery

Hatchlands Park
The Cobbe Collection

A217

Emmetts
Garden

Ightham Mote

alford
Mill

Polesden Lacey

Squerryes Court

Riverhill House

Clandon

Box Hill

Chartwell

A21

Guildford House
Gallery

Tonbridge Castle

A22

Church House

Chiddingstone Castle

Goddards

Leith Hill

Hever Castle

A26

Penshurst Place

A24

Saint Hill
Manor

Sackville
College

Groombridge
Place Gdns

Hammerwood Park

A64

Standen

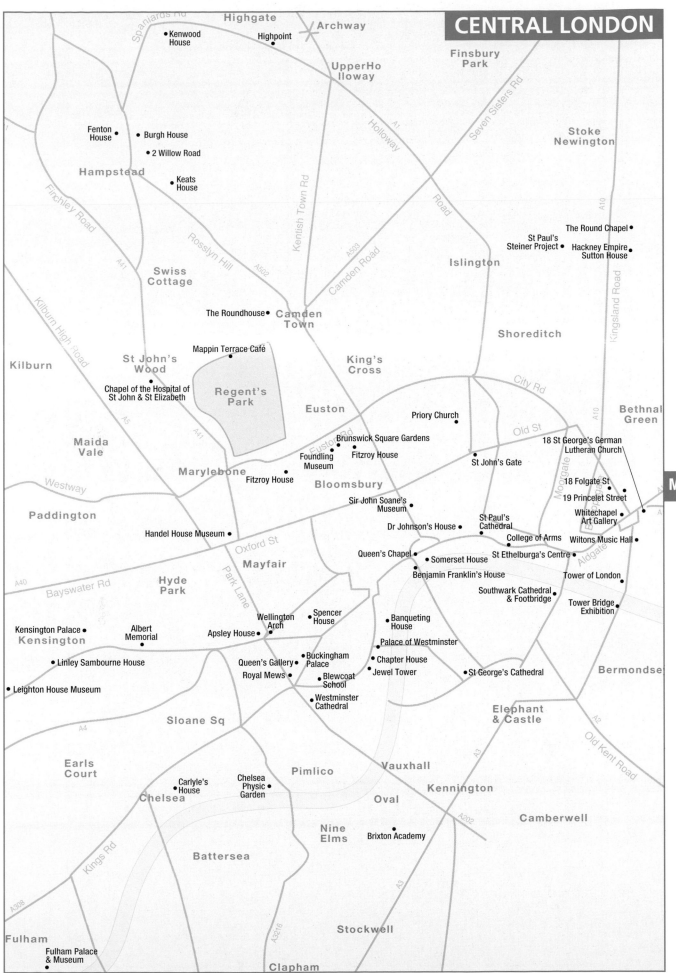

Highgate

Archway

Kenwood House

Highpoint

UpperHo lloway

Finsbury Park

Stoke Newington

Fenton House

Burgh House

2 Willow Road

Hampstead

Keats House

The Round Chapel

St Paul's Steiner Project

Hackney Empire

Sutton House

Swiss Cottage

Islington

Shoreditch

Kilburn

St John's Wood

The Roundhouse

Camden Town

Mappin Terrace Café

Regent's Park

King's Cross

City Rd

Bethnal Green

Chapel of the Hospital of St John & St Elizabeth

Euston

Priory Church

Old St

MAP 20

Maida Vale

Brunswick Square Gardens

18 St George's German Lutheran Church

Foundling Museum

Fitzroy House

Marylebone

Fitzroy House

Bloomsbury

St John's Gate

18 Folgate St

19 Princelet Street

Paddington

Sir John Soane's Museum

Whitechapel Art Gallery

Handel House Museum

Oxford St

Dr Johnson's House

St Paul's Cathedral

College of Arms

Wiltons Music Hall

Westway

Queen's Chapel

Somerset House

St Ethelburga's Centre

Mayfair

Benjamin Franklin's House

Tower of London

Bayswater Rd

Hyde Park

Spencer House

Banqueting House

Southwark Cathedral & Footbridge

Tower Bridge Exhibition

Kensington Palace

Albert Memorial

Wellington Arch

Apsley House

Palace of Westminster

Linley Sambourne House

Queen's Gallery

Buckingham Palace

Chapter House

Jewel Tower

St George's Cathedral

Bermondse

Royal Mews

Blewcoat School

Leighton House Museum

Westminster Cathedral

Elephant & Castle

Sloane Sq

Earls Court

Pimlico

Vauxhall

Carlyle's House

Chelsea Physic Garden

Kennington

Chelsea

Oval

Camberwell

Nine Elms

Brixton Academy

Battersea

Stockwell

Fulham

Fulham Palace & Museum

Clapham

EDINBURGH

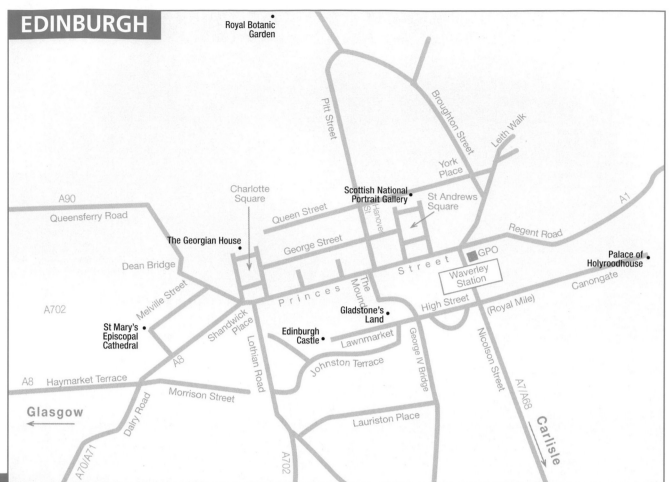

Royal Botanic Garden

Pitt Street

Broughton Street

Leith Walk

York Place

A1

A90
Queensferry Road

Charlotte Square

Scottish National Portrait Gallery

St Andrews Square

Regent Road

The Georgian House

Queen Street

Hanover St

George Street

GPO

Waverley Station

Palace of Holyroodhouse

Dean Bridge

Melville Street

P r i n c e s   S t r e e t

The Mound

High Street

(Royal Mile)

Canongate

A702

Shandwick Place

Gladstone's Land

St Mary's Episcopal Cathedral

Lothian Road

Edinburgh Castle

Lawnmarket

George IV Bridge

Nicolson Street

A7/A68

A8

A8   Haymarket Terrace

Johnston Terrace

Glasgow

Dalry Road

Morrison Street

Lauriston Place

Carlisle

A70/A71

A702

MAP 21

YORK

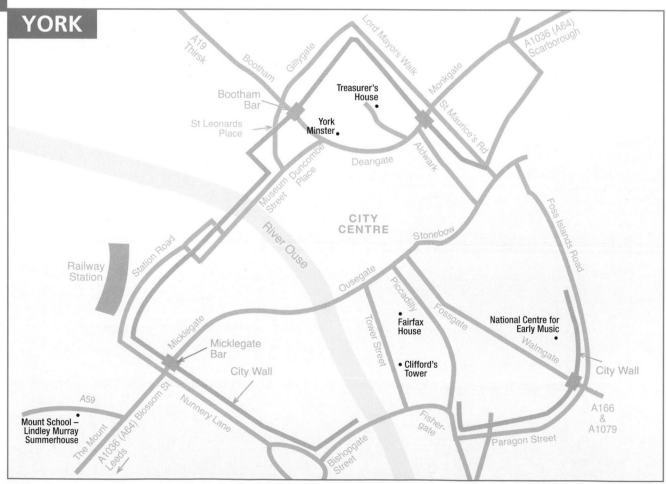

A19 Thirsk

Gillygate

Lord Mayors Walk

A1036 (A64) Scarborough

Bootham

Bootham Bar

Treasurer's House

Monkgate

St Maurice's Rd

St Leonards Place

York Minster

Museum Street

Duncombe Place

Deangate

Aldwark

CITY CENTRE

Foss Islands Road

Railway Station

River Ouse

Stonebow

Station Road

Ousegate

Piccadilly

Fossgate

National Centre for Early Music

Micklegate

Micklegate Bar

City Wall

Tower Street

Fairfax House

Walmgate

City Wall

Clifford's Tower

A59

A1036 (A64) Blossom St

Nunnery Lane

The Mount

Mount School – Lindley Murray Summerhouse

A1036 (A64) Leeds

Fishergate

Bishopgate Street

Paragon Street

A166 & A1079

visit hudsons guide online